Management

Management

Richard L. Daft
Hugh Roy Cullen Professor of Business Administration
Texas A&M University

The Dryden Press
Chicago   New York   San Francisco   Philadelphia
Montreal   Toronto   London   Sydney   Tokyo

Acquisitions Editor: Mary Fischer
Developmental Editor: Penny Gaffney
Project Editor: Cate Rzasa
Design Director: Jeanne Calabrese
Production Manager: Barb Bahnsen
Permissions Editor: Doris Milligan
Director of Editing, Design, and Production: Jane Perkins
Field Sales Rep: Vonalaine Crowe

Text and Cover Designer: Jeanne Calabrese
Photo Researcher: Nancy Moudry
Copy Editor: Nancy Maybloom
Indexer: Sheila Ary
Compositor: York Graphic Services, Inc.
Text Type: 10/12 ITC New Baskerville

Library of Congress Cataloging-in-Publication Data
Daft, Richard L.
   Management.

   Bibliography: p.
   Includes index.
   1. Industrial management. I. Title.
HD31.D134   1988   658   87-6820
ISBN 0-03-009473-9

Printed in the United States of America.
789-036-9876543
Copyright © 1988 by The Dryden Press, a division of
Holt, Rinehart and Winston, Inc.

Address orders:
The Dryden Press
Orlando, Florida 32887

Address editorial correspondence:
The Dryden Press
908 N. Elm St.
Hinsdale, IL 60521

The Dryden Press
Holt, Rinehart and Winston
Saunders College Publishing

Cover Source: *Bal Bullier (Le Bal Bullier)*, by Sonia Delaunay, 1913 oil on canvas,
38³⁄₁₆ × 51¹⁵⁄₁₆ (97 × 132). Kunsthalle Bielefeld, West Germany.

To the Cullen Trust for Higher Education

Nothing is so essential to free government as the general diffusion of knowledge and intelligence of every kind. It is the foundation of civil liberty and constitutes our national strength and glory.

The philosophy of Hugh Roy Cullen, which he adopted from the above quotation by his grandfather

Preface

During the past year, several colleagues asked me, "Why are you writing a management book? There are already lots of management books." My answer was that I was trying to do more than write another management text. I wanted to create a better kind of management text that would convey to students both the intellectual enjoyment of management research and the down-to-earth application of management ideas.

Any textbook is limited as a medium for teaching management. A textbook about management is like a recording of a symphony—the listener isn't really there, and many of the cues and much of the music's intensity are lost. Some people would describe current management texts as rather crude recordings of the management symphony because so little of the excitement, frustration, adventure, and humor of management gets through to the reader. The challenge that The Dryden Press presented to me was to develop the equivalent of a higher-quality "recording" for teaching students about management. Dryden agreed to provide whatever resources were needed, literally creating a far-reaching team of management and publishing experts, to fulfill our shared goal of what a management book could be.

I wrote this management text because the challenge was too exciting to pass up. I have always had a commitment to high-quality instruction and envisioned a book that would create in students both respect for the field of management and confidence that it can be understood and mastered. The "audio" portion of this book has been enhanced through the writing style and in-text examples used to make the concepts realistic and relevant to students. The chapters were rewritten as often as needed to make the language smooth and the ideas appealing to readers.

Much more difficult was the addition of a "visual" component in the form of photo essays illustrating management concepts. We believed that photo essays would significantly expand the amount of management insight to be gained from the text. The photos add a new dimension to student learning just as films have to management training programs and videos to popular music. Well-chosen photographs are unrivaled in their ability to convey vivid descriptions of management scenes, events, and people. The photos are combined with written descriptions that portray how management looks and feels and offer intimate glimpses into management life. They provide a special kind of knowledge through a language all of their own. Some photographs are pleasant, some are disarming, and some are surprising, but all are immensely valuable in helping students penetrate the often abstract and distant world of management.

ORGANIZATION

The chapter sequence in *Management* is organized around the management functions of planning, organizing, leading, and controlling. These four functions effectively encompass both management research and characteristics of the manager's job.

Part One introduces the world of management, including the nature of the manager's job, historical perspectives on management, and the influence of the larger environment on organizations and management.

Part Two presents four chapters on planning. The first two chapters describe goal setting, planning, strategy formulation, and strategy implementation. The next two chapters describe both qualitative and quantitative approaches to making decisions associated with planning.

Part Three focuses on organizing processes. These chapters describe the basic dimensions of structural design, the design alternatives managers can use to achieve strategic objectives, structural designs for promoting innovation and change, and the design and use of the human resource function.

Part Four is devoted to leadership. This section begins with a description of leadership and paves the way for the subsequent topics of employee motivation, communication, and management of small groups. The leading section closes with a chapter unique to management textbooks: It gives a macro view of how leaders influence corporate culture and corporate turnarounds.

Part Five describes the controlling function of management, including basic principles of organization control, the design of control systems, management information systems, and techniques for control of operations management.

Part Six describes two significant management issues—international management and careers. The international chapter provides a comprehensive introduction to the strategies, structure, control systems, and leadership qualities used to manage an organization internationally. The careers chapter describes both individual and organizational strategies for managing careers.

SPECIAL FEATURES

One major goal of this book was to offer better ways of using the text-book medium to convey management knowledge to the reader. To this end, the book includes several special features:

Photo Essays. The most innovative feature of the book is the use of photographs accompanied by detailed captions that describe management events and how they relate to chapter material. Visual media are a predominant form of communication in our society and have the power to convey reality as no written medium can. The photo essays cover a rich assortment of organizations and management events. Many of the photos are beautiful to look at, and all of them convey the vividness, immediacy, and concreteness of management events.

Chapter Outline and Objectives. Each chapter begins with a clear statement of learning objectives and an outline of its contents. These devices provide an overview of what is to come and can also be used by students to see whether they understand and have retained important points.

Management Problem/Solution. The text portion of each chapter begins with a real-life problem faced by organization managers. The problem pertains to the topic of the chapter and will heighten students' interest in chapter concepts. The problem is resolved at the end of the chapter, where chapter concepts guiding the management's actions are highlighted.

Contemporary Examples. Every chapter of the text contains a large number of written examples of management incidents. These are placed at strategic points in the chapter and are designed to demonstrate the application of concepts to specific companies. The examples include well-known companies such as IBM, Hewlett-Packard, McDonald's, Procter & Gamble, General Motors, Ford, Coca-Cola, Walt Disney, and Marriott, as well as less well-known companies and not-for-profit organizations such as Huffy Corporation, New York City Transit Authority, Columbia Gas Systems, Crane Plastics, Parsons Pine Products, a municipal department of sanitation, a medical center, and an elementary school. They put students in immediate touch with the real world of organizations so that they can appreciate the value of management concepts.

Managers Shoptalk. These boxed items contain issues of special interest to management students. They may describe a contemporary topic or problem that is relevant to chapter content or may contain a diagnostic questionnaire or a special example of how managers handle a problem. They also provide specific advice for accomplishing desired organizational outcomes. These boxes will heighten student interest in the subject matter and provide an auxiliary view of management issues not typically available in textbooks.

Focus Boxes. These boxed items pertain to social responsibility, international, and small-business issues. Their purpose is to help students integrate these topics with other concepts in the book. Too often such topics are presented in separate, discrete chapters that have no connection with other materials. Yet concepts in almost every chapter have implications for social responsibility, international management, and small business. The focus boxes will help students understand the relevance of the chapter material for these important management topics.

Glossaries. Learning the management vocabulary is essential to understanding contemporary management. This is facilitated in three ways. First, key concepts are boldfaced and completely defined where they first appear in the text. Second, brief definitions are set out in the margin for easy review and follow-up. Third, a glossary summarizing all key terms and definitions appears at the end of the book for handy reference.

Artwork. Many aspects of management are research based, and some concepts tend to be abstract and theoretical. To enhance students' awareness and understanding of these concepts, many exhibits have been included throughout the book. These exhibits consolidate key points, indicate relationships among variables, and visually illustrate concepts. They also make selective use of color to enhance their imagery and appeal.

Chapter Summary and Discussion Questions. Each chapter closes with a summary of key points to be retained. The discussion questions are a complementary learning tool that will enable students to check their understanding of key issues, to think beyond basic concepts, and to determine areas that require further study. The summary and discussion questions help students discriminate between main and supporting points and provide mechanisms for self-teaching.

Cases for Analysis. Each chapter ends with one or two brief but substantive cases for student analysis and class discussion. Approximately half the cases are about companies whose names students will recognize. The others are based on real management events but disguise the identities of the companies and managers. These cases provide an opportunity for students to apply concepts to real events and to sharpen their diagnostic skills for management problem solving.

SUPPLEMENTARY MATERIALS

Materials that supplement the text have become increasingly important in the teaching of management. Many instructors face large classes with limited resources, and supplementary materials provide a way to expand and improve the student's learning experience. The learning package provided with *Management* was specifically designed to meet the needs of instructors facing a variety of teaching conditions.

Test Bank. The single most important part of the teaching package is the *Test Bank*. The *Test Bank* was given special attention during the preparation of *Management* because instructors desire test questions that accurately and fairly assess student competence in subject material. The *Test Bank* for *Management,* prepared by David W. Chown, Mankato State University; Raymond Cook, University of Texas–Austin; Stan Elsea, Kansas State University; and Trudy G. Verser, Western Michigan University, provides 2,000 excellent multiple-choice, true/false, matching, and essay test items.

The test items have been reviewed and class tested to ensure the highest quality. Each question is keyed to chapter learning objectives, has been rated for level of difficulty, and is designated either as factual or application so that instructors can provide a balanced set of questions for student exams. The Dryden Press will provide an annual update of the *Test Bank*, which will include 1,100 new test questions.

Computerized Test Bank. A *Computerized Test Bank,* designed for either the IBM or Apple microcomputer, is also available free to adopters. The *Computerized Test Bank* allows instructors to select, edit, and add test items and print tests for classroom use.

Instructor's Manual. The *Instructor's Manual* contains an overview of each chapter, a listing of key terms, answers to end-of-chapter discussion questions, and teaching notes for the cases.

Resource Manual. This manual contains detailed chapter outlines, supplementary lecture materials, a detailed description for each transparency acetate and transparency master, and a guide to using many of the videotapes available to adopters. The manual has been designed to provide instructors with innovative instructional material to stimulate classroom participation and student comprehension. James E. Estes, University of South Carolina, and Dale Konicek, Houston Community College, were primary contributors to the manual.

Study Guide with Audio Cassette. This guide is invaluable for helping students to master management concepts. Prepared by Stephen R. Hiatt, Catawba College, the *Study Guide* provides a summary of each chapter, a review of key terms, and a variety of self-test questions. Each chapter also contains management applications for students' use in solving management problems. At the end of each part there is a comprehensive interactive exercise designed to offer students the opportunity to make decisions and learn how decisions impact an organization. These interactive exercises form the basis of a computerized simulation for individual or group activity. A free audio cassette, which accompanies the *Study Guide,* summarizes the major points in each chapter.

Transparency Masters and Acetates. More than 100 transparency masters from text art and 100 all-new color acetates are available to adopters.

Videotapes. One of the exciting innovations for enhancing student learning is the availability of management-related videotapes from the CBS television program "60 Minutes" and the award-winning PBS "Enterprise" series.

The following titles from the "Enterprise" series have been specifically keyed to the text's contents: "Buy-Out," "The Colonel Comes to Japan," "Fired," "The Kyocera Experiment," "The Million Dollar Scan," "Not by Jeans Alone," "Room at the Top," and "Tailspin." As noted previously, a guide to using these titles is included in the *Resource Manual*. Tapes will be provided to adopters.

Management Newsletter. A newsletter, which discusses the latest management trends, will be published three times a year and provided free upon adoption.

Micrograde. This new grading system disk allows instructors to store and analyze student grades on their personal computer.

ACKNOWLEDGMENTS

A project of this magnitude requires the commitment and participation of many people, but none made a greater contribution than Nancy Moudry. Nancy believed absolutely that students' learning could be enriched and deepened through the use of photo essays, and she spent endless hours searching for just the right photographs. The photos she found are about real people in real organizations dealing with real management events. They convey powerful images and insights far beyond what the written word can describe. Nancy's unwavering belief in this book was especially important to me. During the frustrating and difficult days every author faces, Nancy was optimistic and encouraging. She never doubted that we could produce an innovative book that would improve the way management knowledge is conveyed to students. Without Nancy, the book would not have achieved the high level of excellence to which she aspired. Nancy, thanks for the support, thanks for the commitment, thanks for keeping the faith. It was grand "To share a vision evermore, to share a vision evermore."

Another gratifying experience was working with the dedicated team of professionals at The Dryden Press who were determined to produce a first-quality management book. Joan Resler hooked me on the original vision for the book, and her successor, Mary Fischer, kept its spirit alive. I also want to thank Penny Gaffney for her excellent coordination of all of the materials and reviews, Jeanne Calabrese for her elegant design, Doris Milligan for her enthusiastic pursuit of permissions, Cate Rzasa for her superb project coordination, Nancy Maybloom for her skilled copyediting, and Michele McDonald for her coordination and copying of innumerable photos. I also want to thank Jane Perkins for her excellent suggestions and her guidance of the production process and Bill Schoof for putting the Dryden team together. It's not possible to say enough about the caring and commitment of each of these people. I thank you all very much.

Another group of people who made a major contribution to this text were the management experts who provided written materials, cases, and references in topic areas in which I lacked expertise. These materials enabled me to write chapters that were up to date with respect to research findings and management thinking. These contributors were Nikki Paahana, DeVry Institute of Technology, for groups; Bruce Blaylock, Eastern Kentucky University, for management information systems and management science; Barbara Deaux, Santa Fe State University, for motivation and decision making; Jeff Heyl, University of Colorado at Denver, for operations management; Jim Higgins, Rollins College, for strategy and decision making; Chuck Kuehl and Peggy Lambing, University of Missouri at St. Louis, for small business; Janina Latack, Ohio State University, for careers; Marcia Miceli, Ohio State University, for human resource management; Eugene Szwajkowski, University of Illinois at Chicago, for social responsibility; David Van Fleet, Texas A&M University, for leadership; Jim Weekly, University of Toledo, for international management; and Marlin C. Young, Stephen F. Austin State University, and Art Bell, University of Southern California, for communications. I also thank David Van Fleet for preparing Chapter 2, "Foundations of Management Understanding."

Reviewers also played a significant role in developing this text. Several reviewers read and criticized chapters in their areas of expertise. Others read the entire manuscript and made voluminous suggestions for changes, insertions, and clarifications. I want to thank each of these colleagues for their invaluable feedback and suggestions:

Michael Abelson
Texas A&M University

Paul Babrowski
University of Oregon

Jay Barney
Texas A&M University

Gerald Bassford
University of Arizona

Dan Cochran
Mississippi State University

Van Clouse
University of Louisville

Richard Cuba
University of Baltimore

Fran Emory
Northern Virginia Community
College Woodbridge

J.E. Estes
University of South Carolina

Phyllis Fowler
Macomb Community College

Thomas Miller
Memphis State University

Van Miller
Baylor University

David Nagao
Georgia Tech University

Glen Oddou
San Jose State University

Carole Saunders
Texas Christian University

Charles Shrader
Iowa State University

Susan Smith
Central Michigan University

William Smith
Hofstra University

Robert Sullivan
University of Texas—Austin

Mary Thibodeaux
North Texas State University

Lewis Welshofer
Miami of Ohio University

Daniel Wren
University of Oklahoma

I also want to acknowledge a unique debt and extend special appreciation to Phyllis Washburn. Without Phyllis' astonishing typing and secretarial skills, this book could not have been completed. Phyl and I have been working together for three years, and I have come to fully appreciate her significant role in my projects. Every chapter was typed on time and error free. It's still hard to believe we made it. Thanks, Phyl!

In addition, I want to acknowledge an intellectual debt to colleagues and students at Texas A&M. This book has benefited in many ways from my good fortune in having colleagues such as Mike Abelson, Bob Albanese, Jay Barney, Barry Baysinger, Ricky Griffin, Don Hellriegel, Bob Hoskisson, Bill Pride, David Van Fleet, Dick Woodman, and Stu Youngblood. These people are a major reason why Texas A&M is such a wonderful place to work.

Administrators also played a role in this project. Mike Hitt, department head, and Bill Mobley, dean, both supported this project fully and maintained an almost perfect scholarly atmosphere at Texas A&M. I also thank Don Hellriegel, who, in his role as Interim Dean, pursued the scholarly goals and positive work atmosphere we value so highly.

I also want to acknowledge the special support and encouragement provided by my wife, Kathy. The time devoted to this project came out of evenings and weekends that we might have spent together. Kathy understood my need to write this text, and she nudged me back to my writing when we both wanted to do other things. Kathy's love and encouragement were essential. We made the most of the hours we had together, including our Friday meetings at Interurban for hamburgers and our Sunday afternoon breaks to attend the dollar movies. I also want to thank Danielle and Amy, who are now in college and are beginning to understand and appreciate what Dad does for a living. Thanks also to B.J. for his delightful interruptions during the hectic writing schedule.

Finally, I'd like to pay tribute to Hugh Roy Cullen and the Cullen Trust for Higher Education. Hugh Roy Cullen was a generous supporter of Texas civic, educational, medical, and cultural organizations. He established the Cullen Foundation, within which the Cullen Trust for Higher Education has provided generous endowments to Texas A&M and other Texas universities. I especially thank Sidney Smith and the Trustees of the Cullen Trust for the gift of an endowed chair to Texas A&M, of which I am the recipient. The freedom provided by this endowment has enabled me to undertake new research and writing projects in several areas. The endowment has also provided resources for colleagues and students in the Management Department. The Cullen Trust for Higher Education has been most generous to Texas A&M, and I am proud to dedicate this book to them.

Richard L. Daft
College Station, Texas
December 1987

About the Author

Richard L. Daft, Ph.D., holds the Hugh Roy Cullen Chair in Business Administration at Texas A&M University, where he specializes in the study of organization theory and management. Dr. Daft is a Fellow of the Academy of Management and has served on the editorial boards of *Academy of Management Journal* and *Administrative Science Quarterly*. He also served for three years as associate editor of *Administrative Science Quarterly*.

Professor Daft has authored or co-authored six books including *Organization Theory and Design* (West Publishing, 1986) and *What to Study: Generating and Developing Research Questions* (Sage, 1982). He has also authored dozens of scholarly articles, papers, and chapters. His work has been published in *Administrative Science Quarterly, Academy of Management Journal, Academy of Management Review, Strategic Management Journal, Journal of Management, Accounting Organizations and Society, Management Science, MIS Quarterly, California Management Review*, and *Organizational Behavior Teaching Review*. Professor Daft has been awarded several government research grants to pursue studies of organization design, organizational innovation and change, strategy implementation, and organizational information processing.

Dr. Daft also is an active teacher and consultant. He has taught management, organizational change, organizational behavior, organizational theory, and strategic management. He has been actively involved in management development and consulting for many companies and government organizations including the American Banking Association, Bell Canada, NL Baroid, Tenneco, and the United States Air Force.

The Dryden Press Series in Management

Arthur G. Bedeian, Consulting Editor

Bartlett
Cases in Strategic Management for Business

Bedeian
Management

Bedeian
Organizations: Theory and Analysis, Text and Cases
Second Edition

Boone and Kurtz
Contemporary Business
Fifth Edition

Bowman and Branchaw
Business Communication: From Process to Product

Bowman and Branchaw
Business Report Writing
Second Edition

Chen and McGarrah
Productivity Management: Text and Cases

Cullinan
Business English for Industry and the Professions

Daft
Management

Gaither
**Production and Operations Management:
A Problem-Solving and Decision-Making Approach**
Third Edition

Gatewood and Feild
Human Resource Selection

Greenhaus
Career Management

Higgins
Strategy: Formulation, Implementation, and Control

Higgins and Vincze
**Strategic Management and Organizational Policy:
Text and Cases**
Third Edition

Hills
Compensation Decision Making

Hodgetts
Modern Human Relations at Work
Third Edition

Holley and Jennings
**Personnel/Human Resource Management:
Contributions and Activities**
Second Edition

Holley and Jennings
The Labor Relations Process
Third Edition

Huseman, Lahiff, and Penrose
Business Communication: Strategies and Skills
Third Edition

Jauch, Coltrin, Bedeian, and Glueck
**The Managerial Experience:
Cases, Exercises, and Readings**
Fourth Edition

Kuehl and Lambing
Small Business: Planning and Management

Lee
Introduction to Management Science
Second Edition

Miner
Theories of Organizational Behavior

Paine and Anderson
Strategic Management

Robinson
**International Business Management:
A Guide to Decision Making**
Second Edition

Robinson
The Internationalization of Business: An Introduction

Smith
Management Systems: Analyses and Applications

Tombari
**Business and Society: Strategies for the Environment
and Public Policy**

Varner
Contemporary Business Report Writing

Vecchio
Organizational Behavior

Weekly and Aggarwal
**International Business:
Operating in the Global Economy**

Wolters and Holley
Labor Relations: An Experiential and Case Approach

Zikmund
Business Research Methods
Second Edition

Contents

Cases for Analysis
Bethlehem Steel Corporation 28
Pro Line Company 30

Contemporary Examples
United Parcel Service 46
Alcan Aluminum Ltd. 55

Cases for Analysis
Sears, Roebuck & Company 61
Social Service Agency 62

PART ONE 1
Introduction to Management

Chapter 1   The Nature of Management 2

Learning Objectives 2
Management Problem 3
The Definition of Management 5   **The Four Management Functions** 5
Organizational Performance 9   **Management Types** 12   **Management
Skills** 15   **What Is It Like to Be a Manager?** 18   **Learning
Management Skills** 22   **Plan of the Book** 25   **Summary** 26
Management Solution 27
Discussion Questions 27

Chapter 2   Foundations of Management Understanding 32

Learning Objectives 32
Management Problem 33
Historical Forces Shaping Management 35   **Early Management** 37
Classical Perspective 39   **Human Resource Perspective** 46
Focus on International: Bureaucratic Organizing in Egypt 47
Management Science Perspective 52   **Contemporary Extensions** 53
Recent Historical Trends 56   **Summary** 59
Management Solution 60
Discussion Questions 60

Chapter 3   The External Environment and Social Responsibility   *64*

Learning Objectives   *64*
Management Problem   *65*
The External Environment *66* **The Organization-Environment Relationship** *74* **Fundamentals of Social Responsibility** *79* **Evaluating Corporate Social Performance** *81*
Managers Shoptalk: Guidelines for Ethical Decision Making   *83*
Corporate Responses to Social Demands *84* **Organizational Constituencies** *85* **Improving Ethical and Social Responsiveness** *87* **Does Social Responsibility Hurt Economic Performance?** *90* **Summary** *91*
Management Solution   *91*
Discussion Questions *92*

Contemporary Examples
International Business Machines *72*

Cases for Analysis
What Is Right? *93*
Jack Daniel Distillery *94*

PART TWO   *97*
Planning

Chapter 4   Organizational Goal Setting and Planning   *98*

Learning Objectives   *98*
Management Problem   *99*
Overview of Goals and Plans *100* **Goals in Organizations** *104* **Criteria for Effective Goals** *109* **Management-by-Objectives Types of Systems** *112* **Developing Plans for Attaining Goals** *114*
Managers Shoptalk: Ten Steps to Effective Planning   *116*
Planning Time Horizon *119* **Organizational Design for Planning** *120* **Barriers to Organizational Planning** *123* **Summary** *126*
Management Solution   *126*
Discussion Questions *127*

Contemporary Examples
New York City Transit Authority *103*
Employee Development Department *113*
TRW *118*

Cases for Analysis
H.I.D. *127*
Cartier *129*

Chapter 5   Strategy Formulation and Implementation   *130*

Learning Objectives   *130*
Management Problem   *131*
Thinking Strategically *132* **The Strategic Management Process** *136* **Formulating Corporate-Level Strategy** *139* **Formulating Business-Level Strategy** *144*

Contemporary Examples
Deere & Company *138*
Gillette Company *142*
H. J. Heinz Company *150*
Motorola Inc. *152*

Cases for Analysis
People Express *159*
Eastman Kodak *160*

Contemporary Examples
Sperry Corporation *167*
Fiesta Food Marts *173*
Chrysler Corporation *176*
Civil Service Reform Act *179*
Coca-Cola Company *180*
United Technologies *182*

Cases for Analysis
Guardian Engineering *190*
**Commodore International
Ltd.** *191*

Contemporary Examples
Huffy Corporation *199*
CCC Bakeries *205*
Wicker Company *207*
Stotler Associates *211*
Biggers Corporation *214*
National Forest Service *216*

Cases for Analysis
Second National Bank *223*
Gibson Glass Company *224*

Managers Shoptalk: Going on the Pill	*146*

Formulating Functional-Level Strategy *151* **The Human Element in Strategy Formulation** *153* **Implementing Strategies** *154* **Summary** *158*

Management Solution	*158*

Discussion Questions *158*

Chapter 6 Managerial Decision Making   *162*

Learning Objectives	*162*
Management Problem	*163*

Types of Decisions and Problems *164* **Decision-Making Models** *168* **Decision-Making Steps** *172*

Managers Shoptalk: Decision Biases to Avoid	*178*

Group Approaches to Decision Making *181* **Improving Decision-Making Effectiveness** *187* **Summary** *188*

Management Solution	*189*

Discussion Questions *189*

Chapter 7 Management Science Aids for Planning and Decision Making   *192*

Learning Objectives	*192*
Management Problem	*193*

The Nature and Role of Management Science *194* **Forecasting** *196* **Quantitative Approaches to Planning** *203* **Quantitative Approaches to Decision Making** *213* **Strengths and Limitations of Management Science Aids** *220* **Summary** *221*

Management Solution	*222*

Discussion Questions *222*

PART THREE   *227*
Organizing

Chapter 8 Fundamentals of Organizing   *228*

Learning Objectives	*228*
Management Problem	*229*

The Organizing Process *231* **Organizing the Vertical Structure** *232*

Managers Shoptalk: How to Delegate   238

Organizing the Lateral Structure *242* **Balancing Vertical and Lateral Structures** *245*

Focus on Small Business: Can This Business Be Saved?   252

Summary *259*

Management Solution   260

Discussion Questions *260*

Chapter 9 Using Structural Design to Achieve Strategic Objectives   264

Learning Objectives   264
Management Problem   265

Approaches to Structural Design *266* **Functional Approach to Structure** *268* **Functional Approach with Lateral Relationships** *271* **Divisional Approach to Structure** *274* **Hybrid Approach to Structure** *277* **Matrix Approach to Structure** *281* **Using Structural Approaches for Attaining Strategic Objectives** *287*

Managers Shoptalk: Structural Warning Signs   288

Mintzberg's Typology: Integrating Structure and Contingency Factors *290* **Summary** *296*

Management Solution   296

Discussion Questions *297*

Chapter 10 Organizational Change and Development   300

Learning Objectives   300
Management Problem   301

Managing Change Activities *302* **Initiating Change** *305* **Implementing Change** *310*

Managers Shoptalk: Are You an Intrapreneur?   311

Types of Planned Change *317* **Organizational Development** *321* **Summary** *328*

Management Solution   329

Discussion Questions *329*

Chapter 11 Human Resource Management   332

Learning Objectives   332
Management Problem   333

Strategic Human Resource Management *334* **Attracting an Effective Work Force** *337*

Managers Shoptalk: The Right Way to Interview a Job Applicant   347

Developing an Effective Work Force *348* **Maintaining an Effective Work Force** *355* **Summary** *360*

Management Solution   360

Discussion Questions *361*

Contemporary Examples
Sears, Roebuck and USX *236*
Procter & Gamble *248*
Marriott Corporation *258*
Cases for Analysis
Republic National Bank *261*
Malard Manufacturing Company *262*

Contemporary Examples
Ford Motor Company *272*
Apple Computer *278*
Crane Plastics Inc. *285*
Human Resources Administration *294*

Case for Analysis
Tucker Company *297*

Contemporary Examples
Campbell Soup Company *309*
Navistar International *316*
Honeywell Corporation *323*

Cases for Analysis
Southwestern Bell Corporation *330*
Digital Equipment Corporation *331*

Contemporary Examples
EDS *339*
R. H. Macy & Company *349*

Cases for Analysis
Triangle Equipment *361*
Legrande Stores *363*

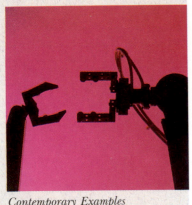

Contemporary Examples
Chick-fil-A, Inc. *374*
Greyhound Corporation *379*
**Fireman's Fund Insurance
Company** *383*
Ko-Rec-Type *385*
Banc One Corporation *389*

Cases for Analysis
Editorial Department *394*
Citicorp *395*

Contemporary Examples
Marquette Electronics *404*
Nucor Corporation *408*
Merrill Lynch *412*
Parsons Pine Products *416*
**Traveler's Insurance
Company** *420*

Cases for Analysis
**Automobile Claims
Department** *425*
Catalog Stores, Inc. *426*

Contemporary Examples
ITT *436*
Delta Air Lines *439*
Borg-Warner *444*
Marriott Corporation *446*
**Training Development
Corporation** *447*

Cases for Analysis
Atlanta Tool and Die Inc. *455*
The Travel Department *456*

PART FOUR   365
Leading

Chapter 12   Leadership in Organizations   366

Learning Objectives   366
Management Problem   367
The Nature of Leadership *368* **Leadership Traits** *370* **Autocratic
versus Democratic Leaders** *371* **Two-Dimensional Approaches** *373*
Contingency Approaches *376* **Inspirational Leadership** *388*
Managers Shoptalk: Are You a Leader?   390
Leadership by Organizational Level *391* **Summary** *392*
Management Solution   393
Discussion Questions *393*

Chapter 13   Motivation in Organizations   396

Learning Objectives   396
Management Problem   397
The Concept of Motivation *398* **Foundations of Motivation** *399*
Content Perspectives on Motivation *401*
*Focus on International:
Japanese versus American Achievement Motivation*   406
Process Perspectives on Motivation *407*
Focus on Small Business: Immigrants as Entrepreneurs   411
Reinforcement Perspective on Motivation *412* **Job Design for
Motivation** *416* **Other Motivational Programs** *421* **Summary** *423*
Management Solution   424
Discussion Questions *424*

Chapter 14   Communicating in Organizations   428

Learning Objectives   428
Management Problem   429
Communication and the Manager's Job *431* **Communicating among
People** *433* **Organizational Communication** *440*
Managers Shoptalk: A Listening Check-up   442
Communicating in Groups *448* **Managing Organizational
Communication** *449*
*Focus on Social Responsibility:
Communication Skills Outside the Organization*   452
Summary *454*
Management Solution   454
Discussion Questions *454*

Chapter 15 Managing Organizational Groups 458

Learning Objectives 458
Management Problem 459
Groups at Work *460* **Types of Groups** *461* **Work Group Characteristics** *463* **Group Processes** *468* **Managing Conflict** *476* **Benefits and Costs of Groups** *478* **Organizational Application of Group Concepts** *481*
Managers Shoptalk: How to Run a Great Meeting 484
Summary *486*
Management Solution 486
Discussion Questions *487*

Contemporary Examples
Medical Center *466*
Federal Reserve Board *470*
Honeywell *475*
Salvo Inc. *477*
Intel *480*
General Motors' Saturn Plant *483*

Cases for Analysis
Special Task Force *487*
Franklin Savings & Loan *488*

Chapter 16 Corporate Culture and Revitalization 490

Learning Objectives 490
Management Problem 491
Corporate Culture *492* **Strategy and Culture** *497*
Managers Shoptalk: Keeping Culture Strong 501
Reshaping Corporate Culture *502* **Techniques for Changing Corporate Culture** *508* **Techniques for Managing Revitalization** *513*
Summary *516*
Management Solution 517
Discussion Questions *517*

Contemporary Examples
PepsiCo Inc. *507*
AM International *509*

Cases for Analysis
Marine Midland Bank *518*
Society of Equals *519*

PART FIVE 523
Controlling

Chapter 17 Effective Organizational Control 524

Learning Objectives 524
Management Problem 525
The Importance of Control *526* **Relationship of Control to Strategic Planning** *529* **Organizational Control Focus** *532* **Multiple Control Systems** *534* **Organizational Control Methods** *536*
Focus on Social Responsibility: The Invisible Supervisor 538
Choosing Your Style of Control *543* **Total Quality Control** *544*
Managers Shoptalk: Ten Keys to Successful Quality Circles 548
Characteristics of Effective Control *550* **Summary** *552*
Management Solution 552
Discussion Questions *553*

Contemporary Examples
Nike Inc. *531*
Scandinavian Design Inc. *535*
Franklin Elementary School *539*
Marquette Electronics *542*
Sonoco Products Company *549*

Case for Analysis
Using Private Eyes at GM *554*

Contemporary Examples
Ford Motor Company *567*
**Thrifty Scott Warehouse
Food Inc.** *578*
**Producers Gas and
Transmission Company** *581*

Cases for Analysis
Apple Computer Inc. *587*
Metallic Finishes Inc. *588*

Chapter 18　Management Control Systems and Techniques

Learning Objectives 556
Management Problem 557
Core Management Control System *558*　**Top Management Financial Control** *561*　**Middle Management Budget Control** *568*
Managers Shoptalk: The Numbers 572
The Budgeting Process *574*　**Controlling through Performance Appraisal** *579*　**Summary** *586*
Management Solution 586
Discussion Questions *587*

556

Contemporary Examples
Western Engine Company *599*
Gromer Supermarket Inc. *600*
**Thermo Electron
Corporation** *603*
Hercules Inc. *610*
McKesson Corporation *614*

Cases for Analysis
Memorial County Hospital *620*
United Way *621*

Chapter 19　Management Information Systems

Learning Objectives 590
Management Problem 591
Focus on International: Kompyuter Use in the Soviet Union 593
Information and Management *593*　**Information Systems for Management** *595*　**CBISs and the Management Hierarchy** *597*　**Other Information Technologies** *604*　**Impact of Information Technology on Organizations** *608*　**Strategic Management and Information Technology** *612*　**Limitations of CBISs** *615*
Managers Shoptalk: Cowboys and Computers 617
Summary *618*
Management Solution 619
Discussion Questions *620*

590

Contemporary Examples
Delco Electronics *642*
Kawasaki *645*

Cases for Analysis
Xaloy Inc. *654*
Blue Bell Inc. *655*

Chapter 20　Operations Management

Learning Objectives 624
Management Problem 625
Organizations as Production Systems *626*　**The Strategic Role of Operations Management** *628*　**Designing Operations Management Systems** *631*　**Inventory Management** *637*　**Purchasing** *645*　**Managing Productivity** *646*
Managers Shoptalk: Managing by the Numbers 648
Organizing the Operations Management Function *651*　**Summary** *653*
Management Solution 653
Discussion Questions *654*

624

PART SIX   *659*
Emerging Management Issues

Chapter 21 Managing in a Multinational World   *660*

Learning Objectives   *660*
Management Problem   *661*

The Nature of International Management *662* **The International Business Environment** *663* **Entry Strategies for International Markets** *671* **The Multinational Corporation** *674* **Multinational Corporate Strategy** *676*

Focus on Social Responsibility: Adhering to the Sullivan Principles   *677*

Multinational Organization Structure *680* **Tailoring Management Style to Cultural Values** *686* **Summary** *688*

Management Solution   *688*

Discussion Questions *689*

Contemporary Examples
Heineken *671*
Dow Chemical Company *675*
Corning Glass Works *685*

Cases for Analysis
Ok Tedi Mining Ltd. *689*
American Telephone and Telegraph Company *691*

Chapter 22 Career Management   *692*

Learning Objectives   *692*
Management Problem   *693*

Changing Scope of Careers *694* **Individual Career Planning** *695*

Focus on Small Business: A Career in Your Own Company   *698*

Focus on International: Japanese Face Up to Stress on the Job   *704*

Organizational Career Management Strategies *707*

Managers Shoptalk: Are You about to Burst into Flames?   *708*

Special Career Management Problems *715* **Focusing Career Management Strategies on Career Stages** *718* **Summary** *720*

Management Solution   *720*

Discussion Questions *721*

Contemporary Examples
Cindy Johnson *699*
International Drug Company *703*
Fred Gabourie Insurance Agency *706*
Sears, Roebuck *711*
Disneyland *714*

Cases for Analysis
Xerox Corporation *721*
American Steel Company *722*

References   *724*

Glossary   *747*

Photo Credits   *764*

Name Index   *767*

Company Index   *774*

Subject Index   *778*

PART ONE

INTRODUCTION TO MANAGEMENT

Source: Bal Bullier (Le Bal Bullier), by Sonia Delaunay, 1913 oil on canvas, 38-$\frac{3}{16}$ × 51-$\frac{15}{16}$ (97 × 132). Kunsthalle Bielefeld, West Germany.

Source: Courtesy of Goulds Pumps, Incorporated.

CHAPTER 1

The Nature of Management

Chapter Outline

The Definition of Management

The Four Management Functions

Planning
Organizing
Leading
Controlling

Organizational Performance

Management Types

Vertical Differences
Horizontal Differences

Management Skills

Conceptual Skills
Human Skills
Technical Skills
Making the Transition

What Is It Like to Be a Manager?

Manager Activities
Manager Roles

Learning Management Skills

AT&T Study
Management Success and Failure

Plan of the Book

Learning Objectives

After studying this chapter, you should be able to:

- Define management and give examples of successful managers.

- Describe the four management functions and the type of management activity associated with each.

- Explain the difference between efficiency and effectiveness and their importance for organizational performance.

- Describe differences in management functions by hierarchical level.

- Define functional and general managers and explain how management functions differ by department.

- Describe conceptual, human, and technical skills and their relevance for managers and nonmanagers.

- Define ten roles that managers perform in organizations.

- Describe the importance of college training versus experience in learning to be a manager and explain why some managers derail.

Management Problem

Edward Esber, Jr., the new chief executive of Ashton-Tate Inc., faced a difficult challenge. Ashton-Tate had lost its two top executives. In recent years the company had been enormously successful in selling a data-based management program, *dBase III*. Sales for 1985 were $140 million. Esber's challenge was clear: The two previous top executives were gone, and the company was in disarray. Earnings had plunged 56 percent because financial controls were lacking. Employee turnover was high. The company's fortunes rested on a single product in an industry where products had short lives. As a manager, Esber was an unknown quantity. He had a Harvard MBA and understood management fundamentals, but in his previous career at another software company he had been demoted three times. In his first weeks as CEO of Ashton-Tate, Esber was spending more than 60 hours a week at the office. He believed his first task was to inject Ashton-Tate with massive doses of "Management 101."[1]

If you were in Esber's position, how would you proceed? How would you infuse Management 101 to reform the company and solve its problems?

Few students have heard of Edward Esber or Ashton-Tate. Most are unfamiliar with the management actions needed to fix Ashton-Tate's problems. The management problem at Ashton-Tate is important because it represents a situation that confronts thousands of managers in hundreds of organizations. Successful organizations don't just happen—they must be managed. Every organization has problems, and every organization needs skilled management.

Why are these managers wearing raincoats? Led by Chairman and CEO Graham Tyson (left), the senior management team at Dataproducts brought the company through the stormy 1985 computer industry recession. These managers saved the company. Three manufacturing plants were closed, the work force was reduced, and product development programs were canceled; customer services, however, were maintained. The severe losses in the first half of 1985 were followed by moderate profits. By 1986 the storm clouds had passed, and the sun was shining on these managers and their new strategic plan that will guide Dataproducts through 1991. These managers made a difference.

Managers like Edward Esber have the opportunity to make a difference. Lee Iacocca made a difference at Chrysler Corporation when he turned it around by reducing internal costs, developing new products, and gaining concessions from lenders, the union, and government. General William Creech made a difference to the huge Tactical Air Command of the U.S. Air Force when he reversed a sortie rate (number of flights flown with tactical aircraft) that had been declining 7.8 percent a year. Within a year of his appointment as TAC commander, the sortie rate increased 11.2 percent and continued to rise at that rate for five years with no additional resources. Kelly Johnson of Lockheed made a difference to an ailing satellite program. Launch effectiveness had been running 12.5 percent, was way behind schedule and over budget, and, as Johnson discovered, one subcontractor was using 1,271 inspectors. Within a year the program was back on schedule, launch effectiveness had improved to 98 percent, and the number of inspectors had been reduced to 35. William Donald Schaefer, mayor of Baltimore, made a difference. He had such a positive impact on that city that he was re-elected against a talented candidate by 94 percent of the vote. He saw a city of dirty parks, housing violations, abandoned cars, dead trees, and uncollected trash. He motivated city workers to clean up the mess and involved citizens in an ownership program that helped pay for and maintain city services.[2]

These managers are not unusual. Every day managers solve difficult problems, turn organizations around, and achieve astonishing performance. Every organization needs skilled managers to be successful. And it's important to remember that managers can make a difference in a negative direction. For example, Harding Lawrence of Braniff Airlines was responsible for a misguided strategy of rapid national and international expansion, and he alienated executives and employees with his domineering, bullying behavior. His influence helped launch Braniff on a flight path to bankruptcy.[3]

The purpose of this book is to define and explain the process of management. By analyzing examples of successful and not-so-successful managers and reviewing systematic studies of management techniques and styles, you will learn the fundamentals of management. The problems Edward Esber faced at Ashton-Tate are not unusual for senior managers. By the end of this chapter, you will already understand the approach Esber should take to get Ashton-Tate back on track. By the end of this book, you will understand what Esber meant by injecting massive doses of "Management 101" into his company. In the remainder of this chapter, we will define the nature of management and look at the roles and activities of managers in today's organizations. We will also outline the building blocks of management knowledge within the book that will help you gain a full understanding of management fundamentals.

THE DEFINITION OF MANAGEMENT

What do managers like Lee Iacocca, General Creech, Kelly Johnson, and Mayor Schaefer have in common? They get things done through their organizations. One early management scholar, Mary Parker Follett, described management as "the art of getting things done through people."[4] Peter Drucker, a noted management theorist, says that managers give direction to their organizations, provide leadership, and decide how to use organizational resources to accomplish goals.[5] Getting things done through people and other resources and providing direction and leadership are what managers do. And not just top executives like Lee Iacocca, General Creech, Kelly Johnson, or Mayor Schaefer—the same activities apply to a new lieutenant in charge of a TAC maintenance squadron, a foreman in the Ontario plant that makes Plymouth minivans, and the head of the Building Inspections Department in Baltimore. Moreover, management often is considered universal because it uses organizational resources to accomplish goals and attain high performance in all types of profit and not-for-profit organizations. Thus, our definition of management is as follows:

> *Management is the attainment of organizational goals in an effective and efficient manner through planning, organizing, leading, and controlling organizational resources.*

management The attainment of organizational goals in an effective and efficient manner through planning, organizing, leading, and controlling organizational resources.

There are two important ideas in this definition: (1) the four functions of planning, organizing, leading, and controlling and (2) the attainment of organizational goals in an effective and efficient manner. Let's start by discussing the four management functions. Exhibit 1.1 illustrates the interrelationships among them.

THE FOUR MANAGEMENT FUNCTIONS

Planning

Planning defines where the organization wants to be in the future and how to get there. **Planning** means defining goals for future organiza-

planning The management function concerned with defining goals for future organizational performance and deciding on the tasks and resource use needed to attain them.

EXHIBIT 1.1

The Four Functions of Management

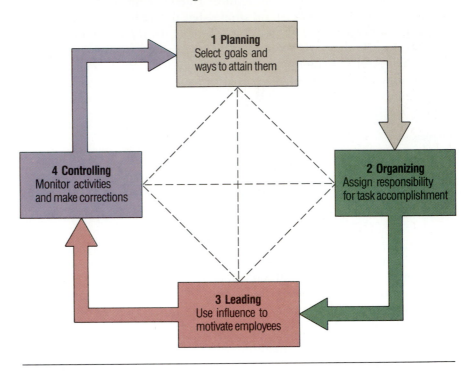

tional performance and deciding on the tasks and use of resources needed to attain them. Senior managers at Bausch & Lomb defined a specific plan: to capture at least 50 percent of every segment of the contact lens market even if prices had to be cut and profits reduced to maintain market share. Senior managers at Chase Manhattan Bank decided to make it the number one service-quality bank in the world and, through extensive planning, to develop a worldwide network of branch banks, implement a sophisticated foreign exchange system, and offer a state-of-the-art electronic funds transfer system. General Creech successfully turned around the Tactical Air Command because he had a specific plan including targets for improved sortie rates and techniques for bringing them about.

A lack of planning—or poor planning—can hurt an organization's performance. Harding Lawrence's unrealistic plan for Braniff was part of the problem that led to Braniff's bankruptcy. When the Airline Deregulation Act became law, Braniff decided—with no planning—to seize every route it could. In one day it applied for more than 300 routes, even though it had nowhere near the resources to fly that many. The flaw in the strategy was that the routes were available because other carriers had found them unprofitable. An even worse planning mistake was the inauguration of new foreign routes to European cities and the Pacific, which are enormously expensive. Lawrence had not foreseen that nationally owned airlines would be relentless price cutters, making it nearly impos-

This is the monthly Operating Board meeting at INTERCO's corporate headquarters in St. Louis. INTERCO has several operating companies that manufacture and distribute apparel, home furnishings, and footwear. The meeting shown here illustrates INTERCO's organizing and planning. The principal officers of the operating companies are organized into the Operating Board, which meets monthly to share financial and market information and solve problems. Moreover, each operating company has its own operating board made up of its management team plus four senior corporate officers. Principal officers and operating boards also plan for their companies, including the development of forecasts and budgets and the preparation of annual profit plans and monthly updates.

sible to earn profits. Other airlines, such as Continental, saw deregulation as a prescription for caution and decided to proceed slowly and carefully. It turned out they were right.[6]

Organizing

Organizing typically follows planning and reflects how the organization tries to accomplish the plan. Organizing involves the assignment of tasks, the grouping of tasks into departments, and the allocation of resources to departments. For example, Hewlett-Packard, Sears, Roebuck, Xerox, and Digital Equipment have all undergone structural reorganizations to accommodate their changing plans. General Creech accomplished his plan for TAC largely through decentralization and the development of small, self-contained maintenance units—a drastic departure from the traditional structures that had encouraged centralization and consolidation of Air Force resources. Kelly Johnson of Lockheed used organizing wizardry to reduce the number of subcontractor inspectors from 1,271 to 35 and still achieve the objective of improved launch effectiveness. Indeed, his organizing was so good that the Air Force insisted that a competitor be allowed to visit Johnson's team. The competitor used 3,750 people to perform a similar task and was years behind and way over budget. Johnson's organization was on schedule and under budget—and with only 126 people.[7]

Likewise, weak organizing facilitated the destruction of Braniff Airlines. Braniff did not have enough departments and offices to handle passengers and airplanes for the new national and international routes. It needed an enormous amount of money to set up a structure to fit its strategy. Even before the expansion Braniff had lacked a strong internal structure with clearly defined roles for accomplishing tasks. The new structure yielded a group of "yes men" who deferred to Lawrence's every decision.[8]

organizing The management function concerned with assigning tasks, grouping tasks into departments, and allocating resources to departments.

leading The management function that involves the use of influence to motivate employees to achieve the organization's goals.

Leading

The third management function is to provide leadership for employees. **Leading** is the use of influence to motivate employees to achieve organizational goals. Leading means communicating goals to employees throughout the organization and infusing them with the desire to perform at a high level. Leading involves motivating entire departments and divisions as well as individuals.

Managers such as Lee Iacocca are exceptional leaders. They are able to communicate their vision throughout the organization and energize employees into action. General Creech was a leader when he improved the motivation of aircraft maintenance technicians in hundreds of maintenance squadrons. Maintenance people previously had been neglected in favor of pilots. Creech set up highly visible bulletin boards displaying pictures of the maintenance crew chiefs, improved their living quarters, and established decent maintenance facilities, complete with paintings and wall murals. He introduced competition among supply and maintenance squadrons. He created trophy rooms to hold plaques and other prizes won in maintenance competitions. This prominent display of concern for maintenance specialists greatly increased their motivation to keep the planes flying.

Mayor Schaefer of Baltimore used a number of techniques to motivate city employees. He sent them action memos that were blunt and direct: "Get the trash off East Lombard Street," "Broken pavement at 1700 Carey," "Abandoned car at 2900 Remington." One action memo said, "There is an abandoned car . . . but I'm not telling you where it is." City crews ran around for a week and towed several hundred cars.[9]

Leadership has a negative side, too. Again consider Harding Lawrence. His leadership of Braniff was said to contribute to employees' *demotivation.* Lawrence won notoriety on Braniff's Flight 6, which he took weekly to visit his wife, who worked in New York City:

His tantrums on Flight 6 are legend. On one flight a stewardess served him an entire selection of condiments with his meal instead of asking him which one he preferred. He slammed his fist into the plate, splattering food on the surrounding seats of the first-class cabin. "Don't you ever assume what I want!" he screamed.

"On several occasions flight attendants came to me in tears, fearful of losing their jobs," says Ed Clements, former director of flight attendant services at Braniff. "I was sickened by what he was doing to the employees."

On one flight Lawrence dumped a trayful of food onto a stewardess's lap because it had gotten cold while he was away from his seat. On another he overturned a champagne bucket that was being used to store fruit. . . . Lawrence's appearance on an aircraft was likely to arouse two emotions in the crew: fear and hatred.[10]

Lawrence also bullied senior executives, making them look bad in front of other managers. The work force was demoralized and hated coming to work. Inevitably, dissatisfied employees led to dissatisfied customers. Marketing surveys indicated that Braniff was unpopular with many of its passengers. Without a loyal customer base, successful expansion and high performance proved impossible.[11]

Leading is the management function that uses influence to motivate employees to achieve organizational goals. Note the attention that these Honeywell employees are giving their manager as he explains a program for quality improvement. He is able to communicate the importance of raising quality levels and reducing scrap and has gained employees' commitment to the program, which will improve both manufacturing and office operations.

Controlling

Controlling is the fourth function in the management process. **Controlling** means monitoring employees' activities, determining whether the organization is on target toward its goals, and making corrections as necessary. Managers must ensure that the organization is moving toward its goals. Controlling often involves using an information system to advise managers on performance and a reward system for employees who make progress toward goals. For example, at Domino's Pizza Distribution Company over 1,200 franchises are measured weekly. A phone survey of customers determines the quality of service at each franchise, which is reported to management. Compensation for all employees is based on the results. Expected performance levels are reviewed every six months and set slightly higher for the next six months. The control system then monitors whether employees achieve the higher targets.

One reason for organization failure is that managers were not serious about control or lacked control information. Harding Lawrence, for example, ignored control system information. Opening new offices and buying new airplanes for Braniff's expanded route system cost several hundred million dollars. The spending spree meant an astronomical climb in the company's debt-to-equity ratio. When one financial officer told Lawrence that the company could not survive this rate of spending, he didn't listen. The officer insisted that Braniff couldn't bring in enough money to pay its bills and had the figures to prove it. After a few months, the red ink flowed so heavily that Lawrence had to listen—but by then it was too late. A few months later Lawrence was fired, but the new management was unable to save the wounded airline.[12]

controlling The management function concerned with monitoring employees' activities, keeping the organization on track toward its goals, and making corrections as needed.

ORGANIZATIONAL PERFORMANCE

The other part of our definition of management is the attainment of organizational goals in an efficient and effective manner. One reason management is so important is that organizations are so important. In an industrialized society where complex technologies dominate, organizations bring together knowledge, people, and raw materials to perform tasks no individual could do alone. Without organizations how could 15,000 flights a day be accomplished without an accident, electricity produced from large dams or nuclear power generators, millions of automobiles manufactured, or hundreds of films, videos, and records made available for our entertainment? Organizations pervade our society. Most college students will work in an organization—perhaps Hospital Corporation of America, Federated Department Stores, Boise Cascade, or Standard Oil. College students already are members of several organizations, such as a university, junior college, YMCA, church, fraternity, or sorority. College students also deal with organizations every day: to renew a driver's license, be treated in a hospital emergency room, buy

The management function of controlling is illustrated by these four managers— Frank Cartier, Ralph Smith, Brian Beckham, and Harold McDonnell—from Aerospace Corporation. They are reviewing progress on the Fleet Satellite Communications spacecraft shown in the background. Management control for this spacecraft follows the planning function, in which targets are set and goals defined for spacecraft performance. Aerospace Corporation also monitors the performance of four operational satellites that serve the Navy, Air Force, and Presidential command networks.

EXHIBIT   1.2

The Organization As a System

Resources From the Environment	Organization Makes Products and Services	Outputs Back to Environment
• Human	• Purchasing	• Products
• Financial	• Manufacturing	• Services
• Raw material	• Marketing	
• Technological	• Maintenance	
• Information	• Personnel	

organization A social entity that is goal directed and deliberately structured.

system A set of interrelated elements that transform inputs into outputs.

effectiveness The degree to which the organization achieves a stated objective.

efficiency The use of minimal resources—raw materials, money, and people—to produce a desired volume of output.

food from a supermarket, eat in a restaurant, or buy new clothes. Managers are responsible for these organizations and for seeing that resources are used wisely to attain organizational goals.

Our formal definition of an **organization** is a social entity that is goal directed and deliberately structured. *Social entity* means being made up of two or more people. *Goal directed* means designed to achieve some outcome, such as make a profit (Boeing, Mack Trucks), win pay increases for members (AFL-CIO), meet spiritual needs (Methodist church), or provide social satisfaction (college sorority). *Deliberately structured* means that tasks are divided and responsibility for their performance assigned to organization members.

The organization can be thought of as a **system,** which is a set of interrelated elements that transform inputs into outputs, as illustrated in Exhibit 1.2. The system idea is important because a system must obtain resources from the environment in order to survive and subsystems within the organization coordinated into an organizational whole.[13] One part of the organization is designated to acquire raw materials (purchasing), another to produce goods or services (manufacturing), others to help maintain the organization's facilities (maintenance) and employees (personnel), and still another to expand the organization's boundary to customers (marketing).

Based on our definition of management, the manager's responsibility is to coordinate these systems such that resources will be used in an effective and efficient manner to accomplish the organization's goals. Organizational **effectiveness** is the degree to which the organization achieves a stated objective. It means that the organization succeeds in accomplishing what it tries to do. Organizational effectiveness pertains to a successful relationship with the external environment by selecting a product or service that customers value. Organizational **efficiency** refers to the amount of resources used to achieve an organizational goal. It is based on how much raw materials, money, and people are necessary for producing a given volume of output. Efficiency can be calculated as the amount of resources used to produce a unit of output.

Efficiency and effectiveness can both be high in the same organization. Consider the Honda plant in Marysville, Ohio, and the AMC Jeep

Campbell Soup Company managers continuously search for ideas and techniques to improve both effectiveness and efficiency. The soudronic welder was introduced into Campbell's major canned food plant to produce better containers and packaging; it makes cans with lead-free seams. Campbell is improving effectiveness through new products such as Creamy Natural Soups, which are increasing consumer demand for Campbell's products.

plant in Toledo, Ohio. The Jeep plant uses 5,400 workers to produce 750 cars per day—an average of 7.2 employees per car. The Honda plant uses 2,423 workers to produce 870 cars per day—only 2.8 employees per car.[14] Honda is far more efficient and also more effective. Customer demand for Honda automobiles is increasing. The Marysville plant continues to grow and add new workers. The AMC plant in Toledo is in decline. Although there is some demand for Jeeps, AMC is less effective because products are not in high demand and the organization is not accomplishing its goals.

Why is Honda's plant both efficient and effective? The answer is in the management of resources. Every organization uses human, financial, raw materials, technological, and information resources to produce outputs. Acquiring excellent resources and managing them in a superior fashion is how Honda attains outstanding performance. Honda employs young workers who are anxious to succeed, while AMC employs workers who are older, unionized, and resistant to company initiatives. Honda has the latest in production technology, including 48 robot welders and a continuous flow production line. Production lines at Jeep are broken in several places, necessitating manual movement of auto bodies. Technology and equipment at Honda are newer and more sophisticated than Jeep's. Jeep's productivity is hampered by work rules and negative tension between workers and managers. Honda's employees help manage the plant and feel no antagonism toward senior management. Managers work hard to keep their positive relationship with employees, enhance workers' skills, and improve assembly line procedures. As Honda's profits have risen, managers have increased wages and holidays for the company's employees.[15]

These first-line supervisors at a Chrysler plant are responsible for the production of automobiles. After an extensive training program, management trainees become first-line supervisors, a position that grooms them for middle- and top-level management jobs. First-line supervisors at Chrysler interact with skilled workers and use technically sophisticated equipment, as shown here, that requires both human and technical skills.

The ultimate responsibility of managers, then, is to achieve high **performance,** which is the attainment of organizational goals by using resources in an efficient and effective manner. Whether managers are responsible for the organization as a whole, such as Roger Smith at General Motors, or for a single department, their ultimate responsibility is performance. Harold Geneen, a legendary manager who transformed ITT into one of the world's largest and best-run corporations, explained it this way:

> *I think it is an immutable law in business that words are words, explanations are explanations, promises are promises—but only performance is reality. Performance alone is the best measure of your confidence, competence, and courage. Only performance gives you the freedom to grow as yourself.*
>
> *Just remember that:* performance is your reality. *Forget everything else. That is why my definition of a manager is what it is: one who turns in the performance. No alibis to others or to one's self will change that. And when you have performed well, the world will remember it, when everything else is forgotten. And most importantly, so will you.[16]*

MANAGEMENT TYPES

The four management functions must be performed in all organizations. But not all managers' jobs are the same. Managers are responsible for different departments, work at different levels in the hierarchy, and meet different requirements for achieving high performance. For example, Gary Smith, age 21, runs a team of 13 assemblers at Honda's Marysville, Ohio, plant. Charles Strang is chief executive officer for Outboard Marine, a manufacturer of outboard motors. Both are managers, and both must contribute to planning, organizing, leading, and controlling their organizations—but in different amounts and ways.

Vertical Differences

An important determinant of the manager's job is hierarchical level. **Top managers** are at the top of the hierarchy and are responsible for the entire organization. They have such titles as president, chairperson, executive director, chief executive officer (CEO), and executive vice-president. Top managers are responsible for setting organizational goals, defining strategies for achieving them, monitoring and interpreting the external environment, and making decisions that affect the entire organization. They look to the future and concern themselves with general environmental trends and the organization's long-term success. They also define the organization's human relations climate and influence internal corporate culture.

Middle managers work at middle levels of the organization and are responsible for major departments. Examples of middle managers are department head, division head, manager of quality control, and director of the research lab. Middle managers typically have two or more management levels beneath them. They are responsible for implement-

performance The organization's ability to attain its goals by using resources in an efficient and effective manner.

top manager A manager who is at the top of the organizational hierarchy and responsible for the entire organization.

middle manager A manager who works at the middle levels of the organization and is responsible for major departments.

E X H I B I T   1.3

Importance of Management Functions by Management Level

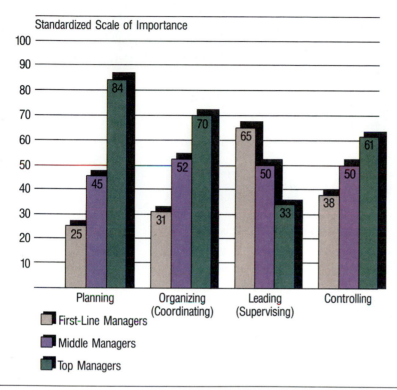

Source: Luis Gomez-Mejia, Joseph E. McCann, and Ronald C. Page, "The Structure of Managerial Behaviors and Rewards," *Industrial Relations* 24(1985), 147–154.

ing the overall strategies and policies defined by top managers. Middle managers set objectives and make decisions for their departments and coordinate activities across departments. They are concerned with the near future, are expected to establish good relationships with peers around the organization, organize their department, encourage teamwork, and resolve conflicts.

First-line managers are directly responsible for the production of goods and services. They are the first or second level of management and have such titles as supervisor, foreman, section chief, and office manager. They are responsible for groups of nonmanagement employees. Their primary concern is the application of rules and procedures to achieve efficient production, provide technical assistance, and motivate subordinates. The time horizon at this level is short, with the emphasis on accomplishing day-to-day objectives.

An illustration of how the three management levels differ hierarchically for one sample of managers is shown in Exhibit 1.3[17] Note that long-range planning is truly the province of top managers, with an "importance" score of 84 compared to 25 for first-line managers. Coordinating, which is often considered part of organizing, also increases with hierarchical level, although not as much as does long-range planning.

first-line manager A manager who is at the first or second management level and directly responsible for the production of goods and services.

E X H I B I T   1.4

Importance of Management Functions by Department

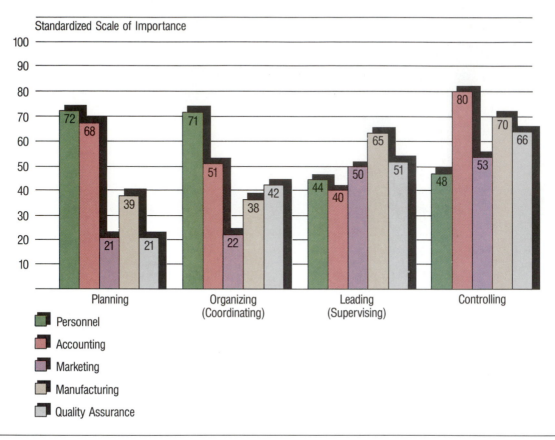

Source: Luis Gomez-Mejia, Joseph E. McCann, and Ronald C. Page, "The Structure of Managerial Behaviors and Rewards," *Industrial Relations* 24(1985), 147–154.

Supervising/leading, in contrast, is highest for first-line managers. A primary concern of first-line managers is the leadership and motivation of technical employees. Note that managers at all three levels are responsible for all four functions, but in different amounts.

Horizontal Differences

functional manager A manager responsible for a department that performs specialized tasks and has employees with similar training and skills.

general manager A manager responsible for several departments that perform different functions.

The other major difference in management jobs occurs horizontally across the organization. **Functional managers** are responsible for departments that perform specialized tasks and have employees with similar training and skills. Functional departments include advertising, sales, finance, personnel, manufacturing, electrical engineering, and accounting. Managers of functional departments usually have technical expertise in the functional area and can provide technical assistance to their subordinates.

General managers are responsible for several departments that perform different functions. A general manager is responsible for a self-

EXHIBIT 1.5

**Relationship of Conceptual, Human, and Technical Skills
to Management Level**

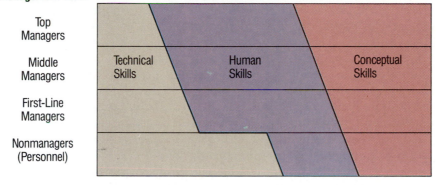

contained division, such as a Dillard's department store, and for all of the functional departments within it. **Project managers** also have general management responsibility, because they coordinate people across several departments to accomplish a specific project. Companies as diverse as consumer products and aerospace firms, for example, use project managers to coordinate across marketing, manufacturing, finance, and production when a new product—breakfast cereal, guidance system—is developed. General managers require excellent human skills because they coordinate a variety of people to attain project or division goals.

Differences in the importance of management functions for a sample of managers from five functional departments are illustrated in Exhibit 1.4. Note that long-range planning and organizing fall more heavily on personnel and accounting than on other functional managers. Supervising/leading is a greater responsibility for manufacturing, where production occurs. Controlling is a somewhat greater responsibility for accounting, manufacturing, and quality assurance than for marketing or personnel. Again, managers in each functional department perform all management functions, but to varying degrees.[18]

project manager A manager who coordinates people across several departments to accomplish a specific project.

MANAGEMENT SKILLS

A manager's job is diverse and complex and, as we shall see throughout this book, requires a range of skills. The necessary skills for planning, organizing, leading, and controlling have been placed into three categories that are especially important if managers are to perform their functions adequately: conceptual, human, and technical.[19] As illustrated in Exhibit 1.5, all managers need each skill, but the amounts differ by hierarchical level.

Conceptual Skills

conceptual skill The cognitive ability to see the organization as a whole and the relationship among its parts.

Conceptual skill is the cognitive ability to see the organization as a whole and the relationship among its parts. Conceptual skill involves the manager's thinking and planning abilities. It involves knowing where one's department fits into the total organization and how the organization fits into the industry and the community. It means the ability to think "strategically"—to take the broad, long-term view.

Conceptual skills are needed by all managers, but are especially important for managers at the top of the organization. They must perceive the significant elements in a situation and make decisions relevant to broad, conceptual patterns. For example, Frances Shane, chairman of SPM Manufacturing, a producer of photo albums and calendars, developed a multiphase strategy to reverse a loss in market share. The strategy tied together elements of cost control, more sales outlets, new manufacturing equipment, and a new company name.

Conceptual skills influence a manager's ability to make difficult decisions. When an important change in production policy is proposed, the decision maker must understand the effects on marketing, finance, and engineering. If managers moving up the hierarchy have limited conceptual skills, their promotability will be limited. A senior engineering manager who is mired in technical matters rather than thinking strategically will not perform well at the top of the organization. Many of the responsibilities of top managers, such as decision making, resource allocation, and innovation, require a broad view.

Human Skills

human skill The ability to work with and through other people and to work effectively as a group member.

Human skill is the manager's ability to work with and through other people and to work effectively as a group member. This skill is demonstrated in the way a manager relates to other people, including the ability to motivate, facilitate, coordinate, lead, communicate, get along with others, and resolve conflicts. A manager with human skills allows subordinates to express themselves without fear of ridicule and encourages participation. A manager with human skills likes other people and is liked by them. Barry Merkin, chairman of Dresher Inc., the largest U.S. manufacturer of brass beds, is a cheerleader for his employees. He visits the plant floor and uses humor and hoopla to motivate them. Employees may have buckets of fried chicken served to them by foremen wearing chef's hats.

Managers who lack human skills often are abrupt, critical, and unsympathetic toward others. Harding Lawrence of Braniff, described earlier, did not excel in human skills. Another example is the executive who walked into a subordinate's office and insisted on talking to him. When the subordinate tried to explain that he was occupied, the manager snarled, "I don't give a damn. I said I wanted to see you now."[20] Managers without human skills are insensitive and arrogant. They often make other people feel stupid and resentful.

In recent years, the awareness of human skills has increased. Books such as *In Search of Excellence, A Passion for Excellence,* and *Theory Z* all stress the need for managers to take care of the human side of the organization. Excellent companies and excellent managers do not take people for granted. For example, one study of mid-sized high-growth companies found the CEOs to be "consummate salesmen who radiate enormous contagious self confidence" and "take pains to communicate their strong sense of mission to all who come in contact with them."[21] In this new view, effective managers are cheerleaders, facilitators, coaches, and nurturers. They build through people. Managers no longer should be cops, referees, and naysayers. Effective human skills enable managers to unleash subordinates' energy and help them grow as people and future managers.

Technical Skills

Technical skill is the understanding of and proficiency in the performance of specific tasks. Technical skill includes mastery of the methods, techniques, and equipment involved in specific functions such as engineering, manufacturing, or finance. Technical skill also includes specialized knowledge, analytical ability, and the competent use of tools and techniques to solve problems in that specific discipline.

Technical skills are concrete and are most important at lower organizational levels. Many managers get promoted into their first management jobs by having excellent technical skills. However, technical skills are less important than human and conceptual skills as managers move up the hierarchy.

Making the Transition

As illustrated in Exhibit 1.5, the major difference between nonmanagers and managers is the shift from reliance on technical skills to focus on human skills. This is perhaps the most difficult transition, because high achievement in the technical area may have been the basis for promotion to a supervisory position. New managers often mistakenly continue to rely on technical skills rather than concentrate on working with others, motivating employees, and building a team. Indeed, some people fail to become managers at all because they let technical skills take precedence over human skills.

Consider Pete Martin, who has a bachelor's degree and has worked for five years as a computer programmer for an oil company. In four short years, he has more new software programs to his credit than anyone else in the department. He is highly creative and widely respected. However, Pete is impulsive and has little tolerance for those whose work is less creative. Pete does not offer to help coworkers, and they are reluctant to ask because he often "puts them down." Pete is also slow to cooperate with other departments in meeting their needs, because he works primarily to enhance his own software writing ability. He spends evenings and weekends working on his programs and analyzing new ones on the market. Pete is a hard-working technical employee, but he sees little need to worry about other people.

Pete received high merit raises but was passed over for promotion and doesn't understand why. His lack of interpersonal skills, inconsideration for coworkers, and failure to cooperate with other departments severely

technical skill The understanding of and proficiency in the performance of specific tasks.

Textron supervisor Tom Winn demonstrates exceptional human, conceptual, and technical skills by communicating in sign language to Robin Smith, who has a hearing impairment. Mr. Winn and other supervisors have learned sign language at Textron-sponsored courses so they can answer technical questions and communicate with all employees. Supervisors with these skills create an environment in which all employees can put forth their best effort. Ms. Smith was named an Employee of the Year in Huntsville, Alabama.

limit his potential as a supervisor. His human skills simply are inadequate for making the transition from worker to supervisor. Another manager, four years older but with the same experience and with fewer software programs to his credit, got the promotion. This person had the conceptual ability to spot programming weaknesses and the human skills to help others within the department and collaborate with other departments. Until Pete is ready to work on human skills, he has little chance of being promoted.

After the initial promotion to supervisory management, changes in skill requirements are more gradual. As managers move up the hierarchy, the need for technical expertise continues to diminish. The need for human skills remains strong at all levels in the hierarchy. The need for conceptual skills increases with hierarchical level, with managers having to take the broad, long-term view to succeed. Top managers must see the interrelationship among parts and make decisions with respect to the organization as a whole rather than to one task or department.

WHAT IS IT LIKE TO BE A MANAGER?

So far we have described how managers perform four basic functions that help insure that organizational resources are used to attain high levels of performance. These tasks require conceptual, human, and technical skills. Unless someone has actually performed managerial work, it is hard to understand exactly what managers do on an hour-by-hour, day-by-day basis. The manager's job is so diverse that a number of studies have been undertaken in an attempt to describe exactly what happens. The question of what managers actually do to plan, organize, lead, and control was answered by Henry Mintzberg, who followed managers around and recorded all of their activities.[22] He developed a description of managerial work that included three general characteristics and ten roles. These characteristics and roles have been supported in subsequent research.[23]

Manager Activities

One of the most interesting findings about managerial activities is how busy managers are and how hectic the average workday can be.

Managerial Activity Is Characterized by Variety, Fragmentation, and Brevity.[24] The manager's involvements are so widespread and voluminous that there is little time for quiet reflection. The average time spent on any one activity is less than nine minutes. Managers shift gears quickly. There is no continuous pattern in their work. Significant crises are interspersed with trivial events in no predictable sequence. One example of the morning activities for a typical general manager, Janet Howard, follows. Note the frequent interruptions, brevity, and variety.

7:30 a.m.	Janet arrives at work, unpacks her briefcase, and begins to plan her day.
7:37 a.m.	A subordinate, Morgan Cook, arrives and stops in Janet's office to discuss a dinner party the previous night.
7:45 a.m.	Janet's secretary, Pat, motions for Janet to pick up the telephone. "Janet, they had serious water damage at the downtown office last night. A pipe broke, causing about $50,000 damage. Everything will be back in shape in three days. Thought you should know."
8:00 a.m.	Another subordinate, Tim Birdwell, stops by. They chat about the water damage. Tim tells a joke. Tim and Morgan both leave, laughing at the story.
8:10 a.m.	Pat brings in the mail. She also asks instructions for typing a report Janet gave her yesterday.
8:30 a.m.	Janet gets a phone call from the accounting manager, who is returning a call from the day before. They talk about an accounting report.
8:45 a.m.	Janet leaves early to attend a regular 9:00 a.m. meeting in her boss's office. She tours the office area and informally chats with people before the meeting starts.
9:45 a.m.	Janet arrives back at her office, and a Mr. Nance is ushered in. Mr. Nance complains that a sales manager mistreats his employees and something must be done. Janet rearranges her schedule to investigate this claim.
10:05 a.m.	Janet begins to read the mail. One letter is from an irate customer who is unhappy with the product and feels the sales engineer was unresponsive. Janet dictates a helpful, restrained reply.
10:20 a.m.	Pat brings in phone messages. Janet makes two phone calls and receives one. She goes back to the mail and papers on her desk.
10:35 a.m.	Another subordinate stops by with a question about how to complete forms requesting a maternity leave.
10:45 a.m.	Janet receives an urgent phone call from Larry Baldwin. They go back and forth talking about lost business, unhappy subordinates, a potential promotion, and what should be done. It is a long conversation, with much exchange of both official information and gossip.[25]

Ed Gresham's job as president of Electronic Realty Associates is characterized by fragmentation, a hectic pace, and frequent communications. Mr. Gresham works 12 hours a day. These 47 telephone messages awaited him after one recent trip despite a stringent screening system that shifts as many calls as possible to others in the company. To keep up with these important communications, Mr. Gresham books daily time on his calendar for returning calls just as he would for an appointment.

The Manager Performs a Great Deal of Work at an Unrelenting Pace.[26] Managers' work is fast paced and requires great energy. The managers observed by Mintzberg processed 36 pieces of mail each day, attended 8 meetings, and took a tour through the building or plant. As

PepsiCo's chairman, Don Kendall, uses the liaison and figurehead roles to build beneficial international relationships for his company. In 1974, he presented Soviet General Secretary Leonid Brezhnev with the first bottle of Pepsi produced in the USSR (top). In 1980, Egyptian president Anwar el Sadat and Kendall dedicated a new Pepsi-Cola bottling plant. In early 1986, Kendall met with Premier Zhao Ziyang following the opening of the second Pepsi-Cola bottling plant in the People's Republic of China.

role   A set of expectations for one's behavior.

soon as a manager's daily calendar is set, unexpected disturbances erupt. New meetings are required. During time away from the office, executives catch up on work-related reading and paperwork.

Sloan Wilson, author of *The Man in the Gray Flannel Suit,* had an opportunity to work with top managers from several companies. He tried to understand how these people had become so famous, rich, and successful. They had no special advantages or influence, because each was a self-made person. Each was intelligent, but no more so than the typical graduate student.

> *So what was the secret? As I attempted to work around the clock on the many projects they undertook in addition to their real jobs, one simple answer came to me: raw energy. Super-abundant, inexhaustible energy— that was the one thing all these very successful men had.*
>
> *They were people who enthusiastically could undertake the fifth rewriting of a speech on education at three in the morning when they were up against a deadline, fly across the continent to deliver it and fly back again, working out of a briefcase on a plane all the time. And when they got to their offices, they were fresh and eager to see what their engagement calendar had to offer for the day and evening ahead. I never understood how they did it, and I was never able to keep up with them.*[27]

The Manager Establishes a Network of Information Contacts.[28]   Managers establish themselves as the center of a large information network. Personal contacts include peers in other departments, senior managers, staff experts, subordinates, and other people throughout the organization. The manager is plugged into formal information and informal gossip. Effective managers also establish personal contacts outside the organization, including suppliers, managers of other organizations, trade organizations, government officials, clients, and people in the community. Eighty percent of a manager's time is spent communicating, and most communication is by telephone and face to face rather than paperwork. Verbal communication is a continuous part of manager activities. Managers work hard to pass on relevant information to others and receive relevant information in turn.

Manager Roles

Mintzberg's observations and subsequent research indicate that diverse manager activities can be organized into ten roles.[29] A **role** is a set of expectations for a manager's behavior. The ten roles are divided into three categories: interpersonal, informational, and decisional. Each role represents activities that managers undertake to ultimately accomplish the functions of planning, organizing, leading, and controlling. The ten roles and brief examples are provided in Exhibit 1.6.

Interpersonal Roles.   Interpersonal roles pertain to relationships with others and are related to the human skills described earlier. The *figurehead* role involves the handling of ceremonial and symbolic activities for the department or organization. The manager represents the organization in his or her formal managerial capacity as the head of the unit. The presentation of awards by a division manager at Taco Bell is an example of the figurehead role. The *leader* role encompasses relationships with

E X H I B I T   1.6

Ten Manager Roles

Category	Role	Activity
Interpersonal	Figurehead	Perform ceremonial and symbolic duties such as greeting visitors, signing legal documents.
	Leader	Direct and motivate subordinates; training, counseling, and communicating with subordinates.
	Liaison	Maintain information links both inside and outside organization; use mail, phone calls, meetings.
Informational	Monitor	Seek and receive information, scan periodicals and reports, maintain personal contacts.
	Disseminator	Forward information to other organization members; send memos and reports, make phone calls.
	Spokesperson	Transmit information to outsiders through speeches, reports, memos.
Decisional	Entrepreneur	Initiate improvement projects; identify new ideas, delegate idea responsibility to others.
	Disturbance handler	Take corrective action during disputes or crises; resolve conflicts among subordinates; adapt to environmental crises.
	Resource allocator	Decide who gets resources; scheduling, budgeting, setting priorities.
	Negotiator	Represent department during negotiation of union contracts, sales, purchases, budgets; represent departmental interests.

Source: Adapted from Henry Mintzberg, *The Nature of Managerial Work* (New York: Harper & Row, 1973), pp. 92–93, and Henry Mintzberg, "Managerial Work: Analysis from Observation," *Management Science* 18 (1971), pp. B97–B110.

subordinates, including motivation, communication, and influence. The *liaison* role pertains to the development of information sources both inside and outside the organization. An example is a face-to-face discussion between a controller and plant supervisor to resolve a misunderstanding about the budget.

Informational Roles.   Informational roles describe the activities used to maintain and develop an information network. The *monitor* role involves seeking current information from many sources. The manager acquires information from others and scans written materials to stay well informed. The *disseminator* role is just the opposite: The manager transmits current information to others, both inside and outside the organization, who can use it. Managers don't hoard information; they pass it around to people who need it. The *spokesperson* role pertains to official statements to people outside the organization about company policies, actions, or plans. The announcement by top management of the name change from United States Steel to USX is an example of the spokesperson role.

Decisional Roles.   Decisional roles pertain to those events about which the manager must make a choice. These roles often require conceptual as well as human skills. The *entrepreneur* role involves the initiation of change. Managers become aware of problems and search for improvement projects that will correct them. One manager studied by Mintzberg had 50 improvement projects going simultaneously. The *disturbance handler* role involves resolving conflicts among subordinates or between the manager's department and other departments. For example, the division manager for a large furniture manufacturer got involved in a personal dispute between two section heads. One section head ultimately was let go because he didn't fit the team. The *resource allocator* role pertains to decisions about how to allocate people, time, equipment, budget, and other resources to attain desired outcomes. The manager must decide which projects receive budget allocations, which of several customer complaints receive priority, and even how to spend his or her own time. The *negotiator* role involves formal negotiations and bargaining to attain outcomes for the manager's unit of responsibility. For example, the manager meets and formally negotiates with others—a supplier about a late delivery, the controller about the need for additional budget resources, or the union about a worker grievance. These formal negotiations are in addition to the many informal and information-sharing conversations in which the manager engages during the normal workday.

Research into manager behavior indicates that all managers perform these ten roles to some extent. The leader role is the most demanding at lower levels, which is consistent with the research on the function of leading.[30] The entrepreneur and disturbance handler roles tend to be equally demanding at all levels of the hierarchy. The figurehead, liaison, monitor, disseminator, spokesperson, resource allocator, and negotiator roles receive greater emphasis at the higher levels of the hierarchy.

LEARNING MANAGEMENT SKILLS

One final question: How do you learn to be a manager? Or, more specifically, does a course in management or a college degree in business help a person to become a manager?

Management is both an art and a science. It is an art because many skills cannot be learned from a textbook. Management takes practice, just like golf, tennis, or volleyball. Studying a book helps, but that's not enough. Many skills, especially the human and, to some extent, the conceptual skills, and roles, such as leader, spokesperson, disturbance handler, and negotiator, take practice. These skills are learned through experience.

Management is also a science because a growing body of knowledge and objective facts describes management and how to attain organizational performance. The knowledge is acquired through systematic research and can be conveyed through teaching and textbooks. Systematic knowledge about planning, organizing, and control system design, for example, helps managers understand the skills they need, the types of roles they must perform, and the techniques needed to manage organizations. Harding Lawrence of Braniff relied solely on his experience and intuition, and he made grave mistakes.

Becoming a successful manager requires a blend of formal learning and practice, of science and art. Practice alone used to be enough to learn how to manage, but no longer. Formal coursework in management can help a manager become more competent and more influential. The study of management enables people to see and understand things about organizations that others cannot. Training that helps one acquire the conceptual, human, and technical skills necessary for management will be a management asset.

AT&T Study

One of the most interesting studies about college training and manager success was conducted by the Human Resources Studies Group of AT&T.[31] This research included two samples of managers studied over many years. The first sample was selected in 1956 and included 422 managers; the second was chosen in 1977 and included 344 managers. The study was designed to determine how five types of college characteristics—education level, grades, quality of undergraduate institution, major field of study, and extracurricular activities—influenced the management level reached by employees 4, 8, and 10 years after employment. The findings were as follows.

Major Field of Study.   Undergraduate major was the strongest predictor of managerial performance and progress. Humanities and social science majors had the best overall records. Their strengths were human and conceptual skills and the motivation to advance. Business majors were a strong second, having sound skills and motivation. Engineering, math, and science majors had strong technical skills but generally were weak in other areas, especially human skills.

Extracurricular Activities.   Extracurricular activities were the second best predictor of managerial performance. Both the sheer number of activities and leadership role in those activities were important. Extracurricular activities were related to better administrative and interpersonal skills.

Level of Education.   Education level also was important. College graduates were more successful than non-college graduates. College graduates had somewhat greater ability and motivation and also were somewhat favored for advancement. People with master's degrees generally were promoted further and faster than were those with bachelor's degrees. Master's-degree people seemed to be bright and motivated, and people with non-business master's degrees had excellent human relations skills.

Grades.   Grades were not related to managerial performance and progress. They were a useful indicator of intellectual ability and of people's high standards for their own work, but they did not predict other manager characteristics or promotion success.

College Quality.   In the initial study, college quality seemed to make a positive difference, but in the second sample it was no longer a sign of manager potential. Attending high-quality schools seemed almost a detriment, because these graduates had motivational and personality characteristics that were not always favorable for managers. College quality was negatively related to primacy of work and career expectations. Graduates from elite universities had less respect for authority and identified less with their organizations. Graduates from colleges of medium quality were more interested in their organizations, displayed less cynicism, and had positive attitudes toward work.

The important conclusion is that preparation in business and social sciences, which includes development of conceptual and human skills, was a positive factor for a management career at AT&T. Although formal training at the university level was of great benefit, it was not everything. Managers who are willing to practice and learn the skill of management also can succeed. The advantage of formal management training is that managers can learn to diagnose their situations and analyze and interpret what is happening around them. Formal study of management helps explain why Lee Iacocca, Mayor Schaefer, Kelly Johnson, and General Creech were excellent managers. But these skills are not learned automatically. The failure to acquire and use management skills explains why Harding Lawrence—and Braniff—failed. Organizations are only as strong as their managers, and a course in management helps provide the tools with which to make Braniff, the city of Baltimore, or the U.S. Air Force more effective.

Management Success and Failure

Another study indicating the importance of acquiring management skills was conducted by the Center for Creative Leadership in Greensboro, North Carolina.[32] This study compared 21 derailed executives with 20 executives who had arrived at the top of the company. The derailed executives were successful people who had been expected to go far but reached a plateau, were fired, or were forced to retire early. These managers were similar in many ways. They were bright and excelled in a technical area such as accounting or engineering. They worked hard, made sacrifices in order to achieve, and established good track records.

Those who arrived at the top, however, had more diverse track records—they didn't rely on a single functional skill. Moreover, they had excellent interpersonal skills. They maintained composure under stress, were able to laugh at themselves, and handled mistakes with poise and grace. They also were conceptually strong and could focus on problems and solve them.

In the managers who had derailed, the single biggest flaw was insensitivity to others. Often this characteristic was associated with other negative personal qualities, such as abrasiveness, aloofness, and arrogance. These managers also failed to display conceptual skills and were unable to think strategically, that is, take a broad, long-term view. One manager was a superb engineer who had advanced rapidly in the early years but

In 1983 Mr. Soichiro Honda visited the United States. He shook hands with the entire 800-member staff at Honda's Gardena plant. As part of the leader role, Mr. Honda reiterated his expectations that manager and company success depends on the positive treatment of employees. Every Honda employee is respected as both an individual and an integral part of a team working toward a common goal. Known as "the Honda way," this philosophy is infused throughout American Honda, a subsidiary of Honda Motor Company Ltd. Mr. Honda demonstrates the people orientation that has made his company so successful.

could go no further. He tended to analyze problems to death and get bogged down in the details. The successful managers were superb negotiators and could confront people and problems without offending anyone. They didn't blame things on others, and if they made a mistake, they didn't dwell on it and kept their sense of humor. Because they readily took responsibility for mistakes, their errors were never fatal.

The ability to deal with others was the most striking difference between the two groups. Only 25 percent of the derailed group were described as having good ability with people, whereas 75 percent of those who had arrived at the top did. Also, some of them had been able to change. One manager had been cold and arrogant and, once he realized these limits to his career, changed almost overnight. He made a genuine effort to develop better human skills—and succeeded.

PLAN OF THE BOOK

We have defined the four primary management functions, key management roles and activities, and the importance of managers to organizational performance. The organization takes in resources from the external environment and transforms them into product and service outputs. The management functions are designed to insure that the organization system works in an effective and efficient way to yield high performance.

The relationship among management functions, organizational resources, and outcomes is illustrated in Exhibit 1.7. The four management functions occur within the organization and provide the mechanisms for transforming inputs into outputs. The framework in Exhibit 1.7 also provides a model for this book. Part One (Chapters 1 through 3) provides an overview of organizations and management. Chapter 3 concerns the environment and its relationship with the organization in obtaining resources and achieving appropriate outputs. Part Two (Chapters 4 through 7) covers planning—how managers define goals, develop strategies and action plans for the organization, and select techniques for making planning decisions. Part Three (Chapters 8 through 11) focuses on organizing, including the fundamentals of organization structure, design alternatives, structuring for innovation, and staffing the organization structure. Part Four (Chapters 12 through 16) is about the leading function; topics covered here are leadership, motivation, communication, managing groups, and managing corporate culture. Part Five (Chapters 17 through 20) examines the topic of control: basic control principles, internal control systems, operations management, and management information systems. Part Six (Chapters 21 and 22) examines recently emerging management issues of multinational management and management as a career.

The book is organized according to the four management functions of planning, organizing, leading, and controlling and describes management techniques and skills for performing them. These functions are the basis for management success and are why some managers get to the top while others derail.

E X H I B I T   1.7

A Dynamic Model of Management

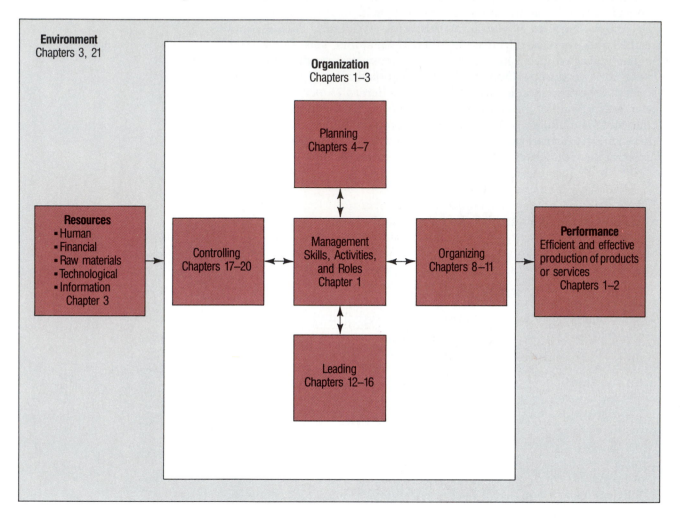

SUMMARY

This chapter introduced a number of important concepts about the nature of management. High performance requires the efficient and effective use of organizational resources through the four management functions of planning, organizing, leading, and controlling. Their importance differs somewhat by hierarchical level and by department. Top and middle managers are most concerned with planning and place greater emphasis on organizing and controlling. First-line managers focus more on leading. In order to perform the four primary functions, managers need three skills—conceptual, human, and technical. Conceptual skills are more important at the top of the hierarchy; human skills are important at all levels; and technical skills are most important for first-line managers.

Three characteristics of managerial work were explained: (1) Managerial activities involve variety, fragmentation, and brevity; (2) managers perform a great deal of work at an unrelenting pace; and (3) managers establish networks of information contacts. Managers also are expected to perform activities associated with ten roles: the interpersonal roles of figurehead, leader, and liaison; the informational roles of monitor, disseminator, and spokesperson; and the decisional roles of entrepreneur, disturbance handler, resource allocator, and negotiator. Learning these roles and the skills required for management can be accomplished through both formal training and experience. The AT&T research indicated that major field of study, participation in extracurricular activities, and level of education were more important than grades or college quality in predicting manager success. The study of manager success and failure by the Center for Creative Leadership found that the biggest single reason for manager derailment was the inability to deal with people. Managers who succeeded had excellent people skills.

Management Solution

Edward Esber, only 33 years old, took over Ashton-Tate, a $140 million software maker that was in disarray. He wanted to inject the company with massive doses of "Management 101." In a nutshell, he improved the planning, organizing, leading, and controlling at Ashton-Tate. He planned a new strategy that broadened the product line to make the company a one-stop "supermarket" for software. Ashton-Tate created new software programs and acquired ANSA Software, which made a compatible product line. The new line strengthened Ashton-Tate's market appeal. In the area of organizing, Esber instituted important procedures, such as formalized task forces for product development. In his leadership capacity, he created a participative approach for employees that increased motivation and reduced turnover. He evidenced control through the increased use of budgets, monthly reports, and rewards for employees who did well. This young, unknown manager understood what needed to be done and did it. Performance was his reality. Profits climbed 146 percent, and today analysts consider Ashton-Tate one of the big surprises in the industry.[33]

DISCUSSION QUESTIONS

1. What similarities do you see among the four management functions of planning, organizing, leading, and controlling? Do you think these functions are related—that is, is a manager who

performs well in one function likely to perform well in the others?

2. Why did a top manager like Harding Lawrence at Braniff fail while a top manager like General Creech of Tactical Air Command succeed? Which of the four management functions best explains this difference? Discuss.

3. What is the difference between efficiency and effectiveness? Which is more important for performance? Can an organization succeed in both simultaneously?

4. What changes in management functions and skills occur as one is promoted from a nonmanagement to a management position and then progresses up the hierarchy? How can managers acquire the new skills?

5. If managerial work is characterized by variety, fragmentation, and brevity, how do managers perform basic management functions such as planning, which would seem to require reflection and analysis?

6. A college professor told her students, "The purpose of a management course is to teach students *about* management, not to teach them to be managers." Do you agree or disagree with this statement? Discuss.

7. How do you interpret the AT&T findings that grades and college quality were less important for manager success than field of study and extracurricular activities? Do you think these findings apply to managers in all organizations?

8. What does it mean to say that management is both an art and a science? Discuss.

9. In the Center for Creative Leadership study, many managers made it to the middle and upper levels of the organization before derailing. How do you think managers got so far if they had flaws that prevented them from reaching the top?

10. Think back to a work situation where you had an excellent supervisor and one where you had a poor supervisor. What skills—conceptual, human, technical—accounted for the supervisors' differences?

CASES FOR ANALYSIS

BETHLEHEM STEEL CORPORATION

Bethlehem Steel, like all steel companies, has had tough times during the 1980s. In 1986 at an executive retreat, several frustrated middle managers claimed that repeated pay cuts had undercut morale. The president, Donald Trautlein, didn't care. He said that was their problem, not his. Executives left the meeting disillusioned. Now Trautlein is leaving Bethlehem's top position under pressure.

Trautlein had gotten the top job because of his financial expertise, which the board of directors believed could help turn the company around. Trautlein's financial expertise did prove valuable for arranging creative financing of Bethlehem's debt, but it didn't solve Bethlehem's deeper problems. Tough conditions in the steel industry required excellent top management, and there is some question about whether Trautlein provided it.

Trautlein basically was a numbers man; he rarely talked shop with either customers or steelworkers. Middle managers were alienated when Trautlein and a few top lieutenants received generous salary increases while other managers had their salaries decreased. Trautlein disrupted the company's emphasis on slow, steady advancement by forcing out several key executives. He seemed to lack personal charisma, and he did not know the steel business. Planning was difficult for him. At one point he wanted to keep the business in steel, and at other times he wanted to diversify. He failed to target a few promising niches on which to concentrate. When Trautlein finally made a diversification move in 1985, the company could barely afford it.

Trautlein attempted some reorganization, but that didn't help either. Bethlehem's firmly entrenched centralized structure was divided into autonomous business units, an approach that had worked at General Electric. Each plant manager became a general manager responsible for everything—labor relations, accounting, and even advertising. The idea seemed good, but it was implemented quickly and had no chance to take hold.

Internal strife increased as blue- and white-collar workers all blamed Trautlein for mounting losses. He periodically issued memos exhorting employees to increase productivity. He never was comfortable dealing with employees face to face or trying to define a broad-based strategy for the corporation.

Questions

1. Of the four management functions—planning, organizing, leading, and controlling—which did Donald Trautlein perform best? Worst?
2. If you were asked to advise Trautlein on which skills to improve, what would you say?
3. Do you see any similarities between Trautlein's approach to management and Harding Lawrence's described in the text?

Source: Based on J. Ernest Beazley and Carol Hymowitz, "Critics Fault Trautlein for Failure to Revive an Ailing Bethlehem," *The Wall Street Journal,* May 27, 1986, 1, 18.

PRO LINE COMPANY

It was almost 6 p.m. and Sally Benson was still at her desk trying to tie up some loose ends with the hope that tomorrow might be a more productive day.

Sally is the western regional sales director, a middle management position, in the Pro Line Company, a manufacturer of a well-known line of sporting goods. As she reads the mail she still has to answer and stacks the phone messages she still has to return, she wonders if being a middle manager is really her kind of job. Selling products, traveling, and meeting with clients seemed much more to her liking than the routine of her present job.

Take today, for example. Sally had come to the office early so she could call Ted Lomax, the eastern regional sales director, to confer on a joint sales forecast they are trying to prepare. Working with Ted isn't the easiest of tasks. Compromise just isn't a word in Ted's vocabulary. She also needs to call the production managers of two of the company's eastern plants to find out what is causing the delay in the receipt of the new product lines. Those production people don't seem to realize that a large inventory is needed to keep sales up. The new product lines were promised two weeks ago and still aren't here. The phone calls took longer than expected, but by mid-morning Sally is finally able to get settled into the major project she has planned for the day. After several days of perusing sales reports of the past several years, she concluded that total sales, as well as productivity of individual salespersons, can be improved if the region is redesigned and the territories of each salesperson adjusted. This is a major project and she needs to have a preliminary proposal ready to present to her district sales managers at her monthly meeting tomorrow afternoon.

Lunch keeps Sally away from the office a little longer than expected and when she returns she finds a half dozen phone messages, including an urgent call from the corporate vice president of personnel, Bill Finley. She returns Finley's call and much to her dismay, she finds she is going to have to allocate a good portion of tomorrow's sales managers' meeting to presenting the company's new benefits program. Bill assured her all the materials she needs will arrive late this afternoon and stressed the need for its immediate dissemination and explanation. After trying unsuccessfully to return several of the other phone calls, she returns to the territory redesign project. She finishes that project just before the 3 p.m. appointment she has with a candidate for a district sales manager position that will open up next week. Sally spends over an hour with the candidate and is impressed enough with him to immediately make some follow-up phone calls to validate the accuracy of some of the information she received.

When 5 p.m. arrives, Sally realizes she won't have much luck with further phone calls. The whole day seems to have gotten away from her, and she still has the materials from Finley to review and she has to prepare the agenda for tomorrow's meeting. She just has to figure a way to motivate better performance from those sales managers. The redesign of the territory was only a partial solution. Sally wonders what else she can do.

Questions

1. Compare Sally's present job to what you think her previous job as a salesperson might have been. How are they similar? How are they different?
2. What major manager roles are depicted in this case?
3. Why do you think Sally might be disenchanted with her present job?

Source: "A Day in the Life of a Middle Manager—Sally Benson," *The Managerial Experience: Cases, Exercises, and Readings,* 4th ed, 24–25, by Lawrence Jauch, Sally A. Coltrin, Arthur G. Bedeian, and William F. Glueck. Copyright © 1983 by CBS College Publishing. Copyright © 1986 by CBS College Publishing. Reprinted by permission of Holt, Rinehart & Winston, Inc.

CHAPTER 2

Foundations of Management Understanding

Chapter Outline

Historical Forces Shaping Management

Social Forces
Political Forces
Economic Forces

Early Management

Ancient Management
Medieval Management

Classical Perspective

Forerunners
Scientific Management
Administrative Principles
Bureaucratic Organizations

Human Resource Perspective

Forerunners
The Hawthorne Studies
The Human Relations Movement
Behavioral Sciences Approach

Management Science Perspective

Contemporary Extensions

Systems Theory
Contingency Views

Recent Historical Trends

Japanese Management
Achieving Excellence

Learning Objectives

After studying this chapter, you should be able to:

- Understand how historical forces in society have influenced the practice of management.

- Identify and explain major developments in the history of management thought.

- Describe the major components of the classical management perspective.

- Describe the major components of the human resource management perspective.

- Discuss the quantitative management perspective.

- Explain the major components of systems theory.

- Discuss the basic concepts underlying contingency views.

- Describe the most recent influences on management in North America.

Management Problem

With drive-in theaters closing and the cost of making movies escalating, would you risk your savings to finance low-budget films? Two Los Angeles lawyers, Lawrence Kuppin and Harry Evans Sloan, bought New World Pictures in 1983 specifically to make B movies. The movie industry is noted for turning out big-budget losers in pursuit of a single smash hit. Moreover, three large competing B-movie companies—Filmways, Avco Embassy, and American International Pictures—have abandoned low-budget films for classier, big-budget productions. New World will make films for an average of $2 million to $4 million, compared to an average of $15 million for a Hollywood film. New World got off to a rocky start, losing almost $5 million in 1983. Investment analysts were wary, believing there was little future for schlock movies. Kuppin and Sloan bet $2 million of their own money plus money borrowed from private investors in the belief they could profit by fighting the trend toward big-budget films.[1]

Do you think Kuppin and Sloan made a wise investment by going into the B-movie business? What historical forces will influence the success or failure of this venture?

Why should history matter to corporate managers? Kuppin and Sloan bought New World Pictures because they were betting on the historical success of B movies, which have had a following since the 1940s. A historical perspective matters to executives because it is a way of thinking, a way of searching for patterns and determining whether they recur across time periods. A historical perspective provides a context or environment in which to interpret problems. Only then does a major problem take on

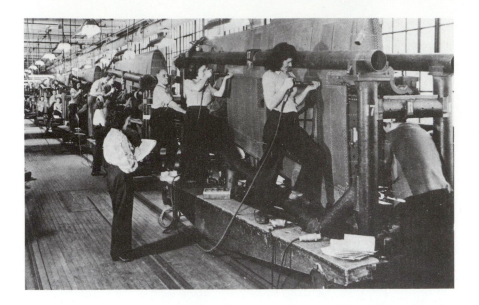

The woman worker celebrated as "Rosie the Riveter" was vital to the war effort during the early 1940s. Prior to World War II, women were not widely accepted in the work force. In this photo, women work alongside men on a Curtiss Helldiver assembly line. Women like these, who entered the work force during the war, started a major historical trend that has persisted until today, when stay-at-home spouses are a small minority. North American businesses and even the military have adapted to this trend by hiring women to perform many jobs.

real meaning, reveal its severity, and point the way toward management actions.[2]

A study of the past contributes to understanding both the present and the future. It is a way of learning: learning from others' mistakes so as not to repeat them; learning from others' successes so as to repeat them in the appropriate situation; and, most of all, learning to understand why things happen to improve things in the future.

For example, an organization faces certain basic changes when it moves from a start-up phase to a rapid growth phase and, finally, into a mature business. Based on the historical development of organizations, specific management techniques are required at each stage. If a manager knows no history, he or she will be unprepared for what is demanded at each new stage of organizational growth. Indeed, the first U.S. business organizations to confront the problem of large size were the railroads during the 1850s. At that time, a small family business could supervise a railroad of only 50 miles in length. The owners had to learn how to develop a structure suitable for a larger railroad and borrowed ideas from the line and staff structures of the military. Since that time, literally thousands of companies have confronted the same problems as they grew and matured. Managers need not reinvent the wheel every time. Companies like Microsoft, Ogilvy & Mather, Ztel Inc., AeroVironment Inc., and People Express have all experienced the need to change management procedures to cope with a new growth stage. When People Express got into trouble by clinging to informal management techniques despite its large size, its managers made a serious mistake by assuming historical trends did not apply to People. It's all a matter of history.

The purpose of this chapter is to provide an overview of the social, political, and economic forces that affect organizations and to examine how the managers' philosophies have changed over the years. This foundation of management understanding illustrates that the value of studying management lies not in learning current facts and research but in developing a perspective that will facilitate the broad, long-term view needed for management success.

HISTORICAL FORCES SHAPING MANAGEMENT

Studying history does not mean merely arranging events in chronological order; it means developing an understanding of the impact of societal forces on organizations. Studying history is a way to achieve strategic thinking, see the big picture, and improve conceptual skills. We will start by examining how social, political, and economic forces have influenced organizations and the practice of management.[3]

Social Forces

Social forces refer to those aspects of a culture that guide and influence relationships among people. What do people value? What do people need? What are the standards of behavior among people? These forces shape what is known as the *social contract*, which comes into play in the human affairs of any culture. The social contract refers to the unwritten, common rules and perceptions about relationships among people and between people and organizations. Expressions such as "a man's as good as his word" and "a day's work for a day's pay" convey the notion of such perceptions.

social forces The aspects of a culture that guide and influence relationships among people—their values, needs, and standards of behavior.

Social forces provide the basis for social trust based on the values that the society holds in high regard. For example, managers who deal with workers and unions need to know about the General Motors Flint strike in Michigan from 1936 to 1937. This strike has been celebrated and commemorated by unions, which keep the memory of that strike and its values alive. Managers should deal with unions by understanding the heritage of disrespect between unions and management and not assume that people across the bargaining table are responding only on the basis of current wage demands.

Political Forces

Political forces refer to the influence of political institutions on people and organizations. Political forces include basic assumptions underlying the political system, such as the desirability of self-government, property rights, contract rights, the definition of justice, and the determination of innocence or guilt of a crime. Further, political forces determine managers' rights relative to those of owners, customers, suppliers, and workers as well as other publics with whom the organization must interact.

political forces The influence of political institutions on people and organizations.

Consider government deregulation in the telecommunications, banking, and transportation industries. Deregulation is a political force that influences the way of doing business in these industries. Managers can understand deregulation by studying the regulations' original impact on corporations and how the new regulations changed the market.

Lewis Hine's famous 1911 "breaker boys" photograph helped promote passage of laws forbidding child labor. These youths were employed in Pittston, Pennsylvania, to pick slate impurities from coal before it was sent to market. Public attitudes became a strong social force against child labor. Political forces prompted Congress to outlaw the employment of children. Economic forces affected the allocation of resources to materials-handling machinery, which reduced the need for children to do this menial task.

economic forces   Forces that affect the availability, production, and distribution of a society's resources among competing users.

Economic Forces

Economic forces pertain to the availability, production, and distribution of resources in a society. Governments, military agencies, churches, schools, and business organizations in every society require resources in order to achieve their objectives, and economic forces influence the allocation of scarce resources. Resources may be human or material, manmade or natural, physical or conceptual, but over time they are scarce and must be allocated among competing users. Economic scarcity is often the stimulus for technological innovation with which to increase resource availability. The perfection of the moving assembly line at Ford in 1913 cut the number of man-hours needed for assembling a Model T from 12 to 1.5. Ford doubled its daily pay rate to $5, shortened working hours, and cut the price of Model Ts until its market share reached 57 percent in 1923.

Every society has mechanisms for allocating scarce economic resources. These include tradition, command, and market.[4] In the *tradition method,* resources are allocated the way they were in the past. In the *command method,* a central agency makes economic decisions that are imposed on the rest of the economy. In the *market method,* economic decisions are decentralized to people and organizations. Most modern societies display a mixture of the three methods of allocating scarce resources. Tradition is behind our doing something "because we have always done it that way." Central agencies direct resources to school systems and local governments. Market forces are at work when organizations freely buy and sell goods and services, sign contracts, and negotiate wages with workers.

E X H I B I T   2.1

The Early Practice of Management

Time Period	Group	Approach
3000–2400 B.C.	Sumerians	Developed written records (cuneiform writing on clay tablets) to assist them; the written laws of the Akkadian ruler, Ur-Nammu, are the oldest in history.
3000–1000 B.C.	Egyptians	Developed the first national government and extensive civilization; built massive buildings and monuments.
2700–500 B.C.	Babylonians	The Code of Hammurabi, an Amorite ruler, developed the oldest, most complete set of laws.
1000–200 B.C.	Greeks	Developed strong form of local government, the *polis*, or city-state; later introduced constitutional democracy.
800 B.C.–500 A.D.	Romans	The Senate advised *consuls* in the Roman Republic and the emperor in the Roman Empire.
1500 B.C.–1300 A.D.	Chinese	Developed extremely capable governments; established a culturally rich civilization emphasizing both art and science.
450–1500 A.D.	Venetians	Center of commercial sea power during the 1400s; developed laws regarding the conduct of commerce.

EARLY MANAGEMENT

The practice of management is as old as civilization itself. The existence of organizations—and, hence, the need for management—perhaps is what distinguishes a civilized from an uncivilized society. The writings from ancient civilizations contain references to events, rules, and regulations that reflect the practice of management. Ancient groups and highlights of their management approaches are summarized in Exhibit 2.1.

Ancient Management

The first known written records suggesting the practice of management are those of the Sumerians, a people who settled along the lowermost section of the Euphrates River.[5] They developed a complex system of commerce, a system of weights and measures for conducting it, and a postal system. The achievements of the ancient Egyptians are perhaps better known. The Egyptians developed the first national government organization and an extensive civilization.[6] And, of course, management must have been involved in the construction of the massive mastaba (tomb) of Imhotep as well as that of the later pyramids.

The Babylonians (Mesopotamians whose ruler's central power was the city of Babel) also developed a common culture and a central govern-

The Laws of Hammurabi are engraved on a shaft of stone nearly 8 feet high. They extend around the entire shaft, occupying over 3,600 lines. King Hammurabi's great contribution was to bring order and system where before there had been confusion. Thus regulated, Babylonia prospered. Merchandising was the chief occupation, and merchants traded across several nations. Early managers were involved in this trade and commerce. Business was even conducted in the temples, which were banking and trading centers.

ment. Its period of greatest glory began with the reign of Hammurabi. His written code of law, the Code of Hammurabi, was carved into an 8-foot-high pillar of hard rock and has survived almost intact. The code regulated trade, profits, and hiring practices for businesses. It specified contract and property rights and attempted to guard against business fraud.

Commerce thrived during this period, and merchants faced many of the same problems collecting past-due bills that they do today. Consider the following letter from Mesopotamia:

> *Thirty years ago you left the city of Assur. You have never made a deposit since, and we have not recovered one shekel of silver from you, but we have never made you feel bad about this. Our tablets have been going to you with caravan after caravan, but no report from you has ever come here. We have addressed claims to your father but we have not been claiming one shekel of your private silver. Please, do come back right away; should you be too busy with your business, deposit the silver for us. We have never made you feel bad about this matter but we are now forced to appear, in your eyes, acting as gentlemen should not. Please, do come back right away or deposit the silver for us.*
>
> *If not, we will send you a notice from the local ruler and the police, and thus put you to shame in the assembly of the merchants. You will also cease to be one of us.[7]*

The ancient Greeks developed a strong form of local government—the *polis*, or city-state—and later introduced the concept of constitutional democracy that underlies the system of government of the United States and many other modern nations. The Romans made many contributions to government as well. The Senate was devised in the Roman Republic to advise the *consuls*. Later, in the Roman Empire, the Senate continued as an advisory group to the emperor, similar to staff advisors in today's organizations. The Chinese also are notable for their contributions to the practice of management. They developed extremely capable government organizations.[8] Their respect for scholarship led to the use of written testing for positions in government organizations, a practice still used in all types of modern organizations.

Medieval Management

Next we come to the medieval period and the influence of the Italians, specifically the Venetians. Venice emerged as a center of commercial sea power during the 1400s and developed extensive laws regarding the conduct of commerce. Bankers in Venice and other major Italian cities were using double-entry accounting that was described in print in 1494.[9] It was just after this time that an out-of-office administrator from Florence wrote a small book describing how to rule successfully; today Machiavelli's *The Prince* is a widely read and much criticized work on management.[10] Machiavelli's ideas flow logically from his assumption that man is bad by nature and that manipulative, deceitful management practices are preferable to those based on morality. This assumption has arisen and been countered repeatedly over the history of management thought.

The Catholic Church dominated medieval life in the West and had great impact on the evolution of management thought. As Christianity spread, the Church faced a growing need for consistency of doctrine and control over membership and religious practices. The Church developed an organizational structure and management practices that permitted rapid growth and large size while achieving standardization and control. One management concept developed in the Catholic Church was **compulsory staff service,** which means that managers must consult with subordinates on important issues. The general concept of participative decision making has been adopted by many business and government organizations for important decisions.

In recent years, the study of management in Europe and North America and the desire of both managers and scholars to develop theories and frameworks for understanding management have led to several distinct perspectives on management. Because elements of each perspective pervade management thinking today, present and future managers should be familiar with the basic concepts of each. The major viewpoints are the classical perspective, the human resource perspective, and the management science perspective, discussed in the following sections.

*Niccolo Machiavelli
(1469–1527)
The Florentine statesman's treatise on ruling,* The Prince, *is considered a management classic today. Machiavelli's assumptions of man's evil nature and tendency toward immoral management practices are still widely read and debated in management circles.*

CLASSICAL PERSPECTIVE

The **classical perspective** on management emerged during the nineteenth and early twentieth centuries. It was grounded in management experiences from manufacturing, transportation, and communication industries, which were heavily staffed by engineers. Firms tended to be small or composed of departments or divisions consisting of small groups. Most organizations produced only one line of product or service. Further, major educational, social, and cultural differences existed among owners, managers, and workers.

Forerunners

The factory system that began to appear in the 1800s posed managerial problems that earlier organizations had not encountered. Large numbers of workers were needed, and machines began performing skilled operations. Managers had to cope with large organization size, retrain workers, and schedule complex manufacturing operations. Managers who solved these problems developed the ideas that were the forerunners of modern management thinking.[11] For example, Charles Babbage (1792–1871) developed a mechanical computer and wrote a successful book on the management of manufacturing organizations.[12] Daniel McCallum (1815–1878), who worked for American railroads, developed management and organization principles during the 1850s and pioneered the systematic study of management. Henry Poor (1812–1905), as editor of the *American Railroad Journal,* became "the conscience of America's first large business."[13]

compulsory staff service A management concept developed in the Catholic Church that required managers to consult with subordinates on important issues.

classical perspective A management perspective that emerged during the nineteenth and early twentieth centuries that emphasized a rational, scientific approach to the study of management and sought to make organizations efficient operating machines.

E X H I B I T   2.2

The Classical Management Perspective

General Approach
- Assumed rationality and sought to improve individual productivity on the further assumption that the effectiveness of the whole organization equals the sum of its parts.
- Strove to make organizations efficient operating machines.

Subfields
- Scientific management, which focused on employees.
- Administrative principles, which focused on internal processes.
- Bureaucratic organizations, which focused on the structure of the organization itself.

Contributions
- Was the formal beginning of the study of management.
- Identified many of the key processes, functions, and skills of management.
- Emphasized a rational, scientific approach to the study of management.

Criticisms
- Relied heavily on self-interest concept of rationality.
- Failed to recognize environmental influences.
- Tended to view workers as tools and as different from managers.

Frederick Winslow Taylor (1856–1915)
Taylor's theory that labor productivity could be improved by scientifically determined management practices earned him the status of "father of scientific management."

scientific management A subfield of the classical management perspective that emphasized scientifically determined changes in management practices as the solution to improving labor productivity.

The work of these forerunners gave rise to the classical perspective, which is summarized in Exhibit 2.2. The thrust of the classical perspective was to make organizations efficient operating machines. Its contribution was the systematic study of management; its weaknesses were its simplistic assumptions about workers and the external environment. This perspective contained three subfields, each with a slightly different emphasis: scientific management, administrative principles, and bureaucratic organizations.

Scientific Management

The early pioneers' somewhat limited success in achieving improvements in labor productivity led a young engineer to suggest that the problem lay more in poor management practices than in labor. Frederick Winslow Taylor (1856–1915) insisted that management itself would have to change and, further, that the manner of change could be determined only by scientific study; hence, the label **scientific management** emerged. Taylor suggested that decisions based on rules of thumb and tradition be replaced with precise procedures developed after careful study of individual situations.

While working at the Midvale Steel Company in Philadelphia, Taylor began experimenting with management methods, procedures, and practices. The American Society of Mechanical Engineers (ASME) was founded in 1880 and, at a few of its meetings, members presented papers dealing with management issues. In 1886, Taylor joined ASME and was strongly influenced by a paper presented that year by the president of Yale and Towne Manufacturing Company entitled "The Engineer as an Economist."[14]

Taylor wrote frequently, had others write under his name, and consulted with businesses to encourage utilization of his ideas.[15] However, it was after the Eastern Railroad Rate Case hearings before the House of Representatives that his work really caught on. The attorney for the shippers, Louis D. Brandeis, used the term "scientific management" and successfully argued the shippers' side of the issue for using these techniques. The popular press picked up the term, and Taylor and his ideas became heralded as the way to prosperity for the United States.[16]

Although known as the "father of scientific management," Taylor was not alone in this area. Numerous colleagues gave momentum to these ideas. Carl Barth (1860–1939) worked with Taylor and applied his ideas in consulting. Henry Gantt (1861–1919), who worked with Taylor at Midvale Steel, later developed the use of graphic techniques in scheduling and recording performance. Harrington Emerson (1853–1931) provided key testimony in the Eastern Rate hearings, asserting that the railroads could save millions of dollars by using scientific management.[17] Morris Cooke (1872–1960) developed and applied scientific management ideas in the public sector.

Two other important pioneers in this area were the husband-and-wife team of Frank B. and Lillian M. Gilbreth. Frank B. Gilbreth (1868–1924) pioneered time and motion study and arrived at many of his management techniques independently of Taylor. He stressed efficiency and was known for his quest for the "one best way" to do work. While he is known for his early work with bricklayers, his work had great impact on medical surgery by drastically reducing the time patients spent on the operating table. Surgeons were able to save countless lives through the application of time and motion study. Lillian M. Gilbreth (1878–1972) was more interested in the human aspect of work. When her husband died at the age of 46, she had 12 children ages 2 to 19. The undaunted "first lady of management" went right on with her work. She presented a paper in place of her late husband, continued their seminars and consulting, lectured, and eventually became a professor at Purdue University.[18] She pioneered in the field of industrial psychology and made substantial contributions to personnel management.

The basic ideas of scientific management are shown in Exhibit 2.3. They include the following:

1. Managers should develop standard methods for doing each job in the organization.
2. Managers should select workers with the appropriate abilities for each job.
3. Managers should train those workers in the standard methods.
4. Managers should support those workers by planning their work and eliminating interruptions.

While scientific management improved productivity, its failure to deal with the social context and workers' needs led to increased conflict between managers and employees. This was in sharp contrast to the harmony and cooperation that Taylor and his followers had envisioned.

Lillian M. Gilbreth (1878–1972) and Frank B. Gilbreth (1868–1924)
This husband-and-wife team contributed to the principles of scientific management. His development of time and motion studies and her work in industrial psychology pioneered many of today's management and human resource techniques.

EXHIBIT 2.3

Characteristics of Scientific Management

General Approach
- Developed standard method for performing each job.
- Selected workers with appropriate abilities for each job.
- Trained workers in standard method.
- Supported workers by planning their work and eliminating interruptions.

Subfields
- Time study.
- Motion study.
- Work study.
- Operations research.
- Industrial engineering.

Contributions
- Demonstrated the importance of compensation for performance.
- Initiated the careful study of tasks and jobs.
- Demonstrated the importance of personnel selection and training.

Criticisms
- Did not appreciate the social context of work and higher needs of workers.
- Did not acknowledge variance among individuals.
- Tended to regard workers as uninformed and ignored their ideas and suggestions.

*Mary Parker Follett
(1868–1933)
Follett was a major contributor to the
administrative principles approach to
management. Her emphasis on shared
goals among managers was embraced by
many businesspeople of her day.*

Administrative Principles

The second major subfield within the classical perspective is known as the **administrative principles** approach. Whereas scientific management focused on the productivity of the individual worker, the administrative principles approach focused on the total organization. The contributors to this approach included Henri Fayol, Mary Parker Follett, and Chester I. Barnard.

Henri Fayol (1841–1925) was a French mining engineer who worked his way up to the head of a major mining group known as Comambault. Comambault survives today as part of Le Creusot-Loire, the largest mining and metallurgical group in central France.[19] In his later years Fayol, based largely on his own management experiences, wrote down his concepts on administration.[20]

In his most significant work, *General and Industrial Management*, Fayol discussed 14 general principles of management. A simplified version of those principles is shown in Exhibit 2.4. Fayol felt that these principles could be applied in any organizational setting. He also identified five basic functions or elements of management: planning, organizing, commanding, coordinating, and controlling. These functions underlie much of the general approach to today's management theory.

Mary Parker Follett (1868–1933) was trained in philosophy and political science at what today is Radcliffe College. She applied herself in

Frederick Taylor's scientific management hit Detroit about 1910, where time and motion techniques became the norm. Henry Ford took the concept one step further by replacing workers with machines and having machines do all heavy lifting and moving. One of the first applications of the moving assembly line was the Magneto assembly operation (top) at Ford's Highland Park plant in 1913. Magnetos were pushed from one worker to the next, reducing production time by about one-half. The same principle was applied to total-car assembly, in which stationary workers performed minuscule tasks. The assembly process became so efficient that the man-hours required to produce a Model-T Ford were cut to fewer than two. A Ford came off the assembly line every ten seconds, creating a huge daily output (bottom).

many fields, including social psychology and management. She stressed the importance of common superordinate goals for reducing conflict in organizations.[21] Her work was popular with businesspeople of her day but was often overlooked by management scholars.[22]

Chester I. Barnard (1886–1961) studied economics at Harvard but failed to receive a degree because he lacked a course in laboratory science.[23] He went to work in the statistical department of AT&T and in 1927 became president of New Jersey Bell. One of Barnard's significant contributions was the concept of the informal organization. The informal organization occurs in all formal organizations and includes cliques and naturally occurring social groupings. Barnard argued that organizations are not machines and informal relationships are powerful forces that can help the organization if properly managed. Another significant contribution was the acceptance theory of authority, which states that

administrative principles A subfield of the classical management perspective that focused on the total organization rather than the individual worker, delineating the management functions of planning, organizing, commanding, coordinating, and controlling.

EXHIBIT 2.4

Fayol's Principles of Administration

1. **Division of work:** The object of division of work is to produce more and better work with the same amount of effort. Managerial and technical work are amenable to specialization. There is, however, a limit to such specialization.

2. **Authority and responsibility:** Authority is needed to carry out managerial responsibilities. This includes the formal authority to command and personal authority deriving from intelligence and experience. Responsibility always goes with authority.

3. **Discipline:** Discipline is absolutely essential for the smooth running of business, but the quality of discipline depends essentially on the worthiness of the organization's leaders.

4. **Unity of command:** Each subordinate receives orders from one—and only one—superior.

5. **Unity of direction:** Similar activities in an organization should be grouped together under one manager.

6. **Subordination of individual interest to general interest:** Individuals' interests should not be placed before the goals of the overall organization.

7. **Remuneration of personnel:** Compensation should be fair to both employees and the organization.

8. **Centralization:** Power and authority tend to be concentrated at upper levels of the organization. Degree of centralization must vary according to the situation; the object is the optimal utilization of all personnel faculties.

9. **Scalar chain:** A chain of authority extends from the top to the bottom of the organization. However, horizontal communication is necessary for swift action.

10. **Order:** A place for everything and everything in its place; a place for everyone and everyone in his or her place.

11. **Equity:** Managers should be kind and fair when dealing with subordinates.

12. **Stability of personnel tenure:** High employee turnover should be prevented.

13. **Initiative:** Subordinates should have the freedom to take initiative.

14. **Esprit de corps:** Harmony, team spirit, and a sense of unity and togetherness should be fostered and maintained.

Source: Adapted from Henri Fayol, *General and Industrial Management*, trans. Constance Storrs (London: Pitman and Sons, 1949), pp. 19–42.

This 1914 photograph shows the initiation of a new arrival at a Nebraska planting camp. This initiation was not part of the formal rules and illustrates the significance of the informal organization described by Barnard. Social values and behaviors were powerful forces that could help or hurt the planting organization depending on how they were managed.

people have free will and can choose whether to follow management orders. People typically follow orders because they perceive positive benefit to themselves, but they do have a choice, and their acceptance of authority may be critical to organization success in important situations.[24]

EXHIBIT 2.5

Characteristics of Weberian Bureaucracy

Elements of Bureaucracy:

1. Labor is divided with clear definitions of authority and responsibility that are legitimatized as official duties.

2. Positions are organized in a hierarchy of authority, with each position under the authority of a higher one.

3. All personnel are selected and promoted based on technical qualifications, which are assessed by examination or according to training and experience.

4. Administrative acts and decisions are recorded in writing. Recordkeeping provides organizational memory and continuity over time.

5. Management is separate from the ownership of the organization.

6. Managers are subject to rules and procedures that will insure reliable, predictable behavior. Rules are impersonal and uniformly applied to all employees.

Source: Adapted from A. M. Henderson and Talcott Parsons, eds. and trans., Max Weber, *The Theory of Social and Economic Organizations* (New York: Free Press, 1947), pp. 328–337.

*Max Weber
(1864–1920)
The German theorist's concepts on bureaucratic organizations have contributed to the efficiency of many of today's corporations.*

Bureaucratic Organizations

The final subfield within the classical perspective is that of **bureaucratic organizations.** Max Weber (1864–1920), a German theorist, introduced most of the concepts on bureaucratic organizations.[25]

During the late 1800s, many European organizations were managed on a "personal," family-like basis. Employees were loyal to a single individual rather than to the organization or its mission. The dysfunctional consequence of this management practice was that resources were used to realize individual desires rather than organizational goals. Employees in effect owned the organization and used resources for their own gain rather than to serve clients. Weber envisioned organizations that would be managed on an impersonal, rational basis.[26] This form of organization was called a *bureaucracy.* Exhibit 2.5 summarizes the characteristics of bureaucracy as specified by Weber.

Weber believed that an organization based on rational authority would be more efficient and adaptable to change because continuity is related to formal structure and positions rather than to particular persons, who may leave or die. To Weber, rationality in organizations meant employee selection and advancement based on competence rather than on "whom you know." The organization relies on rules and written records for continuity. The manager depends not on his or her personality for successfully giving orders but on the legal power invested in the managerial position.

The term *bureaucracy* has taken on a negative meaning in today's organizations and is associated with endless rules and red tape. We have all

bureaucratic organizations A subfield of the classical management perspective that emphasized management on an impersonal, rational basis through elements such as clearly defined authority and responsibility, formal recordkeeping, and separation of management and ownership.

been frustrated by waiting in long lines or following seemingly silly procedures. On the other hand, rules and other bureaucratic procedures provide a standard way of dealing with employees. Everyone gets equal treatment, and everyone knows what the rules are. This has enabled many organizations to become extremely efficient. Consider United Parcel Service, also called the "Brown Giant" for the color of the packages it delivers.

United Parcel Service

United Parcel Service took on the U.S. Postal Service at its own game—and won. UPS specializes in the delivery of small packages. Why has the Brown Giant been so successful? One important reason is the concept of bureaucracy. UPS is bound up in rules and regulations. There are safety rules for drivers, loaders, clerks, and managers. Strict dress codes are enforced—no beards; hair cannot touch the collar; mustaches must be trimmed evenly; and no sideburns. Rules specify cleanliness standards for buildings and other properties. Every manager is given bound copies of policy books and expected to use them regularly.

UPS also has a well-defined division of labor. Each plant consists of specialized drivers, loaders, clerks, washers, sorters, and maintenance personnel. UPS thrives on written records. Daily worksheets specify performance goals and work output. Daily employee quotas and achievements are recorded on a weekly and monthly basis.

Technical qualification is the criterion for hiring and promotion. The UPS policy book says the leader is expected to have the knowledge and capacity to justify the position of leadership. Favoritism is forbidden. The bureaucratic model works just fine at UPS.[27]

HUMAN RESOURCE PERSPECTIVE

human resource perspective A management perspective that emerged during the mid-nineteenth century that emphasized enlightened treatment of workers and power sharing between managers and employees.

America has always had a spirit of human equality. However, this spirit has not always been translated into practice in the form of power sharing between managers and workers. The **human resource perspective** has recognized and directly responded to societal pressures for enlightened treatment of employees.

INTERNATIONAL

Bureaucratic Organizing in Egypt

Organizations throughout the world have taken advantage of the bureaucratic approach to organizing. The bureaucratic organization is designed to be efficient, but too much bureaucracy can cause special problems. Companies wishing to start businesses or make investments in Egypt, for example, find enormous structural barriers that inhibit normal work. The red tape is awesome. It takes up to 34 official signatures to ship an order overseas. Simpler transactions are almost as bad. Eleven different approvals are required to transfer a car registration. Four days and twelve signatures are needed to clear a shipment of books at the post office.

Worse than the red tape is the slow pace of employees. Civil servants work solidly only 20 minutes to 2 hours per day. Only 15 percent of government employees come to work on time. In a typical government office, employees read newspapers and gossip rather than wait on petitioners.

The bureaucratic frustrations slow down economic development and discourage foreign investors. Imports and exports follow circuitous paths, and officials often request "tips" before giving approvals. General Motors waited over three years for approval of its proposal to build a truck plant in Egypt. The government desperately wanted the investment, but officials in several ministries had to approve it. Another company wanted to export a shipment of T-shirts. A government agency approval sheet had to be completed in sextuplicate, with five stamps per page. An inspection team made an on-site visit, inspecting some boxes and sealing others. Laboratories had to certify thread counts and dye content. Months passed.

Scholars explain Egypt's pervasive bureaucracy as a historical tradition established by the Pharaohs 4,000 years ago. Yet the centralized administrative structure that built the pyramids does not seem suited to today's world economy. Citizens have committed suicide out of frustration of having to wait months for a government decision. One westerner waited over six years for a legal decision. The judge required the last court appearance just to see if he was still alive.

Source: Based on Barbara Rosewicz, "Factory Owner Joins Egypt's Export Push but Runs into Hurdles," *The Wall Street Journal*, November 11, 1985, pp. 1, 13; David Ignatius, "The Egyptian Bureaucracy Galls Both the Public and Foreign Investors," *The Wall Street Journal*, March 24, 1983, pp. 1, 20.

Forerunners

Forerunners of the human resource perspective include Hugo Munsterberg (1863–1916), considered the "father of industrial psychology," who established this perspective through his early studies of the human factor at work.[28] Walter Dill Scott (1869–1955) worked on the psychology of persuasion as well as personnel selection and helped formalize the field of personnel management.[29] This early work, however, received little attention because of the prominence of the scientific management approach. Then a series of studies at a Chicago electric company changed all that.

The Hawthorne Studies

Beginning about 1895, a struggle developed between manufacturers of gas and electric lighting fixtures for control of the residential and industrial market.[30] By 1909 electric lighting had begun to win, but the increasingly efficient electric fixtures used less total power. The electric companies began a campaign to convince industrial users that they needed more light to get more productivity. When advertising did not

This is the Relay Room of the Western Electric Hawthorne, Illinois, plant in 1927. Six women worked in this relay assembly test room during the controversial experiments on employee productivity. Professors Mayo and Roethlisberger evaluated conditions such as rest breaks and workday length, physical health, amount of sleep, and diet. Experimental changes were fully discussed with the women and were abandoned if they disapproved. Gradually the researchers began to realize they had created a change in supervisory style and human relations, which they believed was the true cause of the increased productivity.

Hawthorne studies A series of experiments on worker productivity begun in 1924 at the Hawthorne plant of Western Electric Company in Illinois; attributed employees' increased output to managers' better treatment of them during the study.

work, the industry began using experimental tests to demonstrate their argument. Managers were skeptical about the results, so the Committee on Industrial Lighting (CIL) was set up to run the tests. To further add to the tests' credibility, Thomas Edison was made honorary chairman of the CIL. In one test location—the Hawthorne plant of the Western Electric Company—some interesting events occurred. These and subsequent experiments have come to be known as the **Hawthorne studies.**

The major part of this work involved four experimental and three control groups. In all, five different "tests" were conducted. These pointed to the importance of factors *other* than illumination in affecting productivity. To more carefully examine these factors, numerous other experiments were conducted.[31] These were the first Relay Assembly Test Room, the second Relay Assembly Group, the Mica Splitting Group, the Typewriting Group, and the Bank Wiring Observation Room. The results of the most famous study, the first Relay Assembly Test Room (RATR) experiment, were extremely controversial. Under the guidance of two Harvard professors, Elton Mayo and Fritz Roethlisberger, the RATR studies lasted nearly 6 years (May 10, 1927, to May 4, 1933) and involved 24 separate experimental periods. So many factors were changed and so many unforeseen factors uncontrolled for that scholars disagree on the factors that truly contributed to the general increase in performance over that period. Most early interpretations, however, agreed on one thing: Money was not the cause of the increased output.[32] Recent analyses of the experiments, however, suggest that money may well have been the single most important factor.[33] An interview with one of the original participants revealed that just getting into the experimental group had meant a huge increase in income.[34]

From these new data, it is now clear that money mattered a great deal at Hawthorne, but it was not recognized at the time of the experiments. Then it was felt that the factor that best explained increased output was "human relations." Employees' output increased sharply when managers treated them in a positive manner. These findings were published and started a revolution in worker treatment for improving organizational productivity. To be historically accurate, money was probably the best explanation for increases in output, but at that time experimenters believed the explanation was human relations. Despite the inaccurate interpretation of the data, the findings provided the impetus for the human relations movement. That movement shaped management theory and practice for well over a quarter-century, and the belief that human relations is the best approach for increasing productivity persists today.

The Human Relations Movement

One reason that "human relations" interpretation may have been so readily attached to the Hawthorne studies was the Great Depression. An unprecedented number of people were out of work. Emerging social forces supported people's humanitarian efforts to help one another. The **human relations movement** initially espoused a "dairy farm" view of management—contented cows give more milk, so satisfied workers will give more work. Gradually, views with deeper content began to emerge. Two of the best-known contributors to the human relations movement were Abraham Maslow and Douglas McGregor.

Psychologists had been theorizing about human needs and had identified literally hundreds of needs. Some researchers even postulated that human needs could be grouped and arranged into hierarchies.[35] Abraham Maslow (1908–1970), a practicing psychologist, observed that his patients' problems usually stemmed from an inability to satisfy their needs. Thus, he generalized his work and suggested a hierarchy of needs with prepotency as a basic assumption. *Prepotency* means that each step in the hierarchy must be satisfied before the next can be activated. Maslow's hierarchy started with physiological needs and progressed to safety, belongingness, esteem, and, finally, self-actualization needs. Chapter 13 discusses his ideas in more detail.

Douglas McGregor (1906–1964) had become frustrated with the early simplistic human relations notions while president of Antioch College in Ohio.[36] He challenged both the classical perspective and the early human relations assumptions about human behavior. Based on his experiences as a manager and consultant, his training as a psychologist, and the work of Maslow, McGregor formulated his Theory X and Theory Y, which are explained in Exhibit 2.6.[37] McGregor believed that the classical perspective was based on Theory X assumptions about workers. He also felt that a slightly modified version of Theory X fit early human relations ideas. In other words, human relations ideas didn't go far enough. McGregor proposed Theory Y as a more realistic view of workers for guiding management thinking.

human relations movement A movement in management thinking and practice that emphasized satisfaction of employees' basic needs as the key to increased worker productivity.

E X H I B I T   2.6
_____

Theory X and Theory Y

Assumptions of Theory X
- The average human being has an inherent dislike of work and will avoid it if he can. . . .
- Because of the human characteristic of dislike for work, most people must be coerced, controlled, directed, or threatened with punishment to get them to put forth adequate effort toward the achievement of organizational objectives . . . .
- The average human being prefers to be directed, wishes to avoid responsibility, has relatively little ambition, wants security above all.

Assumptions of Theory Y
- The expenditure of physical and mental effort in work is as natural as play or rest. The average human being does not inherently dislike work. . . .
- External control and the threat of punishment are not the only means for bringing about effort toward organizational objectives. Man will exercise self-direction and self-control in the service of objectives to which he is committed.
- Commitment to objectives is a function of the rewards associated with their achievement. The most significant of such rewards, e.g., the satisfaction of ego and self-actualization needs, can be direct products of effort directed toward organizational objectives.
- The average human being learns, under proper conditions, not only to accept but to seek responsibility. Avoidance of responsibility, lack of ambition, and emphasis on security are generally consequences of experience, not inherent human characteristics.
- The capacity to exercise a relatively high degree of imagination, ingenuity, and creativity in the solution of organizational problems is widely, not narrowly, distributed in the population.
- Under the conditions of modern industrial life, the intellectual potentialities of the average human being are only partially utilized.

_____

Source: Douglas McGregor, *The Human Side of Enterprise* (New York: McGraw-Hill, 1960), pp. 33–48.

Behavioral Sciences Approach

behavioral sciences approach
A subfield of the human resource management perspective that applied social science in an organizational context, drawing from economics, psychology, sociology, and other disciplines.

The word *science* is the keyword in the **behavioral sciences approach** (see Exhibit 2.7). Research is the basis for theory development and testing, and its results form the basis for practical applications. The scientific emphasis does not mean that errors are avoided, because the scientific management approach also emphasizes science. It does mean that assumptions are not accepted lightly and that replication (repeating studies to get similar results) is sought before practical applications are suggested.

The behavioral sciences approach can be seen in practically every organization. When General Electric conducts research to determine the best set of tests, interviews, and employee profiles to use when selecting new employees, it is employing behavioral science techniques. Emery Air Freight has utilized reinforcement theory to improve the incentives given to workers and increase the performance of many of its operations. When Westinghouse trains new managers in the techniques of employee motivation, most of the theories and findings are rooted in behavioral science research.

EXHIBIT 2.7

The Behavioral Sciences Approach

General Approach
- Applied social science in an organizational context.
- Drew from an interdisciplinary research base, including anthropology, economics, psychology, and sociology.

Contributions
- Improved our understanding of and practical applications for organizational processes such as motivation, communication, leadership, and group processes.
- Regards members of organizations as human beings, not as chattel or tools.

Criticisms
- Because findings are increasingly complex, applications often are tried incorrectly or not at all.
- Some concepts run counter to common sense, thus inviting managers' rejection.

In the behavioral sciences, economics and sociology have significantly influenced the way today's managers approach organizational strategy and structure. Psychology has influenced management approaches to motivation, communication, leadership, and the overall field of personnel management. The conclusions from the tremendous body of behavioral science research are much like those derived from the natural sciences. While we understand more, that understanding is not simple. Scholars have learned much about the behavior of people at work, but they have also learned that organizational processes are astonishingly complex. The remaining chapters of this book contain research findings and applications that can be attributed to the behavioral sciences approach to the study of organizations and management.

This optimally arranged assembly station is in the Daimler-Benz factory in Düsseldorf, Germany. The behavioral science approach is used to insure that jobs are performed efficiently and also provide responsibility and satisfaction for employees. Note the semicircular arrangement of parts for convenient and quick access during the assembly of steering units. Mechanical lifts relieve workers of heavy manual labor.

MANAGEMENT SCIENCE PERSPECTIVE

management science perspective A management perspective that emerged after World War II and applied mathematics, statistics, and other quantitative techniques to managerial problems.

World War II caused many management changes. The massive and complicated problems associated with modern global warfare presented managerial decision makers with the need for more sophisticated tools than ever before. The **management science perspective** emerged to treat those problems. This view is distinguished for its application of mathematics, statistics, and other quantitative techniques to management decision making and problem solving. During World War II groups of mathematicians, physicists, and other scientists were formed to solve military problems. Since those problems frequently involved moving massive amounts of materials and large numbers of people quickly and efficiently the techniques had obvious applications to large-scale business firms.[38]

Operations research grew directly out of the World War II groups (called *operational research teams* in Great Britain and *operations research teams* in the United States).[39] It consists of mathematical model building and other applications of quantitative approaches to managerial problems.

Operations management refers to the field of management that specializes in the physical production of goods or services. Operations management specialists use quantitative techniques to solve manufacturing problems. Some of the commonly used methods are forecasting, inventory modeling, linear and nonlinear programming, queuing theory, scheduling, simulation, and breakeven analysis.

Management information systems (MIS) is the most recent subfield of the management science perspective. These systems are designed to provide relevant information to managers in a timely and cost-efficient manner. The advent of the high-speed digital computer opened up the full potential of this area for management.

Many of today's organizations have departments of management science specialists to help solve quantitatively based problems. When Sears used computer models to minimize its inventory costs, it was applying a quantitative approach to management. When AT&T performed network analysis to speed up and control the construction of new facilities and switching systems, it was employing another management science tool.

One specific technique used in many organizations is queuing theory. *Queuing theory* uses mathematics to calculate how to provide services that will minimize the waiting time of customers. Queuing theory has been used to analyze the traffic flow through the Lincoln Tunnel and to determine the number of toll booths and traffic officers for a toll road. Telephone systems, including number of operators and switchboard capacity, have been analyzed with queuing techniques. Wesley Long Community Hospital in Greensboro, North Carolina, used queuing theory to analyze the telemetry system used in wireless cardiac monitors. The analysis helped the hospital acquire the precise number of telemetry units needed to safely monitor all patients without overspending scarce resources.[40]

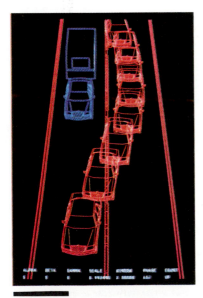

Operations research, a subfield of management science, uses mathematical model building to assist managerial decision making. This road-driving simulation allows calculation of a passing maneuver and shows it on a display unit. Used in the design of Mercedes, calculations are based on a mathematical model that includes all major parameters of vehicle behaviors. With these operations research techniques, engineers can recommend design improvements for management approval.

EXHIBIT 2.8

The Systems View of Organizations

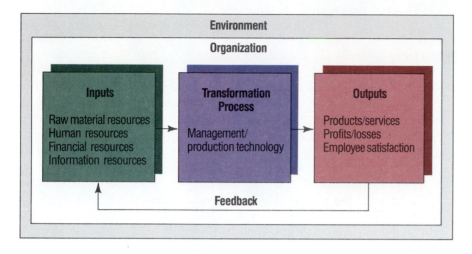

CONTEMPORARY EXTENSIONS

Each of the three major management perspectives discussed still exists. The most prevalent is the human resource perspective, but even it has been undergoing change in recent years. Two major contemporary extensions of this perspective are systems theory and the contingency view. Examination of each will allow a fuller appreciation of the state of management thinking today.

Systems Theory

A **system** is a set of interrelated parts that function as a whole to achieve a common purpose.[41] As described in Chapter 1, a system functions by acquiring inputs from the external environment, transforming them in some way, and discharging outputs back to the environment. Exhibit 2.8 shows the basic **systems theory** of organizations. Here there are five components: inputs, a transformation process, outputs, feedback, and the environment. *Inputs* are the material, human, financial, or information resources used to produce goods or services. The *transformation process* is management's use of production technology to change the inputs into outputs. *Outputs* include the organization's products and services. *Feedback* is knowledge of the results that influence the selection of inputs during the next cycle of the process. The *environment* surrounding the organization includes the social, political, and economic forces that we have noted throughout this chapter.

Some ideas in systems theory have had substantial impact on management thinking. These include open and closed systems, entropy, synergy, and subsystem interdependencies.[42]

system A set of interrelated parts that function as a whole to achieve a common purpose.

systems theory An extension of the human resources perspective that describes organizations as open systems that are characterized by entropy, synergy, and subsystem interdependence.

Executives at Dean Foods Company recognize the open system nature of their organization. Dean Foods is a publicly held company with common stock traded on the New York Stock Exchange. Howard M. Dean, president (left), and Kenneth J. Douglas, chairman of the board, are meeting with financial analysts to report on the company's new developments and progress. Interacting regularly with all aspects of the external environment maintains the flow of resources and prevents entropy, both of which are characteristics of successful companies.

open system A system that interacts with the external environment.

closed system A system that does not interact with the external environment.

entropy The tendency for a system to decay.

synergy The concept that the whole is greater than the sum of its parts.

subsystems Parts of a system that depend on one another for their functioning.

Open systems must interact with the environment to survive; **closed systems** need not. In the classical perspective, organizations were frequently thought of as closed systems. In the management science perspective, closed system assumptions are sometimes used to simplify problems. In reality, however, all organizations are open systems and the cost of ignoring the environment may be failure. A prison tries to seal itself off from its environment; yet it must receive prisoners from the environment, obtain supplies from the environment, recruit employees from the environment, and ultimately release prisoners back to the environment.

Entropy is a universal property of systems and refers to their tendency to decay. If a system does not receive inputs and energy from its environment, it will eventually cease to exist. Organizations must monitor their environments, adjust to changes, continuously bring in new inputs in order to survive and prosper. Managers try to design the organization/environment interfaces to reduce entropy.

Synergy means that the whole is greater than the sum of its parts. When an organization is formed, something new comes into the world. Management, coordination, and production that did not exist before are now present. Organizational units working together can accomplish more than those same units working alone.

Subsystems are parts of a system that depend on one another. Changes in one part of the organization affect other parts. The organization must be managed as a coordinated whole. Managers who understand subsystem interdependence are reluctant to make changes that do not recognize subsystem impact on the organization as a whole. Consider the management decision to remove time clocks from the Alcan Plant in Canada.

Alcan Aluminum Ltd.

A personnel specialist proposed that time clocks be removed from the shop floor. The shop managers agreed but after a few months, several problems emerged. A few workers began to show up late, or leave early, or stay away too long at lunch.

Supervisors had new demands placed upon them to observe and record when workers came and left. They were responsible for reprimanding workers, which led to antagonistic relationships between supervisors and employees. As a consequence, the plant manager found it necessary to reduce the supervisors' span of control. Supervisors were unable to manage as many people because of the additional responsibility.

As Alcan managers discovered, the simple time clock was interdependent with many other parts of the organization system. The time clock influenced worker tardiness and absenteeism, closeness of supervision, the quality of the relationship between supervisors and workers, and span of management. The organization system was more complex than the personnel specialist had realized when he proposed the idea of removing time clocks.[43]

Contingency Views

The second contemporary extension to management thinking is the contingency view. The classical perspective assumes a *universalist* view. Management concepts were thought to be universal—that is, whatever works in one organization will work in another. It proposes the discovery of "one-best-way" management principles that apply the same techniques to every organization. In the area of business education, however, an alternative view exists. This is the *case* view, in which each situation is believed to be unique. There are no universal principles to be found, and one learns about management by experiencing a large number of case problem situations. Managers face the task of determining what will work in every new situation that arises.

To integrate these views the **contingency view** has emerged, as illustrated in Exhibit 2.9.[44] Here neither of the above views is seen as entirely correct. Instead, certain contingencies, or variables, exist for helping management identify and understand situations. The contingency view means that a manager's response depends on identifying key contingencies in a given organizational situation. For example, when managers inadvertently apply the universalist rather than contingency view to their organizations, they make mistakes. A consultant may recommend the same management-by-objectives (MBO) system for a manufacturing firm that was successful in a school system. A central government agency may impose the same rules on a welfare agency that it did in a worker's

contingency view An extension of the human resource perspective in which the successful resolution of organizational problems is thought to depend on managers' identification of key variables in the situation at hand.

E X H I B I T   2.9

The Contingency View of Management

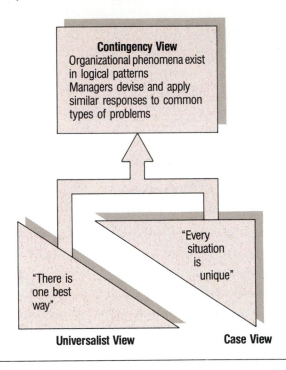

compensation office. A large corporation may take over a chain of restaurants and impose the same organizational charts and financial systems that it used in a banking division. The contingency view tells us that
what works in one setting may not work in another. Management's job is
to search for important contingencies. When managers learn to identify
important patterns and characteristics of their organizations, they can
then fit solutions to those characteristics.

The environment is one important contingency.[45] Management practice in a rapidly changing environment will be very different from that in
a stable one. Other important contingencies that managers must understand are production technology, organization size, and international
culture. A similar organization structure may improve performance for
several firms that use an assembly line technology, but not work at all in
a retail or service firm. The contingency view is important because managers must search for and understand the patterns existing in organizations and their environments.[46]

RECENT HISTORICAL TRENDS

The historical forces that influence management perspectives continue
to change and influence the practice of management. To better understand the changes in management perspectives, consider the views and

E X H I B I T   2.10

Management Perspectives over Time

Perspective on Theory	Began About . . .	Emphasis
Classical perspective	1890	Internal, rational
Human resource perspective	1930	Internal, humanistic
Management science perspective	1940	Internal, rational
Contemporary extensions:		
Systems theory	1950	External/internal, rational
Contingency views	1970	External/internal, humanistic/rational
Japanese management/ achieving excellence	1980	Internal/external, humanistic

their relative emphases as summarized in Exhibit 2.10. The third column of the exhibit shows that the emphasis of each perspective can be either internal or external and either rational or humanistic. *Internal* means that the perspective focused on events and behaviors within the organization; *external* means that it focused on events in the external environment. An emphasis on *rationality* means that the perspective stressed logic and systematic analysis for solving management problems; an emphasis on *humanism* means that the perspective put solutions to problems in the concern for people.

The classical perspective, which evolved around 1890, had an internal focus and stressed the rational aspect of management. Note how the human resource, management science, and contemporary extensions shift emphasis between internal/external and rational/humanistic. The last item in Exhibit 2.10 is another contemporary extension called *Japanese management/achieving excellence*. Important changes in historical forces have continued into the 1980s; these include the increasingly competitive world market that has put new pressures for efficiencies on North American businesses and control of energy resources by OPEC and other oil-producing countries. The effect of these trends has caused the pendulum of American management to swing once again toward humanistic perspective as a way to solve management problems. This represents a major shift from the rational views that characterized management thinking just a few years ago.

Japanese Management

A college student asked a vice-president of a large and respected U.S. corporation, "What, in your opinion, is the key issue facing American business over the next decade?" The answer: "The key issue will not be technology or investment, not regulation or inflation. The key issue will be the way we respond to one fact—the Japanese know how to manage

The success of Japanese management has started what may be a new historical trend in North America. Theory Z recommends integrating Japanese with American management practices. Women employees at the Ito-Yokado corporate office in Japan follow the custom of wearing seifuku, *or identical uniforms, while their male coworkers dress in conservative suits. This dress code, the Japanese feel, contributes to the employees' feeling of teamwork and unity, a quality desired by managers in many American firms.*

better than we do." This statement reflects the impact of Japanese manufacturing on American management. Japanese management practices and techniques have been thought to create more efficient and more effective companies. Japanese products—whether motorcycles, automobiles, or VCRs—have been low priced and of high quality. The problem was dramatized by the reaction of executives of General Motors' Buick division who had visited Japan and a Buick car dealership:

> *The operation appeared to be a massive repair facility, so they asked how he had built up such a large service business. He explained with some embarrassment that this was not a repair facility at all but rather a reassembly operation where newly delivered cars were disassembled and rebuilt to Japanese standards. While many Japanese admire the American automobile, they would never accept the low quality with which they are put together.*[47]

How was American management expected to compete with NEC, Nissan, Sanyo, Sony, Toyota, and Kawasaki? One answer was *Theory Z* by William Ouchi.[48] **Theory Z** is a style of management used by a number of successful U.S. corporations that has characteristics similar to Japanese firms. It emphasized trust and intimacy between employees and the organization. Employees should feel a part of the organization—like a family—and this close relationship and productivity go hand in hand. Once a high-quality, trusting relationship is established with workers, production will increase. For example, at Procter & Gamble's toilet paper factory, an error in one step of the production process may not show up for two days until a whole batch of paper has been ruined, causing a loss of productivity. The solution was the Theory Z idea of involving all workers in the production process and rewarding them for finding any mistakes that occur rather than for just doing their own jobs.

Practicing managers have been enthusiastic about Theory Z. Theory Z shows managers how to modify Japanese techniques to fit the American culture. The book was on the best-seller lists for many months, and several corporations, including Westinghouse, Hewlett-Packard, and Procter & Gamble, have applied its concepts.

Theory Z A management perspective that uses Japanese management techniques of trusting employees and making them feel an intimate part of the organization.

Achieving Excellence

Managements' frustration with the lack of efficiency and quality in U.S. firms has also been revealed in the response to a 1980 *Business Week* article. The article, by Tom Peters, was entitled "Putting Excellence into Management," and it received an overwhelming response. It described characteristics of excellent companies based on McKinsey & Company's research into American corporations. These ideas were expanded in *In Search of Excellence,* which became a runaway best seller.

In Search of Excellence reported a study of U.S. companies based on performance indicators such as average return on capital, equity growth, and innovation. Some of the companies included in the study were Digital Equipment, 3M, McDonald's, Dow, Johnson & Johnson, Caterpillar, Disney, Bechtel, and Hewlett-Packard.[49] The authors condensed their findings into a set of action guidelines that managers can use to stimulate increased excellence within their corporations. For example, one technique is a "bias for action," meaning that people in successful firms make decisions and take action and don't wait for sophisticated quantitative techniques to solve problems. Effective managers get on with it. Another guide is "productivity through people," which means that rank-and-file employees should participate in organizational decisions and managers should seek their commitment to quality and productivity.

Of course, Japanese management characteristics and excellence guidelines are not a panacea.[50] They reflect a management response to pressing historical forces that have increased the need for full utilization of employees. This humanistic approach is currently perceived as more crucial to success than a rational, quantitative approach to management, although most companies use techniques from both. Japanese management and excellence characteristics will be explored in detail in Chapter 16.

Tom Peters (left), author of In Search of Excellence, *confers with William P. Stiritz, chairman and CEO of Ralston Purina Company, at a Creative Management Symposium. Ralston Purina executives realize that superior managers yield superior results. They have instituted the Symposium series to invite well-known authors and educators to challenge managers with new ideas so as to become a more effective management team. Ralston managers aspire to excellence and are action oriented, which are characteristics of managers in the companies reported on in* In Search of Excellence.

SUMMARY

Management is a dominant part of every organization, whether religious, government, education, military, trade, or industry.[51] The practice of management has changed in response to historical conditions. The importance of the ideas in this chapter is that they outline the evolution of the management process so that present and future managers can understand where we are now and continue to progress toward better management.

Three major forces that affect management are social, political, and economic. These forces have influenced management from ancient times to the present. The three major perspectives on management that have evolved since the late 1800s are the classical perspective, the human

This chapter was prepared by David Van Fleet, Professor of Management, Texas A&M University.

resource perspective, and the management science perspective. Each perspective has several specialized subfields.

Two contemporary extensions of management perspectives are systems theory and contingency views. The most recent effect of historical forces has been to produce a renewed concern for the utilization of human resources within organizations, as illustrated by Japanese management techniques and widespread desire for achieving excellence in North American organizations.

Management Solution

Lawrence Kuppin and Harry Evans Sloan took a risk by purchasing New World Pictures to produce B movies when other movie companies were abandoning the B-movie market. But perhaps the risk wasn't so great, because Kuppin and Sloan were tuned to economic and social forces in the external environment and aware of the historical place of B movies in the industry. B movies have always had a market because a large percentage of the population—youngsters, twin-bill theaters—liked low-budget films. Even more important has been the increase in videocassette sales. And since the films are cheaply produced, the risk of loss is low. The films are aimed at 12-to-24-year-olds, who find titles like *Fraternity Vacation* and *Transylvania 6–5000* appealing. What looked like a big risk was no risk at all, because the managers understood the larger historical forces that characterized the industry and saw a vacuum in an attractive market.[52]

DISCUSSION QUESTIONS

1. Why is it important to understand the different perspectives and approaches to management theory that have evolved throughout the history of organizations?
2. To what extent do countries rely on tradition, command, or market methods for allocating economic resources, for example, the United States, Britain, and Russia? Is each method also used within countries?
3. How do societal forces influence the practice and theory of management? Are management perspectives a response to these forces?
4. What change in management emphasis has been illustrated by the interest in "Japanese management" and "achieving excellence"?
5. What is the behavioral science approach? How does it differ from earlier approaches to management?
6. Discuss the basic concepts underlying contingency views.

7. Contrast open and closed systems. Can you give an example of each? Can a closed system survive?
8. Why can an event like the Hawthorne studies be a major turning point in the history of management even if the idea is later shown to be in error? Discuss.
9. Identify the major components of systems theory. Is this perspective primarily internal or external?
10. Which approach to management thought is most appealing to you? Why?
11. Do you think management theory will ever be as precise as theories in the fields of physics, chemistry, or experimental psychology? Why or why not?

CASES FOR ANALYSIS

SEARS, ROEBUCK & COMPANY

In 1886, Richard Warren Sears was a successful railroad station agent in North Redwood, Minnesota. He was a skillful trader; when a consignment of watches was refused, he easily sold them for a profit. He was so successful that he moved to Chicago and expanded the business by hiring Alva H. Roebuck to assemble and repair watches. By 1893, the company had become Sears, Roebuck & Company and gradually moved from watches and jewelry to other products its rural customers desired—firearms, sewing machines, clothing, shoes, wagons, stoves, seeds, and books. In 1895, Sears entered the mail-order business in direct competition with Montgomery Ward and by 1900 had surpassed that company's sales. Despite continued success, by 1924 Sears, Roebuck was still a mail-order business serving the rural market. Thirty years later it had become the largest merchandising organization in the world and remains so today.

The astonishing growth and performance of Sears since 1924 occurred under the direction of Robert E. Wood. Wood studied demographic data on the trends in American society to determine what the customer wanted to buy. Studying the external environment led him to recognize that the rural way of life was giving way to urban life. He replaced the Sears concept of the "American farmer" with the "American mass market." Wood believed that the way to reach the mass market was to offer customers "value," meaning low prices and high-quality merchandise. Since people were migrating to the city, Sears, Roebuck changed its product line and established stores in city and suburban areas. Automobiles were seen as replacing wagons; thus, the company began selling automobiles, although it got out of this line a few years later. Linked to automobiles were automobile repairing and insurance, so Sears offered these services too. Because electricity was competing with gas, Sears began offering electrical appliances.

During the Great Depression, Wood helped Sears respond to changing external conditions. Sears, Roebuck adopted the policy of pricing its merchandise close to actual costs as a service to customers and to the nation. This reflected Wood's belief that profits follow the success of a business, which comes from satisfying customers and employees. Wood believed the company would succeed by placing a high value on customers and employees and placed their interests ahead of stockholders'. This strategy was so successful that stockholders prospered too. No one ever attempted to alter Wood's management practices.

Questions

1. What management perspectives are illustrated in this case? Give examples.
2. Was Wood's management philosophy ahead of its time? Are any of the management perspectives that became prominent after the 1924 to 1954 period reflected in this case?
3. Based on your understanding of historical forces, how has Sears' management adapted to changes in social, economic, and political forces in recent years?

Source: Based on James C. Worthy, *Shaping an American Institution: Robert E. Wood and Sears, Roebuck* (Urbana, Ill.: University of Illinois Press, 1984).

SOCIAL SERVICE AGENCY

Charlotte Hines had been employed for 17 years in a social service agency in a mid-sized city in Illinois. In 1984, she had a rare opportunity to become a supervising clerk in charge of about 20 employees in the typing room, mail room, and security areas. She worked hard at being a good supervisor, paid attention to the human aspects of employee problems, and introduced modern management techniques.

In 1988, the state Civil Service Board required that a promotional exam be taken to find a permanent placement for the supervising clerk position. For the sake of fairness, the exam was an open competition—that is, anyone, even a new employee, could sign up to take it. The person with the highest score would get the job.

More than 50 candidates took the test. Charlotte was devastated. "After I accepted the provisional opening and proved myself on the job, the entire clerical force was deemed qualified to take the same test. My experience counted for nothing."

Charlotte placed twelfth in the field of candidates, and one of her clerks placed first. Now she must forfeit her job to a virtual beginner with no on-the-job supervisory experience.

Questions

1. What management perspective is reflected in the way the Civil Service Board selected people for supervisory jobs? Would another perspective be better for this type of organization?
2. Why did the Civil Service Board pick a permanent supervisor strictly by test results? Is this fair to employees who have supervisory experience? Is it fair to select a supervisor based only on job experience?
3. If you were Charlotte Hines, what would you do? What options would you explore in order to make the best of the situation?

Source: Based on Betty Harrigan, "Career Advice," *Working Woman,* July 1986, 22–24.

CHAPTER 3

The External Environment and Social Responsibility

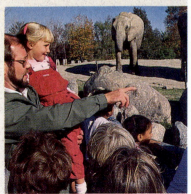

Chapter Outline

The External Environment

Task Environment
General Environment

The Organization-Environment Relationship

Adapting to the Environment
Influencing the Environment

Fundamentals of Social Responsibility

Two Viewpoints

Evaluating Corporate Social Performance

Economic Responsibilities
Legal Responsibilities
Ethical Responsibilities
Discretionary Responsibilities

Corporate Responses to Social Demands

Organizational Constituencies

Improving Ethical and Social Responsiveness

Does Social Responsibility Hurt Economic Performance?

Learning Objectives

After studying this chapter, you should be able to:

- Describe the task and general environments and the dimensions of each.

- Explain how organizations adapt to an uncertain environment and identify techniques managers use to influence and control the external environment.

- Define social responsibility and the two competing viewpoints on its value for corporations.

- Describe how to evaluate corporate social responsibility along economic, legal, ethical, and discretionary criteria.

- Describe four corporate responses to social demands.

- Explain the concept of constituency and identify important constituencies for organizations.

- Describe techniques managers can use to improve their organizations' social responsiveness.

Management Problem

When reports of glass fragments in baby food jars reached Gerber Products Company officials in 1984, they immediately recalled a half-million jars from store shelves. Inspection of the jars revealed no glass fragments. In 1986, when new reports of glass fragments in more than 250 Gerber jars surfaced, senior officials responded more cautiously. They believed the complaints were based on rumor and said a recall was inappropriate. Individual stores were free to remove Gerber products, but an official company recall was postponed. When the government of Maryland banned the sale of some Gerber products, Gerber sued to keep its products on the shelf. A few weeks earlier, Johnson & Johnson had responded to its second Tylenol scare by recalling all pain reliever capsules and publicizing the decision. Johnson & Johnson's response was considered a textbook example of socially responsible behavior. Many people criticized Gerber for not recalling its products.[1]

If you were a senior manager at Gerber, what would you do? What is the socially responsible decision? Could you design your company to respond quickly to unexpected environmental problems?

Gerber Products Company faced a crisis brought on by uncontrollable events in the external environment. Johnson & Johnson faced a similar crisis when cyanide was found in Tylenol capsules. Union Carbide was stunned by the gas leak that killed more than 2,000 people in Bhopal, India. So were managers at the Kansas City Hyatt Regency Hotel when two skywalks collapsed, killing and injuring guests and employees. Officials at Hormel & Company had to respond when someone slipped razor blades into packages of hot dogs. Each of these situations had a common

Deregulation in the legal-political dimension of the general environment led to increased competition in the airline industry. USAir took advantage of the Airline Deregulation Act to redeploy assets to more profitable markets, adopt flexible pricing, and embark on a strategy of controlled growth. The Pittsburgh terminal, shown here, is the hub to 47 cities receiving USAir nonstop service. Not all airlines have done so well responding to changes in regulation and competition; many are losing money or have gone out of business.

organizational environment
All elements existing outside the organization's boundaries that have the potential to affect the organization.

task environment   The layer of the external environment that directly influences the organization's operations and performance.

theme—the events were unexpected, originated in the external environment, and were severe enough to seriously harm the company.

Although few companies experience the crisis of cyanide-laced capsules or a Bhopal tragedy, every organization must cope with changes in the external environment. During the 1970s and early 1980s, for example, high inflation allowed managers to cover up their mistakes with respect to excess inventory and labor costs. Disinflation and mounting competition in the mid-1980s required a new set of organizational actions. Managers at companies such as H. J. Heinz, TRW, Dow Chemical, and General Electric's Medical Systems Group had to discard weak product lines, trim work forces, modernize plants, and keep tight controls on costs, wages, and inventories.[2] Without these internal changes, the companies would no longer have fitted with the reality of the new external environment.

The study of management traditionally has focused on factors within the organization, such as leading, motivating, and controlling employees. The classical, behavioral, and management science schools described in Chapter 2 focused on internal aspects of organizations over which managers have direct control. These views are accurate but incomplete. Most events that affect the organization originate in the external environment. To be effective, managers must monitor and respond to the environment. Contemporary approaches to management acknowledge both events within the organization and the impact of the external environment, whose magnitude and complexity can influence the organization in unexpected ways.

THE EXTERNAL ENVIRONMENT

The reason the environment is so important to organizational survival and success is that organizations are open systems. As described in Chapter 2, an open system consumes resources from the environment and therefore must adapt to changes in it.[3] A closed system, in contrast, is sealed off from the outside world and can function without consuming external resources. If managers act as though their organization is a closed system, they will fail to respond to the external environment and performance ultimately will suffer. Managers should not concentrate on internal efficiency to the exclusion of relationships with customers, competitors, and other elements in the environment.

The definition of **organizational environment** is all elements existing outside the boundary of the organization that have the potential to affect the organization.[4] The environment includes competitors, resources, technology, and economic conditions that influence the organization. It does not include those events so far removed from the organization that their impact is not perceived.

The organizational environment can be further conceptualized as having two layers: the task and general environments.[5] The **task environment** is closer to the organization and includes the sectors that con-

E X H I B I T   3.1

Location of the General, Task, and Internal Environments

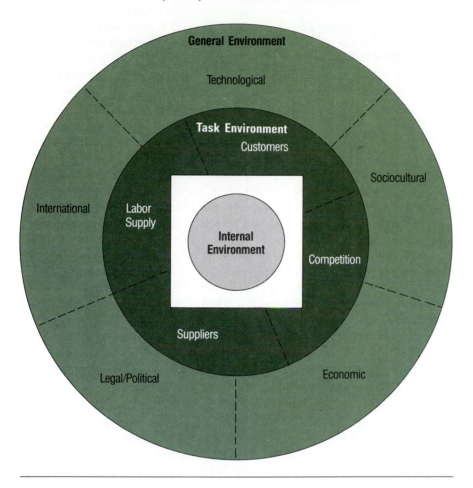

duct day-to-day transactions with the organization and directly influence its basic operations and performance. It is generally considered to include competitors, suppliers, and customers. The **general environment** is the outer layer that is more widely dispersed and affects organizations indirectly. It includes social, demographic, and economic factors that influence all organizations about equally. Increases in the inflation rate or the percentage of women in the work force are part of the organization's general environment. These events do not directly change day-to-day operations, but they do affect all organizations eventually. The organization also has an **internal environment,** which includes the elements within the organization's boundaries. The internal environment is composed of current employees, stockholders, production technology, structure, and corporate culture.

Exhibit 3.1 illustrates the relationship among the task, general, and internal environments. As an open system, the organization draws resources from the external environment and releases goods and service back to it.

general environment The layer of the external environment that affects the organization indirectly.

internal environment The environment within the organization's boundaries.

We will now discuss the two layers of the external environment in more detail; elements of the internal environment will be covered in Parts Three and Four of this book.

Task Environment

As described above, the task environment includes those sectors that have a direct, working relationship with the organization, among them customers, competitors, suppliers, and the labor supply.

customers People and organizations in the environment who acquire goods or services from the organization.

Customers. **Customers** are those people and organizations in the environment who acquire goods or services from the organization. As recipients of the organization's output, customers are important because they determine the organization's success. Patients are the customers of hospitals, students the customers of schools, travelers the customers of airlines, and homemakers the customers of supermarkets. Customers have direct impact on the organization because when their numbers increase the demand for the organization's products rises, and the organization must grow and change to meet the new demand. On the other hand, there are many instances of declining customer demand for an organization's products. Overbuilding in the hotel industry forced companies such as Hyatt and Marriott to spend additional money on advertising, direct mail, giveaways, and expansion into new markets to improve customer demand. Even universities have had to cope with customer decline in certain areas. Enrollment in four-year agricultural programs has dropped 20 percent in the last few years, causing agricultural colleges to reduce their programs while increasing efforts to recruit students.

competitors Other organizations in the same industry or type of business that provide goods or services to the same set of customers.

Competitors. **Competitors** are other organizations in the same industry or type of business that provide goods or services to the same set of customers. Each industry is characterized by specific competitive issues. The recording industry differs from the steel industry and the pharmaceutical industry. Competition in the steel industry, especially from foreign producers, combined with declining demand, has caused some companies to go bankrupt. Companies in the pharmaceutical industry are highly profitable because it is difficult for new firms to enter it. Apple, IBM, and Compaq are competitors in the computer hardware industry. Sometimes industry actions can stir up hot competition in a sleepy industry, such as disposable diapers. The aggressive campaign of Kimberly-Clark increased market share for its Huggies brand but drew a strong response from Procter & Gamble's Pampers. The resulting price war drove Johnson & Johnson and Scott Paper Company out of the business and reduced profits for both P&G and Kimberly-Clark.[6]

suppliers People and organizations who provide the raw materials the organization uses to produce its output.

Suppliers. **Suppliers** provide the raw materials the organization uses to produce its output. A steel mill requires iron ore, machines, and financial resources. A small, private university may utilize hundreds of suppliers for paper, pencils, cafeteria food, computers, trucks, fuel, electricity, and textbooks. Large companies like General Motors, Westinghouse, and Exxon depend on as many as 5,000 suppliers. Normally organizations try to build positive relationships with suppliers so that they will receive preference in the event supplies become tight. The Big Three automakers have decided to acquire a larger share of parts from outside suppliers by 1990. They are trying to build a good relationship with these suppliers so that they will receive high-quality parts as well as low prices. Organizations also depend on banks for capital with which to finance the acquisition of equipment and buildings. The stock and bond markets and insurance companies provide financial resources that permit an organization to grow and expand.

Labor Supply.   The **labor supply** represents the people who can be hired to work for the organization. Every organization needs a supply of trained, qualified personnel. Unions, employee associations, and the availability of certain classes of employees can influence the organization's labor supply. Mary Kay Cosmetics stopped growing when fewer homemakers became available for selling cosmetics door to door due to their entry into the work force as full-time employees.

Three current trends in the labor supply sector of the environment are (1) the pledge by large unions, especially the AFL-CIO, to unionize more companies, (2) the greater expectations by college-educated employees for democracy in the workplace, and (3) the reduced mobility of the labor force. Reasons for these trends are the declining percentage of unionized workers, the increasing number of college graduates, and the high cost of housing that makes it difficult for workers to change locations. Each of these trends can have direct impact on organizations' day-to-day ability to recruit qualified employees.

General Environment

The general environment represents the outer layer of the environment. These dimensions influence the organization over time but often are not involved in day-to-day transactions with it. The dimensions of the general environment include technological, sociocultural, economic, legal-political, and international.

Technological.   The **technological dimension** includes scientific and technological advancements in the industry as well as in society at large. Organizations must incorporate technological advances. In recent years, the most striking advances have been in the computer industry. Computers have enormous power, and many companies are incorporating several computerized systems, including automated offices, robotics, and computer-controlled machines. Exhibit 3.2 illustrates technological advances in the automobile industry. Every auto company must master each new technology. In the photography industry, Japanese developments for a filmless camera may revolutionize picture taking. Polaroid and Kodak are watching closely to see whether electronic images can replace film in today's cameras. A technological development on the horizon that will affect beverage consumption is the self-chilling can. Inside each can is a metal capsule filled with carbon dioxide under high pressure. Opening the can releases the capsule, and the beverage is chilled to 30°F within 90 seconds. These and other technological advances can change the rules of the game; thus, every organization must be ready to respond.

Mud, sweat, and $950 a week. The labor supply sector of the task environment includes the people available to work for an organization. For CP Rail, an increasing number of women are competing for traditionally male jobs, thereby increasing the labor supply. Shelley Emery, 26, one of the handful of women among 1,100 men laboring on the $600 million Rogers Pass Project, empties cement into a bucket. Changes in the sociocultural dimension of the environment, with new norms and values encouraging women to seek nontraditional jobs, have supported this change in the labor supply.

labor supply The people available for hire by the organization.

technological dimension The dimension of the general environment that includes scientific and technological advancements in the industry and society at large.

EXHIBIT   3.2

Chronological Developments in Automobile Technology

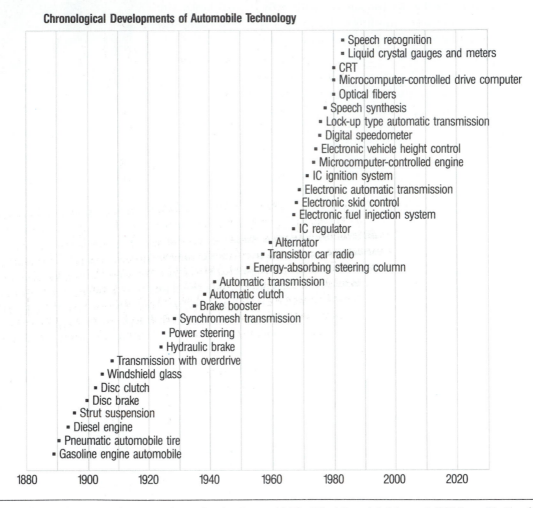

Chronological Developments of Automobile Technology

- Speech recognition
- Liquid crystal gauges and meters
- CRT
- Microcomputer-controlled drive computer
- Optical fibers
- Speech synthesis
- Lock-up type automatic transmission
- Digital speedometer
- Electronic vehicle height control
- Microcomputer-controlled engine
- IC ignition system
- Electronic automatic transmission
- Electronic skid control
- Electronic fuel injection system
- IC regulator
- Alternator
- Transistor car radio
- Energy-absorbing steering column
- Automatic transmission
- Automatic clutch
- Brake booster
- Synchromesh transmission
- Power steering
- Hydraulic brake
- Transmission with overdrive
- Windshield glass
- Disc clutch
- Disc brake
- Strut suspension
- Diesel engine
- Pneumatic automobile tire
- Gasoline engine automobile

1880   1900   1920   1940   1960   1980   2000   2020

Source: Masatoshi Morita, "Does the Lessor Serve for the Greater?" *The Wheel Extended*, 14, no. 1 (1984), p. 21. Reprinted with permission.

sociocultural dimension The dimension of the general environment representing the demographic characteristics, norms, customs, and values of the population within which the organization operates.

Sociocultural.   The **sociocultural dimension** of the general environment represents the demographic characteristics as well as the norms, customs, and values of the population within which the organization functions. Important sociocultural characteristics are geographical distribution and population density, age, and educational levels in the community or region where the organization exists. Also important are the society's norms and values. For example, the Playboy enterprises thrived in the 1960s and 1970s by advocating new values. *Playboy* magazine and Playboy clubs were extremely popular. But changes in the population's values during the 1980s gradually reduced the demand for Playboy products. Magazine sales were off 40 percent, and Playboy clubs were being closed. Other sociocultural trends in recent years that have affected many companies include a shift from a manufacturing to a service economy, an increase in the consumption of chicken and a decrease in that of pork, and a shift toward light wines from hard liquor.

Economic.   The **economic dimension** represents the general economic health of the country or region in which the organization operates. Consumer purchasing power, unemployment rate, and interest rates are part of an organization's economic environment. Not-for-profit organizations such as the Red Cross and the Salvation Army find a greater demand for their services during economic decline but receive smaller contributions. During economic prosperity, contributions are up but demand for their services is reduced. Volunteer organizations must adapt to these changes in economic conditions. The fall in the price of crude oil decimated many small southwestern firms, including Verna Corporation and Crystal Oil Company, which once were the envy of the industry. Today most of their assets are sitting unused in oil industry graveyards. Borden's Dairy Group was adversely affected by the depressed economy in Louisiana, Texas, and Oklahoma during the early 1980s. Borden's managers decided to develop new products and withdraw from businesses that produced only marginal profits. These changes allowed Borden to adapt to the changing economic conditions in the external environment.

Legal-Political.   The **legal-political dimension** includes government regulations at the local, state, and federal levels as well as political activities designed to change legislation and influence company behavior. The U.S. political system encourages capitalism, and the government tries not to overregulate business. However, government laws do specify rules of the game. The federal government influences organizations through the Occupational Safety and Health Administration (OSHA), Environmental Protection Agency (EPA), fair trade practices, libel statutes allowing lawsuits against business, consumer protection legislation, product safety requirements, import and export restrictions, and information and labeling requirements. At the state level, in any given year up to 250,000 bills to control some aspects of organizations will be introduced. Of these, about 50,000 will become law. An additional 50,000 regulations will be proposed, of which about 35,000 will be adopted.[7]

Political action is reflected in the development of special-interest groups that attempt to influence business behavior. Pressure from consumer groups caused McDonald's and other fast-food restaurants to publish information on their products' nutritional content. The Reverend Jesse Jackson joined with Operation PUSH to encourage CBS to hire more minorities. Producers of alcoholic beverages, such as Adolph Coors Company and Anheuser-Busch, are not heavily regulated by the government except for the ingredients that go into beer. A major threat to this industry is legislation pushed by special-interest groups such as Mothers Against Drunk Drivers (MADD) that may reduce consumption of alcoholic beverages.

International.   The **international dimension** of the external environment represents events originating in foreign countries as well as oppor-

Managers at J. P. Morgan need up-to-date information about the economic dimension of the environment to support lending, investment, trading, and advisory activities. Members of the Economic Analysis Department, under the direction of Milton Hudson, carry out wide-ranging analyses of the U.S. economy and financial markets for use throughout the bank. The many charts represent indicators of the U.S. economy and more focused analyses of specific markets in which Morgan companies are involved.

economic dimension   The dimension of the general environment representing the overall economic health of the country or region in which the organization functions.

legal-political dimension   The dimension of the general environment that includes federal, state, and local government regulations and political activities designed to control company behavior.

international dimension   The dimension of the general environment representing events that originate in foreign countries and opportunities for American firms abroad.

tunities for American companies in other countries. The high-quality, low-priced automobiles from Japan and Korea have created a permanent change in the American automobile industry. In addition, many companies have adopted the strategy of having parts manufactured and assembled in other countries, such as Mexico, because of the low price of labor. Changes in the foreign exchange rate can increase or decrease the value of U.S. products overseas as well as the competitiveness of foreign products within the United States. One competitive strategy auto companies have used is to develop joint ventures with auto companies in Japan and Korea. The shift toward capitalism in China promises to open up new markets to U.S. companies. Often, however, the culture of other countries is a puzzle to U.S. managers attempting to market goods overseas. The international dimension has become so important to the management of U.S. and Canadian companies that Chapter 21 is devoted to this topic.[8] IBM has a complex environment that includes international as well as the other sectors discussed above.

International Business Machines

The external environment for IBM is illustrated in Exhibit 3.3. IBM is known for its good treatment of employees and hence has few problems in the labor force sector. Most of IBM's external problems have come from competition and new technology. Competitors such as Compaq have developed cheaper machines that are compatible with IBM products. IBM's strategy has been to follow new developments rather than be the first to introduce a new product. Current economic conditions, such as low interest rates, low unemployment, and reduced inflation, have enhanced the demand for computers. The government has not been a major force in the computer industry, although it has taken steps to regulate software and guarantee information privacy.

One potential problem is an antitrust suit against IBM for being the largest computer manufacturer in the industry. IBM spends about 7 percent of revenues on research and development and uses technology to automate production as a way to cut costs. In the international domain, IBM sells its products in over 130 countries. IBM managers try to integrate operations with the culture of the host country by hiring nationals. IBM also acquires many parts from foreign producers for machines that sell in the United States.[9]

A major responsibility of IBM managers is to scan and monitor environmental events and direct internal operations to fit environmental needs. By monitoring customers, competitors, suppliers, economic con-

E X H I B I T 3.3

The External Environment for IBM

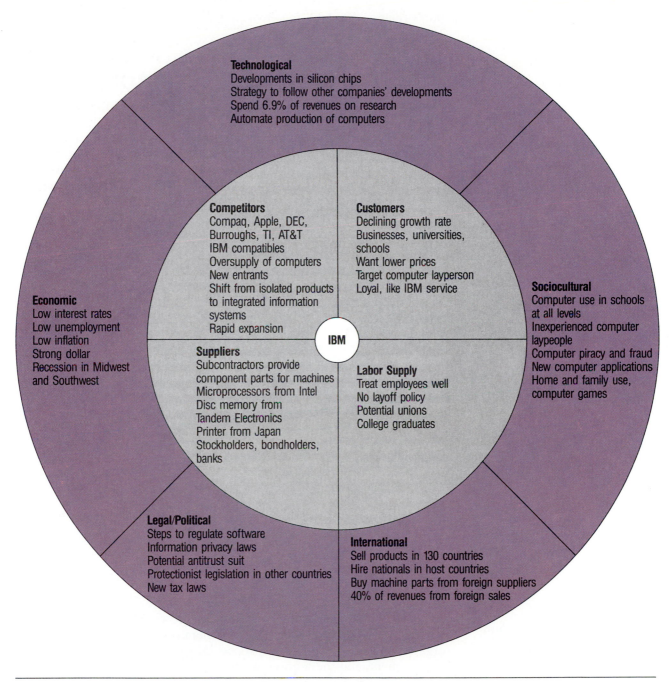

Technological
Developments in silicon chips
Strategy to follow other companies' developments
Spend 6.9% of revenues on research
Automate production of computers

Competitors
Compaq, Apple, DEC,
Burroughs, TI, AT&T
IBM compatibles
Oversupply of computers
New entrants
Shift from isolated products
to integrated information
systems
Rapid expansion

Customers
Declining growth rate
Businesses, universities,
schools
Want lower prices
Target computer layperson
Loyal, like IBM service

Economic
Low interest rates
Low unemployment
Low inflation
Strong dollar
Recession in Midwest
and Southwest

Sociocultural
Computer use in schools
at all levels
Inexperienced computer
laypeople
Computer piracy and fraud
New computer applications
Home and family use,
computer games

IBM

Suppliers
Subcontractors provide
component parts for machines
Microprocessors from Intel
Disc memory from
Tandem Electronics
Printer from Japan
Stockholders, bondholders,
banks

Labor Supply
Treat employees well
No layoff policy
Potential unions
College graduates

Legal/Political
Steps to regulate software
Information privacy laws
Potential antitrust suit
Protectionist legislation in other countries
New tax laws

International
Sell products in 130 countries
Hire nationals in host countries
Buy machine parts from foreign suppliers
40% of revenues from foreign sales

Source: Based on Robert Durand, Teri Fogle, and Matt Stump, "International Business Machines" (Unpublished manuscript, Texas A&M University, December 1985).

ditions, technology, and government regulation, managers can either help IBM adapt to the environment or use the organization's resources to attempt to change it.

We now turn to techniques managers use for managing the organization's relationship with the environment.

THE ORGANIZATION–ENVIRONMENT RELATIONSHIP

How does the environment influence an organization? For each organization, the characteristics of the environment are unique. Depending on the events occurring along each dimension, the organization must have mechanisms with which to learn about the environment and insure that it can obtain the resources needed for its support. The influence of the environment boils down to two essential forces to which the organization must respond: (1) the need for information and (2) the need for resources. Some environmental conditions create a need to gather information in order to understand what is happening; others create a need for scarce material and financial resources.

uncertainty Lack of information about environmental factors that makes it difficult to predict external changes and resource availability.

These forces create uncertainty for the organization. **Uncertainty** means that decision makers lack information about environmental factors and thus find it difficult to predict external changes and resource availability. When uncertainty is high, decision makers are unclear as to what is happening in the environment or whether resources are available.[10] Uncertainty is low when the environment is stable; then managers know what to expect and can obtain necessary resources.

Two basic alternative strategies for coping with environmental uncertainty are to adapt the organization to the amount of uncertainty in the environment or to attempt to control the environment to make it more compatible with organizational needs.

Adapting to the Environment

If the organization faces increased uncertainty with respect to competition, customers, suppliers, or government regulation, managers can use several strategies to adapt to these changes, including boundary-spanning roles, increased planning and forecasting, a flexible structure, and mergers or joint ventures.

boundary-spanning roles Roles assumed by people and/or departments that link and coordinate the organization with key elements in the external environment.

Boundary-Spanning Roles. **Boundary-spanning roles** and departments link and coordinate the organization with key elements in the external environment. Boundary spanners serve two purposes for the organization: They detect and process information about changes in the environment, and they represent the organization's interest to the environment.[11] People in departments such as marketing and purchasing span the boundary to work with customers and suppliers. Many organizations, including corporations and universities, have public affairs personnel charged with monitoring legislative changes in Washington and state capitals. They provide information to managers about impending

Boundary-spanning roles are an important way to gather information and reduce environmental uncertainty. This marketing research focus group is being used by Lotus Development Corporation to obtain customer feedback for use in designing new-product features and documentation. Lotus also spans the boundary to customers with telephone support personnel who answer customer questions, provide in-depth technical assistance, and compile customer call reports for use by Lotus managers. Lotus's introductory software package, 1-2-3®, is one of the most recognized brand names in personal computer software.

changes. When competitive uncertainty increased for Delta Air Lines because of deregulation, managers created a tariff department with the sole purpose of monitoring tariff changes by other airlines. Boundary-spanning employees have computers that monitor fare changes reported by other airlines; posing as customers, they call other airlines to see what prices are offered. The ability to monitor competitors' fares and respond quickly has helped Delta earn a profit during difficult times for the airline industry.[12]

Forecasting and Planning.   Forecasting and planning for environmental changes are major activities in many corporations. Specialized departments often are created when uncertainty is high.[13] Forecasting is an effort to spot trends that enable managers to predict future events. Forecasting techniques range from quantitative economic models of environmental business activity to newspaper clipping services. One of these services, called Burrelle's Information Services Inc., monitors 16,000 newspapers and magazines. Customers such as AT&T Communications use it to keep tabs on competitors and predict their future moves. Companies pay $18,000 a year for the service. Chase investors used reported information about rapidly multiplying television channels in Western Europe to invest in MCA Inc., which had a valuable film library.

   Careful planning also represents an important response to environmental uncertainty.[14] Heinz, United Airlines, and Waste Management Inc., for example, have devised specific management plans for handling crises. Whether the crisis is a hostile takeover attempt or product tampering, an organization that responds without a plan will make mistakes. Planning can soften the adverse impact of rapid shifts in the environment.

Flexible Structure.   An organization's structure should enable it to effectively respond to external shifts. Research has found that a loose, flexible structure works best in an uncertain environment and a tight structure is most effective in a certain environment.[15] The term **organic structure** characterizes an organization that is free flowing, has few rules and regulations, encourages teamwork among employees, and decentralizes decision making to employees doing the job. This type of structure works best when the environment changes rapidly. A **mecha-**

organic structure An organizational structure that is free flowing, has few rules and regulations, encourages employee teamwork, and decentralizes decision making to employees doing the job.

A joint venture is the creation of a new organization through investment by two or more companies. New United Motor Manufacturing, Inc., or NUMMI, is a joint venture in Fremont, California, between Toyota Motor Corporation and General Motors. Established in 1984, NUMMI has become one of the most efficient auto production plants in the United States, representing the best of Japanese and American management techniques. The joint venture integrated people systems with technology systems better than most U.S. companies had done alone and reduced investment risk for both companies.

mechanistic structure   An organizational structure characterized by rigidly defined tasks, many rules and regulations, little teamwork, and centralized decision making.

nistic structure is just the opposite, characterized by rigidly defined tasks, many rules and regulations, little teamwork, and centralization of decision making. This is fine for a stable environment. Dow Chemical and Star-Kist Foods have set up "SWAT" teams that can swing into action if an unexpected disaster strikes. These teams include members from multiple departments who can provide the expertise needed for solving an immediate problem, whether it be a plant explosion or environmental destruction such as that which occurred at Three Mile Island and Love Canal. Organic organizations also create teams to handle changes in supply of raw materials, new products, or the implementation of procedures for adhering to government regulations.

Mergers and Joint Ventures.   Sometimes companies join together to cope with major environmental changes or to undertake risky, expensive projects in response to the environment. A **merger** occurs when two or more organizations combine to become one. Texas Air (owner of Continental Airlines) purchased Eastern Airlines to cope with the increasing competition in the airline industry and gain access to important routes along the Eastern seaboard. General Host acquired Hickory Farms, a retail chain, to become an outlet for General Host's meat products. A **joint venture** involves a mutual investment by two or more organizations that creates a new organization. Several oil companies and automobile manufacturers have engaged in joint ventures. Oil companies have used joint ventures to explore for oil on the Continental Shelf or in inaccessible regions of Alaska and Canada. The risk and expense of oil exploration in these environments are so enormous that they could not go it alone. Sometimes one organization simply buys a partial interest in another company to reduce uncertainty. For example, IBM purchased a stake in MCI Communications and Rolm Corporation to tap into potential new markets and to insure supplies of new technology. Some joint ventures are international in scope. RCA joined with Japan's Sharp Corporation to produce semiconductor chips. Each company hopes to find a greater market in the other's backyard.

merger   The combination of two or more organizations into one.

joint venture   A mutual investment by two or more organizations that creates a new organization.

E X H I B I T 3.4

Organizational Responses to Environmental Changes

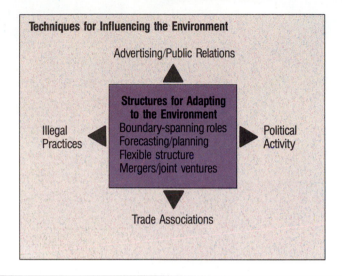

Influencing the Environment

The other major strategy for handling environmental uncertainty is to reach out and change those elements causing problems. Widely used techniques for changing the environment include advertising and public relations, political activity, trade associations, and the use of questionable or illegal practices. Exhibit 3.4 summarizes the techniques organizations can use to adapt to and influence the external environment.

Advertising and Public Relations.   Advertising has become a highly successful way to manage demand for a company's products. Companies spend large amounts of money to influence consumer tastes. Hospitals have begun to advertise through billboards, newspapers, and radio commercials to promote special services. Increased competitiveness among CPA firms has caused them to start advertising for clients, a practice unheard of a few years ago.

Public relations is similar to advertising except that its goal is to change public opinion about the company itself. Much public relations is accomplished through advertising as well as via speeches and press reports. In the 1960s and 1970s, Dow Chemical became infamous for supplying napalm and Agent Orange to the military for use in Vietnam. Even when it stopped making these products the image persisted. Dow started a new advertising campaign—"Dow Lets You Do Great Things"— and used other external communications that emphasized the humanitarian use of its products. As a service to reporters, Dow set up a free, 24-hour hotline to answer questions about the chemical industry. Dow also helped its image by putting up most of the money for a new program to train writers at the University of Missouri School of Journalism.[16]

"Does She . . . or Doesn't She?" Clairol made advertising history when it introduced this line in 1956. Any suggestion of a double-entendre was quickly dispelled with "Hair Color So Natural Only Her Hairdresser Knows for Sure!" Organizations try to control the environment through advertising and public relations, and this advertising campaign, which used models with wholesome, girl-next-door good looks, changed the way women thought about hair color. The campaign was so successful that it increased business for hairdressers at the same time it opened up an entirely new retail market for haircoloring through drugstores.

political activity Organizational attempts, such as lobbying, to influence government legislation and regulation.

Political Activity.   **Political activity** represents organizational attempts to influence government legislation and regulation. Corporations pay lobbyists to express their views to federal and state legislators. Companies in the steel industry, for example, have tried to influence federal legislation to roll back foreign steel imports by 15 percent. For a company like Bethlehem, such a change could result in $250 million of new business. Sometimes senior executives become directly involved in attempting to sway government decisions. The CEO of Du Pont, Irving Shapiro, went directly to President Carter to convince him that a proposed antitrust position was terrible. He succeeded.

Political activity also occurs when large companies influence local governments. Frustrated by disagreement among political units in the Battle Creek, Michigan, area, Kellogg approached the city and township and said that if they wanted to keep Kellogg's corporate headquarters there, the government units must merge. Kellogg claimed it was having trouble recruiting employees to the area. The city merger was put to a citywide vote and unanimously approved.

Trade Associations.   Most organizations join with others having similar interests; the result is a **trade association.** In this way they work together to influence the environment, including federal legislation and regulation. Most manufacturing companies are part of the National Association of Manufacturers. The National Rifle Association has thousands of individual and corporate members whose interests are served by the freedom to use guns. One of the most influential trade associations is the U.S. League of Savings Institutions, which virtually controls government regulations pertaining to the savings and loan industry. It is not uncommon for the League to pay the regulators' expenses to attend association meetings. Federal Home Loan Bank Board officials admit they have taken many actions and changed regulations to suit the League. In 1985, the League met in Chicago and decided that a proposed regulation needed changing. The League called in regulators from Washington and literally rewrote the proposal. This kind of influence has evolved over years of developing a close working relationship with Federal Home Loan Bank Board members.[17]

> **trade association**   An association made up of organizations with similar interests for the purpose of influencing the environment.

Illegal Practices.   Illegal practices are behaviors deemed illegal by government law or regulation. Sometimes an illegal practice is unintentional, such as when a company runs afoul of complex regulations concerning campaign contributions. At other times organizations intentionally engage in unlawful activity. One big scandal concerned electrical contractors charged with rigging bids. Rigging bids is a way to reduce uncertainty and insure that each company gets a share of the work and thus earns a high profit. The ensuing investigation resulted in guilty pleas or convictions of 33 companies and 34 individuals. The companies included top electrical contractors, such as Fischbach & Moore Inc., the nation's largest.[18] Aircraft manufacturers such as McDonnell Douglas were accused of giving kickbacks to foreign governments to secure aircraft sales. Smaller companies may be motivated to undertake illegal practices when low profits or scarce environmental resources lead managers to believe they will not prosper by following the rules of the game.

   We now turn to this very important topic of social responsibility and the ethical dilemmas that confront executives who are trying to succeed in a competitive environment.

FUNDAMENTALS OF
SOCIAL RESPONSIBILITY

Most people agree that deliberate illegal acts on the part of a corporation are not socially responsible behavior.[19] In this sense, the concept of cor-

The Bay Checkerspot butterfly is an endangered species. Waste Management Inc. went beyond the profit-maximizing view to protect this part of its environment. Environmental sensitivity was needed in the development of a new sanitary landfill near San Jose, California, which is located in the Bay Checkerspot's habitat. Company personnel, working with expert consultants, prepared a comprehensive plan designed to protect the butterfly. The plan includes a five-year program of monitoring the Bay Checkerspot butterfly to determine whether the landfill is having any impact on its habitat.

social responsibility The obligation of organization management to make decisions and take actions that will enhance the welfare and interests of society as well as the organization's.

porate social responsibility is easy to understand: It means distinguishing right from wrong and doing right. The formal definition of **social responsibility** is management's obligation to make choices and take actions that will contribute to the welfare and interests of society as well as to the organization's.[20]

As straightforward as this definition seems, social responsibility can be a difficult concept to grasp. The reason is that there are different beliefs as to which actions improve society's welfare.[21] To make matters worse, social responsibility covers a range of issues, many of which are ambiguous with respect to right or wrong. For example, if a bank deposits the money from a trust fund into a low-interest account for 90 days, from which it makes a substantial profit, has it been unethical? How about two companies' engaging in intense competition, such as that between *The Plain Dealer* and *The Cleveland Press* or between American Airlines and Braniff Airlines? Is it socially responsible for the stronger corporation to drive the weaker one into bankruptcy? Or consider companies such as A. H. Robins, maker of the Dalkon shield, Manville Corporation, maker of asbestos, Continental Airlines, or Texaco, the oil company, all of which declared bankruptcy—which is perfectly legal—to avoid mounting financial obligations to consumers, labor unions, or competitors. These examples contain moral, legal, and economic considerations that make ethical behavior hard to define.

Two Viewpoints

One well-known viewpoint on social responsibility was expressed by Nobel economist Milton Friedman, who opposes the concept of broad social responsibility for corporations. He believes in the *profit-maximizing view,* meaning that the corporation should be operated on a profit-oriented basis, with its sole mission being "to use its resources and energy in activities designed to increase its profits so long as it stays within the rules of the game."[22] Friedman's view draws heavily on the writings of Adam Smith, who wrote that market forces—an "invisible hand"—act to direct profit-seeking enterprises toward socially desirable outcomes. In other words, it is to society's advantage to have the organization seek profits.

The other view argues that corporations' responsibility goes beyond the economic. This argument may have begun with the *iron law of responsibility,* which states that in the long run, society will take power away from any organization that uses its influence in a way judged unacceptable or irresponsible.[23] In other words, corporations must consciously try to meet social needs or they will be perceived as illegitimate by society. For example, strip mining is more profitable if the site is abandoned after the ore is extracted. Land reclamation provides a greater benefit to society, but it is less profitable and was not standard practice for many years. Ultimately society responded negatively to mining companies that destroyed the landscape.

EVALUATING CORPORATE SOCIAL PERFORMANCE

A useful model for evaluating corporate social performance is presented in Exhibit 3.5. The model indicates that total corporate social responsibility can be subdivided into four parts—economic, legal, ethical, and discretionary responsibilities.[24] The responsibilities are ordered from bottom to top based on their fundamental role and are cumulative. The proportions in the figure suggest the relative magnitude of each responsibility and the frequency with which managers deal with each issue.

Economic Responsibilities

The first level of social responsibility is *economic responsibility* and includes the profit-maximizing approach advocated by Friedman. The business institution is, above all, the basic economic unit of society. Its responsibility is to produce the goods and services that society wants and to maximize profits for its owners and shareholders.

The purely economic view is no longer considered adequate in Canada, the United States, and Europe. This approach would mean that companies could break the law so long as the behavior served their economic interests. When companies consciously break the law, such as by rigging bids, they will be prosecuted if detected. A notorious example was E. F. Hutton managers' attempt to maximize cash returns from bank deposits. They generated overdrafts in astronomical amounts among hundreds of banks—sometimes totaling more than $1 billion—that in effect created interest-free loans. They also used a technique called "chaining." Managers teamed up and each day passed receipts through accounts in many local banks so that a breakdown anywhere in the chain would create a float for Hutton's use. Hutton used checking accounts as sources of loans without the banks' agreement.[25]

Legal Responsibilities

All modern societies lay down ground rules, laws, and regulations that businesses are expected to follow. *Legal responsibility* defines what society considers important with respect to appropriate corporate behavior.[26] Businesses are expected to fulfill their economic goals within the legal framework. Legal requirements are imposed by local town councils, state legislators, and federal regulatory agencies.

Organizations that knowingly break the law are poor performers in this category. Intentionally manufacturing defective goods or billing a client for work not done is illegal. An example of the punishment given to one company that broke the law is shown in Exhibit 3.6. Sometimes, however, behavior that is economically and legally appropriate still may be perceived as socially irresponsible. In early 1986, interest rates dropped and many lenders "guaranteed" the low rates for a period of 90

EXHIBIT 3.5

Categories of Corporate Social Performance

Source: Archie B. Carroll, "A Three-Dimensional Conceptual Model of Corporate Performance," *Academy of Management Review* 4 (1979), 499.

E X H I B I T   3.6

One Company's Punishment for Breaking the Law

February 12, 1985

American Caster Corporation

Dear Businesses & Residents of the City & County of Los Angeles

Pollution of our environment has become a crisis.

Intentional clandestine acts of illegal disposal of hazardous waste, or "midnight dumping" are violent crimes against the community.

Over the past 2 years almost a dozen Chief Executive Officers of both large and small corporations have been sent to jail by the L.A. Toxic Waste Strike Force.

They have also been required to pay huge fines; pay for cleanups; speak in public about their misdeeds; and in some cases place ads publicizing their crime and punishment.

THE RISKS OF BEING CAUGHT ARE TOO HIGH—
AND THE CONSEQUENCES IF CAUGHT ARE NOT WORTH IT!

We are paying the price. *TODAY,* while you read this ad our President and Vice President are serving time in *JAIL* and we were forced to place this ad.

PLEASE TAKE THE LEGAL ALTERNATIVE AND PROTECT OUR ENVIRONMENT.

Very Truly Yours,

American Caster Corporation
141 WEST AVENUE 34
LOS ANGELES, CA 90031

Source: Barry C. Groveman and John L. Segal, "Pollution Police Pursue Chemical Criminals," *Business and Society Review* 55 (Fall 1985), 41.

Anheuser-Busch developed the "Know When to Say When" program to promote responsible drinking. This behavior represents ethical responsibilities that go beyond the corporation's economic and legal interests. Anheuser-Busch's management has operated with a concern for civic, social, and community responsibilities. Recently Anheuser-Busch contributed more than $600,000 in funds for alcoholism research. The company supports the proposition that anything less than responsible consumption of alcoholic beverages is detrimental to both society and the brewing industry.

days in order to attract mortgage business. However, if the sale of the home was not closed within 90 days, a higher rate was imposed. Some mortgage lenders were accused of intentionally delaying the closing of contracts to force home buyers into higher interest rates. No laws prohibited this practice, and it was economically profitable for the firms.

Ethical Responsibilities

Ethical responsibility includes behaviors that are not necessarily codified into law and may not serve the corporation's direct economic interests. To be *ethical*, organization decision makers should act with equity, fairness, and impartiality, respect the rights of individuals, and provide differential treatment of individuals only when relevant to the organization's goals and tasks.[27] *Unethical* behavior occurs when decisions enable an individual or company to gain at the expense of society.[28]

MANAGERS SHOP TALK

Guidelines for Ethical Decision Making

Below is a list of guidelines that you, the future manager, can apply to difficult social problems and ethical dilemmas you almost surely will face one day. The guidelines will not tell you exactly what to do, but taken in the context of the text discussion they will help you evaluate the situation more clearly by examining your own values and those of your organization. The answers to these questions will force you to think hard about the social and ethical consequences of your behavior.

1. Is the problem/dilemma really what it appears to be? If you are not sure, *find out.*
2. Is the action you are considering legal? Ethical? If you are not sure, *find out.*
3. Do you understand the position of those who oppose the action you are considering? Is it reasonable?

4. Whom does the action benefit? Harm? How much? How long?
5. Would you be willing to allow everyone to do what you are considering doing?
6. Have you sought the opinion of others who are knowledgeable on the subject and who would be objective?
7. Would your action be embarrassing to you if it were made known to your family, friends, co-workers, or superiors? Would you be comfortable defending your actions to an investigative reporter on the evening news?

There are no correct answers to these questions in an absolute sense. Yet, if you determine that an action is potentially harmful to someone, would be embarrassing to you, or if you don't know the ethical or legal consequences, these guidelines will help you clarify whether the action is socially responsible.

Source: Anthony M. Pagano and Jo Ann Verdin, *The External Environment of Business* (New York: Wiley, 1988), Chapter 5.

When Control Data took a chance by building a plant in Minneapolis' inner city, it performed an ethical act because top management wanted to provide equal opportunity for the disadvantaged. Other businesses had built in the ghetto and failed. Chairman Norris insisted that the plant attempt to be profitable, but the company also wanted to provide jobs to inner-city residents. In this case the ethical goals were compatible with the economic goals, and the company achieved both.[29]

From where does a company derive its ethical values? Ethics may come from a variety of sources. **Personal ethics** are adapted from the values of individual managers and may reflect religion, social consciousness, and personal attitudes toward social responsibility. **Corporate ethics** derive from the organization's values and culture. Senior executives help define values that form the corporation's culture. Examples include the policies of IBM and Xerox of lending personnel for community projects. Corporate ethics also reflect standard industry practice. An example is the former prohibition against "naming names" in advertising that compared products with competitors'. That norm was broken with the "Pepsi Challenge." Finally, **professional ethics** are defined by professional occupational groups. The American Medical Association, the American Institute of Certified Public Accountants, and the National Association of Broadcasters define appropriate behavior for member individuals and companies.

The most difficult situation for managers is the ethical dilemma. An *ethical dilemma* arises when all alternative choices or behaviors are unde-

personal ethics Ethics adapted from the values of individual managers; reflect religion, social consciousness, and/or personal attitudes toward social responsibility.

corporate ethics Ethics derived from the organization's own values and culture.

professional ethics Ethics defined by professional occupational groups for member individuals and companies.

EXHIBIT 3.7

**Corporate Responses
to Social Demands**

Organizational responsibility
that is voluntary and guided
by the organization's desire
to make social contributions
not mandated by economics,
law, or ethics.

sirable because of potentially negative ethical consequences. Right and wrong cannot be clearly identified. Consider the case of the bank manager who recruits a black female MBA only to learn that several customers prefer to be served by a white male. Giving the new employee full responsibility to serve customers may hurt the bank's business and reduce employment opportunities for other minority group members. Giving her less challenging duties than other MBAs would be unfair to her. Either way, someone would get hurt. Many businesses face an ethical dilemma with respect to South Africa. For example, if Goodyear pulls out of South Africa, its black employees will be hurt; if it stays, it will be supporting the oppressive government. Goodyear has decided that the responsible choice is to stay in South Africa.

There are no easy answers to ethical dilemmas. Managers must carefully investigate all aspects of the issue and arrive at a decision that will strike the best ethical balance among competing needs.

Discretionary Responsibilities

Discretionary responsibility is purely voluntary and guided by a company's desire to make social contributions not mandated by economics, law, or ethics. Discretionary activities include generous philanthropic contributions that offer no payback to the company and are not expected. An example of discretionary behavior occurred when Pittsburgh Brewing Company helped laid-off steelworkers by establishing and contributing to food banks in the Pittsburgh area. It also started a fund-raising program in which people could drink beer with members of the Pittsburgh Steelers for a $5 contribution to their local food bank. Discretionary responsibility is the highest level of social responsibility, because it goes beyond societal expectations to contribute to the community's welfare.

CORPORATE RESPONSES TO SOCIAL DEMANDS

Confronted with a specific ethical decision, how might a corporation respond? Management scholars have developed a scale of response actions that companies use when a social issue confronts them.[30] These actions are obstructive, defensive, accommodative, and proactive and are illustrated on the continuum in Exhibit 3.7.[31]

Obstructive.   Companies that adopt **obstructive responses** deny all responsibility, claim that evidence of wrongdoing is misleading or distorted, and place obstacles to delay investigation. During the Watergate years, such obstruction was labeled *stonewalling*. A. H. Robins Company reportedly used obstructive actions when it received warnings about its Dalkon shield, an intrauterine device. The company built a wall around itself. It stood against all evidence and insisted to the public that the product was safe and effective. The company spared no effort to resist

obstructive response   A response to social demands in which the organization denies responsibility, claims that evidence of misconduct is misleading or distorted, and attempts to obstruct investigation.

investigation. As word about injuries caused by the Dalkon shield kept pouring in, one attorney was told to search the files and destroy all papers pertaining to the product.[32]

Defensive.   The **defensive response** means that the company admits to some errors of omission or commission. The company cuts its losses by defending itself but is not obstructive. Defensive managers generally believe that "these things happen, but they are nobody's fault." Goodyear adopted a defensive strategy by deciding to keep its South Africa plants open and provided an intelligent argument for why that was the proper action.

Accommodative.   An **accommodative response** means that the company accepts social responsibility for its actions, although it may do so in response to external pressure. Firms that adopt this action try to meet economic, legal, and ethical responsibilities. If outside forces apply pressure, managers agree to curtail ethically questionable activities. Banks that continued to charge high interest rates on credit cards (18 percent and above) even after interest rates had dropped started lowering their rates after a public outcry. As complaints piled up, the House Banking Committee began to consider new regulations, and many banks lowered interest rates to accommodate the public interest.

Proactive.   The **proactive response** means that firms take the lead in social issues. They seek to learn what is in the public interest and respond without coaxing or pressure from outside constituencies. One example of proactive behavior is the Potlatch Corporation. Potlatch makes milk cartons and came up with the idea of printing photographs of missing children on them (see Exhibit 3.8). The company reported that within days after the Alta-Dena Dairy of Los Angeles placed a missing-kids carton in grocery stores, one of the youngsters returned home.[33] Another proactive response is corporate philanthropy. Many companies, including Miller Brewing, Coca-Cola, and Westinghouse, make generous donations to universities, United Way, and other charitable groups as a way of reaching out and improving society.

These four categories of action are similar to the scale of social performance described in Exhibit 3.5. Obstructiveness tends to occur in firms whose actions are based solely on economic considerations. Defensive organizations are willing to work within the letter of the law. Accommodative organizations respond to ethical pressures. Proactive organizations use discretionary responsibilities to enhance community welfare.

ORGANIZATIONAL CONSTITUENCIES

One reason for the difficulty in deciding on social responses is that managers must confront the question "responsiveness to whom?" Enlightened organizations see a variety of constituencies in their external and

EXHIBIT   3.8

Proactive Response at Potlatch Corporation

Source: Courtesy of Potlatch Corporation.

defensive response   A response to social demands in which the organization admits to some errors of commission or omission but does not act obstructively.

accommodative response   A response to social demands in which the organization accepts— often under pressure—social responsibility for its actions in order to comply with the public interest.

proactive response   A response to social demands in which the organization seeks to learn what is in its constituencies' interest and to respond without pressure from them.

EXHIBIT 3.9

Constituencies Relevant to an Organization

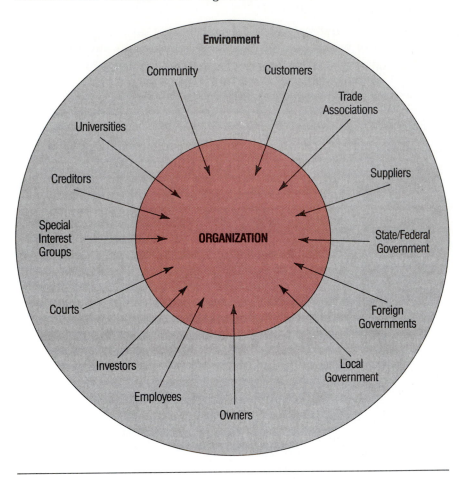

internal environments. A **constituency** is any group within or outside the organization that has a stake in the organization's performance. Each constituency has a different criterion of responsiveness because it has a different interest in the organization.[34]

Exhibit 3.9 illustrates important constituencies, including employees, customers, owners, creditors, suppliers, and investors. Investors', owners', and suppliers' interests are served by managerial efficiency, that is, use of resources to achieve profits. Employees expect work satisfaction, pay, and good supervision. Customers are concerned with decisions about the quality and availability of goods and services.

Other important constituencies are the government and the community. Most corporations exist only under the proper charter and licenses and operate within the limits of safety laws, environmental protection requirements, and other laws and regulations in the government sector. The community includes local government, the natural and physical

Honeywell actively promotes health among an important constituency—employees and their families. A health care advisor program is one of Honeywell's many efforts to insure high-quality health care for employees and at the same time control medical cost increases. The health care advisor helps this family choose doctors and hospitals and offers counseling on healthful life-styles. Employees are made aware of how factors such as blood-fat levels, weight, blood pressure, and stress influence health and longevity. The response to the health needs of Honeywell employees could be considered accommodation or even proaction on the scale in Exhibit 3.7.

environments, and the quality of life provided for residents. Special-interest groups, still another constituency, may include trade associations, political action committees, professional associations, consumerists, and environmentalists. Organizations that use ethical and discretionary considerations pay attention to all constituencies that are affected by its actions.

Lincoln Electric Company is a welding machine and supply firm located in Cleveland. It enjoys the lowest costs in the industry, the highest-rated product quality, and the lowest prices. What is Lincoln's secret? Management is committed to the principle of a moral contract with employees and customers. Employees and customers come first and shareholders last in priority.[35] Managers of Levi Strauss also are concerned with a variety of constituencies. The company won the Lawrence Wien prize for social responsibility in 1984. It donates 2.4 percent of pretax earnings to worthy causes, including social programs in local communities. Levi Strauss even considers international constituencies. It has created 90 community involvement teams around the world, which have built a home for orphans in Argentina and installed new wells in a Philippines village.

IMPROVING ETHICAL AND SOCIAL RESPONSIVENESS

Many managers are concerned about how to improve their companies' social responsiveness. They don't want to be forced into an obstructionist or defensive position. Methods for helping organizations become more responsive include social audits, codes of ethics, ethics committees/ethical advocates, and supporting whistle blowers.

The Social Audit.   Just as a financial audit is designed to depict a company's economic health, the social audit can evaluate a company's social health. The **corporate social audit** is defined as the criteria management develops for evaluating the firm's social contributions—that is, management's attempt to measure, monitor, and evaluate the organization's performance with respect to social programs and objectives.[36]

corporate social audit The criteria management develops for measuring, monitoring, and evaluating the organization's performance with respect to social programs and objectives.

The social audit first must define a list of areas in which corporate performance will be evaluated; such as the following:

1. Ecology and environmental quality
2. Community needs
3. Business philanthropy
4. Minorities and disadvantaged persons
5. Employee relations, benefits, and satisfaction with work
6. Employee safety and health
7. Product safety
8. Marketing practices
9. Stockholder relations
10. Government relations
11. Consumerism[37]

Once the criteria of the social audit have been defined, companies may try to evaluate organizational responsiveness on a cost-benefit basis. This is not always satisfactory, because costs of social programs are more visible and measurable than benefits. The programs tend to look less economical than they really are.[38] Attempting to interpret a social audit in economic terms misses the point that social responsibility goes beyond economics in the attempt to make a contribution to society.

Another method of auditing is simply to evaluate each activity on its own merits and its value to the company rather than on the basis of economic efficiency. The key question is: "Is this worth doing and worth doing by us?" If so, the audit provides a picture of what the firm is doing well.

Social audits are infrequently used in business because they have disadvantages. Social responsiveness is hard to measure accurately, and an audit opens the door to criticism from all sides. Profit-oriented shareholders will criticize money spent on noneconomic programs, and pressure groups will criticize any shortcomings the audit reveals.

code of ethics A formal statement of the organization's values regarding social issues.

Code of Ethics.   A **code of ethics** is a formal statement of the company's values concerning social issues. The purpose of a code of ethics is to communicate to employees in plain language what the company stands for. Codes of ethics are valuable when they explicitly state those behaviors that are expected and those that will not be tolerated and are backed up by management's actions. Without top management support, there is no insurance that the code will be followed. Codes serve to remind employees of existing laws and to tell the public at large what the company stands for.

General Dynamics Corporation uses a successful code of ethics. General Dynamics was in trouble for overcharging on government contracts for a number of years. A new ethics program included a revised code of ethics that prohibited managers from accepting gifts, however small, from vendors. The expanded code of ethics was preached to all 100,000 employees at ethics seminars.

Ethics Committee and Ethical Advocate.   An **ethics committee** is a group of executives appointed to oversee company ethics. Ethical issues are assigned to the committee, and members provide rulings on questionable issues. The ethics committee assumes responsibility for disciplining wrongdoers, which is essential if the organization is to directly influence employee behavior. An **ethical advocate** is a person assigned the role of the organizational conscience, that is, pointing out actual or potential failures of social responsibility.

Ethics committees are not widely used. One survey found that of all the companies having a formal code of ethics, only 14 percent had an ethics committee. General Dynamics has as part of its ethics program an ethics program director whom employees can approach when they are uncomfortable complaining directly to a line supervisor about an ethical issue. General Dynamics also has a steering committee, headed by two vice-presidents, that oversees implementation of appropriate ethical standards within the company. A committee from the board of directors also is concerned with ethics and keeps watch over the internal groups. With this program in place, General Dynamics is able to respond to social issues that arise and sit in judgment on violators.[39]

ethics committee A group of executives assigned to oversee the organization's ethics by ruling on questionable issues and disciplining violators.

ethical advocate An individual assigned to point out actual or potential failures of corporate social responsibility.

Whistle Blowing.   **Whistle blowing** occurs when an employee discloses illegal, immoral, or illegitimate practices on the employer's part.[40] Anyone in the organization can blow the whistle if he or she detects illegal or immoral organizational activities. Whistle-blowers often report wrongdoings to outsiders, such as regulatory agencies, senators, representatives, or newspaper reporters. In enlightened companies, whistle blowers can also report to an ethics advocate or ethics committee.

Whistle blowers must be protected if this is to be an effective ethical safeguard; otherwise, they will suffer and the company may continue its unethical or illegal activity. Helen Guercil noticed something peculiar when she went to work as a secretary to the bankruptcy court of Detroit. The multimillion-dollar cases seemed to be heard by the same judge and handled by the same attorneys. She discovered that one lawyer had been awarded $400,000 in bankruptcy fees from this judge. She blew the whistle when she discovered evidence of special favors bought with lavish trips, expensive gifts, and on-the-job sex. She contacted the chief judge of the district court and called the Justice Department and U.S. courts in Washington. An investigation led to the retirement of two judges, the indictment of the chief clerk, and the conviction of the attorney who had been awarded all the money. However, Helen Guercil received a lot of pressure on the job and was eventually fired.[41]

whistle blowing The disclosure by an employee of illegal, immoral, or illegitimate practices by the organization.

DOES SOCIAL RESPONSIBILITY HURT ECONOMIC PERFORMANCE?

The relationship of a corporation's social responsibility to its financial performance concerns both managers and management scholars and has generated a lively debate.[42] One concern of managers is whether good citizenship will hurt performance—after all, social programs cost money. A number of studies have been undertaken to determine whether heightened social responsiveness increases or decreases financial performance. Studies have provided varying results but generally have found that there is no relationship between social responsibility and financial performance or, at most, a small, positive one.[43] These findings are very encouraging, because they mean that use of resources for the social good does not systematically rebound in a way that would hurt the company.

One reason social responsibility does not hurt performance is that it often has an indirect profit motivation. Profit-motivated philanthropy means that firms do not give money away randomly. They select relevant targets, such as the local community, from which they may receive indirect benefit.[44] In other words, philanthropy can help a firm attain corporate financial goals. Atlantic Richfield supports needy artists in Alaska because it wants the population's blessing for its drilling program on the North Slope. Philip Morris donates thousands of dollars annually to earn the image of a valuable corporate citizen by legislators who ponder questions about tobacco subsidies or required deposits on Miller and 7-Up bottles. The Big Eight accounting firms make large donations to business school accounting departments so they will be able to hire top accounting students, who normally are in short supply.

The important point is that being socially responsible does not hurt a firm. Enlightened firms can use their discretion to contribute to society's welfare and, in so doing, even improve performance. Given the social needs in the United States and Canada, it is important that corporate social involvement does not hurt financial performance.

SUMMARY

This chapter discussed several important points about the organization's relationship to the external environment. The external environment is the single most important influence on organizational behavior and performance. The external environment consists of two layers: the task environment and the general environment. The task environment includes customers, competitors, suppliers, and labor supply. The general environment includes technological, sociocultural, economic, legal-political, and international dimensions. Management techniques for helping the organization adapt to the environment include boundary-spanning roles, forecasting and planning, a flexible structure, and mergers and joint ventures. Techniques managers can use to influence the external environment include advertising and public relations, political activity, trade associations, and illegal practices.

Another important relationship with the external environment pertains to social responsibility. The model for evaluating social performance uses four criteria: economic, legal, ethical, and discretionary. Organizations may use four types of response to specific social pressures: obstructive, defensive, accommodative, and proactive. Evaluating corporate social behavior often requires assessing its impact on organizational constituencies. Techniques for improving social responsiveness include the corporate social audit, code of ethics, ethics committee/ethical advocate, and whistle blowing. Finally, research suggests that socially responsible organizations perform as well as—and sometimes better than—organizations that are not socially responsible.

Management Solution

Gerber executives took a hard line against recalling baby food from the shelves in 1986, because in 1984 consumer reports of crushed glass in containers proved unfounded. A 1986 FDA investigation showed that complaints were unwarranted. After inspecting 40,000 sealed jars of Gerber baby food, the FDA found only harmless glass specks in 9. Gerber plants use state-of-the-art technology, with filters and screening devices. Gerber executives believed it was impossible for a customer to go into a store and find glass slivers in jars. One complainant conceded to the FDA that the jar could have been chipped when she dropped her bag of groceries. Another remembered breaking a glass before she fed the baby.

Based on the problems in 1984, Gerber planned its response carefully. Some people criticized Gerber for not being as responsive as Johnson & Johnson had been in the Tylenol case. However, after carefully analyzing the situation, Gerber executives realized that no one had died or even been injured. Executives did what they believed to be legally and ethically correct for both customers and other constituencies affected by the decision. The planned response, although defensive in nature, was correct for the situation.[45]

DISCUSSION QUESTIONS

1. Which is more important to organizational effectiveness—the external environment or the internal environment? Discuss.
2. How does the task environment differ from the general environment? Would the task environment for a bank contain the same elements as that for a government welfare agency?
3. What are the two forces that influence organizational uncertainty? Would such forces typically originate in the task environment or the general environment?
4. Is it socially responsible for organizations to undertake political activity or join with others in a trade association to influence the government? Discuss.
5. Compare the profit-maximizing view to the iron law of responsibility. Which do you think is correct?
6. The model of corporate social performance suggests that economic responsibilities are of the greatest magnitude, followed by legal, ethical, and discretionary responsibilities. How do these four types of responsibility relate to corporate responses to social demands? Discuss.
7. From where do managers derive ethical values? What can managers do to help define ethical standards for the corporation?
8. Have you ever experienced an ethical dilemma? Evaluate the dilemma with respect to its impact on other people.
9. Lincoln Electric considers customers and employees to be more important constituencies than shareholders. Is it appropriate for management to define some constituencies as more important than others? Should all constituencies be considered equal?
10. Why are corporate social audits seldom used? Do you think a code of ethics combined with an ethics committee would be more effective than a social audit? Explain.

CASES FOR ANALYSIS

WHAT IS RIGHT?

It is often hard for a manager to determine what is "right" and even more difficult to put ethical behavior into practice. A manager's ethical orientation often brings him or her into conflict with people, policies, customers, or bosses. Consider the following examples:

1.   Bob Jones is vice-president of an unprofitable division for a major defense contractor. If the division doesn't land a major defense contract soon, Bob will be fired and many employees and executives laid off. A close friend of Bob's goes to work for a prosperous defense contractor and gains access to proprietary and confidential information. Bob receives an envelope marked "confidential and personal" that contains cost figures for an air-to-air missile contract on which the competitor is bidding. Bob's division is preparing its own bid, and these data could be enormously valuable. Bob suspects that the envelope is from his friend, because he has helped her a number of times in her career. Bob calls in three subordinates to discuss the issue. The marketing vice-president insists that the data should be used because the industry is so competitive; everyone tries to obtain good information on competitors' plans. The engineering executive insists that the data should not be used; it would certainly be immoral because the government assumes the bids will be made independently, and this could amount to collusion. The personnel executive can go either way but is concerned about the enormous human costs if the division lays off employees. What should Bob do?

2.   Jane Smith is president of a $650 million steakhouse chain. This chain, with 650 outlets, is the worst performer among major fast-food restaurants. Jane has been president for 12 years, having gotten this role during a management shakeup following the company's bankruptcy. The steakhouse chain has not kept pace with the environment due to Americans' dietary interest in fish and poultry. McDonald's and other restaurants have taken most of the breakfast business available to fast-food chains. The company is doing so poorly that its stock price is low, and there is a threat of a takeover by U.S.A. Cafes. Jane has gotten the board to approve a golden parachute worth approximately $11 million in case the company is taken over. Five other executives have golden parachutes worth a total of $3 million. Jane's annual salary is $750,000—quite good considering the company's poor performance. The directors, who have been generous with the golden parachutes, are also well compensated. They earn $30,000 a year in their positions ($10,000 more than IBM's directors), and they can retire after 10 years and receive their $30,000 for life. Jane says she deserves the

compensation and the golden parachute as CEO of a large corporation. She plans to open new restaurants and change restaurants to be in tune with consumer demand. Is Jane's management of the steakhouse chain ethical?

3. Junior Bolton drives a truck for a local petroleum plant during the summer. He is between his junior and senior years in college. He was lucky to get the job, because few are available in the depressed Southwest. The job pays well, so he will be able to return to college and finish his degree in business administration. As he was filling out the paperwork after his first delivery, the supervisor said, "Be sure you bill the large companies an extra 5 percent for overhead costs." "What do you mean?" Junior asked. "We don't have a charge for overhead." The supervisor responded, "It's been the practice of this company for years. It's the way business is done. It's not illegal, and it helps us make enough profit to stay in business during these hard times." Junior wondered whether he should blow the whistle on what he considered an unethical practice. What should he do?

Questions

1. Use the guidelines described in "Manager's Shoptalk: Guidelines for Ethical Decision Making" to determine the appropriate behavior in these cases. Do you have all the information you need to make an ethical decision? How would family or friends react to each alternative if you were in these situations?
2. What should be the basis for the decisions—personal ethics, professional ethics, company tradition, industry practices, or laws and regulations?
3. What are the likely consequences for constituencies if the most ethical option is followed? Does the impact on constituencies influence the socially desirable response?

Source: The incidents reported in this case are based on Clinton L. Oaks, "David Kingsbury: Employee vs. Employer Problems and Responsibilities," distributed by HBS Case Services; Alan L. Otten, "Ethics on the Job: Companies Alert Employees to Potential Dilemmas," *The Wall Street Journal*, July 14, 1986, 17; Ruth Simon, "Charred Meat," *Forbes*, April 21, 1986, 93; Steve Buckman, "Doing What's Right," *Management Solutions* (June 1986), 24–25.

JACK DANIEL DISTILLERY

Lynchburg, Tennessee, is where Jack Daniel's whiskey is made. Advertisements feature ducks and oak barrels and leather-faced Tennesseans. But behind the laid back atmosphere, trouble is brewing.

At least 10 local residents charge that Jack Daniel drove them out of the cattle business. "Thick slop," a distillation by-product, makes excellent cattle feed, and Jack Daniel traditionally gave it free to farmers. This went on for decades; then a price was established at $2 a thousand gallons, which was then raised to $4, which was still a bargain. The arrangement was informal, without contracts. Many farmers got into the cattle business or expanded their business because of the cheap cattle feed. So many cattle were being raised that it created a pollution problem for Moore County. Jack Daniel said it would stop delivery unless farmers invested in environmental improvements. Farmers invested heavily in moving feedlots back from creeks, and in building roads, barns, and holding tanks.

Then the slump in whiskey demand hit. Consumers turned to white wine and light beer. Jack Daniel managers had to economize, and switched to a "dry house" method of disposing of slop. This saves a lot of money for Jack Daniel, but leaves no thick slop for farmers—who are angry. Employees are also disgruntled. The business slump forced some layoffs, and angry employees may form a union. Lynchburg draws 300,000 visitors a year, who are shown around by Jack Daniel employees, but they don't see the tension between the farmers, employees, and Jack Daniel. The farmers insist that Jack Daniel assured them a steady supply of thick slop if they solve the water-pollution problem. Jack Daniel denies it, and says the farmers can feed the cattle like farmers everywhere, by buying the feed. Farmers shouldn't expect a free ride forever.

Questions

1. Which environmental sectors and constituencies are involved here? Are these constituencies important to Jack Daniel Distillery? Are other constituencies more important?
2. What is the socially responsible thing to do? Should the Jack Daniel Distillery continue to provide thick slop to farmers at a low price?
3. What are the dilemmas in this case? One part of the environment—customer demand—seems to affect the relationship with other parts. What responses should Jack Daniel managers consider for resolving this problem?

Source: Based on Timothy K. Smith, "Tennessee Cattlemen Are Suin' Jack Daniel Instead of Sippin' It," *The Wall Street Journal,* February 12, 1986, 1, 19.

PART TWO
PLANNING

Source: Art Resource/NY: Rembrandt, Syndic of the Drapers' Guild, Rijksmuseum, Amsterdam.

Source: Courtesy of Honeywell Inc.

CHAPTER 4

Organizational Goal Setting and Planning

Chapter Outline

Overview of Goals and Plans

Goals in Organizations

The Importance of Goals
Organizational Mission
Types of Goals
Hierarchy of Objectives

Criteria for Effective Goals

Goal Characteristics
Goal-Setting Behavior

Management-by-Objectives Types of Systems

MBO Characteristics
Strengths and Weaknesses of MBO Systems

Developing Plans for Attaining Goals

Strategic Plans
Tactical Plans
Operational Plans
Single-Use Plans
Standing Plans

Planning Time Horizon

Organizational Design for Planning

Centralized Planning Department
Decentralized Planning Staff
Planning Task Force

Barriers to Organizational Planning

Specific Barriers
Overcoming Barriers

Learning Objectives

After studying this chapter, you should be able to:

- **Define goals and plans and explain the relationship between them.**

- **Explain the concept of organizational mission and how it influences goal setting and planning.**

- **Describe the types of goals an organization should have and why they resemble a hierarchy.**

- **Define the characteristics of effective goals.**

- **Explain the behavioral approaches to handling multiple and conflicting goals.**

- **Describe how management by objectives can enhance goal setting in organizations.**

- **Explain the difference between single-use plans and standing plans.**

- **Describe the structural designs organizations can use to accomplish planning and goal setting.**

- **Examine the barriers to the organization's planning process.**

Management Problem

Volkswagen was spinning its wheels. The West German carmaker established its reputation during the 1960s and 1970s with witty ads and low prices for the quality Beetle. Then the Beetle lost out to snappier, competitively priced Japanese imports. Volkswagen responded with the Rabbit, but quality problems cut its share of the U.S. market from 6 percent to less than 2 percent. The question facing Volkswagen chairman Carl H. Hahn and other executives was how to get Volkswagen back on track. Volkswagen adopted two significant goals: regain its U.S. market share and become more competitive in the market for small, inexpensive cars. One plan for increasing market share was to redesign the Rabbit into a high-performance automobile called the Golf. To attack the low end of the market, Volkswagen considered having cars produced in South America and teaming up with a carmaker in Spain to build subcompacts.[1]

If you were an advisor to Volkswagen, what goals and plans would you recommend? Do you think the goals and plans contemplated by Volkswagen's executives are feasible?

Times have changed for Volkswagen. Its executives have set new performance objectives and developed new ideas for achieving them. When Volkswagen executives make these decisions, they are planning and goal setting. They are deciding where they want the organization to be in the future and how to get it there. In some organizations, planning is informal and has little impact on the organization. In others, managers follow a well-defined planning framework. The organization establishes a basic mission and develops formal goals and strategic plans for carrying it out.

Each year organizations such as IBM, McDonald's, Royal LaPaige, Mazda, and United Way undertake a strategic planning exercise—reviewing their missions, goals, and plans to meet environmental changes or the expectations of important constituencies such as the community, owners, or stockholders.

Of the four management functions—planning, organizing, leading, and controlling—described in Chapter 1, planning is considered the most important. Everything else stems from planning. Organizing, leading, and controlling all depend on where the organization is trying to go. When planning is done well, the other management functions can be done well.

In this chapter, we explore the process of planning. Special attention is given to goals and goal setting, for that is where the process starts. Then the types of plans organizations can use to achieve those goals are discussed. In Chapter 5, we examine a special type of planning—strategic planning—and a number of strategic options managers can use in a competitive environment. In Chapters 6 and 7, we look at management decision making. Proper decision-making techniques are crucial to selecting the organization's goals, plans, and strategic options.

OVERVIEW OF GOALS AND PLANS

goal A desired future state that the organization attempts to realize.

plan A blueprint specifying the resource allocations, schedules, and other actions necessary for attaining goals.

planning The act of determining the organization's goals and the means for achieving them.

A **goal** is a desired future state that the organization attempts to realize.[2] Goals are important because organizations exist for a purpose and goals define and state that purpose. A **plan** is a blueprint for goal achievement and specifies the necessary resource allocations, schedules, and other actions. Goals specify future ends; plans specify today's means. The term **planning** usually incorporates both ideas; it means determining the organization's goals and defining the means for achieving them. For several years, Owens-Illinois had the goals of being a high-volume glass container manufacturer and having a large market share. Then it changed to a goal of higher profits, even at the risk of losing volume and market share. The new goal led to the creation of a new plan, which included the closing of a recently constructed glass container plant. The plant had fit the previous goals but not the new ones and hence was sold.[3]

When individuals plan, they first do so based on certain assumptions about themselves and their environment; these are called *planning premises*. Then they establish some goals or objectives that are consistent with these premises and formulate plans for achieving them. For example, you plan your career based on assumptions about your abilities, your interests and attitudes, the potential job market for certain specialties, your future needs, and so on. Then you set objectives, perhaps pertaining to future income levels, lifestyle, or where you would like to live. You may set near-term objectives, such as attaining a 3.0 grade point average this semester, and longer-term objectives, such as doing postgraduate

These new McDonnell Douglas Super 80 aircraft are about to be delivered to American Airlines. American took delivery of twenty-three of these fuel-efficient airplanes to achieve its 1985 strategic goals of expansion and cost reduction. Strategic plans to meet the expansion goal included the opening of three new hubs in Nashville, Raleigh/ Durham, and San Juan; the introduction of the "Ultimate Super Saver" fares; and the American Eagle program under which commuter airlines provide convenient connections to American's hubs from smaller cities. The plan for cost reduction was to average down unit costs through lower wages for new employees and the increased use of fuel-efficient aircraft.

work. You may also formulate plans to reach those objectives, such as majoring in marketing or learning about a certain company to increase your chance of being hired there. You make many of your decisions based on this planning process.

Organization managers plan in a similar way. The middle-level manager in a software development company, for example, is expected to accomplish certain objectives, such as "documentation for the new software package completed in six months." Some of the planning premises for this manager might be the following:

- She has an adequate number of personnel.
- Her people are not yet sufficiently trained.
- She will receive the final software package from the programmers in time for her people to write the documentation.
- Her people require 200 hours to do program documentation.

Based on these premises, this manager is able to establish objectives for herself, her department, and individual department members and develop a plan for achieving them. She knows that the documentation must be completed in six months, which is the primary objective. She can then plan to insure having the correct number of adequately trained people to assign to the project. She may develop a schedule that will give people enough hours to complete the project in six months. She may develop a contingency plan in the event the software is not received from the programmers on time. The contingency plan may require additional personnel and perhaps overtime in order to complete the job in six months. All of this planning is done with the understanding that the documentation must be ready to enable the software to be sold in the marketplace and thereby help the organization achieve its overall goals of new-product introduction and profits.

E X H I B I T   4.1

**Relationship between Goals and Plans in the Organizational
Planning Process**

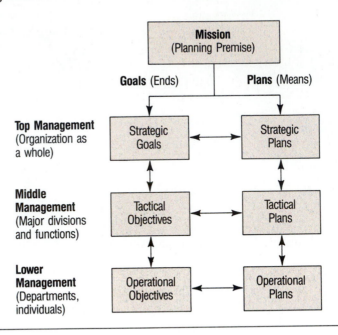

Exhibit 4.1 illustrates the relationship between organizational goals
and plans. Note that the planning process starts with a formal mission,
which sets the planning premises for the organization. Then companywide strategic goals are determined and form the basis for the organization's lower-level objectives. The term **objective** is often used interchangeably with *goal* but usually refers to specific short-term targets for
which measurable results can be obtained. The definition of the organization's goals occurs at three levels: the strategic (company) level, the
tactical (divisional) level, and the operational (department) level.[4] Strategic goals influence the definition of tactical objectives, which in turn
influence operational objectives because the goals and objectives must be
consistent and support one another.

The right-hand side of Exhibit 4.1 shows that the organization's plans
exist in a hierarchy. At the top level, strategic plans define resource allocation and other actions required for achieving the company's strategic
goals. At the middle management level, tactical plans are used to attain
the tactical objectives. At lower organization levels, plans for specific
departments and individuals are used for attaining operational objectives.

Although Exhibit 4.1 suggests that plans are distinct from goals and
that goals and plans exist at three distinct levels, they all occur simultaneously and influence one another. Goals and plans go hand in hand.
Moreover, top-level goals and plans influence those at lower levels, at-

objective   A specific short-term
target for which measurable results can be obtained.

tainment of which determines whether strategic goals and plans will be achieved.

The overall planning process is powerful because it helps managers at all levels crystallize what they are trying to achieve and what they must do. This approach prevents managers from thinking merely in terms of day-to-day work activities and gives them a sense of focus and direction. When organizations drift away from goals and plans, they typically get into trouble. This occurred at the New York City Transit Authority. But new management was able to implement a strong planning system, illustrating the power of planning to improve organizational performance.

The American Egg Board (AEB), a not-for-profit association of egg producers, has defined as its mission "to improve the demand for eggs, egg products, spent fowl, and the products of spent fowl." AEB goals are "to communicate the advantages of increased egg usage to consumers, food service operators, retail food organizations. . ." and "to develop new products and new marketing techniques for the marketing of eggs and spent fowl." The brass egg paperweight here, engraved with the words, "MAKE 'EM EGGS!", was sent to the headquarters of chain restaurants as part of the plan to meet its goals by actively encouraging restaurants to add eggs to their menus.

New York City Transit Authority

In 1984, the New York City Transit Authority was plagued by track fires, the failure of the Flexible Model 870 bus fleet, and the widespread perception of rampant subway crime. The transit authority was trapped in a straitjacket of civil service regulations and union requirements that affected nearly 95 percent of its 5,000 supervisors and 50,000 employees.

When Robert Kiley took over as chairman of the New York City Transit Authority's parent—the Metropolitan Transit Authority—in 1985, his initial steps were to define a mission and several goals. The transit authority's mission was clear: Provide transportation services for New York City. Within that overall mission, Kiley charted a course for the New York City Transit Authority in terms of three strategic goals:

1. A sustained rate of capital investment that would get the transit systems into good repair and keep them there
2. A predictable, assured source of operating revenue
3. An emphasis on recruiting, training, and rewarding good managers and workers and a commitment to shed the anachronistic, demoralizing work practices of the past

David L. Gunn assumed the presidency of the New York City Transit Authority. He and his new management team spent a good part of 1985 developing a system of tactical and operational objectives. They committed themselves to accomplishing more than 340 tactical objectives by the end of the year, including

1. 1,720 (28 percent) of the 6,125 subway cars cleaned, graffiti free, and kept that way
2. 1,169 (31 percent) of the 3,835 buses free of graffiti and body damage and kept that way

3. Working lights and loudspeakers, climate control, accurate destination signs, and readable maps on 90 percent of the subway fleet
4. 450 subway cars overhauled
5. Over 95 percent of requests for replacement parts filled promptly
6. Twice-weekly inspections of all 706 miles of subway track and 126 miles of yard track.

These tactical objectives translated into more specific operational objectives for department managers and their employees. The system of goals and objectives also paved the way for new plans. One plan was to create positions that would be exempt from union and civil service protection. Plans were made to hire up to 1,200 exempt management personnel to meet strategic goal 3. With the influx of new managerial personnel, plans were implemented to decentralize decision making so that managers have the authority to meet their operational objectives. Plans were also made to increase training funds by 27 percent and employee training time by 29 percent.

These goals and plans laid the foundation for rapid operating improvements in the New York City Transit Authority. Planning gave new direction to supervisors and employees. A demoralized, reluctant work force was transformed into one that had a place to go and knew how to get there.[5]

GOALS IN ORGANIZATIONS

Setting goals is a key task for top and middle managers. Goals come first in the planning process and include both a mission statement and goals for the organization as a whole. For example, Uniroyal's recent goal was to revive and expand its ailing tire business. This was the basis for Uniroyal's plan to shut down two U.S. tire plants and sell off foreign and U.S. operations that were only marginally profitable. Goals are the guide by which lower-level personnel set objectives and make plans.

The Importance of Goals[6]

The presence of explicit goals provides several important benefits for the organization.

Source of Motivation and Commitment. Goal statements describe the organization's purpose to employees. They facilitate employees' identification with the organization and help motivate them by reducing uncertainty and clarifying what they should accomplish.

Guides to Action. Organizational goals provide a sense of direction. They focus attention on specific targets and direct employee efforts toward certain outcomes.

Rationale for Decisions. Through goal setting, managers learn what the organization is trying to accomplish. They can then make decisions to insure that internal policies, rules, performance, structure, products, and expenditures will be made in accordance with desired outcomes.

Standard of Performance. Since goals define desired outcomes for the organization, they also serve as performance criteria. They provide a standard of assessment. If an organization wishes to grow by 15 percent and actual growth is 17 percent, managers will have exceeded their prescribed standard.

Organizational Mission

At the top of the goal hierarchy is the **mission**—the organization's reason for existence. The mission describes the organization's values, aspirations, and reason for being. The formal **mission statement** is a broadly stated definition of basic business scope and operations that distinguishes the organization from others of a similar type.[7] The content of a mission statement often focuses on the market and customers and identifies desired fields of endeavor. Some mission statements describe company characteristics such as values, product quality, location of facilities, and attitude toward employees. Mission statements often reveal the company's philosophy as well as purpose. The mission statement for Pillsbury Company is presented in Exhibit 4.2. Note how the explicit mission is to be the best food company in the world. The mission statement also highlights the importance of the company's relationship with employees, product quality, and excellence as the way of doing business.

Many companies' mission statements are short and straightforward, describing basic business activities and purposes. An example of this type of mission statement is that of Columbia Gas System, a gas transmission and distribution company:

> *Columbia Gas System, through its subsidiaries, is active in pursuing opportunities in all segments of the natural gas industry and in related energy resource development. Exemplified by Columbia's three-star symbol, the separately managed companies work to benefit:* system stockholders— *through competitive return on their investment;* customers—*through efficient, safe, reliable service; and* employees—*through challenging and rewarding careers.*[8]

Because of mission statements similar to Pillsbury's and Columbia's, employees, as well as customers, suppliers, and stockholders, know the company's stated purpose.

Types of Goals

Within the organization there are three levels of goals—strategic goals, tactical objectives, and operational objectives—as described in Exhibit 4.1.[9]

mission The organization's reason for existence.

mission statement A broadly stated definition of the organization's basic business scope and operations that distinguish it from similar types of organizations.

E X H I B I T   4.2

The Pillsbury Company Mission Statement

THE PILLSBURY COMPANY
MISSION AND VALUES

The Pillsbury Company exists by public approval and our function is
to serve the public interest. Since 1869, Pillsbury employees have built a tradition of
quality. Our people have brought Pillsbury to the successful position we
hold in the food industry today. We are proud of our heritage,
and we are committed to achieving even greater success.

The Pillsbury Company is a diversified, international, market-oriented organization.

OUR MISSION IS TO BE THE BEST FOOD COMPANY IN THE WORLD.

By the best, we mean a rapidly growing company that supplies
premium quality products and outstanding service to our customers and provides a
superior return to our stockholders. In addition, we are committed
to being an outstanding corporate citizen and creating an environment for our
employees that makes Pillsbury an exceptional place to work.

We will conduct our business with the highest ethical standards and believe the
following values are fundamental to our success.

PEOPLE MAKE THE DIFFERENCE.

It is important that we:
- Attract, motivate and retain the most talented people in our industry.
- Promote mutual trust and respect for each other.
- Encourage promotion from within and provide fully competitive compensation.
- Practice open and timely two-way communication, with the expectation
and confidence that well-informed people will do the right thing.
- Keep an open mind to new ideas and encourage innovation and risk taking with
the knowledge that sometimes we will fail.
- Provide opportunity for all employees to develop their potential and make
the best use of their abilities.

QUALITY IS ESSENTIAL.

This requires that we:
- Define quality as performing up to the
users' expectations and then doing more.
- Make product quality and product safety
the responsibility of every employee.
- Market premium quality, great tasting
products at a fair price.
- Take pride in all the products and
services we provide.

EXCELLENCE MUST BE A WAY OF LIFE.

This demands that we:
- Maintain a dynamic, growth-oriented environment that
promotes teamwork and encourages individual initiative.
- Provide leadership and rewards that
will motivate employees to practice excellence in every
dimension of their job.
- Pursue functional excellence as an integral part of our
total business performance.
- Set priorities and execute plans consistent with our
strategic objectives.

We believe that if we live by these values,
we will establish Pillsbury as a premier company and achieve our long-range objectives.

Pillsbury

Source: People of Pillsbury, *Employee Annual Report,* 1985. Used with permission of
Pillsbury Company.

strategic goals Broad statements of where the organization
wants to be in the future; pertain to the organization as a
whole rather than to specific
divisions or departments.

Strategic Goals. Strategic goals are broad statements of where the organization wants to be in the future. They pertain to the organization as
a whole rather than to specific divisions or departments. Strategic goals
sometimes are called *official goals,* because they are the stated intentions
of what the organization wants to achieve.

EXHIBIT 4.3

Eight Types of Strategic Goals

▪ **Market standing:** Objectives indicating where a company wants to be relative to its competitors with respect to market share and competitive niche.

▪ **Innovation:** Objectives indicating management's commitment to the development of new methods of operation and new products.

▪ **Productivity:** Objectives outlining targeted levels of production efficiency.

▪ **Physical and financial resources:** Objectives pertaining to use, acquisition, and maintenance of capital and monetary resources.

▪ **Profitability:** Objectives specifying the level of profit and other indicators of financial performance.

▪ **Managerial performance and development:** Objectives specifying rates and levels of managerial productivity and growth.

▪ **Worker performance and attitude:** Objectives delineating expected rates of workers' productivity and positive attitudes.

▪ **Public responsibility:** Objectives indicating the company's responsibilities to its customers and society.

Source: Based on Peter F. Drucker, *The Practice of Management* (New York: Harper & Brothers, 1954), pp. 65–83.

What do strategic goals cover? Peter Drucker suggests that business organizations' goals should encompass more than profits, because profits alone lead to short-term thinking. He suggests that organizations focus on eight content areas: market standing; innovation; productivity; physical and financial resources; profitability; managerial performance and development; worker performance and attitude; and public responsibility.[10] A description of each goal is given in Exhibit 4.3.

Drucker's first five goal areas relate to the tangible, impersonal aspect of the organization and its operations. The last three are more subjective and personal. Most organizations have strategic goals in some but not all of these areas. For example, Columbia Gas System set the following four strategic goals for the 1986 to 1990 period to fit the mission described earlier:

1. Meet stockholders' expectations as to total return.
2. Have access to reasonable amounts of capital at reasonable costs at all times.
3. Provide for efficient management of and planned growth in stockholders' equity.
4. Insure the orderly succession of System officers, and enhance employee performance.[11]

These goals relate to profitability and stockholders' return, efficient management, the acquisition of financial resources, and manager/employee performance and development.

One of the strategic goals identified by Peter Drucker is public responsibility. Pacific Gas and Electric Company (PG&E) meets this goal through conservation and load management programs. Here a PG&E employee provides information on efficient use of energy to non-English-speaking customers. In related programs, PG&E helped customers weatherize more than 300,000 homes and provided cash rebates for low-income customers. This public responsibility activity helps keep customers' bills low and also makes PG&E more efficient.

E X H I B I T   4.4

Hierarchy of Objectives for a Manufacturing Organization

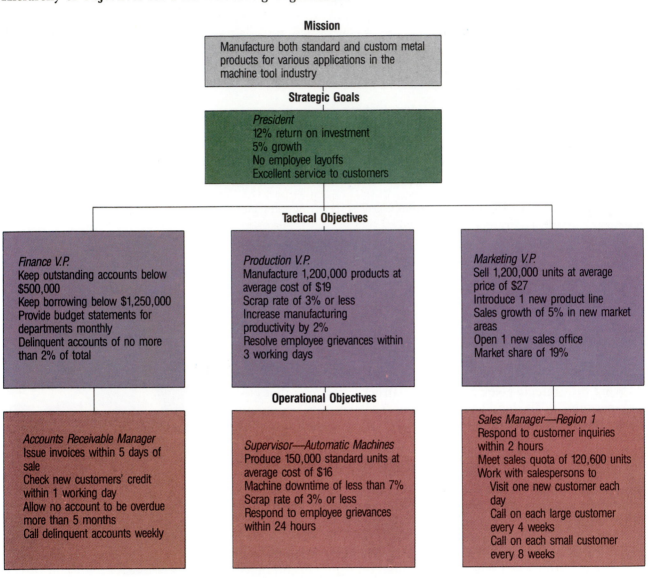

Mission

Manufacture both standard and custom metal products for various applications in the machine tool industry

Strategic Goals

President
12% return on investment
5% growth
No employee layoffs
Excellent service to customers

Tactical Objectives

Finance V.P.
Keep outstanding accounts below $500,000
Keep borrowing below $1,250,000
Provide budget statements for departments monthly
Delinquent accounts of no more than 2% of total

Production V.P.
Manufacture 1,200,000 products at average cost of $19
Scrap rate of 3% or less
Increase manufacturing productivity by 2%
Resolve employee grievances within 3 working days

Marketing V.P.
Sell 1,200,000 units at average price of $27
Introduce 1 new product line
Sales growth of 5% in new market areas
Open 1 new sales office
Market share of 19%

Operational Objectives

Accounts Receivable Manager
Issue invoices within 5 days of sale
Check new customers' credit within 1 working day
Allow no account to be overdue more than 5 months
Call delinquent accounts weekly

Supervisor—Automatic Machines
Produce 150,000 standard units at average cost of $16
Machine downtime of less than 7%
Scrap rate of 3% or less
Respond to employee grievances within 24 hours

Sales Manager—Region 1
Respond to customer inquiries within 2 hours
Meet sales quota of 120,600 units
Work with salespersons to
    Visit one new customer each day
    Call on each large customer every 4 weeks
    Call on each small customer every 8 weeks

tactical objectives Objectives that define the outcomes that major divisions and departments must achieve in order for the organization to reach its overall goals.

Tactical Objectives. **Tactical objectives** define the results that major divisions and departments within the organization intend to achieve. Tactical objectives apply to the middle management. They describe what major subunits must do in order for the organization to achieve its overall goals. For example, one tactical objective for Columbia Gas is to "regain an A long-term debt rating by the end of 1988." This tactical objective pertains to strategic goal 2 regarding access to reasonable amounts of capital. Achieving this objective will increase the organization's ability to borrow money at a reasonable rate.

Operational Objectives.   **Operational objectives** describe specific results expected from departments, work groups, and individuals. Operational objectives are precise and measurable. "Process 150 sales applications each week," "achieve 90 percent of deliveries on time," "reduce overtime by 10 percent next month," and "develop two new elective courses in accounting" are examples of operational objectives.

operational objectives Specific, measurable results expected from departments, work groups, and individuals within the organization.

Hierarchy of Objectives

Effectively designed organizational goals and objectives fit into a hierarchy; that is, the achievement of objectives at lower levels permits the attainment of higher-level goals. This is called a *means-ends chain* because lower-level objectives lead to accomplishment of higher-level goals. Operational objectives lead to the achievement of tactical objectives, which in turn lead to the attainment of strategic goals. Strategic goals typically are the responsibility of top management, tactical objectives that of middle management, and operational objectives that of first-line supervisors and workers.

An example of a goal hierarchy is illustrated in Exhibit 4.4. Note how the strategic goal of "excellent service to customers" translates into "open one new sales office" and "respond to customer inquiries within 2 hours" at lower management levels.

CRITERIA FOR EFFECTIVE GOALS

In order to insure goal-setting benefits for the organization, certain characteristics and guidelines should be adopted. The characteristics of both goals and the goal-setting process are listed in Exhibit 4.5.

Goal Characteristics

The following characteristics pertain to organizational goals at the strategic, tactical, and operational levels.

Specific and Measurable.   When possible, goals should be expressed in quantitative terms, such as increasing profits by 2 percent, decreasing scrap by 1 percent, or increasing average teacher effectiveness ratings from 3.5 to 3.7. Vague goals and objectives have little motivating power for employees. At the top of the organization, goals may be qualitative as well as quantitative. John Reed, CEO of Citicorp, has defined both quantitative and qualitative goals for his organization, including:

- Trim work force from 20,000 to 17,000.
- Clean up loan portfolio; reduce writeoffs.
- Wire 90 trading rooms around the globe.
- Build a merger and acquisition finance group.[12]

Each goal is precisely defined and allows for measurable progress.

E X H I B I T   4.5

Characteristics of Effective Goal Setting

Goal Characteristics
- Specific and measurable
- Cover key dimensions
- Challenging but realistic
- Defined time period
- Linked to rewards

Goal-Setting Behavior
- Coalition building
- Participation

Pier 1 Imports adopted goals in 1985 that illustrate effective goal characteristics. Pier 1's primary strategic goal is to accelerate the growth of the specialty retail business in order to double the square footage of selling space by 1990. Pier 1 also has financial goals that will result in an excellent financial position throughout the remainder of the 1980s. In addition, top management wants to be sensitive to the market and adapt to the changing needs and wants of customers. These goals cover key performance dimensions, are challenging, and specify a defined time period.

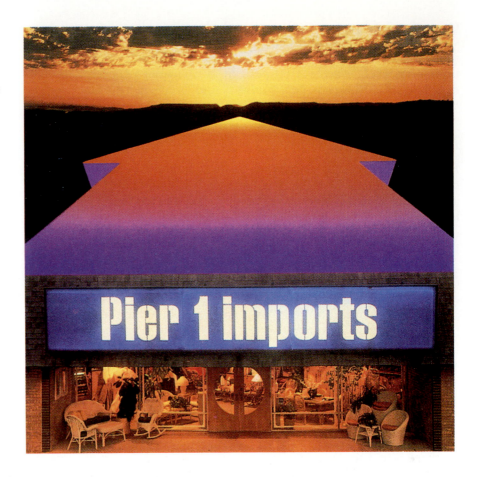

Cover Key Dimensions.   Managers must decide which activities should have explicit goals. Goals cannot be set for every aspect of employee behavior or organizational performance; if they were, their sheer number would render them meaningless. Instead, managers should identify a few critical success areas—perhaps up to four or five for any organizational department or job. For example, Rospatch Corporation makes garment labels, and senior managers have specified four financial goals within which planning takes place: 5 percent return on sales, 10 percent return on assets, 15 percent return on equity, and 20 percent compound annual growth rate.[13]

At the lower levels of the organization, one helpful approach is to limit goals to three categories: *innovation goals,* which pertain to improvement projects; *problem-solving goals,* which are designed to fix areas in which performance is below standard; and *exception goals,* which involve activities outside the normal work flow or that require exceptionally high levels of normal work.

Challenging but Realistic.   Goals should be challenging but not unreasonably difficult. One value of limiting operational goals to innovation, problem-solving, and exception goals is that these offer special challenges to employees. If a goal is too difficult, employees may give up; if too easy, employees may not feel motivated.[14] Managers should also insure that goals are set within the existing resource base and not beyond departments' time, equipment, and financial resources.

Defined Time Period.   Goals and objectives should specify the time period over which they will be achieved. A time period usually is a deadline specifying the date on which goal attainment will be measured. A goal of revising a company's job classification system could have a deadline such as June 30, 1989. If a strategic goal involves a two-to-three-year time horizon, specific dates for achieving parts of it can be set up. For example, strategic sales goals could be established on a three-year time horizon, with a $100 million target in year 1, a $129 million target in year 2, and a $165 million target in year 3.

Linked to Rewards.   The ultimate impact of goals depends on the extent to which salary increases, promotions, and awards are based on goal achievement. People who attain goals should be rewarded. Rewards give meaning and significance to goals and help energize employees to achieve goals. Of course, failure to attain goals often is due to factors outside employees' control. Failure to achieve a financial goal may be associated with a drop in market demand due to industry recession; thus, an employee could not be expected to reach it. Nevertheless, a positive reward may be appropriate if the employee partially achieved goals under difficult circumstances.[15]

Goal-Setting Behavior

In April 1986, President Reagan and the White House staff had decided to retaliate against terrorists in Libya. The specifics of the strike took two to three weeks to hammer out because of major disagreements among Cabinet and staff members on which targets to bomb and how to carry out the mission.[16] Although the overall purpose and mission were defined, establishing strategic goals and tactical objectives was both a political and a social process.

Conflict often occurs during goal setting because key managers disagree over objectives. Yet in order for goals to be effective, commitment is essential. Two techniques for achieving commitment to goals are coalition building and participation.

Coalition Building.   A **coalition** is an informal alliance among managers who support a specific goal. *Coalition building* is the process of forming alliances among managers. In other words, a manager who supports a specific goal, such as increasing the corporation's growth rate through diversification, talks informally to other executives and tries to persuade them to support the goal. Coalition building involves negotiation and bargaining. Without a coalition, a powerful individual or group could derail the goal-setting process. Coalition building gives managers an opportunity to discuss goals and contribute to the goal-setting process, enhancing their commitment to the goals that are finally adopted.[17]

Coalition building occurs most often at the upper levels of the organization, where uncertainty is high. For example, the dean of the business school of one college obtained the pledge of a very large endowment for the college, a major part of which would go to the business school. But

coalition   An informal alliance among managers who support a specific goal.

the donor gave two stipulations: The college had to provide a new degree program whose graduates were needed by the donor, and it had to move part of its campus to 300 acres of designated property so that students of the new program could also provide a part-time labor pool for the donor. The donor agreed to a future endowment to construct a six-building campus at the new location. However, the college president and other deans generally opposed the endowment because they feared that the tail would someday wag the dog—the new campus would become bigger than the old, and the new degree program would take away from the college's liberal arts mission. The business school dean tried to build coalitions with key faculty and administrators in other colleges. In this case, the coalition building attempt was unsuccessful, and the goal of building the new campus was not adopted.

Participation.   At lower levels of the organization, managers and supervisors try to adopt objectives that are consistent with strategic goals. However, if operational objectives are prescribed in a unilateral, top-down fashion, supervisors and employees may not adopt the goals as their own. A more effective process is to encourage subordinates to participate in the goal-setting process. Managers can describe the organization's goals and act as counselors by helping subordinates sort out various goal options, discussing whether the objectives are realistic and specific, and determining whether objectives are congruent with organizational goals. Goal discussions between superior and subordinate take into consideration the subordinate's interests and abilities. With two-way communication, the established objectives are consistent with organizational goals, and employees are committed to them.[18]

MANAGEMENT-BY-OBJECTIVES TYPES OF SYSTEMS

Many organizations adopt management-by-objectives types of systems to facilitate goal setting and coordinate goals at their top and bottom levels. Management by objectives (MBO) was derived from a program called "management by results" first employed by General Motors and described by Peter Drucker.[19] The point of management by objectives is to have all employees focus on the achievement of explicit objectives rather than simply doing day-to-day jobs.

MBO Characteristics

MBO starts with the development of overall goals, which are parceled through the organization in a top-down sequence until middle managers and other employees have been assigned some portion of these objectives as their own. The hierarchy of objectives in Exhibit 4.4 can be developed through a systematic, MBO-type system. Each organization can modify MBO to suit its own needs, but most systems involve the following steps:

1. Overall goals for the organization are established.
2. Major objectives are parceled among departments and managers in a hierarchical fashion and specific objectives in a collaborative manner.
3. Action plans for achieving those objectives are specified and agreed upon by managers and subordinates.
4. The action plans are carried out.
5. Progress toward achieving objectives is periodically reviewed.
6. Overall performance is appraised at the end of a specified time period—generally one year—and new goals are established.

A special advantage of the MBO system is that subordinates are given the latitude to determine how to achieve their objectives. Thus, even if goals are established in a top-down fashion, employees have discretion in determining the work behaviors needed to reach those goals, freeing them to use their skills and creativity.

Strengths and Weaknesses of MBO Systems

The key strengths of an MBO system are as follows: (1) It focuses employees on desired results; (2) it facilitates communication between managers and subordinates regarding goals and action plans; (3) job satisfaction is increased; (4) allowing individuals discretion in achieving goals enhances their growth; (5) both quality and quantity of performance seem to improve; and (6) it provides a vertical linkage between top- and lower-level goals.

However, management-by-objective systems sometimes have drawbacks. One is a large amount of paperwork and recordkeeping. If goal setting becomes detailed and extensive, managers may want to assign goals to subordinates rather than collaborate, and employees may wish to set minimal objectives that they can easily exceed. Moreover, in a large organization an MBO system may stress the paperwork needed to turn in a completed set of goals but offer few monetary or other rewards, thereby discouraging people from achieving goals.

The value of an MBO-type system is illustrated by the California state agency responsible for helping people find jobs.

Employee Development Department

The mission for the Employee Development Department of the state of California was to provide job placement for the unemployed and underemployed. The department had over 100 offices located throughout the state. Senior managers placed special emphasis on the goal of finding jobs for certain groups, such as veterans, unemployment benefit recipients, the handicapped, and minorities. They stressed this outcome in setting organizational goals and allocating goals to the state offices.

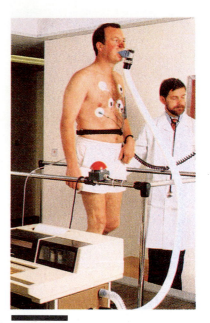

American Medical International (AMI) owns and operates acute care hospitals throughout the United States and abroad. MBO is one component of AMI's motivation and training of its employees. AMI's goal is to build—with its physicians—a company that delivers quality and cost-effective health care services in defensible markets through operational excellence to achieve growth in shareholder value. Clear marketing objectives support this vision. For example, in the United Kingdom, AMI Physiometrics Program shown here provides executive health screening and post-coronary assessment rehabilitation. Specific objectives are established for the marketing of this service to corporations, cardiac patients, and sports enthusiasts in England.

The strategic goal of KeyCorp, a large financial organization, is to provide quality financial services to individuals and small businesses outside major money market cities. The strategic plan to attain that goal included the acquisition of the Alaska Pacific Bancorporation in Alaska and the acquisition of Bank of Oregon to establish a firm base in the Pacific Northwest. KeyCorp reinvests the dollars back into small communities from which people have deposited money. Here employees of one of KeyCorp's clients pour cement in the dead of winter by enclosing the site in a plastic tent. KeyCorp's tactical plans include providing good service to local customers and providing competitive interest rates.

Each state office adopted the objective of trying to place a specific number of employees in new jobs each month. To assess whether state offices were achieving their objectives, actual placements were compared to targeted placements. Moreover, heavier weights were assigned to difficult placements from priority groups such as veterans, minorities, and the handicapped. Each level in the organization adopted a target score, referred to as the "balance placement formula," which was a key part of the MBO system for each employee.

Regular reports were sent from each state office to senior managers at the Employee Development Department, and new goals were set each year.[20]

In addition to providing a coordinated system of goals, management by objectives is an important control technique in organizations when results are properly measured and linked to reward systems. The control implications of MBO will be discussed in Chapter 18.

DEVELOPING PLANS FOR ATTAINING GOALS

Defining organizational goals and objectives is the first step in the planning process. The second step—which is equally important—is to define plans for meeting objectives. Targets mean little if managers don't map out the pathways to them. Managers often find the development of plans difficult. One study found that seven out of ten companies did not carry strategy formulation much beyond general statements of objectives.[21] Managers found it difficult to specify how to reach future targets. Yet detailed planning is an important component of future performance.

In developing plans for attaining objectives managers have several types of plans at their disposal, including strategic plans, tactical plans, operational plans, single-use plans, and standing plans.

Strategic Plans

strategic plans The action steps by which an organization intends to attain its strategic goals.

Strategic plans define the action steps by which a company intends to attain strategic goals. The strategic plan is the blueprint that defines the organizational activities and resource allocations—in the form of cash, personnel, space, and facilities—required for meeting those targets.[22]

Strategic planning tends to be long term and may define organizational action steps from two to five years into the future. The purpose of the strategic plan is to turn organizational goals into realities over that time period. For example, if an organization's goal is to strengthen its service image, the strategic plan may prescribe training for service personnel, identification of products needing quality improvement, and assignment of resources for designing an ad campaign depicting customer satisfaction. As another example, a company may wish to improve its market share from 15 to 20 percent over the next three years. This objective might be achieved through the following strategic plans: (1) commit resources for the development of new, competitive products with high growth potential; (2) improve production methods to achieve higher output at lower cost; and (3) conduct research to develop alternative uses for current products and services.[23] These strategic plans provide the basis for more detailed plans at middle and lower organization levels.

Tactical Plans

Tactical plans are designed to help execute major strategic plans and to accomplish a specific part of the company's strategy.[24] Tactical plans typically have a shorter time horizon than strategic plans—over the next year or so. The term *tactical* derives from the military. For example, strategic weapon systems, such as Intercontinental Ballistic Missiles or the B1 bomber, are designed to deliver major blows to the enemy. Strategic weapon systems reflect the country's overall strategic plans. Tactical weapon systems, such as fighter airplanes, are used to achieve just one part of the overall strategic plan. In a business firm, a new product may be part of the strategic plan to increase profits, but changing the shelf position in the grocery store is part of the tactical plan to call attention to the product.

    Tactical plans define what the major departments and organizational subunits will do to implement the overall strategic plan. Normally it is the middle manager's job to take the broad strategic plan and identify specific tactical actions. For example, Jolt Cola, introduced in 1986, had a strategic plan that called for high levels of sugar and caffeine to appeal to a specific niche in the marketplace for soft drinks. Packaging the product to accommodate this market segment was an important part of the organization's tactical plan. The package had a yellow lightning bolt flashing through a red and white logo. The label looked like something out of a comic book, but its chief tactical purpose was to convey the product's image—a jolt—and this it did.[25]

Operational Plans

Operational plans are developed at the lower levels of the organization to specify action steps toward achieving operational goals and supporting tactical planning activities. The operational plan is the department manager's tool for daily and weekly operations. Objectives are stated in quantitative terms, and the department plan describes how they will be achieved. Operational planning often is the outcome of a management-by-objectives type of system; it specifies plans for supervisors, department managers, and individual employees.

    Schedules are an important component of operational planning. Schedules define precise time frames for the completion of each objective required for the organization's tactical and strategic goals. Operational planning also must be coordinated with the budget, because re-

tactical plans Plans designed to help execute major strategic plans and to accomplish a specific part of the organization's strategy.

operational plans Plans developed at the organization's lower levels that specify action steps toward achieving operational goals and support tactical planning activities.

MANAGERS SHOP TALK

Ten Steps to Effective Planning
Reprinted from Small Business Report

Step 1. Establish a Planning Structure

- Line managers are responsible for designing the plan.
- The CEO provides direction and purpose.
- Staff planners provide assistance and legwork.
- Include provision for long-term corporate plan and shorter term operational plan.

Step 2. Define the Organization's Current Situation

- Where are we now?
- Define the company's mission and purpose.
- Analyze economic and competitive situation, and internal resources.

Step 3. Set Specific Organizational Goals

- Where do we want to go?
- Define measurable goals for desired results in areas such as profitability, market share, productivity, innovation, financial resources, employee development, growth, and environmental responsibility.

Step 4. Devise Possible Courses of Action

- Project current trends into the future.
- Analyze basic planning assumptions.
- Develop scenarios for alternative courses of action.

Step 5. Formulate Strategies

- What will we do to achieve goals?
- Set priorities for strategic alternatives.

- Define specific plans.
- Allocate responsibilities, time, and resource requirements.

Step 6. Analyze Risks and Resources

- Match resources with plan requirements.
- Identify risks associated with products, markets, competition, and employees.

Step 7. Set Timetables

- When will goals be met?
- Define schedules and time frames for key accomplishments.

Step 8. Develop Operational Goals and Plans

- Define short-term objectives in key performance areas.
- Line managers devise short-term action plans.
- Assign responsibilities and schedules.

Step 9. Finalize Strategic Plan

- Reanalyze resources in light of completed plans.
- Consider financing, manpower, facilities, production schedules.
- Involve entire management team.
- Consider contingency plans in case of changes.

Step 10. Implementation and Control

- Coordinate strategic planning system with budgets and other control systems to support managerial actions.
- Schedule periodic reviews.
- Link to rewards and management by objectives systems.

Source: Adapted from "Strategic Planning: Part Three," *Small Business Report* (April 1983), pp. 21–24. *Small Business Report* is a monthly management magazine published for top executives in small and mid-size companies by Business Research & Communications, 203 Calle del Oaks, Monterey, CA 93940.

sources must be allocated for desired activities. For example, an operational plan might describe how the local sales manager is to increase his or her weekly sales quota. It may prescribe a schedule for calling on new customers and budget enough money to cover increased travel expenses.

An example of a project is Chrysler Motors' Liberty Project. One of Liberty's goals is to scour the world for new technologies. Another goal is to produce a new, small, efficient vehicle for introduction in the 1990s. Yet another goal is to reduce the cost of building an average car by $2,500. In this photo, engineers study the stress pattern of a plastic model under polarized light in order to design stronger parts for autos in the future.

Single-Use Plans

Single-use plans are developed to achieve a set of objectives that are not likely to be repeated in the future. Single-use plans typically include both programs and projects.

Program.   A **program** is a complex set of objectives and plans for attaining an important, one-time organizational goal. The program is designed to carry out a major course of action for the organization. An example of such a program is the Pershing missile program at Martin Marietta. Others include the development of the space shuttle for NASA, the Boeing 767 aircraft, and the System 360 computer by IBM. Programs are major undertakings, may take several years to complete, and often require the creation of a separate organization. Programs are large in scope and may be associated with several projects.

Project.   A **project** is also a set of objectives and plans designed to achieve a one-time goal but generally is smaller in scope and complexity. It normally has a shorter time horizon and requires fewer resources.

A project is often one part of a program. Thus, when NASA works to complete its space station program, it will have one project for a rocket booster, one for the environment inside the space station, and one for the station's external shell. A specific project is defined for each major component of the overall program. Within business corporations, projects often are undertaken to perform a specific activity that is not part of the normal production process. For example, the name change from U.S. Steel to USX Corporation was a project. Hundreds of man-hours and millions of dollars were spent researching a name that would characterize the corporation's new mission. Another project at USX evolved from the decision to close some of its steel plants. A project team was created to study the steel plants and decide which ones to close.

single-use plans   Plans that are developed to achieve a set of objectives that are unlikely to be repeated in the future.

program   A complex set of objectives and plans for achieving an important, one-time organizational goal.

project   A set of relatively short-term, narrow objectives and plans for achieving a major, one-time organizational goal.

The agricultural division of CIBA-GEIGY has an explicit policy of taking no short-cuts to gaining acceptance for a new chemical from the Environmental Protection Agency (EPA). This policy means it takes an average of 9 to 12 years to get a proposed chemical from the test tube to acceptance by the EPA at a cost of about $1.5 million per product per year. The agricultural division's policy reflects what management feels is the company's responsibility to its own scientists and to its community.

TRW

An excellent example of a single-use plan was a culture program launched by TRW called "TRW and the 80s." This program had four fundamental objectives:

1. The highest standards of conduct for all employees
2. Superior performance as an economic unit, with emphasis on product quality
3. High-quality internal operations, with emphasis on employees and the quality of work life
4. Continued expansion of social contributions and community involvement by employees and company units

These objectives were followed up with specific plans that helped make the culture program a success. The strategy included action plans for product design, organizational innovation, capital expenditures, job design, and productivity improvement. A productivity college was set up for managers, along with regular productivity workshops for all employees. These action steps helped implement the new culture values within the organization. A further step was to appoint a vice-president for productivity, but this position was eliminated once the program succeeded and employees adopted the new values.[26]

Standing Plans

standing plans Ongoing plans that are used as guidance for tasks performed repeatedly within the organization.

Standing plans are ongoing plans that are used to provide guidance for tasks performed repeatedly within the organization. The major standing plans are organizational policies, procedures, and rules.

policy A general statement based on the organization's overall goals and strategic plans that provides directions for individuals within the company.

Policies.   A **policy** is a general guide to action. It is a general statement based on the organization's overall goals and strategic plans that provides directions for people within the organization. It may define boundaries within which to make decisions. For example, the graduate program of a business school may adopt the goal of increasing the quality of students admitted. It may issue a policy statement requiring applicants to have a minimum general aptitude test score of 500. Thus, the admission officers need not decide which people to eliminate from consideration and can develop a pool of candidates from among those with scores over 500. Another policy may be to mandate that students earn a grade point average of 2.5 or above in required courses before being admitted to the business college for a degree.

procedure A specific series of steps to be used in achieving certain objectives; usually applies to individual jobs.

Procedures.   A **procedure,** sometimes called a *standard operating procedure,* defines a precise series of steps to be used in achieving certain objectives. Procedures are very specific and typically apply to individual jobs. For example, in a hospital the nurse in the orthopedic ward must

E X H I B I T   4.6

Planning Time Horizon

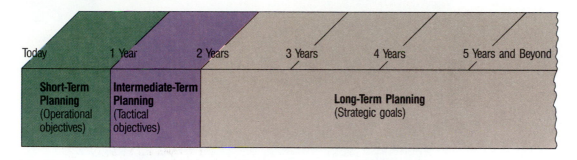

follow strict procedures when treating a patient with a broken leg or one who has just had surgery. These might include having the patient wiggle his or her toes and checking blood pressure and temperature every three hours. Procedures describe how to perform recurring tasks.

Rules. A **rule** describes how a specific action is to be performed. Rules often apply to specific settings, such as a no-smoking rule in areas of the plant where hazardous materials are stored. Universities often have rules pertaining to the receipt of an "incomplete" grade. Such a rule specifies the conditions under which a student can be given an incomplete and requires that the grade be removed within one semester or an F will be given.

Rules and procedures play a similar role in organizations and hence are often confused. Both are narrow in scope and prescribe desired activities. The key difference is that procedures normally describe a series of steps or activities, while rules pertain to one specific action. For example, refraining from smoking in a hazardous area is a single action, but the on-duty nurse in the orthopedic ward follows a procedure involving several steps.

rule A statement describing how a specific action is to be performed.

PLANNING TIME HORIZON

Organizational goals and plans are associated with specific time horizons. The time horizons are long term, intermediate term, and short term as illustrated in Exhibit 4.6. *Long-term planning* includes strategic goals and plans and may extend as far as five years into the future. *Intermediate-term planning* includes tactical objectives and has a time horizon of from one to two years. *Short-term planning* includes operational objectives for specific departments and individuals and has a time horizon of one year or less.

In the early 1980s, Walt Disney Productions was not performing well. Net income had fallen consistently. In 1984, Michael Eisner was brought

Strategic planning at Goulds Pumps, Inc., begins with the strategic planning committee pictured here. President Vincent A. Napolitano (standing) and other top managers use long-range management strategies to direct the company's energies and resources toward long-term sales and profit growth. Goulds' long-term strategic plan sets the basic product, marketing, acquisition, and financial predictions for the next several years. The three-year plan is more specific and drives market planning and capital expenditures. Goulds' annual operating plan is a highly detailed account of planned activities for the coming year. The plan uses budgets and objectives and defines efforts of managers at all levels.

in from Paramount to take over as CEO. One of the major strategic challenges facing Eisner was to turn around a movie division—Touchstone—that was unprofitable and had no track record for producing quality films. One of Eisner's long-term goals was to make Touchstone a major force in the movie industry. This goal had a time horizon of five years and required the implementation of shorter-range plans to bring it into reality. An intermediate-term objective was to increase production from 6 or 7 to 14 or 15 movies a year. This would take about two years to implement and would make Disney a viable industry force. The related short-term plans were to make successful films in the next one to two years. These consisted of bringing in new artists and some of Hollywood's best performers. *Down and Out in Beverly Hills,* with Bette Midler, Nick Nolte, and Richard Dreyfuss, proved to be a successful movie and helped achieve the short-term objectives. *The Color of Money,* starring Paul Newman and Tom Cruise, was another short-term plan that succeeded.

ORGANIZATIONAL DESIGN FOR PLANNING

Chief executive officers and other line managers have primary responsibility for organizational planning. Line managers are responsible for setting goals and objectives and devising plans for achieving them. However, not all line managers have the expertise or skills for doing the analysis required for detailed planning. Thus, three different approaches are used to structure the planning function: centralized planning departments, decentralized planning staff, and planning task forces.

E X H I B I T   4.7

Structural Location of Centralized Planning Department

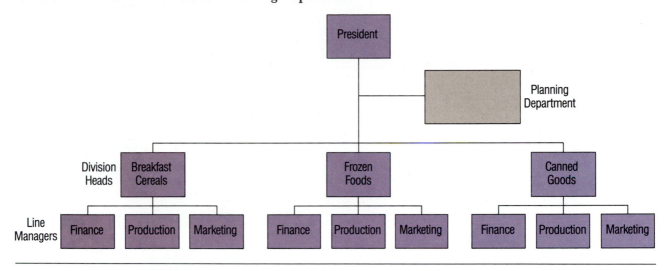

Centralized Planning Department

The traditional approach to corporate planning was to have a **centralized planning department** report to the president or chief executive officer, as illustrated in Exhibit 4.7. This approach became popular during the 1960s and 1970s. Planning specialists were hired at the corporate level to gather data and develop detailed strategic plans. The centralized staff would develop plans for the corporation as a whole and for major divisions and departments. This planning approach was centralized and top down because objectives and plans were assigned to major divisions and departments from the planning department after approval by the president.

This approach is still used and works well in many applications. For example, the Columbia Gas System, described earlier in this chapter, has a Corporate Planning Department with eight full-time specialists. The department has two sections. The Operations Analysis Section is responsible for acquiring and analyzing economic and other data for use in the strategic planning process. The Planning Section prepares the strategic plan for the system and also provides guidance to subsidiary companies for strategic planning activities.[27]

The central planning department has run into trouble in some companies. Line managers often have felt like second-class citizens without the ability to do their own planning. Conflicts have arisen because centralized planning people didn't have detailed knowledge and understanding of the major operating units' activities. In some companies, line managers have begun to rebel against the dictates of strategic planners. Those at GE's Major Appliance Business Group became downright hostile to corporate planners. The latter made mistakes because they had relied on data rather than learning the markets and production processes within GE divisions. In one case, GE's corporate planners analyzed

centralized planning department A group of planning specialists who develop plans for the organization as a whole and its major divisions and departments and typically report to the president or CEO.

EXHIBIT 4.8

Structural Location of Decentralized Planning Staff

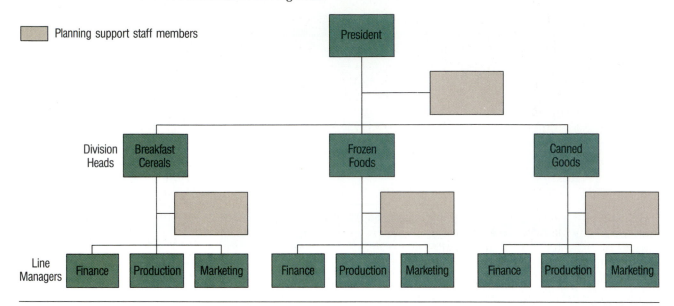

data showing that houses and families were shrinking and concluded that small appliances were the wave of the future. But since the planners had little contact with home builders and retailers, they did not realize that working women wanted *big* refrigerators in order to cut down on trips to the supermarket. GE wasted a lot of time designing smaller appliances because the planning group had failed to see that the data did not tell the true story.[28] Problems like these have caused many companies to reduce the size of their central planning departments and decentralize planning to divisional line managers.

Decentralized Planning Staff

decentralized planning staff A group of planning specialists assigned to major departments and divisions to help managers develop their own strategic plans.

The **decentralized planning staff** evolved when planning experts were assigned to major departments and divisions to help managers develop their own strategic plans, as indicated in Exhibit 4.8. Corporate planners no longer wrote the plans themselves. A small planning staff remained at the corporate level, but it too served a support role. This change helped resolve some of the conflicts between planners and staff, as did the improved strategic planning training of line managers. By the 1980s, business school graduates understood the basics of strategic planning and were able to take on more planning responsibility.

Sonat Inc. started with a system in which planners from headquarters wrote the blueprint for each subsidiary and presented it to the subsidiary's managers. The planning function has since been reorganized such that staff members have been assigned to the operating units to provide a support function for line managers. A centralized strategic staff was introduced at General Motors in 1971. Several years later, planners were assigned to each business unit to act as catalysts for change and provide support for line managers. General Motors has a small staff at headquarters as well as within each division, and their stated goal is to put themselves out of business. By the late 1980s, line managers are expected to have enough expertise to eliminate the need for support planners. At Borg-Warner, the central planning staff has been reduced from ten to three people; these now serve as consultants to business units, giving advice and helping managers write their own plans.[29]

One advantage of having planners in a support role is that it gives the responsibility for planning back to managers. This forces line managers to look at themselves, their business units, and their markets to determine where they are and where they would like to be. Another advantage is that planning experts are still available to provide statistical analyses of environmental data and help coordinate plans at the different levels and business units.

Planning Task Force

The third approach to strategic planning has been the use of planning task forces. A **planning task force** is a temporary group consisting of line managers who have the responsibility of developing a strategic plan. In one study of corporate planning practices, approximately one-third of the companies used an interdepartmental task force to study and make plans for achieving strategic goals. Each team identified and analyzed alternatives for reaching a specific objective and then outlined the major action steps necessary for achieving it. Several teams can be created, one for each major objective. Each task force must deal with the time horizon, the allocation of responsibility to specific individuals and departments, resource requirements, measuring devices to see whether objectives are being met, and possible contingencies and competitor reactions.[30]

Millipore Corporation, a maker of high-tech filtration systems, uses neither centralized nor decentralized corporate planners. Its staff of six was fired and replaced by task forces of operating managers. These meet every 18 months to brainstorm; they pool ideas on current market events and those likely to occur over the next five years. They set long-term and intermediate-term objectives and hammer out action plans for meeting them. Millipore executives claim this approach has helped make the company a leader in the industry because its plans are based on market realities and operational-level activities.[31]

Fleming is a major wholesale food distributor. To answer important strategy and planning questions, the company formed a task force that included key representatives from within the company as well as representatives from an outside consulting firm. The task force concluded that Fleming can maintain its historical growth rate through geographical expansion and continued improvement in its competitive cost position. These plans will help meet the important strategic goal of being an industry leader and providing retailers with a full range of retail services. New services to retailers include the salad bar and non-food products such as video movie cassettes.

planning task force A temporary group consisting of line managers responsible for developing strategic plans.

BARRIERS TO ORGANIZATIONAL PLANNING

Although planning is the primary management function, it does not happen automatically. Planning is difficult because it deals with complex environments and must look toward an uncertain future.

Specific Barriers

Several barriers can interfere with the organizational planning process.

Emphasis on Short-term Results.   Result-oriented managers, who are concerned with outcomes for today and next week, may be reluctant to plan for the future. Often the incentives within the organization reward short-term performance and undercut long-range planning. For example, a strategy adopted by a Tennessee manufacturer of temperature control devices required massive outlays for expensive new assets. Yet managers' bonuses were calculated on profits over a one-year period. In this case, top managers pressured for short-term results and did not take the actions necessary for meeting the organization's long-range planning needs.

Delegation to Staff Specialists.   When the goal-setting and planning functions are assigned to planning specialists, negative things can happen. First, strategic planning may put too much emphasis on numbers. Strategic planners collect large amounts of data, conduct statistical analyses, and create a paper product that may lie unused in line managers' bottom drawers. Second, lack of involvement by line managers may mean the strategic plan is too abstract and inapplicable to the organization's operational and market needs. Third, this approach may result in overemphasis on planning techniques. Although the latest methods may be used, the substance of the plan may not be what the organization needs.

Little Top Management Support.   Top-level managers must provide the direction, scope, and statement of purpose for the strategic plan. They must support the idea of strategic planning, become involved themselves, and encourage the involvement of line managers at middle and lower levels. Sometimes top managers disagree about strategic objectives. They must build a coalition around a specific set of objectives toward which the organization will move. Without top management support, middle management will not allocate time and energy to planning activities.

Lack of Faith in Planning.   Too many managers believe that planning is a waste of time. They may have seen plans become obsolete as soon as they were written. Managers who work under heavy pressure also may feel they have no time to undertake an activity that will produce few results. Lack of faith means that few management resources and little time will be allocated to the planning process.

Limited Line Management Expertise.   Strategic planning requires knowledge of markets and other sectors in the external environment and a thorough understanding of internal operations. Many managers have little expertise in interpreting complex, changing environments or gathering and analyzing data. Managers may feel intimidated by the skills and education associated with planning techniques. Line managers may wish not to be shown up by corporate planning specialists who are good with techniques but don't understand the substance of the company.

Overcoming Barriers

The above barriers are not insurmountable. The following techniques can be used to overcome them.

PepsiCo overcomes barriers to planning by encouraging line management participation and providing planning staff to support each of PepsiCo's business units. The financial planning group shown here helps develop annual plans and provides the analytical support needed to operate a business unit on a sound financial basis. This group also does research on topics related to marketing program decisions, pricing, product changes, and cost-effective measures that are part of management's strategic plan. For long-range plans, the group evaluates financial, marketing, sales, and manufacturing data on the direction of the business over a five-year period.

Start Planning at the Top.   Effective planning must have the explicit support and involvement of top managers. If top managers take the time to plan and involve other line managers in the planning process, many of the barriers will be overcome. Top managers can remove emphasis on short-term results, help increase middle management's faith in planning, and perhaps even provide training opportunities for line managers.

Use Planning Support Staff.   Planning experts who work in an advisory or consulting capacity can help overcome line managers' lack of expertise. Support staff can gather data, perform statistical analyses, use sophisticated scheduling systems, and do other specialized tasks. However, these people perform a support role and do not decide on the substance of goals or plans. Support staff in a consulting role can facilitate line management planning.

Line Management Participation.   Many companies are realizing that planning comes alive for the organization when line managers participate. Managers can have scheduled planning sessions—perhaps a two-to-three-day retreat—to discuss the future or create a task force to define goals and plans. Line management participation in planning deemphasizes techniques such as data analysis and increases the importance of substantive planning issues. It also increases management's faith in planning outcomes.

Recognize Planning Limitations.   Perhaps the biggest barrier to planning is unrealistic expectations. Planning should not be expected to be all encompassing or to allow for every future contingency. Planning is difficult. Planning takes thought and discussion. Planning is subject to Murphy's law—that is, whatever can go wrong with strategic planning probably will. A realistic approach to planning prevents a lack of faith in planning outcomes. Managers should remember that the written plan is far less important than the act of planning. By thinking about, discussing, and developing a plan for the future, managers come to a shared understanding about where the organization is going. That is an important outcome even if the plan itself is eventually scrapped because of unforeseeable circumstances.[32]

SUMMARY

This chapter described several important ideas about organizational planning. Organizational planning involves defining goals/objectives and developing a plan with which to achieve them. An organization exists for a single, overriding purpose known as its mission—the premise for strategic goals and plans. Goals within the organization are defined in a hierarchical fashion, beginning with strategic goals followed by tactical and operational objectives. Plans are defined similarly, with strategic, tactical, and operational plans used to achieve the objectives. Other goal concepts include characteristics of effective goals and goal-setting behavior. Many organizations use management-by-objective types of systems to provide linkages among goals across organization levels.

Several types of plans were described, including strategic, tactical, operational, single-use, and standing plans. Long-term, intermediate-term, and short-term plans have time horizons of from five years down to six months. Organizational design for planning typically includes one of three options: a centralized planning department, a decentralized planning staff, or an interdepartmental task force composed of line managers.

Management Solution

Volkswagen's poor performance in the United States and elsewhere led chairman Carl H. Hahn to adopt the strategic goal of regaining its U.S. and European market share. This goal was to be achieved through a two-part strategic plan. First, Volkswagen's reputation for high quality was to be restored by building a highly automated assembly plant in Germany. This plant could produce the Golf and its sister, the Jetta, more efficiently and with few quality problems. The Golf gained an excellent reputation for quality in Europe and the United States. Second, Volkswagen entered into a production agreement with SEAT in Spain to build subcompact cars. This alliance gave VW the capacity to build up to 400,000 vehicles a year, and SEAT's dealer network was used to distribute VWs throughout Spain. VW's goal setting and planning were very effective. VW cars' prices relative to Japanese cars have dropped 15 percent, and sales volume has increased by 25 percent. Volkswagen now has a new lease on life.[33]

DISCUSSION QUESTIONS

1. Is it possible for an organization to have more than one mission? Discuss.
2. What strategies could the college or university at which you are taking this management course adopt to compete for students in the marketplace? Would these strategies depend on the school's goal?
3. Consider an organization for which you have worked, and evaluate the strategic goals in each of the eight areas identified by Drucker. Were the objectives in each area made explicit or left implicit? Can you infer goals from the organization's behavior?
4. What are the differences among strategic, tactical, and operational objectives? Give an example of each.
5. A famous management theorist proposed that the time horizons for all strategic plans are becoming shorter because of the rapid changes occurring in organizations' external environments. Do you agree? Would the planning time horizon for IBM, a software firm, or Ford Motor Company be shorter than it was 20 years ago?
6. How do managers handle conflicting strategic goals?
7. What are the characteristics of effective goals? Would it be better to have no goals at all than to have goals that do not meet these criteria?
8. What do you think are the advantages and disadvantages of having a centralized planning department to do an organization's planning compared to having decentralized planning groups provide planning support to line managers?
9. Assume Southern University decides to (1) raise its admission standards and (2) initiate a business fair to which local townpeople will be invited. What types of plans would it use to carry out these two activities?
10. What do you think is the single most important barrier to planning in an organization? Second most important? What ways of overcoming these barriers would you recommend?

CASES FOR ANALYSIS

H.I.D.

Dave Collins, president of H.I.D., sat down at the conference table with his management team members, Karen Setz, Tony Briggs, Dave King, and Art Johnson. H.I.D. owns ten Holiday Inns in Georgia, eight hotels of different types in Canada, and one property in the Caribbean. It also owns two Quality Inns in Georgia. Dave Collins and his managers got together to define their mission, goals, and objectives and to set strategic plans. As they began their strategic planning session, the consultant they had hired suggested that each describe what he or she wanted for the company's domestic operations in the next ten years—how many hotels it should own, where to locate them, and who the target market was. Another question he asked them to consider was what the driving force of the company should be—that is, the single characteristic that would separate H.I.D. from other companies.

The team members wrote their answers on flipcharts, and the consultant summarized the results. Dave Collins' goal included 50 hotels in 10 years, with the number increasing to 26 or 27 in 5 years. All the other members saw no more than 20 hotels in 10 years and a maximum of 15 or 16 within 5 years. Clearly there was disagreement among the top managers about long-term goals and desirable growth rate.

With the consultant's direction, the team members began to critique their growth objectives. Dave King, director of operations and development, observed, "We just can't build that many hotels in that time period, certainly not given our current staffing or any reasonable staffing we could afford. I don't see how we could achieve that goal." Art Johnson, the accountant, agreed. Karen Setz then asked, "Could we build them all in Georgia? You know we've centered on the medium-priced hotel in smaller towns. Do we need to move to bigger towns now, such as Jacksonville, or add another to the one we have in Atlanta?" Dave Collins responded, "We have an opportunity out in California, we may have one in New Jersey, and we are looking at the possibility of going to Jacksonville."

The consultant attempted to refocus the discussion: "Well, how does this all fit with your mission? Where are you willing to locate geographically? Most of your operation is in Georgia. Can you adequately support a national building effort?"

Tony Briggs responded, "Well, you know we have always looked at the smaller-town hotels as being our niche, although we deviated from that for the hotel in Atlanta. But we generally stay in smaller towns where we don't have much competition. Now we are talking about an expensive hotel in California."

Dave Collins suggested, "Maybe it's time we changed our target market, changed our pricing strategy, and went for larger hotels in urban areas across the whole country. Maybe we need to change a lot of factors about our company."

Questions

1. What is H.I.D.'s mission at the present time? How may this mission change?
2. What do you think H.I.D.'s mission, strategic goals, and strategic plans are likely to be at the end of this planning session? Why?
3. What goal-setting behavior is being used here to reach agreement among H.I.D.'s managers? Do managers typically disagree about the direction of their organization?

Source: This case was provided by James Higgins.

CARTIER

By 1985 Cartier's president, Alain Perrin, had built his company into the world's leading purveyor of jewelry and related items. Now Perrin is after an even bigger goal: to be the world's first billion-dollar, luxury-goods company by 1990.

How does he plan to achieve this goal? Perrin has many ideas, because in 1985 worldwide sales were $400 million, which means that Cartier must grow by two-and-a-half times by 1990. His plans include opening new stores around the world and developing new products. For example, Cartier has taken over world licenses for Yves St. Laurent and Ferrari Jewelry and Accessories. In another move, Cartier has joined with a U.S. silversmith to make flatware, china, and crystal for distribution through Cartier stores. Perrin also courts the world's rich and famous, including picking up the tab for a huge dinner party at Monaco's sporting club.

Perrin has other goals for Cartier. One is to quadruple U.S. sales to $300 million by 1990. To attain this goal, Perrin has opened 12 Cartier boutiques and 5 full-line jewelry stores. He is also doubling promotion and ad budgets to more than $50 million. Another goal is to maintain an after-tax margin of 15 percent. One way to do this is to find subcontractors, such as for a $600 watch that will cost Cartier only about $125. These high markups will boost profit margins.

New jewelry designs are introduced constantly to attract new customers in stores around the world. Cartier silverware, china, and crystal had its debut in the United States in 1986 and went international in 1987.

Not everyone agrees with Perrin's goals and plans. Some managers argue that when a luxury-goods company gets too big, the magic and personal touch disappear. This is what happened at Tiffany & Company, which lost many upper-crust customers when it broadened its clientele. Perrin is unfazed by the criticisms and is charging ahead to attract customers who are new millionaires and yuppies, particularly in the United States. After all, only 10 to 15 percent of Cartier's revenues in 1985 came from sales to aristocracy and old money.

Source: "For Today's Cartier, Snob Appeal Is Not Enough," *Business Week,* December 16, 1985, 80–81.

Questions

1. Which of Cartier's goals would be considered long range? Intermediate term? What are the strategic plans associated with Cartier's goals?
2. If Cartier's managers develop operational goals and operational plans, what might they be? Give examples.
3. Do you think Cartier displays effective planning? Would you recommend that Alain Perrin create a planning staff? Encourage more participation from lower- and middle-level managers?

Strategy Formulation and Implementation

Chapter Outline

Thinking Strategically

What Is Strategic Management?
Levels of Strategy
Strategy Formulation versus
Implementation

The Strategic Management Process

Situation Analysis

**Formulating Corporate-Level
Strategy**

Grand Strategy
Portfolio Strategy

**Formulating Business-Level
Strategy**

Adaptive Strategy Typology
Porter's Competitive Strategies
Product Life Cycle

**Formulating Functional-Level
Strategy**

**The Human Element in Strategy
Formulation**

Entrepreneurial Mode
Planning Mode
Adaptive Mode

Implementing Strategies

Leadership
Organization Structure
Information and Control Systems
Human Resources
Technology

Learning Objectives

After studying this chapter, you should be able to:

- **Define the components of strategic management.**

- **Describe the strategic planning process and SWOT analysis.**

- **Define corporate-level strategies and explain the portfolio approach.**

- **Describe business-level strategies, including the adaptive model, competitive strategies, and product life cycle.**

- **Explain the major considerations in formulating functional strategies.**

- **Define the three management styles that influence strategy formulation.**

- **Enumerate the organizational dimensions used for implementing strategy.**

Management Problem

Houston's Sakowitz Inc. started out as a small, prestigious menswear store and was transformed into a powerhouse chain of high-fashion specialty stores by Robert Sakowitz, the company's fourth-generation chairman. Riding the booming Sunbelt economy of the 1970s, Sakowitz embarked on an expansion strategy, quickly growing to 17 stores in Texas, Arizona, and Oklahoma. For 33 consecutive months, the chain had sales gains of 10 percent or more. Then the boom ran out. Demand for fancy clothes dropped at a time when strong competitors such as Neiman-Marcus and Marshall Field's moved into Houston and the Southwest. Sakowitz responded by pushing buyers to purchase large inventories at the beginning of the season so that hot lines would not be sold out. He also pushed for continued sales growth by spending heavily on advertising and by marking down merchandise. Following these actions, Sakowitz Inc. found itself short of cash and had difficulty paying suppliers and other lenders.[1]

If you were Robert Sakowitz, what would you do now? What strategy would you adopt to cope with the changing environment and improve profits?

Sakowitz Inc. discovered the need for strategic planning. The environment had changed. With heightened competition and declining demand, Robert Sakowitz's growth strategy caused the chain to go broke. Now it's time for Sakowitz Inc. to do a careful analysis to formulate a strategy that will suit its strengths as well as the changing environment.

Every organization should be concerned with strategy. Hershey developed a new strategy after losing its number one candy bar status to Mars. Hershey's new strategy in the bar wars was to be a fierce product innovator. New products included Take Five, Score, and the Big Block line of

Hershey's standard chocolate bars.[2] The Roman Catholic Church in the United States is faced with the need to reevaluate strategy. Its 115,000 nuns, now with a median age of over 60, have no satisfactory retirement benefits and a depressing medical situation. The nuns who have long served the Catholic Church find themselves on public welfare, clipping coupons in order to eat. Like Sakowitz, the Catholic Church must consider strategies for handling its financial problems. Many large corporations engage in mergers and acquisitions as part of a strategic plan. Philip Morris Inc. purchased General Foods Corporation for $5.7 billion. Procter & Gamble acquired Richardson-Vicks, Nestlé acquired Carnation, and R. J. Reynolds spent almost $5 billion to purchase Nabisco Brands.[3] Coca-Cola has gotten out of the supermarket and into the entertainment industry through acquisitions of Columbia Pictures, Tri-Star Pictures, Embassy Communications, and Merv Griffin Enterprises.[4]

All of these organizations are involved in strategic management—the topic of this chapter. They are finding ways to respond to competitors, cope with difficult environmental changes, and effectively utilize available resources. In Chapter 4, we described the basic ideas associated with goal setting and planning in organizations. In this chapter, we focus on the topic of strategic planning, which pertains to the relationship between the organization and its environment. First we define components of strategic management and then discuss a model of the strategic management process. Next we examine several models of strategy formulation. Then we explore the role of manager style in the formulation of strategy. Finally, we discuss the tools managers use to implement their strategic plans.

THINKING STRATEGICALLY

As discussed in Chapter 4, planning is the most important management function. Although some companies hire strategic planning experts, the responsibility for strategic planning rests with line managers. Senior executives at companies such as General Electric, Westinghouse, and Delta want middle- and lower-level line managers to think strategically. Strategic thinking means to take the long-term view and to see the big picture, including the organization and the environment and how they fit together. As a start toward strategic thinking it is important to understand the strategy concept, the levels of strategy, and strategy formulation versus implementation.

What Is Strategic Management?

strategic management The set of decisions and actions used to formulate and implement strategies that will provide a competitively superior fit between the organization and its environment so as to achieve organizational objectives.

Strategic management is the set of decisions and actions used to formulate and implement strategies that will provide a competitively superior fit between the organization and its environment so as to achieve organizational objectives.[5] Strategic management encompasses the activities associated with planning, including setting goals and objectives and devising plans to achieve them. Strategic management is a process used to help managers answer strategic questions such as "Where is the organi-

CFS Continental's strategy for serving the food service industry with high quality products includes the deployment of more than $80 million to capital improvements. The fast, highly automated bakery here is capable of producing 10,000 dozen hamburger buns per hour. Sesame seeds, which enhance flavor and appearance, are added just before the buns are baked. The deployment of resources to new production technologies helps give CFS a distinctive competence for providing high quality products and exceptional value.

zation now? Where does the organization want to be? What changes and trends are occurring in the external environment? What courses of action will help us achieve our goals?"

Through the process of strategic management executives define an explicit **strategy,** which is the plan of action that describes resource allocation and activities for dealing with the environment and attaining the organization's goals. A strategy has four components: scope, resource deployment, distinctive competence, and synergy.[6]

strategy The plan of action that prescribes resource allocation and other activities for dealing with the environment and helping the organization attain its goals.

Scope. **Scope** pertains to the number of businesses, products, or services that defines the size of the domain within which the organization deals with the environment. General Electric increased its scope in 1986 by acquiring RCA Corporation. International Harvester (now called Navistar) reduced its scope by selling its farm equipment business to Tenneco. ITT had become so large and complex that executives could barely manage the more than 200 divisions, so it reduced its scope by selling off 85 of them.

scope The number of businesses, products, or services that defines the size of the domain within which the organization deals with the environment.

Resource Deployment. **Resource deployment** pertains to the level and pattern of the organization's distribution of physical, financial, and human resources for achieving its strategic goals. For example, one newspaper had to change all employees' work schedules and buy new equipment in order to follow its strategy of shifting from an evening to a morning paper. Taco Bell spent nearly $200 million remodeling existing stores, testing new products, and increasing its marketing emphasis to become more competitive in the fast-food industry. James River Corporation is investing resources in state-of-the-art automation in order to become the lowest-cost producer in the consumer towel and tissue paper business.

resource deployment The level and pattern of the organization's distribution of physical, financial, and human resources for achieving its strategic goals.

Distinctive Competence. **Distinctive competence** refers to the unique position an organization develops vis-à-vis its competitors through its decisions concerning resource deployments or scope. For example, James River Corporation's investment in automation has given it the distinctive competence of being able to produce paper towels and tissues

distinctive competence The unique position the organization achieves with respect to competitors through its decisions concerning resource deployments, scope, and synergy.

more cheaply than Scott Paper Company and Procter & Gamble. Perdue Farms has achieved a competitive advantage by limiting its scope to chickens and by investing resources in quality control to guarantee the highest-quality chickens available in supermarkets. Briggs & Stratton enjoys a distinctive competence because it has concentrated on keeping costs lower than the Japanese and thus is producing more small motors than anyone else.

synergy The condition that exists when the organization's parts interact to produce a joint effect that is greater than the sum of the parts acting alone.

Synergy. **Synergy** occurs when organizational parts interact to produce a joint effect that is greater than the sum of the parts acting alone. The organization may attain a special advantage with respect to cost, market power, technology, or management skill. For example, United Airlines tried to achieve synergy by acquiring Westin Hotels and Hertz Rent-A-Car. UAL fed customers into hotels and car rentals from its airline business, creating more business for the whole corporation than the individual units had when working alone. R. J. Reynolds Industries Inc. achieved synergy when it acquired Nabisco Brands Inc. The product lines were complementary and provided greater clout for supermarket shelf space, better rates from advertisers, and a powerful distribution system for both companies' products in the international market.[7]

Levels of Strategy

Another aspect of strategic management concerns the organizational level to which strategic issues apply. Strategic managers normally think in terms of three levels of strategy—corporate, business, and functional—as illustrated in Exhibit 5.1.[8]

corporate-level strategy The level of strategy concerned with the question: "What business are we in?" Pertains to the organization as a whole and the combination of business units and product lines that make it up.

Corporate-Level Strategy. **Corporate-level strategy** concerns the question: *What business are we in?* Corporate-level strategy pertains to the organization as a whole and the combination of business units and product lines that make up the corporate entity. Strategic actions at this level usually relate to the acquisition of new businesses, additions or divestments of business units, plants, or product lines, and joint ventures with other corporations in new areas. An example of corporate-level strategic management occurred when General Electric purchased 80 percent of Kidder Peabody & Company, the New York securities firm. This was in addition to GE's acquisition of RCA Corporation in December 1985 and purchase of Employer's Reinsurance Corporation from Texaco. Moreover, during the same period General Electric divested its housewares division to Black and Decker, sold its natural resources division, and unloaded its family financial services. Thus, GE redefined its business away from appliances, resources, and family finance toward financial securities, electronics, broadcasting, and insurance.[9]

business-level strategy The level of strategy concerned with the question: "How do we compete?" Pertains to each business unit or product line within the organization.

Business-Level Strategy. **Business-level strategy** concerns the question: *How do we compete?* Business-level strategy pertains to each business unit or product line. It focuses on how the business unit competes within its industry for customers. Strategic decisions at the business level concern amount of advertising, direction and extent of research and development, product changes, new-product development, equipment and

EXHIBIT   5.1

Three Levels of Strategy in Organizations

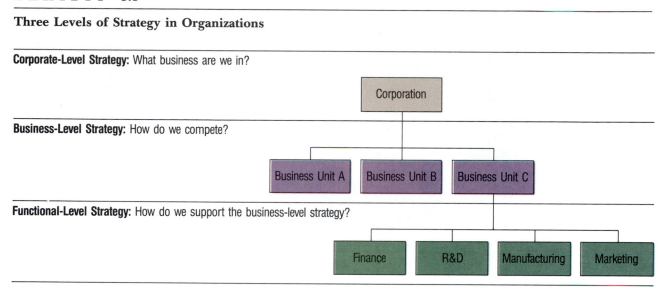

Corporate-Level Strategy: What business are we in?

Business-Level Strategy: How do we compete?

Functional-Level Strategy: How do we support the business-level strategy?

facilities, and expansion or contraction of product lines. For example, Scandinavian Air System (SAS) adopted a business-level strategy of becoming the premier businessperson's airline as a way to compete against SwissAir and Lufthansa. SAS competed by providing superb customer service. Jostens Inc., a Minneapolis producer of high school rings, has a business-level strategy of competing through product innovation. Although students have become less interested in buying class rings over the years, Jostens now offers 23 different stones and 16,000 ring permutations to fit every student's needs. Salespeople visit high schools personally to beat competitors to the student's door.[10]

Functional-Level Strategy.   **Functional-level strategy** concerns the question: *How do we support the business-level competitive strategy?* It pertains to the major functional departments within the business unit. Functional strategies involve all of the major functions, including research and development, marketing, manufacturing, and finance. In order for Hershey to compete on the basis of new-product innovation, its research department must adopt a functional strategy for developing new products. The functional strategy for the marketing department at Jim Beam has been to spend $10 million on magazine ads depicting yuppie couples on boats, in bars, and in elegant apartments. This strategy has helped Jim Beam compete in a market where youthful drinkers are turning to white wine and other light beverages.

Strategy Formulation versus Implementation

The final aspect of strategic management is the stages of formulation and implementation. **Strategy formulation** includes the planning and decision making that lead to the establishment of the firm's goals and the

functional-level strategy The level of strategy concerned with the question: "How do we support the business-level strategy?" Pertains to all of the organization's major departments.

strategy formulation The stage of strategic management that involves the planning and decision making that lead to the establishment of the organization's goals and of a specific strategic plan.

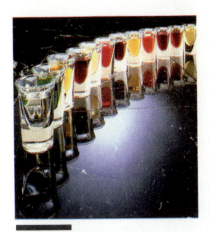

"Make it Schnappy" is the business-level strategy of Heublein Inc., a subsidiary of RJR Nabisco. Heublein pioneered flavored schnapps and now sells eighteen flavors. Peppermint schnapps is still number one, followed by peach and apple. One favorite drink of trendy consumers is the Fuzzy Navel, a combination of peach schnapps and orange juice. Schnapps was originally a working man's drink, but the combination of new flavors and advertising appeals to the yuppie preference for better-tasting, lower-alcohol drinks. The new flavors actually smell and taste like fresh fruit. Heublein's business-level strategy has led to a sharp increase in sales for its Arrow brand of schnapps.

development of a specific strategic plan.[11] Strategy formulation may include assessing the external environment and internal problems and integrating the results into goals and strategy. This is in contrast to **strategy implementation,** which is the use of managerial and organizational tools to direct resources toward accomplishing strategic results.[12] Strategy implementation is the administration and execution of the strategic plan. Managers may use persuasion, new equipment, changes in organization structure, or a reward system to insure that employees and resources are utilized so as to make formulated strategy a reality.

THE STRATEGIC MANAGEMENT PROCESS

The overall strategic management process is illustrated in Exhibit 5.2. Note that it begins when executives evaluate their current position with respect to mission, goals, and strategies. They then scan the organization's internal and external environments and identify strategic factors that may require change. Internal or external events may indicate a need to redefine the mission or goals or to formulate a new strategy at either the corporate, business, or functional level. Once a new strategy is selected, it is implemented through changes in leadership, structure, human resources, information and control systems, or technology.

Situation Analysis

Situation analysis typically includes a search for SWOT—*s*trengths, *w*eaknesses, *o*pportunities, and *t*hreats that affect organizational performance. External information about opportunities and threats may be obtained from a variety of sources, including customers, government reports, professional journals, suppliers, bankers, friends in other organizations, consultants, or association meetings. Many firms hire special scanning organizations to provide them with newspaper clippings and analyses of relevant trends. Some firms use more subtle techniques to learn about the environment, such as asking potential recruits about their visits to other companies, hiring people away from competitors, debriefing former employees of competitors or customers, taking plant tours posing as "innocent" visitors, and even buying competitors' garbage.[13]

Executives acquire internal information about strengths and weaknesses from a variety of reports, including budgets, financial ratios, profit and loss statements, and surveys of employee attitudes and satisfaction. Managers spend 80 percent of their time giving and receiving information from others. Through frequent face-to-face discussions and meetings with people at all levels of the hierarchy, executives build an understanding of the company's internal strengths and weaknesses.

External Opportunities and Threats.   *Threats* are characteristics of the external environment that may prevent the organization from achieving

strategy implementation   The stage of strategic management that involves the use of managerial and organizational tools to direct resources toward achieving strategic outcomes.

situation analysis   Analysis of the strengths, weaknesses, opportunities, and threats (SWOT) that affect organizational performance.

E X H I B I T   5.2

The Strategic Management Process

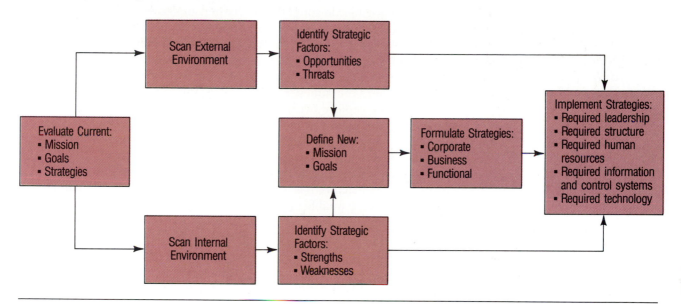

its strategic goals. *Opportunities* are characteristics of the external environment that have the potential to help the organization achieve or exceed its strategic goals. Executives evaluate the external environment with information about the nine sectors described in Chapter 3. The task environment sectors are the most relevant to strategic behavior and include the behavior of competitors, customers, suppliers, and the labor supply. The general environment contains those sectors that have an indirect influence on the organization but nevertheless must be understood and incorporated into strategic behavior. The general environment includes technological developments, the economy, legal-political and international events, and sociocultural changes. Additional areas that might reveal opportunities or threats include pressure groups, interest groups, creditors, natural resources, and potentially competitive industries.

An example of how external analysis can uncover a threat occurred in the Post cereal business of General Foods. A scanning of the environment indicated that Kellogg had increased its market share from 38 to 40 percent while Post's share had dropped from 16 to 14 percent. Information from the competitor and customer sectors indicated that Kellogg had increased advertising and new-product introductions. This threat to Post was the basis for a strategic response. The first step was to throw additional dollars into cents-off coupons and discounts to grocery stores. The next step was to develop new cereals, such as the successful Fruit & Fibre.[14]

Internal Strengths and Weaknesses. *Strengths* are positive internal characteristics that the organization can exploit to achieve its strategic per-

As part of Lucky Stores' situation analysis, surveys indicated that health-conscious consumers choose a food store by the quality of its produce. Traffic studies confirmed that produce is the section shoppers go to first. In response, Lucky Stores moved the fresh produce section to the front of the store and expanded the selection to include imported out-of-season fruits and vegetables, ethnic and exotic varieties, and a broader choice of produce sizes. In addition, Lucky Stores have expanded the fresh fish counters and now sell fresh-cut flowers to match external opportunities.

formance goals. *Weaknesses* are internal characteristics that may inhibit or restrict the organization's performance. Some examples of what executives evaluate to interpret strengths and weaknesses are given in Exhibit 5.3. The information sought typically pertains to specific functions such as marketing, finance, production, and R&D. Internal analysis also examines overall organization structure, management competence and quality, and human resource characteristics. Based on their understanding of these areas, managers can determine their strengths or weaknesses vis-à-vis other companies. For example, Marriott Corporation has been able to grow rapidly because of its financial strength. It has a strong financial base, enjoys an excellent reputation with creditors, and has always been able to acquire financing needed to support its strategy of constructing hotels in new locations.[15] On the other hand, Eastern Airlines has found itself heavily in debt from past purchases of aircraft, and its profit performance has been insufficient to lessen its debt load. Hence Eastern has been unable to acquire the most recent, fuel-efficient aircraft as part of its competitive strategy. Delta has been just the opposite: Its strong financial structure has permitted ready financing of new aircraft, giving Delta the competitive advantage of being one of the most efficient airlines.

The value of situation analysis in helping to formulate the correct strategy is illustrated by John Deere.

Deere & Company

John Deere is considered a contrarian. Despite years of adversity in the American agricultural sector, Deere has continued to invest in more efficient plant and equipment in preparation for the day when agriculture picks up again. John Deere's situation can be neatly characterized with SWOT analysis. Its *strengths* are production efficiency, born of new, automated plants that enable it to be the lowest-cost producer in the industry. It is also innovative and has developed a fierce customer loyalty by letting customers try out new innovations for free. Deere's internal strengths would allow it to weather any price war with other farm implement manufacturers. These strengths have not come without problems, however. Deere's *weaknesses* include massive short-term debt and high inventories that are expensive to service because of the low demand for new farm equipment. Another weakness is underutilized capacity, with some plants running at 50 percent or less of capacity. Finally, Deere lacks expertise and experience in foreign markets, which managers may have to consider because things are not improving in the United States.

John Deere managers see their biggest external *opportunity* as the pent-up demand among U.S. farmers. Once agricultural prices increase, farmers will rush to get rid of their old, gas-guzzling, inefficient tractors and buy the new models. Another opportunity

E X H I B I T   5.3

Checklist for Analyzing Organizational Strengths and Weaknesses

Management and Organization	Marketing	Human Resources
Management quality	Distribution channels	Employee age, education
Staff quality	Market share	Union status
Degree of centralization	Advertising efficiency	Turnover, absenteeism
Organization charts	Customer satisfaction	Work satisfaction
Planning, information, control systems	Product quality	Grievances
	Service reputation	
	Sales force turnover	
Finance	**Production**	**Research and Development**
Profit margin	Plant location	Basic applied research
Debt-equity ratio	Machinery obsolescence	Laboratory capabilities
Inventory ratio	Purchasing system	Research programs
Return on investment	Quality control	New-product innovations
Credit rating	Productivity/efficiency	Technology innovations

Source: Based on Howard H. Stevenson, "Defining Corporate Strengths and Weaknesses," *Sloan Management Review* 17 (Spring 1976), pp. 51–68; M. L. Kastens, *Long-Range Planning for Your Business* (New York: American Management Association, 1976).

exists in foreign markets. Subsidized by governments, the agricultural industry overseas is doing well, and the quality of Deere's products, combined with a favorable foreign exchange rate, would make them very competitive. Yet another opportunity is the use of Deere's sophisticated technology to produce lawn tractors.

The external *threat* that confronts John Deere is the seemingly endless recession in the agricultural sector. Moreover, Deere's competitors, such as Case and International Harvester, have merged, making them more efficient. These competitors now have the backing of Tenneco, a large, wealthy parent company. Another possible threat is the entry of foreign competitors into the United States.

Analysis of these strengths and weaknesses has led to John Deere's strategy of expanding its markets. Its production efficiency and price competitiveness must be utilized. Hence, Deere intends to sell more goods in foreign markets, apply technology to related products, and simply bide its time until the inevitable upturn in agriculture occurs. When that happens, John Deere will make hay.[16]

FORMULATING CORPORATE-LEVEL STRATEGY

Corporate-level strategy typically concerns the mix and utilization of business divisions called **strategic business units (SBUs).** An SBU has a

strategic business unit (SBU) A division of the organization that has a unique business mission, product line, competitors, and markets relative to other SBUs in the same corporation.

unique business mission, product line, competitors, and markets relative to other SBUs in the corporation.[17] Executives in charge of the entire corporation generally define an overall strategic direction—called a *grand strategy*—and then bring together a portfolio of strategic business units to carry it out.

Grand Strategy

grand strategy The general plan or major action by which an organization intends to achieve its long-term objectives.

Grand strategy is the general plan of major action by which a firm intends to achieve its long-term objectives.[18] Grand strategies fall into three general categories: growth, stability, and retrenchment.

Growth. Growth can be promoted internally by investing in the expansion of specific SBUs or externally by acquiring additional business divisions.[19] Internal growth can include development of new or changed products, such as "new, improved Tide," or expansion of current products into new markets, such as Coors' expansion into the Northeast. External growth typically involves *diversification,* which means the acquisition of businesses that are related to current product lines or that take the corporation into new areas. Sometimes expansion involves acquiring competitors, such as Texas Air's acquisition of Eastern Airlines and People Express, or suppliers or distributors, such as Alcan's acquisition of Bauxite mines.

Stability. *Stability,* sometimes called a *pause strategy,* means that the organization wants to remain the same size or grow slowly and in a controlled fashion. The corporation wants to stay in its current business, such as Allied Tire Stores, whose motto is "We just sell tires." After organizations have undergone a turbulent period of rapid growth, executives often focus on a stability strategy to integrate strategic business units and insure that the organization is working efficiently.

Retrenchment. *Retrenchment* means that the organization goes through a period of forced decline by either shrinking current business units or selling off or liquidating entire businesses. The organization may have experienced a precipitous drop in demand for its products, prompting managers to order across-the-board cuts in personnel and expenditures. Apple Computer did so in 1985, and AT&T cut over 20,000 jobs in 1987. *Liquidation* means selling off a business unit for the cash value of the assets, thus terminating its existence. An example is the liquidation of Minnie Pearl fried chicken. *Divestiture* involves the selling off of businesses that no longer seem central to the corporation. When ITT sold business units in 1984 and General Electric sold its family financial services and housewares divisions, both corporations were going through periods of retrenchment, also called *downsizing.*

Portfolio Strategy

portfolio strategy A type of corporate-level strategy that pertains to the organization's mix of SBUs and product lines that fit together in such a way as to provide the corporation with synergy and competitive advantage.

Portfolio strategy pertains to the mix of business units and product lines that fit together in a logical way to provide synergy and competitive advantage for the corporation. For example, an individual may wish to diversify in an investment portfolio, with some high-risk stocks, some

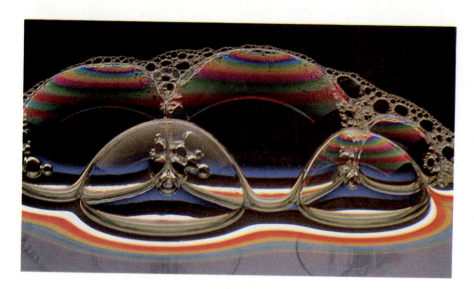

PPG Industries' grand strategy, entitled "Blueprint for the Decade," calls for annual growth in sales volume of 4 percent while maintaining profitability. The chemical portion of the business is positioned for long-term growth by entry into specialty surfactants—materials that facilitate the blending of ingredients in shampoos, detergents, facial creme, plastics, and cement. A surfactant is a wetting agent that lowers the surface tension of water, permitting it to spread out, penetrate fabrics, and remove oil and stains. The cleaning power and rich, foamy lather of bath soaps and shampoos are made possible by surfactants. Avenal S surfactants are developed at PPG's Barberton technical center.

low-risk stocks, some growth stocks, and perhaps a few income bonds. In much the same way, corporations like to have a balanced mix of SBUs.

The BCG Matrix.   The BCG (for Boston Consulting Group) matrix is illustrated in Exhibit 5.4. The **BCG matrix** organizes businesses along two dimensions—business growth rate and market share.[20] *Business growth rate* pertains to how rapidly the entire industry is increasing. *Market share* defines whether a business unit has a larger or smaller share than competitors. The combinations of high and low market share and high and low business growth provide four categories for a corporate portfolio.

The *star* has a large market share in a rapidly growing industry. The star is important because it has additional growth potential, and profits should be plowed into this business as investment for future growth and profits. The star is visible and attractive and will generate profits and a positive cash flow even as the industry matures and market growth slows.

The *cash cow* exists in a mature, slow-growth industry but is a dominant business in the industry, with a large market share. Because heavy investments in advertising and plant expansion are no longer required, the corporation earns a positive cash flow. It can milk the cash cow to invest in other, riskier businesses.

The *question mark* exists in a new, rapidly growing industry but has only a small market share. The question mark is risky: It could become a star, but it could also fail. The corporation can invest the cash earned from cash cows in question marks with the goal of nurturing them into future stars.

The *dog* is a poor performer. It has only a small share of a slow-growth market. The dog provides little profit for the corporation and may be targeted for divestment or liquidation if turnaround is not possible.

The circles in Exhibit 5.4 represent the business portfolio for a hypothetical corporation. Circle size represents the relative size of each business in the company's portfolio. Most organizations, like Gillette, have

BCG matrix   A concept developed by the Boston Consulting Group that evaluates SBUs with respect to the dimensions of business growth rate and market share.

E X H I B I T 5.4

The BCG Matrix

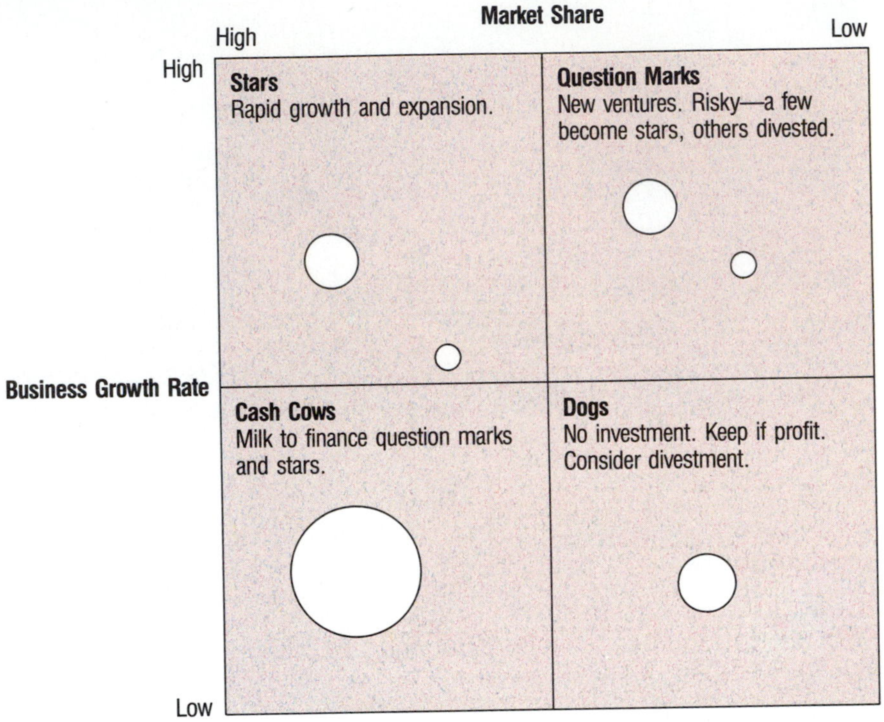

Market Share

High   Low

High

Stars
Rapid growth and expansion.

Question Marks
New ventures. Risky—a few become stars, others divested.

Business Growth Rate

Cash Cows
Milk to finance question marks and stars.

Dogs
No investment. Keep if profit. Consider divestment.

Low

businesses in more than one quadrant, thereby representing different market shares and growth rates.

Gillette Company

Gillette has several cash cows in its corporate portfolio. The most famous is the razor division, which accounts for two-thirds of the company's total profits and holds a large share of a stable market. The Oral-B laboratories division is also a cash cow with its steady sales of toothbrushes and other dental hygiene products. The Papermate division has star status. It has become the world's largest marketer of writing instruments, including Flair, Erasermate, and Liquid Paper, and it shows potential for rapid growth overseas. Gillette's question marks are in the personal care division, which includes the Silkience line of shampoos and conditioners, Mink Difference, and Apri Facial Scrub. Apri has done well, but Mink Difference and Silkience hair conditioners are struggling for a reasonable market share. Without improvement, they may be assigned to the dog category, to which the Cricket line of disposable

Hasbro Inc. has adopted a portfolio strategy for its diverse product lines, which include Milton Bradley board games and puzzles, Playskool® infant and preschool products, and Hasbro's traditional toys such as G.I. Joe.® Hasbro's diversified portfolio includes products that cover the full spectrum of toy users from infants to adults, as well as products in different stages of the product life cycle. For example, games for older children such as Chutes & Ladders are balanced with innovations such as Playskool's Sandwich-Board Aprons for toddlers shown here. Hasbro's balanced portfolio avoids dependence on a single product category and provides long-term growth in a volatile industry.

lighters was relegated. Bic disposable lighters dominated the Cricket line so completely that Cricket became a dog and was eventually put out of its misery through liquidation. Gillette continues to experiment with new products and question marks to insure that its portfolio will include stars and cash cows in the future.[21]

GE Business Screen.   General Electric Company pioneered the development of a more sophisticated portfolio matrix, which is illustrated in Exhibit 5.5. The **GE screen** is used by senior executives to evaluate business units within GE's portfolio in order to determine whether financial investments should be made to expand the business unit or the unit should be left alone or divested. This matrix is also used to evaluate potential business acquisitions.

The business screen has nine categories based on two dimensions: industry attractiveness and business strength. The advantage of the GE matrix is that it provides a list of criteria for evaluating both. Industry attractiveness includes such dimensions as market size and growth rate, industry profit margins, seasonality, and economies of scale. Business strength is evaluated according to such factors as relative market share, profit margins, and technological capability.

By examining each business unit in terms of scores on the two lists of criteria, investment and divestment decisions can be made. Business units that fall into the blue cells of Exhibit 5.5 are considered candidates for divestment, because they rank low in both industry attractiveness and business strength. These SBUs also can be liquidated, or the corporation should find some way to utilize assets but not invest for growth. The three cells in the white section of the exhibit are just the opposite: strong businesses in attractive industries. The corporation should invest in these businesses and encourage market and product development. The gray cells along the diagonal should be handled selectively and investment

GE screen A portfolio matrix developed by General Electric Company that evaluates business units along the dimensions of industry attractiveness and business strength.

EXHIBIT   5.5

GE's Nine-Cell Business Screen

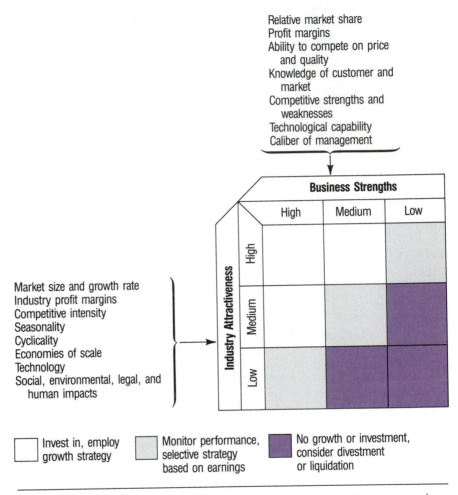

Relative market share
Profit margins
Ability to compete on price
  and quality
Knowledge of customer and
  market
Competitive strengths and
  weaknesses
Technological capability
Caliber of management

Market size and growth rate
Industry profit margins
Competitive intensity
Seasonality
Cyclicality
Economies of scale
Technology
Social, environmental, legal, and
  human impacts

☐ Invest in, employ growth strategy

▨ Monitor performance, selective strategy based on earnings

▧ No growth or investment, consider divestment or liquidation

Source: Based on James H. Higgins and Julian W. Vincze, *Strategic Management and Organizational Policy,* 3d ed. (Hinsdale, Ill.: Dryden Press, 1986).

decisions made with respect to the earning characteristics of each business unit. These businesses normally are kept within the portfolio with the expectation of improved performance, but if they do poorly they may be divested.

FORMULATING BUSINESS-LEVEL STRATEGY

Now we turn to strategy formulation within the strategic business unit, in which the concern is how to compete. The same three generic strategies—growth, stability, and retrenchment—apply at the business level, but they are accomplished through competitive actions rather than the acquisition or divestment of other businesses. The three frameworks in

E X H I B I T 5.6

Miles and Snow's Adaptive Strategy Typology

	Strategy	**Environment**	**Organizational Characteristics**
Prospector	Innovate. Find new market opportunities. Grow. Take risks.	Dynamic, growing	Creative, innovative, flexible decentralized
Defender	Protect turf. Retrench, hold current market.	Stable	Tight control, centralized, production efficiency, low overhead
Analyzer	Maintain current market plus moderate innovation	Moderate change	Tight control and flexibility, efficient production, creativity
Reactor	No clear strategy. React to specific conditions. Drift.	Any condition	No clear organizational approach; depends on current needs

Source: Based on Raymond E. Miles, Charles C. Snow, Alan D. Meyer, and Henry L. Coleman, Jr., "Organizational Strategy, Structure, and Process," *Academy of Management Review* 3 (1978), pp. 546–562.

which business units formulate strategy are the adaptive strategy typology, Porter's competitive strategies, and the product life cycle.

Adaptive Strategy Typology

The adaptive strategy typology was developed from the study of business strategies by Raymond Miles and Charles Snow.[22] The basic idea is that business-level managers seek to formulate strategies that will be congruent with the external environment. Organizations strive to achieve a fit among internal characteristics, strategy, and environmental characteristics. In this way, strategies allow organizations to successfully adapt to the environment. The four strategies that can be adopted based on the environment are the prospector, defender, analyzer, and reactor strategies. These strategies, their environments, and their internal characteristics are summarized in Exhibit 5.6.

Prospector. The *prospector* strategy is to innovate, seek out new opportunities, take risks, and grow. The prospector strategy is suited to a dynamic, growing environment. In such an environment, creativity is more important than efficiency. The internal organization is flexible and decentralized to facilitate innovation. One example of a prospector strategy is Federal Express Corporation, which innovated in both services and production techniques in the rapidly changing overnight mail industry. Another example occurred in the chocolate chip cookie industry: Mrs. Field's Cookies and David's Cookies were both aggressive prospectors that opened many stores, franchised nationally, and attempted to be the dominant producer in the industry.

Defender. The defender strategy is almost the opposite of the prospector: It is concerned with stability or even retrenchment. The *defender* strategy seeks to maintain current market share—that is, hold on to current customers—but it neither innovates nor seeks to grow. The defender is concerned with internal efficiency and control to produce reliable products for steady customers. Defenders can be successful,

MANAGERS SHOP TALK

Going on the Pill

Borden is on the pill. So are the Bank of New York, J. C. Penney, and scores of other companies. These companies are on what the financial community calls a *poison pill*, a legal device that makes it difficult to be acquired by another company. A company takes a poison pill because its management does not want to be taken over by a corporate raider. The raider creates uncertainty for top managers because of the possibility of losing their jobs and pension benefits. The first hostile takeover occurred in the late 1960s. At that time takeovers and mergers were not respectable, but in recent years takeover fever has become a corporate way of life.

In order to understand the merger activity described in business magazines and newspapers, you need to know the language. Merger activity has created its own colorful jargon. Here are some interesting examples:

Black knights: Unfriendly acquirers drawn to a target by news that the target is being considered by other potential acquirers

Golden parachute: Contract requirement for senior executives to receive a huge cash settlement if the firm is acquired by a raider

Greenmail: The buying back of a company's stock from a hostile raider at a premium price not available to other shareholders

Hired guns: Lawyers, merger and acquisition specialists, and other investment bankers employed by either side in a contested takeover

Investment banker: A financial advisor who, in return for a fee and commission, counsels businesspeople on the best ways to make deals and to raise money

Merger: A combination of two companies by the transfer of property to the acquiring firm

Poison pill: A warrant issued by a target company to its stockholders that gives them a legal right to buy shares of an acquiring company at half the market value, thereby making the acquisition unattractive to a raider

Raider: A takeover artist who launches a sudden attack to acquire operating control of a target company

Risk arbitrageurs: People who buy stock in a target company and sell it to the acquiring company to earn a profit on the difference between the two prices

Shark: An extremely predatory raider

Shark repellent: Protective strategies for preventing or combating a raider's tender offer, including divestitures, prohibiting greenmail, or requiring an 80 percent shareholder vote to approve a takeover

Shootout: The climax of a takeover battle, usually conducted by the hired guns

Target company: The firm against which a takeover is planned or executed by a raider

Tender offer: An offer to a target company to sell its shares to a raider, usually contingent on the approval of 51 percent of the stockholders

Unfriendly merger: A merger attempt in which the target company's management does not want to be taken over and puts up a fight both legally and financially

White knight: A company invited by the target firm to make a competing tender offer; if successful, the merger will be friendly

Now, when you read about companies going on the pill or spreading shark repellent, you will know that someone is not pregnant or being thrown overboard. This jargon is the colorful imagery associated with corporate acquisitions and takeover battles.

Source: Paul M. Hirsch and John A. Y. Andrews, "Ambushes, Shootouts, and Knights of the Roundtable: The Language of Corporate Takeovers," in *Organizational Symbolism*, ed. Louis R. Pondy, Peter J. Frost, Gareth Morgan, and Thomas C. Dandridge (Greenwich, Conn.: JAI Press, 1983), pp. 145–155; Joseph Nocera, "It's 'Time to Make a Deal,'" *Texas Monthly* (October 1982), pp. 142–149, 219–254; Alan J. Wax, "Corporations Go on the 'Pill'," *Houston Chronicle*, February 16, 1986, sec. 5, p. 6.

especially when they exist in a declining industry or a stable environment.[23] For example, big advertising agencies such as Ogilvy & Mather and Foote, Cone & Belding Communications Inc. shifted to a defender strategy during 1986 when the advertising industry started to shrink. Growth in ad spending declined sharply; thus, the agencies began cost cutting, which meant leaving open positions unfilled, giving fewer bonuses, and trying to retain current customers.[24] Another example of a defender strategy is PPG (formerly Pittsburgh Plate Glass), which has become a very efficient producer in the stable, commodity-like chemical industry.

Analyzer.   Analyzers are considered to lie midway between prospectors and defenders. The *analyzer* strategy is to maintain a stable business while innovating on the periphery. Some products are targeted toward stable environments, in which an efficiency strategy designed to retain current customers is employed. Others are targeted toward new, more dynamic environments, where growth is possible. The analyzer attempts to balance efficient production for current lines along with the creative development of new product lines. One example is Anheuser-Busch, with its stable beer line and innovation of snack foods as a complementary line. Another is Frito-Lay Inc. Frito-Lay's overall environment is changing moderately. It maintains market share with such stable products as Fritos, Doritos, and Tostitos. However, Frito-Lay also innovates on the periphery to open new markets and has expanded its total product line with O'Grady's Potato Chips and Grandma's Cookies. Frito-Lay is internally efficient, with high-tech plants and state-of-the-art computer information design systems, yet it also has a cadre of creative people who develop a steady flow of new product ideas.[25]

Reactor.   The *reactor* has no strategy at all. Rather than defining a strategy to suit a specific environment, reactors respond to environmental threats and opportunities in ad hoc fashion. Reactors take whatever actions seem likely to meet their immediate needs and have no long-term plan for congruence with the external environment. The reactor strategy could exist in any environment, but the company may have no strategy or internal characteristics suited to it. A reactor strategy seems almost random, because top management has not defined a plan or given the organization an explicit direction. Consequently, reactors often are out of alignment with their environments. Failed companies often are the result of reactor strategies. Schlitz Brewing Company went through a period in which it dropped from first to seventh in the brewing industry due to poor strategic decisions. W. T. Grant, a large retailer, eventually went bankrupt because executives failed to adopt a strategy consistent with the trend toward discount retail stores.

Porter's Competitive Strategies

Michael E. Porter studied a number of business organizations and proposed three effective business-level strategies: differentiation, cost leadership, and focus.[26] The organizational characteristics associated with each strategy are summarized in Exhibit 5.7.

The Pet Foods Division of Quaker Oats uses an analyzer strategy for its Ken-L-Ration and Puss 'n Boots brands. The strategy is to maintain market share for its stable products, while also introducing new products into fast-growing niches in the pet foods industry. Puppy Kibbles 'n Bits dry dog food was successfully introduced in 1985. The dry dog food category is the largest and fastest-growing dog food segment.

EXHIBIT 5.7
_____

Organizational Characteristics for Porter's Competitive Strategies

Strategy	Commonly Required Skills and Resources	Common Organizational Requirements
Differentiation	Strong marketing abilities Product engineering Creative flair Strong capability in basic research Corporate reputation for quality or technological leadership	Strong coordination among functions in R&D, product development, and marketing Subjective measurement and incentives instead of quantitative measures Amenities to attract highly skilled labor, scientists, or creative people
Overall cost leadership	Sustained capital investment and access to capital Process engineering skills Intense supervision of labor Products designed for ease in manufacture Low-cost distribution system	Tight cost control Frequent, detailed control reports Structured organization and responsibilities Incentives based on meeting strict quantitative targets
Focus	Combination of the above policies directed at the particular strategic target	Combination of the above policies directed at the regular strategic target

Source: Reprinted with permission of The Free Press, a Division of Macmillan, Inc., from *Competitive Strategy:* Techniques for Analyzing Industries and Competitors by Michael E. Porter. Copyright © 1980 by The Free Press.

differentiation A type of competitive strategy with which the organization seeks to distinguish its products or services from competitors'.

cost leadership A type of competitive strategy with which the organization aggressively seeks efficient facilities, cuts costs, and employs tight cost controls in order to be more efficient than competitors.

focus A type of competitive strategy that emphasizes concentration on a specific regional market, product line, or buyer group.

Differentiation. The **differentiation** strategy involves an attempt to distinguish the firm's products or services from others in the industry. The organization may use advertising, distinctive product features, exceptional service, or technology to achieve a product perceived as unique. The differentiation strategy can be profitable because customers are loyal and will pay high prices for the product. Examples of products that have benefited from a differentiation strategy include Mercedes-Benz automobiles, Maytag appliances, and Tylenol, all of which are perceived as distinctive in their markets. Beech-Nut developed a strategy to win market share away from Gerber in baby food. Beech-Nut differentiated its products with a new product line called Stages. Each product is color coded to correspond to the stage of the infant's development. The differentiation strategy was so successful that in some areas Stages' market share jumped to 50 percent.[27]

Cost Leadership. **Cost leadership** means that the organization aggressively seeks efficient facilities, pursues cost reductions, and uses tight cost controls to produce products more efficiently than competitors. A low-cost position means that the company can undercut competitors' prices and still offer comparable quality and earn a reasonable profit. Scottish Inns and Motel 6 are low-priced alternatives to Holiday Inn and Ramada Inn. IBP (formerly Iowa Beef Processors) employs state-of-the-art technology and has followed a cost leadership strategy since its founding in 1961. Nothing is wasted, and there is little administrative overhead. The company even processes bones from its slaughtered cattle to make bone charcoal for use in purifying sugar.[28]

Focus. In the **focus** strategy, the organization concentrates on a specific regional market, product line, or buyer group. When focusing on a single target, the company may use either a differentiation or low-cost approach, but only for the narrow target market. The company may seek a competitive cost advantage or perceived differentiation in the target segment. One example of the focus strategy is Fort Howard Paper Company of Green Bay, Wisconsin. It strives for cost leadership by using recycled pulp exclusively, and it focuses on the away-from-home market—office buildings, restaurants, hotels—for tissues, toilet paper, and related products. Its larger competitors, Kimberly-Clark, Scott Paper, and James River, fight for the bigger home market in the grocery stores. Another example is Nucor Corporation, which makes steel from scrap metal and uses an efficient continuous-casting production method for its targeted market in the southeastern United States.[29]

Porter found that many businesses did not consciously adopt one of these three strategies and were stuck in the middle of the pack with no strategic advantage. Without a strategic advantage, businesses earned below-average profits compared to those that used differentiation, cost leadership, or focus strategies. Note the similarity between Porter's strategies and Miles and Snow's adaptive typology. The differentiation strategy is similar to the prospector, the low-cost strategy is similar to the defender, and the focus strategy is similar to the analyzer, which adopts a focus strategy appropriate for each product line. The reactor strategy, which is really not a strategy at all, is similar to that adopted by organizations that Porter found were stuck in the middle of the pack and unable to attain a competitive advantage.

Product Life Cycle

The **product life cycle** is illustrated in Exhibit 5.8. First, a product (or service) is developed within the laboratories of selected companies and then introduced into the marketplace. If the product succeeds, it enjoys rapid growth as consumers accept it. Next is the maturity stage, in which widespread product acceptance occurs but growth peaks. Gradually the product grows out of favor or fashion and enters the decline stage.[30] Digital watches were a big hit when introduced and rapidly accelerated in popularity; now they are in the maturity stage. Personal computers are still a new product and would be considered in the growth stage. Disposable ballpoint pens were an almost overnight success 25 years ago but are now a mature product and may be entering a decline stage. Some products, especially fad items, may take only a few months to go from introduction to decline. Christmas toys and discotheques may have a life cycle of one season to perhaps three years. Other products, such as automobiles, have remained in the maturity stage for 50 years and are not yet in serious decline.

Organizations can take advantage of the product life cycle by tailoring strategy to each stage.[31] During the introduction and growth stages, a prospector or differentiation strategy is appropriate. The organization should stress advertising, develop new customers, seek market growth, and attempt to differentiate the product. It may also invest in research and development to find product variations that will appeal to the marketplace. The company should advertise heavily in order to acquire a dominant share of the new market.

In 1986 Saks Fifth Avenue inaugurated its "Image Campaign" to create the difference that sets Saks apart from other retailers in tradition, service, quality, and selection. The advertisement here is part of the differentiation strategy. The differentiation strategy is explained by Bill Berta, Saks' senior vice-president and sales promotion director: "We wanted to create a new attitude and reinforce our customers' perception of Saks Fifth Avenue."

product life cycle The stages through which a product or service goes: (1) development and introduction into the marketplace, (2) growth, (3) maturity, and (4) decline.

EXHIBIT   5.8

Strategies and Stages of Product Life Cycle

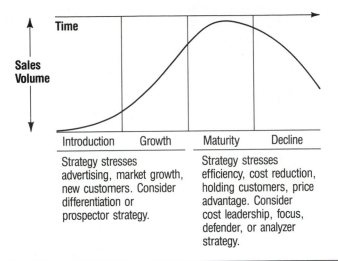

| Strategy stresses advertising, market growth, new customers. Consider differentiation or prospector strategy. | Strategy stresses efficiency, cost reduction, holding customers, price advantage. Consider cost leadership, focus, defender, or analyzer strategy. |

After the product reaches maturity, a change in strategy is warranted. A defender or low-cost strategy is important. By the maturity stage, competitors have developed products that look and perform similarly. The company should stress production efficiency, reduce overhead costs, and seek a price advantage over competitors. A few companies are able to establish brand loyalty during the growth and early maturity stages. Heavy advertising to maintain product differentiation during the maturity stage will work if brand identity is strong. If the product goes into serious decline, the organization may have to consider retrenchment and decline strategies in the form of reducing sales forces, closing plants, or perhaps even terminating the product line.

To summarize, the three models that describe business-level strategies contain similarities. One company that uses these strategies is H. J. Heinz Company.

H. *J. Heinz Company*

Heinz produces a number of mature staples in the consumer food industry and is striving to become the low-cost producer in ketchup, french fries, cat food, tuna, baby food, and soup. At a recent management get-together, called the Low-Cost Operator Conference, chief executive Tony O'Reilly admonished managers to cut costs even further. One technique is to procure cheap raw materials. Another is to hold down manufacturing costs. From 1980 to 1985, Heinz eliminated $4 million in expenses each year with ideas such as removing the back label from large bottles. Consolidation of factories and renegotiation of work rules eliminated 2,000 jobs. The next step

Motor oil is a mature product characterized by slow growth in the 1980s. Quaker State has increased the demand for oil by creating Minit-Lube Centers, a product line in the early stage of the product life cycle. The Quaker State brand name stands for quality and reliability, and this reputation extends to the Minit-Lube Centers. The strategy for Minit-Lube is to penetrate the market, pursue rapid growth, and establish itself as a dominant player as the market matures.

is an automated facility, which competitors are now using to Heinz's disadvantage. Del Monte got into a price battle for market share with Hunt that reduced profit margins for everyone; thus, Heinz will continue cutting costs wherever possible. To keep managers on their toes, O'Reilly plans to eliminate one layer of management if costs can't be cut in other ways.

Heinz has reduced advertising costs by using 15- versus 30-second TV commercials. But Heinz is also working to introduce a few new products. The Weight Watchers frozen entree and dessert lines are doing well, as is a new line of dried instant baby food. Heinz is using the savings made in other areas to increase advertising and development for the new product lines.[32]

Heinz is using a low-cost strategy for mature product lines, and it is working. Market share and profits are increasing. Heinz also is an analyzer because it is innovating on the periphery. Products in the early stages of the life cycle receive heavy advertising and promotion, which is appropriate during the growth stage in order to gain market share.

FORMULATING FUNCTIONAL-LEVEL STRATEGY

Functional-level strategies are the action plans adopted by major functional departments to support the execution of business-level strategy. Major organizational functions include marketing, production, finance, personnel, and research and development. Senior managers in these departments adopt strategies that are coordinated with the business-level strategy to achieve the organization's strategic goals.[33]

For example, consider a company that has adopted a prospector strategy and is introducing new products that are expected to experience rapid growth in the early stages of the life cycle. The personnel department should adopt a strategy appropriate for growth, which would mean recruiting additional personnel and training middle managers for movement into new positions. The marketing department should undertake test marketing, aggressive advertising campaigns, and inducing product trials by consumers. The finance department should adopt plans to borrow money, handle large cash investments, and authorize construction of new production facilities.

A company with mature products or an analyzer strategy will have different functional strategies. The personnel department should develop strategies for retaining and developing a stable work force, including transfers, advancements, and incentives for efficiency and safety. Marketing should stress brand loyalty and the development of established, reliable distribution channels. Production should maintain long production runs, routinization, and cost reduction. Finance should focus on net cash flows and positive cash balances.

Motorola's production and marketing problems in the cellular mobile telephone industry illustrate how functional departments must change their strategies to accommodate new strategies at the business level.

Motorola Inc.

Motorola dominates mobile communication technologies and was expected to be the top firm in cellular communications. This was not to be. As the new cellular phones began to take off in the marketplace, Motorola was left behind. One reason was that the Japanese had developed a high-quality competing technology and slashed prices to reduce inventories and drive U.S. manufacturers out of the new market. Prices went into a free fall, forcing Motorola's marketing and finance divisions to change functional strategies to lower prices and cope with a reduced cash flow. Motorola's legal department adopted a functional strategy of asking the federal government for relief from cutthroat Japanese pricing.

However, customers complained that Motorola's problems were more than pricing. Motorola's quality did not compare with Japanese products' quality. Some phones were D.O.A.—dead right out of the box. Others failed while in service. These problems caused the production department to adopt a new functional strategy for increased quality control. The initial marketing strategies were also poorly conceived, because Motorola sold phones directly to customers through its own sales force as well as through dealers. Thus, dealers were competing with Motorola's salespeople, which prompted many dealers to drop the Motorola line. Marketing's new functional strategy is to eliminate its direct sales force and court dealers as its major distribution channel.

Motorola is working hard to set things right—and is succeeding. The revised strategies within its functional departments have been a major factor in this turnaround.[34]

THE HUMAN ELEMENT IN STRATEGY FORMULATION

So far we have discussed frameworks that relate strategy formulation to characteristics of the environment and the organization. But managers themselves strongly influence strategy formulation. Strategy reflects senior managers' styles and preferences. Research on strategy formulation suggests that it takes place in three modes: entrepreneurial, planning, and adaptive.[35]

Entrepreneurial Mode

The **entrepreneurial mode** is characterized by strong leaders who have a vision for the corporation, a willingness to make bold decisions and take risks, and concern for opportunities rather than problems. Strategic decisions are made to help the organization achieve the leaders' overall vision. H. Ross Perot used the entrepreneurial mode to direct the growth and success of Electronic Data Systems. He had a clear vision and took advantage of new opportunities in the information system service area to realize it. Jack Tramiel, chairman of Atari after leaving Commodore, uses the entrepreneurial style. He has rebuilt Atari by introducing a line

entrepreneurial mode A mode of strategy formulation characterized by strong leaders who have a vision for the organization, are willing to take risks, and emphasize opportunities over problems.

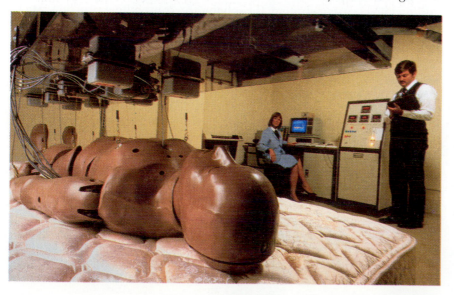

The functional strategy of the research department at Sealy Inc. is to support the business-level strategy of producing superior products. Sealy's DataMan measures and defines sleep surfaces and is considered the most important research tool in the bedding industry. The computer-connected DataMan simulates human weight and movement and affects product design. Sealy's research department has always stressed the strategy of developing better products to maintain high levels of consumer satisfaction, so product research and development is the cornerstone of the marketing effort.

of powerful but inexpensive home computers. He makes decisions quickly and intuitively, such as canceling a million-dollar deal without warning. The next opportunity he sees is the lucrative business market for his inexpensive computers.[36]

Planning Mode

planning mode A mode of strategy formulation that emphasizes a logical and rational rather than intuitive approach.

The **planning mode** reflects a logical, rational approach to strategy formulation. Executives who use this mode often ask strategic management professionals to analyze situational data and make recommendations. Strategic decisions are based on comprehensive analysis rather than intuition. Frank Lorenzo, chairman of Texas Air Corporation, uses a planning mode of strategy formulation. He was a financial analyst at TWA and later moved to Eastern Airlines as a financial planner. Lorenzo is a tough-minded negotiator and never seems unprepared. "He is as rational and intelligent as anyone you can deal with in a negotiation," says one investment banker.[37]

Adaptive Mode

adaptive mode A mode of strategy formulation in which decisions are made solely in response to specific problems as they arise.

The **adaptive mode** is often characterized as "strategy by muddling through." There is neither a visionary leader nor a clear-cut strategic plan. Decisions are made in reaction to specific problems that arise, and the organization could go anywhere the solutions take them. Leaders may focus inwardly on employees rather than outwardly on problems and opportunities. The company moves ahead in incremental steps, which are ad hoc rather than part of a bigger plan. Strategy often appears fragmented, and parts of the organization may appear to be going in different directions. Managers at American LaFrance used an adaptive mode in the manufacture of fire trucks. American LaFrance lost out to Emergency One, a new fire truck manufacturer that had a clear plan. Emergency One used innovations in design, manufacturing, and marketing to give it a clear advantage. American LaFrance was slow to adapt and had no clear-cut strategy for solving the competitive problem. Sticking with tradition and solving problems one step at a time led to American LaFrance's demise.[38]

IMPLEMENTING STRATEGIES

The final step in the strategic management process is strategy implementation. Some people argue that strategy implementation is the most difficult and important part of strategic management.[39] No matter how creative the formulated strategy, the organization will not benefit if it is incorrectly implemented. Implementation involves several dimensions of the organization, as illustrated in Exhibit 5.9. It requires changes in the organization's behavior, which can be brought about by changing one or more dimensions, including management's leadership approach, organization structure, information and control systems, human resources, and production technology.[40]

E X H I B I T   5.9

Organizational Dimensions for Strategy Implementation

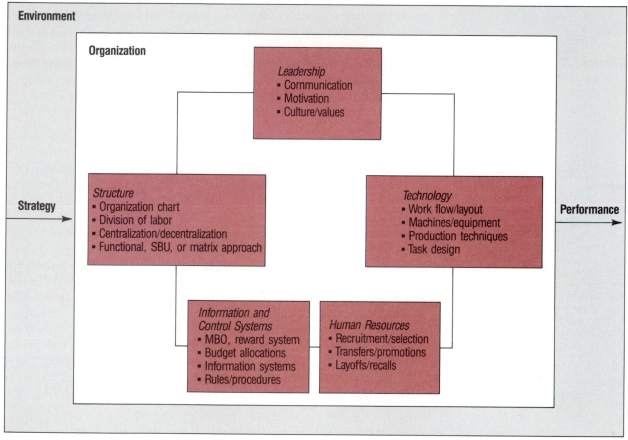

Source: Adapted from Jay R. Galbraith and Robert K. Kazanjian, *Strategy Implementation: Structure, Systems and Process*, 2d ed. (St. Paul, Minn.: West, 1986), p. 115. Used with permission.

Leadership

Leadership is the ability to influence organization members to adopt the behaviors needed for strategy implementation. Leadership includes communication, motivation, and changes in corporate values and culture. Managers seeking to implement a new strategy may make speeches to employees, build coalitions, and persuade middle managers to go along with their vision for the corporation. If leaders involve other managers during strategy formulation, implementation will be easier because managers and employees will already understand and be committed to the new strategy. In essence, leadership is used to motivate employees to adopt new behaviors and, for some strategies, to infuse the required new values and attitudes.

For example, when John Scully became chief executive of Apple Computer, the company's underlying value system needed to be changed. The culture was very informal, and the company was not geared up for serious competition with IBM. Scully's role was to con-

Columbia Gas Distribution Companies (CDC) use leadership to implement competitive strategy. CDC's Safety and Training Director J. Frank Laird presents strategic planning objectives to managers and supervisors. Senior managers barnstormed CDC's eleven districts to inform employees about strategic planning and where the corporation was headed for the next five years. Since employees help carry out the goals and objectives of the strategic plan, CDC top managers believe that "the plan will only be as good as the people trying to make it work." CDC also uses a thoughtful, rational approach prior to implementation, which reflects the "planning" mode of strategy formulation.

vince employees that IBM was a formidable competitor and help them understand that Apple no longer dominated the industry. That change in employee attitude helped him restructure Apple into a more competitive organization.[41] As another example, Q. T. Wiles purchases failing electronics manufacturers and turns them around. His emphasis is on strategy implementation. He uses an almost autocratic leadership style to reinforce a new way of thinking and new values within a firm. To this end, each manager must memorize a 12-item list of "Q. T. disciplines" and the organization's official charter.[42]

Organization Structure

Structure typically is illustrated on the organization chart. It pertains to individual managers' responsibilities, their degree of authority, and the consolidation of jobs into departments and divisions. Structure also pertains to the degree of decentralization and whether to use a functional, divisional, or matrix approach. (These structures will be described in Chapter 9.)

One of the earliest studies of organization structure examined historical changes in General Motors, Du Pont, Standard Oil of New Jersey, and Sears, Roebuck. As these companies grew large and prosperous, they altered their structures to reflect new strategies.[43] Q. T. Wiles also used structural changes to implement strategy in electronic companies. At MiniScribe Corporation he reorganized the work force into small groups, each responsible for a single product, a single customer, or some other narrowly defined target. Each group was an autonomous structural unit with skills and functions necessary to achieve its goals.[44]

Information and Control Systems

Information and control systems include reward systems, incentives, management-by-objective types of systems, budgets for allocating resources, information systems, and the organization's rules, policies, and procedures. Changes in these systems represent major tools for strategy implementation. For example, additional resources can be assigned away from R&D to marketing if a new strategy requires increased advertising but no product changes. Managers and employees must be rewarded for adhering to the new strategy and making it a success.[45]

Again, Wiles immediately clarifies the reward system after taking over a company. He gives plaques and other awards to managers and employees who adhere to his new strategy. He also gives big bonuses to managers who exceed their quarterly goals. These changes in rewards can be quite a shock in an organization whose people expect to be paid regardless of performance. As another example, John Hancock Mutual Life Insurance Company sold whole-life policies that were out of fashion in the wave of new financial instruments and insurance policies that occurred during the 1980s. President John McElwee's strategy was to change Hancock into a financial supermarket, offering banking and investment opportunities along with insurance products. But because insurance agents received bigger commissions from the traditional insurance policies, McElwee had to increase the incentives for selling noninsurance products. Implementing McElwee's strategy also required changes in information systems because new reports had to be developed showing whether agents were meeting their goals in new product areas.[46]

Human Resources

The organization's *human resources* are its employees. The human resource function recruits, selects, trains, transfers, promotes, and lays off employees to achieve strategic goals. For example, training employees can help them understand the purpose and importance of a new strategy or help them develop the necessary specific skills and behaviors. Sometimes employees simply are incompatible with a new strategy and may have to be let go and replaced with new people. One newspaper shifted its strategy from an evening to a morning paper to compete with a large newspaper from a nearby city. The new strategy fostered resentment and resistance among department heads. In order to implement it, 80 percent of the department heads had to be let go because they refused to cooperate. New people were recruited and placed in those positions, and the morning newspaper strategy was a resounding success.[47]

Since the poison gas disaster at a Union Carbide plant in Bhopal, India, many chemical companies have implemented a strategy of increased safety. American Cyanamid requires workers to attend safety classes. The company has had four safety incidents and wants no more. The training consists of 40 hours in the classroom, including courses in basic chemistry to help workers understand plant processes and how to cope with chemical reactions.[48]

Technology

Technology pertains to the knowledge, tools, and equipment used to perform an organization's task. When an organization adopts a strategy of producing new products, managers often must obtain new production equipment, redesign jobs, and construct new buildings and facilities. New, state-of-the-art technology also may be required for implementing a low-cost strategy because of its efficiency. For example, Alcoa poured tons of money into new production technology to produce rigid container sheets used in beer and soda cans. This is one of the most profitable products in the industry, and Alcoa can now manufacture it at lower cost than its competitors, thereby insuring sizable markets and continued high profits.[49] Chemical companies also use technology to implement the strategy of improved safety. American Cyanamid installed a $20,000 control panel simulator to help plant operators identify dangerous conditions promptly. Also in place are new procedures for maintaining equipment to insure that the current technology is reliable.[50]

In summary, strategy implementation is essential for effective strategic management. Managers implement strategy through the five tools of leadership, structure, information and control systems, human resources, and technology. Without implementation, even the most creative strategy will fail. These five organizational dimensions will be discussed in more detail throughout the remainder of this book.

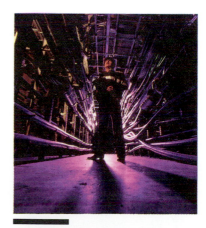

Ohio Bell implements its strategy of cost savings and increased productivity through new technology. Fiberoptic transmission facilities made of optically pure glass are gradually replacing the copper cables shown here. This highly efficient new technology is a major factor for implementing Ohio Bell's goal of becoming the low-cost provider of quality communication products and services.

SUMMARY

This chapter described several important concepts of strategic management. The strategic management process begins with an evaluation of the organization's current mission, goals, and strategy. This is followed by situation analysis (sometimes called SWOT analysis), which examines opportunities and threats in the external environment as well as strengths and weaknesses within the organization. Situation analysis leads to the formulation of explicit strategic plans, which then must be implemented.

Strategy formulation takes place at three levels: corporate, business, and functional. Corporate grand strategies include growth, stability, and retrenchment. Frameworks for accomplishing them include the BCG matrix and the GE business screen. Business-level strategies include the adaptive strategy typology, Porter's competitive strategies, and the product life cycle. Once business strategies have been formulated, functional strategies for supporting them can be developed.

Even the most creative strategies have no value if they cannot be translated into action. Five organizational dimensions used for strategy implementation are leadership, structure, information and control systems, human resources, and technology. The strategic management process is influenced by strategic managers' style: entrepreneurial, planning, or adaptive.

Management Solution

Robert Sakowitz's expansion strategy during a period of decline and his strategy of continued growth through price cuts and large inventories gradually dried up the Sakowitz chain's cash. Suppliers and banks suddenly cut off all credit. The banks called $28 million in loans and grabbed the cash on deposit. Other creditors sued for money owed. Robert Sakowitz's next strategic decision was his most difficult: to file for Chapter 11 bankruptcy. The prospector strategy was not suited to the declining environment.

Sakowitz's new strategy is to just stay in business. A smaller chain of two to three stores located in Houston will offer opportunities for synergy. All stores could take advantage of a single advertising campaign and be monitored by the same managers. It remains to be seen whether the new retrenchment strategy will work. Robert Sakowitz is determined, claiming that "We'll cut back to the profitable trunk of the tree."[51]

DISCUSSION QUESTIONS

1. Which is more important—strategy formulation or strategy implementation? Do they depend on each other? Is it possible for strategy implementation to occur first?

2. If an organization has hired strategic management professionals, during which part of the strategic management process would they play the largest role?

3. Perform a situation (SWOT) analysis for the university you attend. Do you think university administrators consider these factors when devising their strategy?

4. What is meant by the scope and synergy components of strategy? Give examples.

5. Using Porter's competitive strategies and Miles and Snow's adaptive strategy typology, how would you describe the strategies of Wal-Mart, Bloomingdale's, and Kmart?

6. Walt Disney Company has four major strategic business units: movies (Touchstone), theme parks, consumer products, and television (primarily cable). Place each of these SBUs on the BCG matrix and GE business screen based on your knowledge of them.

7. Of the three personal strategy formulation modes, which would you prefer to use as a manager? Are there organizations in which that mode would be most appropriate?

8. As administrator for a medium-size hospital, you and the board of directors have decided to change to a drug dependency hospital from a short-term, acute-care facility. Which organizational dimensions would you use to implement this strategy?

9. How would functional strategies in marketing, research and development, and production departments differ if a business changed from a prospector to a defender strategy?

10. Compare and contrast the adaptive strategy typology of Miles and Snow with Porter's competitive strategies. What are the similarities and differences? Which do you think better describes business-level strategies?

CASES FOR ANALYSIS

PEOPLE EXPRESS

People Express was the darling of participative management proponents in the early 1980s. Chairman Donald Burr believed that the airline's purpose was to enable employees to release their creative energies. Internal control was loose, because Burr believed people did not want to be controlled and would be more productive under self-management. People Express used a low-cost strategy and grew rapidly, becoming an important force in the industry. It changed the way the industry was run, because other airlines had to adapt their strategies in order to compete. Donald Burr likened his airline's mission to that of the *Star Wars* movies— a struggle between good and evil. He saw People Express and his style of management as Luke Skywalker and other airlines as Darth Vader.

But the rags-to-riches story has gone in reverse. In 1986, the company was forced to sell Frontier Airlines for approximately half of what it had paid because People Express was out of money. A few months later, People, struggling to survive, agreed to merge with Texas Air Corporation, which already owned Continental Airlines, Eastern Airlines, and New York Air (a regional airline).

People Express got into trouble when it grew so big so fast. It took on new routes to major cities such as Chicago and Dallas that forced it into competition with big, well-established airlines such as United and American. United and American lowered their fares on these routes to be close to People's. For similar prices, passengers preferred full-service airlines. People Express didn't have the financial strength to endure a rate war, and when it raised prices, more customers left.

When People Express grew large, Burr failed to build a strong management system. There were no sophisticated computers or financial controls. Thus, People couldn't quickly determine how many seats to offer at which prices in order to break even. Also, it had an unwieldy reservation system.

In a last-ditch attempt to turn things around, People's board of directors asked Donald Burr to develop a formal strategy and structure to replace the participative style that had been used early in the airline's life. Burr enforced a specialized division of labor rather than rotating employees among jobs. He also tried to offer more services, but it was too late. People had problems bringing in enough cash to support itself and hence had to be absorbed by Texas Air.

Questions

1. How would you characterize People Express' business-level strategy? Did People have the correct internal structure for this strategy?
2. People Express is now a part of Texas Air's portfolio. What synergy could Texas Air achieve by combining Eastern, People, Continental, and New York Air as business units of one large corporation?
3. Should Texas Air treat People Express as a distinct SBU, or fold it into its established airlines and discontinue the People Express name? Discuss.

Source: Gordon M. Henry, "Air Pocket in the Revolution," *Time,* July 7, 1986, pp. 42–44; James R. Norman, "People Is Plunging but Burr Is Staying Cool," *Business Week,* July 7, 1986, pp. 31–32; William M. Carley, "New Flight Plan: Struggling to Survive, People Express Alters Operations," *The Wall Street Journal,* July 31, 1986, p. 1.

EASTMAN KODAK

During 1984, a marketing consultant working for Kodak commented, "Kodak, today, is a rudderless company, drifting from project to project with little coherent direction." This strategic drift was reflected in declining profits and sales. The question on everyone's mind was "What can Kodak's top managers do to produce a coherent strategy that will yield success in the marketplace?"

For years Kodak had brought products to market that were poorly made or were too late to take advantage of market opportunities. Take instant photography. Kodak's instant camera was never able to make serious inroads into Polaroid's market share. Then, in 1986, the courts ruled that Kodak had infringed upon Polaroid's patents and ordered Kodak to discontinue sales. In 1982 Kodak introduced the Disc camera, but this too proved too little too late. The dramatic improvements in 35mm cameras by Canon and other manufacturers provided a better picture at a similar price. Kodak has even been hurt in film sales, where it has been the leader for years. Japan's Fuji Film launched a determined assault on the U.S. market and walked off with the sponsorship of the Los Angeles Olympics.

Kodak's greatest strength is its technological and research capabilities. It also has a powerful distribution network and huge financial resources. This enables Kodak to undertake the basic research necessary for new technological developments. Despite these strengths, however, Kodak remains out of touch with its environment in many ways. Its huge X-ray film business has been hurt as hospital admissions have declined and insurance companies have reduced the number of diagnostic tests they will cover. The Ektachem blood analyzer was a big failure because it arrived on the market after Du Pont's product and couldn't do as much.

The performance problems have rudely awakened many employees and prompted internal changes. Kodak has embarked on a program of layoffs and voluntary retirements to reduce its work force by 8 percent. This is in sharp contrast to the attention Kodak traditionally has lavished on employees in the form of benefits, recreation facilities, and lifelong employment.

It is felt that Kodak can no longer afford to guess wrong. Kodak must develop products to take advantage of large existing markets before investing in new plants. And the products must get to the market on time. To be innovative, Kodak probably needs to change its internal culture as well. The value of stability should be replaced with the values of change and timely reaction to market opportunities.

Questions

1. What strengths, weaknesses, opportunities, and threats characterize Kodak? What are its current mission and strategy?
2. What strategy would you recommend that Kodak adopt? Why? How should Kodak's senior managers implement this strategy?
3. What mode of strategy making would characterize Kodak's senior managers? Which mode would you recommend for Kodak?

Source: Subrata N. Chakravarty and Ruth Simon, "Has the World Passed Kodak By?" *Forbes,* November 5, 1984, pp. 184–192.

CHAPTER 6

Managerial Decision Making

Chapter Outline

Types of Decisions and Problems

Programmed and Nonprogrammed
Decisions
Certainty, Risk, Uncertainty,
and Ambiguity

Decision-Making Models

Classical Model
Administrative Model

Decision-Making Steps

Recognition of Decision Requirement
Diagnosis and Analysis of Causes
Development of Alternatives
Selection of Desired Alternative
Implementation of Chosen
Alternative
Control and Follow-up

**Group Approaches to Decision
Making**

Coalitions
Task Groups
Group Decision Formats
Advantages and Disadvantages of
Group Decision Making

**Improving Decision-Making
Effectiveness**

Learning Objectives

After studying this chapter, you should be able to:

- Explain why decision making is an important component of good management.

- Explain the difference between programmed and nonprogrammed decisions and the decision characteristics of risk, uncertainty, and ambiguity.

- Describe the classical and administrative models of decision making and their applications.

- Identify the six steps used in managerial decision making.

- Discuss the advantages and disadvantages of using groups to make decisions and the role of coalitions in managerial decision making.

- Identify guidelines for improving decision-making effectiveness in organizations.

Management Problem

Jeff and Pete Coors were expected to lead a comeback for Adolph Coors Company. Coors was getting clobbered in the battle between Anheuser-Busch and Miller, and its efforts to expand sales beyond the Rocky Mountain area had been disappointing. For example, in California Coors' market share had dropped from 44 percent in 1976 to 14 percent in 1985. During that period Coors expanded to 23 new states, but total sales remained the same. Jeff and Pete Coors faced many decisions. The problem of lost market share had to be solved. They considered several alternatives, including diversifying into other businesses such as biotechnology and packaging, introducing new products such as Coors Extra Gold, implementing a more formalized strategic planning process, and increasing advertising budgets. They also considered whether to build a new brewery in the Northeast to achieve market penetration in that region. They were not certain which alternatives would work, because previous attempts at regional expansion and improved advertising had been disappointing, although one new product—Coors Light—was an enormous success and kept the company from losing even more ground to competitors.[1]

If you were Jeff or Pete Coors, what would you do? How would you proceed to gather information and select one or more of the available decision alternatives?

Jeff and Pete Coors must make a number of important decisions, and their decision-making skill will determine whether Coors survives the intense competition in the brewing industry. Organizations grow, pros-

Some decisions don't work. The $100 million ship Columbia *rusts in 18 feet of James River water while awaiting her first—and final—voyage. Destination: a Taiwanese scrapyard. The* Columbia *represents several mistakes resulting from an uncertain and unpredictable decision environment. Built to haul liquefied natural gas, the ship encountered problems when its foam insulation lining cracked. Then the Algerian government reneged on a contract signed by its national oil company. Then the* Columbia *ran aground in a storm off Nova Scotia, irreparably damaging her hull. Her once majestic framework will now be reduced to 70 million pounds of scrap.*

per, or fail as a result of decisions by their managers. Managers often are referred to as *decision makers*. While many of their important decisions are strategic, managers also make decisions about every other aspect of an organization, including structure, control systems, responses to the environment, and human resources. Managers scout for problems, make decisions for solving them, and monitor the consequences to see whether further decisions are required. Good decision making is a vital part of good management because decisions determine how the organization solves its problems, allocates resources, and accomplishes its objectives.

Decision making is not easy. It must be done amid ever-changing factors, unclear information, and conflicting points of view. For example, USX (formerly United States Steel) was hurt by cheap steel from abroad. Top managers at USX made the decision to diversify into chemicals, petroleum, and other areas. This resulted in a costly strike by unionized steelworkers. The strike caused USX's stock price to plummet, and Carl Icahn, a well-known corporate raider, tried to buy the company. David Roderick, chairman of USX, now faces several new choices, including whether to buy back stock, sell the company's oil assets, or search for a white knight.[2]

Consider the issues confronting Ward Hagen when he took over as chief executive of Warner-Lambert. He saw the need to increase spending on drug research, to keep certain consumer product lines, and to move into related, high-tech companies. But what kind of drug research? Which consumer products? Which high-tech medical equipment companies? In order to proceed, Hagen hired a consulting firm to gather information and help his managers plan for these decisions.[3]

Chapters 4 and 5 described strategic planning. The purpose of this chapter is to explore the decision process that underlies strategic planning. Plans and strategies are arrived at through decision making; the better the decision making, the better the strategic planning. First we will examine decision characteristics. Then we will look at decision-making models and the steps executives should take when making important decisions. We will also examine how groups of managers make decisions. Finally, we will discuss techniques for improving decision making in organizations.

TYPES OF DECISIONS AND PROBLEMS

decision A choice made from available alternatives.

decision making The process of identifying problems and opportunities, generating alternatives, selecting an alternative, and implementing the solution.

A **decision** is a choice made from available alternatives. For example, an accounting manager's selection among Bill, Nancy, and Joan for the position of junior auditor is a decision. Many people assume that making a choice is the major part of decision making, but it is only a small part, as illustrated in Exhibit 6.1.

Decision making is the process of identifying problems and opportunities, generating alternatives, selecting an alternative, and implementing the solution. Decision making involves effort both prior to and after the actual choice. Thus, the decision as to whether to select Bill, Nancy, or Joan requires the accounting manager to ascertain whether a new junior auditor is needed, determine the availability of potential job candidates, interview candidates to acquire necessary information, select one candidate, and follow up with the socialization of the new employee into the organization to insure the decision's success.

Programmed and Nonprogrammed Decisions

Management decisions typically fall into one of two categories: programmed and nonprogrammed. **Programmed decisions** involve situations that have occurred often enough to enable decision rules to be developed and applied over and over again.[4] Programmed decisions are made in response to routine, recurring organizational problems. The decision to reorder paper and other office supplies when inventories drop to a certain level is a programmed decision. Other programmed decisions concern the types of skills required to fill certain jobs, the reorder point for manufacturing inventory, exception reporting for expenditures 10 percent or more over budget, and selection of freight routes for product deliveries. Decision rules define exactly how to respond. Once managers formulate decision rules, subordinates and others can make the decision, freeing managers for other tasks.

Nonprogrammed decisions are made in response to situations that are unique, are poorly defined and largely unstructured, and have important consequences for the organization. Nonprogrammed decisions often involve strategic planning, because uncertainty is great and decisions are complex. Nonprogrammed decisions would include decisions to build a new factory, develop a new product or service, enter a new geographical market, or relocate headquarters to a new city. The decisions facing Adolph Coors Company, described at the beginning of this chapter, are examples of nonprogrammed decisions.

Routine decision rules or techniques for solving these problems do not exist. No computer program could have told USX executives how to respond to Icahn's attempt to take over the company or Ward Hagen how to restructure Warner-Lambert. Hundreds of hours were spent analyzing these problems, developing alternatives, and making a choice.

Certainty, Risk, Uncertainty, and Ambiguity

In a perfect world, managers would have all the information necessary for making decisions. In reality, however, some things are unknowable; thus, some decisions will fail to solve the problem or attain the desired outcome. Managers try to obtain information about decision alternatives that will reduce decision uncertainty. Every decision situation can be organized on a scale according to the availability of information and the possibility of failure. The four positions on the scale are certainty, risk, uncertainty, and ambiguity, as illustrated in Exhibit 6.2.

EXHIBIT 6.1

Overview of Decision-Making Activities

1. Managers determine the existence of problems and opportunities

2. Managers generate alternative courses of action

3. Managers choose a course of action

4. Managers implement the course of action

Source: Based on George P. Huber, *Managerial Decision Making* (Glenview, Ill.: Scott, Foresman, 1980).

programmed decision A decision made in response to a situation that has occurred often enough to have generated decision rules that can be applied in each recurrence of the problem.

nonprogrammed decision A decision made in response to a situation that is unique, is poorly defined and largely unstructured, and has important consequences for the organization.

EXHIBIT 6.2

Conditions That Affect the Possibility of Decision Failure

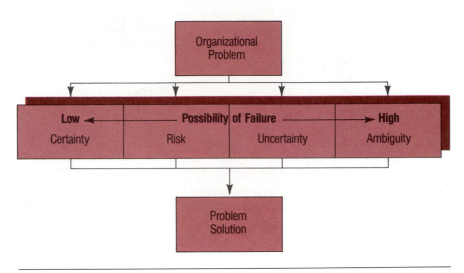

Certainty. *Certainty* means that all the information the decision maker needs is fully available.[5] This situation is considered deterministic because the objective is clear and managers have measurable, reliable data about each alternative for reaching that objective. Managers have information on operating conditions, resource costs or constraints, and each course of action and possible outcome. For example, if a company considers a $10,000 investment in new equipment that it knows for certain will yield $4,000 in cost savings per year over the next five years, managers can calculate a before-tax rate of return of about 40 percent. If managers compare this investment to one that will yield only $3,000 per year in cost savings, they can confidently select the 40 percent return.

Risk. *Risk* means that a decision has clear-cut objectives and good information available but the future events associated with each alternative are subject to chance. However, enough information is available to allow the probability of a successful outcome for each alternative to be expressed quantitatively.[6] Statistical analysis can be used to calculate the probabilities of success or failure. The measure of risk captures the possibility that future events will render the alternative unsuccessful. For example, a petroleum company may bid on a contract to sell 10,000 barrels of a petroleum distillate. After gathering all information, the decision maker settles on two alternatives: a bid to sell at $4.20 a barrel and one to sell at $5 a barrel. The data suggest that the low bid has an 80 percent chance of being successful and the high bid only a 50 percent chance. Using those probabilities, managers can determine which likelihood is more desirable for the company.

Uncertainty. *Uncertainty* means that managers know which objective they wish to achieve but information about alternatives and future events

Ore-Ida made a financially risky, nonprogrammed decision when it decided to establish a national retail brand of frozen potatoes. This was a difficult marketing feat, because commodity foods rarely achieve sizable market penetration nationally. However, managers successfully implemented the decision and later expanded the national product line to include french fries, shredded hash browns, and Tater-Tots®. There were no decision rules to tell Ore-Ida managers how to make this nonprogrammed decision. They took a chance—and succeeded.

is incomplete.[7] Managers do not have enough information to calculate risk. Factors that may affect a decision, such as price, production costs, volume, or future interest rates, are difficult to analyze and predict. This is a difficult decision situation. Managers may have to make assumptions from which to forge the decision even though the decision will be wrong if the assumptions are incorrect. Managers may have to come up with creative approaches to alternatives and use personal judgment to determine which alternative is best.

For example, Time Inc.'s decision to launch a new magazine called *TV–Cable Week* was made under uncertainty. The objective was to increase the magazine group's income by marketing a top-quality weekly through cable operators. Time was unable to get good data on critical variables; thus, it assumed that the magazine would capture a 60 percent market penetration among cable subscribers and that Time would reach distribution agreements with 250 cable systems. These assumptions turned out to be wildly unrealistic. Only a tiny percentage of subscribers were interested in the magazine, and cable operators would not cooperate. The decision to launch the magazine was a failure. It folded in six months because of the uncertainty confronting Time's decision makers.[8]

Ambiguity.   Ambiguity is by far the most difficult decision situation. *Ambiguity* means that the objectives to be achieved or the problem to be solved are unclear, alternatives are difficult to define, and information about outcomes is unavailable.[9] Decision making under ambiguity is equivalent to a decision situation in which virtually nothing is given or easily determined.[10] Ambiguity has been called a "wicked" decision problem. Managers have a difficult time coming to grips with the issues. Wicked problems are associated with manager conflicts over objectives and decision alternatives, rapidly changing circumstances, fuzzy information with multiple interpretations, and unclear linkages among elements relevant to the decision.[11] Fortunately, most decisions are not characterized by ambiguity. But when they are, managers must conjure up objectives and develop reasonable scenarios for decision alternatives in the absence of information. The risk of failure is high because everything is uncertain.

One example of an ambiguous decision situation occurred at Sperry Corporation in 1985.

Gerber executives decided not to recall its baby food jars in 1986 despite reports of broken glass. Although the decision outcomes seemed uncertain, Gerber executives had previously experienced a baby food recall. After calculating the risk, they decided that a negative consumer reaction was unlikely. Gerber adopted the strategy of conveying facts to the public and decided that a recall was unjustified and would not solve the problem. Their prognosis of low-risk consequences for not recalling the baby food turned out to be correct.

Sperry Corporation

Sperry Corporation spent three years at war with itself. Dissenting executives fought over what kind of company Sperry should be, whether it should be kept together or would be worth more if broken up and sold. Sperry had a proud history, but its recent years' performance had been lackluster as it fell to a distant seventh among U.S. computer makers. Everyone seemed dissatisfied with Sperry's performance, but no one was sure what the problem was, what to do, or what objectives to set.

When Gerald Probst became chairman in 1982, Sperry's finances were a disaster. Probst hired an expert, Vincent McLean, as chief financial officer and strategic planner. McLean felt the problem was the computer group and believed those assets should be gradually reduced in favor of aerospace and defense, which would return a higher profit. Managers in the computer group disagreed, and the war began.

McLean eventually lost the battle. A decision was made to keep Sperry in mainframe computers as well as introduce a new line of smaller computers. But executives were still unclear about Sperry's future. Alternatively, senior executives started looking for a merger partner in telecommunications. They considered an alliance with AT&T, ITT, and Hitachi, but nothing clicked. Then Burroughs Corporation, a rival in the mainframe business, showed up as a possible suitor for Sperry. This seemed like an unusual arrangement at first, but the more it was discussed, the more creative and innovative this alternative appeared. In 1986 the deal went through and—to the surprise of many observers—the merged company, named Unisys, is working well.[12]

The Sperry decision was unusual because managers did not agree on what the problems were and had no clear alternatives to evaluate. When the unexpected alternative of a merger with Burroughs surfaced, that was the alternative they tried. It contained a lot of risk, but unlike Time's decision to launch *TV–Cable Week,* this one worked out.

DECISION-MAKING MODELS

The approach managers use to make decisions usually falls into one of two types—the classical model or the administrative model. The choice of model depends on the manager's personal preference, whether the decision is programmed or nonprogrammed, and the extent to which the decision is characterized by risk, uncertainty, or ambiguity.

Classical Model

classical model A model of decision making based on the assumption that managers should make logical decisions that will be in the organization's best economic interests.

The **classical model** of decision making is based on economic assumptions. This model has arisen within the management literature because managers are expected to make decisions that are economically sensible and in the organization's best economic interests. The assumptions underlying this model are as follows:

Weyerhaeuser executives use the classical model of decision making for managing its forests. It takes from 25 to 60 years to grow a crop of trees. The trees at the top of this photograph are nearing harvest age; a young plantation of pine trees is shown in the foreground. Weyerhaeuser manages its commercial forest lands to preserve and enhance shareholders' asset values as well as protect social and environmental values. Its classical decision model incorporates the specific soil, climate, slope, and types of trees in assessing the economics of forestry decisions.

1. The decision maker operates to accomplish objectives that are known and agreed upon. Targeted problems are precisely formulated and defined.
2. The decision maker operates under conditions of certainty, possessing complete information. All alternatives and the potential results of each can be calculated.
3. Criteria for evaluating alternatives are known. The decision maker selects the alternative that will maximize the economic return to the organization.
4. The decision maker is rational and uses logic to assign values, order preferences, evaluate alternatives, and make the decision that will maximize the attainment of organizational objectives.

The classical model of decision making is considered to be **normative,** which means it defines how a decision maker *should* make decisions. It does not try to describe how managers actually make decisions so much as it provides guidelines on how to reach an ideal outcome for the organization. The value of the classical model has been its ability to help decision makers be more rational. For example, many senior managers do not use a systematic process for making decisions but rely solely on intuition and personal preferences.[13] In recent years, the classical approach has been given wider application because of the growth of quantitative decision techniques that use powerful computers. Quantitative techniques (discussed in detail in Chapter 7) include such things as decision trees, pay-off matrices, breakeven analysis, linear programming, forecasting, and operations research models. The use of computerized information systems and databases have increased the power of the classical approach.

In many respects, the classical model represents an "ideal" model of decision making that is quite unattainable by real people in real organizations. It is most valuable when applied to programmed decisions and

normative   An approach that defines how a decision maker should make decisions and provides guidelines for reaching an ideal outcome for the organization.

to decisions characterized by certainty or risk, because relevant information is available and probabilities can be calculated. One value of computer-based decision aids is that decisions previously characterized as uncertain have been converted to decisions under risk because the outcomes of alternatives can be evaluated more accurately.

One example of the classical approach is the decision model developed by Weyerhauser Company for converting a timber harvest into end products. A computer-based model is used to plan stump-to-product activities. The model assesses the economic implications of several short-term and long-term management decision alternatives. It starts with the description of a tree—size and shape—and evaluates such factors as harvesting costs, hauling, mill location, facility operations, expected end products (plywood, dried trim, fiber, lumber), and customer demand. The model helps managers evaluate hundreds of possibilities for moving lumber through the production process to the consumer and choose the most economically efficient alternatives.[14]

Administrative Model

administrative model A decision-making model that describes how managers actually make decisions in situations characterized by nonprogrammed decisions, uncertainty, and ambiguity.

The **administrative model** of decision making describes how managers actually make decisions in difficult situations, such as those characterized by nonprogrammed decisions, uncertainty, and ambiguity. Many management decisions are not sufficiently programmable to lend themselves to any degree of quantification. Thus, managers may be unable to make economically rational decisions even if they want to.[15]

Bounded Rationality and Satisficing.   The administrative model of decision making is based on the work of Herbert A. Simon. Simon proposed two concepts that were instrumental in shaping the administrative model: bounded rationality and satisficing. **Bounded rationality** means that people have limits, or boundaries, on how rational they can be. The organization can be incredibly complex, and managers have the time and ability to process only a limited amount of information with which to make decisions.[16] Since managers do not have the time or cognitive ability to process complete information about complex decisions, they must satisfice. **Satisficing** means that decision makers choose the first solution alternative that satisfies minimal decision criteria. Rather than pursuing all alternatives in order to identify the single solution that will maximize economic returns, managers will opt for the first solution that appears to solve the problem, even if better solutions are presumed to exist. Simon proposed that the environment often did not provide enough information to maximize economic outcomes and the decision maker could not justify the expense of obtaining complete information.[17]

bounded rationality The concept that people have the time and cognitive ability to process only a limited amount of information on which to base decisions.

satisfice To choose the first solution alternative that satisfies minimal decision criteria regardless of whether better solutions are presumed to exist.

An example of both bounded rationality and satisficing occurs when a junior executive on a business trip stains her blouse just prior to an important meeting. She will run to a nearby clothing store and buy the first satisfactory replacement she finds. Having neither the time nor the opportunity to explore all the blouses in town, she satisfices by choosing a blouse that will solve the immediate problem. In a similar fashion, managers generate alternatives for complex problems only until they find one they believe will work. For example, in 1984 Disney chairman

Ray Watson and chief operating officer Ron Miller attempted to thwart takeover attempts. They had limited options. They satisfied with a quick decision to acquire Arivda Realty and Gibson Court Company. The acquisition of these companies had the potential to solve the problem at hand; thus, they looked no further for possibly better alternatives.[18]

The administrative model relies on assumptions different from those of the classical model and focuses on organizational factors that influence individual decisions. It is more realistic than the classical model for complex, nonprogrammed decisions. According to the administrative model,

1. Decision objectives often are vague, conflicting, and lacking in consensus among managers. Managers often are unaware of problems or opportunities that exist in the organization.
2. Rational procedures are not always applied, and when they are, they are confined to a simplistic view of the problem that does not capture the complexity of real organizational events.
3. Managers' search for alternatives is limited because of human, information, and resource constraints.
4. Most managers settle for a satisficing rather than a maximizing solution. This is partly because they have limited information and partly because they have only vague criteria for what constitutes a maximizing solution.

The administrative model is considered to be **descriptive,** meaning that it describes how managers actually make decisions in complex situations rather than dictating how they *should* make decisions according to a theoretical ideal. The administrative model recognizes the human and environmental limitations that affect the degree to which managers can pursue a rational decision-making process.

Intuition.   Another aspect of administrative decision making is intuition. **Intuition** represents a quick apprehension of a decision situation based on past experience but without conscious thought.[19] Intuitive decision making is not arbitrary or irrational, because it is based on years of practice and hands-on experience that enable managers to quickly identify solutions without going through painstaking computations. Managers rely on intuition to determine when a problem exists and to synthesize isolated bits of data and experience into an integrated picture. They also use their intuitive understanding to check the results of rational analysis. If the rational analysis does not agree with their intuition, managers may dig further before accepting a proposed alternative.[20]

Intuition helps managers understand situations characterized by uncertainty and ambiguity that have proven impervious to rational analysis. For example, virtually every major studio in Hollywood turned down the *Star Wars* concept except 20th Century Fox. George Lucas, the creator of *Star Wars,* had attempted to sell the concept to 12 major studios before going to Fox. In each case, the concept had been rejected. All 13 studios saw the same numbers, but only Alan Ladd and his associates at Fox had the right "feel" for the decision. Their intuition told them that *Star Wars* would be a success. The rest is history.[21]

All of these products use NutraSweet® sweetener, the leading low-calorie sweetener in the United States. Richard Mahoney, Monsanto's CEO, made the intuitive decision to acquire G. D. Searle & Company's NutraSweet division while sitting in his Jacuzzi one Sunday. Although expensive, the NutraSweet division promised a strong flow of earnings until its patents would run out in the early 1990s. The threat of an uncomfortable debt level and new competition created high risk. But based on sound business intuition and the necessary homework, Mahoney's decision has been paying off for Monsanto ever since.

descriptive   An approach that describes how managers actually make decisions rather than how they should.

intuition   The immediate apprehension of a decision situation based on past experience but without conscious thought.

EXHIBIT 6.3
_____

**Characteristics of Classical and Administrative
Decision-Making Models**

Classical Model	Administrative Model
Clear-cut problem and objectives	Vague problem and objectives
Condition of certainty	Condition of uncertainty
Full information about alternatives and their outcomes	Limited information about alternatives and their outcomes
Rational choice for maximizing outcomes	Satisficing choice for resolving problem

_____

The key dimensions of the classical and administrative models are listed in Exhibit 6.3. Recent research into decision-making procedures have found rational, classical procedures to be associated with high performance for organizations in stable environments. However, administrative decision-making procedures and intuition have been associated with high performance in unstable environments, in which decisions must be made rapidly and under more difficult conditions.[22]

DECISION-MAKING STEPS

Whether a decision is programmed or nonprogrammed and regardless of managers' choice of the classical or administrative model of decision making, six steps typically are associated with effective decision processes. These are summarized in Exhibit 6.4.

Recognition of Decision Requirement

problem A situation in which organizational accomplishments have failed to meet established objectives.

opportunity A situation in which managers see potential organizational accomplishments that exceed current objectives.

Managers confront a decision requirement in the form of either a problem or an opportunity. A **problem** occurs when organizational accomplishment is less than established objectives. Some aspect of performance is unsatisfactory. An **opportunity** exists when managers see potential accomplishment that exceeds specified current objectives. Managers see the possibility of enhancing performance beyond current levels.

Awareness of a problem or opportunity is the first step in the decision sequence and requires surveillance of the internal and external environment for issues that merit executive attention.[23] This resembles the military concept of gathering intelligence. Managers scan the world around them to determine whether the organization is satisfactorily progressing toward its goals. For example, managers at Wells Fargo & Company in San Francisco survey employees to detect potential human resource

EXHIBIT 6.4

Six Steps in the Managerial Decision-Making Process

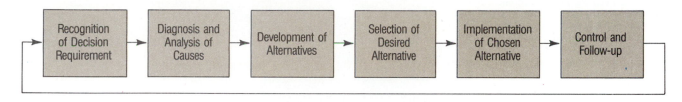

problems. The survey covers effectiveness of company advertising, product quality, and responsibility to the community, as well as internal satisfaction and organizational climate.[24]

Some information comes from formal information systems. Managers are provided with periodic accounting reports, MIS reports, and other sources of information that are designed to discover problems before they become too serious. Managers also take advantage of informal sources. They talk to other managers, gather opinions on how things are going, and seek advice on which problems should be tackled or which opportunities embraced.[25] The manager must be plugged into an information system, whether formal or informal, that gathers these data as a means of identifying problems and opportunities.

Recognizing decision requirements is difficult, because it often means integrating bits and pieces of information in novel ways. Managers should not rely strictly on financial benchmarks that compare this year's performance to last year's or to other companies'.[26] In 1986, IBM had a significant hold on the computer market, but its chief financial officer found himself in a less attractive job. Allen Krowe had been a proponent of IBM's ambitious growth plans and had failed to anticipate the soft computer market or IBM's unimpressive performance. Krowe's inability to sense problems in advance resulted in his demotion from IBM's chief financial officer and head of planning to head of two computer groups in the Rolm Corporation unit.[27]

Failure to find new opportunities can be equally responsible for unimpressive organizational performance. Top managers may be slow to seek new opportunities because doing so entails risk and uncertainty.[28] If managers are willing to take the risk, the payoffs can be high. Some people, such as Donald Bonham of Fiesta Food Marts, see opportunities where others see only problems.

Fiesta Food Marts

Donald Bonham looked around Houston in the early seventies and saw the enormous demographic changes that were taking place. One-fifth of the population were now Hispanic, with an additional 65,000 Southeast Asians, 55,000 Chinese, and sizable Korean, Filipino, and

Decision making begins with a problem or an opportunity. Lever Research and Development uses sophisticated consumer testing to judge the quality of its products and the need for new decisions. From moisturizing soap bars to margarines, Lever measures the products' performance by training employees such as Mike Twitty to be expert judges of sensory intensity. Information from these consumer tests identifies both problems and opportunities that trigger the decision-making process for product changes.

Indian enclaves. Bonham saw an opportunity to supply specialty foods for these groups. Uncertainty was high because he had no way to gauge whether the idea would work, but his information indicated that a need existed.

Bonham has since developed his Fiesta Food Mart stores into "the" place to shop for a little taste of home. He parlayed his supply of specialty foods and his willingness to accept cultural differences into annual sales of $320 million, more than anyone would have anticipated. "Fiesta is the only store in Houston where I can get the products from home and everything else I need," said one Mexican immigrant. A Nigerian commented, "Fiesta has made living here easier." Bonham saw the ethnic population as an opportunity, while other stores considered foreign language, customs, and requests a nuisance.[29]

Diagnosis and Analysis of Causes

Once a problem or opportunity has come to a manager's attention, the understanding of the situation should be refined. **Diagnosis** is the step in the decision-making process in which managers analyze underlying

diagnosis The step in the decision-making process in which managers analyze underlying causal factors associated with the decision situation.

causal factors associated with the decision situation. Managers make a mistake here if they jump right into generating alternatives without first exploring the cause of the problem more deeply.

Kepner and Tregoe, who have conducted extensive studies of manager decision making, recommend that managers ask a series of questions to specify underlying causes, including:

- What is the state of disequilibrium affecting us?
- When did it occur?
- Where did it occur?
- How did it occur?
- To whom did it occur?
- What is the urgency of the problem?
- What is the interconnectedness of events?
- What result came from which activity?[30]

Such questions help specify what actually happened and why. The effort to find the real cause of the problem is critical. Creativity and flexibility in the diagnosis stage are especially important when decisions are nonprogrammable and characterized by uncertainty and ambiguity. Generating an accurate picture guides decision makers to an appropriate set of alternative solutions.

For example, Johnson Controls was a successful company that designed and manufactured equipment used to heat, cool, and light buildings. However, as both buildings and information technology became more sophisticated, Johnson managers began to recognize an opportunity to manage the buildings' internal environments. After careful diagnosis of the opportunity, they realized that customers would welcome a more complete package of services and equipment. Their decision to act was illustrated in the 1986 ad that said, "To you it's another small office building. To us it's creating a more efficient working environment."[31] Johnson managers successfully diagnosed the need for managed facilities because they had supplied the hardware and talked to customers.

Development of Alternatives

Once the problem or opportunity has been recognized and analyzed, decision makers begin to consider taking action. The next stage is to generate possible alternative solutions that will respond to the needs of the situation and correct the underlying causes.

For a programmed decision, feasible alternatives are easy to identify and in fact usually are already available within the organization's rules and procedures. Nonprogrammed decisions, however, require developing new courses of action that will meet the company's needs. For decisions made under conditions of high uncertainty or even ambiguity, managers may develop only one or two custom solutions that will satisfice for handling the problem.

Decision alternatives can be thought of as the tools for reducing the difference between the organization's current and desired performance. Consider Chrysler Corporation.

Chrysler Corporation

After the turnaround led by Lee Iacocca, Chrysler found itself with greater demand for cars in both American and European markets than it could provide. Chrysler executives considered various alternatives such as building new plants, having employees work nights and weekends in existing plants, and renting additional production capacity on a temporary basis.

Chrysler executives dug into the problem and possible alternatives. They saw pending overcapacity in the American market because of stabilized demand, increased foreign imports, and construction of new plants by foreign manufacturers. Thus, if Chrysler built new plants, it might get stuck with high overhead and excess capacity. Because current plants were working at almost full capacity, additional labor hours would not produce many additional cars. The third alternative represented a creative tool for increasing capacity in the short run without incurring the danger of future excess capacity. Chrysler executives rented an American Motors plant in Kenosha, Wisconsin, to build Chrysler automobiles. Chrysler paid for retooling and used AMC workers for assembly. The AMC workers avoided a layoff, and Chrysler fulfilled its requirement of greater short-run production capacity. Developing appropriate alternatives led to a creative idea that helped Chrysler stay efficient and at the same time sell more cars.[32]

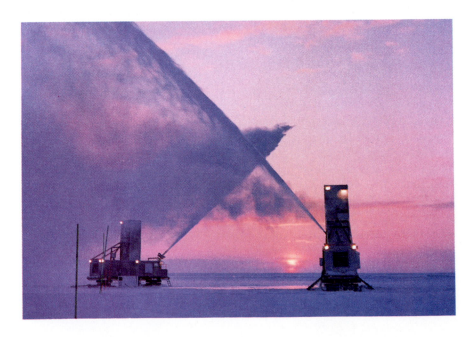

Sea water projected into the Arctic sky instantly freezes into cascading ice crystals. This has created a temporary island in the Beaufort Sea off the northern coast of Alaska. For the drilling of a test well, Amoco executives developed several decision alternatives: Use a drill ship, build an offshore platform, a concrete island, a manmade gravel island, or the temporary island of ice. They selected the ice island alternative because the cost of drilling a test well would be one-third to one-half of that for a gravel island. This alternative would also turn Alaska's forbidding winter into an advantage. Come summer, the ice island will revert to its natural state.

E X H I B I T   6.5

Decision Alternatives with Different Levels of Risk

For each of the following decisions, which alternative would you choose?

1. In the final seconds of a game with the college's traditional rival, the coach of a college football team may choose a play that has a 95 percent chance of producing a tie score or one with a 30 percent chance of leading to victory or to sure defeat if it fails.

2. The president of a Canadian company must decide whether to build a new plant within Canada that has a 90 percent chance of producing a modest return on investment or to build it in a foreign country with an unstable political history. The latter alternative has a 40 percent chance of failing, but the returns would be enormous if it succeeded.

3. A college senior with considerable acting talent must choose a career. She has the opportunity to go on to medical school and become a physician, a career in which she is 80 percent likely to succeed. She would rather be an actress but realizes that the opportunity for success is only 20 percent.

Selection of Desired Alternative

Once feasible alternatives have been developed, one must be selected. This is where the actual decision is made. The decision choice is the selection of the most promising of several alternative courses of action. Managers' goal is to make the choice with the least amount of risk and uncertainty. Through careful discussion, analysis, and diagnosis, managers try to move from uncertainty to risk and, if possible, from risk to certainty to insure a successful outcome. Because some risk is inherent for most nonprogrammed decisions, managers try to gauge prospects for success. Under conditions of uncertainty, they may have to rely on their intuition and experience to estimate whether a given course of action is likely to succeed.

Making choices depends on managers' personality factors and willingness to accept risk and uncertainty. For example, **risk propensity** is the willingness to undertake risk with the opportunity of gaining an increased payoff. The level of risk a manager is willing to accept will influence the analysis of cost and benefits to be derived from any decision. Consider the situations in Exhibit 6.5. In each situation, which alternative would you choose? A person with a low risk propensity would tend to take assured moderate returns by going for a tie score, building a domestic plant, or pursuing a career as physician. A risk taker would go for the victory, build a plant in a foreign country, or embark on an acting career.

Sometimes the high-risk option succeeds. One of the biggest risks of all time occurred when Lee Iacocca took on the challenge of trying to turn around Chrysler Corporation. No one gave him more than a 20 percent chance of success. He entered into negotiations with the government, unions, and bankers and won concessions from all three. He made television commercials that created a new corporate image and con-

risk propensity The willingness to undertake risk with the opportunity of gaining an increased payoff.

MANAGERS SHOP TALK

Decision Biases to Avoid

At a time when decision making is so important, many corporate executives do not know how to make a good choice among alternatives. They may rely on computer analyses or personal intuition without realizing that their own cognitive biases affect their judgment. The complexities of modern corporate life make good judgment more critical than ever.

Many errors in judgment originate in the human mind's limited capacity and in the natural biases most executives display during decision making. To make the best decisions, people must understand their own deficiencies. Awareness of the six biases below can help managers make more enlightened choices:

1. *Ignoring the laws of randomness.* Randomness means that the outcome of one event has nothing to do with the outcome of another. Managers often ignore this principle in making business decisions. For example, even though retail sales should be expected to fluctuate each month, a businessperson decides that a slight sales dip is the beginning of a downward trend and takes significant action, such as increasing the advertising budget. If sales rise

the following month—which would be expected even without a change in advertising—the executive attributes it to the new advertising strategy. Trends should not be interpreted from a single, random event.

2. *Hindsight bias.* Hindsight bias means that people tend to overestimate after the fact the degree to which they could have predicted an event. This is sometimes called the "I-knew-it-all-along effect." One example occurs when you are traveling in an unfamiliar area with your spouse behind the wheel. You reach an unmarked fork in the road, and your spouse decides to turn left. Twenty minutes later you are hopelessly lost, and you exclaim, "I knew you should have turned right at the fork!" Research on hindsight demonstrates that people are not very good at recalling or reconstructing how an uncertain situation appeared beforehand. Managers should be cautious about evaluating decision errors made by themselves and subordinates, because uncertainty may have been greater before the decision than they recall.

3. *Giving too much weight to readily available information.* Decisions often are based on information that is easily available to certain executives, which precludes their digging for additional information that may provide a more balanced view. For example, geologists at a major oil company were asked to estimate the potential yield at several drilling sites. To do so, they relied

vinced people that they could buy a product reminiscent of the Chrysler tradition of quality. Iacocca's willingness to take risks, including the introduction of several new car lines, and to work hard to carry it off created a highly profitable and successful Chrysler Corporation.[33]

Implementation of Chosen Alternative

implementation The step in the decision-making process that involves the employment of managerial, administrative, and persuasive abilities to translate the chosen alternative into action.

The **implementation** stage involves the use of managerial, administrative, and persuasive abilities to insure that the chosen alternative is carried out. This is similar to the idea of strategic implementation described in Chapter 5. The ultimate success of the chosen alternative depends on whether it can be translated into action. Sometimes an alternative never becomes reality because managers lack the resources or energy needed to make things happen. Implementation may require discussion with people affected by the decision. Communication, motivation, and leadership skills must be used to see that the decision is carried out.

One reason Lee Iacocca succeeded in turning Chrysler around was his ability to implement decisions. Iacocca personally hired people from on geological features similar to those of existing oil fields. The results were probably flawed because the geologists failed to consider unproductive fields that had features similar to those of the new sites.

4. *Seeing only one dimension of uncertainty.* In trying to estimate outcome probabilities, executives typically evaluate one dimension of uncertainty at a time and fail to consider their combined effects. For example, a group of subjects were asked to assume that they stood a 1-in-200 chance of being ill. At the same time they were told they had just been given a chest X-ray that was 95 percent accurate and indicated they had tuberculosis. What were the odds of the subjects' actually having TB? Most subjects responded about 90 percent, but the statistically correct answer was less than 9 percent. The subjects had focused on the 95 percent probability of the chest X-ray's accuracy rather than on the 1-in-200 chance of being ill.

5. *Misconception of chance.* When a series of similar events occur, managers may incorrectly gauge the probability of their future recurrence. For example, a manager who is hiring the fifth sales director in two years may feel that the person should work out well. After all, the first four did not work out, and the odds against five failures is small. In truth, the four people who failed have no bearing on the potential performance of the fifth. Each failure was a random event, and the chance of success on the fifth try should not be overestimated.

6. *Overconfidence.* One of the interesting research findings on decision-making biases is that most people overestimate their ability to predict uncertain outcomes. Before making a decision, managers have unrealistic expectations of their ability to understand the risk and make the right choice. Overconfidence is greatest when answering questions of moderate to extreme difficulty. For example, when a group of people were asked to define quantities about which they had little direct knowledge ("What was the dollar value of Canadian lumber exports in 1977?" "What was the amount of taxes collected by the U.S. Internal Revenue Service in 1970?"), they overestimated their accuracy. Evidence of overconfidence is illustrated in cases where subjects were so certain of an answer that they assigned odds of 1,000 to 1 of being correct but in fact were correct only about 85 percent of the time. These findings are especially important for strategic decision making, in which uncertainty is high because managers may unrealistically expect that they can successfully predict outcomes and hence select the wrong alternative.

Source: Based on Max H. Bazerman, *Judgment in Managerial Decision Making* (New York: Wiley, 1986), and Robin H. Hogarth, *Judgment and Choice: The Psychology of Decision* (New York: Wiley, 1981).

Ford to develop new auto models. He hired people who shared his vision and were eager to carry out his decisions. He was able to persuade bankers, the union, and the government to make concessions. All of these were part of the implementation process. Without successful implementation, Iacocca's efforts to turn Chrysler around would have failed.

The decision process does not stop with the selection of an alternative. Sometimes even well-intentioned government decisions fail because of poor implementation.

Civil Service Reform Act

During the Carter administration Congress passed the Civil Service Reform Act, placing 120,000 managers and supervisors on a merit pay system. Their annual pay increases had to be earned, and the amounts of the increases were to be determined via performance appraisals. The administration had made this decision as a way to increase government efficiency.

The new Big Boy sign is one way to implement Marriott's decision to convert over 200 Howard Johnson units to Big Boy restaurants between 1986 and 1989. The implementation of this decision provides a unique opportunity to expand Big Boy into East Coast markets and highway restaurants.

Those charged with implementing the decision created the Merit System Protection Board and met the federally mandated deadline for installation of the performance appraisal system. However, the people charged with implementing the Civil Service Reform Act did not have enough money to provide merit increases. Other parts of the bureaucracy imposed a ceiling on the amount of money to be used for pay raises and reduced the number of employees who could actually benefit. The process of implementation suffered another blow when Ronald Reagan assumed the presidency. The Reagan administration did not enforce implementation, and hence the Civil Service Reform Act failed to have the expected impact. The lack of implementation by the Carter and Reagan administrations prevented the decision to increase efficiency through merit pay from becoming a reality.[34]

Control and Follow-up

In the control stage of the decision process, decision makers gather information that tells them how well the decision was implemented and whether it was effective in achieving its objectives. For example, follow-up and control would have shown that the creators of the Civil Service Reform Act failed to take into account the powerful constituencies that would prevent its full implementation. Performance and efficiency remained unchanged. Follow-up would have shown that implementation was neither complete nor headed in the direction intended when the act was passed.

Control is important because decision making is a continuous, never-ending process. Decision making is not completed when an executive or board of directors votes yes or no. Follow-up provides decision makers with information that can precipitate a new decision cycle. The decision alternative may fail or only partially succeed, thus generating a new analysis of the problem, evaluation of alternatives, and selection of a new alternative. Many big problems are solved by trying several alternatives in sequence, each providing modest improvement. Follow-up is the part of monitoring that assesses whether a new decision needs to be made.

An illustration of the overall decision-making process, including follow-up and control, is Coca-Cola's decision to introduce a "new" Coke flavor.

Coca-Cola Company

"Dear Chief Dodo: What ignoramus decided to change the formula of Coke?" This was one of thousands of letters sent to Coca-Cola chairman Roberto Goizueta after the introduction of the new Coke flavor in 1985. Coca-Cola had made its decision via a cautious, rational decision process. The problem was clear: Pepsi was increasing market share at Coke's expense through supermarket sales. Pepsi was slightly sweeter and tended to beat Coke in blind taste tests. Moreover, the enormous success of Diet Coke—sweeter than regular Coke—reinforced the idea of changing the Coke formula.

The problem led to diagnosis and the development of several alternatives. Coca-Cola spent $4 million to taste-test the new flavor on nearly 200,000 consumers in 30 cities. The test took many forms. Some consumers were asked, "What if this were a new Coke taste?" Others were blind-tested—that is, the emotion-laden brand name was never mentioned. Coca-Cola identified the flavor people most prefered: 55 percent chose the new Coke over the old, and 52 percent chose it over Pepsi.

Yet within three months after the decision was implemented, the old Coke was back in the supermarkets. Why? Because follow-up revealed that brand loyalty is an elusive quality that cannot be measured. People had an emotional attachment to the original Coca-Cola from childhood. Millions of advertising dollars couldn't swing enough people to the new Coke flavor.

Why did the initial decision fail? It was a bold decision—and bold decisions are inherently risky. Coca-Cola tried to measure everything, but it could not measure intangible emotional attachments. On the other hand, the decision should not be considered a total failure. After the old Coke was reintroduced under the name "Coca-Cola Classic," there were two Coke brands with which to battle Pepsi and other competitors. The follow-up and control stage revealed that the two Cokes together had more market share than the original Coke. As chairman Goizueta commented, "Had I known in April what I know today, I definitely would have introduced the new Coke. Then I would have said I planned the whole thing."[35]

Coca-Cola's decision to introduce a new flavor illustrates all the decision steps, and the process ultimately ended in success. Strategic decisions always contain some risk. In this case, the follow-up and incremental changes got Coke back on track with two brands instead of one.

GROUP APPROACHES TO DECISION MAKING

Decision making is something that individual managers often do, but decision makers in the business world also operate as part of a group.

Decisions may be made through a committee, a task group, departmental participation, or an informal group called a *coalition*.

Coalitions

coalition An informal alliance among managers who support a specific decision-making objective.

Chapter 4 described a **coalition** as an informal alliance of managers formed to deal with a specific issue.[36] The coalition concept derives from research that discovered internal alliances among managers formed around "platforms" or issues in much the same way as people join political parties based on positions in a given election year.[37] Through discussion and political negotiations, a group of managers agree that a certain issue needs attention or that a certain course of action is appropriate.

Coalitions are especially important at top levels of the organization, where uncertainty and ambiguity are high. The forces that lead to coalition formation in organizations are illustrated in Exhibit 6.6. Managers jointly discuss goals and problems and build coalitions because of four factors. First, uncertainty is high and each manager has only limited information. Second, people affected by the decision may have conflicting goals, opinions, or values.[38] Third, organization decisions affect many departments, and a coalition is one way to gather inputs and coordinate those departments. Finally, top-level decision making often requires consensus and acceptance, and the coalition serves to get everyone to agree in order to simplify later implementation. One person who didn't build a coalition is Robert Carlson of United Technologies.

United Technologies

Robert Carlson was recruited by United Technologies Corporation because of his marketing ability. He was a "super salesman" and came to United Technologies as president with his mind already made up about its problems. He ignored the need to build a coalition with which to support his ideas.

Existing executives saw him as an unsophisticated outsider because he had spent nearly 30 years at Deere & Company, a farm equipment manufacturer. Carlson's mistake was to bypass existing executives rather than try to win their commitment to his agenda. He brought in several of his own people and ignored the headquarters' financial, legal, and public relations staff. They, in turn, questioned and criticized every decision he made. He created a marketing plan that was considered quite good; it included novel approaches to marketing and cost cutting that United Technologies needed.

However, Carlson went too far in one respect. He proposed to undercut General Electric, a major competitor, by offering an unusual guarantee: If a customer was dissatisfied with the jet engines made by Pratt and Whitney, a major subsidiary, United Technologies

Compaq Computer Corporation uses informal meetings and formal task groups to recognize and solve problems. Several people evaluate in-depth market research to assess the implications of important trends. A formal team of managers from engineering, marketing, manufacturing, sales, and finance must reach consensus on new-product features, performance, and cost before beginning new-product development in response to market opportunities. The effective use of groups and coalitions accounts for Compaq's rapid development of its recently launched DeskPro 386.

EXHIBIT   6.6

Why Coalitions Are Used in Decision Making

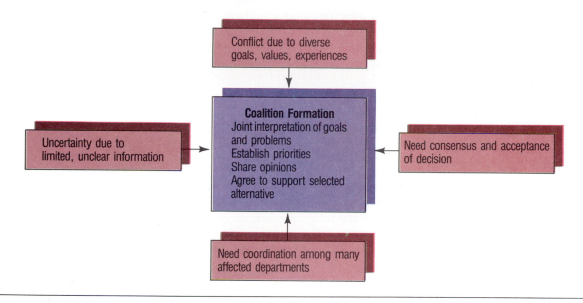

would take them back and refund the purchase price. This was an incredibly risky gamble that could bankrupt the company. This guarantee was later branded as "hairbrained."

With all the distrust and ill will from corporate executives and staff members, there was little support for Carlson's continuing on as president. Carlson was fired because "in a very traditional company, where ideas are approved by layer upon layer of management, Carlson had committed the ultimate sin of not clearing the project. Worst of all, he hadn't cleared it with Harry [Gray, chairman and CEO]." With no coalition to endorse his decisions, Carlson was out.[39]

Task Groups

A task group is formally created by the organization to accomplish a specific task. A task group could consist of departmental employees or a task force or committee formally constructed to look at a specific issue. Managers often ask, "When is it appropriate to let task groups rather than individuals make decisions?"

Many managers believe that the Japanese process of consensual decision making is appropriate for most decisions, pointing to the success of Japanese business organizations. The Japanese involve every person who will be affected by the decision and work until each one's approval has been solicited. It is not unusual for 75 people to formally sign off before a decision is implemented.

E X H I B I T   6.7

When to Use a Group in Decision Making

In general, groups excel at:
- Setting objectives, because more knowledge is available from the combined membership.
- Evaluating alternatives because of the wider range of critical viewpoints.

In situations where:
- The time available is sufficient for an effective group process.
- Enough information is available to group members to make them valuable participants.
- Participants are committed to the decision outcome.
- The decision is nonprogrammed and uncertain.
- Management wishes to develop subordinates' abilities to make decisions.

Source: Based on E. Frank Harrison, *The Managerial Decision-Making Process* (Boston: Houghton-Mifflin, 1975).

interactive group A group decision-making format in which group members are brought together face to face and have a specific agenda and decision objectives.

nominal group A group decision-making format that emphasizes equal participation in the decision process by all group members.

When should managers involve a group in decision making? One set of criteria is presented in Exhibit 6.7. Groups do best at setting objectives and evaluating alternatives because of the broad base of knowledge and viewpoints they make available. Moreover, task groups are an appropriate decision vehicle when there is enough time to use the group process, members have sufficient information to contribute to the decision, implementation requires group members' commitment, the decision is nonprogrammed and uncertain, and management wishes to train participants in decision making.[40]

Group Decision Formats

Three formats generally can be used in group decision making: the interactive group, the nominal group, and the Delphi group. These group formats are similar, but each has unique characteristics that make it more suitable for certain decisions. Most task forces, committees, and work groups fall into the category of interactive groups. Nominal and Delphi groups normally are convened for the purpose of increasing the level of creativity during group decision making.

Interactive Groups. Interactive groups are the most familiar form of task group. An **interactive group** simply means that members are brought together face to face and have a specific agenda and decision objectives. Interactive groups typically begin with a group leader stating a problem and asking for inputs from members. Discussion is unstructured and often even unorganized. The group may meander through problem identification and may require some problem redefinition. Alternatives are generated and evaluated. Eventually participants will vote or perhaps discuss alternatives until they reach a consensus on a desired solution. A staff meeting or departmental meeting formed to discuss next year's goals is a good example of interactive group decision making. Interactive groups will be described in more detail in Chapter 15.

Nominal Groups. The **nominal group** technique was developed to insure that every group participant has equal input in the decision-making process.[41] Because some participants may talk more and dominate group discussions in interactive groups, the nominal group is structured in a series of steps to equalize participation:

1. Each participant writes down his or her ideas on the problem to be discussed. These ideas usually are suggestions for a solution.
2. A round robin in which each group member presents his or her ideas to the group is set up. The ideas are written down on a blackboard for all members to see. No discussion of the ideas occurs until every person's ideas have been presented and written down for general viewing.
3. After all ideas have been presented, there is an open discussion of the ideas for the purpose of clarification and evaluation. This part of the discussion tends to be spontaneous and unstructured.
4. After the discussion, a secret ballot is taken in which each group member votes for preferred solutions. The adopted decision is the one that receives the most votes.

Bev Scott is field operations coordinator for York International Corporation, a subsidiary of Borg-Warner. She is meeting with an interactive group as part of York's Cost Improvement Program. The team came up with 50 ideas in 1985 that saved the company $618,000. The freewheeling discussion among members encourages creativity and brainstorming. Each member gets to talk about his or her ideas; other members elaborate on them until the ideas can be put into practice.

Delphi Groups. The **Delphi group** technique, which originated at the Rand Corporation, is considered to have four major uses: (1) to determine or develop a range of possible alternatives; (2) to examine the situation for underlying assumptions or other unstated vital information; (3) to uncover information that will lead to a consensus among group members; and (4) to combine expert opinions from different perspectives about an ambiguous problem.[42] Unlike interactive and nominal groups, Delphi group participants do not meet face to face—in fact, they never see one another. This technique calls for a group leader to solicit and collate written, expert opinions on a topic through the use of questionnaires. After the answers are received, a summary of the opinions is developed and distributed to participants. Then a new questionnaire on the same problem is circulated. In this second round, participants have the benefit of knowing other people's opinions and can change their suggested answers to reflect this new information. The process of sending out questionnaires and then sharing the results continues until a consensus is reached.

Delphi group A group decision-making format that involves the circulation among participants of questionnaires on the selected problem, sharing of answers, and continuous recirculation/refinement of questionnaires until a consensus has been obtained.

Advantages and Disadvantages of Group Decision Making

Whatever group techniques managers use for decision making, there are clear advantages and disadvantages compared to individual decision making.[43] Since managers often have a choice between making a decision by themselves or including others, they should understand the advantages and disadvantages of group decision making, which are summarized in Exhibit 6.8.

E X H I B I T   6.8

Advantages and Disadvantages of Group Decision Making

Advantages	Disadvantages
1. Broader perspective for problem definition and analysis.	1. Time consuming.
2. More knowledge, facts, and alternatives can be evaluated.	2. Compromise decisions may satisfy no one.
3. Discussion clarifies ambiguous problems and reduces uncertainty about alternatives.	3. Groupthink: Group norms may reduce dissent and opinion diversity.
4. Participation fosters member satisfaction and support for decision.	4. Knowledge overkill and wasted resources if used for programmed decisions.
	5. No clear focus for decision responsibility.

groupthink A phenomenon in which group members are so committed to the group that they are reluctant to express contrary opinions.

Advantages. Groups have an advantage over individuals because they bring together a broader perspective for defining the problem and diagnosing underlying causes and effects. In addition to enriching problem diagnosis, groups offer more knowledge and facts with which to identify potential solutions and produce more decision alternatives. Moreover, people who participate in decision making are more satisfied with the decision and more likely to support it, thereby facilitating implementation. Group discussion also can help reduce uncertainty for decision makers who may be unwilling to undertake a big risk by themselves. Finally, group discussion enhances member satisfaction and produces support for a possibly risky decision.

Disadvantages. Group decisions tend to be time consuming. People must be consulted, and they jointly diagnose problems and discuss solutions. Moreover, groups may reach a compromise solution that is less than optimal for the organization. Another problem is groupthink. **Groupthink** is a "mode of thinking that people engage in when they are deeply involved in a cohesive in-group, and when the members' strivings for unanimity override their motivation to realistically appraise alternative courses of action."[44] Groupthink means that people are so committed to the group that they are reluctant to disagree with one another; thus, the group loses the diversity of opinions essential to effective decision making. Another problem—particularly when groups are used for programmed decisions—is decision overkill due to the task's lack of challenge for group members. Finally, there is no clear focus of decision responsibility because the group rather than any single individual makes the decision.

One example of the disadvantage of group decision making occurred when a coalition at Citibank refused to change the practice of "parking"—the bogus transfer of foreign exchange deposits to shift bank profits to countries with low tax rates. The line between illegal and legal activities was hazy, and people were unwilling to disagree with the current practice because group norms supported high profits and reduced taxes. Group members were willing to compromise their values, groupthink

Pillsbury's Prepared Dough Products plant in East Greenville, Pennsylvania, was nearly forced to close in 1978 and again in 1982 because of declining business demand. Then R&D developed refrigerated dough, and East Greenville production workers helped bring several new ideas to market, including Toaster Strudel™, Pipin' Hot Loaf®, and Spread 'n Bake Fudge Brownies. The Cinnamon Danish was the trickiest. Workers had to make 1,000 dozen for a market sample. They started by spreading the cinnamon filling by hand; then they tried a doughnut maker. They often had to stop the line, unroll the pastry, sprinkle the cinnamon, reroll it, stuff it in a can, and put on the lid. But everybody acted as a team to arrive at the best new-product decisions.

reduced dissent, and there was no clear focus of responsibility because everyone had agreed to the potentially illegal practice.[45]

IMPROVING DECISION-MAKING EFFECTIVENESS

Managers wish to avoid costly mistakes, but at the same time they must occasionally take prudent risks in order for the organization to advance. A number of techniques have been developed to help individual managers and groups arrive at better decisions.

A **devil's advocate** is assigned the role of challenging the assumptions and assertions made by the group.[46] The devil's advocate forces the group to rethink its approach to the problem and to avoid reaching premature consensus or making unreasonable assumptions before proceeding with problem solutions.

Multiple advocacy is similar to a devil's advocate except that more advocates and points of view are presented. Minority opinions and unpopular viewpoints are assigned to forceful representatives, who then debate before the decision makers. An example would be a public hearing on land use at which representatives of the Sierra Club, local hunting organizations, and major lumber concerns all interact before the staff of the Bureau of Land Management.

Dialectical inquiry means that groups are assigned to challenge the underlying values and assumptions associated with problem definition.[47] Dialectical inquiry typically begins by identifying the prevailing view of the problem held within the group. Then another group is asked to

devil's advocate A decision-making technique in which an individual is assigned the role of challenging the assumptions and assertions made by the group in order to prevent premature consensus.

multiple advocacy A decision-making technique that involves several advocates and presentation of multiple points of view, including minority and unpopular opinions.

dialectical inquiry A decision-making technique in which groups are assigned to challenge the underlying values and assumptions associated with each problem definition presented.

challenge these assumptions by defining another problem they believe is equally important and should receive the group's attention. This forces consideration of the assumptions about the problem's importance. For example, as part of a decision on whether to acquire another company, William Ylvisaker, CEO of Gould, staged a full-scale debate by creating a pro and con team of Gould senior managers. In an all-day session, the teams challenged senior management's thinking by trying to create a perspective on new problems, challenge assumptions, and find better alternatives than the prevailing view that the company should acquire the recommended merger candidate.[48]

brainstorming A decision-making technique in which group members present spontaneous suggestions for problem solution, regardless of their likelihood of implementation, in order to promote freer, more creative thinking within the group.

Brainstorming uses a face-to-face, interactive group to spontaneously suggest ideas for problem solution. Brainstorming is perhaps the best-known decision aid; its primary role is to supply additional, creative solutions. Group members are invited to suggest alternatives regardless of their likelihood of being implemented. No critical comments of any kind are allowed until all suggestions have been listed. Members are encouraged to brainstorm possible solutions out loud, and freewheeling is welcomed. The more novel and unusual the idea, the better. The object of brainstorming is to promote freer, more flexible thinking and to enable group members to build on one another's creativity. The typical session begins with a warmup wherein definitional issues are settled, proceeds through the freewheeling idea generation stage, and concludes with an evaluation of feasible ideas.[49]

SUMMARY

This chapter made several important points about the process of organizational decision making. The study of decision making is important because it describes how managers make successful strategic and operational decisions. Managers must confront several different types of decisions, including programmed and nonprogrammed, and decisions differ according to the amount of risk, uncertainty, and ambiguity in the environment.

Two decision-making approaches were described: the classical model and the administrative model. The classical model explains how managers should make decisions so as to maximize economic efficiency. The administrative model describes how managers actually make nonprogrammed, uncertain decisions. Decision making should involve six basic steps: problem recognition, diagnosis of causes, development of alternatives, choice of an alternative, implementation of alternative, and control and follow-up.

In organizations, groups make decisions as well as individuals. The types of groups include coalitions, interactive groups, nominal groups, and Delphi groups. Groups offer a number of advantages and disadvantages compared to individuals. Techniques for improving decision-making quality include devil's advocate, multiple advocacy, dialectical inquiry, and brainstorming. These techniques help managers define problems and develop more creative solutions.

Management Solution

Jeff and Pete Coors faced several nonprogrammed decisions for achieving their goal of increasing market share and profits for Adolph Coors Company. With a number of alternatives before them, they began to act. One risky decision was to build a plant in the Northeast. The decision was extremely successful, because Coors quickly obtained over 10 percent of the market. Next, Coors launched its first national advertising campaign, spending what amounted to $10 per barrel on ads. The ads used actor Mark Harmon to explain why unpasteurized Coors tastes better than the competition. Jeff and Pete Coors are considering further decision alternatives, such as joint ventures with foreign breweries, and they are watching the test market results for Coors Extra Gold, a darker and more robust beer than Coors Banquet. The decisions contain risk and uncertainty, but so far they have been made carefully and thoughtfully, and the results have been impressive. The company's market share increased from 7.1 percent in 1984 to 7.9 percent in 1985—several million dollars' worth. Coors has shown that it can compete with such big boys as Anheuser-Busch and Miller.[50]

DISCUSSION QUESTIONS

1. Why is decision making considered a fundamental part of management effectiveness?
2. Explain the difference among certainty, risk, uncertainty, and ambiguity. How might decision making differ for each situation?
3. Analyze three decisions you made over the last six months. Which of these are programmed and which are nonprogrammed?
4. Why are many strategic decisions made by coalitions rather than by individuals?
5. Think of an organization in which you have worked, and describe a decision in which you participated. Did the decision makers explicitly consider each step of the decision-making process— problem recognition, diagnosis, alternative generation, choice, implementation, and control?
6. Do groups make better decisions than individuals? Why?
7. What are the three major types of decision-making groups? How might each be used to help managers make a decision to market a product in a new geographical territory?
8. What is meant by satisficing and bounded rationality? Why don't managers strive to find the economically best solution for many organizational decisions?
9. What techniques could you use to improve your own creativity and effectiveness in decision making?
10. Which of the six steps in the decision-making process do you think is most likely to be ignored by a manager? Explain.

CASES FOR ANALYSIS

GUARDIAN ENGINEERING

Lew Calderone, engineering manager, was beside himself. The problem he faced was complex and highly personal in nature. Joey Stark had been an employee of Guardian Engineering for 15 years and had a record of reliable, consistent work. Joey had reported to Lew for two years. However, his performance recently had become so poor that Lew felt Joey must be fired. For one thing, Joey was frequently absent on Mondays despite the company's policy against excessive absences. Once or twice Lew had smelled alcohol on Joey's breath while at work, and he suspected that alcohol was the problem. A couple of other employees had commented on Joey's drinking, but Lew had never personally witnessed Joey drinking excessively.

Lew had talked with Joey twice about his absences and declining performance. He had asked Joey about his family life, personal life, and working conditions to learn whether any of these were causing the problem. Joey had simply said everything was okay. After the second conversation, Lew wrote a short memorandum specifying his concerns, and the memo went into Joey's personnel file. Joey improved his performance for a couple of weeks, but nothing seemed to have changed permanently.

If alcoholism was Joey's problem, Lew was thinking about alternative solutions. One would be to fire Joey, because Lew had read that alcoholics lose their jobs and their families before they become motivated to change their behavior. Another would be to confront Joey and accuse him of alcoholism to let him know the company was aware of his drinking problem. A third would be to refer Joey to a private counselor or physician for possible rehabilitation. A fourth would be to give Joey one more warning, making it clear that the next absence or lapse in performance would cost him his job.

Complicating the problem was Lew's feeling that Joey was a friend as well as a senior employee. However, Lew felt he had to proceed with whatever was best for the company. The company had no clearly defined policy on alcoholism, which made choosing a solution somewhat more difficult. Lew wondered whether he should talk to other senior managers about the problem and seek their guidance and agreement. He also wondered if there were some way he could gather more information about the true nature of the problem before deciding on a solution. Frankly, Lew realized he needed to take action, but he just wasn't sure what to do.

Questions

1. Is the decision facing Lew Calderone considered programmed or nonprogrammed?
2. How should Lew proceed to make the decision? Should he investigate the nature of the problem? Should he make a decision among the available alternatives?
3. What would you do in this situation? Why?

COMMODORE INTERNATIONAL LTD.

In 1984, Commodore was on the top of the home computer market. By 1985 the bottom had fallen out, and rumors suggested an impending bankruptcy filing. Part of Commodore's problem was the home computer slump that was hurting the entire industry, including Coleco and Texas Instruments. But there were serious internal problems as well, which were reflected in the decision styles of Jack Tramiel, the founder and president until early 1984, and his successor, Marshall Smith.

Tramiel had a corner-cutting, erratic decision style and short-term focus. He left the company with no clear product strategy or formal controls. Tramiel made decisions on a dime, failed to consult his managers, and often alienated managers, dealers, and suppliers by changing his mind and reversing plans. He had been the sole source of direction at Commodore for 25 years. Smith, his successor, had the opposite decision style. He was slow and deliberate, working through formal reporting channels, ordering detailed analyses, and checking with relevant managers. He spent months establishing lines of authority and decision responsibility. For example, when one vice-president was ready to defect to another company, Smith commissioned an executive pay study before making a counteroffer. Tramiel's style would have been to handle the decision informally, and he had sometimes fired and rehired the same manager several times.

Smith wasn't controversial, but he had no experience in the fast-paced computer market. He made a decision to increase production based on unrealistically high sales estimates. He made a decision to reduce ad spending during a time of falling demand. He made a decision to reject his managers' advice to cut prices in time for Christmas sales. All three decisions turned out to be wrong.

Some people blame the bulk of Commodore's problems on Tramiel's one-man-show approach and lack of a clear decision strategy. Others blame Smith for having made the wrong decisions to help Commodore respond to the slump in the home computer industry.

Questions

1. How would you characterize the decision models used by Tramiel and Smith? Explain.
2. Which decision style do you think was more appropriate for an organization in the rapidly changing home computer industry? Who do you think was more to blame for Commodore's problems?
3. What would you recommend to Smith to improve his decision making at Commodore? How might he avoid decision mistakes in the future?

Source: Based on Dennis Kneale, "Commodore, Betting on a New Computer, Reels from Past Errors," *The Wall Street Journal*, July 19, 1985, pp. 1, 8.

CHAPTER 7

Management Science Aids for Planning and Decision Making

Chapter Outline

The Nature and Role of Management Science

Forecasting

Quantitative Forecasting Techniques
Qualitative Forecasting Techniques

Quantitative Approaches to Planning

Breakeven Analysis
Linear Programming
PERT

Quantitative Approaches to Decision Making

Payoff Matrix
Decision Tree
Game Theory
Simulation Models

Strengths and Limitations of Management Science Aids

Strengths
Limitations

Learning Objectives

After studying this chapter, you should be able to:

- **Define management science and the types of management decisions and problems to which management science techniques apply.**

- **Identify three quantitative methods and three qualitative methods of forecasting future events.**

- **Describe breakeven analysis and explain how it can be used for organizational decisions.**

- **Describe the payoff matrix and decision tree and explain the difference between them.**

- **Discuss the use of PERT in project scheduling and define critical path.**

- **Describe the purpose and application of linear programming.**

- **Discuss the advantages and disadvantages of using management science techniques for planning and decision making.**

Management Problem

The streets of New York City were filthy; almost half were considered unacceptable. The Department of Sanitation faced numerous problems in trying to keep streets clean. A fiscal crisis during the mid-1970s left only 800 street cleaners by 1980 compared to 2,500 in 1975. Employee morale was low because of constant abuse from the public and media blaming them for the city's condition. Managers hardly knew where to start. They did not understand which factors—waste cans, traffic, parking—influenced street cleanliness or the relationship between the number of street cleaners and cleanliness levels. There was no coordination with related departments, and the city council had rejected a Department of Sanitation proposal to expand the cleaning force.[1]

If you were a senior manager in New York City's Department of Sanitation, what decisions would you make for improving street cleanliness with available resources? What information would you gather, and what techniques would you use to make the necessary decisions?

The problem of dirty streets in New York City demonstrates that solving a complex problem often requires more than a general, intuitive approach. Information was not readily available, and the factors influencing street cleanliness were overwhelming.

In previous chapters we have seen how good managers are distinguished from poor ones by how effectively they set goals, develop plans with which to meet those goals, and make the necessary decisions. The purpose of this chapter is to introduce quantitative techniques that can serve as valuable decision aids and planning tools. Management science

Management science uses quantitatively based models to assist managerial decision makers. Exxon specialists use management science techniques to develop better ways to locate hydrocarbons. Robert Heinicke and John E. French, Jr., analyze graphic displays of results from petroleum reservoir simulation models. These displays help petroleum engineers and managers evaluate investment and operating strategies for identifying and utilizing oil and gas reservoirs.

techniques are especially effective when many factors affect a problem, when problems can be quantified, when relationships among factors can be defined, and when the decision maker can control the key factors affecting performance outcomes.[2] This chapter describes some of the more common management science techniques that are applicable to managerial planning and decision making. It discusses quantitative approaches to forecasting, breakeven analysis, linear programming, PERT charting, and the decision aids of payoff matrix and decision tree. These techniques are not covered in depth; managers need to understand the basic approach and be able to communicate with management science experts. Managers need not master the underlying mathematics of these techniques.

THE NATURE AND ROLE OF MANAGEMENT SCIENCE

Management science techniques are designed to supplement managerial planning and decision making. For many decisions, management science leads to better answers. For example, in today's organizations it is not uncommon to find experts who use mathematical and statistical analyses to help managers make capital budgeting decisions, decide whether to open a new factory, predict economic trends or customer demands, determine whether to rent or buy a new computer system, schedule trucks, ships, or aircraft, decide among several proposals for research and development projects, and assess whether a new-product introduction is likely to be profitable.

management science   A set of quantitatively based decision models used to assist management decision makers.

Management science is defined as a set of quantitatively based decision models used to assist management decision makers. There are three key components in this definition.

First, management science is a set of quantitative tools. Mathematically based procedures impart a systematic rigor to the decision process. Certain types of data must be gathered, put into a specific format, and analyzed according to stringent mathematical rules.

Second, management science uses decision models. A *model* is a simplified representation of a real-life situation. For example, small-scale physical models were constructed for every set in the movie *Raiders of the Lost Ark* to diagnose filming problems before constructing the real sets. In a mathematical model, key elements are represented by numbers. A model cannot capture reality in its full complexity, but computer-based models can simulate many of its elements. Mathematical models are difficult for many students and managers because they use a language that is abstract and unfamiliar. However, outcomes from mathematical models can still aid in decision making.

Third, quantitative models *assist* decision makers; they cannot substitute for or replace a manager.[3] Management science models are simply one of many tools in a manager's tool kit. The manager's role is to provide information for use in the models, interpret the information they provide, and carry out the final plan of action.

Sometimes proponents of management science techniques oversell their value for managerial decision making. Managers who are unfamiliar with mathematics may resist the use of management science techniques and hence fail to take advantage of a powerful tool. The best management approach is to attempt to understand the types of problems to which management science aids apply and then work with specialists to formulate the necessary data and analytical procedures.

Exhibit 7.1 lists some of the more common management problems and applicable management science techniques. These techniques apply

E X H I B I T   7.1

Management Problems and Applicable Management Science Tools

Management Problem	Applicable Management Science Tool
Production mix	Linear programming
Scheduling and sequencing	PERT network
Distribution	Simulation
New-product decisions	Payoff matrix Decision tree
Pricing decisions	Payoff matrix Decision tree Game theory
Sales force assignment	Assignment models
Forecasting	Time series Regression analysis Econometric models

Coleco Industries' demographic forecast for its line of Cabbage Patch Kids is favorable. Demographic and sociological trends show that the number of children under age 5 and from 5 to 9 will increase substantially through the early 1990s. Also, almost half of the new babies will be firstborns—for whom parents and grandparents spend more on toys. Due to the rising number of two-income households, toy spending per child is also increasing. Coleco's response to the favorable forecast is to broaden its lines, adding Preemies and 'Koosas, and develop new dolls and accessory items.

sales forecast A forecast of future company sales based on projected customer demand for products or services.

technological forecast A forecast of the occurrence of technological changes that could affect an organization's way of doing business.

demographic forecast A forecast of societal characteristics such as birth rates, educational levels, marriage rates, and diseases.

to problems in production, product distribution, new-product decisions, and sales force assignment. Scores of management science techniques are available. The remainder of this chapter will describe some of the most important management science tools and illustrate their use in managerial planning and decision making.

FORECASTING

Managers look into the future through forecasts. *Forecasts* are predictions about future organizational and environmental circumstances that will influence plans, decisions, and goal attainment. Forecasts are a basic part of the SWOT analysis described in Chapter 5. Virtually every planning decision depends on assumptions about future conditions.

Four types of forecasts are frequently used by managers:

1. *Sales forecasts.* **Sales forecasts** predict future company sales. Sales forecasting is critical, because it defines customers' demands for products or services. Sales forecasts provide a target for production levels for three months, six months, or one year into the future. Managers use them to hire necessary personnel, buy needed raw materials, make plans to finance an expansion, and arrange needed transportation services. Medium- and large-size companies such as Sound Warehouse, Paychex, Wallace Computer Services, and Monsanto use sales forecasts to plan production activities.

2. *Technological forecasts.* **Technological forecasts** attempt to predict the advent of technological changes, especially major technological breakthroughs that could alter an organization's way of doing business. Companies forecast technological changes in order to avoid building plants or acquiring equipment that are out of date and noncompetitive. General Motors has been forecasting the use of robotics in automobile manufacturing so as to remain competitive with other American and Japanese automobile producers. Timex and other watch manufacturers are eyeing developments from a company called AT&E Corporation that has found a high-tech way to transform a standard wristwatch into a paging device. Companies in the pharmaceutical industry attempt to predict the discovery of new drug groups.

3. *Demographic forecasts.* **Demographic forecasts** pertain to the characteristics of society, including birthrates, educational levels, marriage rates, and diseases. For example, the baby boom of the late 1960s and early 1970s has meant fewer young entrants to the labor force in the 1980s, which is a particular concern of labor-intensive companies. However, the baby boom of the 1980s will permit managers in schools and companies that make children's clothing and toys to plan for increased product demand in the near future.

4. *Human resources forecasts.* **Human resources forecasts** predict the organization's future manpower needs. AT&T is predicting a decrease of several thousand employees during the late 1980s. This means that its human resources department must arrange for early retirements and help displaced employees secure jobs elsewhere. Companies in rapidly growing high-tech industries see a need for a large number of additional employees. Thus, senior managers must make arrangements for employee recruitment programs and perhaps locate new plants in areas where employees are available.

human resources forecast A forecast of the organization's future manpower needs.

Forecasts provide information that reduces uncertainty in decision making. Several specific techniques, both quantitative and qualitative, help managers derive forecasts for use in their planning and decision making. Exhibit 7.2 illustrates some of the forecasting techniques, their possible applications, and their degree of accuracy.

Let's now examine both the quantitative and qualitative techniques more closely.

Quantitative Forecasting Techniques

Quantitative forecasts start with a series of past data values and then use a set of mathematical rules with which to predict future values.[4] Quantitative techniques have become widely used by managers for two reasons. First, the techniques have repeatedly demonstrated accuracy, especially in the short and intermediate term, thus earning managers' confidence as a planning aid. Second, improvements in computer technology have increased the efficiency and decreased the expense of using quantitative techniques. A large number of variables can be incorporated into the

quantitative forecast A forecast that begins with a series of past data values and then applies a set of mathematical rules with which to predict future values.

E X H I B I T   7.2

Forecasting Techniques Used by Organizations

		Accuracy		
Quantitative Techniques	**Sample Application**	**Short Term**	**Intermediate Term**	**Long Term**
Time series	Sales, earnings, inventory control	Excellent	Good	Good
Regression analysis	Sales, earnings	Excellent	Excellent	Fair
Econometric models	GNP, sales, demographics, economic shifts	Excellent	Good	Fair
Qualitative Techniques				
Delphi	Product development, technological predictions	Good	Good	Good
Sales force composite	Sales projections, future customer demand	Fair	Fair	Poor
Jury of opinion	Sales, new-product development, earnings	Good	Fair	Poor

Adapted from J. Chambers, S. Mullick, and D. Smith, "How to Choose the Right Forecasting Technique," *Harvard Business Review* (July/August 1971), pp. 55–64.

E X H I B I T **7.3**

Examples of Time Series Forecasting Patterns

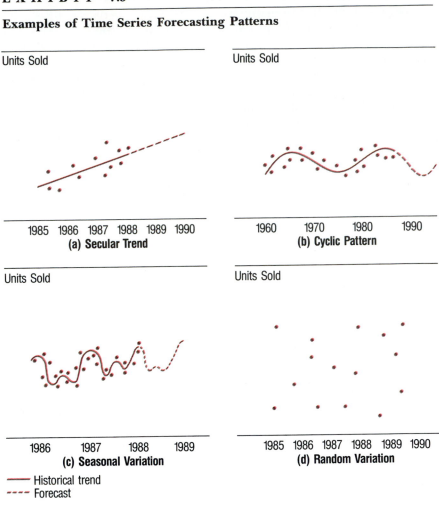

Units Sold

1985 1986 1987 1988 1989 1990
(a) Secular Trend

Units Sold

1960   1970   1980   1990
(b) Cyclic Pattern

Units Sold

1986   1987   1988   1989
(c) Seasonal Variation

Units Sold

1985 1986 1987 1988 1989 1990
(d) Random Variation

——— Historical trend
- - - Forecast

analysis, and statistical refinements have improved the techniques' ability to meet the forecasting needs of company managers.

Quantitative forecasting techniques can be subdivided into two categories: time series analysis and causal models. Time series analyses project past behavior into the future. Causal modeling attempts to unearth past causes of behavior as a way of projecting into the future.[5]

time series analysis A forecasting technique that examines the patterns of movement in historical data.

Time Series Analysis. **Time series analysis** is a forecasting technique that examines the patterns of movement in historical data. It defines patterns in terms of one of four categories:

1. Secular trends
2. Cyclic patterns
3. Seasonal variation
4. Random variation

A *secular trend* is the general behavior of a variable over a long period of time. Panel a of Exhibit 7.3 shows a set of data with an upward trend in unit sales each year. The demand for this company's sales is growing regularly, and managers will project sales for 1990 based on this growth.

A *cyclic pattern* involves a recurring up-and-down movement that is periodic in nature. The pattern extends over several years and cannot always be counted on to repeat with precise regularity. Cyclic patterns are related to general business cycles of growth and recession, which managers find extremely valuable to predict. Panel b of Exhibit 7.3 shows a typical business cycle over several years.

Seasonal variation is a regular variation in behavior that recurs within a period of one year or less. Climatic, social, and religious customs can cause seasonal variation. For example, heating sales increase during the winter and decrease during the summer, while sales of window air conditioners perform in reverse. Bicycle sales normally peak in November and December—prior to Christmas—decline in the winter months, rise in the spring and summer, and decline again in the fall. Panel c of Exhibit 7.3 shows a seasonal pattern that would help a manager predict sales.

The fourth category, random variation, is not a pattern at all. *Random variation* means that there are movements in sales behavior, but they are unpredictable. These movements might be caused by random factors, such as a strike, natural disaster, or changes in government regulations. Panel d of Exhibit 7.3 shows data that have random variation. Managers are unable to use random variation to predict the future.

Time series analysis is used to predict both short-term and intermediate-term behavior. Its power is its ability to account for seasonal changes as well as long-run trends. Time series analysis works best when the business environment is relatively stable, that is, when the past is a good indicator of the future. In environments in which consumer tastes change radically or random occurrences have a great impact on sales, time series models tend to be inaccurate and of little value.

One company that was able to take advantage of time series forecasting is Huffy Corporation.

Huffy Corporation

Huffy Corporation is the largest U.S. producer of bicycles. In 1981, Huffy's plants were producing at maximum capacity in several of its product lines. Huffy executives were concerned about whether they should undertake plans to increase future capacity. Since a major corporate goal was 100 percent customer satisfaction, managers realized that an accurate sales forecasting system was important.

The internal accounting and financial group was commissioned to develop a forecasting system that would have the following characteristics:

1. Usable by managers responsible for all product lines and divisions
2. Use data from the current management information system database

3. Cost efficient
4. Easily maintained and readily understood by nontechnical managers
5. Forecasts based on available sales data
6. Forecasts accurate within ±5 percent for divisions, ±10 percent for each product, and ±10 percent for each brand

After studying many forecasting techniques, Huffy's managers selected a time series model. They found it easy to use because it avoided complex statistics. The final model predicted future sales based on both cyclical and seasonal variation projected from six months of sales history. The time series model was both easy to understand and sufficiently accurate to meet Huffy's forecasting objectives.[6]

causal modeling   A forecasting technique that attempts to predict behavior (the dependent variable) by analyzing its causes (independent variables).

regression analysis   A statistical tool for predicting the value of a dependent variable based on the known values of independent variables.

Causal Forecasting Models.   Causal modeling attempts to predict behavior, called the *dependent variable,* by analyzing its causes, called *independent variables.* Thus, causal modeling may attempt to predict sales (the dependent variable) by examining those factors that cause sales to increase or decrease including amount of advertising expenditure, unit price, competitors' prices, and the overall inflation rate (independent variables). This technique differs from that of simply projecting future sales based on past sales.

Causal modeling is based on the use of statistical regression analysis. **Regression analysis** is a statistical tool for predicting the value of a dependent variable based on the known values of independent variables. The general model for a regression equation is

$$Y = aX_1 + bX_2 + cX_3 + d,$$

where

$$Y = \text{dependent variable being forecasted (sales)}$$

$$X_1, X_2, \text{ and } X_3 = \text{independent variables}$$

$$a, b, \text{ and } c = \text{calculated coefficients of independent variables}$$

$$d = \text{a constant}$$

A regression analysis could be performed to predict a company's sales based on the causal factors of advertising expenditure, unit price, and competitors' prices. The statistical computations would produce the following equation:

$$Y = -24.50 + 1.35X_1 - 0.75X_2 + 0.25X_3,$$

where

Y = sales in hundreds of units

X_1 = advertising expenditure in thousands of dollars

X_2 = product price

X_3 = competitors' average price

From this equation a manager can explore the causal relationships among sales, advertising, product price, and competitors' prices. For example, a $1,000 budget increase for advertising expenditure would cause a 135-unit increase in sales, or a $1 decrease in price would cause a 75-unit increase in sales. These relationships can be used to predict future sales and to influence causal variables that can increase sales.

Many companies use simple regression models. For example, the vice-president of marketing for Pitney Bowes' Data Documents Division has been able to predict sales of business forms based on the growth of the gross national product. Retailers such as Carter Hawley Hale predict future retail sales based on disposable personal income. The producers of big yachts predict sales based on stock market performance, and Mercury Marine predicts outboard motor sales based on the monthly Consumer Confidence Index published by the Conference Board.[7]

Another causal modeling technique is an econometric model. An **econometric model** is a system of regression equations solved simultaneously to take into account the interaction between economic conditions and organizational activities. Econometric models are a complex extension of regression models. They have been used to predict economic conditions such as gross national product, inflation rates, unemployment, and industrial production capacity for the entire country. Econometric models are designed by economists and mathematicians and may include hundreds or even thousands of variables. When managers need to use econometric models to make forecasts, they should hire a consulting firm that specializes in mathematics and economics to construct them.

When choosing between time series predictions and causal modeling, managers should consider that time series predictions are better at describing seasonal sales variations and predicting changes in sales direction while causal models provide better information on how to influence a dependent variable such as sales. Both time series and causal forecasting approaches can produce reliable data if they start with proper data and assumptions. Managers using causal or time series models may wish to work closely with management science experts for maximum benefit.

Qualitative Forecasting Techniques

Qualitative forecasts rely on the opinions of experts. Qualitative techniques are used when precise historical data are unavailable. Three useful forms of qualitative forecasting are the Delphi technique, sales force composite, and jury of opinion.

Hundreds of cans of Glidden Spred® have just come from a high-speed automated line that fills more than 3,500 one-gallon cans an hour. Glidden uses causal forecasting models to predict the demand for its paint and stain products. The independent variables that predict Glidden paint sales are gross national product and disposable personal income. One logical independent variable—new housing starts—has surprisingly little correlation with Glidden's paint sales. The reason is that most Glidden paint is sold through 9,000 retail outlets for use in existing homes and structures.

econometric model A system of regression equations that are solved simultaneously to capture the interaction between economic conditions and the organization's activities.

qualitative forecast A forecast based on the opinions of experts in the absence of precise historical data.

Delphi technique A qualitative forecasting method in which experts reach consensus about future events through a series of continuously refined questionnaires rather than through face-to-face discussion.

sales force composite A type of qualitative forecasting that relies on the combined expert opinions of field sales personnel.

jury of opinion A method of qualitative forecasting based on the average opinions of managers from various company divisions and departments.

Dayton Hudson department stores use a variation of jury of opinion to identify fashion trends. Executives, trend directors, and merchandisers stake out— with cameras in hand—places like Paris' Left Bank, London's King Road, and New York's Soho. A new trend may consist of one hot-selling color, a novel fabric, silhouette, or an innovative theme. Once the information is gathered, the executives meet to decide which styles to acquire for sale to Dayton Hudson's customers. Through this process, Karen Bohnhoff, vice-president of Trend Merchandising, defined the highly successful "pattern play" trend—bold mixes of plaids with stripes and paisleys with tartans.

Delphi Technique.   The **Delphi technique** is a process whereby experts come to a consensus about future events without face-to-face discussion.[8] The Delphi procedure was described in Chapter 6 as a means of group decision making. It is especially effective for technological forecasts, because precise data for predicting technological breakthroughs are not available. Technological experts fill out a questionnaire about future events, and the responses are summarized and returned to participants. They then complete a new questionnaire based on their own previous responses and the estimates of other experts. The process continues until a consensus of opinion is reached. The Delphi technique promotes independent thought and precludes direct confrontations and participants' defensiveness about their ideas. Its biggest advantage is that experts with widely different opinions can share information with one another and reach agreement about future predictions.[9]

Sales Force Composite.   The **sales force composite** relies on the combined expert judgments of field sales personnel. Experienced salespeople know their customers and generally sense fluctuations in customers' needs and buying patterns before these changes are reflected in quantitative data. Salespeople are polled about their customers' expected purchases in the coming time period. Each estimate is reviewed by a district or regional sales manager, who combines these estimates and makes adjustments for expected changes in economic conditions.

The procedure is valuable because it is fast and based on expert knowledge of customer needs. The major disadvantage is that an overzealous sales force or one that wants to make low predictions to easily meet sales quotas can provide incorrect forecasts. If salespeople are aware that they will not be held to these forecasts and that forecasts should be based on business understanding rather than on emotions, the forecasts can be quite accurate. Recent findings by Dun and Bradstreet suggest that businesspeople are good forecasters except in times of unexpected or deep recession. During especially bad periods, both managers and salespeople tend to be overly optimistic about the future.[10]

Jury of Opinion.   A **jury of opinion** is the average opinion of managers from various company divisions and departments. It is similar to a Delphi procedure in that jury members need not meet face to face. Since opinions come from several people, the forecast is less risky than it would be if conducted by a single individual. The method is quick and inexpensive and does not require elaborate statistical analysis. It takes advantage of management's knowledge of the environment based on past experience and good judgment.

All forecasting is based on historical patterns, and qualitative techniques are used when precise, historical data are unavailable. Although biases do creep in, qualitative forecasts often are the only ones available. If managers feel that biases are affecting forecast accuracy, they can use available techniques for detecting biases, measuring them, and correcting future forecasts through instructional feedback. As managers see that their forecasts are too high or too low, they learn to forecast more accurately in future periods.[11]

E X H I B I T   7.4

Breakeven Model

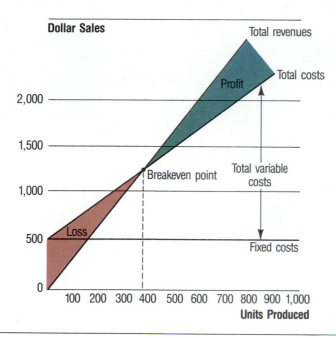

QUANTITATIVE APPROACHES TO PLANNING

Once a sales forecast is produced, managers must incorporate that information into their planning for the firm's future actions. Three quantitative planning techniques tell managers how many units must be sold before a product is profitable, which combination of products can minimize costs, and how to schedule complex projects to be completed in the shortest amount of time. These techniques are called breakeven analysis, linear programming, and PERT.

Breakeven Analysis

Breakeven analysis is a quantitative technique that helps managers determine the level of sales at which total revenues equal total costs and, hence, the firm breaks even.[12] Breakeven analysis portrays the relationships among units of output, sales revenue, and costs, as illustrated in Exhibit 7.4. The following variables are important parts of breakeven analysis:

1. *Fixed costs:* Costs that remain the same regardless of the level of production. Fixed costs, represented by the horizontal line in Exhibit 7.4, remain at $500 whether production is low or high.

breakeven analysis A quantitative technique that helps managers determine the level of sales at which total revenues equal total costs.

BMW uses quantitative approaches to planning to supplement management judgment. Intensive product planning and market research help managers develop the automobiles and motorcycles best suited for the North American market. Statistical quantification of the customer's world is used in conjunction with observing buyer reactions to new prototypes. Quantitative models also help identify and allocate resources to build effective auto air conditioning units and select paint colors for heat reflection. BMW's first goal is quality, and quantitative decision models help achieve it.

2. *Variable costs:* Costs that vary with the number of units produced. These costs increase as production increases and are represented by the difference between total costs and fixed costs in Exhibit 7.4.
3. *Total costs:* The sum of fixed and variable costs, illustrated by the diagonal line in Exhibit 7.4.
4. *Total revenues:* Total revenue dollars for a given unit of production, as illustrated by the steep diagonal line in Exhibit 7.4. Total revenues are calculated as units sold times unit price.
5. *Breakeven point:* The production volume at which total revenues equal total costs, illustrated by the crossover of the two diagonal lines in Exhibit 7.4. As the dashed line indicates, the breakeven point in this particular case is about 380 units.
6. *Profit:* The amount by which total revenues exceed total costs. In Exhibit 7.4, profit occurs at a production volume greater than the breakeven point.
7. *Loss:* The amount by which total costs exceed total revenues, which occurs at a production volume less than the breakeven point in Exhibit 7.4.

The application of these concepts to an organizational situation can be illustrated by the computation of the breakeven point for CCC Bakeries.

CCC Bakeries

The cookie wars have gotten hot in Canada and the United States because profits are terrific. Cookie shops are small and normally have one of the highest sales per square foot of any kind of retail shop. Companies such as the Original Great American Chocolate Chip Cookie Company in Atlanta, Mrs. Fields' Cookies, which originated in Park City, Utah, David's Cookies in New York City, and the Original Cookie Company in Cleveland are four rapidly expanding chocolate chip cookie chains.[13]

Jan Smith started the Chocolate Chip Cookies Bakeries in Northern California. She has two shops and is considering a third in a San Francisco mall. Before opening the shop, she wants to calculate the cost of the operation and the sales volume required for profitability. She has contacted the owners of the San Francisco mall about the cost of rent and equipment rental, and she has a good idea from her other two shops about salary and raw materials costs. Following are her figures:

Fixed costs:	
Rent	$1,000
Salaries:	
Manager	1,000
Part-timers	500
Equipment Rental	800
Total fixed costs	$2,300
Variable costs:	
Cookie mixture	$0.25/cookie
Paper bags and tissue	0.01/cookie
Total variable costs	$0.26/cookie
Estimated revenue	$0.53/cookie

Exhibit 7.5 shows the breakeven analysis for the proposed cookie store. The horizontal line reflects the fixed costs of $2,300. The total cost line is computed by adding the variable costs to the fixed costs. The total revenue line reflects the $0.53 income per cookie. The analysis shows that Jan must sell 8,518 cookies to break even. At this point, Jan's revenue and costs both will be approximately $4,515. If Jan can sell 10,000 cookies a month, she will make a profit of $400. Note in Exhibit 7.5 that the cookie business has high fixed costs relative to variable costs. This means that once the breakeven point is reached, profits will increase rapidly. High profits can be earned as volume increases to a high level.

E X H I B I T   7.5

Breakeven Analysis for Chocolate Chip Cookies Bakeries

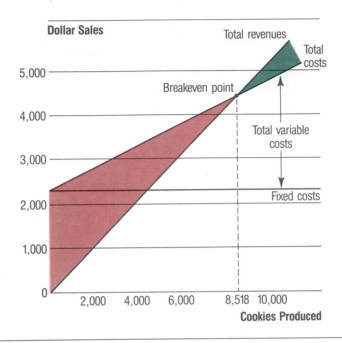

Linear Programming

An important aspect of planning is the allocation of resources across competing demands. For example, a manufacturing company may produce several products, each of which requires use of machines, labor, and raw materials. The manufacturing manager must decide which quantity of each product should be produced to maximize profits. Should they manufacture a large amount of product A and less of product B, or vice versa? Or a political candidate may have to decide how to allocate time and money among television ads, direct mail, and speeches at political rallies. These problems often can be solved through linear programming.[14]

linear programming A quantitative technique that allocates resources so as to optimize a predefined organizational objective.

Linear programming is a mathematical technique that allocates resources so as to optimize a predefined objective. The objective may be a specific profit level, minimizing costs, or maximizing a political candidate's exposure to potential voters. The model must specify a single objective, such as maximizing profits or minimizing costs. Moreover, linear programming assumes that the decision maker has limited resources with which to attain the objective.

The nontechnical manager needs to understand only the three basic steps in formulating a linear programming problem:

- **Step 1:** Define the relevant decision variables. These variables must be controllable by the manager.

EXHIBIT 7.6

Resource Requirements for Wicker Company

	Soaking Time (Hours)	Weaving Time (Hours)	Drying Time (Hours)	Profit
Per basket	0.2	0.4	0.3	$3.25
Per seat	0.4	0.4	0.8	5.00
Available hours	60.0	90.0	108.0	

- **Step 2:** Define the objective in terms of the decision variables. There can be only one objective; thus, it must be chosen carefully.
- **Step 3:** Define the resource restrictions or constraints *first* as word statements and then as mathematical statements.

The following example demonstrates the three steps used in formulating a linear programming model.

Wicker Company

Wicker Company makes wicker baskets and seats. Both products must be processed by soaking, weaving, and drying. A basket has a profit margin of $3.25 and a seat a profit margin of $5. Exhibit 7.6 summarizes the number of hours available for soaking, weaving, and drying and the number of hours required to complete each task. The question confronting Wicker Company's managers is: How many baskets and seats should Wicker make per day in order to maximize profits?

Step 1 is to define the decision variables. What can Wicker managers control in the production process? Two readily controllable variables are the number of baskets and seats to be produced. Thus, we can let X_1 = number of baskets to produce and X_2 = number of seats to produce.

Step 2 is to define an objective function. The objective is clear: Maximize profits. This objective can be described mathematically by using the two decision variables. The profit for each basket is $3.25, or $3.25X_1$. Similarly, the profit for each seat produced is $5, or $5X_2$. Total profits for the firm will be the sum of these two components:

$$\text{Maximize profits} = \$3.25X_1 + \$5.00X_2.$$

Central Soya, a Fortune 500 company, is one of the leading processors of soybeans and related products. Its special feeding and nutrition programs have significantly increased farm yields. Linear programming models automatically reformulate and price an entire line of feed products in response to changes in commodity prices and availability of ingredients. These models insure consistent nutrition at the best possible cost.

Step 3 is to define resource constraints. This is the most difficult step in formulating a linear programming model. Wicker is constrained by three scarce resources, expressed in words as follows:

1. Soaking time cannot exceed 60 hours.
2. Weaving time cannot exceed 90 hours.
3. Drying time cannot exceed 108 hours.

These constraints enable us to state in mathematical terms that total soaking time must be less than or equal to 60 hours. Every basket takes 0.2 hours of soaking time and every seat 0.4 hours. The total production of baskets and seats cannot exceed 60 hours; therefore, our mathematical statement can be:

$$0.2X_1 + 0.4X_2 \leq 60.$$

The remaining constraints can be described in similar fashion. Weaving time cannot exceed 90 hours, which is expressed mathematically as

$$0.4X_1 + 0.4X_2 \leq 90.$$

Drying time cannot exceed 108 hours, which is expressed mathematically as

$$0.3X_1 + 0.8X_2 \leq 108.$$

A final constraint for keeping the mathematical calculations in the correct range is that neither seats nor baskets can be produced in a volume of less than zero. This is expressed mathematically as

$$X_1 \geq 0$$
$$X_2 \geq 0.$$

The completed problem formulation looks like this:

-   Maximize profits = $3.25X_1 + 5X_2$
-   Subject to

    Soaking time: $0.2X_1 + 0.4X_2 \leq 60$

    Weaving time: $0.4X_1 + 0.4X_2 \leq 90$

    Drying time: $0.3X_1 + 0.8X_2 \leq 108$
    Nonnegativity: $X_1 \geq 0$, $X_2 \geq 0$

Exhibit 7.7 graphs the constraints for Wicker Company. Note that each constraint defines a boundary called the *feasibility region,* which is

E X H I B I T   7.7

Graphical Solution to Wicker Company Linear Programming Problem

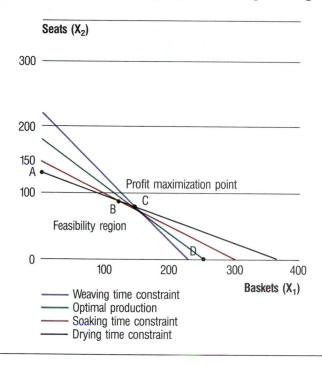

that region bounded by a resource restriction. The optimal solution for maximizing profits is found at the intersection of two or more constraints at the edge of the feasibility region. Those intersections are at point A, B, C, or D.

Management science specialists use high-speed computers and sophisticated software to solve linear programming problems. For a simple problem such as Wicker Company's, the solution can be defined on the graph in Exhibit 7.7. Profit maximization is formally defined as the point (A, B, C, or D) that lies furthest from the origin (0) and through which a line can be drawn that has only one point in common with the feasibility region. In Exhibit 7.7 this is point C, because it is furthest from the origin and the green line drawn through point C touches the feasibility region at only one point. Thus, the production mix to maximize profits is 150 baskets and 75 seats.[15]

Linear programming may seem complicated, but it has many valuable applications in organizations. Managers must understand the basic concepts but need not have the technical skills required for solving complex

PERT network techniques are used to manage and control projects like the Ataturk Dam in southeastern Turkey, the largest construction project in the world today. Project managers must coordinate the moving of 110 million cubic yards of earth and rock, some 400 Caterpillar tractors and trucks, and thousands of employees. Computers help monitor project elements. The project will take seven years to complete.

problems. Linear programming can be used whenever managers find themselves in a planning situation in which they must consider maximizing profits, minimizing costs, and allocating scarce resources across several possible uses.

PERT

Organizations often confront a situation in which they have a large project to complete for which a complicated, single-use plan is developed. A large project may consist of many interrelated activities. In 1958, the U.S. Navy was confronted with the enormous task of coordinating thousands of contractors to build the Polaris nuclear submarine. The Program Evaluation and Review Technique (PERT) was developed to manage the building of submarines.

PERT allows managers to decompose a project into specific activities and to plan far in advance when it is to be completed. PERT can pinpoint bottlenecks and indicate whether resources should be reallocated. It also provides a map of the project and allows managers to control its execution by determining whether activities are completed on time and in the correct sequence.

PERT The Program Evaluation and Review Technique; consists of breaking down a project into a network of specific activities and mapping out their sequence and necessary completion dates.

There are four basic steps required in the use of PERT:

1. Identify all major activities (tasks) to be performed in the project.
2. Determine the sequence in which the tasks must be completed and whether tasks can be performed simultaneously.
3. Determine the amount of time required to complete each task.
4. Draw a PERT network for controlling the project.

EXHIBIT 7.8

Activities Required for Designing a Training Program

Activity	Description	Immediate Predecessor(s)	Estimated Time (Weeks)			
			Optimistic	Most Likely	Pessimistic	Expected
A	Determine topic	—	3.0	4.0	5.0	4.0
B	Locate speakers	A	4.0	5.0	12.0	6.0
C	Find potential meeting sites	—	2.0	4.0	6.0	4.0
D	Select location	C	3.0	4.0	5.0	4.0
E	Arrange speaker travel plans	B, D	1.0	2.0	3.0	2.0
F	Finalize speaker plans	E	2.0	4.0	6.0	4.0
G	Prepare announcements	B, D	2.0	4.0	12.0	5.0
H	Distribute announcements	G	2.0	3.0	4.0	3.0
I	Take reservations	H	6.0	8.0	10.0	8.0
J	Attend to last-minute details	F, I	3.0	4.0	5.0	4.0

A PERT network is a graphical representation of a large project. *Activities* are the tasks that must be completed in order to finish the project. Each activity must have a discrete beginning and ending. Activities are illustrated as solid lines on a PERT network. *Events* represent the beginning and ending of specific activities. Events are represented on the PERT network as circled numbers. *Paths* are strings of activities and events on a network diagram. Project managers determine the sequence of activities that must be performed in order to complete the entire project. A *critical activity* is one that if delayed will cause a slowdown in the entire project. The path with the longest total time is called the **critical path** and represents the total time required for the project.[16]

The application of PERT can best be seen through an illustration.

critical path The path with the longest total time; represents the total time required for the project.

Stotler Associates

Stotler Associates is a consulting firm that provides training seminars for companies all around the country. Planning these seminars can be a difficult project, because each company's requirements are different and a number of factors must be brought together in a timely fashion. Doug Black is director of Executive Training Programs, and he decided to develop a PERT network for the next training seminar. He began by listing all activities to be completed and determined whether each had to be done before or after other activities, as illustrated in Exhibit 7.8.

Doug's next step was to determine the length of time required for each activity. To do this, he and two other managers decided on an optimistic, most likely, and pessimistic estimate of how long each

E X H I B I T   7.9

PERT Network for Designing a Training Program

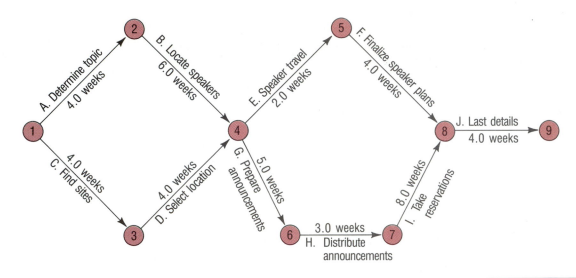

activity would take. The optimistic time indicates how quickly the activity will be completed if there are no problems or obstacles. The pessimistic time indicates the amount of time required if everything goes wrong. The most likely time is the estimate assuming that only a few routine problems will occur.

The expected time is a weighted average of the three estimates. The most likely time is weighted by four. The estimated time is calculated by the following formula:

$$\text{Estimated time} = \frac{\text{Optimistic} + (4)\ \text{Most likely} + \text{Pessimistic}}{6}.$$

The expected time for completing each activity is shown in the right-hand column of Exhibit 7.8.

Based on the information listed in Exhibit 7.8, Doug drew the PERT network illustrated in Exhibit 7.9. This network shows when activities must be completed in order to move on to the next activity. The critical path is the longest path through the network, which for Doug's project is A-B-G-H-I-J. Thus, the project is expected to take 4 + 6 + 5 + 3 + 8 + 4 = 30 weeks to complete.

Laying out a project in a PERT network the way Stotler Associates did has certain advantages for a manager. Analysis of the network may identify slack time along some paths so that resources can be reallocated to the critical path. This would have the effect of shortening the critical path and thereby shortening the length of the entire project. The PERT network also is useful as a control technique. The manager gathers information each week on the status of ongoing activities and determines whether they are on time, behind time, or ahead of time. Activities that are behind time may need additional resources. Activities that are ahead of time may have excess resources that can be allocated to more critical activities.[17]

QUANTITATIVE APPROACHES TO DECISION MAKING

Now we turn to quantitative techniques that help managers make choices under conditions of risk and uncertainty. Recall from Chapter 6 that managerial decision making follows six steps: problem definition, diagnosis, development of alternatives, selection of an alternative, implementation, and control/follow-up. Decision aids focus on the fourth step— selecting an alternative. First we will examine two quantitative decision approaches: the payoff matrix and the decision tree. Then we will discuss two extensions of these ideas: game theory and simulation models.

Payoff Matrix

In order to use the **payoff matrix** as an aid to decision making, a manager must be able to define four variables.

Strategies.   Strategies are the decision alternatives. There can be two strategies or ten depending on the number of alternatives available. For example, a manager wanting to open a new store might consider four different locations, or a university considering an expansion of its football stadium might consider three expansion alternatives of 8,000, 15,000, and 20,000 seats.

States of Nature.   **States of nature** represent future events or conditions that are relevant to decision outcomes. For example, the states of nature for the above store location could be the anticipated sales volume at each site, and those for expanding the football stadium could be the number of additional paying fans at football games.

Probability.   Probability represents the likelihood, expressed as a percentage, that a given state of nature will occur. Thus, the store owner may calculate the probability of making a profit in location 1 as 20 percent, in location 2 as 30 percent, and in location 3 as 50 percent. A probability of 50 percent would be listed in the payoff matrix as 0.5. University administrators would estimate the probability of filling the stadium under each condition of 8,000, 15,000, and 20,000 additional seats. The probabilities associated with the states of nature must add up to 100 percent.

payoff matrix   A decision-making aid comprised of relevant strategies, states of nature, probability of occurrence of states of nature, and expected outcome(s).

state of nature   A future event or condition that is relevant to a decision outcome.

expected value The weighted average of each possible outcome for a decision alternative.

Outcome. The outcome is the payoff calculated for each strategy given the probabilities associated with each state of nature. The outcome is called the **expected value,** which is the weighted average of each possible outcome for a decision alternative. For example, the store owner could calculate the expected profit from each store location, and the university administrators could calculate the expected returns associated with each construction alternative of 8,000, 15,000, and 20,000 seats.

To illustrate the payoff matrix in action, let's consider the problem facing Biggers Corporation's managers, who are trying to decide how to finance the construction of a new plant and its equipment.

Biggers Corporation

The senior managers at Biggers Corporation wish to raise funds to finance the construction and new machinery for a new plant to be located in Alberta, Canada. They have determined that they have three alternative funding sources: to issue common stock, bonds, or preferred stock. The desired decision outcome is the net dollars that can be raised through each financing vehicle. The state of nature that affects the decision is the interest rate at the time the securities are issued, because interest rates influence the firm's ability to attract investment dollars. If interest rates are high, investors prefer bonds; if interest rates are low, they prefer stocks. Biggers' financial experts have advised that if interest rates are high, a common stock issue will bring $1 million, bonds $5 million, and preferred stock $3 million. If interest rates are moderate, common stocks will yield $3.5 million, bonds $3.5 million, and preferred stock $3 million. If interest rates are low, common stock will return $7.5 million, bonds $2.5 million, and preferred stock $4 million. The financial experts also have estimated the likelihood of low interest rates at 10 percent, of moderate interest rates at 40 percent, and of high interest rates at 50 percent.

Biggers' senior managers want to use a logical structure to make this decision, and the payoff matrix is appropriate. The three decision alternatives of stock, bonds, and preferred stock are shown in Exhibit 7.10. The three states of nature—low, moderate, and high interest rates—are listed across the top of the exhibit. The listing of strategy on one side and of states of nature on the other side comprises the payoff matrix. The probability associated with each interest rate is also included in the exhibit.

The decision outcome as defined by the managers is to gain the highest expected monetary value from issuing a security. Thus, the

This helicopter passenger's view is of one of Amoco's two producing platforms off the Gabon-Africa coast. Amoco discovered oil here in 1981. It uses decision models to estimate probabilities and evaluate future oil drilling projects. Using payoff matrix–type computations, Amoco has defined low-, medium-, and high-risk projects. The last are in frontier basins such as those in Africa or its coastal waters. Computations indicate that although the probability of success is small, the potential financial payoff is huge; thus, the expected value is high. Amoco undertakes both high- and low-risk projects to obtain multiple opportunities for finding oil.

EXHIBIT 7.10

Payoff Matrix for Biggers Corporation

Strategy (Decision Alternative)	Event (Interest Rate Level/ State of Nature)		
	Low (0.1)	Moderate (0.4)	High (0.5)
Common stock	$7,500,000	$3,500,000	$1,000,000
Bonds	2,500,000	3,500,000	5,000,000
Preferred stock	4,000,000	3,000,000	3,000,000

managers must calculate the expected monetary return associated with each decision alternative. The calculation of expected value for each decision alternative is performed by multiplying each dollar amount by the probability of occurrence. For the figures in Exhibit 7.10, the expected value of each strategy is calculated as follows:

$$\text{Expected value of common stock} = (0.1)(7.5 \text{ million})$$
$$+ (0.4)(3.5 \text{ million})$$
$$+ (0.5)(1 \text{ million})$$
$$= \$2,650,000$$

$$\text{Expected value of bonds} = (0.1)(2.5 \text{ million})$$
$$+ (0.4)(3.5 \text{ million})$$
$$+ (0.5)(5 \text{ million})$$
$$= \$4,150,000$$

$$\text{Expected value of preferred stock} = (0.1)(4 \text{ million})$$
$$+ (0.4)(3 \text{ million})$$
$$+ (0.5)(3 \text{ million})$$
$$= \$3,100,000.$$

From this analysis, the best decision clearly is to issue bonds. Although managers cannot be certain about which state of nature will actually occur, the expected value calculation weights each possibility and indicates the choice with the highest likelihood of success.

Decision Tree

Management problems often require that several decisions be made in sequence. As the outcome of one decision becomes obvious or as additional information becomes available, another decision is required in order to correct past mistakes or take advantage of new information. For instance, a production manager analyzing the company's product line may decide to add a new product on a trial basis. If customers endorse the product, the manager must then decide how to increase production to meet demand. Conversely, if the new product fails to generate sufficient demand, the manager must then decide whether to drop the product.

This type of decision is difficult to structure into a payoff matrix because of the decision sequence. **Decision trees** are an alternative to payoff tables for decision situations that occur in sequence. The objective of decision tree analysis is the same as for payoff tables: to select the decision that will provide the greatest return to the company. The decision tree approach requires the following variables:

1. The decision tree, which is a pictorial representation of decision alternatives, states of nature, and the outcomes of each course of action
2. Estimated probabilities of each outcome occurring
3. The payoff (profit or loss) associated with each outcome
4. The expected value, which is calculated based on the probabilities and conditional payoffs along each branch of the decision tree

The decision tree consists of a series of nodes and connecting lines. A square node, called a *decision fork,* represents the alternative strategies available to the decision maker *at that time.* From a decision fork the decision maker must choose one branch to follow. A numbered node, called a *chance fork,* represents states of nature over which the decision maker has no control. For branches emanating from a chance fork, the decision maker cannot choose which path to follow and must wait until after the decision has been made to see which state of nature occurred.

The use of a decision tree for decision making can be illustrated by the risks and uncertainties associated with the decision to use fire in contemporary forest management.

National Forest Service

Forest management personnel often use fires under controlled conditions to reduce natural fire hazards and enhance the wildlife habitat. However, decision uncertainties are inherent in the use of fire. For example, the decisions to commit personnel and equipment to the burn site and to actually initiate the burn must be made before weather conditions and fire behavior can be determined with certainty.

For a specific burn there are two basic alternatives, as illustrated in Exhibit 7.11. Decision fork 1 shows that forest managers can either (1) commit resources to the burn or (2) postpone the burn. Two uncertainties are central to this decision. The first is the actual weather conditions on the day of the burn, illustrated in chance fork

decision tree A decision-making aid used for decision situations that occur in sequence; consists of a pictorial representation of decision alternatives, states of nature, and outcomes of each course of action.

E X H I B I T   7.11

Decision Tree for Controlled Forest Fire

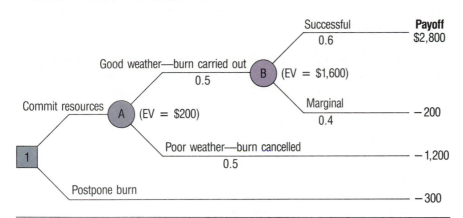

Source: David Cohan, Stephen M. Haas, David L. Radloff, and Richard F. Yancik, "Using Fire in Forest Management: Decision Making under Uncertainty," *Interfaces* 14 (September/October 1984), pp. 8–19. © 1984 The Institute of Management Sciences. Reprinted with permission.

A. There is a 50 percent likelihood that the weather will be poor, in which case the burn will have to be canceled. The second results from the decision to carry out the burn: Will the objectives be met, or will the burn be only marginally successful? This decision is illustrated by chance fork B in Exhibit 7.11. Note that the experts have estimated a 60 percent probability of a successful burn and a 40 percent probability of a marginal burn in that situation.

Given the uncertainties facing National Forest Service managers, should they decide to commit the resources or postpone the burn to await better information? The payoff value of each outcome is listed on the far right in Exhibit 7.11. If everything is successful, the benefit to the forest service will be $2,800. If a marginal burn occurs, there will be a loss of $200. If the burn is canceled after resources have been committed, there will be a loss of $1,200. If the burn is postponed indefinitely, there will be a loss of $300 in management costs.

The way to choose the best decision is through a procedure known as rollback. The *rollback* procedure begins with the end branches and works backward through the tree by assigning a value to each decision fork and chance fork. A fork's value is the expected return from the branches emanating from the fork. Applying the rollback procedure to the data in Exhibit 7.11 produces the following outcomes: The expected value (EV) of chance fork B is

$(0.6)(2,800) + 0.4(-200) = \$1,600$; the expected value of chance fork A is $(0.5)(1,600) + 0.5(-1,200) = \$200$.

These figures provide the information needed for the decision. If the managers decide to commit resources, there is a positive expected value of $200. If they postpone the burn, there is a certain loss of $300. Thus, it is worthwhile to go ahead with the planned burn despite management's uncertainty about the weather and possible outcomes.[18]

Decision tree analysis is one of the most widely used decision analysis techniques.[19] It can be used for any decision situation in which probabilities can be estimated and decisions occur in sequence, such as those concerning new-product introduction, pricing, plant expansion, advertising campaigns, or even acquiring another firm.

Game Theory

game theory A quantitative decision-making aid that helps managers examine the outcomes of their decisions in light of possible competitors' actions.

Many decision situations have an additional complicating factor—the response of competing organizations to the decision. The decision to build a plant or to increase advertising may be countered by a change in competitor strategy. **Game theory** is an extension of the payoff matrix and decision tree methods for helping managers examine the outcomes of their decisions in light of possible actions by their competitors.

Two Atlanta companies—Executive Pools and Leisure Pools—are the sole builders and sellers of in-ground swimming pools. Both companies build similar pools at approximately the same cost. The advertising outlets both companies use are TV advertisements and radio commercials.

The managers at Executive Pools are considering whether to intensify their advertising efforts to increase market share. However, in calculating an expected value for the decision, they also must consider the possibility that Leisure Pools may retaliate with increased advertising. Thus, the managers at Executive Pools must consider (1) the possible outcomes of increasing advertising through either TV or radio and (2) the possible outcomes of increased competitor advertising through each medium. For example, if Executive Pools decides to increase TV advertising and there is no response from Leisure Pools, it can realize a 6 percent market share increase. However, if its competitor responds with more intensive radio spots, the net effect could be only 1 percent gain in market share. Thus, Executive Pools must compute expected values based on its own and its competitor's decision alternatives. The mathematics of game theory are complex because so many possible decision alternatives and responses exist. A computer is needed for detailed analysis.[20]

Simulation Models

simulation model A mathematical representation of the relationships among variables in real-world organizational situations.

Another useful tool for management decision makers is a simulation model. **Simulation models** are mathematical representations of the relationships among variables in real-life organizational situations.[21] For

A unique simulation model based on management science techniques controls movements that simulate driving on real roads. Located at the Berlin-Marienfeld factory of Daimler-Benz, the simulator's computer-controlled range of movement enables the driver's reactions to be monitored and included in important research on automobile design and traffic safety.

example, if an organization is concerned about building a new plant, it could gather information about plant characteristics, such as types of machines, number of required personnel, and transportation costs for raw materials. Before building the plant, it could use a simulation model to indicate the costs associated with building a large versus a small plant and the effects of plant size on the acquisition of raw materials or the number of personnel. Because simulations typically are done by computer, different options can be tried and the effects of decision alternatives can be projected months or even years into the future.

For example, Monsanto Corporation has one ocean-going chemical tanker, and managers wished to have a model that would help them determine the number of trips per year that would provide the most income. Mathematical programming in the form of a simulation model provided the answer. The model included nine ports, fuel prices, operating charges for the tanker, voyage time, amount of fuel used, time in port, time steaming, and voyage itinerary. The simulation model gave operating managers a powerful decision tool. If the vessel manager needed to evaluate the impact of taking on an additional load, he simply simulated the current trip using the model. After completing this analysis, he inserted the data for the additional load and expenses for the extra stop. He could also ask the model if the steaming speed for the voyage could be increased so that the additional stop would not increase total voyage time. He could also compare the cost increase from making the additional stops with increased revenue and simply charge the additional costs plus a reasonable profit to the customer. Using the simulation model to assist management decisions on scheduling the tanker has saved Monsanto an estimated $20,000 per year.[22]

EXHIBIT 7.12

Strengths and Limitations of Management Science Techniques

Strengths	Limitations
• Enhance decision effectiveness in many situations	• Do not fit many situations
• Provide a framework for handling complex problems	• May not reflect reality
• Promote rationality	• Overhead costs
• Inexpensive compared to alternatives	• Are given too much legitimacy

Monte Carlo method A variation of simulation modeling that inserts random occurrences into the model in order to reflect the possibility of real-life problems.

When the outcomes of organizational decisions have random components, a variation of simulation modeling called the Monte Carlo method can be used. The **Monte Carlo method** inserts random possible occurrences into the simulation model, such as a plant fire, a shipping delay, or price cuts by a competitor. Monte Carlo simulations have the advantage of mimicking the occurrence of real-world problems. They have been used in distribution and transportation organizations, inventory management, new-product decisions, and capital investment opportunities.[23]

STRENGTHS AND LIMITATIONS OF MANAGEMENT SCIENCE AIDS

When selectively applied, management science techniques are helpful in both planning and decision making. Many businesses have operations research departments in which experts apply management science techniques to organizational problems. These techniques provide information for improving managerial decision making. In using them, managers should be aware of their basic strengths and limitations, which are summarized in Exhibit 7.12.

Strengths

The primary strength of management science aids is their ability to enhance decision effectiveness in many situations. For example, time series forecasting helps predict seasonal sales variations. Causal models help managers understand the reasons for future sales increases or decreases. Decision trees, payoff matrices, and PERT networks are valuable when data can be organized into the framework the model requires.

Another strength of management science techniques is that they provide a systematic way of thinking about and organizing complex problems. Managers may use these models intuitively, perhaps sketching things out in a decision tree or organizing ideas into a payoff matrix to clarify issues and see how to reach the best decision.

Still another strength is that the models promote management rationality when fully applied. They help managers define a problem, select alternatives, gauge probabilities of alternatives' success, and understand the trade-offs and potential payoffs. Managers need not rely on subjective understanding in order to make a complicated, multidimensional decision.

Finally, management science aids are inexpensive compared to alternatives such as organizational experiments. If an organization actually had to build a new plant to learn whether it would increase profits, a failure would be enormously expensive. Management science models provide a way to experiment with the decision without having to build the plant.

Limitations

The growth of management science has led to some problems. First—and perhaps most important—management science techniques do not yet fit many decision situations. Many management decisions are too ambiguous and subjective. For example, management science techniques have little impact on the poorly structured strategic problems at the top levels of corporations.

A second limitation is that they may not reflect the reality of the organizational situation. The management science model is a simplification, and the outcome can be no better than the numbers and assumptions fed into the model. If these numbers are not good or important variables are left out, the outcome will be unrealistic.

A third limitation is overhead costs. The organization must hire management science specialists and provide computer facilities. If these specialists are not frequently used to help solve real problems, they will add to the organization's overhead costs while providing little return.[24]

Finally, management science techniques can be given too much legitimacy. When managers are trying to make a decision under uncertainty, they may be desperate for a clear and precise answer. A management science model may produce an answer that is taken as fact even though the model is only a simplification of reality and the decision needs the interpretation and intuitive judgment of experienced managers.

The strengths of management science techniques are illustrated at J. P. Morgan Investment Management Inc. Quantitative research is vital to maintaining objectivity and improving investment decisions. Analysts use financial and mathematical skills to analyze the changing structure and dynamics of capital markets, as well as test new theories of market performance. Analyzing a new strategy for equity investment are Thomas M. Luddy (foreground), head of Equity Research; Lisa M. Waller, vice-president; and Michael R. Granito, head of Capital Markets Research.

SUMMARY

This chapter described several important points about management science aids for managerial planning and decision making. Forecasting is the attempt to predict behavior in the future. Forecasting techniques can be either quantitative or qualitative. Quantitative techniques include time series analysis and causal modeling. Qualitative techniques include the Delphi method, sales force composite, and jury of opinion.

Quantitative aids to management planning include breakeven analysis, linear programming, and PERT. Breakeven analysis indicates the volume at which a new product will earn enough revenues to cover costs.

Linear programming helps managers decide which product mix will maximize profits or minimize costs. PERT helps managers plan, monitor, and control project progress.

Management science aids to decision choices also were described. The payoff matrix helps managers determine the expected value of various alternatives. The decision tree is a similar procedure that is used for decisions made in sequence. Game theory considers competitors' responses. Simulation models use mathematics to evaluate the impact of management decisions. All of these techniques have major strengths and limitations.

Management Solution

New York City's Department of Sanitation faced a seemingly impossible problem keeping city streets clean. Management science specialists attacked the problem with management science techniques. The first job was to obtain basic data; thus, they commissioned studies to determine the rate at which litter accumulated in streets, the point at which a street appeared unacceptably dirty, the dirtiest districts, and the effect of manpower and equipment on street cleanliness. Through these data, the specialists analyzed the impact of having litter baskets on sidewalks, alternative-side-of-the-street parking regulations, and using motorized street sweepers. Next they used a regression model to determine how the number of people assigned to a district influenced street cleanliness. Simulation models indicated the effects of changes in litter basket placement, manpower, vehicles, and parades. As a result of these management science aids, manpower was reallocated, litter baskets were strategically placed, and machines were allocated to the neediest districts. The net effect was a reduction of 400 cleaners, a financial saving of $12 million a year, and street cleanliness ratings near record levels.[25]

DISCUSSION QUESTIONS

1. In 1987, the Texas Department of Corrections predicted an increase of almost 20,000 prisoners within 5 years. What forecasting approach do you think was used to arrive at this figure? What approach would you have recommended?

2. Think back to a decision you had to make that was difficult because you were uncertain about the outcomes of each alternative. Attempt to analyze that decision using a payoff matrix or a decision tree. Would either procedure have helped your decision?

3. What is the difference between time series forecasting and causal model forecasting?

4. What is the correct relationship between a nontechnical manager and management science decision tools? Can management science thinking be delegated to staff specialists?

5. If the objective of a business is to maximize profit, what value will breakeven analysis have for a manager?

6. What is the critical path? Why is it especially important for a manager to know which activities lie along the critical path?

7. In linear programming, all inputs to the production process are assumed to be known with certainty and constant. Is this a realistic assumption? If not, why do you suppose linear programming is one of the most frequently used management science techniques?

8. How does game theory differ from a payoff matrix? How does a Monte Carlo simulation differ from other simulation models?

9. Will future managers have an advantage if they are familiar with management science tools and their applications? Explain.

10. Discuss the pros and cons of using management science techniques in organizations.

CASES FOR ANALYSIS

SECOND NATIONAL BANK

You are a member of a notorious bank-robbing gang. The secret of your success is that your robberies are always well planned. For your next caper, you have selected a rural branch of the Second National Bank. From your surveillance, you have discovered that it will take the police 7.5 minutes to reach the bank once the alarm has sounded. You now want to determine if the robbery can be completed successfully in that amount of time.

To complete the robbery, two members of your gang (one gunperson and a safecracker) will be dropped off behind the bank and be responsible for picking the lock on the rear door. The rest of the gang will be driven to the front of the bank to wait. Once the alarm has sounded, the entire gang will enter the bank. The gunpeople will point their weapons at the guards and customers, the counter leaper will leap over the counter and empty the tellers' drawers, and the safecracker will crack or blow open the safe and empty it. Once these things have been accomplished, the gang will leave.

The details are as follows:

Activities

1. Drop off one gunperson and the safecracker in the alley behind the bank.
2. Drop off the other gang members in front of the bank.
3. Everyone enters the bank at the same time.
4. The gunpeople take up their positions and point their weapons at everyone in the bank.

5. The counter leaper leaps over the counter and empties the tellers' drawers.
6. The safecracker cracks open the safe and empties it.
7. All gang members leave the bank at the same time.
8. The driver meets the rest of the gang in front of the bank when the robbery is completed.

Timing

1. 2 minutes to pick the lock on the rear door.
2. The alarm goes off when the back door is picked; the police arrive in 7.5 minutes.
3. 45 seconds to drive from the alley to the front of the bank.
4. 30 seconds for the gunpeople to enter the bank and take up their positions.
5. 60 seconds for the safecracker to reach the safe from the back door.
6. 30 seconds for the counter leaper to leap over the counter and start to empty the drawers.
7. 3 minutes to empty the tellers' drawers.
8. 2 minutes to open the safe.
9. 2 minutes to empty the safe.
10. 45 seconds to exit from the bank and reach the car at the front curb.

Questions

1. Draw a PERT network for the bank robbery scenario.
2. Can the robbery be accomplished in the 7.5 minutes before the police arrive?
3. How quickly can it be accomplished—in other words, what is the critical path?

Source: Adapted from Mark P. Sharfman and Timothy R. Walters, "Robbery: Planning with PERT," Leonard D. Goodstein and J. William Pfeiffer, (Eds.), *The 1983 Annual for Facilitators, Trainers, and Consultants,* San Diego, CA: University Associates, Inc., 1983, pp. 40–44. Used with permission.

GIBSON GLASS COMPANY

Gibson Glass Company opened its doors for business in April 1970. From its small beginnings, the company grew into a large operation. However, the glassmaking technology installed in 1970 has remained essentially unchanged. Because technological innovations adopted by competitors have begun to make Gibson's equipment and processes obsolete, management is considering whether to modernize or to continue operations as is. The choice between these two alternatives depends on anticipated future demand for Gibson's glass bottles and jars. The market forecasters have estimated two possible states of nature to consider. One is high demand for the company's output, which has a 45 percent chance of occurring. The other is moderate demand for the company's products, which has a 55 percent chance of occurring.

According to Gibson's financial analysts, if the company modernizes and demand is high, there will be a positive return of $4 million, and if demand is low, the return will be only $1.5 million. However, if management decides not to modernize, the payoff will be $3 million in the case of high demand and $2.5 million in the case of low demand. With these data, Gibson's managers are trying to determine which choice—to modernize or not—would be the better.

Questions

1. Using a payoff matrix, determine the correct decision.
2. What factors not calculated in the model might the decision makers want to consider? Are these factors strong enough to overrule the decision from the payoff matrix?
3. Is this an appropriate problem for which to use management science decision aids? Discuss.

Source: Adapted from Lawrence R. Jauch, Sally A. Coltrin, Arthur G. Bedeian, and William R. Glueck, "Alcon Canning Company," in *The Managerial Experience: Cases, Exercises, and Readings* (Hinsdale, Ill.: Dryden Press, 1986), p. 102. Used with permission.

PART THREE
ORGANIZING

Source: Art Resource/NY: Turner, the Fighting Temerar, London, National Gallery.

Source: Courtesy of Amoco Corporation.

Fundamentals of Organizing

Chapter Outline

The Organizing Process

Organizing the Vertical Structure

Work Specialization
Chain of Command
Span of Management
Departmentalization
Centralization and Decentralization
Line and Staff
Administrative Intensity
Formalization
Problems with Vertical Structure

Organizing the Lateral Structure

Information Systems
Liaison Roles
Task Forces
Permanent Teams
Integrating Managers

Balancing Vertical and Lateral Structures

Mechanistic versus Organic Organizations
Contingency Factor: The Environment
Contingency Factor: Size and Life Cycle
Contingency Factor: Production Technology

Learning Objectives

After studying this chapter, you should be able to:

- Explain the fundamental characteristics of organizing, including such concepts as work specialization, chain of command, line and staff, and task forces.

- Describe the importance of both vertical and lateral structures, their differences, and their uses.

- Explain when specific structural characteristics such as centralization, span of management, and formalization should be used within organizations.

- Describe how organization structure can be designed to fit environmental uncertainty.

- Define production technology (manufacturing and service) and explain how it influences organization structure.

- Describe four stages of the organizational life cycle and explain how size and life cycle influence the correct structure.

Management Problem

Lotus Development Corporation recently lost several employees, including four of its twelve top officers. Jonathan Sachs, mastermind of *Lotus 1-2-3®*, resigned, as did Raymond Ozzie, a manager on the team that had created the *Symphony* software package. The reason? The managers resented increasing bureaucratic control. As Lotus increased from 90 to 760 employees, tighter controls replaced the freewheeling management style. Official policies, procedures, and organization charts now define many employee tasks. The informal days are gone. "It's difficult to be entrepreneurial in a bureaucracy," said one former employee.[1]

If you were a top manager at Lotus, how would you deal with this dilemma? Would you loosen up the structure to satisfy employees or maintain tighter control despite the loss of key personnel?

The problem confronting Lotus is one of organizing. Senior managers want to establish a tighter, more formal structure, and many employees are resisting. Every firm wrestles with the problem of how to organize and whether to reorganize. Organization structure is never completely settled, because reorganization often is necessary to reflect a new strategy, changing environmental conditions, or innovative production technology. For example, General Motors recently reorganized to consolidate five automobile divisions into two. GM also created teams at both the corporate and plant levels to engender greater cooperation across departments.[2] Greyhound Lines Inc. recently restructured itself from one large company into four independent regional divisions.[3] Even the Defense Department is reorganizing. A realignment has given the chairman of the Joint Chiefs of Staff and regional military commanders more

Structural patterns characterize all aspects of nature. In this froth from a common household detergent, the bubbles divide into segments that meet at 120° angles. Cracks in rocks, mud, and glaze also form a pattern of 120° angles. Systematic patterns likewise exist in the structures of human organizations. These include a vertical hierarchy, specialization, span of management, and formalization. Organization structure research strives to find systematic structural patterns that can be used to solve organizational problems.

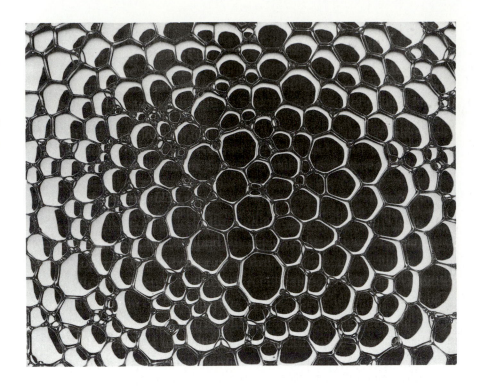

organizing The deployment of organizational resources to achieve strategic objectives.

authority and the Chiefs of Staff of the Army, Navy, and Air Force less.[4] International firms such as Unilever and U.S. Steel have taken steps to decentralize decision making and give middle managers more authority.[5] One small company—the Bloom Advertising Agency in Dallas—developed a structural approach to achieve positive working relationships between people in the creative and marketing departments.[6] Brunswick Corporation restructured in a different way, chopping out many of its headquarters' staff departments and one layer of management to reduce administrative overhead.[7]

Each of these organizations is using fundamental concepts of organizing. **Organizing** is the deployment of organizational resources to achieve strategic objectives. The deployment of resources is reflected in the organization's division of labor into specific departments and jobs, formal lines of authority, and mechanisms for coordinating diverse organization tasks.

Organizing is important because it follows from strategy—the topic of Part Two. Strategy defines *what* to do; organizing defines *how* to do it. Organization structure is a tool that managers use to harness resources for getting things done. The purpose of Part Three is to explain the variety of organizing principles and concepts used by managers. This chapter covers fundamental concepts that apply to all organizations and departments. These ideas are extended in Chapter 9, where we look at how specific structural designs can be used for mission accomplishment. Chapter 10 discusses how organizations can be structured to facilitate innovation and change. Chapter 11 examines how to utilize human resources to the best advantage within the organization structure.

EXHIBIT 8.1

Evolution of Organization Structure

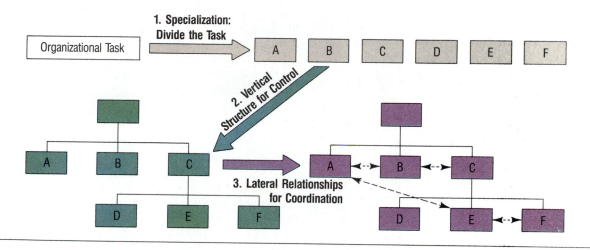

Organization structure is a powerful tool because it is planned and designed. Managers make structure happen. By the end of this chapter, you will understand the dilemma confronting Lotus Development Corporation and how the company should resolve it. You will also understand the logic of the structural changes taking place in such organizations as Brunswick, Bloom Advertising, and the Pentagon.

THE ORGANIZING PROCESS

The organizing process leads to the creation of organization structure, which defines how tasks are divided and resources deployed. **Organization structure** is defined as (1) the set of formal tasks assigned to individuals and departments; (2) formal reporting relationships, including lines of authority, decision responsibility, number of hierarchical levels, and span of managers' control; and (3) the design of systems to insure effective coordination of employees across departments.[8]

The three elements of organization structure are illustrated in Exhibit 8.1. The first element is the division of labor into specific tasks. The second is the installation of a hierarchy of authority to provide for vertical control and communication. The third is the implementation of specific devices for lateral coordination. Vertical channels do not have sufficient capacity to handle every decision or problem that may arise. People in department A often must talk directly to people in department B in order to solve joint problems. Systems and devices for lateral communication include task forces, committees, teams, and project managers. Successful organizing requires that managers use both vertical and horizontal structural tools. In the next section, we will review the basic com-

organization structure The framework in which the organization defines how tasks are divided, resources are deployed, and departments are coordinated.

EXHIBIT 8.2

Organization Chart for a Textile Company

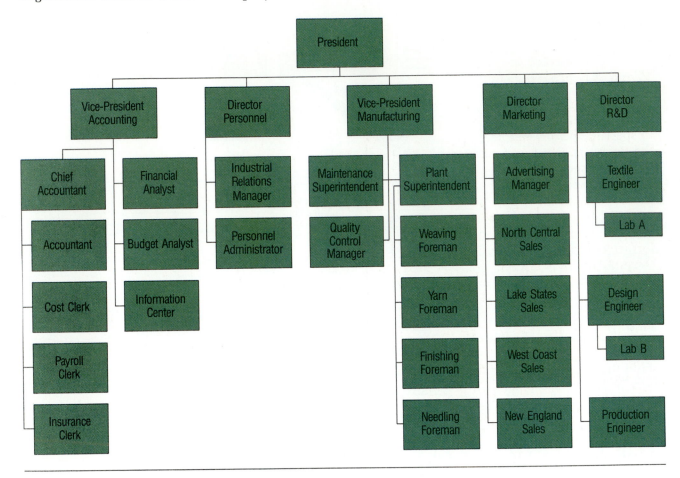

ponents of vertical structure; then we will turn to structural elements used for lateral coordination.

ORGANIZING THE VERTICAL STRUCTURE

Principles of organizing have been established that provide a framework for vertical control of the organization. The characteristics of vertical structure are portrayed in the **organization chart,** which is the visual representation of an organization's structure.

A sample organization chart for a textile mill is illustrated in Exhibit 8.2. The mill has five major departments—accounting, personnel, manufacturing, marketing, and research and development. The organization

organization chart The visual representation of an organization's structure.

chart delineates the chain of command, indicates departmental tasks and how they fit together, and provides order and logic for the organization. Every employee has an appointed task, line of authority, and decision responsibility. The following sections discuss several important features of vertical structure in more detail.

Work Specialization

Organizations perform a wide variety of tasks. A fundamental principle is that work can be performed more efficiently if employees are allowed to specialize.[9] **Work specialization,** sometimes called *division of labor,* is the degree to which organizational tasks are subdivided into separate jobs. Work specialization in Exhibit 8.2 is illustrated by the separation of manufacturing tasks into weaving, yarn, finishing, and needling. Employees within each department perform only the tasks relevant to their specialized function. When work specialization is extensive, employees specialize in a single task. Jobs tend to be small, but they can be performed efficiently. Work specialization is readily visible on an automobile assembly line, where each employee performs the same task over and over again. It would not be efficient to have a single employee build the entire automobile or even perform a large number of unrelated jobs.

Specialization is a fundamental principle of organizing for several reasons. First, production is efficient because employees perform small, well-defined tasks. Second, employees can acquire expertise in their tasks. Third, employees with the appropriate ability and attitude for the task to be performed can be selected. Fourth, the organization achieves standardization across tasks. Managers know what to expect and can easily detect task-related performance problems.

Despite the advantages, however, organizations can overdo work specialization. This leads to the design of tasks wherein employees do only a single, tiny, boring job. Once the task is mastered, it offers no challenge. Specialization, although necessary, should not be carried to such an extreme. If workers become bored and alienated, organizations can enlarge tasks to find the right fit between work specialization and employee motivation. Specific approaches to designing jobs to fit employee needs are described in Chapter 13.

Chain of Command

The **chain of command** is an unbroken line of authority that links all persons in an organization and shows who reports to whom. It is associated with two underlying principles. *Unity of command* means that each employee is held accountable to only one supervisor. The *scalar principle* means a clearly defined line of authority in the organization that includes all employees. Authority and responsibility for different tasks should not overlap. All persons in the organization should know to whom they report as well as the successive management levels all the way to the top. In Exhibit 8.2, the payroll clerk reports to the chief accountant, who in turn reports to the vice-president, who in turn reports to the president.

ARA Services has a separate division, Szabo Correctional Services, which specializes in correctional institutions. Here task specialization permits efficient delivery of hot food to the inmate population. Each person specializes in one task, such as putting a food item on each tray. Employees quickly acquire expertise and Szabo achieves standardization across tasks to insure reliable food service.

work specialization   The degree to which organizational tasks are subdivided into individual jobs; also called *division of labor.*

chain of command   An unbroken line of authority that links all individuals in the organization and specifies who reports to whom.

EXHIBIT 8.3

Reorganization to Increase Span of Management for President of an International Metals Company

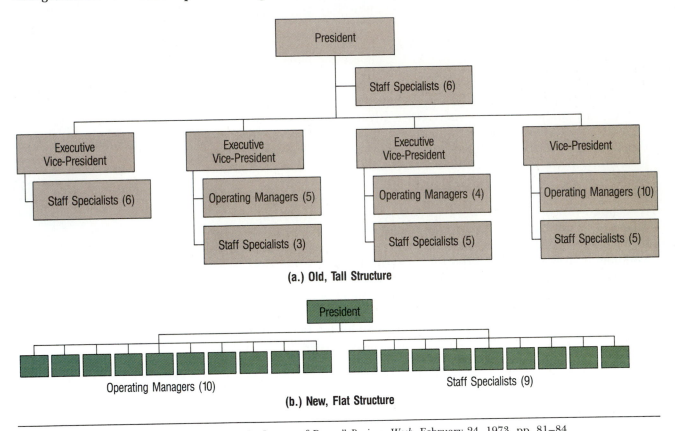

(a.) Old, Tall Structure

(b.) New, Flat Structure

Source: Based on "Kaiser Aluminum Flattens Its Layers of Brass," *Business Week,* February 24, 1973, pp. 81–84.

Span of Management

span of management The number of employees who report to a supervisor; also called *span of control.*

The **span of management** is the number of employees reporting to a supervisor. Sometimes called the *span of control,* this characteristic of structure determines how closely a supervisor can monitor subordinates. Traditional views of organization design recommend a span of management of from four to seven subordinates per manager. However, many organizations have been observed to have larger spans of management and a few smaller. Research on the Lockheed Missile and Space Company and other manufacturing companies has suggested that span of management can vary widely and that several factors influence the correct span.[10] Generally, when supervisors must be closely involved with subordinates the span should be small, and when supervisors need little involvement with subordinates it can be large. The following factors are associated with closeness of supervisor involvement and thus larger spans of control:

1. Work performed by subordinates is stable and routine.
2. Subordinates perform similar work tasks.
3. Subordinates are concentrated in a single location.
4. Subordinates are highly trained and need little direction in performing tasks.
5. Rules and procedures defining task activities are available.
6. Support systems and personnel are available for the manager.
7. Little time is required in nonsupervisory activities such as coordination with other departments or planning.
8. Managers' personal preferences and styles favor a large span.

Tall versus Flat Structure.   The average span of control used in an organization determines whether the structure is tall or flat. A **tall structure** has an overall narrow span and more hierarchical levels. A **flat structure** has a wide span, is horizontally dispersed, and has fewer hierarchical levels. For example, when an international metals company was reorganized during the 1970s, the chief executive officer wanted to shift from a tall to a flat structure. The tall and flat structures are illustrated in Exhibit 8.3. The multilevel set of managers (panel a) was replaced with ten operating managers and nine staff specialists reporting directly to the CEO (panel b). This change meant less time supervising each manager and thus gave managers more independence and responsibility. The CEO welcomed the extremely wide span of 19 management personnel. He understood the importance of quality employees: "I couldn't have 20-odd people working for me if they weren't top people."[11]

Departmentalization

Another fundamental characteristic of organization structure is **departmentalization,** which is the basis for grouping positions into departments and departments into the total organization. How should employees be grouped together to perform their work? Three basic choices are by function, by geographical location, or by product.

Departmentalization by *function* means that employees are grouped together according to common task skills. In the textile mill in Exhibit 8.2, employees in manufacturing are grouped together by function. Quality control people work in one department, maintenance people in another, and production people in others.

Departmentalization by *geographical location* means that employees with diverse skills and tasks are grouped together in the same territory. In Exhibit 8.2, the employees grouped in the North Central sales region belong to the same department. Employees with diverse task skills, including salespersons, clerical personnel, computer technicians, personnel specialists, and financial analysts, may all be grouped together in a regional office.

Departmentalization by *product* means that employees with diverse skills are grouped together to achieve a specific product or project outcome. This is similar to a team approach to structure. At Hewlett-Packard, all employee specialties needed to produce each type of computer or selected software lines are grouped into a single division. At IBM, a separate department had been formed to coordinate the diverse skills

tall structure   A management structure characterized by an overall narrow span of management and a relatively large number of hierarchical levels.

flat structure   A management structure characterized by an overall broad span of control and relatively few hierarchical levels.

departmentalization   The basis on which individuals are grouped into departments and departments into the total organization—by function, geographical location, or product.

Hamilton/Avnet, as part of the Electronic Marketing Group of Avnet Inc., distributes semiconductors. This view of the Hamilton/Avnet sales facility illustrates departmentalization by function: the Sales Support and Communications Departments (center), the Sales & Marketing and Customer Service Departments (far right), and the Product Management Department (far left). Grouping people and positions by function allows employees to exchange ideas, learn from one another, and acquire in-depth expertise.

needed to create and develop the IBM PC. This department was product based because diverse functional skills were brought together to produce a specific product.

Departmental grouping establishes a system of common supervision. The form of departmentalization influences employees' goals and motivations. Specific approaches to designing departmental groupings for attaining organizational goals are discussed in Chapter 9.

Centralization and Decentralization

centralization The location of decision authority near top organizational levels.

decentralization The location of decision authority near lower organizational levels.

Centralization and decentralization pertain to the hierarchical level at which decisions are made. **Centralization** means that decision authority is located near the top of the organization. With **decentralization,** decision authority is pushed downward to lower organization levels. Organizations may have to experiment to find the correct hierarchical level at which to make decisions.

Sometimes decisions should be highly centralized and at other times decentralized. Consider the contrast between Sears and USX.

Sears, Roebuck and USX

Sears, Roebuck recently went through a reorganization in which decision making was centralized to corporate headquarters. Sears' retailing operation had been run as five autonomous territories, which were, in effect, five different retail companies. There was little coordination between headquarters and the field or among the five field regions. The stores carried different lines of merchandise, looked different, and used different advertising. Moreover, the buying organization was uncoordinated with the retail organization. To correct these problems, Sears created a central group at headquarters to supervise all merchandising activities. Decision authority for purchasing and for merchandising were centralized at headquarters. The executive vice-presidents in charge of each region no longer had the freedom to do their own thing.[12]

USX (formerly U.S. Steel), in contrast, has taken steps to decentralize. To help it cope with a changing environment, decisions were pushed down from the top. Previously even routine decisions, such as starting up a blast furnace, "had to be approved on the 61st floor." Production managers ran the business in a militaristic style. With so much hassle required to get a decision made, employees wouldn't bother trying to change things. Decisions on manufacturing, technological improvements, and quality control are now made closer to the plant floor. New freedom at the lower level enables both manufacturing and marketing managers to be more aggressive.[13]

The difference in centralization approaches for Sears and USX illustrates the concept. Sears raised the hierarchical level at which strategic decisions are made, while USX pushed strategic decisions to lower levels.

When should organizations decentralize? In the United States and Canada, the trend over the last 30 years has been toward greater decentralization of organizations. Decentralization is believed to make greater use of human resources, unburden top managers, insure that decisions are made close to the action by well-informed people, and permit more rapid response to external changes.[14]

As Sears illustrated, however, this trend does not mean that every organization should decentralize. Managers should diagnose the organizational situation and select the decision-making level that will best meet the organization's needs. Factors that typically influence centralization versus decentralization are as follows:

1. Greater change and uncertainty in the environment are usually associated with decentralization. More decisions must be made quickly and, hence, are decentralized to lower levels, as occurred at USX.

2. A new organizational strategy may increase the need for decisions to be made at higher or lower organizational levels. Sears' strategy of having the five regional divisions work in concert required centralization. Firms such as Westinghouse and General Electric whose strategy consists of developing new products through internal research decentralize decision making to lower levels.

3. Corporate history and culture socialize managers into a decision approach. The choice between centralization and decentralization often reflects the pattern of decisions made in the past. Senior managers must make a conscious effort to break these patterns in order to change the decision approach.

4. As organizations increase in size, some decentralization is required and a larger number of decisions are made. If over centralized, however, the decision process will slow to a trickle because top managers will be overloaded. Some decision authority must be delegated to middle levels. In a very small organization the top manager can make nearly all decisions, thus centralizing decision authority.

5. Greater cost of decision alternatives or greater risk of failure means that centralization is preferred. Top managers are reluctant to delegate decisions that would put the entire organization at risk.

6. Effective communication and control systems often facilitate centralization. New information and computer technologies enable data to be sent to top management for evaluation and decision making. Less efficient systems provide less data to top management; thus, better decisions can be made at lower levels where information is available.[15]

MANAGERS SHOP TALK

How to Delegate

The attempt by top management to decentralize decision making often gets bogged down because middle managers are unable to delegate. Managers may cling tightly to their decision-making and task responsibilities. Failure to delegate occurs for a number of reasons: Managers are most comfortable making familiar decisions; they feel they will lose personal status by delegating tasks; they believe they can do a better job themselves; or they have an aversion to risk—they won't take a chance on delegating because performance responsibility ultimately rests with them.

Yet decentralization offers an organization many advantages. Decisions are made at the right level, lower-level employees are motivated, and employees have the opportunity to develop decision-making skills. Overcoming barriers to delegation in order to gain these advantages is a major challenge. The following approach can help each manager delegate more effectively:

1. *Delegate the whole task.* A manager should delegate an entire task to one person rather than dividing it among several people. This gives the individual complete responsibility and increases his or her initiative while giving the manager some control over the results.
2. *Select the right person.* Not all employees have the same capabilities and degree of motivation. Managers must match talent to task if delegation is to be effective. They should identify subordinates who have made independent decisions in the past and have shown a desire for more responsibility.
3. *Delegate responsibility and authority.* Merely assigning a task is not effective delegation. The individual must have the responsibility for completing the task and the authority to perform the task as he or she thinks best.
4. *Give thorough instruction.* Successful delegation includes information on what, when, why, where, who, and how. The subordinate must clearly

understand the task and the expected results. It is a good idea to write down all provisions discussed, including required resources and when and how the results will be reported.
5. *Maintain feedback.* Feedback means keeping open lines of communication with the subordinate to answer questions and provide advice, but without exerting too much control. Open lines of communication make it easier to trust subordinates. Feedback keeps the subordinate on the right track.
6. *Evaluate and reward performance.* Once the task is completed, the manager should evaluate results, not methods. When results do not meet expectations, the manager must assess the consequences. When they do meet expectations, the managers should reward employees for a job well done with praise, financial rewards when appropriate, and delegation of future assignments.

Are You A Positive Delegator?

Positive delegation is the way an organization implements decentralization. Do you help or hinder the decentralization process? If you answer "yes" to more than three of the following questions, you may have a problem delegating:

- I tend to be a perfectionist.
- My boss expects me to know all the details of my job.
- I don't have the time to explain clearly and concisely how a task should be accomplished.
- I often end up doing tasks myself.
- My subordinates typically are not as committed as I am.
- I get upset when other people don't do the task right.
- I really enjoy doing the details of my job to the best of my ability.
- I like to be in control of task outcomes.

Source: "Delegation," *Small Business Report* (June 1986), pp. 38–43; Don Caruth and Trazzie Pressley, "Key Factors in Positive Delegation," *Supervisory Management* (July 1984), pp. 6–11; Theodore J. Ein, "How to Improve Delegation Habits," *Management Review* (May 1982), p. 59.

Line and Staff

line department A department that performs tasks related to the organization's mission and primary goal.

Another way to view organization structure is as line and staff departments. **Line departments** are those that perform tasks that reflect the organization's primary goal and mission. In a manufacturing organiza-

EXHIBIT 8.4

Line and Staff Structure for an Automotive Company

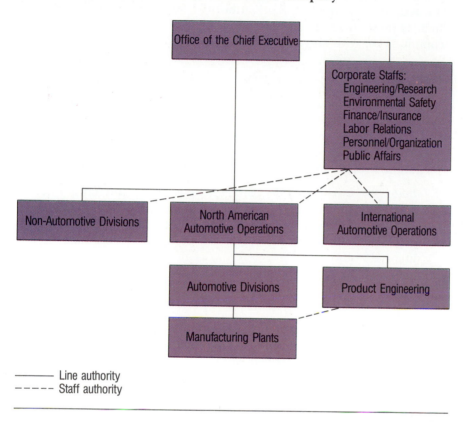

——— Line authority
- - - - - Staff authority

tion, line departments are those that make and sell the product. **Staff departments** include all those that provide specialized skills in support of line departments. Staff departments have an advisory relationship with line departments. Staff departments typically include strategic planning, labor relations, research, accounting, and personnel. Exhibit 8.4 shows a partial organization chart for an automotive manufacturing company such as American Motors or Ford. The line departments follow the line of authority from the office of the chief executive down to the manufacturing plants. Staff departments exist at the corporate and divisional levels and assist company managers in discharging their line responsibilities.

Line and staff positions are related to line and staff authority. *Line authority* means that people in management positions have formal authority to direct and control immediate subordinates. *Staff authority* is narrower and includes the right to advise, recommend, and counsel in the staff specialists' area of expertise. Staff authority often is a communication relationship; staff specialists advise managers in technical areas. Thus, an engineering manager may have authority to define acceptable tolerances for manufacturing machines based on engineering studies.

staff department A department that provides specialized skills in support of line departments.

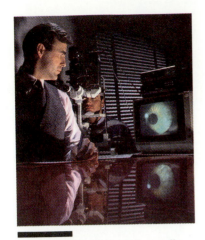

Research and development is a staff department at Bausch & Lomb. Ocular research as shown here is supported by a large in-house staff of optometrists and clinicians, as well as state-of-the-art technology. As part of a staff department, specialists advise marketing and production managers about new technologies and potential new products. Communication and collaboration between R&D and the rest of the company enable Bausch & Lomb to maintain a high rate of innovation in contact lenses and other product areas.

administrative intensity The percentage of resources allocated to administrative and support activities relative to that deployed for line activities.

formalization The amount of written documentation used to direct and control employees.

Accounting specialists may tell line managers which accounting forms to complete so as to facilitate payroll services. Staff authority is confined to the area of staff expertise. Staff authority is represented by dashed lines, such as those in Exhibit 8.4, which imply that corporate staff members communicate with and advise senior line managers.

Administrative Intensity

Since organization structure is the deployment of resources so as to accomplish organizational goals, one characteristic of interest to many managers pertains to the percentage of resources deployed for line activities versus that for administrative and support activities. Two elements of **administrative intensity** can be measured by the following ratios:

1. *Indirect-to-direct-labor ratio.* Direct labor includes line employees who work directly on the organization's product or service. Indirect employees include all other employees—accountants, engineers, clerks—in the organization. This ratio is similar to a line-staff ratio.
2. *Top administrator ratio.* This ratio measures the percentage of total employment made up by top management. For a wide span of control in a flat organization, this percentage would be low.

An example of the importance of administrative intensity is illustrated by comparing major retail firms. One factor precipitating Sears, Roebuck's reorganization described earlier was high expenses for administrative overhead. Sears had the highest administrative cost in the business, running at 29.9 percent of sales. By comparison, K mart had overhead expenses of 23 percent and Walmart 15.3 percent. The low administrative cost at Walmart enabled it to be the low-cost industry leader and to take market share from its less efficient competitors.[16]

Formalization

Formalization is the amount of written documentation used to direct and control employees. Written documentation includes rule books, policies, procedures, job descriptions, and regulations. These documents complement the organization chart by providing descriptions of tasks, responsibilities, and decision authority. The use of rules, regulations, and written records of decisions is part of the bureaucratic model of organizations described in Chapter 2. As proposed by Max Weber, the bureaucratic model defines the basic organizational characteristics that enable the organization to operate in a logical and rational manner.[17]

Although written documentation is intended to be rational and helpful to the organization, it often creates "red tape" that causes more problems than it solves. If an organization tries to do everything through the written word, rules and procedures become burdensome. Consider the government's attempt to define a rule concerning the size of scallops:

A violation of the four-ounce standard occurs if the average of the aggregate weights of the 10 smallest scallops in all the one-pint samples taken fails to meet the four-ounce standard. If a violation of the four-ounce standard is found among those undeclared scallops from a particular vessel and being treated as a separate entity for the purpose of sampling, the entire amount of scallops in possession or control will be deemed in violation. If a violation of the four-ounce standard is found among scallops possessed by a dealer/processor, only those scallops being treated as a separate entity for the purpose of sampling (i.e., the total amount of scallops, up to 10% of which has been drawn as samples) will be deemed in violation.[18]

Problems with Vertical Structure

The above characteristics of structure provide a frame of reference for vertical organizing and control. They impart order and logic to an organization. Every employee has an appointed task, line of authority, and decision responsibility. Thus, these concepts are essential for creating the organization's basic vertical structure, but they also lead to problems. These problems were described by Harold Geneen, who built ITT into one of the world's best-run corporations:

> *The system . . . has in it all the seeds of bureaucracy . . . . In some of our larger companies it can take as long as six months for a decision to be made. Everything must work its way up through the chain of command and back down again. Managers often become paper pushers. Reports stack up, recommendations are made warily, decisions are delayed, actions are not taken. The company stagnates. . . .*
>
> *Without a formal structure and chain of command, there would be chaos. With it, however, there is the danger that each box on the organization chart will become an independent fiefdom, with each vice president thinking of his own terrain, his own people, his own duties and responsibilities, and no one thinking of the company as a whole. What tends to happen is that one man says, "My job is to do this, and that's all I know." The next man says, "My job is to do that and I don't know anything about his. . . ." And so it goes. . . .[19]*

Geneen's experience points out that the vertical structure is necessary and important but too much creates problems:

1. An organization that overdoes vertical structure is brittle and inflexible. Managers prefer order to disorder. Change is difficult. Every decision is made at a high level. Communications are formal and written. Employees follow the rules rather than doing what is needed to serve customers or adapt to change.
2. Vertical organization structure creates barriers among departments. Employees identify with their own departments. They pursue the goals of their own departments even if these conflict with the needs of other departments. People in one department do not appreciate the contributions of others. Conflicts ensue.

Thus, the vertical structure, which is intended to create order, sows seeds of conflict and disagreement. Managers' challenge is to use the vertical structure to achieve order and control without creating negative side effects. The correct use of vertical structure is not just imposing tight control but finding the correct amount of structure for the situation. Moreover, the vertical structure does not exist by itself; it works in conjunction with the lateral structure, which partially offsets the problems of the vertical hierarchy.

ORGANIZING THE LATERAL STRUCTURE

Contemporary research on organizations has defined the existence of lateral structures within organizations. Lateral structure typically evolves from vertical characteristics, such as division of labor and departmentalization. Lateral characteristics keep the organization from becoming rigid and break down barriers across departments. Lateral relationships represent everyday, informal communications among employees. They supply the coordination, agreement, and unity of understanding needed to accomplish the organization's mission.

coordination The quality of collaboration across departments.

The term that best describes lateral relationships is coordination. **Coordination** refers to the quality of collaboration across departments. When coordination is missing, the organization may act like Chrysler Corporation when Lee Iacocca took over:

> *What I found at Chrysler were thirty-five vice presidents, each with his own turf. . . . I couldn't believe, for example, that the guy running engineering departments wasn't in constant touch with his counterpart in manufacturing. But that's how it was. Everybody worked independently. I took one look at that system and I almost threw up. That's when I knew I was in really deep trouble.*
>
> *I'd call in a guy from engineering, and he'd stand there dumbfounded when I'd explain to him that we had a design problem or some other hitch in the engineering-manufacturing relationship. He might have the ability to invent a brilliant piece of engineering that would save us a lot of money. He might come up with a terrific new design. There was only one problem: he didn't know that the manufacturing people couldn't build it. Why? Because he had never talked to them about it. Nobody at Chrysler seemed to understand that interaction among the different functions in a company is absolutely critical. People in engineering and manufacturing almost have to be sleeping together. These guys weren't even flirting![20]*

If lateral relationships do not appear on the organization chart, how can managers insure that coordination will take place? Coordination is the outcome of information and cooperation. Managers can design lateral structures to promote communication. The most important methods for achieving horizontal coordination are information systems, liaison roles, task forces, permanent teams, and integrating managers.

Information Systems

information system A written or electronic internal system for processing data and information among employees.

Information systems are the written and electronically based internal systems for processing data and information among employees. Information systems include memos, bulletins, and written reports, as well as technological systems such as computers, electronic mail, electronic bulletin boards, and teleconferences. Electronic systems have the capacity to process enormous volumes of data among organizational departments, thereby enabling greater coordination.

General Motors acquired Electronic Data Systems (EDS) in the hope of achieving greater internal coordination. GM has many electronic systems, including over 100 IBM mainframe computers. EDS will attempt to get all of these systems to talk to one another.[21] Another application of information systems for coordination was used in the Air Force. A base commander used a portable radio network to link all senior officers. Each officer could overhear conversations among other officers and thus was kept informed of ongoing events. The radio network replaced the telephone and served as a continuous conference medium.

Liaison Roles

A **liaison role** is the assigned formal responsibility for coordinating between two departments. Typically the liaison person is located in one department and acts as a liaison to the other. The liaison role is similar to the staff function that exists in line and staff organizations. The liaison role can be drawn on the organization chart with a dashed line to indicate a communication and coordination responsibility. The computer department in a large university uses two liaison people to coordinate with computer users. One liaison person is responsible for working with the business college and the other with the college of liberal arts. The liaison people carry information back and forth to help design computer systems to fit user needs. General Mills has set up several liaison positions at its corporate headquarters to keep information flowing between headquarters and its five industry groups.[22]

liaison role   A position in one department with designated formal responsibility for coordinating with another department.

Task Forces

A **task force** is a temporary team or committee designed to solve a short-run problem involving several departments.[23] Task force members rep-

task force   A temporary team or committee formed to solve a specific short-run problem involving several departments.

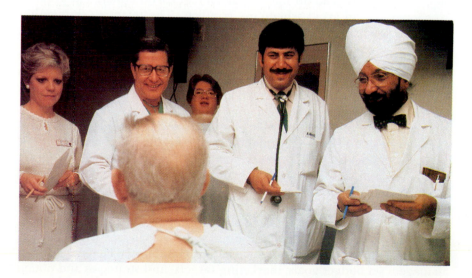

Humana Heart Institute International in Louisville, Kentucky, diagnoses and treats patients with cardiovascular disease and strives to advance research and education. To insure effective horizontal coordination, doctors are assigned to clinical teams and nurses to liaison roles. A registered nurse with the title of Open Heart Coordinator acts as a liaison among the surgeons, nursing staff, and nursing administration to insure their coordination. Here the Open Heart Coordinator meets with a team of doctors examining a patient.

Waste Management Inc. created a task force to plan solid waste collection services for the Los Angeles Coliseum during the 1984 Olympic Games. Los Angeles Olympic Organizing Committee Executive Vice-President Michael Mitchell (left) meets with Waste Management executives Robert Coyle, David Pearre, and John Lavender. These executives work as a task force to provide the planning and coordination needed to insure that all waste disposal needs are met. Meeting face to face allows them to work out problems on the spot.

resent their departments to the committee and carry information from the committee to their departments.

A West Coast bank used a task force to resolve differences among branches. Due to rapid growth, the bank hired branch managers who had different beliefs about how to run it. Conflict ran high, and some branches were in trouble. Top managers decided that the remedy was to bring all branch officers together to examine basic organizational issues. A series of task force meetings were scheduled wherein discrepancies among branches were discussed. After several meetings the problems were solved, and the task force was disbanded.

General Motors uses task forces in its manufacturing plants. A task force is created to solve a problem and then is disbanded. When a shipment of car doors arrived from a fabricating plant with surface imperfections, the plant manager immediately created a task force to resolve the problem: "I got the BOC vice president of manufacturing—who is my boss—the plant manager of the stamping plant, the dye engineers, the quality engineers, the United Auto Workers representatives from both plants, the Olds guy from Lansing, a Cadillac guy, and the Fisher Body guy from the Tech Center. So I had everbody right out there on the floor looking at the exact part that is giving us the problem, and the problem was resolved in about two hours."[24]

Permanent Teams

A **permanent team** is a group of participants from several departments who meet regularly to solve ongoing problems of common interest.[25] The permanent team is similar to a task force except that it works with continuing rather than temporary problems. Teams may exist for several years. An electronics manufacturer created a team whenever a new product had to be developed. Because custom products require help from many departments, the teams include compounding experts, toolmakers, extrusion people, quality control people, and marketing personnel.[26] The teams head off interdepartmental friction. Members are able to cooperate and avoid scheduling conflicts. The teams work together until the products are manufactured, which can take more than a year.

Integrating Managers

An **integrating manager** is a person in a full-time position created for the purpose of coordinating the activities of several departments.[27] The distinctive feature of the integrating position is that the person is not a member of one of the departments being coordinated. These positions often have titles such as product manager, project manager, program manager, or branch manager. The coordinator is assigned to coordinate departments on a full-time basis to achieve desired project or product outcomes.

General Mills, Procter & Gamble, and General Foods all use product managers to coordinate their product lines. A manager is assigned to each line, such as Cheerios, Bisquick, and Hamburger Helper. Product managers set budget goals, marketing targets, and strategies and obtain

permanent team A group of participants from several departments who meet regularly to solve ongoing problems of common interest.

integrating manager An individual responsible for coordinating the activities of several departments on a full-time basis to achieve specific project or product outcomes.

EXHIBIT   8.5

Example of Integrating Manager Relationships to Other Departments

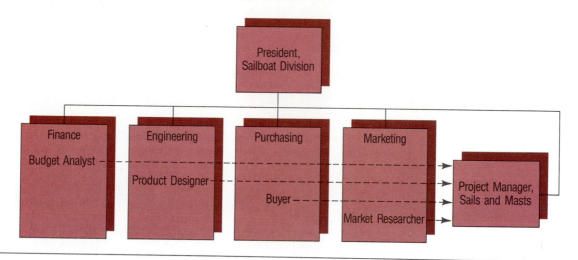

the cooperation from advertising, production, and sales personnel needed for implementing product strategy.

In some organizations project managers are included on the organization chart, as illustrated in Exhibit 8.5. The project manager is drawn to one side of the chart to indicate the lateral relationship. Dashed lines to the project manager indicate formal authority over the project but not over the people assigned to it. Department managers retain line authority over employees.

An interesting variation of the integrator role was developed at Florida Power & Light Company. To keep the construction of a nuclear power plant on schedule, several project managers were assigned the role of "Mothers." The philosophy of the person in charge was, "If you want something to happen, it has to have a mother." The Mothers could nurture their projects on to timely completion. This unusual label worked. Although departmental employees did not report directly to a Mother, the Mothers had a great deal of responsibility, which encouraged departmental managers to listen and cooperate.[28]

BALANCING VERTICAL AND LATERAL STRUCTURES

Recall that the purpose of structure is to organize resources so as to accomplish organizational goals. Organizations use vertical and lateral structures to achieve both the control and coordination necessary for the organization to act as a unified whole. Vertical and lateral structures influence and interact with each other. Increased vertical structure typi-

EXHIBIT 8.6

Differences in Mechanistic versus Organic Organizations

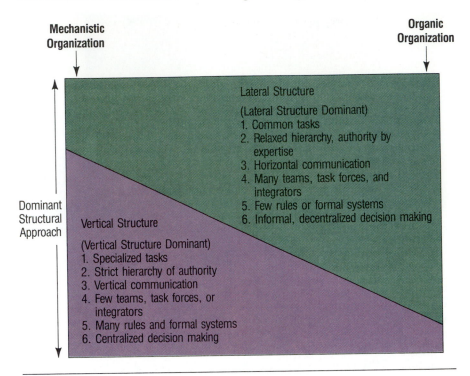

cally will mean less emphasis on lateral structure, and vice versa. Management's responsibility is to achieve the correct degree of each structure and the appropriate balance between them.

Mechanistic versus Organic Organizations

The balance between vertical and lateral structure is similar to the concepts of mechanistic and organic organizations introduced in Chapter 3.[29] When the vertical structure is very strong, the organization is *mechanistic*. The organization emphasizes vertical control. Tasks are broken into routine jobs and are rigidly defined. Voluminous rules exist, and the hierarchy of authority is the major form of control. Decision making is centralized, and communication is vertical. When lateral structures dominate, the organization is *organic*. The organization is informal. Tasks are general, and employees contribute to their department's overall task. Tasks are frequently redefined to fit employee and environmental needs. There are few rules, and authority is based on expertise rather than the hierarchy. Decision making is decentralized. Communication is horizontal and is facilitated through the use of task forces, teams, and liaison personnel. An organic organization may not have job descriptions or even an organization chart. The characteristics of mechanistic versus organic organizations are summarized in Exhibit 8.6.

E X H I B I T   8.7

Contingency Factors That Influence Organization Structure

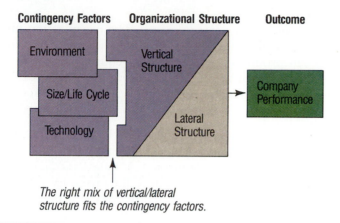

The right mix of vertical/lateral structure fits the contingency factors.

How do managers know whether to emphasize vertical structure, lateral structure, or both? The answer lies in the contingency factors that influence organization structure. *Contingency* pertains to those factors on which structure depends. Research on organization structure shows that the amount of emphasis given to both vertical and lateral characteristics depends on the contingency factors of environment, size/life cycle, and production technology. The right structure is designed to "fit" the contingency factors as illustrated in Exhibit 8.7. Let's look at the relationship between each contingency factor and organization structure in more detail.

Contingency Factor: The Environment

In Chapter 3, we discussed the nature of environmental uncertainty. Environmental uncertainty means that decision makers have a difficult time acquiring good information and predicting external changes. Uncertainty occurs when the external environment is rapidly changing, turbulent, and complex. A certain environment means that external events are stable and simple, permitting decision makers to acquire accurate information and predict changes that do occur.

An uncertain environment causes three things to happen within an organization:

1. *Greater differentiation occurs among departments.* **Differentiation** is the difference in goals and cognitive orientation of members across departments. In an uncertain environment, each major department—marketing, manufacturing, R&D—tailors itself to the needs of the environment and hence distinguishes itself from the others with respect to goals, task orientation, and time horizon.[30] Departments work autonomously. These factors can create barriers among departments.

differentiation The process of distinguishing departments with respect to goals, task orientation, and time horizon.

The vertical alignment of these Marines symbolizes the mechanistic structure that typifies military organizations. Military organizations emphasize vertical control. Tasks are broken into narrow, clearly defined jobs. Many rules exist, and the hierarchy of authority is a major form of control. Military organizations need a mechanistic structure because their mission is relatively stable, and they must have employee compliance when called into action.

2. *The organization needs greater coordination to keep departments working together.* With greater differentiation, more emphasis on lateral structural mechanisms is required in order to link departments together and overcome differences in departmental goals and orientations.

3. *The organization must adapt to change.* The organization must maintain a flexible, responsive posture toward the environment. Changes in products and technology require cooperation among departments, which means a greater emphasis on coordination through the use of teams, task forces, and lateral information processing.[31]

The contingency relationship between environmental uncertainty and structural approach is illustrated in Exhibit 8.8. When the external environment is certain, the organization should have a mechanistic structure that emphasizes vertical control. There is little need for change, flexibility, or intense coordination. The structure can emphasize specialization, centralized decision making, wide spans of control, and low administrative intensity. When environmental uncertainty is high, an organic structure that emphasizes lateral relationships such as teams and task forces is appropriate. Vertical structure characteristics such as specialization, centralization, and formalized procedures should be downplayed. In an uncertain environment, the organization figures things out as it goes along. Departments must cooperate. Decisions should be decentralized to the teams and task forces working on specific problems.

When managers use the wrong structure for the environment, reduced performance will result. A rigid, mechanistic structure in an uncertain environment prevents the organization from adapting. The organization lacks the lateral mechanisms needed for flexibility and coordination. Likewise, a loose, organic structure in a stable environment is inefficient. Too many resources are devoted to meetings and discussions when employees could be more productively focused on specialized tasks.

Many companies are forced to alter their structures as the environment changes. Consider the case of Procter & Gamble.

Procter & Gamble

Procter & Gamble had many traditions—communication by memo, autonomy of divisions, and decisions made at the top. The decision on the color of the cap for Folger's new decaffeinated instant coffee was made by the CEO. But tougher competition and an uncertain environment have led to an internal reorientation. No longer does P&G do everything by the book. The growing bureaucracy is being curtailed. The traditional one-page memo is declining in importance, and a "talk sheet" is encouraging people to use conversation to develop proposals. Business teams have been introduced for making lower-level decisions and facilitating cooperation across divisions. New

E X H I B I T   8.8

Relationship between Environment and Structure

Environment	Structure	
	Mechanistic	**Organic**
Uncertain (Unstable)	Incorrect Fit: Mechanistic structure in uncertain environment Structure too tight	Correct Fit: Organic structure in uncertain environment
Certain (Stable)	Correct Fit: Mechanistic structure in certain environment	Incorrect Fit: Organic structure in certain environment Structure too loose

plants have included rooms for line employees' planning sessions. Professional and administrative staff have been trimmed back. Interdivisional teams now decide on projects over which an autonomous division once had authority. The new stress on lateral relationships has enabled P&G to respond to competitive pressures. One business team designed a cheaper push-up device for Secret deodorant. Ivory shampoo went into national distribution in 4 months instead of the usual 18.

Most Procter & Gamble employees are excited about the new mood. They have more authority, are able to participate in decisions, and can take initiative on desired changes. Managers are excited because they believe the new structural approach will help Procter & Gamble rebound from its earlier setbacks in an increasingly uncertain environment.[32]

Contingency Factor: Size and Life Cycle

The organization's **size** is its scope or magnitude and frequently is measured by number of employees. A large body of research findings has shown that large organizations are structured differently than small ones. Small organizations are informal, have little division of labor, few rules and regulations, ad hoc budgeting and performance systems, and small professional and clerical support staffs. Large organizations have an extensive division of labor, large professional staffs, extensive rules

size The organization's scope or magnitude, typically measured by number of employees.

E X H I B I T   8.9

Structural Characteristics during Organization Life Cycle Stages

	Birth Stage	**Youth Stage**	**Midlife Stage**	**Maturity Stage**
Size Bureaucracy	Small Nonbureaucratic	Medium Prebureaucratic	Large Bureaucratic	Very Large Very Bureaucratic
Structural characteristics:				
Division of labor	Overlapping tasks	Some departments	Many departments, well-defined tasks, organization chart	Extensive—small jobs, written job descriptions
Centralization	One-person rule	Top leaders rule	Decentralization to department heads	Enforced decentralization, top management overloaded
Formalization	No written rules	Few rules	Policy and procedures manuals	Extensive—most activities covered by written manuals
Administrative intensity	Secretary, no professional staff	Increasing clerical and maintenance, little professional staff	Increasing professional support staff	Large—multiple professional and clerical staff departments
Internal systems (information, budget, planning, performance)	Nonexistent	Crude budget and information system	Control systems in place—budget, performance, operational reports	Extensive—planning, financial, and personnel systems added
Lateral teams, task forces for coordination	None	Top leaders only	Some use of liaison and task forces	Frequent at lower levels to break down barriers of bureaucracy

Source: Based on Robert E. Quinn and Kim Cameron, "Organizational Life Cycles and Some Shifting Criteria of Effectiveness: Some Preliminary Evidence," *Management Science* 29 (1983), pp. 31–51; Richard L. Daft and Richard M. Steers, *Organizations: A Micro/Macro Approach* (Glenview, Ill.: Scott, Foresman, 1986).

and regulations, and internal systems for control, rewards, and innovation.[33]

Organizations evolve from small to large by going through stages of a life cycle. Throughout the **organization life cycle,** organizations follow predictable patterns through major developmental stages that are sequential in nature. This is similar to the product life cycle described in Chapter 5 except that it applies to the organization as a whole. Each stage involves changes in the range of organization activities and overall structure.[34] Of course, every organization progresses through the life cycle at its own pace, but most encounter the four stages defined in Exhibit 8.9: birth, youth, midlife, and maturity.

Birth Stage.   In the *birth stage*, the organization is created. The founder is an entrepreneur, who alone or with a handful of employees performs

organization life cycle   The organization's evolution through major developmental stages.

The organizational life cycle follows a predictable pattern through major development stages, and each stage has a different structure. In 1902, when Pepsi-Cola was in the birth stage, the bottling line was an inventive creation in the backroom of owner Caleb Bradham's pharmacy. Structure was informal because Bradham could personally control both production and sales in the pharmacy. Except for a period during World War I, Pepsi's growth has been phenomenal. Today, PepsiCo is a mature organization with an elaborate structure.

all tasks. The organization is very informal, and tasks are overlapping. There is no professional staff, no rules and regulations, and no internal systems for planning, rewards, or coordination. Decision authority is centralized with the owner. Apple Computer was in the birth stage when it was created by Steven Jobs and Stephen Wozniak in Wozniak's parents' garage. Jobs and Wozniak sold their own belongings to raise money to personally build 200 Apple computers. Kentucky Fried Chicken was in the birth stage when Colonel Harland Sanders was running a combination gas station/restaurant in Corbin, Kentucky, before the popularity of his restaurant began to spread.

Youth Stage. In the *youth stage,* the organization has more employees and a product that is succeeding in the marketplace. The organization is growing rapidly. The owner no longer has sole possession. A few trusted colleagues share in the decision making, although control is still relatively centralized. A division of labor is emerging, with some designation of task responsibility to newly created departments. Internal systems remain informal. A few formal rules and policies will appear, and there are few professional and administrative personnel. Apple Computer was in the youth stage during the years of rapid growth from 1978 to 1981, when the major product line was established and over 2,000 dealers signed on to sell Apple computers. Kentucky Fried Chicken was in the

SMALL BUSINESS

Can This Business Be Saved?

Dear Charlotte:
I own a small operation that manu-
factures hand-sewn goods to sell to
retail shops. I started the business
two years ago, doing all the cutting,
sewing and selling myself, and then
when business picked up, I hired two
friends to help out. The three of us
have worked well together—like a
family. Now I plan to hire three new people, and I realize my
old way of managing might not work as the company gets
bigger. I'm reluctant to lose the family atmosphere, though,
and certainly don't want to create a big bureaucracy. What
should I do?

—Resistant in Racine

Every owner who has bootstrapped her business into the marketplace on courage, creativity, and some help from colleagues tends to want to hang on to the "good old days." You forget, though, that new employees will be strangers to the energy and team spirit that was there when you created the company.

You have to create procedures and policies to help new employees understand your way of doing business or else your organization and fabric of the "corporate culture" you have started to create will soon be destroyed. Here are the basic building blocks of a well-run organization:

Policies: Your Organizational Magna Carta. Policies are broad statements outlining your business philosophy. They instruct employees on your standards for quality control, customer service, integrity and ethics, absenteeism, waste, and fraud. They guide managers in hiring, firing, supervising, or rewarding employees. By having written policies, you will be sure everyone in the company is marching to the same drummer without having to make all decisions yourself.

Organization Chart: Your Decision-Making Road Map. A graphic representation of the various positions in your company with indications of who reports to whom in the hierarchy is a valuable managerial tool. When you're hiring a new employee, for instance, looking at an organizational chart will help you keep the big picture in mind. Employees will know whom to go to for certain decisions and will have a better understanding of how departments relate to one another.

Job Descriptions: The Building Blocks of the Organization. Many small businesses resist this basic tool in personnel management because their employees do more than one job at a time. Even if people have several responsibilities, however, it's still important that they understand what their primary tasks are. Like organization charts, job descriptions also help you see the big picture. You'll be able to look at the tasks that need doing and make sure you hire people who can do them.

Reward and Appraisal Systems: The Glue of the Organization. Employees will be more motivated if they understand clearly *how well* they are expected to perform a job and by what standards they will be judged. No small business can afford to carry any deadwood. Your role is to set the standards and then check out the abilities, attitudes, and performance of employees early in their tenure.

Written Procedures: The Rules and Regulations. No matter how small your firm is, you should have a written manual that introduces the company to a new employee and explains policies concerning vacations, sick leave, absenteeism, pay periods, benefits, and so on.

By putting these systems in place, you'll be laying the foundations of a strong, profitable business.

Source: Charlotte Taylor, "Can This Business Be Saved?" *Working Woman*, December 1985, p. 40. Reprinted with permission from *Working Woman* magazine. Copyright © 1985 by HAL Publications.

youth stage when Colonel Sanders convinced over 400 franchises in the United States and Canada to use his original recipe. Although both organizations were growing rapidly, they were still being run in a very informal fashion.

Midlife Stage. By the *midlife stage*, the organization has prospered and grown quite large. At this point, the organization begins to look like a more formalized bureaucracy. An extensive division of labor appears, with statements of policies and responsibilities. Rules, regulations, and job descriptions are used to direct employee activities. Professional and clerical staff are hired to undertake specialized activities in support of manufacturing and marketing. Reward, budget, and accounting control systems are put in place. Top management decentralizes many responsibilities to functional departments, but flexibility and innovation may decline. Apple Computer is now in the midlife stage because it has adopted a host of procedures, internal systems, and staff departments to provide greater control over the organization. Kentucky Fried Chicken moved into the midlife stage when Colonel Sanders sold his company to John Y. Brown, who took the company through a national promotion and building campaign.

Maturity Stage.   In the *maturity stage,* the organization is large and mechanistic—indeed, the vertical structure often becomes too strong. Budgets, control systems, rules, policies, large staffs of engineering, accounting, and finance specialists, and a refined division of labor are in place. Decision making is centralized. At this point, the organization is in danger of stagnation. To offset the rigid vertical hierarchy, inspire innovation, and shrink barriers among departments, the organization may implement lateral structures. To regain flexibility and innovation, managers may decentralize and design teams, task forces, and liaison positions. This is especially true for mature organizations such as Procter & Gamble, Sears, Westinghouse, Deere, and General Motors, which have experienced major changes in the external environment and found that the mature vertical structure inhibited flexible responses.

Moving through the Life Cycle.   Organizations do not progress through the four life cycle stages in a logical, orderly fashion. Stages may lead or lag in a given organization. The transition from one stage to the next is difficult and often promotes crises. Employees who were present at the organization's birth often long for the informal atmosphere and resist the formalized procedures, departmentalization, and staff departments required in maturing organizations. Organizations that prematurely emphasize a rigid vertical structure or that stay informal during later stages of the life cycle will have the wrong structure for their situation. Performance will suffer. The widely reported problems at People's Express occurred because the firm never grew up. Despite its being the fifth largest airline, top management ran it informally without a strong vertical structure. The structure fit neither People's Express' size nor life cycle stage.

Contingency Factor: Production Technology

Technology includes the knowledge, tools, techniques, and activities used to transform organizational inputs into outputs.[35] Technology includes machinery, employee skills, and work procedures. A useful way to think about technology is as "work flow." The production work flow is the organization's major task, whether it be to produce steel castings, television programs, or computer software.

technology The knowledge, tools, techniques, and activities used to transform the organization's inputs into outputs.

Production technology is significant because it has direct influence on the organization structure. Structure must be designed to fit the technology as well as to accommodate the external environment and organization size. Technologies vary between manufacturing and service organizations. In the following paragraphs, we will discuss each characteristic of technology and the structure that best fits it.

Manufacturing Technology.   Before the advent of today's large, sophisticated manufacturing organizations, most products were produced by craftspeople. One or more of these performed al the tasks needed for producing a product such as a musical instrument, kitchenware, or a pair of shoes. With the introduction of machine-based manufacturing technologies, craftspeople played an increasingly smaller role in the production process. Although craftspeople still play a role in certain types of manufacturing, many manufacturing technologies are dominated by machines.

The most influential research into the relationship between manufacturing technology and organization structure was conducted by Joan Woodward, a British industrial sociologist.[36] She gathered data from 100 British firms to determine whether basic structural characteristics, such as administrative intensity, span of control, centralization, and formalization, were different across firms. She found that manufacturing firms could be categorized according to three basic types of work flow technology:

small batch production A type of technology that involves the production of goods in batches of one or a few products designed to customer specification.

1. *Small batch and unit production.* **Small batch production** firms produce goods in batches of one or a few products designed to customer specification. Each customer orders a unique product. This technology also is used to make large, one-of-a-kind products, such as computer-controlled machines. Small batch manufacturing is close to traditional craftsmanship, because human beings are a large part of the process; they run machines to make the product. Examples of small batch manufacturing include custom clothing, special-order machine tools, space capsules, satellites, and submarines.

mass production A type of technology characterized by the production of a large volume of products with the same specifications.

2. *Large batch and mass production.* **Mass production** technology is distinguished by standardized production runs. A large volume of products are produced, and all customers receive the same product. Standard products go into inventory for sale as customers need them. This technology makes greater use of machines than does small batch production. Machines are designed to do most of the physical work, and employees complement the machinery. Examples of mass production are automobile assembly lines and the large batch techniques used to produce Macintosh computers, tobacco products, and textiles.

continuous process production A type of technology involving mechanization of the entire work flow and nonstop production.

3. *Continuous process production.* In **continuous process production,** the entire work flow is mechanized. This is the most sophisticated and complex form of production technology. Because the process runs continuously, there is no starting and stopping. Human operators are not part of the production process, because

Expert clay modelers develop a realistic representation of a new-car proposal. This task is a craft that would be classified as small batch production. Experts make one-of-a-kind products that rely heavily on human knowledge and skill versus machines. Small batch production requires a different organization structure from those of machine-based technologies.

machinery does all of the work. Human operators simply read dials, fix machines that break down, and manage the production process. Examples of continuous process technologies are chemical plants, distilleries, petroleum refineries, and nuclear power plants.

The difference among the three manufacturing technologies is called technical complexity. **Technical complexity** means that machines are more complex and perform more of the work. With a complex work flow technology, employees are hardly needed except to monitor the machines.

technical complexity The degree to which machinery is involved in the production process to the exclusion of people.

The structural characteristics associated with each type of manufacturing technology are illustrated in Exhibit 8.10. Note that formalization and centralization increase as technological complexity increases. More sophisticated machinery requires centralized decision making and well-defined rules and procedures. The administrative ratio and the percentage of indirect labor required also increase with technological complexity. Since the production process is nonroutine, closer supervision is needed. More indirect labor in the form of maintenance people is required because of the machinery's complexity; thus, the indirect–direct labor ratio is high. Span of control for first-line supervisors is greatest for mass production. On an assembly line, jobs are so routinized that a supervisor can handle an average of 48 employees. The number of employees per supervisor in small batch and continuous process production is lower because closer supervision is needed.

Communications also vary by technology. Written communications tend to be stressed in mass production, which is consistent with formalization and standardization. Skilled workers in small batch and continuous process production communicate verbally and in a horizontal direc-

Appleton Papers, a division of BATUS Inc., is the world's largest producer of carbonless copy paper. Appleton has added the latest technology to its Harrisburg, Pennsylvania, plant to meet the increasing demand for its paper products. This machine, which is monitored and controlled by human operators, represents a high level of technical complexity because it performs all work tasks. This paper mill illustrates the continuous process production technology described by Joan Woodward.

service technology Technology characterized by intangible outputs and direct contact between employees and customers.

routine service technology Service technology in which work can be broken down into explicit steps and employees can follow objective procedures for serving customers and solving problems.

tion more than do workers in mass production. Overall, small batch and continuous process firms have organic structures and mass production firms have mechanistic structures.

The important conclusion about manufacturing technology was described by Woodward as follows: "Different technologies impose different kinds of demands on individuals and organizations, and these demands have to be met through an appropriate structure."[37] Woodward found that the relationship between structure and technology was directly related to company performance. Low performing firms tended to deviate from the preferred structural form, often adopting a structure appropriate for another type of technology. High performing organizations had characteristics very similar to those listed in Exhibit 8.10.

Service Technology.   Service organizations are becoming increasingly important in North America. Since 1982, more employees have been employed in service organizations than in manufacturing organizations. Thus, new research has been undertaken to understand the structural characteristics of service organizations. **Service technology** can be defined as follows:

1. *Intangibility.* The output of a service firm is intangible. Services are perishable and, unlike physical products, cannot be stored in inventory. The service is either consumed immediately or lost forever. Manufactured products are produced at one point in time and can be stored until sold at another time.
2. *Direct contact with customers.* Customers and employees interact directly to provide and purchase the service. Production and consumption are simultaneous. Service firm employees have direct contact with customers. In a manufacturing firm, technical employees are separated from customers, and hence no direct interactions occur.[38]

Service organizations work on people; manufacturing organizations work on things. Examples of service firms include consulting companies, law firms, brokerage houses, airlines, hotels, advertising firms, public relations, amusement parks, and educational organizations. Service technology also characterizes many departments in large corporations, even manufacturing firms. In a manufacturing organization such as Ford Motor Company, the legal, personnel, finance, and market research departments provide services. Thus, the structure and design of these departments reflect its own service technology rather than the manufacturing plant's technology. Service technology concepts therefore can be used to structure both service organizations and the many large service departments within manufacturing organizations.

A useful way of characterizing service technology is the extent to which it is routine versus nonroutine.[39] The routine-nonroutine distinction can be used to describe differences across organizational technologies as well as those among various departments within a single organization. A **routine service technology** means that the work can be reduced to a series of explicit steps and employees can follow an objective procedure for serving customers and solving problems. The number of prob-

E X H I B I T   8.10

**Relationship between Manufacturing Technology
and Organization Structure**

	Manufacturing Technology		
	Small Batch	**Mass Production**	**Continuous Process**
Technical complexity of production technology	Low	Medium	High
Structural characteristics:			
Formalization	Low	High	Low
Centralization	Low	High	Low
Top administrator ratio	Low	Medium	High
Indirect–direct labor ratio	1/9	1/4	1/1
Supervisor span of control	23	48	15
Communication:			
Written (vertical)	Low	High	Low
Verbal (lateral)	High	Low	High
Overall structure	Organic	Mechanistic	Organic

Source: Based on Joan Woodward, *Industrial Organizations: Theory and Practice* (London: Oxford University Press, 1965).

lems is low. There is little task variety because the service is provided in a repetitious manner. Day-to-day job requirements are similar, such as those for sales clerks in a discount store. A **nonroutine service technology** means that new problems are encountered every day and variety is high. Moreover, when problems arise there is no specific procedure for telling people what to do. Employees must rely on education, experience, and trial and error, such as lawyers in a defense trial.

In service organizations, routine technologies are used when services are not labor intensive because physical facilities standardize the services. Examples of routine services are sanitation, hotels, airline transportation, and recreation. Nonroutine services typically are labor intensive and provided entirely by individuals. For example, a tax accountant provides a complete tax service for a customer. Nonroutine services include doctors, lawyers, architects, and accountants.[40]

Selected characteristics of organization structure and relationships with service technologies are illustrated in Exhibit 8.11. The nonroutine, people-oriented services tend to be more organic.[41] They are informal and decentralized. These services also are dispersed; hence, each firm is typically small, as in the case of local video stores or doctors' offices. Services cannot be concentrated in a single location because they must be located close to geographically dispersed customers. Routine services have a smaller people component. Organizations such as hotels, banks, and auto repair facilities can be designed with a more mechanistic struc-

nonroutine service technology Service technology in which there are no specific procedures for directing employees, problem situations are varied, and employees must rely on personal resources for problem solving.

EXHIBIT   8.11

Relationship between Service Technology and Organization Structure

	Service Technology	
	Routine	Nonroutine
Labor intensity and complexity of service	Low	High
Structural characteristics:		
Division of labor	High	Low
Formalization	High	Low
Centralization	High	Low
Administrative intensity	Low	Moderate
Span of control	High	Moderate
Employee skill and training	Low	High
Geographical dispersion	High	Low
Overall structure	Mechanistic	Organic

ture. Formalization and division of labor are greater, and decision making can be centralized. As a general pattern, however, even routine service firms have greater variety in the production process than do assembly line manufacturing technologies, and structures tend to be more organic.

An example of how structure should fit technology in a more routine service firm is Marriott Corporation.

Marriott Corporation

Marriott Corporation is now the nation's largest hotel operator, and the president, Bill Marriott, plans to make it even bigger. Marriott's success has come from two strategies: Put hotels where the customers are, and provide excellent service. Putting hotels where the customers are means building hotels downtown and at airports. Convention centers, such as Atlantic City, are another target. Marriott also searches for new niches. The Courtyard is a new type of garden apartment hotel aimed at the moderate-priced segment of the market. Courtyards will be scattered around major metropolitan areas.

At Marriott, the hotel itself is the main service, and a mind-boggling system is used to make the right impression every time. Top managers make no apologies for the tightly centralized system of policies, procedures, and controls for operational details. Chambermaids have 66 things to do in cleaning a room, from

Services are intangible and require direct contact with customers. For example, rides on a roller coaster, like other services, are perishable and cannot be stored in inventory. When a seat goes empty, managers lose forever the opportunity to sell the seat for that ride. A roller coaster is considered a routine service technology because the extensive physical facilities standardize work activities.

dusting the tops of pictures (number 7) to keeping the telephone book and Bibles in a neat condition (number 37). Bill Marriott says, "The more the system works like the Army, the better." The cooks have 6,000 recipes available to them, and they are not allowed to deviate. One rule for chefs says, "Deviations from the standard written specifications may not be made without prior approval and written consent of the vice president of food and beverages."

Marriott Corporation plans to build 9,000 new rooms a year. It routinizes the service as much as possible and builds luxury into the physical structure to insure that guests are treated the same way every time. Rated as one of the five best-managed companies in 1984, Bill Marriott and four executive vice-presidents spend half the year on the road visiting company facilities. The close, personal supervision and careful reading of customer suggestions help Bill Marriott give business travelers the service they expect and deserve.[42]

SUMMARY

This chapter introduced a number of important organizing concepts. Vertical structure for control normally is implemented first and lateral structural devices added to provide coordination across departments. Characteristics of vertical structure include work specialization, chain of command, span of management, departmentalization, centralization and decentralization, line and staff, administrative intensity, and formalization. Lateral structure includes mechanisms designed to achieve coordination across departments, such as information systems, liaison roles, task forces, teams, and integrating managers.

Too much vertical structure can cause problems. Thus, managers should try to achieve the right balance between vertical and lateral organizing. Contingency factors of the environment, size and life cycle, and production technology influence the correct structural balance. When environmental uncertainty is high, lateral relationships are important and the organization should have an organic structure. For manufacturing firms, small batch and continuous process technologies tend to be structured organically, while a mechanistic structure is appropriate for mass production. Service technologies are people oriented, but services such as hotels and transportation are considered routine and can be controlled with a mechanistic structure. People-intensive services, such as universities and medical clinics, tend to be more organically structured.

Finally, as organizations increase in size, they require greater vertical control. Organizations in the birth and youth stages typically are loosely structured. In the midlife stage, a strong vertical structure emerges. In a mature organization the vertical structure may be too strong, necessitating the installation of teams, task forces, and other lateral devices to achieve greater cooperation across departments.

Management Solution

The management problem posed at the beginning of this chapter addressed what managers at Lotus Development Corporation should do about the loss of key people who disliked the new emphasis on rules and tighter control. Lotus started out as a small, informal organization, but its success caused it to grow and move to a new life cycle stage. Moving from one stage to the next is not easy, and employees will miss the informal atmosphere. For the organization to continue to prosper, however, structural changes are needed. As chairman Kapor noted, "People here pine for the good old days, but we're growing up, and we have to grow up organizationally."[43] A stronger top-down emphasis, with new control systems, will provide the control needed to hold a larger organization together.

Equally important, other contingency factors suggest that Lotus should not become overstructured and overmanaged from the top. The software and computer environments are competitive and changing rapidly. An uncertain environment requires a flexible organization and an organic structure. Moreover, software is not a mass production technology; it requires creative people and research and development. Thus, Lotus needs additional vertical structure, but too much could be a mistake. Top managers should add vertical structure in small amounts until they get to the right level. The use of teams, task forces, and other lateral devices will be important to insure that Lotus retains horizontal communication to permit departments to work as a coordinated whole.

DISCUSSION QUESTIONS

1. What problems can arise when too much emphasis is given to vertical structure? How do these problems come about?
2. What are the three major elements in the organizing process? Could these steps overlap? Occur in a different order?
3. Contrast centralization with span of management. Would you expect these characteristics to be related in organizations? Why?
4. What is the difference between a liaison role and an integrating manager? Which would be more effective in achieving coordination?
5. Some observers note that organizations have been making greater use of teams and task forces in recent years. What factors might account for this trend?

6. Discuss why an organization in an uncertain environment requires more lateral relationships than one in a certain environment.

7. To what extent does a small business need a strong vertical structure, including a chain of command, formalized rules and procedures, and clerical and professional support staff?

8. Explain the difference between assembly line and continuous process production. How do these two technologies influence structural characteristics such as indirect–direct labor ratio and span of control?

9. What is the difference between manufacturing and service technology? How would you classify a university, a local discount store, a nursery school? How would you expect the structure of a service organization to differ from that of a manufacturing organization?

10. New manufacturing technologies, called *flexible manufacturing systems*, have been developed to combine elements of both small batch and mass production. These technologies can mass produce products, but variations can be programmed to create customized products. What effect might this new form of technology have on organization structure?

CASES FOR ANALYSIS

REPUBLIC NATIONAL BANK

Republic National Bank was located in a well-to-do suburb in southern California. The population grew rapidly to 250,000, and growth stabilized by the mid-1980s.

The bank began operations in 1958 under the guidance of its founder and president, Richard Johnson. After only five years, deposits grew to $15 million. During those years, the community grew rapidly and the bank grew with it. The organization structure was informal. The bank had no organization chart despite having some thirty employees and two branches. Richard Johnson believed in keeping things informal so that employees could enjoy a family atmosphere.

In 1963, the bank was purchased by Ted White. White immediately imposed a traditional management structure. He asked the personnel director to write job descriptions for all positions and to develop an up-to-date organization chart. He stressed centralized decision making and standard procedures. The two branches and the main bank were urged to offer the same services despite their proximity to different customer groups. One branch was in an ethnic community, the other was near a junior college, and the main branch was in a residential area. Vertical communication and "following the rules" were deemed safe, responsible management approaches for a community bank.

This approach worked successfully for 15 years, but major changes in the late 1970s and early 1980s caused problems within the bank. The bank's assets had grown to over $500 million. Management trainees had been hired from universities and promoted to managerial positions. The new managers began to propose changes. One manager suggested that the bank establish an advisory board to involve residents in bank decisions and provide bank officials with good information about community needs. Another manager urged the creation of several committees to study the effects of government regulation. One committee could study asset/liability management to help the bank make the transition to variable-rate loans and to explore new investment opportunities. Another could work on cost control and the use of new electronic technology to reduce the cost of fund transfers. Yet another could investigate service pricing and the generation of noninterest income, including fees for returned checks, overdrafts, and checking account services.

Ted White resisted these changes. He did not want to create task forces that would decentralize decision making to a lower level. White believed that banks had to have tight control to insure depositors' safety. Within a year, three of the new managers quit in frustration. White also noticed that the bank was not growing and even had lost market share to competitors, some of which were newly created banks run in an informal fashion.

Questions

1. Was it appropriate to develop a stronger vertical structure as the bank grew larger?
2. What are the advantages and disadvantages of implementing lateral relationships in the form of task forces? Do you feel the bank should place greater emphasis on lateral relationships? Why or why not?
3. Would you characterize Republic National Bank's structure as organic or mechanistic? What is the correct structure for the bank's contingency factors of technology, environment, and size/life cycle?

Source: Based on Richard L. Daft and Richard M. Steers, *Organizations: A Micro/Macro Approach* (Glenview, Ill.: Scott, Foresman and Company, 1986), 314–316.

MALARD MANUFACTURING COMPANY

Malard Manufacturing Company produces control valves that regulate flows through natural gas pipelines. Malard has approximately 1,400 employees and has successfully produced a standard line of control valves that are price competitive in the industry. However, whenever the production of a new control valve is required, problems arise. Developments in electronics, metallurgy, and flow control theory required the introduction of new products every year or two. These new products have been associated with interdepartmental conflict and disagreement.

Consider the CV305. As usual, the research and development group developed the basic design and the engineering department converted the designs into a prototype control valve. Now the materials department must acquire parts for the prototype and make plans for obtaining parts needed for production runs. The production department is to manufacture and assemble the product, and marketing is responsible for sales.

Department heads feel that work on the CV305 should be done simultaneously instead of sequentially. Marketing wants to provide input to research and development so that the design will meet customer needs. Production insists that the design fit machine limitations and be cost efficient to manufacture—indeed, it wants to speed up development of the final plans so that it can acquire tooling and be ready for standard production. Engineering, on the other hand, wants to slow down development to insure that specifications are correct and have been thoroughly tested.

All of these controversies with the CV305 exist right now. Department managers are frustrated and becoming uncommunicative. The R&D and engineering departments are keeping their developmental plans secret, causing frustration for the other departments. Moreover, several department managers are new and inexperienced in new-product development. Mr. Crandell, the executive vice-president, likes to keep tight control over the organization. Department managers must check with him before making major decisions. However, with the CV305 he has been unable to keep things running smoothly. The span of control is so large that Crandell has no time to personally shepherd the CV305 through the system.

On November 1, Crandell received a memo from the marketing department head. It said, in part,

The CV305 must go to market immediately. This is urgent. It is needed now because it provides the precision control our competitors' products already have. Three of our salesmen reported that loyal customers are about to place orders with competitors. We can keep this business if we have the CV305 ready for production in 30 days.

Questions

1. What is the balance between vertical and lateral structure in Malard Manufacturing? Is it appropriate that department managers always turn to the executive vice-president for help rather than to one another?
2. If you were Mr. Crandell, how would you resolve this problem? What could you do to facilitate production of the CV305 over the next 30 days?
3. What structural changes would you recommend to prevent these problems in future new-product developments? Would a smaller span of control help? An integrating manager with responsibility for coordinating the CV305? A task force?

Using Structural Design to Achieve Strategic Objectives

Chapter Outline

Approaches to Structural Design

Structural Impact on Employees

Functional Approach to Structure

Advantages and Disadvantages

Functional Approach with Lateral Relationships

Advantages and Disadvantages

Divisional Approach to Structure

Geographically and Customer-Based Divisions
Advantages and Disadvantages

Hybrid Approach to Structure

Advantages and Disadvantages

Matrix Approach to Structure

Key Relationships
Advantages and Disadvantages

Using Structural Approaches for Attaining Strategic Objectives

Mintzberg's Typology: Integrating Structure and Contingency Factors

Simple Structure
Machine Bureaucracy
Professional Bureaucracy
Divisionalized Form
Adhocracy

Learning Objectives

After studying this chapter, you should be able to:

- Explain why departmental grouping impacts on employee goals and motivation.

- Explain the functional approach to structure.

- Explain the functional approach with lateral relationships.

- Explain the divisional approach to structure.

- Explain the hybrid approach to structure.

- Explain the matrix approach to structure and its advantages and disadvantages compared to other structures.

- Describe how each type of structure can be used to achieve the organization's strategic objectives.

- Describe Mintzberg's five organizational forms and the configuration of organizational elements associated with each.

Management Problem

Xerox Corporation's fortunes began to sour in the mid-1970s. Xerox had enjoyed a virtual monopoly on the copier market until the Federal Trade Commission charged Xerox with illegal monopolization. The Japanese were aggressively developing and marketing copiers that were cheaper and more reliable, and International Business Machines had jumped into the copier business. Xerox's share of the market plunged from 82 to 35 percent. By 1980, Xerox was struggling to implement a new strategy that would produce more types of copiers at lower cost and at greater speed. Xerox believed in a centralized, functional organization structure despite having introduced only three new copier products in the previous ten years. But the functional structure that had been successful when Xerox was dominant was no longer working. A once great company was sinking.[1]

If you were the CEO of Xerox, how would you respond? How would you redesign structure to harness organizational resources so as to speed up product development and regain market share?

Managers in organizations like Xerox frequently must rethink structure and may reorganize to meet new conditions in the environment, production technology, or size. In Chapter 8 we examined the fundamental characteristics of structure that apply to all organizations. In this chapter we focus more precisely on structure as a tool, especially on how managers can use the concepts of departmentalization, chain of command, and lateral relationships to achieve specific goals. In recent years many corporations, including American Express, Apple, IBM, Amex Corporation, and Bausch & Lomb, have realigned departmental groupings, chains of command, and teams and task forces to attain new strategic goals. Structure is a very powerful tool for reaching strategic goals, and a strategy's success often is determined by its fit with organization structure. By the end of this chapter, the problem at Xerox will be readily identifiable as a mismatch of structure and strategy. You will understand the different approaches to structure and how Xerox can change its structure to regain competitiveness.

APPROACHES TO STRUCTURAL DESIGN

There are five primary approaches to structural design that reflect differences in departmentalization, chain of command, and lateral relationships. A brief illustration and comparison of the five structural alternatives are given in Exhibit 9.1.

1. *Functional approach.* People are grouped together in departments by common skills and work activities, such as engineering, maintenance, and accounting employees. This is the most common form of structure, and some aspect of it exists in most organizations.
2. *Functional approach with lateral relationships.* Employees are grouped together by common skills as in the functional structure, but an overlay of lateral teams, task forces, and liaison personnel is formally established to provide high-quality coordination across departments.
3. *Divisional approach.* Departments are grouped together into separate, self-contained divisions based on a common product, program, or geographical region. Diverse skills needed to produce a product or program rather than similar skills are the basis of departmentalization. This structure is also referred to as *product* or *program structure.*
4. *Hybrid approach.* This is a mix of functional and divisional structures. In some parts of the organization, all employees with similar skills and tasks are grouped together into a single department. Other parts are divisionalized so as to combine diverse skills for producing a single product or program.
5. *Matrix approach.* Functional and divisional chains of command are implemented simultaneously and overlay one another in the same departments. Two chains of command exist, and some employees report to two bosses.

Each approach to structure serves a distinct purpose for the organization, and each has advantages and disadvantages. The basic difference among structures is the way in which employees are departmentalized and to whom they report. The simple differences in structure illustrated in Exhibit 9.1 have major consequences for employee goals and motivation.

E X H I B I T   9.1

Five Approaches to Structural Design

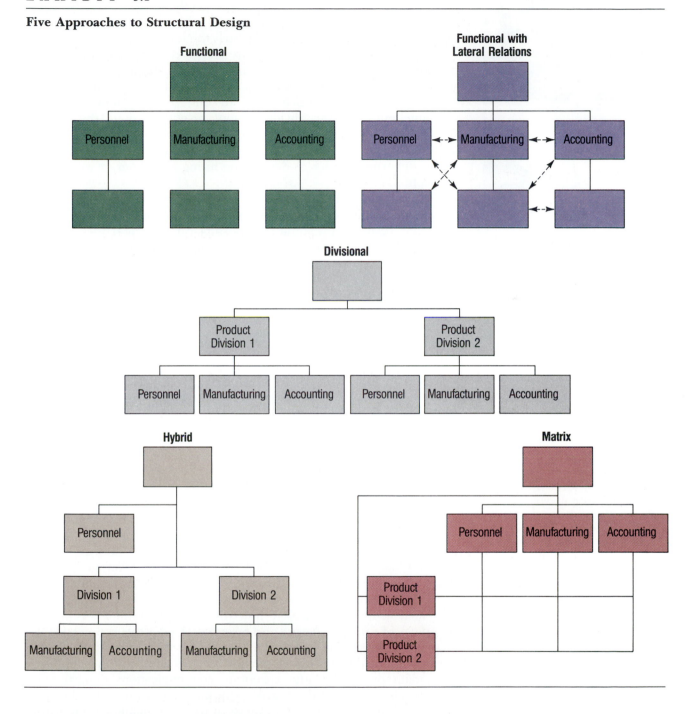

Structural Impact on Employees

Why do structures influence employee goals and motivation? Departmentalization has a powerful impact on employees because it defines the group to which they belong. Employees within a defined de-

Harris Corporation produces information processing, communication, and microelectronics products. Harris is one of the 10 largest producers of integrated circuits in the United States. Here a few of the company's 25,000 employees work in a state-of-the-art clean room where integrated circuits are wire bonded. The clean room reflects the functional approach to structure, with all of its positions located together as one function on the organization chart.

functional structure An organizational structure in which positions are grouped into departments based on similar skills, expertise, and resource use.

partment or group have a common supervisor, share budget resources with which to accomplish their task, are jointly responsible for departmental performance, and tend to identify and collaborate with one another.[2] Departmentalization thus defines the unity of effort for groups. For example, in a functional structure employees who perform personnel tasks are all located in one personnel department. They perform similar tasks, follow the same chain of command, and are motivated to achieve personnel department goals. In contrast, in a product structure personnel employees are divided among several divisions, resulting in smaller personnel groups. Their primary motivation is to achieve the goals of the division rather than those typically associated with the personnel department, such as developing hiring guidelines or writing job descriptions.

Although departmentalization creates a strong unity within groups, it makes coordination across groups more difficult. Thus, lateral relationships may be needed. Lateral relationships can engender the cooperation needed to reach goals for the organization as a whole. As discussed in Chapter 8, the organization tries to find the right balance between vertical and lateral structures to achieve organizational goals. The correct structure encourages communication and joint working relationships among those sets of employees needed to perform the organization's tasks.

Let's now turn to each of the five structural designs and examine their implications for managers.[3]

FUNCTIONAL APPROACH TO STRUCTURE

Functional structure is the grouping of positions into departments based on similar skills, expertise, and resource use. A functional structure can be thought of as departmentalization by organizational resources, because each type of functional activity—personnel, engineering, manufacturing—represents specific resources for performing the organization's task. People and facilities representing a common organizational resource are grouped together into a single department.

An example of a functional structure for an insurance company is presented in Exhibit 9.2. Note how the major departments represent groupings of similar expertise and resources. Under the vice-president–finance are the people responsible for corporate taxes and internal audits. Under the director of information services are the information systems, data processing, and corporate communications departments. Agencies, brokerage, and actuarial departments all exist under the marketing vice-president. Note that no distinctions are made among insurance products. This insurance company handles annuities, life insurance, health insurance, pensions, and group insurance. The tasks relevant to all of these products are handled within each functional de-

EXHIBIT 9.2

Functional Structure for an Insurance Company

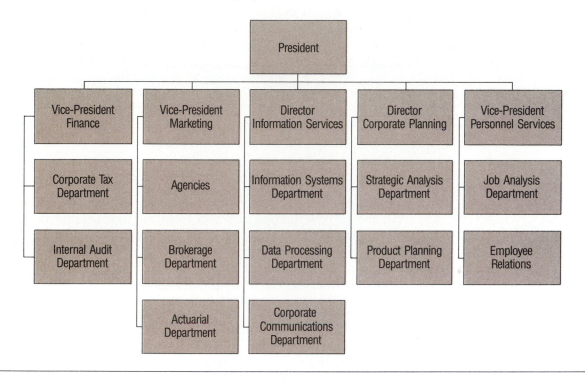

partment. The marketing vice-president is concerned with agents that sell all insurance products, the data processing department handles the data processing for all products, and the actuarial department calculates the statistical tables for all products. This insurance company has a well-defined functional structure.

Advantages and Disadvantages

Grouping employees into departments based on similar skills has many advantages for an organization. Employees who perform a common task are grouped together so as to permit economies of scale and efficient resource use. In the life insurance company in Exhibit 9.2, all data processing people work in the data processing department. They handle data processing for all types of policies and acquire the expertise for handling almost any problem within a single, large department. The larger functional departments enhance the development of in-depth skills because people work on a variety of problems and are associated with other experts. Career progress is based on functional expertise; thus, employees are motivated to develop their skills. Managers and employees are compatible because of similar training and expertise.

E X H I B I T   9.3

Advantages and Disadvantages of Functional Structure

Advantages

- Efficient use of resources, economies of scale
- In-depth skill specialization and development
- Career progress within functional departments
- Top manager direction and control
- Excellent coordination within functions
- High-quality technical problem solving

Disadvantages

- Poor communication across functional departments
- Slow response to external changes, lagging innovation
- Decisions concentrated at top of hierarchy, creating delay
- Responsibility for problems difficult to pinpoint
- Limited view of organizational goals by employees
- Limited general management training for employees

The functional structure also offers a way to centralize decision making and provide unified direction from the top, because the chain of command converges at the top of the organization. Sometimes the functional structure is also associated with wider spans of control because of large departments and common expertise. Communication and coordination among employees within each department are excellent. Finally, functional structure promotes high-quality technical problem solving. The pool of well-trained experts, motivated toward functional expertise, gives the company an important resource, especially those that work with sophisticated technology.

The disadvantages of functional structure reflect the barriers that exist across departments and a slow response to environmental changes. Because people are separated into distinct departments, communication and coordination across functions are often poor. Poor coordination means a slow response to environmental changes, because innovation and change require involvement of several departments. Since the chains of command are separate beneath the top of the organization, decisions involving more than one department may pile up at the top of the organization and be delayed. The functional structure also stresses work specialization and division of labor, which may produce routine, nonmotivating employee tasks.

The functional structure also creates management problems, such as difficulty in pinpointing problems within departments. In the case of the insurance company in Exhibit 9.2, each function works on all products and performs only a part of the task for any product line. Hence, if one life insurance product is not performing well, there is no specific department or group that bears responsibility. In addition, employees tend to focus on the attainment of departmental goals, often to the exclusion of organizational goals. They see only their respective tasks and not the big picture. Because of this narrow task specialization, employees are trained to become experts in their fields and not to manage and coordinate diverse departments. Thus, they fail to become groomed for top management and general management positions.

The advantages and disadvantages of functional structure are summarized in Exhibit 9.3.

FUNCTIONAL APPROACH WITH LATERAL RELATIONSHIPS

Many companies created in the last ten years have adopted a functional structure, but managers have also implemented a lateral team concept. The vertical structure in these organizations would be similar to the functional structure for the insurance company in Exhibit 9.2. However, in a **functional structure with lateral relationships,** top managers deliberately create a series of teams and task forces that include members from several departments. The organization is committed to a functional structure on paper, but the team concept creates a very different organization style.

New, computer-based companies such as Lanier Technology Corporation, Compaq Computer Corporation, Quantum Corporation, and AST Research often seem obsessed with creating a team atmosphere.[4] At Compaq, lateral groups are called "smart teams," which represent an interdisciplinary approach to management. This structural approach assumes that people from the treasurer's office and engineering have ideas to contribute to decisions about marketing and manufacturing. The Deskpro 286 was created by a smart team in response to IBM's super PC. Kevin Ellington, who was in charge of the project, created his own smart team, drawing from every department in the company.[5] Team members worked in parallel: Marketing was positioning the Deskpro in the marketplace, finance was arranging to pay for it, and

functional structure with lateral relationships An organizational structure in which teams and task forces made up of members from several departments are created.

This "Product Business Team" considers a new, cost-saving production technique. General Motors' Harrison Radiator Division incorporates teams and committees as part of its structure. This lateral relations approach achieves cooperation across functional departments. In addition to Product Business Teams, Harrison uses "Standing Committees" at the top and middle management levels, and "Employee Involvement Teams" of hourly workers, first line supervisors, and engineers who work together on product improvements and quality. Harrison executives believe that this structural approach creates a web of relationships that encourages people to work in concert to solve problems and achieve objectives.

manufacturing was figuring out how to produce it. Team members communicated constantly. Within six months, Compaq was shipping its first models—indeed, it beat IBM to the punch because IBM was still suffering production problems. Ellington offers three reasons for the Deskpro 286's success: "The first, second, and third reason was teamwork."[6]

Some organizations that traditionally have stressed the functional structure are adopting the team concept. Ortho-Kinetics, which produces lift chairs and mobility vehicles for the handicapped, was struggling to correct a shipping problem with service parts. It normally took 3 days to ship parts, but customers needed them within 24 hours. The president decided to create a task force. Within a month, the task force had 90 percent of the parts going out in 24 hours, compared to 25 percent previously. In the third month, 100 percent of parts were going out within 24 hours. This type of success created the groundwork for using teams and task forces for other problems.[7]

Even old-line insurance companies can use lateral relationships. An insurance policy normally moves from one work station to the next. Federal Kemper Life Assurance Company decided to group employees from different units into teams, with each team handling several policy-issuing functions. Team members collaborated with one another, and productivity increased.[8]

The adoption of the team concept at Ford Motor Company had striking results.

Ford Motor Company

Ford's—indeed, the North American auto industry's—biggest success in years has been the Ford Taurus and its sister, the Mercury Sable. Ford can't produce cars fast enough to meet demand, and the new models have drawn rave reviews.

How did Ford pull it off? For one thing, it abandoned its traditional organization structure and created a group called Team Taurus. Under the old structure, product planners would come up with a general concept, pass it on to a design department, which passed it on to engineering for developing specifications, which passed it to manufacturing. Each department worked in isolation. Under the Team Taurus concept, representatives from each department worked together as a group. Members took joint responsibility for the vehicle and solved problems early on. Manufacturing suggested productivity-enhancing changes that could be built into the initial design. With the advice of assembly line workers, designers were able to reduce the number of body panels and use bolts with the same head size to speed production and increase quality. They even consulted suppliers during this stage and signed them to long-term contracts.

The Taurus and Sable were huge gambles, but the team concept turned it into an enormous payoff. The team principle worked so well that Ford decided to apply it throughout the company. The head of Team Taurus was promoted to vice-president and given the job of implementing the team concept throughout the company.[9]

Advantages and Disadvantages

Imposing team relationships on a functional structure helps overcome shortcomings in the functional top-down approach to organizing. The organization is able to retain some advantages of a functional structure, such as economies of scale in departments, in-depth training and expertise, and direction from the top while gaining the benefits of lateral relationships. The team concept breaks down barriers across departments. Team members know one another's problems and will compromise rather than blindly pursue their own goals. The team concept also allows the organization to more quickly adapt to environmental change and facilitates decision making because decisions need not go to the top of the hierarchy for approval. Another big advantage is the morale boost. Employees are enthusiastic about their involvement in bigger projects rather than narrow departmental tasks. Jobs are enriched.

But this type of structure has disadvantages. Employees may be enthusiastic about team participation, but they may also experience conflicts and dual loyalties. The team may make different demands on members than their department managers, and members who participate in more than one team must resolve these conflicts. A large amount of time is devoted to meetings, thus increasing overhead costs. Unless the organization truly needs teams in order to coordinate complex projects and adapt to the environment, it will lose production efficiency. Finally, the team approach results in some decentralization. Senior department managers who traditionally made decisions may feel left out if a lower-level team moves ahead on its own. They may sense a loss of power and status, which the organization must deal with.

The advantages and disadvantages of the functional structure with lateral relationships are summarized in Exhibit 9.4.

E X H I B I T   9.4

Advantages and Disadvantages of Functional Structure with Lateral Relationships

Advantages
- Many advantages of functional structure
- Reduced barriers among departments, greater compromise
- Less response time, quicker decisions
- Better morale, enthusiasm from employee involvement

Disadvantages
- Dual loyalties and conflict
- Time and resources spent on meetings
- Unplanned decentralization

EXHIBIT   9.5
_____

Functional versus Divisional Structures

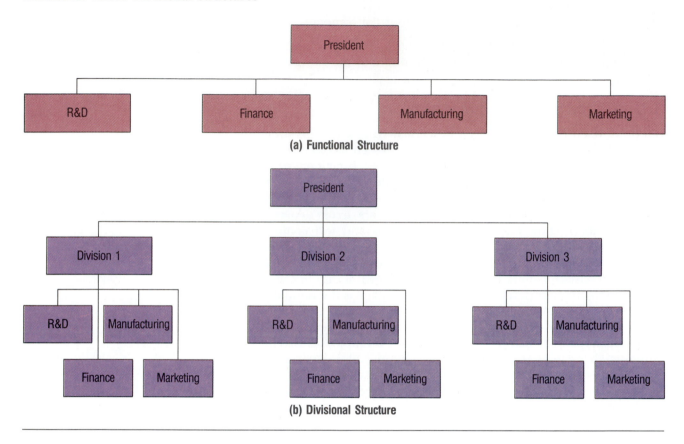

(a) Functional Structure

(b) Divisional Structure
_____

DIVISIONAL APPROACH TO STRUCTURE

divisional structure An organizational structure in which departments are grouped based on similar organizational outputs.

The **divisional structure** occurs when departments are grouped together based on organizational outputs. This is in contrast to the functional approach, in which people are grouped by common skills and resources. The difference between functional and divisional structure is illustrated in Exhibit 9.5. In the divisional structure, divisions are created as self-contained units for producing a single product. Each functional department resource needed to produce the product is assigned to one division. For example, in a functional structure, all engineers are grouped together and work on all products. In a divisional structure, separate engineering departments are established within each division. Each department is smaller and focuses on a single product line. Departments are duplicated across product lines.

The divisional structure is sometimes called a *product structure, program structure,* or *self-contained unit structure.* Each of these terms means essentially the same thing: Diverse departments are brought together to produce a single organizational output, whether it be a product, a program, or service to a single customer. In one sense, the divisional structure formalizes the team approach. An organization using a functional structure may create a team for each product line. The divisional structure brings the functional skills of each team together under the formal chain of command; thus, the team (product) boss has formal authority.

In very large companies, a divisional structure is essential.[10] Most large corporations have separate business divisions that perform different tasks, serve different clients, or use different technologies. When a huge organization produces products for different markets, the divisional structure works because each division is an autonomous business. For example, PepsiCo uses a divisional structure. Frito-Lay, Pizza Hut, Taco Bell, North American Van Lines, and Wilson's Sporting Goods are stand-alone divisions within PepsiCo. Tenneco Inc. also uses a divisional structure. Divisions include J. I. Case, a manufacturer of farm implements, Newport News Shipbuilding, which builds submarines and other ships for the Navy, Tenneco Minerals, and Tenneco Oil Exploration and Production. Each of these companies is best run as a separate division under the overall guidance of Tenneco corporate headquarters.

A major difference between divisional and functional structures is that the chain of command from each function converges lower down in the hierarchy. In Exhibit 9.5, note that differences of opinion among R&D, marketing, manufacturing, and finance would be resolved at the divisional level rather than by the president. Thus, the divisional structure encourages decentralization. Decision making is pushed down at least one level in the hierarchy, freeing up the president and other top managers for strategic planning.

Many small and medium-size companies also use a divisionalized structure. These companies have a clear-cut choice because a functional structure could also work. Kollmorgen Corporation, a manufacturer of electronic circuitry and other goods, believes strongly in the divisional concept because of its motivational factors. The chief executive creates a separate division for each product line with an average of 75 employees. Thus, employees think of themselves as a team—they call it "productization." Kollmorgen's performance jumped dramatically after it shifted to the division concept.[11] W. L. Gore Inc. and 3M Corporation also subscribe to the divisional concept. Their managements' goal is to keep the companies organized into small businesses that are motivated, flexible, and responsive to customer needs.

Geographically and Customer-Based Divisions

Two variations of the divisional structure are the organization of divisions by geography and by customer. Departmentation by customer simply means that all skills needed to service a specific customer are grouped together in a single division. A company may have a very large customer—say, the U.S. government—for a certain line of products. It can create a separate division to serve that customer full time. Another example is a

In 1985, Armstrong Rubber Company reorganized its businesses into separate operating divisions. Each operating unit is treated as a self-managed profit center. The divisional approach to structure enabled Armstrong to respond to changes in the tire business. One innovative outcome was the Formula line of tires developed for the fast-growing high-performance market, which enables performance similar to that of sports vehicles.

supplier that manufactures parts for both General Motors autos and Boeing aircraft. It may create two divisions, one for each major customer. A divisional status provides a common employee focus on the customer's needs. A company such as Macmillan, which produces textbooks, is divided into divisions for the high school, grade school, and college markets. Although the manufacturing technology is the same for all divisons, the writing and selling of textbooks is different for each type of customer.

Geographical divisions are created when an organization serves a national or international area and functional skills need to be located in each geographical region. Sears, Roebuck is organized into five regions, each with its own warehousing, inventory control, distribution systems, and stores. Recent changes in the economy forced Greyhound Lines Inc. to reorganize from a functional to a geographical structure with four regional divisions. The functional structure had worked when bus routes ran from city to city throughout the nation. But competition from low-cost airlines had reduced long-distance bus travel by half; the average bus trip is now less than 250 miles. Greyhound's management decided that four divisions, representing the eastern, central, southern, and western regions, would provide better service and more efficient control. The new geographical structure enables closer coordination of bus routes designed to meet the needs of the customer within the region served by each division.[12]

Advantages and Disadvantages

For medium-size companies, the choice between functional and divisional structure is difficult because each represents different strengths and weaknesses. The advantages and disadvantages of the divisional structure are listed in Exhibit 9.6. By dividing employees and resources along divisional lines, the organization will be flexible and responsive to change because each unit is small and tuned in to its environment. By having employees working on a single product line, the concern for customers' needs is high. Coordination across functional departments is better because employees are grouped together in a single location and committed to one product line. Great coordination exists within divisions. The divisional structure also enables top management to pinpoint responsibility for performance problems in product lines. Since each division is a self-contained unit, poor performance can be assigned directly to the manager of that unit. Finally, employees' goals typically are directed toward product success rather than toward their own functional departments. Employees develop a broader goal orientation that can help them develop into general managers.

The product structure also has well-defined disadvantages. The major disadvantage is duplication of resources and the high cost of running separate divisions. Instead of a single research department in which all research people use a single facility, there may be several. The organization loses efficiency and economies of scale. Because departments within each division are small, there is a lack of technical specialization, expertise, and training. The divisional structure fosters excellent coordination

EXHIBIT   9.6

Advantages and Disadvantages of Divisional Structure

Advantages
- Fast response, flexibility in an unstable environment
- Fosters concern for customers' needs
- Excellent coordination across functional departments
- Easy pinpointing of responsibility for product problems
- Emphasis on overall product and division goals
- Development of general management skills

Disadvantages
- Duplication of resources across divisions
- Less technical depth and specialization in divisions
- Poor coordination across divisions
- Less top management control
- Competition for corporate resources

within divisions, but coordination *across* divisions is often poor. Companies such as Hewlett-Packard and Digital Equipment prided themselves on the divisional structure that gave autonomy to many small divisions. Problems occurred, however, when these divisions went in opposite directions. The software produced in one division did not fit the hardware produced in another. Thus, divisional structures were realigned to establish adequate coordination across divisions. Moreover, divisions may feel themselves in competition with one another, especially for resources from corporate headquarters. This can lead to political behavior that is unhealthy for the company as a whole. Since top management control is somewhat weaker under the divisional structure, top managers must assert themselves in order to get divisions to work together.

Many companies must carefully decide whether the divisional or functional structure better suits their needs. If the efficient use of internal resources, top management control, and employee specialization and expertise are of primary importance, a functional structure is better. If flexibility and adaptability to a changing environment, customer service, and coordination across functions is primary, the divisional structure is preferable, despite its greater cost and duplication of resources. It is not uncommon for a company to try one structure and then switch to another as its needs change. One example is Apple Computer, which went to a divisional structure to insure excellent cooperation within divisions and a rapid response to the external environment. However, a declining market for personal computers made efficiency more important, and Apple reorganized back into a functional structure. The memo on the following pages describes president John Sculley's reasoning for the reorganization.[13]

HYBRID APPROACH TO STRUCTURE

A **hybrid structure** uses both functional and divisional departmentalization. Some departments are functional, with all employees who perform similar tasks grouped together. Other departments are subdivided and

hybrid structure An organizational structure that utilizes both functional and divisional departmentalization.

Apple Computer

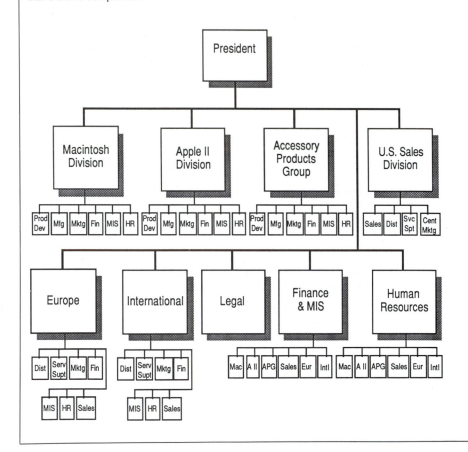

APPLE COMPUTER INTER-OFFICE MEMO

Date: June 14, 1985

To: Board of Directors

From: John Sculley

Subject: **Company Reorganization**

The executive staff, key managers and I have met almost daily over the past several weeks to develop a new organization. As you know, Apple has been a divisionalized company with several highly autonomous profit centers which have acted almost like stand-alone companies:

assigned to each product division. An example of a hybrid structure for Sun Petroleum Products Company is presented in Exhibit 9.7. Sun has three product divisions: fuels, lubricants/waxes, and chemicals. Each division has its own functional departments of marketing, manufacturing, planning, and supply. This permits the close coordination among functions required for serving customers and adapting to environmental change. Sun also has several functional departments, including human

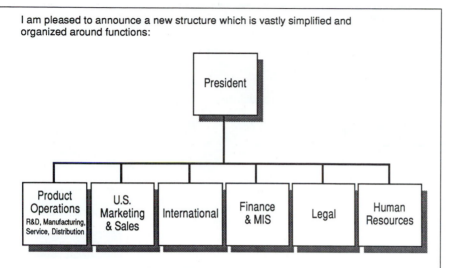

I am pleased to announce a new structure which is vastly simplified and organized around functions:

The new organization will reduce our breakeven point. It should also simplify internal communication of company objectives and allow for greater consistency in their implementation.

We have selected leaders of each functional area who have had considerable experience in their specialty and in managing people.

In the process of moving to this new organization, we will reduce the number of jobs at Apple by 1200. This is a painful and difficult decision. However, this streamlining will allow us to eliminate unnecessary job duplication in the divisional structure. (As shown in the organization chart, each division has had its own product development, manufacturing, finance, management information systems, and human resources staffs.)

The new organization should be more effective at providing products the marketplace wants and at providing them in a more timely manner. In addition to the greater effectiveness of the organization it should also be more efficient -- making us more profitable on lower sales than would have been the case with the former organization.

The reorganization will be costly in the short run. We take such a strong step only because it is clear that the new organization and management team will vastly improve Apple's probability for success as an industry leader.

resources, technology, financial services, resources and strategy, and the chief counsel. These functions are centralized to achieve economies of scale and provide service to the entire organization. The human resource department is concerned with EEOC regulations, union negotiations, and other personnel issues relevant to all three product divisions. Likewise, financial services does the financial and accounting work for the entire corporation. Sun achieves coordination among the three divisions through the efforts of the centralized functional departments.

EXHIBIT 9.7

Sun Petroleum Products Company's Hybrid Structure

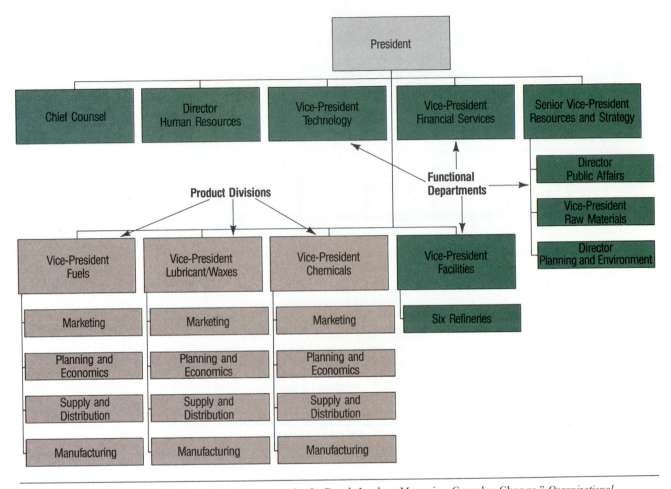

Source: Linda S. Ackerman, "Transition Management: An In-Depth Look at Managing Complex Change," *Organizational Dynamics* (Summer 1982), pp. 46–66.

Advantages and Disadvantages

The purpose of the hybrid structure is to combine functional and divisional departmentalization so as to gain the benefits of each. This structure occurs in medium-size to large organizations that have enough resources to create product divisions but can gain efficiencies by having a few functional departments. The biggest advantage of the hybrid structure is that it encourages coordination both within and between product divisions. Within each product division, departments are located together, goals are shared, and employees coordinate easily with one another. The centralized functional departments provide for uniformity of operations and coordination across the product divisions. Another positive feature is the coalignment of corporate goals with divisional goals.

E X H I B I T   9.8

Advantages and Disadvantages of Hybrid Structure

Advantages
- Some benefits of both functional and divisional structure
- Good coordination both within and between divisions
- Alignment of corporate and division goals
- Flexibility in divisions, efficiency in functional departments

Disadvantages
- Administrative overload—large corporate staffs and duplication of function with divisions
- Conflict between division and headquarters functions

Divisions are not completely autonomous. The corporation is visible and is involved in division activities through the influence of the centralized functional departments. Finally, the organization achieves flexibility and adaptability to the external environment through its divisions and internal efficiency through its functional departments.

There are a couple of major disadvantages to the hybrid approach. First, there is a danger of administrative overhead. When top managers create functional departments at the corporate level, these departments sometimes grow very large. Top management may use these departments to oversee and control divisions, which can make corporate staffs grow large and cumbersome. Moreover, some functions may be duplicated between the divisions and headquarters. The divisions may create their own personnel departments, for example, if they are unhappy with the services from the centralized personnel department. Such duplication of resources lowers efficiency.

The second major weakness is the potential for ongoing conflict between the product divisions and headquarters' departments. Headquarters' functions have no line authority over divisions; yet they attempt to coordinate and influence divisions. Division managers often resent headquarters' intrusions, and headquarters' functional managers resent the lack of cooperation from the divisions. The divisions and headquarters are often geographically separated, which reduces the opportunity for communication and coordination. Headquarters' executives may not understand the unique circumstances of each division, and divisions may not care about the corporate perspective. These differences provide the potential for continuous conflict.

The advantages and disadvantages of the hybrid structure are summarized in Exhibit 9.8.

MATRIX APPROACH TO STRUCTURE

The **matrix structure** utilizes functional and divisional structures simultaneously in the same part of the organization. The matrix actually has dual lines of authority. In Exhibit 9.9, the functional hierarchy of au-

matrix structure An organizational structure that utilizes functional and divisional structures simultaneously in the same part of the organization.

E X H I B I T   9.9

Dual-Authority Structure in a Matrix Organization

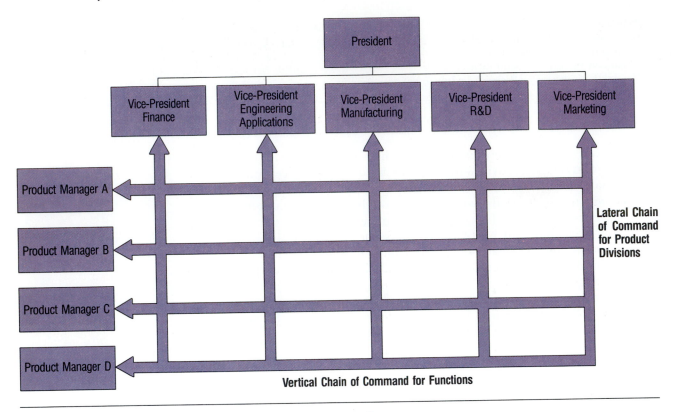

thority runs vertically and the divisional hierarchy of authority runs laterally. The lateral chain of command formalizes the divisional or team-based relationships. Thus, the lateral structure is stronger than in the case of informal teams and task forces, while the matrix structure maintains the vertical chain of command for functional departments. The matrix approach to structure therefore provides a formal chain of command for both the functional and divisional relationships.

The matrix structure typically is used when the organization experiences environmental pressure for both a strong functional departmentalization and a team-based or divisional departmentalization. Thus, the organization may need to have in-depth skills in functional departments (engineering, research) and at the same time the ability to respond flexibly and adaptively to changing environmental demands. The matrix structure enables the organization to achieve greater economies of scale than does the divisional structure, because functional employees can be shared across several divisions. Resource duplication is minimized by having employees work for more than one division or by transferring employees among divisions as personnel requirements change.

E X H I B I T   9.10

Key Positions in a Matrix Structure

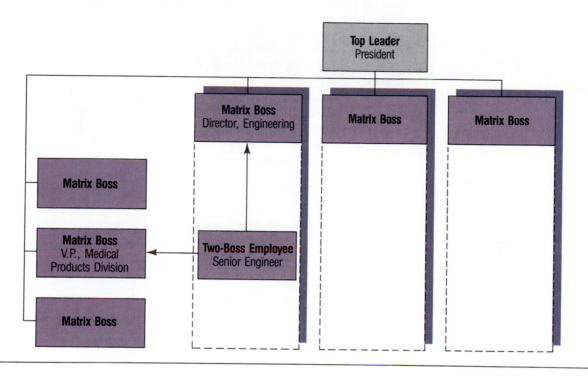

Key Relationships

The success of the matrix structure depends on the abilities of people in key matrix roles. Exhibit 9.10 provides a close-up of the reporting relationships in the dual chain of command. The senior engineer in the medical products division reports to both the medical products vice-president and the engineering director. This violates the unity of command concept described in Chapter 8, but it is necessary to give equal emphasis to both functional and divisional lines of authority. Confusion is reduced by separating responsibilities for each chain of command. The functional boss is responsible for technical and personnel issues, such as quality standards, providing technical training, and assigning technical personnel to projects. The divisional boss is responsible for programwide issues, such as overall design decisions, schedule deadlines, and coordinating technical specialists from several functions.

The senior engineer is called a **two-boss employee** because he or she reports to two supervisors simultaneously. Two-boss employees must resolve conflicting demands from the matrix bosses. They must confront senior managers and reach joint decisions. They need excellent human relations skills with which to confront managers and resolve conflicts.

two-boss employee An employee who reports to two supervisors simultaneously.

matrix boss A product or functional boss, responsible for one side of the matrix.

top leader The overseer of both the product and functional chains of command, responsible for the entire matrix.

Tenneco Inc. has organized its many businesses into a divisional structure. Within the Newport News division a matrix structure is used to coordinate the many functions and ships being built. The Key West *was one of two attack submarines launched during 1985. Newport News also used the matrix structure to develop plans for a new class of submarines and coordinate the 18-month overhaul for the aircraft carrier* Dwight D. Eisenhower. *The matrix structure permits the coordination and sharing of resources needed for these difficult tasks.*

The **matrix boss** is the product or functional boss, who in Exhibit 9.10 is the engineering director and the medical products vice-president. The matrix boss is responsible for one side of the matrix. The top leader is responsible for the entire matrix. The **top leader** oversees both the product and functional chains of command. His or her responsibility is to maintain a power balance between the two sides of the matrix. If disputes arise between them, the problem will be kicked upstairs to the top leader.[14]

Matrix bosses and two-boss employees often find it difficult to adapt to the matrix. The matrix boss has only half of each employee. Without complete control over employees, bosses must consult with their counterparts on the other side of the matrix. This necessitates frequent meetings and discussions to coordinate matrix activities. The two-boss employee experiences problems of conflicting demands and expectations from the two supervisors.

Advantages and Disadvantages

The matrix structure is controversial because of the dual chain of command. However, it has been used successfully in companies such as Dow Chemical. Most important, it makes efficient use of human resources compared to the divisional structure. The functional boss can reassign specialists from one division to another, and people can be assigned half time to two divisions, thus fully utilizing personnel. Moreover, the matrix structure works well in a shifting environment, wherein the organization is expected to be adaptable and innovative. The conflict and frequent meetings generated by the matrix enable new issues to be raised and resolved. The matrix also provides training for both functional and general management skills. People within functional departments have access to in-depth training and specialization and at the same time coordinate with other specialists and programs, which helps them develop a general management perspective. Finally, the matrix structure engages the participation of employees in team meetings and in the achievement of divisional goals. Thus, it challenges and motivates employees, giving them a larger task than would be possible in a functional structure.

The matrix structure also has several disadvantages. The major problem is the confusion and frustration caused by the dual chain of command. Matrix bosses and two-boss employees have difficulty with the dual reporting relationships. The matrix structure also generates high conflict because it pits divisional against functional goals. This leads to the third disadvantage: time lost to meetings and discussions devoted to resolving this conflict. Often the matrix structure leads to more discussion than action because different goals and points of view are being addressed. To survive and perform well in a matrix, employees need human relations training to learn to deal with two bosses, to get by with only "half" of each employee, and to confront and manage conflict. Finally, many organizations find it difficult to maintain the power balances essential for matrix success. The functional and divisional sides of the matrix must have equal power. If one side acquires greater formal au-

EXHIBIT 9.11

Advantages and Disadvantages of Matrix Structure

Advantages	Disadvantages
• More efficient use of resources than divisional structure	• Frustration and confusion from dual chain of command
• Flexibility, adaptability to changing environment	• High conflict between divisional and functional interests
• Development of both general and functional management skills	• Many meetings, more discussion than action
• Interdisciplinary cooperation, expertise available to all divisions	• Needed human relations training
• Enlarged tasks for employees	• Power dominance by one side of matrix

thority, the advantages of the matrix structure will be lost. The organization will then operate like a functional structure with informal lateral relationships.

The advantages and disadvantages of the matrix structure are summarized in Exhibit 9.11.

One company in which the matrix structure works very well is Crane Plastics Inc. in Columbus, Ohio. There is only one matrix boss on the divisional side, but the approach has succeeded because of the skills of Howard Bennett.

Crane Plastics Inc.

Gary Fulmer, executive vice-president of Crane Plastics, hadn't even heard of the matrix structure until he ran across some published articles. The matrix seemed a solution to the intense cooperation needed among departments during a product changeover. "Making the conversion in our large-volume custom products was driving me up a wall," said Fulmer. "Rarely had we done anything that cut across so many departments. It took compounding experts, toolmakers, extrusion people, quality control people—in all, it took about five different disciplines to make this thing work. . . . But it wasn't working." He continued, "People would have a meeting. They'd come back after two or three weeks with all good intentions, but they just didn't get it done, because they had more important things to do in their own functional areas."

Managers resisted the matrix, because team members work for two bosses—team and function—at the same time. Crane Plastics implemented the matrix with one team boss, and it really began to click when Howard Bennett took that position. Bennett understood

EXHIBIT 9.12

Matrix Structure for Crane Plastics Inc.

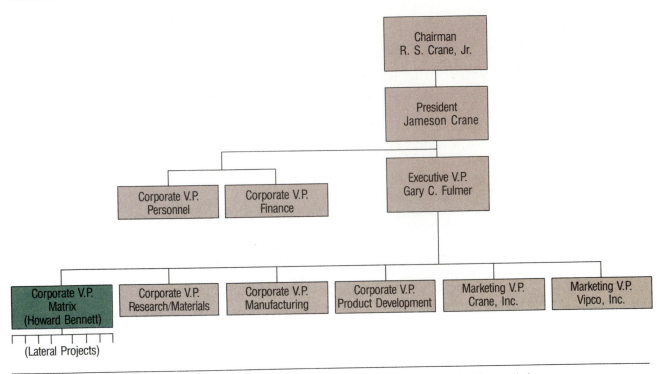

Source: Howard Bennett, Corporate Vice-President, Matrix, Crane Plastics Inc., 1985. Used with permission.

lateral relationships. He guarded against interdepartmental friction by having functional department heads sign an agreement allowing their subordinates' participation in a team. His style encouraged cooperation. But Bennett admits it took some practice: "When I assumed this position, I was totally engrossed in manufacturing. . . . I had no sympathy for marketing, accounting, or most of the other functions. This job gave me a broader outlook."

Bennett was responsible for coordinating all new products, several of which were developed simultaneously, as illustrated by the multiple lines emanating from his position in Exhibit 9.12. His full-time job was to manage these teams, and his rank equaled vice-presidents' of other departments. But it was Bennett's management skill as much as formal rank that made the matrix work. Said one team member, "With other companies, matrix management is reduced to shouting matches. . . . It's inevitable any time you have two bosses." But thanks to Howard Bennett, this didn't happen at Crane Plastics.[15]

USING STRUCTURAL APPROACHES FOR ATTAINING STRATEGIC OBJECTIVES

In Chapter 5, we discussed strategies that business firms can adopt. Two of these are prospector and defender.[16] With a prospector strategy, the organization attempts to develop new, innovative products. With a defender strategy, the organization retrenches, cuts back, and strives for internal efficiency. These two strategies are associated with objectives of innovation versus efficiency, which are mutually exclusive. An **efficiency goal** requires the careful use of scarce resources and often leads to a highly specialized functional structure. An **innovation goal** concerns flexibility, and being on the leading edge of new products and services desired by the society. The needs for efficiency and innovation are difficult to reconcile in the same organization, because they require different skills. Cost cutting inhibits innovation, while innovation makes it difficult to exert the tight control needed for efficiency.[17]

Top managers must set a priority between these strategic objectives and then select the right structure. Exhibit 9.13 illustrates a continuum anchored by the efficiency goal and defender strategy on the left side and by the innovation goal and prospector strategy on the right. As illustrated in Exhibit 9.13, the pure functional structure is appropriate for

efficiency goal An organizational goal that stresses the judicious use of scarce resources.

innovation goal An organizational goal that emphasizes flexibility and leadership in the provision of new products and services.

NIKE, Inc. restructured in 1985 to reflect a changing marketplace and a new strategy. The number of runners had tapered off and the demand for running shoes for fashion and casual wear had declined. One of NIKE's responses was to establish an autonomous division, the New Products Group, that would be lean, quick, and responsive to customers. The division responded quickly to market needs by developing the Air Jordan™ line. The poster here illustrates one marketing approach, and the Jordan line has been highly successful. Creating this autonomous division fits NIKE's strategy of innovation and adaptation.

MANAGERS SHOP TALK

Structural Warning Signs

Managers often have a difficult time knowing when to redesign the organization's structure. When structure is correct, it is hardly noticed. Structural approach, division of labor, reporting relationships, and support personnel are aligned, and performance objectives are met. However, when organization structure is incorrect, certain symptoms appear. Some of the warning signals that a structural change may be needed are as follows:

1. *Changes are occurring in the contingency factors of strategic objectives, production technology, environmental uncertainty, and organization size.* These factors determine the correct structure. When they change, structure may need to be altered. A once stable environment may suddenly shift, such as occurred when the fuel crisis hit airlines and deregulation struck banks. Adoption of a new production technology or major increases in growth also signal the need for a new structure. A new strategy, such as emphasis on production efficiency or innovation, also may require a structural change.

2. *The organization does not respond to the environment.* This occurs because coordination among departments fails to accommodate changes in products or services desired by customers, or departments for scanning, forecasting, and innovation planning may be lacking. Organizational responsiveness requires that departments have assigned responsibilities for dealing with the environment and respond as a coordinated whole.

3. *Too much conflict is evident.* Interdepartmental conflict means employees are identifying too closely with their own departments and do not see the organization's larger goals. Departments may be under pressure to reach their own goals and thus avoid cooperation with others. Departments may be out of step, and lateral relationships in the form of task forces and teams may need strengthening. Reorganization into divisional units may also help.

4. *Top management decision making is too slow and lacks quality.* Top managers may be overloaded with decisions because the hierarchy funnels too many problems to them. Structure may be too centralized. Moreover, information may not reach top managers, keeping them out of touch with operations. Likewise, if decision making is too decentralized, decisions will be fragmented and uncoordinated.

5. *Employee morale and motivation is low.* With the wrong structure, employees may have routine jobs and unclear expectations. They may perceive themselves as having little responsibility or involvement in important activities. Management decisions may appear inconsistent and arbitrary. A clearly defined structure and lateral relationships enabling employees to participate in broader activities will enhance morale.

6. *Personnel costs are too high.* Personnel costs increase when resources are duplicated across divisions or between divisions and headquarters. Perhaps several departments are hiring their own computer programmers rather than using the service available from the information systems department. Some departments may have excess personnel while others don't have enough people, equipment, or facilities to accomplish high-priority tasks. Personnel costs also are high when large professional staffs are created at headquarters to control divisions. If headquarters control is essential, a functional structure is more appropriate than a divisional structure.

7. *Managers are overloaded.* If managers are overloaded, responsibilities may need realignment. Spans of control may be too wide, responsibility may be too broad, and new positions or departments may be needed. Teams and task forces can also reduce overload. Support systems in the form of rules, procedures, and information systems may be needed. Decentralization also may help.

8. *Performance objectives are not being met.* Performance problems may have many causes, but structure is often a culprit. A performance deficiency may be seen in several ways: Specific targets are not being met, or managers feel the organization should be doing better on a variety of dimensions. The perception of performance deficiency may be caused by employee dissatisfaction, too much conflict, slow response, low morale, or poor resource utilization. If structure is severely out of alignment with company needs, reduced performance will result.

Source: Based on John Childs, *Organization: A Guide to Problems and Practice*, 2d. ed. (London: Harper & Row, 1984), Chapters 1, 10.

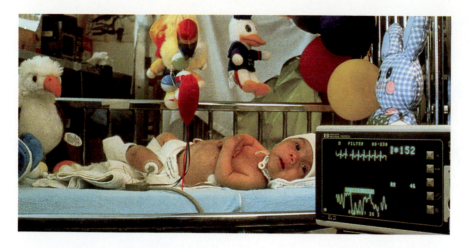

Hewlett-Packard has innovated in the area of microprocessor-based monitoring units for measuring a baby's heart and lung functions. The development and marketing of these products were facilitated through a major corporate restructuring in 1984. HP had many divisions for product development and manufacturing, but their autonomy resulted in overlapping products and a piecemeal approach to key markets. Greater coordination among product divisions was achieved by consolidating them into four major groups within which they work together on major integrated systems.

achieving internal efficiency goals. The functional structure allows efficient use of scarce resources, but it does not enable the organization to be flexible or innovative. In contrast, the divisional structure is most appropriate when the primary goal is innovation and flexibility. Each division is small, able to be responsive, and has the resources necessary for performing its task, although they may be duplicated in other divisions. Divisional structure enables organizations to respond quickly to the demands of a shifting environment, but at the expense of efficient resource use.

Exhibit 9.13 also illustrates how the other forms of structure described in this chapter—functional with lateral relationships, hybrid, and matrix—represent intermediate steps on the organization's path to efficiency and innovation. The functional structure with lateral relationships provides greater coordination and flexibility than the pure functional structure. The hybrid structure is in the middle: Divisions are flexible, and functional departments can achieve efficiency. The matrix structure is designed primarily to facilitate innovation, but it is more efficient than the pure divisional structure. Here the organization has well-defined divisions, but it also has a functional line of authority that minimizes duplication and insures efficient resource utilization across divisions. The array of structures in Exhibit 9.13 balance efficiency and innovation goals, but in differing amounts.

Polaroid president I. M. Booth uses a similar scale to describe his efforts to tear down internal barriers. He uses a structural scale of 1 to 10. A "10" is a structure made up of autonomous groups, each with its own marketing, engineering, and management departments working as a group. A "1" is a totally functional structure, with a single manufacturing division for the whole company, a single marketing division, and so on. Booth claims that Polaroid was a 1 for many years. Its departments were uncoordinated, and little things were being neglected. Booth has been trying to break up Polaroid's functional structure by creating separate divisions for three businesses: magnetics, consumer products, and industrial photography products. Booth feels that the right amount of flexibility and innovation would put Polaroid at a 6 or 7 on the structural scale but admits that it is still only a 2 or 3. He plans to continue pushing until he gets it near the high end of the scale.[18]

EXHIBIT   9.13

Relationship of Strategic Objectives to Structural Approach

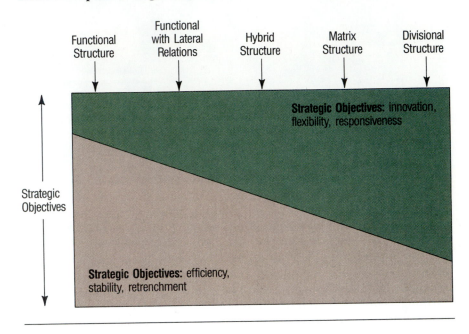

MINTZBERG'S TYPOLOGY: INTEGRATING STRUCTURE AND CONTINGENCY FACTORS

A contemporary approach to organizational design that attempts to integrate many of the ideas about structure in this and the previous chapter was proposed by Henry Mintzberg.[19] Mintzberg suggested that every organization has a configuration of five parts, as illustrated in Exhibit 9.14. Top management is located at the top of the organization. Middle management is at the intermediate level. The technical core includes lower-level managers and employees who do the basic work of the organization. The chain of command from top management to the technical core would be considered the organization's *line* function. The organization also has professional and technical support staff—the researchers, engineers, and system analysts responsible for the formal planning and control of the technical core. The administrative support staff provides indirect services, including maintenance, clerical, and mailroom. The size of each part varies according to organization structure, environment, technology, and goals.

Mintzberg proposed that the organizational parts in Exhibit 9.14 fit together in five basic forms. These forms represent different structures as well as the various contingency factors of technology, size, and envi-

EXHIBIT 9.14

The Five Organizational Parts

Source: Based on Henry Mintzberg, *The Structuring of Organizations: A Synthesis of the Research* (Englewood Cliffs, N.J.: Prentice-Hall, 1979), pp. 215–297, and Henry Mintzberg, "Organization Design: Fashion or Fit?", *Harvard Business Review* 59 (January/February 1981), pp. 103–116.

ronment described in Chapter 8. Mintzberg's research suggests that a number of structural and contingency variables hang together in identifiable clusters to create each organizational form. The five organizational forms are simple structure, machine bureaucracy, professional bureaucracy, divisionalized form, and adhocracy.[20] The structure, configuration, and contingency characteristics associated with each form are summarized in Exhibit 9.15.

Simple Structure

The **simple structure** is an organization that is new, small, and in the entrepreneurial stage of the life cycle. The organization consists of the top manager and a few workers in the technical core. There is no professional/technical staff, and only a small administrative support staff is required. Workers perform overlapping tasks; thus, there is little specialization or formalization. Decision making is centralized to the owner/manager. Coordination is informal and maintained through direct supervision. This organization typically uses a small batch manufacturing or service technology. It is able to adapt to environmental changes and may have been created in response to an unmet environmental need. Goals stress innovation and long-term survival.

simple structure An organization that is new, small, and in the entrepreneurial stage of the life cycle.

EXHIBIT 9.15

Characteristics of Mintzberg's Five Organizational Types

	Simple Structure	Machine Bureaucracy	Professional Bureaucracy	Divisionalized Form	Adhocracy
Structure					
Approach	Functional	Functional	Functional, sometimes hybrid	Divisional, hybrid	Matrix
Formalization	Low	High	Low to moderate	High within divisions	Low
Centralization	High	High	Low to moderate	Decentralized to divisions	Low
Lateral relationships	Few	Few	Many	Some across divisions, many within divisions	Many, built into structure
Configuration					
Technical/professional support staff	None	Many	Few	Many in headquarters departments	Many—part of matrix
Administrative support staff	Few	Many	Many	Many within divisions	Many
Contingency					
Environment	Simple, changing	Stable, certain	Stable, complex	Complex, changing	Unstable, uncertain
Technology	Routine product or service	Routine product or service	Service	Divisible, varies across divisions	Nonroutine, sophisticated
Size, life cycle	Very small, young	Large, mature	Any size, age	Large, mature	Moderate, midlife
Strategic objectives	Innovation, survival	Efficiency	Innovation, quality	Adaptability, efficiency	Innovation, adaptation

Source: Based on Henry Mintzberg, *The Structuring of Organizations: A Synthesis of the Research* (Englewood Cliffs, N.J.: Prentice-Hall, 1979), pp. 466–471.

Machine Bureaucracy

machine bureaucracy A large, functionally structured organization characterized by a high degree of formalization and work specialization.

The **machine bureaucracy** is a large, functionally structured organization. It has many of the characteristics of bureaucracy described in Chapter 2, with a high degree of formalization and work specialization. Technology is mass production manufacturing or routine service. Decisions are centralized as much as possible. A functional structure is used, and little horizontal or lateral coordination is needed. The machine bureaucracy has large professional and administrative support staffs. The former includes engineers, financial analysts, and market researchers, who scrutinize and formalize work in the technical core. The latter handles the paperwork and maintenance associated with a large, bureaucratic organization. Examples of the machine bureaucracy are McDonald's Corporation and government organizations that rigorously standardize work activities. The environment for a machine bureaucracy is typically stable, and the goal is to achieve internal efficiency.

The Chicago Symphony Orchestra, led by Sir Georg Solti, Music Director, is an example of the professional bureaucracy form of organization described by Mintzberg. A professional bureaucracy provides a complex service through highly trained professionals and has a large administrative support staff and small technical support staff. The Orchestral Association reflects this configuration, employing approximately 105 musicians in the technical core, 80 administrative staff members, and 10 technical support employees. The technical support employees include stagehands, an electrician, the director of operations, and the house manager.

Professional Bureaucracy

The **professional bureaucracy** typically is a large, functionally structured organization that has professional employees and uses a nonroutine service technology. Examples are universities, large law firms, hospitals, and consulting firms. While the organization has some formalization, it is decentralized to provide autonomy to the professionals providing nonroutine services. Professional bureaucracies exist in complex but stable environments. Goals are to innovate and provide high-quality services, and size can be moderate to large. Since professional and technical staff are located in the technical core, the technical support staff is small. However, the administrative staff is large to provide clerical and maintenance support for the professional core.

professional bureaucracy A large, functionally structured organization that has professional employees and uses a nonroutine service technology.

Divisionalized Form

The **divisionalized form** of organization is similar to the divisional approach to structure described earlier in this chapter. It is a large organization that is subdivided into product or market divisions. Decision making is decentralized at the divisional level. There are few horizontal coordinating devices among the relatively autonomous divisions. Corporate-level personnel provide some liaison and coordination. The divisionalized form can utilize different technologies within separate divisions, although many divisions have routine manufacturing technologies. The environment for a division tends to be stable, although the total organization serves a complex environment of diverse markets. Technical support staff are located at headquarters to provide services to all divisions. Administrative support staff is located within each division. Large corporations such as Ford, Westinghouse, and Procter & Gamble illustrate the divisionalized form of organization.

divisionalized form A large organization that is subdivided into product or market divisions and decentralizes decision making at the divisional level.

adhocracy A medium-size organization that emphasizes adaptability and is characterized by a low degree of formalization and decentralization of decision making.

Adhocracy

An **adhocracy** is similar to a matrix structure. It develops in complex, dynamic environments in which the technology is sophisticated and coordination in both vertical and lateral directions is required. Adhocracies typically are medium size and must be adaptable and use resources efficiently. The structure is low in formalization and decentralized. Coordination is achieved through dual chains of command. Technical support staffs are small, because technical specialists are involved in the organization's technical core. Clerical support staff is large to support the complex structure. Technology is nonroutine and often is a sophisticated manufacturing technology. The primary goal is innovation and quick adaptation to a changing environment. Adhocracies exist in the aerospace and electronic industries and in R&D firms.

The five organizational forms permit the characteristics described in this chapter and Chapter 8 to fit together in logical patterns. Successful organizations achieve harmony and fit among the elements of structure, configuration, and contingency factors. A neat, orderly machine bureaucracy in a dynamic industry that demands innovation makes no sense, nor does a flexible adhocracy in a stable industry calling for cost efficiency. Structural characteristics should be congruent.

Structure is a powerful management tool when designed to achieve the organizational goal and fit the organization's contingencies, as was that of the Human Resources Administration in New York City.

Human Resources Administration

In late 1971, New York City's welfare operation was totally out of control and heading for sure fiscal disaster. Quality control studies revealed that one-third of all recipients were receiving the wrong amount of money and 15 percent were probably ineligible for any assistance. Approximately $150 million in taxpayer funds was being misappropriated through fraud, error, and mismanagement. Welfare rolls were climbing at the disastrous rate of 10,000 persons a month; costs were increasing at the rate of $120 million per year.

Field operations were in a state of absolute and perpetual chaos. Welfare centers closed their doors routinely at 10:00 or 11:00 o'clock in the morning, unable to handle the crush of desperate recipients. Acts of violence against welfare workers were commonplace, and police measures to protect them proved inadequate. Employee productivity was below 40 percent.

Management was virtually nonexistent. Over one-third of the employees exceeded their allotted lateness limit, at a cost of $1.3

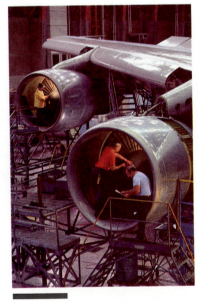

Pan Am mechanics inspect the engines of a Boeing 747 in a maintenance hangar at Pan Am's Jet Center in New York. The presence of a large department of skilled maintenance technicians is part of the machine bureaucracy form of organization described by Mintzberg. Rules and procedures prescribe required activities, and well-trained technical staff support Pan Am's products and services.

million a year to the city. The average employee took eleven and one-half of his twelve days of sick leave, with disproportionate concentrations around holidays and weekends. Although misconduct was prevalent, the agency terminated only nineteen employees for flagrant abuses.

On staff, there were no industrial engineers, less than twenty professional systems analysts, and few professional managers. In short, the system was out of control and the existing organization lacked the capability to bring it back in check.

In late 1971, Mayor Lindsay resolved to overhaul the welfare system and bring the caseload under control. To accomplish this, the mayor brought in a new management team, authorized the expenditure of $10 million a year for professional staff and computer support, and gave the effort full political backing. . . .

Productivity increased by 16 percent. At welfare centers, the lines of waiting clients disappeared and directors regained control of their centers.

The bottom-line result of the overhaul has been a dramatic reversal in welfare expenditures. Whereas in 1971 the welfare rolls were growing at the rate of 10,000 persons a month, in 1972 this growth was arrested; the rolls remained fixed at 1,275,000 persons. In November of that year, the rolls began to decline steadily at an average rate of about 9,000 persons per month. This trend should continue through the end of 1973. The bottom line of the overall effort is a $230 million annual cost turnaround for the City of New York.[21]

The initial design of the Human Resources Administration was all wrong. In terms of Mintzberg's typology, it was run as a decentralized, professional bureaucracy when it should have been designed as a machine bureaucracy. Consider the contingency factors: Processing welfare applicants was a routine service technology, and mass production techniques were needed to handle thousands of people; a large technical support staff was needed to develop and implement efficient management systems; the environment was stable; and the primary goal was internal efficiency. These elements point to a centralized, formalized, machine bureaucracy with a large technical support staff. Once in place, the technical support staff instituted systems and procedures appropriate for the organization's size, technology, and environment. The correct organizational design made an enormous difference.

SUMMARY

The key points in this chapter were the five approaches to structure, their strengths and weaknesses, and their role in attaining strategic objectives. The five approaches are the functional, functional with lateral relationships, divisional, hybrid, and matrix. The functional approach groups positions by common skills and tasks; it is suited for small and medium-size organizations in which internal efficiency is the primary strategic objective. The opposite structure is divisional, which groups people by organizational output such that each division has a mix of functional skills and tasks. This is appropriate for large organizations that can afford the duplication of resources and for the attainment of strategic objectives that require innovation and flexibility. The functional structure with lateral relationships uses teams, task forces, and integrating managers to achieve better coordination across departments than is possible with a pure functional structure. The hybrid structure organizes some departments by function and others by division. The matrix structure uses two chains of command simultaneously, one for functions and one for divisions. Hybrid and matrix structures lie midway between functional and divisional structures and have attributes of each.

Mintzberg's typology of five organizational forms—simple structure, machine bureaucracy, professional bureaucracy, divisionalized form, and adhocracy—integrates several ideas from the structural approaches described in this chapter and the fundamentals of organizing described in Chapter 8. Each structure represents a configuration of structural approach, formalization, centralization, administrative intensity, and contingency factors. Organizations should strive to achieve harmony and fit among the elements of structure, configuration, and contingency factors.

Management Solution

The situation at Xerox presented an opportunity for management to use structure to achieve a new goal. Xerox was organized in a functional structure, which was fine for an organization in a stable environment that was concerned with efficiency. With the shocks administered by IBM, Japanese competition, and the FTC, it was time to change strategy and find an appropriate new structure.

The functional structure was scrapped for a divisional structure. Chairman David Kearns created a series of entrepreneurial divisions. The copier division was split into three divisions, each making and selling a specific type of machine. Each division had its own engineering and marketing personnel. The engineers focused on a specific product and did not have to go to top management for approval. By late 1982, the first new product was out the door and Xerox's recovery was underway. The change in strategy to fit the new, competitive reality was made possible by the new structure.[22]

DISCUSSION QUESTIONS

1. An organizational consultant was heard to say, "Some aspect of functional structure appears in every organization." Do you agree? Explain.
2. Why does the structural approach, especially the difference between function and division, influence employee goals and motivation?
3. The divisional structure is considered almost the opposite of a functional structure because of its underlying purpose. Briefly explain the major differences in these two approaches to structure.
4. One observer of Crane Plastics Inc. (see pages 285 to 286) said that the structure was really a functional approach with lateral relationships, not a matrix. Are these two approaches to structure so similar that they can be mistaken for each other? What do you think are the similarities and differences between them?
5. Why are divisional and hybrid structures frequently used in very large corporations?
6. According to the description of Apple Computer's reorganization (see pages 277 to 279), Apple changed from a divisional to a functional structure. Were the reasons for this change consistent with a shift toward new strategic objectives? Explain.
7. The hybrid and matrix structures are both located near the center of the continuum in Exhibit 9.13. What is the difference in the way these two structural approaches help attain some level of both efficiency and innovation?
8. Which structural approach is most likely to be associated with each of the following organizational forms—(a) machine bureaucracy, (b) professional bureaucracy, (c) divisionalized form, and (d) adhocracy?
9. What are important skills for matrix bosses and two-boss employees in a matrix organization?
10. Some people argue that the matrix structure should be adopted only as a last resort because the dual chains of command can create more problems than they solve. Do you agree or disagree? Why?

CASE FOR ANALYSIS

TUCKER COMPANY

In 1968 the Tucker Company underwent an extensive reorganization that divided the company into three major divisions. These new divisions represented Tucker's three principal product lines. Mr. Harnett, Tucker's president, explained the basis for the new organization in a memo to the board of directors as follows:

> In recent years Tucker has undergone substantial growth and diversification. If we are to meet the new challenges facing us in the marketplace, we must modify our organization. The diversity of our products requires that we reorganize along our major product lines. Toward this end I have established three new divisions: commercial jet engines, military jet engines, and utility turbines. Each division will be headed by a newly appointed vice-president who will report directly to me. I have instructed each of these men to establish profit centers within their organizations so that the responsibilities and cost functions of individual departments can more clearly be identified and performance evaluated. I believe that this new profit center approach will enhance our performance through the commitment of individual managers. It should also help us to identify unprofitable areas where the special attention of the management may be required.
>
> For the most part, each division will be able to operate independently. That is, each will have its own engineering, manufacturing, accounting departments, etc. In some cases, however, it will be necessary for a division to utilize the services of other divisions or departments. This is necessary because the complete servicing with individual divisional staffs would result in unjustifiable additional staffing and facilities. Simple accounting procedures have been established to handle these interdepartmental or interdivisional costs, so that the cost center requiring the service is billed appropriately. . . .

The old companywide laboratory was one such service organization. Functionally it continued to support all of the major divisions through the cost-charging methods described. Administratively, however, the manager of the laboratory reported to the manager of manufacturing in the military jet engine division.

From the time the new organization was initiated until February of 1978, when the laboratory manager Mr. Garfield retired, there was little evidence of interdepartmental or interdivisional conflict. His replacement, Mr. Hodge, unlike Mr. Garfield, was always eager to gain the attention of management. Many of Hodge's peers perceived him as an empire builder who was interested in his own advancement rather than the company's well-being. After about six months in the new position, Hodge became involved in several interdepartmental conflicts over work that was being conducted in his laboratory.

Historically, the engineering departments had used the laboratory as a testing facility to determine the properties of materials selected by the design engineers. Hodge felt that the laboratory should be more involved in the selection of these materials and in the design of experiments and subsequent evaluations of the experimental data. Hodge discussed this with Mr. Franklin of the engineering department of the utility turbine division. Franklin offered to consult with Hodge but stated that the final responsibility of the selection of materials was charged to his department.

In the months that followed, Hodge and Franklin had several disagreements over the implementation of the results. Franklin told Hodge that, because of his position at the testing lab, he was unable to appreciate the detailed design considerations that affected the final decision on materials selection. Hodge claimed that Franklin lacked the materials expertise that he, as a metallurgist, had.

Franklin also noted that the prompt handling of his requests, which he had become accustomed to under Garfield's management, began to take longer and longer under Hodge's management. Hodge explained that military jet engine divisional problems had to be assigned first priority because of his administrative reporting structure. He also told Franklin that if he were more involved in Franklin's problems, he could perhaps appreciate when a true sense of urgency existed and he could revise priorities.

The tensions between Franklin and Hodge reached a peak when one of Franklin's critical projects failed to receive the scheduling that he considered necessary. Franklin phoned Hodge to discuss the need for a schedule change. Hodge suggested that they have a meeting to review the need for the work. Franklin then told Hodge that this was not a matter of his concern and that his function was merely to perform the tests as requested. He further stated that he was not satisfied with the low priority rating that his division's work received. Hodge reminded Franklin that when Hodge had suggested a means for resolving this problem, Franklin was not receptive. At this point, Franklin lost his temper and hung up on Hodge. Franklin's next action was to write the following memo to his supervisor, Mr. Hargove:

> *Since Mr. Hodge assumed responsibility for the laboratory, the commercial turbine division has not received the same degree of prompt service that we enjoyed when Mr. Garfield was the laboratory manager. Projects frequently are difficult to schedule and are not completed within the time span required. Mr. Hodge explains these matters as being due to a lower priority of our division's work compared to the military aircraft division's work. This may be part of the problem; however, I believe that the real reason that we are not receiving cooperation is because I have not permitted Mr. Hodge to assume a shared responsibility for materials selection as he requested. I believe, in short, that he is using his position to try to intimidate our division into giving up its chartered responsibility. I believe this matter can no longer be tolerated. I can directly trace delays in three of our contracts to Mr. Hodge's lack of responsiveness. I believe that you must call this matter to the attention of higher management.*

Questions

1. Sketch out a simple organization chart showing Tucker Company's three divisions, including the location of the laboratory. Why would the laboratory be located in the military jet engine division?
2. Analyze the conflict between Mr. Hodge and Mr. Franklin. Do you think the conflict is based in personalities or on the way in which the organization is structured?
3. Sketch out a new organization chart showing how you would restructure Tucker Company so that the laboratory would provide equal services to all divisions. What advantages and disadvantages do you see in the new structure compared to the previous one?

Source: Reprinted with permission of Macmillan Publishing Company from "The Laboratory," *Organizational Behavior: Readings and Cases,* Second Edition, pp. 385–387, by L. Katz, prepared under the supervision of Theodore T. Herbert. Copyright 1981 by Theodore T. Herbert.

Organizational Change and Development

Chapter Outline

Managing Change Activities

Forces for Change
Need for Change

Initiating Change

Search
Creativity
Intrapreneurs
Venture Teams

Implementing Change

Resistance to Change
Force Field Analysis
Implementation Tactics

Types of Planned Change

Technological Approaches
New-Product Approaches
Structural Approaches
People Approaches

Organizational Development

OD Assumptions
OD Steps
OD Interventions
Effectiveness of OD

Learning Objectives

After studying this chapter, you should be able to:

- Define organizational change and explain the difference between planned and unplanned change.

- Describe the sequence of four change activities that must be performed in order for change to be successful.

- Explain the techniques managers can use to facilitate the initiation of change in organizations, including intrapreneurs and new-venture teams.

- Define sources of resistance to change.

- Explain force field analysis and other implementation tactics that can be used to overcome resistance to change.

- Explain the difference among technology, product, structure, and people changes.

- Explain the change process—bottom up, top down, horizontal—associated with each type of change.

- Define organizational development and explain the steps and techniques used during OD interventions.

Management Problem

General Electric bet heavily on the factory of the future, believing customers would buy automated manufacturing systems to improve quality and productivity. GE's $500 million investment was expected to yield $5 billion annual sales by 1990. GE could make more than 15 component products in its many divisions and thus set itself up as America's factory-of-the-future supermarket. But the dream never materialized. Few customers were willing to sign up for factory automation systems. In numerical controls, for example, GE rushed out with a new device that flopped because poor software turned application into a mess. About the only customers for most of the automation components were GE's other divisions. Rather than making money, GE lost $120 million.[1]

If you were a manager at General Electric, how would you explain the failure to produce and market automation systems? What would you recommend that General Electric do in the future to successfully introduce a new, complex technology?

Top managers at General Electric are frustrated because introducing new products created from sophisticated technology has been extraordinarily difficult. Frito-Lay, in contrast, has been enormously successful at initiating new products. O'Grady's, an extra-thick potato chip, rang up sales of $140 million in its first year. But every organization experiences stress and difficulty undergoing change. Innovation from within is widely recognized as one of the critical problems facing business today in the United States and Canada. To be successful, organizations must embrace many types of changes. Businesses must develop improved production technologies, create new products desired in the marketplace,

3M is one of the world's most innovative companies. To adapt to environmental changes, each division is autonomous and supported by a corporate culture that applauds innovation. The new 3M optical disk can store up to 250,000 pages of data. Optical disks are rooted in the changing technology of thin-film coating and photochemistry. They not only immensely increase storage capacity but eliminate the potential for data-destroying malfunctions.

organizational change The adoption of a new idea or behavior by an organization.

planned change Change that is designed and implemented in an orderly and timely manner to meet current problems and anticipated future needs.

implement new administrative systems, and upgrade employees' skills. Companies such as Westinghouse, Sony, IBM, Honeywell, and General Electric implement all of these changes and more.

How important is organizational change? Consider this: The parents of today's college students grew up without cable television, crease-resistant clothing, personal computers, detergents, VCRs, electronic games, compact disks, frozen entrees, video stores, or laser checkout systems in supermarkets. These changes have not only influenced our way of living but have meant life and death for organizations. Organizations that produce the new products have prospered, while many of those caught in the transition with outdated products and technologies have failed. Every organization is trying to change. Organizations that innovate successfully, such as IBM, Hewlett-Packard, Raychem, 3M, Citicorp, Wang, and Frito-Lay, are both profitable and admired.

Organizational change is defined as the adoption of a new idea or behavior by an organization.[2] In Chapter 9, we discussed alternative forms of organization structure and saw how structure can help an organization be stable or adaptable. In this chapter, we look more closely at how organizations can be designed to respond to the environment through internal innovation and change. First we will examine the basic forces for organizational change. Then we will look closely at how managers facilitate two change requirements: initiation and implementation. Finally, we will discuss the four major types of change—technology, new product, structure, and people—and how the organization can be designed to facilitate each.

MANAGING CHANGE ACTIVITIES

Change can be managed. When organizations are caught flat-footed, failing to anticipate or respond to new needs, management is at fault. **Planned change** is designed and implemented in an orderly and timely fashion to meet current problems and anticipate future needs.[3] Managers should monitor events in the environment and within the organization and make a deliberate attempt to implement changes to meet observed needs.[4] By observing external trends, patterns, and needs, managers use planned change to help the organization adapt to external problems and opportunities.[5]

An overall model for planned change is presented in Exhibit 10.1. Four activities make up the change sequence: (1) Internal and external forces for change exist; (2) organization managers monitor these forces and become aware of a need for change; (3) the perceived need triggers the initiation of change, which (4) is then implemented. How each of these activities is handled depends on the organization and managers' styles.

We now turn to a brief discussion of the specific activities associated with the first two events—forces for change and the perceived need for the organization to respond.

E X H I B I T   10.1

Model of Change Sequence of Events

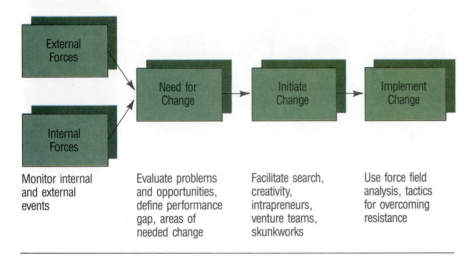

| Monitor internal and external events | Evaluate problems and opportunities, define performance gap, areas of needed change | Facilitate search, creativity, intrapreneurs, venture teams, skunkworks | Use force field analysis, tactics for overcoming resistance |

Forces for Change

Forces for organizational change exist both in the external environment and within the organization.

External Forces. As described in Chapter 3, external forces originate in all environmental sectors, including customers, competitors, technology, economic, and international. For example, the Textile Division of Burlington Industries has been severely affected by international competition. Foreign governments support their export industries through subsidies, tax benefits, and low wages, thus creating formidable competition for North American textile companies. In response to the weak demand for American textiles, Burlington has reduced the size of its apparel fabric business—for instance, it eliminated the Blended Fabrics Division—and redeployed assets into other businesses. McDonald's experienced an external force from the customer sector. Customers were tired of eating hamburgers in their cars, to which top managers responded by incorporating sit-down facilities in McDonald's restaurants. Likewise, major changes in the regulatory, economic, and labor force sectors precipitate response from organizations. New regulations for toxic waste disposal have affected the chemical industry. The increasing number of families with two wage earners has created new opportunities in the child care industry.

Internal Forces. Internal forces for change arise from internal activities and decisions. If top managers decide to seek a higher rate of company growth, internal actions will have to be changed to meet that growth. New departments or technologies will be created. General Motors' senior management, frustrated by poor internal efficiency, designed the Saturn manufacturing plant to solve this internal need. Demands by employees, labor unions and production inefficiencies can all generate a force to which management must respond with change.

Macy's has developed a new concept in retailing as a planned change in response to external forces. "The Cellar" is one of Macy's most creative innovations. Designed to cater to the changing demographics of a new generation of shoppers, the Cellar is a series of small shops, each one geared toward a specific product group. Shown here is the Macy's Atlanta Cellar at the Peachtree Street store in downtown Atlanta.

performance gap A disparity between existing and desired performance levels.

Need for Change

As indicated in Exhibit 10.1, external or internal forces translate into a perceived need for change within the organization. Managers sense a need for change when there is a **performance gap**—a disparity between existing and desired performance levels. The performance gap may occur because current procedures are not up to standard or because a new idea or technology could improve current performance. Management's responsibility is to monitor threats and opportunities in the external environment as well as strengths and weaknesses within the organization to determine whether a need for change exists. Sony managers perceived a need for change when Victor Company of Japan introduced the VCR to compete with Sony's Betamax. The Betamax had dominated the market for several years, but the new VCR was a better system at a lower price. The same thing happened with Sony's famous Walkman and Trinitron color televisions: Competitors came out with imitations that reduced the demand for Sony products. The preceived need for change caused Sony managers to diversify and quickly get into other lines of business in which Sony could recover lost profits.[6]

It is important that managers detect problems and opportunities. The perceived need for change is what sets the stage for subsequent actions that create a new product or technology. Big problems, such as a dramatic fall in market share, are easy to spot. Sensitive monitoring systems are needed in order to detect gradual changes that can fool managers into thinking their company is doing fine. Planned change means that the organization must perceive needs in a slowly changing environment. An organization may be in greater danger when the environment changes slowly, because managers may fail to trigger an organizational response. Failing to use planned change to meet small needs can place the organization in hot water, as illustrated in the following passage:

> *When frogs are placed in a boiling pail of water, they jump out—they don't want to boil to death. However, when frogs are placed in a cold pail of water, and the pail is placed on a stove with the heat turned very low, over time the frogs will boil to death.*[7]

INITIATING CHANGE

The third part of the planned change process is initiating change, a truly critical aspect of change management. This is where the ideas that solve perceived needs are developed. One response an organization can make is to search for a change to adopt.

Search

Search is the process of learning about current developments inside or outside the organization that can be used to meet the perceived need for change. Search typically uncovers existing knowledge that can be applied or adopted within the organization. Many needs, however, cannot be resolved through existing knowledge but require that the organization develop a new response. Initiating a new response means that managers must design the organization so as to facilitate creativity of both individuals and departments, encourage innovative people to initiate new ideas, or create new-venture departments. These techniques have been adopted by corporations such as IBM and Apple with great success.

search The process of learning about current developments inside or outside the organization that can be used to meet a perceived need for change.

Creativity

Creativity is the development of novel solutions to perceived problems.[8] Creative individuals develop ideas that can be adopted by the organization. People noted for their creativity include Edwin Land, who invented the Polaroid camera; Frederick Smith, who came up with the idea for Federal Express' overnight delivery service during an undergraduate class at Yale; and Clarence Birdseye, who invented frozen vegetables after seeing how vegetables reacted to freezing temperatures during an expedition to Labrador. Each of these people saw unique and creative opportunities in a familiar situation.

creativity The development of novel solutions to perceived organizational problems.

One test of creativity is to imagine a block of ice sitting on your desk. What use could you make of it? A creative person might see that it could be used to quench someone's thirst, reduce a patient's fever, crack a victim's skull, or produce steam by boiling.[9] Or consider the person interviewing college graduates for job openings. "Show me a new use for this stapler," the interviewer said. Calmly picking up the scissors on the desk, one creative lady cut the interviewer's tie in half and then stapled it back together. Smiling, she asked, "Now that I've demonstrated my instant mender, how many will you take?"

Each of us has the capacity to be creative. Characteristics of highly creative people are illustrated in the left-hand column of Exhibit 10.2. Creative people often are known for originality, curiosity, openmindedness, a focused approach to problem solving , persistence, a relaxed and playful attitude, and receptiveness to new ideas.[10]

Creativity in organizations can also be attributed to departments. Departments can organize themselves to be creative and initiate changes. The characteristics of creative departments correspond to those of individuals, as illustrated in the right-hand column of Exhibit 10.2. Creative

E X H I B I T   10.2

Characteristics of Creative People and Departments

The Creative Individual	The Creative Department
1. Conceptual fluency Openmindedness	1. Open channels of communication Contact with outside sources Overlapping territories Suggestion systems, brainstorming, nominal group techniques
2. Originality	2. Assigns nonspecialists to problems Allows eccentricity Uses teams
3. Less authoritarian Independent	3. Decentralized; loosely defined positions; loose control Discretionary resources Risk-taking norms
4. Playfulness Undisciplined exploration Curiosity	4. Allows freedom to choose and pursue problems Not run as a tight ship Freedom to discuss ideas; long time horizon
5. Persistent Committed Highly focused	5. Resources allocated to creative personnel and projects without immediate payoff Reward system encourages innovation Absolved of peripheral responsibilities

Source: Based on Gary A. Steiner, ed., *The Creative Organization* (Chicago: University of Chicago Press, 1965), pp. 16–18; Rosabeth Moss Kanter, "The Middle Manager as Innovator," *Harvard Business Review* (July/August 1982), pp. 104–105; James Brian Quinn, "Managing Innovation: Controlled Chaos," *Harvard Business Review* 63 (May/June 1985), pp. 73–84.

departments are loosely structured. People find themselves in a situation of ambiguity, assignments are vague, territories overlap, tasks are poorly defined, and much work is done through teams.[11] Creative organizations energize grass-roots participation.[12] They harness all potential sources of new ideas from within. Many participative management programs are born out of the desire to enhance creativity for initiating changes. People are not stuck in the rhythm of routine jobs.[13] Managers in an insurance company that had been tightly controlled from the top remarked on the changes that enabled them to be more creative:

We used to run by the book and now I don't even know where the book is.

Yesterday's procedures are outdated today.

If you don't like the organization chart, just wait until next week, we'll have a new one.[14]

Open channels of communication, overlapping jobs, discretionary resources, decentralization, and employees' freedom to choose problems and make mistakes can generate unexpected benefits for companies. Creative organizational conditions such as those described in Exhibit 10.2 enabled brand manager Cal Blodgett at General Mills to propose a change for the 6-by-300-foot sheets of granola rolling out of the oven to be crumbled into cereal bits. "Let's cut that into bars," he thought, and

Nature Valley Granola Bars were born. In another General Mills department, Craig Nalen responded to the frustration of developing a new snack food with the idea of turning the food into a product: "Why not peddle the snack food as a toy?" With that idea, Lickety Sticks were born and General Mills entered the toy market.[15]

Intrapreneurs

If creative conditions are successful, new ideas will be generated that must be carried forward for acceptance and implementation. This is where intrapreneurs come in. *Intrapreneur* is a variation on the word *entrepreneur:* a person who starts his or her own business. An intrapreneur is similar, only he or she develops and promotes an idea within an established organization.[16] The formal definition of **intrapreneur** is a person who anticipates the need for and champions productive change within the organization.[17] Remember: Change does not occur by itself. Personal energy and effort are required to successfully promote a new idea. Often a new idea is rejected by management. Intrapreneurs fight to convince managers of the merit of a new idea or line of research. Intrapreneurs are passionately committed to a new product or idea despite rejection by others.

Intrapreneurs may play one of three roles in the initiation of innovations. These roles are illustrated in Exhibit 10.3. The *inventor* develops a new idea and understands its technical value but has neither the ability nor the interest to promote it for acceptance within the organization. The *champion* believes in the idea, visualizes what it can do for the company, and gains the political and financial support needed to bring it to reality. The *sponsor* is a high-level manager who approves the idea, protects it, and removes major organizational barriers to acceptance.[18]

Al Marzocchi was an inventor at Owens-Corning Fiberglass. He invented ways to strengthen fiberglass, developed the fiberglass belted tire in conjunction with Armstrong Tire, and pioneered new ways of using asphalt. One reason Marzocchi thrived was that Owens-Corning's president, Harold Boeschenstein, sponsored his activities. Once Marzocchi went directly to a local contractor and got the company to use an experimental patching compound on city streets. Marzocchi had violated company rules by going directly to an outside firm, but the president protected him and his idea.[19] The film *Top Gun,* a big hit in 1986, would have failed without a champion. A script about Naval air cadets was in limbo because no one at Paramount was interested in producing it. Then someone slipped a copy to Frank Mancuso, the new CEO, and he championed the script for the creators. A revision of the manuscript quickly got the go-ahead. *Top Gun* was the top-grossing movie of the year.[20]

The important point is that managers can directly influence whether intrapreneurs will flourish in their organizations. When Texas Instruments studied 50 of its new-product introductions, a surprising fact emerged: Without exception, every new product that had failed had lacked a zealous champion. The intrapreneur had been missing. In contrast, most of the new products that had succeeded had had an intrapreneur. Texas Instruments' managers made an immediate deci-

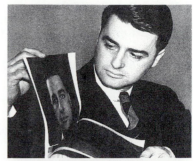

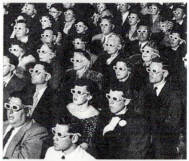

Polaroid has long encouraged creativity. The most creative employee, President Edwin H. Land, demonstrates one-step photography in 1947. In 1952, full-color, stereoscopic movies were made possible by Polaroid products, including the famous 3-D glasses. In 1963, the first color film was introduced. Today Polaroid continues its creative approach by giving researchers the freedom, resources, and open communication with which to develop new-product innovations.

intrapreneur An individual who anticipates the need for productive change and champions it within the organization.

EXHIBIT   10.3

Three Intrapreneurial Roles in Organizational Change

Inventor
Develops and understands technical aspects of idea

Does not know how to win support for idea or make a business of it

Champion
Believes in idea

Visualizes benefits but concerned with organizational realities of costs, benefits, and obtaining financial and political support

Overcomes obstacles

Sponsor
High-level manager who removes organizational barriers

Approves and protects idea within organization

Source: Based on Gifford Pinchot III, *Intrapreneuring* (New York: Harper & Row, 1985), p. 149, and Jay R. Galbraith, "Designing the Innovating Organization," *Organizational Dynamics* (Winter 1982), pp. 5–25.

sion: No new product would be approved unless an intrapreneur championed it. Other companies, such as Hewlett-Packard and 3M, give special awards to successful intrapreneurs, even when they defy management to champion new ideas. The Hewlett-Packard Medal of Defiance was given to Chuck House for championing a new idea despite severe resistance to the idea by knowledgeable people throughout the company.[21]

Venture Teams

A recent idea for facilitating corporate innovation is called venture teams. **Venture teams** are separate from the rest of the organization and are responsible for developing and initiating innovations. Venture teams give free reign to members' creativity because their separate facilities and location protect them from organizational rules and procedures. Peter Drucker advises organizations that wish to innovate to use a separate team or department:

venture team   A group separate from the mainstream of the organization responsible for developing and initiating innovations.

> For the existing business to be capable of innovation, it has to create a structure that allows people to be entrepreneurial. . . . This means, first, that the entrepreneurial, the new, has to be organized separately from the old and the existing. Whenever we have tried to make an existing unit the carrier of the entrepreneurial project, we have failed.[22]

The venture team is quite different from the use of lateral relationships or the matrix structure described in Chapter 9. In those structures, employees remain members of their everyday departments and simply work on a project part time while reporting to their regular boss. Under the venture team concept, employees no longer report through the normal structure.[23] The team exists as a separate departmental entity, as illustrated in Exhibit 10.4. Venture teams are kept small to insure their autonomy and freedom to experiment so that no bureaucracy will emerge.

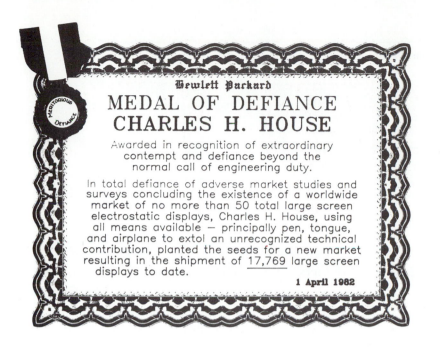

Charles House is an intrapreneur at Hewlett-Packard. He was assigned to develop a Federal Aviation Agency monitor similar to a TV picture tube but with greatly enhanced capacity. It failed to meet government specifications, but House was more interested in other applications. He took a prototype to customers to learn whether it would solve their problems—in violation of HP's rules. He fought for money to support the technology despite no proven market. Finally, the project was ordered killed by Dave Packard himself. House's immediate superior still supported him, however, and gave him one more year. House and his team succeeded, generating $10 million in annual sales because House wouldn't give up.

For a giant corporation such as IBM, venture teams free people from the constraints of the large organization. IBM has started 14 new venture units since 1981. Each is a tiny company-within-a-company that explores areas of customized software, robots, and electrocardiographs. IBM's biggest success—the personal computer—was built by a new venture group.[24]

A variation of venture teams used by some companies is called a skunkworks.[25] **Skunkworks** are small, informal, and sometimes unauthorized groups that create innovations. Companies such as Kollmorgen, IBM, Merck, Philip Morris, and Macy encourage employees to form separate groups, often working nights and weekends, to develop a new idea. If the new venture is successful, group members are rewarded and encouraged to run the new business.

skunkworks A small, informal, and sometimes unauthorized group who creates innovations.

One huge company that felt forces for change and created a new internal structure to increase the initiation of new ideas is Campbell Soup.

Campbell Soup Company

Campbell's size and the success of its traditional soup products made it hard for people to innovate. But president R. Gordon McGovern successfully transformed Campbell into an entrepreneurial company. Why? Campbell was feeling the heat from competitors. "We were scared of getting wiped out," explains McGovern. "We sensed the world was changing. . . . We figured we'd end up like the dinosaurs." The pressure McGovern felt was reflected in the declining shipments

EXHIBIT   10.4

Location of New-Venture Team in an Organization

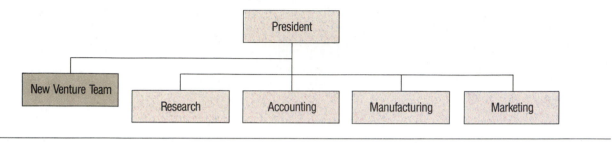

of Campbell's classic line of "red and white" soups and the drop in Swanson TV dinners, a Campbell subsidiary.

To get innovations moving and recapture market share, McGovern broke Campbell into some 50 independent business units and instructed each one to develop its own products. The smaller, decentralized units were no longer constrained by the rules and procedures of the larger company. This was a dramatic shift from the past, but it created a climate for intrapreneurship. In 1984 alone Campbell introduced 92 new products, far more than competitors.

Larry Carpenter, a 29-year-old marketing manager, loved the new freedom to innovate. Carpenter had major responsibility for revitalizing the soup line. One of his new-product introductions was Creamy Natural Soups, which has given old customers new soup products. Things are happening at a frantic pace at Campbell because the president created a series of entrepreneurial divisions within which intrapreneurs like Larry Carpenter flourish.[26]

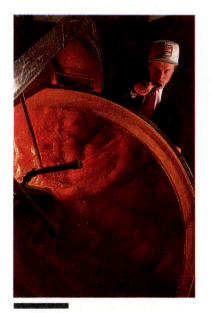

President Gordon McGovern transformed Campbell by decentralizing innovation responsibility to autonomous business units. In 1984 alone the company introduced 92 new products, far more than its competitors. Two products introduced in 1983—Prego spaghetti sauce and Le Menu frozen dinners— have combined sales of $450 million a year. Larry Carpenter is responsible for an entire line of soups and is shown here tasting one of his own creations. Intrapreneurs like Carpenter and decentralized teams are given major resources with which to develop new products.

IMPLEMENTING CHANGE

The final step to be managed in the change process is implementation. If a company has been successful at creating a climate of creativity— facilitating intrapreneurship and establishing separate venture groups— the flow of ideas should be adequate for meeting external and internal pressures for change. The next problem confronting management is to implement change. A new, creative idea will not benefit the organization until it is in place and being fully utilized. One frustration for managers is that employees often seem to resist change for no apparent reason. To effectively manage the implementation process, managers should be aware of the reasons for employee resistance and be prepared to use techniques for obtaining employee cooperation.

Are You an Intrapreneur?

Gifford Pinchot III, author of *Intrapreneuring*, developed the following exam to identify potential intrapreneurs.

Answer "Yes" or "No" to the Following Questions:

1. Does your desire to make things work better occupy as much of your time as fulfilling your duty to maintain them the way they are?
2. Do you get excited about what you are doing at work?
3. Do you think about new business ideas while driving to work or taking a shower?
4. Can you visualize concrete steps for action when you consider ways to make a new idea happen?
5. Do you get in trouble from time to time for doing things that exceed your authority?
6. Are you able to keep your ideas under cover, suppressing your urge to tell everyone about them until you have tested them and developed a plan for implementation?
7. Have you successfully pushed through bleak times when something you were working on looked like it might fail?
8. Do you have more than your share of both fans and critics?
9. Do you have a network of friends at work whom you can count on for help?
10. Do you get easily annoyed by others' incompetent attempts to execute portions of your ideas?
11. Can you consider trying to overcome a natural perfectionist tendency to do all the work yourself and share responsibility for your ideas with a team?
12. Would you be willing to give up some salary in exchange for the chance to try out your business idea if the rewards for success were adequate?

If you have answered yes more often than no, chances are you are already behaving like an intrapreneur. Companies made up of 10 to 15 percent intrapreneurs can be expected to be innovative.

If you are an intrapreneur and want to have your idea accepted, adopt the following approach.

The Intrapreneur's Ten Commandments

1. Come to work each day willing to be fired.
2. Circumvent any orders aimed at stopping your dream.
3. Do any job needed to make your project work, regardless of your job description.
4. Find people to help you.
5. Follow your intuition about the people you choose, and work only with the best.
6. Work underground as long as you can—publicity triggers the corporate immune mechanism.
7. Never bet on a race unless you are running in it.
8. Remember it is easier to ask for forgiveness than for permission.
9. Be true to your goals, but be realistic about the ways to achieve them.
10. Honor your sponsors.

Resistance to Change

Intrapreneurs often discover that other employees are unenthusiastic about their new ideas. Members of a new-venture group may be surprised when managers in the regular organization do not support or approve their innovations. Managers and employees not involved in an innovation often seem to prefer the status quo. There are several reasons why employees appear to resist change, and understanding them helps managers implement change more effectively.

Self-Interest.   Employees typically resist a change they believe will take away something of value. A proposed change in job design, structure, or technology may lead to a perceived loss of power, prestige, pay, or company benefits. The fear of personal loss is perhaps the biggest obstacle to organizational change.[27] When Mesa Oil Corporation tried to buy Phillips Petroleum, Phillips employees started a campaign to prevent the takeover. Employees believed that Mesa would not treat them well and that they would lose financial benefits. Their resistance to change was so effective that the merger failed to take place.

Lack of Understanding and Trust.   Employees often don't understand the intended purpose of a change or distrust the intentions behind it. If previous working relationships with an intrapreneur have been negative, resistance may occur. One manager had a habit of initiating a change in the financial reporting system about every 12 months, then losing interest and not following through. After the third time, employees no longer went along with the change because they did not trust the manager's intention to follow through to their benefit. If an intrapreneur or new-venture group can develop a tradition of positive working relationships and take the time to explain their idea to users, the path of implementation will likely lead to success.[28]

Uncertainty.   *Uncertainty* is the lack of information about future events. It represents a fear of the unknown. Uncertainty is especially threatening for employees who have a low tolerance for change and fear the novel and unusual. Employees may be nervous or anxious because they don't know how an anticipated change will affect them. They may also worry about whether they will be able to meet the demands of a new procedure or technology associated with the change.[29] Union leaders at General Motors' Steering Gear Division in Saginaw, Michigan, were sensitive to the introduction of employee participation programs. They were uncertain about how the program would affect their status and thus initially opposed it. The same thing happened at a Western Electric plant; union leaders resisted so strongly that the company backed away from the innovation.

Different Assessments and Goals.   Another reason for resistance to change is that people who will be affected by innovation may assess the situation differently than an intrapreneur or new-venture group. Often there are legitimate disagreements over the proposed benefits of a change. Managers in each department pursue different goals, and an innovation may detract from performance and goal achievement for some departments. For example, if marketing gets the new product it wants for its customers, the cost of manufacturing may increase and the manufacturing superintendent thus will resist. Resistance based on different assessments can be a positive feature for the organization, however, because it may call attention to problems with the innovation. At the S. C. Johnson & Son Company in Racine, Wisconsin, middle managers resisted the introduction of a new employee program that turned out to be a bad idea. The managers truly believed that the program would do more harm than good. One manager bluntly told his boss, "I've been here longer than you, and I'll be here after you've gone, so don't tell me what really counts at this company."[30]

Uncertainty, misunderstanding, and conflicting goals often make managers and employees resist change. Introducing participative management into autocratic companies is especially difficult, because managers fear loss of power and status. Here Ralph Barra (standing) is using education to teach RCA executives participative methods; participants honk a horn when they think someone is not cooperating. Barra also emphasizes that top managers must support the change if it is to be properly implemented.

These reasons for resistance are legitimate in the eyes of employees affected by the change. The best procedure for managers is not to ignore resistance but to diagnose the reasons and overcome them. Strategies for overcoming resistance to change typically involve two approaches: the analysis of resistance through the force field technique and the use of selective implementation tactics to overcome resistance.

Force Field Analysis

Force field analysis grew from the work of Kurt Lewin, who proposed that change was a result of the competition between *driving* and *restraining forces.*[31] When a change is introduced, some forces drive and other forces resist it. To implement a change, management should analyze the change forces. By selectively removing forces that restrain change, the driving forces will be strong enough to enable implementation, as illustrated by the move from A to B in Exhibit 10.5. As restraining forces are reduced or removed, behavior will shift to incorporate the desired changes.

Just-in-time (JIT) inventory control systems schedule materials to arrive at a company just as they are needed on the production line. In an Ohio manufacturing company, management's analysis showed that the driving forces associated with the implementation of JIT were (1) the large cost savings from reduced inventories, (2) savings from needing fewer workers to handle the inventory, and (3) a quicker, more competitive market response for the company. Restraining forces discovered by managers were (1) a freight system that was too slow to deliver inventory on time, (2) a facility layout that emphasized inventory maintenance over new deliveries, (3) worker skills inappropriate for handling rapid inventory deployment, and (4) union resistance to loss of jobs. The driving forces were insufficient to overcome the restraining forces, and unless managers removed the restraints, JIT would not be implemented.

To shift the behavior to JIT, managers attacked the restraining forces. An analysis of the freight system showed that delivery by truck provided

force field analysis The process of determining which forces drive and which resist a proposed change.

EXHIBIT   10.5

Using Force Field Analysis to Change from Traditional to Just-in-Time Inventory System

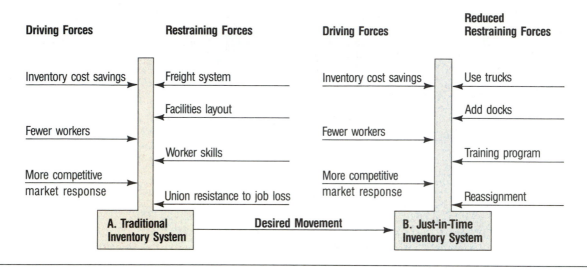

the flexibility and quickness needed to schedule inventory arrival at a specific time each day. The problem with facility layout was met by adding four new loading docks. Inappropriate worker skills were attacked with a training program to instruct workers in JIT methods and in assembling products with uninspected parts. Union resistance was overcome by agreeing to reassign workers no longer needed for maintaining inventory to jobs in another plant. With the restraining forces removed, the driving forces were sufficient to allow the JIT system to be implemented.

Implementation Tactics

The other approach to managing implementation is to adopt specific tactics to overcome employee resistance. For example, resistance to change may be overcome by educating employees or inviting them to participate in implementing the change. Methods for dealing with resistance to change have been studied by researchers. The following five tactics, summarized in Exhibit 10.6, have proven successful.[32]

Communication and Education.   Communication and education are used when solid information about the change is needed by users and others who may resist implementation. Education is especially important when the change involves new technical knowledge or users are unfamiliar with the idea. When Monsanto implemented a new control system for capital spending, the first step was called "education and awareness." People in the accounting department explained the concepts and language of asset management to all management levels. Through education and communication, resistance was overcome. Florida Power & Light Company instituted a change in company procedures that initially

E X H I B I T   10.6

Tactics for Overcoming Resistance to Change

Approach	When to Use
Communication, education	When change is technical; when accurate information and analysis are needed by users to understand change.
Participation	When users need to feel involved; when design requires information from others; when users have power to resist.
Negotiation	When a group has power over implementation; when a group will lose out in the change.
Coercion	When there is a crisis; when initiators clearly have power; when other implementation techniques have failed.
Top management support	When change involves multiple departments or reallocation of resources; when legitimacy of change is doubted by users.

Source: Based on J. P. Kotter and L. A. Schlesinger, "Choosing Strategies for Change," *Harvard Business Review* 57 (March/April 1979), pp. 106–114.

confused managers. Realizing it had implemented the change too quickly, the company stepped back, tailored special training sessions to educate managers, and then reimplemented the new procedures. The training program resolved the difficulty, and implementation was a success.[33]

Participation.   *Participation* involves users and potential resisters in designing the change. This approach is time consuming, but it pays off because users understand and become committed to the change. When General Motors tried to implement a new management appraisal system for supervisors in its Adrian, Michigan, plant, it met with immediate resistance. Rebuffed by the lack of cooperation, top managers proceeded more slowly, involving supervisors in the design of the new appraisal system. Through participation in system design, managers understood what the new approach was all about and dropped their resistance to it.

Negotiation.   Negotiation is a more formal means of achieving cooperation. *Negotiation* uses formal bargaining to win acceptance and approval of a desired change. For example, if the marketing department fears losing power if a new management structure is implemented, top managers may negotiate with marketing to reach a resolution. General Motors, General Electric, and other companies that have strong unions frequently must formally negotiate change with the unions. The change may become part of the union contract reflecting the agreement of both parties.

Coercion.   *Coercion* means that managers use formal power to force employees to change. Resisters are told to accept the change or lose rewards or even their jobs. Coercion is necessary in crisis situations

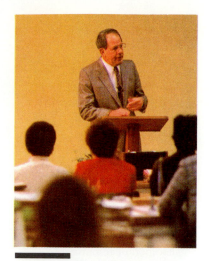

Paul J. Scheel, president of USF&G, is addressing employees of the Richmond, Virginia, branch office regarding new pricing and underwriting guidelines. Scheel facilitated implementation by showing top management support for the changes. Written instructions were circulated among branch offices, a presentation was made at the annual managers' meeting, and regional workshops were held to teach everyone the importance of the new guidelines. Top executives made a series of branch office visits to communicate the changes to every single employee. These tactics insured the new guidelines' successful implementation.

where a rapid response is urgent. When middle managers at TRW Inc.'s Valve Division in Cleveland refused to go along with a new employee involvement program, top management reassigned several first-line supervisors and managers. The new jobs did not involve supervisory responsibility. Further, other TRW managers were told that future pay increases depended on their adoption of the new procedures. The coercive techniques were used as a last resort because managers refused to go along with the change any other way.[34]

Top Management Support.   The visible support of top management also helps overcome resistance to change. Top management support symbolizes to all employees that the change is important for the organization. Top management support is especially important when a change involves multiple departments or when resources are being reallocated among departments. Without top management support, these changes can get bogged down in squabbling among departments. Moreover, when top managers fail to support a project, they can inadvertently undercut it by issuing contradictory orders. This happened at Flying Tiger Lines. In 1984, the airborne freight hauler came up with a plan to eliminate excessive paperwork by changing the layout of offices so that two agents rather than four could handle each shipment. No sooner had part of the change been implemented than top management ordered another system; thus, the office layout was changed again. The new layout was not as efficient, but it was the one that top management supported. Had middle managers informed top managers and obtained their support earlier, the initial change would not have been defeated by a new priority.[35]

By adopting smart implementation techniques, Navistar managers saved a lot of money for the company.

Navistar International

Managers at Navistar International—formerly International Harvester—successfully introduced a maintenance, repair, and operating (MRO) buying program. Purchasing costs were far too high. Buyers were buried under an avalanche of 14,000 requisitions per year, hundreds of suppliers were used, inventory turnover was slow, and there was little coordination between warehousing and purchasing.

James Hall and Pierre Bodeau of the Construction Equipment Group in Melrose Park, Illinois, proposed a redesigned requisition process, including a computerized inventory control system and a new procedure for analyzing vendor capability. They also devised a plan for successful implementation.

Implementation involved several steps: Survey 120 industrial suppliers for accurate information; involve IH employees in discussions to further refine and improve the buying program; undertake internal training to teach employees the new procedures;

E X H I B I T   10.7

Four Types of Organizational Change

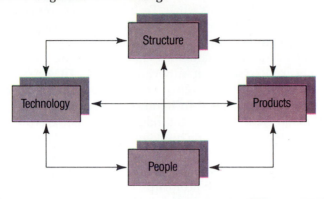

Source: Based on Harold J. Leavitt, "Applied Organizational Change in Industry: Structural, Technical, and Human Approaches," in *New Perspectives in Organization Research,* ed. W. W. Cooper, H. J. Leavitt, and M. W. Shelly II (New York: Wiley, 1964), pp. 55–74.

and analyze other forces for resistance. After the program was fully developed, key employees were already on board because they had participated in program design. Training for other employees went smoothly. The program was launched in June, and by April of the next year 90 percent of the purchases had gone through the MRO system. Cost savings through price reductions amounted to $78,000 the first year, and MRO inventories dropped $1 million in eight months.[36]

TYPES OF PLANNED CHANGE

Now that we have explored how the initiation and implementation of change can be carried out, let us look at the different types of change that occur in organizations. We will address two issues: what parts of the organization can be changed and how managers can apply the initiation and implementation ideas to each type of change.

The four types of organizational change are technology, products, structure, and people, as illustrated in Exhibit 10.7. Organizations may innovate in one or more areas depending on internal and external forces for change. In the rapidly changing toy industry, a manufacturer will have to introduce new products frequently. In a mature, competitive industry, technology changes will be adopted to improve efficiency. Note the arrows connecting the four types of change in Exhibit 10.7; this means that a change in one part may affect other parts of the organization: A new product may require changes in technology, a new technology may require new people skills or a new structure, and so on.

technology change A change that pertains to the organization's production process.

product change A change in the organization's product or service output.

New-product changes are best introduced through a horizontal linkage among departments. This is the Toaster Strudel™ team responsible for the biggest internally generated product success in Pillsbury's history. Originally code named Project Sting, the team includes a process engineer, quality systems coordinator, design engineer, and marketing representative who solve production and distribution problems. Their ingenuity cleared numerous hurdles to allow Pillsbury to introduce the product nationally. Horizontal coordination enabled the team to satisfy customer needs and technical requirements simultaneously.

Technological Approaches

Technology changes pertain to the organization's production process—how the organization does its work. Technology changes are designed to make the production of a product or service more efficient. For example, the adoption of robotics to improve production efficiency at General Motors and Chrysler is a technology change, as is the adoption of laser-scanning checkout systems at supermarkets. At IBM's manufacturing plant in Charlotte, North Carolina, an automated miniload storage and retrieval system was installed to handle production parts. This change provided an efficient method for handling small-parts inventory and constituted a change in the technology of how the IBM plant does its work.

How can managers encourage technology change? The general rule is that technology change is bottom up.[37] The *bottom-up approach* means that ideas are developed at lower organization levels and channeled upward for approval. Lower-level technical experts act as intrapreneurs—they invent and champion technological changes. Employees at lower levels understand the technology and have the expertise needed to propose changes.

Managers can facilitate the bottom-up approach by designing creative departments as described earlier in this chapter. A loose, flexible, decentralized structure provides employees with the freedom and opportunity to initiate changes. A rigid, centralized, standardized structure stifles technology innovation. Anything managers can do to involve the grass roots of the organization—the people who are experts in their parts of the production process—will increase technology change.

A *top-down approach* to technology change usually does not work.[38] Top managers are not close to the production process and lack expertise in technological developments. Mandating technology change from the top produces fewer rather than more technology innovations. The spark for a creative new idea comes from people close to the technology. The rationale behind Motorola's "participative management program," Data General's "pride teams," and Honeywell's "positive action teams" is to extract new technology contributions from lower organization levels.

New-Product Approaches

A **product change** is a change in the organization's product or service output. New-product innovations have major implications for an organization, because they often are an outcome of a new strategy and may define a new market.[39] Examples of new products are Frito-Lay's introduction of O'Grady's potato chips, Hewlett-Packard's introduction of a professional computer, and GE's development of a device for monitoring patients' heart cycles at its Medical Division.

The introduction of a new product is difficult, because it not only involves a new technology but must meet customers' needs. In most industries, only about one in eight new-product ideas are successful.[40] Companies that successfully develop new products usually have the following characteristics:

E X H I B I T   10.8

Horizontal Linkage Model for New-Product Innovation

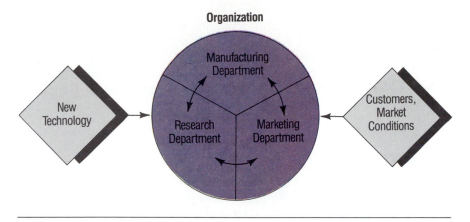

1. People in marketing have a good understanding of customer needs.
2. Technical specialists are aware of recent technological developments and make effective use of new technology.
3. Members from key departments—research, manufacturing, marketing—cooperate in the development of the new product.[41]

These findings mean that the ideas for new products typically originate at the lower levels of the organization just as they do for technology changes. The difference is that new-product ideas flow horizontally among departments. Product innovation requires expertise from several departments simultaneously. A new-product failure is often the result of failed cooperation.[42]

One approach to successful new-product innovation is called the **horizontal linkage model,** which is illustrated in Exhibit 10.8.[43] The model shows that research and development, manufacturing, and marketing must simultaneously develop new products. People from these departments meet frequently in teams and task forces to share ideas and solve problems. Research people inform marketing of new technical developments to learn whether they will be useful to customers. Marketing people pass customer complaints to R&D to use in the design of new products. Manufacturing informs other departments whether a product idea can be manufactured within cost limits. When the horizontal linkage model is used, the decision to develop a new product is a joint one. This is also the case with the use of venture teams described above. Employees from R&D, marketing, and production are assigned to the same venture team; thus, horizontal linkage occurs automatically by having employees jointly do the team's work.

At Convergent Technologies, "Workslate," a portable computer, received accolades when it was introduced. One year later, Workslate was dead. Production problems with the new product had not been worked

horizontal linkage model   An approach to product change that emphasizes shared development of innovations among several departments.

out. Marketing people had not fully analyzed customer needs. The idea had been pushed through without sufficient consultation among research, manufacturing, and marketing. Integrated Genetics Inc. breaks down barriers between scientists and the rest of the company through a series of weekly meetings. Each Friday, one scientist gives a presentation to the company on new developments in biotechnology. On another day, an employee from selling, marketing, or administration speaks to the scientists on ideas and developments in their areas. Other companies use formal linkages, such as the designation of a new-product team or a matrix structure, to insure collaboration sufficient for new-product innovation.

Structural Approaches

structure change   Any change in the way in which the organization is designed and managed.

Structure changes pertain to the hierarchy of authority, goals, structural characteristics, administrative procedures, and management systems.[44] Almost any change in how the organization is managed falls under the category of structural change. At General Telephone & Electronics Corporation, recent structural changes have included a structural reorganization, new pay incentives, a revised performance appraisal system, and affirmative action programs. IBM's change from a functional to a product structure in 1974 was a structural change. In 1981, another restructuring occurred at IBM with the creation of two new divisions in the marketing area, the National Accounts and National Marketing Divisions.

Successful structural change is through a top-down approach, which is distinct from technology change (bottom up) and new products (horizontal).[45] Structural change is top down because the expertise for administrative improvements originates at the middle and upper levels of the organization. The intrapreneurs for structural change are middle and top managers. Lower-level technical specialists have little interest or expertise in administrative procedures. If organization structure causes negative consequences for lower employees, complaints and dissatisfaction alert managers to a problem. Employee dissatisfaction is an internal force for change. The need for change is perceived by higher managers, who then take the initiative to propose and implement it.

The top-down process does not mean that coercion is the best implementation tactic. Implementation tactics include education, participation, and negotiation with employees. Unless there is an emergency, managers should not force structural change on employees. They may hit a resistance wall, and the change will fail. This is exactly what happened at the company for which Mary Kay Ash worked before she started her own cosmetics business. The owner learned that even a top-down change in commission rate needs to incorporate education and participation in order to succeed:

A structure change helped Lewis Grocer Company, a division of Super Valu Stores, Inc., reduce its losses from damaged merchandise. The structure change was a new program called Damage Busters. It began with a letter from the division president to all employees asking for suggestions. Prizes were awarded, and a scoreboard listed weekly damage reports. Although initiated from the top down, this program encouraged technical suggestions from the bottom up. Damage costs were cut significantly ($250,000 annually, first two years), and changes now in effect include forklift and loader operator testing and certification programs.

> *I worked for a company whose owner decided to revise the commission schedule paid to his sales managers. All brochures and company literature were changed accordingly. He then made plans for personally announcing the changes during a series of regional sales conferences. I accompanied him to the first conference. I'll never forget it.*

To an audience of fifty sales managers he announced that the 2 percent override they were presently earning on their units' sales production was to be reduced to 1 percent. "However," he said, "in lieu of that 1 percent, you will receive a very nice gift for each new person you recruit and train."

At that point a sales manager stood up and let him have it with both barrels. She was absolutely furious. "How dare you do this to us? Why, even 2 percent wasn't enough. But cutting our overrides in half and offering us a crummy gift for appeasement insults our intelligence." With that she stormed out of the room. And every other sales manager for that state followed her—all fifty of them. In one fell swoop the owner had lost his entire sales organization in that region—the best in the country. I had never seen such an overwhelming rejection of a change of this kind in my entire life![46]

People Approaches

People change refers to changes in employees' attitudes, skills, beliefs, abilities, styles, and behavior. Sending managers to a leadership training course in order to improve their leadership skills would be an example of people change. Other examples would be improvements in employees' communication, planning, and technical skills. People change is distinct from other types of changes because the primary focus is on employees rather than on technology, products, or administrative structure. Employee retraining programs at IBM are people change, as are the employee involvement programs at General Motors and the quality circle program at Westinghouse. Selection and recruitment programs, early retirement programs, and employee layoffs are still other examples of people change.

The most widely used type of people change is employee training and development. Many companies establish training departments to improve employee skills. Companies such as Tenneco and Exxon hold classes in skills such as machine maintenance, financial procedures, engineering, personnel procedures, machine operation, and drafting. Training departments also focus on upgrading management skills. A class in supervisory management helps employees learn to become first-line managers. Training programs in leadership, strategic planning, and organization design help upper-level managers improve their leadership skills.

Another major approach to people change is organizational development (discussed in the following section). This has evolved as a separate field that is devoted to large-scale people change. Some organization development programs include changes in structure and technology as well as people.

> **people change** A change in employees' attitudes, beliefs, skills, abilities, or behavior.

ORGANIZATIONAL DEVELOPMENT

Organizational development (OD) is the application of behavioral science knowledge to improve an organization's health and effectiveness through its ability to cope with environmental changes, improve internal

> **organizational development (OD)** The application of behavioral science techniques to improve an organization's health and effectiveness through its ability to cope with environmental changes, improve internal relationships, and increase problem-solving capabilities.

In this example of organizational development, employees at Hewitt Associates examine group dynamics and leadership styles. Hewitt management embraces the philosophy that employees thrive on personal growth and development and are capable of taking responsibility for their actions. Following OD assumptions, Hewitt's culture supports employees' development and expression of feelings and attitudes.

relationships, and increase problem-solving capabilities.[47] Organizational development improves working relationships among employees.

The following examples of problems that OD can solve illustrate its value:[48]

1. A product team for the introduction of a new software package is formed at a computer company. Made up of strong-willed individuals, the team makes little progress because members do not agree on the goals of the project.
2. Two managers dislike each other intensely. They argue at meetings, work against each other politically, and inhibit achievement of their departmental goals.
3. Salespeople who have promised delivery dates to customers are in conflict with shop foremen about the priorities for assembling customer orders. Manufacturing foremen are supposed to assemble orders on the basis of cost efficiency, while salespeople insist they be assembled to meet delivery dates regardless of cost.
4. Rapid growth over a three-year period has created a company situation in which managers are unclear about their roles and responsibilities and what to expect in the future.

Organizational development could be used to treat each of these problems. Some problems pertain to working relationships among managers, others to goals within the organization, and still others to interdepartmental relationships and overall company management.

OD Assumptions

Organizational development applies to individuals, departments, and the entire organization. Certain management assumptions must be met in order for OD to be successful.[49]

Individuals

▪ People desire personal growth and development, which can be met in a supportive and challenging work environment.

- People can make greater contributions to the organization than they are normally permitted. People are capable of assuming responsibility for their own actions and of making positive contributions to their work.

Groups

- Work groups can satisfy important needs for individuals and engender feelings of competence and satisfaction.
- Work groups can be helpful or harmful in supporting organizational objectives. They are more effective when their members work in collaboration and use frank and open communication.
- Formal work group leaders cannot possibly perform all leadership duties. In effective groups, leadership is shared.

Organizations

- The culture of the entire organization will affect the expression of individual feelings and attitudes and the contributions of individuals and groups to the organization.
- Resolving differences among departments in such a way that one department wins and one loses will be unhealthy for the organization in the long run.
- Organizations can be designed to meet the needs of individuals and groups and enhance their contributions to organization performance.

The basic value underlying OD is the understanding that people desire personal growth and development and are capable of making a contribution to the organization. The work group meets individual needs when interpersonal trust and support are high and work groups can increase organizational effectiveness. For the entire organization, OD assumes that departments must work together, that successful skills for resolving interdepartmental conflicts can be developed, and that the total organization can be designed to meet the needs of individuals and groups.

The spirit of what OD tries to accomplish is illustrated in Honeywell's use of OD to implement a participative management style.

Honeywell Corporation

For many years a Honeywell division had been an authoritarian entity. Now top managers believed that individuals could contribute to effectiveness if middle- and lower-level managers would allow them to participate more fully:

> Many organizations today want to break out of the beat-'em-up school of management and move toward a more participative management style. But like abused children who grow up to become abusive parents, managers raised in a less enlightened manner may have difficulty operating under a new set of rules.

At Honeywell, we have been working to change from what I call the Patton style of management to a more collaborative way of operating. The way we manage people is still less than perfect. But now our employees can have a real share of the action rather than feeling blocked or frustrated by a rigid bureaucracy.[50]

The implementation of this new way of thinking was not easy. Managers and employees alike had to think in a different way and approach one another with respect and a desire for a positive working relationship. The new values that Honeywell wished to inculcate included the following management principles, published and circulated among all employees:

1. Productivity is a responsibility shared by management and employees.
2. Broadened employee participation in decision making will be fostered.
3. Teamwork, mutual respect, and a sense of ownership will be promoted at all divisional levels.
4. A positive climate for career growth will be supported throughout the division.
5. Work life and personal life have interacting requirements that will be recognized.

Through OD Honeywell created a higher level of participation for employees. Managers learned to think of employees as whole people, not as instruments of production.[51]

OD Steps

unfreezing A step in the diagnosis stage of organizational development in which participants are made aware of problems in order to increase their willingness to change their behavior.

changing A step in the intervention stage of organizational development in which individuals experiment with new workplace behavior.

refreezing A step in the reinforcement stage of organizational development in which individuals acquire a desired new skill or attitude and are rewarded for it by the organization.

Organizational development procedures acknowledge that human behavior in organizations is relatively stable and that companywide changes require major effort. The theory underlying organizational development proposes three distinct steps for widespread behavioral and attitudinal change: (1) unfreezing, (2) changing, and (3) refreezing.[52] In the first step, **unfreezing,** participants must be made aware of problems and be willing to change. Managers and employees must acknowledge difficulties in their current behavior and see new behavior as being more effective. The second, **changing,** occurs when individuals experiment with new behavior. They learn new skills and try them out in the workplace. At Honeywell, the new skill was managers' attempt to involve subordinates in decision making. The third, **refreezing,** occurs when individuals acquire a new attitude or skill and are rewarded for it by the organization.

Organizational development experts have developed specific procedures for each change step:

1. *Diagnosis.* Most organizational development changes are effected in consultation with an outside expert called a change agent. The **change agent** is an OD specialist who contracts with the organization to facilitate change. The change agent performs a systematic diagnosis of the organization and identifies work-related problems. He or she gathers and analyzes data through personal interviews with managers, questionnaires filled out by organization members, observations of meetings and other organizational activities, and analyses of organizational documents. The diagnosis phase is used to determine the extent of organizational problems and help unfreeze managers by making them aware of them.

2. *Intervention.* The intervention stage typically involves action planning for bringing about specific behavioral changes within the organization. The action plan defines objectives for the types of training managers and employees will receive. Intervention also includes workshops and formal classroom training to help managers and employees acquire desired skills.

3. *Reinforcement.* Reinforcement is the process of evaluating the impact of change and helping organization members retain their new behaviors. The change agent can do a follow-up study to determine whether new data show changes in behavior and performance. Positive changes can be rewarded. Managers and employees also participate in refresher courses, held every year or so, to maintain the desired behaviors. Reinforcement is the process of refreezing the organization.

change agent An OD specialist who contracts with an organization to facilitate change.

OD Interventions

Organizational development change programs include a broad range of behavioral science-based techniques. Three popular and important OD intervention techniques are team building, survey feedback, and the managerial grid. Most OD change agents are familiar with and able to utilize these techniques. Moreover, techniques can be selected to facilitate change at the individual, group, or organization level depending on the nature of the organization's problem. Managers can select an intervention to help specific people overcome a problem, one or more departments solve a problem, or change the entire organization.

team building A type of OD intervention that enhances the cohesiveness of departments by helping members to learn to function as a team.

Team Building. **Team building** has the objective of enhancing the cohesiveness and success of organizational departments and teams. A series of exercises are used with department members to help them learn to act and function as a team. Team-building activities often are used for temporary teams that are created in a project or matrix structure. A change agent works with team members to increase their communication skills, facilitate their ability to confront one another, and accept common goals. Team building also increases managers' insight into their own behavior and its impact on other team members.[53] The change agent's activity with the group often is performed off-site so that work distractions will not disturb the team-building process.

The Southland Corporation, known for its 7-Eleven stores, uses team building interventions to improve management effectiveness. In the "Team Building 1" seminar, managers learn about their individual styles and personalities and how these interact in the workplace. An additional course, "Achieving Excellence," helps district managers develop themselves and their employees to their full potential. The team building program helps managers reach their own potential and learn how to help their employees grow as part of the management team.

EXHIBIT   10.9

Examples of Survey Feedback Questions

Answers to the following questions are shared with top managers and members of organizational groups. An OD specialist meets with the groups to explain the findings and to engage them in a discussion on how to solve any shortcomings that appear.

	Never True		Sometimes True		Always True
1. Employees like myself are free to take independent actions as necessary to carry out our jobs.	1	2	3	4	5
2. The leader of my group listens to us in an understanding way.	1	2	3	4	5
3. There is competition and conflict among employees in my department.	1	2	3	4	5
4. Good performance is rewarded in this organization.	1	2	3	4	5
5. There is a strong sense of community among employees in my department.	1	2	3	4	5
6. This organization is slow to experiment with novel ideas and procedures.	1	2	3	4	5
7. People are not focused on goals in this organization.	1	2	3	4	5
8. I have the authority to make decisions relevant to my job activities.	1	2	3	4	5
9. Supervision is considered very good in my department.	1	2	3	4	5
10. People in my department feel free to discuss their feelings about how the department is working.	1	2	3	4	5
11. My supervisor trusts us.	1	2	3	4	5

survey feedback A type of OD intervention in which questionnaires on organizational climate and other factors are distributed among employees and the results reported back to them by a change agent.

Survey Feedback. **Survey feedback** begins with a questionnaire distributed to employees on values, climate, participation, leadership, and group cohesion within the organization.[54] After the survey is completed, an OD change agent meets with groups of employees to provide feedback on their responses.[55] An example of questions used on a survey feedback employee questionnaire is presented in Exhibit 10.9. Answers to these questions provide the basis for group discussions and, hence, organizational change and improvement.

The distinctive feature of this approach is feedback to employee groups. Prior to the survey feedback technique, a company's survey data would be presented to top managers only. The survey feedback technique is powerful because it gives employees at all levels of the organization feedback on results for their departments and engages them in constructive discussions with their bosses for making changes and improvements.

Managerial Grid® An OD intervention technique that assesses management style through the use of a grid that represents concern for production on one axis and concern for people on the other.

Managerial Grid®. The **Managerial Grid** (also called *grid OD*) was developed by Robert Blake and Jane Mouton.[56] It focuses on two aspects of

EXHIBIT 10.10

The Managerial Grid®

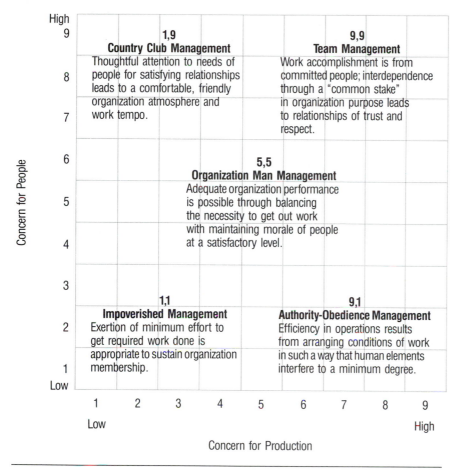

managerial behavior: concern for production and concern for people. Concern for production means getting results and achieving objectives with little regard for the people involved. Concern for people emphasizes healthy interpersonal relationships in the work group over task results. The Managerial Grid and its five major management styles are depicted in Exhibit 10.10. Each axis on the Grid is on a 9-point scale, with 1 meaning low concern and 9 high concern. The combination of management concerns leads to one of the five management styles.

Team management (9,9) is considered the most effective style and is recommended for managers throughout the organization. Organization members work together to accomplish task outcomes. *Country club management* (1,9) occurs when primary emphasis is given to people rather than to work outputs. *Authority-obedience management* (9,1) occurs when efficiency in operations is the dominant orientation. *Organization Man*

Ebasco Services Inc., a huge engineering and construction company, used OD specialists to help employees overcome frictions. A construction project takes several years to complete, and problems may throw schedules off and pit workers against one another. Over 100 formal seminars have helped employees learn to cope with frustrations and conflicts encountered on construction sites. During a two-day session at a Louisiana construction site, personnel were able to vent their resentments and conflicts. The OD interventions were so successful that Ebasco's top echelon participated in planning seminars developed by the OD consultants.

management (5,5) reflects a moderate amount of concern for both people and production. *Impoverished management* (1,1) means the absence of a management philosophy; managers exert little effort toward interpersonal relationships or work accomplishment.

Grid OD involves companywide training to achieve a 9,9 style throughout the organization. In a large organization, Grid OD training will require several years and the participation of hundreds of managers. Many of the world's largest corporations have used Grid OD, including Pillsbury, Union Carbide, and Texas Instruments.

Effectiveness of OD

Organizational development is widely practiced, but whether organizations truly benefit from it is still in question. Many OD consultants evaluate the impact of their intervention to see whether improvement occurred. Some studies suggest that OD improvement is small and relatively short-lived. Others argue that the changes from OD are substantial but are difficult to measure because they represent attitude and behavioral changes. Many companies create their own organizational development departments. Thus, they have in-house OD experts who can provide training for the rest of the organization. Overall, the practice of OD flourishes because companies feel that these interventions meet their needs for improved performance.[57]

SUMMARY

Change is inevitable in organizations. The point of this chapter is that techniques for managing the change process are available. Managers should think of change as having four elements—the forces for change, the perceived need for change, initiation of change, and implementation of change. Forces for change can originate either within or outside the firm, and managers are responsible for monitoring events that may require a planned organizational response. Techniques for initiating changes include designing the organization for creativity, encouraging intrapreneurs, and establishing venture teams or skunkworks. The final step is implementation. Force field analysis is one technique for diagnosing restraining forces, which often can be removed. Managers also should draw on the implementation tactics of communication, participation, negotiation, coercion, or top management support.

This chapter also discussed specific types of change. Technology changes are accomplished through a bottom-up approach that utilizes experts close to the technology. Successful new-product introduction requires horizontal linkage among marketing, research and development, manufacturing, and perhaps other departments. Structural changes tend to be initiated in a top-down fashion, because upper managers are the administrative experts and champion these ideas for approval and implementation. People change pertains to the skills, behaviors, and attitudes of employees. Organizational development is an important type of people change. The OD process entails three stages—diagnosis (unfreezing), intervention (the actual change), and reinforcement (refreezing). Popular OD techniques include team building, survey feedback, and the managerial grid.

Management Solution

Based on the concepts in this chapter, General Electric's problems with making and marketing factory automation systems can be traced to several causes. First, the 15 product lines did not plug together. The close horizontal coordination required among departments did not occur, and thus products were manufactured prematurely. Moreover, marketing tried to sell the products to customers before engineering was ready. As one engineer remembers, "We had our necks stuck out so far . . . [the marketing] was all hype." Even worse, GE discovered that the market for its automation systems was very small. At the end of the first year only nine projects had been sold, half of them to other GE divisions. Market research had not taken place. Realizing these problems, senior executives at GE immediately cut back. Departments and product lines were coordinated. The factory automation project is still alive but has been downsized. Now that the reality of its product innovation is fully appreciated, GE has guarded hopes for the future. Plans are more realistic, and managers are taking the time to coordinate solutions before going to market.[58]

DISCUSSION QUESTIONS

1. What are internal and external forces for change? Which force do you think is the major cause of organizational change?

2. Carefully planned change is assumed to be effective. Do you think unplanned change can sometimes be beneficial to an organization? Discuss.

3. Why do organizations experience resistance to change? What techniques can managers use to overcome resistance?

4. Explain force field analysis. Analyze the driving and restraining forces for a change with which you have been associated.

5. Define the roles of an intrapreneur. Why are intrapreneurs so essential to the initiation of change?

6. To what extent would changes in technology affect products, and vice versa? Compare the process for managing technology and that for product change.

7. Given that structure change is often made top down, should coercive implementation techniques be used?

8. Do the underlying values of organizational development differ from assumptions associated with other types of change? Discuss.

9. Compare and contrast team-building and survey feedback techniques for OD intervention.

10. A manager for an international chemical company said that very few new products in her company were successful. What would you advise the manager to do to help increase the company's success rate?

CASES FOR ANALYSIS

SOUTHWESTERN BELL CORPORATION

Southwestern Bell was a conservative, stable company with a dedicated work force. Suddenly the environment shifted. Sweeping regulatory changes and a flood of new technology and market opportunities washed over the company. The telecommunications world was literally turned upside down.

How did SBC respond? CEO Zane Barnes decided to launch a program to encourage employee "intrapreneurialism." He believed that the response to environmental changes had to come from individual employees: "Our people know this business, and they have good ideas. We want them to know those ideas will be appreciated and used."

Barnes started implementing the concept of intrapreneurialism in several ways. He explained the idea to top managers at the annual corporate policy seminar. He also brought in experts on intrapreneurship to speak to management groups. A new quarterly, *Enterprise,* was devoted to articles celebrating company intrapreneurs. SBC also created small, separate profit centers to give divisions more autonomy. Expenditure decisions were pushed down to low levels. A new management incentive program gave bonuses to exceptional performers.

The next problem concerned reinforcing employees who had helped make the company more efficient or responsive to customers. Barnes decided to create a series of awards. The Rider Service Award was given for creative employee contributions. One winner was a manager whose invention had trimmed average service restoration time from 4 hours to 15 minutes. New procedures were also established for helping employees get financial help and prototypes built.

Intrapreneurialism is working. One subsidiary that publishes yellow pages directories has a hot new product—the Silver Pages discount directory for senior citizens. Another subsidiary, Telecom, radically changed its commission schedule for salespeople. An engineer at Southwestern Bell Mobile Systems devised an ingenious system for monitoring the mobile telephone network 24 hours a day. This saves the company money and is going to be developed and sold to other companies.

Questions

1. Do the changes taking place at Southwestern Bell Corporation follow four stages of forces, need, initiation, and implementation? Explain.
2. What type of change—technology, products, structure, or people— is the shift toward intrapreneurialism? To what extent does the

primary change have secondary effects on other types of change at SBC?

3. What techniques were used for change implementation? Would you recommend additional techniques to further implement the intrapreneurial philosophy at SBC?

Source: Based on "'Intrapreneuring' after the Big Breakup," *Management Review* (July 1986), pp. 8–9.

DIGITAL EQUIPMENT CORPORATION

One black Tuesday in October 1983, the news from Digital Equipment Corporation was devastating: The world's second largest computer company was reeling with late products and a chaotic middle management. On that single day, DEC's stock nosedived 21 points.

DEC's rapid growth had been based upon great engineering skills. Its early minicomputer was an enormous success, but now its products were no longer in synchronization with the industry. New personal computers were not selling well. Why? One engineer said DEC's machines were the "most overengineered and undermarketed in the field." DEC's philosophy seemed to be that all they had to do was make good machines—it didn't worry about how to sell them. To make matters worse, new computer ideas were bogged down in the bureaucracy. Business departments argued among themselves about what products to build, and they lobbied for the backing of the engineering and manufacturing departments.

Some observers believed that DEC's problem was the delay in developing new products because the centralized engineering department was insulated from the marketplace. One former marketer said, "Six of the last eight major projects have been one or two years late." Many managers felt that DEC must become more of a marketing company and design and sell products with the customer in mind. One engineer thought that nothing would change until a new philosophy had been adopted at the top. The rapidly shifting markets in the computer industry can be life threatening, and it was time that DEC learned to respond. One frustration was that president Kenneth Olsen didn't see the need for change. People respected him but felt that he had to recognize the need for change and take the initiative.

Questions

1. With what type of change was Digital Equipment Corporation having trouble? What do you see as the cause of the problem?
2. What would you recommend that president Olsen do to improve the timeliness of new-product innovation and the appeal of new products for computer customers?
3. Was there also a need for structural or administrative change at DEC? If so, who should have initiated it?

Source: Based on Susan Fraker, "How DEC Got Decked," *Fortune,* December 12, 1983, pp. 83–92.

CHAPTER 11

Human Resource Management

Chapter Outline

Strategic Human Resource Management

The Strategic Role of HRM
The HRM Process

Attracting an Effective Work Force

Human Resource Planning
Recruiting
Selection

Developing an Effective Work Force

Training and Development
Performance Appraisal

Maintaining an Effective Work Force

Compensation
External Influences
Terminations

Learning Objectives

After studying this chapter, you should be able to:

- Explain the role of human resource management in organizational strategic planning.

- Describe how human resource professionals work with line managers to attract, develop, and maintain human resources in the organization.

- Explain how organizations determine their future staffing needs through human resource planning.

- Describe the tools managers use to recruit and select employees.

- Describe how organizations develop an effective work force through training and performance appraisal.

- Explain how organizations maintain a work force through the administration of wages and salaries and through terminations.

Management Problem

Au Bon Pain Company is a 40-store, $30-million-a-year gourmet fast-food chain based in Boston. Leonard Schlesinger, executive vice-president, is responsible for coordinating the company's training. Recruitment and training of employees have become serious problems because of Au Bon Pain's success. Sales have been increasing 85 percent a year. Schlesinger commented, "We were growing so fast that we couldn't find enough employees to fill the jobs available." The company's work force increased from 100 employees in 1982 to 800 in 1985. As in any fast-food business, many low-end jobs produce high turnover. Schlesinger has also wrestled with the difficult problem of where to find new store managers and people to build up the ranks of middle- and upper-level executives.[1]

What should Leonard Schlesinger do to cope with the explosive demand for employees? What programs are needed to effectively manage Au Bon Pain's human resource needs?

Au Bon Pain Company illustrates the need for managing human resources. Leonard Schlesinger and other managers must develop the organization's ability to deal with human resources; otherwise, organizational growth will be restricted and performance will decline. The term **human resource management (HRM)** refers to activities undertaken to attract, develop, and maintain an effective work force within an organization. Virtually every large organization has a human resource department. Companies such as IBM, General Electric, and Hewlett-Packard have become famous for their approaches to human resource management. For example, at IBM every manager is expected to pay attention to human resources. Surveys are taken regularly to insure that employee

human resource management (HRM) Activities undertaken to attract, develop, and maintain an effective work force within an organization.

morale is high. Computer programs aid in executive career succession planning. The performance appraisal system evaluates the performances of sales representatives to determine their annual bonuses. Finally, the benefits program encourages lifelong commitment to IBM.[2]

In this chapter, we examine the primary functions of HRM. First we discuss how the human resource department contributes to the corporation's overall strategic planning. Then we examine the components of an effective human resource department, including techniques for attracting, developing, and maintaining an effective work force. Although these topics are discussed separately to enhance clarity, they are in fact related. For example, an organization such as IBM that has an excellent salary and benefit program for maintaining human resources also has better programs for attracting and developing employees. Human resource management is important because it makes a difference in attracting the right people. Job seekers make job choices based on pay and other HRM inducements that vary across organizations.[3]

STRATEGIC HUMAN RESOURCE MANAGEMENT

As the value of human resource management has been increasingly recognized in recent years, HRM departments have contributed to organizations in two ways. First, senior HRM executives participate directly in the formulation and implementation of corporate strategy. Second, HRM professionals provide services to managers and employees throughout the organization.

The Strategic Role of HRM

The human resource management function has evolved in three stages. In the 1920s, HRM was a low-level position charged with insuring that procedures were developed for hiring and firing employees and with implementing benefit plans. By the 1950s unions were a major force, and the HRM manager was elevated to a senior position as chief negotiator. During the 1980s, unions have begun to decline and top HRM managers have become directly involved in corporate strategic management.[4]

Human resource management has increased in strategic significance for three reasons: corporate mergers, downsizing, and government regulations. The 1980s has seen companies acquire other businesses, merge, enter new businesses, and get out of old ones. Such changes have had drastic consequences for personnel, because some new corporate owners have trimmed a layer of management, changed benefit plans, or closed divisions. More than ever strategic decisions for mergers or new businesses have had to be based on human resource considerations, such as whether to keep key personnel after a merger, to solve human problems that arise, and to match skills with jobs.[5]

Downsizing is an attempt to reduce the number of managers and employees in order to make a company more competitive. For example, HRM managers helped Xerox offer early retirement to 4,000 of its 60,000 employees as a way of cutting costs. Downsizing has enormous human consequences, and the human resource department is the problem solver. Government regulation includes equal employment opportunity laws, which prohibit discrimination or pay differentials on the basis of race, national origin, religion, or sex. Emerging issues, such as comparable worth—that people should be paid the same wages for jobs of comparable value—also fall in the lap of human resource management. All of these forces have increased the strategic significance of human resource management.[6]

At progressive corporations such as IBM and GE, HRM managers analyze human resource trends to help chief executives make strategic decisions. IBM's top personnel vice-president develops a five-year strategic plan in the spring and a two-year tactical plan every fall. Major business decisions must have HRM managers' concurrence. Moreover, IBM has a no-layoff policy, meaning that HRM keeps a roster of people for redeployment from slumping divisions to prospering ones. At General Electric, a strategic decision to move one division to a new location was vetoed by the HRM department because too many employees would have quit and their loss would have destroyed the division.[7]

The HRM Process

Most organizations employ human resource professionals to perform the activities of human resource planning, recruiting of potential employees, selection of qualified employees, training and development of

EXHIBIT   11.1

The Human Resource Management Process

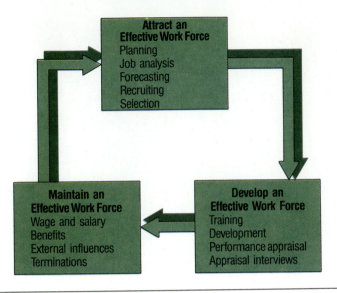

employees, performance appraisal, and compensation administration. A recent survey suggested that for every 1,000 employees, organizations employ about 7 full-time human resource professionals.[8] *Human resource specialists* focus on one of the HRM areas, such as recruitment of professional employees or administration of pension and profit-sharing plans. *Human resource generalists* have responsibility in more than one HRM area.

The three primary goals or activity areas of HRM are illustrated in Exhibit 11.1: to attract, develop, and maintain an effective work force. These goal areas require activities and skills in planning, forecasting, training, performance appraisal, wage and salary administration, and even termination. Each of these areas will be described in this chapter.

However, successful HRM departments nearly always share responsibility for major HRM activities with line managers. Line managers, after all, are directly responsible for human resources. For example, HRM people may establish a pay structure, but line managers have the discretion to award pay raises based on their employees' job performances. HRM people may devise a performance appraisal form, but line managers must use these forms to counsel and develop their employees. General Electric sends HRM specialists to college campuses to interview potential job applicants. The specialists gather information and screen applications for line managers. The line managers within General Electric's more than 100 divisions then decide whom to invite to the divisions for further interviews. Final hiring decisions are made by line managers after site visits by qualified applicants.

E X H I B I T   11.2

Attracting an Effective Work Force

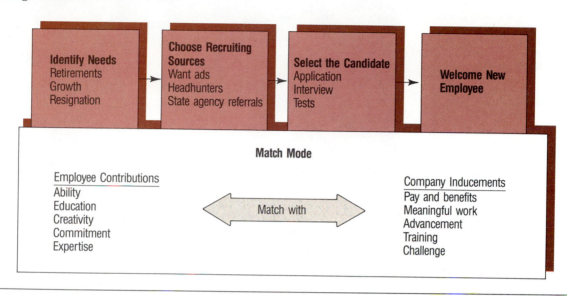

Identify Needs
Retirements
Growth
Resignation

Choose Recruiting Sources
Want ads
Headhunters
State agency referrals

Select the Candidate
Application
Interview
Tests

Welcome New Employee

Match Mode

Employee Contributions
Ability
Education
Creativity
Commitment
Expertise

Match with

Company Inducements
Pay and benefits
Meaningful work
Advancement
Training
Challenge

ATTRACTING AN EFFECTIVE WORK FORCE

The first goal of HRM is to attract individuals who show signs of becoming valued, productive, and satisfied employees. The first step in attracting an effective work force involves human resource planning, in which managers or HRM professionals predict the need for new employees based on the types of vacancies that exist, as illustrated in Exhibit 11.2. The second step is to use recruiting procedures to communicate with potential applicants. The third step is to select from the applicants those persons believed to be the best potential contributors to the organization. Finally, the new employee is welcomed into the organization.

Underlying the organization's effort to attract employees is a matching model. With the **matching model,** the organization and the individual attempt to match the needs, interests, and values that they offer each other. The organization offers "inducements," and the employee offers "contributions."[9] HRM professionals attempt to identify a correct match. For example, a small software developer may require long hours from creative, technically skilled employees. In return, it can offer freedom from bureaucracy, tolerance of idiosyncrasies, and potentially high pay. A large manufacturer can offer employment security and stability, but it may have more rules and regulations and require greater interpersonal skills for "getting approval from the higher-ups." The individual who

matching model   An employee selection approach in which the organization and the applicant attempt to match each other's needs, interests, and values.

The HRM process includes planning, recruitment, selection, training, and employee appraisal and compensation. When BMW built a new plant to employ 3,500 people, these activities were telescoped into a few weeks. Here potential employees take paper-and-pencil selection tests. BMW has found that young people in particular want to work for BMW and that their contributions match the company's inducements.

would thrive working for the software developer might feel stymied and unhappy working for a large manufacturer. Both the company and the employee are interested in finding a good match.

Human Resource Planning

human resource planning   The forecasting of human resource needs and the projected matching of individuals with expected job vacancies.

Human resource planning is the forecasting of human resource needs and the projected matching of individuals with expected vacancies. Human resource planning begins with several questions:

- What will competitors do in response to new government regulations?
- What new technologies are emerging, and how will these affect the work system?
- What is the volume of the business likely to be in the next five to ten years?[10]

The responses to these questions are used to formulate specific questions pertaining to HRM activities, such as the following:

- How many senior managers will we need during this time period?
- What types of engineers will we need, and how many?
- Are persons with adequate computer skills available for meeting our projected needs?
- How many administrative personnel—technicians, secretaries— will we need to support the additional managers and engineers?[11]

Answers to these questions help define the direction for the organization's HRM strategy. For example, if forecasting suggests that there will be a strong need for more technically trained individuals, the organization can (1) define the jobs and skills needed in some detail; (2) hire and train recruiters to look for the specified skills; and/or (3) provide new training for existing employees. By anticipating future HRM needs, the organization can prepare itself to meet competitive challenges more effectively than organizations who react to problems only as they arise.

One of the most successful applications of human resource planning occurred at EDS (Electronic Data Systems) in 1985.

E*DS*

EDS's mission is to assume responsibility for customers' computer information processing needs. Following the merger of EDS into General Motors, EDS's work force grew from 14,000 in 1984 to 40,000 in 1985. The integration into General Motors more than doubled the demand for EDS services, because EDS took over the reshaping of all GM information systems. Specific projects included a computer-aided telemarketing center, a toll-free customer assistance network, and bringing together computers, robots, and other information technologies to improve information efficiencies.

The impact on human resources was dramatic. EDS had to recruit and hire more than 16,000 new employees and assimilate 9,000 of General Motors' information services employees. EDS's human resources nearly tripled in one year.

HRM professionals responded. EDS defined 7,000 new technical development positions and sought applications, which totaled 225,000. The HRM staff increased the number of full-time recruiters from 70 to over 220. EDS line managers provided back-up support and shared the interviewing and selection tasks. One source of pride was that EDS standards were not lowered to meet the enormous hiring goals. Test results showed the new recruits to be among the best qualified ever. Without excellent human resource planning, EDS could not have hired and assimilated this large number of new employees. Human resource management was perhaps the year's single greatest achievement for EDS.[12]

Job Analysis.   To determine the nature of jobs that are changing, HRM professionals often rely on job analysis. **Job analysis** is the process of obtaining accurate and complete information about jobs through a systematic examination of job content. Job analysis provides valuable data for personnel forecasting and other HRM activities. For example, the information collected during job analysis can be used to determine the qualifications applicants need to perform a job adequately, the performance dimensions on which employees should be evaluated, and the worth of jobs for compensation purposes.

Job analysis information can be gathered by observing incumbents as they work, through interviewing incumbents and/or their supervisors, or through the administration of questionnaires. An example of a job analysis questionnaire is presented in Exhibit 11.3. Observation, interviews, and questionnaires have their own advantages; thus, HRM specialists in job analysis often use more than one technique to obtain the most accurate information.[13]

job analysis The process of obtaining accurate and complete information about jobs through a systematic examination of job content.

E X H I B I T   11.3

Sample Job Analysis Questions

The following questions often are used in job analysis. Written answers are provided by the jobholder.

1. **Job purpose:** In one or two sentences, summarize the primary purpose of your job.
   Sample: Technician—Insures the accuracy of mechanical instruments by performing preventive maintenance, repair, and calibration of equipment. Modifies existing equipment and assists higher classified personnel in the development, construction, testing, and installation of new equipment.

2. **Work activities:** List the activities that you must perform in order to successfully complete your job assignments. It may be helpful to think of the things you do beginning with the start of your workday and list in normal sequence each activity you perform during the day.

3. **Job priorities:** Are the activities you perform prescheduled or scheduled on a daily basis? Explain.

4. **Review and approval of work:**
   (a) Other than your immediate supervisor, does anyone regularly provide guidance to you, review your work in progress, or approve your completed work? Explain who and types of approval.
   (b) Do you regularly provide guidance to anyone, assign, review, or approve work? Explain.

5. **Action/decision authority:** What authority do you have to make decisions on your own or to take personal initiative in fulfilling the activities of your job?

6. **Job mobility:** Do you normally remain within your section area in performing your work?

7. **Equipment used:** List the tools or equipment you use in your job.

8. **Work aids:** What kind of specific written guidelines, procedures, protocols, or other aids, such as operating manuals, charts, code lists, catalogs, etc., are utilized in your work?

9. **Physical requirements of job:** In performing your regularly assigned activities, are there any requirements for you to exert significant physical effort, work in a cramped or awkward position, work from heights, etc.? Explain.

10. **Job requirements:** If you were interviewing someone to fill the position you now hold:
    (a) What kind of knowledge, prior experience, formal training, or certifications should that person possess *at a minimum* upon starting on the job?
    (b) What kind of knowledge, skills, and abilities would you expect the newly hired person to gain while *on the job?*
    (c) What knowledge, skills, formal training, or certifications would such a person have to gain in order to advance to the next higher position?

11. **Hardest part of the job:** What do you consider to be the most demanding aspect of your job in terms of planning and completing your work? Give examples.

Source: Based on R. I. Henderson and M. N. Wolfe, *Workbook for Compensation Management: Rewarding Performance,* 4th ed. (Reston, Va.: Reston, 1985).

HRM Forecasting Techniques. A variety of HRM forecasting techniques are in use today.[14] These can be classified as short-range and long-range.

Short-range forecasting frequently uses the following steps:

- The demand for the organization's product or service is anticipated. Major expected external changes (such as demand for a new line of products) are accounted for in this estimation.
- The overall sales forecast is estimated; anticipated internal changes (for example, the conversion to word processors from typewriters) are considered.

The introduction of 125 new Boeing 737-300 aircraft into USAir's fleet involved human resource planning and forecasting. USAir's pilot training included classroom and flight simulator instruction. Training programs also had to be planned for flight attendants, airport personnel, and maintenance workers to familiarize everyone with new job requirements. After the pilots completed flight training, proving flights, with FAA inspectors on board (shown here), were held to review operating procedures and performance.

- Working budgets to reflect the workloads of individual departments are estimated.
- Personnel requirements are determined through conversion of dollars or units into numbers of people.
- Forecasts of labor market conditions or internal organization factors (such as resignation rates) that may affect the future labor supply are considered.

Long-range forecasting ranges from the intuitive to the sophisticated. As described in Chapter 7, some forecasting techniques are based on mathematical extrapolation from past trends. Others involve group decision-making techniques, such as the Delphi method, wherein groups of top managers or other experts use their judgment to make forecasts. Statistical data also are used to project the impact of future employment levels, sales activity, employee turnover, and other variables on the organization's future labor needs.[15]

An example of short-range forecasting occurred when USAir introduced the first Boeing 737-300 into scheduled service. Introducing a new aircraft into an airline operation requires careful planning and coordination. For instance, 737-300 flight simulators had to be obtained and set up in a classroom. Pilots had been trained before the new aircraft was introduced. New pilots with qualifications fitting the 737-300 had to be hired. Long-range planning was illustrated by General Electric in the 1970s when top executives realized that corporate human resources did not fit new products and technologies. General Electric's chairman said, "We were a company with 30,000 electromechanical engineers becoming a company that needed electronics engineers. We didn't plan for this change in 1970, and it caused us big problems by the mid-1970s." As a result of this experience, GE embarked on a sophisticated system of long-range forecasting for human resource needs that today is one of the best in the country. Without planning, a company such as GE could be forced to drain engineers and managers from a stable division to support a growing division, which would propel people into positions above their competence and necessitate a costly rapid-hiring effort.[16]

Recruiting

recruiting The activities or practices that define the desired characteristics of applicants for specific jobs.

Recruiting is defined as "activities or practices that define the characteristics of applicants to whom selection procedures are ultimately applied."[17] While we frequently think of campus recruiting as a typical recruiting activity, many organizations use internal recruiting, or "promote-from-within" policies, to fill their higher-level positions.[18] At Mellon Bank, for example, current employees are given preference when a position opens. Open positions are listed in Mellon's career opportunity bulletins, which are distributed to employees. Internal recruiting has several advantages: It is less costly than an external search, and it generates higher employee commitment, development, and satisfaction, because it offers opportunities for career advancement to employees rather than outsiders.

Frequently, however, it is advantageous to recruit newcomers from outside the organization. A variety of outside sources provide applicants. Organizations use newspaper advertising, state employment services, private employment agencies ("headhunters"), and employee referrals to fill job openings. Some employers even provide cash awards (an average of $388 in 1984) for employees who submit names of people who subsequently accept employment.[19] Studies of recruiting practices suggest that applicants hired from employee referrals tend to have better employment records than those hired from formal sources such as newspaper ads.[20]

realistic job preview (RJP) A recruiting approach that gives applicants all pertinent and realistic information about the job and the organization.

Realistic Job Previews.   One approach to enhancing recruiting effectiveness is called a realistic job preview. A **realistic job preview (RJP)** gives applicants all pertinent and realistic information—positive and negative—about the job and the organization.[21] RJPs enhance employee satisfaction and reduce turnover because they facilitate matching of individuals, jobs, and organizations. Individuals have a better basis on which to determine their suitability to the organization and "self-select" into or out of positions based on full information.[22] When employees choose positions without RJPs, unmet expectations may cause initial job dissatisfaction and increased turnover.[23] Another reason RJPs reduce turnover

The Human Resources Department at CIBA-GEIGY has implemented a policy of promoting from within. Open positions are posted on the bulletin board to encourage job and career changes when these would benefit both the employee and the department. The department also conducts surveys of employee opinions, encourages open communication between bosses and subordinates, and issues publications to inform employees about company activities.

is that applicants often are given training to cope with or adjust to negative aspects of the job. This suggests that when recruiters take care to point out serious negative aspects of a job, HRM professionals also should help newcomers adjust by providing "coping" training that explains what to do when stressful or novel events occur on the job.[24]

Affirmative Action. Organizations must insure that their recruiting practices conform to the law concerning affirmative action. **Affirmative action** refers to the use of goals, timetables, or other methods to promote the hiring, development, and retention of "protected groups"—persons historically underrepresented in the workplace. For example, companies adopting an affirmative action policy may recruit at colleges with large enrollments of black students. A city may establish a goal of hiring one black firefighter for every white firefighter hired until the proportion of black firefighters is commensurate with that in the community. **Equal employment opportunity (EEO) laws** stipulate that recruiting and hiring decisions cannot discriminate on the basis of race, national origin, religion, or sex.

Most large companies try to comply with affirmative action and EEO guidelines. Prudential Insurance Company's policy is illustrated in Exhibit 11.4. Prudential actively recruits employees and takes affirmative action steps to recruit new ones from all walks of life.

Recently the U.S. Supreme Court handed down decisions on three cases that have been called the "affirmative action trilogy."[25] Where a pattern of underutilization of minorities or women is apparent, employers may (or may be ordered to) establish affirmative action plans for recruiting, hiring, or promotions even if those plans would benefit some individuals who have not proven personal suffering from past discrimination. However, the plans should specify that they will be in force only until the underutilization is corrected. Moreover, the Supreme Court decisions emphasized that each situation would be judged on its own merits.[26] Thus, employers should carefully monitor their recruiting practices and implement affirmative action plans where needed.

affirmative action The use of methods to promote the hiring, development, and retention of groups that traditionally have been underrepresented in the workplace.

equal employment opportunity (EEO) laws Legislation that prohibits recruiting and hiring practices that discriminate on the basis of race, national origin, religion, or sex.

E X H I B I T   11.4

Prudential's Corporate Recruiting Policy

An Equal Opportunity Employer

Prudential recruits, hires, trains, promotes, and compensates individuals without regard to race, color, religion or creed, age, sex, marital status, national origin, ancestry, liability for service in the armed forces of the United States, status as a special disabled veteran or veteran of the Vietnam era, or physical or mental handicap.

This is official company policy because:
- we believe it is right
- it makes good business sense
- it is the law

We are also committed to an ongoing program of affirmative action in which members of under-represented groups are actively sought out and employed for opportunities in all parts and at all levels of the company. In employing people from all walks of life, Prudential gains access to the full experience of our diverse society.

Source: Used with permission of Prudential Insurance Company.

Selection

selection The process of determining the skills, abilities, and other attributes needed to perform a particular job.

The next step for managers is to select desired employees from the pool of recruited applicants. In the **selection** process, employers attempt to determine the skills, abilities, and other attributes needed to perform a particular job. Then they assess applicants' characteristics in an attempt to determine the "fit" between the job and applicant characteristics.

Job Descriptions. A good place to start in making a selection decision is the job description. Human resource professionals or line managers who make selection decisions may have little direct experience with the job to be filled. If these persons are to make a good match between job and candidate, they should read the job description before they review applications. An example of a job description appears in Exhibit 11.5.

job description A listing of minimum and desirable qualifications for a particular job.

A **job description** typically contains several sections. The *job specification* section (also called *minimum qualifications*) is the most useful one because it spells out the desired applicant attributes. For example, a recruiter hiring an associate programmer for the position described in Exhibit 11.5 must ascertain that the applicant has a bachelor's degree related to computer science or equivalent experience and several skills and abilities essential to job performance. The job description shown in Exhibit 11.5 also lists qualifications that are believed to enhance the person-job fit but are not essential at the time of hire. The manager or recruiter should determine whether the applicant possesses these attributes.

Selection Devices. Several devices are used for assessing applicant qualifications. The most frequently used are the

- Application form
- Interview
- Paper-and-pencil test
- Physical ability test
- Assessment center

E X H I B I T   11.5

Sample Job Description

Associate Programmer

General Statement of Duties	Perform coding, debugging, testing, and documentation of software under the supervision of a technical superior. Involves some use of independent judgment.
Supervision Received	Works under close supervision of a technical superior or departmental manager.
Supervision Exercised	No supervisory duties required.
Examples of Duties	(Any one position may not include all the duties listed, nor do listed examples include all duties that may be found in positions of this class.)
	Confers with analysts, supervisors and/or representatives of the departments to clarify software intent and programming requirements.
	Performs coding, debugging, and testing of software when given program specifications for a particular task or problem.
	Writes program documentation.
	Seeks advice and assistance from supervisor when problems outside of realm of understanding arise. Communicates any program specification deficiencies back to supervisor.
	Reports ideas concerning design and development back to supervisor.
	Assists in the implementation of the system and training of end users.
	Provides some support and assistance to users.
	Develops product knowledge and proficiency in system usage.
	Assumes progressively complex and independent duties as experience permits.
	Performs all duties in accordance with corporate and departmental standards.
Minimum Qualifications	Education: BA/BS degree in relevant field or equivalent experience/knowledge in computer science, math, or other closely related field.
	Experience: No prior computer programming work experience necessary.
	Knowledge, skills, and abilities: Ability to exercise initiative and sound judgment; knowledge of a structured language; working knowledge of operating systems; ability to maintain open working relationship with supervisor; logic and problem-solving skills; develop system flowcharting skills.
Desirable Qualifications	Exposure to BASIC, FORTRAN, or PASCAL. Some training in general accounting practices and controls; effective written and oral communication skills.

In determining which selection technique to use, human resource professionals consider the extent to which each will produce a valid prediction of employee job performance. **Validity** refers to the relationship between one's score on the selection device and one's future job performance. A valid selection device will provide high scores that corre-

validity The relationship between an applicant's score on a selection device and his or her future job performance.

spond to subsequent high job performance. Researchers have attempted to determine which selection devices produce the most valid scores.

application form A device for collecting information about an applicant's education, previous job experience, and other background characteristics.

Application Form. The **application form** is used to collect information about the applicant's education, previous job experience, and other background characteristics. Research in the life insurance industry shows biographical information inventories can predict future job success.[27]

One pitfall to be avoided is the inclusion of questions that are irrelevant to job success. This is particularly true when a question might adversely affect the employment opportunities of minorities or women.[28] The *Griggs* v. *Duke Power Company* Supreme Court decision of 1971 held that a "facially neutral" practice that had a disproportionate effect on minorities was illegal unless it could be justified by business necessity or job relatedness.[29] Duke Power had required security guard applicants to possess high school diplomas and to pass other tests. Consequently, a smaller proportion of black applicants than white applicants were eligible for hiring. There was no evidence of any relationship between Duke Power's selection policy and job performance. In other words, Duke Power's requirements were invalid because people with diplomas and high test scores are not necessarily better at providing security.

The application form should not ask questions that will create adverse impact on "protected groups" unless the questions are clearly related to the job. For example, employers should not ask whether the applicant rents or owns his or her own home because (1) an applicant's response might adversely affect his or her chances at the job and (2) home-ownership is probably unrelated to job performance. On the other hand, the CPA exam is relevant to job performance in a CPA firm; thus, it is appropriate to ask whether an applicant for employment has passed the CPA exam even if only one-half of all women or minority applicants has done so versus nine-tenths of men applicants.[30]

Interview.[31] The interview is used to hire persons in almost every job category in virtually every organization. The *interview* serves as a two-way communication channel that allows both the organization and the applicant to collect information that would otherwise be difficult to obtain.

Although widely used, the interview as generally practiced is a poor predictor of later job performance. Researchers have identified many reasons for this. Interviewers frequently are unfamiliar with the job. They tend to make decisions in the first few minutes of the interview before all relevant information has been gathered. They also may base decisions on personal biases (such as against minority groups or physically unattractive persons and in favor of those similar to themselves). The interview may be spent discussing matters irrelevant to the job. Finally, interviewers tend to weight negative information too heavily when deciding on the applicant's suitability.

Organizations will continue to use interviews in spite of the pitfalls. Thus, researchers have identified methods for increasing their validity. Advice for effective interviewing is summarized in "Manager's Shoptalk: The Right Way to Interview a Job Applicant."

The first step in selection is to develop a job description. USAir created a new position called Special Assistance Representative to provide personal attention for children, the elderly, and other passengers with special needs. Once the job description was developed, employees were selected and given formal training in providing the service at major airports.

MANAGERS SHOP TALK

The Right Way to Interview a Job Applicant

A so-so interview usually nets a so-so employee. Many hiring mistakes can be prevented during the interview. The following techniques will insure a successful interview:

1. *Know what you want.* Before the interview, prepare questions based on your knowledge of the job to be filled. If you do not have a thorough knowledge of the job, read a job description. If possible, call one or more jobholders and ask them about the job duties and what is required to succeed. Another idea is to make up a list of traits and qualifications for the ideal candidate. Be specific about what it will take to get the job done.

2. *Prepare a road map.* Develop questions that will reveal whether the candidate has the correct background and qualifications. The questions should focus on previous experiences that are relevant to the current job. If the job requires creativity and innovation, ask a question such as "What do you do differently from other sales reps?"

3. *Use open-ended questions in which the right answer is not obvious.* Ask the applicant to give specific examples of previous work experiences. For example, don't ask, "Are you a hard worker?" or "Tell me about yourself." Instead ask, "Can you give me examples from your previous work history that reflect your level of motivation?" or "How did you go about getting your current job?"

4. *Do not ask questions that are irrelevant to the job.* This is particularly important when the irrelevant questions might adversely affect minorities or women. Questions that are considered objectionable during a personal interview are the same as those considered objectionable on application blanks.

5. *Listen, don't talk.* You should spend most of the interview listening. If you talk too much, the focus will shift to you and you may miss important cues. Listen carefully to tone of voice as well as content. Body language also can be revealing; for example, failure to make eye contact is a danger signal.

6. *Allow enough time so that the interview will not be rushed.* Leave time for the candidate to ask questions about the job. The types of questions the candidate asks can be an important clue to his or her interest in the job. Try to delay forming an opinion about the applicant until after the entire interview has been completed.

7. *Avoid reliance on your memory.* Request the applicant's permission to take notes; then do so unobtrusively during the interview or immediately after. If several applicants are interviewed, notes are essential for remembering what they said and the impressions they made.

Paper-and-Pencil Tests. The *Griggs* v. *Duke Power Company* decision described above caused many companies to reconsider their use of **paper-and-pencil tests** such as intelligence tests, aptitude and ability tests, and personality inventories.[32] Managers feared they could not prove the validity of the tests. Unfortunately, this may have resulted in the use of even less valid decision tools, such as interviews. Employers are again beginning to use tests, particularly those shown to be good predictors.[33] For example, a 109-question personality test has been used by independent insurance agents to hire clerical and customer service employees. The test is designed to measure traits such as "motivation to please others" and "people orientation." The insurance agencies feel they need something to better gauge applicants' strengths and weaknesses. The test has been successful, because candidates hired have displayed stronger tendencies to provide service to customers.[34]

Physical Ability Tests. Some jobs require employees to do heavy lifting, move with agility, maintain balance, make precise adjustments, or per-

paper-and-pencil test A written test designed to measure a particular attribute such as intelligence or aptitude.

physical ability test A test that simulates the important physical tasks required for a job and measures the applicant's performance on the simulations.

assessment center A technique for selecting individuals with high managerial potential based on their performance on a series of simulated managerial tasks.

Physical ability tests are important for jobs that require heavy lifting. These tests simulate the on-the-job requirements for strength and endurance. Employees in United Telecom's crews must dig by hand when there is not enough room for a backhoe or trencher. The cable must be at a safe depth of at least 42 inches. Crew members must have excellent physical abilities as well as pass interviews and written tests.

form tasks requiring other physical skills or abilities. Some employers try to assess these skills merely by looking at the applicant, but a far better practice is to administer a test that will directly assess the applicant's suitability. For such jobs industrial psychologists have designed **physical ability tests,** which simulate the important physical tasks involved in a job and measure the applicant's performance on the simulations.[35]

Assessment Centers. The assessment center was developed by psychologists at AT&T several decades ago. Now it is used to select individuals with high potential for managerial careers by such organizations as AT&T, IBM, General Electric, J. C. Penney, and Standard Oil (Ohio).[36] **Assessment centers** present a series of simulated managerial tasks to groups of applicants over, say, a two- or three-day period. Many centers use the in-basket simulation, which requires the applicant to play the role of a manager who must decide how to respond to ten memos in his or her in-basket within a two-hour period. Panels of two or three trained judges observe the applicant's decisions and assess the extent to which they reflect interpersonal, communication, and problem-solving skills.

Assessment centers have proven to be valid predictors of managerial success[37], and some organizations now use them for hiring technical workers. At Kimberly-Clark's newest plants, for example, applicants for machine operator jobs are put through a simulation in which they are asked to play the role of a supervisor. The idea is to see whether candidates have sufficient "people skills" to fit into the participative work atmosphere. A midwestern food products company takes teams of six technician applicants and has them simulate running a plant that produces circuit boards. Then the managers change the type of circuit board to gauge the candidates' flexibility. Company officials credit the assessment center approach for low turnover and low absenteeism at new plants and for production running at 170 percent of projected capacity.[38]

DEVELOPING AN EFFECTIVE WORK FORCE

Following selection, the major goal of HRM is to develop employees into an effective work force. Development includes training and performance appraisal.

Training and Development

Training and development represent a planned effort by an organization to facilitate employees' learning of job-related behaviors.[39] Some authors distinguish the two forms of intervention by noting that the term *training* usually refers to teaching lower-level or technical employees how to do their present jobs, while *development* refers to teaching managers and professionals the skills needed for both present and future jobs.[40] For simplicity, we will refer to both interventions as training.

It is estimated that organizations spend nearly $100 billon each year on training.[41] Training may occur in a variety of forms. The most common method is on-the-job training.[42] In **on-the-job training (OJT),** an experienced employee is asked to take a new employee "under his or her wing" and show the newcomer how to form job duties. OJT has many advantages, such as few out-of-pocket costs for training facilities, materials, or instructor fees and easy transfer of learning back to the job. The learning site is the work site. On the other hand, the one-on-one or small-group instruction provided in OJT requires that the organization be willing to free the trainer from normal duties. The trainer must be willing and able to help newcomers and not feel threatened by them.[43]

Other frequently used training methods include

- *Orientation training,* in which newcomers are introduced to the organization's "culture"
- *Classroom training,* including lectures, films, audiovisual techniques, and simulations
- *Programmed and computer-assisted instruction,* in which the employee works at his or her own pace to learn material from a text that includes exercises and quizzes to enhance learning
- *Conference and case discussion groups,* in which participants analyze cases or discuss topics assisted by a training leader

The literature on training suggests that organizations frequently omit two important steps that would increase the effectiveness of training.[44] First, a needs analysis should precede the planning and execution of a training program. In a **needs analysis,** the HRM specialist determines exactly what the training needs are before designing a program to meet them. While this seems an obvious step, many training programs are initiated simply because "Marie over in Production Materials heard a good speaker last week; she thought we should bring the guy in to talk to Marketing." Such programs may be entertaining for employees, but they do not address the real needs of the organization or department. Further, they may be a wasteful use of the training budget.

A second step in the effective management of training is known as **training program evaluation,** in which the HRM specialist determines the program's effectiveness in terms of participant learning. Training is given to some groups but not others. Tests are given to all groups to measure whether those who received training score higher on test performance. If not, the training program is redesigned or replaced.

on-the-job training (OJT) A type of training in which an experienced employee "adopts" a new employee for the purpose of teaching him or her how to perform job duties.

needs analysis A professional assessment of a company's training needs and development of a program designed to meet them.

training program evaluation A control-group technique designed to measure the effectiveness of a training program on participants' job performance.

R. *H. Macy & Company*

Macy's runs an executive training program so famous that *The Wall Street Journal* has compared it to Harvard University. The prestigious training program is called "training squad." It is so good that it attracts top-notch business graduates to work at Macy's. Macy's is a Fortune 500 service company and operates 95 stores. At Macy's New York, potential trainees spend an entire day at an assessment center to qualify for the training squad program. The assessors are Macy's senior executives.

USF&G has made a major investment in classroom training to facilitate employees' learning of job-related behavior. The USF&G School of Insurance is held in technologically sophisticated classrooms at the Mt. Washington Center. The classroom provides personal contact between student and teachers and the latest audiovisual aids. Often classroom programs are evaluated for effectiveness by testing graduates' progress.

The typical training squad lasts 11 weeks. The program focuses on the basics of Macy's organization and merchandise, and trainees spend several days in stores with sales managers. After more classes, the trainees spend three weeks in the buying office. Then they return to the classroom for workshops, this time conducted by high-level executives. Aspiring managers thus receive both classroom and on-the-job training. Robyn Payne, a graduate of Wellesley College, said, "Training squad was an intense and exciting learning experience. Within three months I had gained significant business and retailing skills." She also noted, "There is a tremendous amount of pressure and responsibility right from the start, just as they promised. But there is also a real sense of assurance in discovering first-hand that Macy's is the kind of company which teaches you exactly what you need to know to perform your duties."[45]

Performance Appraisal

performance appraisal   The process of observing and evaluating an employee's performance, recording the assessment, and providing feedback to the employee.

Performance appraisal is another important technique for developing an effective work force. **Performance appraisal** comprises the steps of observing and assessing employee performance, recording the assessment, and providing feedback to the employee. Managers use performance appraisal to describe and evaluate the employees' performances. Performance appraisal plays a critical HRM role when jobs do not lend themselves to simple productivity "counts."

During performance appraisal, skillful managers give feedback and praise concerning the acceptable elements of the employee's performance. They also describe performance areas that need improvement. Employees can use this information to change their job performance. Performance appraisal can also serve a "maintenance" function in the sense that high performers identified through it can be rewarded through merit pay, recognition, and other rewards.

Research on performance appraisal is extensive. Generally it has focused on (1) the accurate assessment of performance through the training of raters and the development of assessment systems such as rating scales and (2) the performance appraisal interview, in which managers can provide feedback that will reinforce good performance and motivate development.

Assessing Performance Accurately.   To obtain an accurate performance rating, managers must acknowledge that jobs are multidimensional and performance thus may be multidimensional as well. For example, a sports broadcaster may perform well on the job knowledge dimension; that is, she or he may be able to report facts and figures about the players and describe which rule applies when there is a questionable play on the field. But the same sports broadcaster may not perform as well on another dimension, such as communication. She or he may be unable to express the information in a colorful way that interests the audience or may interrupt the other broadcasters.

The dimensions of a job can be derived from job analysis information as described earlier. If performance is to be rated accurately, the performance appraisal form should require the rater—usually the supervisor—to assess each relevant performance dimension and not those that are inapplicable to a given job. A multidimensional form increases the usefulness of the performance appraisal for giving rewards and facilitates employee growth and development.

Although we would like to believe that every manager carefully assesses employees' performances, researchers have identified several rating errors.[46] For example, **halo error** occurs when an employee receives the same rating on all dimensions even if his or her performance is good on some dimensions and poor on others, as in the case of the sports broadcaster described above. **Homogeneity** occurs when a rater gives all employees a similar rating even if their performances are not equally good.

Human resource professionals can use two approaches to overcome management performance evaluation errors. The first is to use a behavior-based rating technique, such as the behaviorally anchored rating scale. The **behaviorally anchored rating scale (BARS)** is developed from critical incidents pertaining to job performance. Each job performance scale is anchored with specific behavioral statements that describe varying degrees of performance. By relating employee performance to specific incidents, it is possible to evaluate an employee's performance accurately.[47]

halo error   A type of rating error that occurs when an employee receives the same rating on all dimensions regardless of his or her performance on individual ones.

homogeneity   A type of rating error that occurs when a rater gives all employees a similar rating regardless of their individual performances.

behaviorally anchored rating scale (BARS)   A rating technique that relates an employee's performance to specific job-related incidents.

EXHIBIT 11.6

Example of a Behaviorally Anchored Rating Scale

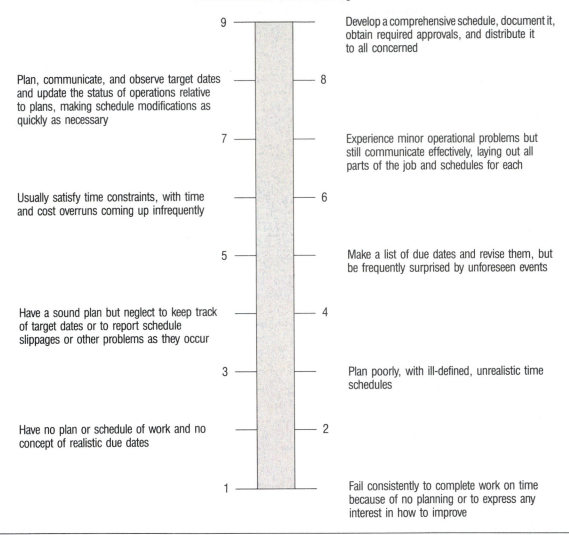

Job: Production Line Supervisor
Work Dimension: Work Scheduling

9 — Develop a comprehensive schedule, document it, obtain required approvals, and distribute it to all concerned

Plan, communicate, and observe target dates and update the status of operations relative to plans, making schedule modifications as quickly as necessary — 8

7 — Experience minor operational problems but still communicate effectively, laying out all parts of the job and schedules for each

Usually satisfy time constraints, with time and cost overruns coming up infrequently — 6

5 — Make a list of due dates and revise them, but be frequently surprised by unforeseen events

Have a sound plan but neglect to keep track of target dates or to report schedule slippages or other problems as they occur — 4

3 — Plan poorly, with ill-defined, unrealistic time schedules

Have no plan or schedule of work and no concept of realistic due dates — 2

1 — Fail consistently to complete work on time because of no planning or to express any interest in how to improve

Source: Based on J. P. Campbell, M. D. Dunnette, R. D. Arvey, and L. V. Hellervik, "The Development and Evaluation of Behaviorally Based Rating Scales," *Journal of Applied Psychology,* 57; 1973, 15–22, and "Behaviorally Anchored Rating Scales: A Method for Effective Management," *Small Business Report* (February 1986), 71–77.

Exhibit 11.6 illustrates the BARS method for evaluating a production line supervisor. The production supervisor's job can be broken down into several dimensions, such as equipment maintenance, employee training, or work scheduling. A behaviorally anchored rating scale should be developed for each dimension. The dimension in Exhibit 11.6 is work scheduling. Good performance is represented by a 7, 8, or 9 on the scale and unacceptable performance as a 1, 2, or 3. If a production supervisor's job has eight dimensions, the total performance evaluation will be the sum of the scores for each of eight scales.[48]

The second approach to correcting performance rating errors is for HRM professionals to train management raters to observe performance closely and to motivate them to correct rating errors. One training method involves manager workshops that use videotapes of employees performing their jobs.[49] Raters rate a videotaped performance and then compare their ratings with other raters' and with the correct ratings. After each videotaped rating, raters discuss the errors that caused them to rate performance inaccurately and the steps to be taken to avoid making errors back on the job. As the process is repeated, raters become aware of their own tendencies and their rating accuracy improves.

For example, when John Zimmermann joined MCI Communications Corporation to build a human resource department that would support a high-technology, rapid-growth company, one priority was to develop a system to assess performance accurately and thoroughly. He studied the performance assessment system and made sure managers understood it. The motivating factor for managers and HRM employees alike was MCI employees' desire to be measured accurately. They wanted feedback and the opportunity to be rewarded accordingly. As the performance appraisal system improved, employees were rewarded more equitably and thus became more responsive.[50]

Performance Appraisal Interview.   Most corporations provide formal feedback in the form of an annual **performance appraisal interview** with the employee.[51] Too often, however, this meeting between boss and subordinate does not stimulate better job performance.[52] Managers may be unaware of the true causes of performance problems because they have not carefully observed employee job activities. They may have a number of useful ideas for subordinates but present them in a threatening manner. As a result, employees may feel defensive and reject suggestions for improvement.

Research into the performance appraisal interview suggests a number of steps that will increase its effectiveness:[53]

> **performance appraisal interview** A formal review of an employee's performance conducted between the superior and the subordinate.

1. Raters (usually supervisors) should be knowledgeable about the subordinates' jobs and performance levels.
2. Raters should welcome employee participation during the interview rather than "tell and sell" their views by lecturing to subordinates.[54] This is particularly true when the employee is knowledgeable and accustomed to participating with the supervisor.
3. A contingency approach to feedback based on the characteristics of the subordinate, the job, and his or her performance level is useful. For example:

   —With difficult, nonroutine jobs, high performers need feedback that is given at flexible time intervals and focused on development.

   —With routine jobs, satisfactory performers need infrequent feedback (positive or negative) that is focused only on deviations from acceptable performance.

   —Newer employees need more frequent feedback.

Performance appraisal is an excellent opportunity for communication between managers and employees. However, some managers find it difficult to provide negative feedback during a performance appraisal interview. In this role-play sequence designed to build supervisory skills for employees of Varian Associates Inc., managers practice performance appraisal interviewing. Employees take turns in roles of manager and subordinate. Managers learn to assess performance accurately and give the positive and negative feedback necessary for their subordinates' continued development.

4.   Training is needed to help supervisors devise interview strategies for different situations. This training should include the observation and rating of performance. Role playing that involves practice appraisal interviews is helpful for this purpose.

Researchers also have studied ways in which feedback itself can be effective. Giving specific examples of good and bad performance is more helpful than general statements. For example, "Your attendance record shows that you were here on time nearly every day this month, and this is a great improvement over last month" is more specific and helpful than "You seem to have a much better attitude these days about your work." Some experts suggest that managers keep diaries of employee performance so they will not have to rely on their memories to generate specific examples.[55] In situations in which more than one rater gives feedback to the same employee, all the raters should discuss the feedback before meeting with the subordinate because employees tend to discount negative feedback if it is given inconsistently.[56]

Performance Appraisal Documentation.   When employee performance has been poor and is the reason for no raise or even dismissal, the performance appraisal is especially important. Employees are legally entitled to be forewarned of the consequences of unsatisfactory performance. Unexcused absences, tardiness, or other violations call for progressive discipline that begins with written warnings, suspensions, and eventually termination. The employee's performance must be documented and placed in his or her performance evaluation file. Managers should be honest with subordinates and put their observations in writing; they should not offer good evaluations just to avoid conflict. Good evaluations may be the basis for a lawsuit that the employee will win if written documentation does not support employer actions against him or her.

MAINTAINING AN EFFECTIVE WORK FORCE

Now we turn to the topic of how managers and HRM professionals maintain a work force that has been recruited and developed. Maintenance of the current work force involves compensation, the management of potentially disruptive external influences, and occasional terminations.

Compensation

The term **compensation** refers to (1) all monetary payments and (2) all goods or commodities used in lieu of money to reward employees.[57] An organization's compensation structure includes wages and/or salaries and fringe benefits such as health insurance, paid vacations, or employee fitness centers.

Ideally, management's goals and strategies for the organization should be a critical determinant of the features and operations of the pay system. Organization leaders' goals for the pay system should be linked with the organization's strategy.[58] For example, managers may have the goal of maintaining or improving profitability or market share by stimulating employee performance. Thus, they should design and use a merit pay system rather than a system based on nonperformance criteria such as seniority. As another example, managers may have the goal of attracting and retaining desirable employees. Here they can use a pay survey to determine competitive wages in comparable companies and adjust pay rates to meet or exceed the going rates.[59]

Sibson & Company studied 66 firms to determine whether high-performing companies designed management compensation plans differently from others. The high-performing companies were distinguished by having clear performance priorities set by top management and financial rewards that recognized employee contributions to performance priorities. An interesting additional finding was that financial rewards were used to communicate priorities to employees. Thus, the pay system not only rewarded high performance but told employees what counts with respect to organizational goals and priorities. As goals and strategies shifted, the distribution of financial rewards became an important channel for telling employees how to respond. Moreover, successful firms' compensation systems emphasized teamwork rather than competition among individual employees. In low-performing companies, compensation systems tended to focus on individuals rather than groups, top management priorities were unclear or conflicting, and rewards were given for reasons unrelated to high performance.[60]

Managers often wish to maintain a sense of fairness and equity within the pay structure and thereby fortify employee morale. **Job evaluation** refers to the process of determining the value or worth of jobs within an organization through an examination of job content. Job evaluation techniques enable managers to compare similar and dissimilar jobs and to determine internally equitable pay rates—that is, pay rates that em-

compensation Monetary payments (wages, salaries) and nonmonetary goods/commodities (fringe benefits, vacations) used to reward employees.

job evaluation The process of determining the values of jobs within an organization through an examination of job content.

EXHIBIT 11.7

Steps in Building a Point-Based Wage and Salary Structure

1. Create or update job descriptions by performing a job analysis.

2. Choose a point-based job evaluation method and evaluate the job descriptions.

3. Select the key jobs and obtain a pay survey to determine their market pay rates.

4. Calculate the pay-trend line and assign average pay rates to the nonkey jobs.

5. Group jobs into classes and establish pay ranges within each class.

point system   A job evaluation system that assigns a predetermined point value to each compensable job factor in order to determine the worth of a given job.

Honeywell has a formal salary and benefits compensation plan to attract and motivate productive employees. When this photograph was taken in 1935, however, performance appraisal and compensation took a different form. Honeywell thermostats were sold door to door, and performance was assessed according to the number sold each month. A salesman's clothing indicated how well he was meeting his quota. This informal method of appraisal and compensation was effective in the days preceding compensation specialists and salary surveys.

ployees believe are fair compared to those for other jobs in the organization. Managers also may want to provide income security so that their employees need not be overly concerned with the financial consequences of disability or retirement. The inclusion of pension and other income security programs can shield employees from a variety of risks.

Building the Wage and Salary Structure.   Large organizations typically employ HRM compensation specialists to establish and maintain a pay structure. They may also hire outside consultants, such as the Hay Group or PAQ (Position Analysis Questionnaire) Associates, whose pay systems have been adopted by many companies and government organizations. The majority of large public- and private-sector U.S. employers use some formal process of job evaluation.[61]

The most commonly used job evaluation system is the **point system.**[62] The steps typically followed when using point systems are summarized in Exhibit 11.7.

First, compensation specialists must insure that job descriptions are complete, up to date, and accurate. If, for example, a computer programmer's duties have changed since the last update, a pay value based on the old job description will probably be too low or too high. The process of job analysis described earlier is used to maintain accurate job descriptions.

Next, a job evaluation system for assessing the job descriptions is chosen. The system should allow top managers to select compensable job factors (such as skill, effort, and responsibility) and decide how each factor will be weighed in establishing job worth. These factors are described in a point manual, which is used to assign point values to each job. An example of a point manual description for the responsibility factor is given in Exhibit 11.8.

The compensation specialist then compares the extent of responsibility apparent in a given job description to that specified in the point manual. This process is repeated until the job has been evaluated on all factors. Then the compensation specialist evaluates a second job and repeats the process until all jobs have been evaluated.

The job evaluation process can establish an internal hierarchy of job worth. However, in order to determine competitive market pay rates,

EXHIBIT 11.8

Point Manual Description of Responsibility

Degree	Description of Characteristics and Measures
0	Routine work performed under close supervision or in accordance with specific detailed instructions. *Benchmark:* File Clerk.
1	Error may result in minor confusion or damage, causing a minor expense for correction or repair. *Benchmark:* Billing Clerk, General Secretary.
2	Error generally confined to a single department or phase of activities and may result in moderate expense for correction or unfavorable public relationship. *Benchmark:* Administrative Secretary, Statistical Clerk, Purchasing Clerk.
3	Error may be serious, involving loss of time, money, damage to property, waste of materials, and/or unfavorable public relationship. *Benchmark:* Staff Social Worker, Nurses, Intake Technician, School Therapist.
4	Error may be difficult to detect initially and may result in serious consequences, such as significant property damage, loss of money or time and materials, or physical injury to the incumbent. *Benchmark:* Team Leaders, Coordinators, Psychologists, Clinical Manager.
5	Error may have extreme consequences, and can be potentially dangerous to public safety, in addition to significant property damage, loss of money, or time and materials. *Benchmark:* Executive Director.

Source: R. W. Beatty and C. E. Schneier, *Personnel Administration: An Experiential Skill Building Approach,* 2d ed. © 1981 Addison-Wesley Publishing Company, Inc., Reading, Massachusetts. Reprinted with permission.

most organizations obtain one or more pay surveys. **Pay surveys** show what other organizations pay incumbents in jobs that match a sample of "key" jobs selected by the organization. Pay surveys are available from many sources, including consulting firms and the U.S. Bureau of Labor Statistics.[63]

The compensation specialist then compares the survey pay rates for key jobs with their job evaluation points by plotting them on a graph as illustrated in Exhibit 11.9. The **pay-trend line** shows the relationship between pay and total point values. The compensation specialist can use the pay-trend line to determine the pay values of all jobs for which point values have been calculated.

Jobs are then grouped into classes based on similarity in pay rates. The number of classes reflects the number of levels in the organization structure, because most managers expect to be compensated in a higher pay range than the persons they supervise. Ranges of pay for each job class are established, enabling a newcomer or lower performer to be paid less than other people in the same job class. The organization must then specify how individuals in the same job class can advance from the low to the high end of the range. For example, the organization can reward merit, seniority, or a combination of both.

Benefits. The wage and salary structure is an important part of the compensation package that maintains a productive work force, but equally important are the benefits offered by the organization. Benefits were once called "fringe" benefits, but this term is no longer accurate because they are now a central rather than peripheral part of the pay

pay survey A study of what other companies pay employees in jobs that correspond to a sample of key positions selected by the organization.

pay-trend line A graph that shows the relationship between pay and total job point values for the purpose of determining the worth of a given job.

E X H I B I T   11.9

Pay-Trend Line

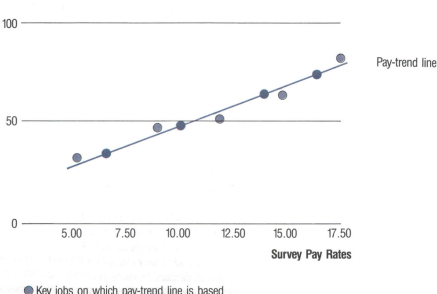

Job Evaluation Points

Pay-trend line

Survey Pay Rates

● Key jobs on which pay-trend line is based
● Other jobs placed on pay-trend line to determine pay rate

Comerica Inc. is a huge bank holding company in Michigan. One goal of its compensation package is to provide employees with excellent benefits. The CustomComp Flexible Benefits Program allows employees to select combinations of benefits that best meet their needs and lifestyles. One option is the child care reimbursement plan, which shares with parents the cost of obtaining high-quality child care.

structure. A U.S. Chamber of Commerce survey has revealed that benefits in general comprise more than one-third of labor costs and in some industries nearly two-thirds.[64]

A major reason why benefits make up a large portion of the compensation package is that until very recently health care costs were increasing more quickly than the inflation rate. Since employers frequently provide health care insurance as an employee benefit, these costs are important in the management of benefits. A recent survey showed that more than 70 percent of responding employers plan to place a major emphasis on health care cost containment in the next one to three years.[65] Employers control health care costs through a variety of methods, such as requiring second opinions for major surgery, increasing the cost borne by employees, and participating in Health Maintenance Organizations (HMOs). HMOs provide health care for a flat fee that may be less than the costs paid to independent physicians or hospitals.

Organizations that want to provide cost-effective benefits should be sensitive to changes in employee lifestyles.[66] Several years ago, benefits were based on the assumption that the typical worker was a married man with a dependent wife and two school-age children. The benefits packages provided life insurance coverage for the worker, health insurance coverage for all family members, and no assistance with child care expenses. But today fewer than 10 percent of American workers fit the description of the so-called typical worker.[67] Far more workers are single, and both spouses in most families are working. These workers are not likely to value the traditional benefits package.[68] In response, some companies are establishing cafeteria-style benefits packages that allow employees to select the benefits of greatest value to them. Other companies use surveys to determine which combination of fixed benefits is most desirable.[69] The benefits packages provided by large companies attempt to meet the needs of all employees.

External Influences

Two external factors that influence corporate compensation practices are unions and equal employment opportunity laws. Employers must deal with these factors when developing compensation systems.

Unions. The National Labor Relations Act of 1935 provides that employees may elect to be represented by unions in negotiations with employers over "wages, hours and other terms and conditions of employment."[70] Currently about one-fourth of all workers are covered by collective bargaining agreements. Where unions represent workers, union officials research the needs of the bargaining unit, the elements of the pay package, and the employer's financial condition. When a contract expires, union officials negotiate on behalf of the members of the bargaining unit for desired pay components and may also play an active role in the job evaluation process.[71]

Just the threat of a union may cause employers to adjust pay and benefits. At Cannon Mills Company, three mills had to be closed because of overseas competition and productivity standards were increased without pay increases. As a result, some employees tried to unionize. Cannon's management struck back at the unionization attempts by persuading employees that the union would not improve benefits and would simply take part of employees' paychecks in the form of union dues.[72]

Equal Employment Opportunity Laws. There are many laws affecting compensation systems. The Equal Pay Act of 1963 and the Civil Rights Act of 1964 are two of the most important ones. The Equal Pay Act provides that persons of opposite genders who perform substantially similar work must be paid the same rate unless the pay differential can be justified on the basis of (1) merit, (2) seniority, (3) quantity or quality of production, or (4) any factor other than sex.[73] The Civil Rights Act is broader: It outlaws discrimination in any employment decision, including pay, on the basis of race, national origin, religion, or sex. When employees or a union feel the company has broken the law, they can take the company to court and seek compensation.

Terminations

Despite the best efforts of line managers and HRM professionals, the organization will lose employees. Some will retire, others will depart voluntarily for other jobs, and still others will be forced out through involuntary termination. The value of terminations for maintaining an effective work force is twofold. First, employees who are poor performers can be dismissed. Productive employees often resent disruptive, low-

"A good way to do bad time." Best Western developed an innovative response to an external influence—the high volume of incoming phone calls during peak periods, nights, and holidays. The company uses prison inmates to take reservations over the phone. Managers came up with this idea because of the readily available prison labor force. Best Western pays inmates the same wages as other reservation agents. Now inmates like Jolinda look forward to a day of productive employment. Callers don't know where Jolinda is working when she answers the phone, "Good Morning, Best Western."

exit interview An interview conducted with departing employees to determine the reasons for their termination.

performing employees who are allowed to stay with the company and receive pay and benefits comparable to theirs. Second, employers can use exit interviews. An **exit interview** is an interview conducted with departing employees to determine why they are leaving. The exit interview is an excellent and inexpensive tool for reducing turnover and for learning about pockets of dissatisfaction within the organization. Exit interviews are most effective when they are conducted for all departing employees. Retiring employees can use them to reflect on their work experiences within the organization and provide valuable insights for managers. Voluntary departures of valued employees provide good information on the reasons for their leaving. Exit interviews with fired employees can also provide useful feedback. Such employees may feel they were dismissed unfairly or that weaknesses exist in discipline or termination procedures.

Exit interviews can have a positive affect on departing employees, because they demonstrate fair, consistent application of in-house policies and an interest in departing employees. A monthly or quarterly report about the reasons for employee terminations can be summarized and passed on to top managers so that they can initiate policy changes for solving human resource problems.[74]

SUMMARY

This chapter described several important points about human resource management in organizations. All managers are responsible for human resources, and most organizations have a human resource department that works with line managers to insure a productive work force. The first goal of the human resource department is to attract an effective work force through human resource planning, recruiting, and employee selection. The second is to develop an effective work force. Newcomers are introduced to the organization and to their jobs through orientation and training programs. Moreover, employees are appraised through performance appraisal programs. The third goal is to maintain an effective work force. Human resource managers retain employees with wage and salary systems, with benefits packages, by dealing with unions and government regulations, and by using exit interviews.

Management Solution

The problem Leonard Schlesinger faced at Au Bon Pain Company was growth from 100 to 800 employees in 3 years. Au Bon Pain recruited employees but was unable to develop them quickly enough to fill all the vacant management positions. Managers decided that the answer was to develop a training program that would enable the company to develop managers from within. Schlesinger began by interviewing vendors who could supply prepackaged management training programs. Because of their expense, Au Bon Pain decided to do its own employee education. This meant tripling the training budget and expanding the human resource department. The training program included a job rotation system that rotated store employees to corporate headquarters and back for 12 to 24 months. The training program for store operators was expanded from two to six weeks. A general management skills program was also offered for all employees. The HRM training programs helped Au Bon Pain meet its strategic goals of growth and expansion.[75]

DISCUSSION QUESTIONS

1. What does it mean to say that human resource management should reflect corporate goals and strategy? How are the human resource activities of planning, recruiting, performance appraisal, and compensation related to corporate strategy?
2. Think back to your own job experience. What human resource management activities described in this chapter were performed for the job you filled? Which ones were absent?
3. What are the three major goal areas of human resource management? Are activities related to these goals performed by HRM professionals or by line managers?
4. Why are planning and forecasting necessary for human resource management? Discuss.
5. Job analysis is a central HRM activity. How does job analysis contribute to (a) planning, (b) recruiting, (c) selection, (d) training, (e) performance appraisal, and (f) compensation?
6. What techniques can managers adopt to improve their recruiting and interviewing practices?
7. How does affirmative action differ from equal employment opportunity in recruiting and selection?
8. Why should companies make it a point to perform a needs analysis and an evaluation as part of employee training programs?
9. How can exit interviews be used to maintain an effective work force?
10. Describe the procedure used to build a wage and salary structure for an organization.

CASES FOR ANALYSIS

TRIANGLE EQUIPMENT

In 1986, Jane Foster joined Triangle Equipment, a small Kansas manufacturer of farm equipment. Triangle employed 1,700 people, most of whom were welders, machine operators, and assemblers in the plant. The company was successful despite a downturn in the farm economy because of a loyal clientele, committed employees, and efficient production methods.

Jane was in charge of administrative services, but she had a problem. She had reviewed her first-level managers for merit pay. She had worked hard on the performance appraisal and kept records about employee performance. She believed in rewarding those who contributed the most to the organization. However, before holding the appraisal interview with each employee, she was required to get approval from her boss, Frank Galloway, before implementing the promised raises.

Frank was a vice-president, a close personal friend of the president, and was well liked by many employees. Unfortunately, Frank wanted to change the recommended merit pay increases for each of Jane's managers. Frank told Jane that this year's performance was not as important as the individual's potential, attitude, years to retirement, age, and family situation. Since Jane was still new, Frank decided to overrule her in each case.

The following information reflects Jane's notes about the performance of three employees as well as Frank's response.

David Thompson had had 18 years with Triangle but had never been an outstanding performer. His recent poor effort had held up the assembly operation, and Jane had sent several memos requesting improvement. David was a close personal friend of Frank Galloway and had several children, two of whom were in college. Jane recommended a salary increase from $30,000 to $31,000, but Frank believed David's salary should be increased to $35,000.

Dolores Rodriguez had shown remarkable improvement over the last year. She was a hard worker and had been coming to work early and staying late. She had spent many hours untangling problems created by others and had clearly found her position in the organization. Jane could always rely on Dolores to do whatever was needed and do it in an efficient manner. Dolores was unmarried and a high school graduate. Jane's salary increase recommendation was from $22,000 to $26,500. Frank would approve only a $1,500 increase.

Ray Sanders had always been an outstanding employee. However, during the last year Ray had experienced family problems, including a divorce, followed by his former wife and children moving out of state. His performance had declined markedly; his misspecified equipment drawings had cost the company time and money. Jane recommended a small salary increase from $41,000 to $42,500. Frank believed that Ray's salary should be increased to $46,000.

Questions

1. Frank believed his recommended raises reflected the company's goals. Do you agree?
2. Do any of Frank's recommendations violate laws concerning equitable pay for employees?
3. If you were a personnel specialist consulting with Jane, what would you recommend that Jane do?

LEGRANDE STORES

Chief buyer Ruth Brown called management trainee Carla Hume into her office. "Carla, you've been with us only six months," Ruth began, "but in that time you've progressed very fast. I'm delighted with your work, and I appreciate the effort you've put into it."

Carla was pleased. When she had come to Legrande Stores fresh out of college, she was at first very disappointed. The job was different than she had expected, with long hours and little glamour. But now she had been there six months, and she was getting adjusted to it. Her boss said she was doing splendidly.

Three months later, however, Carla was in for another letdown. When an opening for assistant buyer occurred in the lingerie division, someone else was hired. No one had even mentioned the opening to Carla.

Upset and annoyed, Carla went to visit her friend Howard Price, a buyer in the men's division. Howard was someone in whom Carla could confide. "My boss said I was doing well and had a great future here. So why didn't they promote me?"

"Well, for one thing," Howard said, "you weren't ready."

"That's not true," Carla responded. "I've learned everything there is to know about fabrics, inventory control, and fashion forecasting. What else is there to learn?"

"I thought you knew the policy of this company, Carla," Howard began hesitantly. "The company wants to be a fashion leader. Being a buyer isn't simply knowing how to get the best item for the cheapest price. It also takes creativity—such as finding new fashion items that will be a big hit. You have to be ahead of the customers. You are competent, Carla, but you haven't come up with any new ideas." Carla was disappointed. She walked dejectedly out of Howard's office.

The next day Carla phoned in sick. Over the next few months, her performance gradually declined and she made several purchasing and accounting errors. Concerned that Carla was failing to meet minimum performance standards, Ruth asked her what was wrong.

"Oh, nothing," Carla answered. "It's just that I don't feel like working so hard if I'm not going to get rewarded."

Questions

1. How would you evaluate the performance appraisal system at Legrande Stores?
2. What mistakes did Ruth and Legrande Stores make with respect to human resource management? What changes would you recommend to prevent these mistakes in the future?
3. What can Ruth do now to restore Carla's motivation and get her back on track?

Source: Reprinted by permission of the publishers, from "Let's Get Down to Cases," *Supervisory Management,* March 1974. Copyright 1974 by AMACOM, a division of American Management Association. All rights reserved.

PART FOUR
LEADING

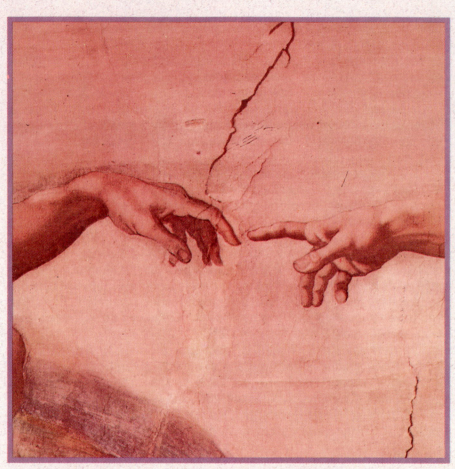

Source: © *Thatcher + Poulides.*

Leadership in Organizations

Chapter Outline

The Nature of Leadership

Sources of Leader Influence
The Use of Power

Leadership Traits

Autocratic versus Democratic Leaders

Two-Dimensional Approaches

Ohio State Studies
Michigan Studies
The Managerial Grid

Contingency Approaches

Fiedler's Contingency Theory
Path-Goal Theory
Vroom-Yetton Model
Substitutes for Leadership

Inspirational Leadership

Leading versus Managing
Inspirational Leaders

Leadership by Organizational Level

Learning Objectives

After studying this chapter, you should be able to:

- Define leadership and explain its importance for organizations.

- Identify personal characteristics associated with effective leaders.

- Explain the five sources of leader influence and how each causes different subordinate behavior.

- Describe the leader behaviors of initiating structure and consideration and when they should be used.

- Explain the path-goal model of leadership.

- Describe the Vroom-Yetton model and its application to subordinate participation in leader decisions.

- Explain how leadership fits the organizational situation and how organizational characteristics can substitute for leadership behaviors.

- Describe inspirational leadership and when it should be used.

Management Problem

Once perceived as easygoing and amiable, James L. Dutt, CEO of Beatrice Companies, developed into a hot-tempered autocrat who relentlessly pushed his vision for a new Beatrice. Dutt is said to deliver tirades at management meetings, haranguing his subordinates mercilessly and insisting they don't work hard enough. During one speech, he threatened that three top executives would lose their jobs if goals weren't met. He is considered vindictive and intolerant of dissent or debate. Executive turnover within Beatrice has been high, and Dutt apparently drove top executives out of Esmark, a recent acquisition. Dutt's vision is to create a national marketing juggernaut that will allow Beatrice's many regional brands to acquire national identity and sales. But with so many alienated executives, it is not clear whether Dutt is an ogre or a misunderstood genius.[1]

How would you characterize James Dutt's leadership style? Is his style helping or hurting Beatrice? What leadership style would you recommend?

James Dutt is the leader of a giant corporation, and his style seems unusual for that position. However, many styles of leadership can be successful in organizations. Rod Canion, cofounder and chief executive officer of Compaq Computer, stresses that in his company "the casual—and often idiosyncratic—clothing seen at California personal computer makers is out, and employees are encouraged to work normal hours." Canion has no private parking space at his company and flies coach like other employees when he travels. John Gutfreund, CEO of brokerage giant Salomon Brothers, influences his company by throwing imaginatively extravagant parties: "Cigar in hand, he constantly prowls [his company]

Leadership is the ability to influence other people toward the attainment of goals. In the U.S. Army, primary sources of leader influence are legitimate, reward, and coercive power. The military has a well-defined leadership structure. These women undergoing basic training accept the sergeant's legitimate right to issue commands. The sergeant also has the authority to bestow rewards such as praise and recognition and punish subordinates for failure to perform. While these sources of influence will gain recruits' compliance, they are unlikely to engender their personal commitment to a course of action.

leadership The ability to influence other people toward the attainment of organizational goals.

power The potential ability to influence others' behavior.

legitimate power Power that stems from a formal management position in an organization and the authority granted to it.

reward power Power that results from the leader's authority to reward others.

. . . , springing impromptu quizzes on young employees." Jesse Aweida, the entrepreneur who built Storage Technology Corporation into a $1 billion company, still "works 10 to 12 hours a day and also finds time to jog 4 miles. When he isn't working, he's either skiing in Vail, Colorado (where he owns a condominium), or toodling around Boulder in a red Porsche or an orange motorcycle."[2]

The purpose of this chapter is to explore leadership, one of the most widely discussed and researched topics in management. Here we will define leadership and explore the sources of leadership influence. We will discuss trait, behavioral, and contingency theories of leadership effectiveness. We will also explore a new type of leader, called the *inspirational leader,* who creates a vision, inspires loyalty, and leads corporate transformations. Chapters 13 through 16 deal with many of the functions of leadership, including employee motivation, communication, leading groups, and leading corporate culture and revitalization.

THE NATURE OF LEADERSHIP

Among all the ideas and writings about leadership, three images stand out—people, influence, and goals. Leadership occurs between people, involves the use of influence, and is used to attain goals. Influence means that the relationship among people is not passive. Moreover, influence is designed to achieve some end or goal. Thus, our formal definition of leadership is: **Leadership** is the ability to influence other people toward the attainment of goals. This definition captures the idea that leaders are involved with other people in the achievement of objectives. Leadership is a "people" activity, distinct from administrative paper shuffling or problem-solving activities. Leadership is dynamic and involves the use of power. Power is important for influencing others, because it determines whether a leader is able to command compliance from followers.

Sources of Leader Influence

Power is the potential ability to influence the behavior of others.[3] Power represents the resources with which a leader effects changes in employee behavior. Leadership is the actual use of that power. Within organizations, leaders typically have five sources of power: legitimate, reward, coercive, expert, and referent.[4]

Legitimate Power.   **Legitimate power** comes from a formal management position in an organization and the authority granted to it. For example, once a person has been selected as a supervisor, most workers understand that they are obligated to follow his or her direction with respect to work activities. Subordinates accept this source of power as legitimate, which is why they comply.

Reward Power.   **Reward power** stems from the leader's authority to bestow rewards on other people. Leaders may have access to formal rewards, such as pay increases or promotions. They also have at their dis-

E X H I B I T   12.1

Outcomes of the Use of Leader Influence

| | Outcomes | | |
Source of Influence	Commitment	Compliance	Resistance
Legitimate power	Possible	Likely	Possible
Reward power	Possible	Likely	Possible
Coercive power	Unlikely	Possible	Likely
Expert power	Likely	Possible	Possible
Referent power	Likely	Possible	Possible

Source: G. Yukl and T. Taber, "The Effective Use of Managerial Power," *Personnel* (March/April 1983), pp. 37–44. Reprinted with the permission of *Personnel Journal*, Inc., Costa Mesa, CA. All rights reserved.

posal rewards such as praise, attention, and recognition. Leaders can use rewards to influence subordinates' behavior.

Coercive power.   Coercive power is the opposite of reward power: It refers to the leader's authority to punish or recommend punishment. Leaders have coercive power when they have the right to fire or demote employees, criticize, or withdraw pay increases. For example, if Paul, a salesman, does not perform as expected, his supervisor has the coercive power to criticize him, reprimand him, put a negative letter in his file, and hurt his chance for a raise.

coercive power   Power that stems from the leader's authority to punish or recommend punishment.

Expert Power.   Expert power is the result of a leader's special knowledge or skill regarding the tasks performed by followers. When the leader is a true expert, subordinates go along with recommendations because of his or her superior knowledge. Leaders at supervisory levels often have experience in the production process that gains them promotion. At top management levels, however, leaders may lack expert power because subordinates know more about technical details than they do.

expert power   Power that stems from the leader's special knowledge of or skill in the tasks performed by subordinates.

Referent Power.   Referent power comes from leader personality characteristics that command subordinates' identification, respect, and admiration so they wish to emulate the leader. When workers admire and respect a supervisor because of the way she deals with them, the influence is based on referent power. Referent power depends on the leader's personal characteristics rather than formal title or position.

referent power   Power that results from leader characteristics that command subordinates' identification with, respect and admiration for, and desire to emulate the leader.

The Use of Power

Leaders use the above five sources of power to affect the behavior and performance of followers. But how do followers react to each source? Exhibit 12.1 presents research findings on the impact of the five types of power.[5] Each can influence the commitment, compliance, or resistance of followers. *Commitment* means workers will share the leader's point of view and enthusiastically carry out instructions. *Compliance* means workers will obey orders and carry out instructions, although they may personally disagree with the instructions and will not be enthusiastic. *Resist-*

The trait approach to leadership suggests that a leader needs certain personal and social characteristics. One of the traits required for a leadership position at Price Waterhouse is the ability to advise and guide new staff members. Movement to higher management levels draws on such traits as facility in public speaking and in dealing with clients and senior partners, which require self-confidence and desire for responsibility.

traits The distinguishing personal characteristics of a leader, such as intelligence, values, and appearance.

ance means that workers will deliberately try to avoid carrying out instructions and attempt to disobey orders.

When leaders use legitimate power and reward power, the most likely outcome will be compliance. This means that workers will do as they are told so long as the leader can reward them and has a legitimate company position, but workers may not agree with or be committed to the course of action. Coercive power is most likely to produce employee resistance. People hate to be forced to do things through punishment and will resist at every opportunity. They will try to avoid carrying out the instructions and to dodge the punishment. Expert power and referent power have a positive impact, because they lead to subordinate commitment. Subordinates will comply because they trust the leader's knowledge and ability or because they believe in and identify with the leader. They will perform as instructed because they want to.

For example, Glenn Van Pelt worked himself up from junior apprentice to production supervisor. He was respected by everyone for his knowledge of the production process and his pleasant attitude. One day Glenn asked John Simmons, one of his foremen, to reassign one of his people to help finish a project in another department. John felt he didn't have enough people, but he knew the boss used good judgment and trusted his expertise. Thus, he agreed to lend one employee to Glenn and committed himself to making it work. However, had Glenn threatened John with punishment, John would have found a reason why he could not get along without the employee. Had Glenn used his formal position or reward power to force John's agreement, John would have complied, but without commitment.

LEADERSHIP TRAITS

Early efforts to understand leadership success focused on the leader's personal characteristics or traits. **Traits** are the distinguishing personal characteristics of a leader, such as intelligence, values, and appearance. The early research focused on leaders who had achieved a level of greatness and hence was referred to as the "great man" approach. The idea was relatively simple: Find out what made these people great, and select future leaders who already exhibited the same traits or could be trained to develop them. Generally, research found only a weak relationship between personal traits and leader success.[6] For example, Tom Osborne, football coach at Nebraska, and Bo Schembechler, football coach at the University of Michigan, have different personality traits, but both are successful leaders of their football programs.

One review of the trait studies concluded that successful leadership traits depend on the situation.[7] For example, the traits that described a great religious leader were not necessarily the same ones associated with great business executives or political leaders. In other words, the situation as well as leader traits determines whether a leader is effective.[8] Recent studies suggest that both personal traits and the nature of the situation are important for understanding why a leader succeeds.[9]

EXHIBIT   12.2

Personal Characteristics of Leaders

Physical characteristics:
   Activity
   Energy

Social background:
   Mobility

Intelligence and ability:
   Judgment, decisiveness
   Knowledge
   Fluency of speech

Personality:
   Alertness
   Originality, creativity
   Personal integrity, ethical conduct
   Self-confidence
   Work-related characteristics
   Achievement drive, desire to excel
   Drive for responsibility
   Responsible in pursuit of objectives
   Task orientation

Social characteristics:
   Ability to enlist cooperation
   Cooperativeness
   Popularity, prestige
   Sociability, interpersonal skills
   Social participation
   Tact, diplomacy

Source: Adapted with permission of The Free Press, a Division of Macmillan, Inc. from *Stogdill's Handbook of Leadership,* Revised Edition, by Bernard M. Bass, pp. 75–76. Copyright © 1974, 1981 by The Free Press. This adaptation appeared in R. Albanese and D. D. Van Fleet, *Organizational Behavior: A Managerial Viewpoint.* Hinsdale, IL: The Dryden Press, 1983 and is used with permission.

In addition to personality traits, physical, social, and work-related characteristics of leaders have been studied. Exhibit 12.2 summarizes the physical, social, and personal leader characteristics that have received the greatest research support.[10] However, it is important to understand that these characteristics do not stand alone. The appropriateness of a trait or set of traits depends on the leadership situation. The same traits do not apply to every organization.

For example, Sarah Brown is the manager of Far Eastern imports for a major steel corporation. There is an opening for a subordinate manager in her department who will supervise the field sales personnel. For this position, the personal characteristic of intelligence and a working knowledge of steel product marketing are important, as are desire for responsibility, a task orientation, and supervisory skills. Sarah Brown's ability to understand the situation and the type of leader who will succeed in it will help her select the appropriate person for the job.

AUTOCRATIC VERSUS DEMOCRATIC LEADERS

One way to approach leader characteristics is to examine autocratic and democratic leaders. An **autocratic leader** is one who tends to centralize authority and rely on legitimate, reward, and coercive power. A **democratic leader** delegates authority to others, encourages participation, and relies on expert and referent power to influence subordinates.

The first studies on these leadership characteristics were conducted at Iowa State University by Kurt Lewin and his associates.[11] These studies compared autocratic and democratic leaders and produced some interesting findings. The groups with autocratic leaders performed highly so long as the leader was present to supervise them. However, group members were displeased with the close, autocratic style of leadership, and

autocratic leader A leader who tends to centralize authority and rely on legitimate, reward, and coercive power to manage subordinates.

democratic leader A leader who delegates authority to others, encourages participation, and relies on expert and referent power to manage subordinates.

E X H I B I T   12.3

Leadership Continuum

| Manager makes decision and announces it | Manager "sells" decision | Manager presents ideas and invites questions | Manager presents tentative decision subject to change | Manager presents problem, gets suggestions, makes decision | Manager defines limits, asks group to make decision | Manager permits subordinates to function within limits defined by superior |

Source: Reprinted by permission of the *Harvard Business Review*. An exhibit from "How to Choose a Leadership Pattern" by Robert Tannenbaum and Warren Schmidt (May/June 1973). Copyright © 1973 by the President and Fellows of Harvard College; all rights reserved.

feelings of hostility frequently arose. The performance of groups who were assigned democratic leaders was almost as good, and these were characterized by positive feelings rather than hostility. In addition, under the democratic style of leadership group members performed well even when the leader was absent and the group left on its own.[12] The participative techniques and majority rule decision making used by the democratic leader trained and involved group members such that they performed well with or without the leader present.

This early work suggested that leaders were either autocratic or democratic in their approach. However, further work by Tannenbaum and Schmidt indicated that leadership could be a continuum reflecting different amounts of employee participation.[13] Thus, one leader might be autocratic (boss centered), another democratic (subordinate centered), and a third a mix of the two styles. The leadership continuum is illustrated in Exhibit 12.3.

Tannenbaum and Schmidt suggested that the extent to which leadership is boss centered or subordinate centered depends on organizational circumstances. For example, if there is time pressure on a leader or if it takes too long for subordinates to learn how to make decisions, the leader will tend to use an autocratic style. When subordinates are able to learn decision-making skills readily, a participative style can be used. Another situational factor is the skill difference between subordinates and leader. The greater the skill difference, the more autocratic the leader approach, because it is difficult to bring subordinates up to the leader's expertise level.[14]

Henry Henley, CEO of Cluett, Peabody & Company, Inc., uses a democratic, subordinate-centered style.[15] Cluett, Peabody is an apparel maker, whose best-known brand is Arrow. Henley's management philosophy is that of dealing primarily with people. He tries to find the best individual for a job and then leave him or her alone to do it. He doesn't harass or direct his managers on a day-to-day basis but feels that people should be left on their own. This leadership style works well at the top management levels of this giant apparel maker. In contrast, Stephen Fleming uses an autocratic style as a marketing manager in an oil products company. He is being groomed for a higher position because his marketing department has performed so well. However, this has meant time spent at meetings away from his group, and the performance of his department has declined. This situation is not uncommon for autocratic managers, because they reserve decision making for themselves and their subordinates have not learned to function independently.

IBM frequently joins in partnerships with government organizations to meet its social responsibilities. Students at the Urban League Job Training Center prepare for jobs in areas such as word processing and data entry. Here the IBM trainer demonstrates "consideration." She is friendly, provides open communication, and respects subordinates' emotional needs.

TWO-DIMENSIONAL APPROACHES

The autocratic and democratic styles suggest that it is the "behavior" of the leader rather than a personality trait that determines leadership effectiveness. Perhaps any leader can adopt the correct behavior with appropriate training. The focus of recent research has shifted from leader personality traits toward the behaviors successful leaders display. Important research programs on leadership behavior were conducted at Ohio State University[16] and the University of Michigan.[17]

Ohio State Studies

Researchers at Ohio State University surveyed leaders to study hundreds of dimensions of leader behavior. They identified two major behaviors, called consideration and initiating structure.

Consideration is the extent to which the leader is mindful of subordinates, respects their ideas and feelings, and establishes mutual trust. Considerate leaders are friendly, provide open communication, develop teamwork, and are oriented toward their subordinates' welfare.

Initiating structure is the extent to which the leader is task oriented and directs subordinate work activities toward goal attainment. Leaders with this style typically give instructions, spend time planning, emphasize deadlines, and provide explicit schedules of work activities.

Consideration and initiating structure are independent of each other, which means that a leader with a high degree of consideration may be either high or low on initiating structure. The two dimensions are illustrated in Exhibit 12.4. A leader may have any of four styles reflecting the four combinations of consideration and initiating structure. The Ohio State research found that the high consideration–high initiating structure style achieved better performance and greater satisfaction than the other leader styles. However, new research has found that effective leaders may be high on consideration and low on initiating structure or low on consideration and high on initiating structure depending on the situation. Thus, the "high-high" style is not always the best.[18]

consideration   A type of leader behavior that describes the extent to which a leader is sensitive to subordinates, respects their ideas and feelings, and establishes mutual trust.

initiating structure   A type of leader behavior that describes the extent to which a leader is task oriented and directs subordinates' work activities toward goal achievement.

EXHIBIT   12.4

Two-Dimensional Model of Leadership Behavior

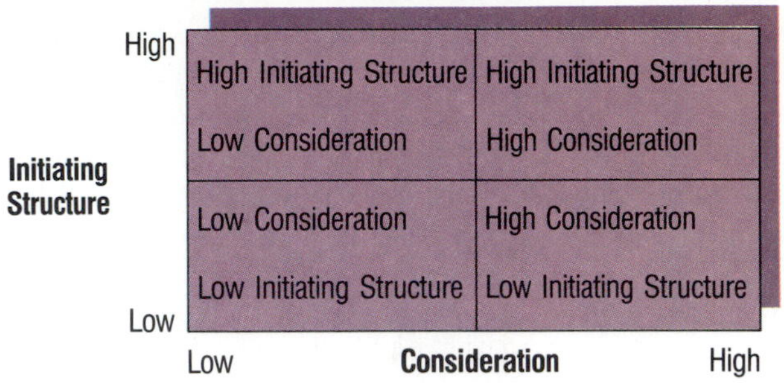

Michigan Studies

Studies at the University of Michigan at about the same time took a different approach by comparing the behavior of effective and ineffective supervisors.[19] The most effective supervisors were those who focused on the subordinates' human needs in order to "build effective work groups with high performance goals." The Michigan researchers used the term *employee-centered leaders* for leaders who established high performance goals and displayed supportive behavior toward subordinates. The less effective leaders were called *job-centered leaders;* these tended to be less concerned with goal achievement and human needs in favor of meeting schedules, keeping costs low, and production efficiency.

The Managerial Grid

managerial grid A two-dimensional leadership theory that measures a leader's concern for people and concern for production.

Blake and Mouton of the University of Texas proposed a two-dimensional leadership theory called the **managerial grid.**[20] The managerial grid is similar to Exhibit 12.4 except that consideration behavior is called "concern for people" and initiating structure behavior is called "concern for production."

Exhibit 12.4 is an interpretation of all three streams of research on leader behavior. The significance of the research is that each stream discovered similar dimensions of leadership style. The effectiveness of leaders depends on the types of behavior they display. The Ohio State, Michigan, and Texas research programs suggested that leader behavior is more complex than the simple autocratic versus democratic behavior described earlier. The two dimensions of leadership are illustrated in the following examples.

Chick-fil-A, Inc.

Samuel Truett Cathy is founder and president of Chick-fil-A, Inc. Cathy has been remarkably successful, and one of the keys is his people orientation. "Truett Cathy is probably the most person-

oriented individual I've ever known," says a close friend. "He honestly believes his highest obligation is to help people reach their highest potential. . . . He's one of the most tolerant persons I've known." The executive vice-president of Chick-fil-A calls his boss "the most patient man I've ever encountered, and one totally committed to individual development. He delegates easily, lets people grow by trusting them."

Of course, to be successful Cathy also had to set goals and provide direction for his company. But the reason he succeeded was that he was an outstanding encourager of other people.[21]

Compare Cathy's leadership style with that of Ross B. Kenzie, who pushes change from the top at Buffalo Savings Bank. As new chairman of Buffalo Savings, he fired 15 percent of the managers and has pushed relentlessly for growth. He is quick to get rid of people who don't meet his standards. He provides clear goals and direction for subordinates. One plan was to acquire financially weak thrift institutions with the help of the Federal Deposit Insurance Corporation. He also initiated the construction of a new headquarters building and imposed the idea of shifting people from job to job to see if they did well. If not, they were fired.[22]

Truett Cathy's leadership style is characterized by a high level of consideration and a moderate level of initiating structure. Ross Kenzie, in contrast, is high on initiating structure and low on consideration. Both managers are successful because of their situations.

contingency approach   A model of leadership that describes the relationship between leadership styles and specific organizational situations.

LPC scale   A questionnaire designed to measure relationship-oriented versus task-oriented leadership style according to the leader's choice of adjectives for describing the "least preferred coworker."

Daryl Johnson is food service sales manager at Stilwell Foods Inc., a subsidiary of Flowers Industries. Johnson cites his greatest enjoyment as helping people, both in his job at Stilwell and as scoutmaster of a local Boy Scout troop. According to Fiedler's contingency theory, Johnson would have a high LPC score, indicating a relationship-oriented leader. This leadership style is especially appropriate in organizational situations of intermediate favorability. Johnson gives 100 percent to the task, which helps solve on-the-job problems.

CONTINGENCY APPROACHES

Several models of leadership that explain the relationship between leadership styles and specific situations have been developed. These are termed **contingency approaches** and include the leadership model developed by Fiedler and his associates, the path-goal theory presented by Evans and House, the Vroom-Yetton model, and the substitutes-for-leadership concept.

Fiedler's Contingency Theory

An early, extensive effort to combine leadership style and organizational situation into a comprehensive theory of leadership was made by Fiedler and his associates.[23] The basic idea is simple: Match the leader's style with the situation most favorable for his or her success. By diagnosing leadership style and the organizational situation, the correct fit can be arranged.

Leadership Style.   The cornerstone of Fiedler's contingency theory is the extent to which the leader's style is relationship oriented or task oriented. A *relationship-oriented leader* is concerned with people, as in the consideration style described earlier. A *task-oriented leader* is primarily motivated by task accomplishment, which is similar to the initiating structure style described earlier.

Leadership style was measured with a questionnaire known as the least preferred coworker (LPC) scale. The **LPC scale** has a set of 16 bipolar adjectives along an 8-point scale. Examples of the bipolar adjectives used by Fiedler on the LPC scale are as follows:

open	__	__	__	__	__	__	__	__	guarded
quarrelsome	__	__	__	__	__	__	__	__	harmonious
efficient	__	__	__	__	__	__	__	__	inefficient
self-assured	__	__	__	__	__	__	__	__	hesitant
gloomy	__	__	__	__	__	__	__	__	cheerful

If the leader describes the least preferred coworker using positive concepts, he or she is considered relationship oriented, that is, cares about and is sensitive to other people's feelings. Conversely, if a leader uses negative concepts to describe the least preferred coworker, he or she is considered task oriented, that is, sees other people in negative terms and places greater value on task activities than on people.

Situation.   Leadership situations can be analyzed in terms of three elements: the quality of leader-member relationships, task structure, and positional power.[24] Each of these elements can be described as either favorable or unfavorable for the leader.

1. *Leader-member relations* refers to group atmosphere and represents members' attitude toward and acceptance of the leader. When the group of subordinates trust, respect, and have confidence in the leader, leader-member relations are considered good. When

EXHIBIT   12.5

Fiedler's Classification of Situation Favorableness

	Very Favorable		Intermediate				Very Unfavorable	
Leader-Member Relations	Good	Good	Good	Good	Poor	Poor	Poor	Poor
Task Structure	High		Low		High		Low	
Leader Position Power	Strong	Weak	Strong	Weak	Strong	Weak	Strong	Weak
Situations	I	II	III	IV	V	VI	VII	VIII

Source: Fred E. Fiedler, "The Effects of Leadership Training and Experience: A Contingency Model Interpretation," *Administrative Science Quarterly* 17 (1972), p. 455. Reprinted by permission of *Administrative Science Quarterly*.

subordinates distrust, do not respect, and have little confidence in the leader, leader-member relations are poor.

2. *Task structure* refers to the extent to which tasks performed by the group are defined, involve specific procedures, and have clear, explicit goals. Routine, well-defined tasks, such as those of assembly line workers, have a high degree of structure. Creative, ill-defined tasks, such as research and development or strategic planning, have a low degree of task structure. When task structure is high, the situation is considered favorable to the leader; when low, the situation is less favorable.

3. *Position power* is the extent to which the leader has formal authority over subordinates. Position power is high when the leader has the power to plan and direct the work of subordinates, evaluate it, and reward or punish them. Position power is low when the leader has little authority over subordinates and cannot evaluate their work or reward them. When position power is high, the situation is considered favorable for the leader; when low, the situation is unfavorable.

Combining the three situational characteristics yields a list of eight leadership situations, which are illustrated in Exhibit 12.5. Note that situation I is most favorable to the leader because leader-member relations are good, task structure is high, and leader position power is strong. Situation VIII is most unfavorable to the leader because leader-member relations are poor, task structure is low, and leader position power is weak. All other octants represent intermediate degrees of favorableness for the leader.

Contingency Theory.   When Fiedler examined the relationships among leadership style, situational favorability, and group task performance, he found the pattern shown in Exhibit 12.6. Task-oriented leaders are more effective when the situation is either highly favorable or highly unfavora-

E X H I B I T   12.6

How Leader Style Fits the Situation

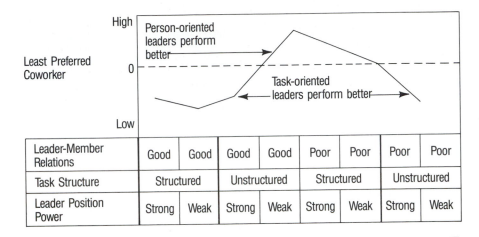

Leader-Member Relations	Good	Good	Good	Good	Poor	Poor	Poor	Poor
Task Structure	Structured		Unstructured		Structured		Unstructured	
Leader Position Power	Strong	Weak	Strong	Weak	Strong	Weak	Strong	Weak

Source: Fred E. Fiedler, "The Effects of Leadership Training and Experience: A Contingency Model Interpretation," *Administrative Science Quarterly* 17 (1972), p. 455. Reprinted by permission of *Administrative Science Quarterly*.

ble. Relationship-oriented leaders are more effective in situations of moderate favorability.

The reason the task-oriented leader excels in the favorable situation is that when everyone gets along, the task is clear, and the leader has power, all that is needed is for someone to take charge and provide direction. Similarly, if the situation is highly unfavorable to the leader, a great deal of structure and task direction is needed. A strong leader defines task structure and can establish authority over subordinates. Since leader-member relations are poor anyway, a strong task orientation will make no difference in the leader's popularity.

The reason the relationship-oriented leader performs better in situations of intermediate favorability is that human relations skills are important in achieving high group performance. In these situations the leader may be moderately well liked, have some power, and supervise jobs that contain some ambiguity. A leader with good interpersonal skills can create a positive group atmosphere that will improve relationships, clarify task structure, and establish position power.

A leader, then, needs to know two things in order to use Fiedler's contingency theory. First, the leader should know whether he or she has a relationship- or task-oriented style. Second, the leader should diagnose the situation and determine whether leader-member relations, task structure, and position power are favorable or unfavorable. If a leader discovers that his or her style does not match the situation, the leader should try to change the situation in order to increase effectiveness.[25] The leader may be able to increase or decrease task structure or change the amount of position power. Consider the relationship between leader style and the situation at Greyhound.

Greyhound Corporation

John Teets, chairman of Greyhound, has found himself in a situation that fits his leadership style. Teets is a very tough, task-oriented leader. As one vice-president said, "He'd rather kick a door down than turn the handle." Teets fires questions at top executives to see whether they know the details of their operations. He has been known to shout during meetings and rip pages out of financial reports. He exhorts managers to work harder and to achieve a 15 percent return. When the union refused to cut wages, he shut down 29 plants in one day.

Because of Teets' fierce style, Greyhound is shaping up. The company was a sleepy, poor performer and did not provide a good situation for any leader. Teets sold off some divisions, insisted on higher performance in others, and has fought with managers and the union. His task-oriented style has been just right for Greyhound Corporation and has been largely responsible for whipping it back into shape.[26]

John Teets, chairman of Greyhound Corporation, is considered a tough, task-oriented leader. Every morning he climbs 19 flights of stairs to his office and offers prizes to other managers who become stair climbers. Setting performance goals for subordinates illustrates his leadership style. Teets does not become personally involved with employees, preferring to set goals and show confidence in their ability to achieve them.

John Teets's experience at Greyhound illustrates Fiedler's model: A task-oriented style works in an unfavorable situation.

An important contribution of Fiedler's research is that it goes beyond the notion of leadership styles to show how styles fit the situation to improve organizational effectiveness. On the other hand, the model has also been criticized.[27] Using the LPC score as a measure of relationship- or task-oriented behavior seems simplistic, and it's unclear how the model works over time. For example, if a task-oriented leader is matched with an unfavorable situation and is successful, the organizational situation is likely to improve and become more favorable to the leader. In other words, as Greyhound's performance improves, the formal position power, leader-member relations, and task structure will improve and become more positive for the leader, and the hard-nosed style of John Teets may no longer be appropriate. Teets may have to change his style or go to a new situation to find the same challenge for his task-oriented leader style.

Path-Goal Theory

Another contingency approach to leadership is called the path-goal theory.[28] According to the **path-goal theory,** the leader's responsibility is to increase subordinates' motivation to attain personal and organizational goals. As illustrated in Exhibit 12.7, the leader increases their motivation by either (1) clarifying the subordinates' path to the rewards that are available or (2) increasing the rewards that they value and desire. Path clarification means that the leader works with subordinates to help them identify and learn the behaviors that will lead to successful task accom-

path-goal theory A contingency approach to leadership specifying that the leader's responsibility is to increase subordinates' motivation by clarifying the behaviors necessary for task accomplishment and rewards.

EXHIBIT   12.7

Leader Roles in the Path-Goal Model

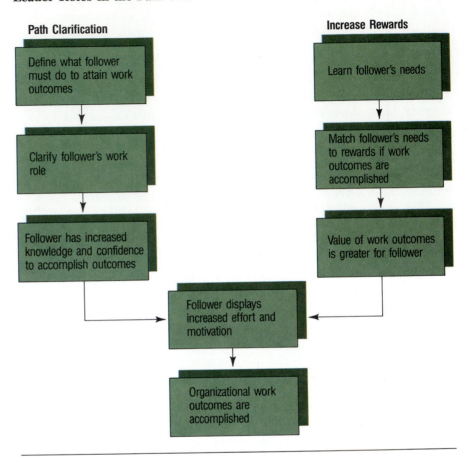

Source: Based on Bernard M. Bass, "Leadership: Good, Better, Best," *Organizational Dynamics* 13 (Winter 1985), pp. 26–40.

plishment and organizational rewards. Increasing rewards means that the leader talks with subordinates to learn which rewards are important to them—that is, whether they desire intrinsic rewards from the work itself or extrinsic rewards such as raises or promotions. The leader's job is to increase personal payoffs to subordinates for goal attainment and to make the paths to these payoffs clear and easy to travel.[29]

This model is called a contingency theory because it consists of three sets of contingencies—leader behavior and style, situational contingencies, and the use of rewards to meet subordinates' needs.[30]

Leader Behavior.   The path-goal theory suggests a fourfold classification of leader behaviors.[31] These classifications are the types of leader behavior the leader can adopt and include supportive, directive, achievement-oriented, and participative styles.

Supportive leadership involves leader behavior that shows concern for subordinates' well-being and personal needs. Leadership behavior is open, friendly, and approachable, and the leader creates a team climate and treats subordinates as equals. Supportive leadership is similar to the consideration leadership described earlier.

Directive leadership occurs when the leader tells subordinates exactly what they are supposed to do. Leader behavior includes planning, making schedules, setting performance goals and behavior standards, and stressing adherence to rules and regulations. Directive leadership behavior is similar to the initiating structure leadership style described earlier.

Participative leadership means that the leader consults with his or her subordinates about decisions. Leader behavior includes asking for opinions and suggestions, encouraging participation in decision making, and meeting with subordinates in their workplaces. The participative leader encourages group discussion and written suggestions.

Achievement-oriented leadership occurs when the leader sets clear and challenging objectives for subordinates. Leader behavior stresses high-quality performance and improvement over current performance. Achievement-oriented leaders also show confidence in subordinates and assist them in learning how to achieve high goals.

The four types of leader behavior are not considered ingrained personality traits; rather, they reflect types of behavior that every leader is able to adopt depending on the situation.

Situational Contingencies.   The two important situational contingencies in the path-goal theory are (1) the personal characteristics of group members and (2) the work environment. Personal characteristics of subordinates include such factors as ability, skills, needs, and motivations. For example, if an employee has a low level of ability or skill, the leader may need to provide additional training or coaching in order for the worker to improve performance. If a subordinate is self-centered, the leader must manipulate rewards to motivate him or her. Subordinates who want clear direction and authority require a directive leader who will tell them exactly what to do. Craftworkers and professionals, however, may want more freedom and autonomy and work best under a participative leadership style.

The work environment contingencies include the degree of task structure, the nature of the formal authority system, and the work group itself. The task structure is similar to the same concept described in Fiedler's contingency theory; it includes the extent to which tasks are defined and have explicit job descriptions and work procedures. The formal authority system includes the amount of legitimate power used by managers and the extent to which policies and rules constrain employees' behavior. Work group characteristics are the educational level of subordinates and the quality of relationships among them.

Use of Rewards.   Recall that the leader's responsibility is to clarify the path to rewards for subordinates or to increase the amount of rewards to enhance satisfaction and job performance. In some situations, the leader works with subordinates to help them acquire the skills and confidence needed to perform tasks and achieve rewards already available. In oth-

Owners John and Marie Bouchard launched a small business called Wild Things with a unique leadership style. John Bouchard's leadership differs from the more traditional approaches he learned while earning an MBA and working as an auditor for a Big Eight accounting firm. He gives employees complete control over their tasks, hours, and workloads. Each day employees and owners talk shop during company-paid lunch. Bouchard finds that being a supportive and participative leader enables employees to meet both individual and company goals. Because sales were ahead of projections, the Bouchards rewarded six staffers with a company-paid week's vacation climbing in Yosemite.

EXHIBIT 12.8

Path-Goal Situations and Preferred Leader Behaviors

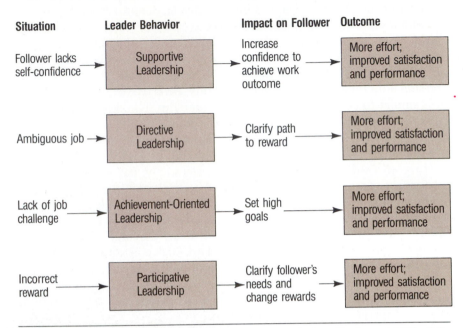

Source: Adapted from Gary A. Yukl, *Leadership in Organizations* (Englewood Cliffs, N.J.: Prentice-Hall, 1981), pp. 146–152.

ers, the leader may develop new rewards to meet the specific needs of a subordinate.

Exhibit 12.8 illustrates four examples of how leadership behavior is tailored to the situation. In situation 1, the subordinate lacks confidence; thus, the supportive leadership style provides the social support with which to encourage the subordinate to undertake the behavior needed to do the work and receive the rewards. In situation 2, the job is ambiguous and the employee is not performing effectively. Directive leadership behavior is used to give instructions and clarify the task so that the follower will know how to accomplish it and receive rewards. In situation 3, the subordinate is unchallenged by the task; thus, an achievement-oriented behavior is used to set higher goals. This clarifies the path to rewards for the employee. In situation 4, an incorrect reward is given to a subordinate and the participative leadership style is used to change this. By discussing the subordinate's needs, the leader is able to identify the correct reward for task accomplishment. In all four cases, the outcome of fitting the leadership behavior to the situation produces greater employee effort by either clarifying how subordinates can receive rewards or changing the rewards to fit their needs.

In some organizations, such as Fireman's Fund Insurance Company, leaders display complementary leadership styles to meet subordinates' needs.

Fireman's Fund Insurance Company

John Byrne and William McCormick have been called the "odd couple of insurance." McCormick is in charge of Fireman's Fund Insurance Company, and Byrne is his boss. McCormick is somewhat of an intellectual and repeats his vision for the company to employees at every opportunity. McCormick confronts employees when they are the cause of performance problems and rewards them when performance is high. He sets challenging goals and provides rewards accordingly. When he joined the company, the difference between the best and worst branch managers' bonus was only $3,000. Now it is $42,000.

Byrne, in contrast, is at home backslapping with employees. Byrne likes small talk, attends cocktail parties, and dislikes a stiff, memo-writing, policy-setting style. He is a people person and provides support whenever he can—indeed, as McCormick's boss, he gives McCormick the freedom to run Fireman's Fund as he likes.[32]

McCormick's leadership style is achievement oriented, but it also includes some elements of directive behavior. This is appropriate because of Fireman's Fund's difficulties in recent years. Strong direction and high goals are improving performance. Byrne's style is considered supportive leadership behavior, which gives McCormick the support to overcome obstacles and achieve higher performance.

Path-goal theorizing can be complex, but much of the research on it has been encouraging.[33] It's difficult to specify precise relationships and make exact predictions about employee outcomes based on the model. But the four types of leader behavior and the ideas for fitting them to situational contingencies provide a useful way for leaders to think about motivating subordinates.

Vroom-Yetton Model

Vroom and Yetton extended the earlier Iowa State studies and the work of Tannenbaum and Schmidt to develop a model of participation in decision making that provides guidance for practicing managers.[34] The **Vroom-Yetton model** helps the leader gauge the appropriate amount of participation for subordinates. It has three major components: leader participation styles, a set of diagnostic questions with which to analyze a decision situation, and a series of decision rules.

Leader Participation Styles. The model employs five levels of subordinate participation in decision making ranging from highly autocratic to highly democratic, as illustrated in Exhibit 12.9. Autocratic leadership styles are represented by AI and AII, consulting style by CI and CII, and a group decision by GII. The five styles fall along a continuum, and the manager should select one depending on the situation. If the situation

Vroom-Yetton model A model designed to help leaders identify the appropriate amount of subordinate participation in decision making.

EXHIBIT 12.9

Five Leader Participation Styles

	Decision Style	**Description**
Highly Autocratic	AI	You solve the problem or make the decision yourself using information available to you at that time.
	AII	You obtain the necessary information from your subordinates, then decide on the solution to the problem yourself.
	CI	You share the problem with relevant subordinates individually, getting their ideas and suggestions without bringing them together as a group. Then you make the decision.
	CII	You share the problem with your subordinates as a group, collectively obtaining their ideas and suggestions. Then you make the decision.
Highly Democratic	GII	You share a problem with your subordinates as a group. Your role is much like that of chairman. You do not try to influence the group to adopt "your" solution, and you are willing to accept and implement any solution that has the support of the entire group.

Note: A = autocratic; C = consultative; G = group.
Source: Reprinted, by permission of the publisher, from "A New Look at Managerial Decision-Making," by Victor H. Vroom, *Organizational Dynamics*, Spring 1973, pp. 67, 70. © 1973 AMACOM, a division of American Management Association, New York. All rights reserved.

warrants, the manager could make the decision alone (AI), share the problem with subordinates individually (CI), or let group members make the decision (GII).

Diagnostic Questions.   How does a manager decide which of the five decision styles to use? The appropriate degree of decision participation depends on the responses to seven diagnostic questions. These questions deal with the problem, the required level of decision quality, and the importance of having subordinates accept the decision. Each should be given a "yes" or "no" answer:

1. *Does the problem possess a decision requirement for high quality?* If a high-quality decision is important for group performance, the leader has to be actively involved.
2. *Do I have enough information to make a high-quality decision?* If the leader does not have sufficient information or expertise, the leader should involve subordinates to obtain that information.
3. *Is the decision problem well structured?* If the problem is ambiguous and poorly structured, the leader will need to interact with subordinates to clarify the problem and identify possible solutions.
4. *Is acceptance of the decision by subordinates important for effective implementation?* If implementation requires that subordinates agree with the decision, leaders should involve the subordinates in the decision process.
5. *If I were to make the decision by myself, is it reasonably certain that it would be accepted by my subordinates?* If subordinates typically go

along with whatever the leader decides, their involvement in the decision process will be less important.

6. *Do subordinates share the organizational goals to be attained in solving this problem?* If subordinates do not share the goals of the organization, the leader should not allow the group to make the decision alone.

7. *Is conflict over preferred solutions likely to occur among subordinates?* Disagreement among subordinates can be resolved by allowing their participation and discussion.

These questions seem detailed, but they quickly narrow the options available to managers and point to the appropriate level of group participation in the decision.

Selecting a Leadership Style.   The decision flowchart in Exhibit 12.10 allows a leader to adopt a participation style by answering the questions in sequence. The leader begins at the left side of the chart with question A: Does the problem possess a quality requirement? If the answer is yes, the leader proceeds to question B. If the answer to question A is no, the leader proceeds to question D, since questions B and C are irrelevant if quality is a requirement. Managers can quickly learn to use the basic model to adapt their leader styles to fit the decision problem and the situation.

Several decision styles are equally acceptable in many situations. When this happens, Vroom and Yetton recommend using the most autocratic style because this will save time without reducing decision quality or acceptance.

The Vroom-Yetton model is useful to leaders, and while it has been criticized as less than perfect,[35] there is a growing body of supportive research.[36] One application of the model occurred at Barouh-Eaton Allen Corporation.

Employees discuss ways to improve production in a quality circle meeting at Goodyear's Lincoln, Nebraska, industrial product plant. This leader is using a GII group decision-making approach (Vroom-Yetton model) by turning the problem over to the group. This style is especially effective when the leader lacks sufficient information, the decision problem is poorly structured, and subordinates share organizational goals.

Ko-Rec-Type

Barouh-Eaton Allen started prospering when owner Vic Barouh noticed that a typist kept a piece of white chalk by her machine. To erase an error, she would lightly rub over it with the chalk. It took several passes, but the correction was neatly made. Barouh's company already made carbon paper, so he tried rubbing chalk on one side of a sheet of paper, putting the paper between the error and typewriter, and striking the same key. Most of the error disappeared under a thin coating of chalk dust. Thus, Ko-Rec-Type was born. Demand for the product was enormous, and the company prospered.

Then IBM invented the self-correcting typewriter. Within two days after IBM's announcement, nearly 40 people told Barouh that the company was in trouble. Nobody was going to buy Ko-Rec-Type again.

E X H I B I T 12.10

Decision Tree for Determining Participation in Decision Making

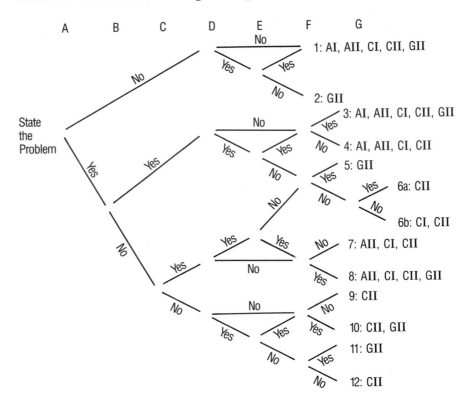

A. Does the problem possess a quality requirement? Does it matter what the answer is?
B. Do I have sufficient information to make a high-quality decision?
C. Is the problem structured? Do I know what information I need and where it is located?
D. Is acceptance of the decision by subordinates important for effective implementation?
E. If I were to make the decision by myself, am I reasonably certain that it would be accepted by my subordinates?
F. Do subordinates share the organizational goals to be attained in solving this problem?
G. Is conflict among subordinates likely in preferred solutions?

Source: Reprinted, by permission of the publisher, from "A New Look at Managerial Decision-Making," by Victor H. Vroom, *Organizational Dynamics*, Spring 1973, pp. 67, 70. © 1973 AMACOM, a division of American Management Association, New York. All rights reserved.

Barouh bought a self-correcting typewriter, took it to the plant, called everybody together, and told them what they had to do. To survive, the company had to learn to make this ribbon. They also had to learn to make the cartridge that held the ribbon, because cartridges could not be purchased on the market. They also had to learn to make the spools that held the tape. They had to learn to make the ink, the machine that puts on ink, injection-molding to make the spools, and so on. It was an enormous challenge. Barouh got everyone involved regardless of position or education.

To everyone's astonishment, Ko-Rec-Type produced the first self-correcting ribbon in only six months. Moreover, it was the only company in the world to produce that product. Barouh later learned that it took IBM six years to make the self-correcting ribbon. With the new product, Ko-Rec-Type's sales remained high and the company avoided disaster.[37]

The Vroom-Yetton model shows that Vic Barouh used the correct decision style. Moving from left to right in Exhibit 12.10, the questions and answers are as follows. (A) *Did the problem possess a quality requirement?* Definitely yes. (B) *Did Barouh have sufficient information to make a high-quality decision?* Definitely no. (C) *Was the decision well structured?* Definitely no. (D) *Was the acceptance of the decision by subordinates important for effective implementation?* Probably not, because subordinates had a great deal of respect for Barouh and would do whatever he asked. Question E is not relevant. (F) *Did subordinates share the organizational goals?* Yes. Thus, the decision tree leads to alternative 10: Use either CII or GII decision styles. Barouh should have used a participative style—and did.

Substitutes for Leadership

The contingency leadership approaches considered so far have focused on the leaders' style, the subordinates' nature, and the situation's characteristics. The final contingency approach suggests that situational variables can be so powerful that they actually substitute for or neutralize the need for leadership.[38] This approach outlines those organizational settings in which a leadership style is unimportant or unnecessary.

Exhibit 12.11 shows the situational variables that tend to substitute for or neutralize leadership characteristics. A **substitute** for leadership makes the leadership style unnecessary or redundant. For example, highly professional subordinates who know how to do their tasks do not need a leader who initiates structure for them and tells them what to do.

substitute A situational variable that makes a leadership style redundant or unnecessary.

These researchers are working in a new, state-of-the-art pharmaceutical development facility of Schering-Plough, a pharmaceutical and consumer products manufacturer. The leadership style used here will differ from that used in other company areas because the high levels of employee training, professionalism, and autonomy reduce the need for both task- and people-oriented leadership styles. The situation substitutes for leaders in research settings because the task and people needs are met in other ways.

EXHIBIT 12.11

Substitutes and Neutralizers for Leadership

Variable		Task-Oriented Leadership	People-Oriented Leadership
Macro variables:	Group cohesiveness	Substitutes	Substitutes
	Formalization	Substitutes	
	Inflexibility	Neutralizes	
	Low positional power	Neutralizes	Neutralizes
	Physical separation	Neutralizes	Neutralizes
Task characteristics:	Highly structured task	Substitutes	
	Automatic feedback	Substitutes	
	Intrinsically satisfying		Substitutes
Group characteristics:	Professionalism	Substitutes	Substitutes
	Trained/experienced	Substitutes	
	Low value of rewards	Neutralizes	Neutralizes

neutralizer A situational variable that counteracts a leadership style and prevents the leader from displaying certain behaviors.

A **neutralizer** counteracts the leadership style and prevents the leader from displaying certain behaviors. For example, if a leader has absolutely no position power or is physically removed from subordinates, the leader's ability to give directions to subordinates is greatly reduced.

Note in Exhibit 12.11 that situational variables include characteristics of the subordinate, the task, and the organization itself. For example, when subordinates are highly professional and experienced, both leadership styles are less important. The employees do not need as much direction or consideration. With respect to task characteristics, highly structured tasks substitute for a task-oriented style and a satisfying task substitutes for a people-oriented style. With respect to the organization itself, group cohesiveness substitutes for both leader styles. Formalized rules and procedures substitute for leader task orientation. Physical separation of leader and subordinate neutralizes both leadership styles.

The value of the situations described in Exhibit 12.11 is that they help leaders avoid leadership overkill. Leaders should adopt a style with which to complement the organizational situation. For example, the work situation for bank tellers provides a high level of formalization, little flexibility, and a highly structured task. The head teller should not adopt a task-oriented style, because the organization already provides structure and direction. The head teller should concentrate on a people-oriented style. In other organizations, if group cohesiveness or previous training meet employees' social needs, the leader is free to concentrate on task-oriented behaviors. The leader can adopt a style complementary to the organizational situation to insure that both task needs and people needs of the work group will be met.

INSPIRATIONAL LEADERSHIP

In Chapter 1, we defined management to include the management functions of leading, planning, organizing, and controlling. But recent work on leadership has begun to distinguish leadership as something more: a quality that inspires and motivates people beyond their normal levels of performance. The difference between traditional management and inspirational leadership is illustrated in Exhibit 12.12.

Leading versus Managing

The traditional management function of leading has been called transactional leadership.[39] **Transactional leaders** clarify the role and task requirements of subordinates, initiate structure, provide appropriate rewards, and try to be considerate to and meet the social needs of subordinates. Transactional leaders help satisfy subordinates to improve productivity. Transactional leaders excel at management functions. They are hard working, tolerant, and fair-minded. They take pride in keeping things running smoothly and efficiently. Transactional leaders often stress the impersonal aspects of performance, such as plans, schedules, and budgets. They have a sense of commitment to the organization and conform to organizational norms and values.

Inspirational Leaders

Inspirational leadership goes beyond traditional leadership techniques. The **inspirational leader** has the capacity to motivate people to do more than normally expected. Inspirational leaders raise subordinates' consciousness about new outcomes and motivate them to transcend their own interests for the sake of the department or organization. Inspirational leaders tend to be less predictable than transactional leaders. They create an atmosphere of change, and they may be obsessed by visionary ideas that excite, stimulate, and drive other people to work hard. Inspirational leaders have emotional impact on subordinates. They stand for something, have a vision of the future, are able to communicate that vision to subordinates, and motivate them to realize it.[40] One employee described the inspirational activities of his leader:

> My supervisor held a meeting to talk about how vital the new contract is for the company and said he was confident we could handle it if we all did our part. My boss told us we were the best design group he had ever worked with and he was sure that this new product was going to break every sales record in the company.[41]

Inspirational leaders sometimes are called *charismatic leaders* because of their unique ability to influence others through speaking, writing, and personal actions. Charismatic leaders include Mother Theresa, Martin Luther King, Adolf Hitler, and Jim Jones of Jonestown, Guyana. The true charismatic leader often does not fit within a traditional organization and may lead a social movement rather than a formal organization.

Some established companies, such as Banc One Corporation, have succeeded by nurturing inspirational leaders.

Banc One Corporation

Banc One Corporation in Columbus, Ohio, adopted a conscious strategy of thrusting "zealot"-style executives to the forefront. Banc

---

EXHIBIT 12.12

Leaders versus Managers

Let's Get Rid of Management

People don't want to be managed. They want to be led. Whoever heard of a world manager? World leader, yes. Educational leader. Political leader. Religious leader. Scout leader. Community leader. Labor leader. Business leader. They lead. They don't manage. The carrot always wins over the stick. Ask your horse. You can *lead* your horse to water, but you can't *manage* him to drink. If you want to manage somebody, manage yourself. Do that well and you'll be ready to stop managing. And start leading.

Source: Courtesy of United Technologies Corporation, Hartford, CT 06101.

transactional leader A leader who clarifies subordinates' role and task requirements, initiates structure, provides rewards, and displays consideration for subordinates.

inspirational leader A leader who has the ability to motivate subordinates to transcend their expected performance; also called a *charismatic leader*.

Are You a Leader?

If you were the head of a major department in a corporation, how important would each of the following activities be to you? Answer yes or no to indicate whether you would strive to perform each activity.

1. Help subordinates clarify goals and how to reach them.
2. Give people a sense of mission and overall purpose.
3. Help get jobs out on time.
4. Look for the new product or service opportunities.
5. Use policies and procedures as guides for problem solving.
6. Promote unconventional beliefs and values.
7. Give monetary rewards in exchange for high performance from subordinates.
8. Command respect from everyone in the department.
9. Work alone to accomplish important tasks.
10. Suggest new and unique ways of doing things.
11. Give credit to people who do their jobs well.
12. Inspire loyalty to yourself and to the organization.
13. Establish procedures to help the department operate smoothly.
14. Use ideas to motivate others.
15. Set reasonable limits on new approaches.
16. Demonstrate social nonconformity.

The even-numbered items represent behaviors and activities of inspirational leaders. Inspirational leaders are personally involved in shaping ideas, goals, and direction of change. They use an intuitive approach to develop fresh ideas for old problems and seek new directions for the department or organization. The odd-numbered items are considered more traditional management activities, or what would be called transactional leadership. Managers respond to organizational problems in an impersonal way, make rational decisions, and coordinate and facilitate the work of others. If you answered yes to more even-numbered than odd-numbered items, you may be a potential inspirational leader.

Based on Bernard M. Bass, *Leadership and Performance Beyond Expectations* (New York: Free Press, 1985), and Lawton R. Burns and Selwyn W. Becker, "Leadership and Managership," in *Health Care Management*, ed. S. Shortell and A. Kaluzny (New York: Wiley, 1986).

One has grown into the largest banking organization in Ohio. The inspirational leaders are combined with other managers who excel at implementation and control. One zealot is John Fisher, senior vice-president, who is expected to clear new paths in consumer banking. Other managers will follow the path, implement important details, and watch closely in case anything drastically goes wrong.

Harnessing inspirational leadership has worked, because Banc One is considered a pioneer in consumer banking, controlling 21 banks and $7.3 billion in assets. The inspirational leaders' nonconformity has created shock waves within the organization. For example, one television commercial featured comedienne Phyllis Diller stuffing a furry stole into an overnight deposit box and acting zany. The board of directors felt it communicated the wrong image. But the chief executive, John McCoy, let it go with the admonition that his people were free to try things as long as they did them right. As CEO, McCoy has been an inspirational leader himself by creating and communicating a vision of what the bank could become.[42]

Inspirational leaders rely on personal style and charisma to motivate others to transcend their own interests for the sake of a larger mission. Gandhi, shown here in 1947 with his two granddaughters, was an inspirational leader. Although he held no formal government position, he led a social movement that defeated the British Empire in India. Gandhi stood for a larger cause and was able to communicate it to others.

One variation of the inspirational leader is called the *transformational leader,* who brings about a major strategic change in an organization.[43] Transformational leaders emerge to take an organization through a major change, such as revitalization. They have the ability to make the necessary changes in the organization's mission, structure, and human resource management. Employees are persuaded to go along. In recent years a number of firms, such as General Electric, Campbell Soup, and Coca-Cola, have undergone transformation after appointing a new chief to act in the leadership role. John Welch of General Electric, Gordon McGovern of Campbell Soup, and Roberto Goizuta of Coca-Cola helped invigorate and revitalize their firms.

Another variation of inspirational leadership is called entrepreneurial leadership. The *entrepreneurial leader* initiates major improvement projects or may even create an entirely new organization.[44] Entrepreneurial leaders have a strong need for independence and do not like to submit to others' authority. Thomas Watson of IBM, David Packard of Hewlett-Packard, Edwin Land of Polaroid, and Walt Disney of Walt Disney Productions all provided entrepreneurial leadership that created a new organization and went beyond the normal leadership expected of managers.

LEADERSHIP BY ORGANIZATIONAL LEVEL

Leadership is important throughout every organization. However, leader approaches depend on organizational level. The ideas described in this chapter often follow the pattern in Exhibit 12.13.

EXHIBIT   12.13

Levels of Leadership in Organizations

		Leadership Emphasis
Organizational Levels	**Sources of Influence**	**Leadership Approaches**
Top	Referent power Legitimate power	Inspirational leadership; contingency approaches
Middle	Legitimate power Expert power Reward power	Contingency approaches (Fiedler's, path-goal, Vroom-Yetton model)
Lower	Expert power Reward power Coercive power Legitimate power	Two-dimensional approaches (autocratic versus democratic, consideration and initiating structure)

The inspirational leadership style becomes more important at top organizational levels. In this class at GE's Management Development Institute in Ossining, New York, managers are taught how to be inspirational leaders. Learning to use referent power as a source of influence and to inspire others through vision, courage, and commitment is critical for advancement to top organizational levels. Although managers in this class have a variety of traits and leadership styles, they are being taught how to express themselves most effectively and motivate others to accomplish GE's mission.

Lower-level leaders spend time training and coaching subordinates and seeing that they follow rules and procedures. Expert power is based on technical knowledge. Because the time horizon often is short, leaders must get quick results through the use of reward power and coercive power. The two-dimensional leadership approaches apply at this level. The supervisor can concentrate on being autocratic or democratic or on displaying task-oriented or people-oriented behaviors.

Middle-level leaders have a somewhat broader responsibility. They are responsible for larger groups and entire departments. Legitimate power is an important source of influence, as are expert power and reward power. Leadership tends to reflect the contingency approach, with the leader tailoring personal behavior and style to the needs of subordinates and the organizational situation.

At the top level of the organization, the pattern changes once again. These leaders spend time on strategic activities. The important sources of influence are referent power and legitimate power. Top leaders develop a vision for their organizations. Leader approaches at this level incorporate inspirational leadership. Senior executives must articulate a vision, provide direction, and motivate the organization toward desired goals. Contingency approaches are also used at this level, depending on the leader's style and situation.

SUMMARY

This chapter covered several important ideas about leadership. The early research on leadership focused on personal traits such as intelligence, energy, and appearance. Since that time, research attention has shifted to leadership behaviors that are appropriate to the organizational situation. Two-dimensional approaches dominated the early work in this area; consideration and initiating structure were suggested as behaviors that lead work groups toward high performance. Contingency approaches include Fiedler's theory, the path-goal model, the Vroom-Yetton model, and the substitutes-for-leadership concept.

A recent concept is that of inspirational leadership, which is the ability to articulate a vision and motivate employees to make it a reality. Inspirational leadership is similar to charisma. Inspirational leaders are especially important during periods of organizational transformation and for the creation of new organizations.

Management Solution

James Dutt's fiery style and relentless haranguing of followers have created a lot of hard feelings at Beatrice Companies. However, despite the resentment from many executives, others feel his leadership style is highly effective. They believe he is doing what he ought to be doing: being an inspirational leader. Dutt has a strong vision for the company, namely to consolidate its diffuse operations into a single national marketing juggernaut. He is forcing all subsidiaries into a single Beatrice mold. As one board member said, "People who sit around and don't do anything are not leaders." Corporate transformations are difficult and require strong leaders who are committed to a single vision. Moreover, Dutt's style agrees with Fiedler's contingency theory, which says that a task-oriented style is better than a people-oriented style in an unfavorable organizational situation. Dutt must deal with an unfavorable Beatrice situation until performance improves and investors find Beatrice more attractive.[45]

DISCUSSION QUESTIONS

1. Suggest some personal traits that you believe would be useful to a leader. Are these traits more valuable in some situations than in others?
2. What is the difference between trait theories and behavioral theories of leadership?
3. Suggest the sources of power that would be available to a leader of a student government organization.
4. Would you recommend that a leader adopt a consideration or initiating structure leadership style? Discuss the reasons for your recommendation.
5. The Vroom-Yetton model suggests five decision styles. How should a manager go about choosing the style to use?
6. What do you think are the primary strengths and weaknesses of Fiedler's contingency theory?
7. What is inspirational leadership? Differentiate between

inspirational leadership and transactional leadership. Give an example of each.

8. Do you think leadership style is fixed and unchangeable for a leader or flexible and adaptable? Discuss.

9. Consider the leadership position of a senior partner in a law firm. What task, subordinate, and organizational factors might serve as substitutes for leadership in this situation?

CASES FOR ANALYSIS

EDITORIAL DEPARTMENT

Toni Ramsey just learned that she was not getting a replacement for her editorial assistant, who had resigned. Her boss said, "With the salary and hiring freezes in effect, you'll have to give her work to others." Toni spent the afternoon deciding how to divide the work among her other subordinates in the editorial department.

The next morning, Toni announced to her seven staff members that Dianne had resigned and would not be replaced. Toni had divided Dianne's job into seven categories, with one person responsible for each. Toni informed each person of the additional work required from Dianne's resignation.

Toni noticed grumbling as she announced the assignments. The next day, she found Ed waiting in her office. "Why did you assign the press lunches to me?" he asked. "I hate listening to boring speeches. Can't you give this to someone else?"

The next person at her door was James. "Can't you reassign the traveling interviews to someone else? Just because my wife likes to travel on vacations doesn't mean I enjoy it."

Complaints came in all day. Toni attempted to juggle and switch assignments until it nearly drove her crazy. She called another staff meeting and said, "I've tried to accommodate you, but it can't be done. Take the assignments I've given you and do your best."

In the meantime, Ernest said to James, "I know you hate the traveling interviews, so I'll do them if you'll take the proofreading." Rose Marie told Ed, "I'll give you my research work if you'll do the copyediting." Other people started to trade jobs also, and the voices began to get loud. Toni came out of her office to see what the noise was about.

When Toni learned about the trading of assignments, she was upset. She went to her boss and said, "Several of the staff members seem happy with their trades, but the ones who didn't trade are unhappy. How should I have handled this?"

Questions

1. What leadership style did Toni Ramsey use? Was it appropriate for the situation?

2. Based on the Vroom-Yetton model, should Toni have been more participative? What style should she have adopted?
3. Since her approach did not work, what should Toni do now?

Source: Based on "The Case of the Missing Staffer," *Supervisory Management* (December 1985), pp. 36–37.

CITICORP

John S. Reed assumed the chairmanship and chief executive officer position of Citicorp in 1984. He was so different from his predecessor, Walter B. Wriston, that people inside and outside the organization wondered what would happen.

Reed has left the broad goals for the bank unchanged but in many other ways is establishing himself as a force in his own right. Reed is accommodative in contrast to Wriston's combative style. Reed focuses on internal efficiency and execution, while Wriston focused on rapid expansion. Reed avoids public attention, while Wriston enjoyed public debates. Reed works hard to cooperate with institutional investors and regulators, while Wriston sometimes came across as belligerent.

Reed's background was in the main operations of Citicorp. During the 1970s, he automated and streamlined the operating group that processes checks within the company. He succeeded in keeping costs constant while transactions grew at 15 percent a year. The results were impressive, but Reed earned a reputation for getting these results "no matter whom he hurt."

After Reed was named chairman, it was expected that his main rival, Thomas C. Theobald, would resign. The resignation has not occurred. Reed is working hard to keep Theobald's talent and experience available to Citicorp. At a public meeting, for instance, Reed made only a brief luncheon appearance, letting Theobald be the primary attention getter. Reed has also named Theobald to head Citicorp's fastest-growing division.

Questions

1. Can leadership style change with different jobs? Do the apparent changes in Reed's behavior seem appropriate for his position?
2. Of the four types of leadership described in the path-goal model, which ones has Reed used? Can a leader such as Reed realistically be expected to display more than one type of leadership behavior?
3. How successful do you think Citicorp will be under Reed's leadership? Why?

Source: Based on Carrie Gottlieb, "Citicorp: What the New Boss Is Up to," *Fortune,* February 17, 1986, pp. 40–44.

Motivation in Organizations

Chapter Outline

The Concept of Motivation

Foundations of Motivation

Traditional Approach
Human Relations Approach
Human Resource Approach
Contemporary Approaches

Content Perspectives on Motivation

Hierarchy of Needs Theory
Two-Factor Theory
Acquired Needs Theory

Process Perspectives on Motivation

Equity Theory
Expectancy Theory

Reinforcement Perspective on Motivation

Reinforcement Tools
Schedules of Reinforcement

Job Design for Motivation

Job Simplification
Job Rotation
Job Enlargement
Job Enrichment
Job Characteristics Model

Other Motivational Programs

Merit Pay
Modified Work Schedules
Lump Sum Salary Increases
Open Salary Information

Learning Objectives

After studying this chapter, you should be able to:

- **Define motivation and explain the difference between current approaches and traditional approaches to motivation.**

- **Identify and describe content theories of motivation based on employee needs.**

- **Identify and explain process theories of motivation.**

- **Describe reinforcement theory and how it can be used to motivate employees.**

- **Discuss major approaches to job design and how job design influences motivation.**

- **Discuss current management applications of motivation theories.**

Management Problem

Ted Gaebler arrived in Visalia, California, a month before Proposition 13 reduced total municipal government tax income by $7 billion. Gaebler had worked in five city governments and now was facing an uphill battle with limited funds in Visalia. Visalia was a good community and had benefited from farsighted city councils and effective planning. But with the sharp decrease in tax revenues, how could Gaebler challenge city managers and workers to take risks and find ways to provide better city services? Gaebler wanted to motivate employees to think like owners, not bureaucrats. He wanted to motivate people to think, "If this were my money, would I really spend it this way?" Gaebler's challenge was to motivate employees to try new ideas for reducing costs, increasing revenues, and satisfying city residents.[1]

If you were Ted Gaebler, how would you motivate city managers and workers to adopt new actions that would both save money and improve services?

The challenge facing Ted Gaebler is to motivate a large number of employees to display behaviors consistent with organizational objectives. Motivation is a challenge for managers because it requires that managers understand how employees think. Motivation arises from within employees, and motivational factors differ for each employee. For example, Joan Harding is a soft-spoken, almost shy real estate salesperson. But she loves to talk about houses and in one recent year made $180,000 in sales commissions. Greg Storey is a skilled machinist who is challenged by writing programs for numerically controlled machines. After dropping out of college, he swept floors in a machine shop and was motivated to

EXHIBIT   13.1

A Simple Model of Motivation

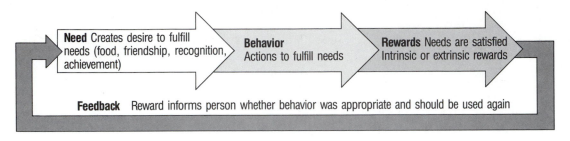

Need Creates desire to fulfill needs (food, friendship, recognition, achievement)

Behavior Actions to fulfill needs

Rewards Needs are satisfied Intrinsic or extrinsic rewards

Feedback   Reward informs person whether behavior was appropriate and should be used again

learn to run the machines. Frances Blais sells *World Book Encyclopedia.* She is a top salesperson, but she doesn't care about the $50,000-plus commissions: "I'm not even thinking money when I'm selling. I'm really on a crusade to help children read well." In stark contrast, Rob Michaels gets sick to his stomach before he goes to work. Rob is a telephone salesperson who spends all day trying to get people to buy products they don't need, and the rejections are painful. His motivation is money, because he earned $120,000 in the past year and can't make nearly that much doing anything else.[2]

Rob is motivated by money, Joan by her love of houses, Frances by the desire to help children read, and Greg by the challenge of mastering numerically controlled machinery. Each person is motivated to perform, yet each has different reasons for performing. With such diverse motivations, it is a challenge for managers to motivate employees toward common organizational goals.

The purpose of this chapter is to review theories and models of employee motivation. First we will review traditional approaches to motivation. Then we will cover models that describe the employee needs and processes associated with motivation. Finally, we will discuss the designing of jobs to increase employee motivation.

THE CONCEPT OF MOTIVATION

Most of us get up in the morning, go to school or work, and behave in ways that are predictably our own. We respond to our environment and the people in it with little thought as to why we work hard, enjoy certain classes, or find some recreational activities so much fun. Yet all of these behaviors are motivated by something. **Motivation** generally is defined as the arousal, direction, and persistence of behavior.[3] The study of motivation concerns what prompts people to initiate action, what influences their choice of action, and why they persist in doing it over time.

A simple model of human motivation is illustrated in Exhibit 13.1. People have basic *needs*, such as for food, achievement, or monetary gain,

motivation The arousal, direction, and persistence of behavior.

that translate into an internal tension that motivates specific behaviors with which to fulfill the need. To the extent that the behavior is successful, the person is rewarded in the sense that the need is satisfied. The reward also informs the person that the behavior was appropriate and can be used again in the future.

Rewards are of two types: intrinsic and extrinsic. **Intrinsic rewards** are received as a direct consequence of a person's actions. The completion of a complex task may bestow a pleasant feeling of accomplishment. **Extrinsic rewards** are given by another person, typically a manager, and include promotions and pay increases. For example, Frances Blais sells encyclopedias for the intrinsic reward of helping children read well. Rob Michaels, who hates his sales job, nevertheless is motivated by the extrinsic reward of high pay.

The importance of motivation as illustrated in Exhibit 13.1 is that it can lead to behaviors that reflect high performance within organizations.[4] Managers can use motivation theory to help satisfy employees' needs and simultaneously encourage high work performance.

intrinsic reward A reward received as a direct consequence of a person's actions.

extrinsic reward A reward given by another person.

FOUNDATIONS OF MOTIVATION

A manager's assumptions about employee motivation and use of rewards depend on his or her perspective on motivation. Three distinct perspectives on employee motivation that have evolved are the traditional approach, the human relations approach, and the human resources approach.[5] The most recent theories about motivation represent a fourth perspective called contemporary approaches.

Traditional Approach

The study of employee motivation really began with the work of Frederick W. Taylor on scientific management. Recall from Chapter 2 that scientific management pertains to the systematic analysis of an employee's job for the purpose of increasing efficiency. Economic rewards are provided to employees for high performance. Taylor boasted that "under scientific management, the initiative of the workmen—that is, their hard work, their goodwill, their ingenuity—is obtained practically with absolute regularity."[6] On what did Taylor base this claim? Money. Taylor believed in economic incentives and that employees would respond to greater pay. The emphasis on pay evolved into the perception of workers as *economic men*—people who would work harder for higher pay. This approach led to the development of incentive pay systems, in which people were paid strictly on the quantity and quality of their work outputs.

Human Relations Approach

The economic man was gradually replaced by a more sociable employee in managers' minds. Beginning with the landmark Hawthorne studies at a Western Electric plant, noneconomic rewards, such as congenial work

Employee motivation has always been a management concern. The traditional approach stresses extrinsic rewards and punishments administered by the boss. Although the management style shown here seems old-fashioned, many managers still prefer punishment over improved motivational techniques. Contemporary approaches explore employees' needs and their behaviors for meeting them. These ideas can be built into job design and used in other ways to more effectively motivate employees.

groups who met social needs, seemed more important than money as a motivator of work behavior.[7] For the first time workers were studied as people, and the concept of *social man* was born. Further study led researchers to conclude that simply paying attention to workers could change their behavior for the better; this was called the *Hawthorne effect.*

Elton Mayo, the man behind the Hawthorne studies, believed that the discovery of social needs meant the downfall of economic man. This turned out not to be the case, because employee motivation was found to include both social and economic needs.[8]

Human Resource Approach

The human resource approach carries the concepts of economic man and social man further to introduce the concept of the *whole person.* Human resource theory suggests that employees are complex and motivated by many factors. The work by McGregor on Theory X and Theory Y described in Chapter 2 argued that people want to do a good job and that work is as natural and healthy as play. Proponents of the human resource approach felt that earlier approaches had tried to manipulate employees through economic or social rewards. From a human resource perspective, employees should be encouraged to participate in organizational decisions and given challenging, meaningful work. By assuming that employees are competent and able to make major contributions, managers can enhance organizational performance. The human resource approach laid the groundwork for contemporary perspectives on employee motivation.

Contemporary Approaches

Contemporary approaches to employee motivation are dominated by three types of theories, each of which will be discussed in the remaining sections of this chapter. The first are *content theories,* which stress the analysis of underlying human needs. Content theories provide insight into the needs of people in organizations and help managers understand how they can be satisfied in the workplace. *Process theories* concern the thought processes that influence behavior. They focus on how employees seek rewards in work circumstances. *Reinforcement theories* focus on

EXHIBIT   13.2

Maslow's Hierarchy of Needs

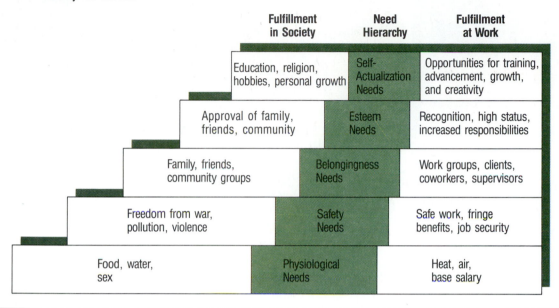

Fulfillment in Society	Need Hierarchy	Fulfillment at Work
Education, religion, hobbies, personal growth	Self-Actualization Needs	Opportunities for training, advancement, growth, and creativity
Approval of family, friends, community	Esteem Needs	Recognition, high status, increased responsibilities
Family, friends, community groups	Belongingness Needs	Work groups, clients, coworkers, supervisors
Freedom from war, pollution, violence	Safety Needs	Safe work, fringe benefits, job security
Food, water, sex	Physiological Needs	Heat, air, base salary

employee learning of desired work behaviors. In Exhibit 13.1, content theories focus on the concepts in the first box, process theories on those in the second, and reinforcement theories on those in the third.

CONTENT PERSPECTIVES ON MOTIVATION

Content theories emphasize the needs that motivate people. At any point in time, people have basic needs such as those for food, achievement, or monetary reward. These needs translate into an internal drive that motivates specific behaviors in an attempt to fulfill the needs. An individual's needs are like a hidden catalog of the things he or she wants and will work to get. To the extent that managers understand worker needs, the organization's reward systems can be designed to meet them and reinforce employees for directing energies and priorities toward attainment of organizational goals.

content theories A group of theories that emphasize the needs that motivate people.

Hierarchy of Needs Theory

Probably the most famous content theory was developed by Abraham Maslow.[9] Maslow's **hierarchy of needs** theory proposes that humans are motivated by multiple needs and that these needs exist in a hierarchical order as illustrated in Exhibit 13.2. Maslow identified five general types of motivating needs in order of ascendance:

hierarchy of needs theory A content theory that proposes that people are motivated by five categories of needs—physiological, safety, belongingness, esteem, and self-actualization—that exist in a hierarchical order.

Chem-Nuclear Systems, a subsidiary of Waste Management Inc., provides low-level radioactive waste management services. Meeting the employees' safety needs is especially important in this type of business. Here a Chem-Nuclear technician decontaminates tools and plant components inside a specially designed decontamination unit. His suit is part of the decontamination technology that protects workers while decontaminating equipment for reuse by customers.

1. *Physiological needs.* These are the most basic human physical needs, including food, water, and sex. In the organizational setting, these are reflected in the needs for adequate heat, air, and base salary to insure survival.
2. *Safety needs.* These are the needs for a safe and secure physical and emotional environment and freedom from threats, that is, for freedom from violence and for an orderly society. In an organizational workplace, safety needs reflect the needs for safe jobs, fringe benefits, and job security.
3. *Belongingness needs.* These needs reflect the desire to be accepted by one's peers, have friendships, be part of a group, and be loved. In the organization, these needs influence the desire for good relationships with coworkers, participation in a work group, and a positive relationship with supervisors.
4. *Esteem needs.* These needs relate to the desire for a positive self-image and to receive attention, recognition, and appreciation from others. Within organizations, esteem needs reflect a motivation for recognition, increases in responsibility, high status, and credit for contributions to the organization.
5. *Self-actualization needs.* These represent the need for self-fulfillment, which is the highest need category. They concern developing one's full potential, increasing one's competence, and becoming a better person. Self-actualization needs can be met in the organization by providing people with opportunities to grow, be creative, and acquire training for challenging assignments and advancement.

According to Maslow's theory, lower-order needs take priority—they must be satisfied before higher-order needs are activated. The needs are satisfied in sequence: Physiological needs come before safety needs, safety needs before social needs, and so on. A person desiring physical safety will devote his or her efforts to securing a safer environment and will not be concerned with esteem needs or self-actualization needs. Once a need is satisfied, it declines in importance and the next higher need is activated. When a union wins good pay and working conditions for its members, basic needs are met; union members may then desire to get belongingness and esteem needs met in the workplace.

ERG Theory.   Alderfer proposed a modification of Maslow's theory in an effort to simplify it and respond to criticisms of its lack of empirical verification.[10] His **ERG theory** identified three categories of needs:

1. *Existence needs.* These are the needs for physical well-being.
2. *Relatedness needs.* These pertain to the need for satisfactory relationships with others.
3. *Growth needs.* These focus on the development of human potential and the desire for personal growth and increased competence.

The ERG model and Maslow's need hierarchy are similar because both are in hierarchical form and presume that individuals move up the hierarchy one step at a time. However, Alderfer reduced the number of

ERG theory A modification of the needs hierarchy theory that proposes three categories of needs: existence, relatedness, and growth.

need categories to three and proposed that movement up the hierarchy is more complex, reflecting a **frustration-regression principle,** namely, that failure to meet a higher-order need may trigger a regression to an already fulfilled lower-order need. Thus, a worker who cannot fulfill a need for personal growth may revert to a lower-order social need and redirect his or her efforts toward making a lot of money. The ERG model therefore is less rigid than Maslow's need hierarchy, suggesting that individuals may move down as well as up the hierarchy depending on their ability to satisfy needs.

For example, need hierarchy theory partly explains why sales organizations in recent years have shifted from commissions to straight salaries for compensating salespeople. Commissions put the emphasis on making money to meet safety and physiological needs but expose salespeople to high risk during periods of economic downturn. Fixed salaries guarantee that basic needs will be met, thus freeing individuals to pursue work activities that will fulfill higher-level belongingness or esteem needs.

Two-Factor Theory

Frederick Herzberg developed another popular theory of motivation called the *two-factor theory*.[11] Herzberg interviewed hundreds of workers about times when they were highly motivated to work and other times when they were dissatisfied and unmotivated at work. His findings suggested that the work characteristics associated with dissatisfaction were quite different from those pertaining to satisfaction, which prompted the notion that two factors influence work motivation.

The general idea of the two-factor theory is illustrated in Exhibit 13.3. The center of the scale is neutral, meaning that workers are neither satisfied nor dissatisfied. Herzberg believed that two entirely separate dimensions contribute to an employee's behavior at work. The first, called **hygiene factors,** involves the presence or absence of job dissatisfiers, such as working conditions, pay, company policies, and interpersonal relationships. When hygiene factors are poor, work is dissatisfying. However, good hygiene factors simply remove the dissatisfaction; they do not in themselves cause people to become highly satisfied and motivated in their work.

The second set of factors does influence job satisfaction. **Motivators** are higher-level needs and include achievement, recognition, responsibility, and opportunity for growth. Herzberg believed that when motivators are absent workers are neutral toward work, but when motivators are present, workers are highly motivated and satisfied. Thus, hygiene factors and motivators represent two distinct factors that influence motivation. Hygiene factors work only in the area of dissatisfaction. Abundant hygiene factors will remove dissatisfaction but will not be a major employee motivator. Unsafe working conditions or a noisy work environment will cause people to be dissatisfied; their correction will not lead to a high level of motivation and satisfaction. Motivators such as challenge, responsibility, and recognition must be in place before employees will be highly motivated to excel at their work.

The Limited Inc. is considered the most successful specialty apparel retailer in the United States thanks to the motivational philosophy of management. Michael Weiss, president of Limited Express, a division of The Limited, tries to supply Herzberg's motivational factors to meet employees' higher-level needs. "The company has acknowledged that the No. 1 incentive is not money, but self-realization and recognition." Weiss' management philosophy is that work is an uplifting experience, and the motivation of employees has put The Limited in first place in the specialty apparel industry.

frustration-regression principle The idea that failure to meet a higher-order need may cause a regression to an already satisfied lower-order need.

hygiene factors Factors that involve the presence or absence of job dissatisfiers, including working conditions, pay, company policies, and interpersonal relationships.

motivators Factors that influence job satisfaction based on fulfillment of higher-level needs such as achievement, recognition, responsibility, and opportunity for growth.

E X H I B I T   13.3

Herzberg's Two-Factor Theory

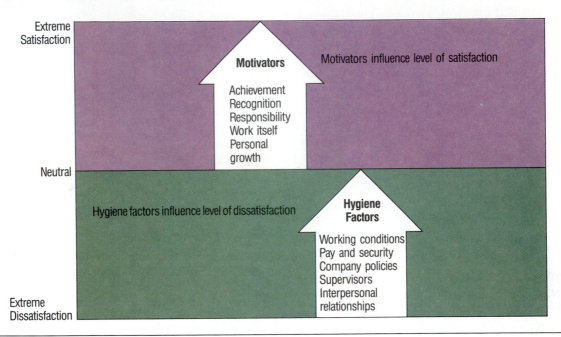

The implication of the two-factor theory for managers is clear. Providing hygiene factors will eliminate employee dissatisfaction but will not motivate workers to high achievement levels. On the other hand, recognition, challenge, and opportunities for personal growth are powerful motivators and will promote high satisfaction and performance. The manager's role is to remove dissatisfiers—that is, provide hygiene factors sufficient to meet basic needs—and then use motivators to meet higher-level needs and propel employees toward greater achievement and satisfaction.

Marquette Electronics

Michael Cudahy, president of Marquette Electronics, knows about motivation. Cudahy does not skimp on hygiene factors—50 cents on top of every dollar in salary goes to benefits such as savings, insurance, and day care.

Higher-level needs also are given priority: "You can't put people in boxes, telling them what they can do, when they can do it and who's going to get rid of them if they don't do it. You've got to give people a voice in their jobs. You've got to give them a piece of the action, and a chance to excel." Cudahy works hard to insure that employees have a chance for recognition, to belong to a group, and for personal growth, all of which meet the higher level needs of Marquette employees.

Does it work? Marquette holds 80 percent of the market for centralized electrocardiograph management systems, 26 percent of the stress-testing market, and 20 percent of the market for patient monitoring devices. Marquette has been profitable since its third year of operations, and recent earnings were nearly $7 million.[12]

Acquired Needs Theory

The final content theory was developed by David McClelland. The *acquired needs theory* proposes that certain types of needs are acquired during the individual's lifetime. In other words, people are not born with these needs but may learn them through their life experiences.[13] The three needs most frequently studied are:

1. *Need for achievement:* the desire to accomplish something difficult, attain a high standard of success, master complex tasks, and surpass others.
2. *Need for affiliation:* the desire to form close personal relationships, avoid conflict, and establish warm friendships.
3. *Need for power:* the desire to influence or control others, be responsible for others, and have authority over others.

Early life experiences determine whether people acquire these needs. If children are encouraged to do things for themselves and receive reinforcement, they will acquire a need to achieve. If they are reinforced for forming warm human relationships, they will develop a need for affiliation. If they get satisfaction from controlling others, they will acquire a need for power.

For over 20 years, McClelland studied human needs and their implication for management. People with a high need for achievement tend to be entrepreneurs. They like to do something better than competitors and take sensible business risks. On the other hand, people who have a high need for affiliation are successful "integrators," whose job is to coordinate the work of several departments in an organization.[14] Integrators, as will be described in Chapter 17, include brand managers and project managers who must have excellent people skills. People high in need for affiliation are able to establish positive working relationships with others.

A high need for power often is associated with successful attainment of top levels in the organizational hierarchy. For example, McClelland studied managers at AT&T for 16 years and found that those with a high need for power were more likely to follow a path of continued promotion over time. Over half of the employees at the top levels had a high need for power. In contrast, managers with a high need for achievement but a low need for power tended to peak earlier in their careers and at a

FOCUS

INTERNATIONAL

Japanese versus American Achievement Motivation

Although underlying human needs are similar in all countries, their intensity may differ across countries and across organizations in other countries. This is especially true for acquired needs, such as the need for achievement. A study by A. J. Diaz examined whether a firm's motivational spirit could be assessed by coding the chief executive's annual letters to stockholders. For example, the level of achievement motivation may explain differences in the performances of automobile companies, especially between such countries as Japan and the United States. The performance of Japanese auto companies was far superior during the late 1970s and early 1980s on almost every dimension. The average Japanese plant had a work force of 2,360, was able to produce 550 parts per hour, and required only 30.8 hours to build a small car. The average U.S. firm had 4,250 employees, could stamp 325 parts per hour, and required 59.9 hours to build a small car. Absenteeism was nearly twice as great in American firms.

One explanation for the success of Japanese firms is revealed in Exhibit 13.4. The three Japanese manufacturers, Nissan, Toyota, and Honda, scored higher in achievement motivation levels at nearly every point in time than did their U.S. counterparts, General Motors and Chrysler. High need for achievement generally is associated with greater entrepreneurial spirit and greater efficiency. The strength of achievement need in a company or a nation determines performance because managers and employees alike

EXHIBIT 13.4

Level of Achievement Concern in CEO's Letters to Stockholders in Japanese and U.S. Automobile Companies

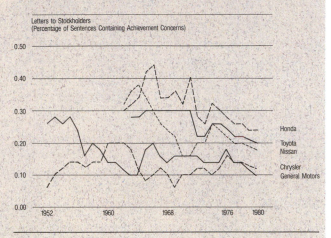

Source: From *Human Motivation* by David C. McClelland, p. 453. Copyright © 1985 by Scott, Foresman and Company. Reprinted by permission.

strive to meet achievement needs. There are many reasons why Japanese firms have established a competitive advantage over U.S. firms, but achievement motivation seems the most important. The underlying achievement motivation of Japanese executives may be one reason why Japanese automobile makers have done so much better than their U.S. counterparts.

Source: Based on David C. McClelland, *Human Motivation*, (Glenview, Ill.: Scott, Foresman, 1985) p. 452.

lower level. The reason is that achievement needs can be met through the task itself, but power needs can be met only by ascending to a level at which a person has power over others.

In summary, content theories focus on people's underlying needs and label those that motivate people to behave. Maslow's need hierarchy, ERG theory, Herzberg's two-factor theory, and the acquired needs theory all help managers to understand what motivates people. In this way, managers can design work to meet needs and hence elicit appropriate and successful work behaviors.

PROCESS PERSPECTIVES ON MOTIVATION

Process theories explain how workers select behavioral actions to meet their needs and determine whether their choices were successful. There are two basic process theories: equity theory and expectancy theory.

Equity Theory

Equity theory focuses on individuals' perceptions of how fairly they are treated compared to others. Developed by J. Stacey Adams, equity theory proposes that people are motivated to seek social equity in the rewards they expect for performance.[15]

According to equity theory, if people perceive their compensation as equal to what others receive for similar contributions, they will believe that their treatment is fair and equitable. People evaluate equity by a ratio of inputs to outcomes. Inputs to a job include education, experience, effort, and ability. Outcomes from a job include pay, recognition, benefits, and promotions. The input to outcome ratio may be compared to another person in the work group, or to a perceived group average. A state of **equity** exists whenever the ratio of one person's outcomes to inputs equals the ratio of another's outcomes to inputs.

Inequity occurs when the input-outcome ratios are out of balance, such as when a person with a high level of education or experience receives the same salary as a new, lesser educated employee. It is interesting to note that perceived inequity also occurs in the other direction. Thus, if an employee discovers she is making more money than other people who contribute the same inputs to the company, she may feel the need to correct the inequity by working harder, getting more education, or accepting lower pay. Perceived inequity creates tensions within individuals that motivate them to bring equity into balance.[16]

The most common methods for reducing a perceived inequity are:

- *Change inputs.* A person may choose to increase or decrease his or her inputs to the organization. For example, underpaid individuals may reduce their level of effort or increase their absenteeism. Overpaid people may increase effort on the job.
- *Change outcomes.* A person may change his or her outcomes. An underpaid person may request a salary increase or a bigger office. A union may try to improve wages and working conditions in order to be consistent with a comparable union whose members make more money.
- *Distort perceptions.* Research suggests that people may distort perceptions of equity if they are unable to change inputs or outcomes. They may artificially increase the status attached to their jobs or distort others' perceived rewards to bring equity into balance.

process theories A group of theories that explain how employees select behaviors with which to meet their needs and determine whether their choices were successful.

equity theory A process theory that focuses on individuals' perceptions of how fairly they are treated relative to others.

equity A situation that exists when the ratio of one person's outcomes to inputs equals that of another's.

These sugar free candies are made by Philadelphia's Sorbee International. Equity theory predicts that if these women bring similar inputs, such as education, experience, and ability, to the job, they can expect similar outcomes in the form of pay, benefits, and recognition. If not, the employees receiving fewer outcomes will be motivated to reduce their effort and, in cases of extreme inequity, even quit. Maintaining equity among employees is an important source of motivation.

▪ *Leave the job.* People who feel inequitably treated may decide to leave their jobs rather than suffer the inequity of being under- or overpaid. In their new jobs, they expect to find a more favorable balance of rewards.

The implication of equity theory for managers is that employees indeed evaluate the perceived equity of their rewards compared to others'. An increase in salary or a promotion will have no motivational effect if it is perceived as inequitable relative to other employees. Some organizations, for example, have created a two-tier wage system to reduce wage rates. New employees make far less than experienced ones, which creates a basis for inequity. Chris Boschert, who sorts packages for United Parcel Service, was hired after the two-tier wage system took effect. "It makes me mad," Boschert said. "I get $9.68 an hour, and the guy working next to me makes $13.99 doing exactly the same job." The inequity works both ways: An employee who had worked 16 years at a supermarket and earned $10.30 an hour literally cried when new employees were hired at $4.00 an hour. The inequity was almost too great to bear.[17]

Smart managers try to keep feelings of equity in balance in order to keep their work forces motivated. Consider Nucor Corporation.

Nucor Corporation

Ken Iverson, CEO at Nucor Corporation, goes one step beyond apparent equity to get the results he wants. Because of his commitment not to lay people off during hard times, everyone at Nucor Minimills feels the pain during bad times so that everyone can stay employed. In Iverson's "share-the-pain" program, the cuts get stiffer as they go *up* the corporate ladder. In order for everyone to remain employed, a worker might lose 25 percent of his or her salary; however, the worker's department head could lose 35 to 40 percent. The officers, whose compensation is tied to return on stockholders' equity, might lose 60 or 70 percent. These cuts are severe, but they are perceived as more than equitable by the work force. Iverson claims he heard no complaints from the production floor when workers were forced to go to a three-and-a-half-day week in order to avoid layoffs. Iverson correctly anticipated the workers' perception of relative inputs and outputs. As he put it, "Management should take the biggest drop in pay because they have the most responsibility."[18]

Expectancy Theory

expectancy theory A process theory that proposes that motivation depends on individuals' expectations about their ability to perform tasks and receive desired rewards.

Expectancy theory suggests that motivation depends on individuals' expectations about their ability to perform tasks and receive desired rewards. Expectancy theory is associated with the work of Victor Vroom,

E X H I B I T   13.5

Major Elements of Expectancy Theory

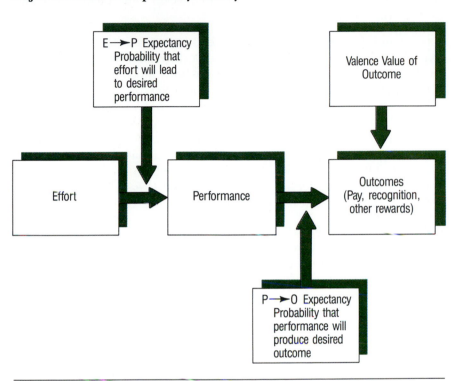

although a number of scholars have made contributions in this area.[19] Expectancy theory is concerned not with identifying types of needs but with the thinking process that individuals use to achieve rewards. Consider Bill Bradley, a university student with a strong desire for a B in his accounting course. Bill has a C+ average and one more exam to take. Bill's motivation to study for that last exam will be influenced by (1) the expectation that hard study will lead to an A on the exam and (2) the expectation that an A on the exam will result in a B for the course. If Bill believes he can't get an A on the exam or that receiving an A will not lead to a B for the course, he will not be motivated to study extra hard.

Expectancy theory is based on the relationship between the individual's *effort*, the individual's *performance,* and the desirability of *outcomes* associated with high performance. These elements and the relationships among them are illustrated in Exhibit 13.5. The keys to expectancy theory are the expectancies for the relationships among effort, performance, and outcomes and the value of the outcomes to the individual.

Expectancy That Effort Will Lead to Performance.   E → P expectancy involves whether putting effort into a task will lead to high performance. For this expectancy to be high, the individual must have the ability, previous experience, and necessary machinery, tools, and opportunity to perform. For Bill Bradley's getting a B in the accounting course, the

E → P expectancy   Expectancy that putting effort into a given task will lead to high performance.

P → O expectancy   Expectancy that successful performance of a task will lead to the desired outcome.

E → P expectancy is high if Bill truly believes that with hard work he can get an A on the final exam. If Bill believes he has neither the ability nor the opportunity to achieve high performance, the expectancy will be low, and so will his motivation.

Expectancy That Performance Will Lead to Desired Outcome.   P → O expectancy involves whether successful performance will lead to the desired outcome. In the case of a person who is motivated to win a job-related award, this expectancy concerns the belief that high performance will truly lead to the award. If the P → O expectancy is high, the individual will be more highly motivated. If the expectancy is that high performance will not produce the desired outcome, motivation will be lower. If an A on the final exam is likely to produce a B in the accounting course, Bill Bradley's P → O expectancy will be high. Bill may talk to the professor to see whether an A will be sufficient to earn him the B in the course. If not, he will be less motivated to study hard for the final exam.

valence   The value of outcomes for the individual.

Valence of Outcomes.   Valence is the value of outcomes for the individual. If the outcomes that are available from high effort and good performance are not valued by employees, motivation will be low. Likewise, if outcomes have a high value, motivation will be higher.

Note that expectancy theory attempts not to define specific types of needs or rewards but only to establish that they exist and may be different for every individual. One employee may want to be promoted to a position of increased responsibility, and another may have high valence for good relationships with peers. Consequently, the first person will be motivated to work hard for a promotion and the second for the opportunity for a team position that will keep him or her associated with a group.

A simple sales department example will explain how the expectancy model in Exhibit 13.5 works. If Jane Anderson, a salesperson at the Diamond Gift Shop, believes that increased selling effort will lead to higher personal sales, we can say that she has a high E → P expectancy. Moreover, if Jane also believes that higher personal sales will lead to a bonus or pay raise, we can say that she has a high P → O expectancy. Finally, if Jane places a high value on the bonus or pay raise, valence is high and Jane will have a high motivational force. On the other hand, if either the E → P or P → O expectancy is low, or if the money or promotion has low valence for Jane, the overall motivational force will be low. In order for an employee to be highly motivated, all three factors in the expectancy model must be high.[20]

Mary Kay Cosmetics Inc. has specialized at helping women find the path of financial success—a form of expectancy theory. Mary Kay sales directors train new employees to channel their efforts toward successful cosmetic sales (E → P expectancy). Once employees are ringing up sales, Mary Kay follows up with valued outcomes (P → O expectancy), including lavish financial rewards and prizes such as diamonds, furs, luxury trips, and the pink Cadillacs shown here. Promotions are based strictly on performance, and every employee has an equal opportunity to advance along the "ladder of success."

Implications for Managers.   The expectancy theory of motivation is similar to the path-goal theory of leadership described in Chapter 12. Both theories are personalized to subordinates' needs and goals. Managers' responsibility is to help subordinates meet their needs and at the same time attain organizational goals. Managers must try to find a match between a subordinate's skills and abilities and the job demands. To increase motivation, managers can clarify individuals' needs, define the outcomes available from the organization, and insure that each individ-

SMALL BUSINESS

Immigrants as Entrepreneurs

Why are immigrants so often motivated to start their own businesses? In many areas of the country an entire industry is dominated by immigrants of a single nationality. For example, consider Koreans in the produce industry. In New York City, Korean-run outlets account for 85 percent of the independent fruit and vegetable stores. These stores have been so effective that supermarket sales of produce have been reduced by 20 percent.

Young Jun Kwon, a Korean-born entrepreneur, is part of the Green Grocer Industry. He begins each day at 2:00 a.m., selects and loads 3,000 pounds of fresh produce into his van, and hauls it to his store. Young's wife and brother help scrub and stack the vegetables and prepare the store for opening at 8:00 a.m. Young then manages the business all day, leaving at 8:00 p.m. to get a few hours of sleep before the next day's work begins. Young has maintained this routine for ten years but now finds it necessary to take naps during the day.

Although Koreans dominate New York City's produce industry, 70 percent of the newsstand business is dominated by Indians and Pakistanis. One of the most successful newsstand entrepreneurs is Bhawnesh Kapoor, whose company operates more than 200 outlets and has gross sales of approximately $17 million per year. Kapoor came to the United States in 1972 with only $68. He began with one newsstand but by 1983 had obtained a license to run all newsstands in the city's subway system. Kapoor employs many other Indians who work long hours saving money to establish their own newsstands.

Miami's garment district has recently become dominated by Cubans. One of the clothing manufacturers, Antonio Acosta, left Cuba for Miami in 1960 when he was 16 years old. He had no money but found a job as a sweeper, cleaning a factory. Seven years later he started his own garment cutting service and after three years established his own line of clothing. His company, called Tony and Toni Fashions, manufactures sportswear and has gross annual sales of approximately $500,000.

Most immigrants start new businesses at a tremendous disadvantage compared to American-born entrepreneurs. Immigrants confront a new culture, new customs, and a different language. They often arrive with little money and must build a business using few financial resources.

In the face of such adversity, why are immigrants so motivated to start their own businesses? One answer is that immigrants choose entrepreneurship because they have no other alternative for earning a living. Starting a business is the only path to a goal of survival and eventual prosperity. Another reason is that immigrants are used to working long hours for low wages. They do not have immediate needs for luxuries that money can buy and so devote themselves to achieving a long-term goal. Many immigrants also bring values from their native cultures that support high achievement. Indeed, many of these immigrants would have been successful entrepreneurs in their own countries. Because of their drive for success, instinct for business, and willingness to work long hours, these immigrants are able to overcome great difficulties to start successful businesses in their new country.

Source: Provided by Charles R. Kuehl and Peggy A. Lambing, authors of *Small Business: Planning and Management* (Chicago: The Dryden Press, 1987).

ual has the ability and support (namely, time and equipment) needed to attain outcomes.

Some companies use expectancy theory principles by designing incentive systems with which to identify desired organizational outcomes and give everyone the same shot at getting the big rewards. Consider Merrill Lynch's change in its pay system, which is discussed on the following page.

Merrill Lynch

Merrill Lynch wanted its brokers to do more for its customers than just trade their securities. Providing more services would strengthen the tie between client and company and reduce the chances of losing customers to other financial supermarkets. Top brokers at Merrill Lynch had been earning about $2 million, but under the new system they can earn even more because they will be rewarded for increasing the assets under Merrill Lynch management as well as for stock and bond transactions. For example, brokers get paid if the customer takes out a second mortgage with Merrill Lynch, buys securities on margin, or increases the value of their accounts.

Another major change has been to provide the biggest incentives for the star salespeople. The commission paid to the most productive brokers has increased to 42 percent of fees generated. At the same time, poor performers are punished by having their commissions reduced from 30 to 25 percent. Thus, the people who generate the most fees for Merrill Lynch now get a higher percentage of those fees to keep.[21]

Merrill Lynch's incentive system works because employees have sufficient ability to keep the $E \rightarrow P$ expectancy high. If they perform well, the $P \rightarrow O$ expectancy is guaranteed by the commission schedule. The problem occurs for those who do not place a high value on earning big bucks. These people simply are unwelcome at the company because their motivations are out of alignment with Merrill Lynch's needs.

REINFORCEMENT PERSPECTIVE ON MOTIVATION

The reinforcement approach to employee motivation sidesteps the issues of employee needs and thinking processes described in the content and process theories. **Reinforcement theory** simply looks at the relationship between behavior and its consequences. It focuses on changing or modifying the employees' on-the-job behavior through the appropriate use of immediate rewards and punishments.

Reinforcement Tools

Behavior modification is the name given to the set of techniques by which reinforcement theory is used to modify human behavior. The

reinforcement theory A motivation theory based on the relationship between a given behavior and its consequences.

behavior modification The set of techniques by which reinforcement theory is used to modify human behavior.

basic assumption underlying behavior modification is the **law of effect,** which states that behavior that is positively reinforced tends to be repeated, while behavior that is not reinforced tends not to be repeated. **Reinforcement** is defined as anything that causes a certain behavior to be repeated or inhibited. The four reinforcement tools are positive reinforcement, avoidance learning, punishment, and extinction.[22] Each type of reinforcement is a consequence of either a pleasant or unpleasant event being applied or withdrawn following a person's behavior. The four types of reinforcement are summarized in Exhibit 13.6.

Positive Reinforcement. *Positive reinforcement* is the administration of a pleasant and rewarding consequence following a desired behavior. A good example of positive reinforcement is immediate praise for an employee who arrives on time or does a little extra in his or her work. The pleasant consequence will increase the likelihood of the excellent work behavior occurring again.

Avoidance Learning. *Avoidance learning* is the removal of an unpleasant consequence following a desired behavior. Avoidance learning is sometimes called *negative reinforcement.* Employees learn to do the right thing by avoiding unpleasant situations. Avoidance learning occurs when a supervisor stops harassing or reprimanding an employee once the incorrect behavior has stopped.

Punishment. *Punishment* is the imposition of unpleasant outcomes on an employee. Punishment typically occurs following undesirable behavior. For example, a supervisor may berate an employee for performing a task incorrectly. The supervisor expects that the negative outcome will serve as a punishment and reduce the likelihood of the behavior recurring. The use of punishment in organizations is controversial and often criticized because it fails to indicate the correct behavior.

Extinction. *Extinction* is the withdrawal of a positive reward, meaning that behavior is no longer reinforced and hence is less likely to occur in the future. If a perpetually tardy employee fails to receive praise and pay raises, he or she will begin to realize that the behavior is not producing desired outcomes. The behavior will gradually disappear if it is continually nonreinforced.

Some executives use reinforcement theory very effectively to shape employees' behavior. Jack Welch, chairman of General Electric, has made it a point to reinforce behavior. As an up-and-coming group executive, Welch reinforced purchasing agents by having someone telephone him whenever an agent got a price concession from a vendor. Welch would stop whatever he was doing and call the agent to say, "That's wonderful news; you just knocked a nickel a ton off the price of steel." He would also sit down and scribble out a congratulatory note to the agent. The effective use of positive reinforcement and the heightened

law of effect The assumption that positively reinforced behavior tends to be repeated while unreinforced or negatively reinforced behavior tends to be inhibited.

reinforcement Anything that causes a given behavior to be repeated or inhibited.

A novel approach to reinforcement at York's Restaurant in Canton, Ohio, was to give employees a chance to throw a pie in their manager's face. Two teams of employees competed for the "prize." Each winning team member got to throw a pie in the losing manager's face. Here team captain Gary Jones gets hit by Ann Bourquin. The great time had by employees served as positive reinforcement for their successful selling behavior.

E X H I B I T   13.6

Changing Behavior with Reinforcement

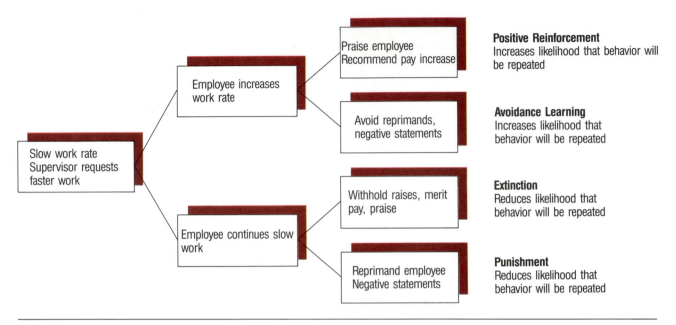

Source: Based on Richard L. Daft and Richard M. Steers, *Organizations: A Micro/Macro Approach* (Glenview, Ill.: Scott, Foresman, 1986), p. 109.

motivation of purchasing employees marked Jack Welch as executive material in the organization.[23]

Schedules of Reinforcement

A great deal of research into reinforcement theory suggests that the timing of reinforcement impacts on the speed of employee learning. **Schedules of reinforcement** pertain to the frequency with and intervals over which reinforcement occurs. A reinforcement schedule can be selected to have maximum impact on employees' job behavior. There are five basic types of reinforcement schedules.

Continuous and Partial Reinforcement.   With a **continuous reinforcement schedule,** every occurrence of the desired behavior is reinforced. This schedule can be very effective in the early stages of learning new types of behavior, because every attempt has a pleasant consequence.

However, in the real world of organizations it is often impossible to reinforce every correct behavior. With a **partial reinforcement schedule,** the reinforcement is administered only after some occurrences of the correct behavior. There are four types of partial reinforcement schedules: fixed-interval, fixed-ratio, variable-interval, and variable-ratio.

Fixed-Interval Schedule.   The *fixed-interval schedule* rewards employees at specified time intervals. If an employee displays the correct behavior

schedule of reinforcement   The frequency with and intervals over which reinforcement occurs.

continuous reinforcement schedule   A schedule in which every occurrence of the desired behavior is reinforced.

partial reinforcement schedule   A schedule in which only some occurrences of the desired behavior are reinforced.

E X H I B I T   13.7

Schedules of Reinforcement

Schedule of Reinforcement	Nature of Reinforcement	Effect on Behavior When Applied	Effect on Behavior When Withdrawn	Example
Continuous	Reward given after each desired behavior	Leads to fast learning of new behavior	Rapid extinction	Praise
Fixed-interval	Reward given at fixed time intervals	Leads to average and irregular performance	Rapid extinction	Weekly paycheck
Fixed-ratio	Reward given at fixed amounts of output	Quickly leads to very high and stable performance	Rapid extinction	Piece-rate pay system
Variable-interval	Reward given at variable times	Leads to moderately high and stable performance	Slow extinction	Performance appraisal and awards given at random times each month
Variable-ratio	Reward given at variable amounts of output	Leads to very high performance	Slow extinction	Sales bonus tied to number of sales calls, with random checks

each day, reinforcement may occur every week. Regular paychecks or quarterly bonuses are examples of a fixed-interval reinforcement.

Fixed-Ratio Schedule.   With a *fixed-ratio schedule,* reinforcement occurs after a specified number of desired responses, say, after every fifth. For example, paying a field hand $1.50 for picking 10 pounds of peppers is a fixed-ratio schedule. Most piece-rate pay systems are considered fixed-ratio schedules.

Variable-Interval Schedule   With a *variable-interval schedule,* reinforcement is administered at random times that cannot be predicted by the employee. An example would be a random inspection by the manufacturing superintendent of the production floor, at which time he or she commends employees on their good behavior.

Variable-Ratio Schedule.   The *variable-ratio schedule* is based on a random number of desired behaviors rather than on variable time periods. Reinforcement may occur after 5, 10, 15, or 20 displays of behavior. One example is the attraction of slot machines for gamblers. People anticipate that the machine will pay a jackpot after a certain number of plays, but the exact number of plays is variable.

The schedules of reinforcement available to managers are illustrated in Exhibit 13.7. Continuous reinforcement is most effective for establishing new learning, but behavior is vulnerable to extinction. Partial reinforcement schedules are more effective for maintaining behavior over extended time periods. The most powerful is the variable-ratio schedule, because employee behavior will persist for a long time due to the administration of reinforcement only after a long interval.[24]

One example of an organization that successfully uses reinforcement theory is Parsons Pine Products.

Parsons Pine Products

Parsons Pine Products has only 75 employees, but it is the world's largest manufacturer of slats for louvered doors and shutters. Managers have developed a positive reinforcement scheme for motivating and rewarding workers. The plan includes the following:

1. *Safety pay.* Every employee who goes for a month without a lost-time accident receives a bonus equal to four hours' pay.
2. *Retro pay.* If the company saves money when its worker's compensation premiums go down because of a lower accident rate, the savings are distributed among employees.
3. *Well pay.* Employees receive monthly well pay equal to eight hours' wages if they have been neither absent nor tardy.
4. *Profit pay.* All company earnings above 4 percent after taxes go into a bonus pool, which is shared among employees.

The plan for reinforcing correct behaviors has been extraordinarily effective. Parsons's previous accident rate had been 86 percent above the state average; today it is 32 percent below it. Turnover and tardiness are minimal, and absenteeism has dropped to almost nothing. The plan works because the reinforcement schedules are strictly applied, with no exceptions. Owner James Parsons has said, "One woman called to say that a tree had fallen, and she couldn't get her car out. She wanted me to make an exception. If I did that, I'd be doing it all the time."[25]

Reinforcement also works at such organizations as HUD, Emery Air Freight, Michigan Bell, and General Electric because managers reward appropriate behavior. They tell employees what they can do to receive reinforcement, tell them what they are doing wrong, distribute rewards equitably, tailor rewards to behaviors, and keep in mind that failure to reward deserving behavior has an equally powerful impact on employees.[26]

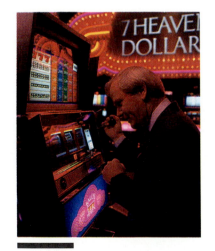

Bally Manufacturing Corporation has several divisions, including lottery products, casino hotels, and gaming equipment. Its slot machine is shown here. One reason slot machines are fun is that they pay rewards randomly, which is a variable-ratio reinforcement schedule. Reinforcement may occur after 5, 10, or 20 coins. Large jackpots occur less frequently. Variable-ratio reinforcement schedules are powerful learning devices in other applications, because behavior extinguishes slowly.

JOB DESIGN FOR MOTIVATION

A *job* in an organization is a unit of work that a single employee is responsible for performing. A job could include writing tickets for parking violators in New York City or doing long-range planning for ABC television. Jobs are important because their components may provide intrinsic and extrinsic rewards that meet employees' needs. An assembly line worker may install the same bolt over and over, while an emergency room physician may provide each trauma victim with a unique treatment package. Managers need to know what aspects of a job provide motivation as well as how to compensate for routine tasks that have little inherent satisfaction. **Job design** is the application of motivational theories to the structure of work for the purpose of improving productivity and satisfaction. Approaches to job design are generally classified as job simplification, job rotation, job enlargement, and job enrichment.

Job Simplification

Job simplification pursues task efficiency by reducing the number of tasks one person must do. Job simplification is based on principles drawn from scientific management and industrial engineering. Tasks are designed to be simple, repetitive, and standardized. As complexity is stripped from a job, the worker has more time to concentrate on doing more of the same routine task. Workers with low skill requirements can perform the job, and the organization achieves a high level of efficiency. Indeed, workers are interchangeable, since they need little training or skill and exercise little judgment. As a motivational technique, however, job simplification has failed. People dislike routine and boring jobs and react in a number of negative ways, including sabotage, absenteeism, and unionization. Job simplification is compared to job rotation and job enlargement in Exhibit 13.8.

Job Rotation

Job rotation systematically moves employees from one job to another, thereby increasing the number of different tasks an employee performs without increasing the complexity of any one job. For example, an autoworker may install windshields one week and front bumpers the next. Job rotation still takes advantage of engineering efficiencies, but it provides variety and stimulation for employees. However, while employees may find the new job interesting at first, the novelty soon wears off as the repetitive work is mastered.

Job rotation has greater motivational potential when the jobs are challenging rather than simplified. Swissair, one of the most profitable airlines, periodically rotates managers to different departments. The program is designed to insure that managers remain productive and stimulated. Exposure to unfamiliar areas gives managers an opportunity to expand their knowledge of corporate operations and to learn another area of the company through hands-on experience.[27]

Job Enlargement

Job enlargement combines a series of tasks into one new, broader job. This is a response to the dissatisfaction of employees with oversimplified jobs. Instead of only one job, an employee may be responsible for three or four and will have more time to do them. Job enlargement provides

EXHIBIT   13.8

Types of Job Design

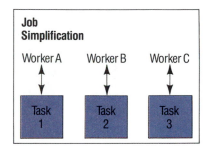

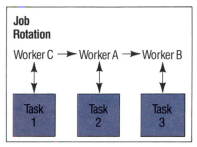

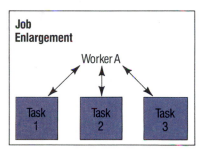

job design   The application of motivational theories to the structure of work for the purpose of improving productivity and satisfaction.

job simplification   A job design whose purpose is to improve task efficiency by reducing the number of tasks a single person must perform.

job rotation   A job design that systematically moves employees from one job to another for the purpose of providing them with variety and stimulation.

U.S. Shoe uses job enlargement to increase employee motivation and satisfaction. Modular work areas such as the one shown here have replaced production lines in over half of its factories. In these areas, workers perform two or three shoe-making steps instead of only one as in traditional production lines. As a consequence of heightened employee involvement in manufacturing, footwear is produced more efficiently and with greater attention to quality.

job enlargement A job design that combines a series of tasks into one new, broader job for the purpose of giving employees variety and challenge.

job variety and a greater challenge for employees. At Maytag, jobs were enlarged when work was redesigned such that workers assembled an entire water pump rather than doing each part as it reached them on the assembly line. When General Motors opened new assembly plants in 1986, the assembly lines were gone. In its place was a motorized carrier that transports a car through the assembly process. The carrier allows a vehicle to stop, and a group of workers perform logical blocks of work, such as installing an engine and its accessories. The workers get to perform an enlarged job on a stationary automobile rather than a single task on a large number of automobiles.

Job Enrichment

job enrichment A job design that incorporates achievement, recognition, and other high-level motivators into the work.

Recall the discussion of Maslow's need hierarchy and Herzberg's two-factor theory. Rather than just changing the number and frequency of tasks a worker performs, **job enrichment** incorporates high-level motivators into the work, including job responsibility, recognition, and opportunities for growth, learning, and achievement. In an enriched job, employees have control over the resources necessary for performing it, make decisions on how to do the work, experience personal growth, and set their own work pace. Many companies, including AT&T, IBM, and General Foods, have undertaken job enrichment programs to increase employees' motivation and job satisfaction.

Job Characteristics Model

work redesign The altering of jobs to increase both the quality of employees' work experience and their productivity.

The most recent work on job design is the job characteristics model developed by Richard Hackman and Greg Oldham.[28] Hackman and Oldham's research concerned **work redesign,** which is defined as altering jobs to increase both the quality of employees' work experience and their productivity. Hackman and Oldham's research into the design of

E X H I B I T   13.9

The Job Characteristics Model

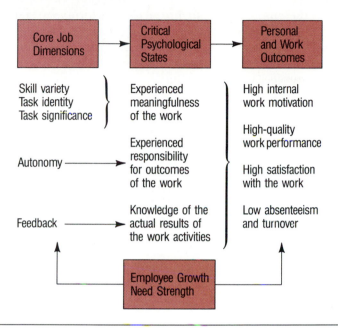

Source: Adapted from J. R. Hackman and G. R. Oldham, "Motivation through the Design of Work: Test of a Theory," *Organizational Behavior and Human Performance* 16 (1976), p. 265. Academic Press, Orlando, Florida.

hundreds of jobs yielded the **job characteristics model,** which is illustrated in Exhibit 13.9. The model consists of three major parts: core job dimensions, critical psychological states, and employee growth-need strength.

Core Job Dimensions.   Hackman and Oldham identified five dimensions that determine a job's motivational potential:

1. *Skill variety* is the number of diverse activities that comprise a job and the number of skills used to perform it. A routine, repetitive assembly line job is low in variety, while an applied research position that entails working on new problems every day is high in variety.
2. *Task identity* is the degree to which an employee performs a total job with a recognizable beginning and ending. A chef who prepares an entire meal has more task identity than a worker on a cafeteria line who ladles mashed potatoes.
3. *Task significance* is the degree to which the job is perceived as important and having impact on the company or consumers. People who distribute penicillin and other medical supplies during times of emergencies would feel they have significant jobs.
4   *Autonomy* is the degree to which the worker has freedom, discretion, and self-determination in planning and carrying out

job characteristics model   A model of job design comprised of core job dimensions, critical psychological states, and employee growth-need strength.

Bell Atlantic employees are responsible for providing dependable service. Repairing cable 75 feet above the waters of the New River in Fayetteville, West Virginia, is all in a day's work for Bob Boughman, an outside plant technician with C&P Telephone of West Virginia. According to the job characteristics model, work that scores high on core job dimensions provides greater employee satisfaction. How would you rate Bob Boughman's job on the dimensions of skill variety, task identity, task significance, autonomy, and feedback?

tasks. A house painter can determine how to paint the house; a paint sprayer on an assembly line has little autonomy.

5. *Feedback* is the extent to which doing the job provides information back to the employee about his or her performance. Jobs vary in their ability to let workers see the outcomes of their efforts. A football coach knows whether the team won or lost, but a basic research scientist may have to wait years to learn whether a research project was successful.

The job characteristics model says that the more these five core characteristics can be designed into the job, the more motivation employees will have and the higher will be performance quality and satisfaction.

Critical Psychological States.   The model posits that core job dimensions are more rewarding when individuals experience three psychological states in response to job design. Note in Exhibit 13.9 that skill variety, task identity, and task significance tend to influence the employee's psychological state of *experienced meaningfulness of work.* The work itself is satisfying and provides intrinsic rewards for the worker. The job characteristic of autonomy influences the worker's *experienced responsibility.* The job characteristic of feedback provides the worker with *knowledge of actual results.* The employee thus knows how he or she is doing and can change work performance to increase desired outcomes. The impact of the five job characteristics on the psychological states of experienced meaningfulness, responsibility, and knowledge of actual results leads to the personal and work outcomes of high work motivation, high work performance, high satisfaction, and low absenteeism and turnover.

Employee Growth-Need Strength.   The final component of the job characteristics model is called *employee growth-need strength,* which means that people have different needs for growth and development. If a person wants to satisfy lower-level needs, such as safety and belongingness, the job characteristics model has less effect. When a person has a high need for growth and development, including the desire for personal challenge, achievement, and challenging work, the model is especially effective. People with a high need to grow and expand their abilities respond very favorably to the application of the model and to improvements in core job dimensions.

One application of the job characteristics model that worked extremely well took place at Traveler's Insurance Company.

Traveler's Insurance Company

Traveler's Insurance Company executives wanted to increase the motivation and job satisfaction of keypunch operators. The company was experiencing absenteeism and turnover and felt that employees' needs were not being met. The keypunch operator's job consisted of a single skill—the ability to accurately punch data onto cards. Employees punched cards continuously and did not have identifiable, whole jobs. Once a batch was completed, it disappeared and the workers received no feedback on performance quality. Operators were isolated from the rest of the company and had little knowledge about how their work was used.

Researchers investigated the job and recommended several changes. First, instead of being assigned a random set of cards, each operator was given responsibility for a computer user account. In addition, each was given the opportunity for direct contact with clients when problems arose. The operators also were allowed to do planning and control in addition to keypunching. They were asked to correct obvious errors on their own and to set their own daily work schedules. Finally, all incorrectly punched cards were returned to operators for correction, along with weekly printouts of error rates.

These changes dramatically increased the motivating potential of the keypunch operator's job. The job now had greater variety, task identity, and perceived significance. Autonomy and task feedback also were increased.

What were the consequences of the work redesign? Productivity increased 39.6 percent. The error rate dropped from 1.53 to 0.99 percent. Absenteeism declined 24.1 percent. Reported job satisfaction increased 16.5 percent. Moreover, because operators had greater responsibility, supervision was reduced, providing more freedom for keypunch operators and greater savings for Traveler's.[29]

OTHER MOTIVATIONAL PROGRAMS

Organizations have adopted a number of programs for applying motivational theory to improve employees' satisfaction and performance. These include merit pay, modified work schedules, lump sum salary increases, and open salary information.

Merit Pay

Merit pay rewards employees in proportion to their performance contributions. Sometimes called *pay for performance* or *incentive systems*, merit pay is a logical outgrowth of such motivational concepts as expectancy theory and reinforcement theory because rewards are tied to work behavior. However, the implementation of merit pay requires study and answers to several questions: Whose performance is to be measured? Will merit pay be given for an individual's personal performance, for a

merit pay A motivational program that rewards employees in proportion to their contributions to the organization.

Nationwide Insurance believes that productivity is based on incentives that reward employee performance. This merit pay approach rewards people for what they do rather than for their seniority. Nationwide has a merit pay system, called Improved Methods Plan, through which employees make suggestions for cost savings. For Thelma Pearson, the plan provided more than pennies from heaven: Her suggestions have saved Nationwide $88,697 and earned her more than $1,700.

work group's performance, or for the performance of the organization as a whole?[30]

One company developed a merit pay plan that rewarded employees for both individual and company success. At Woodward Governor Company of Rockford, Illinois, all employees are ranked according to their contributions during the year. Supervisors spend hours ranking each of their subordinates, and senior managers rank everyone below them. Eventually a top committee produces a list that ranks each of the 2,750 workers according to their contributions to the corporation. Each employee is then given a bonus based on company profits and his or her ranking. People receive the greatest reward when the company is successful and when they have made a major contribution to that success.[31]

Modified Work Schedules

Modified work schedules drop the restriction that employees work the normal eight-hour workday from 8 a.m. to 5 p.m. These modifications include the four-day workweek, flex time, and job sharing.

With the *four-day workweek* employees work four days for ten hours each instead of five days for eight hours. The motivational factor is that of meeting the needs of workers who want more leisure time. The four-day workweek has been adopted in close to 2,000 companies. Olin Ski Company of Middletown, Connecticut, initiated the four-day workweek in 1972 to compete more effectively for skilled workers.[32] Employees work ten hours a day, Monday through Thursday. Employee response has been positive because workers love three-day weekends.

Flex time allows employees to determine their workday schedules. People can choose starting and quitting times. For example, a company may have core hours during which employees must be present, perhaps from 9 a.m. to 4 p.m. Employees then are free to start work anywhere from 7 a.m. to 9 a.m. and to finish anywhere from 4 p.m. to 6 p.m., depending on their own needs and desires. Flex time, like the four-day workweek, does not alter the basic nature of the job but gives employees discretion concerning when to work in order to meet their individual needs.

Job sharing involves two or more persons jointly covering one job over a forty-hour week. Job sharing allows part-time workers, such as a mother with small children, to work only part of a day without having to create a special job. Job sharing also relieves job fatigue if work is routine or monotonous. Like the other modified work schedules, job sharing does not change the basic nature of the job but makes the job more attractive for potential employees and gives workers the opportunity to meet needs and desires outside the workplace.

Lump Sum Salary Increases

lump sum salary increase   A salary increase that is paid as a bonus at one or more times during the year in order to enhance its motivational value.

Often salary increases do not seem very large when spread over an entire year's worth of paychecks. **Lump sum salary increases** are paid as a bonus at one or more times during the year in order to increase their motivational value. For example, a 10 percent raise for an employee earning $20,000 would be a one-time $2,000 payment. Lump sum payments can be given three or four times a year to more frequently reinforce employees' outstanding performances. For example, one Texas oil service company devised a plan in which field engineers were given their merit increases in cash during the performance appraisal interview. The program was successful, and engineers reported increased satisfaction with pay. In return, the company received improved job performance and reduced turnover.[33]

Open Salary Information

Many companies keep their managers' salaries secret. In such cases, managers may overestimate the amount of pay other people in the organization receive, creating feelings of inequity. When people overestimate others' pay, they become more dissatisfied with their own. Moreover, by not knowing the pay of others and the potential salary available for hard work and high performance, the motivating impact of pay is reduced. *Open salary information* is a policy of openness regarding salaries. Salaries can be published for all employees to see. An open salary policy helps clarify for employees the relationship between performance and pay and creates a climate of trust. It also encourages managers to make salary increases equitable and to reward people for obvious good performance rather than on the basis of friendship or seniority.[34]

SUMMARY

This chapter introduced a number of important ideas about the motivation of people in organizations. The content theories of motivation focus on the nature of underlying employee needs. Maslow's hierarchy of needs, Alderfer's ERG theory, Herzberg's two-factor theory, and McClelland's acquired needs theory all suggest that people are motivated to meet a range of needs. Process theories examine how people go about selecting rewards with which to meet needs. Equity theory says that people compare their contributions and outcomes to others' and are motivated to maintain a feeling of equity. Expectancy theory suggests that people calculate the probability of achieving certain outcomes. Managers can increase motivation by treating employees fairly and by clarifying employee paths toward meeting their needs. Still another motivational approach is reinforcement theory, which says that employees learn to behave in certain ways based on the availability of reinforcements.

The application of motivational ideas is illustrated in job design and other motivational programs. Job design approaches include job enrichment and work redesign, which provide an opportunity for employees to meet higher-level needs. Other motivational programs include modified work schedules, merit pay, lump sum salary increases, and open salary information.

Management Solution

Ted Gaebler confronted the challenge of making the Visalia, California, city government innovative despite a decrease in tax revenues. His approach seemed revolutionary, but it consisted of basic motivational principles. First, he rewarded city departments for cutting costs by letting them keep any savings, thus eliminating the rush to spend the entire budget at the end of the year. A new system, called "Expenditure-Control Budgeting," was implemented to motivate employees to further improve performance. For example, the police department adopted a system of having officers take their own cars home, which improved maintenance by motivating them to take care of their cars. The average car now lasts 5 years compared with 18 months previously. To further motivate employees, Gaebler initiated the Employee Development Program, designed to help talented people move up within the organization. Further motivation came from the bonus program. Department heads are eligible for unlimited bonuses, while other employees can earn up to $1,000 each year. Moreover, if an employee saves the city money, he or she gets to keep 15 percent with no cap on the total amount. The result of these motivational techniques is a city government in which morale is high, employees work hard, and new ideas are constantly being proposed.[35]

DISCUSSION QUESTIONS

1. Discuss the similarities and differences among the content theories of Maslow, Alderfer, and Herzberg.
2. If an experienced secretary discovered that she made less money than a newly hired janitor, how would she react? What inputs and outcomes might she evaluate to make this comparison?
3. Would you rather work for a supervisor high in need for achievement, need for affiliation, or need for power? Why? What are the advantages and disadvantages of each?
4. A survey of teachers found that two of the most important rewards were the belief that their work was important and a feeling of accomplishment. Is this consistent with the content theories? With Hackman and Oldham's job characteristics model?
5. The teachers in question 4 also reported that pay and fringe benefits were poor; yet they continued to teach. Use Herzberg's two-factor theory to explain this finding.
6. Some companies are using what they call "positive discipline," meaning that they send "difficult workers" home for a day with pay as a last resort before firing them. These companies report

that behavior often improves after this positive discipline. How could reinforcement theory and expectancy theory be used to explain this improvement?

7. Many organizations use sales contests and motivational speakers to motivate salespeople to overcome frequent rejections and turndowns. How would these devices help motivate salespeople?

8. Which employee needs are met by innovative reward systems such as lump sum salary increases, merit pay, and open salary information?

9. What characteristics of individuals determine the extent to which work redesign will have a positive impact on work satisfaction and work effectiveness?

10. With which motivational theory would you be most comfortable as a manager? Why?

CASES FOR ANALYSIS

AUTOMOBILE CLAIMS DEPARTMENT

Ellen Richards supervised 30 stenographers in the automobile claims department of a large insurance company. She spent much of her time assigning dictation to the staffers who handled correspondence arising out of accident claims against the company. Some of this correspondence was fairly routine, but letters involving litigation were quite complicated. As a rule, Ellen gave the most difficult dictation to the most experienced stenographers.

She tried to remind herself of this as it became time to announce the annual merit raises. She used her records on attendance, lateness, and daily letter output to determine the size of each raise. After she had made her decisions, Ellen called each person to her desk individually to report the amount of the raise. The next day, Annette Simmons came up to Ellen's desk, obviously upset. "Ellen," she said, trying to control her voice, "could you please tell me why Jason got a bigger raise than I did? I have had very few absences and I'm never late. You often compliment me on my work, and you give me some of the hardest assignments." Ellen got out her records and looked at them. "You're a good worker, Annette," she said, "but your letter output is just a little below average. If you could raise your output, next time I'm sure you'll get a bigger raise."

"But I get the hardest dictation!" Annette said angrily. "And when Gene came into our section, you put him next to me and told me to help him until he got familiar with the work. I don't mind helping someone new, but he still interrupts me with questions about things he should know by now. Don't you take things like that into consideration before deciding how much of a raise I deserve?"

"In a section as large as ours," Ellen explained, "I have to use objective standards like output and attendance to determine each person's raise. Here productivity is everything. I'm sorry you're upset, because I know how helpful you are to the less experienced workers, and I know how much they appreciate your giving them a hand."

"Evidently they are the only ones who appreciate my giving them a hand. From now on, I'll just attend to my own work" With that, Annette turned away and went back to her desk before Ellen could reply.

Questions

1. Is Ellen Richards successfully motivating her staff? What mistake is she making?
2. Use expectancy theory to analyze Annette's motivation. What are the $E \rightarrow P$ and $P \rightarrow O$ expectancies?
3. If you were Ellen, what would you do now?

Source: Adapted by permission of the publisher, from "I Deserve a Bigger Raise," *Management Solutions,* June 1986, pp. 43–44. © 1986 American Management Association, New York. All rights reserved.

CATALOG STORES, INC.

Joe Beck is manager of one store in a chain of catalog stores. The catalogs are distributed nationally, and people in the region can write or telephone Joe's store to place catalog orders.

Some employees are assigned to telephone orders, others handle mail orders. Each employee sits at a computer terminal. The order processing is rather routine, consisting of typing orders into the computer-based information system. Each order must have the same information, including the catalog number, unit price, customer name and address, credit card number, expiration date, color, and size. Each order is assigned an invoice number, and everything must be typed accurately.

Joe has noticed that the employees who take orders over the telephone are more satisfied than those who handle mail orders. The mail orders seem more routine and are handled in batches of 40 to 50 at a time. The telephone orders provide people with a chance to visit with customers, and each order takes longer to process. Speed and accuracy are necessary performance indicators for both telephone and written orders. Punctuality and reliable attendance are also important, because employees are hard to replace on short notice. Typing skill and the ability to pay attention to details and spot errors are also helpful.

The catalog store is located in a nice shopping mall, and employees enjoy the surroundings. The building is new, and the equipment is excellent, with few breakdowns. Employees spend their noon break shopping in the mall and frequently spend time discussing new purchases after returning from lunch. There are a variety of restaurants in which employees can get a bite to eat, and parking is close to the store.

In recent months, Joe has noticed that the productivity of his catalog store is below average for the chain. He feels that part of the problem is the dissatisfaction of employees who handle written orders. Those employees have slightly higher rates of absenteeism and tardiness that reduce productivity. He has been considering trying to establish specific goals for both groups of employees, but is unsure how to proceed.

Most of the employees seem to be friends; during breaks and slow periods, they are free to visit with one another. A few socialize together outside the workplace.

Questions

1. What could Joe Beck do to increase the motivation and job satisfaction of his workers?
2. Which of the various approaches to job design for motivation could be used to make these jobs more satisfying and also increase productivity?
3. Which worker needs are being met? Which are not?

CHAPTER 14
Communicating in Organizations

Chapter Outline

Communication and the Manager's Job

What Is Communication?
The Communication Process

Communicating among People

Perception and Communication
Communication Channels
Nonverbal Communication
Listening

Organizational Communication

Formal Communication Channels
Informal Communication Channels

Communicating in Groups

Managing Organizational Communication

Barriers to Communication
Overcoming Communication
Barriers

Learning Objectives

After studying this chapter, you should be able to:

- Explain why communication is essential for effective management.

- Define the basic elements of the communication process.

- Describe how perception, nonverbal behavior, and listening affect communication among people.

- Describe the concept of channel richness and explain how communication channels influence the quality of communication among managers.

- Explain the difference between formal and informal organizational communications and the importance of each for organization management.

- Describe group communications and how structure influences communication outcomes.

- Describe barriers to organizational communications and suggest ways to avoid or overcome them.

Management Problem

New CEO John Egan was given a simple mandate: Either make Jaguar Cars profitable or shut it down. Customer surveys indicated that quality ratings for Jaguar autos and service were among the lowest in the industry. An already small market share was getting smaller. A major part of the problem was communication. Production employees did not appreciate the goal of high quality set by top management. Top managers did not understand the problems or concerns of supervisors and shop floor employees trying to produce cars. Dealers did not understand the customers' wishes or how to communicate them back to the factory. John Egan faced the challenge of improving Jaguar quality and productivity, but to do so meant improving communication in all directions.[1]

If you were a consultant to John Egan, what would you recommend for improving communications? How could you smooth the flow of information throughout the company?

CEO John Egan knows the importance of communication but sees a big problem breaking down communication barriers at Jaguar. Senior executives at many companies are striving to improve communication. The president of Syntex Corporation, a pharmaceuticals maker, eats breakfast at 7:30 each morning in the employee cafeteria. He asks employees what's going on in the organization. He in turn is asked many questions and gives employees information from top management's perspective. The president of Banc One Corporation in Columbus, Ohio, keeps track of employees' feelings by reading exit interviews with departed employees. John Scully, the CEO of Apple Computer, insists that top executives listen to customer complaints on the toll-free number. Although senior

Roast beef sandwiches and vienna sausages were on the menu when Ed Addison, president of Southern Company, lunched with a line crew in Columbus, Georgia. Addison likes to visit plants around Southern's utility system to chat with employees and meet with managers. This gives him a chance to explain what the company is doing from a top management perspective and learn about issues and concerns within the company. Communication is a major part of a manager's job, and informal lunches are Ed Addison's way of facilitating it.

executives often lack the technical expertise to solve customers' problems, they quickly learn customers' concerns about Apple computers.[2]

These executives are interested in getting at the truth. They want to be in touch with employees and customers, and they do so through personal communications. Nonmanagers often are amazed at how much energy successful executives put into communication. Consider Robert Strauss, former chairman of the Democratic National Committee:

His network is probably as large as any around, and he works hard to keep it. One of his friends says, "His network is everywhere. It ranges from bookies to bank presidents. . . . Hamilton Jordan said to me recently, "Strauss is all over the damn place. He's got contacts on the Hill, he's got contacts in the business community, he's got contacts in the press. . . .

He seems to find time to make innumerable phone calls to "keep in touch;" he cultivates secretaries as well as senators; he will befriend a middle-level White House aide whom other important officials won't bother with. Every few months, he sends candy to the White House switchboard operators.[3]

The purpose of this chapter is to explain why executives like Robert Strauss, John Scully, and the presidents of Banc One Corporation and Syntex Corporation are effective communicators. First we will see how managers design organizations to facilitate communication. Next, we will define communication and describe a model of the communication process. Then we will consider the interpersonal aspects of communication, including perception, channels, and listening skills, that affect managers' ability to communicate. Next, we will look at the organization as a whole and consider formal upward and downward communications as well as informal communications. Finally, we will examine barriers to communication and how managers can overcome them.

E X H I B I T   14.1

Forms of Communication Used by Managers

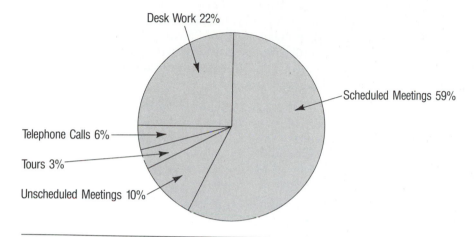

Source: Henry Mintzberg, *The Nature of Managerial Work* (New York: Harper & Row, 1973).

COMMUNICATION AND THE MANAGER'S JOB

How important is communication? Consider this: Managers spend over 80 percent of every working day communicating. How do they communicate? One survey broke down managers' communication time as illustrated in Exhibit 14.1. Scheduled and unscheduled face-to-face meetings accounted for 69 percent of managers' time, telephone calls another 6 percent, and walk-around tours another 3 percent. The remaining 22 percent was spent reading and writing at their desks.[4]

Communication permeates every management function.[5] For example, when managers perform the planning function, they gather information, write letters, memos, and reports, and then meet with other managers to explain the plan. When managers lead, they communicate with subordinates to motivate them to do certain tasks. When managers organize, they gather information about the the state of the organization and communicate a new structure to others. Communication skills are a basic part of every managerial activity.

What Is Communication?

Before going further, let's determine what communication is. A professor at Harvard once asked a class to define communication by drawing pictures. Most students drew a manager speaking or writing. Some placed "speech balloons" next to their characters; others showed pages flying from a typewriter. "No," the professor told the class, "none of you have captured the essence of communication." He went on to explain that communication means "to share"—not "to speak" or "to write."

communication The process by which information is exchanged and understood by two or more people, usually with the intent to motivate or influence behavior.

Communication thus can be defined as the process by which information is exchanged and understood by two or more people, usually with the intent to motivate or influence behavior. Communication is not just sending information. This distinction between *sharing* and *proclaiming* is crucial for successful management. A manager who does not listen is like a used-car salesperson who claims, "I sold a car—they just did not buy it." Management communication is a two-way street that includes listening and other forms of feedback. Effective communication, in the words of one expert, is as follows:

> When two people interact, they put themselves into each other's shoes, try to perceive the world as the other person perceives it, try to predict how the other will respond. Interaction involves reciprocal role-taking, the mutual employment of empathetic skills. The goal of interaction is the merger of self and other, a complete ability to anticipate, predict, and behave in accordance with the joint needs of self and other.[6]

It is the desire to share understanding that motivates executives to visit employees on the shop floor or eat breakfast with them. The things managers learn from direct communication with employees shape their understanding of the corporation.

The Communication Process

Many people think communication is rather simple because they communicate without conscious thought or effort. However, communication is usually quite complex, and the opportunities for sending or receiving the wrong messages are innumerable. How often have you heard someone say, "But that's not what I meant"? Have you ever given people directions in what you thought was a clear fashion and they still got lost? How often have you wasted time on misunderstood instructions?

To more fully understand the complexity of the communication process, note the key elements outlined in Exhibit 14.2. Two common elements in every communication situation are the sender and the receiver. The *sender* is anyone who wishes to convey an idea or concept to others, to seek information, or to express a thought or emotion. The *receiver* is the person to whom the message is sent. The sender **encodes** the idea by selecting symbols with which to compose a message. The **message** is the tangible formulation of the idea that is sent to the receiver. The message is sent through a **channel,** which is the communication carrier. The channel can be a formal report, a telephone call, or a face-to-face meeting. The receiver **decodes** the symbols to interpret the meaning of the message. Encoding and decoding are potential sources for communication errors, because knowledge, attitudes, and background act as filters and create "noise" when translating from symbols to meaning. Finally, **feedback** occurs when the receiver responds to the sender's communication with a return message. Without feedback, the communication is one-way; with feedback, it is two-way. Feedback is a powerful aid to communication effectiveness, because it enables the sender to determine whether the receiver correctly interpreted the message.

Managers who are effective communicators understand and use the circular nature of communication. For example, James Treybig of Tan-

encode To select symbols with which to compose a message.

message The tangible formulation of an idea to be sent to a receiver.

channel The carrier of a communication.

decode To translate the symbols used in a message for the purpose of interpreting its meaning.

feedback A response by the receiver to the sender's communication.

EXHIBIT 14.2

A Model of the Communication Process

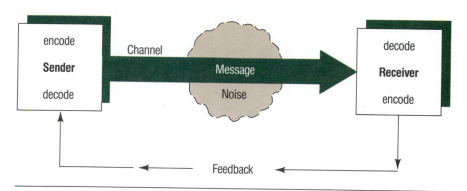

dem Computers Inc. has widened the open-door policy in order to communicate with employees. Treybig appears on a monthly television program broadcasted over the company's in-house TV station. Employees around the world watch the show and call in their questions and comments. The television is the channel through which Treybig sends his encoded message. Employees decode and interpret the message and encode their feedback, which is sent through the channel of the telephone hookup. The communication circuit is complete. Similarly Tom Monaghan, president of Domino's Pizza, maintains communication channels with employees when he fields complaints for two hours during a monthly "call-in." Monaghan also maintains toll-free numbers with which employees call him directly. Treybig and Monaghan understand the elements of communication and have developed systems that work.[7]

COMMUNICATING AMONG PEOPLE

The communication model in Exhibit 14.2 illustrates the components that must be mastered for effective communication. Communications can break down if sender and receiver do not encode or decode language in the same way.[8] The selection of communication channels can determine whether the message is distorted by noise and interference. The listening skills of both parties can determine whether a message is truly shared. Thus, in order for managers to be effective communicators, they must understand how interpersonal factors such as perception, communication channels, nonverbal behavior, and listening all work to enhance or detract from communication.

Perception and Communication

The way we perceive people is the starting point for how we communicate. When one person wishes to share an idea with another, the message is formulated based on references constructed from past events, experiences, expectations, and current motivations. When a receiver hears a

Effective communication leads to shared understanding among people. Here two nurses confer in a passageway of the Baystate Medical Center. Such face-to-face communications comprise a substantial portion of information sharing in organizations. While such discussion is informal, it includes encoding, message, channel, decoding, and feedback. Understanding the communication process allows people to be better communicators.

perception   The process of making sense out of one's environment.

perceptual selectivity   The screening and selection of objects and stimuli that compete for one's attention.

perceptual organization   The categorization of an object or stimulus according to one's frame of reference.

stereotype   A widely held generalization about a group of people that assigns attributes to them solely on the basis of a limited number of categories.

message, he or she relies on a particular frame of reference for decoding and understanding it. The more similar the frames of reference between people, the more easily they can communicate.

Perception is the process one uses to make sense out of the environment. However, perception in itself does not always lead to an accurate picture of the environment.[9] **Perceptual selectivity** means that various objects and stimuli that vie for our attention are screened and selected by individuals. Certain stimuli catch their attention, and others do not. Once a stimulus is recognized, individuals organize or categorize it according to their frame of reference, that is, **perceptual organization.** Only a partial cue is needed to enable perceptual organization to take place. For example, all of us have spotted an old friend from a long distance and, without seeing the face or other features, recognized the person from the body movement.

The most common form of perceptual organization is stereotyping. A **stereotype** is a widely held generalization about a group of people that assigns attributes to them solely on the basis of one or a few categories, such as age, race, or occupation. For example, young people may assume that older people are old-fashioned or conservative. Students may stereotype professors as absent-minded or as political liberals.

How do perceptual selectivity and organization affect manager behavior? Consider the following comment from Joe, a staff supervisor, on his expectations about the annual budget meeting with his boss, Charlie:

> *About a month before the meetings are to begin, I find myself waking up around 4:00 a.m., thinking about Charlie and the arguments I'm going to have with him. I know he'll accuse me of trying to "pad" my requests and, in turn, I'll accuse him of failing to understand the nature of my department's needs. I'll be trying to anticipate every little snide remark he can generate and every argument that he's likely to propose, and I'll be getting ready with snide remarks and arguments of my own. This year, as always, I've got to be sure to get him before he gets me.[10]*

Joe's selective perception will cause him to immediately recognize any cues that resemble snide remarks. He will also organize these remarks to fit his belief that Charlie's motivation is to reduce his budget. No matter what frame of mind Charlie brings to the communication, Joe is set to perceive in his own way, which will surely harm the opportunity for open and honest communication.

Perceptual differences and perceptual mistakes also occur when people perceive simple objects in dissimilar ways. Typical examples are illustrated in Exhibit 14.3. In panel a, many people see a sad old woman, but others see a beautiful young lady with a large head covering. The two lines in panel b are commonly used in psychological research. Are the lines the same length? Most people perceive line segment b as being longer than line segment a even though both are exactly the same length. People think that b is longer because of perceptual organization. The images are arranged according to past experience with similar lines, and perceptions are distorted by irrelevant information such as the V-shaped lines, which seem to expand or contract the line segments.

An important point for managers to understand is perceptual differences are natural but can distort messages and create noise and interfer-

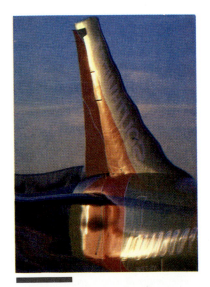

Things are not always what they seem. Although this picture suggests that the airplane is distorted, the phenomenon of perceptual organization tells us that this is not true. The mind interprets the cues and assumes that the airplane is intact. Perceptual organization helps people acquire an accurate picture of the world despite limited or inconsistent perceptual cues.

E X H I B I T   14.3

Perception: What Do You See?

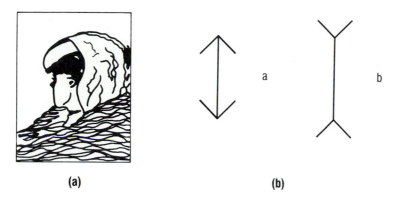

(a)   (b)

ence for communications. Managers should remember words can mean different things to different people and should not assume they already know what the other person or the communication is about.

Communication Channels

Managers have a choice of many channels through which to communicate to other managers or employees. A manager may discuss a problem face to face, use the telephone, write a memo or letter, or put an item in a newsletter, depending on the nature of the message. Recent research has attempted to explain how managers select communication channels to enhance communication effectiveness.[11] The research has found that channels differ in their capacity to convey information. Just as a pipeline's physical characteristics limit the kind and amount of liquid that can be pumped through it, a communication channel's physical characteristics limit the kind and amount of information that can be conveyed among managers. The channels available to managers can be classified into a hierarchy based on information richness. **Channel richness** is the amount of information that can be transmitted during a communication episode. The hierarchy of channel richness is illustrated in Exhibit 14.4.

channel richness The amount of information that can be transmitted during a communication episode.

The capacity of an information channel is influenced by three characteristics: (1) the ability to handle multiple cues simultaneously; (2) the ability to facilitate rapid feedback; and (3) the ability to establish a personal focus for the communication. Face-to-face discussion is the richest medium, because it permits direct experience, multiple information cues, immediate feedback, and personal focus. Face-to-face discussions facilitate the assimilation of broad cues and deep, emotional understanding of the situation. Telephone conversations and interactive electronic media, such as video conferencing and electronic mail (discussed in more detail in Chapter 19), lack the element of "being there." Eye contact, gaze, blush, posture, and body language cues are eliminated. Written media that are personalized, such as memos, notes, and letters, can be personally focused, but they convey only the cues written on paper and are slow to provide feedback. Impersonal written media, including fliers, bulletins, and standard computer reports, are the lowest in richness.

E X H I B I T   14.4

Hierarchy of Channel Richness and Application to Messages

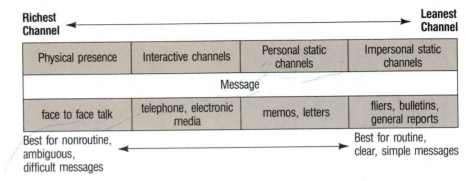

These channels are not focused on a single receiver, use limited informa-tion cues, and do not permit feedback.

Channel selection depends on whether the message is routine or non-routine. *Nonroutine messages* typically are ambiguous, concern novel events, and impose great potential for misunderstanding. Nonroutine messages often are characterized by time pressure and surprise. Mana-gers can communicate nonroutine messages effectively only by selecting rich channels. On the other hand, routine communications are simple and straightforward. *Routine messages* convey data or statistics or simply put into words what managers already agree on and understand. Misin-terpretation is unlikely. Routine messages can be efficiently communi-cated through a channel lower in richness.[12]

Most managers experience surprise and time pressure on the job. Consider a CEO trying to work out a press release with his public rela-tions people about a plant explosion that injured 15 employees. If the press release must be ready in three hours, the communication is truly nonroutine and forces a rich information exchange. The group will meet face to face, brainstorm ideas, register multiple cues, and provide rapid feedback to resolve disagreement and convey the correct information. If the CEO has three days to prepare the release, high information capacity is less essential. The CEO and public relations people might begin devel-oping the press release with an exchange of memos and telephone calls.

The key is to select a channel to fit the message. One successful man-ager who understood channel selection was Harold Geneen of ITT.

ITT

Harold Geneen was at the helm of ITT from 1959 to 1977. He strove to make ITT a unified organization despite its huge size. One of his first decisions was to create ITT-Europe, which would serve as headquarters for European operations. ITT's strategy was to grow by acquisition, eventually increasing to more than 200 subsidiary companies around the world. One of Geneen's most difficult problems was how to get French, German, Italian, and American managers to go along with central decisions. Initial executive sessions sounded like a United Nations meeting. Gradually, Geneen solved the communication problem by relying on face-to-face channels:

> *One of the first things I learned in those early days was that when I responded to a question or request from Europe while sitting in New York, my decision was often different from what it would have been had I been in Europe. In New York, I might read a request and say no. But in Europe, I could see the man's face, hear his voice, understand the intensity of his conviction, and the answer to the same question might be yes. So, early on, I decided that if I and my headquarters' team intended to monitor and oversee the European operations, I owed it to the European managers to be there on the spot. . . . It became our policy to deal with problems on the spot, face-to-face.[13]*

Geneen discovered that the face-to-face channel was needed for handling difficult communications among managers from different countries. Thus, for 17 years Geneen and his senior staff went to Europe for one week every month to deal personally with the European managers' requests and needs. It worked: ITT went on to become one of the best-managed companies in the world.

Nonverbal Communication

Nonverbal communication refers to messages sent through human actions and behaviors rather than through words.[14] Although most nonverbal communication is unconscious or subconscious on our part, it represents a major portion of the messages we send and receive. Most managers are astonished to learn that words themselves carry little meaning. Major parts of the shared understanding from communication come from the nonverbal messages of facial expression, voice, mannerisms, posture, and dress.

Nonverbal communication occurs mostly face to face. One researcher found three sources of communication cues during face-to-face communication: the verbal, which are the actual spoken words; the vocal, which include the pitch, tone, and timber of a person's voice; and facial expressions. According to this study, the relative weights of these three factors in message interpretation are as follows: verbal impact, 7 percent; vocal impact, 38 percent; and facial impact, 55 percent.[15]

This research strongly implies that "it's not what you say, but how you say it." Nonverbal messages convey thoughts and feelings with greater force than do our most carefully selected words. Body language often communicates our real feelings eloquently. Thus, while the conscious mind may be formulating vocal messages such as "I'm happy" or "Congratulations on your promotion," the body language may be signaling true feelings through blushing, perspiring, glancing, crying, or avoiding eye contact. When the verbal and nonverbal messages are contradictory, the receiver may be confused and usually will give more weight to behavioral actions than to verbal messages.[16]

nonverbal communication A communication transmitted through actions and behaviors rather than through words.

Ed Czapor, General Motors' vice-president of quality and reliability, plans to visit every GM division to get a hands-on assessment of quality implementation. The face-to-face channel is sufficiently rich to enable Czapor to gain a full understanding of such nonroutine topics as new manufacturing concepts, engineering lab activities, strategic planning, and new manufacturing designs. Face-to-face communication also allows Czapor to assess the togetherness and enthusiasm that employees demonstrate.

Nonverbal messages can be a powerful asset to communication if they complement and support verbal messages. Nonverbal communications relate to verbal messages in six ways:

1. *Repeating:* Someone says, "She walked toward the administration building" and physically points in that direction.
2. *Contradicting:* Someone says, "I'm not nervous about this interview" as he fidgets in his chair.
3. *Substituting:* Someone makes a statement that you do not believe, and you say nothing but peer at her with head down and eyebrows raised. This posture clearly says, "Are you serious?"
4. *Complementing:* Someone says, "You're wonderful!" with a big smile on her face and a quick wink.
5. *Accenting:* Someone says, "I don't want you to do that again!" and points angrily at you.
6. *Relating and regulating:* Someone raises her hand, indicating that she wants to speak.[17]

Managers should pay close attention to nonverbal behavior when communicating. They must learn to coordinate their verbal and nonverbal messages and at the same time be sensitive to what their peers, subordinates, and supervisors are saying nonverbally.[18]

Listening

The final characteristic associated with successful interpersonal communication is *listening*. The listener is responsible for message reception, which is a vital link in the communication process. The listener must actively try to grasp facts and feelings and interpret the message's genuine meaning. Only then can the receiver provide the feedback with which to complete the communication circuit. Listening requires attention, energy, and skill.

Many people do not listen effectively. They concentrate on formulating what they are going to say next rather than on what is being said to them. Our listening efficiency, as measured by the amount of material understood and remembered by subjects 48 hours after listening to a 10-minute message, is, on average, no better than 25 percent.[19]

What constitutes good listening? Exhibit 14.5 illustrates a number of ways to distinguish a bad from a good listener. A good listener finds areas of interest, is flexible, works hard at listening, and uses thought speed to mentally summarize, weigh, and anticipate what the speaker will say. Some companies, such as IBM and Delta, take listening very seriously. Managers know they are expected to *listen* to employees.

Delta Air Lines

At Delta, managers spend an extraordinary amount of time listening to people. Every year senior managers meet with all employees in an "open forum," in which direct communications take place between the highest and lowest organizational levels. Top managers also hold four full days of meetings a year just to listen to flight attendants based in Atlanta. Senior vice-presidents spend more than 100 days a year on the road learning what people have to say; these days include time on the flight line at 2 a.m. The total amount of management time devoted to listening is staggering.

At Delta, the concern for listening starts at the top. Every Monday morning all the company's problems, finances, and programs are reviewed at a staff meeting. Afterward senior executives take their department heads to lunch to bring them up to date; thus, news is quickly passed throughout the company.

There are other examples of how seriously Delta managers take listening. A committee of flight attendants chooses uniforms for Delta's 6,000 stewardesses and stewards and tells management what they want. "It's important that management listen," says one flight attendant, "because we have to live in the uniforms." Mechanics have a say in choosing their immediate supervisors. It is little wonder that Delta has an almost unblemished record of successful employee relations and profit performance.[20]

Nonverbal communication refers to messages sent through human action and behavior and includes facial expression, poise, mannerisms, posture, and dress. The facial expressions in this photo provided by Alco Health Services Corporation certainly indicate what these people are feeling—even better than words. Research on nonverbal communication suggests that body language accurately communicates feelings and accounts for 55 percent of message interpretation.

E X H I B I T   14.5

Ten Keys to Effective Listening

Keys	Poor Listener	Good Listener
Listens actively	Passive, laid back	Asks questions, paraphrases what is said
Finds areas of interest	Tunes out dry subjects	Looks for opportunities, new learning
Resists distractions	Easily distracted	Fights or avoids distractions; tolerates bad habits; knows how to concentrate
Capitalizes on the fact that thought is faster than speech	Tends to daydream with slow speakers	Challenges, anticipates, mentally summarizes; weighs the evidence; listens between the lines to tone of voice
Is responsive	Little involvement	Nods; shows interest, give and take, positive feedback
Judges content, not delivery	Tunes out if delivery is poor	Judges content; skips over delivery errors
Holds one's fire	Preconceptions, starts to argue	Does not judge until comprehension is complete
Listens for ideas	Listens for facts	Listens for central themes
Works at listening	Shows no energy output; faked attention	Works hard, exhibits active body state, eye contact
Exercises one's mind	Resists difficult material in favor of light, recreational material	Uses heavier material as exercise for the mind

Source: Adapted from Sherman K. Okum, "How to Be a Better Listener," *Nation's Business* (August 1975), p. 62, and Philip Morgan and Kent Baker, "Building a Professional Image: Improving Listening Behavior," *Supervisory Management* (November 1985), pp. 34–38.

ORGANIZATIONAL COMMUNICATION

Another aspect of management communication concerns the organization as a whole. Organizationwide communications typically flow in three directions—downward, upward, and horizontally. Managers are responsible for establishing and maintaining formal channels of communication in these three directions. Managers also use informal channels, which means they get out of their offices and mingle with employees.[21]

Formal Communication Channels

formal communication channel
A communication channel that flows within the chain of command or task responsibility defined by the organization.

downward communication
Messages sent from top management down to subordinates.

Formal communication channels are those that flow within the chain of command or task responsibility defined by the organization. The three formal channels and the types of information conveyed in each are illustrated in Exhibit 14.6.[22]

Downward Communication. The most familiar and obvious flow of formal communication, **downward communication,** is the messages and

E X H I B I T   14.6

Downward, Upward, and Horizontal Communication in Organizations

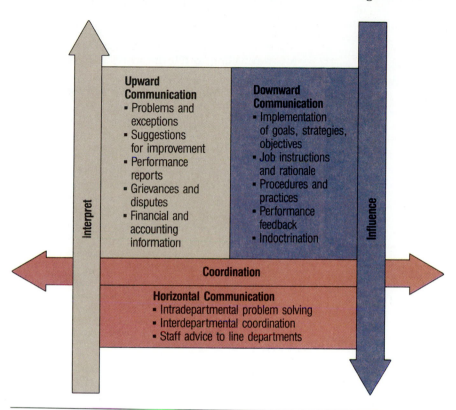

Upward Communication
- Problems and exceptions
- Suggestions for improvement
- Performance reports
- Grievances and disputes
- Financial and accounting information

Downward Communication
- Implementation of goals, strategies, objectives
- Job instructions and rationale
- Procedures and practices
- Performance feedback
- Indoctrination

Interpret

Influence

Coordination

Horizontal Communication
- Intradepartmental problem solving
- Interdepartmental coordination
- Staff advice to line departments

Source: Adapted from *Organizations: A Micro/Macro Approach* by Richard L. Daft and Richard M. Steers, p. 538. Copyright © 1986 by Scott, Foresman and Company. Used by permission.

information sent from top management to subordinates in a downward direction. The president of Tenneco, for example, sends bulletins to his vice-presidents, who in turn send memos to their subordinates. Management communicates downward to employees through speeches, messages in company publications, information leaflets tucked into pay envelopes, material on bulletin boards, and policy and procedure manuals.

Downward communication in an organization usually encompasses the following topics:

1. *Implementation of goals, strategies, and objectives.* Communicating new strategies and goals provides information about specific targets and expected behaviors. It gives direction for lower levels of the organization. Example: "The new quality campaign is for real. We must improve product quality if we are to survive."

2. *Job instructions and rationale.* These are directives on how to do a specific task and how the job relates to other organizational activities. Example: "Purchasing should order the bricks now so the work crew can begin construction of the building in two weeks."

A Listening Check-up

What is your listening competency? Managers must be active listeners, but they seldom realize whether they are perceived by others as active listeners. The only way to know whether listening skills are sufficient is to ask someone else. For this listening check-up, select a friend or colleague with whom you communicate frequently and ask him or her to candidly answer the questions below. Communication may be easier if you agree to take turns answering the questions about one another.

1. On a 1 to 10 scale, with 10 excellent, how do you rate me as a listener? Why?
2. Can you recall any situations where I apparently wasn't listening to you?
3. Do I usually give you my full attention when you are talking?
4. Do you generally feel comfortable talking with me?
5. Do I ever cut you off, appear to be disinterested, or avoid eye contact?
6. Am I usually open to your feedback? Do I sometimes react defensively?
7. Do you feel that I'm genuinely interested in you as well as in what you are saying?
8. Are you willing to tell me when you feel I am not listening?
9. Do you have any specific listening suggestions for me now?
10. Would you be willing to do this again in six months?

Managers are encouraged to add, delete, or modify the above list of questions to suit their specific needs. The important thing is that by hearing answers to these questions, you will be able to assess and refine your listening skills.

Source: *Tuning In: A Guide to Effective Listening* by Robert Maidment. Copyright © 1984 by Robert Maidment, used by permission of the publisher, Pelican Publishing Company, Inc.

3. *Procedures and practices.* These are messages defining the organization's policies, rules, regulations, benefits, and structural arrangements. Example: "After your first 90 days of employment, you are eligible to enroll in our company-sponsored savings plan."
4. *Performance feedback.* These messages appraise how well individuals and departments are doing their jobs. Example: "Joe, your work on the computer network has greatly improved the efficiency of our ordering process."
5. *Indoctrination.* These messages are designed to motivate employees to adopt the company's mission and cultural values and to participate in special ceremonies, such as picnics and United Way campaigns. Example: "The company thinks of its employees as family and would like to invite everyone to attend the annual picnic and fair on March 3."

Although formal downward communications are a powerful way to reach all employees, much information gets lost—25 percent or so each time a message is passed from one person to the next. In addition, the message can be distorted if it travels a great distance from its originating source to the ultimate receiver. A tragic example is the following:

A reporter was present at a hamlet burned down by the U.S. Army 1st Air Cavalry Division in 1967. Investigations showed that the order from the Division headquarters to the brigade was: "On no occasion must hamlets be burned down."

*The brigade radioed the battalion: "Do not burn down any hamlets
unless you are absolutely convinced that the Viet Cong are in them."*

*The battalion radioed the infantry company at the scene: "If you think
there are any Viet Cong in the hamlet, burn it down."*

*The company commander ordered his troops: "Burn down that
hamlet."[23]*

*The event was known as Hands Across
America. Its cause was combating hunger
in the United States. Monsanto executives
used this opportunity for downward
communication of company values by
picking up the tab for a two-mile stretch
of employees. Monsanto also benefited
from upward communication in the form
of notes from employees describing their
wonderful feelings about Monsanto's
participation in the event.*

Upward Communication.   Formal **upward communications** include
messages that flow from the lower to the higher levels in the organization's hierarchy. Most organizations take pains to build in healthy channels for upward communication. Employees need to air grievances, report progress, and provide feedback on management initiatives.
Coupling a healthy flow of upward and downward communication insures that the communication circuit between managers and employees
is complete.[24] Five types of information communicated upward are:

1. *Problems and exceptions.* These messages describe serious problems
   with and exceptions to routine performance in order to make
   senior managers aware of difficulties. Example: "The printer has
   been out of operation for two days, and it will be at least a week
   before a new one arrives."
2. *Suggestions for improvement.* These messages are ideas for
   improving task-related procedures to increase quality or
   efficiency. Example: "I think we should eliminate step 2 in the
   audit procedure because it takes a lot of time and produces no
   results."
3. *Performance reports.* These messages include periodic reports that
   inform management how individuals and departments are
   performing. Example: "We completed the audit report for Smith
   & Smith on schedule but are one week behind on the Jackson
   report."
4. *Grievances and disputes.* These messages are employee complaints
   and conflicts that travel up the hierarchy for a hearing and
   possible resolution. Example: "The manager of operations
   research cannot get the cooperation of the Lincoln plant for the
   study of machine utilization."
5. *Financial and accounting information.* These messages pertain to
   costs, accounts receivable, sales volume, anticipated profits, return
   on investment, and other matters of interest to senior managers.
   Example: "Costs are 2 percent over budget, but sales are 10
   percent ahead of target, so the profit picture for the third
   quarter is excellent."

upward communication Messages transmitted from the lower
to the higher levels in the organization's hierarchy.

Many organizations make a great effort to facilitate upward communication. Mechanisms include suggestion boxes, employee surveys, open-
door policies, management information system reports, and face-to-face
conversations between workers and executives.

Despite these efforts, however, barriers to accurate upward communication exist. Managers may resist hearing about employee problems, or
employees may not trust managers sufficiently to push information upward.[25] In organizations such as Borg-Warner, innovations are being
tried for facilitating rather than stifling the upward flow of information.

Recognizing the challenges ahead in the financial services industry, IDS Financial Services, an American Express Company subsidiary, has created task forces to examine a broad range of topics and make recommendations for the future. These task forces have encouraged horizontal communication and opened new communication lines between product management personnel and the field force. Another form of horizontal communication among IDS employees, shown here, is a periodic lunch group made up of people from different departments. Facilitating communication among IDS employees is one of president Harvey Golub's top priorities.

horizontal communication The lateral or diagonal exchange of messages across peers or coworkers.

Borg-Warner

"Something had to be done to get management to listen," said a worker at Borg-Warner's Bellwood, Illinois, plant. The worker was referring to a Borg-Warner innovation called a *peer-review panel.* Peer-review panels have been installed at 11 Borg-Warner plants. They provide an outlet for employee complaints and a mechanism for resolving disputes with direct supervisors.

In a typical case, three names are selected randomly by the aggrieved employee from a pool of workers who have volunteered for peer-review duty. Each panel member receives up to 12 hours of training in peer-review guidelines. The panel also includes the plant manager and an employee relations representative. The panel hears the case and hands down a decision signed by all five members.

The system is working well. From the workers' perspective, peer review provides a useful communication channel: "If you've got another peer listening to you, you think you can get a better shot." Managers like it because they learn about problems quickly. Workers like it because they feel they get a fair hearing and it is a vehicle through which managers can learn about worker gripes.[26]

Horizontal Communication. **Horizontal communication** is the lateral or diagonal exchange of messages across peers or coworkers. It may occur within or across departments. The purpose of horizontal communication is not only to inform but to request support and coordinate activities. Horizontal communication falls into one of three categories:

1. *Intradepartmental problem solving.* These messages take place between members of the same department and concern task accomplishment. Example: "Betty, can you help us figure out how to complete this medical expense report form?"
2. *Interdepartmental coordination.* Interdepartmental messages facilitate the accomplishment of joint projects or tasks. Example: "Bob, please contact marketing and production and arrange a meeting to discuss the specifications for the new subassembly. It looks like we may not be able to meet their requirements."
3. *Staff advice to line departments.* These messages often go from specialists in operations research, finance, or computer services to line managers seeking help in these areas. Example: "Let's go talk to the manufacturing supervisor about the problem he's having interpreting the computer reports."

Recall from Chapter 8 that many organizations build in horizontal communications in the form of task forces, committees, liaison personnel, or even a matrix structure to encourage coordination. For example, Carol Taber, publisher of *Working Woman,* was bothered by the separa-

EXHIBIT   14.7

Formal and Informal Organizational Communication Channels

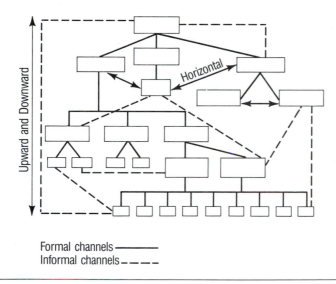

Formal channels ————
Informal channels – – – –

tion of departments at her magazine. She instituted frequent meetings among department heads and a monthly report to keep everyone informed and involved on a horizontal basis.[27]

Informal Communication Channels

Informal communication channels exist outside the formally authorized channels and do not adhere to the organization's hierarchy of authority. Informal communications coexist with formal communications but may skip hierarchical levels, cutting across vertical chains of command to connect virtually anyone in the organization. For example, Jim Treybig of Tandem Computers uses informal channels by letting any employee reach him through his computer terminal. Treybig also holds Friday afternoon beer busts at each of Tandem's 132 offices worldwide. The idea is to create an informal communication channel for employees. Treybig says, "Over beer and popcorn, employees are more willing to talk openly."[28] An illustration of both formal and informal communications is given in Exhibit 14.7. Note how formal communications can be vertical or horizontal depending on task assignments and coordination responsibilities.

Two types of informal channels used in many organizations are "management by wandering around" and the "grapevine."

Management by Wandering Around. **Management by wandering around (MBWA)** has been made famous as a communication technique by the books *In Search of Excellence* and *A Passion for Excellence*.[29] These books describe executives who talk directly with employees to learn what is going on. MBWA works for managers at all levels. They mingle with employees, develop positive relationships with them, and learn directly

informal communication channel   A communication channel that exists outside formally authorized channels without regard for the organization's hierarchy of authority.

management by wandering around (MBWA)   A communication technique in which managers interact directly with workers to exchange information.

Management by wandering around is one of the most powerful communication devices available to executives. Here Kenneth A. Macke, chairman and CEO of Dayton Hudson Corporation, walks around the Eden Prairie, Minnesota, Target store with store manager Jane Hanzlik. Mr. Macke appreciates the importance of being close to customers and employees: "You have to do a lot of looking and listening when you visit stores. . . . You have to talk to management people—but you also have to make it a point to talk with those who have the last contact with the customer. Generally it's the people at the end of the production line who really know what our customers are thinking."

from them about their department, division, or organization. For example, the president of ARCO had a habit of visiting a district field office and immediately going to a routine meeting of junior geologists discussing a minor property. Rather than schedule a big strategic meeting with the district supervisor, he would come in unannounced and chat with the lowest-level employees. Andy Pearson of PepsiCo starts his tours from the bottom up: He goes directly to a junior assistant brand manager and asks, "What's up?" In any organization both upward and downward communication are enhanced with MBWA. Managers have a chance to describe key ideas and values to employees and in turn learn about the problems and issues confronting employees.

When managers fail to take advantage of MBWA, they become aloof and isolated from employees. For example, Peter Anderson, president of Ztel Inc., a maker of television switching systems, preferred not to personally communicate with employees. He managed at arm's length. As one manager said, "I don't know how many times I asked Peter to come to the lab, but he stayed in his office. He wasn't that visible to the troops." This formal management style contributed to Ztel's troubles and eventual bankruptcy.[30]

In contrast, MBWA has been a tradition at Marriott, where Bill Marriott logs 200,000 miles a year visiting the chain's hotels and resorts.

Marriott Corporation

Mr. Marriott wanders around and checks out his hotels at odd hours. He may be in the kitchen at midnight and in the laundry room at 5 a.m. On one recent visit, Mr. Marriott went directly to the manager and congratulated him on clearing up an unwaxed strip at the base of a pillar in the lobby. "Looks good," he said approvingly. When he visited the kitchen, he addressed a few of the old-timers by their first names. During a typical two-hour tour, he will check the loading dock, exercise spa, storage lockers, and a half-dozen rooms and suites. He likes to greet workers, shake hands, and chat. Mr. Marriott also pays unexpected calls on customers to learn about their experiences with Marriott. Wandering around as a management style keeps his managers sharp and his employees happy.[31]

grapevine An informal, person-to-person communication network of employees that is not officially sanctioned by the organization.

The Grapevine. The **grapevine** is an informal, person-to-person communication network of employees that is not officially sanctioned by the organization.[32] The grapevine links employees in all directions, ranging from the president through middle management, support staff, and line employees. The grapevine will always exist in an organization, but it can become a dominant force when formal channels are closed. In such cases, the grapevine is actually a service because the information it provides helps make sense of an unclear or uncertain situation. Employees use grapevine rumors to fill in information gaps and clarify management

E X H I B I T   14.8

Two Grapevine Chains in Organizations

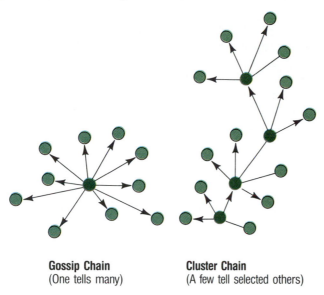

Gossip Chain
(One tells many)

Cluster Chain
(A few tell selected others)

Source: Based on Keith Davis and John W. Newstrom, *Human Behavior at Work: Organizational Behavior*, 7th ed. (New York: McGraw-Hill, 1985).

decisions.[33] The grapevine tends to be more active during periods of change, excitement, anxiety, and sagging economic conditions.

Research suggests that a few people are primarily responsible for the grapevine's success. Exhibit 14.8 illustrates the two most typical grapevines.[34] In the *gossip chain*, a single individual conveys a piece of news to many other people. In a *cluster chain*, a few individuals each convey information to several others. Having only a few people conveying information may account for the accuracy of grapevines. If every person told one other person in sequence, distortions would be greater.

Surprising aspects of the grapevine are its accuracy and its relevance to the organization. About 80 percent of grapevine communications pertain to business-related topics rather than personal, vicious gossip. Moreover, from 70 to 90 percent of the details passed through a grapevine are accurate.[35] Many managers would like the grapevine to be destroyed because they consider its rumors to be untrue, malicious, and harmful to personnel. Typically this is not the case; however, managers should be aware that almost five of every six important messages are carried to some extent by the grapevine rather than through official channels. When official communication channels are closed, destructive rumors can occur. Consider the events at Training Development Corporation.

Training Development Corporation

A bad-news rumor swept to tidal wave proportions among workers at Training Development Corporation (TDC) in California. Two vice-

The grapevine is an informal, person-to-person communication network of employees that is not officially sanctioned by the organization. It communicates information of special importance to employees. Grapevines tend to be more active during periods of organizational change, excitement, and uncertainty. In most grapevines, a few individuals actively convey information to several others. Although many managers would prefer not to have them, grapevines tend to be accurate and pertinent to business-related topics.

presidents and the president of the corporation joined in a brief conversation about the possibility of moving company headquarters some 300 miles to northern California. The idea, it turned out, was just talk and came to nothing. A secretary, however, passed word to her close friends in the work group that "a big move is underway—they've already picked the site. How many of us will even be asked to make the move?"

Management, of course, was silent on the topic because they had given up the idea. But workers interpreted their silence in the worst possible light: "Not only are they planning to move the company, but they're not even telling us. A big layoff must lie ahead after all we've given to this company." Workers expressed their fears around water coolers, over after-work drinks, and at social gatherings. A petition was finally circulated listing workers who pledged to quit the company if moving expenses and housing allowances were not offered to all employees with at least two years of employment. This petition was presented, with apparent hostility, to management. Every worker turned eyes and ears toward management's reaction.

That reaction, of course, was shock. How could a brief, dead-end idea have grown into such a monster? It started from a brief conversation overheard by a secretary. Since there had been no formal downward communication about the supposed move and it had created uncertainty, it was important news on which employees felt compelled to act. There was no formal channel of upward communication through which employees could express their concerns and learn whether the rumor was true or false. The grapevine pointed out the defects in the formal systems for downward and upward communication.

COMMUNICATING IN GROUPS

centralized network A group communication structure in which group members communicate through a single individual to solve problems or make decisions.

decentralized network A group communication structure in which group members freely communicate with one another and arrive at decisions together.

Frequent organizational communication occurs within groups and departments. Employees work together to accomplish tasks, and the group's communication structure influences both group performance and employee satisfaction. Research into group communication has focused on two characteristics: the extent to which group communications are centralized and the nature of the group's task.[36] The relationship between these characteristics is illustrated in Exhibit 14.9. In a **centralized network,** group members must communicate through one individual to solve problems or make decisions. In a **decentralized network,** individuals can communicate freely with other group members. Members process information equally among themselves until all agree on a decision.[37]

In laboratory experiments, centralized communication networks achieved faster solutions for simple problems. Members could simply pass relevant information to a central person for a decision. Decentralized communications were slower for simple problems because information was passed among individuals until someone finally put the pieces together and solved the problem. However, for more complex problems, the decentralized communication network was faster. Because all necessary information was not restricted to one person, a pooling of information through widespread communications provided greater input into the decision. Similarly, the accuracy of problem solving was related to problem complexity. The centralized networks made fewer errors on simple problems but more errors on complex ones. Decentralized networks were less accurate for simple problems but more accurate for complex ones.[38]

Research into the relationship between communication and task complexity has also been undertaken in business and government organizations.[39] When the complexity of the departmental task is high, a decentralized communication process, in which all members share information to solve problems, works best. Departments with complex tasks are research and development and strategic planning, and these should be organized for decentralized communications. When departmental tasks are simple and routine, such as for assembly line workers or bank tellers, communication can be centralized to a single person for efficient problem solving and decision making.[40]

Group communication processes have several implications for the design of organizational departments. Groups who deal with difficult, nonroutine problems need a free flow of communication in all directions. Members should be encouraged to discuss problems with one another and a large percentage of employee time should be devoted to information processing. Groups who perform routine tasks spend less time processing information, and thus communications can be centralized. Data can be channeled to a supervisor for decisions, freeing workers to spend a greater percentage of time on task activities.

E X H I B I T   14.9

Effectiveness of Group Communication Network

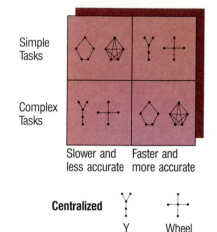

Source: Adapted from A. Bavelas and D. Barrett, "An Experimental Approach to Organization Communication," *Personnel* 27 (1951) pp. 366–371; M. E. Shaw, *Group Dynamics: The Psychology of Small Group Behavior* (New York: McGraw-Hill, 1976); E. M. Rogers and R. A. Rogers, *Communication in Organizations* (New York: Free Press, 1976).

MANAGING ORGANIZATIONAL COMMUNICATION

Many of the ideas described in this chapter pertain to barriers to communication and how to overcome them. Barriers can be categorized as those that exist at the individual level and those that exist at the organizational level. First we will examine communication barriers; then we will look at techniques for overcoming them. These barriers and techniques are summarized in Exhibit 14.10.

Barriers to Communication

Barriers to communication can exist within the individual or as part of the organization.

E X H I B I T   14.10

Communication Barriers and Ways to Overcome Them

Barriers	**How to Overcome**
Individual	
1. Interpersonal dynamics	1. Active listening
2. Channels and media	2. Selection of appropriate channel
3. Semantics	3. Knowledge of other's perspective
4. Inconsistent cues	4. MBWA
Organizational	
1. Status and power differences	1. Climate of trust
2. Departmental needs and goals	2. Development and use of formal channels
3. Communication network unsuited to task	3. Encouragement of multiple channels, formal and informal
4. Lack of formal channels	4. Changing organization or group structure to fit communication needs

Individual Barriers.   First, there are interpersonal barriers; these include problems with emotions and perceptions held by group participants. For example, if people are more concerned with their own feelings and emotions than with the people with whom they are communicating, communication will be difficult. Rigid perceptual labeling or categorizing of others prevents modification or alteration of opinions. If a person's mind is made up before the communication starts, communication will fail. Moreover, people with different backgrounds or knowledge may interpret communications in different ways.

Second, selecting the wrong channel or medium for sending a communication can be a problem. For example, when a message is emotional, it is better to transmit it face to face rather than in writing. On the other hand, writing works best for routine messages but lacks the capacity for rapid feedback and multiple cues needed for difficult messages.

semantics   The meaning of words and the way they are used.

Third, semantics often causes communication problems. **Semantics** pertains to the meaning of words and the way they are used. A word such as "effectiveness" may mean achieving high production output to a production superintendent but providing for employee satisfaction in the mind of a personnel staff specialist. Many common words have an average of 28 definitions; thus, communicators must take care to select the words that will accurately encode ideas.[41]

Fourth, sending inconsistent cues between verbal and nonverbal communications will confuse the receiver. If one's facial expression does not match one's words, the communication will contain noise and uncertainty. The tone of voice and body language should be consistent with the words, and actions should not contradict words.

Organizational Barriers.   Organizational barriers pertain to factors for the organization as a whole. First is the problem of status and power differences. Low-power people may be reluctant to pass bad news up the hierarchy, thus giving the wrong impression to upper levels.[42] High-power people may not pay attention or may feel that low-status people have little to contribute.

Second, differences across departments in terms of needs and goals interfere with communications. Each department perceives problems in its own terms. The production department is concerned with production schedules and may not fully understand the marketing department's need to get the product to the customer in a hurry. The engineering department's specialized jargon may make it difficult for engineers to communicate with less educated foremen on the shop floor.

Third, the communication flow may not fit the group's or organization's task. If a centralized communication structure is used for a non-routine task, there will not be enough information circulated to solve problems. When a decentralized, wide-open communication style is used for solving simple tasks, excess communication takes place. The organization, department, or group is most efficient when the amount of communication flowing among employees fits the nature of the task.

Fourth, the absence of formal channels reduces communication effectiveness. Organizations must provide adequate upward, downward, and horizontal communication in the form of employee surveys, open-door policies, newsletters, memos, task forces, and liaison personnel. Without these formal channels, the organization cannot communicate as a whole.

Overcoming Communication Barriers

Managers can design the organization so as to encourage positive, effective communication. Designing involves both individual skills and organizational actions.

Individual Skills.   Perhaps the most important individual skill is active listening. Active listening means asking questions, showing interest, and occasionally paraphrasing what the speaker has said to insure that one is interpreting accurately. Active listening also means providing feedback to the sender to complete the communication loop.

Second, individuals should select the appropriate channel for the message. A complicated message should be sent through a rich channel, such as face-to-face discussion or telephone. Routine messages can be sent through memos, letters, or electronic mail, because there is little chance of misunderstanding.

Third, senders and receivers should make a special effort to understand each other's perspective. Managers can sensitize themselves to the information receiver so that they will be better able to target the message, detect bias, and clarify missed interpretations. By understanding others' perspectives, semantics can be clarified, perceptions understood, and objectivity maintained.

The fourth individual skill is management by wandering around. Managers must be willing to get out of the office and check communications with others. Through direct observation and face-to-face meetings, managers will develop an understanding of the organization and be able to communicate important ideas and values directly to others.

Organizational Actions.   Perhaps the most important thing managers can do for the organization is to create a climate of trust and openness. This will encourage people to communicate honestly with one another. Subordinates will feel free to transmit negative as well as positive mes-

Ford has undertaken "participative management" and "employee involvement" programs to change from a centralized to a decentralized communication structure within groups. The major barrier to improved group communication is lack of trust, as shown in the top photo. Training programs help people overcome barriers and communicate in teams. In one office, managers were hesitant to provide quality and cost performance data to employees. But once employees were informed, they suggested actions that have saved millions of dollars. A decentralized communication structure is Ford's way of solving organization problems.

SOCIAL RESPONSIBILITY

Communication Skills Outside the Organization

The Equitable Life Assurance Society of the United States encourages its employees to make contributions outside the organization. For example, Jim Santangelo knows that communication problems exist outside an organization as well as within. Jim is a director in Equitable's Individual Financial Management Group. At night, he steps into a totally different role at Aurora Concept, a Flushing, New York, organization, whose volunteer staff helps children and their parents deal with a broad range of behavioral problems, from alcoholism and drug addiction to child abuse (see photograph below).

"On the surface, it seems the kids are the problem," says Santangelo, who serves as the liaison between the program and Aurora's Parents Association, "but one thing I've learned is that nobody exists in a vacuum.

Frustrations, tensions, and lack of communication can inhibit entire families.

"There are any number of examples; here's one. You begin to probe a little and maybe you find that the mother of the 15-year-old you're working with can't make it through the day without her Darvon, and Dad puts away a 6-pack every night—yet they get on their son's case for using pills. You understand why the boy is confused, so you call in his mother and father and get communication going among the three of them. When the people involved begin talking to each other, problems start turning into solutions."

Dozens of Equitable people devote large amounts of their free time to volunteer work. One employee, for example, spends weekends working for Emergency Medical Services. In Alaska, an employee helps deliver emergency food to the poor. Others work with retired people, youth organizations, mentally handicapped people, and hospitals.

Each of these employees uses skills learned at Equitable to help others. For Jim Santangelo, these skills pertain to interpersonal communication. Helping others is a great satisfaction. As Santangelo says when he looks on his work with Aurora Concept, "As much as I've given—I've gotten it all back tenfold."

Source: "Equitable in Review," Equitable Life Assurance Society of the United States, 1985.

sages without fear of retribution. Efforts to develop interpersonal skills among employees can be made to foster openness, honesty, and trust.

Second, managers should develop and use formal information channels in all directions. Scandinavian Design uses two newsletters to reach employees. Interstate Van Lines uses a daily training session at which

Phillips Petroleum Company has made a major move toward information sharing among employees by giving high status to local company newsletters, a formal information channel. There are now more than 30 field publications that employees prepare as part of their jobs. Jean Knight, a compensation aide at the Philtex plant in Borger, Texas, edits the Philtex News Letter. With the support of Phillips' management, these employee-editors provide a vital information link at the local level.

managers address workers concerning the business. Bank of America uses programs called "Innovate" and "Idea Tap" to get ideas and feedback from employees. Other techniques include direct mail, bulletin boards, and employee surveys.

Third, managers should encourage the use of multiple channels, including both formal and informal communications. Multiple communication channels include written directives, face-to-face discussions, MBWA, and the grapevine. Sending messages through multiple channels increases the likelihood that they will be properly received. In some cases, it is desirable to bypass the formal channel and go directly to intended receivers.

Fourth, the structure should fit communication needs. For example, interdepartmental task forces can be created to overcome communication barriers among departments. The organization can be designed to use teams, task forces, liaison personnel, or a matrix structure as needed to facilitate the horizontal flow of information for coordination and problem solving. Structure should also reflect group information needs. Where task complexity is high, a decentralized structure should be implemented to encourage discussion and participation. In a routine department, the structure can be centralized with a single person making most decisions.

SUMMARY

This chapter described several important points about communicating in organizations. Communication takes up 80 percent of a manager's time. Communication is a process of encoding an idea into a message, which is sent through a channel and decoded by a receiver. Communication among people can be affected by perceptions, communication channels, nonverbal communication, and listening skills.

At the organizational level, managers are concerned with managing formal communications in a downward, upward, and horizontal direction. Informal communications also are important, especially management by wandering around and the grapevine. Moreover, research shows that communication structures in groups and departments should reflect the underlying tasks.

Finally, several barriers to communication were described. These barriers occur at both individual and organizational levels, as do the skills and actions with which to overcome them.

Management Solution

Jaguar's quality problems were leading the company into bankruptcy despite having an attractive product with a venerable history. Led by president John Egan, communication was the key to a turnaround. To attack problems in production quality, senior executives met face to face with supervisors in task forces to discuss ways to reduce defects. Management also created a direct communication channel to employees—bypassing the union—by stopping the line each week to brief the troops. The most telling communication strategy was to record telephone conversations with several hundred buyers each month. Senior and middle managers appreciated the intensity of customers' feelings about dirty waiting rooms, incompetent mechanics, indifferent dealers, and "service that stinks." Hearing the customers' own words energized managers to do something about it. Top management also sent an unambiguous message to dealers: "You'd better satisfy the customer, because we are not going to be content with anything else." Two years later, Jaguar made the biggest one-year leap in customer satisfaction in history: It moved into sixth place, between Honda and Mazda.[43]

DISCUSSION QUESTIONS

1. Describe the elements of the communication process. Give an example of each part of the model as it exists in the classroom during communication between teacher and students.

2. How might perception influence communication accuracy? Is perception more important for ambiguous or unambiguous messages? Explain.

3. Should the grapevine be eliminated? How might managers control information that is processed through the grapevine?

4. What do you think are the major barriers to upward communication in organizations? Discuss.

5. What is the relationship between group communication and group task? For example, how should communications differ in a strategic planning group and a group of employees who stack shelves in a grocery store?

6. Some senior managers believe they should rely on written information and computer reports because these yield more accurate data than do face-to-face communications. Do you agree?

7. Why is management by wandering around considered effective communication? Consider channel richness and nonverbal communications in formulating your answer.

8. Is speaking accurately or listening actively the more important communication skill for managers? Discuss.

9. Assume you have been asked to design a training program to help managers become better communicators. What would you include in the program?

10. What should a manager consider when choosing a channel through which to send a message?

CASES FOR ANALYSIS

ATLANTA TOOL AND DIE INC.

The president of Atlanta Tool and Die Inc., Rich Langston, wanted to facilitate upward communication. He believed an open-door policy was a good place to start. He announced that his own door was open to all employees, and encouraged senior managers to do the same. He felt this would give him a way to get early warning signals that would not be filtered or redirected through the formal chain of command. Langston found that many employees who used the open-door policy had been with the company for years and were comfortable talking to the president. Sometimes messages came through about inadequate policies and procedures. Langston would raise these issues and explain any changes at the next senior managers' meeting.

The most difficult complaints to handle were those from people who were not getting along with their bosses. One employee, Leroy, complained bitterly that his manager had overcommitted the department and put everyone under too much pressure. Leroy argued that long hours and low morale were major problems. But he would not allow Rich Langston to bring the manager into the discussion nor to seek out other employees to confirm the complaint. Although Langston suspected that Leroy might be right, he couldn't let the matter sit and blurted out, "Have you considered leaving the company?" This made Leroy realize that a meeting with his immediate boss was unavoidable.

Before the three-party meeting, Langston contacted Leroy's manager and explained what was going on. He insisted that the manager come to the meeting willing to listen and without hostility toward Leroy. During the meeting, Leroy's manager listened actively and displayed no ill will. He learned the problem from Leroy's perspective and realized he was over his head in his new job. After the meeting, the manager said he was relieved. He had been promoted into the job from a technical position just a few months earlier and had no management or planning experience. He welcomed Rich Langston's offer to help him do a better job of planning.

Questions

1. What techniques increased Rich Langston's communication effectiveness? Discuss.
2. Do you think that an open-door policy was the right way to improve upward communications? What other techniques would you suggest?
3. What problems do you think an open-door policy creates? Do you think many employees are reluctant to use it? Why?

Source: Based on Everett T. Suters, "Hazards of an Open-Door Policy," *INC.*, January 1987, pp. 99–102.

THE TRAVEL DEPARTMENT

Helen Wesley runs the travel department for a large Fortune 500 corporation. Helen is a devoted employee and prefers written communications because they are precise and accurate, which she feels is necessary for making travel arrangements. April Faulk is the new advertising department head. She hasn't had time to meet other department heads, but she travels extensively. April didn't have the luxury of a travel department in her previous job, so she made all of her own flight and hotel reservations. When her bills arrived at accounting, they were forwarded to Helen for approval and explanation. Company policy states that travel requests are to be made in writing two weeks in advance and that all travel be scheduled through the travel department. Realizing that April had not read the travel policies given to her when she was hired, Helen wrote a terse memo: "I am enclosing another copy of the company's policy on travel. I'm sure this will help us handle your future travel needs more efficiently." Helen also sent a copy of the memo to April's boss.

For April's next trip, the travel department was contacted by her secretary, secured the best prices on air travel and hotels, and delivered the tickets to April's office. But on the morning of the trip, April's secretary called to request a different travel time, a different airline, a limo at the airport, and a different hotel. This caused last-minute work and doubled the price of the trip.

Helen asked one of her reservationists to talk to April's secretary and explain the policy again. This did little good. Last-minute requests from April's secretary continued to be phoned in, and written requests were incomplete and changed before the trip. Helen was truly upset about the complaints from her reservationists and the extra money these changes were costing the company.

Questions

1. What mistakes have Helen and April made with respect to their communications?
2. Are last-minute changes in travel arrangements to be expected in advertising work? If so, how might communications be structured differently between the advertising and travel departments?
3. If you were Helen, how would you handle this problem? Discuss.

Source: Based on "When a Peer Steps on Your Toes," *Savvy,* April 1986, pp. 16–18.

CHAPTER 15

Managing Organizational Groups

Chapter Outline

Groups at Work

What Is a Group?
Model of Work Group Effectiveness

Types of Groups

Formal Groups
Informal Groups

Work Group Characteristics

Size
Member Roles

Group Processes

Stages of Group Development
Group Cohesiveness
Group Norms

Managing Conflict

Causes of Conflict
Resolving Conflicts

Benefits and Costs of Groups

Potential Benefits of Groups
Potential Costs of Groups

Organizational Application of Group Concepts

Task Forces and Committees
Autonomous Work Groups

Learning Objectives

After studying this chapter, you should be able to:

- Identify the types of groups in organizations.

- Identify roles within groups and the type of role you could play to help a group be effective.

- Explain the general stages of group development.

- Explain the concepts of group cohesiveness and group norms and their relationship to group performance.

- Understand the causes of conflict within and among groups and how to reduce conflict.

- Discuss the assets and liabilities of organizational groups.

- Discuss organizational applications of group concepts.

Management Problem

William Gamblin, superintendent of production control for GM's Delco Electronics Division, saw the need for a new inventory management system. The new system had to reduce inventory yet provide reliable service for nearly 50 departments. It also had to maintain an accurate, secure inventory while providing an automated picking system that would minimize use of people. Its performance requirements were extraordinary, because it had to meter materials to departments based on their own assembly schedules. Developing the system would require knowledge of mechanical design, computers, computer software, machine controls, and production control. The puzzle facing William Gamblin was how to accomplish such a difficult task, obtain cooperation from multiple departments, and utilize expertise from several specialties.[1]

If you were William Gamblin, how would you proceed? Would you hire outside consultants, assign a project specialist to the task, or perhaps create an in-house team?

The issue facing William Gamblin is whether to create a team or task force to develop and implement a new inventory system. In making that decision, Gamblin must weigh the benefits and costs of using a group rather than an individual or outside consultant to accomplish the task. Groups are a major part of organizational life. The creation of groups, both permanent and temporary, is an important technique for achieving organizational goals. Groups are a basic building block of organizations, because most employees are assigned to some type of group. Employees also belong to groups outside the organization, such as a softball team, a dinner group, or the Jaycees.

The purpose of this chapter is to focus on groups that exist within organizations. We will define various types of groups, explore group stages of development, and examine such characteristics as size, cohesiveness, and norms. We will discuss how individuals can make contributions to groups and review the benefits and costs associated with groups in organizations. We will examine new applications of group concepts in organizations. Groups are an important aspect of organizational life, and the ability to manage them is an important component of manager and organization success.

GROUPS AT WORK

In this section, we will first define groups and then discuss a model of group effectiveness that summarizes important group concepts.

What Is a Group?

group A unit of two or more people who interact with and influence each other to accomplish a shared purpose.

A **group** is a unit of two or more people who interact with and influence each other to accomplish a shared purpose.[2] This definition has three components. First, two or more people are required. Groups can be quite large, running to as many as 100 people. Second, people in a group must have an opportunity for regular interaction. People who do not interact, such as when standing in line at a lunch counter or riding in an elevator, do not comprise a group. Third, people in a group have a shared purpose, whether it be to design a new type of hand calculator or write a textbook. Students often are assigned to groups to do classwork assignments, in which case the purpose is to perform the assignment and receive an acceptable grade.

Model of Work Group Effectiveness

This Pan Am crew at London's Heathrow Airport prepares to board a Boeing 747. It is considered a group because it consists of people who interact with and influence one another to accomplish a shared purpose. Contextual factors such as group structure, composition, size, and roles may all influence the cohesiveness and norms that have evolved within the flight crew. Passengers, however, are not considered part of a group because they need not interact to accomplish a common purpose.

Some of the factors associated with group effectiveness are illustrated in Exhibit 15.1. Note that work group effectiveness is based on two outcomes—productive output and personal satisfaction. *Satisfaction* pertains to the group's ability to meet the personal needs of its members and hence maintain their membership and commitment. *Productive output* pertains to the quality and quantity of task outputs as defined by group goals.

The factors that influence group effectiveness begin with the organizational context.[3] The organizational context in which the group operates is described in other chapters and includes such factors as structure, strategy, environment, and control systems. Within that context, managers define groups. Important group characteristics are the type of group, the group structure, and group composition. Managers must decide when to create permanent groups within the formal command structure and when to use a temporary task group. Group size and roles also are important. Managers must also consider whether a group is the best way to do a task. If costs outweigh benefits, managers may wish to assign an individual employee to the task.

EXHIBIT 15.1

Work Group Effectiveness Model

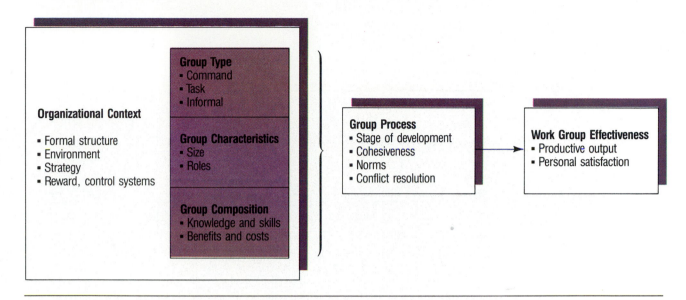

These group characteristics influence processes internal to the group, which in turn affect output and satisfaction. Group leaders must understand and manage stages of development, cohesiveness, norms, and conflict in order to establish an effective team. These processes are influenced by group and organizational characteristics and by the ability of group members and leaders to direct these processes in a positive manner.

The model of group performance in Exhibit 15.1 is the basis for this chapter. In the following sections, we will examine types of organizational groups, group structure, internal processes, and group benefits and costs.

TYPES OF GROUPS

Many types of groups exist within organizations. The easiest way to classify groups is in terms of those created as part of the organization's formal structure and those that arise informally within the organization.

Formal Groups

Formal groups are created by the organization to perform a specific task. Two common types of formal group are command groups and task groups.

A **command group** is composed of a manager and his or her subordinates in the formal chain of command. Sometimes called a *functional*

formal group A group created by the organization to perform a specific task.

command group A formal group composed of a manager and his or her subordinates in the organization's formal chain of command.

E X H I B I T   15.2

The Organization as a Series of Overlapping Groups

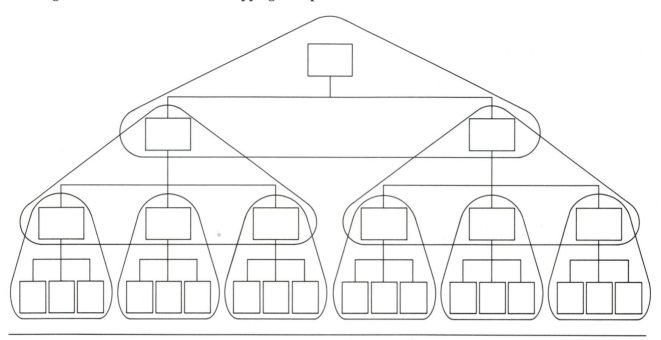

Source: Based on Rensis Likert, *New Patterns of Management* (New York: McGraw-Hill, 1961), p. 113.

group, a command group represents a specific department or work unit in the organization. The third-shift nursing group on the second floor of St. Luke's Hospital is a command group working under a nursing supervisor. A financial analysis department, a quality control department, an accounting department, and a personnel department are all command groups. Each is created by the organization to attain specific goals through members' joint activities and interactions. An illustration of one type of command group structure is presented in Exhibit 15.2. Note that middle-level managers are a part of two command groups and hence serve as "linking pins" between them. The command structure defines a series of groups that serve as building blocks to create the organization as a whole.

task group   A formal group created to achieve a specific goal within a limited time period.

A **task group** is created by the organization to achieve a specific goal within a limited time period. Task groups do not reflect the organization's command structure. Group members may be drawn from several departments, given a specific task, and disbanded after the task is completed. Task groups are known as teams, task forces, project groups, and committees.

A task group's short-term goal often involves coordination across several departments. IBM created a large task force to develop the System 360. Although it was formed for a specific project, the team remained in existence for several years. Contact among members was intense, and principal players met every day. Honda used a task force to create the

Civic automobile. Canon created a task group of 200 senior engineers to develop the Canon AE-1 camera. One of the largest task groups was formed when General Motors decided to downsize its automobiles during the 1970s. A project center was created to which 1,200 key people from the five GM auto divisions were assigned. The center lasted four years until the downsizing of autos was complete.[4]

Informal Groups

An **informal group** is created by employees themselves rather than by the organization and is designed to meet their mutual interests. Informal groups can be created on the basis of friendship or shared interests. **Interest groups** evolve because of a common personal interest among members. Examples of interest groups include groups for discussing current events, pursuing a hobby or sport such as model airplane flying or softball, or working on an invention that the company has not authorized. Chapter 10 described a *skunkworks*, in which employees get together in a group without company permission to pursue new ideas and innovations. A **friendship group** evolves because members enjoy personal interactions with one another. These groups exist for social interaction, such as shopping, lunching, or enjoying a Saturday evening gourmet dinner.

One interest group was formed when the president of Milwaukee's Brown Deer Bank, impressed with the book *In Search of Excellence*, initiated a discussion series for bank employees. The discussions took place at 7:30 on Thursday mornings and were entirely voluntary. Normally about 20 of the bank's 50 employees showed up. Discussing ideas in this informal atmosphere provided an opportunity for employees to talk about their feelings toward the company and a forum for their ideas. These discussions led to the creation of a formal task force to evaluate the bank's fringe benefit policy. The task force came up with a much better policy than that which company officers had originally established.[5]

Informal groups can include any employees in the organization, as illustrated in Exhibit 15.3. Note how formal task forces and informal groups both cut across the vertical command structure. Formal task groups often have members at the same organizational level, but informal groups can have members from any level or department. In the discussion group at Brown Deer Bank, for example, the president and first-level employees enjoyed a common interest.

WORK GROUP CHARACTERISTICS

Groups in organizations take on characteristics that are important to internal processes and group performance. Two characteristics of concern to managers are group size and member roles.

informal group A group created by employees rather than by the organization and designed to meet their mutual interests.

interest group An informal group formed on the basis of a common personal interest among members.

friendship group An informal group based on members' enjoyment of personal interactions with one another.

Pennwalt's assistant treasurer, Paul J. Clark (center), meets with the Payroll Department every other Friday to discuss new methods and equipment that will help streamline their operation. These employees are a command group, because they consist of a manager and his subordinates in the formal chain of command. Group meetings have produced significant improvements in the Payroll Department. Morale is high and turnover has been virtually eliminated because employees both contribute fully to the group and get something out of it.

E X H I B I T   15.3

Task and Informal Groups in an Organization

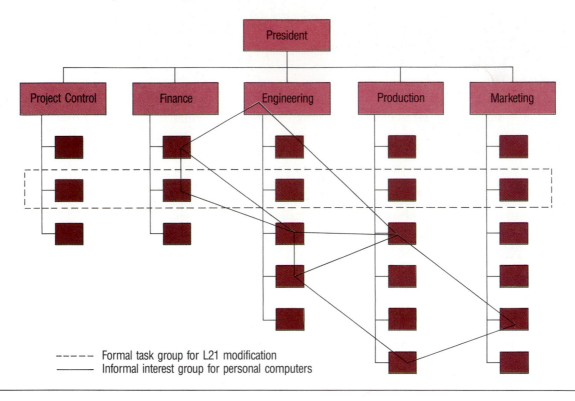

------- Formal task group for L21 modification
———— Informal interest group for personal computers

Size

The ideal size of work groups is often thought to be 7, although variations of from 5 to 12 are typically associated with good group performance. These groups are large enough to take advantage of diverse skills,
enable members to express good and bad feelings, and aggressively solve
problems. They are also small enough to permit members to feel an
intimate part of the group and to serve everyone's needs.

In general, as a group increases in size it becomes harder for each
member to interact with and influence the others. A summary of research on group size suggests the following:

1. Small groups (two to four members) show more agreement, ask
   more questions, and exchange more opinions. Members want to
   get along with one another. Small groups report more satisfaction
   and enter into more personal discussions. They tend to be
   informal and make few demands on group leaders.
2. Large groups (12 or more) tend to have more disagreements and
   differences of opinion. Subgroups often form, and conflicts
   among them occur. Demands on leaders are greater because
   there is more centralized decision making and less member
   participation. Large groups also tend to be less friendly. Turnover

This fitness center at Wetterau Incorporated was designed to promote employees' physical well-being, but it also provides a setting for the creation of informal groups. Sharing a personal interest, such as basketball, enables employees throughout the corporation to engage in informal group activities during lunch hours, after work, or on weekends. Providing opportunities for the formation of interest and friendship groups helps achieve communication and cooperation across departments.

and absenteeism are higher in a large group, especially for blue-collar workers. Because less satisfaction is associated with the specialized tasks and poor communication, group members have fewer opportunities to participate and feel an intimate part of the group.[6]

As a general rule, large groups make need satisfaction for individuals more difficult; thus, there is less reason for people to remain with the group or be committed to its goals. Groups of from 5 to 12 seem to work best. If a group grows larger than 20, managers should divide it into subgroups, each with its own members and goals.

Member Roles

In order for a group to be successful over the long run, it must be structured so as to both maintain its members' social well-being and accomplish the group's task. In successful groups, the requirements for task performance and social satisfaction are met by the emergence of two roles: task specialist and socioemotional.[7]

People who play the **task specialist role** spend time and energy helping the group reach its goal. They often display the following behaviors:

- *Initiation:* Propose new solutions to group problems.
- *Give opinions:* Offer opinions on task solutions; give candid feedback on others' suggestions.
- *Seek information:* Ask for task-relevant facts.
- *Summarize:* Relate various ideas to the problem at hand; pull ideas together into a summary perspective.
- *Energize:* Stimulate the group into action when interest drops.[8]

People who adopt a **socioemotional role** support group members' emotional needs and help strengthen the social entity. They display the following behaviors:

- *Encourage:* Are warm and receptive to others' ideas; praise and encourage others to draw forth their contributions.

task specialist role A role in which the individual devotes personal time and energy to helping the group accomplish its task.

socioemotional role A role in which the individual provides support for group members' emotional needs and social unity.

This product management task group at Dryden Press is meeting to coordinate activities for one of Dryden's books. With seven members, the group is small enough to allow everyone to express opinions, ask questions, and feel an intimate part of things. Members must actively fill both task specialist and socioemotional roles in order to insure the group's long-term success.

dual role   A role in which the individual both contributes to the group's task and supports members' emotional needs.

nonparticipator role   A role in which the individual contributes little to either the task or members' social-emotional needs.

- *Harmonize:* Reconcile group conflicts; help disagreeing parties reach agreement.
- *Reduce tension:* May tell jokes or in other ways draw off emotions when group atmosphere is tense.
- *Follow:* Go along with the group; agree to other group members' ideas.
- *Compromise:* Will shift own opinions to maintain group harmony.[9]

Exhibit 15.4 illustrates task specialist and socioemotional roles in groups. When most individuals in a group play a social role, the group is socially oriented. Group members do not criticize or disagree with one another and do not forcefully offer opinions or try to accomplish group tasks, because their primary interest is to keep the group happy. Groups with mostly socioemotional roles can be very satisfying, but they also can be unproductive. At the other extreme, a group made up primarily of task specialists will tend to have a singular concern for group task accomplishment. This group will be effective for a short period of time but will not be satisfying for members over the long run. Task specialists convey little emotional concern for one another, are unsupportive, and ignore group members' social and emotional needs. The task-oriented group can be humorless and unsatisfying.

As seen in Exhibit 15.4, some group members may play a dual role. People with **dual roles** both contribute to the task and meet members' emotional needs. Such people may become group leaders because they satisfy both types of needs and are looked up to by other members. Exhibit 15.4 also shows the final type of role, called the nonparticipator role. People in the **nonparticipator role** contribute little to either the task or the social needs of group members. They typically are held in low esteem by the group because they do not help meet group needs.

The important thing for managers to remember is that effective groups must have people in both roles. Humor and social concern are as important to group effectiveness as are facts and problem solving. Managers also should remember that some people perform better in one type of role; some are inclined toward social concerns and others toward task concerns. A well-balanced group will do best over the long term because it will be personally satisfying for group members and permit the accomplishment of group tasks.

Medical Center

The need for both the task specialist and socioemotional roles is illustrated in the management team from a major medical center. The team consists of Arnold, the hospital director, and his immediate subordinates, the directors of nursing, finance, the clinic, personnel, facilities, and the assistant hospital director. The hospital had been under probation by the state accrediting agency for two years. Nine months earlier, this administrative team had set up a crash program

E X H I B I T   15.4

Group Member Roles

	Low ← **Member Social Behavior** → High	
High **Member Task Behavior** **Low**	**Task Specialist Role** Focuses on task accomplishment over human needs Important role, but if adopted by everyone, group's social needs won't be met	**Dual Role** Focuses on task and people May be a group leader Important role, but not essential if members adopt task specialist and socioemotional roles
	Nonparticipator Role Contributes little to either task or people needs of group Not an important role—if adopted by too many members, group will disband	**Socioemotional Role** Focuses on people needs of group over task Important role, but if adopted by everyone, group's task won't be accomplished

Source: Based on Don Hellriegel and John W. Slocum, Jr., *Management*, 4th ed. (Reading, Mass.: Addison-Wesley, 1986), p. 523.

to deal with the major accreditation problems. The team held a meeting just after a recent accreditation visit and unofficially learned that the evaluation would be positive.

Arnold called a special meeting to share this information and have the group assess how they had worked together during the preceding months. The first half hour of the meeting was spent in mutual congratulations. Members complimented one another and traded examples of departments' solutions to problems. Then the team shifted to a task focus. They examined in detail how they had worked together. The task-oriented members were quite specific. Arnold's administrative assistant was criticized for not meeting deadlines. The director of nursing played a social role by asking whether the assistant's feelings were hurt. The group identified other potential problems, such as coordination between the facilities manager and the director of the clinic. After these problems were solved, the group knew it could work together to face future challenges, meeting both social and task needs of members.[10]

E X H I B I T   15.5

**Five Stages of Group
Development**

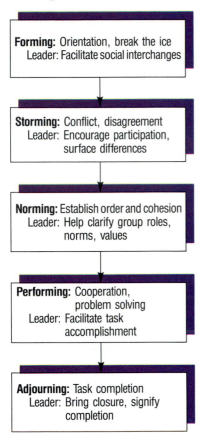

┌─────────────────────────────────┐
│ **Forming:** Orientation, break the ice
│ Leader: Facilitate social interchanges
└─────────────────────────────────┘

┌─────────────────────────────────┐
│ **Storming:** Conflict, disagreement
│ Leader: Encourage participation,
│   surface differences
└─────────────────────────────────┘

┌─────────────────────────────────┐
│ **Norming:** Establish order and cohesion
│ Leader: Help clarify group roles,
│   norms, values
└─────────────────────────────────┘

┌─────────────────────────────────┐
│ **Performing:** Cooperation,
│   problem solving
│ Leader: Facilitate task
│   accomplishment
└─────────────────────────────────┘

┌─────────────────────────────────┐
│ **Adjourning:** Task completion
│ Leader: Bring closure, signify
│   completion
└─────────────────────────────────┘

forming   The stage of group
development characterized by
orientation and acquaintance.

storming   The stage of group
development in which individual
personalities and roles, and
resulting conflicts, emerge.

GROUP PROCESSES

Now we turn our attention to internal group processes. Group processes pertain to those dynamics that change over time and can be influenced by group leaders. In this section, we will discuss the group processes of stages of development, cohesiveness, and norms. The fourth type of group process, conflict, will be covered in the next section.

Stages of Group Development

After an organization group has been created, there are distinct stages through which it develops. New groups are different from mature groups. Recall a time when you were a member of a new group, such as a fraternity or sorority pledge class, a committee, or a small group formed to do a class assignment. Over time the group changed. In the beginning, group members had to get to know one another, establish roles and norms, divide the labor, and clarify the group's task. In this way, members became parts of a smoothly operating team.

   In organizations, new task forces, teams, and committees are constantly being created. In addition, established command groups may have an influx of new members that creates conditions similar to those for a new group. The challenge for leaders is to understand the stage of the group's development and take action that will help the group improve its functioning.

   Research suggests that group development is not random but evolves over the five definitive stages illustrated in Exhibit 15.5. The five stages typically occur in sequence. In groups that are under time pressure or will exist for only a few days, these stages may occur rapidly. Each stage confronts group leaders and members with unique problems and challenges.[11]

Forming.   The **forming** stage of development is a period of orientation and getting acquainted. Members break the ice and test one another for friendship possibilities and task orientation. Group members find which behaviors are acceptable to others. Uncertainty is high during this stage, and members usually accept whatever power or authority is offered by either formal or informal leaders. Members are dependent on the group until they find out what the ground rules are and what is expected of them. During this initial stage, members are concerned about such things as "What is expected of me?" "What is acceptable?" "Will I fit in?" During the forming stage, the group leader should provide time for group members to get acquainted with one another and encourage them to engage in informal social discussions.

Storming.   During the **storming** stage, individual personalities emerge. People become more assertive in clarifying their roles and what is expected of them. This stage is marked by conflict and disagreement. People may disagree over their perceptions of the group's mission. Members may jockey for positions, and coalitions or subgroups based on common interests may form. One subgroup may disagree with another over the

This drilling crew for Panhandle Eastern is in the performing stage of group development. Crew members are committed to the group's task and coordinate with one another. This group's manager concentrates on maintaining high task performance. Because disruption or disunity on a drilling rig could result in severe injuries, the group must work through differences of opinion and establish roles prior to the actual drilling task.

total group's goals or how to achieve them. The group is not yet a cohesive team and may be characterized by a general lack of unity. Unless groups can successfully move beyond this stage, they may get bogged down and never become a high-performing team. During the storming stage, the group leader should encourage participation by each group member. Members should propose ideas, disagree with one another, and work through the uncertainties and conflicting perceptions about group tasks and goals.

Norming.   During the **norming** stage, conflict is resolved and group harmony and unity emerge. Consensus develops on who has the power, who is the leader, and members' roles. Members come to accept and understand one another. Differences are resolved, and members develop a sense of group cohesion. This stage typically is of short duration. During the norming stage, the group leader should emphasize oneness within the group and help clarify group norms and values.

norming The stage of group development in which conflicts developed during the storming stage are resolved and group harmony and unity emerge.

Performing.   During the **performing** stage, the major emphasis is on problem solving and accomplishing the assigned task. Members are committed to the group's mission. They are coordinated with one another and handle disagreements in a mature way. They confront and resolve problems in the interest of task accomplishment. They interact frequently and direct discussion and influence toward achieving group goals. The performing stage is associated with a mature, well-managed team. During this stage, the leader should concentrate on managing high task performance. Both socioemotional and task specialists should contribute.

performing The stage of group development in which members focus on problem solving and accomplishing the group's assigned task.

Adjourning.   The **adjourning** stage occurs in committees, task forces, and teams that have a limited task to perform and are disbanded afterward. During this stage, there is an emphasis on wrapping up and gear-

adjourning The stage of group development in which members prepare for the group's disbandment.

ing down associated with task completion. Task performance is no longer a top priority because the task has been completed or is within easy reach. Members may feel heightened emotionality, strong cohesiveness, and depression or even regret over the group's disbandment. At the same time, they may feel happy about mission accomplishment and sad about the loss of friendship and associations. At this point the leader may wish to signify the group's disbanding with a ritual or ceremony, perhaps giving out plaques and awards to signify closure and completeness for group members.

Sometimes a group will move to the performing stage only to revert to the storming stage when it is infused with new members. This happened at the Federal Reserve Board, which had to work its way back to the performing stage.

Federal Reserve Board

The Federal Reserve Board is composed of seven independent governors. Paul Volcker, chairman from 1979 to 1987, had a single mission: to stop inflation. Group members agreed with Volcker's direction until four new members were appointed during the mid-1980s. In 1986, Board members had to start over. They got into a big battle over the Board's priorities and ways to achieve them. In the first vote, the new Board members voted against Volcker's position on a discount-rate cut that had the potential to stimulate growth and hasten inflation.

Volcker's initial reaction to the dissenting vote was strong. It even raised speculation that he might resign. But that speculation was premature, because as the governors continued to work together, passions cooled. Members came to understand one another, and Volcker and his dissenters reached an understanding. Volcker even praised one dissenter as "a man of strong and independent views, as befits the Board." Volcker found that establishing a good working relationship with the new Board members needed just a little time. Volcker showed more tolerance for dissent, and his former opponents began to appreciate his view.[12]

Group Cohesiveness

group cohesiveness The extent to which group members are attracted to the group and motivated to remain in it.

Another important aspect of the group process is cohesiveness. **Group cohesiveness** is defined as the extent to which group members are attracted to the group and motivated to remain in it.[13] Members of highly cohesive groups are committed to group activities, attend meetings, and are happy when the group succeeds. Members of less cohesive groups are less concerned about the group's welfare and success. High cohesiveness is normally considered an attractive feature of groups.

Determinants of Group Cohesiveness.   Three characteristics of internal group structure and activities influence cohesiveness. First is group interaction. The greater the amount of contact among group members and the more time spent together, the more cohesive the group. Through frequent interactions members get to know one another and become more devoted to the group.[14] Second is the concept of shared goals. If group members agree on goals, they will be more cohesive. Agreeing on purpose and direction binds the group together. Disagreement over group goals decreases cohesiveness. Third is personal attraction to the group, meaning that members have similar attitudes and values and enjoy being together.

Two other factors that influence group cohesiveness come from outside the group. The first is the presence of competition. When a group is in direct competition with other groups, its cohesiveness increases as it strives to win. Whether competition is among sales groups to attain the top sales volume or among manufacturing departments to reduce rejects, competition increases group solidarity and cohesiveness.[15] Finally, group success and favorable evaluation of the group by outsiders adds to cohesiveness. When a group succeeds in its task and others in the organization recognize the success, members feel good and their commitment to the group will be high.

For example, Compaq Computer, the astoundingly successful personal computer maker in Houston, encourages team cohesiveness. Compaq managers believe it is not individual superstars who make the company great but a bunch of bright people who are committed to the team. The team commitment was put to the test in 1983 when a senior manager wanted to produce a laptop computer that would be small enough to fit inside a briefcase. Mary Dudley, a market researcher, surveyed the market and concluded that there weren't enough customers to justify manufacturing a laptop computer. Dudley pushed her negative assessment because she was committed to the group. Compaq's history of frequent interactions, shared goals and values, and product success enabled Dudley to disagree with top management. Her point prevailed—and it was a good thing for Compaq, because laptop computers put out by other companies at that time were market flops.[16]

Consequences of Group Cohesiveness.   The outcome of group cohesiveness can fall into two categories—morale and productivity. As a general rule, morale is higher in cohesive groups. There are several reasons for high morale, including increased communication among members, a friendly group climate, maintenance of membership because of commitment to the group, loyalty, and member participation in group decisions and activities. High cohesiveness has almost uniformly good effects on the satisfaction and morale of group members.[17]

With respect to group performance, cohesiveness can have several effects. First, in a cohesive group, group members' productivity tends to be more uniform. Productivity differences among members is small be-

Frequent group interaction and shared goals increase group cohesiveness. Steelcase encourages free exchange of ideas among group members at all organizational levels. Employees participate in discussions and programs on improving productivity, profitability, and product quality. Because of the groups' good relationship with management, their cohesiveness is associated with excellent performance.

E X H I B I T   15.6

**Relationship among Group Cohesiveness,
Performance Norms, and Productivity**

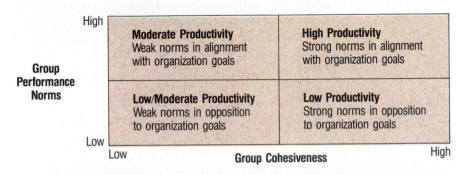

cause the group exerts strong pressure toward conformity. Noncohesive groups do not have this control over member behavior and hence tend to have wider variation in member productivity.

With respect to the productivity of the group as a whole, research findings suggest that cohesive groups have the potential to be productive, but the degree of productivity depends on the relationship between management and the working group. Thus, group cohesiveness does not necessarily lead to higher group productivity. One study surveyed over 200 work groups and correlated job performance with their cohesiveness.[18] Highly cohesive groups were more productive when group members felt management supported them and less productive when they sensed management hostility and negativism. Management hostility led to group norms and goals of low performance, and the highly cohesive groups performed poorly, in accordance with their norms and goals.

The relationship between performance outcomes and cohesiveness is illustrated in Exhibit 15.6. Note how the highest productivity occurs when the group is cohesive and also has a high performance norm, which is a result of its positive relationship with management. Moderate productivity occurs when cohesiveness is low, because group members are less committed to performance norms. The lowest productivity occurs when cohesiveness is high and the group's performance norm is low. Thus, cohesive groups are able to attain their goals and enforce their norms, which can lead to either very high or very low productivity.

As an example of the ability of cohesive groups to reduce differences in their members' productivity and restrict production when they are at odds with management, consider the new employee in a furniture factory. He worked too fast and also found finished parts in the sawdust. He announced to one operator, "Hey, look what I found," but got into trouble with the other employees and was told to stay away:

*Confused, troubled, almost in tears, not knowing what to do or where to go,
I lit a cigarette and began pacing up and down, puffing at my Camel.
While I'm pacing and puffing, Sam comes in, saying, "Lissen, kid, don't
get sore. I was trying to set you straight. Let me tell you what it's all about.*

The guys around, that is, the machine operators, agree on how much we are gonna turn out. And that's what the boss gets, no more, no less. Now sometimes any one of us might just fall behind a little, so we always keep some finished stuff hidden away just in case." The more he talked, the more I really began to feel like the enemy. I tried to apologize, but he just went on. "Look, kid, the boss always wants more and he doesn't give a damn if we die giving it to him, so we agree on how much we're going to give him— no more, no less. You see, kid, if you keep running around, moving the stuff too fast, the boss will get wise to what's going on."[19]

The kid understood, and he no longer worked faster than what was necessary for meeting the group norms. The group had norms of low performance because they had a poor relationship with management.

Group Norms

A group **norm** is a standard of conduct that is shared by group members and guides their behavior.[20] Norms are informal. They are not written down as are rules and procedures. Norms are valuable because they define boundaries of acceptable behavior. They make life easier for group members by providing a frame of reference for what is right and wrong. Norms identify key group values, clarify role expectations, and facilitate group survival. For example, union members may develop a norm of not cooperating with management because they don't trust management's motives. In this way, norms protect the group and express key values.

Norms begin to develop in the first interactions among members of a new group.[21] Norms that apply to both day-to-day behavior and employee output and performance gradually evolve. Norms thus tell members what is acceptable and direct members' actions toward acceptable productivity or performance. Four common ways in which norms develop for controlling and directing behavior are illustrated in Exhibit 15.7.[22]

Critical Events.   Often there are *critical events* in a group's history that establish an important precedent. One example occurred when Arthur Schlesinger, despite his serious reservations about the Bay of Pigs invasion, was pressured by Attorney General Robert Kennedy not to raise his objections to President Kennedy. This critical incident helped create a norm in which group members refrained from expressing disagreement with the President.

Any critical event can lead to the creation of a norm. In one organization, a department head invited the entire staff to his house for dinner. The next day people discovered that no one had attended, and this resulted in a norm prohibiting outside entertaining.[23]

Primacy.   *Primacy* means that the first behaviors that occur in a group often set a precedent for later group expectations. For example, members often expect to sit in the same seats at the second and third meetings as they did in the first. If the first meeting is very informal, people expect later meetings to also be informal, and that becomes the norm. Managers should be aware of the importance of primacy and design group meetings to establish norms that will support correct behavior and performance goals.

norm   A standard of conduct that is shared by group members and guides their behavior.

E X H I B I T   15.7

Four Sources of Group Norms

Source: Based on D. C. Feldman, "The Development and Enforcement of Group Norms," *Academy of Management Review* 9 (1984), pp. 47–53.

Carryover Behaviors.   *Carryover behaviors* bring norms into the group from other, similar groups. When students attend job interviews in one company, they learn behavioral norms that apply to interviews with other companies. When an audit team develops a norm for interviewing one company, it applies for audits of others. University students do not have to continually learn new norms from class to class; there are norms that regulate basic behaviors. The same is true for small groups created to do classwork. Norms brought into the group from outside indicate that students should participate equally and help members get a reasonable grade.

Explicit Statements.   With *explicit statements,* leaders or group members can initiate norms by articulating them to the group. Explicit statements by formal and informal leaders can have considerable impact. In one organization, the supervisor advises new recruits to be seen and not heard. In another, recruits are told that they are expected to be fully participating members of the department. Such explicit statements make a big difference in member behavior and define norms for the group.

Making explicit statements is probably the most effective way for managers to change norms in an established group. Richard Boyle of Honeywell wrote a memo to create a new norm.

A norm is a standard of conduct that is shared by group members and guides their behavior. Columbia Gas managers are attempting to establish a no-smoking norm. This photo is from a video program that explicitly depicts the problems associated with smoking. The developing norm is also influenced by carryover behaviors from outside the company that have emerged to protect nonsmokers' rights. The new norm will be further encouraged by a task force that is studying Columbia's situation and may recommend smoking restrictions.

Honeywell

Honeywell undertook a major change program to relax the company's traditional militaristic style of management and substitute a more participative approach. The absence of clear guidelines called for explicit statements from management. One norm of the company was excessive formality. Richard Boyle, vice-president and group executive for Honeywell Defense and Marine Systems Group in Minneapolis, wrote a memo called "Loosening Up the Tie." The memo said in part:

> *To conserve energy, thermostat settings are higher in the summer and lower in the winter than previously experienced. To compensate, more comfortable clothing appropriate to the summer season in Minnesota will help make the working environment more pleasant and comfortable.*
>
> *I wish to announce a relaxed wearing apparel policy, and loosen my tie for the summer. Let's try it starting on May 15th and tentatively ending on September 15th. Since departments vary in customer contact and, depending on location, may even vary slightly in temperature, Department Heads are hereby given authority to allow variations. . . .*
>
> *This change requires each of us to use good judgment. On the one extreme it means you do not have to wear a tie; on the other tennis shoes, shorts, and a t-shirt is too relaxed. Have a comfortable, enjoyable summer. I hope to.*

The tie memo helped demonstrate management's interest in developing a relaxed, more casual atmosphere at Honeywell. Employee response suggested that the freedom to exercise common sense over arbitrary rules was healthy for the organization. When Mr. Boyle showed up at the office without a tie, people really began to believe that the new dress code was okay.[24]

MANAGING CONFLICT

The final characteristic of group process is conflict. Whenever people work together in groups, some conflict is inevitable. Conflict can arise among members within a group or between one group and another. **Conflict** refers to antagonistic interaction in which one party attempts to block the intentions or goals of another.[25] Competition, which is rivalry between individuals or groups, can have a healthy impact because it energizes people toward higher performance. However, too much conflict can be destructive, tear relationships apart, and interfere with the healthy exchange of ideas and information.[26]

conflict Antagonistic interaction in which one party attempts to thwart the intentions or goals of another.

Causes of Conflict

Several factors can cause people to engage in conflict.[27]

Scarce Resources.   Resources include money, information, supplies. In their desire to achieve goals, individuals may wish to increase their resources, which throws them into conflict. Whenever individuals or departments must compete for scarce or declining resources, conflict is almost inevitable.

Jurisdictional Ambiguities.   Conflicts also emerge when job boundaries and responsibilities are unclear. When task responsibilities are well defined and predictable, people know where they stand. When they are unclear, people may disagree about who has responsibility for specific tasks or who has a claim on resources.

Communication Breakdown.   Communication, as described in Chapter 14, is sometimes faulty. Poor communications result in misperceptions and misunderstandings of other people and groups. In some cases information may be intentionally withheld, which can jeopardize trust among groups and lead to long-lasting conflict.

Personality Clashes.   A personality clash occurs when people simply do not get along with one another and do not see eye to eye on any issue. Personality clashes are caused by basic differences in personality, values, and attitudes. Often it's a good idea to simply separate the parties so that they need not interact with one another.

Power and Status Differences.   Power and status differences occur when one party has disputable influence over another. Low-prestige individuals or departments may resist their low status. People may engage in conflict to increase their power and influence in the organization.

Goal Differences.   Conflict often occurs simply because people are pursuing conflicting goals. Goal differences are natural in organizations.

Individual salespeople's targets may put them in conflict with one another or with the sales manager. Moreover, the sales department may have goals that conflict with those of manufacturing. A salesperson may promise delivery next Monday to satisfy a customer, yet manufacturing may wait for a long production run that will reduce costs.

Salvo Inc.

An interesting example of conflict occurred within a product marketing team at Salvo, a designer of computer software programs. Product marketing teams developed demonstration tapes of their new games or programs for use in dealer stores. The tapes are filled with sound, color, and clever graphics that are successful sales tools. The marketing person on the team works up an outline for a tape based on product content. The outline is then submitted to the team member from the information systems department to work out displays and graphics.

Larry from marketing is energetic, has a good sense of humor, and has a high standard for excellence. He knows what a computer can do, but he is not a programmer. Larry submitted an outline of a new videotape to Eric in information systems for development. Eric, a new member of the team, is serious and somewhat introverted. He sent a highly technical memo to Larry explaining why the project wouldn't work as requested. Larry was upset because he didn't understand the memo or why Eric had written a memo instead of talking to him face to face. Eric is technically oriented and has a difficult time communicating with noncomputer people.

Larry and Eric had a blowup at their first meeting because of their different goals and personalities. Miscommunication further aggravated the situation. Also, it was unclear who was responsible for each task in the development of the demonstration tapes, because Eric was new and unaccustomed to taking orders from another team member. Although both Eric and Larry supposedly had the same team goal, the problems with personality, communication, jurisdictional ambiguity, and individual goals led to a severe conflict between them.[28]

Resolving Conflicts

What does a manager or team leader do when a conflict erupts within a group or among groups? Research suggests several helpful techniques for confronting and resolving conflicts.

superordinate goal A goal that cannot be reached by a single party.

Superordinate Goals. **Superordinate goals** are goals that cannot be attained by a single party.[29] A superordinate goal requires the cooperation of the conflicting parties for achievement. People must pull together. To the extent that employees can be focused on group or organization goals, the conflict will decrease because they see the big picture and realize they must work together to achieve it.

Bargaining/Negotiation. Bargaining and negotiation mean that the parties engage one another in an attempt to systematically reach a solution. They attempt logical problem solving to identify and correct the conflict. This approach works well if the individuals can set aside personal animosities and deal with the conflict in a businesslike way.

mediation The process of using a third party to settle a dispute.

Mediation. **Mediation** means using a third party to settle a dispute. A mediator could be a supervisor, higher-level manager, or someone from the personnel department. The mediator can discuss the conflict with each party and work toward a solution. If a solution satisfactory to both sides cannot be reached, the parties may be willing to turn the conflict over to the mediator and abide by his or her solution.

Providing Well-Defined Tasks. When conflict is a result of ambiguity, managers can reduce it by clarifying responsibilities and tasks. In this way, all parties will know the tasks for which they are responsible and the limits of their authority.

Facilitating Communication. Managers can facilitate communication to insure that conflicting parties hold accurate perceptions. Providing opportunities for the disputants to get together and exchange information reduces conflict. Efforts can be made to increase the dialogue among parties. As they learn more about one another, suspicions diminish and improved teamwork becomes possible.

For example, the conflict between Larry and Eric at Salvo Inc. over the demonstration tape was eventually resolved by improved communication, clear definition of their respective tasks, and stronger commitment to the superordinate goal of finishing the tape. Larry went to see Eric and discussed the problem with him. The discussion revealed that they were pursuing different goals because Larry wanted the tape right away and Eric wanted to keep it until he could perfect it. Discussing each point of view was the key to their solution. Debbie, another team member, agreed to help them so that the tape could be of high quality and still be finished in two weeks. Larry and Eric also worked out a schedule that specified their respective responsibilities and tasks.

Although some conflict is inevitable, superordinate goals and well-defined tasks help resolve conflict in high-performing groups. For example, Pier 1 Imports uses groups to set up new stores. Called Visual Merchandising Teams, these groups ready each new store by laying out the sales floor, creating crate, shelf, and free-standing displays, and arranging the lighting to enhance merchandise appeal. The groups are so efficient that the store is transformed from an empty shell to a grand opening in only two weeks.

BENEFITS AND COSTS OF GROUPS

In deciding whether to use groups to perform specific tasks, managers must consider both benefits and costs. Groups may have positive impact on both the output productivity and satisfaction of members. On the other hand, groups may also create a situation in which motivation and performance are actually decreased. When groups can take advantage of their members' abilities and motivation, they can come close to achieving their potential.[30]

Potential Benefits of Groups

Groups come closest to achieving their full potential when they enhance individual productivity through increased member effort, members' personal satisfaction, and integration of diverse abilities and skills.[31]

Level of Effort.   Early researchers noticed that cyclists achieved better times when they raced against others. This observation led to research on whether working in the presence of a group increased an individual's motivation and performance. **Social facilitation** refers to the tendency for the presence of others to enhance an individual's motivation and performance. Simply being in the presence of other people has an energizing effect.[32] The impact is even more important when others are evaluating an individual's performance. Thus, observation by managers is expected to increase employees' level of work intensity.

Social facilitation, however, does not always work in a positive direction. In some cases, people are inhibited and work less hard in the presence of others. They may waste energy simply trying to look busy. The presence of others may make the performance of cognitive tasks more difficult because it affects concentration. Social facilitation has its greatest positive effect on physical and routine tasks that require less concentration.

Satisfaction of Members.   As described in Chapter 13, employees have needs for belongingness and affiliation. Working in groups can help meet these needs. People who have a satisfying group environment cope better with stress and enjoy their jobs. Moreover, group involvement provides a means of participation, making employees feel they have more influence over their jobs. Working in a group makes the work more enjoyable. Satisfaction with coworkers is still another important outcome of group activities.

Job Knowledge and Skills.   The third major benefit of using groups to perform organizational tasks is the diversity of knowledge, abilities, and skills brought to the tasks. Groups have the resources of several members who can suggest shortcuts, offer alternative points of view for group decisions, and increase the level of participation and feedback available to individual members. Group members also learn from one another, thereby increasing everyone's knowledge and skills. The opportunity to increase skills combined with the diverse resources available to the group are major benefits of group work.

The willingness of group members to pitch in and help solve problems is illustrated in the following description by Andrew Grove of a decision made at Intel.

social facilitation   The tendency for the presence of others to influence an individual's motivation and performance.

This telephonics quality circle group at Knight-Ridder's Philadelphia Daily News *illustrates the benefits and costs of groups. The group meets regularly to discuss improved techniques for selling newspapers and can take advantage of social facilitation, member satisfaction, and diverse job knowledge to improve performance. However, if costs such as free riding or diffusion of responsibility get too great, the group may not be worthwhile. But so far the benefits outweigh the costs, and Knight-Ridder has created 58 teams in a program designed to encourage employees to contribute solutions to operational problems.*

Intel

"I just don't understand how your new way of measuring things around here will help us at all," the plant manager said, grimacing. Others at the meeting merely looked puzzled. The vice-president of manufacturing, the plant manager's direct superior, had just finished vigorously urging the use of a particular statistical indicator to determine whether the company's plants were delivering products on time. Faced with the plant manager's incredulity, the vice-president redoubled his efforts, trying again to win over everyone in the room.

The plant manager remained unconvinced. His colleagues then jumped into the fray. Arguments generated rebuttals, numbers collided with other numbers. New ideas began to surface, most of them to be immediately rejected, until eventually the heated exchanges dissipated. The still-animated group of people in the room suddenly realized, with considerable satisfaction, that they had now come up with the right statistical measure.

As the meeting ended, the vice-president shook his head in mock dismay. "It's too bad," he said, "that you people are so reticent." He put away his papers somewhat ruefully—his hours of preparation for the meeting had not resulted in his proposal being adopted. But he also knew that the solution was better than his original idea.[33]

Potential Costs of Groups

When managers decide whether to use groups, they must also assess certain costs or liabilities associated with group work. Sometimes groups don't work very well. The major reasons are free riding, coordination costs, and diffusion of responsibility.

free rider A person who benefits from group membership but does not make a proportionate contribution to the group's work.

Free Riding. The term **free rider** refers to a group member who attains benefit from group membership but does not do a proportionate share of the work.[34] Free riding is sometimes called *social loafing,* because members do not exert equal effort. In large groups, some people are likely to work less. For example, research found that the pull exerted on a rope was greater by individuals working alone than by individuals in a group. Similarly, people who were asked to clap and make noise made more noise on a per person basis when working alone or in small groups than they did in a large group.[35] The problem of free riding has been experienced by people who have participated in student project groups. Some students put more effort into the group project than others, and often it seems that no members work as hard for the group as they do for their individual grades.

coordination costs The time and energy needed to coordinate the activities of a group to enable it to perform its task.

Coordination Costs. **Coordination costs** include the time and energy required to coordinate the activities of a group to enable it to perform its task. Groups must spend time getting ready to do work and lose productive time in deciding who is to do what and when.[36] Once again student project groups illustrate coordination costs. Members must meet after class just to decide when they can meet to perform the task. Schedules must be checked, telephone calls made, and meeting times arranged in order to get down to business. Hours may be devoted to the administration and coordination of the group. Students often feel they could do the same project by themselves in less time.

Diffusion of Responsibility.   The final problem associated with group activities is the loss of individual responsibility. **Diffusion of responsibility** means that a single individual cannot be assigned responsibility for group outcomes. Because each person may be expected to do a part of the group task, no one is to blame if the group fails and no one gets the credit if it succeeds. Diffusion of responsibility also occurs when group members believe that other members will perform an undesirable task. Salespersons may not like to handle exchanges of merchandise because they get commissions only on new sales and hence will try to pass this duty to someone else. Likewise, dusting the shelves during slack periods may be avoided; no one does it because no one thinks it is his or her responsibility. Diffusion of responsibility can be resolved if group members are assigned specific responsibility for undesirable tasks. These tasks can be passed around in a logical way as long as everyone knows who is responsible.[37]

> **diffusion of responsibility**   The lack of individual responsibility for group outcomes.

ORGANIZATIONAL APPLICATION OF GROUP CONCEPTS

Group concepts are applied in many organizations through decisions to perform more activities through groups. These organizations establish task forces, committees, and other work groups as the best way to accomplish organizational tasks.

Task Forces and Committees

Some managers believe that committees and task forces are a waste of time. Groups are criticized for taking too long to perform a simple task or for reaching a compromise decision that satisfies no one. However, task forces and committees have considerable value.

Task forces are groups of employees formed to deal with specific tasks and existing only until the task is completed. For example, the tasks of creating a new product in a manufacturing organization and creating a new history curriculum in a university are complex because several departments are involved and there are many views to consider. A task force can be created with people who have the expertise to solve the problem. The task force provides a way to deal with a complicated issue, resolve conflicting points of view from several departments, and coordinate the diverse needs of the organization or university.

> **task force**   A group of employees formed to deal with a specific task and existing only until the task is completed.

Committees often are a permanent part of an organization's structure, and membership is usually based on organizational positions. J. P. Morgan's Credit Policy Committee meets weekly to review significant credit developments. The committee is responsible for seeing that credit quality is maintained and problems identified and dealt with immediately. Members include Morgan vice-presidents and senior vice-presidents.

committee   A long-lasting, sometimes permanent group in the organization structure created to deal with tasks that recur regularly.

A **committee** is generally long-lived and may even be a permanent part of the organization's structure. Committees often are formed to deal with tasks that recur on a regular basis. For example, a grievance committee handles employee grievances; an advisory committee makes recommendations in the areas of employee compensation, work practices, or company policies; a safety committee improves on-the-job safety; a recruiting committee handles the recruitment of professional employees; a loan approval committee approves bank loans. Membership on a committee may come from election by coworkers in the case of a grievance committee or appointment by management in the case of an advisory or safety committee.

Committees offer several advantages to the organization: (1) They allow organization members to exchange information; (2) they generate suggestions that can be offered to other organizational units; (3) they develop new ideas for solving existing organizational problems; and (4) they assist in the development of organizational policies.[38]

Membership on a committee is usually decided by the person's title or position rather than by personal expertise. Official representation is needed on a committee, while task force selection is based on personal qualifications for solving a specific problem. To get the best performance out of a committee, goals should be clearly defined, preferably in writing. The committee's authority should be clearly specified, and a chairperson with the ability to run an efficient meeting should be selected.[39]

Autonomous Work Groups

To take advantage of groups, organizations in recent years have been redesigned to emphasize group rather than individual work. IBM creates teams to work on new projects, one of which created the highly successful personal computer. Kollmorgen, a manufacturer of printed circuits, took a noticeable jump in success when president Bob Swiggett reorganized the company into a series of 75-person units. Seventy-five people are too many to work face to face, but each team was subdivided into smaller groups and each overall team was responsible for a single product line. W. L. Gore and Associates limits the size of its plants to 100 to 150 people. By keeping each plant small it has a family atmosphere, allowing people to identify with the plant as well as with their own work groups. Milliken & Company maintains that the right number for plants is about 100.[40]

Even giant corporations such as General Motors are trying to integrate group approaches into their production plans. When designing the new Saturn automobile, General Motors had a blank slate to design the plant structure as it wished and gave high priority to groups.

General Motors' Saturn Plant

In GM's new Saturn facility, work teams operate without foremen. Teams are created at all levels to replace the old hierarchy of bosses. Higher-level teams consist of representatives from management and the union. In its old-style assembly plants, GM had six levels of

EXHIBIT   15.8

Group Structure at GM's Saturn Plant

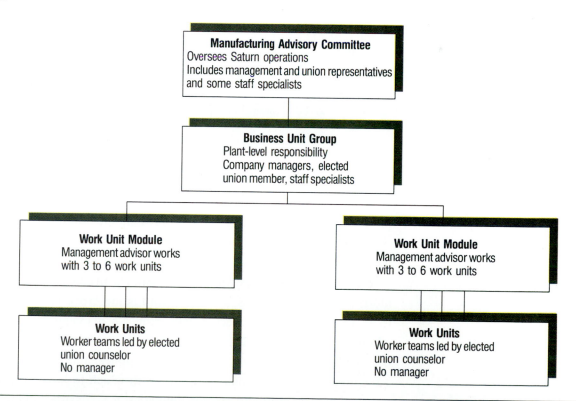

Source: Based on "How Power Will Be Balanced on Saturn's Shop Floor," *Business Week*, August 5, 1985, pp. 65–66.

MANAGERS SHOP TALK

How to Run a Great Meeting

Many executives believe that meetings are a waste of time. Busy executives may spend up to 70 percent of their time in meetings at which participants doodle, drink coffee, and think about what they could be doing back in their offices.

Meetings need not be unproductive. Most meetings are called to process important information or to solve a problem. The key to success is what the chairperson does. Most of the chairperson's contributions are made before the meeting begins. He or she should make sure discussion flows freely and follow up the meeting with agreed-upon actions. The success of a meeting depends on what is done in advance of, during, and after it.

Prepare in Advance.   Advance preparation is the single most important tool for running an efficient, productive meeting. Advance preparation should include the following:

1. *Define the objective.* Is the objective to communicate critical information? To discuss a difficult problem? To reach a final decision? If the purpose of the meeting is to "discuss the reduction of the 1989 research and development budget," then say so explicitly in the memo sent out to members.

2. *Circulate background papers.* Any reading materials relevant to the discussion should be given to each member in advance. These can be circulated with the agenda or with the minutes of the previous meeting. Members as well as the chairperson must be prepared, so make sure members know their assignments and have background materials.

3. *Prepare an agenda.* The agenda is a simple list of the topics to be discussed. It's important because it keeps the meeting on track. The agenda provides order and logic and gives the chairperson a means of control during the meeting if the discussion starts to wander.

4. *Issue invitations selectively.* If the group gets too big, the meeting won't be productive. If members with little to learn or contribute are invited, they will be bored. If everyone is expected to participate, membership between four and seven is ideal. Twelve is the outside limit; above twelve, many people will just sit and listen.

5. *Set a time limit.* A formal meeting should have a specified amount of time. The ending time should be announced in advance, and the agenda should require the meeting to move along at a reasonable pace. Unexpected issues can be handled if they will take little time; otherwise, they should be postponed until another meeting.

During the Meeting.   If the chairperson is prepared in advance, the meeting will go smoothly. Moreover, certain techniques will bring out the best in people and make the meeting even more productive:

6. *Start on time.* This sounds obvious—but do not keep busy people waiting. Some companies have a norm of waiting five minutes for everyone to arrive

---

authority, beginning with the plant manager and followed by the production manager, the general superintendent, the production superintendent, the general supervisor, and the foremen. There were 90 foremen per shift, each responsible for several workers.

The new structure has four rather than six primary levels, as illustrated in Exhibit 15.8. At the bottom is the Work Unit of from 6 to 15 workers led by an elected counselor. No manager is assigned. The team decides who does which job. It is almost self-sufficient, because it maintains equipment, orders supplies, and sets vacation schedules. It has a personal computer with which to keep tabs on production schedules and freight deliveries.

and then beginning the meeting even if some people are absent. Starting on time also has symbolic value, because it tells people that the topic is important.

7. *State the purpose.* The chairperson should start the meeting by stating the explicit purpose and clarifying what should be accomplished by the time the meeting is over. Members should already know the purpose, but this restatement helps refocus everyone's attention on the matter at hand.

8. *Encourage participation.* Good meetings contain lots of discussion. If the chairperson merely wants to present one-way information to members, he or she should send a memo. A few subtle techniques go a long way toward increasing participation:

a. *Draw out the silent.* This means saying, "Bob, what do you think of Nancy's idea?"

b. *Control the talkative.* Some people overdo it and dominate the discussion. The chairperson's job is to redirect the discussion toward other people. This is more effectively done by drawing other people into the discussion than by trying to quiet the talkative people.

c. *Encourage the clash of ideas.* A good meeting is not a series of dialogues but a cross-current of discussion and debate. The chairperson guides, mediates, stimulates, and summarizes this discussion. Many effective chairpeople refuse to participate in the debate, preferring to orchestrate it instead.

d. *Call on the most senior people last.* Sometimes junior people are reluctant to disagree with senior people, so it is best to get the junior people's ideas on the table first. This will provide wider views and ideas.

e. *Give credit.* Make sure that people who suggest ideas get the credit, because people often make someone else's ideas their own. Giving due credit encourages continued participation.

f. *Listen.* The chairperson should not preach or engage in one-on-one dialogue with group members. The point is to listen and to facilitate discussion. If the chairperson really listens, he or she will be able to lead the meeting to a timely conclusion and summarize what has been accomplished.

After the Meeting. The actions following the meeting are designed to summarize and implement agreed-upon points. Post-meeting activities are set in motion by a call to action.

9. *End with a call to action.* The last item of the meeting's agenda is to summarize the main points and make sure everyone understands his or her assignments. Deadlines should be prescribed. The chairperson should also commit to sending out minutes, organizing the next meeting, and mailing other materials that participants may need.

10. *Follow-up.* Mail minutes of the meeting to members. Use this memorandum to summarize the key accomplishments of the meeting, suggest schedules for agreed-upon activities, and start the ball rolling in preparation for the next meeting.

Source: Based on Daniel Stoffman, "Waking Up to Great Meetings," *Canadian Business,* November 1986, pp. 75–79; Antony Jay, "How to Run a Meeting," *Harvard Business Review* (March/April 1976), pp. 120–134; Andrew S. Grove, "How (and Why) to Run a Meeting," *Fortune,* July 11, 1983, pp. 132–140.

Management input comes at the next level up, which is called the Work Unit Module. Each consists of three to six work units and a management advisor. The advisor acts as a liaison to technical experts in engineering and personnel. The next level up is the Business Unit, which includes the plant manager, union representatives, and staff specialists. A fourth group, called the Manufacturing Advisory Committee, is responsible for the entire Saturn complex. It consists of UAW representatives, company officials, and staff specialists from the business units. This committee reaches consensus on decisions relevant to all Saturn employees, such as changes in salaries and benefits.

The new structure is a dramatic change from the old line of authority. To get a job in this plant, people are interviewed by teams of workers. The workers must feel the right chemistry and see that candidates have skills relevant to the group's requirements. Everything is structured around teams, and although this involves risks, GM managers feel it is worth it.[41]

SUMMARY

Several important points about the management of work groups were described in this chapter. Organizations have both formal and informal groups. The most common formal groups are command groups, task forces, and committees. These groups go through systematic stages of development: forming, storming, norming, performing, and adjourning. Group characteristics that can influence organizational effectiveness are size, cohesiveness, norms, and members' adopted roles. Advantages of using groups include increased motivation, diverse knowledge and skills, and satisfaction of group members. Potential costs of using groups are free riding, coordination costs, and diffusion of responsibility. All groups experience some conflict because of scarce resources, ambiguous responsibility, communication breakdown, personality clashes, power and status differences, and goal conflicts. Techniques for resolving these conflicts include superordinate goals, bargaining, clear definition of task responsibilities, mediation, and communication.

Management Solution

William Gamblin, superintendent of production control, faced the challenge of developing an automated inventory system. The system had to be sophisticated enough to provide reliable parts service for nearly 50 departments, reduce inventory, and anticipate possible materials shortages. Gamblin's solution was to establish a project team. The team included four members. Don DeMotte, an engineering specialist, worked on the computer systems and software needs. Evan Yoder was responsible for handling system machine controls. Tim Garner was responsible for racks, storage containers, and conveyor components. Gene King, a production control specialist, determined what was needed to improve the accuracy and efficiency of inventory management and storage. The engineers gathered data and wrote functional specifications. The team worked well together and coordinated the needs of several departments— indeed, teamwork was the key to developing a sophisticated system that solved Delco Electronics' inventory management problem. Group benefits far outweighed costs.[42]

DISCUSSION QUESTIONS

1. Why is it important for managers to understand groups? Discuss.
2. During your own work experience, have you been part of a command group? A task force? A committee? How did your work experience differ in each type of group?
3. What are the five stages of group development? What happens during each stage?
4. What factors influence group effectiveness? Are these factors within the control of group members or leaders?
5. Assume you are part of a student project group and one member is not doing his or her share. Which conflict resolution strategy would you use? Why?
6. Do you think some level of conflict might be healthy for an organization? Discuss.
7. When you are a member of a group, do you adopt a task specialist or socioemotional role? Which role is more important for a group's effectiveness? Discuss.
8. What is the relationship between group cohesiveness and group performance?
9. Describe the advantages and disadvantages of groups. In what situations might the disadvantages outweigh the advantages?
10. What is the difference between a task force and a committee?
11. What is a group norm? What norms have developed in groups to which you have belonged?

CASES FOR ANALYSIS

SPECIAL TASK FORCE

Phil Douglas, supervisor of the Special Task Force, was proud of the amount and quality of work that the members of the force had done in the few weeks they had been working together. He remembered the time one of the task force members had an idea about one problem that was costing the company a lot of money. It was close to lunchtime, so the group decided to discuss the idea over lunch. They were so excited and optimistic over the chance of success that they had spent two-and-a-half hours at the restaurant discussing possible results, problems, and implementation. But the idea was a success, and no one on the task force complained about all the nights spent working on the project.

However, Ted Young, Phil's boss, told Phil that some of the engineers in Fred Jacobi's department were griping about unfair treatment. "I'm sorry that some of our brainstorming and other creative techniques are being misunderstood, Ted," Phil replied, "but look at what we've been able to accomplish—we've improved the production methods and quality of our products, bringing in many more orders." Phil started to suggest, "Perhaps if Fred tried some of our methods, his engineers would be more content . . ."

"Try to see this from another point of view, Phil," Ted interrupted. "You and I know that your people are actually working when they take a two-and-a-half-hour lunch to discuss some new idea, but it doesn't look that way. Fred's engineers see them laughing and talking in a restaurant at 12 and then see them coming back to the office at 2:30. How do you think that looks to them?

"In their department, keeping regular hours is crucial. I think the only fair solution is to insist that the Special Task Force people keep the same hours, lunch hours, and coffee breaks as everyone else," Ted concluded.

"But Ted, no one's here to see them when they work on past 5:00. It's their freedom from a rigid schedule that has brought such good results."

"I'm sorry to interrupt, Phil, but I have to make a management meeting at two."

Phil left Ted's office and stepped into an elevator with several workers from Fred Jacobi's department. "Must be nice to get back from coffee break in time to go home," one engineer commented. Phil laughed and replied, "It's none of your business, but I'm going to the library."

"Yeh. He's going to check out the new librarian," another man rejoined. The group laughed, and Phil left the elevator more troubled than before. He hadn't realized how much the other departments resented his group.

Questions

1. What accounts for the high level of motivation on the Special Task Force? Evaluate other benefits and costs of using the task force.
2. What norms seem to have evolved on this task force? Is the group cohesive? If so, does this help or hurt productivity?
3. If you were Ted, how would you handle Fred Jacobi's complaint?

Source: Adapted by permission of the publisher, from "'Special' Task Force," *Supervisory Management,* August 1983, pp. 44–45, © 1983 American Management Association, New York. All rights reserved.

FRANKLIN SAVINGS & LOAN

The early 1980s was not a good time for most savings and loans, but Franklin was an exception. Located in a rapidly growing Florida city, Franklin prospered under deregulation. The number of branches increased from two to ten in just four years. In order to accommodate the rapid growth, the bank hired several new middle managers and loan officers to staff the new branches.

Because the branch managers came from various backgrounds and held different beliefs about how to manage a savings and loan, branch performance was uneven. Moreover, conflict across branches was high because branch managers disagreed with one another on proper strategies and operating procedures. The central operations staff was confused because of the different approaches within the branches. Top managers were puzzled because they felt that a branch is a branch and each manager should know how to run one. But top management also recognized that business objectives were not being met.

An analysis of Franklin's situation indicated that a team approach did not exist. Even within branches there was disagreement about lending and operations. The divergent opinions on how to run the savings and loan was blocking the development of teams.

Top management decided to attack the problem by bringing branch officers together to examine basic organizational issues. Branch managers met with top managers until they had hammered out a set of strategies and operating procedures with which everyone agreed. Follow-up branch meetings helped bring about unanimity in approach. Training was arranged where needed, and a reporting system was developed for indicating how well each branch was doing with respect to achieving Franklin's overall goals.

The key to the successful outcome was developing a feeling of collective respect within each branch and making branch managers feel part of a team working to accomplish Franklin's goals. This change came about because top management invested the time required for people to get to know one another as human beings. As one of the top managers said, "People are looking for something to belong to, and a cohesive work group is a very attractive base on which to build an organization."

Questions

1. How do you account for the success of groups at Franklin Savings & Loan?
2. Do you feel top managers handled emerging conflict correctly? What other strategies would you suggest?
3. What costs may arise with the new emphasis on teams in this organization?

Source: Based on Jac Fitz-Enz, "White-Collar Effectiveness," *Management Review* (May 1986), pp. 52–53.

CHAPTER 16

Corporate Culture and Revitalization

Chapter Outline

Corporate Culture

Symbols
Stories
Heroes
Slogans
Ceremonies

Strategy and Culture

Tough-Guy, Macho Culture
Work Hard/Play Hard Culture
Bet-Your-Company Culture
Process Culture

Reshaping Corporate Culture

Theory Z
Achieving Excellence

Techniques for Changing Corporate Culture

Symbolic Management
Change Tools

Techniques for Managing Revitalization

Revitalization Stages
Revitalization Framework

Learning Objectives

After studying this chapter, you should be able to:

- **Define corporate culture and give organizational examples.**

- **Explain the difference between underlying values and the surface characteristics that illustrate them.**

- **Explain organizational symbols, stories, heroes, slogans, and ceremonies and how they relate to corporate culture.**

- **Describe how corporate culture relates to strategy and the environment.**

- **Describe the characteristics of Theory Z and organizational excellence.**

- **Define a symbolic manager and explain the tools a symbolic manager uses to change corporate culture.**

- **Describe techniques other than culture that can be used to revitalize a corporation.**

Management Problem

Remember Harley-Davidson? It used to make motorcycles, and still does, but was nearly driven off the face of the earth by the onslaught of high-quality, low-priced Japanese motorcycles. In the late 1970s, Honda, Suzuki, Yamaha, and Kawasaki saturated the United States with inexpensive motorcycles. Honda took up to 56 percent of the U.S. market, leaving Harley with only 3.86 percent. Harley specialized in big bikes but sold only 26,000 in 1985 compared to 50,000 in 1979. All four Japanese manufacturers were found guilty of "dumping" bikes in the United States at low cost to win market share. Harley got a reprieve in 1983 with a law prohibiting the importing of large motorcycles for five years. But Harley-Davidson had been badly wounded, and management realized the company was inefficient. Harley used outdated production technology, managers fought with the union, employees were unmotivated, and product quality was terrible. President Vaughn Beals had five years in which to transform Harley into a super-efficient company: The Japanese were gearing up to export big bikes to the United States in 1988.[1]

If you were Vaughn Beals, how would you transform Harley-Davidson into a competitive company? What could you do to improve its structure, technology, and corporate culture?

President Vaughn Beals faces the challenge of installing a new value system, improved management, and updated technology to revitalize Harley-Davidson. Many North American corporations face similar problems. Competitive pressures on many businesses have increased. In industries such as airlines, trucking, and banking, deregulation has changed the ground rules. Perhaps the most serious threat has been tough foreign competition, especially from Japan, Korea, and Europe. North America has lost its leadership in radios, television, steel, home appliances, machine tools, watches, motorcycles, and, to some extent, automobiles.

The purpose of this chapter is to explore how organizations change their internal value systems and revitalize themselves. Harley-Davidson is just one example of hundreds of companies that need to catch fire in order to survive. The management field has responded to the need for improved management with best-selling books that propose techniques based on Japanese management *(Theory Z, The Art of Japanese Management)*, books on influencing corporate cultural values *(Corporate Cultures)*, and books on harnessing and motivating human resources *(In Search of Excellence, A Passion for Excellence)*. The ideas of corporate culture, Japanese management, and corporate revitalization are important because they help organizational leaders renew and revitalize their companies. In this final chapter on leading, we will discuss the important topics of changing cultural values and leading a poorly performing company toward improved performance.

CORPORATE CULTURE

culture The set of key values, beliefs, understandings, and norms that members of an organization share.

Culture can be defined as the set of key values, beliefs, understandings, and norms shared by members of an organization.[2] Culture represents the unwritten, informal norms that bind organization members together. Culture can be analyzed at two organizational levels, as illustrated in Exhibit 16.1.[3] At the surface level are visible artifacts, which include manners of dress, stories, physical symbols, organizational ceremonies, and office layout. The surface level represents the cultural patterns observable within an organization. At a deeper level are the values and norms that govern behavior. Values cannot be observed directly, but they can be interpreted from the stories, language, and symbols that represent them. These values are held by organization members who jointly understand their importance.

One organization with a strong culture is J. C. Penney Company. James Cash Penney believed in the golden rule: Treat employees and customers as you would like to be treated. He shunned the term *employee*, preferring to call workers *associates* because they were treated as partners. The dominant values in Penney's corporate culture are customer satisfaction and happy associates. Mr. Penney even wrote down the underlying values in seven guiding principles called "The Penney Idea." These values determined employee behavior. One store manager was reprimanded for making too much profit at customers' expense. Layoffs are avoided at all costs.[4]

Some companies put underlying values in writing so they can be passed on to new generations of employees. Hewlett-Packard created a list of cultural concepts that were central to its success in 1975. Called "The H-P Way," the list includes the following values: belief in people, freedom, and recognition; shared benefits and responsibility; helping

E X H I B I T   16.1

Two Levels of Corporate Culture

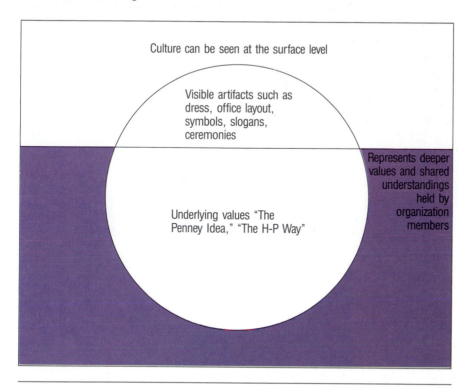

Culture can be seen at the surface level

Visible artifacts such as dress, office layout, symbols, slogans, ceremonies

Underlying values "The Penney Idea," "The H-P Way"

Represents deeper values and shared understandings held by organization members

one another; informality and first names; open communication; and performance and enthusiasm. These underlying values are reflected in day-to-day surface attributes and activities, such as having no time clocks, keeping units small so that individuals can be recognized, open office partitions, and a belief that managers should walk around and mingle with employees.[5] Visible organizational activities that illustrate corporate culture include symbols, stories, heroes, slogans, and ceremonies. Managers can influence corporate culture by attacking values directly or attacking surface behaviors.

Symbols

A **symbol** is an object, act, or event that conveys meaning to others. Symbols associated with corporate culture convey the organization's deeper values. Some organizations use a piece of art or a mission statement to symbolize important values. Eastern Airlines made paperweights that included metal from each aircraft it had flown during its history. The paperweights were distributed to key employees and symbolized Eastern's commitment to them. At Mary Kay Cosmetics, pink Cadillacs symbolize a top sales year. Sequint Computers Systems Inc. symbolized its family orientation by starting a yearbook and by installing a computer terminal in every employee's home so that family members

symbol An object, act, or event that conveys meaning to others.

Corporate culture is the set of values, beliefs, understandings, and norms shared by organization members. This painting, "The Spirit of Service," inspired the AT&T culture for nearly a century. It shows one of the company's first linemen, Angus MacDonald, checking the wires during the Great Blizzard of 1888. This painting symbolizes for employees the long-standing cultural value of dedication to service.

could talk to one another during the day. Another important symbol was the red buttons worn by people who performed tasks critical to the production of hardware that was behind schedule yet essential to company survival. The red buttons symbolized the gravity of the situation, and all Sequint employees were expected to pitch in and help anybody wearing one.[6]

Stories

story A narrative based on true events that is repeated frequently and shared by organizational employees.

Stories are narratives based on true events that are repeated frequently and shared among organizational employees. Stories are told to new employees to keep the organization's primary values alive. At Sony Corporation, a favorite story concerns the reason why every employee wears a corporate smock. After World War II, when Sony was small and struggling, its employees were struggling too. Since many could not afford a change of clothes, smocks were issued to prevent any damage to employees' clothing. The story symbolizes Sony's difficult beginnings and concern for employees.[7] Two popular stories at Hewlett-Packard communicate the values of the founders, David Packard and Bill Hewlett. After work hours one evening, Packard was wandering around the Palo Alto lab. He discovered a prototype constructed of inferior materials. Packard destroyed the model and left a note saying, "That's not the H-P way, Dave." Similarly, Bill Hewlett is said to have gone to a plant one Saturday and found a lab stockroom door locked. He cut the padlock and left a note saying, "Don't ever lock this door again. Thanks, Bill." Hewlett wanted engineers to have free access to components—even take them home—to stimulate the creativity that was part of "The H-P way." These stories are widely told at Hewlett-Packard; every employee knows them and the values they represent.[8]

Heroes

Heroes are figures who exemplify the deeds, character, and attributes of a strong culture. Heroes are role models for employees to follow. Sometimes heroes are real, like Lee Iacocca, and sometimes they are symbolic, such as the mythical sales representative at Robinson Jewelers who delivered a wedding ring directly to the church because the ring had been ordered late. The deeds of heroes are out of the ordinary but not so far out as to be unattainable by other employees. Heroes show how to do the right thing in the organization.

Some heroes are corporate founders and signify the corporation's history as well as values. Mary Kay Ash of Mary Kay Cosmetics is a hero, as are Dave Packard of Hewlett-Packard, H. Ross Perot, founder of Electronic Data Services Corporation, and Tom Watson of IBM. Other heroes are anointed by their peers in recognition of some special accomplishment. Companies with strong cultures take advantage of these achievements to define heroes who uphold key values.

At Minnesota Mining and Manufacturing (3M), top managers keep alive the heroes who developed projects that were killed by top management. One hero was a vice-president who was fired early in his career for persisting at a new product even after his boss had told him, "That's a stupid idea. Stop!" After the worker was fired, he wouldn't leave. He stayed in an unused office, working without a salary on the new product idea. Eventually he was rehired, the idea succeeded, and he was promoted to vice-president. The lesson of this hero as a major element in 3M's culture is: Persist at what you believe in. This hero reminds employees to keep plugging away even if they feel frustrated and discouraged, because they are not the first to overcome considerable odds in the process of innovation.[9]

On the first day Leo Burnett opened for business—August 5, 1935—the receptionist set out a bowl of fresh apples to welcome visitors to the advertising agency. Since then, apples have symbolized the warm, friendly, down-to-earth atmosphere of Leo Burnett and welcomed visitors and clients from all over the world. In 1985, Leo Burnett gave away 440,713 apples—more than 1,700 apples each day its offices were open. Here 660 Burnetters strike an apple pose to celebrate the agency's 25th anniversary.

hero A figure who exemplifies the deeds, character, and attributes of a corporate culture.

Slogans

A **slogan** is a phrase or sentence that succinctly expresses a key corporate value. Many companies use a slogan or saying to convey special meaning to employees. H. Ross Perot of Electronic Data Systems established the philosophy of hiring the best people he could find and noted how difficult it was to find them. His motto was "Eagles don't flock. You have to find them one at a time." Edward Carlson, president of United Airlines during the 1970s, coined phrases to indicate values that he wanted managers to adopt. One was "NETMA" ("Nobody ever tells me anything"), which encouraged managers to send information down the ranks.[10] T. J. Watson, Jr., son of the founder of International Business Machines, used the metaphor "wild ducks" to describe employees IBM valued. Wild ducks symbolized the freedom and opportunity needed to keep creative employees from being tamed. The moral of the "wild ducks" slogan was: You can make wild ducks tame, but you can never make tame ducks wild again.[11]

Slogans communicate cultural values because they can be used in public statements by senior executives. Slogans enable a philosophy to be widely communicated. "Everybody at Northrop is in marketing" and

slogan A phrase or sentence that succinctly expresses a key corporate value.

No company gives better ceremonies than Mary Kay Cosmetics. The sparkling display of pageantry and prizes inspires everyone and rewards the best performers of the previous year. At each ceremony, the top consultants and directors in sales, recruiting, and leadership take their places onstage. Queens are crowned and gifts showered in a dazzling tribute to employees' achievements. Mary Kay's ceremonies are the highlight of the year and communicate its values to all employees.

"The 11th commandment is never kill a new product idea" (3M) are slogans used to symbolize what the company stands for to employees and to people outside the organization.

Ceremonies

ceremony A planned activity that makes up a special event and is conducted for the benefit of an audience.

Ceremonies are planned activities that make up a special event and are conducted for the benefit of an audience. Managers hold ceremonies to provide dramatic examples of company values. Ceremonies are special occasions that reinforce valued accomplishments, create a bond among people by allowing them to share an important event, and anoint and celebrate heroes.[12]

The value of a ceremony can be illustrated by the presentation of a major award for meritorious sales or for developing a new product. The award can be bestowed secretly by mailing it to the employee's home or, if a check, by depositing it in a bank. But such procedures would not make the bestowal of rewards a significant organizational event and would be less meaningful to the employee. For example, an important annual event at McDonald's Corporation is its nationwide contest to determine the best hamburger cooking team in the country. Competition takes place among teams at the local level and gradually narrows down to a few teams at the national level. The cooking teams are judged on minute details that determine whether the hamburgers are cooked to perfection. The ceremony is highly visible, and McDonald's makes sure all employees know about it. The ceremony communicates to all employees the value of hamburger quality.[13]

A Philadelphia advertising agency uses an elaborate annual breakfast meeting as its major ceremony. Executives make speeches, jokes are told, and a feeling of togetherness is created. Gifts are presented to employees for long service. Promotions are announced and honors given for special accomplishments. Goals for the next year are established. Many events

E X H I B I T   16.2

Relationship between Underlying Cultural Values and Their Indicators

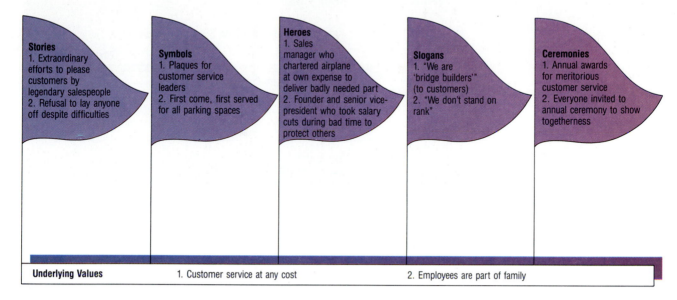

Stories
1. Extraordinary efforts to please customers by legendary salespeople
2. Refusal to lay anyone off despite difficulties

Symbols
1. Plaques for customer service leaders
2. First come, first served for all parking spaces

Heroes
1. Sales manager who chartered airplane at own expense to deliver badly needed part
2. Founder and senior vice-president who took salary cuts during bad time to protect others

Slogans
1. "We are 'bridge builders'" (to customers)
2. "We don't stand on rank"

Ceremonies
1. Annual awards for meritorious customer service
2. Everyone invited to annual ceremony to show togetherness

Underlying Values	1. Customer service at any cost	2. Employees are part of family

are consolidated into a single ceremony to increase their significance and to socialize new employees into the corporate culture.[14]

In summary, organizational culture represents the values and understandings that employees share, and these values are signified by symbols, stories, heroes, slogans, and ceremonies, as illustrated in Exhibit 16.2. The shared values help define important symbols, stories, and heroes, and cultural displays help determine company values. Managers can manipulate symbols to create the appropriate culture. Cultural values can be modified to be congruent with organizational strategy.

STRATEGY AND CULTURE

A big influence on shaping corporate culture is corporate strategy. Corporate strategy reflects the needs of the larger business environment. Corporate culture should embody what it takes to succeed in that environment. If the external environment and strategy require extraordinary customer service, the culture should encourage good service; if they call for careful technical decision making, cultural values should reinforce managerial decision making.

Deal and Kennedy, two researchers and consultants on corporate culture, have proposed that the relationship between environmental strategy and internal culture leads to four cultural categories, which are illustrated in Exhibit 16.3.[15] These categories are based on two strategic factors: (1) the degree of risk associated with the company's strategic

**Relationship of Strategy and Environmental
Feedback to Corporate Culture**

Feedback on Strategic Performance

		Fast	Slow
Strategic Decisions	High Risk	**Tough-Guy, Macho Culture** Construction, cosmetics, movies, advertising	**Bet-Your-Company Culture** Aerospace, new ventures, research and development, capital-intensive projects
	Low Risk	**Work Hard/Play Hard Culture** Fashion, marketing, consumer goods, electronics	**Process Culture** Government, utilities, insurance, financial services

Source: Based on Terrence E. Deal and Allan A. Kennedy, *Corporate Cultures: The Rights and Rituals of Corporate Life* (Reading, Mass.: Addison-Wesley, 1982), pp. 107–108.

decisions and (2) the speed with which the company receives feedback on the strategy's success. The four cultural types associated with these strategic differences are the tough-guy, macho culture, the work hard/play hard culture, the bet-your-company culture, and the process culture.

Tough-Guy, Macho Culture

tough-guy, macho culture A type of corporate culture that emerges in a strategic situation characterized by high-risk decision making, rapid feedback, and large-scale projects.

The **tough-guy, macho culture** emerges in a strategic situation with high-risk decision making and fast feedback. Decision makers quickly learn whether their risks were right or wrong. This culture often exists in organizations involved with large construction projects, cosmetics, movie production, venture capital, and advertising. Financial stakes are high. Decision makers bet their own futures on a $30 million movie project, a risky construction project in South America, or a new advertising campaign for a major customer. These industries move rapidly, and feedback on a new movie's or Broadway show's success is quick to come.

One example of a tough-guy, macho culture is the Crescent Engineering Company in Houston. Crescent provides construction and maintenance of pipelines and refineries around the world. This may seem a rather safe endeavor, but each new project is high in risk. Many unknowns influence the cost of providing these services in foreign countries. A serious mistake can ruin the company, and managers quickly learn if they have under- or overbidden on a project.

Heroes in a tough-guy, macho culture tend to be individualists. This culture does not inspire a team approach. Individuals take big risks in a fast-paced industry, and those who succeed become stars. A hero is the genius who pulls off the unexpected deal that becomes movie of the year or who submits the low bid on a huge contract and makes it work. The culture values tough guys who cry alone if they fail. Culture stories eulogize past risks that paid off. Ceremonies tend to focus on solving problems and avoiding the big mistake. Stars may band together to congratulate one another on their performances and to give awards for outstanding successes.

Work Hard/Play Hard Culture

The **work hard/play hard culture** is also characterized by rapid feedback, but strategic decisions are low risk. Strategy is characterized by many small decisions rather than a few big ones. This creates an internal culture in which fun, action, and fast pace dominate. The culture encourages people to be creative and to undertake a high level of activity and decision making.

Work hard/play hard values often arise in marketing-oriented firms and sales organizations. Mary Kay Cosmetics, Frito-Lay, PepsiCo, retail stores, and many computer manufacturers exist in this environment. The people in these companies make frequent decisions, each one fairly low risk, but the pace is fast and feedback is immediate. The new line of merchandise either sells or it doesn't. The salesperson either makes his or her quota or not. Values emphasize the fast pace and serving customer needs. Strategic decisions often pertain to finding a customer need and filling it. Because the environment changes, a stream of new products and services are required. The company must never stand still.

The heroes in the work hard/play hard culture are "super-salespeople." They conduct an extraordinary volume of activity and often help the team succeed, unlike heroes in a tough-guy, macho culture, who succeed alone by taking big risks. Ceremonies reinforce the values of hard work and high volume. Frequent sales conventions, meetings, and contests offer opportunities to blow off steam, party, and change the pace. Tandem Computers' weekly beer busts and Mary Kay's extravagant annual conventions serve this purpose.

One example of a work hard/play hard culture is Jay Jacobs Stores in Seattle. J. J. is a fashion store, and employees dress the "Jay Jacobs way." The emphasis is on thinking and looking young, hard work, creativity, and staying ahead of the crowd in the fast-moving fashion industry. Fashions change at a dizzying speed. Salesmanship and fashion savvy are more important than seniority, age, and seasoning. Employees work at a feverish pitch to promote new lines of merchandise and do it all over again. The dominant value is: The customer is number one. A team feeling predominates, as does a can-do attitude. Important ceremonies include issuing the *Encore* newsletter, which features top performers' stories, and giving people plaques after five years of service to initiate them as members of the J. J. family. People who make major sales are congratulated on the spot in front of other employees.[16]

Bet-Your-Company Culture

The **bet-your-company culture** is characterized by decisions that involve big stakes and several years before decision makers know whether they were correct. This is a high-risk, slow-feedback strategic environment.

work hard/play hard culture A form of corporate culture characterized by low-risk decision making, rapid feedback, and many small-scale decisions.

bet-your-company culture A form of corporate culture characterized by a high-risk, high-stake, slow-feedback strategic environment.

The computer-software firm of Microrim is a high-energy place where employees take two stairs at a time as Product Manager Daryl Care does here. Microrim has a "work hard/play hard" culture. Employees are high-achieving, hard-driving types who like sports. Once a month, everyone knocks off at 3 p.m. for a beer bust in the shipping department. Microrim is a powerful marketing firm with a strong people orientation. Managers work hard to maintain the camaraderie existing since Microrim's earliest days.

Companies involved in multimillion-dollar investments that take years to develop have this culture. Boeing Aircraft spent hundreds of millions of dollars to build the Boeing 757 and Boeing 767. Aerospace firms invest millions of dollars in new weapon systems in the hope of successful government and private sector sales. Oil companies such as Gulf and Exxon spend millions to explore for oil off shore and wait years before learning whether the risk has paid off. Companies in the capital-goods industry, such as Caterpillar Tractor, and mining companies, such as Alcoa, must invest millions in new products or new mining ventures, and knowledge of results is slow to come. A new biotechnology research company developed a bet-your-company culture because it was created without a single product. The company spent years doing research to produce a successful product before the money ran out.

The heroes in the bet-your-company culture are the wise, seasoned players. Length of tenure and experience with slow-feedback decisions are valued. Unlike in the work hard/play hard culture, young people are not expected to work hard and excel early. Heroic figures are people who persisted on a big project for years until it succeeded. These heroes provide emotional support for employees undergoing the uncertainty of taking a big risk and not knowing whether it will succeed. Ceremonies and rituals tend to emphasize formal meetings and uncertainty reduction. Seniority counts, and ceremonies give accolades to people whose projects pay off. Newer, youthful employees typically are not acknowledged or rewarded during these events. Ceremonies resemble business meetings for evaluating company progress rather than the hoopla and party-like events of the work hard/play hard culture.

Process Culture

process culture A type of corporate culture characterized by low-risk decision making, little or no feedback, and low-stake decisions.

The **process culture** is characterized by low-risk decisions and little or no feedback to employees about decision effectiveness. Outcomes are hard to measure; hence, employees concentrate on how decisions are made

MANAGERS SHOP TALK

Keeping Culture Strong

A strong corporate culture enables people to feel good about what they do. They are committed to a higher purpose and are likely to work harder. Being able to say "I'm with Morgan Guaranty Trust" rather than "I work at a bank" is important. An often overlooked way to strengthen corporate culture is through the selection and socialization of new employees. Recruits need to understand what makes their company's culture tick. Great American companies that pass a strong culture from one generation to the next include Delta Air Lines, Procter & Gamble, and Morgan Guaranty Trust.

Seven steps for cultural socialization are as follows:

1. *Subject employment candidates to a selection process so rigorous that it seems designed to discourage rather than encourage individuals to take the job.* Recruits should not be oversold. They should be grilled and told the bad as well as the good side of the job. At P&G, recruits are interviewed twice by line managers and must pass a test of general knowledge. Survivors go through additional interviews at headquarters. Morgan Stanley, a New York investment banking house, encourages people to discuss with family and friends the demands of sometimes working 100 hours a week.

2. *Subject newly hired individuals to experiences calculated to induce humility and to make them question prior behavior, beliefs, and values.* New recruits get little glory and work long hours at mundane tasks. At Procter & Gamble, a recruit might color in a map of sales territories. Morgan Stanley associates work 12- to 14-hour days and most weekends, and lunches are 30 minutes long in a very unplush cafeteria.

3. *Send newly humbled recruits into the trenches, pushing them to master one of the core disciplines of the company's business.* It takes 6 years to become an IBM marketing representative, 12 years to become a controller. There is no quick way to jump ranks and reach the top. Progress is slow and based on performance.

4. *At every stage of new managers' careers, measure the operating results they have achieved and reward them accordingly.* At P&G, new professionals are measured on three central factors: building volume, building profits, and conducting plant change. At IBM, managers track adherence to the core value of respecting the decency of the individual. Climate surveys and open-door procedures let IBM management know whether new employees are on the right track.

5. *Repeatedly promote adherence to the company's transcendent values—those overarching purposes that rise above the day-to-day imperative to make a buck.* The important thing at Delta is the "Delta family feeling." New employees hear about the sacrifices required. Managers take a pay cut during lean times, and senior flight attendants and pilots voluntarily work fewer hours to avoid laying off junior people. Before AT&T's divestiture, new employees learned about the transcendent value of guaranteeing phone service through any emergency.

6. *Constantly harp on watershed events in the organization's history that reaffirm the importance of your firm's culture.* Folklore and stories reinforce key values and the code of conduct for "how we do things around here." Stories have a moral that teach employees about key values. One story at Procter & Gamble concerns how the top brand manager was fired for overstating the product's features. The point is that honesty comes ahead of making money.

7. *Supply role models.* Exemplary individuals—the heroes—convey the traits the culture values most. Role models can be current employees, recognized as winners, whom the new employees can imitate. McDonald's has an obsessive concern for quality control, IBM for customer service, and 3M for innovation. Role models demonstrate these values for aspiring professionals. Role models are the most powerful culture training program available.

Source: Richard Pascale, "Fitting New Employees into the Company Culture," *Fortune*, May 28, 1984, pp. 28–39; Richard Pascale, "The Paradox of 'Corporate Culture': Reconciling Ourselves to Socialization," *California Management Review* 27 (Winter 1985), pp. 26–41.

and how work is accomplished. An important value here is that of following the procedures that management believes will get the job done. Low-risk, slow-feedback companies often include government organizations, insurance companies, and heavily regulated industries such as utilities. The financial stakes are low, and decision makers get little feedback concerning their impact.

The lack of feedback and difficulty of measuring outcomes focus cultural values on how work is done rather than on work outputs. Values consist of technical perfection and following procedures. Accounting firms and insurance companies cannot make mistakes despite slow feedback. This culture may foster red tape that specifies correct procedures.

Heroes in a process culture are those who devise new procedures and help meet employees' social and emotional needs. Ceremonies reinforce work patterns and procedures. Public awards call attention to formal titles and promotions. A major event is promotion from a class-30 technician to a class-35 supervisor. Movement up the formal hierarchy is a sign of success. Promotions also stimulate other cultural status symbols, such as a bigger desk, an improved office location, an extra chair, and perhaps a credenza.

One example of a process culture is Safeco Insurance Company. Safeco is stuffy and regimented, and working there is a lot like being in the Army. All employees take their coffee breaks at an assigned time (10 to 10:15 a.m. and 3 to 3:15 p.m.). The dress code specifies white shirts and suits for men and no beards. But the starchy culture is just what management wants: The company must be trusted to deliver on insurance policies. Reliability counts. No fads or fashions here; nonconformists need not apply. Employment is stable; the company values employees to the point where it eschews layoffs. However, extra work is not required either; people go home at 4:30 and are expected to work no more. Employees like the culture and feel that it's appropriate for the insurance industry, although it radically differs from cultures that exist in tough-guy, macho, work hard/play hard, and bet-your-company organizations.[17]

RESHAPING CORPORATE CULTURE

What happens when corporate culture is not in alignment with the organization's strategy and environment? Culture often reflects values that worked in the past. Cultures are slow to change and often lag behind environmental or strategy changes.[18] For example, Texas Instruments developed a strong internal culture of self-reliance and thus tended to be a closed organization. If TI didn't produce a product, it didn't exist. When TI built its own computer for the home computer market, it used only chips produced by other TI divisions and ignored the Z-80, an eight-byte chip made by another company that was used in most home computers. The TI culture became TI's weakness; it kept TI insulated from rapidly changing external markets in the home computer industry.

Playful, life-size sculptures of working people, such as this one by Stephen Hansen, add to the corporate culture at Herman Miller Inc., the innovative office furniture manufacturer. Along with vibrant wall art, the sculptures add to a physical environment designed to express cultural values that nurture creativity. Herman Miller executives seek participation of all employees in management decisions, and they encourage employees to try new things and make mistakes. Herman Miller has shaped its culture to fit an external environment that calls for innovative designs in office furniture and office environments.

For this market, a work hard/play hard culture was better than a process culture. TI had to change.[19]

Many organizations run into problems with culture when the bureaucratic, process form of culture dominates. Organizations become preoccupied with internal processes and lose touch with the marketplace. Two approaches to cultural change that have become popular in recent years are the adoption of Japanese management techniques and the adoption of excellence characteristics. Both of these approaches are directed toward greater participation by and utilization of the organization's human resources.

Theory Z

The Japanese perspective on human resource management has been influenced by William Ouchi's *Theory Z* and Richard Pascale and Anthony Athos' *The Art of Japanese Management.*[20] The success of Japanese firms is often attributed to their group orientation. The Japanese culture focuses on trust and intimacy within the group and family. In North America, in contrast, the basic cultural orientation is toward the individual and stresses individual rights and achievements. These differences in the two societies are reflected in how companies are managed.

Exhibit 16.4 illustrates differences in the management approaches used in America and Japan. American organizations are called Type A and Japanese organizations Type J. However, it is impractical to take a management approach based on the culture of one country and apply it directly to that of another country. **Theory Z** proposes a hybrid form of management that incorporates techniques from both Japanese and North American management practices. Type Z is a blend of American and Japanese characteristics that can be used to revitalize and strengthen corporate cultures in North America.[21]

Theory Z A management perspective that incorporates techniques from both Japanese and North American management practices.

E X H I B I T   16.4

Characteristics of Theory Z Management

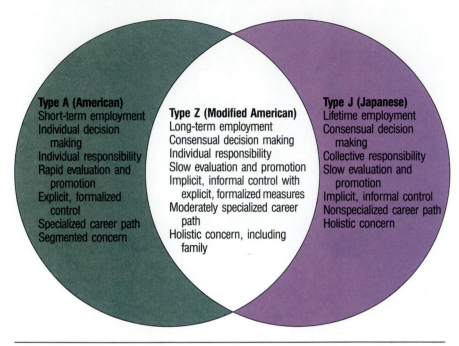

Type A (American)
Short-term employment
Individual decision
  making
Individual responsibility
Rapid evaluation and
  promotion
Explicit, formalized
  control
Specialized career path
Segmented concern

Type Z (Modified American)
Long-term employment
Consensual decision making
Individual responsibility
Slow evaluation and promotion
Implicit, informal control with
  explicit, formalized measures
Moderately specialized career
  path
Holistic concern, including
  family

Type J (Japanese)
Lifetime employment
Consensual decision
  making
Collective responsibility
Slow evaluation and
  promotion
Implicit, informal control
Nonspecialized career path
Holistic concern

Source: Adapted from William G. Ouchi and Alfred M. Jaeger, "Type Z Organizations: Stability in the Midst of Mobility," *Academy of Management Review* 3 (1978), pp. 308–311.

As illustrated in Exhibit 16.4, the Type Z organization uses long-term employment, a characteristic similar to the Type J organization. Long-term employment rather than rapid mobility across firms means that employees become familiar with the organization and are committed to and fully integrated into it. The Type Z organization also uses slow evaluation and promotion for employees as does the Type J organization. Individuals are expected to soak up corporate values and become fully integrated into the organization. Likewise, the highly specialized American convention of a narrow career path is modified to reflect career training in multiple departments and functions.

In the Theory Z approach, control over employees combines the U.S. preference for explicit and precise performance measures and the Japanese approach to control based on social values. The Theory Z approach also encourages the Type J characteristic of consensual decision making—that is, managers discuss decisions among themselves and with subordinates until everyone is in agreement. Responsibility for outcomes, however, is based on the American approach of providing responsibilities and rewards for individuals. Finally, Theory Z adopts the holistic concern for employees' total personal lives that is typical of Japanese management.[22]

Fujitsu Limited, the largest computer and telecommunications company in Japan, has created a cross-cultural Theory Z approach in its

Theory Z combines Japanese and American management techniques. The Japanese approach to employee welfare is illustrated by Toyota, which endeavors to make a positive contribution to the quality of life of employees and their families. Toyota provides employee social clubs and sports facilities, as shown here. Dormitories and apartments are available to employees at modest rent. Employees and their families have access to the Toyota hospital, as well as to Toyota's resort facilities throughout Japan. This concern for the "total employee" is being adopted by increasing numbers of North American companies in an attempt to improve quality and productivity.

American subsidiary. Mid-level managers work in interactive teams composed of senior managers, workers, and peers. The decision-making approach is consensual, and commitment to employees is long term. Managers are individually responsible for achieving goals, but they are also expected to encourage employee participation and communication. Recreational condominiums in locations such as California's Lake Tahoe, for example, show a holistic concern for employees' family and recreational needs. The hybrid management style used in America reinforces the Japanese understanding that employees *are* the company.[23]

Achieving Excellence

Perhaps spurred by ideas from Japanese management, American managers have reawakened an interest in attaining high-quality products through human resource management. The most notable publication in this area is *In Search of Excellence* by Peters and Waterman.[24] The book reported a study of U.S. companies selected on the basis of sustained high performance. The companies included Digital Equipment, 3M, Bechtel, Dow, Johnson & Johnson, Disney, Fluor, Caterpillar, Procter & Gamble, and McDonald's. These companies showed above-average performance for several years, and Peters and Waterman's research sought to uncover why. The findings revealed eight **excellence characteristics** that reflected these companies' management values and corporate culture.

excellence characteristics A group of eight features found to typify the highest-performing U.S. companies.

1. Bias toward Action.   Successful companies value action, doing, and implementation. They don't talk problems to death or spend all their time creating exotic solutions. Managers in these companies "do it, fix it, try it." The CEO of a computer peripherals company put it this way: "We tell our people to make at least 10 mistakes a day. If you are not making 10 mistakes a day, you are not trying hard enough."[25] H. Ross Perot, after selling his company, EDS, to General Motors and serving on GM's board, remarked on the action differences between the two companies: "The first EDSer to see a snake kills it. At GM, the first thing you do is organize a committee on snakes. Then you bring in a consultant who

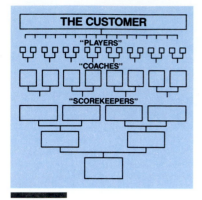

This unusual organization chart is AM International's way of achieving excellence. The importance of "closeness to the customer" is stressed in training programs, allocation of talented people for meeting customer needs, and placement of the customer at the top of the organization chart. The Players are the people who design, make, sell, and service products to insure customer satisfaction. Lower on the organization chart are the Coaches and Scorekeepers, who support the Players. Employees who are closest to the customer are at the highest level on the chart.

knows a lot about snakes. The third thing you do is talk about it for a year."[26]

2. Closeness to the Customer.   Successful companies are customer driven. A dominant value is customer need satisfaction, whether through excellent service or through product innovation. Managers often call customers directly and learn their needs. Successful companies value sales and service overkill. J. Willard Marriott, Sr., read every single customer complaint card—raw and unsummarized. Tom McAvoy, president of Corning Glassware, personally sifts through hundreds of proposals each year to help identify projects that will have a "significant strategic impact on the company."

3. Autonomy and Entrepreneurship.   Organization structure in excellent corporations is designed to encourage innovation and change. Technical people are located near marketing people so that they can lunch together. Organizational units are kept small to create a sense of belonging and adaptability. W. L. Gore & Associates will not let a plant grow larger than about 150 employees. Although large plants are technically efficient, president Bill Gore values human relations even more. The small plants encourage a family atmosphere, and it works. Companies such as IBM, 3M, and Hewlett-Packard give freedom to idea champions and create separate venture groups to provide the autonomy needed to generate creative new products.

4. Productivity through People.   Rank-and-file employees are considered the roots of quality and productivity. People are encouraged to participate in production, marketing, and new-product decisions. Conflicting ideas are encouraged rather than suppressed. The ability to move ahead by consensus preserves trust and a sense of family, increases motivation, and facilitates both innovation and efficiency. Even giant General Motors has learned that it cannot build high-quality cars with an antagonistic work force. At IBM, managers are told to spend a large portion of their time on individual employees' problems. IBM's culture respects the individual. IBM employees respond with commitment, goodwill, and quality work.

5. Hands On, Value Driven.   Excellent companies are clear about their value system. Managers and employees alike know what the company stands for. Leaders provide a vision of what can be accomplished and give employees a sense of purpose and meaning. Leadership is often "hands-on." Leaders are willing to roll up their sleeves and become involved in problems at all levels. They lead by example. At McDonald's, the norms of quality, cleanliness, value, and service are repeatedly stressed to all employees. Employees in excellent companies do not receive mixed signals or suffer doubts about important cultural values and what the organization is trying to accomplish.

6. Sticking to the Knitting.   Successful firms stay close to the business they know and understand. Successful firms are highly focused. For example, IBM, Boeing, Intel, and Genentech confine themselves to a single product line of computer products, commercial aircraft, integrated circuits, and genetic engineering, respectively. Similarly, 80 percent of

Kodak's sales come from photographic products, and 80 percent of Xerox's sales come from duplicating machines. Management in successful companies stresses the cultural value of doing what one knows best.

7. Simple Form, Lean Staff.   The underlying structural form and systems of excellent companies are elegantly simple, and few personnel are employed in staff positions. Large companies are subdivided into small divisions that allow each to do its job. For example, when Jack Reichert took over Brunswick Corporation, his job was to pump new life into a slow-moving, bureaucratic company. Two corporate planes were sold, the executive dining room was closed, and $20 million of administrative overhead was eliminated. The headquarters' staff was reduced from 560 to 230 people. The vertical hierarchy was reduced to only five layers of management between Reichert and the lowest employee. The simple structure and leaner staff reinforced the new cultural value of risk taking and decentralized decision making. Brunswick's stock value jumped 30 percent in one year.[27]

8. Simultaneous Loose-Tight Properties.   This may seem like a paradox, but excellent companies use tight controls in some areas and loose controls in others. Tight, centralized control is used for the firm's critical core values. At McDonald's, no exceptions are made to the core values of quality, service, cleanliness, and value. At IBM, top management will tolerate no disagreement with the cultural value of respect for the individual. Yet in other areas employees are free to experiment, to be flexible, to innovate, and to take risks in ways that will help the organization achieve its goals. Employees are not allowed to deviate from basic cultural values but have great freedom while working within them.

In Peters and Waterman's study, not every company scored high on all eight values, but a preponderance of these values was part of their management culture. Managers were intensely committed to implementing and living these values every day. One company that displays many characteristics of excellence is PepsiCo Inc.

PepsiCo Inc.

PepsiCo is on a roll. Pepsi-Cola is now the best-selling soft drink in supermarkets, and its new lemon-lime Slice is selling like mad.

What makes Pepsi excel is a fast-moving, risk-oriented management philosophy. As president D. Wayne Calloway puts it, the underlying philosophy is "ready, fire, aim." Pepsi is biased toward action rather than toward studying things to death.

Decentralization and autonomy create a highly charged atmosphere that pressures people to perform. High performers are well compensated. Low performers are fired. Calloway also believes that senior managers must look, listen, and learn. "Walk through the hallway at Pepsi, and you hear a lot of conversations about what's going on at the supermarket, what the competition is doing," which reflects the customer orientation.

Pepsi rewards autonomy and risk taking. It made a quick decision to purchase 7-Up Company in order to compete with Coca-Cola's Sprite brand, but the merger was not approved. Pepsi also got the jump on Coca-Cola by being the first to introduce a 100 percent Nutrasweet formula in 1984. To avoid tipping off Coca-Cola, Pepsi didn't test the product in advance. Diet Pepsi's sales volume soared 25 percent to $1.2 billion. As one manager says, "We believe it's more important to do something than sit around and worry about it."[28]

TECHNIQUES FOR CHANGING CORPORATE CULTURE

Japanese management approaches and the excellence characteristics represent important management values to which organizations can aspire. The logical next question is: How do managers actually change the culture? The organization's underlying value system cannot be managed in traditional ways using conventional techniques.

Symbolic Management

symbolic manager A manager who defines and uses signals and symbols to influence corporate culture.

To effect cultural change, managers must adopt a "symbolic manager" approach. **Symbolic managers** define and use signals and symbols to influence corporate culture. They are aware of both the underlying values to be encouraged and the surface artifacts that represent those values. An effective symbolic manager must master both ends of the spectrum, as follows:

1. *The symbolic manager must articulate and communicate a lofty vision that will generate excitement and enthusiasm for hundreds of employees.* A symbolic manager defines and communicates the central values that employees believe in and will rally around.
2. *The symbolic manager heeds the mundane, day-to-day details that provide the reinforcement for the lofty ideal.* The symbolic leader is a stickler for detail and directly instills the new cultural value through deeds as well as words. No opportunity is too small.[29]

The reason symbolic management works is that executives are watched by their employees. Employees attempt to read signals from what executives *do,* not just from what they say. For example, W. Scott Thompson, division general manager at Advanced Technology Inc., was amazed to learn that he had been sending the wrong signals to employees. He was extremely busy but finally found time to take departmental employees to lunch. He learned that employees were confused about where the company was going because he had not taken time to commu-

Jerry Kalov (front row with beard) is a symbolic manager. Kalov is president and CEO of Dynascan and is responsible for the climate of excitement illustrated here. He has articulated a vision for new products and innovation that will broaden Dynascan's approach to electronic markets. He also keeps pace with the day-to-day details that keep employees happy, satisfied, motivated, and focused on company goals.

nicate the company's mission and key values. Thompson learned that he "was being constantly watched by these people. My slightest facial expressions were always being evaluated. When I closed my door, people assumed something was wrong." When the division moved from one office to another, many employees assumed they were being manipulated without being told so. In another company a senior manager told how employees always knew in advance when someone was to be laid off. Employees noticed that he always dressed in his pink shirt and matching tie when layoffs were to be announced. Employees watch executives just as students watch professors. Students look for signals on important exam topics, the professor's likes, and how to get a good grade.

Symbolic managers take advantage of being watched to signal new values. Consider Roy Ash at AM International.

AM International

Roy Ash used symbolic techniques to change the culture at Addressograph-Multigraph. His goal was to break down the stifling bureaucratic culture. He wanted to get people talking to one another face to face, reduce paperwork, decentralize decision making, and have people pay attention to the customer rather than to internal procedures. To accomplish this cultural change, Ash did the following:

1. He spent several months visiting widely scattered operations and asking a lot of searching questions. This was the opposite of what his predecessors had done, which was to summon subordinates to headquarters.

2. He left his office door open and encouraged people to drop by and discuss problems face to face. He also placed his own calls to arrange meetings and always talked with people in person rather than in writing.

3. He removed several of the company's copying machines to stop breeding so much paperwork.

4. He flew off to visit an important customer in Minneapolis and solved the customer complaint on the spot.

5. He changed the corporation's name to AM International and moved its headquarters from Cleveland to Los Angeles.

The change in the company's name and the move to Los Angeles were part of the new, lofty vision that AM would be a progressive leader in the office products industry. Visiting widely scattered spots helped create a sense of decentralization and autonomy, because people no longer had to trek to headquarters. Leaving his door open, placing his own calls, and speaking with people face to face helped Ash break down the bureaucratic convention of communicating through written memos. Removing the copying machines symbolized the devaluation of paperwork. Flying to Minneapolis to solve a customer complaint was an effective signal that customers count. Within just a few days everyone in the company had heard about the trip, and field representatives learned that they should solve customer complaints themselves.

Through symbolic actions, Ash communicated the new corporate values to thousands of employees. For Ash the symbolic manager, actions spoke louder than words.[30]

Change Tools

The change tools available to managers stem directly from the need to state lofty ideals and manage symbolic details. One key to using culture change tools is the theory of "small wins." Through hundreds of small deeds and actions, managers gradually change corporate culture. Symbolic managers should strive for a pattern of small, consistent, clear-cut outcomes. The other key is persistence. Managers must be patient and allow the organization time to change. Symbolic managers persistently nudge the organization toward the new cultural values.[31] The change tools that symbolic managers can use to foster new values are public statements to infuse lofty visions and overall values and symbols, ceremonies, slogans, stories, and heroes to cement these values in day-to-day activities.

Public Statements. *Public statements* include both oral and written communications to the organization as a whole. Public statements are the

E X H I B I T   16.5

Johnson & Johnson's Credo

Our Credo

We believe our first responsibility is to the doctors, nurses and patients,
to mothers and all others who use our products and services.
In meeting their needs everything we do must be of high quality.
We must constantly strive to reduce our costs
in order to maintain reasonable prices.
Customers' orders must be serviced promptly and accurately.
Our suppliers and distributors must have an opportunity
to make a fair profit.

We are responsible to our employees,
the men and women who work with us throughout the world.
Everyone must be considered as an individual.
We must respect their dignity and recognize their merit.
They must have a sense of security in their jobs.
Compensation must be fair and adequate,
and working conditions clean, orderly and safe.
Employees must feel free to make suggestions and complaints.
There must be equal opportunity for employment, development
and advancement for those qualified.
We must provide competent management,
and their actions must be just and ethical.

We are responsible to the communities in which we live and work
and to the world community as well.
We must be good citizens — support good works and charities
and bear our fair share of taxes.
We must encourage civic improvements and better health and education.
We must maintain in good order
the property we are privileged to use,
protecting the environment and natural resources.

Our final responsibility is to our stockholders.
Business must make a sound profit.
We must experiment with new ideas.
Research must be carried on, innovative programs developed
and mistakes paid for.
New equipment must be purchased, new facilities provided
and new products launched.
Reserves must be created to provide for adverse times.
When we operate according to these principles,
the stockholders should realize a fair return.

Johnson & Johnson

Source: Courtesy of Johnson & Johnson.

major tool for communicating a path-finding vision and the values essential for attaining it. A strong leader who articulated a lasting vision seemed to account for the extraordinary success of Dana, Wang, Walmart, Disney, McDonald's, Digital Equipment, and Levi-Strauss. Written statements often take the form of corporate credos or mission statements. Companies such as Johnson & Johnson and Pillsbury have crystallized their values in written form. The Johnson & Johnson credo is shown in Exhibit 16.5. This credo is given to all employees. Employee "Credo challenge meetings" are held to refresh these values.[32]

U S West is a large telecommunications company that has changed its culture to place new emphasis on competitiveness, innovation, and greater responsibility to customers. Senior executives have adopted the slogan "Bring on the competition!" to reflect the new corporate values. As symbolized by the bronco rider, U S West favors more competition and less regulation in the telephone and related industries.

Symbols, Ceremonies, and Slogans. As discussed earlier, symbols are objects, behaviors, or events that serve as vehicles for conveying cultural meaning. Almost anything can serve as a symbol for establishing new cultural values. For example, Roy Ash's behaviors symbolized the changes he desired at AM International. Ceremonies, both formal and informal, also provide opportunities to signal and provide positive reinforcement for new values. An informal ceremony used by a research vice-president was to congratulate a junior manager about her new product design in front of other managers in the coffee room. Slogans, when repeated frequently, can also become the carriers of new corporate values. When president of ITT, Harold Geneen captured his new value for the corporation in a few words: "Search for the unshakeable facts." He believed in cutting through the smokescreens and political games that often characterize management decision making.

Stories and Heroes. Stories and heroes often emerge on their own from within the corporation, but symbolic managers can help. As described earlier, top managers at 3M repeat the stories and acclaim the heroes who defied management and persisted with a new invention until it succeeded. One famous story used by Mars' executives to illustrate the company's concern for employees relates Mr. Mars' mid-summer visit to a chocolate factory:

> *He went up to the third floor, where the biggest chocolate machines were placed. It was hotter than the hinges of hell. He asked the factory manager, "How come you don't have air conditioning up here?" The factory manager replied that it wasn't in his budget, and he darn well had to make the budget. While Mr. Mars allowed that was a fact, he nonetheless went over to the nearby phone and dialed the maintenance people downstairs and asked them to come up immediately. He said, "While we (he and the factory manager) stand here, would you please go downstairs and get all (the*

factory manager's) furniture and other things from his office and bring them up here? Sit them down next to the big chocolate machine up here, if you don't mind." Mr. Mars told him that once the factory had been air conditioned, he could move back to his office any time he wanted.[33]

Stories such as these can be found in most companies and used to enhance the desired culture. The value of stories depends not on whether they are precisely true but whether they are repeated frequently and convey the correct values.

To summarize, symbolic managers can bring about cultural change through the use of public statements, ceremonies, stories, heroes, symbols, and slogans. To change culture, executives must learn ceremonial skills and how to use speech, symbols, and stories to influence company values. Executives do not drive trucks or run machines. Symbolic managers' task is to manage symbols, ceremonies, labels, and images.[34] Symbolic activities provide information about what counts in the company.

TECHNIQUES FOR MANAGING REVITALIZATION

Revitalization is the infusion of renewed strength, vigor, and competitiveness into an organization. In addition to changes in corporate culture, many companies use other approaches to revitalization. Recall from earlier chapters that organization structure can be changed to meet new strategic needs, and that the introduction of new technologies and products is an important part of organizational response to the environment. Revitalization often relies on improvements that extend beyond corporate culture.

For example, Scott Paper Company experienced a dramatic revitalization from 1982 to 1985. Scott's chief executive, Philip Lippincott, changed a corporate culture that had perpetuated a bureaucratic, hold-the-fort mentality. Decisions were decentralized, and more people were given a stake in the strategy. But beyond culture, Lippincott altered the incentive system to base managers' pay on contribution to profits rather than on the size of the departments they manage. Structure was changed to reduce 11 layers of management to 7. The work force was reduced by nearly 20 percent. New equipment was acquired to make the company self-sufficient in producing energy. Now scrap wood is burned to produce steam that provides low-cost energy for running the plant. A new wood-handling system allows Scott to enjoy the lowest raw materials costs in the industry. Now that Scott has recovered from its earlier profit difficulties, it is embarking on a new road to growth.[35]

Revitalization Stages

Broad-based revitalization strategies typically include three phases. The first is *contraction,* in which managers reduce organizational size and lower production costs. This may involve salary reductions, personnel

revitalization Infusion of renewed strength, vigor, and competitiveness into an organization.

A&P has undergone a major cultural change and revitalization. An important part of this change was the slogan "We built a proud new feeling," which was followed by a series of communications to enlighten shoppers on employees' renewed excitement and positive attitude. This photograph is a scene from a television commercial in which Anthony Guglieono helps a customer with her order. To further implement cultural change, A&P designated 1986 as "The Year of the Customer" and initiated customer orientation sessions for employees as part of its "Reach Out" program.

As part of Scott Paper Company's revitalization program, a corporate culture has been created that encourages all employees to become fully involved in their work and attain higher standards of performance. These employees are celebrating their recognition as Plant of the Year. Scott Paper's revitalization included better training programs, competitive reward and recognition programs, new production technology, changes in organization structure, and open two-way communications. These changes have carried Scott Paper through the three stages of revitalization and transformed it into a more profitable and productive company.

layoffs, and elimination of noncritical expenditures. Managers articulate new values during this stage. The second phase is *consolidation*, which is the stabilization of a leaner corporation. After the cutbacks, managers identify areas of strength and weakness and make plans to seek an organizational balance. Managers stress the new cultural values during this stage. In some respects, this is a post-contraction healing period. The third stage is *rebuilding*, wherein the organization once again begins to grow. In contrast to the focus on efficiency during the contraction and consolidation phases, the organization tries to innovate by implementing new technology and new products to foster controlled growth.[36]

Revitalization Framework

A framework for understanding organizational revitalization is presented in Exhibit 16.6. Its value is that it includes both cultural and noncultural change techniques that managers can use to improve corporate performance. The model has two dimensions. The first is the focus of change, which can be on either behavior or values within the organization. Behavior is considered a surface characteristic. Values pertain to the deeper structure of corporate culture and are related to employees' attitudes and beliefs. The other dimension in Exhibit 16.6 pertains to control over change. The concern here is whether the change effort is organizationally based or controllable by managers. Many activities, such as the choice of symbol or slogan or the use of incentives or scheduling, can be controlled by a single manager. However, changes in technology, structure, or major new training programs require organizational support and participation.

Cell 1 of Exhibit 16.6 includes organization-controlled changes that influence employee behavior. Changes in technology, structure, infor-

E X H I B I T 16.6

Framework for Revitalization Techniques

Source of Control over Change

	Organizational	Personal
Employee Behavior	**(1)** Manipulate: Structure Technology Information and control systems Manpower	**(2)** Manipulate: Incentives, rewards Resource allocation Planning, priorities Scheduling Negotiation
Employee Values	**(3)** Manipulate: Training, O.D. Retreats, workshops Programs Selection Socialization	**(4)** Manipulate: Public statements Symbols Stories, heroes Slogans Ceremonies

Focus of Change (row label at left)

mation and control systems, products, and manpower can increase efficiency and improve performance. Lawrence and Dyer studied revitalization in industries such as hospitals, autos, and steel that have been under severe pressure and need improved efficiency.[37] They found that organizations improved performance by making several organizational changes: A new organization structure established specialization as well as effective horizontal coordination; control systems stressed both measurable outcomes and employee commitment; employees participated in decision making; and the organization reduced staff personnel and product lines to fit intermediate environmental demands.

For example, Continental Steel Corporation, like other companies, suffered in the early 1980s. Modernization was essential. One step toward modernization was new technology, including a new rod mill and a continuous caster. A new union agreement was negotiated that reduced manpower and wage rates. Employee commitment was increased. Inefficiencies had caused the company to give up lucrative market areas, such as high carbon wire, and the new structure and technology overcame that shortcoming. The revitalization was reflected in both better efficiency—on-time delivery increased from 60 to 87 percent—and high-quality ratings from customers.[38]

Techniques for changing employees' behavior that are under managers' personal control are in cell 2. Managers can manipulate such things as incentives, rewards, and allocation of resources under their control. Individual managers also can change planning and scheduling and engage in negotiations to effect changes in job design, work priorities, and strategy.

Cells 3 and 4 describe techniques for changing deeper cultural values. Cultural change is typically slower than behavioral change and requires greater persistence. Organization-based changes in cell 3 include the manipulation of training programs, organizational development efforts, and the use of companywide retreats, workshops, and programs. The organization can also use selection and socialization procedures to insure that new employees have the attitudes and values appropriate to the desired corporate culture. Cell 4 represents techniques individual managers can use to affect the values within their departments. These are the techniques described earlier in this chapter and include managers' use of public statements, symbols, stories, heroes, slogans, and ceremonies. The impact of these changes is to shift employees' underlying values to fit the new efficiency and innovation needs of a more competitive organization.

SUMMARY

This chapter discussed several important ideas about corporate culture. Corporate culture includes the key values, beliefs, understandings, and norms that organization members share. Organizational activities that illustrate corporate culture include symbols, stories, heroes, slogans, and ceremonies. In order to be effective, corporate culture should be in alignment with corporate strategy and the needs of the external environment. Corporate culture is influenced by the degree of risk associated with strategic decisions and the speed of environmental feedback on the strategy's success. The four cultures are the tough-guy, macho culture, the work hard/play hard culture, the bet-your-company culture, and the process culture.

Two recent perspectives on corporate culture that suggest how to break down bureaucratic barriers and create a more positive culture for employees are Theory Z and excellence characteristics. Theory Z applies ideas from Japanese corporations to North American management; excellence characteristics define eight ways to improve management.

Techniques for changing corporate culture work at two levels: the symbolic managers must (1) communicate a lofty vision to employees and (2) pay attention to day-to-day details to reinforce it. Change tools take advantage of cultural characteristics and include public statements, ceremonies, slogans, symbols, stories, and heroes. Finally, many corporate revitalizations include changes that go beyond cultural values. Organizations may have to go through stages of contraction, consolidation, and rebuilding during which major changes in structure, technology, and manpower occur. A revitalization model identifies techniques to use depending on the focus of the change effort and managers' control over it.

Management Solution

The dumping of motorcycles into the U.S. market in the early 1980s nearly killed Harley-Davidson. Ironically, the first thing CEO Vaughn Beals did was take his top executives to visit Japan's motorcycle factories. They were impressed and made dramatic changes to revitalize Harley-Davidson. The vertical hierarchy was replaced with a series of small, self-contained units so that employees could feel deeply involved with the product. Employees participated in improving the manufacturing process. Harley-Davidson also responded with Theory Z concern for the whole employee, guarantees of job stability, job security, cross-training, and a variety of employee assistance programs. Employees also gained better promotion opportunities because of renewed promotion from within and a peer review system that built social and cultural norms for high-quality motorcycles. New technology for handling inventory and new CAD/CAM equipment and robots helped improve production efficiency. The top management team created a new culture based on Japanese ideas that is now positioning Harley-Davidson to beat the Japanese at their own game. They have created a new corporate philosophy and discovered the real secret of Japanese manufacturing success.[39]

DISCUSSION QUESTIONS

1. Define corporate culture and explain its importance for managers.
2. Why are symbols important to a corporate culture? Do stories, heroes, slogans, and ceremonies also have symbolic value? Discuss.
3. Explain the relationship between underlying cultural values and visible manners of dress, stories, symbols, and ceremonies. Do values influence visible behaviors, or vice versa?
4. Describe cultural values for a company at which you have worked. What was the source of those values?
5. What type of environmental situation and strategy is associated with a tough-guy, macho culture? How does this culture differ from the work hard/play hard culture?
6. Describe the key characteristics of Theory Z. Do you think American firms are able to adopt management practices that have worked in Japanese firms despite the differences in national culture?

7. Compare and contrast the characteristics of Theory Z with the excellence characteristics of "bias toward action," "productivity through people," and "simultaneous loose-tight properties."

8. What is a symbolic manager? What does it mean to say that a symbolic manager must deal at two levels?

9. Do you think a strong culture leads to greater organizational effectiveness? Are there times when a strong culture can reduce effectiveness?

10. What is revitalization? What are the three stages organizations typically go through to achieve revitalization?

11. Within the revitalization framework, can managers ignore corporate culture if they want to implement organization-based change in employee behavior? Discuss.

CASES FOR ANALYSIS

MARINE MIDLAND BANK

Marine Midland Bank embarked on an ambitious program to change its culture, structure, and policies to improve its financial performance and image. Although a huge bank, Marine Midland has not been a high performer, and executives in Buffalo, New York, were ready for a change. They coined the phrase the "New Marine" to symbolize the lean, dynamic organization. The New Marine would be characterized by risk taking, competitiveness, and boldness.

The grand strategy was devised by chairman Duffy and president Petty. They began by defining new performance goals. By examining the performance of peer banks, they decided that Marine's return on assets should be 0.6 percent, return on equity 15 percent, and equity 4 percent of assets. To make the goals perfectly clear, management adopted the slogan "60-15-4—you'll make the difference." The slogan was engraved on desk clocks presented to the bank's officers. Ballpoint pens inscribed with the numbers were distributed to vice-presidents.

The senior executive met with the planning group and hammered out a formal "Statement of Corporate Style" listing 17 practices and principles that were to characterize the New Marine Midland. These principles defined the philosophy, innovation, decision making, communication, performance appraisal, and reward systems that would characterize the new culture. These principles were written down and displayed on top managers' desktops. One principle was: "Decisions will be made no higher in the organization than necessary." Another was: "Compensation will be fully competitive with comparative banks."

In another efficiency move, Marine cut more than 700 employees from the payroll and closed 26 branches. These efficiencies would also improve performance.

Not everyone at Marine Midland is convinced of the new culture. Some old-timers are skeptical because many new, fast-track employees who believe in the new philosophy have been hired. About 450 outsiders have been hired as managers. Old-timers feel it's unfair for the new people to succeed so quickly. Another concern is that the new culture has not infiltrated below the top management level. The 135 senior vice-presidents are true believers, but the 400 or so vice-presidents are unclear about the cultural change. Many of the 9,500 employees below that level are unaware that cultural change is taking place. One executive vice-president has taken it upon himself to spread the word at four meetings to audiences of about 500 supervisors. Still, the planning director is concerned that cultural change won't be implemented until people downstream get the message—and so far they seem to have been left out of the change process.

Questions

1. What symbolic management techniques are being used by Marine Midland senior managers? Are they appropriate for the desired cultural change?
2. Of the four cultures described in Exhibit 16.3, which characterizes Marine Midland before the cultural change? Which culture do executives hope to have after the change?
3. Why do you think cultural change has not reached the bottom levels of the organization? How can management reach the lower levels with the new values?

Source: Based on Arthur M. Louis, "In Search of Style at the 'New Marine'," *Fortune*, July 26, 1982, pp. 40–45.

SOCIETY OF EQUALS

Ted Shelby doesn't make very many mistakes, but . . .

"Hey, Stanley," said Ted Shelby, leaning in through the door, "you got a minute? I've just restructured my office. Come on and take a look. I've been implementing some great new concepts!"

Stanley is always interested in Ted Shelby's new ideas. For if there is anyone Stanley wants to do as well as, it is Edward W. Shelby IV. Stanley follows Ed back to his office and stops, nonplussed.

Restructured is right! Gone are Ted's size B (Junior Exec.) walnut veneer desk and furniture, and his telephone table. In fact, the room is practically empty save for a large, round, stark white cafeteria table and the half-dozen padded vinyl swivel chairs that surround it.

"Isn't it a beauty! As far as I know, I'm the first executive in the plant to innovate this. The shape is the crucial factor here—no front or rear, no status problems. We can all sit there and communicate more effectively."

We? Communicate? Effectively? Well, it seems that Ted has been attending a series of Executive Development Seminars given by Dr. Faust. The theme of the seminars was—you guessed it—"participative management." Edward W. Shelby IV has always liked to think of himself as a truly democratic person.

"You see, Stanley," says Ted, managing his best sincere/intense attitude, "the main thing wrong with current mainstream management practice is that the principal communication channel is down-the-line oriented. We on the top send our messages down to you people, but we neglect the feedback potential. But just because we have more status and responsibility doesn't mean that we are necessarily (Stanley duly noted the word, "necessarily") better than the people below us. So, as I see the situation, what is needed is a two-way communication network: down-the-line and up-the-line.

"That's what the cafeteria table is for?" Stanley says.

"Yes!" says Ted. "We management people don't have all the answers, and I don't know why I never realized it before that seminar. Why . . . let's take an extreme example . . . the folks who run those machines out there. I'll bet that any one of them knows a thing or two that I've never thought of. So I've transformed my office into a full-feedback communication net."

"That certainly is an innovation around here," says Stanley.

A few days later Stanley passed by Ted Shelby's office and was surprised that Ted's desk, furniture, and telephone table were back where they used to be.

Stanley, curious about the unrestructuring, went to Bonnie for enlightenment. "What," he asked, "happened to Shelby's round table?"

"That table we were supposed to sit around and input things?" she said. "All I know is, about two days after he had it put in, Mr. Drake came walking through here. He looked in that office, and then he sort of stopped and went back—and he looked in there for a long time. Then he came over to me, and you know how his face sort of gets red when he's really mad? Well, this time he was so mad that his face was absolutely white. And when he talked to me, I don't think he actually opened his mouth; and I could barely hear him, he was talking so low. And he said, 'Have that removed. Now. Have Mr. Shelby's furniture put back in his office. Have Mr. Shelby see me.'"

My, my. You would think Ted would have known better, wouldn't you? But then, by now you should have a pretty firm idea of just why it is those offices are set up as they are.

Questions

1. How would you characterize the culture in this company? What are the dominant values?
2. Why did Ted Shelby's change experiment fail? To what extent did Ted use the appropriate change tools to increase employee communication and participation?

3. What would you recommend Ted do to change his relationship
    with subordinates? Is it possible for a manager to change cultural
    values if the rest of the organization, especially top management,
    does not agree?

Source: R. Richard Ritti and G. Ray Funkhouser, *The Ropes to Skip & The Ropes to Know*, 3d. (New York: Wiley, 1987), pp. 176–177. Reprinted by permission of John Wiley & Sons, Inc.

PART FIVE
CONTROLLING

Source: The Houses of Parliament, Sunset; *Claude Monet; National Gallery of Art, Washington; Chester Dale Collection.*

Source: Courtesy of Amoco Corporation.

CHAPTER 17
Effective Organizational Control

Chapter Outline

The Importance of Control

Steps in the Control Process

Relationship of Control to Strategic Planning

Environmental Change and Control Types

Organizational Control Focus

Feedforward Control
Concurrent Control
Feedback Control

Multiple Control Systems

Organizational Control Methods

Bureaucratic Control
Clan Control

Choosing Your Style of Control

Total Quality Control

Quality Circles
QC Contingency Factors

Characteristics of Effective Control

Learning Objectives

After studying this chapter, you should be able to:

- Define organizational control and explain why it is a key management function.

- Explain the four steps in the control process.

- Describe how organizational control relates to strategic planning.

- Describe differences in control focus, including feedforward, concurrent, and feedback control.

- Describe bureaucratic and clan control approaches and the methods used within the organization to implement each.

- Diagnose the type of control you should use as a manager.

- Describe the concept of total quality control and explain how quality circles can be used to improve quality control in organizations.

- Describe the characteristics of effective organizational controls.

Management Problem

The Electromagnetic Division of Spectrum Control Inc. makes 75,000 tubular ceramic capacitors a week. If the solder that holds the terminal to the ceramic capacitors doesn't stick, the division has a problem . . . perhaps thousands of problems. Recently the division's reject rate had begun to climb. At one point, nearly a third of the capacitors would not hold solder. Rejects of incoming material jumped to 32 percent; over 50 percent of the division's engineering time was diverted to this problem. To make matters worse, filled orders weren't being shipped on the correct dates. An order shipped too early was simply returned by the customer, at a cost of up to $400 for transshipping and paperwork. At about the same time Department Number Nine, which produces shielded windows, saw its reject rate climb to 15 percent, which was far too high to be profitable.[1]

At this point, Spectrum's managers were struggling to improve quality control in the Electromagnetic Division. If you were a top manager at Spectrum, what would you do to improve control over the production process? Where would you start, and what changes would you make?

Spectrum was a solid, $22 million company with some 1,500 customers, including Hewlett-Packard and IBM. Yet even in this well-run company, rejection rates were way above target. Assembly was not going as planned. Spectrum's problem shows how vital control is to organizational success and how difficult it is to achieve effective control.

Control is an issue facing managers in every organization. Campbell Taggart Inc., for example, achieved cost control over bakeries spread

Organizational control is the process through which managers regulate company activities to make them consistent with plans, targets, and standards of performance. In this novel form of control, Goodyear's "Gorilla" hose is field tested by Timmy of Cleveland's Metroparks Zoo. Timmy's torture test indicates to managers whether the hose performs to the toughness standards set for its applications in agriculture, mining, and construction. If the hose fails in any of these applications, managers take corrective action.

organizational control The systematic process through which managers regulate organizational activities to make them consistent with the expectations established in plans, targets, and performance standards.

across several states by implementing a fast, accurate, cost control system. A computer printout reaches the president's desk by 10 a.m. each Wednesday showing each bakery's profit and loss for the week ended Tuesday night. If anything is out of line, the president phones the local bakery by Wednesday afternoon.[2] Stix & Company, a St. Louis brokerage firm, failed to achieve control, and an employee and several cohorts embezzled more than $16 million. A later investigation showed that small securities firms were vulnerable to fraud and embezzlement because they lacked the formal management controls used by some large firms such as Salomon Brothers.[3]

THE IMPORTANCE OF CONTROL

Control is the fourth major management function. The four chapters in Part Five describe important areas of management control. This chapter defines basic control concepts, the control cycle, and organizational strategies for internal control. Chapter 18 describes control systems and gives particular attention to budgets and performance evaluation systems. Chapter 19 describes new developments in management information systems and how they can be used to improve managers' control. Chapter 20 discusses operations management techniques that can be used to control both manufacturing and service production activities.

Organizational control is defined as the systematic process through which managers regulate oganizational activities to make them consistent with the expectations established in plans, targets, and standards of performance.[4] In order to effectively control an organization, managers must plan and set performance standards, implement an information system that will provide knowledge of actual performance, and take action to correct deviations from the standard. Spectrum Control's managers understood the standard of performance and had information that the rejection rates were too high. They did not, however, have a way to implement corrections that would change behavior to meet the standard. Stix's management had no system for monitoring employee behavior and calling attention to performance deviations. Campbell Taggart, by comparison, has a control system that provides timely information on performance, compares it to standards, and permits management to immediately correct any deviation.

Steps in the Control Process

Based on our definition of organizational control, a well-designed control system consists of four steps, which are illustrated in Exhibit 17.1.

Establish Standards of Performance. Managers define goals for organizational departments in specific, operational terms that comprise a *standard of performance* against which to compare organizational activities. A standard of performance could include "reducing the reject rate from

E X H I B I T   17.1

Steps in the Control Process

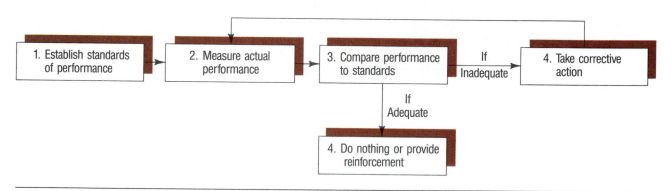

15 to 3 percent," "increasing the corporation's return on investment to 7 percent," or "reducing the number of accidents to 1 per each 100,000 hours of labor." American Airlines sets standards for such activities as acquiring additional aircraft for its fleet, designing discount fares to attract price-conscious travelers, improving passenger load factors, and increasing freight business by 15 percent. Standards must be defined in such a way that managers can determine whether activities are on target. Standards can then be communicated to the people in the organization responsible for achieving them.

Measure Actual Performance.   Many organizations develop quantitative measurements similar to Campbell Taggart's that can be reviewed on a daily, weekly, or monthly basis. For example, Richard Simmons, chief executive of Allegheny Ludlum Steel Corporation, explained why his company has a fanatical system for measuring internal operations. "It's simple," says Simmons. "If you can't measure it, you can't manage it."[5] Allegheny has 26,000 recipes for making steel and thus needs a vast computer system to maintain the tight cost control for each order filled. In most companies, however, managers do not rely exclusively on quantitative measures. They get out into the organization to see how things are going. People's Express established a standard of commitment to employee growth, which cannot be quantitatively measured. Top managers had to observe for themselves whether employees were being treated fairly and allowed opportunities for growth and development.

Compare Performance to Standards.   The third step is the explicit comparison of actual activities to performance standards. Managers take time to read computer reports or walk through the plant and thereby compare actual performance to standards. At Campbell Taggart, targeted performance standards are right on the computer printout along with the actual performance for the previous week and the previous year. This makes the comparison easy for managers. A. O. Smith manufactures heavy metal frames for automobiles. With changes in the design of automobiles, it adopted a goal of diversification. In 1983, Smith's

EXHIBIT   17.2

**Example of Actual Performance Compared to
Standard for an Airline's Central Division**

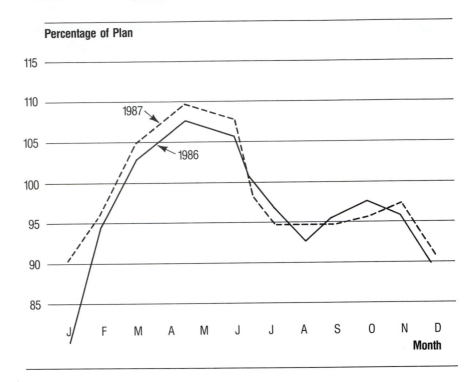

managers obtained data revealing that 20 percent of sales were from products not made five years earlier, indicating they were on target for diversification.

Exhibit 17.2 illustrates how a major airline used a computer reporting system to monitor performance and compare actual performance against standards. Productivity plans are developed a year in advance, and each month the comparison with actual productivity is provided for senior managers. Note that Exhibit 17.2 is designed as a percentage of plan so that anything above 100 percent means that performance exceeded targets. Performance seems to be highest during the spring months. When divisional productivity is below target, managers may wish to take corrective action.

However, interpreting the comparison between standards and actual performance is not always easy. Managers are expected to dig beneath the surface and find the cause of the problem. If the sales goal is to increase the number of sales calls by 10 percent and a salesperson achieved an increase of 8 percent, where did she fail to achieve her goal? Perhaps several businesses on her route closed, or additional salespeople were assigned to her area by competitors, or she needs training in making cold sales calls. Management should take an inquiring approach to deviations in order to gain a broad understanding of factors that influenced performance. Effective management control involves subjective judgment as well as objective analysis of performance data.

Take Corrective Action. *Corrective action* is a change in work activities to bring them back to acceptable performance standards. In this step, managers exercise their formal authority to make necessary changes. Managers may encourage employees to work harder, redesign the production process, or fire employees. One Friday night, the night shift at the Toledo, Ohio, AMC Jeep plant had a 15 percent no-show rate for workers, which is below the acceptable absenteeism standard of 10 percent. Management's corrective action was to shut the plant down and send the other 85 percent of workers home without pay.

In a few cases, corrective managers may consider changing performance standards. They may realize that standards are too high or too low if departments continuously fail to meet or exceed standards. If contingency factors that influence organizational performance change, performance standards may need to be altered to be more realistic and provide positive motivation for employees.

Managers may wish to provide positive reinforcement when performance meets or exceeds targets. They may reward a department that has exceeded its planned goals or simply congratulate employees for a job well done. Managers should not ignore high-performing departments in favor of working on corrective actions elsewhere.

RELATIONSHIP OF CONTROL TO STRATEGIC PLANNING

In order to exert effective control over the organization, management must integrate control with the strategic planning ideas described in Part Two. If control simply monitors internal activities, it may not help the organization achieve its strategic objectives. The linkage of strategy to control is important because strategy reflects changes in the problems and opportunities that appear in the external environment.

Environmental Change and Control Types

Environments create uncertainty for organizations because of change. Social, economic, technological, and political forces all can influence an organization.[6] Sometimes environmental change is gradual, permitting organizations to shift internal controls in an incremental fashion. At other times changes are **environmental discontinuities,** which are large changes over a short time period. Organizations may need to respond almost overnight. The banking business, for example, used to be straightforward. Interest rates and the number of banks were deter-

environmental discontinuity A large change in the organization's environment over a short time period.

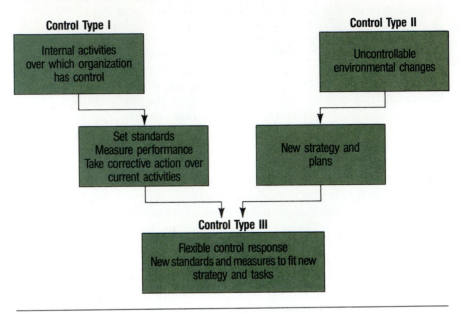

EXHIBIT   17.3

Relationship of Organizational Control to Strategic Planning

Source: Based on Peter Lorange, Michael F. Scott Morton, and Sumantra Ghoshal, *Strategic Control* (St. Paul, Minn.: West, 1986), Chapter 1.

Control Type I   The control of stable, internal organizational activities.

Control Type II   The adaptation to unpredictable factors in the organization's external environment through strategic planning.

Control Type III   The control of unpredictable environmental factors through the adoption of new strategic objectives and performance standards.

mined by the government. Suddenly—within a few months—the financial services industry spewed forth new organizations. Banks now compete with insurance companies and retailers such as Sears, Roebuck and Company. Nonbanks provide services such as electronic funds transfer systems, automatic tellers, and investment opportunities.[7]

What do environmental discontinuities mean for organizational control? Organizations can control stable, internal activities, which is called **Control Type I** in Exhibit 17.3. However, many factors in the external environment are uncontrollable, which is **Control Type II.**[8] The firm adapts to these events through strategic planning. As described in the chapters on planning, the organization scans the environment and develops strategic plans that reflect opportunities and potential threats. Internal control systems must change to reflect new strategic objectives and new standards of performance, which is **Control Type III.** The internal control system accommodates factors considered uncontrollable by adapting to them. Control Type III also reflects stable activities internal to the organization over which managers have power. Control Type III reflects both today's activities that are measurable and definable and new activities identified in strategies needed for tomorrow.

As illustrated in Exhibit 17.3, uncontrollable events lead to the creation of new strategic plans, which in turn lead to new standards of performance, activities, and feedback systems. Likewise, ongoing internal activities influence the design of Control Type III. Control systems reflect the balance between planning for uncontrollable external changes and current internal activities. Thus, the control cycle, which establishes standards, measures performance, and takes corrective action, is continuously changing. This cycle encourages adjustments that lead to new plans, new standards of performance, new activities, and so on. If managers do not carefully link control to strategy, the organization may exert tight control over current tasks—which are the wrong tasks for successful performance.

Nike Inc. recently experienced major changes in the external environment and adapted its strategic planning and internal control systems accordingly.

Nike Inc.

Nike started making its own running shoes in 1972 and is now the biggest U.S. athletic shoe and apparel maker. Nike grew with the running fad. In the 1980s, however, the interest in running has been leveling off, and new competitors have driven down Nike's market share from 36 to 32 percent in two years. Nike's net income is down, and sales are growing slowly. In response to these environmental changes, Nike's strategy reflects a new philosophy of internal control. One new control standard is to cut bloated inventories that had increased to 22 million pairs of shoes; the new target is 12 million. Another standard is to give better service to Nike's large national accounts, such as J. C. Penney. Nike managers also plan to refocus the product line. They are being more choosy about which products carry the Nike label.

Some aspects of Nike's control system will remain the same. Nike will continue to make nearly 95 percent of the footwear overseas and will monitor costs carefully. It will also continue using big-name athletes to promote its products, because these advertisements have generated excellent performance in the past.

Nike's new strategy reflects changes in the environment. The internal control system will keep tighter rein on costs, inventories, and proliferation of shoe models. The linkage between strategy and internal control is a strong plus for Nike. Nike officials feel that there are enough runners to forecast a bright future. "People are still pretty active out there," said one executive. It's just a matter of Nike's meeting the challenge.[9]

A major environmental change that confronted USAir was the abrupt fuel cost increases of the 1970s and early 1980s. USAir adapted to this change by developing new internal control systems to reflect revised strategic objectives and performance standards, which are Control Type III. The new control systems responded to changes in strategy and the external environment. Since fuel represents over one-fourth of USAir's operating expenses, it initiated fuel storage and conservation. In addition, flight plans developed in this System Control Center contributed to annual savings of thousands of gallons of fuel.

ORGANIZATIONAL CONTROL FOCUS

When managers design and implement the four steps of control described above, on which part of the organization should they focus? The organization is a production process, and control can focus on events before, during, or after this process.[10] For example, a local automobile dealer can focus control on activities before, during, or after sales of new cars. Careful inspection of new cars and cautious selection of sales employees would be examples of control that occurs before sales take place. Monitoring how salespeople act with customers and providing rules and procedures for guiding the sales process would be considered control during the sales task. Counting the number of new cars sold during the month or telephoning buyers about their satisfaction with sales transactions would constitute control after sales have taken place. These three types of control are formally called feedforward, concurrent, and feedback and are illustrated in Exhibit 17.4.

Feedforward Control

feedforward control Control that focuses on human, material, and financial resources flowing into the oganization; also called *preliminary* or *preventative control.*

Feedforward control focuses on human, material, and financial resources that flow into the organization. Sometimes called *preliminary* or *preventative control,* its purpose is to insure that input quality is sufficiently high to prevent problems when the organization performs its tasks.[11] Feedforward control is anticipatory and attempts to identify and prevent deviations before they occur.

Feedforward controls are evident in the selection and hiring of new employees. Westinghouse selects only 5 percent of job applicants for its College Station plant, because only a certain type of person fits the plant's culture. Tandem Computer Company subjects potential middle managers to 20 grueling hours of interviews with both top-level managers and prospective peers.[12] These interviews are designed to insure that the right person is selected and no problems will occur after hiring. The Air Force uses feedforward control when it specifies rigid quality standards for replacement parts for the F-16 fighter aircraft. Procter & Gamble used feedforward control when it set a policy of hiring only college graduates to participate in its sales and management training programs. The requirement that professional football, basketball, and baseball players pass a physical exam before their contracts are validated is still another form of feedforward control.

Concurrent Control

concurrent control Control that consists of monitoring ongoing employee activities to insure their consistency with established standards.

Concurrent control monitors ongoing employee activities to insure that they are consistent with planned standards. Concurrent control is a common form of control because it assesses the organization's ongoing activities. It relies on performance standards and includes rules and regulations for guiding employee tasks and behaviors. Concurrent control is designed to insure that employee work activities produce the correct results.

E X H I B I T   17.4

Organizational Control Focus

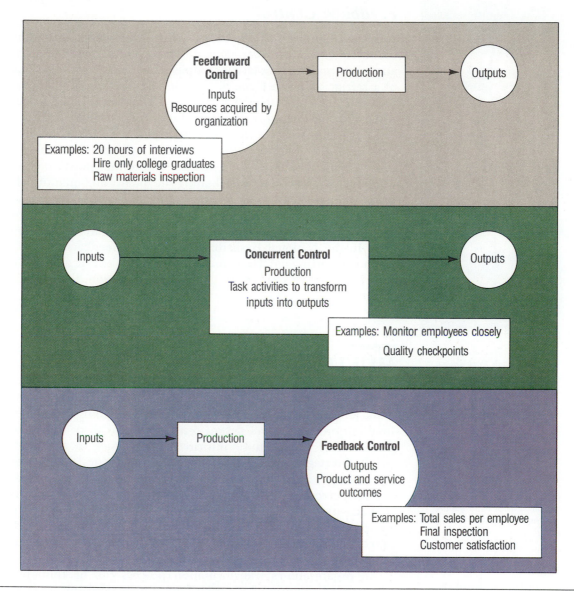

At a construction company, the construction superintendent may hire laborers with little screening. Employees are given a chance to perform, and the superintendent monitors their behavior. If employees obey the rules and work effectively, they are allowed to stay; if they do not, they are let go. In a manufacturing firm, it is not unusual for production managers to have a series of quality checkpoints. A sample of products is examined at each checkpoint to see whether the production steps have been completed satisfactorily. The use of concurrent control in professional sports focuses on players' performance during a game. When Bos-

The Photographic Quality Services Department at the Kodak Park Division uses concurrent control to insure the high quality of large rolls of Kodak Ektachrome Film. Here a workman checks film in the film-winding take-up area at the Park Division's coating facility. Bill Hackett, Photographic Quality Services Manager, receives continuous information from roll-coating, emulsion-coating, finished-film, spooling, and other departments to insure that only the finest-quality film goes out the door. Concurrent control helps build quality into every product so that final inspection is hardly needed.

feedback control   Control that focuses on the organization's outputs; also called *post-action* or *output control*.

multiple control system   A control system involving the simultaneous use of feedforward, concurrent, and feedback control.

strategic control point   An activity that is especially important for achieving the organization's strategic objectives.

ton Celtics managers use performance on the basketball court as the performance criterion, they are using concurrent control.

Feedback Control

Feedback control focuses on the organization's outputs. Sometimes called *post-action* or *output control*, it focuses on the end product or service after the organization's task is completed.[13] An intensive final inspection of a refrigerator at a General Electric assembly plant is an example of feedback control. Caterpillar Tractor Company uses feedback control when it surveys customers after 300 and 500 hours of product use.

Sales organizations often rely on feedback control. Salespeople are permitted wide latitude in their choice of style and sales techniques, because evaluation is based on total sales and commissions. The sales organization is concerned with evaluating the quality and quantity of the end result and pays less attention to recruiting salespeople (feedforward control) or monitoring their daily sales activities (concurrent control). Feedback control is directed toward reaching the organization's output targets. In the National Basketball Association, feedback control is used when team managers focus on games won or lost. If a basketball team wins the targeted number of games for the season, the organization is considered effective.

MULTIPLE CONTROL SYSTEMS

Most organizations use **multiple control systems** simultaneously. Thus, managers are able to control resource inputs, ongoing task activities, and final outputs. Managers design control systems to define standards of performance and acquire information feedback at strategic control points. **Strategic control points** are those activities that are especially important for achieving strategic objectives. An organization may decide that 60 percent of its total success comes from its ability to control current activities. Thus, a strategic control point would be the monitoring of the production process. Another firm may feel that it can achieve 50 percent of its strategic objectives if it acquires the right people and materials. Thus, resource inputs would be a strategic control point.

An organization's transformation process can be thought of as a value-added chain in which each department performs work that adds value to the final product. A simple value-added chain for a manufacturing firm is illustrated in Exhibit 17.5.[14] This firm uses feedforward, concurrent, and feedback control simultaneously. The control linkage to inbound people and supplies establishes performance standards and monitors the rejection rate for raw materials inventory. No direct control is used for parts drilling and machining on the shop floor, except for the presence of supervisors. Component assembly, however, is monitored. Standards can be set for the number and quality of components to be assembled on a daily basis. This is concurrent control. Feedback control is provided at the strategic points of final inspection and by the sales

E X H I B I T   17.5

Strategic Control Points Using Multiple Control Systems

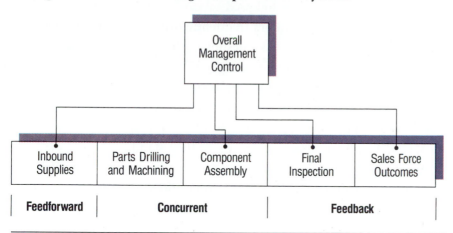

Source: Based on Peter Lorange, Michael F. Scott Morton, and Sumantra Ghoshal, *Strategic Control* (St. Paul, Minn.: West, 1986), Chapter 5.

force. Final inspection reveals rejection rates and provides feedback regarding changes in either raw materials acquisition or the production process. Sales force control indicates success rates in selling products.

The implementation of multiple controls in organizations can be complex, but each control system plays a logical part. The system can be designed to anticipate problems through feedforward control, monitor ongoing activities through concurrent control, or inspect final output for feedback control. The three types of control also work in service organizations, as illustrated by Scandinavian Design Inc.

Scandinavian Design Inc.

Scandinavian Design is a profitable furniture retailer located in Natick, Massachusetts. It is rapidly growing and was the twenty-second largest U.S. furniture retailer in 1983. Scandinavian Design's success is largely due to the management and control of employees. Management first tries to select employees who will be more knowledgeable, dedicated, and productive than competitors'. After selecting good employees, managers emphasize the training and monitoring of employees within stores. Scandinavian Design University was created as a training center for both salespeople and managers. The training center teaches employees the written rules and standards of performance. Employees learn specific techniques for dealing with customers. They also learn unwritten rules, such as

Anheuser-Busch uses multiple control systems to insure high-quality products. A strategic control point is the acquisition of quality raw materials. This requires feedforward control in the form of testing ingredients before brewing even begins. In addition, numerous flavor panels meet daily at company headquarters to judge each product's aroma, appearance, and taste, which is feedback control. Samples are flown into St. Louis from each brewery for taste evaluation, thus insuring the quality of every bottle, can, and keg of beer.

standards of dress and conduct. Trainers act as role models to give employees examples of correct behavior.

Emphasis on training is followed by close control of store operations. Top administrators frequently drop into stores to observe employee behavior and to ask questions. Administrators enlist friends to call on stores and critique employee behavior toward customers. Moreover, each employee's sales performance is carefully monitored by computer. Sales figures are charted by the month and the year to date and compared with previous months and years. The figures are posted to let all employees know where they stand.

Senior managers also monitor total store outcome figures, such as total sales, net profits, and sales per square foot. They know that the average furniture retailer generates about $60 in sales per square foot annually and stock turns over about twice a year. Scandinavian Design does much better, selling an average of $377 per square foot and turning over inventory eight times a year.

Multiple control systems help managers control the rapidly growing company. Managers feel that the strategic control point is employees' daily sales activity. Managers thus concentrate on training employees and helping them become expert salespeople. If each employee learns how to deal with customers one on one, everything else falls into place. The few employees who seem unable to master good customer relationships are shifted into nonsales jobs or let go.[15]

Scandinavian Design stresses concurrent control, but it also utilizes feed-forward and feedback control. The combination of control systems fits Scandinavian Design's strategic needs and helps it to achieve its outstanding sales record.

ORGANIZATIONAL CONTROL METHODS

Regardless of whether the organization focuses control on inputs, production, or outputs, another choice must be made between bureaucratic and clan control methods. These two control methods represent different philosophies. Most organizations display some aspects of both bureaucratic and clan control, but many managers emphasize one or the other as the prominent form of control in their organizations.

Bureaucratic Control

Bureaucratic control is the use of rules, policies, hierarchy of authority, written documentation, reward systems, and other formal mechanisms to influence employee behavior and assess performance.[16] Bureaucratic control relies on the organization's administrative system. It assumes that targets can be defined and that employees' work behavior will conform to those targets if formal rules and regulations are provided. The following control elements are typically associated with bureaucratic control.

Rules and Procedures.   Rules and procedures include the standard operating procedures and policies that prescribe correct employee behavior. Rules are based on organizational experience and newly defined strategies. They indicate acceptable behaviors and standards for employee performance.

Management Control Systems.   Management control systems include those internal organization systems, such as budgeting, financial reporting, reward systems, operations management, and performance appraisal, that monitor and evaluate performance. These systems are normally quantitative in nature and sometimes measure performance on a daily or even hourly basis. Control systems will be discussed in detail in Chapters 18 through 20.

Hierarchy of Authority.   Hierarchy of authority relies on central authority and personal supervision for control. Managers are responsible for the control of subordinates through direct surveillance. The supervisor has formal authority for control purposes. Lower-level employees are not expected to participate in the control process.

Selection and Training.   Under bureaucratic control methods, selection and training are highly formalized. Objective written tests are administered to see if employees meet hiring criteria. Demographic characteristics, such as education and work experience, are quantified to see whether applicants qualify. Formalized selection procedures are intended to allow broad opportunities for employment, but they are associated with extensive paperwork.

Technology.   Technology extends bureaucratic control in two ways. First, it can control the flow and pace of work.[17] In an assembly line manufacturing plant, for example, the technology defines the speed and standards at which workers must perform. Second, computer-based technology can be used to monitor employees. This occurs frequently in service firms. AT&T has a monitoring system that counts the number of seconds that elapse prior to answering each call and the number of seconds spent on each call. American Express uses electronic techniques to monitor data entry personnel who record account payments as well as operators who answer phone queries from credit cardholders. The system reports daily productivity data for each operator and each department. To supplement the electronic monitoring system, supervisors often listen in on telephone calls or personally observe data entry personnel.[18]

bureaucratic control   The use of rules, policies, hierarchy of authority, reward systems, and other formal devices to influence employee behavior and assess performance.

Elements of bureaucratic control are used in Rockwell International's Graphic Systems Division in Reading, Pennsylvania, which manufactures newspaper printing presses. Using computer-based technology, the management control system monitors factory time, attendance, and labor productivity. Terminals on the factory floor supply factory managers with control information and employees with timely data on job status, job cost, and payroll. This control system is part of a factory data collection system developed by Honeywell.

SOCIAL
RESPONSIBILITY

The Invisible Supervisor

Vaughn Foster is a truck driver for Leprino Foods in Denver, and he is in a hurry to get home. His wife and kids are waiting, but he will not drive more than 50 miles an hour. Why? The computer. It's a black box under the hood from which management will pull a cartridge to tell the complete story of his trip. Speeding or other deviations could lead to Foster's dismissal. Like thousands of other employees, he dislikes computer surveillance.

Managers love the control provided by the computer, which is called the "invisible supervisor." Jerry Sheehan, vice-president of transportation for Leprino Foods, was unable to accomplish much in the way of controlling drivers without the computer. Lower speeds now have increased gas mileage 25 percent. Maintenance costs have declined 20 percent, and the reduced accident rate has saved $50,000 in insurance premiums.

Computer control is revolutionizing management throughout North America. In word processing pools, the computer keeps track of how many keystrokes a typist produces in one minute. In production plants, computer terminals tell foremen which machine operators are ahead of schedule and which are behind. In Canada, the computer is used to monitor meter readers—and faithfully reports the time meter readers take between calls and how many calls they make each day.

But employees don't like being watched. Many union leaders argue that working to please the machine is stressful, aggravates already tension-filled jobs, and is an affront to human dignity. In both Canada and the United States, unions are preparing to fight the computer watchdog. At the Ontario Health Insurance Plant in Ontario, keystrokes count. When one employee's keystrokes declined from 15,000 to 12,000 per hour, she was moved off by herself. She was having personal problems, but no one seemed to be interested. "All that mattered was that I was capable of 15,000 strokes and wasn't producing it." She thinks computer surveillance creates dissatisfaction. "You wouldn't feel so guilty about being a minute late from lunch and knowing that it's recorded. As it is, you feel like a robot."

Some companies use electronic surveillance to pit workers against one another. This supposedly improves productivity. In one Pacific Western Airlines office, a poster urged employees to "Compare yourself to your friends. Are you pulling your weight in the office?"

Air Canada measures performance in such areas as tickets booked per hour, revenue per hour, and number of typing errors. One reservation clerk claims Air Canada uses the statistics to threaten its workers. Although officials deny it, the potential for abuse exists in all organizations that use computers for surveillance and control.

In the United States, the Communications Workers of America sought to ban monitoring in its 1986 contract with AT&T. The Service Employees International Union is supporting legislation in several states that would outlaw computer monitoring. The Labour Canada Task Force on Micro-Electronics and Employment has recommended that computer surveillance be banned: "Surveillance is based on mistrust and lack of respect for basic human dignity. . . . An infringement on the rights of the individual. . . ." Telephone monitoring in Sweden has been prohibited since 1972. In Denmark, point-of-sale cash registers are no longer permitted to tally a cashier's revenue and number of customers per shift.

The Ontario Public Service Employees Union feels one solution may be to monitor employees in groups rather than individually. This would protect workers who can't keep up with the rest of the office. "The current monitoring situation is stressful, and some people realize their best is not good enough. The quotas keep going up, and they fall further behind."

Yet there is no denying the beneficial aspects from management's perspective. In almost every application of electronic surveillance, productivity increases. What is the socially responsible solution? Before long, managers' answer may be based on surveillance of their own activities. Plastic, computer-linked ID cards that open doors and even deduct the cost of meals in company cafeterias are now a fact of life for many managers. The cards provide a picture of the manager's workday: time of arrival, time and length of washroom use, time at lunch, and departure time. The question is whether computers will continue to be such a great management tool if they make managers and workers alike feel like organization robots.

Source: Based on Lawrence Archer, "I Saw What You Did and I Know Who You Are," *Canadian Business*, November 1985, pp. 76–83, and Michael W. Miller, "Computers Keep Eye on Workers and See If They Perform Well," *The Wall Street Journal*, June 3, 1985, pp. 1, 12.

Although many managers effectively use bureaucratic control, too much control can backfire. Employees resent being watched too closely, and they may try to sabotage the control system. However, too little bureaucratic control also can backfire. Finding the right level is the challenge. Bureaucratic control methods can be implemented and used in many kinds of organizations, even elementary schools.

Franklin Elementary School

In response to the public's demand for improved student performance scores, Franklin Elementary School has adopted formalized control techniques. First, precise educational objectives are set forth for both teachers and students. One objective for first-grade students is to "write complete sentences, using periods correctly." The principal also visits each teacher's classroom and monitors what each child actually does minute by minute. These observations show that students are now engaged in direct learning 83 percent of the time compared with 60 percent two years ago.

The school principal also provides a rigid disciplinary code. In the school cafeteria, rules are enforced with three lights. The green light demands "total silence"; the yellow light allows students to "whisper softly"; the red light means that five minutes remain in the lunch period. Rigid rules define the response to violations. On the third cafeteria violation, the rule is: "Student stands against wall during red light if lunch completed, otherwise at recess." Rules even extend to the homework regimen. Teachers no longer accept excuses, and missed homework must be made up during the lunch hour or a free period.

Most schools that have established bureaucratic control programs have reported improved student achievement, attendance, and discipline. Barbara Martin, Franklin's principal, doesn't want the school to become too impersonal and rule bound. She stresses a nurturing, warm environment between teachers and students. Equipped with rules for defining appropriate behavior, teachers are free to create a more positive working relationship with students.[19]

Clan Control

Clan control is almost the opposite of bureaucratic control. **Clan control** relies on social values, traditions, shared beliefs, and trust to foster compliance with organizational goals. Employees are trusted, and managers believe employees are willing to perform correctly without extensive

clan control The use of social values, traditions, common beliefs, and trust to generate compliance with organizational goals.

rules or supervision. Given minimal direction and standards, employees are assumed to perform well—indeed, they even participate in setting standards and designing the control system. Clan control is usually implemented through the following techniques.

Corporate Culture.   Corporate culture was described in Chapter 16 as the norms and values shared by organization members. If the organization has a strong corporate culture and the established values are consistent with its goals, corporate culture will be a powerful control device. The organization is like a large family, and each employee is committed to activities that will best serve it. Corporate traditions such as IBM's 100% Club and Mary Kay's pink Cadillac awards instill values in employees that are consistent with the goals and behaviors needed for corporate success.

Delta Air Lines, for example, has a strong corporate culture that induces employees to work toward company goals. In fact, during a recent downturn, employees made voluntary contributions to buy Delta a multimillion-dollar airplane.

Peer Group.   In Chapter 15, we saw that norms evolve in working groups and that cohesive groups influence employees. If peer control is established, less top-down bureaucratic control is needed. Employees are likely to pressure coworkers into adhering to group norms and achieving departmental goals.

Self-Control.   No organization can control employees 100 percent of the time. Self-discipline and self-control are what keep employees performing their tasks up to standard. Most employees bring to the job a belief in doing a fair day's work and a desire to contribute to the organization's success in return for rewards and fair treatment. To the extent that managers can take greater advantage of employee self-control, bureaucratic controls can be reduced. Employees high in self-control often are those who have had several years of training and hence have internal standards of performance. It is common to see departments of attorneys, researchers, or doctors at large corporations such as General Motors, Reynolds Metals, Phillips Petroleum, and Penn Central. The experience, training, and socialization of professionals provide internal standards of performance that allow for self-control.

Employee Selection and Socialization.   Clan methods of selection use personal evaluations rather than the formal testing procedures associated with bureaucratic control. For example, companies that use clan control methods often subject employment candidates to a rigorous selection process. We mentioned earlier that Tandem Computer subjects managers to 20 grueling hours of interviews. For an entry-level position at Procter & Gamble, the person is interviewed at length by a line manager; people from the personnel department are not involved. The line managers have been trained to probe deeply into the applicant's qualities. The candidate also goes through a second interview of similar depth and takes a test of general knowledge. Then there is a full day of one-on-one interviews at corporate headquarters and a group interview over lunch.[20] After candidates are hired, they are subjected to intensive train-

Clan control relies on social values, traditions, shared beliefs, and trust to foster employee compliance with organizational goals. At this U.S. Caterpillar plant employees from all departments work together on cost-cutting and quality improvement projects. The shared cultural values of improving efficiency and interdepartmental trust are typical of clan control. These machine shop employees as a group have greatly reduced machine setup time, resulting in reduced costs and improved efficiency.

EXHIBIT 17.6

Bureaucratic and Clan Methods of Control

	Bureaucratic	Clan
Purpose	Employee compliance	Employee commitment
Techniques	Rules, formal control systems, hierarchy, selection and training, technology	Corporate culture, peer group, self-control, selection and socialization
Performance expectations	Measurable standards define minimum performance; fixed indicators	Emphasis on higher performance and oriented toward dynamic marketplace
Organization structure	Tall structure, top-down controls	Flat structure, mutual influence
	Rules and procedures for coordination and control	Shared goals, values, traditions for coordination and control
	Authority of position	Authority of knowledge and expertise
Rewards	Based on employee's achievement in own job	Based on group achievements and equity across employees
Participation	Formalized and narrow (e.g., grievance procedures)	Informal and broad, including control systems design and organizational governance

Source: Based on Richard E. Walton, "From Control to Commitment in the Workplace," *Harvard Business Review* (March/April 1985), pp. 76–84.

ing in company values, standards, and traditions. Rigorous selection and socialization activities are an effective way to insure that candidates believe in the company's values, goals, and traditions.

In summary, clan control utilizes methods different from those of bureaucratic control. The important point is that both methods provide organizational control. It is a mistake to assume that clan control is weak or represents the absence of control simply because visible rules, procedures, and supervision are absent. Indeed, some people believe that clan control is the stronger form of control because it engages employees' commitment and involvement.

Exhibit 17.6 compares bureaucratic and clan control methods. Bureaucratic control is concerned with compliance and clan control with employee commitment.[21] Bureaucratic methods define explicit standards that translate into minimum performance and use top-down control. Compensation is based on individual performance. Employees rarely participate in the control process. With clan methods, employees strive to achieve standards beyond explicitly stated objectives. Influence is mutual, with employees having a say in how tasks are performed and even in determining standards of performance and design of control systems. Shared goals and values replace rules and procedures. Compensation is based on group, departmental, and organizational success rather than on individual performance. This induces individuals to help rather than compete against one another. Employees participate in a wide range of issues, including company governance, objective setting, and performance standards.

An example of how far clan control can go is Marquette Electronics.

Marquette Electronics

Marquette Electronics makes sophisticated medical devices that doctors use to make life-or-death decisions. Considering the seriousness of its task, it is surprising to see the company characterized by disorder. Some employees wear Hawaiian shirts and have a boom box playing in the background. In the company cafeteria, employees may enjoy a beer. The day care center takes care of employees' children, and employees can take time off to play with them. Managers at Marquette Electronics do not overcontrol. "The truth is, we're all quite bad managers," says the engineering vice-president. "Maybe we're not managers at all."

The company is well managed, but management consciously delegates important responsibilities to employees. Marquette's approach to human resources is one that scorns policies and procedures and eschews memos and directives. Employees are believed to act in the company's best interest, and a harmonious relationship between company and employees flourishes.

The guiding philosophy, as expressed by Mike Cudahy, is: "People want to love their job, their boss, and their company. They want to perform. But that happens only when you've taken the yuck, the real drudgery out of working. You can't put people in boxes, telling them what they can do, when they can do it, and who's going to get rid of them if they don't do it. That only gets their noses bent out of shape. You've got to give people a voice in their jobs. You've got to give them a piece of the action and a chance to excel. You've got to give them the freedom to have fun."

Marquette employees enjoy a generous profit-sharing plan. They begin work anywhere from 6 to 9 a.m.; the flex time program allows them to select their own hours of work.

The Marquette culture is fluid and informal, but that doesn't mean a lack of control. People are not bound by traditional rules, but the group norms and the company culture demand a high standard of performance. Everyone shares a simple but strong expectation: Make good products, give good customer service, and do it all fast. This may seem an unusual approach to management, but as one former employee has said, "Boy, does it work."[22]

E X H I B I T   17.7

Choosing Your Control Style

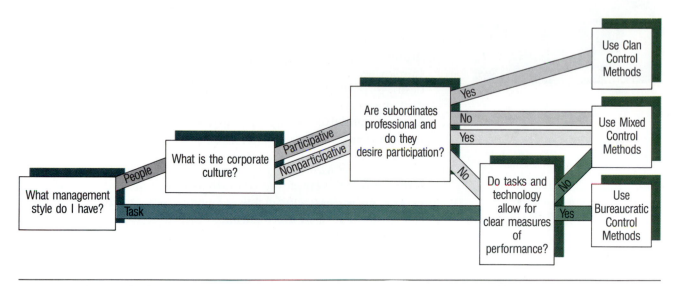

Source: Based on Cortlandt Cammann and David A. Nadler, "Fit Control Systems to Your Managerial Style," *Harvard Business Review* (January/February 1976), pp. 65–72.

CHOOSING YOUR STYLE OF CONTROL

Managers often are confronted with the dilemma of whether to adopt a bureaucratic or clan control style or a style that uses elements of each. One approach for answering this question is illustrated in Exhibit 17.7. By analyzing four factors, managers are able to decide on the correct control method to use. The four factors are (1) individual management style, (2) corporate culture, (3) employee professionalism and desire to participate, and (4) performance measures.[23] Each of these factors can be diagnosed by answering specific questions.

1. *What kind of management style do I have?* This simply asks whether you have a personal inclination toward a people- or task-oriented leadership style as described in Chapter 12. Generally, the extent to which a manager likes to consult with subordinates, share information, and encourage them to disagree suggests a clan control approach. The more a manager prefers to make decisions alone and provide close supervision and direction for subordinates, the more appropriate is a bureaucratic style.

2. *What kind of corporate culture does my organization have?* Manager style and approach toward employees should be consistent with corporate culture. Are employees through the organization

Sam Walton, founder and CEO of Wal-Mart, has a distinct personal control style. Wal-Mart's concern for its people reflects Walton's own inclination toward a people-oriented leadership style. Walton has also fostered a corporate culture that encourages participative decision making, and most employees adopt a professional orientation. These factors explain why Sam Walton prefers clan control. However, tasks and technology in the retail business enable clear measures of performance; thus, the overall control process also employs bureaucratic methods, including specific performance measures and rules and procedures.

encouraged to participate in decisions? Does the reward system encourage participation and the establishment of shared values and norms? Are employees trusted? If so, a clan control style will fit well. If the corporate culture limits decision making to those at the top and avoids employee participation, bureaucratic control will fit better.

3. *Are my subordinates highly professional, and do they desire to participate?* Employees who have extensive training, are professional, and desire to participate in management decisions are more likely to display self-control. They respond to group norms and to their internal standards for high performance. If employees do not have professional experience or training and do not desire to participate, formal, bureaucratic control is appropriate.

4. *Do the task and technology allow for accurate and reliable measures of performance?* Are employee tasks discrete and quantifiable? If explicit measures are available, a bureaucratic approach to control can be used. If tasks are difficult to measure, as in the case of scientists in a research laboratory, managers should encourage norms and values with which to control employee behavior.

The answers to these four questions indicate whether managers should adopt bureaucratic or clan methods. When management style and corporate culture support participation and employee professionalism is high, clan control is preferred. When management style is directive, tasks are quantifiable, and subordinates desire not to participate, a bureaucratic control style is appropriate. Note that in several situations a mixed control style is preferable. If both the manager and the corporation encourage a participative style but subordinates desire not to participate, the manager should use elements of both strategies. Over time, employees may learn to accept responsibility and thrive in a clan control setting.

The framework in Exhibit 17.7 is a useful guideline for helping managers understand when bureaucratic and clan control methods can be given priority. It is not appropriate for diagnosing the organization as a whole. It contains useful ideas for practicing managers by showing that a personal approach to control is a function of one's own management style, corporate culture, subordinates' desire to participate, and the ability to measure performance.

TOTAL QUALITY CONTROL

A recent trend in the United States and Canada has been companies' adoption of a concept called *total quality control*. This approach to control was successfully implemented by Japanese companies and gave Japanese products an international reputation for quality.[24] Ironically, the concept originally was introduced in an American book by A. V. Feigenbaum called *Total Quality Control*.[25] The Japanese borrowed the ideas that Americans had ignored for years. A more recent book, *Quality Is Free:*

The Art of Making Quality Certain by Philip Crosby, helped reawaken North American commitment to quality.[26]

The theme of **total quality control** is simple: "The burden of quality proof rests . . . with the makers of the part."[27] In other words, workers, not managers, are responsible for achieving standards of quality. Quality control departments and control systems no longer have primary control responsibility. Some Japanese companies prefer the term "companywide quality control" to convey the idea of total employee involvement. Everyone from top management to the janitor, including both line and staff personnel, must make quality control happen.

Sanyo, a Japanese company that practices total quality control, purchased a TV manufacturing plant in the United States that had a notorious reputation for poor quality. Sanyo employed the same workers and transformed the plant to produce high-quality output. Its first step was to make the former chief of quality control the new chief of manufacturing. This appointment signaled to everyone that quality was to become an integral part of manufacturing and would no longer be handled by a separate quality control department.

The emphasis on total participation in quality control is a significant departure from the philosophy of most companies in Canada and the United States. These companies traditionally have practiced the western notion of achieving an "acceptable quality level." This allows a certain percentage of defects and engenders a mentality that imperfections are okay and only those caught by a quality control department need be corrected. Total quality control not only engages the participation of all employees but has a target of zero defects. Everyone strives for perfection. A rejection rate of 2 percent will lead to a new quality control target of 1 percent. This approach instills a habit of continuous improvement rather than the traditional western approach of attempting to meet the minimum acceptable standard of performance.

The approach to total quality as advocated in *Quality Is Free* consists of four precepts:

1. Quality must be defined as conformity to requirements, not as goodness.
2. The system for creating quality is prevention, not appraisal.
3. The performance standard must be zero defects, not "that's close enough."
4. The measurement of quality is the price of nonconformity, not indexes.[28]

Quality control thus becomes part of the day-to-day business of every employee. Management needs to evaluate quality in terms of lost sales and total company performance rather than as a percentage indicator from a management control system. Each employee must internalize the value of preventing defects. Crosby's book calls for management to define, quantify, measure, and guarantee conformity to requirements. "Do it right the first time" is the motto.

This approach to control represents a shift from a bureaucratic to a clan method of control. The bureaucratic method does not fully engage

total quality control A control concept that gives workers rather than managers responsibility for achieving standards of quality.

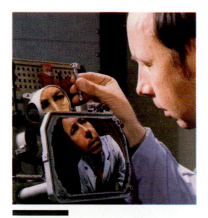

Hughes Aircraft Company has a written commitment signed by the chairman and the president that makes total quality control the number one operating priority. Each employee is obligated to strive for error-free performance. Each manager is required to provide systems and training to enable employees to perform to their highest capability. These quality standards are reflected in the flexible design of the thermal imaging system shown here, which was designed for the M1 tank. The system projects TV-like pictures into the gunners' eyepieces, indicating which objects radiate body heat.

Burlington Industries' commitment to quality has been implemented with new equipment, procedures, and training. In addition, employee involvement programs such as the quality circle shown here tap workers' creativity. The quality circles bring employees together and give them greater operational responsibilities and a sense of "ownership" of work activities. Quality control is successful at Burlington because contingency factors are positive, including highly skilled tasks, enriched jobs, and the challenge of significant problems.

employees' commitment to achieving control standards. Total quality uses clan methods to gain employees' commitment as described in Exhibit 17.6.

The implementation of total quality control is similar to that of other control methods. Targets must be set for employee involvement and for new quality standards. Employees must be trained to think in terms of prevention, not detection, and they must be given the responsibility of correcting their own errors and exposing any quality problems they discover. In the Kawasaki plant in Lincoln, Nebraska, the implementation of the new approach caused a substantial decrease in the size of the quality control department and its role in inspections. Kawasaki shifted from feedback to feedforward control. Quality control inspectors were assigned to the receiving dock to inspect items to be used by Kawasaki workers. If workers had good materials to work with, the final output would be of high quality.[29]

Quality Circles

quality circle A group of from six to twelve volunteer employees who meet regularly to discuss and solve problems that affect their common work activities.

Another approach to implementing a total control philosophy and engaging the work force in a clan approach is that of quality circles. A **quality circle** is a group of from six to twelve volunteer employees who meet regularly to discuss and solve problems affecting their common work activities.[30] Time is set aside during the workweek for these groups to meet, raise problems, and try to find solutions. The key idea is that people who do the job know the job better than anyone else and can make recommendations for improved performance. QCs also push control decision making to a lower organizational level. Circle members are free to collect data and take surveys. In some companies, team members are given training in team building, problem solving, and statistical quality control to enable them to confront problems and solutions more readily. The groups do not focus on personal gripes and problems. Often a facilitator is present to help guide the discussion. The quality circle process as used in most American companies is illustrated in Exhibit 17.8.

The quality circle concept has spread to the United States and Canada from Japan. Originally quality circles were a way for Japanese companies

E X H I B I T   17.8

The Quality Circle Process

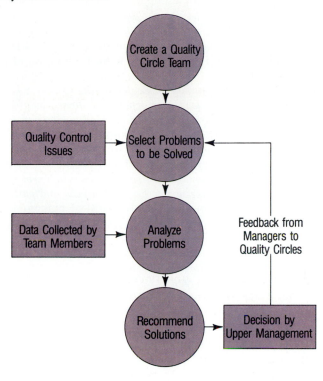

Source: Adapted from Burlington Industries, Inc., *1985 Annual Report*, p. 9.

to gain employees' commitment to high standards. They spread to the United States when executives from Lockheed visited Japan and were impressed by how well quality circles worked. Such North American companies as Westinghouse Electric Corporation, Digital Equipment, Martin Marietta Corporation, and Baltimore Gas & Electric Company have adopted quality circles. In several of these companies, managers attest to the improved performance and cost savings. Westinghouse has over 100 quality circles; a single innovation proposed by one group saved the company $2.4 million. In some cases, workers who participated in on-the-job quality circle groups posed fewer absentees and grievances than coworkers.[31]

QC Contingency Factors

Despite their promise, quality circles don't always work. A few firms have had disappointing results. Generally, the organizational contingency factors in Exhibit 17.9 will influence the chance for QC success.[32] A positive contingency factor is the task skill demands on employees in the QC. When skill demands are great, the quality circle can further enhance productivity. When tasks are simple and require low skills, improved skills from QC meetings will have little impact on output. Quality circle success also increases when the circle serves to enrich jobs and improve

MANAGERS SHOP TALK

Ten Keys to Successful Quality Circles

1. *Explain the quality control QC concept to managers and supervisors, and solicit volunteers.* Assert that quality is a primary objective rather than a side issue. Before any circles are formed, all employees must thoroughly understand what QCs are and what they can do.

2. *Train management volunteers in the QC philosophy so that they can set up circles, train circle members, and maintain the program.* Companies with unions will find it important to treat the QC program as a cooperative venture between the company and the union.

3. *Trained managers present the idea to their work groups and solicit volunteers.* Initial meetings teach employees basic QC techniques. Circle leaders must be skilled in the techniques of team building, motivation, and problem solving.

4. *Trained facilitators coordinate the program's overall structure and provide support to groups.* Facilitators should be people oriented, good communicators, and willing to engage in challenging discussions with individuals from all company levels.

5. *Established circles meet regularly to identify, analyze, and solve work-related problems.* Meetings should be scheduled for one hour to insure a problem focus. Problem areas are easy to identify, but deciding which problem to address first is difficult.

6. *Quality is defined and measured in concrete terms so that positive steps to improve quality control can be taken.* Both statistical (for example, scrap rate) and general (such as consumer response) measurements can be taken.

7. *As circles acquire problem-solving skills, they split, disband, and reform, with experienced members serving as group leaders.* Group leaders may be provided training in motivation, team building, and problem solving.

8. *Responsibility for coordinating QCs may be assigned to a single person or department, and standard operating procedures are developed to avoid overlaps in QC responsibilities.* The responsible manager or department should also monitor QCs to insure they are properly motivated and producing results.

9. *Top management supplies the reinforcement and feedback necessary to keep enthusiasm and participation high.* Recognition in the form of management acknowledgment, trophies, T-shirts, or a special luncheon is appropriate.

10. *A committee composed of top managers studies the proposals from the circles and takes action to implement favorable suggestions.* An explanation is provided for the rejection of a recommendation. Some companies award circle members 10 percent of the money saved from QC suggestions. Others pay participants overtime for the time spent in meetings.

Source: Based on "Quality Circles," *Business Update,* vol. 1, no. 8, pp. 12–18; Mark Bomster, "Quality Circles Help Solve Job Problems," *Houston Chronicle,* May 4, 1986, sec. 5, p. 12; Gerald R. Ferris and John A. Wagner III, "Quality Circles in the United States: A Conceptual Reevaluation," *Journal of Applied Behavioral Science* 21 (1985), pp. 155–167.

employee motivation. In addition, when the quality circle improves workers' problem-solving skills, productivity is likely to increase. Finally, when the participation and teamwork aspects of QCs are used to tackle significant, nonprogrammed problems, such as how to keep metal parts free of oil film, the outcome is better. QCs should not be used to tackle simple, routine problems, such as where to locate the water cooler.

Quality circles often have trouble when senior management's expectations are too high. Managers quickly become disaffected if they are expecting immediate jumps in quality. QC success comes through a series of small, incremental gains. Moreover, middle- and upper-level managers sometimes are dissatisfied because problem-solving opportunities are taken from them and given to employees on the shop floor. Also, when workers are dissatisfied with their organizational lives outside the quality

E X H I B I T   17.9

Quality Circle Contingency Factors

Positive Factors	Negative Factors
Tasks make high skill demands on employees.	Management expectations are unrealistically high.
The QC serves to enrich jobs and motivate employees.	Middle managers frequently are dissatisfied.
Problem-solving skills are improved for team participants.	Workers are dissatisfied with other aspects of organizational life.
Participation and teamwork are used to tackle significant, nonprogrammed problems.	Union leaders are left out of QC discussions.
	Highly automated plants limit improvements in personal productivity.

circle, the QC will have a smaller chance of success. Union leaders can also upset the quality circle program if they feel left out of the discussions between workers and management. Finally, in highly automated plants where machines do most of the work, quality circles have less impact because worker improvements add little to productivity.

When correctly applied, quality circles generate enormous savings. At Lockheed, savings of $3 million were documented. At the Norfolk Naval Shipyard, savings of $3.41 for every dollar invested in a QC program were reported over an 18-month period. Another organization that succeeded with quality circles as a way of implementing a total quality control program is the Sonoco Plant in Texas.

Sonoco Products Company

In mid-1983, Sonoco's Arlington, Texas, plant recorded 48 incidents of defects in production, making it one of Sonoco's most troubled operations. The plant manager, Dan Hause, decided to implement a total quality program. Sonoco would no longer tolerate any defective products. The quality control people were to reject any product not in total compliance with customer requirements, and employees were given the responsibility to police their own efforts.

The zero-defect quality program was based on Philip Crosby's book *Quality Is Free*. Sonoco found that the price of poor quality was enormous. Inspections, rework, lost time for repairs, warranty costs, and reinspection could run 20 to 30 percent of gross sales. It followed Crosby's precepts of making quality the day-to-day requirement, of preventing rather than correcting problems, of setting the standard at zero defects rather than "that's close enough," and of measuring the total cost of nonconformity.

The first step was to set new quality standards and communicate them to all employees. The next step was to form a quality improvement team. This got employees involved. Employees throughout the plant attended a training program on zero defects. Representatives from marketing, production, sales, shipping, and maintenance met regularly to discuss common problems and improve quality levels.

As the teams developed lists of nonconformity areas, the company began posting problem areas, along with their costs, for all employees to see. Sharing information helped involve employees in both the process and the solutions. Open communications fostered honesty and trust between management and employees.

The program's success surprised everyone. In one recent period, rejects were cut by 78 percent. Indeed, after totaling the plant's production records for one production period, Sonoco found there were *no* defects, *no* return orders, and *no* production errors. Profits had increased by 10 percent.

Employees learned that it is their responsibility to maintain quality standards. "The idea that we were now expected to do our job right the very first time was scary at first," said a machine operator. "But when you finally realize the management is serious about not allowing defects and they are really trying to help you, you know the program can work."[33]

CHARACTERISTICS OF EFFECTIVE CONTROL

Whether organizational control focuses on feedforward or feedback activities or whether control emphasizes the bureaucratic or clan methods, certain characteristics should be present. In order for organizational controls to be effective, they should be tailored to the organization's needs and facilitate the accomplishment of its task. Effective controls share the following traits:[34]

1. *Linked to strategy.* The control system should not simply measure what was important in the past or be tailored to current operations. It should reflect where the organization is going and adapt to new strategies. Moreover, the organization should focus on strategic control points that are most relevant for strategic objectives. If the dominant competitive issue facing a company is to develop innovative products, the control system should not emphasize raw materials cost, which is unrelated to innovation.

2. *Uses all control steps.* The control steps consist of setting standards of performance, gathering information about actual performance, comparing standards to real performance, and taking corrective action. The control system will not be effective unless it completes each step. Assuming that people know what standard is expected, for example, is a mistake. Managers should make standards explicit and then identify and obtain relevant information on performance. With valid information on performance, managers can take action to redirect activities to correct deficiencies.

3. *Accepted by members.* The total quality control approach is effective because managers concentrate first on involving the entire organization membership in the control process. The more committed employees are to control standards, the more successful the control system will be. The control system should motivate rather than demotivate. It should set standards and provide information feedback that is meaningful to employees.

4. *Balance objective and subjective data.* Managers can be misled when control system data are either completely numeric or based solely on subjective opinion. Control should be perceived as objective, but quantitative information alone tells only part of the story. Easily measured activities will receive more weight unless managers balance quantitative and qualitative performance indicators. Good control systems are objective and unbiased and incorporate both hard and soft data to provide a well-rounded picture of performance for managers.

5. *Accurate.* Upward communication, especially about performance, often is influenced by what employees feel management wants to hear. Subordinates may distort communications to present a positive image of themselves.[35] Junior managers tend to filter upward communications to highlight positive messages and downplay negative ones.[36] The control system must encourage accurate information in order to detect deviations. If the system is too rigid or oppressive to employees, inaccurate information will be fed into it. The senior management of the Boy Scouts of America learned that membership figures had been exaggerated in response to the pressures of a national membership drive. This campaign led people to feed inaccurate data into the system, and top managers mistakenly believed that the drive was successful.[37]

6. *Flexible.* Organizations exist in changing environments. Internal goals and strategies change over time in response to the environment. The control system must be flexible enough to make adaptations from one year to the next. Managers who rely too heavily on existing controls will find themselves out of synchronization with changing external events. The control system should allow for changing standards and for allocating additional resources to critical activities.

7. *Timely.* The control system should provide information soon enough to permit a management response. Corrective action is of no value if performed too late. A study of air conditioner manufacturers in Japan and the United States found that control

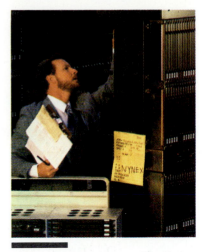

Quality Assurance Manager Tom Rogers of NYNEX Materiel Enterprises inspects a digital switch at a northern telecom plant. Materiel Enterprises was established as a separate unit to evaluate and purchase equiment for NYNEX companies. The unit performs an effective control function—to handle procurement to meet strategic objectives. Subjective data from personal observations are balanced with objective indicators of performance. Relying heavily on feedforward control, the unit uses all four control steps by setting standards, gathering information, comparing standards to actual performance, and taking corrective action with vendors as needed.

data were received twice as fast in Japanese companies and management's responses were quicker.[38] Organizations such as Campbell Taggart in the United States use computer-based control systems to get performance reports to managers on the same day the information is obtained.

SUMMARY

This chapter introduced a number of important concepts about organizational control. Organizational control is the systematic process through which managers regulate organizational activities to meet planned standards of performance. The implementation of control includes four steps: establishing standards of performance, measuring actual performance, comparing performance to standards, and taking corrective action. The relationship of control to strategic planning was discussed. Changes in the environment require that internal control systems adapt to strategic changes; control systems must not continue measuring what was important in the past.

The focus of organizational control can be on resource input, the production process, or product and service outputs. These forms of control are called, respectively, feedforward, concurrent, and feedback control. Most organizations use all three types simultaneously but emphasize the form that most closely corresponds to their strategic objectives.

Organizational control techniques used by managers can emphasize either bureaucratic or clan methods. Bureaucratic control uses the organization's formal rules, procedures, and systems. Clan control involves employee commitment and relies on trust, shared values, and traditions of high performance. Managers can emphasize either control method depending on personal management style, corporate culture, performance measures, and employees' professionalism and desire to participate.

Total quality control is a new approach to control being widely adopted in Canada and the United States that reflects clan control ideas. Everyone in the organization is involved and committed to the control function. Quality circles, which are teams of six to twelve employees who raise quality problems and discuss solutions, are one means of implementing a total quality control philosophy in an organization.

Finally, effective organizational control consists of several characteristics, including a link to strategy, using all four control steps, acceptance by members, balancing objective and subjective data, and the qualities of accuracy, flexibility, and timeliness.

Management Solution

The Electromagnetic Division of Spectrum Control Inc. was suffering high rejection rates for ceramic capacitors and shielded windows. Ted Leofsky, a department manager, took an extraordinary action: He shut the department down cold. This was unexpected, because the department accounted for 40 percent of the division's sales. The dramatic action called everyone's attention to the problem of quality control. Next, Leofsky made a major investment in feedforward control by purchasing $7,000 worth of new gauges with which to evaluate incoming material. Then he established a vendor selection committee to identify the vendors that provided the best products. Next, management got the employees involved. It adopted a total quality control approach, drawing heavily from the book *Quality Is Free*. The new philosophy is "Why not do things right the first time?" The book's author, Philip Crosby, was hired as a consultant to develop quality education courses for every employee.

Simple standards, such as shipping the customer's order on time to avoid transshipping and return costs, were established. One by one the quality problems were solved. Rejection rates took a nosedive. The 32 percent rejection rate for capacitors was reduced to 7 percent and is still dropping. The 15 percent rejection rate for shielded windows was reduced to a scant 0.8 percent. Sales returns to the plant from dissatisfied customers dropped 75 percent. The value of a good control system is evident when Leofsky says, "Life here is a lot more pleasant these days."[39]

DISCUSSION QUESTIONS

1. Why is control an important management function? How does it relate to the other management functions of planning, organizing, and leading?
2. Briefly describe the four steps of control. Give an example of each step from your own organizational work experience.
3. What does it mean to say that organizational control should be linked to strategic planning?
4. How does feedforward control differ from feedback control? Do both types of control use the four control steps?
5. How do organizations that use multiple control systems decide which control elements are most important?
6. What is the difference between bureaucratic and clan control? Which do you think is the stronger form?
7. Think back to an organizational work experience, and diagnose the appropriate control style for that situation.
8. What are the four precepts of *Quality Is Free*, and what do they mean?
9. The theme of total quality control is "The burden of quality proof rests . . . with the makers of the part." How does this differ from traditional North American approaches to quality?
10. What is a quality circle? How can it be used to improve organizational quality control?

CASE FOR ANALYSIS

USING PRIVATE EYES AT GM

Crime in the workplace is a problem faced by practically every major U.S. corporation. Pilferage, drug abuse, and drinking cost companies billions of dollars in lost productivity, absenteeism, and sickness benefits.

Recently at General Motors' Mansfield, Ohio, plant, the drug abuse problem went too far. Although no systematic data were available, the plant manager felt he had to do something. Marijuana and cocaine were being used on the plant floor, in the parking lot, and near the cafeteria. Supposedly at least one out of every ten workers was using drugs or alcohol on the job. A community resident complained that narcotics were flooding the community. One worker received a death threat. Another worker's son died of an opium overdose.

GM's action was extreme: It hired undercover agents to work on the assembly line. The agents worked with law enforcement officials to identify and arrest drug pushers. Users were given disciplinary action or treatment.

How do companies like General Motors control this problem? Some of the tactics used by Fortune 500 companies include compulsory urinalysis, lie detectors, drug-sniffing dogs, counseling and treatment programs, and undercover detectives. GM chose the last option in an effort to destroy the drug culture at the Mansfield and eight other plants.

The detectives were astonished at what they found. They purchased "dime bags" of marijuana easily and pretended to snort cocaine through dollar bills behind machinery on the plant floor. Drug use was difficult to control because the Mansfield plant is huge and employs 4,000 workers. Traditional control techniques didn't work. Security guards were supposed to monitor illegal activities, but one worker attempted to sell cocaine to an undercover agent while security guards were less than 20 feet away. A $4,000 cocaine purchase took place as unsuspecting security guards cruised by.

GM's approach was partially successful. Nearly 200 people were arrested, most of them employees. One arrest of 21 people on the plant floor was applauded by other employees.

Not everyone agrees that the use of private detectives for monitoring employee behavior is appropriate. Some people even feel it is unethical. One union official charged that the operation unfairly concentrated on union members instead of management: "These narcs were strictly sent out to get the union people by GM, but management was doing it too."

Questions

1. Which of the four steps in the control process—setting standards, gathering information on performance, comparing performance to the standard, and taking corrective action—is the most difficult to implement in the case of drug use by employees?

2. Would companies such as General Motors be better off using feedforward rather than concurrent or feedback control to control drugs? Explain. Would clan control work if a drug culture existed in a company?
3. What would be the advantages and disadvantages of other control techniques such as lie detectors, compulsory urinalysis, or drug counseling? Which of these techniques would you consider unethical with respect to employees' rights?

Source: Based on Bryan Burrough, "How GM Began Using Private Eyes to Fight Drugs, Crime," *The Wall Street Journal,* February 27, 1986, pp. 1, 17.

CHAPTER 18

Management Control Systems and Techniques

Chapter Outline

Core Management Control System

Top Management Financial Control

Financial Statements
Financial Forecasts
Financial Analysis
Financial Audits
Management Use of Financial
Controls

**Middle Management Budget
Control**

Responsibility Centers
Operating Budgets
Financial Budgets

The Budgeting Process

Top-down or Bottom-up
Zero-Based Budgeting
Advantages and Disadvantages of
Budget Control

**Controlling through Performance
Appraisal**

Management by Objectives
Assessing MBO Effectiveness
Statistical Process Control

Learning Objectives

After studying this chapter, you should be able to:

- **Identify the components of the core management control system.**

- **Describe financial statements, financial forecasts, financial analysis, and financial audits used for top management controls.**

- **Explain the concept of responsibility centers and their relationship to operating and financial budgets.**

- **Explain the advantages of top-down, bottom-up, and zero-based budgeting.**

- **Define the four essential steps in the MBO process.**

- **Explain the advantages and disadvantages of using MBO for management control.**

- **Describe the procedures used to implement statistical process control and how SPC helps supervisors evaluate subordinates' performances.**

Management Problem

Elling Brothers Mechanical Contractors sprung a leak. On a single construction contract, money was draining out fast enough to bankrupt the company. Elling Brothers was a 53-year-old, well-managed business. But the lush, plush days of easy profits for contractors were over. Industry profit margins were low. This single 15-month job to install industrial piping was a nightmare. It took 30 months to complete, at a loss of $250,000—half of the company's net worth. Elling Brothers was in trouble and needed a solution—fast.[1]

If you were CEO Clifford Elling, what would you do to stop the financial leaks that are about to bankrupt the company? What types of control systems would help you solve this problem, and how would you proceed?

Elling Brothers Mechanical Contractors illustrates a specific type of control problem—expenditures far in excess of budgeted cost targets. In Chapter 17, we described basic control concepts. Now we will look at specific control systems and techniques managers use to steer the organization toward its goals. These control systems include financial ratios, budgets, performance evaluation systems, management by objectives, and statistical reports. Elling Brothers' problem is the budget system, and it can be solved only through improved budget control.

Internal management control systems are part of the bureaucratic method of control described in Chapter 17. Management control systems provide formal data and reports for management evaluation and corrective action. However, the use of management control systems does not mean that organizations cannot use clan methods. Japanese organizations that pioneered quality circles and other clan approaches also rely on good numbers. One study showed that managers in Japanese firms had more quantitative information available from formal control systems than did managers in American firms.[2]

Every organization needs basic systems for allocating financial resources, approving and developing human resources, analyzing financial performance, and evaluating operational productivity. In long-established organizations such as Cummins Engine, Lever Brothers, Mack Trucks, and the U.S. Department of Housing and Urban Development, these systems are already in place. Managers' responsibility is to know how to use these control systems and improve them. In new organizations—especially those that have grown rapidly, such as Culver Personnel Agency, Record Exchange of Roanoke, and Central Petroleum Transport—managers' responsibility is to design new control systems.

Control system design is different for top managers than for middle- and lower-level managers. We will begin by explaining how multiple control systems fit together to provide overall control for top managers and then examine control systems used by middle managers.

CORE MANAGEMENT CONTROL SYSTEM

core control system The strategic plans, financial forecasts, budget, performance appraisal system, operations management techniques, and MIS reports that form an integrated system for directing and monitoring organizational activities.

Research into the makeup of control systems across organizations has revealed the existence of a core management control system. The **core control system** consists of the strategic plans, financial forecasts, budget, performance evaluation system, operations management techniques, and MIS reports that together provide an integrated system for directing and monitoring organizational activities.[3] The elements of the core control system and their relationship to one another are illustrated in Exhibit 18.1. Note how the strategic plan and financial forecast provide guidance for the budget, performance evaluation, and operations management systems used at middle management levels. The definition of each element in the core control system is as follows:

1. *Strategic plan.* The strategic plan consists of the organization's strategic objectives, as discussed in Chapters 4 and 5. It is based on in-depth analysis of the organization's industry position, internal strengths and weaknesses, and environmental opportunities and threats. The written plan typically discusses company products, competition, economic trends, and new business opportunities.

2. *Financial forecast.* The financial forecast consists of a one- to five-year projection of company financial statements. This forecast is number based and includes projected revenues, income statements, balance sheets, and departmental expenditures. This is the company's financial projection based on the overall strategic plan. Companies such as W. R. Grace, Teledyne, and Union Carbide use projected financial statements to estimate their future financial positions.

E X H I B I T   18.1

Core Control System Components

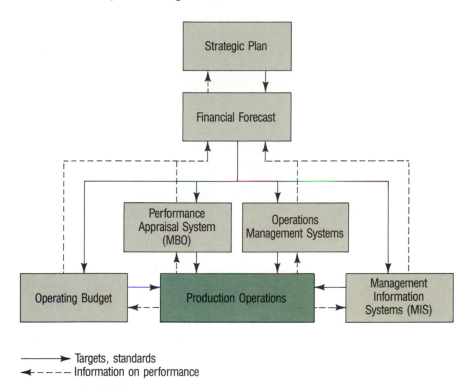

Targets, standards
- - - - Information on performance

3. *Operating budget.* The operating budget is an annual projection of estimated expenses, revenues, assets, and related financial figures for each operating department for the coming year. Budget reports typically are issued monthly and include comparisons of expenditures with budget targets. Budget reports are developed for all divisions and departments.

4. *Performance appraisal.* Performance appraisal is the formal method of evaluating and recording the performances of managers and employees. Chapter 11 described the basic design of the performance evaluation system. It typically includes standard forms and rating scales that evaluate employee skills and abilities. Many companies also use management by objectives (MBO) to direct employee activities toward corporate objectives. MBO is integrated into the performance appraisal system and enhances management control.

5. *Operations management systems and reports.* Operations management systems pertain to inventory (economic order quantity, just-in-time), purchasing and distribution systems, and project management (PERT charts). Using operations management systems for control is the topic of Chapter 20.

The strategic plan and financial forecast guide other elements of an organization's core control system. At Tasty Baking Company, senior managers cooperate in developing plans and forecasts. Senior managers from the corporate planning, finance, and legal departments, shown here, are reviewing the annual budget. They provide planning and control support for all areas of the business.

E X H I B I T   18.2

Application of Control Systems to Management Levels

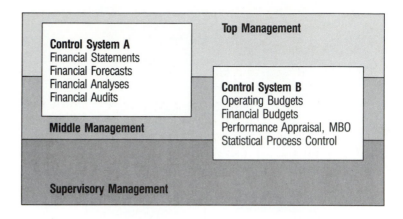

6. *Management information system (MIS) reports.* MIS reports are
    composed of statistical data, such as personnel complements,
    volume of orders received, delinquent account ratios, percentage
    sales returns, and other statistical data relevant to the
    performance of a department or division. MIS reports typically
    contain nonfinancial data, while operating budgets contain
    financial data. MIS reports are issued weekly and monthly, and
    their exact content depends on the nature of task activities and
    available measures. A sales department MIS report may describe
    the number of new sales, while an assembly department MIS may
    record the number of parts assembled per hour. Management
    information systems will be discussed in Chapter 19.[4]

  Each control system component is separate and distinct from the others. The overall strategic plan is top management's responsibility and the
financial forecast the controller's. The budget is concerned with the financial figures and is also the controller's responsibility. The performance appraisal system is usually the responsibility of the personnel department. Operations management techniques are the responsibility of
the production department. MIS reports are produced and distributed
by the information system department. Although each control system
element is distinct, a successful core control system combines them into
an integrated package of controls.
  In this chapter, we discuss control systems as they are used by top and
middle management levels, as illustrated in Exhibit 18.2. Top management control systems concern financial performance for the organization as a whole and include financial statements, forecasts, financial analyses, and audits. Middle managers are responsible for departments and
rely heavily on budgets and performance evaluation systems, especially
MBO, for control. They are also involved, to some extent, in the financial control issues of top managers as well as statistical process control to

evaluate employee performance. The other components of the core control system—MIS reports and operations management techniques—will be discussed in Chapters 19 and 20, respectively.

TOP MANAGEMENT FINANCIAL CONTROL

Based on the overall strategic plan, top management must define a financial forecast for the organization, perform financial analyses of selected ratios to reveal business performance, and use financial audits to evaluate internal operations. Each of these controls is based on financial statements—the building blocks of financial control.

Financial Statements

Financial statements provide the basic information used for financial control of a company. Two major financial statements—the balance sheet and the income statement—are the starting points for financial control.

The **balance sheet** shows the firm's financial position with respect to assets and liabilities at a specific point in time. An example of a balance sheet is presented in Exhibit 18.3. The balance sheet provides three

balance sheet A financial statement showing the firm's financial position with respect to assets and liabilities at a specific point in time.

EXHIBIT 18.3

Balance Sheet

Lester's Clothiers
Consolidated Balance Sheet
December 31, 1988

Assets			Liabilities and Owners' Equity		
Current assets:			**Current liabilities:**		
Cash	$ 25,000		Accounts payable	$200,000	
Accounts receivable	75,000		Accrued expenses	20,000	
Inventory	500,000		Income taxes payable	30,000	
Total current assets		$ 600,000	Total current liabilities		$ 250,000
Fixed assets:			**Long-term liabilities:**		
Land	250,000		Mortgages payable	350,000	
Buildings and fixtures	1,000,000		Bonds outstanding	250,000	
Less depreciation	200,000		Total long-term liabilities		$ 600,000
Total fixed assets		1,050,000	**Owners' equity:**		
			Common stock	540,000	
			Retained earnings	260,000	
			Total owners' equity		800,000
Total assets		$1,650,000	Total liabilities and net worth		$1,650,000

income statement A financial statement that summarizes a company's financial performance over a given time interval.

EXHIBIT 18.4

Income Statement

Lester's Clothiers
Statement of Income
For the Year Ended December 31, 1988

Gross sales	$3,100,000	
Less sales returns	200,000	
Net sales		$2,900,000
Less expenses and cost of goods sold:		
Cost of goods sold	2,110,000	
Depreciation	60,000	
Sales expenses	200,000	
Administrative expenses	90,000	2,460,000
Operating profit		440,000
Other income		20,000
Gross income		460,000
Less interest expense	80,000	
Income before taxes		380,000
Less taxes	165,000	
Net income		$ 215,000

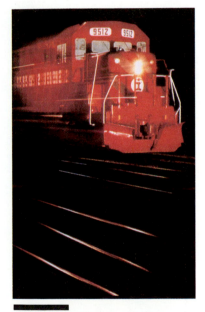

The balance sheet shows the firm's financial position with respect to assets and liabilities at a specific point in time. The Illinois Central Gulf Railroad, a subsidiary of IC Industries, discontinued uneconomical lines of business while spending over $1.5 billion to rebuild its mainline track and high-volume branch lines. This financial reconfiguration influenced the assets, liabilities, and owners' equity reported on the balance sheet. It also improved the income statement, with pretax income increasing to $73 million in 1984. The financial forecast calls for new locomotives and other future capital improvements.

types of information: assets, liabilities, and owners' equity. *Assets* are what the company owns and include *current assets* (assets that can be converted into cash in a short time period) and *fixed assets* (assets that are long term in nature). *Liabilities* are the firm's debts. Liabilities include both *current debt* (obligations that will be paid to the company in the near future) and *long-term debt* (obligations payable over a long period). *Owners' equity* is the difference between assets and liabilities and is the company's net worth in stock and retained earnings.

The **income statement,** sometimes called a *profit-and-loss statement,* summarizes the firm's financial performance for a given time interval, usually one year. A sample income statement is given in Exhibit 18.4. Some firms calculate the income statement at three-month intervals during the year to see if they are on target for sales and profits. The income statement shows revenues coming into the organization from all sources and subtracts all expenses, including cost of goods sold, interest, taxes, and depreciation. The bottom line indicates the net income—profit or loss—for the given time period.

For example, Jim Greenwood, founder of Aahs!, a specialty retailing chain in California, used the income statement to detect that sales and profits were dropping during the summer months. He immediately evaluated company activities and closed two money-losing stores. He also began a new education program to teach employees how to increase sales and decrease costs to improve net income. During the last three months of 1985, the Aahs! gross profit margin was 3 percent ahead of budget.[5]

E X H I B I T   18.5

Financial Forecast for Dowell Motor Supply

Income Statement	1988	1989	1990
Revenue	$480,000	$530,000	$585,000
Cost of sales	390,000	400,000	497,000
Expenses	30,000	40,000	50,000
Depreciation	15,000	38,000	38,000
Gross income	45,000	52,000	60,000
Taxes	20,000	22,000	25,000
Net income	$ 25,000	$ 30,000	$ 35,000
Balance Sheet			
Cash	$ 10,000	$ 12,000	$ 14,000
Inventory	45,000	53,000	65,000
Land and buildings	200,000	190,000	180,000
Total assets	$255,000	$255,000	$259,000
Current liabilities	45,000	45,000	50,000
Long-term liabilities	100,000	90,000	82,000
Owners' equity	110,000	120,000	127,000
Total liabilities and equity	$255,000	$255,000	$259,000

Financial Forecasts

The first step toward financial control is to prepare a financial forecast and compare actual financial statements with forecasted financial statements. Based on the overall strategic plan, the controller's office can calculate income statement and balance sheet forecasts based on anticipated new products, sales, and expansion. The strategic plan for Dowell Motor Supply in Exhibit 18.5 shows an expected revenue increase for the next two years of 22 percent. This forecast can be used by each department to prepare for increases in revenues, personnel, supplies, equipment, and buildings. The acquisition of new personnel, supplies, and equipment will have to move rapidly in order to meet the rising demand for the parts manufactured by Dowell. The financial forecast provides top management with the information needed for diagnosing problems and making corrections to keep the entire corporation on track toward meeting its financial targets.[6]

Financial Analysis

Another step in financial control is to use the data in the financial statements to calculate ratios that will reveal in detail how the company is performing. A *financial ratio* is the comparison of two financial numbers. Several financial ratios can be used to illustrate company performance. Those most frequently calculated are the liquidity, leverage, activity, and profitability ratios. Actual ratios are compared to budget targets and to

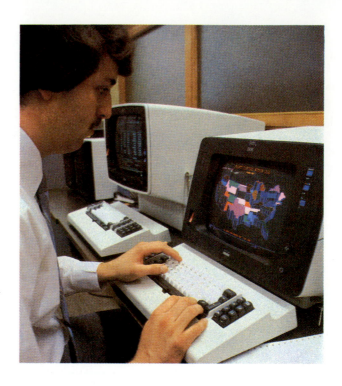

Goodyear financial analysts are involved in analyzing financial data for corporate planning and decision making. The computer graphics shown here have been developed to portray financial information in concise, pictorial form. Financial analysts examine liquidity, leverage, activity, and profitability ratios. They also forecast balance sheet information, cash requirements, profit performance, and inventory and expense controls. These data are also analyzed by product line, market, and profit centers for use in top management's strategic planning.

industry averages to evaluate company performance. Key indicators for each of these ratios for a company called Oceanographics Inc. are illustrated in Exhibit 18.6.

liquidity ratio A financial ratio that indicates the company's ability to meet its current debt obligations.

Liquidity Ratio.   A **liquidity ratio** indicates the organization's ability to meet its current debt obligations. The *current ratio* tells whether there are sufficient assets to convert into cash to pay off debts if needed. In the case of Oceanographics Inc. in Exhibit 18.6, the current ratio is 2.4. This is the same as budgeted and is slightly below the industry average. Since financial ratios vary widely across industries, many companies compare their performances to those of other firms in the same industry as well as to their own budget targets.

leverage ratio A financial ratio that indicates the amount of financing of company operations available from creditors.

Leverage Ratio.   A **leverage ratio** indicates the amount of financing of company operations provided by creditors. This ratio also indicates the organization's ability to meet its financial obligations—that is, whether it has sufficient assets to pay off its liabilities. The most frequently used measure is the *total-debt-to-total-assets ratio,* as illustrated in Exhibit 18.6. For Oceanographics Inc. the ratio is 50 percent, which is high compared to both the budget target and the industry average. The company is highly leveraged because a large part of its operations are financed with borrowed money.

activity ratio A ratio that measures the firm's internal performance with respect to inventory and collection of customer receivables.

Activity Ratio.   An **activity ratio** measures internal performance with respect to activities such as inventory and collection of customer payments. *Inventory turnover* is calculated by dividing total sales by average inventory. This ratio tells how many times the inventory is turned over to meet the total sales figure. For Oceanographics Inc., inventory turnover

EXHIBIT   18.6

Financial Ratios for Oceanographics Inc.

Ratio	Formula	Calculation	Budget Target	Industry Average	Evaluation
Liquidity					
Current ratio	$\dfrac{\text{Current assets}}{\text{Current liabilities}}$	$\dfrac{\$600,000}{\$250,000} = 2.4$ times	2.4	2.5	Satisfactory
Leverage					
Total debt to total assets	$\dfrac{\text{Total debt}}{\text{Total assets}}$	$\dfrac{\$750,000}{\$1,500,000} = 50\%$	40%	40%	Satisfactory
Activity					
Inventory turnover	$\dfrac{\text{Sales}}{\text{Inventory}}$	$\dfrac{\$2,500,000}{\$250,000} = 10$ times	9	9	Good
Average collection period	$\dfrac{\text{Receivables}}{\text{Sales per day}}$	$\dfrac{\$200,000}{\$6,950} = 29$ days	21 days	23 days	Poor
Profitability					
Profit margin on sales	$\dfrac{\text{Net income}}{\text{Sales}}$	$\dfrac{\$200,000}{\$2,500,000} = 8\%$	10%	9%	Satisfactory
Return on total assets	$\dfrac{\text{Net income}}{\text{Total assets}}$	$\dfrac{\$200,000}{\$1,500,000} = 13\%$	12%	11%	Good

is 10, which compares favorably to both the budget and industry standards. The *average collection period* measures the amount of customer receivables divided by the average sales per day. The average collection period for Oceanographics is 29 days, which is unsatisfactory.

Profitability.   Profitability ratios describe the organization's profits. One important profitability ratio is the *profit margin on sales,* which is calculated as net income divided by sales. For Oceanographics Inc., the profit margin on sales is 8 percent. Another profitability measure is *return on total assets (ROA),* which is the percentage return to investors on assets. It is a valuable yardstick of the returns adequacy compared to other investment opportunities. Return on total assets for Oceanographics is 13 percent, which compares well with the budget target and the industry average. Oceanographics' senior managers are making good use of assets to earn profits; thus, the owners are unlikely to sell the company and invest their money elsewhere. Each dollar invested in Oceanographics returns 13 percent, which is more than investors could earn in investments such as U.S. savings bonds or money market accounts.

profitability ratio   A financial ratio that describes the firm's profits.

Financial Audits

Financial audits are independent appraisals of the organization's financial records. Audits are of two types—external and internal.[7] An *external audit* is conducted by experts from outside the organization, typically certified public accountants (CPAs) or CPA firms. An *internal audit* is

financial audit   An independent appraisal of the organization's financial records conducted by external or internal experts.

handled by experts within the organization. Large companies such as Allis-Chalmers, American Can, Boise Cascade, and Boeing have an accounting staff assigned to the internal audit function. The internal auditors evaluate departments and divisions throughout the corporation to insure that operations are efficient and conducted according to prescribed company financial practices.

Both external and internal audits should be thorough. Their purpose is to examine every nook and cranny to verify that the financial statement represents actual company operations. Some of the areas examined by auditors are:

- *Cash:* Go to banks and confirm bank balances; review cash management procedures.
- *Receivables:* Obtain guarantees from customers concerning amounts owed and anticipated payments; confirm balances.
- *Inventory:* Conduct physical count of inventory and compare to financial statement; review for obsolescence.
- *Fixed assets:* Make physical observation, evaluate depreciation; determine whether insurance is adequate.
- *Loans:* Review loan agreements; summarize obligations.
- *Revenues and expenses:* Evaluate timing, propriety, and proper matching.[8]

Management Use of Financial Controls

The financial controls used by top management follow the control steps described in Chapter 17: Targets are set, actual performance is measured, and performance is compared to targets. A more difficult control function is corrective action. Managers must look beneath the numbers to decide exactly what is causing the financial problem and to devise and implement a solution. A financial performance shortfall often has several causes, and managers must be familiar with a range of operations and activities in order to make an accurate diagnosis. The diagnosis must be followed with action plans that will change activities so as to meet financial goals. The financial control tools described so far in this chapter provide top managers with information for analysis that is the start of the control process. Managers then must dig beneath the figures to find the sources of the numbers. After defining the causes, they must initiate programs that will rectify the problem and bring the financial figures back into line.

Lee Iacocca is best known for his turnaround of Chrysler Corporation. But Iacocca learned to analyze financial statements, dig beneath the figures, and initiate corrective programs while he was president of Ford. In Iacocca's own words, here is how he used financial statements as the starting point for solving a number of deeply rooted problems at Ford.

Ford Motor Company

When I became president, the Ford Motor Company had approximately 432,000 employees. In North America alone, we were building close to 2.5 million cars a year and 750,000 trucks. Our total sales for 1970 added up to $14.9 billion, on which we made a profit of $515 million.

Now, while $515 million was certainly nothing to sneeze at, it represented only 3.5 percent of total sales. In the early 1960s, our return on sales had never dipped below 5 percent. I was determined to get it back up.

One of the first moves I made as president was to convene a meeting of top managers to establish a cost-cutting program. I called it "four fifties," as its purpose was to cut operating expenses by $50 million in each of four areas—timing foul-ups, product complexity, design costs, and outmoded ways of doing business. If we could reach our goal within three years, we could improve our profits by $200 million—a gain of almost 40 percent—even before selling a single additional car.

There was plenty of room for improvement. For example, it took us two weeks out of each year to prepare our factories for the production of the next year's models. Through more vigorous computer programming and more sophisticated scheduling, it was possible to reduce the changeover period from two weeks to two days.

Another area where we cut costs was shipping. We began packing the freight cars much more tightly. At one point, I recall, we trimmed a fender design by two inches to allow a few more cars to fit onto each train. With huge sums of money at stake, the last thing I wanted was to be shipping air. When you're dealing with figures like $500 million for freight, even a minuscule saving of half of one percent came to $2.5 million.

I also instituted a program called Shuck the Losers. In a company as large as ours, there were dozens of operations that either lost money or made only minimal profits. And so I announced that managers had three years to either make their departments profitable or sell them off. It was simple common sense, like a large department store whose manager says: "We're losing a ton of money in that boutique over there, so let's close it."[9]

MIDDLE MANAGEMENT BUDGET CONTROL

Budgets are a primary control device for middle management. Of course, top managers too are involved with budgets for the company as a whole, but middle managers are responsible for the budget performance of their departments or divisions. Budgets identify both planned and actual expenditures for cash, assets, raw materials, salaries, and other resources departments need. Budgets are the most widely used control system, because they plan and control the dollar value of resources and revenues essential to the firm's health and survival.[10]

A budget is created for every division or department within the organization, no matter how small, so long as it performs a distinct project, program, or function. In order for budgets to be used, the organization must define each department as a responsibility center.

Responsibility Centers

A responsibility center is the fundamental unit of analysis of a budget control system. A **responsibility center** is defined as any organizational department under the supervision of a single person who is responsible for its activity.[11] A three-person appliance sales office in Watertown, New York, is a responsibility center, as is General Electric's entire refrigerator manufacturing plant. The manager of each unit has budget "responsibility."

There are four major types of responsibility center—cost centers, revenue centers, profit centers, and investment centers. The budget focus for each type of cost center is illustrated in Exhibit 18.7.

Cost Center. A *cost center* is a responsibility center in which the manager is held responsible for controlling cost inputs.[12] The manager is responsible for salaries, supplies, and other costs relevant to the department's operation. Staff departments such as personnel, legal, and research typically are organized as cost centers.

responsibility center Any organizational department under the supervision of a single individual who is responsible for its activity.

E X H I B I T   18.7

Types of Responsibility Centers

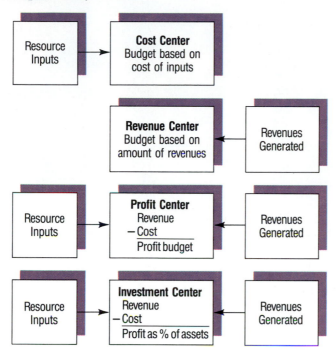

Revenue Center.   In a *revenue center*, the budget is based on generated revenues or income. Sales and marketing departments frequently are revenue centers. The department has a revenue goal, such as $3,500,000. Assuming each salesperson can generate $250,000 of revenue per year, the department can be allocated 14 salespeople. Revenue budgets can also be calculated as the number of items to be sold rather than as total revenues. For example, the revenue budget for an appliance shop might include 50 refrigerators, 75 washers, 60 dryers, and 40 microwaves to be sold for 1988.

Profit Center.   In a *profit center*, the budget measures the difference between revenues and costs. For budget purposes, the profit center is defined as a self-contained unit to enable a profit to be calculated. In Kollmorgen Corporation, each division is a profit center. Control is based on profit targets rather than on cost or revenue targets.

Investment Center.   An *investment center* is based on the value of assets employed to produce a given level of profit. Profits are calculated in the same way as in a profit center, but for control purposes managers are concerned with return on the investment in assets for the division. For example, Exxon may acquire a gasoline refinery for a price of $40 million. If Exxon managers target a 10 percent return on investment, the gasoline refinery will be expected to generate profits of $4 million a year.

Individual businesses within Quaker Oats Company are organized as profit centers. The Profit Center Award is highly coveted in the Quaker organization because it recognizes and symbolizes operating excellence. In 1985, William Smithburg (left), chairman and CEO, presented the award to Jon Grant, president, and all employees of Quaker-Canada for achieving excellent returns and growth. From 1981 to 1985, the profit center's sales were up 57 percent, operating income up 87 percent, and return on invested capital up 26.5 percent.

Exxon managers are not concerned with the absolute dollar value of costs, revenues, or profits so long as the budgeted return on assets reaches 10 percent.

Relationship to Structure.   Responsibility centers are closely related to the types of organization structure described in Chapter 9.[13] Cost centers and revenue centers typically exist in a functional structure. The production, assembly, finance, accounting, and personnel departments each make up part of the organizational whole, and managers control expenditures through cost budgets for each department. Marketing or sales departments, however, often are controlled as revenue centers. Profit centers typically exist in a divisional structure. Each self-contained division can be evaluated on the basis of total revenues minus total costs, which equals profits. Finally, very large companies in which each division is an autonomous business use investment centers. Frito-Lay and Taco Bell are investment centers for PepsiCo. PepsiCo managers are concerned with the return on investment from these companies, and each business is left alone so long as investment goals are met.

Operating Budgets

An **operating budget** is the financial plan for each organizational responsibility center for the budget period. The operating budget outlines the financial resources allocated to each responsibility center in dollar terms, typically calculated for a year in advance. The most common types of operating budgets are expense, revenue, and profit budgets.

Expense Budget.   An **expense budget** outlines the anticipated expenses for each responsibility center and for the total organization. Expense budgets apply to cost centers, as described above. The department of management at the University of Illinois may have a travel budget of $24,000; thus, the department head knows that the expense budget can be spent at approximately $2,000 per month. Three different kinds of expenses normally are evaluated in the expense budget—fixed, variable, and discretionary.

operating budget The plan for the allocation of financial resources to each organizational responsibility center for the budget period under consideration.

expense budget An operating budget that outlines the anticipated expenses for each responsibility center and for the organization as a whole.

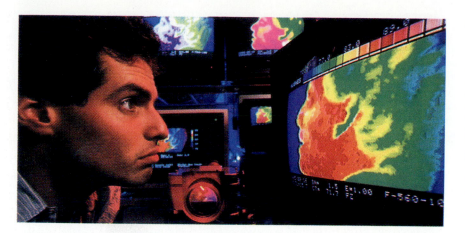

This highly sensitive equipment identifies minute variations in body temperature. Thermography equipment was acquired by Warner-Lambert to develop new over-the-counter pharmaceuticals such as cough/cold, sinus, dental, and oral hygiene products. This is an example of the type of equipment whose purchase is planned for in the capital expenditure budget. The cost of the equipment purchased is recorded as a fixed asset and depreciated or spread over a number of years as a fixed cost in the operating expense budget.

Fixed costs are based on a commitment from a prior budget period and cannot be changed. Expensive machinery purchased three years ago that is paid over a period of 10 years is a fixed cost. The same is true for the annual mortgage payments on a building amortized over 15 years.

Variable costs, often called *engineered costs,* are based on an explicit physical relationship with the volume of departmental activity. Variable costs are calculated in manufacturing departments when a separate cost can be assigned for each product produced. A variable cost budget might allocate two hours of machine time for each turbine blade or $3 in supplies for each integrated circuit board. The greater the volume of production, the greater the expense budget the department will have.

Discretionary costs are based on management decisions. They are not based on a fixed, long-term commitment or on volume of items produced, because such costs cannot be calculated with certainty. In the judgment of top management, an expense budget of $120,000 might be assigned to the inspection department to pay the salaries of four inspectors, one assistant, and one secretary. This budget could be increased or decreased the following year depending on whether management feels this responsibility center is needed.

Revenue Budget. A **revenue budget** identifies the revenues required by the organization. The revenue budget is the responsibility of a revenue center, such as marketing or sales. The revenue budget for a small manufacturing firm could be $3 million, based on sales of 600,000 items at $5 each. The revenue budget of $6 million for a local school district would be calculated not on sales to customers but on the community's current tax rate and property values.

Profit Budget. A **profit budget** combines both expense and revenue budgets into one statement to show gross and net profits. Profit budgets apply to profit and investment centers. If a bank has budgeted income of $2 million and budgeted expenses of $1,800,000, the estimated profit will be $200,000. If the budget profit is unacceptable, managers must develop a plan for increasing revenues or decreasing costs to achieve an acceptable profit return.

fixed costs Costs that are based on a commitment from a previous budget period and cannot be altered.

variable costs Costs that are based on an explicit physical relationship with the volume of departmental activity; also called *engineered costs.*

discretionary costs Costs based on management decisions and not on fixed commitments or volume of output.

revenue budget An operating budget that identifies revenues required by the organization.

profit budget An operating budget that combines both expense and revenue budgets into one statement showing gross and net profits.

MANAGERS SHOP TALK

The Numbers

Harold Geneen, trained as an accountant, used accounting numbers to understand ITT when he was president. In his view, numbers were essential to diagnosing problems. Here is what he said:

Too many people mistakenly believe that large American corporations, like ITT, are run (heartlessly) by the numbers. They make that mistake because most people read words better than they do numbers. They may understand the complex novels of Henry James or James Joyce or Marcel Proust, but they read columns of numbers as they would a vocabulary list of strange, esoteric words. As symbols of what is going on in business, numbers represent measurements, not the business activity itself. René Magritte, the surrealist artist, painted a picture of a man's pipe and on the canvas he wrote, "This is not a pipe." It wasn't. It was a picture of a pipe. So I say: The numbers are not the business; they are only pictures of the business.

Nevertheless, no business could run without them. Numbers serve as a sort of thermometer which measures the health and well-being of the enterprise. They serve as the first line of communication which informs management what is going on, and the more precise the numbers are, the more they are based upon "unshakable facts," the clearer the line of communication.

When a manager makes up a budget for the coming year, he is putting down on paper a series of expectations, expressed in numbers. They include the whole gamut of costs of the product or products—design, engineering, supplies, production, labor, plants, marketing, sales, distribution—and also anticipated income from sales based upon market share, back orders, and what have you. . . . When all the figures are pulled together for one

company or one division, you have its budget. At ITT we had 250 of these profit centers and their annual budgets, replete with numbers, when lined up side by side, occupied thirty-odd feet of shelf space.

Any significant variation between your expectations and what is actually happening in the marketplace, as expressed in those numbers, is a signal for action. The sooner you see the numbers, the sooner you can take action, if needed. However—and this is most important—the numbers themselves will not tell you what to do. They are only a signal for action, a trigger to thinking. It is akin to the man with the divining rod who points to the spot where there is water underground. But to get the water, you have to dig for it. The key issue in business is to find out what is happening behind those numbers.

Once you start digging into the areas which the numbers represent, then you get into the guts of your business. If sales are off, is it because of the design of your product? Its cost? Marketing? Distribution? Financing? What? The search goes on not only at the top of the company but also at the operating levels. . . . You don't want to manage the numbers; you don't want to push sales or receivables from one quarter to another, for the truth will always catch up with you. That is like treating the thermometer instead of the patient. If a thermometer registers above 98.6 degrees, it is telling you the patient has a fever; he is sick. It is not telling you what is wrong, only that something is wrong. You can put the thermometer in a glass of ice water or dunk the whole patient into a bathtub of cold water, and that will bring the number down. But it won't cure him. In business, you want to manage and control the elements of the business itself, not the numbers on your profit-and-loss statement.

Source: Excerpts from *Managing* by Harold Geneen with Alvin Moscow, pp. 182–184, copyright © 1984 by Harold S. Geneen and Alvin Moscow. Reprinted by permission of Doubleday & Company, Inc.

Financial Budgets

financial budget A budget that defines where the organization will receive its cash and how it will spend it.

Financial budgets define where the organization will receive its cash and how it intends to spend it. Three important financial budgets are the cash, capital expenditure, and balance sheet budgets.

cash budget A financial budget that estimates cash flows on a daily or weekly basis to insure that the company has sufficient cash to meet its obligations.

Cash Budget.   The **cash budget** estimates cash flows on a daily or weekly basis to insure that the organization has sufficient cash to meet its obligations. The cash budget shows the level of funds flowing through the organization and the nature of cash disbursements. If the cash budget shows that the firm has more cash than necessary, the company can

E X H I B I T   18.8

Relationships among Budgets

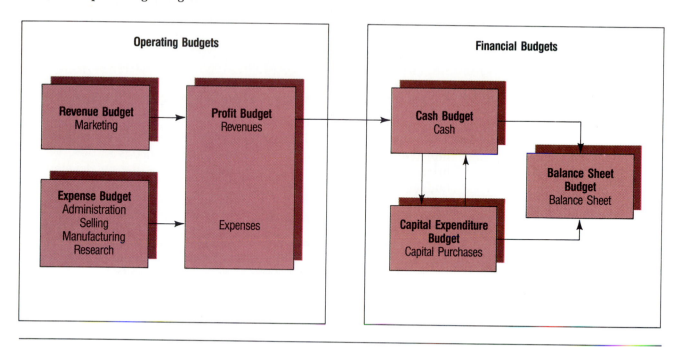

arrange to invest the excess cash in Treasury bills to earn interest income. If the cash budget shows a payroll expenditure of $20,000 coming at the end of the week but only $10,000 in the bank, the controller must borrow cash to meet the payroll.

Capital Expenditure Budget.   The **capital expenditure budget** plans future investments in major assets such as buildings, trucks, and heavy machinery. *Capital expenditures* are major purchases that are paid for over several years. Capital expenditures must be budgeted to determine their impact on cash flow and whether revenues are sufficient to cover capital expenditures and annual operating expenditures. Large corporations such as Navistar, Scott Paper, and Joseph E. Seagram & Sons assign financial analysts to work exclusively on the development of a capital expenditure budget. The analysts also monitor whether actual capital expenditures are being made according to plan.

capital expenditure budget A financial budget that plans future investments in major assets to be paid for over several years.

Balance Sheet Budget.   The **balance sheet budget** plans the amount of assets and liabilities for the end of the time period under consideration. It indicates whether the capital expenditures and cash management, revenues, and operating expenses will mesh into the financial results desired by senior management. The balance sheet budget shows where future financial problems may exist. Financial ratio analysis can be performed on the balance sheet and profit budgets to see whether important ratio targets, such as debt to total assets and ROA, will be met.

balance sheet budget A financial budget that plans the amount of assets and liabilities for the end of the time period under consideration.

The relationships among the operating and financial budgets are illustrated in Exhibit 18.8. All company budgets are interconnected. The revenue budget combined with the cost budget leads to the profit budget. The profit budget influences the amount of cash available, which in turn determines the amount of capital purchases the company can afford. The data from these budgets enable calculation of the balance sheet budget.

The budgeting process is concerned with how budgets are actually formulated and implemented in an organization. In this section, we will briefly describe the procedure many companies use to develop the budget for the coming year.

Top-down or Bottom-up

top-down budgeting A budgeting process in which middle- and lower-level managers set departmental budget targets in accordance with overall company revenues and expenditures specified by top management.

Many traditional companies use **top-down budgeting.** The budgeted amounts for the coming year are literally imposed on middle- and lower-level managers.[14] The top-down process has certain advantages: Top managers have information on overall economic projections; they know the financial goals and forecasts; and they have reliable information about the amount of resources available in the coming year. Thus, the top-down process enables managers to set budget targets for each department within the framework of overall company revenues and expenditures.

The problem with the top-down budgeting process is that lower managers often are not committed to achieving budget targets. They are excluded from the budgeting process and resent their lack of involvement in deciding the resources available to their departments in the coming year.[15]

bottom-up budgeting A budgeting process in which lower-level managers budget their departments' resource needs and pass them up to top management for approval.

In response to these negative outcomes, many organizations adopt **bottom-up budgeting.** Lower managers anticipate their departments' resource needs, which are passed up the hierarchy and approved by top management. The advantage of the bottom-up process is that lower managers are able to identify resource requirements about which top managers are uninformed, have information on efficiencies and opportunities in their specialized areas, and are motivated to meet the budget because the budget plan is their responsibility.[16]

However, the bottom-up approach also has problems. Managers' estimates of future expenditures may be inconsistent with realistic economic projections for the industry or with company financial forecasts and objectives. A university accounting department may plan to increase the number of professors by 20 percent, which is too much if the university plans to increase accounting student enrollment by only 10 percent.

The result of these advantages and disadvantages is that many companies use a joint process. Top managers and the controller define economic projections and financial goals and forecasts and then inform lower managers of the anticipated resources available to them. Once these overall targets (for example, a resource increase of 4 to 7 percent)

E X H I B I T   18.9

Top-down and Bottom-up Budgeting

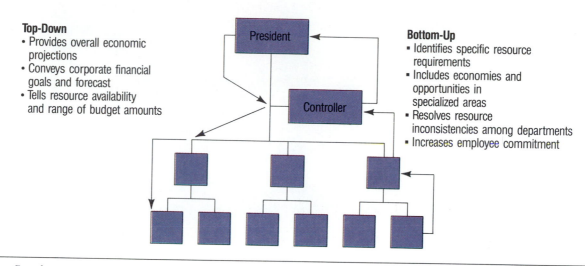

Top-Down
- Provides overall economic projections
- Conveys corporate financial goals and forecast
- Tells resource availability and range of budget amounts

President

Controller

Bottom-Up
- Identifies specific resource requirements
- Includes economies and opportunities in specialized areas
- Resolves resource inconsistencies among departments
- Increases employee commitment

Source: Based on Neil C. Churchill, "Budget Choice: Planning vs. Control," *Harvard Business Review* (July/August 1984), 150–164.

are made available to each department, department managers can develop their budgets within them. Each department can take advantage of special information, resource requirements, and opportunities. The budget is then passed up to the next management level, where inconsistencies across departments can be removed.

The combined top-down and bottom-up process is illustrated in Exhibit 18.9. Top managers begin the cycle. They also end it by giving final approval to all departmental budgets. Departmental budgets fall within the guidelines provided by top management, and the overall company budget reflects the specific knowledge, needs, and opportunities within each department.

Zero-Based Budgeting

In most organizations, the budgeting process begins with the previous year's expenditures; that is, managers plan future expenditures as an increase or decrease over the previous year. This procedure tends to lock departments into a stable spending pattern that is difficult to adapt to environmental changes. **Zero-based budgeting (ZBB)** was designed to overcome this rigidity by having each department start from zero in calculating resource needs for the new budget period.[17] Based on next year's plans and priorities rather than on last year's budget, each responsibility center justifies its work activities and needed personnel, supplies, and facilities for the next budget period. Responsibility centers that cannot justify expenditures for the coming year will receive fewer resources or be disbanded altogether. In zero-based budgeting, each year is viewed as bringing a new set of goals. It forces department managers to thoroughly examine their operations and justify their departments' activities

zero-based budgeting (ZBB) A budgeting process in which each responsibility center calculates its resource needs based on the coming year's priorities rather than on the previous year's budget.

Quaker Oats Company employs a top-down, bottom-up approach to planning and budgeting. Its overall financial objectives, including earnings, dividends, growth rates, and profits, are established at the top and passed down to divisions. Specific budget plans and operating strategies within divisions, such as Quaker-Canada, are defined bottom-up. The two sets of plans are reviewed by senior management and integrated to meet the needs of divisions and the overall corporation.

based on their direct contribution to the achievement of organizational goals.[18]

The zero-based budgeting technique was originally developed for use in government organizations as a way to justify cost requests for the succeeding year. The U.S. Department of Agriculture was the first to use zero-based budgeting in the 1960s. ZBB was adopted by Texas Instruments in 1970 and by many government and business corporations during the 1970s and 1980s. Companies such as Ford, Westinghouse, Owens-Illinois, and New York Telephone, as well as government agencies at both the federal and state levels, use zero-based budgeting techniques.

The specific steps used in zero-based budgeting are as follows:

1. Managers develop a *decision package* for their responsibility centers. The decision package includes written statements of the department's objectives, activities, costs, and benefits, alternative ways of achieving objectives, consequences of not performing each activity, and personnel, equipment, and resources required during the coming year.

2. Each manager ranks the activities for which he or she is responsible. Then senior managers rank the decision packages from the responsibility centers according to their degree of benefit to the organization. These rankings involve widespread management discussions and may culminate in a voting process in which managers rate activities from "essential" to "would be nice to have" to "not needed."

3. Top management allocates organizational resources based on activity rankings. Budget resources are distributed according to the activities rated as essential to meeting organizational goals. Some departments may receive large budgets and others nothing at all.

E X H I B I T   18.10

Advantages and Disadvantages of Budgets

Advantages	Disadvantages
▪ Facilitate coordination across departments	▪ Can be used mechanically
▪ Translate strategic plans into departmental actions	▪ Lack of participation can demotivate employees
▪ Record organizational activities	▪ Can cause perceptions of unfairness
▪ Improve communication with employees	▪ Can create competition for resources and politics
▪ Improve resource allocation	▪ Can limit opportunities for innovation and adaptation
▪ Reallocations provide a tool for corrective action	

Advantages and Disadvantages of Budget Control

Budgeting is the most widely used control system in North American organizations. It offers several advantages to managers but can also create problems. The advantages and disadvantages of budgets are summarized in Exhibit 18.10.

The first major strength of budgeting is that it coordinates activities across departments. The budget ties together resource requirements from each responsibility center into a financial blueprint for the entire firm. Second, budgets translate strategic plans into action. They specify the resources, revenues, and activities required to carry out the strategic plan for the coming year. Third, budgets provide an excellent record of organizational activities. Fourth, budgets improve communication, because they provide information to employees. Budgets let people see where the organization is going and their role in that mission. Fifth, budgets improve resource allocation, because all requests are clarified and justified. Senior managers get a chance to compare budget requests across departments and set priorities for resource allocation. Finally, budgets provide a way of implementing corrective action. For example, when personal computer sales declined in 1985, IBM used a budget to reduce expenditures for PC manufacturing and increase budgeted resources for other computer lines.

Budgets can also cause headaches for managers when improperly used. The major problem occurs when budgets are applied mechanically and rigidly. The budgeting process is then only an exercise in filling out paperwork, with each department getting the same percentage increase or decrease as the others. Second, when managers and employees are not allowed to participate in the budget-setting process, budgeting is demotivating. If budgets are arbitrarily imposed top down, employees will not understand the reason for budgeted expenditures and will not be committed to them. A third weakness occurs when budget perceptions differ across hierarchical levels. Supervisors also may feel they did not receive a fair share of resources if top managers do not explain corporate priorities and budget decisions. Fourth, budgets may pit departments against one another. Managers may feel their own activities are essential and even resort to politics to get more resources. Finally, a rigid budget structure reduces initiative and innovation at lower levels, making it impossible to obtain money for new ideas. Some companies, such as 3M, set discretionary resources aside to prevent this problem.

Skilled managers who understand budgets and how to use them have a powerful control tool with which to attain departmental and organizational goals. One manager who knows how to use budgets to achieve goals is the CEO of a grocery store chain in Orlando, Florida.

Thrifty Scott Warehouse Food Inc.

Bob Popaditch, CEO of Thrifty Scott Warehouse Food, likes to talk about cost control and profit margins. He understands budget matters and has learned how to use them to motivate managers.

In a talk to several of his store managers, he reviewed budget performance. "Let's talk about the last 36 weeks," he began. "You could say that things looked pretty good. Sales were just 2.9 percent off budget. Not bad. Payroll was over budget a bit, but only by 0.24 percent. Pretty close."

Popaditch knows that overall budget figures are abstract and boring for his managers. He has learned that budgets motivate people when "spoken" in their language. Thus, the 2 percent shortfall in sales amounts to $244,000 for the 36 weeks. Popaditch went on breaking down the sales shortfall. That comes down to $26.85 in sales per hour. The average number of customers per hour is 87, which is just $0.31 more sales per customer. Store managers understand this. They simply need to get each customer to buy $0.31 more while in the store.

What about payroll? Over budget by 0.24 percent is pretty close, but it amounts to $9,163 per store, or $254 per week for each store. That's about 52 hours of labor. Since each store has about 50 employees, that's one hour per employee per week.

So that's how Bob Popaditch gets his managers to look at the problem: "$0.30 per customer, 60 minutes per employee." A small increase in income and an easily manageable decrease in costs will lead to 100 percent attainment of budget targets and a tidy increase of $65,804 in net profit. Budget figures are not abstract numbers drawn out of the air. When used by effective managers, they translate into action that produces better performance.[19]

CONTROLLING THROUGH PERFORMANCE APPRAISAL

In addition to budgets, middle managers can use performance appraisal to control their departments. The performance appraisal system is designed to provide "the systematic description of the job-relevant strengths and weaknesses of employees."[20] As discussed in Chapter 11, the performance appraisal system is important because it provides a basis for rewarding and developing employees in all departments—marketing, advertising, finance, quality control, and industrial engineering.

The performance appraisal system has the potential to be a control device for management. A variation, called management by objectives (MBO), was developed to strengthen the control aspect of performance appraisal. With MBO, the performance appraisal system is a means with which to set targets for employees, monitor their performance, compare performance to targets, and take corrective action—the four steps in the organizational control process.

Management by Objectives

Management by objectives (MBO) is related to goal- and objective-setting ideas described in Chapter 4. Management by objectives concept is credited to Peter Drucker and has been widely adopted in American and Canadian corporations. Traditional performance appraisal systems focus on employee characteristics, such as strengths and weaknesses, but MBO focuses on the achievement of explicit objectives.[21] **Management by objectives** assists managers in defining objectives for every department, project, and employee and uses those objectives to control subsequent performance.

A model of the essential steps of the MBO process is presented in Exhibit 18.11. The four major activities that must occur in order for MBO to be successful are setting objectives, developing action plans, reviewing progress, and appraising overall performance.[22]

Setting Objectives. Setting objectives is the most difficult step in MBO. Objective setting looks beyond day-to-day activities to answer the question "What are we trying to accomplish?" Objective setting involves employees at all levels. Top managers set overall corporate objectives that define priorities for middle managers. Middle managers define objectives for the departments and divisions for which they are responsible. Corporate and departmental objectives are used to set objectives for individual employees.

Objectives may be both quantitative and qualitative depending on whether outcomes are measurable. Quantitative goals typically are described in numerical terms, such as "Obtain 16 new sales accounts," "Hire 3 new financial analysts," or "Increase the occupancy rate to 80 percent." Qualitative objectives use terms such as "Improve customer

management by objectives (MBO) A variation of performance appraisal in which managers define objectives for each department, project, and employee and use them to control subsequent performance.

EXHIBIT 18.11

Model of the MBO Process

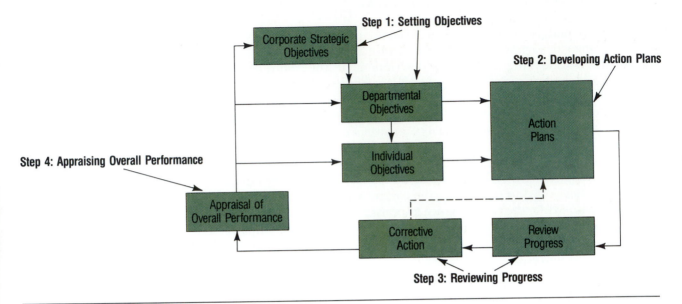

service," "File reports promptly," and "Increase minority hiring." The qualitative statements must be sufficiently precise to permit realistic appraisal and evaluation.

Objectives should be mutually derived. Mutual agreement between subordinate and supervisor results in the strongest commitment to achieving objectives. If employees have no voice in objective setting, they will resist MBO control and be unmotivated to achieve their objectives. Mutual agreement is crucial for obtaining total commitment and a shared responsibility for achieving results.

action plan A step in MBO that defines the course of action needed to achieve stated objectives.

Developing Action Plans.   An **action plan** defines the course of action needed to achieve the stated objectives. Action plans are made for both individuals and for departments. A department may undertake an entirely new work activity because of a new corporate objective. If a university decides to raise $5 million in donations, the college of arts and sciences will have to start fund-raising activities. The action plan would define exactly how fund raising should be performed to achieve the objective. Likewise, each employee must develop an action plan for achieving his or her personal objectives. If a marketing manager is given the objective of increasing the sales volume by 6 percent, the following action plan might be undertaken: (1) Start a sales discount program for high-volume buyers; (2) work with salespeople to increase sales performance by 5 percent; (3) seek a 10 percent increase in the advertising budget; and (4) hire one additional salesperson.

Reviewing Progress.   A periodic progress review is important to insure that action plans are working. These reviews can occur informally between managers and subordinates, or the organization may wish to conduct three-, six-, and nine-month reviews during the year. This periodic checkup allows managers and employees to see whether they are on target and whether corrective action is necessary. If the sales manager finds that quantity discounts are having no impact on sales, that idea may be dropped and the resources transferred to advertising. Managers and employees should not be locked into predefined behavior and must be willing to undertake whatever actions are necessary to produce meaningful results. The point of MBO is to achieve objectives. The action plan can be changed whenever objectives are not being met.

Appraising Overall Performance.   The final step in MBO is to evaluate whether annual objectives have been achieved for both individuals and departments. This appraisal carefully evaluates whether 16 new sales accounts were obtained, 3 new financial analysts were hired, or the organization achieved an 80 percent occupancy rate. Qualitative objectives, such as filing reports in a timely fashion or increasing minority hiring, also are carefully appraised. Success or failure to achieve objectives can become part of the performance appraisal system and the designation of salary increases and other rewards.

The appraisal of departmental and overall corporate performance shapes objectives for the next year. The MBO cycle repeats itself on an annual basis. The specific application of MBO must fit the needs of each company. An example of how one company used MBO to solve a safety problem follows.

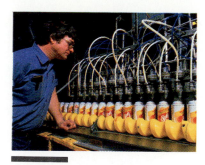

Gillette Company uses management by objectives. Corporate objectives include (1) profitable growth and (2) improved cost control. The cost control objective has been a continuing effort, and the action plans and annual appraisal have decreased cost of sales as a percentage of net sales from 47.4 percent in 1979 to 41.9 percent in 1984, representing an annual savings of $126 million, based on 1984 sales. A principal contributor to lower cost of sales has been a program to reduce direct product costs by 4 percent annually. An important element in achieving this objective has been new machinery and equipment for improving productivity, as shown here.

Producers Gas and Transmission Company

Producers Gas and Transmission Company is a medium-size refinery and distributor of gasoline and other refinery products. A major concern of top management was an unusually high employee accident rate during the previous year. Ten employees had minor injuries, four were severely injured, and one was killed. The company lost 112 employee days of work due to accidents. Top management discussed the accident rate and decided on a corporate objective of a 50 percent reduction in all accidents for 1988. Based on discussions with top managers, department managers also adopted the objective of a 50 percent reduction in accidents.

Middle managers developed an action plan that included (1) the establishment of an employee safety training program, (2) the creation of a companywide safety committee, and (3) a new system of safety recognition. Also, (4) line supervisors were asked to develop safety training sessions for their departments within 60 days, and (5) middle managers were given 30 days to nominate supervisors to the safety committee. Finally, (6) the safety committee had 30 days in which to design a safety recognition program, including awards.

Progress was reviewed through the compilation of quarterly safety reports measuring percentage of accidents compared to the previous year. The action plan could be revised if obstacles were discovered. The safety committee appraised the safety performance of each department every 90 days and posted the results for all employees to see. Letters of commendation were given to departments that met or exceeded the 50 percent reduction objective.

At the end of the year, an overall performance appraisal was held for individuals, departments, and the corporation as a whole. Departments that had successfully reduced accidents by 50 percent were given awards (wall plaques). Information about safety procedures and accident rates was used to set a new safety objective for 1989. Delinquent departments were given stringent objectives. Most important, the company achieved its 1988 objective of reducing accidents by 50 percent. The MBO system energized employee actions companywide toward a goal deemed critical by top management. MBO got all employees working toward the same end.[23]

Assessing MBO Effectiveness

Research findings have reported no dramatic increases in performance by organizations that use MBO.[24] However, many companies, such as Intel, Tenneco, Black and Decker, and DuPont, have adopted MBO, and most managers feel that MBO is effective.[25] Managers believe they are better oriented toward goal achievement when MBO is used. Like any system, MBO has many benefits when used properly and is associated with management problems when used improperly.

Benefits of MBO.   Major benefits to companies that use MBO include the following:

1. Corporate objectives are achieved by focusing manager and employee efforts on specific activities that will lead to their attainment.
2. Performance can be improved at all company levels because employees are committed to attaining objectives.
3. Employees are motivated because they know what is expected and are free to be resourceful in accomplishing their objectives.
4. Departmental and individual objectives are aligned with company objectives. Objectives at lower levels enable the attainment of objectives at top management levels.
5. Relationships between managers and subordinates are improved by having explicit discussions about objectives, defining activities that will help achieve them, and assigning responsibility.

6. Control procedures are improved because systems for reporting on progress toward objective achievement are developed and used. Managerial attention is focused on activities critical for goal attainment rather than on every activity within their departments.[26]

Problems with MBO. MBO does not work in every situation. Some of the problems that can occur with MBO are as follows:

1. Constant change prevents MBO from taking hold. The environment and internal activities must have some stability in order for performance to be measured and compared against goals. If new objectives are defined every few months, the implementation of action plans and appraisal will have no time to take effect before the objectives are abandoned and new ones established.

2. An environment of poor employer-employee relations reduces MBO effectiveness. If management lacks confidence in subordinates or feels that they will not be committed to objectives, the objective-setting process will be ineffective.

3. Organizational values that discourage participation can harm the MBO process. Managers may lack the training or ability to jointly set objectives with employees. Training must be undertaken to help employees at all levels learn participative MBO skills.

4. Lack of top management support will undercut MBO efforts. The initiative for MBO must come from the top of the organization as a clear statement of corporate objectives. If top managers take no steps to define corporate goals and appraise whether they are being reached, the MBO program will not work.

5. Too much paperwork saps MBO energy. If MBO becomes a process of routinely filling out annual forms rather than energizing employees to achieve explicit goals, MBO will be an empty exercise. Once the routine paperwork is completed, employees will forget about the objectives and go about their daily activities—only to have to fill out paperwork again the following year.

Statistical Process Control

Another technique for performance evaluation is statistical process control. **Statistical process control (SPC)** is the use of carefully gathered data and statistical analyses to evaluate the quality and productivity of employee activities. Statistical process control increases a manager's ability to measure employee outputs. It is widely used in manufacturing departments, where worker activities are measurable. Statistical process techniques can also be used in any department in which outputs can be defined and employee tasks can be subdivided into discrete, measurable elements.

The basic principles of statistical process control can be realized through the following procedures:

statistical process control (SPC) A type of managerial control that employs carefully gathered data and statistical analysis to evaluate the quality and productivity of employee activities.

AMP is the leading producer of electrical/electronic connection devices. AMP has adopted statistical process control to improve quality in its 85,000 types and sizes of connection devices. Here an AMP statistical process control specialist instructs suppliers on the latest quality control techniques. Statistical process control is used to evaluate supplier as well as employee performance. SPC is helping AMP achieve a tenfold improvement in quality in five years.

1. *Define the characteristics of a high-quality output.* The output can be a hamburger produced by a Wendy's restaurant, a job description written by an employee in the personnel department, or a radial tire produced at a Firestone plant. The supervisor must provide an exact definition of a high-quality output or service.

2. *Decompose the work activities into the discrete elements required for producing a high-quality output.* For making a hamburger, one discrete element is forming the raw hamburger patty, a second is cooking it, and a third is garnishing it. The quality associated with each discrete element must be defined.

3. *Each work element must have a standard that is current and reasonable.* If standards for work elements are not already available, they must be developed. The standard is the basis for comparison of worker performance.

4. *Specific performance expectations for every job must be communicated to workers.* It's important that each worker understand what the supervisor expects with respect to his or her work elements and quality outputs. Workers should be given a chance to agree or disagree and know how their performances will be measured.

5. *Make checksheets and collect data for each task element.* The supervisor must develop written documents that reflect performance and teach machine operators to collect data and assess whether their performances are up to standard. Likewise, supervisors can monitor employee performance by gathering data on their outputs.

6. *Employee progress must be evaluated against standards at frequent intervals.* In some manufacturing situations, the supervisor should check the output records for every worker several times during the day. If employees are involved in running several different batches of material, different standards will apply. If planned quality and quantity standards are not being met, changes can be made before the end of the work period.

E X H I B I T   18.12

Documents for Statistical Output Control

Chart A: Daily Record

Work Assignment			Follow-Up			Report	
Name	Job	Target	Period 1	Period 2	Period 3	Actual	% Target

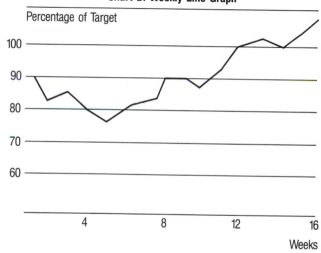

Chart B: Weekly Line Graph

Tridon Ltd., an Oakville, Ontario, manufacturer of windshield wiper blades, implemented an SPC program in 1983. It discovered that 25 percent of the output from the rubber extrusion line was defective. The rubber couldn't be reworked and thus was lost. To set up its program, Tridon conducted a feasibility study to identify the dimensions of high-quality parts. After defining standards for performance, it taught operators how the production line functioned and how to collect data that would indicate whether quality standards were being met. Setting up the SPC program cost almost $30,000 for studies, analysis, and training. Since implementing the SPC program, Tridon's scrap rate has decreased 10 percent. Each part produced is better but costs less because supervisors are able to gather output data on workers' performance at each stage of the manufacturing process.[27]

The charts in Exhibit 18.12 illustrate statistical records that supervisors can gather and use. Chart A describes employee output and is completed daily by a supervisor or employee. Note that the day is divided into three periods, but for some jobs this is too frequent; one observation a day may be sufficient. Chart B shows a simple line graph that illustrates whether the employee met quality and production standards for the previous three months. Line graphs can also be calculated for the department as a whole to show whether departmental goals were met. Supervisors at General Electric use charts such as those in Exhibit 18.12 to gather output data on production activities.[28]

SUMMARY

This chapter introduced a number of important concepts about management control systems and techniques. Organizations have a core management control system consisting of the strategic plan, financial forecast, operating budget, performance appraisal system, operations management system, and management information system. Top management financial control uses the balance sheet, income statement, and financial forecast and financial analyses of these documents.

At the middle levels of the organization, budgets are an important control system. Departments are responsibility centers, each with a specific type of operating budget—expense, revenue, or profit. Financial budgets are also used for organizational control and include the cash, capital expenditure, and balance sheet budgets. The budget process can be either top down or bottom up, but a budget system that incorporates both seems most effective. Zero-based budgeting is a variation of the budget process and requires that managers start from zero to justify budget needs for the coming year. Management by objectives is another important control device used by middle managers. MBO involves four steps: setting objectives, developing action plans, reviewing progress, and appraising overall performance. Finally, statistical process control is the use of statistical data to evaluate employee outputs.

Management Solution

Elling Brothers Mechanical Contractors found itself losing an enormous amount of money on building projects. President Cliff Elling decided it was time to plug the leaks. Elling Brothers had to cut costs quickly and scrounge for every penny just to stay alive. The top six executives took salary cuts. Bonuses and profit sharing were eliminated. Purchasing was rationed, with only urgent deliveries accepted. Things were so desperate that Elling and other stockholders pledged their homes and personal assets to borrow operating capital.

The firm gradually came back as managers were able to develop a budgeting and cost-monitoring system that would blow the whistle on costs. First, they implemented a system that provided budget information quickly. Next, they developed a targeted cost-monitoring system. The budget focused attention on items for which costs were most likely to get out of hand. The new philosophy was to have a good, detailed analysis with rapid feedback. Then "you concentrate your energy where the danger is," says Elling. Now Elling can pinpoint problems quickly. "We're making more money than ever before, not because of fatter markups or less competition, but because we know in a timely way about any problems. . . . We have found it is critical to know where we stand, and the only way to do this is by having reasonable control over the budget and schedule."[29]

DISCUSSION QUESTIONS

1. What is the core control system? How do its components relate to one another for control of the production process?
2. What are the four types of responsibility centers, and how do they relate to organization structure?
3. What types of analyses can be performed on financial statements to help managers diagnose a company's financial condition?
4. When using financial analyses, which do you think is more important: diagnosing organizational problems or taking corrective action to solve them? Discuss.
5. Explain the difference among fixed costs, variable costs, and discretionary costs. In which situation would each be used?
6. What are the advantages of top-down versus bottom-up budgeting? Why is it better to combine the two approaches?
7. According to zero-based budgeting, a department that cannot justify a budget will cease to exist. Do you think this actually happens under zero-based budgeting? Discuss.
8. If you were a top manager of a medium-size real estate sales agency, would you use MBO? What types of objectives would you set for managers and sales agents?
9. What are action plans? Why are they so important for MBO effectiveness?
10. Can statistical process control help a manager establish clan control within a department? Explain.

CASES FOR ANALYSIS

APPLE COMPUTER INC.

During the last quarter of 1984, Apple Computer made a strong finish. Five hundred thousand computers were sold during that period. Unfortunately, a slowdown in the computer industry was masked by strong Christmas sales. Consumer interest in portable computers was declining, and Apple got the first bad news in January of 1985. The finance department reported that dealers had an average of 7.2 weeks' worth of inventory, well above the normal average of 4.1 weeks. Excess dealer inventory was forecasted to slow sales during the first six months of 1985. Dealers would have to sell off inventory before reordering from Apple.

Sales for the first quarter of 1985 were only $435 million and profits $10 million, both well below Apple's business plan. The slowdown in sales hurt profits badly, because costs decreased at a slower rate than sales. Apple's expense budget was difficult to reduce because of the large proportion of fixed costs—people and facilities.

President John Scully issued a memo urging employees to control spending. Actions to be taken included (1) shutting down all manufacturing facilities for one week, (2) asking all employees to take one week of vacation time, and (3) asking all employees to reduce expenses wherever possible. Moreover, efforts were made to increase sales without increasing costs. Expensive network television advertising was replaced with local radio and newspaper advertising.

These measures helped but were not enough. Finally, Scully initiated a major cost reduction program. The cost reduction eliminated 1,200 jobs and closed 3 factories. Budgets for remaining departments were kept tight. It was a traumatic experience, but it put Apple on a profitable footing.

Questions

1. Discuss the Apple Computer situation in terms of the budget and finance concepts described in this chapter. Which concepts seem most relevant for explaining financial control systems at Apple?
2. The approach used by John Scully seems to have been top-down budgeting. Do you think this was appropriate? Should top-down have been combined with bottom-up budgeting in this situation?
3. Based on the information available in this case, would you say that Apple had an adequate budget system?

Source: Based on Apple Computer Inc., 1985 Annual Report, pp. 6–22.

METALLIC FINISHES INC.

Metallic Finishes Inc. is a producer of chrome finishes and specialty metals. In 1987 the new executive vice-president, Stuart Galante, was committed to using the latest management techniques. His first step was to install a new management-by-objectives system for middle and senior managers. The plan was to appraise managers on goal achievement rather than on general activities. Each manager met with his or her superior to set objectives through mutual discussion.

One day Galante had lunch with Dr. Hank Gilman, vice-president for research and development. One of the topics discussed was whether the

MBO system was working in the R&D department. Galante was concerned that Metallic Finishes would fail to achieve its long-term goal of having 25 percent of all sales come from new products by 1990.

Gilman reassured Galante that there was no problem. He explained that it took several years to produce a new product and top management should have confidence in the research team. To illustrate, Gilman said they had data showing an increase in the number of technical papers written and conferences attended and that equipment purchases were down 5 percent. Moreover, the waste rate on experimental materials had dropped 12 percent. The R&D department also was employing one less researcher and one less lab technician than in the previous year. "All in all," said Gilman, "we are running a very efficient operation, and I don't see how we can do much more under this new MBO system of yours."

Questions

1. Do you agree with Gilman's conclusions about the successful performance of the research and development department?
2. How does this MBO system fit the MBO model as summarized in Exhibit 18.11? What improvements would you make? Which aspects seem satisfactory?
3. Do you think the executive vice-president, Stuart Galante, did a good job of implementing the MBO system? Explain.

Source: Based on "Metallic Finishes, Inc.," in Richard L. Daft, *Organization Theory and Design* (St. Paul, Minn.: West, 1983), pp. 320–321, and "Goals and Gripes," in Richard N. Farmer, Barry M. Richman, and William G. Ryan, *Incidents for Studying Management and Organization* (Belmont, Cal.: Wadsworth, 1970), p. 83.

CHAPTER 19

Management Information Systems

Chapter Outline

Information and Management

Data versus Information
Characteristics of Useful Information

Information Systems for Management

Information System Components
Hardware and Software

CBISs and the Management Hierarchy

Transaction Processing Systems
Management Information Systems
Decision Support Systems

Other Information Technologies

Telecommunications
Artificial Intelligence
Networking
Automated Offices

Impact of Information Technology on Organizations

Management Efficiency
Social Relationships
Organization Structure

Strategic Management and Information Technology

Low-Cost Strategy
Differentiation Strategy

Limitations of CBISs

Learning Objectives

After studying this chapter, you should be able to:

- **Describe the importance of information systems for management and the characteristics of useful information.**

- **Describe the components of an information system.**

- **Explain how computer-based information systems are designed to meet the needs of managers at different levels in the organizational hierarchy.**

- **Explain transaction processing, MIS, and DSS and the role of each in organizations.**

- **Describe other new information technologies being used in organizations.**

- **Discuss the impact of information technology on manager efficiency, social relationships, organization structure, and organizations' business strategy.**

- **Discuss the limitations of computer-based information systems.**

Management Problem

Bank of America has a problem. Strategic managers lack enough customer information to launch a marketing campaign to compete against Merrill Lynch, Sears, and other financial institutions that have entered the banking arena since deregulation. For example, Bank of America finances 250,000 California home buyers each year, but it has no database to show whether these high-potential customers use other bank services. In an effort to hold down costs, Bank of America invested little in new technologies during the 1970s. Moreover, BofA has a huge network of 950 branches and international units, each operating as an independent business and using different reporting methods and incompatible computer systems. President Armacost has put it this way: "We've been sitting here with a gigantic battleship that was built to compete before nuclear subs and long-range fighter aircraft ever came along."[1]

What recommendations would you make for improving information systems at Bank of America? What systems might help BofA reduce costs and become more competitive in the marketplace?

The problem confronting Bank of America is to develop internal databases and information systems to help senior executives manage a huge, decentralized banking organization. Information management is a challenge facing every organization. New information products and services available for use in organizations include teleconferencing, microcomputers, software packages, distributed data processing, artificial intelligence, automated offices, electronic mail, voice mail, networking, and database management systems.

Ready or not, the computer revolution is bringing changes to organizations. Several years ago personal computers were introduced to universities, where required computer courses are now common. These Apple PCs are being used at the grade school level, which means that future generations of managers will be computer literate from an early age. With so much of the work force involved in information products and services, computer literacy is expected to be a major requirement for management success.

The proliferation of information technology can be overwhelming. Tomorrow's managers will have to understand the applications of these technologies in order to improve organizational competitiveness and performance. We are in the midst of an information revolution. Over half of the U.S. work force is now involved in information products or services. Since the first computer was built in 1942, technological developments have been breathtaking. Had the automobile industry experienced a similar rate of development, one could buy a Rolls Royce for $280 and drive it 1 million miles on a gallon of gas.

The computer revolution is bringing changes to organizations, whether they like it or not. For example, Hercules Inc. is using electronic technologies to reduce the number of managers. Digital Equipment Corporation uses artificial intelligence systems to determine how its customers' equipment should fit together. First Boston Corporation has electronic linkage to real estate agents who check for mortgage rates and availability, thereby facilitating the lending process. Large companies such as American Airlines, AT&T, and American Express could not account for their operations, control their assets, or manage projects without computers. American Express has 16 major information processing centers, 10 worldwide data networks, 90 mainframe computer systems, 400 minicomputer systems, and 30,000 individual work stations to support its data processing requirements.

The purpose of this chapter is to describe the basic principles of management information systems and their impact on managers. As discussed in Chapters 17 and 18, management information systems represent one control system component in organizations. To effectively manage and control organizations in an information-dominated world,

FOCUS

INTERNATIONAL

Kompyuter Use in the Soviet Union

During one of his first Politburo meetings, General Secretary Gorbachev launched a campaign to computerize the Soviet economy. The Soviets have about 100,000 mainframe and minicomputers in place—only a fraction of America's 1.3 million. They are in even worse shape in the area of micro- and personal computers, with only a few thousand compared with the 25 million in the United States. One Soviet goal is to place 1 million personal computers in secondary schools by 1990.

Why are the Soviets so far behind? One reason is the decision made in the late 1960s to copy western computer designs rather than develop their own computer industry. This allowed the Soviets to copy huge amounts of western hardware and software, but it provided no Soviet infrastructure for computer design and manufacturing. The Soviet bureaucracy also inhibits development, because many ministries try to control computer technology, and each must approve computer-related decisions. Yet another reason is alleged "psychological barriers." For example, a plant manager may receive an expensive computer system but leave it in the warehouse for fear of losing more control to a central authority. Managers want to process their own financial data so that they can fudge plans if they have to. The plan to place computers in high schools may be delayed because only two textbooks have been written, and one of those is for schools that do not have computers.

A few computer devotees are getting hold of personal computers, but they must construct their own keyboards and wiring harnesses and use TV screens for monitors. Moreover, Soviet personal computers will never be able to talk to one another as they do in the United States, because the telephone lines are of insufficient quality to support data channels. However, the Soviet Union does have one similarity with the United States: a phenomenon known as "hackers," who in the Soviet Union are called "fanatiky." Parents often call the computer center to find out why their children aren't home for dinner.

One reason for the computer lethargy is the Soviet's penchant for control. The equipment needed for word processing, for example, is not readily available. Since xeroxing carries a seven-year prison sentence, the government bureaucracy is not about to start giving away printing presses. Copying machines are closely regulated because they threaten the state's publishing monopoly. Moreover, Soviet organizations treat most information as secret, no matter how mundane. Widespread use of personal computers would threaten that control and cause undesirable changes in Soviet society. However, in order to achieve computer adoption, Soviet society may *have* to change. A new school computer will soon go into production, and a computer "superministry" may come into being to allow decisions to be made in one location. The revolution in information technology taking place in the United States may yet occur in the Soviet Union. The two important questions about the future of computer technology in the Soviet Union are: Can computerization in the Soviet Union simply be decreed by the government like everything else? If computerization does take place, will it change the structure of a closed society?

Based on Alex Beam, "Atari Bolsheviks," *The Atlantic*, March 1986, pp. 28–32.

managers must understand the technology of the Information Age and how it can be used.

INFORMATION AND MANAGEMENT

In a very realistic sense, information is the lifeblood of organizations. To appreciate how managers use information in control and decision making, we must first distinguish data from information and then look at the characteristics of useful information.

EXHIBIT 19.1

Characteristics of Useful Management Information

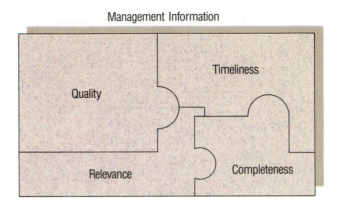

Data versus Information

data Raw, unsummarized, and unanalyzed facts.

information Data that are meaningful and alter the receiver's understanding.

The terms *data* and *information* often are used interchangeably. Yet there is an important difference. **Data** are raw, unsummarized, and unanalyzed facts. **Information** is data that are meaningful and alter the receiver's understanding.[2] Information is the data that managers actually use to interpret and understand events in the organization and the environment. For example, the Boddie brothers have an information system for controlling their 200 Hardee's restaurants. Thousands of data transactions are fed into the information system, including food sales, sales tax, water and electricity usage, and movement of inventory items. However, these raw data have no meaning, and in unsummarized form are worthless. Data require proper organization to produce meaningful information, such as total sales for the 200 Hardee restaurants, sales by store and by region, and profit per store.[3]

Characteristics of Useful Information

What makes information valuable? Information has many attributes, such as verifiability, accessibility, clarity, and precision. Four factors that are especially important for management information are quality, timeliness, completeness, and relevance, as illustrated in Exhibit 19.1.[4]

quality The degree to which information accurately portrays reality.

Quality.   **Quality** means that information accurately portrays reality. The data are accurate and reliable. If the data say that a valve in a nuclear power plant is open, such quality is important to management decision making. A police officer in San Jose, California, runs a license plate check by tapping into the state license plate records system. If the data were inaccurate, an innocent person could be stopped or a guilty one let go.[5] Quality is what makes any information system work. Once a system is known to have errors, managers will no longer use it and its value for decision making will decrease.

Timeliness.   **Timeliness** means that information is available soon after events occur. Managers work at a fast pace, and things change quickly. In order for information to be valuable, it must arrive on time and pertain to the problem to be solved now. Information that arrives two weeks from now will not help, because managers will have had to make their decisions and move on. At Oxford Industries, an Atlanta clothing company, workers' activities are clocked to a thousandth of a minute. Oxford has figured, for instance, that a stitcher should spend 3.4 seconds on each front pocket and may work on 5,000 pockets a day. The information system gives running updates throughout the day of each worker's pace so that problems can be solved immediately.[6]

Completeness   Information **completeness** refers to the proper quantity of data. Too much data lead to information overload; too little fail to tell the complete story. As described in Chapters 17 and 18, managers exercise control by recognizing deviations from targets and instituting necessary changes. Managers need the correct amount of information so that they can make decisions based on an understanding of key events and issues.

Relevance.   Information **relevance** means that the information must pertain to the problems, decisions, and tasks for which a manager is responsible. Information relevance is a difficult problem for an information system to solve, because every manager's situation is unique. Production managers need data on scrap rates, production volume, and employee productivity. Personnel managers need data on employee background, work experience, insurance programs, employee demographics, and position descriptions. Marketing managers need data on customer accounts, sales forecasts, sales activity, and individual salespeople's commissions.

timeliness   The degree to which information is available soon after events occur.

completeness   The extent to which information contains the appropriate amount of data.

relevance   The degree to which information pertains to the problems, decisions, and tasks for which a manager is responsible.

information system   A mechanism for collecting, organizing, and distributing data to organizational employees.

INFORMATION SYSTEMS FOR MANAGEMENT

Now that we understand the characteristics of useful information, we will discuss how a system for providing information to managers can be devised. An **information system** is a mechanism that collects, organizes, and distributes data to organizational personnel.

Information System Components

Any information system must have five basic components: input, processing (also called *computation*), storage, control, and output. *Inputs* are the raw data that enter the information system, such as data on inventory levels, lists of sales invoices, and records of personnel absences. *Processing* involves the abilities to manipulate, organize, sort, and perform calculations on the data. Processing transforms the data into a form useful for managers. *Storage* is the system function in which data are stored in an

Information is data that are meaningful and useful to receivers. In the dealing room at the Morgan Guaranty Ltd. London office, these Capital Markets Research managers discuss market reception of a new Eurobond issue. Morgan's sophisticated information system provides high-quality, timely, complete, and relevant information about bond prices and yield patterns in tabular or graphic form for easy interpretation. With its global capability, it transmits useful data to offices anywhere in the world.

EXHIBIT   19.2

Components of an Information System

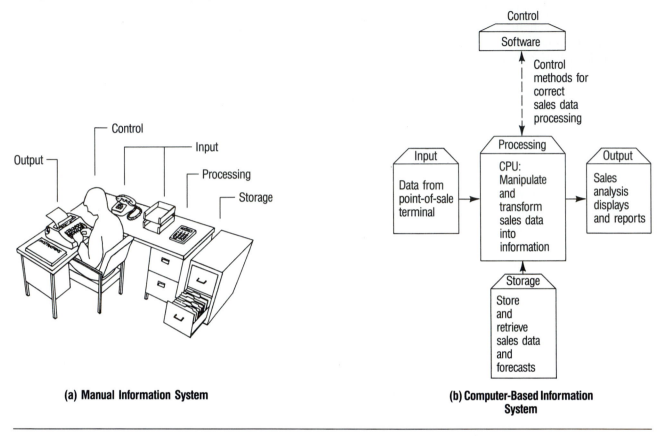

(a) Manual Information System

(b) Computer-Based Information System

Source: J. A. O'Brian, *Computers in Business* (Homewood, Ill.: Irwin, 1985). Used with permission.

computer-based information system (CBIS) An information system that uses electronic computing technology to create the various system components.

organized manner for future processing or until needed by system users. *Control* is a system monitoring and evaluation device for determining whether the information system is delivering information of sufficient quality, timeliness, completeness, and relevance for users. The control function also must have the capability to change the output. *Output* includes the reports and other organized information produced by the information system for users.

These five components must be part of every information system, whether manual or computer based, as illustrated in Exhibit 19.2. A *manual information system* is one in which people perform the information activities by hand. A **computer-based information system (CBIS)** is a system that uses electronic computing technology to create the five system components. Thus, a CBIS differs from a manual system only in the physical components that perform the functions. Input into a CBIS may be done through a terminal, punched cards, or automatic scanning systems. The data processing function is handled by a *central processing unit (CPU),* which manipulates data according to previously defined procedures. Most storage is outside the CPU in the form of magnetic tapes and disks that can store huge volumes of data. Control over the system is provided by a software program that contains specific instructions for organizing data needed by users. Outputs are computer reports generated for users.

For example, Best Western developed a system called TIS (Total Information System) to provide high-quality, timely, complete, and relevant information for managers. Inputs are raw data on reservations, personnel, finance, and marketing; these are kept in the storage component until needed. The system uses an on-line directory as the central brain and control system. Software prescribing data access, security, integrity, and outputs is written for managers. Output information is available to managers through their own terminals.

Hardware and Software

Hardware is the name given to the physical equipment used in a computer-based information system. Hardware used for inputs includes terminals with keyboards, cash registers, optimal character readers, and voice input devices. Output hardware includes printers, video screens, and voice synthesizers. The central processing unit is the hardware that performs the processing function. Storage hardware includes the CPU, which has some primary storage called *core memory* and secondary storage in the form of tape drives, magnetic disks, or floppy disks.

Software is the set of instructions that control and direct computer processing. It is the primary device used for controlling an information system. Software transforms raw data into usable information reports. Thousands of software programs are available for purchase, and programs can be written by in-house staff to suit special applications. For example, in 1983 over 200 packages were available just for handling accounts receivable.[7] Some of the popular application software programs managers use include *VisiCalc* and *Lotus 1-2-3* (electronic spreadsheets) and *dBASE III* (database management system).

CBISs AND THE MANAGEMENT HIERARCHY

Recall from Chapter 1 that management activities differ according to top, middle, and first-line management levels in the hierarchy as illustrated in Exhibit 19.3. Hierarchical differences mean that managers need different kinds of information. For example, strategic planning is a primary responsibility at the top level, while operational control is a primary responsibility of first-line supervisors. Top managers work on nonprogrammable problems, such as new-product development, marketing plans, and acquisition of other companies. First-line managers, in contrast, deal with programmable decisions arising from well-defined problems, such as inventory control, production scheduling, and sales analysis.

E X H I B I T   19.3

Information Requirements and CBISs by Management Level

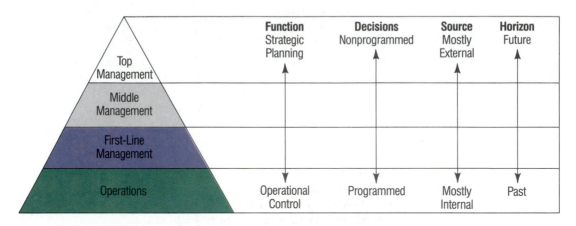

Source: Adapted from Rolland Hurtubise, *Managing Information Systems: Concept and Tools* (West Hartford, Conn.: Kumarian Press, 1984), p. 57, and G. Anthony Gorry and Michael S. Scott Morton, "A Framework for Management Information Systems," *Sloan Management Review* 13 (1971), pp. 55–70.

The information top managers use pertains mostly to the external environment. It is broad in scope to cover unanticipated problems that may arise and is oriented toward the future, including trends and forecasts. First-line managers need information on internal operations that is narrowly focused on specific activities and deals with past performance.

To meet the different information needs along the hierarchy, three types of computer-based information systems have evolved. At the lower organization level, transaction processing systems (TPSs) assist first-line supervisors with recordkeeping, routine calculations, and data sorting. Middle-managers use management information systems (MISs). Top managers use decision support systems (DSSs) to provide information for strategic and nonprogrammable decisions. DSSs may be used by middle managers and MIS reports by both top and first-line managers. We will now discuss each system in more detail.

Transaction Processing Systems

transaction processing system (TPS) A type of CBIS that performs the organization's routinely occurring transactions.

The initial purpose of business computing in the 1960s was to reduce clerical costs by computerizing the flow of day-to-day business transactions. The **transaction processing system (TPS)** performs the organization's routine, recurring transactions. Examples of transactions include sending bills to customers, depositing checks in the bank, placing orders, recording receipts and payments in accounting ledgers, and paying invoices. A transaction processing system typically performs one or more of the following operations:

1. Storing transaction data to create a file of transaction records
2. Sorting, sequencing, or arranging records

A unique transactions processing system provides the parents of these boys at a nursery school in Toyama, Japan, with a report on their activities, including how much they ate for lunch and when they were picked up at the end of the day. The system enables the school to keep detailed records on its 100 youngsters, handles accounting functions and salary records for the staff, and tracks nutritional content of school meals. Developed by IBM, the software can also provide MIS data to nursery school managers for making decisions about school activities.

3. Merging the contents of two or more files
4. Performing calculations on file data
5. Accumulating amounts to develop summary totals
6. Sorting data for future use
7. Retrieving stored data
8. Displaying or printing out data from files for use by employees or supervisors[8]

Transaction processing systems thus are typically used when there are many transactions and transactions are repeated several times during the day. The computer technology focuses on simple tasks such as payroll, which includes recording worker hours, establishing pay rates, calculating tax withholdings and other deductions, and issuing paychecks. Efficiency and accuracy of transactions is the system's primary goal, because data typically are not used for management decision making.[9]

An example of an excellent transaction processing system is that of Western Engine Company.

Western Engine Company

When a trucker's diesel breaks down on the road, getting replacement parts fast is of primary importance. If the breakdown occurs in Illinois, chances are the trucker will call one of 102 Western Engine Company dealers. "Service is crucial in our business," says the controller. Further, the company has installed an exceptionally swift order-handling procedure that allows emergency orders to be turned around within 24 hours. However, just as important as high service is low inventory cost. The transaction processing system saves the company at least $1 million a year in reduced inventory investment.

The transaction processing system runs round the clock. Some 10,000 customer orders a month flow through the system, drawing on a combined inventory of 32,000 diesel engine parts. Sixty display terminals and eight printers are used to support data entry, order processing, and customer inquiries. The system tracks every order from receipt to delivery, billing, and payment. After the order is entered, the system allocates the stock, reviews customer records, and sends orders for shipment. The system also summarizes the demand for each part so that inventory levels can be adjusted to achieve the best inventory balance.[10]

Management Information Systems

management information system (MIS) A form of CBIS that collects, organizes, and distributes the data managers use in performing their management functions.

A **management information system (MIS)** is a mechanism that collects, organizes, and distributes data used by managers in performing their management functions. As information systems evolved, management information systems were the next stage of evolution beyond transaction processing systems. As databases accumulated, managers began visualizing ways in which the computer could help them make important decisions. Managers needed information in summary form that pertained to specific management problems. The lists of thousands of daily organizational transactions were useless for planning, controlling, or decision making.

MISs provided information reports designed to help managers make decisions. For example, when a production manager needs to make decisions about production scheduling, he or she may need data on the anticipated number of orders in the coming month based on trends, current inventory levels, and availability of equipment and personnel. The MIS can provide these data.

The MIS required more complex software that would instruct computers to translate data into useful reports. Computer hardware also became more complex and sophisticated because it needed greater capacity and the ability to integrate diverse databases. For example, thousands of transactions take place daily in supermarkets. One leader in developing management information systems is Gromer Supermarket Inc.

Gromer Supermarket Inc.

Gromer's is a huge superstore in Elgin, Illinois. The laser scanners at Gromer's ten checkout counters speed shoppers through the checkout lines, but more important, they provide tons of information. Millions of transactions are recorded, and a quarter of a million dollars' worth of computer hardware and software are used to provide management reports on everything from checker efficiency, bagging speed, and

This computer library at Campbell Soup Company illustrates the scope of computer data used in organizations. These tapes represent multiple databases that support executive decision making as well as routine transactions such as ordering and bill paying. Computer technology has affected practically every segment of Campbell, resulting in increased efficiency, greater productivity, and improved customer service. The data must be readily available, especially for those managers who use DSS to retrieve, manipulate, and display information needed for specific decisions.

food turnover. Take cereal, for example. The MIS data showed that Rice Krispies had six size categories, but two were slow movers and thus were eliminated.

In the meat department, MIS reports tell the meat manager how much gross margin a side of beef will produce. The system also describes the cuts from a pork loin that will maximize gross profits. Labor cost decisions are made efficiently because the number of baggers scheduled to work is chosen to fit the number of customers coming through the store and the known rate at which a bagger can bag. The millions of numbers crunched through the MIS system help managers make better decisions on how to display products, which products to stock, and how to make storage and delivery more efficient.[11]

Decision Support Systems

Decision support systems represent the final and most sophisticated level of CBIS support developed for managers. These were developed because managers wanted more help for unanticipated and unstructured problems, which MISs were not flexible enough to provide.

A **decision support system (DSS)** is an interactive, computer-based information system that retrieves, manipulates, and displays information needed for making specific decisions.[12] A DSS allows managers to make inquiries and receive answers to pressing questions rather than just periodic reports.[13] Moreover, it gives managers access to any of multiple databases depending on their immediate information needs, as illustrated in Exhibit 19.4.

Decision support systems deal with nonprogrammed decisions such as strategic planning. Consequently, the hardware and software technologies are very sophisticated. Indeed, to be accessible to top managers who are not computer experts, up to 75 percent of the computer system's

decision support system (DSS)
An interactive CBIS that retrieves, manipulates, and displays information needed for making specific management decisions.

EXHIBIT   19.4

Elements of a Decision Support System

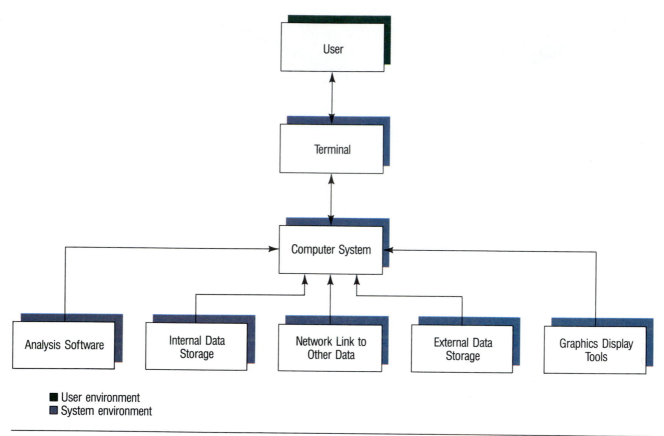

capacity may be used for software that permits managers to "talk" to the system in everyday English. This frees the remaining 25 percent to handle multiple databases, translate inquiries into simple graphs and charts, and provide an instant answer to almost any question.

The essential characteristics of a decision support system include the following:

1. Supports semistructured or unstructured executive decision making
2. Data and models organized around executives' decisions rather than available databases
3. Easy-to-use software that utilizes natural language
4. Interactive processing that allows rapid responses
5. Use and control determined by the user rather than by the computer systems department or the transaction processing data in the system

6. Flexible and adaptable to changes in the external environment and the decision maker's style
7. Includes data on the external environment as well as those pertaining to internal activities and operations[14]

American Airlines uses a decision support system for pricing and route selection, Champlin Petroleum for corporate planning and forecasting, First United BankCorporation for investment evaluation, and Zales Corporation for assessment of store sites. Another company that uses a DSS successfully is Thermo Electron.

Thermo Electron Corporation

Senior managers at Thermo Electron peck away at their own computer terminals to monitor business operations. Using decision support systems, the executives discover for themselves how the company is doing. Executives can ask a specific question, such as the name of a bank officer who authorized a specific loan, or can gather general data, such as corporate sales over the last six months. Some executives don't sit at the terminal themselves but ask an assistant to fetch the data they want. Thermo Electron's chairperson is among the direct users: "When I sit down at a terminal, I get ideas on how to analyze things that I'd never get otherwise."

Top executives have data available almost beyond their imagination. Databases include consumer surveys and census reports as well as vast amounts of economic, marketing, and financial data. The decision support system allows an executive to test theories, challenge assumptions, and selectively analyze information. Current numbers can be compared with last month's, last year's, or an average of year-to-date figures. Trends can be examined and projected out to make forecasts. For example, a forecast of furnace sales to the auto industry used to take two weeks to produce; with the DSS, it takes five minutes. Some questions used to be so hard to answer that they were never asked. Now senior executives can ask anything they want, because the system is organized to provide the answer quickly and in easily understandable form.[15]

Exhibit 19.5 summarizes the evolution of computer-based information systems used in organizations. Transaction processing came first; it used simple hardware and software for use at lower organization levels. Management information systems represented a higher level of complexity. Decision support systems represent the latest and most complex technology applicable to top managers' nonprogrammed decisions. DSSs

EXHIBIT   19.5

**Evolution of Information Applications and Computer
Technology Used for CBISs**

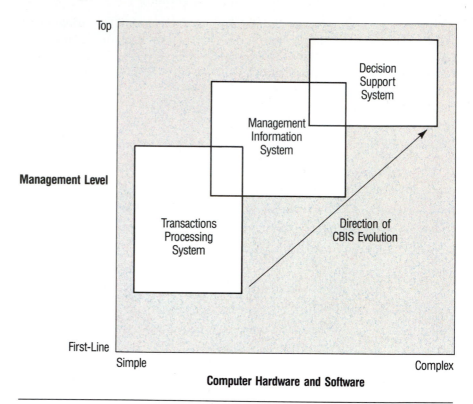

Source: Based on D. W. Krober and H. J. Watson, *Computer-Based Information Systems: A Managerial Approach* (New York: Macmillan, 1984).

are interactive, can address broad issues concerning the external environment, and can help managers formulate strategic plans.

OTHER INFORMATION TECHNOLOGIES

Developments in MISs and DSSs have paralleled advances in other information processing technologies. Developments in telecommunications have sped up the flow of data and information around corporations. Advances such as artificial intelligence have made the computer itself an organizational decision maker.

Telecommunications

Telecommunications represent a host of communication and conferencing devices based on technological developments such as long-distance fiber optics that reduce communication costs to one-tenth of traditional circuitry.[16] The best known of these communications technologies are as follows.

Electronic Mail. *Electronic mail* is the use of electronic circuitry to transmit written messages instantaneously to other people within the organization or to other organizations around the world. Electronic mail is cheaper than long-distance telephoning and faster than a letter. The message sits at the receiver's terminal to be read when the computer is turned on. Electronic mail is basically a form of one-to-one communication. It is also effective for mass communications, because a message can be sent to several people on a mailing list. Many corporations have acquired their own electronic mail systems. The only drawback is that sender and receiver both need computer terminals.

Voice Messaging. In *voice messaging,* the computer acts as a giant answering machine because the computer answers a manager's phone, relays memos, gives out information, and takes messages.[17]

Computer Conferencing. *Computer conferencing* is an extension of electronic mail that allows multiparty communications, that is, communications conducted among members of a group. Each member sits at a terminal. Messages can be sent to the entire group, and members can cross-talk with one another. Hewlett-Packard has thousands of engineers in more than 70 divisions. It had become increasingly difficult to get engineers across divisions to share their knowledge in order to avoid unnecessary duplication of effort. In an experiment, 1,000 employees used a computer conferencing system and discovered it to be easy and fun to share technological developments with one another. Hewlett-Packard now has about 60 conferences running simultaneously.[18]

Videoconferencing. *Videoconferencing* uses a live television hookup so that group members can see one another during their conference. Aetna Life and Casualty Company uses full videoconferencing to link its offices in Hartford and Windsor, Connecticut. Videoconferences at NASA sometimes involve hundreds of people at scores of locations and often last up to six hours. Without videoconferencing, NASA could not integrate ideas from so many engineers and other professionals.[19]

Electronic Bulletin Boards. An *electronic bulletin board* disseminates routine information on fringe benefits, job openings, and corporate events through the organization's computer system. Moreover, the technology can be expanded to serve as a corporate library, storing policy manuals, job descriptions, telephone directory listings, and other documentation to which managers and employees need access. With documents stored electronically, paperwork is reduced. Ford Motor Credit Company has a system that includes both an electronic library and an

telecommunications A set of communication and conferencing devices based on electronic communications technology.

Dave Smith will retire some day, but his abilities as GE's top locomotive field service engineer will stay with the company—housed in a computer. A team of computer specialists from the R&D Center succeeded in translating Smith's thought processes into a computer-aided trouble-shooting system for guiding other locomotive mechanics. This expert system duplicates Smith's thinking and serves as an advisor to other engineers.

artificial intelligence (AI)   Information technology that attempts to make computers think, talk, see, and listen like people.

expert system   An area of AI that attempts to program a computer to duplicate an expert's decision-making and problem-solving strategies.

networking   The linking together of groups and departments within or across organizations for the purpose of sharing information resources.

electronic bulletin board. Terminals are available to employees, who can tap into the library from their desks and catch up on job postings and bulletin board announcements.[20]

Artificial Intelligence

Artificial intelligence (AI) is information technology whose ultimate goal is to make computers think, see, talk, and listen like humans. Concepts from psychology, linguistics, and computer science have been combined to create programs that can perform tasks never before done by machines. For example, Hal, the supercomputer in the movies *2001* and *2010*, was the ideal result of AI technology; it could think, talk, and make decisions like a human being.

The area of AI that has had the greatest impact on organizations is called the expert system. An **expert system** duplicates the thinking process that professionals and managers use when making decisions. An expert system is developed by codifying a specialist's knowledge into decision rules that are written into a computer program to mimic the expert's problem-solving strategy.[21] For example, Campbell was about to experience a serious loss when Aldo Cimino retired. He knew more than anyone about maintaining the seven-story soup sterilizers and kettles used in Campbell's kitchens. Campbell's solution was to develop an expert system that could duplicate Cimino's thought processes. Developing the expert system was painstaking and difficult. A programmer from Texas Instruments interviewed Cimino day after day to obtain the minutest details on what he thought and why he took every step. It took seven months to boil Cimino's experience down to 151 "if-then" rules that a computer could understand. Now whenever a problem comes up with a huge kettle, the expert system tells managers how Cimino would have responded.[22]

Artificial intelligence is a major departure from MISs and DSSs. The reason is that MISs and DSSs support the human being who makes decisions, while an AI system operates as an advisor to, or even replaces, the human decision maker. With a DSS, the human asks questions of the machine system. With artificial intelligence, the machine asks questions of the human and accumulates responses that lead to a decision. AI systems give machines the capacity to infer the right conclusion or make the correct choice.[23] Companies such as General Electric, Schlumberger, Digital Equipment Corporation, and Arthur D. Little have developed artificial intelligence to assist in expert activities such as analyzing oil-drilling logs, diagnosing diesel locomotives, and telling managers what machinery is needed to manufacture a new product.[24]

Networking

Networking is the linking together of groups and departments within or among organizations to share information resources such as databases. Networking requires that computers in each part of the organization use the same programs, formats, and computer languages. Once this is achieved, managers across the network have access to the databases and resources of all participants. For example, General Motors' acquisition of

E X H I B I T   19.6

An Interorganizational Computer Network

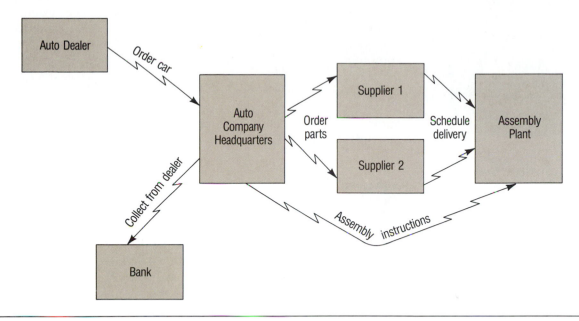

Source: Based on Joel Dreyfuss, "Networking: Japan's Latest Computer Craze," *Fortune,* July 7, 1986, p. 95.

Electronic Data System Company was partially motivated by the desire to establish common computer resources for use in networking. Networking greatly enhances the computer resources available to managers and facilitates coordination across departments and divisions.[25]

Interorganizational networks are now being created to link the information systems of two or more organizations. Organizations that regularly do business with one another can now do so more efficiently and with less paperwork by communicating with computers. One example of an interorganizational network is illustrated in Exhibit 19.6. This network is similar to those used by Japanese automakers.[26] The computer at the auto company headquarters electronically receives a car order specifying model, color, and options. It automatically orders the required parts from suppliers and coordinates the shipping of parts to arrive at the plant at the same time. The computer issues instructions for building a car to the computer at the assembly plant. The computer at company headquarters can electronically invoice the dealer and pay suppliers through the network linkage to the bank. Interorganizational networking systems are highly efficient; however, the computer hardware and software are complex and require standardization among companies.

Automated Offices

The **automated office** is the integration of multiple electronic technologies to automate managerial work. The automated office starts with a personal computer that gives managers word processing and local data

automated office The integration of multiple electronic technologies to automate managerial work.

These bankers' work stations are part of J. P. Morgan's automated office approach that uses electronic technology to automate managerial work. In the foreground are vice-presidents Lynn Allegert and Jeffrey B. Westcott. Their personal computers are linked to a large mainframe system that gives them access to an array of analytical programs and data for developing financial product strategies suited to clients' needs. The nearby terminals also give these New York managers access to data that serve clients in other states.

analysis capabilities and connects them with MIS and DSS support. Managers also have access to one another via electronic mail, computer conferencing, and videoconferencing. Databases are networked to give managers broad access to information resources. For example, the vice-president for production and engineering at Burroughs Wellcome Company is moving toward an automated office. He uses a personal computer to route documents among his senior managers. Six senior managers report to the vice-president, and their subordinates in turn are hooked up together electronically. They can share messages during group meetings or send one-to-one communications confidentially. The automated office utilizes many facets of electronic technology to make managers super-efficient.[27]

IMPACT OF INFORMATION TECHNOLOGY ON ORGANIZATIONS

The adoption of MISs, DSSs, computer conferencing, electronic mail, and automated offices has both intended and unintended consequences for organizations. The desired consequence is improved organizational efficiency, especially with respect to the management functions of decision making and controlling. Unintended consequences are changes in social relationships among employees and in organization structure. New information technology also presents senior managers with new strategic options. In order to properly manage computer resources, managers must appreciate the impact of computers on organizations. The consequences of information technologies are illustrated in Exhibit 19.7. We will discuss each in turn.

Management Efficiency

The impact of information technology falls primarily on the functions of decision making and control. Information technology provides faster, more comprehensive, and more accurate knowledge of operations for timely problem diagnoses and decisions. For the most part, these benefits seem to be greatest at lower organizational levels.

The positive impact on first-line managers is that they spend more time performing programmable functions. Information technology is easily adapted to production scheduling, inventory management, and office procedures. At middle organizational levels, desktop terminals have given managers access to more information than ever before, including outside databases, production schedules, marketing orders, pricing, and demand forecasts. Electronic mail and teleconferencing provide opportunities for coordination and rapid communication. The outcome of these technologies is improved manager productivity and decision making.[28]

Computer-based technologies have had less impact on top management. The unstructured nature of top-level planning and decision making and reluctance to use management science models are two reasons

E X H I B I T   19.7

Areas of Information Technology Impact

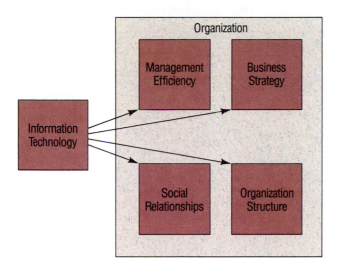

why top executives have been slower to embrace the new technologies. However, when senior people do use computers, their efficiency often increases. One senior bank executive commented, "Everything I do on the computer I do ten times faster than I used to." An executive at Mobil's New York headquarters remarked on his increased efficiency: "When I shave in the morning, I find myself contemplating all the ways I can solve a problem using the computer instead of worrying if there's a solution at all."[29]

Social Relationships

Interesting research findings suggest that information technology changes how people relate to one another in organizations. Computer-mediated communications differ from face-to-face and telephone interactions in three important respects.[30]

Greater Sense of Anonymity.   When a person sits at a terminal to communicate, information exchanges tend to be impersonal. Subtle cues, such as tone of voice and eye contact, are missing, and people feel less bound by status and norms. Their behavior may be impulsive and self-centered, and they may feel less emotion and concern for others. This anonymity is an advantage in that all participants in the computer network feel like equals and participate more readily than they would in face-to-face groups. On the negative side, they ignore social status and may engage in **flaming**—an emotional outburst that can have a negative impact on other people.

flaming   An emotional outburst with a potentially negative impact on others sent via electronic communication technology.

Creation of New Groups.   Groups created by electronic technology cut across traditional organizational boundaries. Whoever is interested in

One impact of information technology has been to improve management decision making and control, especially for first-line managers. Federal Express uses the Digitally Assisted Dispatch System shown here to provide unprecedented efficiency in communicating with its ground courier fleet. Packages are tracked by computer. The system uses a video display terminal in each delivery van. Couriers can call up information on the screen to determine their next assigned stop. Managers can reassign couriers as needed to respond to incoming requests for pickup or delivery.

the same problem, whether a technical project or the intricacies of Chinese cooking, can find others and communicate through electronic mail and bulletin boards. People may become more committed to the computer group than to their own departments.

Computer "Addiction."   After managers have spent the 40 or so hours needed to learn to use a personal computer and telecommunications technology, they may find it fun. Many executives have purchased a second computer to use at home, and hence they spend less time at the office. Some executives do not even come into the office unless there is an important meeting. Using computers to accomplish their work may make managers less social and less available for needed face-to-face conversations.[31]

Organization Structure

Another consequence of information technology has been a gradual change in organization structure. Although the widespread use of information technology is so recent that definitive findings are not available, a few trends have been discerned.

Creation of New Departments.   For smaller companies, the explosion in information often leads to the creation of a chief information officer (CIO) who is responsible for managing organizational databases. Another structural innovation has been the creation of an information center.[32] The *information center* mediates between users and the computer department. It helps managers become end users so they can solve their own data processing needs. At Rayovac, for example, information center personnel have expertise in computer hardware and software. They work as consultants with clients to teach them sufficient computer skills to meet their own business needs.

Smaller Management Structure.   The general outcome of information technology has been to reverse the trend of hiring new managers. By speeding up information routing, the number of managers in many organizations has been reduced. This reduction has been felt through an increased span of control and a decrease in the number of levels in the management hierarchy.[33] Automated offices allow managers to increase their spans of control.

One organization that has gone heavily into information technology and benefited from fewer managers is Hercules Inc.

Hercules Inc.

Hercules Inc. is a Delaware-based chemical company in which a sophisticated combination of electronic and voice mail, videoconferencing, word processing, and high-speed communications have led to a leaner management structure. Hercules started with a satellite dish on the roof and five videoconferencing rooms on different floors. It then introduced a network of more than 400 word processing terminals and 205 personal computers. Under the system memos and text can be routed electronically through any company office worldwide. This has led to a 40 percent reduction in secretarial hours.

Hercules' voice mail and videoconferencing technology has saved the company over $4 million a year in time and travel expenses. These improvements have enabled Hercules to trim 1,800 jobs. It has eliminated assistant department managers, assistant plant managers, and a level of vice-presidents. Every top manager now has a terminal in his office and, with fewer managers, the information-handling technology has become even more important. Managers need hands-on familiarity in order to keep up with their responsibilities. The cost savings have more than paid for the high investment in new technology.[34]

Improved Coordination.   Another outcome of information technology has been to break down barriers among departments and across hierarchical levels. Managers who are wired into a computer system communicate with anyone who can help solve problems. Consider the problem Citicorp had in trying to control its many independent businesses scattered around the globe. A client of one Citicorp bank would seek advice from a Citicorp bank in another part of the world. To insure that advice offered to clients by all divisions is consistent, Citicorp installed a computer conferencing system. Citicorp managers now can expedite communications with their clients as well as with one another.[35]

Network Corporations.   Perhaps the most dramatic impact on information technology has been the creation of the network corporation structure, which many experts believe will be the wave of the future. In a **network corporation** the company, rather than being a single entity with manufacturing, engineering, sales, and accounting as its components, is disaggregated. The organization itself is a small, central broker electronically connected to other organizations or subsidiaries that perform each function, as illustrated in Exhibit 19.8.

A small, centralized group of people can coordinate functions around the world. For example, Schwinn Bicycle Company reorganized into a network structure. Rather than manufacturing products, Schwinn imports its bicycles from Asia and distributes them through a set of independent dealers who are coordinated electronically. Another example is Lewis Galoob Toys Inc., which sold $58 million worth of toys with only 115 employees. Galoob farms out manufacturing and packaging to contractors in Hong Kong. Independent inventors and entertainment companies are charged with designing new toys. When manufactured toys land in the United States, they are distributed by independent sales representatives. Galoob never touches a product and doesn't even collect the money. The company is held together with phones, telexes, and other electronic technology.[36]

Important consequences of computer technology have been streamlined organization structure and improved coordination across departments. Here buyers from a department store chain based in Los Angeles use a computer system to improve inventory coordination among stores. The company links its six department store divisions and four specialty store chains through a centralized data processing center. The computer network coordinates 300 locations through 17,000 terminals that have access to relevant databases.

network corporation   An organization that is electronically connected to other companies or subsidiaries that perform each of its functions.

EXHIBIT   19.8

A Network Corporation

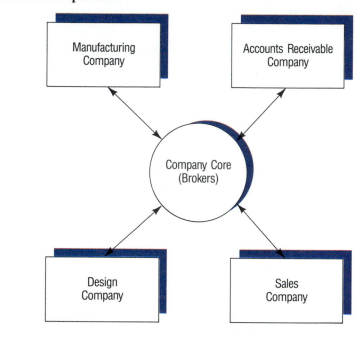

telecommuting A network corporation whose employees work from their homes via terminals that connect them with the office.

A variation on the network corporation is telecommuting. With **telecommuting,** employees stay at home and perform their work via terminals that connect them with the office. Telecommuting deploys people away from the office but links them electronically to a central location. Telecommuting is a great advantage for employees who need to be at home, such as working parents, and it saves commuting and travel costs for both employees and organizations.[37]

STRATEGIC MANAGEMENT AND INFORMATION TECHNOLOGY

One of the most significant influences of computer-based information systems is on competitive strategy. Managers can use information technology to further the organization's strategic goals.

Consider American Hospital Supply Corporation, a health goods manufacturer. Starting in the late 1970s, senior executives decided to give computer terminals free to hospitals around the country. These terminals linked hospital purchasers with American Hospital Supply and enabled them to directly place orders for any of more than 100,000 products. This corporate strategy linked the company directly to its customers, and it was a strategic breakthrough. AHS gained sales and market share at competitors' expense. Hospitals had the advantage of low-

E X H I B I T   19.9

**Information Technology Applications That Support
Competitive Business Strategies**

Low-Cost Leader	Differentiation
• Lock in suppliers	• Lock in customers
• Telemarketing	• Customer service
• Cut training costs	• Improved product development
• More efficient financial management	• Gather market intelligence, find new niches
• Operational efficiency: inventory control, production scheduling	• Customize products
• Office automation for staff reduction	• Quality monitoring systems

ered inventory carrying costs, since they were confident that orders with AHS would be processed quickly. AHS was one of the first companies to use information technology in corporate strategy. Customers were locked in because they could not switch to another supplier without losing efficiency and convenience.[38]

Recall from Chapter 5 that businesses can excel at either low-cost leadership or product differentiation. Examples of how information technology can facilitate low-cost and differentiation strategies are presented in Exhibit 19.9.

Low-Cost Strategy

Several uses of CBISs can help a company become a low-cost leader.[39] First, a CBIS makes it possible to lock in suppliers. This means having a terminal in the purchasing department from which to order from suppliers, which reduces inventory costs, purchasing paperwork, and delivery times. Second, marketing departments can use telemarketing to reduce salesperson costs. For example, Louisiana Oil & Tire Company took ten salespeople off the road and made them into *telemarketers*—people who use telephone and other electronic devices to reach customers. Sales expenses fell by 10 percent, and sales volume doubled. Third, personnel department training costs can be reduced by using videodisks and computer programs to help employees learn at their own speed and by decreasing the need for classrooms and teachers. Fourth, better financial management can be gained by setting up computer links between the company treasurer's office and its banks. Deposits can be made instantly, and the treasurer can receive timely financial information. Fifth, a CBIS can make the shop floor more efficient through programs that control inventory levels and track products through the production process. The computers can make production scheduling more efficient. Finally, the adoption of automated office equipment can shrink the size of the management hierarchy by increasing spans of control and reducing the number of management levels.[40]

Differentiation Strategy

Information technology can give a company a competitive edge in products and services. First, a strategy such as that used by American Hospital Supply can help lock in customers. By putting terminals in customers' offices, a company can differentiate itself from competitors. Second, customer service and loyalty can be increased by letting customers tap into the company's database to track orders and determine scheduled delivery dates. Third, sophisticated aspects of information technology can be used in product development. Computer-based designs enhance product differentiation, such as Coleco's use of computers to design millions of their wildly successful Cabbage Patch dolls, each of which was unique. Fourth, market intelligence provides data on competitors, demographics, customers, and census factors to spot unutilized niches and detect needs for new products. Fifth, information technology can help customize products to meet specific customer needs. For example, Sulzer Brothers, which makes marine diesel engines, used information technology to increase from five to eight the number of cylinder bore sizes available. Finally, information technology is useful as a control device because it can monitor quality at all stages of the production process. Quality enhancement is often one of the most desirable features of a differentiated product.[41]

In summary, managers should adopt information technology with a clear vision of how it will influence business strategy in order to reap the greatest return. Consider McKesson Corporation.

McKesson Corporation

McKesson Corporation is a wholesale drug distributor that had a record of mediocre returns and modest market position until it turned to information technology. McKesson gambled $125 million on automation. In the purchasing departments, information technology gathered accurate data on the demand for individual items and compared incoming items to invoices. Information technology helped employees handle more items, thus turning over inventory more frequently and increasing profits. The biggest innovation was to create electronic linkages to drugstore customers so that they could enter orders from their terminals. McKesson went so far as to help design information systems for drugstore managers to use to control their own inventories. The systems helped pharmacists

Burlington Industries uses its computer system to gain a strategic advantage over competitors. It provides an electronic linkage to customers in the form of this interactive computer that gives apparel manufacturers access to Burlington's databases. By tapping Burlington's computers for fabric length, width, and shade data, customers can prepare their patterns and cutting and sewing equipment before Burlington's fabric is delivered. This linkage enables Burlington to differentiate its product by locking in customers and providing excellent customer service.

organize data on patients, track payments to insured medical plans, provide customers with records of drug purchases, and process insurance forms. The payoff to McKesson came in two forms. First, once a drugstore signed on, McKesson's share of business immediately doubled or tripled because pharmacists would order more products through McKesson. Second, customers began requesting new items, in response to which McKesson broadened its product line, obtaining a further increase in profit and market share. By adopting information technology as a strategic weapon, McKesson realized greater returns than did companies that acquired technology without an overall plan.[42]

LIMITATIONS OF CBISs

Although information technology has undergone a revolution and can enhance corporate strategy as well as improve manager efficiency, the CBIS still suffers a number of limitations. Some of these pertain to the nature of the technology and its inability to perform many informational tasks. Other limitations are behavioral and pertain to its lack of acceptance and use within organizations.

Significant applications of computer technology are of little value unless the technology is carefully implemented and actually used. At the National Institute for Deaf Children, children learn to speak more clearly with the aid of a speech training system developed at the IBM France Scientific Center. Here a child working with a therapist matches his speech to a prototype pattern displayed on an IBM PC screen. Visual feedback allows the child to adjust his pitch until he makes the correct sound. This computer application is well tailored to user needs, is suited to the specific task, and was properly implemented.

systems development life cycle The sequence of events that CBIS designers follow in developing and implementing a new system.

Unsuitability for Many Tasks.   CBISs have not yet become the primary source of management information. Recall from Chapter 1 that a manager's job is characterized by variety and fragmentation. Managers do not spend time sitting at their desks analyzing data. Managers—especially top managers—work in an informal, reactive manner that is unsuited to the design of MISs or even of sophisticated decision support systems. Moreover, as described in Chapter 14, managers need rich, face-to-face communications in order to interpret ambiguous events. Face-to-face communication conveys social cues, establishes personal relationships, and enables managers to build coalitions for important decisions, none of which can be accomplished through a CBIS.[43]

Unrealistic Expectations.   Most organizations adopt new information technology with high expectations. Yet new information systems merely work within the organization's current information structure. Moreover, some managers have always received enough information to do their jobs adequately. Thus, if an information system suddenly provides data ten times as fast or provides ten times the volume of data, the improvement in manager performance will be only modest—say, 10 percent—because all that additional data and speed are unnecessary. Further, if the previous manual system did not provide useful data, the same worthless data will come through the computer system. An inventory control system with poor ordering rules will simply reorder the wrong quantities more quickly with a computer. Computers provide only a modest improvement in manager efficiency or strategic competitiveness, and managers should not expect more.[44]

Underused or Sabotaged Systems.   The implementation of a new, computer-based information system has consequences for power and control—indeed, one motivation for adopting a new system is to increase management's control over the organization. The new system has the potential to provide data that will measure and monitor the performances of both individuals and departments. In response, operating personnel in some organizations have deliberately distorted or destroyed input data such as time cards and production control information.[45] In one case, corporate accountants took the initiative of introducing the new system as a way of tightening control over organizational divisions. Division managers fought cooperation with the new system, attacking it for design, technical, and feasibility limitations. The most frequent problem is not sabotage but employees who avoid or bypass the new system. Senior-level managers may be reluctant to learn how to use a terminal, feeling they will lose power and influence by taking over clerical or middle management functions.

Improper Implementation.   As discussed in Chapter 10, any new technology must be implemented properly in order for it to be successful. An effective strategy for developing and implementing a CBIS is called the **systems development life cycle,** which is the sequence of events that system designers should use to bring a new system to reality.[46] The life cycle starts with a feasibility study that ascertains user needs. Then the technology requirements are determined, followed by the system's de-

MANAGERS SHOP TALK

Cowboys and Computers

Salam Qureishi would like to call plays for the Dallas Cowboys—or at least he would like his computer to call the plays. Back in 1960, when Dallas finally got an NFL football franchise, there was no system for evaluating player talent. Tex Schramm wondered if computers could improve on old-fashioned hunches and meaningless statistics. Qureishi worked for IBM and agreed to help the Cowboys use computers to draft players. He spent months talking to coaches and scouts and extracted a list of phrases to describe player qualities. Examples were:

- "He would hate his mother if she were on the other side." (*competitiveness*)
- "He would just as soon miss practice." (*character*)
- "He is strong as a bull." (*strength and explosion*)

After years of development, the Cowboys put the computer program to the test in 1964. After crunching scouts' evaluations of players, a list of players were ranked from 1 to 100. As it turned out, 87 of the top 100 prospects became pros. Eighty-seven percent accuracy was Super Bowl potential.

With the computer's help, the Cowboys improved to a 7 win/7 loss record in 1965 and a 10 win/3 loss/1 tie record in 1966. In 1968, Qureishi used the computer to develop the first of the modern-day game plans. By using the computer to analyze other teams, he could tell coaches how often the Giants would try a quarterback sneak in a short-yardage situation or whether the Steelers were likely to pass the ball on first down.

Qureishi left the Cowboys in 1970. The computer programs were not kept up to date, and the quality of the Cowboys' draft selections deteriorated. The software was supposed to be tuned up each year by checking the quality of the scouts' ratings. The computer could be used to determine which scouts had correctly identified the players who would hate their mothers. Without this follow-up analysis, the program would grind bad data, which translated into bad answers.

By 1984, Salam Qureishi was back with the Cowboys. He had been enormously successful in his other ventures and was willing to help the Cowboys for free. He started by evaluating the scores given to players in recent drafts by the scouts and how well they reflected the players' success in the NFL. Qureishi is confident that with the developments in computer information technology, he will have the Cowboys back on the winning track. As the first person to use a computer to prepare a game plan, he now wants to develop software to update the game plan during a game. If the plan needs to be revised after the kickoff, the coach can do it in his head. Qureishi points out, "But the human mind blanks out with too many choices. That's where the computer can help. . . . Somebody is going to win a Super Bowl with it. I think it will be the Cowboys."

Based on Aaron Latham, "The Cowboys, the Indian, and the Computer that Fumbled," *Texas Monthly*, September 1986, pp. 118–121, 181–184.

---

sign and physical construction. Physical construction consists of the design of appropriate software and acquisition of hardware. Next, the system is implemented. Implementation requires user participation, education, and communication. The more users are involved in the system's design, the more they will understand, accept, and use it.

Another variation for implementation used by some system designers is prototyping. A **prototype** is a working version of an information system developed to test the system's features.[47] The prototype provides samples of output to users and gives managers a chance to work with the output. A good implementation strategy is to insure that management users are involved throughout all stages of development.[48]

Information Not Tailored to User Needs. One of the biggest problems for both new and ongoing computer-based information systems is that

prototype A working model of an information system developed to test the system's features.

information may not precisely fit what managers need to make decisions or control a large corporation. This is a continuing dilemma because as management problems change, the data provided by information systems also must change. Too often data end up being designed to satisfy machine requirements or design specialists rather than the managers who will use it. Specialists may be enamored with the volume of data a system can produce and overlook the need to provide small amounts of data in a timely and useful format for decision making.

Three techniques that help bridge the gap between information system specialists and managers' needs have been identified:

key indicator system A technique for determining managers' information needs based on key business indicators, exception reporting, and the use of graphics packages.

1. *Key indicator system.* A **key indicator system** is based on the selection of key business indicators, exception reporting, and the use of graphics packages. The key indicator system emphasizes managers' control needs and provides those data rapidly and selectively.

total study A process that attempts to assess information requirements at all management levels.

2. *Total study.* The **total study** is a process of assessing information needs at all levels of the management hierarchy. Managers are interviewed about their information requirements. Interview results are compared with available databases, and priorities for information reports are set. The difficulty with this system is that it is time consuming and tries to meet all managers' needs from the same information system, which may mean that no information needs are fully satisfied.

critical success factors (CSFs) The particular areas in which satisfactory results will enhance the organization's overall performance.

3. *Critical success factors.* **Critical success factors (CSFs)** are the "limited number of areas in which results, if they are satisfactory, will ensure successful and competitive performance for the organization."[49] CSFs are obtained through lengthy interviews with individual managers, which define the managers' goals and methods for assessing goal attainment. Then, depending on the level of responsibility—department, division, or entire organization—the interviews are used to define which information will keep the managers apprised of key performance areas. CSFs differ from company to company and among managers within a firm. They force managers to consider only important information needs, thus eliminating useless data. Periodic interviews with managers allow for changing information needs. The information system is designed to provide data to meet individual managers' needs rather than those of the organization as a whole.

SUMMARY

This chapter discussed several important points about management information systems. Nontechnical managers need not understand hardware and software technologies, but they should be aware of how information technology can enhance organizational efficiency and effectiveness. We are becoming an information society, and computer-based information systems are an important part of most organizations today.

Information systems process huge amounts of data and transform them into useful information for managers. Useful management information has the characteristics of quality, timeliness, completeness, and relevance. The five components of an information system, whether manual or computer-based, are input, processing, storage, control, and output.

Computer-based information systems include three types: transaction processing, management information systems, and decision support systems. Transaction processing is used at lower organizational levels; MISs provide information for middle managers; and DSSs help senior managers answer strategic questions. Other new technologies being adopted by organizations include electronic mail, voice messaging, videoconferencing, artificial intelligence, and networking.

Information technology impacts on management efficiency, social relationships, organization structure, and business strategy. The effect on strategy is most important. Information systems should be adopted and implemented in congruence with the organization's strategic objectives. Finally, computer-based information systems have some limitations, including unsuitability for many tasks, unrealistic expectations, underused or sabotaged output, improper implementation, and difficulty of tailoring systems to managers' specific needs.

Management Solution

Huge Bank of America found that it had no strategic customer information or data with which to coordinate its 950 operating units. Its solution was to launch a program of improved, computer-based information systems. Max Hopper was recruited from American Airlines to serve as executive vice-president in charge of systems development. The Bank's information technology policies now will come from a central source. The first new technology was focused on transaction processing. Hopper says BofA can now process cash transactions and fund transfers five times faster than and at one-third the cost of standard banking systems. Additional money is being invested to consolidate 20 different telecommunication systems into a single, flexible network. New MIS and DSS programs have been installed in Europe, where corporate lending officers can now pull electronic files on customers' current accounts, loans, and other data anywhere in Europe and, eventually, around the world. Supervisors can also detect any unauthorized currency trades and exceeding of credit limits, thereby improving control. BofA officers feel that the push in information technology is worth the investment, because BofA will achieve a strategic advantage with lower transaction costs than other banks.[50]

DISCUSSION QUESTIONS

1. What are four characteristics of useful information? How can information systems be designed to include these characteristics?
2. Define an information system. What are the five components of all information systems? How do these components differ for manual and computer-based information systems?
3. How do information needs for control and decision making differ by hierarchical level?
4. What are the limitations of computer-based information systems? Are they due to characteristics of technology or human behavior?
5. If you were asked to help design and implement an information system for a department at your university, how would you proceed? How would you overcome limitations and possible resistance?
6. What is a decision support system? How does a DSS differ from an MIS?
7. Many experts have proposed that in the future organizations will be characterized by a network structure. What do you think will be the benefits and costs of this form of organization?
8. Describe artificial intelligence and expert systems. How do these systems differ from other computer-based information systems?
9. What are the possible effects of information technologies on social relationships and organization structure? Are these effects related? Discuss.
10. Recent thinking suggests that CBISs should be adopted to further competitive strategy. How might information system applications be used to enhance low-cost or differentiation strategies?

CASES FOR ANALYSIS

MEMORIAL COUNTY HOSPITAL

In 1984, Memorial County Hospital was hit by the same changes in Medicare reimbursement as all other hospitals. For years, the longer patients were hospitalized, the more Memorial County got paid. Now the government uses a fixed-fee system, under which hospitals are paid a specific amount for each disease. If the hospital's cost is less than the amount paid, the hospital keeps the profit; if too high, it takes the loss.

Memorial County is scrambling to implement a series of new information systems. An information systems department has been created, and an MIS expert, Jack Grant, has been hired to run it. The challenge facing Grant is awesome: Memorial County must be able to track costs patient by patient, doctor by doctor, and disease by disease. Memorial County never needed this information before because it simply did a rough approximation of overhead costs for each patient before billing Medicare.

The system Grant wants to design will have several characteristics. When a pharmacist fills a prescription, the data will also go into the patient's computer file so that the hospital will know the cost immediately. Similarly, doctors will be expected to file information on patient treatments directly into the computer through terminals in their offices. The hospital has a strong incentive to treat patients as quickly and inexpensively as possible and expects doctors to help in the process. Grant also envisions a cost-tracking system that will follow each doctor's use of the X-ray department, laboratory tests, and other hospital resources. The information system also will report the consumption of all hospital resources per each patient and each disease. Weekly and monthly reports will reveal the different patterns among attending physicians and give Memorial County's senior managers a chance to buttonhole doctors to be aware of costs.

Another change Grant envisions is to integrate financial and medical records. These records were always kept separately, but now the medical record has financial implications, and both medical and financial data will be accessible from a patient's file.

The new technologies will cost Memorial County Hospital several hundred thousand dollars over the next three years. Administrators hope the new computer-based information systems will make the hospital more efficient. Managers will be able to determine, for example, if a cataract treatment costs $2,356 when reimbursement is only $2,128. With such information, administrators can concentrate on shortening hospital stays, reducing the number of tests, or treating some cases as outpatient.

Questions

1. Has the change in Medicare reimbursement altered Memorial County Hospital's competitive strategy? Will information systems help implement that strategy?
2. What impact do you think the increase in information systems will have on structure, social relationships, and management functions within Memorial County Hospital? Discuss.
3. Would you characterize the new information systems as transaction processing, MIS, or DSS? Explain.

UNITED WAY

In September 1986, Mark Mechanic, the director of a university computer center in upstate New York, was working at his desk when the phone rang. On the other end was Paul Powers, an executive in charge of evaluation at the local United Way. Paul wondered if Mark would help design a consolidated information system that would help center directors cut paperwork and also give the United Way more objective performance data for agency evaluation and control. Mark Mechanic indicated that he was very interested. A week later, he had his first meeting with the directors of eight neighborhood centers and executives from three funding agencies. The directors all had similar problems. Most of the centers had evolved from local settlement houses to neighborhood centers that provided a number of services to local residents. Services varied widely but usually included housing, employment, recreation, food, clothing, child care, health services, and referrals and transportation to other agencies. Each had its own unique variety of funding sources, and each was inundated with paperwork.

During the discussion of a potential information system, Mechanic explained what might be done to reduce the paperwork. He pointed out that the current narrative reports written by the caseworkers and the wide variety of forms could be reduced to several standardized forms. From the information on the standardized forms, the computer could produce summaries that would eliminate 80 percent of the paperwork that the directors were doing. The presentation generated considerable enthusiasm, and it was agreed that Mechanic's staff would begin to wade through the numerous forms used in each of the agencies.

After three months, the computer staff had conducted over 100 interviews with people from all levels of the eight agencies and had gathered 190 forms that were currently in use. By the end of five months, the computer staff members felt that they had a rough understanding of information needs, and . . . they scheduled interviews with each of the eight center directors. Shortly thereafter, Mechanic met with the members of his staff. At one point in the meeting, the following discussion took place.

Mechanic: *Up until now you have all been enthusiastic. All of a sudden you seem discouraged. What happened?*

Bill Meadows (project director): *"Mark, the directors of the centers are idiots. They don't understand the first thing about information systems.*

Mechanic: *Idiots! What do you mean?*

Meadows: *We go in and ask them what information they need. They get a shocked look on their face, like they never had thought of such a question. They hem and haw. They have no vision of what an information system is or what it might do for them. No matter how many times we go back, they still cannot deal with the questions we need answered. Whenever we are around the directors disappear.*

Mechanic: *If they disappear, what do you do?*

Meadows: *Well, it is sort of a tacit agreement. We don't bother them with questions and they don't bother us with objections. We show them the forms and they look at them and say O.K.*

Questions

1. What type of information system—transaction processing, MIS, or DSS—will be most appropriate for the United Way agency?
2. Do the United Way agencies truly need a computer-based information system? What limitations do you see in the ability of a CBIS to meet its information needs?
3. How would you characterize the procedure being used to design and implement the information system? What techniques should Bill Meadows use to help managers define their information needs and overcome their resistance?

Source: Robert E. Quinn, "Computers, People, and the Delivery of Services: How to Manage the Management Information System," in John E. Diettrich and Robert A. Zawacki, *People & Organizations,* 2d ed. (Plano, Tex.: Business Publications, 1985), pp. 226–232. Used with permission of Robert Quinn.

CHAPTER 20

Operations Management

Chapter Outline

Organizations as Production Systems

Manufacturing and Service Operations

The Strategic Role of Operations Management

Designing Operations Management Systems

Product and Service Design
Facilities Layout
Production Technology
Facility Location
Capacity Planning

Inventory Management

The Importance of Inventory
Economic Order Quantity
Materials Requirement Planning
Manufacturing Resource Planning
Just-in-Time Inventory

Purchasing

Managing Productivity

Measuring Productivity
Productivity and Quality
Improving Productivity

Organizing the Operations Management Function

Materials Management Approach
Structural Location

Learning Objectives

After studying this chapter, you should be able to:

- **Define operations management and describe its area of application within manufacturing and service organizations.**

- **Explain the role of operations management strategy in the company's overall competitive strategy.**

- **Discuss product, process, and fixed-position layouts and their relative advantages.**

- **Explain why small inventories are preferred by most organizations.**

- **Discuss the differences among EOQ, MRP, and JIT for the management of material and inventory.**

- **Define productivity and explain its relationship to quality.**

- **Describe alternative structural arrangements for the operations management function.**

Management Problem

Roger Schipke, the new chief of General Electric's Appliance Division, was concerned. Dishwashers had been the division's big seller, but its market share had steadily decreased, taking profits with it. A recent survey indicated that GE dishwashers had fallen to second place in market share and that customers perceived them as in third place in product quality. All signs indicated that General Electric was not making as good a dishwasher as its competitors, and the Japanese appeared on the verge of entering the home appliance market. GE's problem was that manufacturing operations in the dishwasher plants were not providing high-quality dishwashers and costs were not low enough.[1]

If you were a senior executive in GE's Appliance Division, what would you do? How would you attack the manufacturing problem to improve quality and efficiency?

The problems confronting GE's Appliance Division are not unusual. Many companies have discovered that success or failure is contingent on well-managed manufacturing operations. During the 1970s, manufacturing operations seemed to lose their primary role in business. Marketing, strategic planning, and finance were held in high esteem and considered the keys to corporate success.

But no longer. For example, Hewlett-Packard Company, which has always been known for its innovative products, has realized that manufacturing excellence is equally important. HP has increased manufacturing automation, introduced just-in-time inventory, and committed itself to new quality standards. Inmed Corporation began as a distributor of medical and surgical supplies and then moved into manufacturing. Executives quickly realized that an efficient, well-managed manufacturing operation was essential and earmarked $5 million to improve its manufacturing processes—a lot for a small company.[2]

The importance of operations to company success partly reflects their large share of resources. Operations management claims some 70 percent of production employees, payroll, and total company assets.[3] Using these resources wisely is a major reason for company efficiency and effectiveness. In addition, manufacturing operations represent the company's basic purpose—indeed, its reason for existence. Without the ability to produce products and services that are competitive in the marketplace, companies cannot expect to succeed in an increasingly competitive environment.[4]

The purpose of this chapter is to describe techniques for the planning and control of manufacturing and service operations. The three preceding chapters described overall control concepts, including management information systems. In this chapter, we will consider the management and control of production operations. First we define operations management and describe the transformation process for producing manufacturing and service outputs. Then we look at how some companies bring operations into strategic decision making. Finally, we consider specific operational design issues such as plant layout, location planning, inventory management, purchasing, scheduling, manufacturing productivity, and organization of the operations management function.

ORGANIZATIONS AS PRODUCTION SYSTEMS

In Chapter 1, the organization was described as a system used for transforming inputs into outputs, as illustrated in Exhibit 20.1. At the center of this transformation process is the **technical core,** which is the heart of the organization's production of its product or service.[5] In an automobile company, the technical core includes the plants that manufacture automobiles. In a university, the technical core includes the academic activities of teaching and research. In a restaurant, the technical core is where the food is prepared. Inputs into the technical core include human resources, land, equipment, buildings, and technology. Outputs from the technical core include the goods and services that are provided for customers and clients. Feedback and control include information on the quality of outputs and on the efficiency of operations within the technical core. This information is used to make control adjustments to increase manufacturing or service efficiency.

The topic of operations management pertains to the day-to-day management of the technical core. **Operations management** is formally defined as the application of special tools and techniques to the operation and control of the technical core for transforming resource inputs into goods and services. In essence, operating managers are concerned with all production activities within the organization.

technical core   The heart of the organization's production of its product or service.

operations management   The application of special tools and techniques to the operation and control of the organization's technical core for transforming resource inputs into goods and services.

E X H I B I T   20.1

The Organization as an Operations Management System

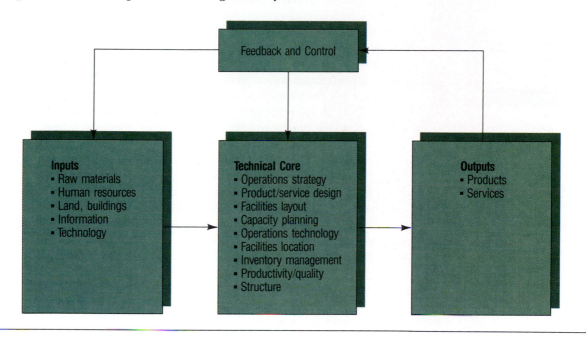

Manufacturing and Service Operations

While terms such as "production" and "operations" seem to imply manufacturing organizations, operations management applies to all organizations. In recent years, most new businesses have provided services rather than products. The service sector has increased three times as fast as the manufacturing sector in the North American economy. Today more than one-half of all businesses are service organizations. Operations management tools and techniques apply to services as well as manufacturing.

Manufacturing organizations are those that produce physical goods. Ford Motor Company, which produces automobiles, and Levi Strauss, which makes clothing, are both manufacturing companies. In contrast, **service organizations** produce nonphysical outputs, such as medical, educational, or transportation services provided for customers. Airlines, doctors, lawyers, and the local barber all provide services. Services also include the sale of merchandise. Although merchandise is a physical good, the service company does not manufacture it but merely sells it as a service to the customer. Retail stores such as Sears and McDonald's are service organizations.

Services differ from manufactured products in two ways. First, the service customer is involved in the actual production process.[6] The patient actually visits the doctor to receive the service, and it's difficult to

manufacturing organization An organization that produces physical goods.

service organization An organization that produces nonphysical goods that require customer involvement and cannot be stored in inventory.

Operations management concerns the operation and control of the organization's technical core. At H&R Block, the technical core involves the provision of income tax service to clients. H&R Block is designed to provide personal, one-to-one service because customers are involved in the service firm production process. Moreover, it locates its more than 8,000 offices close to clients for their convenience and easy access.

operations strategy The recognition of the importance of operations to the firm's success and the involvement of operations managers in the organization's strategic planning.

imagine a barber or a beautician providing services without direct customer contact. The same is true for hospitals, restaurants, and banks. Second, manufactured goods can be placed in inventory while service outputs, being intangible, cannot be stored. Manufactured products such as clothes, food, cars, and VCRs can all be put in warehouses and sold at a later date. However, a beautician cannot wash, cut, and set hair in advance and leave it on the shelf for the customer's arrival, nor can a doctor place examinations in inventory. The service must be created and provided for the customer exactly when he or she wants it.

However, despite the differences between manufacturing and service firms, they face similar operational problems. First, each kind of organization needs to be concerned with scheduling. A medical clinic must schedule appointments so that doctors' and patients' times will be used efficiently, just as a manufacturing plant must schedule workers and raw materials. Second, both manufacturing and service organizations must obtain materials and supplies. Third, both types of organization should be concerned with quality and productivity. Neither wants to produce an output that doesn't work or doesn't satisfy the customer. Since many operational problems are similar, operations management tools and techniques can and should be applied to service organizations as readily as they are to manufacturing.

THE STRATEGIC ROLE OF OPERATIONS MANAGEMENT

Many operations managers are involved in day-to-day problem solving on the shop floor and lose sight of the fact that the best way to control operations is through strategic planning. The more operations managers become enmeshed in operational details, the less likely they are to see the big picture with respect to inventory buildups, parts shortages, and seasonal fluctuations.[7] Indeed, one reason suggested for the Japanese' success is their direct involvement of operations in strategic management. To manage operations effectively, managers must understand operations strategy.

Operations strategy is the recognition of the important role of operations in organizational success and the involvement of operations managers in the organization's strategic planning. Exhibit 20.2 illustrates four stages in the evolution of operations strategy.

Many companies are at stage 1, where strategy is set without considering the capability of operations. The operations department plays no direct role in strategy formulation. For example, a major electronics instrument producer experienced a serious mismatch between strategy and the ability of operations to manufacture products. Because of fast-paced technological changes, the company was changing its products and developing new ones. However, the manufacturer had installed a materials-handling system in the operations department that could not handle diversity and change of this magnitude. Operations managers

EXHIBIT 20.2

Four Stages of Operations Strategy

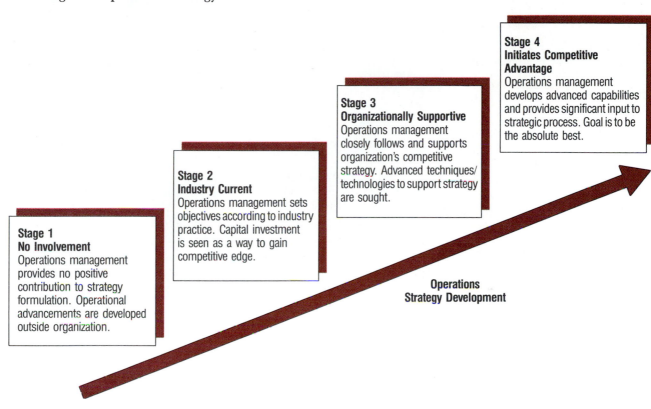

Stage 1
No Involvement
Operations management provides no positive contribution to strategy formulation. Operational advancements are developed outside organization.

Stage 2
Industry Current
Operations management sets objectives according to industry practice. Capital investment is seen as a way to gain competitive edge.

Stage 3
Organizationally Supportive
Operations management closely follows and supports organization's competitive strategy. Advanced techniques/technologies to support strategy are sought.

Stage 4
Initiates Competitive Advantage
Operations management develops advanced capabilities and provides significant input to strategic process. Goal is to be the absolute best.

Operations Strategy Development

Source: Based on R. H. Hayes and S. C. Wheelwright, *Restoring Our Competitive Edge: Competing Through Manufacturing* (New York: Wiley, 1984).

were blamed for the company's failure to achieve strategic objectives even though the operations department's capacity had never been considered during strategy formulation.[8]

At stage 2, the operations department sets objectives according to industry practice.[9] The organization tries to be current with respect to operations management techniques and views capital investment in new plant and equipment as one way to be competitive.

At stage 3, operations managers are more strategically active. Operations strategy is in concert with company strategy, and the operations department will seek new operational techniques and technologies to enhance strategy. For example, Fireplace Manufacturers Inc., a small California company, suddenly found itself facing competitors that were undercutting its prices by as much as 50 percent. The company's strategy was to retrench and become more efficient, and operations managers played a key role. The company made technological improvements in manufacturing that brought major payoffs. Machine setup times were reduced from 2 hours to 15 minutes. Inventory was cut 52 percent.

Allen-Bradley has reached the stage 4 level of operations strategy. It used its operations knowledge to develop a fully automated manufacturing system for producing world-class products. Note the absence of employees—only a few technicians are needed. Larry Yost, vice-president of operations for the Industrial Control Group, was in charge of the project. Here Yost is holding an IEC-standard contactor and relay made in the computer-integrated manufacturing facility. Orders are shipped the day after receipt. This facility is the best in the business and serves as a showcase for customer visits.

Scrap rates alone dropped from 20 to 9 percent, representing a one-year savings of $300,000.[10]

At the highest level of operations strategy, stage 4, operations managers pursue new technologies on their own in order to do the best possible job of delivering the product or service. At stage 4, operations can be a genuine competitive weapon.[11] Operations departments develop new strategic concepts themselves. With the use of new technologies, operations management becomes a major force in overall company strategic planning. Operations can originate new products and processes that will add to or change company strategy.

Why will a company that operates at stage 3 or 4 be more competitive than those that rely on marketing and financial strategies? The reason is that operations differences often determine which organization gets the customer's order. Many orders are won through better price, quality, performance, delivery, or responsiveness to customer demand. These factors are affected by operations, which help the company win orders in the marketplace.[12] Thus, company strategy and success depend on the willingness of operations to seize the initiative in providing better quality, performance, price, delivery, and responsiveness.

One recent example of operations strategy influencing company strategy is the GM Saturn automobile. While the actual details of the car have yet to be decided on, the process by which it will be made has already been studied. GM's goal is to provide a better production system through which to gain more orders and defeat the productive Japanese at their own game. An example of how operations strategy has influenced service organizations is the use of automated teller machines (ATMs) in banking. The rapid adoption of the new operations technology indicated banks' willingness to explore new ways to deliver services to customers. With ATMs, banks now provide services to customers at all hours of the day or night in an amazing variety of locations. Banks thus have embraced operations in their strategic planning.

DESIGNING OPERATIONS MANAGEMENT SYSTEMS

Every organization must design its production system. This starts with the design of the product or service to be produced. A restaurant designs the food items on the menu. An automobile manufacturer designs the cars it produces. Once products and services have been designed, the organization turns to other design considerations, including facilities layout, production technology, facilities location, and capacity planning.

Product and Service Design

Operations management has four major concerns with respect to product design: producibility, cost, quality, and reliability. *Producibility* is the degree to which a product or service can actually be produced for the customer within the firm's existing operational capacity. Producibility is an important strategic consideration because corporate strategy should not anticipate products or services that the firm cannot actually produce. Deere & Company's decision to produce lawn and garden tractors required a major reorganization of the operations management function. Traditional farm tractors had a higher level of producibility for Deere.

The issue of *cost* simply means the sum of the materials, labor, design, transportation, and overhead expense associated with a product or service. Organizations must keep product and service designs within reasonable costs.

The third issue is *quality,* which is the excellence of the product or service. Quality represents the serviceability and value that customers gain by purchasing the product.

Reliability, the fourth issue, is the degree to which the customer can count on the product or service to fulfill its intended function. The product should function as designed for a reasonable length of time. Highly complex products often have lower reliability than simple ones because more things can go wrong.

The IBM personal computer is an excellent example of a product that has all of these design attributes. It is simple and effective in design, is very reliable, and can be made at low cost. The IBM PC is high on producibility because IBM had all of the technology necessary for producing the personal computer along with its other computer lines. The IBM personal computer gains its simplicity and reliability through the use of proven technology and simple design. In addition, low cost is not the same as low price. The IBM PC is sold at a reasonably high price relative to its competition because of its perceived superior quality and

Product design must be concerned with producibility, cost, quality, and reliability. The Italian textile industry, working in conjunction with IBM, has developed a system that allows designers to view simulated woven cloth patterns on a color display screen. Viewing the cloth reduces cost by eliminating the need for preproduction samples. Moreover, patterns can be designed for producibility, quality, and reliability while providing a rapid response to customer requirements.

reliability. These characteristics mean that it can be sold for a high price and yield high profits for IBM.

The design of services also should reflect producibility, cost, quality, and reliability. However, services have one additional design requirement: timing. *Timing* is the degree to which the provision of a service meets the customer's delivery requirements. Recall that a service cannot be stored in inventory and must be provided when the customer is present. If you take your friend or spouse to a restaurant for dinner, you expect the meal to be served in a timely manner. Service organizations must organize their operations to provide the service when the customer wants and needs it. In contrast, manufacturing organizations can produce products for inventory that can later be distributed according to customer demand.

For example, when Pizza Hut announced a special lunch menu that could be served in five minutes or less, the timing required that operations—the kitchen—develop a small list of special items that could consistently be made in five minutes or less. Indeed, pizzas had to be redesigned to accommodate the five-minute requirement. Each step in the delivery of pizza items to customers had to be streamlined to insure that the timing promise was kept.

Facilities Layout

Once a product or service has been designed, the organization must plan for the actual production. The three most common types of layout are process, product, and fixed-position. Exhibit 20.3 illustrates these three layouts.

Process Layout.   A **process layout,** as illustrated in panel a of Exhibit 20.3, is one in which machines are grouped together because they perform a similar function or task. In a machine shop, the lathes perform a

process layout A facilities layout in which machines that perform the same function are grouped together in one location.

E X H I B I T   20.3

Basic Production Layouts

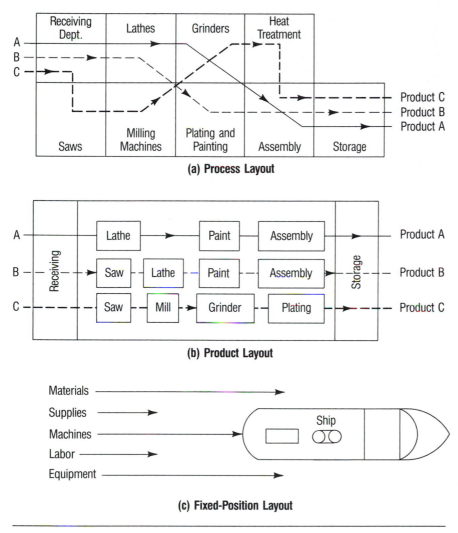

(a) **Process Layout**

(b) **Product Layout**

(c) **Fixed-Position Layout**

Source: Based on J. T. Black, "Cellular Manufacturing Systems Reduce Setup Time, Make Small Lot Production Economical," *Industrial Engineering* (November 1983), pp. 36–48.

similar function and are located together in one section. The grinders are in another section of the shop. Equipment that performs similar "processes" is grouped together. Service organizations also use process layouts. In a bank, the loan officers are in one area, the tellers in another, and managers in a third.

The advantage of the process layout is that it has the potential to reduce costs. For example, having all painting done in one spray-painting area means that fewer machines and people are required to paint all products for the organization. In a bank, having all tellers located together in one carefully controlled area provides increased security. Placing all operating rooms together in a hospital makes it possible to control the environment for all rooms simultaneously.

The drawback to the process layout, as illustrated in Exhibit 20.3a, is that the actual path a product or service takes through the organization can be long and complicated. A product may need several different processes performed on it and thus must travel through many different areas before production is complete.

product layout A facilities layout in which machines and tasks are arranged according to the sequence of steps in the production of a single product.

Product Layout. A **product layout,** illustrated in panel b of Exhibit 20.3, is one in which machines and tasks are arranged according to the progressive steps in producing a single product. The automobile assembly line is a classic example, because it produces a single product starting from the raw materials to the finished output. The product layout at Ford is so carefully tailored to each product line that Ford can make Mustangs only on the Mustang assembly line and cannot use it to make Thunderbirds. Many fast-food restaurants also use the product layout, with activities arranged in sequence to produce hamburgers or chicken depending on the products available.

The product layout is efficient when the organization produces huge volumes of identical products. Note in Exhibit 20.3 that two lines have paint areas. This duplication of functions can be economical only if the volume is high enough to keep each paint area busy working on specialized products.

Harley-Davidson reorganized its motorcycle plant from a process to a product layout. The functions of tapping, drilling, grinding, and assembly are now conducted in the same area. Instead of having all similar activities grouped together, many engine and transmission parts are now completed by just a few people working in a small area with all of the tools and machines they need to make them.[13]

fixed-position layout A facilities layout in which the product remains in one location and the required tasks and equipment are brought to it.

Fixed-Position Layout. The **fixed-position layout,** shown in panel c of Exhibit 20.3, is one in which the product remains in one location, and tasks and equipment are brought to it. The fixed-position layout is used to create a product or service that is either very large or one of a kind, such as aircraft, ships, and buildings. The product cannot be moved from function to function or along an assembly line; rather, the people, materials, and machines all come to the fixed-position site for assembly and processing, as illustrated in Exhibit 20.3. This layout is not good for high volume but it is necessary for large, bulky products and custom orders.

Production Technology

One goal of many operations management departments is to move toward more sophisticated technologies for producing products and services. New technology is sometimes called the "factory of the future." Extremely sophisticated systems that can work almost unaided by employees are being designed.[14] For example, Apple Computer produces the Macintosh in an astonishing new plant. The plant can produce 500,000 Macintosh computers a year with just 200 production workers.

A product layout is one in which machines and tasks are arranged in the sequence of operations used to produce a single product. Chrysler's automobile assembly line (left) uses robotic equipment tailored to the manufacture of Chrysler autos. This layout is efficient for high-volume manufacturing. In contrast, a fixed-position layout is one in which the product remains in one location, as shown by the aircraft body at Lockheed (right). This layout is used when the product is very large, is one of a kind, and cannot be moved.

Labor accounts for only 1 percent of computer manufacturing; robots and computer-guided assembly processes do most of the work.[15]

Two types of production technologies that are becoming more widely used in operations management are flexible manufacturing systems and CAD/CAM.

Flexible Manufacturing Systems.   The **flexible manufacturing system (FMS)** can be viewed as a small or medium-size automated production line.[16] The machinery uses computers to coordinate and integrate the automated machines. Functions such as loading, unloading, storing parts, changing tools, and machining are done automatically. Moreover, the computer can instruct the machines to change parts, machining, and tools when a new product must be produced. This is a breakthrough compared to the product layout, in which a single line is restricted to a single product. With a flexible manufacturing system, a single line can be readily readapted to different products based on computer instructions. Cummins Engine, Chrysler, Caterpillar, and Rockwell have acquired FMSs.

FMSs are most efficient when small batches of products are run on the production line. The computer reprograms the line to run each batch of products. The flexibility for producing different products has increased the utilization of FMS machinery to approximately 80 percent, compared to 30 percent for traditional production lines.

CAD/CAM.   CAD (computer-aided design) and CAM (computer-aided manufacturing) represent new uses of computers in operations management.

CAD enables engineers to develop new-product designs in about half the time required with traditional methods. Computers provide a visual display for the engineer and illustrate the implications of any design change. For example, CAD systems have helped a sportswear manufacturer adjust to rapidly changing product lines. Products change five times a year, and each new season's line requires new production stand-

flexible manufacturing system (FMS)   A small or medium-size automated production line.

CAD   A production technology in which computers perform new-product design.

ards, new bills of material for use on the shop floor, and new cutting patterns. Engineers can use the CAD system to design the pattern layouts and then determine the manufacturing changes needed to produce new sizes and styles, expected labor standards, and bills of material.[17]

CAM is similar to the use of computers in flexible manufacturing systems. The computer is harnessed to help guide and control the manufacturing system. For example, for the above sportswear manufacturer, the entire sequence of manufacturing operations—pattern scaling, layout, and printing—has now been mechanized through the use of computers. Computer-controlled cutting tables have been installed. Once the computer has mathematically defined the geometry, it guides the cutting blade, eliminating the need for paper patterns. Fabric requisitions, production orders for cutting and sewing operations, and sewing line work can also be directed by computer programs.

CAM A production technology in which computers help guide and control the manufacturing system.

Facility Location

At some point, almost every organization must make a decision concerning the location of facilities. A bank may need to open a new branch office, Wendy's needs to find locations for some of the 100 or so new stores opened each year, or a manufacturer needs to build a warehouse. When these decisions are made unwisely, they are expensive and troublesome for the organization. For example, Modulate Corporation moved its head office six times in seven years because it had incorrectly anticipated its building requirements.

The most common approach to selecting a site for a new location is to do a cost-benefit analysis. For example, a bank may identify four possible locations. The costs associated with each location are the land (purchase or lease), transportation from the current facility, and construction, including zoning laws, building codes, land features, and size of the parking lot. Taxes, utilities, rents, and maintenance are other cost factors to be considered in advance. Each possible bank location also will have certain benefits. Benefits to be evaluated are accessibility of customers, location of major competitors, general quality of working conditions, and nearness to restaurants and shops, which would be desirable for both employees and customers.

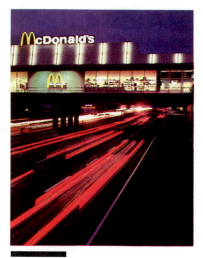

Facility location is a major concern of McDonald's executives. One innovation was to locate restaurants on tollways. The cost-benefit analysis revealed that greater construction costs for tollway locations were more than offset by increased sales. Tollway restaurants such as this one on the Illinois tollway at Des Plaines have sales of from two to ten times greater than those of previous food service operations on the same sites. McDonald's has targeted more tollway and interstate sites for the future.

Once the bank managers have evaluated the worth of each benefit, the cost-benefit analysis becomes relatively simple. Total benefits can be divided by total costs for each location, and managers can select the location with the highest ratio. If benefits cannot be precisely calculated, the choice may be made on the basis of cost analysis, with managers choosing the location with the lowest cost. Sophisticated techniques that can aid in location decisions were described in Chapter 7. These include linear programming, the payoff matrix, and decision tree analysis, each of which provides a useful framework for making a location decision.

Capacity Planning

capacity planning The determination and adjustment of the organization's ability to produce products and services to match customer demand.

Capacity planning is the determination and adjustment of the organization's ability to produce products or services to match demand. For example, if a bank anticipates a customer increase of 20 percent over the next year, capacity planning is the procedure whereby it will insure that it has sufficient capacity to service that demand.

Organizations can do several things to increase capacity. One is to create additional shifts and hire people to work on them. A second is to ask existing people to work overtime to add to capacity. A third is to subcontract extra work to other firms. A fourth is to build a larger plant with more equipment. Each of these techniques will increase the organization's ability to meet demand.

One major difference in these approaches is in their feasibility for long- versus short-term capacity planning. Having employees work overtime can solve a short-term capacity problem. Constructing a new building can solve a long-term capacity requirement. The responsibility of operations managers is to determine how far in advance they need to plan for capacity. In a fast-food restaurant, one to two weeks' advance planning is probably sufficient. Changes in capacity are handled primarily through the number of people employed during that period. However, the capacity of an automobile plant must be considered several years in advance, because it takes a long time to design a car, acquire the necessary tooling, and modify the assembly line.

An interesting capacity plan was undertaken by Chrysler. Chrysler leased a manufacturing plant from AMC, including AMC's work force. The leased plant produces Chrysler New Yorkers and has significantly increased Chrysler's capacity for three years. Since Chrysler and other American manufacturers expect a glut of new cars in the future, Chrysler won't be stuck with a new plant. Ford's capacity plan was to simply refuse to increase capacity despite the popularity of its automobiles. It has decided to accept fewer sales in the short term rather than suffer from overcapacity in the long run.

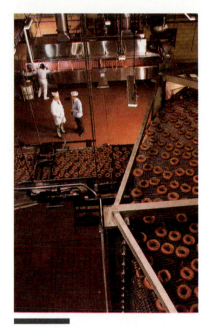

Tasty Baking's donut manufacturing plant is a direct result of the company's strategic plan to increase capacity for making and selling donuts. Because the new donut line was successful, executives planned an addition to the existing bakery building. The additional capacity will produce a full line of mini-, powdered, honey wheat, and chocolate-covered donuts as well as the regular line of full-size premium donuts.

INVENTORY MANAGEMENT

A large portion of the operations manager's job consists of inventory management. **Inventory** is the goods the organization keeps on hand for use in the production process. Most organizations have three types of inventory—finished-goods, work-in-process, and raw materials.

Finished-goods inventory includes items that have passed through the entire production process but have not been sold. This is highly visible inventory. The new cars sitting in the storage lot of an automobile factory are finished-goods inventory, as are the hamburgers and french fries waiting under the lamps at a McDonald's restaurant. Finished-goods inventory is expensive, because the organization has invested labor and other costs to make the finished product.

Work-in-process inventory includes the materials moving through the stages of the production process that are not yet a completed product. Work-in-process inventory in an automobile plant includes engines, wheel and tire assemblies, and dashboards waiting to be installed. In a fast-food restaurant, the french fries in the fryer and hamburgers on the grill are work-in-process inventory.

inventory The goods that the organization keeps on hand for use in the production process.

finished-goods inventory Inventory consisting of items that have passed through the complete production process but have yet to be sold.

work-in-process inventory Inventory composed of the materials that are still moving through the stages of the production process.

E X H I B I T   20.4

Large Inventories Hide Operations Management Problems

Source: R. J. Schonberger, *Japanese Manufacturing Techniques: Nine Hidden Lessons in Simplicity* (New York: The Free Press, 1982).

raw materials inventory Inventory consisting of the basic inputs to the organization's production process.

Raw materials inventory includes the basic inputs to the organization's production process. This inventory is cheapest because the organization has not yet invested labor in it. Steel, wire, glass, and paint are raw materials inventory for an auto plant. Meat patties, buns, and raw potatoes are the raw materials inventory in a fast-food restaurant.

The Importance of Inventory

Why is inventory management so important to organizations? Simply put, inventory costs money. Many years ago a firm's wealth was measured by its inventory. Today inventory is recognized as an unproductive asset. Most organizations strive to keep inventories to a minimum, and management effectiveness is often measured by low inventory levels. Dollars not tied up in inventory can be used in other productive ventures. One hundred thousand dollars in inventory is money that cannot be used for capital improvements, investment, or research and development.

The Japanese analogy of rocks and water describes the current management attitude toward the importance of inventory.[18] As illustrated in Exhibit 20.4, the water in the stream is the inventory in the organization.

The higher the water, the less managers have to worry about the rocks, which represent problems. In operations management, these problems apply to scheduling, plant layout, product design, and quality. When the water level goes down, managers see the rocks and must deal with them. When inventories are reduced, the problems of a poorly designed and managed production process also are revealed. The problems then must be solved. When inventory can be kept at an absolute minimum, operations management is considered excellent.

Ed Heard, a consultant who specializes in inventory management, has the following message:

The best criterion for gauging the effectiveness of a manufacturing operation is inventory. If you have a lot of it sitting on the floor, you are probably not doing as good a job as you could be. Inventory is simply the best indicator of manufacturing performance that we have. There is no problem, no screw-up, that doesn't show up in the inventory number. Both raw materials and work-in-process are supposed to be where they are needed in the right quantity at the right time. Too much too soon and money invested in inventory is wasted. Too little too late and the production process is held up waiting for more inventory.[19]

Today most companies recognize inventories as unproductive assets and strive to keep them to a minimum. Noxell Corporation has implemented computer-based inventory control systems to decrease the amount of inventory on hand. The computer helps managers continuously monitor inventory to reduce purchase volume and improve component quality. In addition, vendor delivery procedures have been established so that products arrive only as needed. A substantial reduction in inventory has occurred without compromising excellent customer service.

Poor management decisions cause inventory to increase beyond acceptable levels. For example, at the end of the 1986 car model year, General Motors found itself with a large number of unsold cars. The cars were tying up a great deal of money and the 1987 models were about to be introduced, making the 1986 cars obsolete. General Motors chose to dramatically cut interest rates on car loans to stimulate sales. It worked and dramatically reduced finished-goods inventory. The reduced interest rates on car loans meant that GM made less money on car sales, but the cost of carrying the excess inventory would have been greater than the cost of the reduced rates.

Let's now consider specific techniques for inventory management. Four important ones are economic order quantity, materials requirement planning, manufacturing resource planning, and just-in-time inventory systems.

Economic Order Quantity

Two basic decisions that can help minimize inventory are how much raw material to order and when to order from outside suppliers. Ordering the minimum amounts at the right time keeps the raw materials, work-in-process, and finished-goods inventory at low levels. One popular technique is **economic order quantity (EOQ),** which is designed to minimize the total of ordering costs and holding costs for inventory items. *Ordering costs* are the costs associated with actually placing the order, such as postage, receiving, and inspection. *Holding costs* are costs associated with keeping the item on hand, such as storage space charges, finance charges, and materials-handling expenses.

The EOQ calculation indicates the order quantity size that will minimize holding and ordering costs based on the organization's use of inventory. The EOQ formula includes ordering costs (C), holding costs

economic order quantity (EOQ)   An inventory management technique designed to minimize the total of ordering and holding costs for inventory items.

EXHIBIT 20.5

Inventory Control of Surgical Dressings by EOQ

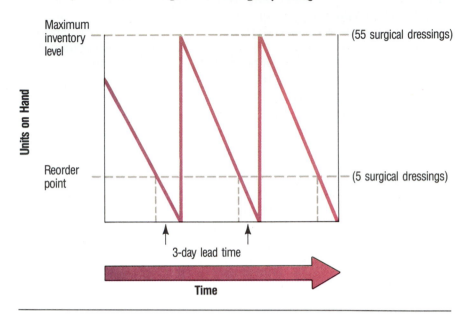

(H), and annual demand (D). For example, consider a hospital's need to order surgical dressings. Based on hospital records, the ordering costs for surgical dressings are $15, the annual holding cost is $6, and the annual demand for dressings is 605. The formula for the economic order quantity is:

$$EOQ = \sqrt{\frac{2DC}{H}} = \sqrt{\frac{2(605)(15)}{6}} = 55.$$

The EOQ formula tells us that the best quantity to order is 55.

The next question is when to make the order. For this decision a different formula, called **reorder point (ROP),** is used. ROP is calculated by the following formula, which assumes that it takes three days to receive the order after the hospital has placed it:

$$ROP = \frac{D}{Time} \text{ (Lead time)} = \frac{605}{365} (3) = 4.97, \text{ or } 5.$$

reorder point (ROP) The most economical level at which an inventory item should be reordered.

The reorder point tells us that since it takes three days to receive the order, at least five dressings should be on hand when the order is placed. As nurses use surgical dressings, operations managers will know that when the level reaches the point of 5, the new order should be placed for a quantity of 55.

This relationship is illustrated in Exhibit 20.5. Whenever the reorder point of 5 dressings is reached, the new order is initiated, and the 55 arrive just as the inventory is depleted. In a typical hospital, however, some variability in lead time and use of surgical dressings will occur. Thus, a few extra items of inventory, called *safety stock,* are used to insure that the hospital does not run out of surgical dressings.

Materials Requirement Planning

The EOQ formula works well when inventory items are not dependent on one another. For example, in a restaurant the demand for hamburgers is independent of the demand for milkshakes; thus, an economic order quantity is calculated for each item. A more complicated inventory problem occurs with **dependent demand inventory,** meaning that item demand is related to the demand for other inventory items. For example, if Ford Motor Company decides to make 100,000 cars, it will also need 400,000 tires, 400,000 rims, and 400,000 hubcaps. The demand for tires is dependent on the demand for cars. Dependent demand inventory requires a complex formulation that will determine the demand for all dependent inventory items simultaneously.

dependent demand inventory Inventory in which item demand is related to the demand for other inventory items.

The most common inventory control system used for handling dependent demand inventory is **materials requirement planning (MRP).** MRP is a dependent demand inventory planning and control system that schedules the exact amount of all materials required to support the desired end product. MRP is computer based and requires sophisticated software to coordinate information on inventory location, bill of materials, purchasing, production planning, invoicing, and order entry.

materials requirement planning (MRP) A dependent demand inventory planning and control system that schedules the precise amount of all materials required to support the production of desired end products.

MRP relies on three basic documents. The *master production schedule* is a forecast of the number of end products to be produced for the next period—say, one month. The *bill of materials* is a list of all parts and inventory pieces that make up each end product. The *inventory status file* is the record of parts currently in inventory.[20]

The MRP system operates in response to the master production schedule, which specifies when end products must be ready. The MRP software issues instructions to either order raw materials or take materials from inventory as needed to assemble products for sale. MRP also calculates the minimum inventories on hand required for meeting future production schedules. MRP results in precise coordination between inventory requirements and production schedules. Unlike with EOQ, inventory levels are not based on past consumption; rather, they are based on precise estimates of future orders. With MRP, inventory costs can be cut dramatically.

For example, consider the hospital described earlier using an MRP approach. The hospital would set up the surgical schedule for the coming week—the equivalent of a master production schedule. For each scheduled surgery, a bill of materials would be issued listing the dressings and other needed items. The inventory status file would show how many surgical dressings the hospital has on hand. Now assume that the master production schedule shows that 20 surgeries will be performed next week and the inventory status file shows 5 surgical dressings on hand. MRP would then calculate that the hospital needs 20 surgical dressings, less the 5 on hand; thus, 15 would be ordered. They arrive, are used in the 20 operations, and the entire inventory is used up. There are no extra inventory carrying costs and no risk of needing to scrap excess or obsolete inventory. In the meantime, the schedule of surgeries for the following week has been fed into the MRP system, the need for surgical dressings identified, and the inventory ordered. Inventory flows into the hospital as it is needed, thereby minimizing inventory storage and handling costs.

The essential requirement for successful MRP is that every employee—whether computer operator, purchasing agent, or inventory analyst—be diligent about feeding accurate data into the system. If the MRP system starts accumulating errors concerning stock on hand or future needs, it will break down. If the master production schedule anticipates more production than will actually occur, excess inventory will be ordered. If the inventory status file shows the hospital has five surgical dressings when in fact there are only three, the hospital will be two short when it comes time for surgery. MRP systems require 99 percent data accuracy in order for their full potential to be realized.[21] Consider the implementation of MRP at Delco Electronics.

Delco Electronics

A sophisticated MRP system was installed at Delco Electronics because "We needed a more efficient materials handling and storage system to support increased production of radios, heater/air controls, and electronic engine controls utilizing billions of components a year," said J. L. Moore, materials management director. "We now have a reliable system that practically 'spoon feeds' processing, sub-assembly, and final assembly operations. The new system should pay for itself within a year."

The MRP system drives the inventory system, which includes automated retrieval of inventory items. Machines go down the aisles permitting touch terminals to direct "picking" and "put-away" operations. The centralized storage and picking system is designed to store or retrieve a load every 30 seconds in a 16-hour workday. Terminal screens provide a list of parts required for each end product as well as direct the storage of new raw materials. The displayed list shortens as workers put parts away. Then the terminal display indicates the number of items on hand for future assembly.

The MRP system has created a $12 million reduction in inventory. The savings is based partly on the fact that only two days' inventory, on average, is kept on hand. Additional floor space from reduced inventory has provided an extra savings of $133,000 a year. Labor savings from the automated picking and put-away operations have saved nearly $14 million.[22]

Manufacturing Resource Planning

Manufacturing resource planning, called **MRP II,** represents a major development beyond MRP. MRP is a technique for managing inventory, while MRP II reaches into every company operation to control all resources. MRP II creates a model of the overall business that allows senior managers to control production scheduling, cash flow, manpower planning, capacity planning, inventory, distribution, and materials purchasing. MRP II also supports marketing and engineering and provides financial information. It unites business functions by translating all operations into financial data and provides the entire company with access to the same set of numbers. In the ideal application, it is a computer-based model of the company's operations.

Although MRP II evolved from MRP, it plays more of a strategic planning role for senior managers. The hardware and software for MRP II are sophisticated and complex and typically are used only in larger companies. Under MRP II, the entire company's efforts are analyzed and the computer produces corporate plans and solves corporate problems. MRP II starts with the company's business plan, which is translated into sales objectives by product line. Sales objectives, in turn, are translated into forecasts of materials requirements, inventory needs, and production schedules.[23]

manufacturing resource planning (MRP II)   An extension of MRP to include the control of resources pertaining to all operations of the organization.

Just-in-Time Inventory

Just-in-time (JIT) inventory systems are designed to reduce the level of an organization's inventory to zero. Sometimes these systems are referred to as *stockless systems, zero inventory systems,* or *Kanban systems.* Each system centers on the concept that suppliers deliver materials only at the exact moment needed, thereby reducing raw material inventories to zero. Moreover, work-in-process inventories are kept to a minimum because goods are produced only as needed to service the next stage of production. Finished-goods inventories are minimized by matching them exactly to sales demand.

Just-in-time inventory requires that the production system be simple and well coordinated, as illustrated in Exhibit 20.6.[24] Each part of the production process produces and moves goods forward only when the next stage requires them. JIT is called a *demand pull* system because each work station produces its product only when the next work station says it is ready to receive more input. This is in contrast to the traditional *batch-push system,* in which parts are made in large, supposedly efficient batches and pushed to the next operation on a fixed schedule, where they sit until used. In a push system, each work station produces at a constant rate regardless of the actual requirement of the next work station. The demand-pull system can result in reduced inventories, improved quality, and better responsiveness, but it requires excellent coordination among all parts of the production sequence.

Recall the Japanese analogy of the rocks and the water. To reduce inventory levels to zero means that all management and coordination problems will surface and must be resolved. Scheduling must be scrupu-

just-in-time (JIT) inventory system   An inventory control system that schedules materials to arrive precisely when they are needed on a production line.

Lear Siegler Inc. recently completed this plant for making upholstered car seats near Flint, Michigan, which is a model for just-in-time plants. Because of the innovative layout, incoming parts are used immediately and completed seats shipped hourly to a nearby General Motors plant for immediate installation. The surrounding work area is uncluttered. The only inventory on hand is either being worked on or within a few minutes of production or delivery.

EXHIBIT 20.6

Just-in-Time Inventory System

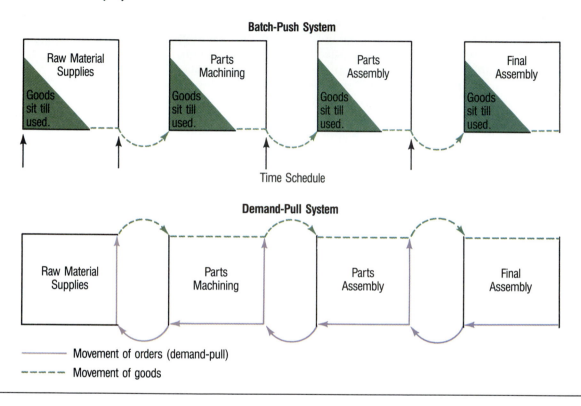

lously precise. For example, Johnson Controls makes automobile seats two hours before they are to be installed in an automobile on Chrysler's assembly line. After production, the seats are driven to the Chrysler plant 75 miles away and taken directly to the moving assembly line for installation. If the seats don't arrive on time, the entire assembly line has to stop, generating enormous expense.[25]

Just-in-time inventory systems also require excellent employee motivation and cooperation. Workers are expected to perform at their best because they are entrusted with the responsibility and authority to make the zero inventory system work. Employees must help one another when they fall behind and must be capable of doing different jobs. Workers experience the satisfaction of being in charge of the system and making useful improvements in the company's operations.[26]

Just-in-time systems have tremendous advantages. The reduced inventory level frees productive capital for other company uses. For example, Omark Industries, a $300 million corporation in Oregon, saved an estimated $7 million in inventory carrying costs. It calls its version the Zero Inventory Production System (ZIPS).[27] General Motors has used the approach since 1980 and has slashed its annual inventory-related costs from $8 billion to $2 billion. Appliance makers such as Westinghouse and RCA are experimenting with just-in-time inventory systems in some of their plants.

One illustration of cost savings from inventory flexibility occurred in a Kawasaki motorcycle plant.

Kawasaki

The Kawasaki plant in Lincoln, Nebraska, installed a JIT system and found that scheduling had to be absolutely precise. Workers on the line needed to know that every KZ100 motorcycle would be followed by two KZ750 motorcycles and thus have the necessary parts available for assembly. With such precise scheduling, there was little need to have inventory sitting on the floor or in bins.

After the system was successfully implemented, Kawasaki managers found that the most important benefit was the increased flexibility and responsiveness to the marketplace. For example, at one point the Kawasaki plant had planned for and was making both blue and red motorcycles. However, the blue motorcycles were not selling well. The marketing people investigated and found out that black was the hot new color and that Kawasaki should be making black rather than blue motorcycles. In a plant with lots of work-in-process and finished-goods inventory, it could have taken weeks or even months to work off the inventory of blue tanks and other parts. During those weeks, Kawasaki would be shipping blue motorcycles to stores that did not want and could not sell them. However, with the JIT system in place, the change in color took Kawasaki less than one day. By nightfall they were shipping new, black motorcycles to customers. The change in color resulted in dramatically increased sales.[28]

PURCHASING

The purchasing function has long been overlooked as a major contributor to the organization's overall profit plan. However, with the increased sophistication of inventory management techniques such as MRP and JIT, the purchasing role has become more prominent. A business spends about 58 percent of its cost of sales on purchases outside the organization.[29] Considering its large scope and the need to purchase materials suitable for sophisticated inventory control systems, purchasing is an excellent function for enhancing organizational profitability.

The **purchasing function** involves finding and acquiring the right goods, at the right price, on time, in the needed quantity, and with the desired quality characteristics. In a hospital, purchasing obtains drugs,

purchasing function The organizational function concerned with finding and obtaining the right goods at the desired price and time, in the needed quantity, and of the correct quality.

surgical equipment, oxygen, bed linens, X-ray film, and thousands of other supplies. A municipal government purchases computer services, trucks, paper, pencils, cement, traffic lights, and electrical energy.

With the advent of MRP and JIT, the role of the purchasing department has changed.[30] For example, just-in-time purchasing requires long-term, stable supply relationships. The organization no longer goes out for the most competitive bids for each new batch of raw materials. Since the supplier's production is closely linked to the buyer's consumption of inventory, the organization cannot rely on annual rebidding to decrease costs. Other changes include sole-source contracts and localized buying, both of which facilitate transportation and coordination with production. At Zebco, the Brunswick unit that makes fishing reels, 80 percent of purchased parts were defective. Purchasing got tough and bought only if quality was guaranteed. With a reduced number of suppliers, defects are down to 2.5 percent.

The role of purchasing requires more than just buying goods and services cheaply and seeing that they arrive on time. The responsibility of the purchasing department is to establish *vendor relations,* that is, a strong, sound, cooperative relationship between the company and its vendors.[31]

Establishing a good relationship with a vendor can pay important dividends in times of difficulty. Maintaining good vendor relations is not always easy; thus, highly skilled purchasing agents are valuable assets to the organization. They are responsible for monitoring the introduction of new materials and products that could be useful for production. In addition, skilled purchasing agents anticipate when a major supplier is likely to suffer a long strike or the flow of supplies will be interrupted for some other reason. The purchasing department's responsibility is to insure that these problems do not upset the organization's smooth, efficient production process.

MANAGING PRODUCTIVITY

People have argued that the United States is in the midst of a productivity crisis because U.S. growth and productivity have declined while sharp productivity increases have been reported in Japan, West Germany, Canada, and other countries.[32] Productivity is significant because it influences the well-being of the entire society as well as of individual companies. The only way to increase the output of goods and services to society is to increase organizational productivity.

Measuring Productivity

productivity The organization's output of products and services divided by its inputs.

What is productivity, and how is it measured? In simple terms, **productivity** is the organization's output of goods and services divided by its inputs. This means that productivity can be improved by either increasing the amount of output using the same level of inputs or reducing the number of inputs required to produce the output. As a simple example,

Lone Star Industries Inc. is the country's leading cement producer, a position that is attributed to its flexibility and productivity. Lone Star's improved productivity is illustrated in the trend from 1980 to 1985, when improvements reduced the average number of kilowatt-hours per ton by 2 percent; BTUs per ton by 20 percent; and man-hours per ton by 33 percent. Lone Star has improved productivity in labor, capital, materials, and energy, leading to improved ratios for both total factor and partial productivity.

assume that a small trucking company is able to provide $400,000 worth of transportation services to customers using three trucks during 1987. In 1988 the company, using improved scheduling procedures, provides services worth $450,000 with the same three trucks. The trucking company has experienced an increase in productivity.

However, the actual measurement of productivity is somewhat more complex than simply dividing inputs by outputs. First we must define these components. Two approaches for measuring productivity are total factor productivity and partial productivity.[33] **Total factor productivity** is the ratio of total outputs to the inputs from labor, capital, materials, and energy:

$$\text{Total factor productivity} = \frac{\text{Output}}{\text{Labor} + \text{Capital} + \text{Materials} + \text{Energy}}.$$

total factor productivity The ratio of total outputs to the inputs from labor, capital, materials, and energy.

Total factor productivity represents the best measure of how the organization is doing. Often, however, managers need to know about productivity with respect to certain inputs. **Partial productivity** is the ratio of total outputs to a major category of inputs. For example, many organizations are interested in the idea of labor productivity. Labor productivity would be measured as follows:

$$\text{Productivity} = \frac{\text{Output}}{\text{Labor dollars}}.$$

partial productivity The ratio of total outputs to inputs from a single major input category.

Calculating this formula for labor, capital, or materials provides information on whether improvements in each element are occurring. How-

MANAGERS SHOP TALK

Managing by the Numbers

W. Edwards Deming is known as the "father of statistical quality control." He knows the value of numbers, but he also believes numbers are secondary to good management and employee commitment. Compare his comments with those of Harold Geneen in the Manager's Shoptalk in Chapter 18:

Some of you are students of finance. You learn how to figure and how to run a company on figures. If you run a company on figures alone you will go under. . . . Why? Because the most important figures are not there. You [must] learn that the most important figures are those that are unknown or unknowable.

What about the multiplying effects of a happy customer, in either manufacturing or in service? Is he in your figures? What about the multiplying effect of an unhappy customer? Is that in your figures? Did you learn that in your school of finance? What about the multiplying effect of getting better material to use in production? What about the multiplying effect that you get all along the production line? Do you know that figure? You don't! If you run your company without it, you won't have a company. What about the multiplying effect of doing a better job along the line?

People all over the world think that it is the factory worker that causes problems. He is not your problem. . . . Yet he cannot do a good job. He is not allowed to do it because the management wants figures, more product, and never mind the quality. They measure only in figures. The factory worker is forced to make defective products, forced to turn out defective items. He is forced to work with defective material, so no matter what he does, it will still be wrong. The worker can't do anything about it. He is totally helpless. If he tries to do something about it, he might as well talk to the wall. Nobody listens.

The foreman better not stop the line. He'll hurt production if he does, and he may not be here tomorrow. . . . A millwright, feeling a bearing, informed the foreman that it was getting warm. He suggested that they stop and take care of it before the bearing froze up and scored the shaft. If that happened, they would be down for sure. The foreman knew that the proper thing for the company to do was to stop and work on the bearing. His answer was, "We can't stop now, we must get these castings out today." He didn't make it. The bearing froze and scored the shaft. The line was down four days, but the foreman did his job.

Source: W. Edwards Deming, from a lecture given at Utah State University. Used with permission of Mr. Deming. (Quoted in Tom Peters and Nancy Austin, *A Passion for Excellence: The Leadership Difference* [New York: Random House, 1985], pp. 102–105.)

ever, partial productivity measures can be misleading. Operations managers should not fall into the trap of mistaking partial productivity measures for an indicator of total productivity. For example, labor productivity may show an increase as a result of improvements in capital equipment. Partial productivity measures can cause operations managers to misinterpret productivity improvements because the measures fail to consider important production elements.

Productivity and Quality

In the United States, managers traditionally have viewed productivity and quality as opposing forces. The organization can increase productivity, but only at the expense of quality, and vice versa. Under this assumption, productivity was really conceptualized as total output. In the new way of thinking, quality and productivity have a positive relationship. The reason is that improved quality reduces waste and reduced waste improves productivity.

For example, consider a company that makes brass figurines. Each worker may average 100 figurines per hour, but through carelessness

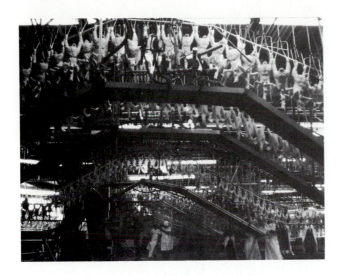

five figurines may be defective. Assume that through increased worker involvement in quality control and improved management techniques, the five defective figurines are reduced to one. This is an improvement of four brass figurines with no increase in labor or materials inputs. Through improved quality, what has hapened to productivity? Quality has increased from 95 to 99 percent, at no additional cost, and productivity has improved by the same amount.

In Chapters 17 and 18, we talked about two quality concepts that are helpful to operations managers. The first is *total quality control,* which means that all elements of the organization participate in improving the quality of products and services.[34] The other concept is *statistical quality control,* which uses the powerful tools of probability and statistics to monitor the manufacturing process's conformity to quality specifications.

Perdue Farms Inc. is a world leader in productivity and quality. Eight lines run continuously in this processing plant at Accomac, Virginia (left). Every chicken is checked for 54 quality specifications. To insure fresh products, incoming chickens are prepared for the marketplace in just 75 minutes and arrive at distributors and stores in a few hours. Compare Perdue's operation with the poultry inspection systems used around 1910 (right). Advances by companies such as Perdue use technology, workers, and management to improve both quality and productivity.

Improving Productivity

Quality problems plague many firms. One Ford engine plant had so much variation in pistons for the same engine that they were classified into 13 sizes. Quality improvements over five years reduced the sizes to three and then to one. Now any piston fits any engine block, as in Japan.[35]

When an organization decides that it's important to improve productivity, there are three places to look: technological productivity, worker productivity, and managerial productivity.

Technological productivity means the use of more efficient machines, robots, computers, and other technologies to increase outputs. The flexible manufacturing and CAD/CAM systems described earlier in this chapter are technological improvements that enhance productivity. Computer-based MRP is another example.

Worker productivity means having workers produce more output in the same time period. Improving worker productivity is a real challenge for American companies, because too often workers have an antagonistic

E X H I B I T   20.7

Deming's 14 Points for Management Productivity

1. Create constancy of purpose toward improved product and service.

2. Adopt a new philosophy, because the old ones no longer work.

3. Cease dependence on mass inspection and require statistical evidence of design quality.

4. End the practice of awarding business on price alone. Quality must also be recognized.

5. Find problems by monitoring the system continually.

6. Institute modern methods of on-the-job training.

7. Institute modern methods of supervision.

8. Drive out fear so that everyone is working for the company.

9. Break down barriers between parts of the organization.

10. Eliminate numerical goals and slogans asking for higher levels of output without providing methods.

11. Eliminate standards that prescribe numerical quotas.

12. Remove the barriers between the worker and pride in the job.

13. Institute vigorous programs of education and retraining.

14. Create a management structure that will work on the above 13 points every day.

Source: Reprinted from *Quality, Productivity and Competitive Position* by W. Edwards Deming by permission of MIT and W. Edwards Deming. Published by MIT, Center for Advanced Engineering Study, Cambridge, MA 02139. Copyright 1982 by W. E. Deming.

relationship with management. At Corning Glass, workers are formed into temporary "corrective action teams" to solve specific problems. Employees also fill out "method improvement requests," which are promptly reviewed. Zebco got its workers involved by taking them to a trade show to see how good the Japanese fishing reels are. With workers' efforts, Zebco's productivity doubled in four years.[36]

Managerial productivity simply means that managers do a better job of running the business. Leading experts in the field of productivity and quality have often stated that the real reason for productivity problems in the United States is poor management.[37] One of these authorities went so far as to propose specific points for telling management how to improve productivity. These points are listed in Exhibit 20.7.

Management productivity improves when managers emphasize quality over quantity, break down barriers between themselves and their employees, and do not overmanage using numbers. Managers must learn to use reward systems, management by objectives, and other management techniques that have been described throughout this book. For example, in a recent look at Honda and Jeep automobile assembly plants in Ohio, a dramatic difference in quality and productivity was found. The Honda plant produced 870 cars a day with 2,423 workers, and the Jeep plant produced 750 cars with 5,400 workers. The greater productivity in the Honda plant was attributed to better management.[38]

Hughes Aircraft Company uses a materials management approach. It even has a producibility laboratory for ironing out potential production snags before a product design is released to the factory floor. Design and assembly specialists work together to coordinate production flow. Moreover, paperless documentation of assembly steps as shown here displays a color-coded graphical representation of the part, cautionary measures, and assembly instructions. Hughes' materials management departments improve manufacturing effectiveness.

ORGANIZING THE OPERATIONS MANAGEMENT FUNCTION

Our final topic concerns the organization of operations management activities to achieve the greatest impact on the firm's productivity and effectiveness. Operations management includes many departmental activities, such as inventory management, purchasing, materials handling, distribution, traffic, receiving, scheduling, and plant layout. In many organizations, these departments are widely disbursed. Inventory management and materials handling may report to a production control manager. Distribution and traffic may be part of the marketing department. Receiving may be part of quality control.

Departmental separation leads to poor communication and coordination, higher than necessary inventories, and lower productivity. Thus, the choice of organization structure should consider two factors: whether to group all materials management activities together into a single department and to whom this department should report.

Materials Management Approach

The first step is to group the materials management departments together into a single function, which is called the materials management concept. **Materials management** is the total integration of all organizational departments and activities that contribute to the cost of materials.[39] The materials management concept suggests that it is in the organization's interest to effectively coordinate and control the acquisition and use of materials. Grouping all materials-handling activities together under one senior materials manager heightens the emphasis given to achieving operations management objectives and improves communication among departments.

materials management The complete integration of all organizational departments and activities that contribute to the cost of materials.

Structural Location

The second aspect of structure pertains to whom the materials manager should report. One alternative is for the materials manager to report to the CEO just like the head of marketing, finance, engineering, and manufacturing, as illustrated in panel a of Exhibit 20.8. Having the materials manager report to such a high level has the advantage of infusing operations into the organization's strategic planning.

The second alternative is for the materials manager to report to the head of manufacturing, as illustrated in panel b. As a practical matter, this structure typically is easier to achieve. Some of the materials management activities probably already report to manufacturing; thus, the

E X H I B I T   20.8

Two Reporting Levels for Materials Management Department

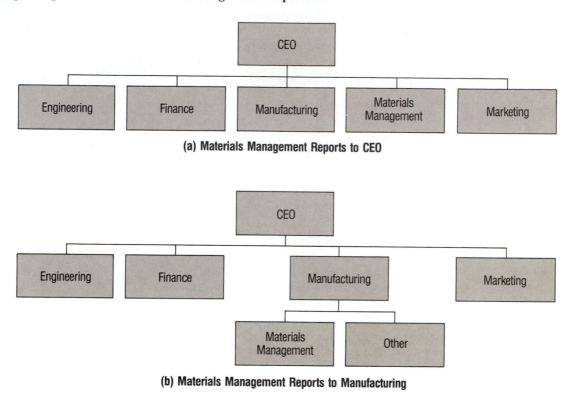

(a) Materials Management Reports to CEO

(b) Materials Management Reports to Manufacturing

changes necessary for bringing all materials management activities together are not great. Also, since the structural changes are occurring at a lower level, the power and political dynamics will be easier to handle. The drawback to reporting to the manufacturing manager is the reduced visibility and impact of materials management on top management. Many ideas described in this chapter—layout, capacity, new technology, MRP, JIT, and FMS—are less likely to be infused into the organization's overall strategic planning.

Although Exhibit 20.8 applies to manufacturing businesses, the materials management concept is also relevant for service organizations.[40] For example, the huge size and geographical dispersion of fast-food chains has required sophisticated materials management to keep each restaurant supplied without bearing undue inventory expense. With the rapidly escalating cost of health care and increasing resistance to hospital price increases, many hospitals have incorporated a materials management department to handle the diverse problems of inventory management, shipping, purchasing, and distribution. In service firms, grouping together all activities into a materials management department effects improved coordination, and having the department report to a high-level administrator provides input into the strategic planning process.

SUMMARY

This chapter described several important points about operations management. Operations management pertains to the tools and techniques used to manage the organization's core production process. These techniques apply to both manufacturing and service organizations. Operations management has great impact when it influences competitive strategy. Areas of operations management described in the chapter include product and service design, location of facilities, facilities layout, capacity planning, and the use of new technologies.

The chapter also discussed inventory management. Three types of inventory are raw materials, work-in-process, and finished goods. Economic order quantity, materials requirement planning, and just-in-time inventory are techniques for minimizing inventory levels.

Another important concept is that operations management can enhance organizational productivity. Total factor productivity is the best measurement of organizational productivity. Managers can improve both quality and productivity through technology, management, and the work force.

Finally, operations management's effectiveness can be enhanced through organization structure. The materials management concept suggests that all departments that contribute to the cost of materials be grouped together under a single materials manager. The materials manager can report either to the manufacturing manager or to the president of the organization.

Management Solution

The Appliance Division of General Electric had to confront the problem of declining quality, market share, and profits. As a first step, the division president called in the operations vice-president for a long talk. Their goal was to become a stage 4 company, wherein innovative operations techniques would make them a leader in the field. This approach was implemented through several activities. First, a new dishwasher was designed using new plastic material that the purchasing department had found for the tub and microelectronics to control the machine. The design of the new dishwasher made it possible to automate production. The plant also set a goal for using just-in-time inventory, and managers instituted a new quality and productivity program. All of this happened just four years ago. Today, GE's Appliance Division is the number one dishwasher manufacturer in both market share and quality. Profits are up, and so is employee morale. The attention given to operations management paid off.[41]

DISCUSSION QUESTIONS

1. What is the difference between manufacturing and service organizations? Which has the greater need for operations management techniques?
2. Briefly explain the difference between process and product layout. What do you see as the advantages and disadvantages of each?
3. If you were asked by a local video store owner to help identify a location for a second video store, how would you proceed? How might you help the owner plan for the new store's capacity?
4. What are the three types of inventory? Which of these are most likely to be affected by the just-in-time inventory system? Explain.
5. What is materials requirement planning? How does it differ from using economic order quantity to reduce inventory?
6. Why is purchasing an important, if unheralded, aspect of operations management? How do purchasing requirements change if a company introduces a just-in-time inventory system?
7. Many managers believe that improvements in product quality reduce plant productivity. Why do you think managers feel this way? Are they correct?
8. Assume that a local manufacturing manager asks you about ways to improve productivity. What would you advise the manager?
9. What is the appropriate strategic role for operations management? Should operations management take the initiative in influencing competitive strategy?
10. What are the two structural issues relevant to operations management? How might the solution to these issues influence operations strategy?

CASES FOR ANALYSIS

XALOY INC.

Xaloy Inc., located in the Blue Ridge Mountains of Southwest Virginia, manufactures steel and alloy cylinders used to extrude plastics and other materials. The cylinders begin as logs of steel that are bored out, filled with a special metal alloy, and then heated to 2,000°F. After cooling, the cylinders are straightened, ground smooth, and machined so that they can be connected to an extrusion machine. The cylinders are used to produce food products such as puffed rice and puffed wheat.

Plant manager Kelley Nunley and materials manager Danny Porter were concerned about a number of problems on the shop floor that indicate materials management inefficiencies. There were huge piles of cylinders stacked among the boring machines and latches; other giant cylinders hung from cranes above the shop floor. In all, some 2,000 cylinders were waiting to be worked on. One reason was that the bandsaw that cut the cylinders was the fastest machine in the place, so cylinders were stacked everywhere waiting to go on to other production stages.

A related problem was that workers liked to have lots of inventory sitting around. They associated accumulated cylinders with good times and no awaiting stacks of work with bad times. Workers thus had achieved comfort with high work-in-process inventory.

Another problem was plant layout. Xaloy made several cylinder sizes, each of which had to travel around the 96,000-square-foot plant because the machines that performed similar operations were located together. This created the potential for accidents and damage. Sometimes a cylinder would go back and forth in the plant several times in one week.

Still another problem was purchasing. A salesperson had offered a quantity discount, at which one of the senior managers jumped. Nearly 400,000 pounds of steel—a five- or six-month supply—arrived at the back door, overwhelming the raw materials inventory storage area. The manager believed that buying material cheaply in huge amounts was a smart way to save money.

The final problem that concerned Nunley and Porter was the cylinder-straightening process. They could not understand why the steel came into the plant straight and was precisely machined, yet was getting bent and necessitating later straightening. Something must have been happening to the steel during the production process.

Questions

1. To what extent can the problems faced by Nunley and Porter be solved with operations management techniques?
2. Which operations management ideas described in this chapter are most appropriate to the Xaloy situation?
3. What suggestions would you make to help Xaloy improve productivity and quality?

Source: Craig R. Waters, "Profit and Loss," *INC.,* April 1985, pp. 103–112.

BLUE BELL INC.

Blue Bell Inc. is one of the world's largest manufacturers of wearing apparel. Sales in 1983 totaled $1.2 billion and net income $48 million. Blue Bell is headquartered in Greensboro, North Carolina, and employs over 27,000 people worldwide. In the United States, Blue Bell has 80 plants and 32 distribution centers. Blue Bell is organized into three major businesses: the Wrangler Group, which manufactures denim and corduroy jeans; Red Kap, which makes durable garments for on-the-job wear; and Jantzen, which manufactures sportswear.

Apparel manufacturing is a working capital-intensive business. Inventory and accounts receivable comprise three-fourths of Blue Bell's asset base. In 1982, Blue Bell's management became concerned about the high investment in working capital. These concerns were legitimate. Over the previous 12 months, inventory had averaged over $371 million, or more than 50 percent of Blue Bell's assets. Annual charges for maintaining inventory, including warehousing, short-term borrowing, and product obsolescence, totaled at least 25 percent of the investment in inventory. Moreover, short-term interest rates were near 20 percent. Thus, the cost of carrying inventory had become acute. The interest expense for Blue Bell had ballooned from $1.1 million in 1979 to $21.9 million in 1982. Simply financing the inventory had pushed up Blue Bell's cost of doing business and sharply increased retail prices.

Accompanying these inventory and working capital problems were changing customer expectations. Blue Bell's major customers included national and regional chain stores, mass merchandisers, and catalog houses. These customers were making new demands on apparel manufacturers:

1. Lead time on orders was decreasing. Retailers were sensitive to the high cost of financing their own inventory and thus ordering products closer to the time of actual sale. This meant Blue Bell had a shorter lead time and less opportunity to plan production. This led some managers to believe they should produce more apparel for finished-goods inventory to meet the uncertainties regarding customer orders.
2. Service demands were increasing. Retailers were becoming increasingly concentrated as major chains and discounters took a larger share of the business. These powerful retailers exerted pressure on Blue Bell for immediate product availability, on-time shipments, and delivery of complete orders. Recognizing the competitive advantage of superior customer service, Blue Bell was reluctant to reduce inventory at its expense.
3. The pressures on Blue Bell's management caused them to consider a new planning process. Managers saw the need to coordinate sales, marketing, manufacturing, operations, and finance. One manager proposed that a task force be created to include representatives of each function to develop a plan for reducing inventories yet maintaining customer service.

Questions

1. At what stage is Blue Bell in its operations strategy? At what stage is it striving to be?
2. Which techniques described in this chapter would help Blue Bell manage its huge inventories?

3. What could Blue Bell do to reduce inventory without impairing customer relations? Will lower inventories require better management? Discuss.

Source: Jerry R. Edwards, Harvey M. Wagner, and William P. Wood, "Blue Bell Trims Its Inventory," *Interfaces* 15 (January/February 1985), pp. 34–52.

PART SIX
EMERGING MANAGEMENT ISSUES

Source: Stella, Joseph. Brooklyn Bridge. *Reprinted by permission of the Yale Art Gallery. Gift of Collection Société Anonyme.*

Source: Luis Villota 1985 © The Stock Market of NY.

CHAPTER 21

Managing in a Multinational World

Chapter Outline

The Nature of International Management

The International Business Environment

The Economic Environment
The Legal-Political Environment
The Sociocultural Environment
Summary of the International Environment

Entry Strategies for International Markets

Exporting
Licensing
Foreign Production

The Multinational Corporation

Characteristics of Multinational Corporations

Multinational Corporate Strategy

Grand Strategies
Strategic Planning

Multinational Organization Structure

International Division
Product-Based Structure
Geographic-Based Structure
Functional-Based Structure
Matrix Structure
Centralization versus Decentralization

Tailoring Management Style to Cultural Values

Leadership
Decision Making
Motivation
Control

Learning Objectives

After studying this chapter, you should be able to:

- **Define international management and explain how it differs from the management of domestic business operations.**

- **Indicate how dissimilarities in the economic, sociocultural, and legal-political environments throughout the world can affect business operations.**

- **Describe entry strategies that business firms use to develop foreign markets.**

- **Describe the characteristics of a multinational corporation and the generic strategies available to them.**

- **Explain the steps in the strategic planning process for multinational corporations.**

- **Identify the organizational structures that multinationals use and factors that determine the appropriate structure.**

Management Problem

Black and Decker has a 50 percent share of the world market for power tools, but new competitors are making rapid gains. Black and Decker's strategy has been to customize products for individual markets: The British subsidiary makes tools for Britons, the Italian subsidiary makes tools for Italians, and so on. The subsidiaries' autonomy has caused problems. Dustbuster, the cordless vacuum cleaner, was a runaway best seller in the United States, but the Australians refused to introduce it in their market. The European managers refused to sell Black and Decker housewares, maintaining that the products were strictly for Americans. The decision facing Black and Decker's managers is whether to centralize control and develop standard products for sale around the globe or continue with autonomous operations in each country.[1]

If you were a consultant to Black and Decker, would you recommend selling standard products worldwide? What structural changes would you recommend in order to achieve better coordination across foreign operations?

Black and Decker is a well-established, international competitor facing changes in strategy and structure. Companies such as McDonald's, IBM, Coca-Cola, Kellogg, Boeing, General Motors, and Caterpillar Tractor all rely on international business for a substantial portion of sales and profits. These companies face special problems in trying to tailor their products to the unique needs of foreign countries—but when they succeed, the whole world is their marketplace.

How important is international business to the study of management?

Consider this: In 1984, 24 states had a unitary tax, which taxed a percentage of worldwide profits for companies residing within the state. Companies from Japan and other countries insisted that the states change the laws or they would not build plants within those states. Governments in states such as Florida, California, and Oregon knuckled under to pressure from foreign companies. Today only three states have active unitary tax laws.[2]

Also, consider this: Many managers are selected for top positions in U.S. and Canadian firms because they have international experience. Edward Jefferson, president of Du Pont, is from England. Roberto Goizueta, a Cuban, is president of Coca-Cola. Michel Bergerac, a Frenchman, is CEO of Revlon. British-born and Chinese-bred William Anderson is president of NCR Corporation. Anthony O'Reilly, president of H. J. Heinz Company, is from Ireland.[3]

The purpose of this chapter is to introduce some basic concepts pertaining to international management. International management is no longer a one-way street through which U.S. and Canadian companies sell goods overseas. Foreign competitors have been more successful selling in the North American market than the other way around. In this chapter, we consider the difficulties of operating in foreign environments. We then discuss multinational corporations and the types of strategies and structures they use to compete effectively on a global scale. Finally, we examine international management issues associated with leadership, decision making, motivation, and control.

THE NATURE OF INTERNATIONAL MANAGEMENT

international management The management of business operations conducted in more than one country.

International management is the management of business operations conducted in more than one country. The fundamental tasks and processes associated with business management, including the financing, production, and distribution of products and services, do not change in any substantive way when a firm is transacting business across international borders. The basic management functions of planning, organizing, leading, and controlling are the same whether a company operates domestically or internationally. It is very likely, however, that managers will experience greater difficulties and risks when performing these management functions on an international scale. For example, managers at one American company were shaken when they discovered that the brand name of the cooking oil they had introduced in Latin America translated into Spanish as "jackass oil." Still another company tried to sell its toothpaste in Southeast Asia by stressing that it whitens teeth. Managers were chagrined to discover that local people chew betel nut to blacken their teeth because they find the result attractive.[4]

The problems confronted by most companies are attributable to novel environmental conditions in foreign countries. Environmental conditions are more diverse and volatile when business is conducted in many

International management is the management of business operations in more than one country. The Bristol-Myers International Group markets pharmaceutical, nutritional, and consumer products in more than 100 countries. Bristol-Myers' nutritional research often has application in developing countries. Although not produced by Bristol-Myers, the special nutritional drink shown here is prepared for young mothers in Gambia by Dunn Nutrition Laboratories doctors. The liquid is a wheat and soy flour blend to which vitamins, minerals, and other ingredients have been added. International companies must carefully tailor products to the cultural and nutritional needs of groups in each country.

different countries simultaneously. The first thing to understand in international management, then, is the nature of environments in other countries.

THE INTERNATIONAL BUSINESS ENVIRONMENT

Environmental factors that affect international business are similar to the task and general environmental sectors described in Chapter 3. However, when comparing country to country, the economic, legal-political, and sociocultural sectors present the greatest differences. Key factors in each part of the environment are summarized in Exhibit 21.1.

The Economic Environment

The economic environment represents the economic conditions in the country where the international organization operates. This part of the environment includes such factors as economic development; resource and product markets; infrastructure; exchange rates; and inflation, interest rates, and economic growth.

Economic Development.   Economic development differs widely among the countries and regions of the world. Countries can be categorized as either "developing" or "developed." The developing countries are referred to as *less-developed countries (LDCs)*. The criterion traditionally used to classify countries as developed or developing is *per capita income,* which is the income generated by the nation's production of goods and services divided by total population. The developing countries have low per

EXHIBIT   21.1

Key Factors in the International Environment

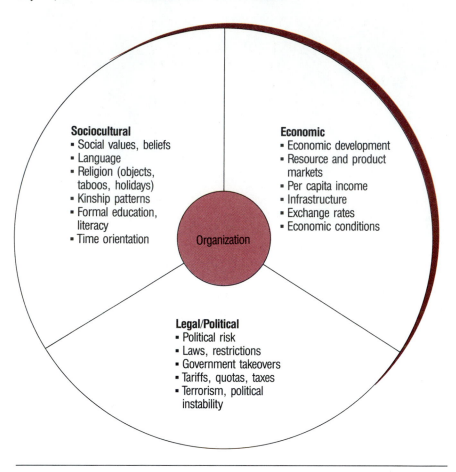

Sociocultural
- Social values, beliefs
- Language
- Religion (objects, taboos, holidays)
- Kinship patterns
- Formal education, literacy
- Time orientation

Economic
- Economic development
- Resource and product markets
- Per capita income
- Infrastructure
- Exchange rates
- Economic conditions

Organization

Legal/Political
- Political risk
- Laws, restrictions
- Government takeovers
- Tariffs, quotas, taxes
- Terrorism, political instability

capita incomes. LDCs generally are in the Southern Hemisphere, including Africa, Asia, and South America, while developed countries tend to be in the Northern Hemisphere, including North America, Europe, and Japan.[5]

Most international business firms are based in the developed countries. They show a preference for confining their operations to the wealthier and economically advanced nations. However, based on the number of prospective customers, developing countries constitute an immense and largely untapped market.

infrastructure   A country's physical facilities that support economic activities.

Infrastructure.   Infrastructure refers to a country's physical facilities that support economic activities. The infrastructure includes transportation facilities such as airports, highways, and railroads; energy-producing facilities such as utilities and power plants; and communication facilities such as telephone lines and radio stations. LDCs typically have poor infrastructures and cannot support rapid economic growth because of the potential strain on their communication, transportation, and energy industries. Companies operating in LDCs must contend with lower levels of technology and perplexing logistical, distribution, and communication problems.

For example, Lionel Trains moved its manufacturing plant to Tijuana, Mexico, to take advantage of the $0.55-an-hour wages. Lionel managers didn't foresee the difficulty in getting telephone lines, nor did it realize there were no Mexican subcontractors for some manufacturing processes. Thus, many parts had to be shuttled back and forth from California, and the labor savings soon evaporated. Lionel could deliver only one-third of its orders, and its share of the track market dropped from 75 to 25 percent. Lionel managers decided to cut their losses and move manufacturing operations back to Michigan.[6]

Resource and Product Markets.   When operating in another country, managers must evaluate the market demand for its products. If market demand is high, it may choose to export products to establish sales offices in that country. To develop manufacturing plants, however, resource markets for providing needed raw materials and labor must also be available. For example, McDonald's has had great success in finding market demand for its more than 2,000 restaurants around the world. The greatest challenge for McDonald's managers is to obtain supplies of everything from potatoes to hamburger buns to plastic straws. Often supplies that meet McDonald's exacting standards are unavailable. The hamburger bun was the most difficult item to procure in Britain, because local bakeries would not meet their standards. In Thailand, McDonald's actually helped farmers cultivate Idaho Russet potatoes of sufficient quality to produce their golden french fries.[7]

Exchange Rates.   *Exchange rates* are the rate at which one country's currency is exchanged for another country's. Exchange rates typically are set by a country's monetary policies as well as the international supply and demand for its currency. Changes in the exchange rate can have major implications for the profitability of international operations.[8] For example, assume that the American dollar is exchanged for 8 French francs. If the dollar increases in value to 10 francs, U.S. goods will be more expensive in France because it will take more francs to buy a dollar's worth of U.S. goods. It will be more difficult to export American goods to France, and profits will be slim. If the dollar drops to a value of 6 francs, on the other hand, U.S. goods will be cheaper in France and can be exported at a profit.

In the early 1980s, when the dollar was very strong compared to the Japanese yen, Japanese products flooded the U.S. markets. Lawn mowers, automobiles, consumer electronics, and construction equipment were all attractively priced, making Japanese goods very competitive. However, the value of the dollar dropped in the mid-1980s, making it attractive for U.S. firms to become more aggressive in exporting goods to foreign countries.[9]

This deliveryman arrives at the Aga Khan Hospital in a suburb of Nairobi, Kenya, with a consignment of Beecham antibiotics. Beecham Research International's headquarters are in the United Kingdom, but the company succeeds in less developed countries because of its flexibility. Many host countries suffer from economic difficulties. Imports, even of medicines, frequently depend on sales of indigenous crops or foreign aid. The establishment of local packaging operations has helped Beecham adapt to these markets.

The Legal-Political Environment

Businesses must deal with unfamiliar political systems when they go international, as well as with more government supervision and regulation. Government officials and the general public often view foreign companies as outsiders or even intruders and are suspicious of their impact on economic independence and political sovereignty. Some of the major legal-political concerns affecting international business are political risk, laws and restrictions, and political instability.

political risk A company's risk of loss of assets, earning power, or managerial control due to politically motivated events or actions by host governments.

Political Risk. **Political risk** is defined as a company's risk of loss of assets, earning power, or managerial control due to events or actions by host governments that are politically based.[10] Political risk includes acts of violence directed against a firm's properties or employees. Because such acts are not uncommon, companies must formulate special plans and programs to guard against unexpected losses. For example, Hercules Inc., a large chemical company, has increased the number of security guards at several of its European plants. Monsanto Corporation canceled a ceremony to celebrate the opening of a new plant in England. Bombs were exploded in the Lyon, France, offices of American Express and Control Data.[11]

Government takeovers of property are another manifestation of political risk. There are various ways to take over a company's property, ranging from outright seizure of a company's facilities by armed forces to gradual government encroachment into their management or ownership. Outright seizure occurred by the revolutionary government of Ayatollah Khomeini following the overthrow of the Shah of Iran in 1979. R. J. Reynolds, United Technologies, and Xerox were all forced to abandon their Iranian operations.[12] Chesebrough-Pond reduced its holding in its wholly owned branch in India to 40 percent by issuing equity exclusively to Indian investors. This negotiation gave greater ownership to the host country and enabled Chesebrough to continue operating.[13]

Laws and Regulations. Government laws and regulations differ from country to country and make manufacturing and sales a true challenge for international firms. Goods and services must meet each country's regulations despite the problems they pose, especially for manufacturing organizations. For example, N. V. Phillips Gloelampenfabrieken makes electrical plugs and cords. Some plugs have three prongs, others have two, and the prongs may be straight or right angled, round or rectangular, and fat or thin depending on the European country to which it is sold. Phillips also makes circular plug faces, squares, pentagons, and hectagons. One French plug has a niche like a keyhole. British plugs carry fuses. The variety of standards across European countries is partially designed to insure safety and compliance with different voltages and cycles, but it is also a way of protecting host country manufacturers by increasing the costs of international companies.[14]

Host governments also have myriad laws concerning libel statutes, consumer protection, information and labeling, employment and safety, and wages. International companies must learn these rules and regulations and abide by them.

A sign saying "Mickey, don't touch our land" sprouts in a farm field in Romainvilliers, France, near where Euro Disneyland may be located. Lovable Mickey Mouse has spawned intense conflict. Many people are enthusiastic about the potential for jobs and economic development, but farmers, organized labor, and politicians who want to protect French culture are resisting a French Disneyland. This political risk delayed development, but construction eventually was approved with a maximum American ownership of 30 percent. New laws and regulations were passed to give Disneyland the right to schedule flexible worker hours.

Political Instability.   Still another frequently cited problem for international organizations is political instability, which includes riots, revolutions, civil disorders, and frequent changes in government personnel. Political instability increases uncertainty and makes operations more difficult. International firms can operate effectively under almost any political system that is stable, including right-wing dictatorships, socialistic or capitalistic democracies, and even authoritarian communist regimes. However, sudden, drastic changes in the political system will make operations in any country very risky.

The Sociocultural Environment

A nation's **culture** includes the shared knowledge, beliefs, and values, as well as the common modes of behavior and ways of thinking, among members of a society. Cultural factors are more perplexing than political and economic factors in foreign countries. Culture is intangible, pervasive, and difficult to learn. It is absolutely imperative that international businesses comprehend the significance of local cultures and deal with them effectively.

culture The shared knowledge, beliefs, values, behaviors, and ways of thinking among members of a society.

Social Values.   Research by Geert Hofstede on thousands of employees in 40 countries identified four dimensions of national value systems that influence organizational and employee working relationships:[15]

1. *Power distance.* High **power distance** means that people accept inequality in power among institutions, organizations, and people. Low power distance means that people expect equality in power. Countries that value high power distance are Malaysia, the Philippines, and Panama. Countries that value low power distance are Denmark, Austria, and Israel.

power distance The degree to which people accept inequality in power among institutions, organizations, and people.

2. *Uncertainty avoidance.* High **uncertainty avoidance** means that members of a society feel uncomfortable with uncertainty and ambiguity and thus support beliefs that promise certainty and conformity. Low uncertainty avoidance means that people have high tolerance for the unstructured, the unclear, and the unpredictable. High uncertainty avoidance countries include

uncertainty avoidance A value characterized by people's intolerance for uncertainty and ambiguity and resulting support for beliefs that promise certainty and conformity.

individualism   A preference for a loosely knit social framework in which individuals are expected to take care of themselves.

collectivism   A preference for a tightly knit social framework in which individuals look after one another and organizations protect their members' interests.

masculinity   A cultural preference for achievement, heroism, assertiveness, and material success.

femininity   A cultural preference for modesty, tending to the weak, and quality of life.

Greece, Portugal, and Uruguay. Countries with low uncertainty avoidance values are Singapore and Jamaica.

3. *Individualism and collectivism.* **Individualism** reflects a value for a loosely knit social framework in which individuals are expected to take care of themselves. **Collectivism** means a preference for a tightly knit social framework in which individuals look after one another and organizations protect their members' interests. Countries with individualist values include the United States, Canada, Great Britain, and Australia. Countries with collectivist values are Guatemala, Ecuador, and Panama.

4. *Masculinity/femininity.* **Masculinity** stands for preference for achievement, heroism, assertiveness, and material success. **Femininity** reflects the values of relationships, modesty, caring for the weak, and quality of life. Societies with strong masculine values are Japan, Austria, Mexico, and Germany. Countries with feminine values are Sweden, Norway, Denmark, and Yugoslavia. Both men and women subscribe to the dominant value in masculine and feminine cultures.

Social values influence organizational functioning and management styles. For example, organizations in France and Latin and Mediterranean countries tend to be hierarchical bureaucracies. Germany and other central European countries have organizations that strive to be impersonal, well-oiled machines. In India, Asia, and Africa, organizations are viewed as large families.

Cultural problems occur with the wrong combination of manager and organization. An African doctor who works in a Belgian hospital will expect the organization to yield to personal authority, and it will take a long time for this person to learn to work in a rigid Belgian bureaucracy. A German manager who is appointed to run a civil engineering project in Indonesia may discover that nobody pays attention to his rules and procedures and that he must use personal and social influence to get the job done. U.S. managers in Denmark will be frustrated by the lack of individual competitiveness and the concern for collective welfare.[16]

ethnocentrism   A cultural attitude marked by the tendency to regard one's own culture as superior to others.

Other Cultural Characteristics.   Other cultural characteristics that influence international organizations are language, religion, attitudes, social organization, and education. Some countries, such as India, are characterized by *linguistic pluralism,* meaning that several languages exist there. Other countries rely heavily on spoken versus written language. Religion includes sacred objects, philosophical attitudes toward life, taboos, and rituals. Attitudes toward achievement, work, and time can all affect organizational productivity. An attitude called **ethnocentrism** means that people have a tendency to regard their own culture as superior and to downgrade other cultures. Ethnocentrism within a country makes it difficult for foreign firms to operate there. Social organization includes status systems, kinship and families, social institutions, and opportunities for social mobility. Education influences the literacy level, the availability of qualified employees, and the predominance of primary or secondary degrees.

Managers in international companies have found that cultural differences cannot be ignored if international operations are to succeed.[17] For example, Procter & Gamble ran into unanticipated cultural barriers when marketing its Cheer laundry soap in Japan. Cheer initially prospered by discounting its price, but that alienated wholesalers who were not used to having reduced margins. P&G discovered too late that unlike in Europe and the United States, once you discount a product in Japan it's hard to raise the price later. Also, since most Japanese walk and carry, they shop close to home at small mom-and-pop stores, which have limited shelf space and thus don't carry discounted goods. The Japanese also were repulsed by Cheer's hard-sell TV ads.[18] As another example, Bank of America got into a jam in the Middle East because managers didn't realize that the legal system offered little recourse to a bank when borrowers default. The cultural environment leaves moneylenders open to being taken, a fact of life that BofA should have understood.[19]

On the other hand, organizations that manage cultural differences report major successes. Kellogg introduced breakfast cereals into Brazil, where the traditional breakfast is coffee and a roll. Through carefully chosen advertising, many Brazilians were won over to the American breakfast. Many families now start the day with Kellogg's Sucrilhos (Frosted Flakes) and Crokinhos (Cocoa Krispies).[20] Perhaps the companies most effective at bridging culture gaps are those from Japan. When Honda Motor Company introduced the little CRX in the United States, it was an immediate hit. But the Japanese didn't design the CRX, relying instead on U.S.-born executives to make design decisions. Nippon Light Metal Company developed an ice cream maker that used no electricity, ice, or salt. It was turned over to U.S. businesspeople, who remade the one-pint device into a one-quart size to accommodate American ice cream appetites. A special recipe book catering to American tastes was also developed. In the first year, over 400,000 ice cream makers were sold.[21]

Summary of the International Environment

Some of the complexities of operating in diverse countries are illustrated in Exhibit 21.2. The upper portion of the exhibit shows a firm operating

E X H I B I T   21.2

Environmental Influences on an International Firm

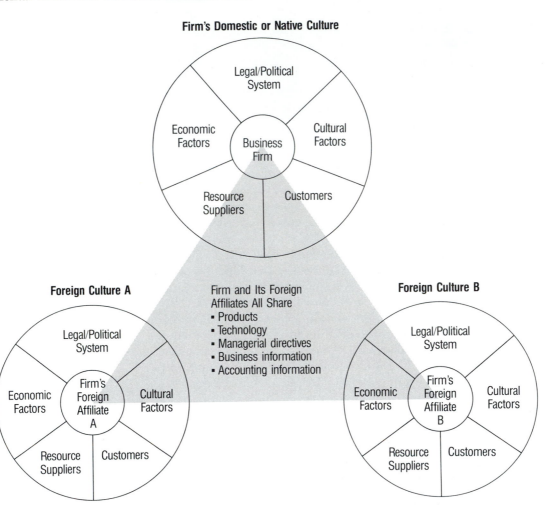

in its domestic market and native culture. The lower portion shows how complicated business operations can become when operating in several countries simultaneously. Through its foreign affiliates, the organization must carry on the same basic types of relationships in other countries, but to do so it must adapt to their cultural environments. Moreover, the organization must transcend the boundaries of separate cultures to transfer resources and products between the firm and foreign affiliates. The organization must also coordinate technological know-how, advertising, and managerial directives across cultural boundaries. The affiliates will be restricted by different legal-political systems, cultural values, and economic incentives.

One company that has transcended foreign boundaries and thrives internationally is Heineken.

Heineken

Heineken, once an obscure beermaker in the Netherlands, is now the fourth largest beer producer in the world. Three-fourths of its beer sales are international, conducted through its distributors in 150 countries.

Heineken produces a beer that looks and tastes the same everywhere and markets it as a high-class product that is worth a premium price. At the same time, Heineken tailors its advertising, sales pitch, and brand names to what it sees as the cultural idiosyncrasies of each national market. A television commercial for the French market shows a sophisticated, middle-aged gentleman holding a glass of beer to the light and murmuring about its "finesse." The Heineken ads in Italy link beer drinking to "romantic" occasions. In Japan, the commercials associate Heineken beer with the "refined" European lifestyle. In the United States, advertising presents Heineken beer as a status symbol—"the Rolls Royce of beers."

Heineken now depends on its success in foreign markets and is continuing to expand. It is moving into South America and other developing regions where beer consumption is rising. Heineken has made use of selective international marketing strategies and continues to enter new foreign markets successfully.[22]

ENTRY STRATEGIES FOR INTERNATIONAL MARKETS

Corporations wishing to develop markets outside their home country have a number of approaches available, including exporting, licensing, and foreign production. These are called **entry strategies,** since they represent alternative ways to enter foreign markets. Most firms begin with exporting and eventually work up to foreign production, although some employ all three strategies simultaneously. Exhibit 21.3 shows the strategies companies can use to enter foreign markets.

entry strategy An organizational strategy for entering a foreign market.

Exporting

With **exporting,** the corporation maintains its production facilities within the home nation and transfers its products for sale in foreign countries. Exporting enables a country to market its products in other countries at small resource cost and with limited risk. Exporting does entail numerous problems based on physical distances, government regulations, foreign currencies, and cultural differences, but it is less expen-

exporting An entry strategy in which the organization maintains its production facilities within its home country and transfers its products for sale in foreign markets.

E X H I B I T   21.3

Strategies for Entering International Business Operations

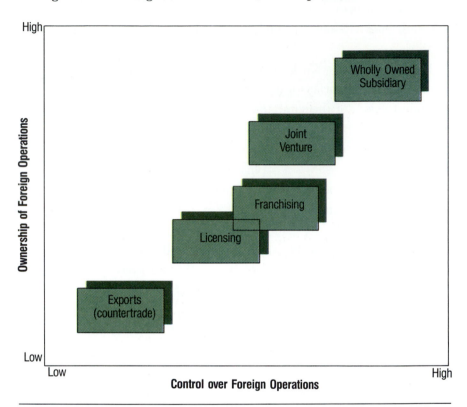

sive than committing the firm's own capital to building plants in host countries. A form of exporting to less developed countries is called **countertrade,** which is the barter of products for products rather than the sale of products for currency. Many less developed countries have products to exchange but have no foreign currency. An estimated 20 percent of world trade is countertrade.

Many U.S. firms rely on exports even when the dollar is high relative to foreign currencies. Graco Inc., a manufacturer of spray guns and finishing machinery, had built up long-term relationships with foreign distributors and refused to give them up despite low profit margins. Ionics Inc. sells desalination plans overseas for about half its total revenues. Exporting is second nature to this firm, although it does require determination and finding customers who want the product badly enough.[23]

Licensing

With **licensing,** a corporation (the licensor) in one country makes certain resources available to companies in another country (the licensee). These resources include technology, managerial skills, and/or patent and trade-

countertrade The barter of products for other products rather than their sale for currency.

licensing An entry strategy in which an organization in one country makes certain resources available to companies in another in order to participate in the production and sale of its products abroad.

mark rights. They enable the licensee to produce and market a product similar to what the licensor has been producing. This arrangement gives the licensor an opportunity to participate in the production and sale of products outside its home country. Hasbro has licensing agreements with companies in several Latin American countries and Japan. Hasbro builds brand identity and consumer awareness by contracting with toy companies to manufacture products locally. Glidden has licensing arrangements for its coating technology with manufacturers in over 25 countries. The most widely licensed products are based on water-borne and electrocoating technologies. Many of Glidden's international customers want products made in overseas plants to have the same consistent high quality as those made in domestic plants, and licensing is the answer.

Franchising is a form of licensing in which the franchisor provides foreign franchisees with a complete package of materials and services, including equipment, products, product ingredients, trademark and trade name rights, managerial advice, and a standardized operating system. Some of the best known international franchisers are the fast-food chains. Kentucky Fried Chicken, Burger King, Wendy's, and McDonald's outlets are found in almost every large city in the world. The story is often told of the Japanese child visiting Los Angeles who excitedly pointed out to his parents, "They have McDonald's in America too!"

Licensing and franchising offer a business firm relatively easy access to international markets, but they limit its participation in and control over the development of those markets.

Foreign Production

A higher level of involvement in international trade is direct investment in manufacturing facilities in a foreign country. **Direct investment** means that the company directly manages the productive assets, which distinguishes it from other entry strategies that permit less managerial control.

A partial form of direct investment is a **joint venture,** through which the company shares costs with a firm in the host country to build a manufacturing facility. This option is frequently used in countries whose laws prohibit complete foreign ownership of economic enterprises. For example, General Electric signed a joint venture with France's state-owned SNECMA to produce a low-pollution engine for high-performance aircraft. Both sides will share the $800 million development cost. Toyota Motor Corporation engaged in a joint venture in the United States with General Motors called New United Motor Manufacturing Inc. (NUMMI). The joint venture produces approximately 250,000 subcompact cars a year that are marketed by both Toyota and Chevrolet, which split the profits.[24]

The other choice is to have a **wholly owned foreign affiliate,** over which the company has complete control. Direct investment provides cost savings over exporting by shortening distribution channels and reducing storage and transportation costs. Local managers also have heightened awareness of economic, cultural, and political conditions.

Exporting heavy equipment from the United States is a major source of Caterpillar's business, with international sales amounting to $3.3 billion in 1986, almost equaling U.S. sales. For its business in China, Caterpillar moved to a licensing agreement in 1985 for the local manufacture of power-shift transmissions for use in Chinese-built construction equipment. Mechanics receive training at this Machimpex Distribution Center for Caterpillar parts near Beijing. The warehouse provides 75 percent of the heavy equipment parts available within China.

franchising A form of licensing in which an organization provides its foreign franchisees with a complete assortment of materials and services.

direct investment An entry strategy in which the organization directly manages its productive facilities in a foreign country.

joint venture A variation of direct investment in which an organization shares costs with a host-country firm to build a local facility.

wholly owned foreign affiliate A foreign subsidiary over which an organization has complete control.

The company must expend capital funds and human resources in order to acquire productive assets that will be exposed to risks from the host country's economic, legal-political, and sociocultural environments.

Recent examples of companies that have invested directly in foreign countries are in the advertising industry. Foote Cone & Belding acquired advertising agencies in Europe, South America, and Asia. Saatchi & Saatchi, based in London, has taken over 12 companies in Europe and the United States. Such mergers create wholly owned subsidiaries that enable advertising agencies to coordinate the advertising for multinational clients. Direct investment gives them complete control over agencies in host countries.[25]

THE MULTINATIONAL CORPORATION

The size and volume of international business are so large that it is hard to comprehend. Merchandise exports for the world as a whole total more than $2 trillion. U.S. companies alone have direct investments in more than 25,000 overseas affiliates employing over 7 million people. The value of the annual output of U.S. overseas affiliates has exceeded the gross national product of every world nation except the United States and Soviet Union.[26]

The massive volume of international business has largely been carried out by a rather small number of very large business firms called *multinational corporations (MNCs)*. MNCs have been the subject of tremendous attention and concern. MNCs can move assets from country to country and influence nations' economies, politics, and cultures. A large multinational can have sales revenues exceeding $10 billion per year—more than most countries' gross national products.

Characteristics of Multinational Corporations

multinational corporation (MNC) An organization that receives more than 25 percent of its total sales revenues from operations outside the parent company's home country.

Although there is no precise definition, a **multinational corporation (MNC)** typically receives more than 25 percent of its total sales revenues from operations outside the parent's home country. MNCs also have the following distinctive managerial characteristics:

1. An MNC is managed as an integrated worldwide business system. This means that foreign affiliates act in close alliance and cooperation with one another. Capital, technology, and people are transferred among affiliates. The MNC can acquire materials and manufacture parts wherever in the world it is most advantageous to do so.

2. An MNC is ultimately controlled by a single management authority that makes key, strategic decisions relating to the parent and all affiliates. The centralization of management is imperative

for maintaining worldwide integration and profit maximization for the enterprise as a whole.

3. MNC top managers are presumed to exercise a "global perspective." They regard the entire world as the relevant frame of reference for strategic decisions, resource acquisition, location of production, and marketing efficiency.

In a few cases, the MNC management philosophy may differ from that described above. For example, some researchers have distinguished among *ethnocentric companies,* which place emphasis on their home countries, *polycentric companies,* which are oriented toward the markets of individual foreign host countries, and *geocentric companies,* which are truly world oriented and favor no specific country.[27] In general, a multinational corporation can be thought of as a business enterprise that is composed of affiliates located in different countries and whose top managers make decisions primarily on the basis of global business opportunities and objectives.

Dow Chemical and NEC are multinational companies.

Dow Chemical Company

Dow Chemical Company is the seventh largest chemical company in the world and the second largest in the United States. Net sales total approximately $10 billion, of which sales outside the United States exceed 50 percent of the total. Dow makes over 2,000 products in the areas of chemicals, plastics, metals, pharmaceuticals, and consumer products.

In 1979 Dow had 55,900 employees, 21,800 of them outside the United States. It had 121 manufacturing locations at 162 sales offices around the world. To manage this huge, global enterprise, management is organized according to six geographic areas—the United States, Europe/Africa, Canada, Pacific, Latin America, and Brazil. All of these divisions are responsible to senior managers, who are based in the United States.

Another international corporation is Nippon Electric Company Ltd. (NEC). NEC began international business operations after World War II. Its operations include radio communications, electronic devices, consumer electronics, and electronic data processing. Sales in 1980 were $4 billion, of which 30 percent were outside of Japan. NEC has 15 manufacturing facilities in 10 countries and 12 marketing affiliates in 7 countries. International operations have grown dramatically since World War II. All foreign affiliates report to a senior executive vice-president located in Japan.[28]

When Phillips Petroleum Company was founded in 1917, it was a small producer of crude oil and natural gas. Today Phillips is an MNC with more than $12 billion in assets. This map in the Phillips Exhibit Hall pinpoints Phillips' worldwide operations. Almost half of Phillips' international crude oil production and one-third of its gas production come from outside the United States. Phillips is divided into three operating groups, each with worldwide operating responsibility for exploration, petroleum products and chemicals, or gas and gas liquids.

MULTINATIONAL CORPORATE STRATEGY

In today's multinational corporations, senior executives try to formulate coherent strategies to provide synergy among worldwide operations for the purpose of fulfilling common objectives. A systematic strategic planning process for deciding on the appropriate strategic alternative should be used.

Grand Strategies

Recall from Chapter 5 that growth and retrenchment are two grand strategies available to large corporations. In the international arena, MNCs face an additional dilemma between global integration and national responsiveness. Organizations must decide whether they want each affiliate to act autonomously or whether activities should be standardized and centralized across countries. This choice leads managers to select basic strategic alternatives: globalization versus multidomestic strategy and growth versus retrenchment.

globalization The standardization of product design and advertising strategies throughout the world.

Globalization. **Globalization** means that product design and advertising strategies are standardized throughout the world. This approach is based on the assumption that global markets exist for most consumer and industrial products. People around the world watch television, use similar technologies, and hence will buy common goods.[29] Ford Motor Company sells the same Escort car around the world. Ford assembly plants in different countries all use standard products, which provide great efficiencies compared to designing unique cars for each country or region.

Globalization enables marketing departments to save hundreds of thousands of dollars by adopting similar advertising campaigns in each country. For example, International Playtex developed a single advertising campaign for selling its Wow bra in 12 countries. It decided to avoid the more expensive approach of assigning ad agencies in each country the job of developing a marketing campaign.[30] Another example was the worldwide introduction of diet Coke. The brand name, concentrate formula, positioning, and advertising theme were standardized worldwide. The only factors tailored to individual countries were packaging and choice of artificial sweetener to meet local regulations.[31]

multidomestic strategy The modification of product design and advertising strategies to suit the specific needs of individual countries.

Multidomestic Strategy. A **multidomestic strategy** means that competition in each country is handled independently of industry competition in other countries. Thus, the MNC is present in many countries, but it encourages marketing, advertising, and product design to be modified and adapted to the specific needs of each country.[32] For example, Hewlett-Packard changes its computer keyboards to meet European traditions and adapts business software to reflect different accounting principles in the user country. Du Pont produces customized herbicides for problems with weeds that are unique to countries such as Brazil and Japan. Avon found that its door-to-door sales strategy would not work in Japan and thus customized a soft-sell approach.[33]

SOCIAL RESPONSIBILITY

Adhering to the Sullivan Principles

A major force in the debate over whether businesses should remain in South Africa is the list of principles developed by Leon H. Sullivan, a Baptist minister from Philadelphia. These principles represent a voluntary code of conduct for U.S. companies doing business under the controversial system called *apartheid*:

1. Nonsegregation of races in all eating, comfort, locker room, and work facilities
2. Equal and fair employment practices for all employees
3. Equal pay for all employees doing equal or comparable work for the same period of time
4. Initiation and development of training programs that will prepare substantial numbers of blacks, coloreds, and Asians for supervisory, administrative, clerical, and technical jobs
5. Increasing the number of blacks, coloreds, and Asians in management and supervisory positions
6. Improving the quality of employees' lives outside the work environment in such areas as housing, transportation, schooling, recreation, and health facilities

Of the 240 American firms remaining in South Africa, about one-half have signed the Sullivan code. Each year participating companies are graded on their progress. They pay dues and complete paperwork that support the administrative structure behind the code. Companies can get two passing grades: "making good progress" or "making progress." Companies reported as making good progress in 1986 included FMC Corporation, Fluor Corporation, Johnson & Johnson, Kellogg Company, McGraw-Hill Inc., SmithKline Beckman Corporation, and Union Carbide. Companies in the second category included Amdahl Corporation, Eli Lilly & Company, Dresser Industries Inc., Champion Spark Plug Company,

Black and Decker Corporation, Tenneco Inc., and RJR Nabisco Inc. Companies fail the code if they don't meet the first three principles concerning workplace equality.

The Sullivan principles have generated controversy. The workplaces of virtually all Sullivan companies are now desegregated, and employers have spent additional money to educate some 50,000 workers. Social assistance costs the companies a great deal of money, making them less competitive than their rivals that are not part of the Sullivan club.

Moreover, companies have been under pressure to withdraw from South Africa. By the end of 1986, some 70 had departed. The most recent were General Motors, IBM, and Warner Communications. Others expected to leave are Honeywell, Xerox, and RJR Nabisco. The bad publicity associated with operations in South Africa, combined with activist tactics of selling off stocks and bonds of firms doing business there, are having a profound effect.

The argument for pressuring firms to leave South Africa is that without American businesses the South African economy would shut down, causing depression, hardship, and starvation. This would eventually bring down the current government and allow a new one to be established. Many companies and politicians, however, disagree. They feel that even if the country were characterized by depression and starvation, the psychology of the Afrikaners would keep them from supporting an overthrow of apartheid. Even worse, complete divestment would undercut black unions, which are one source from which blacks can gain an equal say in the country's affairs. American companies can have more impact by staying in South Africa guided by the Sullivan principles rather by withdrawing. Until recently even Reverend Sullivan encouraged companies to use their influence to bring about peaceful reform rather than leave South Africa. Pressures are mounting, however, and Reverend Sullivan and other leaders are now encouraging more companies to leave.

Source: Based on Stratford P. Sherman, "Scoring Corporate Conduct in South Africa," *Fortune*, July 9, 1984, pp. 168–172; "Pull Out Parade," *Time*, November 3, 1986, pp. 32–34; Marq DeVilliers, "The Case for Staying Put," *Canadian Business* (March 1986), pp. 38–40.

Growth. The grand strategy of *growth* is a major motivation for moving into the international arena. Each country or region represents a new market with the promise of increased sales and profits. McDonald's built more than 2,000 restaurants outside the United States because the domestic market was becoming saturated. Procter & Gamble has established marketing components in Europe and Japan as a way to compete in new markets. PepsiCo signed a contract to distribute Pepsi in the Soviet Union and is now moving to distribute in China, where the potential for growth is huge. At a price equivalent to about $0.15 per 12-ounce bottle, many Chinese can afford Pepsi.[34]

Retrenchment.   Through a *retrenchment* strategy, an MNC tries to become extremely efficient so that it can make its products at lower costs. A technique for reducing costs is **outsourcing,** which is direct investment to build plants in foreign countries for supplying consumers in the home country. For example, Apple Computer transferred the bulk of its Apple II production to Singapore. The Dallas plant was closed because costs were too high compared to the low wage rates overseas. Ingersoll-Rand Company closed its iron foundry in New York and outsourced castings from overseas at half the cost. General Electric, AT&T, USX Corporation, Goodyear, Emerson Radio, and Cincinnati Milacron have all replaced domestic plants with overseas plants to reduce costs and maintain a competitive edge in the U.S. marketplace.[35]

outsourcing   A retrenchment strategy in which an organization directly invests in plants in foreign countries for supplying consumers in its home country.

Strategic Planning

Intense international competition has increased MNCs' requirement for strategic planning. Moreover, management must systematically assess political risks and fashion overall corporate strategies with which to counter them. The strategic planning process should enable MNC affiliates to support one another as well as the goals of the enterprise. It is desirable to have managers at all locations involved in developing corporate strategy. Combined top-down and bottom-up strategy making provides strategic flexibility for the MNC and insures the availability of appropriate information for making the best strategic decisions.

Multinational strategic planning is similar to the processes described in Chapters 4 and 5, although its horizon is broader. Strategic planning in most MNCs contains the elements outlined in Exhibit 21.4.[36]

Environmental Analysis.   The first step in environmental analysis is a global screening procedure in which the firm scans the entire world and selects or rules out countries on the basis of broad criteria. A firm might establish some minimum standards in terms of population size, per capita income, political stability, or stage of industrialization essential for successful operations. Additional analysis would encompass economic, legal-political, and cultural environments within the target country or region.

Environmental analysis is used to target potential new markets and to determine whether to expand or contract existing marketing or production facilities. Environmental analysis also provides valuable guidance for deciding whether exporting, licensing, a joint venture, or a wholly owned subsidiary would be the best approach in a specific country. Political instability and competitive intensity, for example, might indicate that exporting is preferable to building a new plant.

Coca-Cola's grand strategy includes both growth and globalization. Coke has a 44 percent share of the international market but nevertheless plans significant growth in the future. Management's strategy is based on three factors: increasing availability, enhancing affordability, and broadening acceptability of its soft-drink products. Coke uses the same product formula and similar advertising around the globe. Since 1979, Coke has been available, affordable, and acceptable to consumers such as this Chinese soldier and is becoming more so to an increasing share of that market.

E X H I B I T   21.4

Multinational Strategic Planning Process

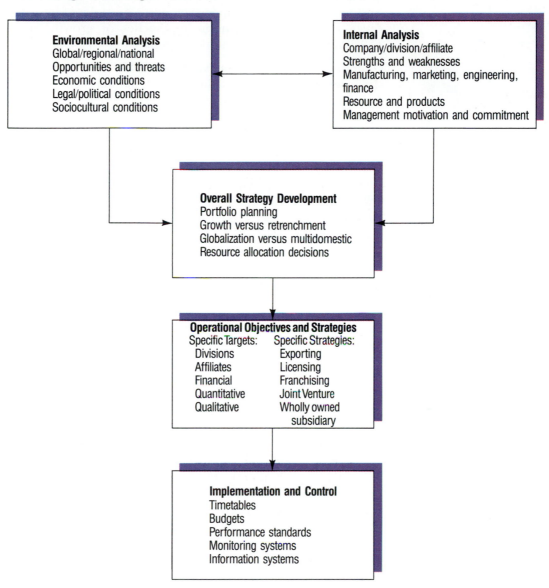

Environmental Analysis
Global/regional/national
Opportunities and threats
Economic conditions
Legal/political conditions
Sociocultural conditions

Internal Analysis
Company/division/affiliate
Strengths and weaknesses
Manufacturing, marketing, engineering, finance
Resource and products
Management motivation and commitment

Overall Strategy Development
Portfolio planning
Growth versus retrenchment
Globalization versus multidomestic
Resource allocation decisions

Operational Objectives and Strategies
Specific Targets: Specific Strategies:
Divisions   Exporting
Affiliates   Licensing
Financial   Franchising
Quantitative   Joint Venture
Qualitative   Wholly owned
               subsidiary

Implementation and Control
Timetables
Budgets
Performance standards
Monitoring systems
Information systems

Internal Analysis.   The second requirement for strategic planning is to look inward and evaluate strengths and weaknesses of the organization itself. This analysis should consider the multinational corporation as a complete entity and extend to individual divisions and affiliates. Internal analysis appraises the quality of the firm's products, production capability and efficiency, management competence, financial resources, and managers' commitment to international operations.

The BOC Group, headquartered in Britain, produces nitrogen, oxygen, and other gases for industrial use. The ratio of nitrogen to oxygen sales is BOC's measure of each country's industrial development; for example, Bangladesh is considered an emergent economy with 30 percent nitrogen and 70 percent oxygen consumption. Workers are involved in agriculture-related industries, such as these working with jute fibers (top). In more advanced countries, such as India (bottom), which BOC classifies as a smokestack economy, the industrial gas use is 50 percent nitrogen and 50 percent oxygen. In highly advanced economies, such as Canada and the United States, 70 percent of gas consumption is nitrogen.

Overall Strategy Development.   The next step is to decide on an overall mission and strategy. The organization can consider its own strengths as well as international opportunities. This decision pertains to overall opportunities and risks and may extend to a portfolio of business opportunities as well as the generic approaches of growth, retrenchment, globalization, or multidomestic strategies.

Operational Objectives and Strategies.   The next step is to focus in on strategies that can be operationalized. This step involves setting objectives for each MNC affiliate and making decisions on whether to export, license, or directly invest in other countries. The operational statement of objectives will include expected financial targets, such as rate of return on assets or sales, or the expected year-to-year rate of growth. Specific targets may also be qualitative, such as to establish goodwill in a new country. PepsiCo did this in China by distributing cases of Pepsi to officials in cities where it was to conduct business.

Implementation and Control.   The final step is implementation and control. Specific timetables are set, courses of action defined, and resources allocated. Budgets and timetables may be drawn up for each affiliate as well as for regional organization groupings. In addition, control systems are created to monitor progress toward desired objectives. Because each affiliate is geographically distant from top management, monitoring and information systems are valuable tools for determining whether performance standards are being met.

For example, Best Western International has over 1,000 hotels located outside the United States and Canada. To maintain control, Best Western uses a 1,000-point inspection list and employs 14 full-time inspectors to check every Best Western property twice a year for cleanliness and quality. Best Western also uses a computerized reservation and control system. This helps coordinate hotels worldwide and also provides information for headquarters on each affiliate's activities.

The strategic planning process is difficult and time consuming, but many MNCs use it to enhance strategic effectiveness. Companies such as Bausch & Lomb Inc., Borden, Mobil Oil, Firestone, Dow Corning, Kellogg, Colgate-Palmolive, Signa, Upjohn, and Chase Manhattan try to use some elements of formal planning for their international operations. A great majority of international firms have found that comprehensive, long-range plans are essential for keeping their worldwide operations intact and profitable in the face of enormous environmental diversity and uncertainties.

MULTINATIONAL ORGANIZATION STRUCTURE

Multinational strategy is closely linked to MNCs' organization structure.[37] Organization structure typically falls into two general categories. The first is a separate *export department,* which may grow into an interna-

E X H I B I T   21.5

International Division Structure

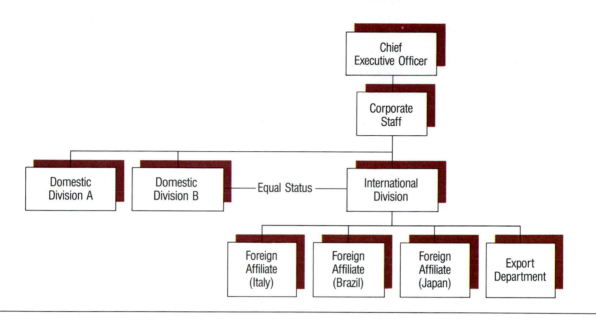

tional division. The second is a *global management structure* that combines domestic and foreign operations. Global management structures include product-based, geographic-based, functional-based, and matrix structures.[38]

International Division

Organizations typically start international operations by appointing an individual to coordinate exports. As the volume of foreign sales increases, the MNC establishes a separate export department. This department has specialists who are responsible for the export portion of the firm's manufacturing and sales. When the organization's strategy moves to foreign production or foreign licensing, more complex structures are required because a greater commitment of organizational resources and management attention is needed.

Historically, firms that have gone beyond exporting have established an international division, which is illustrated in Exhibit 21.5. An **international division** is set up alongside one or more domestic divisions and has equal status in the management hierarchy. The international division supervises and coordinates all business operations outside the company's home country. For example, Coca-Cola got started in international business around 1900 by exporting soft drinks to Cuba, Puerto Rico, and England because managers knew of potential customers there. Exports were handled by an export department, which in 1930 was replaced by a "foreign department."

An international division provides a clear focus for the company's strategy of increasing foreign operations. It consolidates management of

international division An organizational division that is established alongside one or more domestic divisions and has equal status in the management hierarchy.

EXHIBIT   21.6

Product-Based Global Organization Structure

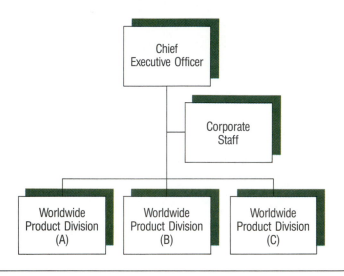

overseas activities and establishes clear lines of authority between foreign affiliates and the parent company. On the negative side, however, an international division splits the company into rival segments and perpetuates the separation of domestic and foreign operations. This may cause duplication of functions and personnel and may interfere with the smooth coordination and exchange of resources among domestic and foreign divisions. To overcome these problems, some organizations have moved to one of the global management structures.

Product-Based Structure

product-based structure A global organization structure in which an MNC establishes product divisions whose managers plan, organize, and control all functions for producing and distributing their products at home and worldwide.

Many multinational companies assign managerial responsibility on the basis of products or product groups, as illustrated in Exhibit 21.6. Under a **product-based structure,** the firm sets up product divisions and each division manager plans, organizes, and controls all functions that produce and distribute its products domestically and around the world. The product approach is appropriate for firms that make products that are technologically similar within a group but technologically distinct across groups. It is essential that managers be thoroughly familiar with technical and performance capabilities and equipped to manufacture and sell the products in all countries where business is conducted. Companies in the capital goods, chemical, and electronics industries tend to use the product-based structure.

Geographic-Based Structure

geographic-based structure A global organization structure in which all of an MNC's products and functions in a particular country or region report to the same division manager.

An alternative for assigning management responsibility is to group the MNC's activities by geographic region, as illustrated in Exhibit 21.7. Under a **geographic-based structure,** all products and functions in a

EXHIBIT 21.7

Geographic-Based Global Organization Structure

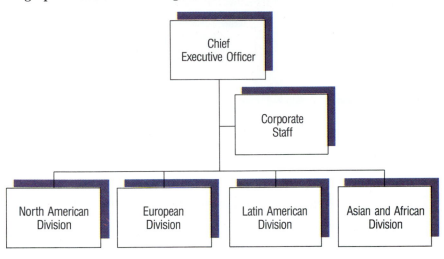

specific country or region report to the same division manager. The geographic approach is ideal for companies with a line of similar products that are sensitive to local market conditions. Specific techniques for the production or sale of the product can be adapted to a given geographical area. Organizations that produce foods, beverages, cosmetics, and other consumer staples often use the geographic structure. For example, at LSI Logic Corporation, a semiconductor company based in California, management's strategy is to divide the world into three geographical markets—Japan, the United States, and Europe—with autonomous operations in each division. This way each division is able to focus on the fierce competition from Japanese semiconductor manufacturers in its part of the world.[39]

Coca-Cola first created an international division, called the Foreign Department, in 1926. The Foreign Department started bottling operations in such countries as Belgium, Italy, Mexico, and Spain. Today Coke's international operations are organized into a geographically-based structure. The three major geographical groups are Latin America, the Pacific group, and Europe and Africa. Many food and beverage manufacturers use this structure because such products must be marketed under local conditions.

EXHIBIT 21.8

Functional-Based Global Organization Structure

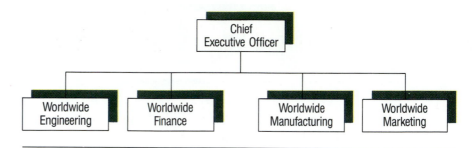

Functional-Based Structure

functional-based structure A global organization structure in which managers' responsibility and authority are assigned along functional lines.

The worldwide **functional-based structure** divides management responsibility and authority along functional lines. A senior executive at the parent corporation is responsible for worldwide manufacturing operations. Another executive is responsible for worldwide marketing of the firm's product. Still another is in charge of engineering, finance, and so on, as illustrated in Exhibit 21.8. The functional structure has been criticized for being rigid and inflexible, and it tends to limit communication and coordination across functions. A manufacturing manager in Manila reports directly to the manufacturing vice-president in the United States and may fail to coordinate manufacturing with local marketing conditions in the Philippines. The advantage of the functional structure is that it overcomes duplication and provides a clear chain of command.

Matrix Structure

matrix structure A global organization structure that permits an MNC to achieve vertical control and horizontal coordination simultaneously.

The problems that occur when a structure emphasizes a single dimension, such as functional or product, can be overcome with a matrix structure. Designing a multinational corporation is a difficult task, and a **matrix structure** provides a way to achieve vertical control and horizontal coordination simultaneously. Matrix structures used by MNCs are similar to those described in Chapter 9 except that geographical distances for communication and coordination are greater.

The most typical matrix structure has two lines of authority—geographic and product—as illustrated in Exhibit 21.9. The product executives and regional executives all report to the MNC president. Managers of affiliates report to two superiors. In Exhibit 21.9, the general manager of a plant producing plastic containers in Venezuela reports to both the head of the plastic products division and the head of Latin American operations.

The matrix structure creates the potential for confusion because of the dual lines of authority, but it also encourages both product and regional concerns to be considered in production and marketing decisions. For example, Westinghouse disbanded its product division structure because of poor coordination across divisions and product managers' insensitivity to the needs of individual nations. In 1980, a matrix structure

EXHIBIT 21.9

Global Matrix Structure

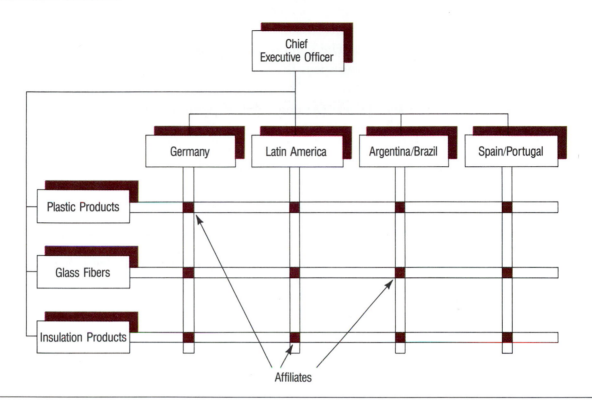

was put in place that gave regional managers authority equal to product managers'. The matrix structure helped Westinghouse overcome the one-dimensional bias built into the global product structure and respond to national differences while simultaneously coordinating its worldwide businesses.[40]

Managing a worldwide matrix structure is not easy. Consider Corning Glass Works.

Corning Glass Works

Corning is a $1 billion-plus worldwide manufacturer of specialized glass and ceramic products. Approximately 33 percent of its sales are international. In 1975, the company faced a worldwide recession, soaring costs, and poor profits. Its geographic structure was ineffective, because domestic and foreign subsidiaries were competing with one another in the same markets. Managers needed a coordinated global strategy and believed the matrix structure would help achieve that goal.

Corning's product lines were clustered into seven divisions—electrical, electronic, science, medical, consumer, technical, and ceramics products. The geographic part of the matrix structure included three regions—Europe, Latin America/Far East, and North America. The regions were responsible for all geographic matters.

Corning spent five years installing and getting the kinks out of its matrix structure. Strategic meetings were held for each business unit, and the product and regional executives participated jointly. When they agreed on a plan, they presented it to corporate management for approval. Although Corning initially had underestimated the complexity of a matrix structure, executives were able to adapt it to Corning's personality and unique circumstances.[41]

Centralization versus Decentralization

One of the issues facing managers using any type of structure is the extent to which their decision authority should be centralized or decentralized. Many managers believe that the diversity of international operating environments and the regional dispersion of operations make a strong case for decentralizing managerial decision making. Local managers are familiar with the economic and cultural milieu in each country.

On the other hand, there are persuasive arguments for centralizing managerial authority. A major one is the benefit derived from close cooperation and interdependence among parent and affiliates worldwide. Central control allows the organization to respond to business opportunities on a worldwide basis and reallocate resources as needed rather than giving local managers authority over this function. Centralization of decision making also is conducive to the development and implementation of uniform worldwide policies and procedures, products, and business practices. Globalization strategy, for example, requires centralized decision making.

TAILORING MANAGEMENT STYLE TO CULTURAL VALUES

Managers in the international arena deal with employees from different cultures. What one culture sees as participative management another sees as incompetence. Before undertaking an assignment in a foreign culture, managers must understand the subtleties of culture and how to provide proper leadership, decision making, motivation, and control.[42]

Leadership

In relationship-oriented societies, leaders should take a strong personal interest in employees. In Asia, the Arab world, and Latin America, managers should use a warm, personalized approach, appearing at soccer games and birthday parties. In Latin America and China, managers should have periodic social visits with workers, inquiring about morale and health.

Leaders should be especially careful about criticizing others. To Asians, Africans, Arabs, and Latin Americans, the loss of self-respect brings dishonor to themselves and their families. Public criticism is intolerable. In a moment of exasperation, an American supervisor on an oil rig in Indonesia shouted at his timekeeper to take the next boat to shore. A mob of outraged Indonesians grabbed fire axes and went after the supervisor. He escaped and barricaded himself in his quarters. The moral: One simply never berates an Indonesian in public.

Managers in foreign countries must receive special training in order to understand the subtleties of culture and perform their functions of leadership, decision making, motivation, and control. In this class at Mazda, managers are receiving English-language training to help prepare them to live and work in the United States and Canada. Mazda vehicles are built in 17 countries. The Japanese leadership preference for group decision making, nonconfrontation, and no individual competition is ineffective in some cultures.

Decision Making

European managers frequently use centralized decision making. American employees might discuss a problem and give the boss a recommendation, but German managers expect the boss to issue specific instructions. East Indian and Latin American employees typically do not understand participatory decision making. Deeply ingrained social customs suggest that a supervisor's effort toward participation signifies ignorance and weakness.

In Arab and African nations, managers are expected to use consultative decision making in the extreme. Arabs prefer one-on-one consultation and make decisions in an informal and unstructured manner.

The Japanese prefer a bottom-up style of decision making, which is consistent with Far Eastern cultures that emphasize group harmony. In Taiwan, Hong Kong, and South Korea, managers are paternalistic figures who guide and help employees.

Motivation

Motivation must fit the incentives within the culture. In Japan, employees are motivated to satisfy the company. A financial bonus for star performance would be humiliating for Japanese, Chinese, or Yugoslav employees. An American executive in Japan offered a holiday trip to the top salesperson, but employees were not interested. After he realized that Japanese are motivated in groups, he changed the reward to a trip for everyone if together they achieved the sales target. They did.

In Latin America, employees work for an individual rather than for a company. Among Turks and Arabs the individual is supreme, and employees are evaluated on their loyalties to superiors more so than on job performance.

Control

When things go wrong, managers in foreign countries often are unable to get rid of employees who don't work out. In Europe, Mexico, and Indonesia, to hire and fire on performance seems unnaturally brutal. Workers are protected by strong labor laws and union rules. In Mexico, employees are considered permanent after a 30-day work period. British

A Japanese Buddhist priest enjoys McDonald's world-famous french fries on the stone steps of a temple in Kamakura, one of Japan's ancient centers of Buddhist culture. McDonald's of Japan became Japan's largest food service organization in 1983. Local employees and managers work in each restaurant to prevent Americanization of foreign cultures. However, McDonald's maintains control over its worldwide franchises through standardization of menu, food preparation, and quality.

and Belgian labor laws dramatically favor employees, and in the USSR workers are guaranteed jobs. Managers must find creative ways of dealing with unproductive employees.

In foreign cultures, managers also should not control the wrong things. A Sears manager in Hong Kong insisted that employees come to work on time instead of 15 minutes late. The employees did exactly as they were told, but they also left on time instead of working into the evening as they had previously. A lot of work was left unfinished. The manager eventually told the employees to go back to their old ways. His attempt at control had a negative effect.

In another case, a Japanese manager was told to criticize an American employee's performance. It took the manager five tries before he could be direct enough to confront the American on his poor performance. Japanese managers are unused to confrontations.

SUMMARY

This chapter covered several important ideas about international management. International business involves risk and difficulty because of complicated economic, legal-political, and sociocultural forces. Companies wishing to develop and serve foreign markets can do so in several ways. The major alternatives are exporting, licensing, franchising, and foreign production through joint ventures or wholly owned subsidiaries.

Much of the growth in international business has been carried out by large businesses called MNCs. Generic strategies for MNCs are growth versus retrenchment and globalization versus multidomestic strategy. Organization structure of MNCs should be selected to reflect strategic objectives. Major structures include an international division, product-based structure, geographic-based structure, functional-based structure, and matrix structure.

Finally, we discussed several key points for management success in foreign cultures. Successful leadership, decision making, motivation, and control depend on understanding the specific culture and tailoring management style to its values.

Management Solution

Black and Decker faced increasing worldwide competition in power tools. Its solution was globalization. Similar products would be designed and sold in all countries, providing enormous savings in manufacturing and marketing. However, implementing the strategy was not easy because affiliates were used to autonomy. President Laurence Farley fired 25 European managers and closed the Brussels headquarters to demonstrate the importance of the new strategy. Black and Decker recently unveiled 50 new power tool models, each standardized for world production and marketing. The home appliance business purchased from General Electric is the next candidate for globalization. Black and Decker will use its worldwide distribution system for standard toasters, can openers, and coffee makers.[43]

DISCUSSION QUESTIONS

1. Why do you think international businesses traditionally prefer to operate in industrialized "First World" countries? Discuss.
2. What considerations in recent years have led international businesses to expand their activities into less developed Third World countries?
3. What policies or actions would you recommend to an MNC for reducing political risk in foreign operations?
4. What steps could a company take to avoid making product design and marketing mistakes when introducing new products into a foreign country?
5. Compare the advantages associated with the foreign market entry strategies of exporting, licensing, and wholly owned subsidiaries.
6. Should a multinational corporation operate as an integrated, worldwide business system, or would it be more effective to let each subsidiary operate autonomously?
7. Are formulation and implementation of corporate strategies likely to be more difficult in a multinational firm than in a domestic firm? Explain.
8. Compare a product-based organization structure with a geographic-based structure. When would each be more appropriate for a multinational corporation?
9. What might managers do to avoid making mistakes concerning leadership, motivation, control, and decision making when operating in a foreign culture?
10. What is meant by the cultural values of individualism and masculinity/femininity? How might these values affect organization design and management processes?

CASES FOR ANALYSIS

OK TEDI MINING LTD.

Ok Tedi (pronounced "Owk teddy") is a joint venture headed by Standard Oil Company of Indiana and Broken Hill Proprietary Company of Australia that was formed in the early 1980s to mine gold and copper in Papua, New Guinea. Papua, New Guinea, is a newly independent "developing" country that needed advanced foreign technology for extracting its mineral ores. The Ok Tedi mine was expected to help develop a remote and poor region of the country that is rich in natural resources. The minerals were expected to be easily mined, since all that Ok Tedi had to do was bulldoze Mount Fublian, a 6,000-foot mountain of copper ore capped by a crown of gold-bearing ore. The joint venture was put together quickly during a period of rapidly rising metal prices. There was no time to conduct detailed engineering studies or to purchase insurance against political risk.

Local tribes believe that Mount Fublian is the haunt of evil spirits, and the western engineers working on the project no longer laugh at this belief. The region surrounding the mine is one of the wettest on earth; yet as soon as Ok Tedi began bringing heavy equipment up river by barge, the rains stopped for five months and equipment had to be airlifted to the mine site. When the rains returned, they did so with a vengeance, washing away roads and equipment. Just after work on a tailings dam was started, 50 million tons of soft, black mud slid down the mountainside and covered the dam site. The estimated cost of building the dam jumped from $50 million to $350 million. To start mining gold, Ok Tedi tried a chemical method of neutralizing wastes. Two accidents released untreated cyanide into nearby streams. Alarmed villagers found dead fish and crocodiles, and the government became concerned about the villagers' health.

Ok Tedi managers believe that local unhappiness has caused additional problems with the government. Because of simultaneous cost overruns and falling metal prices, the company decided to concentrate on producing gold, which has higher profit potential. The government of Papua, New Guinea, regarded this as a violation of its agreement with Ok Tedi, which called for both copper and gold production. The government insisted that Ok Tedi build processing lines for copper ore, hydroelectric facilities, and a permanent dam to contain the mine tailings, despite an additional cost of $800 million, which managers could not afford.

In February 1985, the government ordered the mine closed. The company can resume gold production if it agrees to proceed with the construction of the waste dam and one copper processing line.

Questions

1. Did senior managers at Ok Tedi do insufficient strategic planning, or can the project's problems be attributed to uncontrollable circumstances?
2. Discuss the interplay among economic, political, and cultural factors in this situation. Do you think that unanticipated problems like these could occur in any less developed country?
3. What do you think Ok Tedi's managers should do now?

Source: "Ok Tedi Can Stay Open If Foreign Owners Guarantee Completion of Copper-Gold Mine," *The Wall Street Journal,* February 13, 1985, p. 34; "Government of Papua New Guinea Orders Ok Tedi Mine Closed," *The Asian Wall Street Journal,* February 4, 1985, p. 2; "Ok Tedi Will Start Up Its Gold and Copper Mine in Papua New Guinea in May, 1984," *American Metal Markets,* January 1, 1984, p. 2; "Papua New Guinea Goes for the Gold," *Business Asia,* February 10, 1984, p. 46.

AMERICAN TELEPHONE AND TELEGRAPH COMPANY

American Telephone and Telegraph Company (AT&T) expanded rapidly into international markets since divesting the 13 Bell companies in the United States and Canada. AT&T had limited international involvement and managers lacked international experience, but the company utilized its technology and strong financial position to quickly establish a world-wide presence. AT&T moved into some of the world's most competitive technology markets through joint ventures with large foreign companies such as Italy's Olivetti, the Netherlands' Phillips, and South Korea's Lucky Gold-Star Group.

One strategy AT&T is using to market computer technology in foreign countries is to present itself as an alternative to IBM. Although its over-seas experience in operations are minuscule compared to IBM's, AT&T is playing on fears that IBM is so dominant that customers will be locked into a single supplier. AT&T scored a notable success in Europe when six top European computer makers adopted its Unix software operating sys-tem to counter IBM's dominant position in their market. AT&T is now building on that success by entering the telephone switching equipment market in France. It has offered to sell French-made telephone switches in the United States in exchange for a share of the French market.

AT&T is putting big money and big risks into its global expansion. In Japan it joined Mitsui, the giant trading company, and 15 other Japanese firms to create a massive computer communications network to compete with a similar project planned by IBM and Mitsubishi Electric Corpora-tion. Although a similar idea flopped in the United States, AT&T hopes to succeed by "Japanizing" its software. In Thailand, it won a bidding con-test to publish the nation's telephone directories. In order to win, it had to guarantee the Thais $45 million in profits over five years—twice the guar-antee offered by GTE, which had published the directory for 17 years.

AT&T's international ventures have not been without setbacks. In Tai-wan, it is stuck with part ownership of a manufacturing facility that has had no sales because of delays in government orders for digital tele-phone switches. A joint venture with Phillips in Europe lost a key contract to a British competitor and has had few orders from other customers. The head of Olivetti, another joint venture partner, openly criticized AT&T for slow sales of Olivetti products in the United States. Others have criticized AT&T for putting together business deals without a clear overall plan and for trying to do too many things with too few experienced people.

Questions

1. How would you characterize the principal components of AT&T's strategy for international expansion?
2. Are AT&T's global objectives and strategies consistent with its resources and capabilities? Discuss.
3. Would a strategy of globalization make sense for AT&T? Would it be appropriate to target less developed nations? Discuss.

Source: "AT&T Starts to Lose Its Innocence Abroad," *Business Week,* July 22, 1985, pp. 80–81.

CHAPTER 22
Career Management

Chapter Outline

Changing Scope of Careers

Career versus Job
A Career Management Perspective

Individual Career Planning

Steps in Career Planning
Avoiding Overplanning
Stages of Career Development
Mentor Relationships
Managing Career Stress

Organizational Career Management Strategies

Evaluation of Career Potential
Training and Management Development
Human Resource Information Systems
Career Paths, Career Ladders, and Succession Planning
Career Planning Programs
Facilitation of Mentoring

Special Career Management Problems

Women and Minorities
Dual-Career Couples
Plateaued Employees

Focusing Career Management Strategies on Career Stages

Learning Objectives

After studying this chapter, you should be able to:

- **Explain the importance of career management for both individuals and organizations.**

- **Describe the difference between careers and jobs.**

- **Discuss the steps needed for individual career planning and the stages through which people progress while pursuing careers.**

- **Describe sources of management stress and coping strategies for reducing stress.**

- **Define mentors and their role in career management.**

- **Describe a model organizations can use to help manage employees' careers.**

- **Define career paths, career ladders, and succession planning.**

- **Explain the special career needs of women, minorities, dual-career couples, and plateaued employees.**

Management Problem

Bonnie Freeman started her career as an elementary school teacher. Like many young professionals, she found herself frustrated in her career. After three years of teaching, Freeman "wanted more sense of achievement, a better salary, and a chance to use skills that were wasted in education." At 28, Freeman wanted to leave her Long Beach, California, school and break into a new career without having to start from square one. She was unsure, however, how to proceed in selecting and starting a new career.[1]

If you were Bonnie Freeman, what would you do now? What steps would you take to determine the right career and launch it with a first job?

Bonnie Freeman has an important decision to make, and she is not alone. Most working people must make decisions about jobs and careers. These decisions determine whether their work lives will be satisfying, rewarding, and productive. Roger Smith started as an accounting clerk for GM, making $3,540 a year, and is now president of General Motors. Hamish Maxwell, CEO of Phillip Morris, started as a $2,000-a-year travel agent for Thomas Cook in Paris. Michael Dickens started out as a $2.30-an-hour lifeguard for a Guest Quarters hotel; he progressed through 9 jobs over 16 years, including maintenance man and hotel general manager, and is now president of Guest Quarters.[2]

Careers is currently a "hot" topic in management. It is important to both individuals striving to succeed in organizations and organizations that want to manage the careers of hundreds of employees. The right fit between person and career makes a difference. For example, a recent survey of vice-presidents found that the most important criterion for career success is love of work: "People don't get to the top unless they really love what they are doing and are willing to work very, very hard."[3] Sometimes a career causes problems. Suzanne is so obsessed with career success that she blocks out all aspects of her life other than work. She is cool, impersonal, aloof, and attractive and has easily reached the upper middle management of a major corporation, but she is really not happy.[4] Media coverage of career problems highlights career burnout and mid-career crisis.

Senior managers in organizations are concerned about career paths for employees and aspiring managers. Issues confronting organizations are especially acute with respect to working mothers, early retirement of employees, the need to downsize—reduce the number of middle managers—and ways of handling excess employees after corporate mergers. Growth in many sectors of the economy is slow, and pressures for organizations to remain competitive influence employee careers through staff consolidations and retraining. Moreover, new legal issues relating to wrongful discharge and age discrimination affect careers. Employees are pressuring organizations for greater self-determination in addition to employee rights, job security, and earning equity. These trends place considerable pressure on managers to pay attention to career development and to manage both their own and their subordinate careers' effectively.[5]

The purpose of this chapter is to explore the topic of career management in organizations. First we examine the scope of career issues in today's organizations. Then we discuss individuals' career planning, including steps for self-analysis and career selection, stages in a successful career, how to cope with stress, and the use of mentors. We also examine career management strategies from the organization's perspective, including career development systems, job matching, career paths, and succession planning. Finally, we will examine the special career problems of women, minorities, dual-career couples, and plateaued employees.

CHANGING SCOPE OF CAREERS

Career versus Job

What does it mean to have a career? Most people don't want to just "go to work"; they want to "pursue a career." To some people having a career requires successful movement up the corporate ladder, marked by boosts in salary and status. To others, a career means having a profession—doctors and professors have careers, while secretaries and blue-collar workers have jobs. Still others will tell you that no matter what the occupation, the difference between a career and a job is about 20 hours a week—that is, people who have careers are so involved in their work that they extend beyond its requirements.[6] For these people, it is psychological involvement in their work that defines a career.

The formal definition of a **career** is a sequence of work-related activities and behaviors over the life span viewed as both movement through different job experiences and the person's attitudes toward involvement in those experiences.[7] A **job** is a specific task performed for an organization. A career has a long-term perspective and includes a series of jobs. Moreover, to understand careers, we must look not only at people's work histories or resumes but also at their attitudes toward their work. People may have more or less money or power, be professional or blue collar, and vary in the importance they place on the work in relation to the rest of their lives—yet all may have careers.

A Career Management Perspective

Career development refers to employee progress or growth over time as a career unfolds. Career development is the result of two important activities: career planning and career management. *Career planning* emphasizes individual activities helpful in making career-related decisions. *Career management* focuses on organizational activities that foster employees' career growth.[8]

A career management perspective means adopting a "big picture" of work in the total context of people's lives and recognizing that each person's work experiences add up to a career. More importantly, as long as people are employed with an organization, they have an *organizational career,* which is the sequence of work-related activities and experiences they accumulate during their time with the organization. As a manager, you will be responsible for developing people and helping manage their organizational careers.

INDIVIDUAL CAREER PLANNING

"Work hard and you will be rewarded." When it comes to your career, the advice to work hard makes sense, but it is not enough. Although many organizations take great interest in the management of their employees' careers, you cannot expect to work hard and let the organization take care of your career. The responsibility for your career is yours alone. People who plan their careers improve their chance of having successful ones.

Career planning is the self-assessment, exploration of opportunities, goal setting, and other activities necessary for making informed career-related choices. It is a crucial step in linking your personal needs and capabilities with career opportunities. Career planning involves systematic thinking and attention to short-term and long-term career goals. Career planning is an ongoing activity, not something limited to high school and college graduates making an initial job choice. Because the world and organizations change, a periodic review of your career plans and progress is a must.

career   A sequence of work-related activities and behaviors over a person's life span viewed as movement through various job experiences and the individual's attitudes toward involvement in those experiences.

job   A specific task performed for an organization.

career development   Employee progress or growth over time as a career unfolds.

career planning   The self-assessment, exploration of opportunities, goal setting, and other activities necessary for making informed career-related decisions.

Debbie Glick has a career rather than a job at Pfizer Inc. She began her career after a self-assessment and exploration for opportunities. Her investigation attracted her to Pfizer: "I knew that Pfizer's lean management structure meant exposure to top management very quickly. Within six months I had full profit and loss responsibility for an in-line product. Pfizer has a reputation for strong and innovative marketing." Debbie Glick's career planning paid off. Since joining Pfizer in 1981, she was promoted to assistant product manager and then product manager. She is also attending classes for a JD degree in preparation for the next stage in her career.

Steps in Career Planning

There are five steps involved in career planning.

1. Self-Assessment. The first step is gathering data on yourself—your values, interests, skills, abilities, and preferred activities. You must learn to see yourself clearly and objectively. Consider what makes you happy in work, how closely your self-image is tied to your occupation, and rewards that are important to you. Self-assessment exercises designed to clarify abilities and interests are provided in Exhibit 22.1. The questionnaire inventories for values and interests can be compared to those of people with similar interests who have successful careers. Richard K. Bernstein, a corporate vice-president for a housewares company, answered the following question as part of a self-assessment: "If you had two million dollars, how would you spend it?" Bernstein immediately pictured himself in medical school. Despite being 45 years old, he knew what he wanted and went on to study medicine and specialize in research and teaching on diabetes.[9]

2. Explore Opportunities. Step 2 involves gathering data on your opportunities and potential choices both within and outside your organization. Evaluate the job market and economic conditions. Also, find out about training and development opportunities offered by your organization, including chances to move into different jobs and departments. For example, when Sharon Burklund wanted to move from communications research into sales, her superiors were not interested. Thus, she used an industry directory and called possible employers directly. Through direct contact, she discovered some opportunities. Sharon got her big break when she talked to the head of a trade paper who was about to launch a new publication and needed help in sales.[10]

3. Make Decisions and Set Goals. Once you have evaluated yourself and available opportunities, you must make decisions about short-term

E X H I B I T   22.1

Self-Assessment Exercises

1. Write an autobiographical summary including a general scenario of your life, the people in your life, feelings about the future, the major changes that have occurred, the turning points, and the pros and cons of various career-related decisions and different jobs you have held.

2. Develop an inventory of your functional/transferable skills along such dimensions as machine or manual, athletic/outdoor/traveling, detail/follow-through, numerical/financial/accounting, influencing/persuading, leadership, developing/planning, language/reading, instructing/interpreting, serving/helping, intuitional and innovating, artistic, and so forth. Use data from your autobiographical summary.

3. Complete the Allport, Vernon, and Lindsey (AVL) *Study of Values*. The values indexed are theoretical, economic, aesthetic, social, political, and religious.[a]

4. Maintain a 24-hour diary of what you do over one (or more) 24-hour periods.

5. Complete the *Strong-Campbell Interest Inventory* or the *Self-Directed Search*.

6. Develop a representation of your lifestyle (i.e., a pictorial, graphic, or written representation of your current lifestyle).

7. Write down your memories about the past and your feelings about the present. Stimulate visions about the future. Review themes and images in your writing for clues to your true interests and abilities.

8. Examine your life space concerns—activities, thoughts, and feelings that shape how you are relating to work, family, community, outside activities, and self.

[a] See M. London and S. A. Stumpf, *Managing Careers* (Reading, Mass.: Addison-Wesley, 1982) or your college counseling office for information on obtaining these instruments.

Source: Adapted from M. London and S. A. Stumpf, *Managing Careers* (Reading, Mass.: Addison-Wesley, 1982); J. G. Clawson, J. P. Kotter, V. A. Faux, and C. C. McArthur, *Self-Assessment and Career Development* (Englewood Cliffs, N.J.: Prentice-Hall, 1985); R. M. Bolles, *What Color Is Your Parachute?* (Berkeley, Cal.: Ten Speed Press, 1986).

and long-term goals. What do you want to accomplish in the next year? To which areas of the organization do you desire exposure? What skills do you want to acquire? Decide which target jobs or departments will help you get the necessary exposure and accomplish your goals. Define projects and work assignments that will provide growth opportunities.

4. Action Planning.   This is the "how-do-I-get-there" part of career planning. It involves setting deadline dates, defining needed resources, and making plans to get around barriers. For example, when Sharon Burklund could not get the sales job in her own organization, she made action plans to find out about opportunities in other companies.

5. Follow Up.   Once your plan is in place, periodic review and updating are needed. Take it out every six months and ask yourself, "How am I

A Career in Your Own Company

Victoria Johnson had just graduated from college. She worked for a year and had little savings but was disillusioned working for a large organization. Victoria decided to investigate the possibility of starting her own business. A friend suggested that she check with the local office of the Small Business Administration (SBA). She told an SBA officer of her dissatisfaction with her job and asked him what line of business she might enter. She left the meeting feeling discouraged because of the complexities of small business ownership. She wanted to start a business anyway and decided to see if her parents would provide financial support.

Will Victoria succeed in the difficult world of small business? Probably not. She does not have technical skills that provide the basis for a new business, she is unaware of any customer need to be fulfilled, and she has not yet gained management experience. Furthermore, Victoria visited the SBA office because a friend suggested she do so, not because she sought out someone to assist her. Victoria seems to lack initiative. She also is using business ownership as a substitute for a boring job, which is not a good reason to start a business.

How do people know whether they should pursue a career running their own business or working for a corporation? There is no single answer but entrepreneurs do display certain personality characteristics, which differ from managers in large organizations. Some of the more prominent entrepreneurial personality traits are as follows:

Internal Locus of Control. This means a person feels autonomous and independent and can exert personal control over situations. Internal locus of control is important because the tasks of starting and running a small business require planning, and entre-preneurs must believe they can plan and have control over events. People with an external locus of control believe that future developments are controlled by events over which they have no influence, so planning is futile.

Energy Level. A business start-up requires great effort. For most people, working twelve hours a day is simply too demanding, yet the entrepreneur thrives on long hours. The entrepreneur finds starting and running a business invigorating, while other people would find the total commitment exhausting.

Need to Achieve. Entrepreneurs have high achievement needs. They like to set their own goals, which tend to be difficult, and they enjoy feedback on how well they perform. The high achiever does not like things too easy or unrealistically difficult and gets great satisfaction from business success.

Self-Confidence. Individuals who start and run a business must act decisively. Self-confidence is the belief in your ability to deal with anything the future holds. The entrepreneur believes that even complex, unanticipated problems can be handled and pushes ahead to solve them as they occur.

Background Factors. Entrepreneurs often are the first-born within their families. Also, if the father was successful as an entrepreneur, there is a likelihood that the individual will follow in his footsteps. In addition, fathers who are absent for part of an individual's childhood seem to have children who are more interested in starting their own businesses.

In summary, entrepreneurs tend to be unusual people. They exhibit a cluster of personality traits not typically found in the rest of the population. These factors explain why Victoria Johnson should not start her own business. Victoria did not seem to have exceptional self-confidence, high energy, or an internal locus of control. The right career for Victoria is in someone else's organization.

Source: Based on Charles R. Kuehl and Peggy A. Lambing, *Small Business: Planning and Management* (Chicago: The Dryden Press, 1987).

doing? Am I growing? Did I accomplish what I wanted? Are there new target jobs or work assignments that would be better for me?" For example, Cindy Johnson, general manager of the Hotel Sofitel in Chicago, credits planning with helping her career.

Cindy Johnson

Cindy Johnson started in the hotel business as a part-time waitress at a Holiday Inn at a time when few women were in motel management. Her climb up the corporate ladder was facilitated because she had made plans and prepared herself.

After deciding on the hotel business, she worked part-time in every department of the Holiday Inn while attending the University of Minnesota. She gained experience in everything from housekeeping and reservations to banquets and catering. After rising through the ranks of the Holiday Inn after graduation, she reassessed herself and adopted new action plans. Her plan was to move to a larger hotel and broaden her experience even more by acquiring a better foundation in banquets and catering. First she moved to the Radisson hotel in Minneapolis. After two years, she became director of catering for Jumer's Castle Lodge in Davenport, Iowa. At that point she was ready to become a general manager and began looking for openings in other hotels. Hotel Sofitel recognized her years of experience and appointed her general manager of the Hotel Sofitel in Houston. From there she moved on to become general manager of the new hotel in Chicago, where she is responsible for the entire operation and a staff of 300. Understanding her own strengths and weaknesses, seeking opportunities, making decisions, and adopting action plans provided a valuable assist to Cindy Johnson's career.[11]

Avoiding Overplanning

Career planning should not be rigid, narrow one's options, or chart a single course at the expense of unexpected opportunities. No one can see 10 to 15 years into the future. The point of the plan is to assess yourself and chart a course consistent with your strengths.

Walter B. Wriston, who served 14 years as CEO of CitiBank, calls life a series of accidents. People must be prepared for opportunities. A big part of having a successful career is the corner you are standing on when the bus comes. If an organization is so static and employees so rigid that they know where they will be in five years, their jobs aren't worth much. Every job Wriston had at the bank before becoming CEO didn't exist when he joined it.[12] Likewise, the student newspaper of a large midwestern university ran the headline "Students Shouldn't Plan Their Careers"

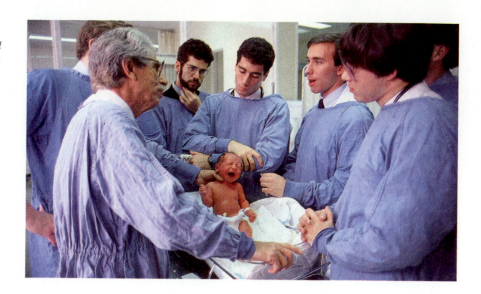

This group of young pediatricians in training at New York University Medical Center are in the first stage—exploration and trial—of the four stages of career development. By going on rounds conducted by pediatrician Dr. Sidney Cohlan, the young pediatricians receive on-the-job training, develop an image of their profession, and confront early job challenges and feedback—all part of the learning associated with the exploration and trial stage. Dr. Cohlan, by contrast, is in the mid-career stage in which he enjoys professional accomplishments and the opportunity to teach new doctors.

based on an interview with the university president. The president cautioned students against deciding too early on just one interest area and closing off other options.

The policy of paying careful attention to career planning is intended to do just the opposite. Career planning enables you to consider a broad range of options, identify several that will be satisfying, and choose the path that seems best at the time. Career planning provides you with self-insight to help you adjust your plans as you go along. Career planning gives you a criterion against which to evaluate unplanned opportunities so that you will know which ones to accept.

Stages of Career Development

As their careers unfold, people pass through predictable stages that signify the course of career development over time. Most careers go through four distinct stages, each associated with different issues and tasks. Dealing successfully with these stages leads to career satisfaction and growth. The four stages are illustrated in Exhibit 22.2.[13]

exploration and trial stage The stage of career development during which a person accepts his or her first job and perhaps tries several jobs.

Stage 1: Exploration and Trial. The **exploration and trial stage** usually occurs between the ages of 15 and 25. A person accepts his or her first job and may try several jobs, some part-time. People must decide whether to stay with an organization or try a job with another company. Job training, developing an image of a preferred occupation, job interviews, and early job challenges and feedback are all part of the learning process associated with this stage.

establishment and advancement stage The stage of career development during which the individual experiences progress with the organization in the form of transfers, promotions, and/or high visibility.

Stage 2: Establishment and Advancement. During the **establishment and advancement stage**—typically from age 25 to 45—people experience progress within the organization. They are transferred and promoted, establish their worth to the organization, and become visible to those at higher levels. Many people form a specific career strategy, de-

EXHIBIT 22.2

Stages of Career Development

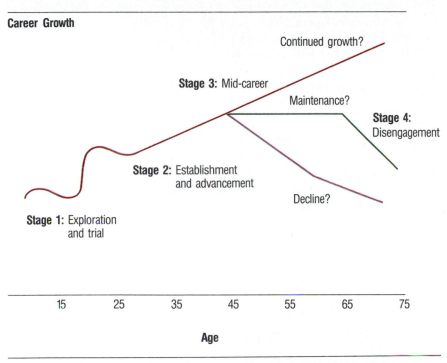

Career Growth

Continued growth?

Stage 3: Mid-career

Maintenance?

Stage 4: Disengagement

Stage 2: Establishment and advancement

Decline?

Stage 1: Exploration and trial

15   25   35   45   55   65   75

Age

Source: Adapted from *Careers in Organizations* by Douglas Hall, p. 57. Copyright © 1976 by Scott, Foresman and Company. Used by permission.

cide on a field of specialization, and find a mentor to support them. A person may receive offers from other organizations.

Stage 3: Mid-Career. The **mid-career stage** often occurs from ages 45 to 65. Mid-career may move in three directions. If characterized by *growth*, the individual continues to progress, receiving promotions and increasing responsibility. The person may have a feeling of "making it" but fear stagnation and thus seek new challenges. If mid-career is characterized by *maintenance*, the person tends to remain in the same job or be transferred at the same level. The individual has job security and is loyal to the organization but stops progressing up the hierarchy. He or she enjoys professional accomplishments and may become a mentor. The person may also consider a second career. If the mid-career stage is characterized by *decline*, the individual is not valued by the organization. As a "surplus" employee, demotion is possible. Decline is characterized by insecurity, crisis, a feeling of failure, and possible early retirement.

mid-career stage The stage of career development characterized by either growth, maintenance, or decline.

Stage 4: Disengagement. The **disengagement stage** comes toward the end of every career. The person prepares for retirement and begins to disengage from both the organization and the occupation. During this stage, a person may feel a need to mentor or teach others, find new interests, and prepare for retirement and a reduced role.

disengagement stage The stage of career development during which the person prepares for retirement and begins to disengage from both the organization and the occupation.

Here a senior executive in the mid-career stage interacts with young professionals in the establishment and advancement stages of their careers. Peter Tombros, senior vice-president, Pfizer Pharmaceuticals, talks with Todd Greeno and Lyn Wiesinger. These opportunities for interaction give young people visibility and access to key decision makers to enhance their professional and career development.

mentor   A senior employee who acts as a sponsor and teacher to a younger, less experienced employee.

For example, Sarah Dickenson, 36, is in the establishment and advancement stage of her career with Hewlett-Packard. The company has grown rapidly, and Sarah has grown with it, receiving three promotions in six years to become research and development manager for Advanced Manufacturing Systems. She expects to reach the level of division manager shortly. In a few years Sarah will enter the mid-career stage, which may be characterized by continued growth, maintenance, or decline.[14]

Mentor Relationships

A **mentor** is a senior employee who acts as a sponsor and teacher to a younger, less experienced protégé.[15] The concept of mentor is derived from Greek mythology. Odysseus trusted the education of his son Telemachus to Mentor, a trusted counselor and friend. In today's organizations, mentors are senior, experienced employees who help younger, newer ones navigate the organization. A mentor relationship typically lasts from two to five years and goes through periods of initiation, cultivation, and separation.[16] The *initiation stage* is a period of six months or so during which mentor and protégé get to know each other. *Cultivation* is the major period, during which the mentor "supports, guides and counsels the young adult."[17] During this period, the mentor-protégé relationship can be described by terms such as "master-apprentice" and "teacher-student." During the *separation* period, which lasts six months or so, the protégé may no longer want guidance and the mentor is likely to move on to other junior employees.

Mentoring has career and social implications.[18] Some of the characteristics of a mentor relationship are listed in Exhibit 22.3. The relationship often goes beyond coaching and training to become a close, personal friendship that includes mutual respect and affection, helping the protégé understand organizational norms, using power on the protégé's behalf, and taking the protégé along when the mentor moves to a new position. The mentor is a friend, counselor, and source of support.

A survey of top executives found that nearly two-thirds had a mentor at some point in their careers. The benefits of a mentoring relationship are substantial. Executives who had mentors received higher salaries, bonuses, and total compensation than did those who had not.[19] Mentors can be an important source of career development because they help new managers learn the ropes and benefit from their experience.[20]

Although it seems like senior managers generally initiate mentoring relationships, there are steps that young managers can take to develop a mentoring relationship with experienced managers:

1. Determine who is successful and well thought of, and get to know him or her professionally and socially.
2. Seek out opportunities for exposure and visibility—committees and special projects—that will provide opportunities to work with experienced, successful people.
3. Inform experienced colleagues of your interests and goals; let your activities and successes be known to these people; seek specific feedback on your performance from experienced colleagues other than your boss.

E X H I B I T   22.3

Characteristics of a Mentor Role

- Trusted counselor, guide, role model, and teacher

- Press agent/parent

- Respect with affection/caring

- Use of power on protégé's behalf

- Taking protégé along when moving to new position

- Sharing of value system, personal feelings, and political strategies

- Enduring relationship

4. Keep in mind that it may not be necessary to find a single, powerful senior manager to fulfill the mentor role. You may be able to develop mentoring relationships with a variety of experienced managers, including peers, during your career.[21]

Mentoring relationships can be confusing and misunderstood by new employees. When understood, they are marvelous opportunities for planning and managing a career.

Consider the following letter indicating how the initiation period of a mentor relationship appeared to one young protégé at International Drug Company.

International Drug Company

"A little over a year ago, I was suddenly asked if I wanted to move from the low-priority project I was working on to the company's top-priority project. It happened quickly and outside the company's system of job posting and bidding. . . . Much later I found out that the middle-aged senior vice president of my division had hand-selected me for the assignment. He had read reports I'd written and was impressed after watching me assist my supervisor at meetings.

The transition to the new team was terrible. The existing team . . . seemed to resent me. During that period, the senior vice president stopped by my office on two occasions to see how I was doing. . . . It was apparent that he held me in some kind of special regard. At business functions, he seeks me out for a brief visit. . . .

He seems to be an admirer. Recently I received a routine and anticipated promotion and I noticed that he had signed the approval letter."[22]

A mentor is a senior employee who acts as a sponsor and teacher to a younger, less experienced one. Colt Industries' Management Career System (MCS) helps individuals develop their talents. MCS staff choose employee assignments to pair younger employees with strong managers. Experienced mentors help develop new managers' skills. Here Dan Burke, an industrial engineer, assists Andrew McMeeking, designer of plant layout at France Compressor Products Division.

The writer of this letter is unsure of how to react to the mentor's actions. The protégé's best bet is to work hard and take advantage of what the mentor can contribute to career development and growth.

Managing Career Stress

Recall from Chapter 1 that managerial work is characterized by brevity, variety, and discontinuity. In other chapters we have seen that managers are responsible for organizing, controlling, and leading the organization. Successful managers are action oriented and responsible for high performance. Considering the nature of managerial work, stress is part of the job—indeed, many people have a stereotype of executives as harried, stressed-out, coronary-prone individuals.

stress The physiological and emotional response to demands, constraints, and opportunities that create uncertainty when important outcomes are at stake.

Stress is defined as the physiological and emotional response to demands, constraints, and opportunities that create uncertainty when important outcomes are at stake.[23] A key notion concerning stress is that people perceive the situation as taxing or as beyond their resources for responding appropriately.[24] Thus, you experience stress if your workload is too heavy for the available time, a deadline is rapidly approaching and you need more information to make a decision, or your boss is dragging his feet on approving a project important to your career. Even

EXHIBIT   22.4

Sources of Management Stress

- Work overload, excessive time demands, and "rush" deadlines

- Erratic work schedules and take-home work

- Ambiguity regarding work tasks, territory, and role

- Constant change and daily variability

- Role conflict (e.g., with immediate supervisor)

- Job instability and fear of unemployment

- Negative competition (e.g., "cutthroat," "one-upmanship," "zero-sum game," and "hidden aggression")

- Type of vigilance required in work assignments

- Ongoing contact with "stress carriers" (e.g., workaholics, passive-aggressive subordinates, anxious and indecisive individuals)

- Sexual harassment

- Accelerated recognition for achievement (e.g., the Peter Principle)

- Detrimental environmental conditions of lighting, ventilation, noise, and personal privacy

Source: Based on K. R. Pelletier, *Healthy People in Unhealthy Places: Stress and Fitness at Work* (New York: Dell, 1984).

positive events, such as a promotion or a new baby, can induce stress because of the adjustments they require.[25]

Sources of Stress.   There are many sources of stress for managers. Some common ones are listed in Exhibit 22.4. Factors such as work overload, erratic schedules, job instability, and cutthroat competition influence the level of stress.[26] Managers also feel stress in the transition from one career stage to the next. Turbulence and uncertainty associated with the establishment and mid-career stages can be great, especially if the career is perceived as not going well or if there is no mentor relationship.

In recent years, a key source of stress for middle managers has been the threat of termination brought about by retrenchment, shifts in corporate strategy based on competitive pressures, and mergers and acquisitions. The fear and uncertainty surrounding possible job loss often create stress as great as that from actual job loss. Job insecurity and job loss are sources of stress that will be particularly relevant to managers' careers in the coming decade.[27]

However, not all stress is bad. Hans Selye, one of the originators of stress research, observed that the only people who have no stress are dead![28] As illustrated in Exhibit 22.5, a moderate amount of stress has a positive effect on performance, but extremely high stress contributes to performance decline. Extended periods of high stress can lead to **burnout,** which is the emotional exhaustion arising from overexposure to stress.[29] Moderate job stress is a natural part of managerial work. Although executives may complain of stress, few want lower-pressure jobs.[30]

burnout   The emotional exhaustion resulting from extended periods of stress.

Symptoms of Stress.   How do managers manifest too much stress? Common stress symptoms are anxiety and tension, depression, and physical disorders such as headache, low back pain, hypertension, and gastrointestinal problems. Behavioral symptoms include difficulty sleep-

E X H I B I T   22.5

Relationship of Stress Level to Performance

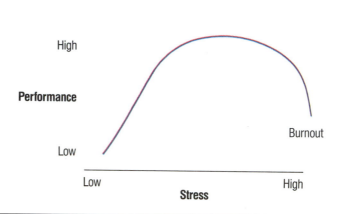

ing, loss of creativity, and alcohol or drug abuse.[31] The impact of stress is revealed in the increasing number of workers' compensation awards made based on psychological distress on the job.[32]

Coping with Stress.   Research on effective ways of coping with managerial stress is just now emerging, but some trends have been identified. For example, coping is effective for reducing tension when it consists of activities such as planning, organizing, and requesting resources needed to remove the cause of stress.[33] Other effective behaviors are building resistance to stress through regular sleep, good health habits, and discussing the situation with coworkers.[34]

Recent data indicate that factors under managerial control, such as performance feedback and clear job expectations, job decision latitude, and social support, are key factors in helping subordinates cope effectively with job stress.[35] In the end, however, each person must find his or her own strategies for coping with stress. For example, a survey of senior executives revealed a variety of techniques, including having other interests, keeping in shape, keeping a balance in their lives, deciding not to let things bother them, and not taking matters too seriously.[36]

Sometimes it's hard to take personal responsibility for dealing with stress. This happened to Fred Gabourie, who managed his own business.

Fred Gabourie Insurance Agency

Fred Gabourie jogged at 6:00 every morning to alleviate his stress, but it wasn't enough. Gabourie won a contract to represent Sovereign Life Insurance. In 1979, his agency wrote $77 million in new policies and increased it to $330 million in 1980. But Gabourie was ridden with anxiety. He said, "The more we did, the more pressure I felt."

For Gabourie, it was all business. He was always on the go. One brokerage representative said, "We felt absolutely pushed by him. We felt guilty when it came time for vacations." Gabourie tried to do everything himself, and when things piled up he would feel a constriction in his upper back. He also felt emotional pangs about how he was going to get all of his work done. He was often so impatient that he would boil over when others didn't see his point at meetings.

His intense style caused him to lose his wife and children. He now says, "Anybody who had any degree of consciousness would have seen the signs. My wife did everything in her power to have me understand what was happening in our marriage. The divorce was a cumulative effort of paying 95 percent of my energy and attention to business and 5 percent to my family life."

Gabourie seemed addicted to telephones. When he went on a vacation, he spent his time on the telephone back to the office. His problems kept him awake. He hadn't had a good night's sleep in years. He'd wake up at 2 a.m. and spend the night working.

Finally, Fred went to the doctor about a physical problem and learned he had a heart irregularity. He had to have major surgery and was suddenly made aware of his mortality. Fred knew he had to learn to do the right things for himself. He tried to cut back on work but was unsuccessful, so he sold the business. That was the breakthrough. He now works as a consultant to other insurance agencies, dresses casually, and often has business meetings at the gym. He greets former employees from his agency with a big hug. Gabourie now believes that executives should realize that high stress is not necessarily a part of the job. "People like me, who take business so seriously, usually just drop dead," he says. "But this is chapter two of my life. I feel like I've been reincarnated without having to die."[37]

ORGANIZATIONAL CAREER MANAGEMENT STRATEGIES

Up to this point, we have been dealing with career planning from the viewpoint of the individual employee. Now we turn to career manage-

MANAGERS SHOP TALK

Are You about to Burst into Flames?

Review the past six months. Have you been noticing changes in yourself or in the world around you? Think of the office . . . the family . . . social situations. Allow about 30 seconds for each answer. Then assign it a number from one (little or no change) to five (for a great deal of change) to designate the degree of change you perceive.

1. Do you tire more easily? Feel fatigued rather than energetic?
2. Are people annoying you by telling you, "You don't look so good lately"?
3. Are you working harder and harder and accomplishing less and less?
4. Are you increasingly cynical and disenchanted?
5. Are you often invaded by a sadness you can't explain?
6. Are you forgetting (appointments, deadlines, personal possessions)?
7. Are you increasingly irritable? More short tempered? More disappointed in the people around you?
8. Are you seeing close friends and family members less frequently?
9. Are you too busy to do even routine things, like make phone calls or read reports or send out your Christmas cards?
10. Are you suffering from physical complaints (aches, pains, headaches, a lingering cold)?
11. Do you feel disoriented when the activity of the day comes to a halt?
12. Is joy elusive?
13. Are you unable to laugh at a joke about yourself?
14. Does romance seem like more trouble than it's worth?
15. Do you have very little to say to people?

Very roughly, now, place yourself on the burnout scale. Keep in mind that this is merely an approximation of where you are, useful as a guide on your way to a more satisfying life. Don't let a high total alarm you, but pay attention. Burnout is reversible, no matter how far along it is. The higher number signifies that the sooner you start being kinder to yourself, the better.

15–25: You're doing fine.
26–35: There are things you should be watching.
36–50: You're a candidate.
51–60: You are burning out.
More than 65: You're threatening your physical and mental well-being.

Source: Excerpts from *Burnout* by Herbert J. Freudenberger and Geraldine Richelson. Copyright © 1980 by Herbert J. Freudenberger and Geraldine Richelson. Reprinted by permission of Doubleday, a division of Bantam, Doubleday, Dell Publishing Group, Inc.

ment strategies that organizations can use to promote effective employee career development.

career management Organizational activities designed to promote employees' career development.

Career management refers to organizational activities designed to promote employees' career development. These activities should function as a "system designed to meet individual needs—for job advancement, extension of skill or the enhancement of human experience on the job—and to relate these needs to the future requirements of the organization."[38] A career development system is created by coordinating various personnel functions, such as recruiting, performance appraisal, and training, while providing a variety of special policies and programs focusing specifically on employee career development.

Exhibit 22.6 illustrates the key components and functions of a career development system. The formal responsibility for career development is usually housed in the human resource management/personnel department. As with most human resource management programs, however,

E X H I B I T   22.6

A Model for an Organizational Career Development System

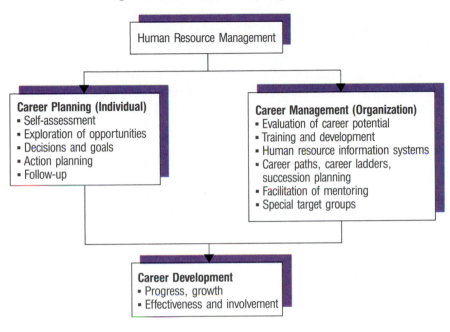

the success of career development depends on line managers' adoption of a career development perspective on a cooperative relationship with the human resource staff. The two dimensions in Exhibit 22.6 are career planning and career management. As described earlier, career planning emphasizes individual actions, while career management emphasizes organizational initiatives. Moreover, as the arrows in Exhibit 22.6 indicate, individual and organizational activities should jointly influence career development. Employees are more likely to do systematic career planning if the organization provides opportunities and structure for this purpose. Organizationally prescribed performance feedback and discussion of career potential are an important impetus to individual efforts. Organizations can provide career planning programs such as workshops and counseling, but individuals must choose to invest energy and time in action planning and follow-up if career development is to take place.

The major components of the organization's career management system are an evaluation of potential, training and development, human resource information systems, career paths, career planning programs, and the facilitation of mentoring.

Evaluation of Career Potential

A critical input into career development is the performance appraisal process described in Chapter 11. Feedback on job performance is important in all aspects of individual career planning, providing valuable data

Career management at Price Waterhouse promotes career development through performance evaluation and individual counseling. In this counseling session, performance is evaluated along with key components of the employee's professional development. The supervisor provides a written job performance, on-the-job training, and suggestions for continuing education. The performance evaluation covers categories ranging from technical skills and knowledge to judgment, leadership, and speaking and writing skills. The career management policy insures that new employees are never uncertain about how they are doing with Price Waterhouse.

human resource inventory A database that summarizes individuals' skills, abilities, work experiences, and career interests.

on skills and strengths and assisting employees in identifying realistic future goals.

The appraisal process also helps the organization assess future potential—the individual's probability of moving upward in the organization. Organizations may use a variety of tools to assess potential, such as commercially prepared tests and inventories, internally developed questionnaires, succession planning, or an assessment center. Often, however, it is the manager's role to determine future career potential using personal judgment. A section of the formal performance appraisal rating form can ask the manager to rate the employee's "future potential" or "promotability."

Training and Management Development

The backbone of a career management program is organizational commitment to training and employee development. *Training* programs focus on the immediately applicable, technically oriented skills required for the next level of job. *Management development* suggests a longer-term view of expanding a person's confidence and growth. Many organizations have a wide range of training and development programs that employees can attend. Some send employees to management training programs sponsored by universities and the American Management Association.

Another important aspect of training and development is internal job moves. The organization should consider other types of moves besides upward promotion, such as lateral transfers and downward moves.[39] The most frequently used job moves for broadening and increasing an employee's potential for advancement are vertical and horizontal:

- *Vertical:* Moving up and down the organizational pyramid; job moves in this category involve changes in rank or organizational level.

- *Horizontal:* Lateral movement to a different function, division, or product line in the organization, such as from sales to marketing or from personnel to public relations.

Human Resource Information Systems

Effective career development systems depend on information. Data on organizational human resource planning and individual career planning must be available to managers and employees. These data usually come from job analysis and job matching systems.

Job Analysis. *Job analysis* was referred to in Chapter 11 as the systematic collection of information about the purpose, responsibilities, tasks, knowledge, and abilities needed for a job. Data are collected by the personnel staff through interviews with job incumbents and supervisors.

Human Resource Inventory. The **human resource inventory** is a database that summarizes individuals' skills, abilities, work experiences, and career interests. These data are made available to both managers and personnel specialists.

Job Matching Systems.   The component for bringing together both job data and human resource interests is a **job matching system,** which links individuals with career opportunities within the organization. The job matching system brings together the human resources inventory as well as the job characteristics, descriptions, and profiles derived from the job analysis. The job matching system searches through all potentially qualified or interested employees and matches them with present or future openings.

job matching system   A method that links qualified individuals with career opportunities within the organization.

Sears, Roebuck

Sears' philosophy of management development is to rotate managers from job to job as they advance from lower ranks. Sears uses a job evaluation system to measure required job competencies: know-how, problem solving, and accountability. Combined with the human resource inventory, Sears is able to construct possible career paths based on individual qualifications. This system also specifies when a manager will need training in a new skill area. In some cases, Sears uses lateral and even downward moves for people needing additional development and wishing to develop expertise in a new functional area. The job matching system enables managers with vacancies in their units to search the organization's personnel files for individuals who are ready for a move into these openings.[40]

Career Paths, Career Ladders, and Succession Planning

Career paths are job progression routes along which employees can advance through the organization. Career paths typically are developed for specific employees, or they may be drawn up by the organization as general routes for employee advancement. They consist of a series of target jobs or functional areas that indicate future job moves appropriate for the individual's career. Career paths may include horizontal moves and an occasional downward move in order to obtain needed experience.

career path   A job progression route along which an employee can advance through the organization.

Career ladders are formalized job progression routes based on jobs that are logically connected. Career ladders tend to be more precisely and objectively determined than career paths. Career ladders are based on data collected through job analysis and examination of personnel records showing historical patterns of employee job moves. An example of a career ladder for Link Flight Simulator Division of the Singer Company is illustrated in Exhibit 22.7. This career ladder charts the normal progression for engineers. After an engineer advances through the first four stages, a decision must be made. The person can concentrate on

career ladder   A formalized job progression route based on logically connected jobs.

E X H I B I T   22.7

Career Ladder for Engineers at the Link Flight Simulation Division of The Singer Company

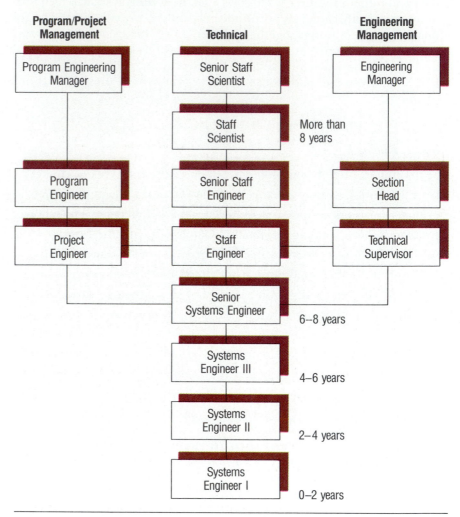

This chart indicates normal career pattern mobility, recognizing some people may progress at different rates depending upon individual capability.

Source: Courtesy of Link Flight Simulation Division, The Singer Company.

technical challenges and remain in the staff engineering track, or he or she may decide to pursue a management track.

There are two ladders associated with management—functional management within the engineering department and program management that involves the coordination of entire projects. The decision to pursue a specific track will be based on the individual's self-assessment and interest in becoming either a staff scientist or a manager.

Succession planning is the process used to create a plan for moving people into the higher levels of the organization. Succession planning applies to a specific group of employees who have the development potential to become top-level managers. "Top level" usually is defined as two to four levels below the CEO. Organizations with progressive career development systems have extended succession planning for all professional and managerial positions.

Succession planning defines both present and future job requirements and determines the availability of candidates and their readiness to move into top jobs.[41] It utilizes career paths and career ladders for a particular group of managers and managerial jobs. The succession planning time horizon is usually 12 to 36 months and is periodically updated. The appropriate emphasis in succession planning is on developing a pool of talent rather than selecting a "crown prince" to assume a top position.

Career Planning Programs

Career planning programs offered by the organization can take the form of career planning workshops and individual career counseling sessions. Group workshops can be conducted by personnel department staff or outside consultants. The workshops take employees through the systematic steps of individual career planning by using individual assessment exercises, small-group discussions, and providing information on organizational opportunities.

Individual career counseling may be provided by the personnel department, but a major part takes place during career planning discussions with supervisors. Supervisors must be trained and knowledgeable about career planning and opportunities. Career counseling requires that a manager assume the role of coach and counselor. Sometimes it is difficult to do career planning during a performance appraisal session because employees become defensive. Some organizations resolve this problem by asking supervisors to hold separate sessions—the first for performance evaluation and the second for creating a career plan.[42]

Facilitation of Mentoring

As we discussed earlier, mentoring provides many advantages to the career development of junior managers. Although mentoring is usually thought of as something that managers undertake on their own, mentor relationships can be an important organizational tool for career development.[43]

Organizations can use two strategies to encourage and facilitate mentoring: education and structural change.[44] Educational programs help senior managers understand mentoring and its importance in career management and help establish norms and cultural values in support of mentoring. Structural changes that facilitate mentoring include adjusting the reward system to place greater emphasis on mentoring, modifying the work design, adapting performance management systems, and even introducing a formal mentoring program. In this way, senior man-

succession planning   The process of creating a plan for moving people into higher organizational levels.

Goodyear Tire & Rubber Company provides a human resource information system to match employees to job openings. Employees are encouraged to prepare inventories of their education, experience, special skills, and interests, which are entered in a computer. When job openings occur, the skills bank supplies information about qualified personnel regardless of their current assignments. Goodyear also has adopted a dual-career ladder that enables employees to remain in scientific work while advancing parallel to management levels in salary and responsibility. Here a chemical engineer and her associate review test results.

Company career planning programs can take the form of career planning workshops or career counseling sessions. Smith Kline & French laboratories have a staff of human resources experts dedicated to the development of the R&D staff. This is an R&D workshop called "Managing Personal Growth" that focuses on career development. The human resources staff also provides individual career counseling.

agers can be encouraged and rewarded for mentoring and may even be assigned junior managers to support and assist. Organizational efforts to facilitate mentoring are important because informally developed, one-to-one relationships may not be available to all promising junior employees. One outcome of mentoring programs is to foster multiple developmental relationships between junior managers and more experienced senior people.

One organization that has developed an effective career management system is Disneyland.

Disneyland

Walt Disney Productions' Anaheim, California, facility employs up to 8,000 people during the summer. Its career management program began in 1976 and is administered by the employee relations department.

The career management program has several parts. First is the intern program, which lasts six months. Approximately 30 individuals start the program twice each year. The program includes weekly classes as well as in-depth, on-the-job training to establish a core of qualified, high-potential management personnel.

Second, a career counseling program is managed by a full-time professional career counselor. A series of meetings can be set up between the counselor and employees at which the counselor helps them define educational objectives, career directions, and possible career changes.

Third, a series of career planning workshops help employees define career objectives and how to achieve them. Workshops are held on career orientation, goal setting, job satisfaction, resume preparation, job interviewing, and worker effectiveness.

Fourth, Disneyland has both job posting and skills inventory systems. The job posting system informs employees of available openings. The skills inventory system is computer based and contains data on all employees who have used the services of the career planning department. When an opening occurs, a listing of those individuals who either have the potential or have been recommended for such positions is produced.

Presently, most career development is handled by the personnel department. Line managers have not been heavily involved. In the future, career development services will be expanded through supervisory training so that line managers too can boost their employees' careers.[45]

SPECIAL CAREER MANAGEMENT PROBLEMS

Because of current social, economic, and legal pressures, organizational career management strategies may be focused on the unique needs of special target groups. Concerns about career development for women and minorities is a direct outgrowth of equal employment opportunity legislation. Although women and minorities are advancing within corporations, they are still underrepresented in middle- and top-level management.[46] The increasing number of dual-career couples has pressured organizations to solve the problems unique to this group of employees. Further, as organizations face increasing competition and are forced to streamline management structures, many management employees find they have plateaued because there are fewer opportunities to move up the hierarchy.

Women and Minorities

Because of common issues faced by women and minorities, recommended career development management strategies often consider these two target groups together.[47] Organizations must confront issues related to assimilating and developing these two groups. For example, since minorities and women have only recently entered management ranks, they may have difficulty developing the social networking and mentoring helpful to career development.

Issues that women face include balancing multiple roles of career and family and sexual harassment.[48] A recent survey found that nearly one out of three women who received MBAs from the nation's top business schools ten years ago have left the managerial work force.[49] Because many of these women left to devote more time to their families, some companies are experimenting with innovative programs that respond to family pressures and offer more flexibility for both men and women.

The pressures are so great that some women must make difficult choices. Linda Searl, a managing partner in her own architectural firm, made the decision not to marry. She was afraid of being distracted and wanted to be able to focus completely on her job. She has succeeded but feels some regret about having no husband and children. Sarah Nesper Brewster, a divorced mother with two daughters, has made a conscious decision not to travel. This has hurt her career progress, but she feels it is essential for her children. She feels guilty because she is always pulled between her children and her job.[50]

To respond to these needs, Mellon Bank allows women to work flexible hours, work at home, and engage in job sharing. At Peat Marwick Mitchell, women can opt for a lighter client load and a less than 40-hour workweek for two to three years. Procter & Gamble gives women eight weeks' paid maternity leave and six months' unpaid child care leave to either parent.[51]

The biggest barrier facing minorities, especially black managers, is in advancement into upper management. Minorities must learn the "difficult, lonely and threatening way to navigate in a basically white environ-

The biggest barrier facing minorities is advancement into upper management. At Pfizer Inc., presentations to peers and management are a routine part of professional activities. This type of training and development helps minority group members develop their careers as well as meet top managers. These opportunities help young professionals develop social networking and mentoring skills helpful to career development.

Roy Morrow and Candace Carruthers are a dual-career couple. Managing their joint careers has involved trade-offs, negotiation, and compromise. When Morrow's employer, Westinghouse Electric Corporation, offered him a promotion to the West Coast, he told his superiors that his wife's career had to figure in his decision. Carruthers found an acceptable job just before Morrow's decision deadline. Her salary was reduced, and the new job required a change in career goals from television station management to production and script writing. Westinghouse helped by recognizing dual-career problems and by giving the couple time to work out a satisfactory solution.

ment." This environment is characterized by white executives' discomfort with nonwhites as well as the tendency to promote managers with backgrounds similar to their own.[52] A recent survey of black managers revealed that many of them perceived the organizational climate for black managers in their organization as indifferent, patronizing, and reluctant to accept blacks. On the positive side, some organizational climates were seen as encouraging, supportive, and trusting.[53]

Recommendations for addressing the unique needs of women and minorities include providing them with access to information, allowing nontraditional career moves, and providing better assessment and coaching skills for potential managers.[54] Organizations should pay particular attention to assisting women and minorities in identifying and examining career paths and the requirements for advancement. Training programs should emphasize the job skills women and minorities need as well as the unique problems they face when advancing within the corporation.

Dual-Career Couples

The growing number of dual-career couples has prompted organizational career management programs to focus on the corporate problems posed by this expanding group of employees.[55] Traditionally it was assumed that if a wife worked, her own career took second place to her husband's. Today women are increasingly likely to place equal importance on their career involvement and are no longer expected to fit their careers to their husbands' career needs. As a result, more couples face the issue of having both a committed personal relationship and careers that are central to each spouse.

Dual-career relationships involve trade-offs, and both employees and managers are realizing that most people cannot "have it all"—happy marriage, children, charming home, many friends, and intense commitment to a career.[56] Organizations are concerned because the pressures experienced by dual-career couples may harm productivity or morale and can pose difficulties when recruiting new employees or transferring current employees to new locations.

There is a strong link between the career problems facing women and the problems of dual-career couples. Women MBAs who left the work force did so because of work-family conflicts. In the final analysis, in most families the responsibility for balancing work and family responsibilities falls disproportionately on the woman.[57]

These issues are difficult to resolve. Suppose, for example, that you have just been promoted to manager of market development for a fast-growing computer software firm in Chicago. Your spouse is offered a big promotion that requires a move to Dallas. What criteria would you use to decide whether to give up your new position or make your spouse pass up the promotion? Will you consider a commuting relationship? If so, for how long?

Ted Koppel resolved a dual-career dilemma by taking ten months off from his newscasting job at ABC to be at home with the children so that his wife, Grace Anne, could start law school at Georgetown University.

Many lesser known couples make similar compromises. Others take turns promoting each other's careers. For example, Peter Briggs left a challenging job as data processing manager in a Minneapolis bank to move with his family to Burlington, Vermont, so that his wife, Barbara Grant, could become an assistant professor of medicine at the University of Vermont. Following his spouse to a new city was an excruciating experience, because he had no job to look forward to. He found a new job at a bank in Burlington, but at a lower level.[58] Some couples end up taking jobs in separate locations and having a "commuter marriage." Robert and Marina Whitman live in Princeton, New Jersey. He commutes to Pittsburgh three days a week, where he teaches English at the University of Pittsburgh, and she commutes to New York and Detroit, where she is chief economist and vice-president for General Motors. Whenever they are in the same city, they always have dinner together.[59]

Organizations try to help dual-career couples in order to maintain productivity, alleviate stress, and retain competent people. Career management programs directed at these people include flexible work schedules, transfer policies, career planning assistance, and local support services such as day care for children. For example, at General Motors when one spouse is hired by the company and relocated, the other gets counseling and referral help in finding a new job. Sometimes the spouse is hired too. At Lotus Development, more than 70 percent of the married people are part of two-career families; thus, generous parental leave benefits are available.[60]

Plateaued Employees

A **career plateau** is "a point in a career from which the likelihood of additional hierarchical promotion, in the judgment of the organization, is very low."[61] Due to the high value most people place on upward mobility, plateauing has come to be viewed by organizations as a problem and may lead to the employee being written off or ignored with respect to career development opportunities. As a practical matter, there is nothing inherently negative about reaching a career plateau. It is a natural consequence of the narrowing pyramid shape of organizations, and many employees experience a career plateau somewhere during mid-career.

Plateaued employees can fall into one of two categories. "Solid citizens" are plateaued employees rated as performing satisfactorily. "Deadwood" are plateaued employees whose performance has fallen below the satisfactory level.[62] Since many plateaued employees are effective performers, it is important not to stereotype them as unmotivated or performing inadequately.[63]

Many organizations anticipate a larger number of plateaued employees in the future. Fewer promotional opportunities will be available because of leaner management staffs. This may also mean that plateauing will occur earlier than in mid-career for some employees. Most managers will have plateaued employees on their staffs and will need to devote attention to developing and maintaining these people's competence.

One study found that plateaued managers performed better when they and their bosses agreed on clear performance objectives and when

career plateau A point in a career from which the opportunities for further promotion are scarce.

E X H I B I T   22.8

Techniques for Renewing Plateaued Managers

- Rotate people laterally among existing jobs.

- Use lateral or downward transfers to other departments.

- Increase job scope to require new knowledge and skills.

- Create temporary work units to solve specific problems.

- Provide training in current technical or administrative skills.

- Encourage development of mentoring, counseling, and advisory skills.

- Reward supplemental contributions such as mentoring and community or government relations.

- Use individuals as internal consultants in different parts of the organization.

Source: Based on J. M. Bardwick, "Plateauing and Productivity," *Sloan Management Review* (Spring 1983), pp. 67–73.

the managers received feedback on specific tasks and overall performance. Other factors that helped plateaued employees' performances were whether they knew the basis on which their performances were being evaluated and whether they had challenging, satisfying, and clearly defined jobs that were important to the company.[64]

A number of career management techniques organizations can use to help plateaued employees are listed in Exhibit 22.8. One is to enhance job challenge and task accomplishment opportunities. This can be done through transfers or by changing the scope of the present job.[65] Other techniques include job changes, training programs that provide mentoring and career counseling, and managerial and technical updating.[66.]

FOCUSING CAREER MANAGEMENT STRATEGIES ON CAREER STAGES

To make organizational career management strategies more effective, the organization can focus on employee career stages. Rather than providing a program for all employees, each program can match the needs of specific employee groups. Examples of career management strategies associated with each of the four career stages described earlier are illustrated in Exhibit 22.9.

In the exploration/trial stage, one concern is how to deal with *reality shock,* which is the upsetting experience and stress brought about by unmet expectations of organizational newcomers.[67] Reality shock can lead to early career dissatisfaction and high turnover. Thus, one career management strategy is to give new recruits *realistic job previews* that

EXHIBIT   22.9

Stage-Related Career Development Focus

STAGE 1
Exploration/Trial
- Deal with reality shock
- Varied job activities and job challenges
- Opportunity for self-exploration
- Gain organizational knowledge

STAGE 2
Establishment/Advancement
- Develop competence in a specialty area
- Develop creativity and innovation
- Gain familiarity with different organizational areas
- Display special skills and expertise

STAGE 3
Mid-Career
- Combat obsolescence
- Develop skills in coaching and mentoring
- Minimize deadwood
- Upward mobility for top performers
- Renewal opportunities such as lateral transfer

STAGE 4
Disengagement
- Change from role of power to one of guidance and wisdom
- Select and develop key subordinates
- Integrate efforts of others rather than making day-to-day decisions
- Preretirement programs
- Begin activities outside the organization

Source: Adapted from T. Gutteridge, *Career Planning and Management* (New York: Little, Brown, in press, 1987); Douglas T. Hall and Marilyn A. Morgan, "Career Development and Planning," in *Contemporary Problems in Personnel*, rev. ed., ed. W. Clay Hammer and Frank Schmidt (Chicago: St. Clair Press, 1977), pp. 205–225; Edgar H. Seatin, *Career Dynamics* (Reading, Mass.: Addison-Wesley, 1978), pp. 40–46.

present job interviewees with the full picture of the organization without selling or "sugar coating" job opportunities. Other strategies during the early career stage are to provide varied job activities, opportunities for self-exploration, and opportunities to gain organizational knowledge.

For employees in the establishment/advancement stage, career management should focus on helping them gain competence in a specialty and develop personal creativity and innovation skills. People at this level should be encouraged to gain familiarity with different organizational areas, possibly through horizontal transfers. They should also be given an opportunity to develop and display their skills and expertise for potential mentor relationships and promotability.

For employees in mid-career, the organization should provide **mid-career renewal strategies,** which are designed to provide upward mobility for those who merit it while maximizing the contributions of plateaued employees who continue to perform satisfactorily. For employees who experience mid-career crises, planning workshops and support groups can help redirect career goals. The organization also can help managers combat obsolescence by providing technical and managerial skill training programs.

For employees in the disengagement stage of their careers, an increasingly popular career management strategy is to provide preretirement programs.[68] **Preretirement programs** assist employees in managing the stress of the transition from work to retirement. Some educational areas that facilitate the transition are financial planning, leisure activities, work/career alternatives, and health.[69] Other ways to keep disengaging managers contributing to the organization are to help them shift from a role of power and decision making to one of consultation, guidance, and

mid-career renewal strategy A strategy designed to provide advancement opportunities for deserving mid-career employees while maximizing the contributions of plateaued employees who continue to perform satisfactorily.

preretirement program A strategy designed to assist employees in coping with the stress of the transition from work to retirement.

development of key subordinates. The organization can also help disengaging people find meaningful activities outside the organization.

Focusing on employees' needs relative to their career stages coordinates the organization's career management strategies with the varied needs of all personnel. The potential bottom-line payoffs to the organization for effective career management are substantial. Productivity, satisfaction, retention and commitment of valued employees, stress reduction, and a flexible work force will help the organization remain competitive in our global economy.

To make career management programs more effective, the Columbia Gas Distribution Company targets programs to the needs of specific employee groups. Here Francis J. Martin, a town serviceman at Cumberland, Maryland, and his wife Margaret listen attentively to lifestyle planning information given during Columbia's retirement planning program, which assists employees in managing the transition from work to retirement. The program deals with financial planning, social security, company benefits, and the emotional, psychological, and social needs of employees when they retire. Spouses attend the program so couples can make retirement decisions together.

SUMMARY

This chapter covered several important issues about the management of careers. Career management was discussed from two perspectives: the individual who wants to have a successful career and the organization that wishes to provide career opportunities for its employees.

Individual career planning normally entails five steps—self-assessment, exploring opportunities, making decisions and setting goals, action planning, and follow-up. Individual careers follow predictable stages that include exploration and trial, establishment and advancement, mid-career, and disengagement. Other issues of concern to individual career planning are mentors and coping with stress.

Career management from the organization's viewpoint involves several systems and techniques. These include evaluation of career potential, training and development programs, human resource information systems, career paths and succession planning, career planning programs, and facilitation of mentoring. Other organizational concerns pertain to women and minorities, dual-career couples, and plateaued employees. Dealing effectively with these target groups can enhance the organization's human resource base. Finally, effective career management programs target individuals' needs at each stage in their career.

Management Solution

Bonnie Freeman was frustrated in her job as an elementary school teacher. She sought advice from a counseling and career management firm, where counselors helped her with career planning. Through testing and self-assessment exercises, Freeman identified the field of "promotion" as her preferred skill. She also identified several personal strengths, including public speaking, persuasion, and problem solving, that she had developed through teaching. During her next summer vacation, Freeman conducted 35 information interviews to pinpoint the work she wanted. Her search gradually focused on the Long Beach Convention and Visitors Council. Freeman secured an internship the following summer, and six months later she was hired as convention-services manager. Less than two years later, she was approached by an aerospace firm and negotiated a position doing public affairs work. Her new salary is substantially higher than her top earnings in education. Career planning made the difference by helping her assess her own strengths and identify new career opportunities.[70]

DISCUSSION QUESTIONS

1. What is the difference between a career and a job? What satisfaction might come with having a job rather than a career?
2. What is job stress? What are the symptoms of high stress? Of moderate stress?
3. Think of someone you know, such as a parent or relative, who has been in a career for several years. In which career stage is this person? Have there been any problems with the transition from one stage to another?
4. What is the organization's responsibility toward a plateaued employee who has become deadwood? Was the individual or the organization the likely cause of this problem?
5. Many people go through a mid-life crisis between the ages of 40 and 50. What career factors might be associated with this crisis?
6. What career planning steps have you taken? What additional steps will you take as you get closer to graduation?
7. Some managers claim, "Individuals should not plan careers. They should remain open to opportunities." How do you respond to this statement?
8. Discuss some of the special problems of women, minorities, and dual-career couples. Is it fair for the organization to offer special programs or make exceptions for people in these groups?
9. Is it imperative to have a mentor for career success? Should you find a mentor or let a mentor find you?
10. Is career management an individual or organizational concern? What types of systems can organizations adopt to facilitate employees' career development?

CASES FOR ANALYSIS

XEROX CORPORATION

Xerox Corporation has over 60,000 employees in Canada and the United States. Xerox established a career systems program in 1975 designed to help employees plan their careers, provide them with information about jobs and opportunities for advancement at Xerox, and help them resolve career conflicts. Xerox's career development programs originally had a strong focus on minorities and women but have been expanded to include all employees except senior executives. The program's philosophy is that career program responsibility rests with line managers, who are assisted by consultants from the personnel department.

The career planning system has several parts. First is the career planning workbook, which is a self-paced primer that helps employees formalize their thoughts and work through the steps of self-analysis, setting job goals, and contingency planning. Second, the career information center provides videotapes addressing such issues as career planning, special problems of minorities and women, and interviews with senior department managers. Third, the managers' career planning handbook helps each manger hold an annual career discussion with his or her subordinates. The workbook is designed to help managers provide effective career counseling for their people. Fourth, career planning workshops provide information about career planning tools. The workshops last one day and are held whenever enough employees sign up.

Personnel department counselors believe that career workshops and workbooks are the most effective career management tools. One drawback is that the workshop reaches only a small number of employees. Counselors are disappointed with the career information system because it is hard to keep the videotapes up to date. The managers' career planning handbook is adequate but by itself does not really teach managers how to handle career planning for subordinates. Xerox's career planning has lost its focus on selected groups, such as handicapped employees, and the personnel department would like to do a better job of serving special target groups. Overall, however, senior management is satisfied with the career planning system for encouraging employees to take responsibility for their own career development.

Questions

1. How do you evaluate the performance of Xerox's career management system?
2. If you were in charge of the personnel department, what changes would you make? Would you add additional programs?
3. Does this system benefit Xerox as well as employees? How?

Source: Based on "Xerox Corporation," in T. Gutteridge, *Career Planning and Management* (Boston: Little, Brown, 1987).

AMERICAN STEEL COMPANY

When Jeff Orr began job hunting during his senior year at a state university, he received four job offers. He accepted the offer at American Steel Company as an assistant to the plant manager. He felt this would give him an opportunity to learn all phases of the plant while utilizing the financial and accounting expertise he had acquired in college.

Three years later—when Jeff was only 25—the plant controller died and Greg McDonald, plant manager, offered him the controller's job. It was a big responsibility, but the plant manager felt Jeff could handle it; besides, there was no one else who could take the job on such short notice. Jeff accepted and worked many 12-hour days. But it was challenging and exciting. He loved the responsibility and felt he was making a difference in plant decisions.

After only two years as controller, Greg McDonald called him to his office. "Headquarters in Philadelphia needs another person in their financial planning group. They've looked throughout the company and feel you have the right combination of training and experience. Headquarters wants you to take a position with the headquarters' financial planning group. Although I hate to lose you, I recommended you highly and do not want to stand in your way."

Jeff took the job and loved it. It utilized his ability to explain complex financial data to unsophisticated listeners. He could organize data logically, and he spoke well. His presentations at headquarters were always well received.

Jeff was disappointed when his new boss, Gilbert Clark, said that Jeff would not make the annual capital budget presentation to the board of directors. Clark told him, "It's customary for the financial planning department head to appear before the board. You'll have to brief me thoroughly before I present next week." The briefing did not go well, because Clark was ignorant of many details and could not answer some questions. One proposal for remodernizing plants was shot down, which angered Greg McDonald and other plant managers, who had thought Jeff would help them get the equipment they needed to improve productivity.

Jeff suddenly found himself agonizing over his career. "What should I do about Mr. Clark?" Jeff mused. "He's a real roadblock. He doesn't understand capital budgeting or financial planning or what I'm trying to do. He's still wearing a green eyeshade so far as new financial planning techniques are concerned. Should I sit tight until he retires in seven years? Or would it be better to transfer back to plant management? Maybe I should try to sneak around him in the hierarchy." Jeff felt he had made excellent progress in his career up to this point but now felt blocked and frustrated.

Questions

1. In what career stages are Jeff Orr and Gilbert Clark? Do you see any special problems associated with either career from the organization's perspective?
2. How well has Jeff planned his career? Do you think he should do more systematic planning? Explain.
3. What should Jeff do now?

Source: Inspired by John L. Snook, Jr., "Sanford Jarvis Case" UVA-H-75 (Colgate Darden Graduate School of Business Administration, University of Virginia, 1976).

REFERENCES

Chapter 1

1. "The Dark Horse Who Has Ashton-Tate Galloping Again," *Business Week*, February 10, 1986, 89–92.
2. Tom Peters and Nancy Austin, *A Passion for Excellence: The Leadership Difference* (New York: Random House, 1985).
3. Byron Harris, "The Man Who Killed Braniff," *Texas Monthly*, July 1982, 116–120, 183–189.
4. James A. F. Stoner and Charles Wankel, *Management*, 3d ed. (Englewood Cliffs, N.J.: Prentice-Hall, 1986).
5. Peter F. Drucker, *Management: Tasks, Responsibilities, Practices* (New York: Harper & Row, 1974).
6. Harris, "The Man Who Killed Braniff."
7. Peters and Austin, *A Passion for Excellence*, 11–12.
8. Harris, "The Man Who Killed Braniff."
9. Peters and Austin, *A Passion for Excellence*.
10. Harris, "The Man Who Killed Braniff." 118–120.
11. Ibid.
12. Ibid.
13. L. von Bertalanffy, "The History and Status of General Systems Theory," *Academy of Management Journal* 15 (1972), 407–426.
14. John Merwin, "A Tale of Two Worlds," *Forbes*, June 16, 1986, 101–106.
15. Ibid.
16. Harold Geneen with Alvin Moscow, *Managing* (Garden City, N.Y.: Doubleday, 1984), 285.
17. Luis Gomez-Mejia, Joseph E. McCann, and Ronald C. Page, "The Structure of Managerial Behaviors and Rewards," *Industrial Relations* 24 (1985), 147–154.
18. Ibid.
19. Robert L. Katz, "Skills of an Effective Administrator," *Harvard Business Review* 52 (September/October 1974), 90–102.
20. Morgan W. McCall, Jr., and Michael M. Lombardo, "Off the Track: Why and How Successful Executives Get Derailed" (Technical Report No. 21, Center for Creative Leadership, Greensboro, N.C., January 1983).
21. A. Levitt, Jr., and J. Albertine, "The Successful Entrepreneur: A Personality Profile," *The Wall Street Journal*, August 29, 1983, 12.
22. Henry Mintzberg, *The Nature of Managerial Work* (New York: Harper & Row, 1973).
23. Robert E. Kaplan, "Trade Routes: The Manager's Network of Relationships," *Organizational Dynamics* (Spring 1984), 37–52; Rosemary Stewart, "The Nature of Management: A Problem for Management Education," *Journal of Management Studies* 21 (1984), 323–330; John P. Kotter, "What Effective General Managers Really Do," *Harvard Business Review* (November/December 1982), 156–167; Morgan W. McCall, Jr., Ann M. Morrison, and Robert L. Hannan, "Studies of Managerial Work: Results and Methods" (Technical Report No. 9, Center for Creative Leadership, Greensboro, N.C., 1978).
24. Henry Mintzberg, "Managerial Work: Analysis from Observation," *Management Science* 18 (1971), B97–B110.
25. Based on John P. Kotter, "What Effective General Managers Really Do," *Harvard Business Review* (November/December 1982), 156–167; Mintzberg, "Managerial Work."
26. Mintzberg, "Managerial Work."
27. Sloan Wilson, "What Do Successful Men Have in Common? Raw Energy," *Houston Chronicle*, March 30, 1980, section 6, 11.
28. Mintzberg, "Managerial Work."
29. Lance B. Kurke and Howard E. Aldrich, "Mintzberg was Right!: A Replication and Extension of *The Nature of Managerial Work*," *Management Science* 29 (1983), 975–984; Cynthia M. Pavett and Alan W. Lau, "Managerial Work: The Influence of Hierarchical Level and Functional Specialty," *Academy of Management Journal* 26 (1983), 170–177; Colin P. Hales, "What Do Managers Do? A Critical Review of the Evidence," *Journal of Management Studies* 23 (1986), 88–115.
30. Pavett and Lau, "Managerial Work."
31. Ann Howard, "College Experiences and Managerial Performance" (Unpublished manuscript, Human Resources Studies Group, AT&T, December 1984).
32. McCall and Lombardo, "Off the Track."
33. "The Dark Horse."

Chapter 2

1. Peter Nulty, "New World's Boffo B Movie Script," *Fortune*, February 17, 1986, 48–50.
2. Alan M. Kantro, ed., "Why History Matters to Managers," *Harvard Business Review* 64 (January/February 1986), 81–88.
3. Daniel A. Wren, *The Evolution of Management Thought*, 2d ed. (New York: Wiley, 1979), 6–8. Much of the discussion of these forces comes from Arthur M. Schlesinger, *Political and Social History of the United States, 1829–1925* (New York: Macmillan, 1925), and Homer C. Hockett, *Political and Social History of the United States, 1492–1828* (New York: Macmillan, 1925).
4. Robert L. Heilbroner, *The Making of Economic Society* (Englewood Cliffs, N.J.: Prentice-Hall, 1962).
5. Much of this discussion is based on Isaac Asimov, *The Near East: 10,000 Years of History* (Boston: Houghton Mifflin, 1968), Chapter 1. See also Richard E. Leakey and Roger Lewin, *Origins: The Emergence and Evolution of Our Species and Its Possible Future* (New York: Dutton, 1977), and Claude S. George, Jr., *The History of Management Thought* (Englewood Cliffs, N.J.: Prentice-Hall, 1968).
6. Isaac Asimov, *The Egyptians* (Boston: Houghton Mifflin, 1967), 36. See also George, *History of Management Thought*, 4–9.
7. Letter of Silla-Labbum and Elani, Old Assyrian., *Inc.*, January 1986, 16.
8. Daniel J. Boorstin, *The Discoverers: A History of Man's Search to Know His World and Himself* (New York: Random House, 1983).
9. Wren, *Evolution of Management Thought*, 26; see also George, *History of Management Thought*, 30–39.
10. Nicolo Machiavelli, *The Prince*, trans. Luigi Ricci (New York: New American Library, 1952).
11. The following is based on Wren, *Evolution of Management Thought*, Chapters 4, 5, and George, *History of Management Thought*, Chapter 4.
12. Charles Babbage, *On the Economy of Machinery and Manufactures* (London: Charles Knight, 1932).
13. Wren, *Evolution of Management Thought*, 98.
14. Arthur G. Bedeian, "1986 Calendar of Management Scholars' Birthdays," The Academy of Management, 1985; and George, *History of Management Thought*, 80.

15. Charles D. Wrege and Ann Marie Stoka, "Cooke Creates a Classic: The Story behind F. W. Taylor's Principles of Scientific Management," *Academy of Management Review* (October 1978), 736–749.

16. John F. Mee, "Pioneers of Management," *Advanced Management—Office Executive* (October 1962), 26–29, and W. J. Arnold and the editors of *Business Week, Milestones in Management* (New York: McGraw-Hill, vol. I, 1965; vol. II, 1966).

17. Wren, *Evolution of Management Thought*, 181; George, *History of Management Thought*, 103–104.

18. Wren, *Evolution of Management Thought*, 171; George, *History of Management Thought*, 103–104.

19. Wren, *Evolution of Management Thought*, 227; George, *History of Management Thought*, 105–110.

20. Henri Fayol, *Industrial and General Administration*, trans. J. A. Coubrough (Geneva: International Management Institute, 1930); Henri Fayol, *General and Industrial Management*, trans. Constance Storrs (London: Pitman and Sons, 1949); Arnold, "Milestones in Management."

21. Mary Parker Follett, *The New State: Group Organization: The Solution of Popular Government* (London: Longmans, Green, 1918), and Mary Parker Follett, *Creative Experience* (London: Longmans, Green, 1924).

22. Henry C. Metcalf and Lyndall Urwick, eds., *Dynamic Administration: The Collected Papers of Mary Parker Follett* (New York: Harper & Row, 1940), and Arnold, "Milestones in Management."

23. Wren, *Evolution of Management Thought*, 335–345.

24. William B. Wolf, *How to Understand Management: An Introduction to Chester I. Barnard* (Los Angeles: Lucas Brothers, 19), and David D. Van Fleet, "The Need-Hierarchy and Theories of Authority," *Human Relations* 9 (Spring 1982), 111–118.

25. Max Weber, *General Economic History*, trans. Frank H. Knight (London: Allen & Unwin, 1927); Max Weber, *The Protestant Ethic and the Spirit of Capitalism*, trans. Talcott Parsons (New York: Scribner, 1930); and Max Weber, *The Theory of Social and Economic Organizations*, eds. and trans. A. M. Henderson and Talcott Parsons (New York: Free Press, 1947).

26. Wren, *Evolution of Management Thought*, 249.

27. Richard L. Daft, *Organization Theory and Design*, 2d ed. (St. Paul, Minn.: West, 1986), 180–181; Kathy Goode, Betty Hahn, and Cindy Seibert, "United Parcel Service: The Brown Giant" (Unpublished manuscript, Texas A&M University, 1981).

28. Hugo Munsterberg, *Psychology and Industrial Efficiency* (Boston: Houghton Mifflin, 1913).

29. Wren, *Evolution of Management Thought*, 216; see also George, *History of Management Thought*, 121–122.

30. Charles D. Wrege, "Solving Mayo's Mystery: The First Complete Account of the Origin of the Hawthorne Studies—The Forgotten Contributions of Charles E. Snow and Homer Hibarger" (Paper presented to the Management History Division of the Academy of Management, August 1976).

31. Ronald G. Greenwood, Alfred A. Bolton, and Regina A. Greenwood, "Hawthorne a Half Century Later: Relay Assembly Participants Remember," *Journal of Management* 9 (Fall/Winter 1983), 217–231.

32. F. J. Roethlisberger, W. J. Dickson, and H. A. Wright, *Management and the Worker* (Cambridge, Mass.: Harvard University Press, 1939).

33. H. M. Parson, "What Happened at Hawthorne?" *Science* 183 (1974), 922–932.

34. Greenwood, Bolton, and Greenwood, "Hawthorne a Half Century Later," 219–221.

35. W. C. Langer, *Psychology and Human Living* (New York: Appleton-Century-Crofts, 1937).

36. Warren G. Bennis, "Revisionist Theory of Leadership," *Harvard Business Review* 39 (January/February 1961), 26–28.

37. Douglas McGregor, *The Human Side of Enterprise* (New York: McGraw-Hill, 1960), 16–18.

38. Mansel G. Blackford and K. Austin Kerr, *Business Enterprise in American History* (Boston: Houghton Mifflin, 1986), Chapters 10, 11, and Alex Groner and the editors of *American Heritage* and *Business Week, The American Heritage History of American Business and Industry* (New York: American Heritage Publishing, 1972), Chapter 9.

39. Larry M. Austin and James R. Burns, *Management Science* (New York: Macmillan, 1985).

40. Tom Scott and William A. Hailey, "Queue Modeling Aids Economic Analysis at Health Center," *Industrial Engineering* (February 1981), 56–61.

41. Ludwig von Bertalanffy, Carl G. Hempel, Robert E. Bass, and Hans Jonas, "General System Theory: A New Approach to Unity of Science," *Human Biology* 23 (December 1951), 302–361, and Kenneth E. Boulding, "General Systems Theory—The Skeleton of Science," *Management Science* 2 (April 1956), 197–208.

42. Fremont E. Kast and James E. Rosenzweig, "General Systems Theory: Applications for Organization and Management," *Academy of Management Journal* (December 1972), 447–465.

43. Daft, *Organization Theory*, 14–15.

44. Fred Luthans, "The Contingency Theory of Management: A Path Out of the Jungle," *Business Horizons* 16 (June 1973), 62–72, and Fremont E. Kast and James E. Rosenzweig, *Contingency Views of Organization and Management* (Chicago: Science Research Associates, 1973).

45. H. E. Aldrich, *Organizations and Environments* (Englewood Cliffs, N.J.: Prentice-Hall, 1979), and T. Burns and G. M. Stalker, *The Management of Innovation* (London: Tavistock Publications, 1961).

46. Jay W. Lorsch, "Making Behavioral Science More Useful," *Harvard Business Review* 57 (March/April 1979), 171–180.

47. William Ouchi, *Theory Z: How American Business Can Meet the Japanese Challenge* (Reading, Mass.: Addison-Wesley, 1981).

48. Ouchi, *Theory Z*. See also R. Pascale and A. Athos, *The Art of Japanese Management: Applications for American Executives* (New York: Simon and Schuster, 1981), and Peter F. Drucker, "Behind Japan's Success," *Harvard Business Review* 59 (January/February 1981), 83–90.

49. Thomas J. Peters and Robert H. Waterman, Jr., *In Search of Excellence: Lessons from America's Best-Run Companies* (New York: Harper & Row, 1982); Tom Peters and Nancy Austin, *A Passion for Excellence: The Leadership Difference* (New York: Random House, 1985); and Tom Peters, "Putting Excellence into Management," *Business Week*, July 21, 1980, 196–201.

50. "Who's Excellent Now?", *Business Week*, November 5, 1984, 76+; Daniel T. Carroll, "A Disappointing Search for Excellence," *Harvard Business Review* 61 (November/December 1983), 78–79+; Jeremiah J. Sullivan, "A Critique of Theory Z," *Academy of Management Review* (January 1983), 132–142; William Bowen, "Lessons from Behind the Kimono," *Fortune*, June 15, 1981, 247–250.

51. Harold E. Pollard, *Trends in Management Thinking, 1960–1970* (Houston: Gulf, 1978), 291.

52. Peter Nulty, "New World's Boffo B Movie Script," *Fortune*, February 17, 1986, 48–50.

Chapter 3

1. John Bussey, "Gerber Takes Risky Stand as Fears Spread about Glass in Baby Food," *The Wall Street Journal*, March 6, 1986, 21; Felix Kessler, "Tremors from the Tylenol Scare Hit Food Companies," *Fortune*, March 31, 1986, 59–62; John Gorman, "Gerber Decides to Fight Back," *Chicago Tribune*, March 16, 1986, sec. 7, p. 3.
2. Arthur M. Louis, "America's New Economy: How to Manage in It," *Fortune*, June 23, 1986, 21–25.
3. James D. Thompson, *Organizations in Action* (New York: McGraw-Hill, 1967).
4. Richard L. Daft, *Organization Theory and Design*, 2d ed. (St. Paul, Minn.: West, 1986).
5. L. J. Bourgeois, "Strategy and Environment: A Conceptual Integration," *Academy of Management Review* 5 (1980), 25–39.
6. John Bussey, "P & G's New Disposable Diaper Intensifies Marketing Battle with Kimberly-Clark," *The Wall Street Journal*, January 4, 1985, 13.
7. "State Regulators Rush in Where Washington No Longer Treads," *Business Week*, September 19, 1983, 124–131.
8. See Arvind P. Phatak, *International Dimensions of Management* (Boston: Kent, 1983).
9. Robert Durand, Teri Fogle, and Matt Stump, "International Business Machines" (Unpublished manuscript, Texas A&M University, December 1985); "IBM Sees Selectric with New Features as More Competitive," *The Wall Street Journal*, October 16, 1985, 17; Randall Smith, "IBM Adds Features to Sierra Model to Increase Speed," *The Wall Street Journal*, October 3, 1985, 10.
10. Dave Ulrich, "Specifying External Relations: Definition of an Actor in an Organization's Environment," *Human Relations* 37 (1984), 245–262.
11. David B. Jemison, "The Importance of Boundary Spanning Roles in Strategic Decision-Making," *Journal of Management Studies* 21 (1984), 131–152, and Marc J. Dollinger, "Environmental Boundary Spanning and Information Processing Effects on Organizational Performance," *Academy of Management Journal* 27 (1984), 351–368.
12. John Koten, "In Airlines' Rate War, Small Daily Skirmishes Often Decide Winners," *The Wall Street Journal*, August 24, 1984, 1, 8.
13. R. T. Lenz and Jack L. Engledow, "Environmental Analysis Units and Strategic Decision-Making: A Field Study of Selected 'Leading Edge' Corporations," *Strategic Management Journal* 7 (1986), 69–89.
14. Mansour Javidan, "The Impact of Environmental Uncertainty on Long-Range Planning Practices of the U.S. Savings and Loan Industry," *Strategic Management Journal* 5 (1984), 381–392.
15. Tom Burns and G. M. Stalker, *The Management of Innovation* (London: Tavistock, 1961).
16. "Dow Chemical: From Napalm to Nice Guy," *Fortune*, May 12, 1986, 75–78.
17. Monica Langley, "Thrifts' Trade Group and Their Regulators Get Along Just Fine," *The Wall Street Journal*, July 16, 1986, 1, 14.
18. Andy Pasztor, "Electrical Contractors Reel under Charges That They Rigged Bids," *The Wall Street Journal*, November 29, 1985, 1, 5.
19. Eugene W. Szwajkowski, "The Myths and Realities of Research on Organizational Misconduct," in *Research in Corporate Social Performance and Policy*, ed. James E. Post (Greenwich, Conn.: JAI Press, 1986), 9:103–122.
20. Keith Davis, William C. Frederick, and Robert L. Blostrom, *Business and Society: Concepts and Policy Issues* (New York: McGraw-Hill, 1979).
21. Douglas S. Sherwin, "The Ethical Roots of the Business System," *Harvard Business Review* 61 (November/December, 1983), 183–192.
22. Milton Friedman, *Capitalism and Freedom* (Chicago: University of Chicago Press, 1962), 133, and Milton Friedman and Rose Friedman, *Free to Choose* (New York: Harcourt Brace Jovanovich, 1979).
23. Henry L. Gantt, *Organization for Work* (New York: Harcourt Brace Jovanovich, 1919).
24. Archie B. Carroll, "A Three-Dimensional Conceptual Model of Corporate Performance," *Academy of Management Review* 4 (1979), 497–505.
25. Roy Rowan, "E. F. Hutton's New Man on the Hot Seat," *Fortune*, November 11, 1985, 130–136.
26. Eugene W. Szwajkowski, "Organizational Illegality: Theoretical Integration and Illustrative Application," *Academy of Management Review* 10 (1985), 558–567.
27. David J. Fritzsche and Helmut Becker, "Linking Management Behavior to Ethical Philosophy—An Empirical Investigation," *Academy of Management Journal* 27 (1984), 165–175.
28. Carroll, "A Three-Dimensional Model."
29. James J. Chrisman and Archie B. Carroll, "Corporate Responsibility—Reconciling Economic and Social Goals," *Sloan Management Review* 25 (Winter 1984), 59–65.
30. Elizabeth Gatewood and Archie B. Carroll, "The Anatomy of Corporate Social Response: The Rely, Firestone 500, and Pinto Cases," *Business Horizons* 24 (September/October 1981), 9–16.
31. Carroll, "A Three-Dimensional Model"; Ian Wilson, "What One Company Is Doing about Today's Demands on Business," in *Changing Business-Society Interrelationships*, ed. George A. Steiner (Los Angeles: Graduate School of Management, UCLA, 1975); Terry W. McAdam, "How to Put Corporate Responsibility into Practice," *Business and Society Review/Innovation* 6 (1973), 8–16.
32. John Kenneth Galbraith, "Behind the Wall," *New York Review of Books*, April 10, 1986, 11–13.
33. Milton R. Moskowitz, "Company Performance Roundup," *Business and Society Review* 53 (Spring 1985), 74–77.
34. Terry Connolly, Edward J. Conlon, and Stuart Jay Deutsch, "Organizational Effectiveness: A Multi-Constituency Approach," *Academy of Management Review* 5 (1980), 211–217, and Frank Friedlander and Hale Pickle, "Components of Effectiveness in Small Organizations," *Administrative Science Quarterly* 13 (1968), 289–304.
35. Adapted from Eugene W. Szwajkowski, "The Odd Couple: Employee Misconduct and the Work Ethic" (Paper presented at the Fifth Annual Business and Professional Ethics Conference, Chicago, August 1986).
36. Archie B. Carroll and George W. Beiler, "Landmarks in the Evolution of the Social Audit," *Academy of Management Journal* 18 (September 1975), 589–599, and Robert J. DeFilippi, "Conceptual Frameworks and Strategies for Corporate, Social Involvement Research," *Research and Corporate Social Performance* 4 (1982), 35–56.
37. Keith Davis and Robert L. Blomstrom, *Business and Society: Environment and Responsibility*, 3d ed. (New York: McGraw-Hill, 1975).
38. Susan J. Tolchin, "Equity Abandoned," in "Can Socially Responsible Societies Compete Economically?" *Business and Society Review* 52 (Winter 1981), 11–14.

39. "Where Business Goes to Stock Up on Ethics," *Business Week,* October 14, 1985, 63–66.

40. Marcia Parmarlee Miceli and Janet P. Near, "The Relationship among Beliefs, Organizational Positions, and Whistle-Blowing Status: A Discriminant Analysis," *Academy of Management Journal* 27 (1984), 687–705.

41. Clair Safran, "Women Who Blew the Whistle," *Good Housekeeping,* April 1985, 25, 216–219.

42. Philip L. Cochran and Robert A. Wood, "Corporate Social Responsibility and Financial Performance," *Academy of Management Journal* 27 (1984), 42–56.

43. Cochran and Wood, "Corporate Social Responsibility," and Kenneth E. Aupperle, Archie B. Carroll, and John D. Hatfield, "An Empirical Examination of the Relationship between Corporate Social Responsibility and Profitability," *Academy of Management Journal* 28 (1985), 446–463.

44. Louis W. Fry, Gerald D. Keim, and Roger E. Meiners, "Corporate Contribution: Altruistic or For-Profit?" *Academy of Management Journal* 25 (1982), 94–106.

45. "Why Gerber Is Standing Its Ground," *Business Week,* March 17, 1986, 50–51, and Felix Kessler, "Tremors from the Tylenol Scare Hit Food Companies," *Fortune,* March 31, 1986, 59–62.

Chapter 4

1. Louis S. Richman, "Volkswagen Regains Some Beetle Magic," *Fortune,* March 31, 1986, 38–45, and "Can VW Regain Its Magic Touch?" *Business Week,* August 6, 1984, 50–58.

2. Amitai Etzioni, *Modern Organizations* (Englewood Cliffs, N.J.: Prentice-Hall, 1984), 6.

3. "Owens-Illinois: Giving Up Market Share to Improve Profits," *Business Week,* May 11, 1981, 81–82.

4. Max D. Richards, *Setting Strategic Goals and Objectives,* 2d ed. (St. Paul, Minn.: West, 1986).

5. "Building Better Transit," *Metropolitan Transportation Authority Annual Report,* 1984.

6. This discussion is based on Richard L. Daft and Richard M. Steers, *Organizations: A Micro/Macro Approach* (Glenview, Ill.: Scott, Foresman, 1986), 319–321; Herbert A. Simon, "On the Concept of Organizational Goals," *Administrative Science Quarterly* 9 (1964), 1–22; Charles B. Saunders and Francis D. Tuggel, "Corporate Goals," *Journal of General Management* 5 (1980), 3–13.

7. Jerome H. Want, "Corporate Mission: The Intangible Contributor to Performance," *Management Review* (August 1986), 46–50; Philip Kotler, *Marketing Management: Analysis, Planning and Control* (Englewood Cliffs, N.J.: Prentice-Hall, 1980), 50–54; John A. Pearce II, "The Company Mission as a Strategic Tool," *Sloan Management Review* (Spring 1982), 15.

8. "Preparing for the Unexpected," *Columbia Today* (Winter 1985/1986), 2–4.

9. Richard, *Setting Strategic Goals,* 1986, and Charles Perrow, "Analysis of Goals in Complex Organizations," *American Sociological Review* 26 (1961), 854–866.

10. Peter F. Drucker, *The Practice of Management* (New York: Harper & Brothers, 1954), 65–83.

11. "Preparing for the Unexpected," 2.

12. Sarah Bartlett, "John Reed's Citicorp," *Business Week,* December 8, 1986, 90–96.

13. Tom Richman, "What Business Are You Really In?" *INC.,* August 1983, 77–86.

14. Carl R. Anderson, *Management* (Dubuque, Iowa: Wm. C. Brown, 1984), 262.

15. Daft and Steers, *Organizations.*

16. "ABC News," special news telecast, April 14, 1984, 9:30 p.m. EST.

17. William B. Stevenson, Jon L. Pearce, and Lyman W. Porter, "The Concept of 'Coalition' in Organization Theory and Research," *Academy of Management Review* 10 (1985), 256–268.

18. Miriam Erez, P. Christopher Early, and Charles L. Hulin, "The Impact of Participation on Goal Acceptance and Performance: A Two-Step Model," *Academy of Management Journal* 28 (1985), 50–66, and Miriam Erez and Frederick H. Kanfer, "The Role of Goal Acceptance in Goal Setting and Past Performance," *Academy of Management Review* 8 (1983), 454–463.

19. For a history of management by objectives, see Peter F. Drucker, *Managing for Results* (New York: Harper & Row, 1964), and George S. Odiorne, "MBO: A Backward Glance," *Business Horizons* (October 1978), 14–24.

20. Barry P. Keating, "Goal Setting and Efficiency in Social Service Agencies," *Long Range Planning* 14 (February 1981), 40–48.

21. Daniel H. Gray, "Uses and Misuses of Strategic Planning," *Harvard Business Review* 64 (January/February 1986), 89–97.

22. Ibid.

23. "Strategic Planning: Part 2," *Small Business Report* (March 1983), 28–32.

24. Paul Meising and Joseph Wolfe, "The Art and Science of Planning at the Business Unit Level," *Management Science* 31 (1985), 773–781.

25. "Jolt Cola Has It All—Sugar, Caffeine, and Strategy," *The Orlando Sentinel,* June 15, 1986, D3.

26. Jac Fitz-Enz, "White-Collar Effectiveness," *Management Review* (June 1986), 52–56.

27. "Preparing for the Unexpected," 2–4.

28. "The New Breed of Strategic Planner," *Business Week,* September 17, 1984, 62–68.

29. Ibid.

30. Daniel H. Gray, "Uses and Misuses of Strategic Planning," *Harvard Business Review* 64 (January/February 1986), 89–97.

31. "The New Breed."

32. "Strategic Planning: Part 1," *Small Business Report* (February 1983), 28–32.

33. J. E. Pluenneke, "VW Rejoins Race to Sell Superchief Cars," *Business Week,* January 27, 1986, 56, and Richman, "Volkswagen Regains Magic."

Chapter 5

1. James R. Norman and Amy Dunkin, "How Bobby Sakowitz Took an Escalator to the Basement," *Business Week,* August 19, 1985, 54–55.

2. Steve Lawrence, "Bar Wars: Hershey Bites Mars," *Fortune,* July 8, 1985, 52–57.

3. "New? Improved? The Brand-Name Mergers," *Business Week,* October 21, 1985, 108–110.

4. "Columbia Pictures: Are Things Really Better with Coke?" *Business Week,* April 14, 1986, 56–58.

5. John E. Prescott, "Environments as Moderators of the Relationship between Strategy and Performance," *Academy of Management Journal* 29 (1986), 329–346; John A. Pearce II

and Richard B. Robinson, Jr., *Strategic Management: Strategy, Formulation, and Implementation,* 2d ed. (Homewood, Ill.: Irwin, 1985); David J. Teece, "Economic Analysis and Strategic Management," *California Management Review* 26 (Spring 1984), 87–110.

6. Charles W. Hofer and Dan Schendel, *Strategy Formulation: Analytical Concepts* (St. Paul, Minn.: West, 1979), 25.

7. "Why Nabisco and Reynolds Were Made for Each Other," *Business Week,* June 17, 1985, 34–35.

8. Milton Leontiades, *Strategies for Diversification and Change* (Boston: Little, Brown, 1980), 63, and Dan E. Schendel and Charles W. Hofer, eds., *Strategic Management: A New View of Business Policy and Planning* (Boston: Little, Brown, 1979), 11–14.

9. Janet Guyon, Scott McMurray, and James B. Stewart, "General Electric, Kidder Peabody Announce Pact," *The Wall Street Journal,* April 25, 1986, 2.

10. Jaclyn Fierman, "How to Make Money in Mature Markets," *Fortune,* November 25, 1985, 47–53.

11. Milton Leontiades, "The Confusing Words of Business Policy," *Academy of Management Review* 7 (1982), 45–48.

12. Lawrence G. Hrebiniak and William F. Joyce, *Implementing Strategy* (New York: Macmillan, 1984).

13. Steven Flax, "How to Snoop on Your Competitors," *Fortune,* May 14, 1984, 28–33.

14. Pamela Sherrid, "Fighting Back at Breakfast," *Forbes,* October 7, 1985, 126–130.

15. Steve Swartz, "Basic Bedrooms: How Marriott Changes Hotel Design to Tap Mid-Priced Market," *The Wall Street Journal,* September 18, 1985, 1.

16. Kathleen Deveny, "Thinking Ahead Got Deere in Big Trouble," *Business Week,* December 8, 1986, 69, and Jill Bettner with Lisa Gross, "Planting Deep and Wide at John Deere," *Forbes,* March 14, 1983, 119–122.

17. Frederick W. Gluck, "A Fresh Look at Strategic Management," *Journal of Business Strategy* 6 (Fall 1985), 4–19.

18. John A. Pearce II, "Selecting among Alternative Grand Strategies," *California Management Review* (Spring 1982), 23–31.

19. Michael A. Hitt, R. Duane Ireland, and K. A. Palia, "Industrial Firms' Grand Strategy and Functional Importance: Moderating Effects of Technology and Uncertainty," *Academy of Management Journal* 25 (1982), 265–298.

20. William L. Shanklin and John K. Ryans, Jr., "Is the International Cash Cow Really a Prize Heifer?" *Business Horizons* 24 (1981), 10–16.

21. Bobbie Holbrook, Sondra Rodgers, and Greg Lock, "Gillette Company" (Unpublished manuscript, Texas A&M University, 1986).

22. Raymond E. Miles and Charles C. Snow, *Organizational Strategy, Structure, and Process* (New York: McGraw-Hill, 1978).

23. Donald C. Hambrick, "Some Tests of the Effectiveness and Functional Attributes of Miles and Snow's Strategic Types," *Academy of Management Journal* 26 (1983), 5–26.

24. "How Adversity Is Reshaping Madison Avenue," *Business Week,* September 15, 1986, 142–147.

25. Bill Hale and Paula Boudreaux, "Frito Lay Inc.: A Case Study" (Unpublished manuscript, Texas A&M University, 1986).

26. Michael E. Porter, *Competitive Strategy* (New York: Free Press, 1980), 36–46.

27. Thomas L. Wheelen and J. David Hunger, *Strategic Management and Business Policy* (Reading, Mass.: Addison-Wesley, 1986), and J. Fierman, "Beech-Nut Bounces Up in the Baby Food Market," *Fortune,* December 24, 1984, 56.

28. Bill Saporito, "Heinz Pushes to Be the Low-Cost Producer," *Fortune,* June 24, 1985, 44–54.

29. Ibid., 54.

30. C. R. Wasson, *Dynamic Competitive Strategy and Product Life Cycles,* 3d ed. (Austin, Tex.: Austin Press, 1978).

31. Carl R. Anderson and Carl P. Zeithaml, "Stage of the Product Life Cycle, Business Strategy, and Business Performance," *Academy of Management Journal* 27 (1984), 5–24.

32. Saporito, "Heinz Pushes."

33. Harold W. Fox, "A Framework for Functional Coordination," *Atlanta Economic Review* (now *Business Magazine*) (November/December 1973).

34. Ford S. Worthy, "A Phone War that Jolted Motorola," *Fortune,* January 20, 1986, 43–46.

35. Henry Mintzberg, "Strategy-Making in Three Modes," *California Management Review* 16 (Winter 1973), 44–53.

36. "Father Knows Best—Just Ask the Tramiel Boys," *Business Week,* December 15, 1986, 106–108.

37. Kenneth Labich, "The New Master of the Skies," *Fortune,* January 5, 1987, 72–73.

38. "The Limits of Tradition," *Forbes,* May 20, 1985, 112–115.

39. L. J. Bourgeois III and David R. Brodwin, "Strategic Implementation: Five Approaches to an Elusive Phenomenon," *Strategic Management Journal* 5 (1984), 241–264, and Anil K. Gupta and V. Govindarajan, "Business Unit Strategy, Managerial Characteristics, and Business Unit Effectiveness at Strategy Implementation," *Academy of Management Journal* (1984), 25–41.

40. Jay R. Galbraith and Robert K. Kazanjian, *Strategy Implementation: Structure, Systems and Process,* 2d ed. (St. Paul, Minn.: West, 1986).

41. Joel Dreyfuss, "John Scully Rises in the West," *Fortune,* July 9, 1984, 180–184.

42. Michael W. Miller, "Q. T. Wiles Revives Sick High-Tech Firms with Strong Medicine," *The Wall Street Journal,* June 23, 1986, 1, 12.

43. Alfred V. Chandler, *Strategies and Structures* (Cambridge, Mass: MIT Press, 1962).

44. Miller, "Q. T. Wiles."

45. Gupta and Govindarajan, "Business Unit Strategy," and Bourgeois and Brodwin, "Strategic Implementation."

46. Alex Beam, "Can the Boston Brahmin of Insurance Shake Off the Cobwebs?" *Business Week,* August 26, 1985, 51.

47. James E. Skivington and Richard L. Daft, "A Study of Organizational 'Framework' and 'Process' Modalities for the Implementation of Business-Level Strategies." (Unpublished manuscript, Texas A&M University, 1987).

48. Barry Meier, "Under Public Pressure, Chemical Firms Push Plant Safety Programs," *The Wall Street Journal,* November 11, 1985, 1, 17.

49. Saporito, "Heinz Pushes," 54.

50. Meier, "Under Public Pressure."

51. Norman and Dunkin, "Bobby Sakowitz."

Chapter 6

1. "Can Pete and Jeff Coors Brew Up a Comeback?" *Business Week,* December 16, 1985, 86–88, and "Coors Comes Bubbling Back," *Fortune,* March 17, 1986, 51–53.

2. Gregory Miles and Matt Rothman, "David Roderick Puts Icahn's Patience to a Test," *Business Week,* November 10, 1986, 41, and J. Ernest Beazley, "USX Corp. Agrees to Resume Bargaining with Union in Effort to End Steel Strike," *The Wall Street Journal,* October 27, 1986, 3.

3. Myron Magnet, "How Top Managers Make a Company's Toughest Decision," *Fortune*, March 18, 1985, 52–57.

4. Herbert A. Simon, *The New Science of Management* (Englewood Cliffs, N.J.: Prentice-Hall, 1977), 47.

5. Samuel Eilon, "Structuring Unstructured Decisions," *Omega* 13 (1985), 369–377, and Max H. Bazerman, *Judgment in Managerial Decision Making* (New York: Wiley, 1986).

6. Inga Skromme Baird and Howard Thomas, "Toward a Contingency Model of Strategic Risk Taking," *Academy of Management Review* 10 (1985), 230–243, and Philip A. Roussel, "Cutting Down the Guesswork in R&D," *Harvard Business Review* 61 (September/October 1983), 154–160.

7. Eilon, "Structuring Unstructured Decisions," and Roussel, "Cutting Down the Guesswork."

8. Mark N. Vamos, "Time Inc.'s $47 Million Belly Flop," *Business Week*, February 17, 1986, 14–15.

9. Eilon, "Structuring Unstructured Decisions," and Richard L. Daft and Robert H. Lengel, "Organizational Information Requirements, Media Richness and Structural Design," *Management Science* 32 (1986), 554–571.

10. Henry Mintzberg, D. Raisinghani, and A. Theoret, "The Structure of 'Unstructured' Decision Processes," *Administrative Science Quarterly* 21 (1976), 246–275.

11. David M. Schweiger, William R. Sandberg, and James W. Ragan, "Group Approaches for Improving Strategic Decision Making: A Comparative Analysis of Dialectical Inquiry, Devil's Advocacy, and Consensus," *Academy of Management Journal* 29 (1986), 51–71, and Richard O. Mason and Ian I. Mitroff, *Challenging Strategic Planning Assumptions* (New York: Wiley Interscience, 1981).

12. Peter Petre, "The Struggle over Sperry's Future," *Fortune*, December 9, 1985, 78–84.

13. Earnest R. Acher, "How to Make a Business Decision: An Analysis of Theory and Practice," *Management Review* 69 (February 1980), 54–61.

14. Douglas A. Hay and Paul N. Dahl, "Strategic and Midterm Planning of Forest-to-Product Flows," *Interfaces* 14 (September/October 1984), 33–43.

15. Herbert A. Simon, *The New Science of Management Decision* (New York: Harper & Row, 1960), 5–6; Peer Soelberg, "Unprogrammed Decision Making," *Proceedings of the Academy of Management* (1966), 3–16; E. Frank Harrison, *Managerial Decision Making*, 2d ed. (Boston: Houghton Mifflin, 1981), 9–13.

16. James G. March and Herbert A. Simon, *Organizations* (New York: Wiley, 1958).

17. Herbert A. Simon, *Models of Man* (New York: Wiley, 1957), 196–205, and Herbert A. Simon, *Administrative Behavior*, 2d ed. (New York: Free Press, 1957).

18. John Taylor, "Project Fantasy: A Behind-the-Scenes Account of Disney's Desperate Battle against the Raiders," *Manhattan* (November 1984).

19. Weston H. Agor, "The Logic of Intuition: How Top Executives Make Important Decisions," *Organizational Dynamics* 14 (Winter 1986), 5–18.

20. Daniel J. Isenberg, "How Senior Managers Think," *Harvard Business Review* 62 (November/December 1984), 80–90.

21. David Frost and Michael Deakin, *David Frost's Book of the World's Worst Decisions* (New York: Crown, 1983), 60–61.

22. James W. Fredrickson, "Effects of Decision Motive and Organizational Performance Level on Strategic Decision Processes," *Academy of Management Journal* 28 (1985), 821–843, and James W. Fredrickson, "The Comprehensiveness of Strategic Decision Processes: Extension, Observations, Future Directions," *Academy of Management Journal* 27 (1984), 445–466.

23. Arkalgud Ramaprasad and Ian I. Mitroff, "On Formulating Strategic Problems," *Academy of Management Review* 9 (1984), 597–605, and Simon, *The New Science*, 40.

24. Larry Reibstein, "A Finger on the Pulse: Companies Expand Use of Employee Surveys," *The Wall Street Journal*, October 27, 1986, 27.

25. Richard L. Daft, Juhani Sormumen, and Don Parks, "Chief Executive Scanning, Environmental Characteristics, and Company Performance: An Empirical Study" (Unpublished manuscript, Texas A&M University, 1987).

26. W. E. Pounds, "The Process of Problem Finding," *Industrial Management Review* (Fall 1969), 1–19.

27. Paul B. Carroll, "IBM Reassigns Financial Chief Krowe: Analysts Cite Failure to Foresee Slump," *The Wall Street Journal*, October 20, 1986, 5.

28. H. H. Stevenson, "Defining Corporate Strengths and Weaknesses," *Sloan Management Review* (Spring 1976), 51–66, and Harold E. Klein and Robert E. Linneman, "Strategic Environmental Assessment: An Emerging Typology of Corporate Planning Practice," *Contribution of Theory and Research to the Practice of Management* (Proceedings of the Southern Management Association, New Orleans, November 1982), 4–9.

29. Matt Moffett, "Attention to Area's Demographic Change Makes Houston's Fiesta Stores a Success," *The Wall Street Journal*, October 23, 1986, 35.

30. C. Kepner and B. Tregoe, *The Rational Manager* (New York: McGraw-Hill, 1965).

31. "Johnson Controls Advertisement," *Business Week*, November 3, 1986, 47.

32. William J. Hampton, "The Next Ace at Chrysler," *Business Week*, November 3, 1986, 66.

33. Maynard M. Gordon, *The Iacocca Management Technique* (New York: Ballatine Books, 1985), 172.

34. Barbara Deaux, "From Equity to Performance: Some Lessons from Uncle Sam" (Unpublished manuscript, Santa Fe State University, 1984).

35. Ann B. Fisher, "Coke's Brand-Loyalty Lesson," *Fortune*, August 5, 1985, 44–46; "How Coke Decided a New Taste Was It," *Fortune*, May 27, 1985, 80; "Voices," *Working Woman*, November 1985, 85.

36. William B. Stevenson, Jon L. Pearce, and Lyman W. Porter, "The Concept of 'Coalition' in Organization Theory and Research," *Academy of Management Review* 10 (1985), 256–268.

37. Michael Murray, *Decisions: A Comparative Critique* (Marshfield, Mass.: Pitman, 1986); Richard Cyert and James March, *A Behavioral Theory of the Firm* (Englewood Cliffs, N.J.: Prentice-Hall, 1963); March and Simon, *Organizations*.

38. Anna Grandori, "A Prescriptive Contingency View of Organizational Decision Making," *Administrative Science Quarterly* 29 (1984), 192–209.

39. William M. Carley, "How Dissension Jolted United Technologies, Led to Carlson's Exit," *The Wall Street Journal*, May 20, 1986, 1, 16.

40. E. Frank Harrison, *The Managerial Decision-Making Process* (Boston, Mass.: Houghton Mifflin, 1975).

41. Andre Delbecq, Andrew Van de Ven, and D. Gustafson, *Group Techniques for Program Planning* (Glenview, Ill.: Scott, Foresman, 1975), and L. Richard Hoffman, "Improving the Problem-Solving Process in Managerial Groups," in *Improving Group Decision Making in Organizations*, ed. Richard A. Guzzo (New York: Academic Press, 1982), 95–126.

42. John F. Preble, "The Selection of Delphi Panels for Strategic Planning Purposes," *Strategic Management Journal* 5 (1984), 157–170, and N. Delkey, *The Delphi Method: An Ex-*

perimental Study of Group Opinion (Santa Monica, Cal.: Rand Corporation, 1969).

43. Norman P. R. Maier, "Assets and Liabilities in Group Problem Solving: The Need for an Integrated Function," *Psychological Review* 47 (1967), 239–249; Linda M. Jewell and H. Joseph Reitz, *Group Effectiveness in Organizations* (Glenview, Ill.: Scott, Foresman, 1981); Walter C. Swap, "Destructive Effects of Groups on Individuals" in *Group Decision Making*, ed. Walter C. Swap and Associates (Beverly Hills, Cal.: Sage, 1984).

44. Irving L. Janis, *Group Think*, 2d ed. (Boston: Houghton Mifflin, 1982), 9.

45. Roy Rowan, "The Maverick Who Yelled Foul at Citibank," *Fortune*, January 10, 1983, 46–56.

46. David M. Schweiger and Phyllis A. Finger, "The Comparative Effectiveness of Dialectical Inquiry and Devil's Advocate: The Impact of Task Biases on Previous Research Findings," *Strategic Management Journal* 5 (1984), 335–350, and Charles R. Schwenk, "Effects of Planning Aids and Presentation Media on Performance and Affective Responses in Strategic Decision-Making," *Management Science* 30 (1984), 263–272.

47. Michael N. Chanin and Harris J. Shapiro, "Dialectical Inquiry in Strategic Planning: Extending the Boundaries," *Academy of Management Review* 10 (1985), 663–675.

48. Magnet, "Top Managers."

49. A. Osborn, *Applied Imagination* (New York: Scribner, 1957).

50. "Coors Comes Bubbling Back" and "Pete and Jeff Coors."

Chapter 7

1. Lucius J. Riccio, Joseph Miller, and Ann Litke, "Polishing the Big Apple: How Management Science Has Helped Make New York Streets Cleaner," *Interfaces* 16 (January/February 1986), 83–88.

2. H. Watson and P. Marett, "A Survey of Management Science Implementation Problems," *Interfaces* 9 (August 1979), 124–128.

3. For further explanation of management science techniques, see B. Render and R. Stair, *Quantitative Analysis for Management*, 2d ed. (Boston: Allyn & Bacon, 1985), and S. Lee, L. Moore, and B. Taylor, *Management Science* (Dubuque, Iowa: W. C. Brown, 1981).

4. S. C. Wheelwright and S. Makridakis, *Forecasting Methods for Management* (New York: Wiley, 1973).

5. Ibid.

6. Robert F. Reilly, "Developing a Sales Forecasting System," *Managerial Planning* (July/August 1981), 24–30.

7. Dexter Hutchins, "And Now, the Home-Brewed Forecast," *Fortune*, January 20, 1986, 53–54.

8. N. Dalkey, *The Delphi Method: An Experimental Study of Group Opinion* (Santa Monica, Cal.: Rand Corporation, 1969).

9. Bruce Blaylock and L. Reese, "Cognitive Style and the Usefulness of Information," *Decision Sciences* 15 (Winter 1984), 74–91.

10. J. Duncan, "Businessmen Are Good Sales Forecasters," *Dun's Review* (July 1986).

11. M. Moriarty, "Design Features of Forecasting Systems Involving Management Judgments," *Journal of Marketing Research* 22 (November 1985), 353–364, and D. Kahneman, B. Slovic, and A. Tversky, eds., *Judgment under Uncertainty: Heuristics and Biases* (Cambridge, Mass: Cambridge Press, 1982).

12. M. Anderson and R. Lievano, *Quantitative Management: An Introduction*, 2d ed. (Boston: Kent, 1986).

13. Kevin McManus, "The Cookie Wars," *Forbes*, November 7, 1983, 150–152.

14. Anderson and Lievano, *Quantitative Management;* J. Byrd and L. Moore, "The Application of a Product Mix Linear Programming Model in Corporate Policy Making," *Management Science* 24 (September 1978), 1342–1350; D. Darnell and C. Lofflin, "National Airlines Fuel Management and Allocation Model," *Interfaces* 7 (February 1977), 1–16.

15. P. Williams, "A Linear Programming Approach to Production Scheduling," *Production and Inventory Management* 11 (3d Quarter, 1970), 39–49.

16. W. J. Erikson and O. P. Hall, *Computer Models for Management Science* (Reading, Mass.: Addison-Wesley, 1986).

17. "Network Models," *Small Business Report* (February 1986), 37–40.

18. David Cohan, Stephen M. Haas, David L. Radloff, and Richard F. Yancik, "Using Fire in Forest Management: Decision Making under Uncertainty," *Interfaces* 14 (September/October 1984), 8–19.

19. J. W. Ulvila and R. V. Brown, "Decision Analysis Comes of Age," *Harvard Business Review* (September/October 1982), 130–141.

20. Erikson and Hall, *Computer Models*, Anderson and Lievano, *Quantitative Management*.

21. B. Render and R. Stair, *Quantitative Analysis for Management*, 2d ed. (Boston: Allyn & Bacon, 1985).

22. Raymond F. Boykin and Reuven R. Levary, "An Interactive Decision Support System for Analyzing Ship Voyage Alternatives," *Interfaces* 15 (March/April 1985), 81–84.

23. William G. Sullivan and R. Gordon Orr, "Monte Carlo Simulation Analyzes Alternatives in Uncertain Economy," *IE*, November 1982, 43–49.

24. T. Naylor and H. Schauland, "A Survey of Users of Corporate Planning Models," *Management Science* 22 (1976), 927–937.

25. Riccio, Miller, and Litke, "Polishing the Big Apple," and Lucius J. Riccio, "Management Science in New York's Department of Sanitation," *Interfaces* 14 (March/April 1984), 1–13.

Chapter 8

1. Based on "Coming of Age at Lotus: Software's Child Prodigy Grows Up," *Business Week*, February 25, 1985, 100–101.

2. Michael Brody, "Can GM Manage It All?", *Fortune*, July 8, 1985, 22–28.

3. "Greyhound Splitting into Four to Go After Short-Haul Trade," *Chicago Tribune*, April 30, 1986, sec. 3, p. 8.

4. "Bill To Restructure Pentagon, Boost Role of Joint Chiefs' Chairman, Clears Senate," *The Wall Street Journal*, May 8, 1986, 5.

5. Andrew C. Brown, "Unilever Fights Back in the U.S.," *Fortune*, May 26, 1986, 32–38, and "The Toughest Job in Business: How They're Remaking U.S. Steel," *Business Week*, February 25, 1985, 50–55.

6. Sara Delano, "Managing the Right Side of the Brain," *Inc.*, December 1982, 85–90.

7. "A Slimmed-Down Brunswick Is Proving Wall Street Wrong," *Business Week*, May 28, 1984, 90–98, and J. Vettner, "Bowling for Dollars," *Forbes*, September 12, 1983, 138.

8. John Child, *Organization: A Guide to Problems and Practice*, 2d ed. (London: Harper & Row, 1984).

9. Adam Smith, *The Wealth of Nations* (New York: Modern Library, 1937).

10. Paul D. Collins and Frank Hull, "Technology and Span of Control: Woodward Revisited," *Journal of Management Studies* 23 (March 1986), 143–164; David D. Van Fleet and Arthur G. Bedeian, "A History of the Span of Management," *Academy of Management Review* 2 (1977), 356–372; David D. Van Fleet, "Span of Management Research and Issues," *Academy of Management Review* 26 (1983), 546–552; C. W. Barkdull, "Span of Control—A Method of Evaluation," *Michigan Business Review* 15 (May 1963), 25–32; John Udall, "An Empirical Test of Hypotheses Relating to Span of Control," *Administrative Science Quarterly* 12 (1967), 420–439.

11. "Kaiser Aluminum Flattens Its Layers of Brass," *Business Week*, February 24, 1973, 81–84.

12. Edward R. Telling, "How Sears Restructured for Growth in Financial Services," *Management Review* (May 1986), 31–41.

13. "The Toughest Job in Business: How They're Remaking U.S. Steel," *Business Week*, Vol. 2882; pp. 50–56; Feb. 25, 1985.

14. James A. F. Stoner and Charles Wankel, *Management*, 3d ed. (Englewood Cliffs, N.J.: Prentice-Hall, 1986), 311–314.

15. Ernest Dale, *Organization* (New York: American Management Association, 1967), and Stoner and Wankel, *Management*, 312–313.

16. "How Sears Became a High Cost Operator," *Business Week*, February 16, 1981, 52–57, and Jeremy Main, "Kmart's Plan to Be Born Again," *Fortune*, September 21, 1981, 78–85.

17. W. Graham Astley, "Organization Size and Bureaucratic Structure," *Organization Studies* 6 (1985), 201–228, and Max Weber, *The Theory of Social and Economic Organization*, trans. A. M. Henderson and T. Parsons (New York: Free Press, 1927).

18. From a final rule published by the U.S. Department of Commerce, effective January 1, 1986.

19. Harold Geneen with Alvin Moscow, *Management* (Garden City, N.Y.: Doubleday, 1984), 81–82.

20. Lee Iacocca with William Novak, *Iacocca: An Autobiography* (New York: Phantom Books, 1984), 152–153.

21. Brody, "Can GM Manage?"

22. "How to Manage Entrepreneurs," *Business Week*, September 7, 1981, 66–69.

23. William J. Altier, "Task Forces—An Effective Management Tool," *Sloan Management Review* 27 (Spring 1986), 69–76.

24. Brody, "Can GM Manage?"

25. Henry Mintzberg, *The Structuring of Organizations* (Englewood Cliffs, N.J.: Prentice-Hall, 1979).

26. Ellen Wojahn, "Will the Company *Please* Come to Order," *Inc.*, March 1986, 78–86.

27. Paul R. Lawrence and Jay W. Lorsch, "New Managerial Job: The Integrator," *Harvard Business Review* (November/December 1967), 142–151.

28. Ron Winslow, "Utility Cuts Red Tape, Builds Nuclear Plant Almost on Schedule," *The Wall Street Journal*, February 22, 1984, 1, 18.

29. Tom Burns and G. M. Stalker, *The Management of Innovation* (London: Tavistock, 1961).

30. Paul R. Lawrence and Jay W. Lorsch, *Organization and Environment* (Homewood, Ill. Irwin, 1969).

31. Robert B. Duncan, "Characteristics of Organizational Environments and Perceived Environmental Uncertainty," *Administrative Science Quarterly* 17 (1972), 313–327; W. Alan Randolph and Gregory G. Dess, "The Congruence Perspective of Organization Design: A Conceptual Model and Multivariate Research Approach," *Academy of Management Review* 9 (1984), 114–127; Masoud Yasai-Ardekani, "Structural Adaptations to Environments," *Academy of Management Review* 11 (1986), 9–21.

32. Jolie B. Solomon and John Bussey, "Pressed by Its Rivals, Procter & Gamble Co. Is Altering Its Ways," *The Wall Street Journal*, May 20, 1985, 1–18, and John Smale, "Behind the Brands at P&G," *Harvard Business Review* 63 (November/December 1985), 78–90.

33. Astley, "Organization Size"; John B. Cullen, Kenneth S. Anderson, and Douglas D. Baker, "Blau's Theory of Structural Differentiation Revisited: A Theory of Structural Change or Scale?", *Academy of Management Journal* 29 (1986), 203–229; Richard L. Daft, *Organization Theory and Design*, 2d ed. (St. Paul, Minn.: West, 1986); Peter M. Blau and Richard Schoenherr, *The Structure of Organizations* (New York: Basic Books, 1971).

34. Robert E. Quinn and Kim Cameron, "Organizational Life Cycles and Shifting Criteria of Effectiveness: Some Preliminary Evidence," *Management Science* 29 (1983), 33–51, and John R. Kimberly, Robert H. Miles, and associates, *The Organizational Life Cycle* (San Francisco: Jossey-Bass, 1980).

35. Denise M. Rousseau and Robert A. Cooke, "Technology and Structure: The Concrete, Abstract, and Activity Systems of Organizations," *Journal of Management* 10 (1984), 345–361; Charles Perrow, "A Framework for the Comparative Analysis of Organizations," *American Sociological Review* 32 (1967), 194–208; Denise M. Rousseau, "Assessment of Technology in Organizations: Closed versus Open Systems Approaches," *Academy of Management Review* 4 (1979), 531–542.

36. Joan Woodward, *Industrial Organizations: Theory and Practice* (London: Oxford University Press, 1965), and Joan Woodward, *Management and Technology* (London: Her Majesty's Stationary Office, 1958).

37. Woodward, *Industrial Organizations*, vi.

38. Peter K. Mills and Thomas Kurk, "A Preliminary Investigation into the Influence of Customer-Firm Interface on Information Processing and Task Activity in Service Organizations," *Journal of Management* 12 (1986), 91–104; Peter K. Mills and Dennis J. Moberg, "Perspectives on the Technology of Service Operations," *Academy of Management Review* 7 (1982), 467–478; Charles A. Snyder, James F. Cox, and Richard R. Jesse, Jr., "A Dependent Demand Approach to Service Organization Planning and Control," *Academy of Management Review* 7 (1982), 455–466; Roger W. Schmenner, "How Can Service Businesses Survive and Prosper?", *Sloan Management Review* 27 (Spring 1986), 21–32.

39. Michael Withey, Richard L. Daft, and William C. Cooper, "Measures of Perrow's Work Unit Technology: An Empirical Assessment and a New Scale," *Academy of Management Journal* 25 (1983), 45–63.

40. Schmenner, "How Can Service Businesses Survive?"

41. Richard B. Chase and David A. Tansik, "The Customer Contact Model for Organization Design," *Management Science* 29 (1983), 1037–1050, and Gregory B. Northcraft and Richard B. Chase, "Managing Service Demand at the Point of Delivery," *Academy of Management Review* 10 (1985), 66–75.

42. "Marriott: The Fearless Host," *Dun's Business Month*, December 1984, 36–37, and Thomas Moore, "Marriott Grabs for More Rooms," *Fortune*, October 31, 1983, 107–122.

43. "Coming of Age at Lotus."

Chapter 9

1. Gary Jacobson and John Hillkirk, *Xerox: American Samurai* (New York: Macmillan, 1986).

2. Henry Mintzberg, *The Structuring of Organizations* (Englewood Cliffs, N.J.: Prentice-Hall, 1979).

3. The following discussion of structural alternatives draws heavily on Jay R. Galbraith, *Designing Complex Organizations* (Reading, Mass.: Addison-Wesley, 1973); Jay R. Galbraith, *Organization Design* (Reading, Mass.: Addison-Wesley, 1977); Robert Duncan, "What Is the Right Organization Structure?", *Organizational Dynamics* (Winter 1979), 59–80; J. McCann and Jay R. Galbraith, "Interdepartmental Relations," in *Handbook of Organizational Design*, eds. P. Nystrom and W. Starbuck (New York: Oxford University Press, 1981), 60–84.

4. Joel Kotkin, "The 'Smart-Team' at Compaq Computer," *Inc.*, February 1986, 48–56.

5. Ibid., 50.

6. Ibid., 56.

7. Susan Benner, "Three Companies in Search of an Author," *Inc.*, August 1984, 49–55.

8. William A. Bowen, "The Puny Payoff from Office Computers," *Fortune*, May 25, 1986, 20–24.

9. Based on "How Ford Hit Bulls-eye with Taurus," *Business Week*, June 30, 1986, 69–70, and Anne B. Fisher, "Ford Is Back on the Track," *Fortune*, December 23, 1985, 18–22.

10. Richard P. Rumelt, *Strategy, Structure, and Economic Performance* (Cambridge, Mass.: Harvard University Press, 1974).

11. Lucien Rhodes, "The Passion of Robert Swiggett," *Inc.*, April 1984, 121–140.

12. "Greyhound Splitting into Four to Go after Short-Haul Trade," *Chicago Tribune*, April 30, 1986, sec. 3, p. 8, and Rick Gladstone, "Highway Blues," *Bryan-College Station Eagle*, May 18, 1986, 6F.

13. Apple Computer, Inc., *Annual Report*, 1985. Reproduced with permission of Apple Computer, Inc.

14. Stanley M. Davis and Paul R. Lawrence, *Matrix* (Reading, Mass.: Addison-Wesley, 1977).

15. Ellen Kolton, "Team Players," *Inc.*, September 1984, 140–144, and personal communication from Howard Bennett, matrix vice-president.

16. Raymond E. Miles and Charles C. Snow, *Organizational Strategy, Structure, and Process* (New York: McGraw-Hill, 1978).

17. Paul R. Lawrence and Davis Dyer, *Renewing American Industry* (New York: Free Press, 1983).

18. Clem Morgello, "Booth: Creating a New Polaroid," *Dun's Business Month*, August 1985, 51–52.

19. Henry Mintzberg, *The Structuring of Organizations: A Synthesis of the Research* (Englewood Cliffs, N.J.: Prentice-Hall, 1979), 215–297, and Henry Mintzberg, "Organization Design: Fashion or Fit?", *Harvard Business Review* 59 (January/February 1981), 103–116.

20. Ibid.

21. From Kenneth L. Harris, "Organizing to Overhaul a Mess." Copyright © 1975 by the Regents of the University of California. Reprinted from *California Management Review*, vol. XVII, no. 3, pp. 40–49. By permission of the Regents.

22. Jacobson and Hillkirk, *Xerox*.

Chapter 10

1. Peter Petre, "How GE Bobbled the Factory of the Future," *Fortune*, November 11, 1985, 52–63.

2. Richard L. Daft, "Bureaucratic vs. Nonbureaucratic Structure in the Process of Innovation and Change," in *Perspectives in Organizational Sociology: Theory and Research*, ed. Samuel B. Bacharach (Greenwich, Conn.: JAI Press, 1982), 129–166.

3. Ricky W. Griffin, *Management* (Boston: Houghton Mifflin, 1984).

4. Ibid.

5. Andre L. Delbecq and Peter K. Mills, "Managerial Practices That Enhance Innovation," *Organizational Dynamics* 14 (Summer 1985), 24–34.

6. William Burpeau, Theresa McMurray, and Mike Clifford, "Sonyvision: A Report on the Sony Corporation" (Unpublished manuscript, Texas A&M University, 1986); "Sony Shifts Electronic Gears," *Time*, October 22, 1984, 79; John Burgess, "Sony Shifts Focus to 'Non-Consumers,'" *The Washington Post*, October 31, 1984, G1.

7. Attributed to Gregory Bateson in Andrew H. Van de Ven, "Central Problems in the Management of Innovation," *Management Science* 32 (1986), 595.

8. Charles Pearlman, "A Theoretical Model for Creativity," *Education* 103 (1983), 294–305, and Robert R. Godfrey, "Tapping Employees' Creativity," *Supervisory Management* (February 1986), 16–20.

9. Craig R. Hickman and Michael A. Silva, "How to Tap Your Creative Powers," *Working Woman*, September 1985, 26–30.

10. Gordon Vessels, "The Creative Process: An Open-Systems Conceptualization," *Journal of Creative Behavior* 16 (1982), 185–196, and Pearlman, "A Theoretical Model."

11. James Brian Quinn, "Managing Innovation: Controlled Chaos," *Harvard Business Review* 63 (May/June 1985), 73–84; Howard H. Stevenson and David E. Gumpert, "The Heart of Entrepreneurship," *Harvard Business Review* 63 (March/April 1985), 85–94; Marsha Sinetar, "Entrepreneurs, Chaos, and Creativity—Can Creative People Really Survive Large Company Structure?", *Sloan Management Review* 6 (Winter 1985), 57–62.

12. Rosabeth Moss Kanter, *The Change Masters* (New York: Simon and Schuster, 1983).

13. Ibid.

14. Ibid.

15. Paula Doody, Pat Hall, and Mike Nelson, "General Mills" (Unpublished paper, Texas A&M University, 1983), and "Look Who's Playing with Toys!", *Forbes*, December 15, 1981, 22.

16. Gifford Pinchot III, *Intrapreneuring* (New York: Harper & Row, 1985).

17. Pinchot, *Intrapreneuring;* Kanter, *The Change Masters.*

18. David H. Gobeli and William Rudelius, "Managing Innovation: Lessons from the Cardiac-Pacing Industry," *Sloan Management Review* 26 (Summer 1985), 29–43, and Jay R. Galbraith, "Designing the Innovating Organization," *Organizational Dynamics* (Winter 1982), 5–25.

19. Pinchot, *Intrapreneuring.*

20. Laura Landro, "The Movie 'Top Gun' and Deft Management Revive Paramount," *The Wall Street Journal*, July 14, 1986, 1, 11.

21. Pinchot, *Intrapreneuring.*

22. Peter F. Drucker, *Innovation and Entrepreneurship* (New York: Harper & Row, 1985).

23. Michael Tushman and David Nadler, "Organizing for Innovation," *California Management Review* 28 (Spring 1986), 74–92.

24. "How the PC Project Changed the Way IBM Thinks," *Business Week*, October 3, 1983, 86–90, and Erik Larson and Carrie Dolan, "Large Computer Firms Sprout Little Divisions for Good, Fast Work," *The Wall Street Journal*, August 19, 1983, 1, 11.

25. Tom Peters and Nancy Austin, *A Passion for Excellence: The Leadership Difference* (New York: Random House, 1985).

26. Joel Kotkin, "The Revenge of the Fortune 500," *Inc.*, August 1985, 39–44.

27. John P. Kotter and Leonard A. Schlesinger, "Choosing Strategies for Change," *Harvard Business Review* 57 (March/April 1979), 106–114.

28. Paul R. Lawrence, "How to Deal with Resistance to Change," in *Organizational Change and Development,* ed. G. W. Dalton, R. P. Lawrence, and L. E. Greiner, (Homewood, Ill.: Irwin & Dorsey, 1970), 181–197.

29. G. Zaltman and R. Duncan, *Strategies for Planned Change* (New York: Wiley Interscience, 1977).

30. Leonard M. Apcar, "Middle Managers and Supervisors Resist Moves to More Participatory Management," *The Wall Street Journal,* September 16, 1985, 25.

31. Kurt Lewin, *Field Theory in Social Science: Selected Theoretical Papers* (New York: Harper & Brothers, 1951).

32. Paul C. Nutt, "Tactics of Implementation," *Academy of Management Journal* 29 (1986), 230–261; Kotter and Schlesinger, "Choosing Strategies"; Richard L. Daft and Selwyn Becker, *Innovation in Organizations: Innovation Adoption in School Organizations* (New York: Elsevier, 1978); Richard Beckhard, *Organization Development: Strategies and Models* (Reading, Mass.: Addison-Wesley, 1969).

33. Patricia J. Paden-Bost, "Making Money Control a Management Issue," *Management Accounting* (November 1982), 48–56, and Apcar, "Middle Managers."

34. Apcar, "Middle Managers."

35. Jeremy Main, "The Trouble with Managing Japanese-Style," *Fortune,* April 2, 1984, 50–56.

36. Jabby Lowe, Greg Millsap, and Bill Breedlove, "International Harvester" (Unpublished manuscript, Texas A&M University, 1982), and Barbara Marsh, *A Corporate Tragedy: The Agony of International Harvester Company* (Garden City, N.Y.: Doubleday, 1985).

37. Richard L. Daft, *Organization Theory and Design* (St. Paul, Minn.: West, 1986), and Tom Burns and G. M. Stalker, *The Management of Innovation* (London: Tavistock Publications, 1961).

38. Richard L. Daft, "A Dual-Core Model of Organizational Innovation," *Academy of Management Journal* 21 (1978), 193–210, and Kanter, *The Change Masters.*

39. Harold J. Leavitt, "Applied Organizational Change in Industry: Structural, Technical, and Human Approaches," in *New Perspectives in Organization Research*, ed. W. W. Cooper, H. J. Leavitt, and M. W. Shelly II (New York: Wiley, 1964), 55–74.

40. Edwin Mansfield, J. Rapoport, J. Schnee, S. Wagner, and M. Hamburger, *Research and Innovation in Modern Corporations* (New York: Norton, 1971).

41. Andrew H. Van de Ven, "Central Problems in the Management of Innovation," *Management Science* 32 (1986), 590–607; Daft, *Organization Theory;* Science Policy Research Unit, University of Sussex, *Success and Failure in Industrial Innovation* (London: Centre for the Study of Industrial Innovation, 1972).

42. William L. Shanklin and John K. Ryans, Jr., "Organizing for High-Tech Marketing," *Harvard Business Review* 62 (November/December 1984), 164–171; Arnold O. Putnam, "A Redesign for Engineering," *Harvard Business Review* 63 (May/June 1985), 139–144.

43. Daft, *Organization Theory.*

44. F. Damanpour and W. M. Evan, "Organizational Innovation and Performance: The Problem of 'Organizational Lag'," *Administrative Science Quarterly* 29 (1984), 392–409.

45. Daft, "Bureaucratic vs. Nonbureaucratic Structure," and Daft, "A Dual-Core Model."

46. Mary Kay Ash, *Mary Kay on People Management* (New York: Warner, 1984), 75.

47. Edgar F. Huse and Thomas G. Cummings, *Organization Development and Change*, 3d ed. (St. Paul, Minn.: West, 1985).

48. Hugh J. Arnold and Daniel C. Feldman, *Organizational Behavior* (New York: McGraw-Hill, 1986).

49. The following assumptions are based on Huse and Cummings, *Organization Development,* and Arthur G. Bedeian, *Management* (Hinsdale, Ill.: Dryden Press, 1986).

50. Richard J. Boyle, "Wrestling with Jelly Fish," *Harvard Business Review* (January/February 1984), 74–83.

51. Ibid.

52. Kurt Lewin, "Frontiers in Group Dynamics: Concepts, Method, and Reality in Social Science," *Human Relations* 1 (1947), 5–41, and Huse and Cummings, *Organization Development.*

53. L. P. Bradford, J. R. Gibb, and K. D. Benne, *T-Group Theory and Laboratory Method* (New York: Wiley, 1964), 15–44.

54. David A. Nadler, *Feedback and Organizational Development: Using Data-Based Methods* (Reading, Mass.: Addison-Wesley, 1977).

55. Wendell L. French and Cecil H. Bell, Jr., *Organization Development: Behavioral Science Interventions for Organization Improvement,* 3d ed. (Englewood Cliffs, N.J.: Prentice-Hall, 1984).

56. Robert R. Blake and Jane Srygley Mouton, *The Managerial Grid III* (Houston: Gulf, 1985).

57. John M. Nicholas, "The Comparative Impact of Organization Development Interventions on Hard Criteria Measures," *Academy of Management Review* 7 (1982), 531–542; David E. Terpstra, "The Organization Development Evaluation Process: Some Problems and Proposals," *Human Resource Management* 20 (1981), 24–29; Jerry I. Porras and T. L. Berg, "The Impact of Organization Development," *Academy of Management Review* 3 (April 1978), 249–266.

58. Petre, "How GE Bobbled."

Chapter 11

1. Joseph P. Kahn and Susan Buchsbaum, "The Training Imperative," *Inc.*, March 1986, 119–120.

2. D. Kneale, "Working at IBM: Intense Loyalty in a Rigid Culture," *The Wall Street Journal,* April 7, 1986, 17.

3. S. L. Rynes, D. P. Schwab, and H. G. Heneman II, "The Role of Pay and Market Pay Variability in Job Application Decisions," *Organizational Behavior and Human Performance* 31 (1983), 353–364.

4. "Human Resources Managers Aren't Corporate Nobodies Any More," *Business Week*, December 2, 1985, 58–59, and Raymond E. Miles and Charles C. Snow, "Designing Strategic Human Resources Systems," *Organizational Dynamics* 13 (Summer 1984), 36–52.

5. D. Quinn Mills, "Planning with People in Mind," *Harvard Business Review* 63 (July/August 1985), 97–105.

6. Myron Magnet, "Help! My Company Has Just Been Taken Over," *Fortune,* July 9, 1984, 44–51; John Nielsen, "Management Layoffs Won't Quit," *Fortune,* October 28, 1985, 46–56; "Comparable Worth: It's Already Happening," *Business Week,* April 28, 1986, 52–56.

7. "Human Resources Managers Aren't Corporate Nobodies Any More," *Business Week,* December 2, 1985, 58–59.

8. L. Schein, "Current Issues in Human Resource Management," *The Conference Board Research Bulletin,* no. 190 (New York: The Conference Board, 1986).

9. James G. March and Herbert A. Simon, *Organizations* (New York: Wiley, 1958).

10. E. H. Burack and R. D. Smith, *Personnel Management: A Human Resource System Aproach* (New York: Wiley, 1982).

11. Ibid.

12. Electronic Data Systems Corporation, *1985 Annual Report*, 4–12.

13. Richard I. Henderson, *Compensation Management: Rewarding Performance*, 4th ed. (Reston, Va.: Reston, 1985).

14. Details concerning these techniques can be found in Burack and Smith, *Personnel Management*.

15. Ibid.

16. D. Quinn Mills, "Planning with People in Mind," *Harvard Business Review* 63 (July/August 1985), 97–105, and USAir, *1985 Annual Report*, 5.

17. J. W. Boudreau and S. L. Rynes, "Role of Recruitment in Staffing Utility Analysis," *Journal of Applied Psychology* 70 (1985), 354–366.

18. P. B. Doeringer and M. J. Piore, *Internal Labor Markets and Manpower Analysis* (Lexington, Mass.: Heath, 1971).

19. P. Farish, "HRM Update: Referral Results," *Personnel Administrator* 31 (1986), 22.

20. P. G. Swaroff, L. A. Barclay, and A. R. Bass, "Recruiting Sources: Another Look," *Journal of Applied Psychology* 70 (1985), 720–728.

21. J. P. Wanous, *Organizational Entry* (Reading, Mass.: Addison-Wesley, 1980).

22. Ibid.

23. Paula Popovich and John P. Wanous, "The Realistic Job Preview as a Persuasive Communication," *Academy of Management Review* 7 (1982), 570–578.

24. For a discussion of the pros and cons of RJPs, see J. Breaugh, "Realistic Job Previews: A Critical Appraisal and Future Research Directions," *Academy of Management Review* 8 (1983), 612–619; G. M. McEvoy and W. F. Cascio, "Strategies for Reducing Employee Turnover: A Meta-Analysis," *Journal of Applied Psychology* 70 (1985), 342–353; M. P. Miceli, "Why Realistic Job Previews Cannot Meet Our Unrealistically High Expectations" (Proceedings of the 43rd Annual Meeting of the Academy of Management, 1983); S. L. Premack and J. P. Wanous, "A Meta-Analysis of Realistic Job Preview Experiments," *Journal of Applied Psychology* 70 (1985), 706–719; S. L. Rynes, "Recruitment, Organizational Entry, and Early Work Adjustment" (Working paper, Cornell University, 1986, to appear in *Handbook of Industrial and Organizational Psychology*, ed. M. D. Dunnette; M. P. Miceli, "Effects of Realistic Job Previews on Newcomer Affect and Behavior: An Operant Perspective," *Journal of Organizational Behavior Management* (1988) (in press).

25. L. Z. Lorber and R. Kirk, "Direction Shifts with Bias Ruling," *Resource* 1 (August 1986), 6.

26. Ibid.

27. P. W. Thayer, "Somethings Old, Somethings New," *Personnel Psychology* 30 (1977), 513–524.

28. J. Ledvinka, *Federal Regulation of Personnel and Human Resource Management* (Boston: Kent, 1982); Civil Rights Act, Title VII, 42 U.S.C. Section 2000e *et seq.* (1964).

29. *Griggs v. Duke Power Company*, 401 U.S. 424, 91 S. Ct. 849, 3 FEP Cases 175.

30. For other examples of possibly objectionable questions, see R. S. Lowell and J. A. DeLoach, "Equal Employment Opportunity: Are You Overlooking the Application Form?" *Personnel* 59 (1982), 49–55.

31. The material in this section is largely drawn from R. D. Arvey and J. E. Campion, "The Employment Interview: A Summary and Review of Recent Research," *Personnel Psychology* 35 (1982), 281–322.

32. A. Brown, "Employment Tests: Issues without Clear Answers," *Personnel Administrator* 30 (1985), 43–56.

33. Ibid.

34. Larry Reibstein, "More Firms Use Personality Tests for Entry-Level, Blue-Collar Jobs," *The Wall Street Journal*, January 16, 1986, 25.

35. For example, see R. R. Reilly, S. Zedeck, and M. L. Tenopyr, "Validity and Fairness of Physical Ability Tests for Predicting Performance in Craft Jobs," *Journal of Applied Psychology* 64 (1979), 262–274.

36. W. C. Byham, "Assessment Centers for Spotting Future Managers," *Harvard Business Review* (July/August 1970), 150–167.

37. G. F. Dreher and P. R. Sackett, "Commentary: A Critical Look at Some Beliefs about Assessment Centers," in *Perspectives on Employee Staffing and Selection*, ed. G. F. Dreher and P. R. Sackett (Homewood, Ill.: Irwin, 1983), 258–265.

38. Reibstein, "Personality Tests."

39. K. N. Wexley and G. P. Latham, *Developing and Training Human Resources in Organizations* (Glenview, Ill.: Scott, Foresman, 1981).

40. G. Dessler, *Personnel Management*, 2d ed. (Reston, Va.: Reston, 1981).

41. L. Lien, "Reviewing Your Training and Development Activities," *Personnel Journal* 58 (1979), 791–807.

42. Wexley and Latham, *Developing and Training*.

43. Ibid.

44. Ibid.

45. Barbara Koeth, "The Making of Merchandising Executives: Macy's," *Management Review* (June 1985), 28–34.

46. H. J. Bernardin and R. W. Beatty, *Performance Appraisal: Assessing Human Behavior at Work* (Boston: Kent, 1984).

47. Ibid.

48. "Behaviorally Anchored Rating Scales," *Small Business Report* (February 1986), 71–77.

49. G. P. Latham, K. N. Wexley and E. D. Pursell, "Training Managers to Minimize Rating Errors in the Observation of Behavior," *Journal of Applied Psychology* 60 (1975), 550–555.

50. John H. Zimmerman, "Human Resource Management at MCI," *Management Review* (April 1986), 49–51.

51. M. G. Miner, *Management Performance Appraisal Programs*, PPF Survey No. 104 (Washington, D.C.: Bureau of National Affairs, 1974).

52. D. Cederblom, "The Performance Appraisal Interview: A Review, Implications, and Suggestions," *Academy of Management Review* 7 (1982), 219–227.

53. Ibid.

54. N. R. F. Maier, *The Appraisal Interview: Three Basic Approaches* (La Jolla, Cal.: University Associates, 1976).

55. H. J. Bernardin and P. C. Smith, "A Clarification of Some Issues Regarding the Development and Use of Behaviorally Anchored Rating Scales," *Journal of Applied Psychology* 66 (1981), 458–463.

56. D. L. Stone and E. F. Stone, "The Effects of Feedback Favorability and Feedback Consistency on Self-Perceived Task Competence and Perceived Feedback Accuracy," (Proceedings of the 43rd Annual Meeting of the Academy of Management, 1983), 178–182.

57. Henderson, *Compensation Management*.

58. Renée F. Broderick and George T. Milkovich, "Pay Planning, Organization Strategy, Structure and 'Fit': A Prescriptive Model of Pay" (Paper presented at the 45th Annual Meeting of the Academy of Management, San Diego, August 1985).

59. George E. Mellgard, "Achieving External Competitiveness through Survey Use," in *Handbook of Wage and Salary Administration,* ed. Milton L. Rock (New York: McGraw-Hill, 1984), Chapter 34.

60. Jay R. Schuster, "Compensation Plan Design," *Management Review* (May 1985), 21–25.

61. L. R. Burgess, *Wage and Salary Administration* (Columbus, Ohio: Merrill, 1984), and E. J. McCormick, *Job Analysis: Methods and Applications* (New York: AMACOM, 1979).

62. B. M. Bass and G. V. Barrett, *People, Work, and Organizations: An Introduction to Industrial and Organizational Psychology,* 2d ed. (Boston: Allyn & Bacon, 1981), and D. Doverspike, A. M. Carlisi, G. V. Barrett, and R. A. Alexander, "Generalizability Analysis of a Point-Method Job Evaluation Instrument," *Journal of Applied Psychology* 68 (1983), 476–483.

63. For descriptions of available surveys, see Henderson, *Compensation Management,* and M. L. Rock, ed., *Handbook of Wage and Salary Administration* (New York: McGraw-Hill, 1984), Chapters 32–42.

64. U.S. Chamber of Commerce, *Employee Benefits 1983* (Washington, D.C.: U.S. Chamber of Commerce, 1984).

65. D. C. Stone and E. G. S. Reitz, "Health Care Cost Containment and Employee Relations," *Personnel Administrator* 29 (1984), 27–33.

66. "New Benefits for New Lifestyles," *Business Week,* February 11, 1980, 111–112.

67. J. A. Haslinger, "Flexible Compensation: Getting a Return on Benefit Dollars," *Personnel Administrator* 30 (1985), 39–46, 224.

68. M. Wilson, G. B. Northcraft, and M. A. Neale, "The Perceived Value of Fringe Benefits," *Personnel Psychology* 38 (1985), 309–320.

69. R. B. Dunham and R. A. Formisano, "Designing and Evaluating Employee Benefit Systems," *Personnel Administrator* 27 (1982), 29–35.

70. Section 8(d) of the National Labor Relations Act, as amended June 23, 1947, 61 Stat. 136.

71. Integrated Job Evaluation at Continental Can, IR-RR 291, March 8, 1983, pp. 9–15.

72. "Why David Murdock Is So Afraid of a Union," *Business Week,* October 14, 1985, 43.

73. Equal Pay Act, 29 U.S.C. Section 206(d)(1), 1963.

74. "Exit Interviews: An Overlooked Information Source," *Small Business Report* (July 1986), 52–55.

75. Kahn and Buchsbaum, "The Training Imperative."

Chapter 12

1. Arthur M. Louis, "The Controversial Boss of Beatrice," *Fortune,* July 22, 1985, 110–116.

2. "The Newsmakers," *Business Week,* April 18, 1986, 194; D. D. Van Fleet, "Changing Patterns of Significant Authors on Leadership and Managerial Effectiveness," *Journal of Management* 1 (1975), 39–44; R. M. Stogdill, "The Evolution of Leadership Theory," *Proceedings of the Academy of Management* (1975), 4–6.

3. Henry Mintzberg, *Power in and around Organizations* (Englewood Cliffs, N.J.: Prentice-Hall, 1983); Jeffrey Pfeffer, *Power in Organizations* (Marshfield, Mass.: Pitman, 1981); R. L. Kahn and E. Boulding, eds., *Power and Conflict in Organizations* (New York: Basic Books, 1964); M. L. Tushman,

"A Political Approach to Organizations: A Review and a Rationale," *Academy of Management Review* 2 (1977), 207.

4. J. R. P. French, Jr., and B. Raven, "The Bases of Social Power," in *Group Dynamics,* ed. D. Cartwright and A. F. Zander (Evanston, Ill.: Row, Peterson, 1960), 607–623. For examples of possibly dysfunctional uses of power, see Steven Flax, "The Toughest Bosses in America," *Fortune,* August 6, 1984, 18–23.

5. G. A. Yukl and T. Taber, "The Effective Use of Managerial Power," *Personnel* (March/April 1983), 37–44.

6. G. A. Yukl, *Leadership in Organizations* (Englewood Cliffs, N.J.: Prentice-Hall, 1981), and S. C. Kohs and K. W. Irle, "Prophesying Army Promotion," *Journal of Applied Psychology* 4 (1920), 73–87.

7. W. O. Jenkins, "A Review of Leadership Studies with Particular Reference to Military Problems," *Psychological Bulletin* 44 (1947), 54–79.

8. H. H. Jennings, "Leadership: A Dynamic Redefinition," *Journal of Educational Sociology* 17 (1944), 431–433; R. M. Stogdill, "Personal Factors Associated with Leadership: A Survey of the Literature," *Journal of Psychology* 25 (1948), 35–71; C. A. Gibb, "Leadership," in *Handbook of Social Psychology,* ed. G. Lindzey (Cambridge, Mass.: Addison-Wesley, 1954); R. D. Mann, "A Review of the Relationship between Personality and Performance in Small Groups," *Psychological Bulletin* 56 (1959), 241–270; L. F. Carter, "Leadership and Small Group Behavior," in *Group Relations at the Crossroads,* eds. M. Sherif and M. O. Lindzey (New York: Harper, 1953).

9. R. M. Stogdill, *Handbook of Leadership* (New York: Free Press, 1974).

10. R. Albanese and D. D. Van Fleet, *Organizational Behavior: A Managerial Viewpoint* (Hinsdale, Ill.: Dryden Press, 1983).

11. During the studies, a third form of leader behavior occurred when one of the leaders forgot his role and did essentially nothing—laissez-faire or "hands-off" leadership. This obviously was ineffective and has not become part of the general theory of leadership. For reports of these studies, see K. Lewin, "Field Theory and Experiment in Social Psychology: Concepts and Methods," *American Journal of Sociology* 44 (1939), 868–896; K. Lewin and R. Lippitt, "An Experimental Approach to the Study of Autocracy and Democracy: A Preliminary Note," *Sociometry* 1 (1938), 292–300; K. Lewin, R. Lippitt, and R. K. White, "Patterns of Aggressive Behavior in Experimentally Created Social Climates," *Journal of Social Psychology* 10 (1939), 271–301.

12. R. K. White and R. Lippitt, *Autocracy and Democracy: An Experimental Inquiry* (New York: Harper, 1960).

13. R. Tannenbaum and W. H. Schmidt, "How to Choose a Leadership Pattern," *Harvard Business Review* 36 (1958), 95–101.

14. F. A. Heller and G. A. Yukl, "Participation, Managerial Decision-Making and Situational Variables," *Organizational Behavior and Human Performance* 4 (1969), 227–241; F. A. Heller, *Managerial Decision-Making: A Study of Leadership Styles and Power-Sharing among Senior Managers* (London: Tavistock, 1971); F. A. Heller, "Leadership, Decision Making, and Contingency Theory," *Industrial Relations* 12 (1973), 183–199.

15. Jack Hyde, "Henry H. Henley, Jr.," *SKY,* April 1985, 70–76.

16. C. A. Schriesheim and B. J. Bird, "Contributions of the Ohio State Studies to the Field of Leadership," *Journal of Management* 5 (1979), 135–145, and C. L. Shartle, "Early Years of the Ohio State University Leadership Studies," *Journal of Management* 5 (1979), 126–134.

17. R. Likert, "From Production- and Employee-Centeredness to Systems 1-4," *Journal of Management,* 5 (1979), 147–156.

18. P. C. Nystrom, "Managers and the High-High Leader Myth," *Academy of Management Journal* 21 (1978), 325–331; L. L. Larson, J. G. Hunt, and R. N. Osborn, "The Great High-High Leader Behavior Myth: A Lesson from Occam's Razor," *Academy of Management Journal* 19 (1976), 628–641; E. W. Skinner, "Relationships between Leadership Behavior Patterns and Organizational-Situational Variables," *Personnel Psychology* 22 (1969), 489–494; E. A. Fleishman and E. F. Harris, "Patterns of Leadership Behavior Related to Employee Grievances and Turnover," *Personnel Psychology* 15 (1962), 43–56.

19. R. Likert, "From Production- and Employee-Centeredness to Systems 1-4," *Journal of Management* 5 (1979), 147–156.

20. Robert R. Blake and Jane S. Mouton, *The Managerial Grid* (Houston: Gulf, 1964).

21. Jasper Dorsey, "S. Truett Cathy," *SKY,* February 1985, 45–50.

22. Julie Salamon, "Acquisitive Chief of Buffalo Savings Buys Time, Cleans House—and Makes Big Splash," *The Wall Street Journal,* April 23, 1982, 33, 36.

23. F. E. Fiedler, "Assumed Similarity Measures as Predictors of Team Effectiveness," *Journal of Abnormal and Social Psychology* 49 (1954), 381–388; F. E. Fiedler, *Leader Attitudes and Group Effectiveness* (Urbana, Ill.: University of Illinois Press, 1958); F. E. Fiedler, *A Theory of Leadership Effectiveness* (New York: McGraw-Hill, 1967).

24. F. E. Fiedler and M. M. Chemers, *Leadership and Effective Management* (Glenview, Ill.: Scott, Foresman, 1974).

25. F. E. Fiedler, "Engineer the Job to Fit the Manager," *Harvard Business Review* 43 (1965), 115–122, and F. E. Fiedler, M. M. Chemers, and L. Mahar, *Improving Leadership Effectiveness: The Leader Match Concept* (New York: Wiley, 1976).

26. Brian O'Reilly, "A Body Builder Lifts Greyhound," *Fortune,* October 28, 1985, 124–134.

27. R. Singh, "Leadership Style and Reward Allocation: Does Least Preferred Co-worker Scale Measure Task and Relation Orientation?", *Organizational Behavior and Human Performance* 27 (1983), 178–197, and D. Hosking, "A Critical Evaluation of Fiedler's Contingency Hypotheses," *Progress in Applied Psychology* 1 (1981), 103–154.

28. M. G. Evans, "The Effects of Supervisory Behavior on the Path-Goal Relationship," *Organizational Behavior and Human Performance* 5 (1970), 277–298; M. G. Evans, "Leadership and Motivation: A Core Concept," *Academy of Management Journal* 13 (1970), 91–102; B. S. Georgopoulos, G. M. Mahoney, and N. W. Jones, "A Path-Goal Approach to Productivity," *Journal of Applied Psychology* 41 (1957), 345–353.

29. Robert J. House, "A Path-Goal Theory of Leader Effectiveness," *Administrative Science Quarterly* 16 (1971), 321–338.

30. M. G. Evans, "Leadership," in *Organizational Behavior,* ed. S. Kerr (Columbus, Ohio: Grid, 1974), 230–233.

31. Robert J. House and Terrence R. Mitchell, "Path-Goal Theory of Leadership," *Journal of Contemporary Business* (Autumn 1974), 81–97.

32. "The Team Pushing Fireman's Up the Ladder," *Business Week,* August 4, 1986, 50–51.

33. Charles Greene, "Questions of Causation in the Path-Goal Theory of Leadership," *Academy of Management Journal* 22 (March, 1979), 22–41, and C. A. Schriesheim and M. A. von Glinow, "The Path-Goal Theory of Leadership: A Theoretical and Empirical Analysis," *Academy of Management Journal* 20 (1977), 398–405.

34. V. H. Vroom and P. W. Yetton, *Leadership and Decision-Making* (Pittsburgh: University of Pittsburgh Press, 1973).

35. R. H. G. Field, "A Test of the Vroom-Yetton Normative Model of Leadership," *Journal of Applied Psychology* (October 1982), 523–532, and R. H. G. Field, "A Critique of the Vroom-Yetton Contingency Model of Leadership Behavior," *Academy of Management Review* 4 (1979), 249–257.

36. Edwin A. Locke, David M. Schweiger, and Gary P. Latham, "Participation in Decision Making: When Should It Be Used?" *Organizational Dynamics* 14 (Winter 1986), 65–79; Arthur G. Jago, "Leadership: Perspectives in Theory and Research," *Management Science* 28 (1982), 315–336; Madeline E. Heilman, Harvey A. Hornstein, Jack H. Cage, and Judith K. Herschlag, "Reactions to Prescribed Leader Behavior as a Function of Role Perspective: The Case of the Vroom-Yetton Model," *Journal of Applied Psychology* (February 1984), 50–60; Arthur G. Jago and Victor H. Vroom, "Some Differences in the Incidence and Evaluation of Participative Leader Behavior," *Journal of Applied Psychology* (December 1982), 776–783; V. H. Vroom and A. G. Jago, "On the Validity of the Vroom-Yetton Model," *Journal of Applied Psychology* 63 (1978), 151–162; A. G. Jago and V. H. Vroom, "An Evaluation of Two Alternatives to the Vroom-Yetton Normative Model," *Academy of Management Journal* 23 (1980), 347–355.

37. Tom Richman, "One Man's Family," *INC.,* November 1983, 151–156.

38. S. Kerr and J. M. Jermier, "Substitutes for Leadership: Their Meaning and Measurement," *Organizational Behavior and Human Performance* 22 (1978), 375–403, and Jon P. Howell and Peter W. Dorfman, "Leadership and Substitutes for Leadership among Professional and Nonprofessional Workers," *Journal of Applied Behavioral Science* 22 (1986), 29–46.

39. The terms *transactional* and *transformational* come from James M. Burns, *Leadership* (New York: Harper & Row, 1978), and Bernard M. Bass, "Leadership: Good, Better, Best," *Organizational Dynamics* 13 (Winter 1985), 26–40.

40. Robert J. House, "Research Contrasting the Behavior and Effects of Reputed Charismatic vs. Reputed Non-Charismatic Leaders" (Paper presented as part of a symposium, "Charismatic Leadership: Theory and Evidence," Academy of Management, San Diego, 1985). See also Gary A. Yukl and David D. Van Fleet, "Cross-Situational, Multimethod Research on Military Leader Effectiveness," *Organizational Behavior and Human Performance* (January 1982), 87–108.

41. Bass, "Leadership," 35.

42. Wisocki, "The Chief's Personality."

43. Noel M. Tichy and David O. Ulrich, "The Leadership Challenge—A Call for the Transformational Leader," *Sloan Management Review* 26 (Fall 1984), 59–68.

44. G. A. Yukl, *Leadership in Organizations* (Englewood Cliffs, N.J.: Prentice-Hall, 1981), 79–82; David McClelland, *Power: The Inner Experience* (New York: Irvington, 1975); David McClelland and D. H. Burnham, "Power Is the Great Motivator," *Harvard Business Review* (March/April 1976), 100–110.

45. Louis, "The Controversial Boss."

Chapter 13

1. David Osborne, "The Most Entrepreneurial City in America," *INC.,* September 1985, 54–62.

2. "Meet the Savvy Supersalesmen," *Fortune*, February 4, 1985, 56–62; Michael Brody, "Meet Today's Young American Worker," *Fortune*, November 11, 1985, 90–98; Tom Richman, "Meet the Masters. They Could Sell You Anything . . . ," *INC.*, March 1985, 79–86.

3. Richard M. Steers and Lyman W. Porter, eds., *Motivation and Work Behavior*, 3d ed. (New York: McGraw-Hill, 1983).

4. Terence R. Mitchell, "Motivation: New Directions for Theory, Research, and Practice," *Academy of Management Review* 7 (1982), 80–88.

5. Steers and Porter, *Motivation*.

6. Frederick W. Taylor, *Scientific Management* (New York: Harper & Row, 1947), 39–73.

7. J. F. Rothlisberger and W. J. Dickson, *Management and the Worker* (Cambridge, Mass.: Harvard University Press, 1939).

8. W. A. Medina, "Managing People to Perform," *The Bureaucrat* (Spring 1985), 52.

9. Abraham F. Maslow, "A Theory of Human Motivation," *Psychological Review* 50 (1943), 370–396.

10. Clayton Alderfer, *Existence, Relatedness and Growth* (New York: Free Press, 1972).

11. Frederick Herzberg, "One More Time: How Do You Motivate Employees?" *Harvard Business Review* (January/February 1968), 53–62.

12. Ellen Wojan, "Will the Company Please Come to Order," *INC.*, March 1986, 78–86.

13. David C. McClelland, *Human Motivation* (Glenview, Ill.: Scott, Foresman, 1985).

14. David C. McClelland, "The Two Faces of Power," in *Organizational Psychology*, ed. D. A. Colb, I. M. Rubin, and J. M. McIntyre (Englewood Cliffs, N.J.: Prentice-Hall, 1971), 73–86.

15. J. Stacy Adams, "Injustice in Social Exchange," in *Advances in Experimental Social Psychology*, 2d ed., ed. L. Berkowitz (New York: Academic Press, 1965), and J. Stacy Adams, "Toward an Understanding of Inequity," *Journal of Abnormal and Social Psychology* (November 1963), 422–436.

16. Ray V. Montagno, "The Effects of Comparison to Others and Primary Experience on Responses to Task Design," *Academy of Management Journal* 28 (1985), 491–498, and Robert P. Vecchio, "Predicting Worker Performance in Inequitable Settings," *Academy of Management Review* 7 (1982), 103–110.

17. "The Double Standard That's Setting Worker against Worker," *Business Week*, April 8, 1985, 70–71.

18. George Gendron, "Steel Man Ken Iverson," *INC.*, April 1986, 41–48.

19. Victor H. Vroom, *Work and Motivation* (New York: Wiley, 1964); B. S. Gorgopoulos, G. M. Mahoney, and N. Jones, "A Path-Goal Approach to Productivity," *Journal of Applied Psychology* 41 (1957), 345–353; E. E. Lawler III, *Pay and Organizational Effectiveness: A Psychological View* (New York: McGraw-Hill, 1981).

20. Richard L. Daft and Richard M. Steers, *Organizations: A Micro/Macro Approach* (Glenview, Ill.: Scott, Foresman, 1986).

21. "The Rich Get Richer at Merrill Lynch," *Fortune*, March 31, 1986, 93.

22. H. Richlin, *Modern Behaviorism* (San Francisco: Freeman, 1970), and B. F. Skinner, *Science and Human Behavior* (New York: Macmillan, 1953).

23. Tom Peters and Nancy Austin, *A Passion for Excellence: The Leadership Difference* (New York: Random House, 1985), 267.

24. L. M. Sarri and G. P. Latham, "Employee Reaction to Continuous and Variable Ratio Reinforcement Schedules Involving a Monetary Incentive," *Journal of Applied Psychology* 67 (1982), 506–508, and R. D. Pritchard, J. Hollenback, and P. J. DeLeo, "The Effects of Continuous and Partial Schedules of Reinforcement on Effort, Performance, and Satisfaction," *Organizational Behavior and Human Performance* 25 (1980), 336–353.

25. "Creating Incentives for Hourly Workers," *INC.*, July 1986, 89–90.

26. W. Clay Hamner, "Reinforcement Theory and Contingency Management in Organizational Settings," in *Organizational Behavior in Management: A Contingency Approach*, rev. ed., Henry L. Tosi and W. Clay Hamner (New York: Wiley, 1977), 93–112.

27. "Job Rotation Keeps Swissair Flying High," *Management Review*, August 1985, 10.

28. J. Richard Hackman and Greg R. Oldham, *Work Redesign* (Reading, Mass.: Addison-Wesley, 1980), and J. Richard Hackman and Greg Oldham, "Motivation through the Design of Work: Test of a Theory," *Organizational Behavior and Human Performance* 16 (1976), 250–279.

29. J. Richard Hackman, Greg R. Oldham, R. Janson, and K. Purdy, "A New Strategy for Job Enrichment," *California Management Review* 17 (1975), 57–71, and Daft and Steers, *Organizations*, 173–174.

30. Hugh J. Arnold and Daniel C. Feldman, *Organizational Behavior* (New York: McGraw-Hill, 1986), 344–345.

31. Robert McGaugh, "How to Win the Class Struggle," *Forbes*, November 3, 1986, 153–156.

32. "Workers Love Four-Day Week," *Eugene Register-Guard*, July 22, 1984, 4C.

33. J. W. Annas, "The Up-Front Carrot," *Compensation Review* (1985), 45–49.

34. Arnold and Feldman, *Organizational Behavior*.

35. Osborne, "The Most Entrepreneurial City."

Chapter 14

1. Michael H. Dale, "How We Rebuilt Jaguar in the U.S.," *Fortune*, April 28, 1986, 110–120; and Minda Zetlin, "John Egan: Tough Leadership Turns Jaguar Around," *Management Review* (May 1986), 20–22.

2. Thomas F. O'Boyle and Carol Hymowitz, "More Corporate Chiefs Seek Direct Contact with Staff, Customers," *The Wall Street Journal*, February 27, 1985, 1, 12.

3. Elizabeth B. Drew, "Profile: Robert Strauss," *The New Yorker* May 7, 1979, 55–70.

4. Henry Mintzberg, *The Nature of Managerial Work* (New York: Harper & Row, 1973).

5. Fred Luthans and Janet K. Larsen, "How Managers Really Communicate," *Human Relations* 39 (1986), 161–178; and Larry E. Penley and Brian Hawkins, "Studying Interpersonal Communication in Organizations: A Leadership Application," *Academy of Management Journal* 28 (1985), 309–326.

6. D. K. Berlo, *The Process of Communication* (New York: Holt, Rinehart and Winston, 1960), 24.

7. Nelson W. Aldrich, Jr., "Lines of Communication," *INC.*, June 1986, 140–144.

8. Bruce K. Blaylock, "Cognitive Style and the Usefulness of Information," *Decision Sciences* 15 (Winter 1984), 74–91.

9. Richard L. Daft and Richard M. Steers, *Organizations: A Micro/Macro Approach* (Glenview, Ill.: Scott, Foresman, 1986).

10. James R. Wilcox, Ethel M. Wilcox, and Karen M. Cowan, "Communicating Creatively in Conflict Situations," *Management Solutions* (October 1986), 18–24.

11. Richard L. Daft and Robert H. Lengel, "Organizational Information Requirements, Media Richness and Structural Design," *Management Science* 32 (May 1986), 554–572, and Richard L. Daft and Robert H. Lengel, "Information Richness: A New Approach to Managerial Behavior and Organization Design," in *Research in Organizational Behavior*, vol. 6, eds. Barry Staw and Larry L. Cummings (Greenwich, Conn. JAI Press, 1984), 191–233.

12. Richard L. Daft, Robert H. Lengel, and Linda Klebe Trevino, "The Relationship among Message Equivocality, Media Selection, and Manager Performance: Implications for Information Support Systems," *MIS Quarterly* (1987), in press.

13. Harold Geneen with Alvin Moscow, *Managing* (New York: Doubleday, 1984), 46–47.

14. I. Thomas Sheppard, "Silent Signals," *Supervisory Management* (March 1986), 31–33.

15. Albert Mehrabian, *Silent Messages* (Belmont, Cal.: Wadsworth, 1971), and Albert Mehrabian, "Communicating without Words," *Psychology Today*, September 1968, 53–55.

16. Sheppard, "Silent Signals."

17. Mark Knapp, *Nonverbal Communication in Human Interaction* (New York: Holt, Rinehart and Winston, 1972), 9–12.

18. Gerald M. Goldhaber, *Organizational Communication*, 4th ed. (Dubuque, Iowa: Wm. C. Brown, 1986), 189.

19. Ibid.

20. Thomas J. Peters and Robert H. Waterman, Jr., *In Search of Excellence* (New York: Harper & Row, 1982), 254–255.

21. Corwin P. King, "Keep Your Communication Climate Healthy," *Personnel Journal* (April 1978), 206.

22. Daft and Steers, *Organizations*, and Daniel Katz and Robert Kahn, *The Social Psychology of Organizations*, 2d ed. (New York: Wiley, 1978).

23. J. G. Miller, "Living Systems: The Organization," *Behavioral Science* 17 (1972), 69.

24. Michael J. Glauser, "Upward Information Flow in Organizations: Review and Conceptual Analysis," *Human Relations* 37 (1984), 613–643, and "Upward/Downward Communication: Critical Information Channels," *Small Business Report* (October 1985), 85–88.

25. Mary P. Rowe and Michael Baker, "Are You Hearing Enough Employee Concerns?", *Harvard Business Review* 62 (May/June 1984), 127–135; W. H. Read, "Upward Communication in Industrial Hierarchies," *Human Relations* 15 (February 1962), 3–15; Daft and Steers, *Organizations*.

26. Jonathan Tasini, "Letting Workers Help Handle Workers' Gripes," *Business Week*, September 15, 1986, 82–86.

27. Jacqueline Kaufman, "Carol Taber, Working Woman," *Management Review* (October 1986), 60–61.

28. Thomas F. O'Boyle and Carol Hymowitz, "More Corporate Chiefs Seek Direct Contact with Staff, Customers," *The Wall Street Journal*, February 27, 1985, 1, 12.

29. Peters and Waterman, *In Search of Excellence*, and Tom Peters and Nancy Austin, *A Passion for Excellence: The Leadership Difference* (New York: Random House, 1985).

30. Lois Therrien, "How Ztel Went from Riches to Rags," *Business Week*, June 17, 1985, 97–100.

31. O'Boyle and Hymowitz, "More Corporate Chiefs."

32. Keith Davis and John W. Newstrom, *Human Behavior at Work: Organizational Behavior*, 7th ed. (New York: McGraw-Hill, 1985).

33. Donald B. Simmons, "The Nature of the Organizational Grapevine," *Supervisory Management* (November 1985), 39–42.

34. Goldhaber, *Organizational Communication*, and Philip V. Louis, *Organizational Communication*, 3d ed. (New York: Wiley, 1987).

35. Simmons, Organizational Grapevine," and Davis and Newstrom, *Human Behavior*.

36. E. M. Rogers and R. A. Rogers, *Communication in Organizations* (New York: Free Press, 1976), and A. Bavelas and D. Barrett, "An Experimental Approach to Organization Communication," *Personnel* 27 (1951), 366–371.

37. This discussion is based on Daft and Steers, *Organizations*.

38. Bavelas and Barrett, "An Experimental Approach," and M. E. Shaw, *Group Dynamics: The Psychology of Small Group Behavior* (New York: McGraw-Hill, 1976).

39. Richard L. Daft and Norman B. Macintosh, "A Tentative Exploration into the Amount and Equivocality of Information Processing in Organizational Work Units," *Administrative Science Quarterly* 26 (1981), 207–224.

40. Michael L. Tushman, "Technical Communication in Research and Development Laboratories: The Impact of Project Work Characteristics," *Academy of Management Journal* 21 (1978), 624–645.

41. James A. F. Stoner and Charles Wankel, *Management*, 3d ed. (Englewood Cliffs, N.J.: Prentice-Hall, 1986).

42. Janet Fulk and Sirish Mani, "Distortion of Communication in Hierarchical Relationships," in *Communication Yearbook*, vol. 9, ed. M. L. McLaughlin (Beverly Hills, Cal.: Sage, 1986), 483–510.

43. Dale, "How We Rebuilt Jaguar," and Zetlin, "John Egan."

Chapter 15

1. "Teamwork Was the Key in Developing Our System," *Modern Materials Handling*, August 5, 1983, 42–47.

2. A. Fuhreman, S. Dreshler, and G. Burlingame, "Conceptualizing Small Group Process," *Small Group Behavior* 15 (1984), 427–440, and Linda N. Jewell and H. Joseph Reitz, *Group Effectiveness in Organizations* (Glenview, Ill.: Scott, Foresman, 1981).

3. Deborah L. Gladstein, "Groups in Context: A Model of Task Group Effectiveness," *Administrative Science Quarterly* 29 (1984), 499–517.

4. Thomas J. Peters and Robert H. Waterman, Jr., *In Search of Excellence* (New York: Harper & Row, 1982), 132–134.

5. Susan Benner, "Three Companies in Search of an Author," *INC.*, August 1984, 49–55.

6. For research findings on group size, see M. E. Shaw, *Group Dynamics*, 3d ed. (New York: McGraw-Hill, 1981); J. W. O'Dell, "Group Size and Emotional Interaction," *Journal of Personality and Social Psychology* 8 (1968), 75–78; B. Burelson and G. Steiner, *Human Behavior: An Inventory of Scientific Findings* (New York: Harcourt Brace, 1964); G. Manners, "Another Look at Group Size, Group Problem-Solving and Member Consensus," *Academy of Management Journal* 18 (1975), 715–724; Richard M. Steers and Susan R. Rhodes, "Major Influences on Employee Attendance: A Process Model," *Psychological Bulletin* 63 (1978), 391–407; Lyman W. Porter and Richard M. Steers, "Organizational, Work, and Personal Factors in Employee Turnover and Absenteeism," *Psychological Bulletin* 80 (1973), 151–176.

7. K. D. Benne and P. Sheats, "Functional Roles of Group Members," *Journal of Social Issues* 4 (1948), 41–49, and R. F. Bales, *SYMOLOG Case Study Kit* (New York: Free Press, 1980).

8. Robert A. Baron, *Behavior in Organizations*, 2d ed. (Boston: Allyn & Bacon, 1986).

9. Ibid.

10. Based on David L. Bradford and Allan R. Cohen, *Managing for Excellence* (New York: Wiley, 1984), 178–179.

11. Bruce W. Tuckman and Mary Ann C. Jensen, "Stages of Small-Group Development Revisited," *Group and Organizational Studies* 2 (1977), 419–427, and Bruce W. Tuckman, "Developmental Sequences in Small Groups," *Psychological Bulletin* 63 (1965), 384–399. See also Jewell and Reitz, *Group Effectiveness.*

12. Blanca Reimer, "A Dose of Dissent Won't Damage the Fed," *Business Week*, April 7, 1986, 38.

13. Shaw, *Group Dynamics.*

14. Daniel C. Feldman and Hugh J. Arnold, *Managing Individual and Group Behavior in Organizations* (New York: McGraw-Hill, 1983).

15. Ricky W. Griffin, *Management* (Boston: Houghton Mifflin, 1984).

16. Joel Kotkin, "The 'Smart Team' at Compaq Computer," *INC.*, February 1986, 48–56.

17. Dorwin Cartwright and Alvin Zander, *Group Dynamics: Research and Theory*, 3d ed. (New York: Harper & Row, 1968), and Elliot Aronson, *The Social Animal* (San Francisco: W. H. Freeman, 1976).

18. Stanley E. Seashore, *Group Cohesiveness in the Industrial Work Group* (Ann Arbor, Mich.: Institute for Social Research, 1954).

19. R. Schrank, *Ten Thousand Working Days* (Cambridge, Mass.: MIT Press, 1978), 7.

20. J. Richard Hackman, "Group Influences on Individuals," in *Handbook of Industrial and Organizational Psychology*, ed. M. Dunnette (Chicago: Rand McNally, 1976).

21. Kenneth Bettenhausen and J. Keith Murnighan, "The Emergence of Norms in Competitive Decision-Making Groups," *Administrative Science Quarterly* 30 (1985), 350–372.

22. The following discussion is based on Daniel C. Feldman, "The Development and Enforcement of Group Norms," *Academy of Management Review* 9 (1984), 47–53.

23. Hugh J. Arnold and Daniel C. Feldman, *Organizational Behavior* (New York: McGraw-Hill, 1986).

24. Reprinted by permission of the *Harvard Business Review.* Excerpts from "Wrestling with Jellyfish" by Richard J. Boyle (January/February 1984). Copyright © 1984 by the President and Fellows of Harvard College; all rights reserved.

25. Stephen P. Robbins, *Managing Organizational Conflict: A Nontraditional Approach* (Englewood Cliffs, N.J.: Prentice-Hall, 1974).

26. Dean Tjosvold, "Making Conflict Productive," *Personnel Administrator* 29 (June 1984), 121.

27. This discussion is based in part on Richard L. Daft, *Organization Theory and Design* (St. Paul, Minn.: West, 1986), Chapter 11.

28. Based on Mary Jean Parson, "The Peer Conflict," *Supervisory Management* (May 1986), 25–31.

29. Robbins, *Managing Organizational Conflict.*

30. I. D. Steiner, "Models for Inferring Relationships between Group Size and Potential Group Productivity," *Behavioral Science* 11 (1966), 273–283.

31. This discussion draws heavily from Feldman and Arnold, *Managing Behavior*, 486–488.

32. R. B. Zajonc, "Social Facilitation," *Science* 149 (1965), 269–274.

33. Andrew S. Grove, "How to Make Confrontation Work for You," *Fortune*, July 23, 1984, 73–74. © 1984 Time Inc. All rights reserved.

34. Robert Albanese and David D. Van Fleet, "Rational Behavior in Groups: The Free-Riding Tendency," *Academy of Management Review* 10 (1985), 244–255.

35. Baron, *Behavior in Organizations.*

36. H. J. Reitz, *Behavior in Organizations*, 2d ed. (Homewood, Ill.: Irwin, 1981).

37. Based on Feldman and Arnold, *Managing Behavior.*

38. "Committees: Their Role in Management Today," *Management Review* 46 (October 1957), 4–10.

39. Ethel C. Glenn and Elliott Pood, "Groups Can Make the Best Decisions If You Lead the Way," *Supervisory Management* (December 1978), 2–6.

40. Tom Peters and Nancy Austin, *A Passion for Excellence: The Leadership Difference* (New York: Random House, 1985).

41. "How Power Will Be Balanced on Saturn's Shop Floor," *Business Week*, August 5, 1985, 65–66.

42. "Teamwork Was the Key."

Chapter 16

1. Rod Willis, "Harley-Davidson Comes Roaring Back," *Management Review* (March 1986), 20–27.

2. Ralph H. Kilmann, Mary J. Saxton, and Roy Serpa, "Issues in Understanding and Changing Culture," *California Management Review* 28 (Winter 1986), 87–94, and Linda Smircich, "Concepts of Culture and Organizational Analysis," *Administrative Science Quarterly* 28 (1983), 339–358.

3. Edgar H. Schein, "Coming to a New Awareness of Organizational Culture," *Sloan Management Review* (Winter 1984), 3–16, and Vijay Sathe, "Implications of Corporate Culture: A Manager's Guide to Actions," *Organizational Dynamics* (Autumn 1983), 5–23.

4. "Corporate Culture," *Business Week*, October 27, 1980, 148–160.

5. "15 Great Companies to Work For," *Management Review* (August 1985), 39–43.

6. Susan Benner, "Culture Shock," *INC.*, August 1985, 73–82.

7. William Burpeau, Theresa McMurray, and Mike Clifford, "Sonyvision: A Report on the Sony Corporation" (Unpublished manuscript, Texas A&M University, 1985).

8. Charlotte B. Sutton, "Richness Hierarchy of the Cultural Network: The Communication of Corporate Values" (Unpublished manuscript, Texas A&M University, 1985).

9. Terrence E. Deal and Allan A. Kennedy, *Corporate Cultures: The Rights and Rituals of Corporate Life* (Reading, Mass.: Addison-Wesley, 1982).

10. Edward E. Carlson, "Visible Management at United Airlines," *Harvard Business Review* 53 (July/August 1975), 90–97.

11. Richard L. Daft, *Organization Theory and Design* (St. Paul, Minn.: West, 1986).

12. Harrison M. Trice and Janice M. Beyer, "Studying Organizational Cultures Through Rites and Ceremonials," *Academy of Management Review* 9 (1984), 653–669.

13. Thomas J. Peters and Robert H. Waterman, Jr., *In Search of Excellence* (New York: Harper & Row, 1982).

14. Michael Rosen, "Breakfast at Spiro's: Dramaturgy and Dominance," *Journal of Management* 11 (1985), 31–48.

15. This discussion is based on Deal and Kennedy, *Corporate Cultures*, Chapter 6.

16. Carey Quan Jelernter, "Corporate Culture," *The Seattle Times*, June 5, 1986, sec. D, pp. 1, 8.

17. Carey Quan Jelernter, "Safeco: Success Depends Partly on Fitting the Mold," *The Seattle Times*, June 5, 1986, sec. D. p. 8.

18. Jay W. Lorsch, "Managing Culture: The Invisible Barrier to Strategic Change," *California Management Review* 28 (Winter 1986), 95–109, and Howard Schwartz and Stanley M.

Davis, "Matching Corporate Culture and Business Strategy," *Organizational Dynamics* (Summer 1981), 30–48.

19. Joseph Nocera, "Death of a Computer," *Texas Monthly* (April 1984), 136–139, 216–231.

20. William G. Ouchi, *Theory Z: How American Business Can Meet the Japanese Challenge* (Reading, Mass.: Addison-Wesley, 1981), and Richard Pascale and Anthony Athos, *The Art of Japanese Management* (New York: Warner Books, 1981).

21. William G. Ouchi and Alfred M. Jaeger, "Type Z Organizations: Stability in the Midst of Mobility," *Academy of Management Review* 3 (1978), 305–314.

22. Ibid.

23. Art Gemmell, "Fujitsu's Cross-Cultural Style," *Management Review* (June 1986), 7–8; James Cook, "We Started from Ground Zero," *Forbes,* March 12, 1984, 104.

24. Thomas J. Peters and Robert H. Waterman, Jr., *In Search of Excellence* (New York: Harper & Row, 1982).

25. Tom Peters, "An Excellent Question," *INC.,* December 1984, 155–162.

26. "Ross Perot's Crusade," *Business Week,* October 6, 1986, 60–65.

27. "A Slimmed-Down Brunswick Is Proving Wall Street Wrong," *Business Week,* May 28, 1984, 90–98.

28. "Pepsi's Marketing Magic: Why Nobody Does It Better," *Business Week,* February 10, 1986, 52–57.

29. Peters and Waterman, *In Search of Excellence,* 287.

30. Louis Kraar, "Roy Ash Is Having Fun at Addressogrief-Multigrief," *Fortune,* February 27, 1978, 47–52, and Thomas J. Peters, "Symbols, Patterns, and Settings: An Optimistic Case for Getting Things Done," *Organizational Dynamics* (Autumn 1978), 3–23.

31. Peters and Waterman, *In Search of Excellence.*

32. Tom Peters and Nancy Austin, *A Passion for Excellence: The Leadership Difference* (New York: Random House, 1985).

33. Peters and Austin, *A Passion for Excellence,* 278.

34. Karl E. Weick, "Cognitive Processes in Organizations," in *Research in Organizations,* vol. 1, ed. B. M. Staw (Greenwich, Conn.: JAI Press, 1979).

35. Bill Saporito, "Scott Isn't Lumbering Anymore," *Fortune,* September 30, 1985, 48–55.

36. Donald C. Hambrick, "Turnaround Strategies," in *Handbook of Business Strategy,* ed. W. D. Guth (Boston: Warren, Gorham & Lamont, 1985), 10.1–10.32, and Thomas L. Wheelen and J. David Hunger, *Strategic Management and Business Policy,* 2d ed. (Reading, Mass.: Addison-Wesley, 1986).

37. Paul R. Lawrence and Davis Dyer, *Renewing American Industry* (New York: Free Press, 1983).

38. Joel Kotkin, "A Commitment Forged in Steel," *INC.,* June 1983, 82–93.

39. Willis, "Harley-Davidson."

Chapter 17

1. Craig R. Waters, "Quality Begins at Home," *Inc.,* August 1985, 68–71.

2. Ann M. Morrison, "A Big Baker that Won't Live by Bread Alone," *Fortune,* September 7, 1981, 70–76.

3. John Curley, "How a Clerk Built Up a Brokerage Business by Hook or by Crook," *The Wall Street Journal,* February 7, 1985, 1, 22.

4. Kenneth A. Merchant, *Control in Business Organizations* (Marshfield, Mass.: Pitman, 1985), and Robert J. Mockler, *The Management Control Process* (Englewood Cliffs, N.J.: Prentice-Hall, 1972).

5. Bill Saporito, "Allegheny Ludlum Has Steel Figured Out," *Fortune,* June 25, 1984, 40–44.

6. Peter Lorange, Michael F. Scott Morton, and Sumantra Ghoshal, *Strategic Control* (St. Paul, Minn.: West, 1986), Chapter 1.

7. Ibid.

8. Ibid.

9. Mike Tharp, "Easy-Going Nike Adopts Stricter Controls to Pump Up Its Athletic-Apparel Business," *The Wall Street Journal,* November 6, 1984, p. 29.

10. William H. Newman, *Constructive Control* (Englewood Cliffs, N.J.: Prentice-Hall, 1975).

11. Edward P. Gardner, "A Systems Approach to Bank Credential Management and Supervision: The Utilization of Feed Forward Control," *Journal of Management Studies* 22 (1985), 1–24.

12. Myron Magnet, "Managing by Mystique at Tandem Computers," *Fortune,* June 28, 1982, 84–91.

13. James H. Donnelly, Jr., James L. Gibson, and John M. Ivancevich, *Fundamentals of Management* 5th ed. (Dallas: Business Publications, 1984).

14. Lorange, Scott Morton, and Ghoshal, *Strategic Control,* 105–107.

15. Ellen Wojahn, "A Touch of Class," *Inc.,* September 1983, 79–86.

16. William G. Ouchi, "Markets, Bureaucracies, and Clans," *Administrative Science Quarterly* 25 (1980), 129–141, and B. R. Baligia and Alfred M. Jaeger, "Multinational Corporations: Control Systems and Delegation Issues," *Journal of International Business Studies* (Fall 1984), 25–40.

17. Nestor K. Oballe II, "Organizational/Managerial Control Processes: A Reconceptualization of the Linkage between Technology and Performance," *Human Relations* 37 (1984), 1047–1062.

18. "Corporate Big Brother Is Watching You," *Dun's Business Month,* January 1984, 36–39.

19. Burt Schorr, "Schools Use New Ways to Be More Efficient and Enforce Discipline," *The Wall Street Journal,* December 15, 1983, 1, 16.

20. Richard Pascale, "Fitting New Employees into the Company Culture," *Fortune,* May 28, 1984, 28–40.

21. Richard E. Walton, "From Control to Commitment in the Workplace," *Harvard Business Review* (March/April 1985), 76–84.

22. Ellen Wojahn, "Will the Company Please Come to Order," *Inc.,* March 1986, 78–86.

23. Cortlandt Cammann and David A. Nadler, "Fit Control Systems to Your Managerial Style," *Harvard Business Review* (January/February 1976), 65–72.

24. Richard J. Schonberger, "Production Workers Bear Major Quality Responsibility in Japanese Industry," *Industrial Engineering* (December 1982), 34–40.

25. A. V. Feigenbaum, *Total Quality Control: Engineering and Management* (New York: McGraw-Hill, 1961).

26. Philip B. Crosby, *Quality Is Free: The Art of Making Quality Certain* (New York: McGraw-Hill, 1979).

27. Schonberger, "Production Workers."

28. Crosby, *Quality Is Free.*

29. Schonberger, "Production Workers."

30. Edward E. Lawler III and Susan A. Mohrman, "Quality Circles after the Fad," *Harvard Business Review* (January/February 1985), 65–71, and George Munchus III, "Employer-Employee Based Quality Circles in Japan: Human Resource Policy Implications for American Firms," *Academy of Management Review* 8 (1983), 255–261.

31. Mark Bomster, "Quality Circles Help Solve Job Problems," *Houston Chronicle,* May 4, 1986, sec. 5, p. 12.

32. Robert Wood, Frank Hull, and Koya Azumi, "Evaluating Quality Circles: The American Application," *California Management Review* 26 (Fall 1983), 37–53, and Gregory P. Shea, "Quality Circles: The Danger of Bottled Change," *Sloan Management Review* 27 (Spring 1986), 33–46.

33. "Doing Things Right at GE and Sonoco," *Management Review* (September 1985), 11–12.

34. James A. F. Stoner and Charles Wankel, *Management* (Englewood Cliffs, N.J.: Prentice-Hall, 1986), and Peter Lorange and Declan Murphy, "Considerations in Implementing Strategic Control," *Journal of Business Strategy* 4 (Spring 1984), 27–35.

35. W. H. Read, "Upward Communication in Industrial Hierarchies," *Human Relations* 15 (February 1962), 3–15, and Michelle J. Glauser, "Factors Which Facilitate or Impede Upward Communication in Organizations" (Paper presented at the Academy of Management meeting, New York, August 1982).

36. Ibid.

37. Cammann and Nadler, "Fit Control Systems."

38. David A. Garbin, "Quality on the Line," *Harvard Business Review,* 61 (September-October 1983), pp. 65–75.

39. Waters, "Quality Begins at Home."

Chapter 18

1. Matthew Berke, "Elling Bros. Got Costs under Control," *INC.,* January 1982, 45–50.

2. David A. Garvin, "Quality on the Line," *Harvard Business Review* (September/October 1983), 65–75.

3. E. G. Flamholtz, "Accounting, Budgeting and Control Systems in Their Organizational Context: Theoretical and Empirical Perspectives," *Accounting, Organizations and Society* 8 (1983), 153–169.

4. Richard L. Daft and Norman B. Macintosh, "The Nature and Use of Formal Control Systems for Management Control and Strategy Implementation," *Journal of Management* 10 (1984), 43–66.

5. Bruce G. Posner, "How to Stop Worrying and Love the Next Recession," *INC.,* April 1986, 89–95.

6. Michael F. van Breda, "Integrating Capital and Operating Budgets," *Sloan Management Review* (Winter 1984), 49–58.

7. Arthur W. Holmes and Wayne S. Overmeyer, *Basic Auditing,* 5th ed. (Homewood, Ill.: Irwin, 1976).

8. John J. Welsh, "Pre-Acquisition Audit: Verifying the Bottom Line," *Management Accounting* (January 1983), 32–37.

9. Lee Iacocca with William Novak, *Iacocca: An Autobiography* (New York: Bantam Books, 1984), 92–94. Used with permission.

10. Daft and Macintosh, "Formal Control Systems," and Robert N. Anthony, John Dearden, and Norton M. Bedford, *Management Control Systems,* 5th ed. (Homewood, Ill.: Irwin, 1984).

11. This discussion is based on Peter Lorange, Michael F. Scott Morton, and Sumantra Ghoshal, *Strategic Control* (St. Paul, Minn.: West, 1986), Chapter 4; Anthony, Dearden, and Bedford, *Management Control Systems;* Richard F. Vancil, "What Kind of Management Control Do You Need?" *Harvard Business Review* (March/April 1973), 75–85.

12. Lorange et al., *Strategic Control.*

13. Vancil, "What Kind of Management Control?"

14. Anthony, Dearden, and Bedford, *Management Control Systems.*

15. Participation in budget setting has been described in a number of studies, including Peter Brownell, "Leadership Style, Budgetary Participation and Managerial Behavior," *Accounting, Organizations and Society* 8 (1983), 307–321; Paul J. Carruth and Thurrell O. McClandon, "How Supervisors React to 'Meeting the Budget' Pressure," *Management Accounting* 66 (November 1984), 50–54; Chris Argyris, "Human Problems with Budgets," *Harvard Business Review* 31 (January 1953), 97–110; Selwyn W. Becker and David Green, Jr., "Budgeting and Employee Behavior," *Journal of Business* (October 1962), 392–402.

16. Neil C. Churchill, "Budget Choice: Planning vs. Control," *Harvard Business Review* (July/August 1984), 150–164.

17. Peter A. Pyhrr, "Zero-Based Budgeting," *Harvard Business Review* (November/December 1970), 111–121, and Peter A. Pyhrr. *Zero-Based Budgeting: A Practical Management Tool for Evaluating Expense* (New York: Wiley, 1973).

18. "Zero-Based Budgeting: Justifying All Business Activity from the Ground Up," *Small Business Report* (November 1983), 20–25, and M. Dirsmith and S. Jablonsky, "Zero-Based Budgeting as a Management Technique and Political Strategy," *Academy of Management Review* 4 (1979), 555–565.

19. Based on Tom Richman, "Talking Cost," *INC.,* February 1986, 105–108.

20. Randy Schuler, *Personnel and Human Resource Management* (St. Paul, Minn.: West, 1984).

21. George S. Odiorne, "MBO: A Backward Glance," *Business Horizons* 21 (October 1978), 14–24.

22. W. Giegold, *Volume II: Objective Setting and the MBO Process* (New York: McGraw-Hill, 1978).

23. "Delegation," *Small Business Report* (July 1986), 71–75.

24. Jack N. Kondrasuk, "Studies in MBO Effectiveness," *Academy of Management Review* 6 (1981), 419–430, and Jan P. Muczyk, "Dynamics and Hazards of MBO Applications," *Personnel Administrator* 24 (May 1979), 52.

25. John Ivancevich, J. Timothy McMahon, J. William Streidl, and Andrew D. Szilagyi, "Goal Setting: The Tenneco Approach to Personnel Development and Management Effectiveness," *Organizational Dynamics* (Winter 1978), 48–80.

26. "Delegation," *Small Business Report* (July 1986), 71–75, and Robert C. Ford and Frank S. McLaughlin, "Avoiding Disappointment in MBO Programs," *Human Resource Management* 21 (Summer 1982), 44–49.

27. Sherrie Posesorski, "Here's How to Put Statistical Process Control to Work for You," *Canadian Business* (December 1985), p. 163.

28. Harlan R. Jessup, "Front Line Control," *Supervisory Management* (October 1985), 12–20.

29. Berke, "Elling Bros."

Chapter 19

1. Jonathan B. Levine, "Bank of America Rushes into the Information Age," *Business Week,* April 15, 1985, 110–112.

2. Steven L. Mandell, *Computers and Data Processing* (St. Paul, Minn.: West, 1985), and Richard L. Daft and Norman B. Macintosh, "A Tentative Exploration into the Amount and Equivocality of Information Processing in Organizational Work Units," *Administrative Science Quarterly* 26 (1981), 207–224.

3. Craig R. Waters, "Franchise Capital of America," *INC.,* September 1984, 99–108.

4. Charles A. O'Reilly III, "Variations in Decision Makers' Use of Information Sources: The Impact of Quality and Accessibility of Information" *Academy of Management Journal* 25

(1982), 756–771; R. H. Gregory and R. L. Van Horn, "Value and Cost of Information," in *Systems Analysis Techniques,* ed. J. Daniel Cougar and Robert W. Knapp (New York: Wiley, 1974), 473–489; Niv Ahituv and Seev Neumann, *Principles of Information Systems for Management,* 2d ed. (Dubuque, Iowa: Wm. C. Brown, 1986).

5. Erik Larson, "After Long Hesitancy, Police Departments Use Computers More," *The Wall Street Journal,* November 12, 1984, 1, 25.

6. Michael W. Miller, "Computers Keep Eye on Workers and See If They Perform Well," *The Wall Street Journal,* June 3, 1985, 1, 12.

7. W. L. Harrison, *Computers and Information Processing* (St. Paul: West, 1985).

8. Raymond McLeod, *Management Information Systems,* 2d ed. (Chicago: Science Research Associates, 1983).

9. John C. Camillus and Albert L. Lederer, "Corporate Strategy and the Design of Computerized Information Systems," *Sloan Management Review* 26 (Spring 1985), 35–42.

10. "Maintaining Profitability," *Viewpoint,* March/April 1983.

11. Gary Geipel, "At Today's Supermarket, the Computer Is Doing It All," *Business Week,* August 11, 1986, 64–65, and Tom Richman, "Supermarket," *INC.,* October 1985, 115–120.

12. Eric D. Carlson, "Decision Support Systems: Personal Computing Services for Managers," *Management Review* (January 1977), 5–11.

13. David Davis, "Computers and Top Management," *Sloan Management Review* 25 (Spring 1984), 63–67.

14. Jack T. Hogue and Hugh J. Watson, "Management's Role in the Approval and Administration of Decision Support Systems," *MIS Quarterly* (June 1983), 15–26.

15. Mary Bralove, "Direct Data," *The Wall Street Journal,* January 12, 1983, 1.

16. Robert I. Benjamin, John F. Rockart, Michael S. Scott Morton, and John Wyman, "Information Technology: A Strategic Opportunity," *Sloan Management Review* 25 (Spring 1984), 3–10.

17. "Let a Computer Do the Walking (and the Talking)," *Working Woman,* April 1986, 104.

18. Henry C. Mishkoff, "The Network Nation Emerges," *Management Review* (August 1986), 29–31.

19. Robert Johansen and Christine Bullen, "What to Expect from Teleconferencing," *Harvard Business Review* 62 (March/April 1984), 164–174, and John Tyson, "Cutting Costs with Video; Making Hay with Horses," *Management Review* (January 1986), 5–6.

20. Melinda Grenier Guiles, "Bulletin Boards Go High-Tech at More Firms," *The Wall Street Journal,* April 9, 1986, 29.

21. T. J. O'Leary and Brian K. Williams, *Computers and Information Processing* (Menlo Park, Cal.: Benjamin Cummings, 1985).

22. Emily T. Smith, "Turning an Expert's Skills into Computer Software," *Business Week,* October 7, 1985, 104–108; David E. Whiteside, "Artificial Intelligence Finally Hits the Desktop," *Business Week,* June 9, 1986, 68–70; Mary A. C. Fallon, "Losing an Expert? Hire an Expert System," Bryan-College Station *Eagle,* September 7, 1986, sec. E, p. 1.

23. Efraim Turban and Paul R. Watkins, "Integrating Expert Systems and Decision Support Systems," *MIS Quarterly* 10 (June 1986), 1, 121–138, and John F. Magee, "What Information Technology Has in Store for Managers," *Sloan Management Review* 26 (Winter, 1985), 45–49.

24. Karl W. Wiig, "AI: Management's Newest Tool," *Management Review* (August 1986), 24–28.

25. James A. F. Stoner and Charles Wankel, *Management,* 3d ed. (Englewood Cliffs, N.J.: Prentice-Hall, 1986), 638.

26. Joel Dreyfuss, "Networking: Japan's Latest Computer Craze," *Fortune,* July 7, 1986, 94–96.

27. Michael W. Miller, "In This Futuristic Office, Intimacy Exists between Workers Separated by 500 Miles," *The Wall Street Journal,* June 27, 1986, 29; and "Office Automation," *American Way Magazine Special Section,* 1985, 16.

28. Davis, "Computers."

29. Peter Nulty, "How Personal Computers Change Managers' Lives," *Fortune,* September 3, 1984, 38–48, and John Dearden, "Will the Computer Change the Job of Top Management?" *Sloan Management Review* (Fall 1983), 57–60.

30. Sara Kiesler, "The Hidden Messages in Computer Networks," *Harvard Business Review* 64 (January/February 1986), 46–60.

31. Nulty, "Personal Computers."

32. John P. Murray, "How an Information Center Improved Productivity," *Management Accounting* (March 1984), 38–44; "Information Centers: A Great Resource If Run Properly," *Dun's Business Month,* October 1985, 109–110; "Helping Decision Makers Get at Data," *Business Week,* September 13, 1982, 118–123; "Chief Information Officer," *Small Business Report* (December 1986), 30–34.

33. E. B. Swanson, "Information in Organization Theory: A Review" (*Information Systems* working paper, UCLA, 1986); John F. Magee, "What Information Technology Has in Store for Managers," *Sloan Management Review* (Winter 1985), 45–49; John Child, "New Technology and Developments in Management Organization," *OMEGA* 12 (1984), 211–223.

34. "Office Automation Restructures Business," *Business Week,* October 8, 1984, 118–125.

35. Henry C. Mishkoff, "The Network Nation Emerges," *Management Review* (August 1986), 29–31.

36. Raymond E. Miles and Charles C. Snow, "Organizations: New Concepts for New Forms," *California Management Review* 28 (Spring 1986), 62–73, and "And Now, the Post-Industrial Corporation," *Business Week,* March 3, 1986, 64–74.

37. Boas Shamir and Ilan Salomon, "Work-at-Home and the Quality of Working Life," *Academy of Management Review* 10 (1985), 455–464, and Miriam K. Mills, "Teleconferencing—Managing the 'Invisible Worker'," *Sloan Management Review* 25 (Summer 1984), 63–67.

38. Laton McCartney, "Companies Get a Competitive Edge Using Strategic Computer Systems," *Dun's Business Month,* December 1985, 13–14, and Robert I. Benjamin, John F. Rockart, Michael S. Scott Morton, and John Wyman, "Information Technology: A Strategic Opportunity," *Sloan Management Review* 25 (Spring 1984), 3–10.

39. John F. Rockart and Michael S. Scott Morton, "Implications of Changes in Information Technology for Corporate Strategy," *Interfaces* 14 (January/February 1984), 84–95.

40. Catherine L. Harris, "Information Power," *Business Week,* October 14, 1985, 108–114; Gregory L. Parsons, "Information Technology: A New Competitive Weapon," *Sloan Management Review* 25 (Fall 1983), 3–14; Michael E. Porter and Victor E. Millar, "How Information Gives You Competitive Advantage," *Harvard Business Review* 63 (July/August, 1985), 149–160.

41. Porter and Millar, "Competitive Advantage"; Harris, "Information Power"; Parsons, "Information Technology"; John Diebold, "Taking Stock of the Information Age," *Management Review* (September 1985), 18–21; Camillus and Lederer, "Corporate Strategy."

42. Joan O'C. Hamilton, "For Drug Distributors, Information is the Rx for Survival," *Business Week*, October 14, 1985, p. 116; J. F. Rockart and M. S. Scott Morton, "Implications of Changes in Information Technology for Corporate Strategy," *Interfaces*, 14 (January-February 1984), pp. 84–95.

43. Dearden, "Will the Computer Change?"

44. Dearden, "Will the Computer Change?"; Richard L. Van Horn, "Don't Expect Too Much from Your Computer System," *The Wall Street Journal*, October 25, 1982, 24.

45. Michael Newman and David Rosenberg, "Systems Analysts and the Politics of Organizational Control," *OMEGA* 13 (1985), 393–406.

46. David R. Hampton, *Management*, 3d ed. (New York: McGraw-Hill, 1986), 723–725.

47. Ibid. 725.

48. John F. Rockart and Adam D. Crescenzi, "Engaging Top Management in Information Technology," *Sloan Management Review* 25 (Summer 1984), 3–16.

49. Andrew C. Boynton and Robert W. Zmud, "An Assessment of Critical Success Factors," *Sloan Management Review* 25 (Summer 1984), 17–27, and John F. Rockart, "Chief Executives Define Their Own Data Needs," *Harvard Business Review* 57 (March/April 1979), 81–93.

50. Levine, "Bank of America."

Chapter 20

1. Douglas R. Sease, "How U.S. Companies Devise Ways to Meet Challenge from Japan," *The Wall Street Journal*, September 16, 1986, 1, 19.

2. Craig R. Waters, "New! Improved! Manufacturing," *INC.*, January 1986, 73–76.

3. Charles G. Andrew and George A. Johnson, "The Crucial Importance of Production and Operations Management," *Academy of Management Review* 7 (1982), 143–147.

4. Everett E. Adam, "Towards a Typology of Production and Operations Management Systems," *Academy of Management Review* 8 (1983), 365–375.

5. James D. Thompson, *Organizations in Action* (New York: McGraw-Hill, 1967).

6. Gregory B. Northcraft and Richard B. Chase, "Managing Service Demand at the Point of Delivery," *Academy of Management Review* 10 (1985), 66–75, and Richard B. Chase and David A. Tansik, "The Customer Contact Model for Organization Design," *Management Science* 29 (1983), 1037–1050.

7. Harlan C. Meal, "Putting Production Decisions Where They Belong," *Harvard Business Review* (March/April 1984), 102–111.

8. Ibid.

9. W. Skinner, "Manufacturing: The Missing Link in Corporate Strategy," *Harvard Business Review* (May/June 1969), 136–145.

10. Waters, "New! Improved!."

11. R. H. Hayes and S. C. Wheelwright, *Restoring Our Competitive Edge: Competing Through Manufacturing* (New York: Wiley, 1984).

12. T. Hill, *Manufacturing Strategy: The Strategic Management of the Manufacturing Function* (London: Macmillan, 1985).

13. Rod Willis, "Harley-Davidson Comes Roaring Back," *Management Review* (March 1986) 20–27.

14. Robert Kreitner, *Management*, 3d ed. (Boston: Houghton Mifflin, 1986).

15. John S. DeMott, "Manufacturing Is in Flower," *Time*, March 26, 1984, 50–51.

16. Sumer C. Aggarwal, "MRP, JIT, OPT, FMS?", *Harvard Business Review* 63 (September/October 1985), 8–16, and Paul Ranky, *The Design and Operation of Flexible Manufacturing Systems* (New York: Elsevier, 1983).

17. Kurt H. Schaffir, "Information Technology for the Manufacturer," *Management Review* (November 1985), 61–62.

18. R. J. Schonberger, *Japanese Manufacturing Techniques: Nine Hidden Lessons in Simplicity* (New York: Free Press, 1982).

19. Craig R. Waters, "Profit and Loss," *INC.*, April 1985, 103–112.

20. "Materials Requirement Planning," *Small Business Report* (June 1985), 37–40.

21. Sumer C. Aggarwol, "MRP, JIT, OPT, FMS?", *Harvard Business Review* 63 (September/October 1985), 8–16.

22. "MRP 'Drives' AS/RS—Cuts Inventory $12 Million," *Modern Materials Handling*, August 5, 1983, 38–41.

23. "Manufacturing Resource Planning," *Small Business Report* (August 1985), 37–40, and Kenneth A. Fox, "MRP-II Providing a Natural 'Hub' for Computer-Integrated Manufacturing System," *Industrial Engineering* (October 1984), 44–50.

24. R. W. Hall, *Zero Inventories* (Homewood, Ill.: Dow Jones-Irwin, 1983).

25. Dexter Hutchins, "Having a Hard Time with Just-in-Time," *Fortune*, June 9, 1986, 64–66.

26. "Kanban: The Just-in-Time Japanese Inventory System," *Small Business Report* (February 1984), 69–71, and Richard C. Walleigh, "What's Your Excuse For Not Using JIT?", *Harvard Business Review* 64 (March/April 1986), 38–54.

27. Aggerwal, "MRP."

28. J. Claunch, "Implementing JIT" (Paper presented at the Spring Seminar of the Purchasing Management Association of Denver, Denver, 1985).

29. U.S. Bureau of the Census, *Annual Survey of Manufacturers* (Washington, D.C.: U.S. Government Printing Office, 1978).

30. Richard J. Schonberger and James P. Gilbert, "Just-in-Time Purchasing: A Challenge for U.S. Industry," *California Management Review* 26 (Fall 1983), 54–68.

31. D. W. Dobler, L. Lee, Jr., and D. N. Burt, *Purchasing and Materials Management: Text and Cases* (New York: McGraw-Hill, 1984).

32. *Benchmarks* (American Productivity Center, 1982).

33. E. E. Adam, Jr., J. C. Hershauer, and W. A. Ruch, *Productivity and Quality: Measurement as a Basis for Improvement*, 2d ed. (Columbia, Mo.: Research Center, College of Business and Public Administration, University of Missouri–Columbia, 1986).

34. A. V. Fiegenbaum, *Total Quality Control*, 3d ed. (New York: McGraw-Hill, 1983).

35. Jeremy Main, "Detroit's Cars Really Are Getting Better," *Fortune*, February 2, 1987, 90–98.

36. Maggie McComas, "Cutting Costs without Killing the Business," *Fortune*, October 13, 1986, 70–78.

37. W. E. Deming, *Quality, Productivity, and Competitive Position* (Cambridge, Mass.: Center for Advanced Engineering Study, MIT, 1982), and P. B. Crosby, *Quality Is Free* (New York: McGraw-Hill, 1979).

38. J. Merwin, "A Tale of Two Worlds," *Forbes*, June 16, 1986.

39. Dobler, Lee, and Burt, *Purchasing and Materials Management*.

40. H. David Sherman, "Improving the Productivity of Service Businesses," *Sloan Management Review* 25 (Spring 1984), 11–23.

41. Sease, "U.S. Companies," and Herb Schneider, "Implementation of Operations Strategy" (Presentation to the Fourth Annual Meeting of the Operations Management Association, Tempe, Arizona, November 1985).

Chapter 21

1. Bill Saporito, "Black & Decker's Gamble on 'Globalization'," *Fortune*, May 14, 1984, 40–48.
2. Thane Peterson, "The Unitary Tax: May It Rest in Peace," *Business Week*, September 15, 1986, 62.
3. Douglas Ramsey, "Making It in America," *Newsweek*, May 4, 1981, 24–30.
4. John S. Hill and Richard R. Still, "Adapting Products to LDC Tastes," *Harvard Business Review* 62 (March/April 1984), 92–101, and David A. Ricks, *Big Business Blunders: Mistakes in Multinational Marketing* (Homewood, Ill.: Dow Jones-Irwin, 1983).
5. Karen Paul and Robert Barbarto, "The Multinational Corporation in the Less Developed Country: The Economic Development Model versus the North-South Model," *Academy of Management Review* 10 (1985), 8–14.
6. Cynthia F. Mitchell, "Some Firms Resume Manufacturing in U.S. after Foreign Fiascos," *The Wall Street Journal*, October 14, 1986, 1–27.
7. Kathleen Deveny, "McWorld?" *Business Week*, October 13, 1986, 78–86.
8. Bruce Kogut, "Designing Global Strategies: Profiting from Operational Flexibility," *Sloan Management Review* 27 (Fall 1985), 27–38.
9. Edward Boyer, "Let Down by the Drooping Dollar," *Fortune*, June 9, 1986, 95–98, and Paul Ingrassian and Damon Darlin, "Japanese Auto Makers Find the Going Tough Because of Yen's Climb," *The Wall Street Journal*, December 15, 1986, 1–20.
10. Mark Fitzpatrick, "The Definition and Assessment of Political Risk in International Business: A Review of the Literature," *Academy of Management Review* 8 (1983), 249–254.
11. "Multinational Firms Act to Protect Overseas Workers from Terrorism," *The Wall Street Journal*, April 29, 1986, 31.
12. James B. Stewart and Peter Truell, "U.S. Firms Win Some, Lose Some at Tribunal Arbitrating $5 Billion in Claims against Iran," *The Wall Street Journal*, November 15, 1984, 38.
13. Dennis J. Encarnation and Sushil Vachani, "Foreign Ownership: When Hosts Change the Rules," *Harvard Business Review* 63 (September/October 1985), 152–160.
14. Gary Putka, "Phillips Finds Obstacles to Intra-Europe Trade Are Costly, Inefficient," *The Wall Street Journal*, August 7, 1985, 1–12.
15. Geert Hofstede, "The Interaction between National and Organizational Value Systems," *Journal of Management Studies* 22 (1985), pp. 347–357; Geert Hofstede, "The Cultural Relativity of the Quality of Life Concept," *Academy of Management Review* 9 (1984), 389–398.
16. Hofstede, "Interaction."
17. Ricks, *Big Business Blunders*.
18. Jeffrey A. Trachtenberg, "They Didn't Listen to Anybody," *Forbes*, December 15, 1986, 168–169.
19. Jonathan B. Levine, "How Bank of America Blew It in Jakarta," *Business Week*, August 4, 1986, 40.
20. Kenneth Labich, "America's International Winners," *Fortune*, April 14, 1986, 34–46.

21. Douglas R. Sease, "Japanese Firms Use U.S. Designers to Tailor Products to Local Tastes," *The Wall Street Journal*, March 4, 1986, 29.
22. Richard L. Hudson, "Competition Gets Scrappy in Heineken's Beer Markets," *The Wall Street Journal*, August 24, 1984, 20.
23. Jeffrey A. Trachtenberg, "Against All Odds," *Forbes*, February 11, 1985, 54–59.
24. Howard V. Perlmutter and David A. Hennan, "Cooperate to Compete Globally," *Harvard Business Review* 64 (March/April 1986), 136–152.
25. Janice Castro, "Heavy-Duty Mergers," *Time*, May 12, 1986, pp. 72–73.
26. Bureau of Economic Analysis, U.S. Department of Commerce, "1977 Benchmark Survey of U.S. Direct Investment Abroad," *Survey of Current Business* (April 1981), 29–37.
27. Howard V. Perlmutter, "The Torturous Evolution of the Multinational Corporation," *Columbia Journal of World Business* (January/February), 1969, 9–18, and Youram Wind, Susan P. Douglas, and Howard V. Perlmutter, "Guidelines for Developing International Marketing Strategies," *Journal of Marketing* (April 1973), 14–23.
28. *New Directions in Multinational Corporate Organizations* (New York: Business International, 1981).
29. Theodore Levitt, "The Globalization of Markets," *Harvard Business Review* 61 (May/June 1983), 92–102.
30. Christine Dugas, "Playtex Kicks Off a One-Ad Fits All Campaign," *Business Week*, December 16, 1985, 48–49.
31. John A. Quelch and Edward J. Hoff, "Customizing Global Marketing," *Harvard Business Review* 64 (May/June 1986), 59–68.
32. Michael E. Porter, "Changing Patterns of International Competition," *California Management Review* 28 (Winter 1986), 40.
33. Labich, "America's International Winners."
34. Louis Kraar, "Pepsi's Pitch to Quench Chinese Thirsts," *Fortune*, March 17, 1986, 58–64.
35. Ellen James, "International Outsourcing Becoming Necessity," *Houston Chronicle*, April 27, 1986, sec. 5, p. 12.
36. The following discussion is based on William A. Dymsza, "Global Strategic Planning: A Model and Recent Developments," *Journal of International Business Studies* (Fall 1984), 169–183; Arvand P. Phatak, *International Dimensions of Management* (Boston: Kent, 1983), 39–62; S. B. Prasad and Y. Kirshna Shetty, *An Introduction to Multinational Management* (Englewood Cliffs, N.J.: Prentice-Hall, 1976), 67–82.
37. William G. Egelhoff, 'Strategy and Structure in Multinational Corporations: An Information Processing Approach," *Administrative Science Quarterly* 27 (1982), 435–458.
38. John D. Daniels, Robert A. Pitts, and Marietta J. Tretter, "Strategy and Structure of U.S. Multinationals: An Exploratory Study," *Academy of Management Journal* 27 (1984), 292–307, and Theodore T. Herbert, "Strategy and Multinational Organization Structure: An Interorganizational Relationships Perspective," *Academy of Management Review* 9 (1984), 259–271.
39. Mike Tharp, "LSI Logic Corp. Does as the Japanese Do," *The Wall Street Journal*, April 17, 1986, 6.
40. Christopher A. Bartlett, "MNCs: Get Off the Organization Merry-Go-Round," *Harvard Business Review* 61 (March/April 1983), 138–146.
41. "New Directions in Multinational Corporate Organizations," prepared and published by Business International Corporation (New York: 1981).

42. The following discussion is based on Lennie Copeland and Lewis Griggs, "Getting the Best from Foreign Employees," *Management Review* (June 1986), 19–26, and Amanda Bennett, "American Culture Is Often a Puzzle for Foreign Managers in the U.S.," *The Wall Street Journal,* February 12, 1986, 29.

43. Saporito, "Black & Decker's Gamble."

Chapter 22

1. Andrea Fooner, "Three Ways to Break Out of a Dead-End Job," *Working Woman,* February, 1986, 82–85.

2. Janet Bamford, "Everyone Has to Start Somewhere," *Forbes,* July 14, 1986, 98–100.

3. R. Ricklafs, "Many Executives Complain of Stress, But Few Want Less-Pressure Jobs," *The Wall Street Journal,* September 29, 1982, 1.

4. William G. Flannigan, "What Makes Suzanne Run?" *Forbes,* October 7, 1985, 152.

5. C. Stein, "A Glut Economy," *Boston Globe,* July 27, 1986; B. W. Su, "The Economic Outlook to 1995: New Assumptions and Projections," *Employment Projections for 1995: Data & Methods* (Washington, D.C.: U.S. Bureau of Labor Statistics, April 1986); J. Naisbitt, *Megatrends: Ten New Directions Transforming Our Lives* (New York: Warner, 1982).

6. Robert Kreitner, *Management,* 3 ed. (Boston: Houghton Mifflin, 1986).

7. T. Gutteridge, *Career Planning and Management* (Boston: Little, Brown, 1987), and D. T. Hall, *Careers in Organizations* (Santa Monica, Cal: Goodyear, 1976).

8. Gutteridge, *Career Planning.*

9. Scott Bronestein, "Past Forty and Back to Square One," *The New York Times,* October 20, 1985, 6F.

10. Fooner, "Three Ways to Break Out."

11. Edie Gibson, "Fast Track Often Starts at Bottom," *Chicago Tribune,* December 15, 1986, sec. 4, p. 15.

12. "Expert View," *Working Woman,* October 1985, 154.

13. The discussion of career stages is based on M. London and S. A. Stumpf, "Individual and Organizational Development in Changing Times," in Douglas T. Hall and associates, *Career Development in Organizations* (San Francisco: Jossey-Bass, 1986).

14. Irene Pave, "A Woman's Place is at GE, Federal Express, P&G . . . ," *Business Week,* June 23, 1986, 75–77.

15. Kathy E. Kram, *Mentoring at Work: Developmental Relationships in Organizational Life* (Glenview, Ill.: Scott, Foresman, 1985).

16. Kathy E. Kram, "Phases of the Mentor Relationship," *Academy of Management Journal* 26 (1983), 608–625.

17. Kram, *Mentoring at Work.*

18. David Marshall Hunt and Carol Michael, "Mentorship: A Career Training and Development Tool," *Academy of Management Review* 8 (1983), 475–485.

19. G. R. Roche, "Much Ado about Mentors," *Harvard Business Review* (January/February 1979), 14–28.

20. Kathy E. Kram and L. Isabella, "Mentoring Alternatives: The Role of Peer Relationships in Career Development," *Academy of Management Journal* 28 (1985), 110–132.

21. Rosabeth Moss Kanter, *Men and Women of the Corporation* (New York: Basic Books, 1977).

22. Adapted from Betty Harrigan, "Career Advice," *Working Woman,* October 1985, 44–46.

23. T. A. Beehr and R. S. Bhagat, *Human Stress and Cognition in Organizations: An Integrated Perspective* (New York: Wiley, 1985).

24. R. S. Lazarus and S. Folkman, *Stress, Appraisal and Coping* (New York: Springer, 1984).

25. T. Homes and R. Rahe, "The Social Readjustment Rating Scale," *Journal of Psychosomatic Research* 11 (1967), 213–218.

26. K. R. Pelletier, *Healthy People in Unhealthy Places: Stress and Fitness at Work* (New York: Dell, 1984).

27. J. C. Latack, "After the Ax Falls: Job Loss as a Career Transition," *Academy of Management Review* 11 (1986), 375–392, and L. Greenhalgh and Z. Rosenblatt, "Job Insecurity: Toward Conceptual Clarity," *Academy of Management Review* 9 (1984) 438–446.

28. Hans Selye, *The Stress of Life* (New York: McGraw-Hill, 1956).

29. Jeannie Gaines and John M. Jermier, "Emotional Exhaustion in a High Stress Organization," *Academy of Management Journal* 26 (1983), 567–586.

30. Ricklafs, "Many Executives Complain."

31. Pelletier, *Healthy People.*

32. S. Dentzer, J. McCormick, and D. Tsuruoka, "A Cure for Job Stress," *Newsweek,* June 2, 1986, 46–47.

33. S. Parasuraman and M. A. Cleek, "Coping Behaviors and Managers' Affective Reactions to Role Stressers," *Journal of Vocational Behavior* 24 (1984), 179–193.

34. R. J. Burke and M. L. Belcourt, "Managerial Role Stress and Coping Responses," *Journal of Business Administration* 5 (1974), 55–68.

35. J. C. Latack, R. J. Aldag, and B. Joseph, "Job Stress: Determinants and Consequences of Coping Behaviors" (Working paper, Ohio State University, 1986), and R. A. Karasek, Jr., "Job Demands, Job Decision Latitude, and Mental Strain: Implications for Job Redesign," *Administrative Science Quarterly* 24 (1979), 285–308.

36. Ricklefs, "Many Executives Complain."

37. Joshua Hyatt, "All Stressed-Up and Nowhere to Go," *INC.,* January 1987, 74–79.

38. E. H. Burack, *Career Planning and Management: A Managerial Summary* (Lake Forest, Ill.: Brace-Park Press, 1983).

39. D. T. Hall, "An Overview of Current Career Development Theory, Research, and Practice," in Douglas T. Hall and Associates, *Career Development in Organizations* (San Francisco: Jossey-Bass, 1986).

40. M. London and S. A. Stumpf, *Managing Careers* (Reading, Mass.: Addison-Wesley, 1982).

41. M. London, *Developing Managers* (San Francisco: Jossey-Bass, 1985).

42. D. T. Wight, "The Split Role in Performance Appraisal," *Personnel Administrator* (May 1985), 83–87, and A. H. Soerwine, "The Manager as Career Counselor: Some Issues and Approaches," in D. H. Montross and C. J. Shinkman, (eds.), *Career Development in the 1980s* (Springfield, Ill.: Charles C. Thomas, 1981).

43. Hunt and Michael, "Mentorship."

44. Kram, *Mentoring at Work.*

45. Gutteridge, *Career Planning.*

46. London and Stumpf, "Individual and Organizational Development."

47. Hall, "An Overview."

48. J. R. Turborg, "Women in Management: A Research Review," *Journal of Applied Psychology* 62 (1977), 647–664.

49. A. Taylor, "Why Women Managers Are Bailing Out," *Fortune,* August 18, 1986, 16–23.

50. Rochelle Distelheim, "The New Shoot-out at Generation Gap," *Working Woman,* March 1986, 113–117.
51. Taylor, "Women Managers."
52. L. Riebstein, "Many Hurdles, Old and New, Keep Black Managers Out of Top Jobs," *The Wall Street Journal,* July 10, 1986, 1.
53. Ibid.
54. Hall, "An Overview."
55. U. Sekaran, *Dual Career Families: Implications for Organizations and Counselors* (San Francisco: Jossey-Bass, 1986).
56. F. S. Hall and D. T. Hall, *The Two-Career Couple* (Reading, Mass.: Addison-Wesley, 1979).
57. D. T. Hall, "Career Development in Organizations: Where Do We Go from Here?" in Douglas T. Hall and Associates, *Career Development in Organizations* (San Francisco: Jossey-Bass, 1986).
58. Denies Weil, "Husbands Who Star in Supporting Roles," *Working Woman,* June 1986, 114–116.
59. "The Uneasy Life of the Corporate Spouse," *Fortune,* August 20, 1984, 26–32.
60. Taylor, "Why Women Managers are Bailing Out," *Fortune,* August 18, 1986, 16–23.
61. J. A. F. Stoner, T. P. Ference, E. K. Warren, and H. K. Christensen, *Managerial Career Plateaus: An Exploratory Study* (New York: Center for Research and Career Development, Columbia University, 1980).
62. Ibid.
63. J. W. Slocum, W. L. Cron, R. W. Hansen, and S. Rawlings, "Business Strategy and the Management of the Plateaued Performer" (Working paper, Southern Methodist University, 1986).
64. J. P. Carnazza, A. K. Korman, T. P. Ference, and J. A. F. Stoner, "Plateaued and Non-Plateaued Managers: Factors in Job Performance," *Journal of Management* 7 (1981), 7–25.
65. London, *Developing Managers.*
66. J. M. Bardwick, "Plateauing and Productivity," *Sloan Management Review* (Spring 1983), 67–73.
67. J. P. Wanous, *Organizational Entry: Recruitment, Selection, and Socialization of Newcomers* (Reading, Mass.: Addison-Wesley, 1980).
68. S. E. Sullivan, "Is the Best Yet to Be? A Critical Examination of the Design and Evaluation of Pre-Retirement Preparation Programs" (Paper presented at the National Academy of Management Meeting, Chicago, August 1986).
69. W. Arnone, "Preretirement Planning: An Employee Benefit That Has Come of Age," *Personnel* 61 (1982), 760–763.
70. Fooner, "Three Ways to Break Out."

Glossary

accommodative response A response to social demands in which the organization accepts—often under pressure—social responsibility for its actions to comply with the public interest.

achievement-oriented leadership Leadership behavior that involves setting clear and challenging objectives for subordinates.

acquired needs theory A content theory of motivation that proposes that individuals develop certain types of needs through their life experiences rather than being born with them.

action plan A step in MBO that defines the course of action needed to achieve stated objectives.

activity (PERT) One of the tasks that must be completed in order to finish the project.

activity ratio A ratio that measures the firm's internal performance with respect to inventory and collection of customer receivables.

adaptive mode A mode of strategy formulation in which decisions are made solely in response to specific problems as they arise.

adhocracy A medium-size organization that emphasizes adaptability and is characterized by a low degree of formalization and decentralization of decision making.

adjourning The stage of group development in which members prepare for the group's disbandment.

administrative intensity The percentage of resources allocated to administrative and support activities relative to that deployed for line activities.

administrative model A model of decision making that describes how managers actually make decisions in situations characterized by nonprogrammed decisions, uncertainty, and ambiguity.

administrative principles A subfield of the classical management perspective that focused on the total organization rather than the individual worker,

delineating the management functions of planning, organizing, commanding, coordinating, and controlling.

affirmative action The use of methods to promote the hiring, development, and retention of groups that traditionally have been underrepresented in the workplace.

ambiguity A situation in which the desired objectives or problem at hand are unclear, alternatives are difficult to define, and information about future outcomes is unavailable.

analyzer A type of adaptive strategy emphasizing a combination of status quo in existing, stable markets and innovation in new, dynamic markets.

application form A device for collecting information about an applicant's education, previous job experience, and other background characteristics.

artificial intelligence (AI) Information technology that attempts to make computers think, talk, see, and listen like people.

assessment center A technique for selecting individuals with high managerial potential based on their performance on a series of simulated managerial tasks.

assets Everything that the company owns.

autocratic leader A leader who tends to centralize authority and rely on legitimate, reward, and coercive power to manage subordinates.

automated office The integration of multiple electronic technologies to automate managerial work.

autonomy The extent to which an employee has freedom, discretion, and self-determination in planning and performing tasks.

average collection period An activity ratio that measures the amount of customer receivables divided by average sales per day.

avoidance learning The removal of an

unpleasant consequence following the performance of a desired behavior.

balance sheet A financial statement showing the firm's financial position with respect to assets and liabilities at a specific point in time.

balance sheet budget A financial budget that plans the amount of assets and liabilities for the end of the time period under consideration.

batch-push system An inventory control system in which each work station produces at a constant rate regardless of the next work station's input requirements.

BCG matrix A concept developed by the Boston Consulting Group that evaluates SBUs with respect to the dimensions of business growth rate and market share.

behaviorally anchored rating scale (BARS) A rating technique that relates an employee's performance to specific job-related incidents.

behavioral sciences approach A subfield of the human resource management perspective that applied social science in an organizational context, drawing from economics, psychology, sociology, and other disciplines.

behavior modification The set of techniques by which reinforcement theory is used to modify human behavior.

belongingness needs The needs for peer acceptance, friendships, and love.

bet-your-company culture A form of corporate culture characterized by a high-risk, high-stake, slow-feedback strategic environment.

birth stage The phase of the organization life cycle in which the company is created.

bottom-up approach An approach to innovation in which ideas are developed at lower organizational levels and proposed upward for approval.

Note: The glossary contains definitions for the terms in text that appear either in boldface or italic type.

bottom-up budgeting A budgeting process in which lower-level managers budget their departments' resource needs and pass them up to top management for approval.

boundary-spanning roles Roles assumed by people and/or departments that link and coordinate the organization with key elements in the external environment.

bounded rationality The concept that people have the time and cognitive ability to process only a limited amount of information on which to base decisions.

brainstorming A decision-making technique in which group members present spontaneous suggestions for problem solution, regardless of their likelihood of implementation, in order to promote freer, more creative thinking within the group.

breakeven analysis A quantitative technique that helps managers determine the level of sales at which total revenues equal total costs.

bureaucratic control The use of rules, policies, hierarchy of authority, reward systems, and other formal devices to influence employee behavior and assess performance.

bureaucratic organizations A subfield of the classical management perspective that emphasized management on an impersonal, rational basis through elements such as clearly defined authority and responsibility, formal recordkeeping, and separation of management and ownership.

burnout The emotional exhaustion resulting from extended periods of stress.

business-level strategy The level of strategy concerned with the question: "How do we compete?" Pertains to each business unit or product line within the organization.

CAD A production technology in which computers perform new-product design.

CAM A production technology in which computers help guide and control the manufacturing system.

capacity planning The determination and adjustment of the organization's ability to produce products and services to match customer demand.

capital expenditure budget A financial budget that plans future investments in major assets to be paid for over several years.

career A sequence of work-related activities and behaviors over a person's life span viewed as movement through various job experiences and the individual's attitudes toward involvement in those experiences.

career development Employee progress or growth over time as a career unfolds.

career ladder A formalized job progression route based on logically connected jobs.

career management Organizational activities designed to promote employees' career development.

career path A job progression route along which an employee can advance through the organization.

career planning The self-assessment, exploration of opportunities, goal setting, and other activities necessary to make informed career-related decisions.

career plateau A point in a career from which the opportunities for further promotion are scarce.

cash budget A financial budget that estimates cash flows on a daily or weekly basis to insure the company has sufficient cash to meet its obligations.

cash cow A BCG matrix classification for an SBU that exists in a mature, slow-growth industry but holds a dominant position and large market share.

causal modeling A forecasting technique that attempts to predict behavior (the dependent variable) by analyzing its causes (independent variables).

centralization The location of decision authority near top organizational levels.

centralized network A group communication structure in which group members communicate through a single individual to solve problems or make decisions.

centralized planning department A group of planning specialists who develop plans for the organization as a whole and its major divisions and de-

partments and typically report to the president or CEO.

central processing unit (CPU) The CBIS component that manipulates data based on previously defined procedures.

ceremony A planned activity that makes up a special event and is conducted for the benefit of an audience.

certainty A situation in which all the information needed by the decision maker is fully available.

chain of command An unbroken line of authority that links all individuals in the organization and specifies who reports to whom.

champion An intrapreneur who believes in a new idea and gains the political and financial support needed to bring it to reality.

chance fork A numbered node on a decision tree that represents states of nature over which the decision maker has no control.

change agent An OD specialist who contracts with an organization to facilitate change.

changing A step in the intervention stage of organizational development in which individuals experiment with new workplace behavior.

channel The carrier of a communication.

channel richness The amount of information that can be transmitted during a communication episode.

charismatic leader *See* inspirational leader.

clan control The use of social values, traditions, common beliefs, and trust to generate compliance with organizational goals.

classical model A model of decision making based on the assumption that managers should make logical decisions that will be in the organization's best economic interests.

classical perspective A management perspective that emerged during the nineteenth and early twentieth centuries that emphasized a rational, scientific approach to the study of management and sought to make organizations efficient operating machines.

closed system A system that does not interact with the external environment.

coalition An informal alliance among managers who support a specific decision-making objective.

code of ethics A formal statement of the organization's values regarding social issues.

coercion Managers' use of formal power to force employees to accept a proposed change.

coercive power Power that stems from the leader's authority to punish or recommend punishment.

collectivism A preference for a tightly knit social framework in which individuals look after one another and organizations protect their members' interests.

command group A formal group composed of a manager and his or her subordinates in the organization's formal chain of command.

command method A mechanism for allocating resources in which a central agency makes economic decisions that are imposed on the rest of the economy.

commitment Subordinates' devotion to the leader's point of view and enthusiasm in carrying out instructions and obeying orders.

committee A long-lasting, sometimes permanent group in the organization structure created to deal with tasks that recur regularly.

communication The process by which information is exchanged and understood by two or more people, usually with the intent to motivate or influence behavior.

compensation Monetary payments (wages, salaries) and nonmonetary goods/commodities (fringe benefits, vacations) used to reward employees.

competitors Other organizations in the same industry or type of business that provide goods or services to the same set of customers.

completeness The extent to which information contains the appropriate amount of data.

compliance Subordinates' willingness to obey orders and instructions despite personal disagreement.

compulsory staff service A management concept developed in the Roman Catholic Church that required managers to consult with subordinates on important issues.

computer-based information system (CBIS) An information system that uses electronic computing technology to create the various system components.

computer conferencing An extension of electronic mail to include multiparty communications.

conceptual skill The cognitive ability to see the organization as a whole and the relationship among its parts.

concurrent control Control that consists of monitoring ongoing employee activities to insure their consistency with established standards.

conflict Antagonistic interaction in which one party attempts to thwart the intentions or goals of another.

consideration A type of leader behavior that describes the extent to which a leader is sensitive to subordinates, respects their ideas and feelings, and establishes mutual trust.

consolidation The stage in the organization revitalization process in which managers seek to stabilize the streamlined corporation and stress appropriate new cultural values.

constituency Any group within or outside the organization that has a stake in the organization's performance.

content theories A group of theories that emphasize the needs that motivate people.

contingency A condition such as environment, organization size and life cycle stage, or production technology that determines managers' choice between a vertical and lateral organization structure.

contingency approach A model of leadership that describes the relationship between leadership styles and specific organizational situations.

contingency view An extension of the human resource perspective in which the successful resolution of organizational problems is thought to depend on managers' identification of key variables in the situation at hand.

continuous process production A type of technology involving mechanization of the entire work flow and nonstop production.

continuous reinforcement schedule A schedule in which every occurrence of the desired behavior is reinforced.

contraction The stage in the organization revitalization process in which managers reduce corporation size, production costs, and nonessential expenditures.

control An information system monitoring and evaluation mechanism for assessing the quality, timeliness, completeness, and relevance of the information produced by the system.

controlling The management function concerned with monitoring employees' activities, keeping the organization on track toward its goals, and making corrections as needed.

Control Type I The control of stable, internal organizational activities.

Control Type II The adaptation to unpredictable factors in the organization's external environment through strategic planning.

Control Type III The control of unpredictable environmental factors through the adoption of new strategic objectives and performance standards.

coordination The quality of collaboration across departments.

coordination costs The time and energy needed to coordinate the activities of a group to enable it to perform its task.

core control system The strategic plans, financial forecasts, budget, performance appraisal system, operations management techniques, and MIS reports that form an integrated system for directing and monitoring organizational activities.

corporate ethics Ethics derived from the organization's own values and culture.

corporate-level strategy The level of strategy concerned with the question: "What business are we in?" Pertains to the organization as a whole and the combination of business units and product lines that make it up.

corporate social audit The criteria management develops for measuring, monitoring, and evaluating the organization's performance with respect to social programs and objectives.

corrective action A change in work activities to restore them to acceptable performance standards.

cost The sum of the materials, labor, design, transportation, and overhead expense associated with a product or service.

cost center A responsibility center in which the manager is responsible for controlling cost inputs.

cost lag The condition that exists when costs cannot be reduced as rapidly as sales.

cost leadership A type of competitive strategy with which the organization aggressively seeks efficient facilities, cuts costs, and employs tight cost controls in order to be more efficient than competitors.

countertrade The barter of products for other products rather than their sale for currency.

creativity The development of novel solutions to perceived organizational problems.

critical activity (PERT) An activity whose delay would cause a slowdown in the overall project.

critical path The path with the longest total time; represents the total time required for the project.

critical success factors (CSFs) The particular areas in which satisfactory results will enhance the organization's overall performance.

culture The set of key values, beliefs, understandings, and norms that members of an organization share.

current assets Assets that can be converted into cash over a short period of time.

current debt Obligations that are payable in the near future.

current ratio A liquidity ratio that determines whether the firm has sufficient assets to convert into cash to pay off debts as necessary.

customers People and organizations in the environment who acquire goods and services from the organization.

cyclic pattern A periodically recurring up-and-down movement in the behavior of a variable.

data Raw, unsummarized, and unanalyzed facts.

decentralization The location of decision authority near lower organizational levels.

decentralized network A group communication structure in which group members freely communicate with one another and arrive at decisions together.

decentralized planning staff A group of planning specialists assigned to major departments and divisions to help managers develop their own strategic plans.

decision A choice made from available alternatives.

decision fork A square node on a decision tree that represents the alternative strategies available to the decision maker at a given moment.

decision making The process of identifying problems and opportunities, generating alternatives, selecting an alternative, and implementing the solution.

decision support system (DSS) An interactive CBIS that retrieves, manipulates, and displays information needed for making specific management decisions.

decision tree A decision-making aid used for decision situations that occur in sequence; consists of a pictorial representation of decision alternatives, states of nature, and outcomes of each course of action.

decode To translate the symbols used in a message for the purpose of interpreting its meaning.

defender A type of adaptive strategy for a stable environment emphasizing stability, maintenance of current market share, and possibly retrenchment.

defensive response A response to social demands in which the organization admits to some errors of commission or omission but does not act obstructively.

Delphi group A group decision-making format that involves the circulation among participants of questionnaires on the selected problem, sharing of answers, and continuous recircula-

tion/refinement of questionnaires until a consensus has been obtained.

Delphi technique A qualitative forecasting method in which experts reach consensus about future events through a series of continuously refined questionnaires rather than through face-to-face discussion; used in a Delphi group.

demand-pull system An inventory control system in which each work station produces its product only when the next work station says it is ready to receive more input.

democratic leader A leader who delegates authority to others, encourages participation, and relies on expert and referent power to manage subordinates.

demographic forecast A forecast of societal characteristics such as birth rates, educational levels, marriage rates, and diseases.

departmentalization The basis on which individuals are grouped into departments and departments into the total organization—by function, geographical location, or product.

dependent demand inventory Inventory in which item demand is related to the demand for other inventory items.

descriptive model A model that describes how managers actually make decisions rather than how they should.

development The process of teaching managers and professionals the skills needed for their present and future jobs.

devil's advocate A decision-making technique in which an individual is assigned the role of challenging the assumptions and assertions made by the group in order to prevent premature consensus.

diagnosis The step in the decision-making process in which managers analyze underlying causal factors associated with the decision situation.

dialectical inquiry A decision-making technique in which groups are assigned to challenge the underlying values and assumptions associated with each problem definition presented.

differentiation A type of competitive strategy with which the organization seeks to distinguish its products or services from competitors'.

diffusion of responsibility The lack of individual responsibility for group outcomes.

direct investment An entry strategy in which the organization directly manages its productive facilities in a foreign country.

directive leadership Leadership behavior that emphasizes telling subordinates precisely what they are supposed to do.

discretionary costs Costs based on management decisions and not on fixed commitments or volume of output.

discretionary responsibility Organizational responsibility that is voluntary and guided by the organization's desire to make social contributions not mandated by economics, law, or ethics.

disengagement stage The stage of career development during which the person prepares for retirement and begins to disengage from both the organization and the occupation.

disseminator A type of informational role that concerns transmitting current information to others, both inside and outside the organization, who can use it.

distinctive competence The unique position the organization achieves with respect to competitors through its decisions concerning resource deployments, scope, and synergy.

disturbance handler A type of decisional role that concerns the resolution of conflicts among subordinates or between the manager's department and other departments.

divestiture A form of retrenchment in which the organization sells off a business that is no longer central to its operations.

divisional structure An organizational structure in which departments are grouped based on similar organizational outputs.

divisionalized form A large organization that is subdivided into product or market divisions and decentralizes decision making at the divisional level.

division of labor See work specialization.

dog A BCG matrix classification for an SBU in a slow-growth market with only a small market share and offering little profit or promise of recovery.

downward communication Messages sent from top management down to subordinates.

driving force A force that propels a proposed change.

dual role A role in which the individual both contributes to the group's task and supports members' emotional needs.

econometric model A system of regression equations that are solved simultaneously to capture the interaction between economic conditions and the organization's activities.

economic dimension The dimension of the general environment representing the overall economic health of the country or region in which the organization functions.

economic forces Forces that affect the availability, production, and distribution of a society's resources among competing users.

economic order quantity (EOQ) An inventory management technique designed to minimize the total of ordering and holding costs for inventory items.

economic responsibility The organization's responsibility to produce the goods and services desired by society while seeking to maximize profits for its owners and shareholders.

effectiveness The degree to which the organization achieves a stated objective.

efficiency The use of minimal resources—raw materials, money, and people—to produce a desired volume of output.

efficiency goal An organizational goal that stresses the judicious use of scarce resources.

electronic bulletin board A device that disseminates routine information through the organization's computer system.

electronic mail The use of electronic circuitry to transmit written messages instantaneously to people within the organization or to other organizations.

employee-centered leader A type of leader who establishes high performance goals and behaves supportively toward subordinates.

employee growth-need strength A component of the job characteristics model that emphasizes different people's needs for growth and development.

encode To select symbols with which to compose a message.

engineering costs See variable costs.

entrepreneur A type of manager decisional role that involves the initiation of changes in order to correct problems.

entrepreneurial leader A type of inspirational leader who initiates major improvement projects or perhaps an entirely new organization.

entrepreneurial mode A mode of strategy formulation characterized by strong leaders who have a vision for the organization, are willing to take risks, and emphasize opportunities over problems.

entropy The tendency for a system to decay.

entry strategy An organizational strategy for entering a foreign market.

environmental discontinuity A large change in the organization's environment over a short period.

E → P expectancy Expectancy that putting effort into a given task will lead to high performance.

equal employment opportunity (EEO) laws Legislation that prohibits recruiting and hiring practices that discriminate on the basis of race, national origin, religion, or sex.

equity A situation that exists when the ratio of one person's outcomes to inputs equals that of another's.

equity theory A process theory that focuses on individuals' perceptions of how fairly they are treated relative to others.

ERG theory A modification of the needs hierarchy theory that proposes three categories of needs: existence, relatedness, and growth.

establishment and advancement stage The stage of career development during which the individual experiences progress with the organization in the form of transfers, promotions, and/or high visibility.

esteem needs The needs for a positive self-image, responsibility, recognition from others, and high status.

ethical advocate An individual assigned to point out actual or potential failures of social responsibility.

ethical dilemma A situation that arises when all alternative choices or behaviors have been deemed undesirable because of potentially negative ethical consequences, making it difficult to distinguish right from wrong.

ethical responsibility The organization's responsibility to act with equity, fairness, and impartiality, and respect individuals' rights.

ethics advocate An individual assigned to point out actual or potential failures of corporate social responsibility.

ethics committee A group of executives assigned to oversee the organization's ethics by ruling on questionable issues and disciplining violators.

ethnocentric company An MNC that places emphasis on its home country.

ethnocentrism A cultural attitude marked by the tendency to regard one's own culture as superior to others.

event (PERT) The beginning and ending of a specific activity.

excellence characteristics A group of eight features that have been found to typify the highest-performing U.S. companies.

exit interview An interview conducted with departing employees to determine the reasons for their termination.

expectancy theory A process theory that proposes that motivation depends on individuals' expectations about their ability to perform tasks and receive desired rewards.

expected value The weighted average of each possible outcome for a decision alternative.

expense budget An operating budget that outlines the anticipated expenses for each responsibility center and for the organization as a whole.

expert power Power that stems from the leader's special knowledge of or skill in the tasks performed by subordinates.

expert system An area of AI that attempts to program a computer to du-

plicate an expert's decision-making and problem-solving strategies.

exploration and trial stage The stage of career development during which a person accepts his or her first job and perhaps tries several jobs.

exporting An entry strategy in which the organization maintains its production facilities within its home country and transfers its products for sale in foreign markets.

external audit A financial audit conducted by experts from outside the organization.

extinction The withdrawal of a reward for the purpose of inhibiting future occurrences of a behavior.

extrinsic reward A reward given by another person.

feedback The degree to which doing the job provides information back to the employee regarding his or her performance; a response by the receiver to the sender's communication.

feedback control Control that focuses on the organization's outputs; also called *post-action* or *output control*.

feedforward control Control that focuses on human, material, and financial resources flowing into the organization; also called *preliminary* or *preventative control*.

femininity A cultural preference for modesty, tending to the weak, and quality of life.

figurehead A type of interpersonal role that involves the handling of ceremonial and symbolic activities for the department or organization.

financial audit An independent appraisal of the organization's financial records, conducted by external or internal experts.

financial budget A budget that defines where the organization will receive its cash and how it will spend it.

financial ratio The comparison of two financial numbers for the purpose of illustrating company performance.

finished-goods inventory Inventory consisting of items that have passed through the complete production process but have yet to be sold.

first-line manager A manager who is at the first or second management level and directly responsible for the production of goods and services.

fixed assets Assets that are long term in nature.

fixed costs Costs that are based on a commitment from a previous budget period and cannot be altered.

fixed-interval schedule A schedule that administers reinforcement for a desired behavior at specified time intervals.

fixed-position layout A facilities layout in which the product remains in one location and the required tasks and equipment are brought to it.

fixed-ratio schedule A schedule that administers reinforcement after a specified number of desired responses.

flaming An emotional outburst with a potentially negative impact on others sent via electronic communications technology.

flat structure A management structure characterized by an overall broad span of control and relatively few hierarchical levels.

flexible manufacturing system (FMS) A small or medium-size automated production line.

flex time A modified work schedule that allows employees to determine their workday schedules based on their own needs and desires.

focus A type of competitive strategy that emphasizes concentration on a specific regional market, product line, or buyer group.

force field analysis The process of determining which forces drive and which resist a proposed change.

forecast A prediction about future organizational and environmental circumstances that will influence plans, decisions, and goal achievement.

formal communication channel A communication channel that flows within the chain of command or task responsibility defined by the organization.

formal group A group created by the organization to perform a specific task.

formalization The amount of written documentation used to direct and control employees.

forming The stage of group development characterized by orientation and acquaintance.

four-day workweek A modified work schedule under which employees work four days for ten hours each day.

franchising A form of licensing in which an organization provides its foreign franchisees with a complete assortment of materials and services.

free rider A person who benefits from group membership but does not make a proportionate contribution to the group's work.

friendship group An informal group based on members' enjoyment of personal interactions with one another.

frustration-regression principle The idea that failure to meet a higher-order need may cause a regression to an already satisfied lower-order need.

functional-based structure A global organization structure in which managers' responsibility and authority are assigned along functional lines.

functional-level strategy The level of strategy concerned with the question: "How do we support the business-level strategy?" Pertains to all of the organization's major departments.

functional manager A manager responsible for a department that performs specialized tasks and has employees with similar training and skills.

functional structure An organizational structure in which positions are grouped into departments based on similar skills, expertise, and resource use.

functional structure with lateral relationships An organizational structure in which teams and task forces made up of members from several departments are created.

game theory A quantitative decision-making aid that helps managers examine the outcomes of their decisions in light of possible competitors' actions.

general environment The layer of the external environment that affects the organization indirectly.

general manager A manager responsible for several departments that perform different functions.

generic strategy *See* grand strategy.

geocentric company An MNC that is completely world oriented and favors no particular country.

geographic-based structure A global organization structure in which all of an MNC's products and functions in a particular country or region report to the same division manager.

GE screen A portfolio matrix developed by General Electric Company that evaluates business units along the dimensions of industry attractiveness and business strength.

globalization The standardization of product design and advertising strategies throughout the world.

goal A desired future state that the organization attempts to realize.

grand strategy The general plan or major action by which an organization intends to achieve its long-term objectives; also called a *generic strategy*.

grapevine An informal, person-to-person communication network of employees that is not officially sanctioned by the organization.

group A unit of two or more people who interact with and influence each other to accomplish a shared purpose.

group cohesiveness The extent to which group members are attracted to the group and motivated to remain in it.

groupthink A phenomenon in which group members are so committed to the group that they are reluctant to express contrary opinions.

halo error A type of rating error that occurs when an employee receives the same rating on all dimensions regardless of his or her performance on individual ones.

hardware The physical equipment used in a CBIS.

Hawthorne studies A series of experiments on worker productivity begun in 1924 at the Hawthorne plant of Western Electric Company in Illinois; attributed employees' increased output to managers' better treatment of them during the study.

hero A figure who exemplifies the deeds, character, and attributes of a corporate culture.

hierarchy of needs theory A content theory that proposes that people are motivated by five categories of needs—physiological, safety, belongingness, esteem, and self-actualization—that exist in a hierarchical order.

holding costs Costs associated with keeping an inventory item on hand, such as storage space, finance, and materials-handling expenses.

homogeneity A type of rating error that occurs when a rater gives all employees a similar rating regardless of their individual performances.

horizontal communication The lateral or diagonal exchange of messages across peers or coworkers.

horizontal linkage model An approach to product change that emphasizes shared development of innovations among several departments.

human relations movement A movement in management thinking and practice that emphasized satisfaction of employees' basic needs as the key to increased worker productivity.

human resource generalist A person responsible for more than one HRM area.

human resource inventory A database that summarizes individuals' skills, abilities, work experiences, and career interests.

human resource management (HRM) Activities undertaken to attract, develop, and maintain an effective work force within an organization.

human resource perspective A management perspective that emerged during the mid-nineteenth century that emphasized enlightened treatment of workers and power sharing between managers and employees.

human resource planning The forecasting of human resource needs and the projected matching of individuals with expected job vacancies.

human resources forecast A forecast of the organization's future manpower needs.

human resource specialist A person responsible for a single HRM area.

human skill The ability to work with and through other people and to work effectively as a group member.

hybrid structure An organizational structure that utilizes both functional and divisional departmentalization.

hygiene factors Factors that involve the presence or absence of job dissatisfiers, including working conditions, pay, company policies, and interpersonal relationships.

implementation The step in the decision-making process that involves the employment of managerial, administrative, and persuasive abilities to translate the chosen alternative into action.

income statement A financial statement that summarizes a company's financial performance over a given time interval.

individualism A preference for a loosely knit social framework in which individuals are expected to take care of themselves.

informal communication channel A communication channel that exists outside formally authorized channels without regard for the organization's hierarchy of authority.

informal group A group created by employees rather than by the organization and designed to meet their mutual interests.

information Data that are meaningful and alter the receiver's understanding.

information system A written or electronic internal system for processing data and information among employees.

infrastructure A country's physical facilities that support economic activities.

initiating structure A type of leader behavior that describes the extent to which a leader is task oriented and directs subordinates' work activities toward goal achievement.

innovation goal An organizational goal that emphasizes flexibility and leadership in the provision of new products and services.

inputs The raw data that enter the organization's information system.

inspirational leader A leader who has the ability to motivate subordinates to transcend their expected performance; also called a *charismatic leader.*

integrating manager An individual responsible for coordinating the activities of several departments on a full-time basis to achieve specific project or product outcomes.

interactive group A group decision-making format in which group members are brought together face to face and have a specific agenda and decision objectives.

interest group An informal group formed on the basis of a common personal interest among members.

intermediate-term planning Planning that includes tactical objectives and has a time horizon of from one to two years.

internal audit A financial audit performed by experts within the organization.

internal environment The environment within the organization's boundaries.

international dimension The dimension of the general environment representing events that originate in foreign countries and opportunities for American firms abroad.

international division An organizational division that is established alongside one or more domestic divisions and has equal status in the management hierarchy.

international management The management of business operations conducted in more than one country.

intrapreneur An individual who anticipates the need for productive change and champions it within the organization.

intrinsic reward A reward received as a direct consequence of a person's actions.

intuition The immediate apprehension of a decision situation based on past experience but without conscious thought.

inventor An intrapreneur who develops and technically understands a new idea but lacks the ability and interest to fight for its acceptance.

inventory The goods that the organization keeps on hand for use in the production process.

inventory turnover An activity ratio that indicates the number of times inventory is turned over to meet total sales figures.

investment center A responsibility center based on the value of assets employed to produce a given level of profit.

iron law of responsibility The belief that society eventually will remove power from any organization that uses its influence in an unacceptable or irresponsible manner.

job A unit of work that a single employee is responsible for performing.

job analysis The process of obtaining accurate and complete information about jobs through a systematic examination of job content.

job-centered leader A type of leader who emphasizes schedules, low costs, and production efficiency over goal achievement and human needs.

job characteristics model A model of job design comprised of core job dimensions, critical psychological states, and employee growth-need strength.

job description A listing of minimum and desirable qualifications for a particular job.

job design The application of motivational theories to the structure of work for the purpose of improving productivity and satisfaction.

job enlargement A job design that combines a series of tasks into one new, broader job for the purpose of giving employees variety and challenge.

job enrichment A job design that incorporates achievement, recognition, and other high-level motivators into the work.

job evaluation The process of determining the values of jobs within an organization through an examination of job content.

job matching system A method that links qualified individuals with career opportunities within the organization.

job rotation A job design that systematically moves employees from one job to another for the purpose of providing them with variety and stimulation.

job sharing A modified work schedule that involves two or more people jointly covering one job over a forty-hour week.

job simplification A job design whose purpose is to improve task efficiency by reducing the number of tasks a single person must perform.

joint venture A mutual investment by two or more organizations that creates a new organization.

jury of opinion A method of qualitative forecasting based on the average opinions of managers from various company divisions and departments.

just-in-time (JIT) inventory control system An inventory control system that schedules materials to arrive precisely when they are needed on a production line.

key indicator system A technique for determining managers' information needs based on key business indicators, exception reporting, and the use of graphics packages.

labor supply The people available for hire by the organization.

law of effect The assumption that positively reinforced behavior tends to be repeated while unreinforced or negatively reinforced behavior tends to be inhibited.

leader A type of interpersonal role that encompasses relationships with subordinates, such as motivation, communication, and influence.

leader-member relations A representation of subordinates' attitude toward and acceptance of a leader.

leadership The ability to influence other people toward the attainment of organizational goals.

leading The management function that involves the use of influence to motivate employees to achieve the organization's goals.

legal-political dimension The dimension of the general environment that includes federal, state, and local government regulations and political activities designed to control company behavior.

legal responsibility The organization's obligation to conduct its activities according to society's legally defined standards of appropriate corporate behavior.

legitimate power Power that stems from a formal management position in an organization and the authority granted to it.

leverage ratio A financial ratio that indicates the amount of financing of company operations available from creditors.

liabilities The firm's debts.

liaison A type of manager interpersonal role that concerns the development of information sources both inside and outside the organization.

liaison role A formal position in one department with designated responsibility for coordinating with another department.

licensing An entry strategy in which an organization in one country makes certain resources available to companies in another in order to participate in the production and sale of its products abroad.

linear programming A quantitative technique that allocates resources so as to optimize a predefined organizational objective.

line authority A form of authority in which individuals in management positions have the formal power to direct and control immediate subordinates.

line department A department that performs tasks related to the organization's mission and primary goal.

liquidation A form of retrenchment in which the organization sells off a business unit for the cash value of its assets, thus terminating its existence.

liquidity ratio A financial ratio that indicates the company's ability to meet its current debt obligations.

long-term debt Obligations that are payable over a long period.

long-term planning Planning that includes strategic goals and plans and has a time horizon of up to five years.

LPC scale A questionnaire designed to measure relationship-oriented versus task-oriented leadership style according to the leader's choice of adjectives for describing the "least preferred coworker."

lump sum salary increase A salary increase that is paid as a bonus at one or more times during the year in order to enhance its motivational value.

machine bureaucracy A large, functionally structured organization characterized by a high degree of formalization and work specialization.

management The attainment of organizational goals in an effective and efficient manner through planning, organizing, leading, and controlling organizational resources.

management by objectives (MBO) A variation of performance appraisal in which managers define objectives for each department, project, and employee and use them to control subsequent performance.

management by wandering around (MBWA) A communication technique in which managers interact directly with workers to exchange information.

management information system (MIS) A system, often computerbased, designed to provide managers with relevant information in a timely and cost-efficient manner.

management science A set of quantitatively based decision models used to assist management decision makers.

management science perspective A management perspective that emerged after World War II and applied mathematics, statistics, and other quantitative techniques to managerial problems.

managerial grid An OD intervention technique that assesses management style through the use of a grid that represents concern for production on one axis and concern for people on the other.

manual information system An information system whose activities are performed by people.

manufacturing organization An organization that produces physical goods.

manufacturing resource planning (MRP II) An extension of MRP to include the control of resources pertaining to all operations of the organization.

market method A mechanism for allocating resources in which economic decisions are decentralized to people and organizations.

masculinity A cultural preference for achievement, heroism, assertiveness, and material success.

mass production A type of technology characterized by the production of a large volume of products with the same specifications.

matching model An employee selection approach in which the organization and the applicant attempt to match each other's needs, interests, and values.

materials management The complete integration of all organizational departments and activities that contribute to the costs of materials.

materials requirement planning (MRP) A dependent demand inventory planning and control system that schedules the precise amount of all materials required to support the production of desired end products.

matrix boss A product or functional boss, responsible for one side of the matrix.

matrix structure An organizational structure that utilizes functional and divisional structures simultaneously in the same part of the organization.

maturity stage The phase of the organization life cycle in which the organization has become exceedingly large and mechanistic.

means-ends chain The process by which the achievement of lower-level objectives leads to the attainment of higher-level goals.

mechanistic structure An organizational structure characterized by rigidly defined tasks, many rules and regulations, little teamwork, and centralized decision making.

mediation The process of using a third party to settle a dispute.

mentor A senior employee who acts as a sponsor and teacher to a younger, less experienced employee.

merger The combination of two or more organizations into one.

merit pay A motivational program that rewards employees in proportion to their contributions to the organization.

message The tangible formulation of an idea to be sent to a receiver.

mid-career renewal strategy A strategy designed to provide advancement opportunities for deserving mid-career employees while maximizing the contributions of plateaued employees who continue to perform satisfactorily.

mid-career stage The stage of career development characterized by either growth, maintenance, or decline.

middle manager A manager who works at the middle levels of the organization and is responsible for major departments.

midlife stage The phase of the organization life cycle in which the firm has reached prosperity and grown substantially large.

mission The organization's reason for existence.

mission statement A broadly stated definition of the organization's basic business scope and operations that distinguish it from similar types of organizations.

model A simplified representation of a real-life situation.

monitor A type of informational role that involves seeking current information from many sources for the purpose of keeping well informed.

Monte Carlo method A variation of simulation modeling that inserts random occurrences into the model in order to reflect the possibility of real-life problems.

motivation The arousal, direction, and persistence of behavior.

motivators Factors that influence job satisfaction based on fulfillment of higher-level needs such as achievement, recognition, responsibility, and opportunity for growth.

multidomestic strategy The modification of product design and advertising strategies to suit the specific needs of individual countries.

multinational corporation (MNC) An organization that receives more than 25 percent of its total sales revenues from operations outside the parent company's home country.

multiple advocacy A decision-making technique that involves several advocates and presentation of multiple points of view, including minority and unpopular opinions.

multiple control system A control system involving the simultaneous use of feedforward, concurrent, and feedback control.

need A desire that translates into an internal drive that motivates a specific behavior with which to fulfill it.

need for achievement The desire to accomplish difficult tasks, attain a high standard of success, and surpass others.

need for affiliation The desire to form close personal relationships and avoid conflict.

need for power The desire to influence, control, and have authority over others.

needs analysis A professional assessment of a company's training needs and development of a program designed to meet them.

negotiation The use of formal bargaining to win acceptance and approval of a proposed change.

negotiator A type of decisional role that involves formal negotiations and bargaining to attain outcomes for the manager's unit of responsibility.

network corporation An organization that is electronically connected to other companies or subsidiaries that perform each of its functions.

networking The linking together of groups and departments within or across organizations for the purpose of sharing information resources.

neutralizer A situational variable that counteracts a leadership style and prevents the leader from displaying certain behaviors.

nominal group A group decision-making format that emphasizes equal participation in the decision process by all group members.

nonparticipator role A role in which the individual contributes little to either the task or members' social-emotional needs.

nonprogrammed decision A decision made in response to a situation that is unique, is poorly defined and largely unstructured, and has important consequences for the organization.

nonroutine service technology Service technology in which there are no specific procedures for directing employees, problem situations are varied, and employees must rely on personal resources for problem solving.

nonverbal communication A communication transmitted through actions and behaviors rather than through words.

norm A standard of conduct that is shared by group members and guides their behavior.

normative model A model that defines how a decision maker should make decisions and provides guidelines for reaching an ideal outcome for the organization.

norming The stage of group development in which conflicts developed during the storming stage are resolved and group harmony and unity emerge.

objective A specific short-term target for which measurable results can be obtained.

obstructive response A response to social demands in which the organization denies responsibility, claims that evidence of misconduct is misleading or distorted, and attempts to obstruct investigation.

on-the-job training (OJT) A type of training in which an experienced employee "adopts" a new employee for the purpose of teaching him or her how to perform job duties.

open salary information A policy of disclosing all employees' salaries to all organization members.

open system A system that interacts with the external environment.

operating budget The plan for the allocation of financial resources to each organizational responsibility center for the budget period under consideration.

operational objectives Specific, measurable results expected from departments, work groups, and individuals within the organization.

operational plans Plans developed at the organization's lower levels that specify action steps toward achieving operational goals and support tactical planning activities.

operations management The field of management that specializes in the physical production of goods or services and uses quantitative techniques for solving manufacturing problems.

operations research A subfield of the management science perspective consisting of mathematical model building and other applications of quantitative approaches to management problems.

operations strategy The recognition of the importance of operations to the firm's success and the involvement of operations managers in the organization's strategic planning.

opportunity A characteristic of the external environment that has the potential to help the organization achieve or exceed its strategic goals.

ordering costs Costs associated with placing an order for an inventory item, including postage, receiving, and inspection.

organic structure An organizational structure that is free flowing, has few rules and regulations, encourages employee teamwork, and decentralizes decision making to employees doing the job.

organization A social entity that is goal directed and deliberately structured.

organizational change The adoption of a new idea or behavior by an organization.

organizational control The systematic process through which managers regulate organizational activities to make them consistent with the expectations established in plans, targets, and performance standards.

organizational development (OD) The application of behavioral science techniques to improve an organization's health and effectiveness through its ability to cope with environmental changes, improve internal relationships, and increase problem-solving capabilities.

organizational environment All elements existing outside the organization's boundaries that have the potential to affect the organization.

organization chart The visual representation of an organization's structure.

organization life cycle The organization's evolution through major developmental stages.

organization structure The framework in which the organization defines how tasks are divided, resources are deployed, and departments are coordinated.

organizing The management function concerned with assigning tasks, grouping tasks into departments, and allocating resources to departments.

output The reports and other organized information that the information system produces for its users.

outsourcing A retrenchment strategy in which an organization directly invests in plants in foreign countries for supplying consumers in its home country.

owners' equity The difference between assets and liabilities.

paper-and-pencil test A written test designed to measure a particular attribute such as intelligence or aptitude.

partial productivity The ratio of total outputs to the inputs from a single major input category.

partial reinforcement schedule A schedule in which only some occurrences of the desired behavior are reinforced.

participation A change implementation tactic that involves users and potential resisters in the design of a change.

participative leadership Leadership behavior that involves consultation with subordinates over decisions.

path (PERT) A specified sequence of activities and events on a network diagram.

path-goal theory A contingency approach to leadership specifying that the leader's responsibility is to increase subordinates' motivation by clarifying the behaviors necessary for task accomplishment and rewards.

pause strategy A temporary stability strategy adopted to consolidate activities prior to a new growth stage.

payoff matrix A decision-making aid comprised of relevant strategies, states of nature, probability of occurrence of states of nature, and expected outcome(s).

pay survey A study of what other companies pay employees in jobs that correspond to a sample of key positions selected by the organization.

pay-trend line A graph that shows the relationship between pay and total job point values for the purpose of determining the worth of a given job.

people change A change in employees' attitudes, beliefs, skills, abilities, styles, or behavior.

perception The process of making sense out of one's environment.

perceptual organization The categorization of an object or stimulus according to one's frame of reference.

perceptual selectivity The screening and selection of objects and stimuli that compete for one's attention.

performance The organization's ability to attain its goals by using resources in an efficient and effective manner.

performance appraisal The process of observing and evaluating an employee's performance, recording the assessment, and providing feedback to the employee.

performance appraisal interview A formal review of an employee's performance conducted between the superior and the subordinate.

performance gap A disparity between existing and desired performance levels.

performing The stage of group development in which members focus on problem solving and accomplishing the group's assigned task.

permanent team A group of participants from several departments who meet regularly to solve ongoing problems of common interest.

personal ethics Ethics adapted from the values of individual managers; reflect religion, social consciousness, and/or personal attitudes toward social responsibility.

PERT The Program Evaluation and Review Technique consists of breaking down a project into a network of specific activities and mapping out their sequence and necessary completion dates.

physical ability test A test that simulates the important physical tasks required for a job and measures the applicant's performance on the simulations.

physiological needs The most basic human needs, such as for food, water, and sex.

plan A blueprint specifying the resource allocations, schedules, and other actions necessary for attaining goals.

planned change Change that is designed and implemented in an orderly and timely manner to meet current problems and anticipated future needs.

planning The management function concerned with defining goals for future organizational performance and deciding on the tasks and resource use needed to attain them.

planning mode A mode of strategy formulation that emphasizes a logical and rational rather than intuitive approach.

planning task force A temporary group consisting of line managers responsible for developing strategic plans.

P → O expectancy Expectancy that successful performance of a task will lead to the desired outcome.

point system A job evaluation system that assigns a predetermined point value to each compensable job factor in order to determine the worth of a given job.

policy A general statement based on the organization's overall goals and strategic plans that provides directions for individuals within the company.

political activity Organizational attempts, such as lobbying, to influence government legislation and regulation.

political forces The influence of political institutions on people and organizations.

political risk A company's risk of loss of assets, earning power, or managerial control due to politically motivated events or actions by host governments.

polycentric company An MNC that is oriented toward individual host country markets.

portfolio strategy A type of corporate-level strategy that pertains to the organization's mix of SBUs and product lines that fit together in such a way as to provide the corporation with synergy and competitive advantage.

position power The extent of a leader's formal authority over subordinates.

positive reinforcement The administration of a rewarding consequence following performance of a desired behavior.

post-action control *See* feedback control.

power The potential ability to influence others' behavior.

power distance The degree to which people accept inequality in power among institutions, organizations, and people.

preliminary control *See* feedforward control.

preretirement program A strategy designed to assist employees in coping with the stress of the transition from work to retirement.

preventative control *See* feedforward control.

proactive response A response to social demands in which the organization seeks to learn what is in its constituencies' interest and to respond without pressure from them.

problem A situation in which organizational accomplishments have failed to meet established objectives.

procedure A specific series of steps to be used in achieving certain objectives; usually applies to individual jobs.

process culture A type of corporate culture characterized by low-risk decision making, little or no feedback, and low-stake decisions.

process layout A facilities layout in which machines that perform the same function are grouped together in one location.

process theories A group of theories that explain how employees select behaviors with which to meet their needs and determine whether their choices were successful.

processing The manipulation, organization, sorting, and utilization of data.

producibility The degree to which a product or service can be produced for a customer within the organization's existing operational capacity.

product-based structure A global organization structure in which an MNC establishes product divisions whose managers plan, organize, and control all functions for producing and distributing their products at home and worldwide.

product change A change in the organization's product or service output.

productivity The organization's output of products and services divided by its inputs.

product layout A facilities layout in which machines and tasks are arranged according to the sequence of steps in the production of a single product.

product life cycle The stages through which a product or service goes: (1) development and introduction into the marketplace, (2) growth, (3) maturity, and (4) decline.

professional bureaucracy A large, functionally structured organization that has professional employees and uses a nonroutine service technology.

professional ethics Ethics defined by professional occupational groups for member individuals and companies.

profitability ratio A financial ratio that describes the firm's profits.

profit budget An operating budget that combines both expense and revenue budgets into one statement showing gross and net profits.

profit center A responsibility center in which the budget is used to measure the difference between revenues and costs.

profit margin on sales A profitability ratio calculated by dividing net income by sales.

profit-maximizing view The belief that an organization's responsibility is to operate in a manner that will increase its profits while staying within the rules of the game.

program A complex set of objectives and plans for achieving an important, one-time organizational goal.

programmed decision A decision made in response to a situation that has occurred often enough to have generated decision rules that can be applied in each recurrence of the problem.

project A set of relatively short-term, narrow objectives and plans for achieving a major, one-time organizational goal.

project manager A manager who coordinates people across several departments to accomplish a specific project.

prospector A type of adaptive strategy for a changing environment emphasizing innovation, discovery of new opportunities, risk taking, and growth.

prototype A working model of an information system developed to test the system's features.

public statement An oral or written communication expressing the organization's mission and values.

punishment The administration of an unpleasant consequence, usually following the peformance of an undesirable behavior.

purchasing function The organizational function concerned with finding and obtaining the right goods at the desired price and time, in the needed quantity, and of the correct quality.

qualitative forecast A forecast based on the opinions of experts in the absence of precise historical data.

quality The degree to which information accurately portrays reality; the excellence of a product or service.

quality circle A group of from six to twelve volunteer employees who meet regularly to discuss and solve problems that affect their common work activities.

quantitative forecast A forecast that begins with a series of past data values and applies a set of mathematical rules with which to predict future values.

question mark A BCG matrix classification for an SBU that exists in a new, rapidly growing industry but has only a small market share and thus is considered a risky investment.

queuing theory A management science technique that uses mathematics to calculate ways of providing services that will minimize customers' waiting time.

random variation An unpredictable variation in the behavior of a variable.

raw materials inventory Inventory consisting of the basic inputs to the organization's production process.

reactor A type of adaptive "nonstrategy" that involves ad hoc responses to environmental threats and opportunities rather than definitive strategies for specific environments.

realistic job preview (RJP) A recruiting approach that gives applicants all pertinent and realistic information about the job and the organization.

rebuilding The stage in the organization revitalization process characterized by innovation for the purpose of achieving controlled growth.

recruiting The activities or practices that define the desired characteristics of applicants for specific jobs.

referent power Power that results from leader characteristics that command subordinates' identification with, respect and admiration for, and desire to emulate the leader.

refreezing A step in the reinforcement stage of organizational development in which individuals acquire a desired new skill or attitude and are rewarded for it by the organization.

regression analysis A statistical tool for predicting the value of a dependent variable based on the known values of independent variables.

reinforcement Anything that causes a given behavior to be repeated or inhibited.

reinforcement theory A motivation theory based on the relationship between a given behavior and its consequences.

relationship-oriented leader A leader who is concerned primarily with people.

relevance The degree to which information pertains to the problems, decisions, and tasks for which a manager is responsible.

reliability The degree to which a product or service can be counted on to fulfill its intended purpose.

reorder point (ROP) The most economical level at which an inventory item should be reordered.

resistance Subordinates' attempt to avoid carrying out instructions and disobey orders.

resource allocator A type of decisional role that pertains to decisions on how to allocate the organization's resources to attain desired outcomes.

resource deployment The level and pattern of the organization's distribution of physical, financial, and human resources for achieving its strategic goals.

responsibility center Any organizational department under the supervision of a single individual who is responsible for its activity.

restraining force A force that resists a proposed change.

retrenchment A type of grand strategy in which the organization reduces current business units or sells off or liquidates entire businesses in response to a period of forced decline.

return on total assets (ROA) The percentage return on assets to investors.

revenue budget An operating budget that identifies the revenues required by the organization.

revenue center A responsibility center in which the budget is based on generated revenues or income.

revitalization The infusion of renewed strength, vigor, and competitiveness into an organization.

reward power Power that results from the leader's authority to reward others.

risk A situation in which the decision to be made has clear-cut objectives and sufficient information available but the future outcomes associated with each alternative are subject to chance.

risk propensity The willingness to undertake risk with the opportunity of gaining an increased payoff.

role A set of expectations for one's behavior.

rollback A decision-making procedure that begins with the end branches of a decision tree and works backward by assigning a value to each decision fork and chance fork.

routine service technology Service technology in which work can be broken down into explicit steps and employees can follow objective procedures for serving customers and solving problems.

rule A statement describing how a specific action is to be performed.

safety needs The needs for a safe physical and emotional environment.

sales force composite A type of qualitative forecasting that relies on the combined expert opinions of field sales personnel.

sales forecast A forecast of future company sales based on projected customer demand for products or services.

satisfice To choose the first solution alternative that satisfies minimal decision criteria regardless of whether better solutions are presumed to exist.

scalar principle The concept of a clearly defined line of authority in the organization that includes all employees.

schedule of reinforcement The frequency with and intervals over which reinforcement occurs.

scientific management A subfield of the classical management perspective that emphasized scientifically determined changes in management practices as the solution to improving labor productivity.

scope The number of businesses, products, or services that defines the size of the domain within which the organization deals with the environment.

search The process of learning about current developments inside or outside the organization that can be used to meet a perceived need for change.

seasonal variation A regular variation in the behavior of a variable that recurs within a period of one year or less.

secular trend The general behavior of a variable over a long period of time.

selection The process of determining the skills, abilities, and other attributes needed to perform a particular job.

self-actualization needs The needs for self-fulfillment, personal growth, creativity, challenge, and advancement.

semantics The meaning of words and the way they are used.

service organization An organization that produces nonphysical goods that require customer involvement and cannot be stored in inventory.

service technology Technology characterized by intangible outputs and direct contact between employees and customers.

short-term planning Planning that includes operational objectives for specific departments and individuals and has a time horizon of one year or less.

simple structure An organization that is new, small, and in the entrepreneurial stage of the life cycle.

simulation model A mathematical representation of the relationships among variables in real-world organizational situations.

single-use plans Plans that are developed to achieve a set of objectives that are unlikely to be repeated in the future.

situation analysis Analysis of the strengths, weaknesses, opportunities, and threats (SWOT) that affect organizational performance.

size The organization's scope or magnitude, typically measured by number of employees.

skill variety The number of diverse activities that make up a job and the number of skills used to perform it.

skunkworks A small, informal, and sometimes unauthorized group who creates innovations.

slogan A phrase or sentence that succinctly expresses a key corporate value.

small batch production A type of technology that involves the production of goods in batches of one or a few products designed to customer specification.

social contract The unwritten, common rules and perceptions about relationships among people and between people and organizations.

social facilitation The tendency for the presence of others to influence an individual's motivation and performance.

social forces The aspects of a culture that guide and influence relationships among people—their values, needs, and standards of behavior.

social responsibility The obligation of organization management to make decisions and take actions that will enhance the welfare and interests of society as well as the organization's.

sociocultural dimension The dimension of the general environment representing the demographic characteristics, norms, customs, and values of the population within which the organization operates.

socioemotional role A role in which the individual provides support for group members' emotional needs and social unity.

software The set of instructions that control and direct computer processing.

span of control *See* span of management.

span of management The number of employees who report to a supervisor; also called *span of control*.

spokesperson A type of informational role that pertains to official statements to people outside the organization about company policies, actions, or plans.

sponsor A high-level manager who approves and protects a new idea and removes major organizational barriers to its acceptance.

staff authority A form of authority granted to staff specialists in their areas of expertise.

staff department A department that provides specialized skills in support of line departments.

standards of performance Departmental goals expressed in specific operational terms to permit comparison with organizational activities.

standing plans Ongoing plans that are used as guidance for tasks performed repeatedly within the organization.

star A BCG matrix classification for an SBU that has a large market share in a rapidly growing industry and thus offers the promise of future growth and profits.

state of nature A future event or condition that is relevant to a decision outcome.

statistical process control (SPC) A type of managerial control that employs carefully gathered data and statistical analysis to evaluate the quality and productivity of employee activities.

stereotype A widely held generalization about a group of people that assigns attributes to them solely on the basis of a limited number of categories.

storage The information system function in which data are stored in an organized manner for future processing or until needed by users.

storming The stage of group development in which individual personalities and roles, and resulting conflicts, emerge.

story A narrative based on true events that is repeated frequently and shared by organizational employees.

strategic business unit (SBU) A division of the organization that has a unique business mission, product line, competitors, and markets relative to other SBUs in the same corporation.

strategic control point An activity that is especially important for achieving the organization's strategic objectives.

strategic goals Broad statements of where the organization wants to be in the future; pertain to the organization as a whole rather than to specific divisions or departments.

strategic management The set of decisions and actions used to formulate and implement strategies that will provide a competitively superior fit between the organization and its environment so as to achieve organizational objectives.

strategic plans The action steps by which an organization intends to attain its strategic goals.

strategy The plan of action that prescribes resource allocation and other activities for dealing with the environment and helping the organization attain its goals.

strategy formulation The stage of strategic management that involves the planning and decision making that lead to the establishment of the organization's goals and of a specific strategic plan.

strategy implementation The stage of strategic management that involves the use of managerial and organizational tools to direct resources toward achieving strategic outcomes.

strength A positive internal characteristic that the organization can exploit to achieve its strategic goals.

stress The physiological and emotional response to demands, constraints, and opportunities that create uncertainty when important outcomes are at stake.

structure change Any change in the way in which the organization is designed and managed.

substitute A situational variable that makes a leadership style redundant or unnecessary.

subsystems Parts of a system that depend on one another for their functioning.

succession planning The process of creating a plan for moving people into higher organizational levels.

superordinate goal A goal that cannot be reached by a single party.

suppliers People and organizations who provide the raw materials the organization uses to produce its output.

supportive leadership Leadership behavior that indicates concern for subordinates' well-being and personal needs.

survey feedback A type of OD intervention in which questionnaires on organizational climate and other factors are distributed among employees and the results reported back to them by a change agent.

symbol An object, act, or event that conveys meaning to others.

symbolic manager A manager who defines and uses signals and symbols to influence corporate culture.

synergy The condition that exists when the organization's parts interact to produce a joint effect that is greater than the sum of the parts acting alone.

system A set of interrelated parts that function as a whole to achieve a common purpose.

systems development life cycle The sequence of events that CBIS designers follow in developing and implementing a new system.

systems theory An extension of the human resource perspective that describes organizations as open systems that are characterized by entropy, synergy, and subsystem interdependence.

tactical objectives Objectives that define the outcomes that major divisions and departments must achieve in order for the organization to reach its overall goals.

tactical plans Plans designed to help execute major strategic plans and to accomplish a specific part of the organization's strategy.

tall structure A management structure characterized by an overall narrow span of management and a relatively large number of hierarchical levels.

task environment The layer of the external environment that directly influences the organization's operations and performance.

task force A temporary team or committee formed to solve a specific short-run problem involving several departments.

task group A formal group created to achieve a specific goal within a limited time period.

task identity The extent to which an employee performs an entire job with a distinct beginning and ending.

task-oriented leader A leader who is concerned mainly with task accomplishment.

task significance The degree to which the job is perceived as important and impactful on the organization or consumers.

task specialist role A role in which the individual devotes personal time and energy to helping the group accomplish its task.

task structure The extent to which subordinates' tasks are defined, involve specific procedures, and have clear, explicit goals.

team building A type of OD intervention that enhances the cohesiveness of departments by helping members to learn to function as a team.

technical complexity The degree to which machinery is involved in the production process to the exclusion of people.

technical core The heart of the organization's production of its product or service.

technical skill The understanding of and proficiency in the performance of specific tasks.

technological dimension The dimension of the general environment that includes scientific and technological advancements in the industry and society at large.

technological forecast A forecast of the occurrence of technological changes that could affect an organization's way of doing business.

technology The knowledge, tools, techniques, and activities used to transform the organization's inputs into outputs.

technology change A change that pertains to the organization's production process.

telecommunications A set of communication and conferencing devices based on electronic communications technology.

telecommuting A network corporation whose employees work from their homes via terminals that connect them with the office.

Theory Z A management perspective that uses Japanese management techniques of trusting employees and making them feel an intimate part of the organization.

threat A characteristic of the external environment that may prevent the organization from achieving its strategic goals.

timeliness The degree to which information is available soon after events occur.

time series analysis A forecasting technique that examines the patterns of movement in historical data.

timing The extent to which the provision of a service meets the customer's delivery requirements.

top-down approach An approach to innovation in which ideas are developed at upper organizational levels and implemented downward.

top-down budgeting A budgeting process in which middle- and lower-level managers set departmental budget targets in accordance with overall company revenues and expenditures specified by top management.

top leader The overseer of both the product and functional chains of command, responsible for the entire matrix.

top manager A manager who is at the top of the organizational hierarchy and responsible for the entire organization.

total-debt-to-total-assets ratio A leverage ratio calculated by dividing the firm's total debts by its total assets.

total factor productivity The ratio of total outputs to the inputs from labor, capital, materials, and energy.

total quality control A control concept that gives workers rather than managers the responsibility for achieving standards of quality.

total study A process that attempts to assess information requirements at all management levels.

tough-guy, macho culture A type of corporate culture that emerges in a strategic situation characterized by high-risk decision making, rapid feedback, and large-scale projects.

trade association An association made up of organizations with similar interests for the purpose of influencing the environment.

tradition method A mechanism for allocating resources based on how they were distributed in the past.

training The process of teaching lower-level or technical employees the skills needed to do their present jobs.

training and development An organizational intervention with the purpose of facilitating employees' mastery of job-related behaviors.

training program evaluation A control-group technique designed to measure the effectiveness of a training program on participants' job performance.

traits The distinguishing personal characteristics of a leader, such as intelligence, values, and appearance.

transactional leader A leader who clarifies subordinates' role and task requirements, initiates structure, provides rewards, and displays consideration for subordinates.

transaction processing system (TPS) A type of CBIS that performs the organization's routinely occurring transactions.

transformational leader A type of inspirational leader who effects a major strategic change in the organization.

two-boss employee An employee who reports to two supervisors simultaneously.

two-factor theory A motivation theory developed by Herzberg suggesting that the work factors associated with satisfaction differ from those pertaining to dissatisfaction.

uncertainty Lack of information about environmental factors that makes it difficult to predict external changes and resource availability.

uncertainty avoidance A value characterized by people's intolerance for uncertainty and ambiguity and resulting support for beliefs that promise certainty and conformity.

unfreezing A step in the diagnosis stage of organizational development in which participants are made aware of problems in order to increase their willingness to change their behavior.

unity of command The principle that every employee be held accountable to only one supervisor.

upward communication Messages transmitted from the lower to the higher levels in the organization's hierarchy.

valence The value of outcomes for the individual.

validity The relationship between an applicant's score on a selection device and his or her future job performance.

variable costs Costs that are based on an explicit physical relationship with the volume of department activity; also called *engineered costs.*

variable-interval schedule A schedule that administers reinforcement at random, unpredictable time intervals.

variable-ratio schedule A schedule that administers reinforcement following a random number of desired responses.

venture team A group separate from the mainstream of the organization who is responsible for developing and initiating innovations.

videoconferencing A mechanism that uses a live television hookup to allow group members to see one another during a conference.

voice messaging A mechanism by which a computer answers phones, relays and records messages, and transmits information.

Vroom-Yetton model A model designed to help leaders identify the appropriate amount of subordinate participation in decision making.

weakness A negative internal characteristic that may inhibit or restrict the organization's performance.

whistle blowing The disclosure by an employee of illegal, immoral, or illegitimate practices by the organization.

wholly owned foreign affiliate A foreign subsidiary over which an organization has complete control.

work hard/play hard culture A form of corporate culture characterized by low-risk decision making, rapid feedback, and many small-scale decisions.

work-in-process inventory Inventory composed of the materials that are still moving through the stages of the production process.

work redesign The altering of jobs to increase both the quality of employees' work experience and their productivity.

work specialization The degree to which organizational tasks are subdivided into individual jobs; also called *division of labor.*

youth stage The phase of the organization life cycle in which the organization is growing rapidly and has a product enjoying some marketplace success.

zero-based budgeting (ZBB) A budgeting process in which each responsibility center calculates its resource needs based on the coming year's priorities rather than on the previous year's budget.

Photo Credits

Chapter 1

Page 2: Courtesy of Dataproducts Corporation. Page 4: Courtesy of Dataproducts Corporation. Page 7: Courtesy of Interco Incorporated. Page 8: Courtesy of Honeywell Incorporated. Page 9: Courtesy of TRW Incorporated. Page 11: Courtesy of Campbell Soup Company. Page 12: Courtesy of Chrysler Motors Corporation. Page 17: Courtesy of Textron Incorporated. Page 19: Courtesy of *Working Woman* Magazine. Page 20: Courtesy of Pepsico Incorporated. Page 24: Courtesy of American Honda Motor Company, Incorporated.

Chapter 2

Page 32: National Archives. Page 34: Courtesy of Baker Library, Harvard Business School. Page 36: National Archives. Page 38: Historical Pictures Service, Chicago. Page 39: Historical Pictures Service, Chicago. Page 40: Frederick W. Taylor Collection, S.C. Williams Library, Stevens Institute of Technology. Page 41: Courtesy of Ronald G. Greenwood. Page 42: Courtesy of Ronald G. Greenwood. Page 43: (top) Courtesy of Ford Motor Company; (bottom) From the Collections of Henry Ford Museum and Greenfield Village. Page 44: National Archives. Page 45: Courtesy of German Information Center. Page 48: Courtesy of Western Electric Photographic Services. Page 51: Courtesy of Daimler-Benz AG. Page 52: Courtesy of Daimler-Benz AG. Page 54: Reprinted with permission of Dean Foods Corporation. Page 58: © 1986 Jonathan Selig for Southland Corporation. Page 59: © Ralson Purina Company 1985. Reprinted by permission.

Chapter 3

Page 64: Courtesy of J. P. Morgan & Company Incorporated. Page 66: Ira Wexler for U.S. Air. Page 69: © Deborah MacNeill. Page 71: Courtesy of J. P. Morgan & Company Incorporated. Page 75: © Lotus Development Corporation 1987. Used with permission. Page 76: Courtesy of Toyota Motor Corporation. Page 78: Courtesy of Clairol. Page 80: Courtesy of Waste Management, Incorporated. Page 82: Courtesy of Anheuser-Busch Companies, Incorporated. Page 87: Courtesy of Honeywell Incorporated. Page 90: Courtesy of J. P. Morgan & Company Incorporated.

Chapter 4

Page 98: Courtesy of Pier 1 Imports. Page 101: Courtesy of American Airlines. Page 103: Courtesy of American Egg Board. Page 107: Courtesy of Pacific Gas & Electric Company. Page 110: Courtesy of Pier 1 Imports. Page 113: Courtesy of American Medical International, Incorporated. Page 114: © Ken Graham for KeyCorp. Page 117: Courtesy of Chrysler Motors Corporation. Page 118: Courtesy of Agricultural Division, Ciba-Geigy Corporation. Page 120: Courtesy of Goulds Pumps, Incorporated. Page 123: Courtesy of Fleming Companies, Incorporated. Page 125: Courtesy of PepsiCo Incorporated.

Chapter 5

Page 130: Courtesy of Ohio Bell, an Ameritech Company. Page 133: Courtesy of Staley Continental Incorporated. Page 136: Reprinted with permission from the quarterly publication of RJR Nabisco. Page 138: Ed Young for Lucky Stores, Incorporated. Page 141: © Robert Arnold Photographer. Page 143: © Hasbro, Incorporated. Page 147: Courtesy of The Quaker Oats Company. Page 149: Courtesy of Batus, Incorporated. Page 151: Courtesy of Quaker State Corporation. Page 153: Courtesy of Sealy, Incorporated. Page 156: Hayes L. Hemphill, Columbia Gas Distribution Companies. Page 157: Courtesy of Ohio Bell, an Ameritech Company.

Chapter 6

Page 162: Courtesy of Weyerhaeuser Company. Page 164: Lynn Johnson/Black Star. Page 166: Courtesy of Ore-Ida Foods Incorporated. Page 167: © Kathryn Lambert. Page 169: Courtesy of Weyerhaeuser Company. Page 171: Erich Hartmann/Magnum Photos, Incorporated. Page 174: Courtesy of Lever Brothers Company. Page 176: Courtesy of Amoco Corporation. Page 180: Courtesy of Marriott Corporation. Page 182: Courtesy of Compaq Computer Corporation. Page 185: Courtesy of Borg Warner. Page 187: Courtesy of The Pillsbury Company.

Chapter 7

Page 192: Courtesy of BMW of North America, Incorporated. Page 194: Courtesy of Exxon Corporation. Page 196: © 1987 CABBAGE PATCH KIDS® and all related trademarks are owned by and licensed from Original Appalachian Artworks, Incorporated, Cleveland, Georgia, U.S.A. All Rights Reserved. Page 199: Courtesy of The Glidden Company, Huron, Ohio. Page 201: Courtesy of Dayton Hudson Department Store. Page 204: Courtesy of BMW of North America, Incorporated. Page 208: Courtesy of Central Soya Company, Incorporated. Page 210: Courtesy of Caterpillar Incorporated. Page 216: Courtesy of Amoco Corporation. Page 219: Courtesy of Daimler-Benz AG. Page 221: © J. P. Morgan & Company Incorporated. Photography by Tom Hollyman.

Chapter 8

Page 228: Appleton Papers Incorporated. Courtesy of the BATUS Group of Companies. Page 230: John T. Urban/Stock, Boston. Page 233: Courtesy of ARA Services. Page 235: Courtesy of Avnet, Incorporated. Page 240: © 1985 Ted Kawalerski for Bausch & Lomb. Page 243: Courtesy of Humana Hospital. Page 244: Courtesy of Waste Management, Incorporated. Page 248: U.S. Marine Corps. Page 251: Courtesy of PepsiCo Incorporated. Page 255: Courtesy of Ford Motor Company. Page 256: Appleton Papers Incorporated. Courtesy of the BATUS Group of Companies. Page 259: Courtesy of Bally Manufacturing Corporation.

Chapter 9

Page 264: Photography by Jeff Smith for Pan Am. Page 268: Courtesy of Harris Corporation. Page 271: Courtesy of Harrison Radiator Division, General Motors Corporation. Page 275: Photo by Barry Tenin. Courtesy of Armstrong Rubber Company. Page 284: Courtesy of Tenneco Incorporated. Page 287: By permission of NIKE, Incorporated and ProServ, Incorporated. Page 289: Courtesy of Hewlett-Packard Company. Page 293: Courtesy of the Orchestral Association, Chicago Symphony Orchestra. Page 294: Photography by Jeff Smith for Pan Am.

Chapter 10

Page 300: Reprinted with permission, *Inc.* Magazine, August 1985, p. 10. Copyright © 1985 by Inc. Publishing Company, 38 Commercial Wharf, Boston, MA 02110. Page 302: Mark Joseph, Chicago, for 3M Company. Page 304: Courtesy of R. H. Macy & Company, Incorporated. Page 307: Courtesy of Polaroid Corporation. Page 309: Courtesy of Hewlett-Packard Company. Page 310: Reprinted with permission, *Inc.* Magazine, August 1985, p. 10. Copyright © 1985 by Inc. Publishing Company, 38 Commercial Wharf, Boston, MA 02110. Page 313: J. Ross Baughman/Visions. Page 316: Courtesy of USF&G Corporation, 1984 Annual Report. Page 318: Courtesy of The Pillsbury Company. Page 320: Courtesy of Super Valu Stores, Incorporated. Page 322: Richard L. Smith for Hewitt Associates. Page 325: © 1986 David Lawrence. Page 328: Courtesy of Ebasco Services Incorporated.

Chapter 11

Page 332: Mike Mitchell for USAir. Page 335: National Archives. Page 338: Courtesy of BMW AG. Page 341: Mike Mitchell for USAir. Page 343: Courtesy of Ciba-Geigy Corporation. Page 346: Ira Wexler for USAir. Page 348: Courtesy of United Telecom. Page 350: Courtesy of USF&G Corporation, 1984 Annual Report. Page 354: Courtesy of Varian Associates, Incorporated. Page 356: Courtesy of Honeywell, Incorporated. Page 358: Comerica Incorporated/Richard Hirneisen Photography. Page 359: Courtesy of Best Western International.

Chapter 12

Page 366: U.S. Army Recruitment Brochure. Page 368: U.S. Army Recruitment Brochure. Page 370: Gary Gladstone for Price Waterhouse. Page 373: Courtesy of International Business Machines Corporation. Page 375: U.S. Marine Corps. Page 376: Courtesy of Flowers Industries, Incorporated. Photo by Ed Lallo. Page 379: © Terry Husebye. Page 383: © Richard Howard. Page 385: Courtesy of The Goodyear Tire & Rubber Company. Page 387: Photo by Ted Horowitz. Courtesy of Schering-Plough Corporation. Page 391: The Bettmann Archive. Page 392: Joe McNally for General Electric Corporation.

Chapter 13

Page 396: Courtesy of Waste Management, Incorporated. Page 399: Courtesy of David Wojdyla. Page 400: Courtesy of Pennwalt Corporation, Philadelphia, Pennsylvania. Page 402: Courtesy of Waste Management, Incorporated. Page 403: Courtesy of The Limited, Inc. Page 408: John Blaustein for McKesson Corporation. Page 410: Courtesy of Mary Kay Cosmetics, Incorporated. Page 413: © York Restaurants. Page 416: Courtesy of Bally Manufacturing Corporation. Page 418: Courtesy of United States Shoe Corporation. Page 420: Alen MacWeeney for Bell Atlantic. Page 422: Courtesy of Nationwide® Insurance.

Chapter 14

Page 428: Courtesy of Southwest Airlines. Page 430: Courtesy of Georgia Power Company. Page 433: © 1985 John Madere. Page 434: Courtesy of Southwest Airlines. Page 438: Courtesy of New Departure Hyatt's *Communicator*, Volume 13, Number 3. Page 439: © 1987 Tony Ward, photographer for Alco Health Services Corporation. Page 443: © 1986 James Visser. Page 444: © Steve Krongard for American Express Company. Page 446: Photograph by Keeler. Reprinted with permission of Dayton Hudson Corporation. Page 448: Courtesy of Medi-Plus Laboratories, Division of Arvey Corporation, Sander Allen Advertising, Chicago, Illinois. Page 451: Courtesy of Ford Motor Company. Page 453: Wyatt McSpodden for Phillips Petroleum Company.

Chapter 15

Page 458: Courtesy of Wetterau Incorporated. Page 460: Photography by Jeff Smith for Pan Am. Page 463: Courtesy of Pennwalt Corporation, Philadelphia, Pennsylvania. Page 465: Courtesy of Wetterau Incorporated. Page 466: Photograph by Cindy Wheaton for The Dryden Press. Page 469: Joe Baraban Photography, Incorporated. Page 471: Courtesy of Steelcase Incorporated. Page 475: Courtesy of Hayes L. Hemphill of Columbia Gas of Ohio, Incorporated. Page 478: Courtesy of Pier 1 Imports. Page 480: Courtesy of Knight-Ridder, Incorporated. Page 482: Courtesy of J. P. Morgan & Company Incorporated.

Chapter 16

Page 490: Courtesy of US West, Incorporated. Page 494: Reproduced with permission of AT&T Corporate Archive. Page 495: Courtesy of Leo Burnett Company. Page 496: Gary Blokley/Mary Kay Cosmetics, Incorporated. Page 500: Alan Berner/*Seattle Times*. Page 503: Courtesy of Herman Miller, Incorporated. Page 505: Courtesy of Toyota Motor Corporation. Page 506: Courtesy of AM International, Incorporated. Page 509: Courtesy of Dynascan Corporation. Page 512: Courtesy of US West, Incorporated. Page 513: Courtesy of A&P. Page 514: Courtesy of Scott Paper Company.

Chapter 17

Page 524: Courtesy of Honeywell, Incorporated. Page 526: Courtesy of The Goodyear Tire & Rubber Company. Page 531: Ira Wexler for USAir. Page 534: Reprinted courtesy of Eastman Kodak Company. Page 535: Courtesy of Anheuser-Busch Companies, Incorporated. Page 537: Courtesy of Honeywell, Incorporated. Page 540: Courtesy of Caterpillar Incorporated. Page 544: Courtesy of Wal-Mart Stores, Incorporated. Page 545: Courtesy of Hughes Aircraft Company. Page 546: Courtesy of Burlington Industries Incorporated. Page 551: Courtesy of NYNEX/Roger Tully.

Chapter 18

Page 556: Courtesy of Tasty Baking Company. Page 559: Courtesy of Tasty Baking Company. Page 562: Mark Joseph/Chicago for IC Industries. Page 564: Courtesy of The Goodyear Tire & Rubber Company. Page 566: Gary Gladstone for Price Waterhouse. Page 570: Courtesy of The Quaker Oats Company. Page 571: Courtesy of Warner-Lambert Company. Page 576: Courtesy of The Quaker Oats Company. Page 581: Courtesy of The Gillette Company. Page 584: Courtesy of AMP Incorporated.

Chapter 19

Page 590: Courtesy of International Business Machines Corporation. Page 592: Used by permission of Apple Computer, Incorporated. Page 595: Courtesy of J. P. Morgan & Company Incorporated. Page 599: Courtesy of International Business Machines Corporation. Page 601: Courtesy of Campbell Soup Company. Page 606: Ken Regan/Camera 5. Page 608: Courtesy of J. P. Morgan & Company Incorporated. Page 610: Courtesy of Federal Express Corporation. All rights reserved. Page 611: Courtesy of International Business Machines Corporation. Page 615: Courtesy of Burlington Industries, Incorporated. Page 616: Courtesy of International Business Machines Corporation.

Chapter 20

Page 624: Courtesy of Tasty Baking Company. Page 628: Courtesy of H&R Block, Incorporated. Page 630: Courtesy of Allen Bradley Company Incorporated. Page 632: Courtesy of International Business Machines Corporation. Page 635: (left) Courtesy of Chrysler Motors Corporation; (right) Courtesy of Lockheed Corporation. Page 636: Courtesy of McDonald's Corporation. Page 637: Courtesy of Tasty Baking Company. Page 639: Courtesy of Noxell Corporation. Page 643: Courtesy of Lear Siegler, Incorporated. Page 647: Copyright Mason Morfit 1986 for Lone Star Industries, Incorporated. Page 649: (left) Courtesy of Perdue Farms Incorporated; (right) Courtesy of History office, U.S. Food & Drug Administration. Page 651: Photo by Hughes Aircraft photographer Gary Panton.

Chapter 21

Page 660: Courtesy of Bristol-Myers Company. Page 663: Courtesy of Bristol-Myers Company. Page 665: Courtesy of Beecham Group p.l.c. Page 667: Reuters/The Bettmann Archive. Page 669: Courtesy of The Gillette Company. Page 673: Courtesy of Caterpillar Incorporated. Page 675: Courtesy of Phillips Petroleum Company. Page 678: Courtesy of The Coca-Cola Company. Page 680: Courtesy of the BOC Group. Page 683: Courtesy of The Coca-Cola Company. Page 687: Courtesy of Mazda Motor Company. Page 688: Courtesy of McDonald's Corporation.

Chapter 22

Page 692: Dana Duke for Colt Industries Incorporated. Page 696: Courtesy of Pfizer Incorporated. Page 700: Courtesy of Bristol-Myers Company. Page 702: Courtesy of Pfizer Incorporated. Page 703: Dana Duke for Colt Industries Incorporated. Page 710: © Charles Moore. Page 713: Courtesy of Goodyear Tire & Rubber Company. Page 714: Courtesy of Smith Kline Beckman Corporation, Philadelphia, PA. Page 715: Courtesy of Pfizer Incorporated. Page 716: © Ron Shuman. Page 720: Hayes L. Hemphill, Columbia Gas Distribution Companies.

Name Index

Acher, Ernest R., 719 *n*
Ackerman, Linda S., 280 *n*
Acosta, Antonio, 411
Adam, Everett E., Jr., 743 *n*
Adams, J. Stacy, 407, 737 *n*
Aggarwal, Sumer C., 743 *nn*
Agor, Weston H., 729 *n*
Ahituv, Niv, 742 *n*
Albanese, Robert, 371 *n*, 735 *n*, 739 *n*
Albertine, J., 724 *n*
Aldag, R. J., 745 *n*
Alderfer, Clayton, 402, 737 *n*
Aldrich, Howard E., 724 *n*, 725 *n*
Aldrich, Nelson W., Jr., 737 *n*
Alexander, R. A, 735 *n*
Altier, William J., 731 *n*
Anderson, Carl R., 727 *n*, 728 *n*
Anderson, Kenneth S., 731 *n*
Anderson, M., 730 *n*
Anderson, Peter, 446
Anderson, William, 662
Andrew, Charles G., 743 *n*
Andrews, John A. Y., 146 *n*
Annas, J. W., 737 *n*
Anthony, N., 741 *nn*
Apcar, Leonard M., 733 *n*
Archer, Lawrence, 538 *n*
Argyris, Chris, 741 *n*
Arnold, Hugh J., 733 *n*, 737 *nn*, 739 *nn*
Arnold, W. J., 725 *n*
Arnone, W., 746 *n*
Aronson, Elliot, 739 *n*
Arvey, R. D., 734 *n*
Ash, Mary Kay, 320, 495, 733 *n*
Ash, Roy, 509–510
Asimov, Isaac, 724 *nn*
Astley, W. Graham, 731 *nn*
Athos, Anthony, 725 *n*, 740 *n*
Aupperle, Kenneth E., 727 *n*
Austin, Larry M., 725 *n*
Austin, Nancy, 648 *n*, 724 *nn*, 725 *n*,
    732 *n*, 737 *n*, 738 *n*, 739 *n*, 740 *n*

Aweida, Jesse, 368
Azumi, Koya, 741 *n*

Babbage, Charles, 39, 724 *n*
Bacharach, Samuel B., 732 *n*
Baird, Inga Skromme, 729 *n*
Baker, Douglas D., 731 *n*
Baker, Kent, 440 *n*
Baker, Michael, 738 *n*
Bales, R. F., 738 *n*
Baligia, B. R., 740 *n*
Balke, Robert R., 736 *n*
Bamford, Janet, 745 *n*
Barbato, Robert, 744 *n*
Bardwick, J. M., 718 *n*, 746 *n*
Barkdull, C. W., 731 *n*
Barnard, Chester I., 43–44
Baron, Robert A., 738 *nn*, 739 *n*
Barouh, Vic, 385–387
Barrett, D., 449 *n*, 738 *nn*
Barrett, G. V., 735 *n*
Barslay, L. A., 734 *n*
Barth, Carl, 41
Bartlett, Christopher A., 744 *n*
Bartlett, Sarah, 727 *n*
Bass, A. R., 734 *n*
Bass, Bernard M., 380 *n*, 390 *n*, 735 *n*,
    736 *nn*
Bass, Robert E., 725 *n*
Bateson, Gregory, 732 *n*
Bavelas, A., 449 *n*, 738 *nn*
Bazerman, Max H., 179 *n*, 729 *n*
Beals, Vaughn, 491, 517
Beam, Alex, 593 *n*, 728 *n*
Beatty, R. W., 357 *n*, 734 *nn*
Beazley, J. Ernest, 29 *n*, 728 *n*
Becker, Helmut, 726 *n*
Becker, Selwyn W., 390 *n*, 733 *n*, 741 *n*
Beckhard, Richard, 733 *n*
Bedeian, Arthur G., 31 *n*, 225 *n*, 724 *n*,
    731 *n*, 733 *n*
Bedford, Norton M., 741 *nn*

Beehr, T. A., 745 *n*
Beiler, George W., 726 *n*
Belcourt, M. L., 745 *n*
Bell, Cecil H., Jr., 733 *n*
Benjamin, Robert L., 742 *nn*
Benne, K. D., 733 *n*, 738 *n*
Benner, Susan, 732 *n*, 738 *n*, 739 *n*
Bennett, Amanda, 744 *n*
Bennett, Howard, 285–286, 286 *n*
Bennis, Warren G., 725 *n*
Berg, T. L., 733 *n*
Bergerac, Michel, 662
Berke, Matthew, 741 *nn*
Berkowitz, L., 737 *n*
Berlo, D. K., 737 *n*
Bernardin, H. J., 734 *nn*
Bertalanffy, Ludwig von, 724 *n*, 725 *n*
Bettenhausen, Kenneth, 738 *n*
Bettner, Jill, 728 *n*
Beyer, Janice M., 739 *n*
Bhagat, R. S., 745 *n*
Bird, B. J., 735 *n*
Birdseye, Clarence, 305
Black, Doug, 211
Black, J. T., 633 *n*
Blackford, Mansel G., 725 *n*
Blake, Robert R., 327 *n*, 374, 733 *n*
Blau, Peter M., 731 *n*
Blaylock, Bruce K., 730 *n*, 737 *n*
Blodgett, Cal, 306
Blomstrom, Robert L., 726 *nn*
Boeschenstein, Harold, 307
Bolles, R. M., 697 *n*
Bolton, Alfred A., 725 *nn*
Bomster, Mark, 548 *n*, 741 *n*
Bonham, Donald, 173–174
Boorstin, Daniel J., 724 *n*
Booth, I. M., 289
Boschert, Chris, 408
Boudreau, J. W., 734 *n*
Boudreaux, Pamela, 728 *n*
Boulding, E., 735 *n*

Boulding, Kenneth E., 725 *n*
Bourgeouis, L. J. III, 726 *n*, 728 *n*
Bowen, William A., 725 *n*, 732 *n*
Boyer, Edward, 744 *n*
Boykin, Raymond F., 730 *n*
Boyle, Richard J., 475, 733 *nns*, 739 *n*
Boynton, Andrew C., 743 *n*
Bradford, David L., 739 *n*
Bradford, L. P., 733 *n*
Bralove, Mary, 742 *n*
Brandeis, Louis D., 41
Breaugh, J., 734 *n*
Breedlove, Bill, 733 *n*
Brezhnev, Leonid, 20
Broderick, Renee F., 734 *n*
Brodwin, David R., 728 *n*
Brody, Michael, 730 *n*, 731 *nns*, 737 *n*
Bronestein, Scott, 745 *n*
Brown, Andrew C., 730 *nns*, 734 *nns*
Brown, R. V., 730 *n*
Brown, Sarah, 371
Brownell, Peter, 741 *n*
Buchsbaum, Susan, 735 *n*
Buckman, Steve, 94 *n*
Bullen, Christine, 742 *n*
Burack, E. H., 734 *nns*, 745 *n*
Burelson, B., 738 *n*
Burgess, John, 732 *n*
Burgess, L. R., 735 *n*
Burke, R. J., 745 *n*
Burlingame, G., 738 *n*
Burnham, D. H., 736 *n*
Burns, James M., 736 *n*
Burns, James R., 725 *n*
Burns, Lawton R., 390 *n*
Burns, Tom, 725 *n*, 726 *n*, 733 *n*
Burpeau, William, 732 *n*, 739 *n*
Burr, Donald, 159–160
Burrough, Bryan, 555 *n*
Burt, D. N., 743 *nns*
Bussey, John, 726 *nns*, 731 *n*
Byham, W. C., 734 *n*
Byrne, John, 383

Cage, Jack H., 736 *n*
Calloway, D. Wayne, 507
Cameron, Kim, 250 *n*, 731 *n*
Camillus, John C., 742 *n*
Cammann, Cortlandt, 543 *n*, 740 *n*, 741 *n*
Campion, J. E., 734 *n*
Canion, Rod, 367
Carley, William M., 160 *n*, 729 *n*
Carlisi, A. M., 735 *n*
Carlson, Edward E., 495, 739 *n*
Carlson, Eric D., 742 *n*
Carlson, Robert, 182–183
Carnazza, J. P., 746 *n*
Carrol, Daniel, 725 *n*
Carroll, Archie B., 81 *n*, 726 *nns*, 727 *n*
Carroll, Paul B., 729 *n*
Carruth, Paul J., 741 *n*
Carter, L. F., 735 *n*
Cartwright, Dorwin, 735 *n*, 739 *n*
Caruth, Don, 238 *n*
Cascio, W. F., 734 *n*
Castro, Janice, 744 *n*
Cathy, Samuel Truett, 374–375

Cederblom, D., 734 *nns*
Chakravarty, Subrata N., 161 *n*
Chambers, J., 197 *n*
Chandler, Alfred V., 728 *n*
Chandler, John S., 602 *n*
Chanin, Michael N., 730 *n*
Chase, Richard B., 731 *n*, 743 *n*
Chemers, M. M., 736 *nns*
Child, John, 289 *n*, 730 *nns*
Chrisman, James J., 726 *n*
Christensen, H. K., 746 *nns*
Churchill, Neil C., 575 *n*, 741 *n*
Cimino, Aldo, 606
Claunch, J., 743 *n*
Clawson, J. G., 697 *n*
Cleek, M. A., 745 *n*
Clifford, Mike, 732 *n*, 739 *n*
Cochran, Philip L., 727 *nns*
Cohen, Allan R., 739 *n*
Cohen, David, 217 *n*, 704 *n*, 730 *n*
Colb, D. A., 737 *n*
Coleman, Henry L., Jr., 145 *n*
Collins, Dave, 127–128
Collins, Paul D., 731 *n*
Coltrin, Sally A., 31 *n*, 225 *n*
Conlon, Edward J., 726 *n*
Connolly, Terry, 726 *n*
Cook, James, 740 *n*
Cooke, Morris, 41
Cooke, Robert A., 731 *n*
Cooper, W. W., 733 *n*
Cooper, William C., 731 *n*
Coors, Jeff, 163, 189
Coors, Pete, 163, 189
Copeland, Lennie, 745 *n*
Cougar, J. Daniel, 742 *n*
Cowan, Karen M., 738 *n*
Cox, James F., 731 *n*
Creech, William, 4, 5, 6, 7, 8
Crescenski, Adam D., 743 *n*
Cron, W. L., 746 *n*
Crosby, Philip B., 545, 549, 740 *nns*, 743 *n*
Cudahy, Michael, 404
Cullen, John B., 731 *n*
Cummings, Larry L., 738 *n*
Cummings, Thomas G., 733 *nns*
Curley, John, 740 *n*
Cyert, Richard, 729 *n*

Daft, Richard L., 250 *n*, 262 *n*, 414 *n*,
    441 *n*, 589 *n*, 725 *nns*, 726 *n*, 727 *nns*,
    728 *n*, 729 *nns*, 731 *nns*, 732 *n*,
    733 *nns*, 737 *nns*, 738 *nns*, 739 *nns*,
    741 *nns*
Dahl, Paul N., 729 *n*
Dale, Michael H., 737 *n*, 738 *n*
Dalkey, N., 730 *n*
Dalton, G. W., 733 *n*
Damanpour, F., 733 *n*
Dandridge, Thomas C., 146 *n*
Daniels, John D., 744 *n*
Darlin, Damon, 744 *n*
Darnell, D., 730 *n*
Davis, David, 742 *nns*
Davis, Keith, 447 *n*, 726 *nns*, 738 *nns*
Davis, Stanley M., 732 *n*, 740 *n*
Deakin, Michael, 729 *n*

Deal, Terrence E., 498, 499 *n*, 739 *nns*
Dearden, John, 741 *nns*, 742 *n*, 743 *nns*
Deaux, Barbara, 729 *n*
Delano, Sara, 730 *nns*
Delbecq, Andre L., 729 *n*, 732 *n*
DeLeo, P. J., 737 *n*
Delkey, N., 729 *n*
Deloach, J. D., 734 *n*
Deming, W. Edwards, 648, 650 *n*, 743 *n*
DeMott, John S., 743 *n*
Dentzer, S., 745 *n*
Dess, Gregory G., 731 *n*
Dessler, G., 734 *n*
Deutsch, Stuart Jay, 726 *n*
Deveny, Kathleen, 728 *n*, 744 *n*
DeVilliers, Marq, 677 *n*
Dickson, W. J., 725 *n*, 737 *n*
Diebold, John, 742 *n*
Diettrich, John E., 623 *n*
Dirsmith, M., 741 *n*
Distelheim, Rochelle, 746 *n*
Dobler, D. W., 743 *nns*
Doeringer, P. B., 734 *n*
Dolan, Carrie, 732 *n*
Dollinger, Marc J., 726 *n*
Donelly, James H., Jr., 740 *n*
Doody, Paula, 732 *n*
Dorfman, Peter W., 736 *n*
Dorsey, Jasper, 736 *n*
Douglas, Susan P., 744 *n*
Doverspike, D., 735 *n*
Dreher, G. F., 734 *n*
Dreshler, S., 738 *n*
Drew, Elizabeth B., 737 *n*
Dreyfuss, Joel, 607 *n*, 728 *n*, 742 *n*
Drucker, Peter F., 5, 107 *n*, 107, 112,
    724 *n*, 725 *n*, 727 *nns*, 732 *n*
Dudley, Mary, 471
Dugas, Christine, 744 *n*
Duncan, J., 730 *n*
Duncan, Robert B., 731 *n*, 732 *n*, 733 *n*
Dunham, R. B., 735 *n*
Dunkin, Amy, 727 *n*, 728 *n*
Dunnette, M. D., 734 *n*, 739 *n*
Durand, Robert, 73 *n*, 726 *n*
Dutt, James L., 367, 393
Dyer, Davis, 515, 732 *n*, 740 *n*
Dymsza, William A., 744 *n*

Early, P. Christopher, 727 *n*
Edwards, Jerry R., 657 *n*
Egan, John, 429, 455
Egelhoff, William G., 744 *n*
Eilon, Samuel, 729 *nns*
Ein, Theodore J., 238 *n*
Eisner, Michael, 119–120
Elling, Clifford, 557, 586–587
Ellington, Kevin, 271–272
Emerson, Harrington, 41
Encarnation, Dennis J., 744 *n*
Engledow, Jack L., 726 *n*
Erez, Miriam, 727 *n*
Erikson, W. J., 730 *n*
Esber, Edward, Jr., 3, 27
Etzioni, Amitai, 727 *n*
Evan, W. M., 733 *n*
Evans, M. G., 736 *nns*

Fallon, Mary A. C., 742 *n*
Farish, P., 734 *n*
Farley, Lawrence, 688
Farmer, Richard N., 589 *n*
Faux, V. A., 697 *n*
Fayol, Henri, 42, 44 *n*, 725 *n*
Feigenbaum, A. V., 544, 740 *n*
Feldman, Daniel C., 474 *n*, 733 *n*, 737 *n*, 739 *nn*
Ference, T. P., 746 *nn*
Ferris, Gerald R., 548 *n*
Fiedler, F. E., 376–379, 377 *n*, 378 *n*, 736 *nn*
Fiegenbaum, A. V., 743 *n*
Field, R. H. G., 736 *n*
Fierman, Jaclyn, 728 *nn*
Finger, Phyllis A., 730 *n*
Fisher, Anne B., 729 *n*, 732 *n*
Fisher, John, 390
Fitz-Enz, Jac, 491, 727 *n*
Fitzpatrick, Mark, 744 *n*
Flamholtz, E. G., 741 *n*
Flannigan, William G., 745 *n*
Flax, Steven, 728 *n*, 735 *n*
Fleishman, E. A., 736 *n*
Fleming, Stephen, 373
Fogle, Teri, 73 *n*, 726 *n*
Folkman, S., 745 *n*
Follett, Mary Parker, 5, 42–43, 725 *n*
Fooner, Andrea, 745 *nn*, 746 *n*
Ford, Robert C., 741 *n*
Formisano, R. A., 735 *n*
Fox, Harold W., 728 *n*
Fox, Kenneth A., 743 *n*
Fraker, Susan, 331 *n*
Frederick, William C., 726 *n*
Fredrickson, James W., 729 *n*
Freeman, Bonnie, 693, 720
French, J. R. P., Jr., 735 *n*
French, Wendell L., 733 *n*
Freudenberger, Herbert J., 708 *n*
Friedlander, Frank, 726 *n*
Friedman, Milton, 80, 726 *n*
Friedman, Rose, 726 *n*
Fritzsche, David J., 726 *n*
Frost, David, 729 *n*
Frost, Peter J., 146 *n*
Fry, Louis W., 727 *n*
Fuhreman, A., 738 *n*
Fulk, Janet, 738 *n*
Fulmer, Gary, 285
Funkhouser, G. Ray, 521 *n*

Gabourie, Fred, 706–707
Gaebler, Ted, 397, 423
Gaines, Jeannie, 745 *n*
Galbraith, Jay R., 155 *n*, 308 *n*, 728 *n*, 732 *nn*
Galbraith, John Kenneth, 726 *n*
Gamblin, William, 459, 486
Gantt, Henry L., 41, 726 *n*
Gardner, Edward P., 740 *n*
Garvin, David A., 741 *n*
Gatewood, Elizabeth, 726 *n*
Geipel, Gary, 742 *n*
Gemmell, Art, 740 *n*
Gendron, George, 737 *n*

Geneen, Harold, 12, 241, 436–437, 512, 572 *n*, 724 *n*, 731 *n*, 738 *n*
George, Claude S., Jr., 724 *nn*
Georgopolous, B. S., 736 *n*, 737 *n*
Ghandi, Mahatma, 391 *illus.*
Ghoshal, Sumantra, 530 *n*, 740 *nn*, 741 *nn*
Gibb, C. A., 735 *n*
Gibb, J. R., 733 *n*
Gibson, Edie, 745 *n*
Gibson, James L., 740 *n*
Giegold, W., 741 *n*
Gilbert, James P., 743 *n*
Gilbreth, Frank B., 41
Gilbreth, Lillian M., 41
Gladstein, Deborah L., 738 *n*
Gladstone, Rick, 732 *n*
Glauser, Michelle J., 738 *n*, 741 *nn*
Glenn, Ethel C., 739 *n*
Gluck, Frederick W., 728 *n*
Glueck, William R., 31 *n*, 225 *n*
Gobeli, David H., 732 *n*
Godfrey, Robert R., 732 *n*
Goizueta, Roberto, 662
Goldhaber, Gerald M., 738 *nn*
Gomez-Mejia, Luis, 13 *n*, 14 *n*, 724 *nn*
Goode, Kathy, 725 *n*
Gorman, John, 726 *n*
Gorry, G. Anthony, 598 *n*
Gottlieb, Carrie, 395 *n*
Govindarajan, V., 728 *nn*
Grandori, Anna, 729 *n*
Gray, Daniel H., 727 *nn*
Green, David, Jr., 741 *n*
Greene, Charles, 736 *n*
Greenhalgh, L., 745 *n*
Greenwood, Jim, 562
Greenwood, Regina A., 725 *nn*
Greenwood, Ronald G., 725 *nn*
Gregory, R. H., 742 *n*
Greiner, L. E., 733 *n*
Griffin, Ricky W., 732 *n*, 739 *n*
Griggs, Lewis, 744 *n*
Groner, Alex, 725 *n*
Gross, Lisa, 728 *n*
Grove, Andrew S., 485 *n*, 739 *n*
Groveman, Barry C., 82 *n*
Guercil, Helen, 89
Guiles, Melinda Grenier, 742 *n*
Gumpert, David E., 732 *n*
Gupta, Anil K., 728 *nn*
Gustafson, D., 729 *n*
Gutfreund, John, 367
Guth, W. D., 740 *n*
Gutteridge, T., 719 *n*, 722 *n*, 745 *n*
Guyon, Janet, 728 *n*
Guzzo, Richard A., 729 *n*

Haas, Stephen M., 217 *n*, 730 *n*
Hackman, J. Richard, 418, 419 *n*, 737 *nn*, 739 *n*
Hagen, Ward, 164
Hahn, Betty, 725 *n*
Hahn, Carl H., 99, 126
Hailey, William A., 725 *n*
Hale, Bill, 728 *n*
Hales, Colin P., 724 *n*

Hall, Douglas T., 200 *n*, 701 *n*, 718 *n*, 719 *n*, 745 *nn*, 746 *nn*
Hall, F. S., 746 *n*
Hall, O. P., 730 *n*
Hall, Pat, 732 *n*
Hall, R. W., 743 *n*
Hambrick, Donald C., 728 *n*, 740 *n*
Hamburger, M., 733 *n*
Hamilton, Joan O'C., 743 *n*
Hamner, W. Clay, 719 *n*, 737 *n*
Hampton, David R., 743 *nn*
Hampton, William J., 729 *n*
Hannan, Robert L., 724 *n*
Hansen, R. W., 746 *n*
Harrigan, Betty, 63 *n*,*745 *n*
Harris, Byron, 724 *nn*
Harris, Catherine L., 742 *nn*
Harris, E. F., 736 *n*
Harris, Kenneth L., 732 *n*
Harrison, E. Frank, 184 *n*, 729 *n*
Harrison, W. L., 742 *n*
Haslinger, J. A., 735 *n*
Hatfield, John D., 727 *n*
Hawkins, Brian, 737 *n*
Hay, Douglas A., 729 *n*
Hayes, R. H., 629 *n*, 743 *n*
Heard, Ed, 637
Heilbroner, Robert L., 724 *n*
Heilman, Madeline E., 736 *n*
Heller, R. F., 735 *n*
Hellriegel, Don, 467 *n*
Hempel, Carl G., 725 *n*
Henderson, A. M., 45 *n*
Henderson, Richard I., 340 *n*, 734 *nn*, 735 *n*
Heneman, H. G. II, 733 *n*
Henley, Henry, 372–373
Hennan, David A., 744 *n*
Henry, Gordon M., 160 *n*
Herbert, Theodore T., 299 *n*, 744 *n*
Herschlag, Judy K., 736 *n*
Hershauer, J. C., 743 *n*
Herzberg, Frederick, 403, 737 *n*
Hewlett, Bill, 494
Hickman, Craig R., 732 *n*
Higgins, James H., 128 *n*, 144 *n*
Hill, John S., 744 *n*
Hill, T., 743 *n*
Hillkirk, John, 731 *n*, 732 *n*
Hirsch, Paul M., 146 *n*
Hitt, Michael A., 728 *n*
Hockett, Homer C., 724 *n*
Hofer, Charles W., 728 *nn*
Hoff, Edward J., 744 *n*
Hoffman, L. Richard, 729 *n*
Hofstede, Geert, 667, 744 *nn*
Hogarth, Robin M., 179 *n*
Hogue, Jack T., 742 *n*
Holbrook, Bobbie, 728 *n*
Hollenback, J., 737 *n*
Holmes, Arthur W., 741 *n*
Homes, T., 745 *n*
Honda, Soichiro, 24
Hornstein, Harvey A., 736 *n*
Hosking, D., 736 *n*
House, Robert J., 736 *nn*
Howard, Ann, 724 *n*

Howell, Jon P., 736 *n*
Hrebiniak, Lawrence G., 728 *n*
Huber, George P., 165 *n*
Hudson, Richard L., 744 *n*
Hulin, Charles L., 727 *n*
Hull, Frank, 731 *n*, 741 *n*
Hunger, J. David, 728 *n*, 740 *n*
Hunt, David Marshall, 745 *nn*
Hunt, J. G., 736 *n*
Hurtubise, Rolland, 598 *n*
Huse, Edgar F., 733 *nn*
Hutchins, Dexter, 730 *n*, 743 *n*
Hyatt, Joshua, 745 *n*
Hyde, Jack, 735 *n*
Hymowitz, Carol, 29 *n*, 737 *n*, 738 *nn*

Iacocca, Lee, 4, 5, 8, 177–179, 495, 567, 731 *n*, 741 *n*
Icahn, Carl, 164
Ignatius, David, 47 *n*
Ingrassian, Paul, 744 *n*
Ireland, R. Duane, 728 *n*
Irle, K. W., 735 *n*
Isabella, I., 745 *n*
Isenberg, Daniel J., 729 *n*
Ivancevich, John M., 740 *n*, 741 *n*
Iverson, Ken, 408

Jablonsky, S., 741 *n*
Jacobson, Gary, 731 *n*, 732 *n*
Jaeger, Alfred M., 504 *n*, 740 *n*
Jago, Arthur G., 736 *n*
James, Ellen, 744 *n*
Janis, Irving L., 730 *n*
Janson, R., 737 *n*
Jauch, Lawrence R., 31 *n*, 225 *n*
Javidan, Mansour, 726 *n*
Jay, Antony, 485 *n*
Jefferson, Edward, 662
Jelernter, Carey Quan, 739 *nn*
Jemison, David D., 726 *n*
Jenkins, W. O., 735 *n*
Jennings, H. H., 735 *n*
Jensen, Mary Ann C., 739 *n*
Jermier, John M., 736 *n*, 745 *n*
Jesse, Richard R., Jr., 731 *n*
Jessup, Harlan R., 741 *n*
Jewell, Linda N., 730 *n*, 738 *n*
Jobs, Steven, 251
Johansen, Robert, 742 *n*
Johnson, Cindy, 699
Johnson, George A., 743 *n*
Johnson, Kelly, 4, 5, 7
Johnson, Richard, 260
Johnson, Victoria, 698
Jonas, Hans, 725 *n*
Jones, N. W., 736 *n*, 737 *n*
Joseph, B., 745 *n*
Joyce, William F., 728 *n*

Kahn, Joseph P., 733 *n*, 735 *n*
Kahn, Robert L., 735 *n*, 738 *n*
Kahneman, D., 730 *n*
Kanfer, Frederick H., 727 *n*
Kanter, Rosabeth Moss, 306 *n*, 732 *nn*, 733 *n*, 745 *n*
Kantro, Alan M., 724 *n*

Kaplan, Robert E., 724 *n*
Kapoor, Bhawnesh, 411
Karasek, R. A., Jr., 745 *n*
Kast, Fremont E., 725 *nn*
Kastens, M. L., 139 *n*
Katz, Daniel, 738 *n*
Katz, Robert L., 724 *n*
Katz, L., 299 *n*
Kaufman, Jacqueline, 738 *n*
Kazanjian, Robert K., 155 *n*
Keating, Barry P., 727 *n*
Keim, Gerald D., 727 *n*
Kendall, Don, 20
Kennedy, Allan A., 498, 499 *n*, 739 *nn*
Kenzie, Ross, 375
Kepner, C., 729 *n*
Kerr, K. Austin, 725 *n*
Kerr, S., 736 *n*
Kessler, Felix, 726 *n*, 727 *n*
Kiesler, Sara, 742 *n*
Kilmann, Ralph H., 739 *n*
Kimberly, John R., 731 *n*
King, Corwin P., 738 *n*
Kirk, R., 734 *n*
Klein, Harold E., 729 *n*
Knapp, Mark, 738 *n*
Knapp, Robert W., 742 *n*
Kneale, Dennis, 191 *n*, 733 *n*
Kobuta, Hiroto, 704
Kogut, Bruce, 744 *n*
Kohs, S. C., 735 *n*
Kolton, Ellen, 732 *n*
Kondrasuk, Jack N., 741 *n*
Korman, A. K., 746 *n*
Koten, John, 726 *n*
Kotkin, Joel, 732 *nn*, 733 *n*, 739 *n*, 740 *n*
Kotler, Philip, 727 *n*
Kotter, John P., 315 *n*, 697 *n*, 724 *nn*, 733 *nn*
Kraar, Louis, 740 *n*, 744 *n*
Kram, Kathy E., 745 *nn*
Kreitner, Robert, 743 *n*, 745 *n*
Krober, D. W., 604 *n*
Kuehl, Charles R., 411 *n*, 698 *n*
Kuppin, Lawrence, 33, 60
Kurk, Thomas, 731 *n*
Kurke, Lawrence B., 724 *n*
Kwon, Young Jun, 411

Labich, Kenneth, 728 *n*, 744 *nn*
Lacke, Edwin A., 736 *n*
Lambing, Peggy A., 411 *n*, 698 *n*
Land, Edwin, 305
Landro, Laura, 732 *n*
Langer, W. C., 725 *n*
Langley, Monica, 726 *n*
Langston, Rich, 455–456
Larsen, Janet K., 737 *n*
Larson, Erik, 732 *n*, 742 *n*
Larson, L. L., 736 *n*
Latack, J. C., 745 *n*, 745 *n*
Latha, Aaron, 617 *n*
Latham, Gary P., 734 *nn*, 736 *n*, 737 *n*
Lau, Alan W., 724 *nn*
Lawler, Edward E. III, 740 *n*
Lawrence, Harding, 4, 6, 7, 8, 9, 23

Lawrence, Paul R., 515, 731 *nn*, 732 *nn*, 733 *n*, 740 *n*
Lawrence, R. P., 733 *n*
Lawrence, Steve, 727 *n*
Lazarus, R. S., 745 *n*
Leakey, Richard E., 724 *n*
Leavitt, Harold J., 317 *n*, 733 *n*
Lederer, Albert L., 742 *n*
Ledvinka, J., 734 *n*
Lee, L., Jr., 743 *nn*
Lee, S., 730 *n*
Lengel, Robert H., 729 *n*, 738 *nn*
Lenz, R. T., 726 *n*
Leofsky, Ted, 553–554
Leontiades, Milton, 728 *nn*
Levary, Reuven R., 730 *n*
Levine, Jonathan B., 741 *n*, 743 *n*, 744 *n*
Levitt, A., Jr., 724 *n*
Levitt, Theodore, 744 *n*
Lewin, Kurt, 733 *nn*, 735 *n*
Lewin, Roger, 724 *n*
Lien, L., 734 *n*
Lievano, R., 730 *n*
Likert, Rensis, 462 *n*, 736 *nn*
Lindzey, G., 735 *n*
Lindzey, M. O., 735 *n*
Linneman, Robert E., 729 *n*
Lippincott, Philip, 513
Lippitt, R., 735 *nn*
Litke, Ann, 730 *nn*
Lock, Greg, 728 *n*
Lofflin, C., 730 *n*
Lombardo, Michael M., 724 *nn*
London, M., 697 *n*, 745 *nn*, 746 *n*
Lorange, Peter, 530 *n*, 740 *nn*, 741 *nn*
Lorber, L. Z., 734 *n*
Lorenzo, Frank, 154
Lorsch, Jay W., 725 *n*, 731 *nn*, 739 *n*
Louis, Arthur M., 519 *n*, 726 *n*, 735 *n*
Lowe, Jabby, 733 *n*
Lowell, R. S., 734 *n*
Luthans, Fred, 725 *n*, 737 *n*

McAdam, Terry W., 726 *n*
McArthur, C. C., 697 *n*
McAvoy, Tom, 506
McCall, Morgan W., Jr., 724 *nn*
McCallum, Daniel, 39
McCann, Joseph E., 13 *n*, 14 *n*, 724 *nn*, 732 *n*
McCartney, Laton, 742 *n*
McClandon, Thurrell O., 741 *n*
McClelland, David C., 405, 406 *n*, 736 *n*, 737 *nn*
McComas, Maggie, 743 *n*
McCormick, E. J., 735 *n*
McCormick, J., 745 *n*
McCormick, William, 383
McCoy, John, 391
McElwee, John, 156
McEvoy, G. M., 734 *n*
McGaugh, Robert, 737 *n*
McGovern, R. Gordon, 309–310
McGregor, Douglas, 49–50, 725 *n*
Machiavelli, Nicolo, 38, 39, 724 *n*
Macintosh, Norman B., 738 *n*, 741 *nn*
McIntyre, J. M., 737 *n*

McLaughlin, Frank S., 741 *n*
McLaughlin, M. L., 738 *n*
McLean, Vincent, 168
McLeod, Raymond, 742 *n*
McMahon, J. Timothy, 741 *n*
McManus, Kevin, 730 *n*
McMurray, Scott, 728 *n*
McMurray, Theresa, 732 *n*, 739 *n*
Magee, John F., 742 *nn*
Magnet, Myron, 729 *n*, 730 *n*, 733 *n*, 740 *n*
Mahar, L., 736 *n*
Mahoney, G. M., 736 *n*, 737 *n*
Mahoney, Richard, 171
Maidment, Robert, 442 *n*
Maier, N. R. F., 734 *n*
Maier, Norman P. R., 730 *n*
Main, Jeremy, 731 *n*, 733 *n*, 743 *n*
Makridakis, S., 730 *n*
Mancuso, Frank, 307
Mandell, Steven L., 741 *n*
Mani, Sirish, 738 *n*
Mann, R. D., 735 *n*
Manners, G., 738 *n*
Mansfield, Edwin, 733 *n*
March, James G., 729 *nn*, 734 *n*
Marett, P., 730 *n*
Marriott, Bill, 258, 259, 446
Marriott, J. Willard, Sr., 506
Marsh, Barbara, 733 *n*
Martin, Pete, 17–18
Marzocchi, Al, 307
Maslow, Abraham F., 49, 401–403, 737 *n*
Mason, Richard O., 729 *n*
Maynard, M. Gordon, 729 *n*
Mayo, Elton, 48, 400
Meal, Harlan C., 743 *nn*
Medina, W. A., 737 *n*
Mee, John F., 725 *n*
Mehrabian, Albert, 738 *n*
Meier, Barry, 728 *nn*
Meiners, Roger E., 727 *n*
Meising, Paul, 727 *n*
Mellgard, George E., 735 *n*
Merchant, Kenneth A., 740 *n*
Merwin, John, 724 *nn*, 743 *n*
Metcalf, Henry C., 725 *n*
Meyer, Alan D., 145 *n*
Miceli, Marcia Parmarlee, 727 *n*, 734 *n*
Michael, Carol, 745 *nn*
Miles, Gregory, 728 *n*
Miles, Raymond E., 145 *n*, 728 *n*, 732 *n*, 733 *n*, 742 *n*
Miles, Robert H., 731 *n*
Milkovich, George T., 734 *n*
Millar, Victor E., 742 *nn*
Miller, Joseph G., 730 *nn*, 738 *n*
Miller, Michael W., 538 *n*, 728 *nn*, 742 *nn*
Mills, D. Quinn, 733 *n*, 734 *n*
Mills, Miriam K., 742 *n*
Mills, Peter K., 731 *n*, 732 *n*
Millsap, Greg, 733 *n*
Miner, M. G., 734 *n*
Mintzberg, Henry, 18, 21 *n*, 290–291, 291 *n*, 292 *n*, 431 *n*, 724 *nn*, 728 *n*, 729 *n*, 731 *nn*, 732 *nn*, 735 *n*, 737 *n*
Mishkoff, Henry C., 742 *nn*
Mitchell, Cynthia F., 744 *n*

Mitchell, Terence R., 736 *n*, 737 *n*
Mitroff, Ian I., 729 *nn*
Moberg, Dennis J., 731 *n*
Mockler, Robert J., 740 *n*
Moffett, Matt, 729 *n*
Mohrman, Susan A., 740 *n*
Monaghan, Tom, 433
Montagno, Ray V., 737 *n*
Montross, D. H., 745 *n*
Moore, L., 730 *n*
Morgan, Gareth, 146 *n*
Morgan, Marilyn A., 719 *n*
Morgan, Philip, 440 *n*
Morgello, Clem, 732 *n*
Moriarty, M., 730 *n*
Morita, Masatoshi, 70 *n*
Morrison, Ann M., 724 *n*, 740 *n*
Moscow, Alvin, 572 *n*, 724 *n*, 731 *n*, 738 *n*
Moskowitz, Milton R., 726 *n*
Mouton, Jane Srygley, 327 *n*, 374, 733 *n*, 736 *n*
Muczyk, Jan P., 741 *n*
Mullick, S., 197 *n*
Munchus, George III, 740 *n*
Munsterberg, Hugo, 47, 725 *n*
Murninghan, J. Keith, 739 *n*
Murphy, Declan, 741 *n*
Murray, John P., 742 *n*
Murray, Michael, 729 *n*

Nadler, David A., 543 *n*, 732 *n*, 733 *n*, 740 *n*, 741 *n*
Naisbitt, J., 745 *n*
Nalen, Craig, 307
Naylor, T., 730 *n*
Neale, M. A., 735 *n*
Near, Janet P., 727 *n*
Nelson, Mike, 732 *n*
Neumann, Seev, 742 *n*
Newman, Michael, 743 *n*
Newman, William H., 740 *n*
Newstrom, John W., 447 *n*, 738 *nn*
Nicholas, John M., 733 *n*
Nielsen, John, 733 *n*
Nocera, Joseph, 146 *n*, 740 *n*
Norman, James R., 160 *n*, 727 *n*, 728 *n*
Northcraft, Gregory B., 731 *n*, 735 *n*, 743 *n*
Novak, William, 731 *n*, 741 *n*
Nulty, Peter, 724 *n*, 725 *n*, 742 *nn*
Nutt, Paul C., 733 *n*
Nystrom, P. C., 732 *n*, 736 *n*

Oaks, Clinton L., 94 *n*
Oballe, Nestor K. II, 740 *n*
O'Boyle, Thomas F., 737 *n*, 738 *nn*
O'Brian, J. A., 596 *n*
O'Dell, J. W., 738 *n*
Odiorne, George S., 727 *n*, 741 *n*
Okum, Sherman K., 440 *n*
Oldham, Greg R., 418, 419 *n*, 737 *nn*
O'Leary, T. J., 742 *n*
O'Reilly, Anthony, 662
O'Reilly, Brian, 736 *n*
O'Reilly, Charles A. III, 741 *n*
Orr, R. Gordon, 730 *n*
Osborn, A., 730 *n*
Osborn, R. N., 736 *n*

Osborne, David, 736 *n*, 737 *n*
Osborne, Tom, 370
Otten, Alan L., 94 *n*
Ouchi, William G., 58, 503, 504 *n*, 725 *nn*, 740 *nn*
Overmeyer, Wayne S., 741 *n*
Ozzie, Raymond, 229

Packard, David, 494, 495
Paden-Bost, Patricia J., 733 *n*
Pagano, Anthony M., 83 *n*
Page, Ronald C., 13 *n*, 14 *n*, 724 *nn*
Palia, K. A., 728 *n*
Parasuraman, S., 745 *n*
Parks, Don, 729 *n*
Parson, H. M., 725 *n*
Parson, Mary Jean, 739 *n*
Parsons, Gregory L., 742 *nn*
Parsons, Talcott, 45 *n*
Pascale, Richard, 501 *n*, 725 *n*, 740 *nn*
Pasztor, Andy, 726 *n*
Paul, Karen, 744 *n*
Pave, Irene, 745 *n*
Pavett, Cynthia M., 724 *nn*
Payne, Robyn, 350
Pearce, John A. II, 727 *nn*, 728 *n*
Pearce, Jon L., 727 *n*, 729 *n*
Pearlman, Charles, 732 *nn*
Pearson, Andy, 446
Pelletier, K. R., 705 *n*, 745 *nn*
Penley, Larry E., 737 *n*
Penney, James Cash, 492
Perlmutter, Howard P., 744 *nn*
Perot, H. Ross, 153–154, 495, 505
Perrin, Alain, 129
Perrow, Charles, 727 *n*, 731 *n*
Peters, Thomas J., 59, 505, 648 *n*, 724 *nn*, 725 *n*, 732 *n*, 737 *n*, 738 *nn*, 739 *n*, 740 *nn*
Peterson, Thane, 744 *n*
Petre, Peter, 729 *n*, 732 *n*, 733 *n*
Phatak, Arvand P., 726 *n*, 744 *n*
Pickle, Hale, 726 *n*
Pinchot, Gifford III, 308 *n*, 732 *n*
Piore, M. J., 734 *n*
Pitts, Robert A., 744 *n*
Pluenneke, J. E., 727 *n*
Pollard, Harold E., 725 *n*
Pondy, Louis R., 146 *n*
Pood, Elliott, 739 *n*
Poor, Henry, 39
Popaditch, Bob, 578
Popovich, Paula, 734 *n*
Porras, Jerry I., 733 *n*
Porter, Lyman W., 727 *n*, 729 *n*, 737 *nn*, 738 *n*
Porter, Michael E., 147, 148 *n*, 728 *n*, 742 *nn*, 744 *n*
Posesorski, Sherrie, 741 *n*
Posner, Bruce G., 741 *n*
Post, James E., 726 *n*
Pounds, W. E., 729 *n*
Prasad, S. B., 744 *n*
Preble, John F., 729 *n*
Premack, S. L., 734 *n*
Prescott, John E., 727 *n*
Pressley, Trazzie, 238 *n*

Pritchard, R. D., 737 n
Probst, Gerald, 168
Purdy, K., 737 n
Pursell, E. D., 734 n
Putka, Gary, 744 n
Putnam, Arnold O., 733 n
Pyhrr, Peter A., 741 n

Quelch, John A., 744 n
Quinn, James Brian, 306 n, 732 n
Quinn, Robert E., 250 n, 623 n, 731 n
Qureishi, Salam, 617

Radloff, David L., 217 n, 730 n
Ragan, James W., 729 n
Rahe, R., 745 n
Raisinghami, D., 729 n
Ramaprasad, Arkalgud, 729 n
Ramsey, Douglas, 744 n
Randolph, W. Alan, 731 n
Ranky, Paul, 743 n
Rapoport, J., 733 n
Raven, B., 735 n
Rawlings, S., 746 n
Read, W. H., 738 n, 741 nn
Reese, L., 730 n
Reibstein, Larry, 729 n, 734 nn, 746 n
Reichert, Jack, 507
Reilly, R. R., 734 n
Reilly, Robert F., 730 n
Reimer, Blanca, 739 n
Reitz, E. G. S., 735 n
Reitz, H. Joseph, 730 n, 738 n, 739 nn
Render, B., 730 nn
Rhodes, Lucien, 732 n
Rhodes, Susan R., 738 n
Riccio, Lucius J., 730 nn
Richards, Max D., 727 nn
Richlin, H., 737 n
Richman, Barry M., 589 n
Richman, Louis S., 727 n
Richman, Tom, 727 n, 736 n, 737 n, 741 n,
    742 n
Ricklafs, R., 745 nn
Ricks, David A., 744 nn
Ritti, R. Richard, 521 n
Robbins, Stephen P., 739 nn
Robinson, Richard B., Jr., 728 n
Roche, G. R., 745 n
Rock, Milton L., 735 nn
Rockart, John F., 742 nn, 743 nn
Roderick, David, 164
Rodgers, Sondra, 728 n
Roebuck, Alva H., 61
Roethlisberger, F. J., 48, 725 n
Rogers, E. M., 449 n, 738 n
Rogers, R. A., 449 n, 738 n
Rosen, Michael, 739 n
Rosenberg, David, 743 n
Rosenblatt, Z., 745 n
Rosenzweig, James E., 725 nn
Rosewicz, Barbara, 47 n
Rothlisberger, J. F., 737 n
Rothman, Matt, 728 n
Rousseau, Denise M., 731 n
Roussel, Philip A., 729 n
Rowan, Roy, 726 n, 730 n

Rowe, Mary P., 738 n
Rubin, I. M., 737 n
Ruch, W. A., 743 n
Rudelius, William, 732 n
Rumelt, Richard B., 732 n
Ryan, William G., 589 n
Ryans, John K., Jr., 728 n, 733 n
Rynes, S. L., 733 n, 734 nn

Sachs, Jonathon, 229
Sackett, P. R., 734 n
Safran, Claire, 727 n
Sakowitz, Robert, 131, 158
Salomon, Ilan, 742 n
Sandberg, William R., 729 n
Sanders, Colonel Harland, 251
Santangelo, Jim, 452
Saporito, Bill, 728 nn, 740 nn, 744 n, 745 n
Sarri, L. M., 737 n
Sathe, Vijay, 739 n
Saunders, Charles B., 727 n
Saxton, Mary J., 739 n
Schaefer, William Donald, 4, 5, 8
Schaffir, Kurt H., 743 n
Schauland, H., 730 n
Schein, Edgar H., 739 n
Schein, L., 733 n
Schembechler, Bo, 370
Schendel, Dan, 727 nn
Schipke, Roger, 625
Schlesinger, Arthur M., 724 n
Schlesinger, Leonard A., 315 n, 333, 361–
    362, 733 nn
Schmidt, Frank, 719 n
Schmidt, Warren, 372 n
Schnee, J., 733 n
Schneider, Herb, 744 n
Schneier, C. E., 357 n
Schonberger, Richard J., 731 n, 740 nn,
    743 nn
Schorr, Burt, 740 n
Schrank, R., 739 n
Schriesheim, C. A., 735 n, 736 n
Schuler, Randy, 741 n
Schuster, Jay R., 735 n
Schwab, D. P., 733 n
Schwartz, Howard, 739 n
Schweiger, David M., 729 n, 730 n, 736 n
Schwenk, Charles R., 730 n
Scott, Tom, 725 n
Scott, Walter Dill, 47
Scott Morton, Michael F., 530 n, 598 n,
    740 nn, 741 nn, 742 nn, 743 nn
Scully, John, 155, 429
Sears, Richard Warren, 61
Sease, Douglas R., 743 n, 744 nn
Seashore, Stanley E., 739 n
Segal, John L., 82 n
Sekaran, U., 746 n
Selye, Hans, 705 n, 745 n
Serpa, Roy, 739 n
Shamir, Boas, 742 n
Shanklin, William L., 728 n, 733 n
Shapiro, Harris J., 730 n
Sharfman, Mark P., 224 n
Shartle, C. L., 735 n
Shaw, M. E., 449 n, 738 nn, 739 n

Shea, Gregory P., 741 n
Sheats, P., 738 n
Shelly, M. W. II, 733 n
Sheppard, I. Thomas, 738 nn
Sherif, M., 735 n
Sherman, H. David, 743 n
Sherman, Stratford P., 677 n
Sherrid, Pamela, 728 n
Sherwin, Douglas S., 726 n
Shetty, Y. Kirshna, 744 n
Shinkman, C. J., 745 n
Siebert, Cindy, 725 n
Silva, Michael A., 732 n
Simmons, Donald B., 738 nn
Simmons, Richard, 527
Simon, Herbert A., 170, 727 n, 729 nn,
    734 n
Simon, Ruth, 94 n, 161 n
Sinetar, Marsha, 732 n
Singh, R., 736 n
Skinner, B. F., 737 n
Skinner, E. W., 736 n
Skinner, W., 743 n
Skivington, James E., 728 n
Sloan, Harry Evans, 33, 60
Slocum, John W., Jr., 467 n, 746 n
Slovic, B., 730 n
Smale, John, 731 n
Smircich, Linda, 739 n
Smith, Adam, 80, 730 n
Smith, D., 197 n
Smith, Emily T., 742 n
Smith, Frederick, 305
Smith, Jan, 205
Smith, P. C., 734 n
Smith, R. D., 734 nn
Smith, Randall, 726 n
Smith, Timothy K., 95 n
Snook, John L., Jr., 723 n
Snow, Charles C., 145 n, 728 n, 732 n,
    733 n, 742 n
Snyder, Charles A., 731 n
Soelberg, Peer, 729 n
Soerwine, A. H., 745 n
Solomon, Julie B., 731 n, 736 n
Sormumen, Juhani, 729 n
Stair, R., 730 nn
Stalker, G. M., 725 n, 726 n, 733 n
Starbuck, W., 732 n
Staw, B. M., 738 n, 740 n
Steers, Richard M., 250 n, 262 n, 414 n,
    441 n, 727 nn, 737 nn, 738 nn
Stein, C., 745 n
Steiner, Gary A., 306 n
Steiner, George A., 726 n, 738 n
Steiner, I. D., 739 n
Stevenson, Howard H., 139 n, 729 n,
    732 n
Stevenson, William B., 727 n, 729 n
Stewart, James B., 728 n, 744 n
Stewart, Rosemary, 724 n
Still, Richard R., 744 n
Stoffman, Daniel, 485 n
Stogdill, R. M., 735 nn
Stoka, Ann Marie, 725 n
Stone, D. C., 735 n
Stone, D. L., 734 n

Stone, E. F., 734 n
Stoner, James A. F., 724 n, 731 nn, 738 n, 741 n, 742 n, 746 nn
Strauss, Robert, 430
Streidl, J. William, 741 n
Stump, Matt, 73 n, 726 n
Stumpf, S. A., 697 n, 745 nn
Su, B. W., 745 n
Sullivan, Jeremiah J., 725 n
Sullivan, S. E., 746 n
Sullivan, William G., 730 n
Suters, Everett T., 456 n
Sutton, Charlotte B., 739 n
Swanson, E. B., 742 n
Swap, Walter C., 730 n
Swarof, P. G., 734 n
Swartz, Steve, 728 n
Swiggett, Bob, 482
Szilyagi, Andrew D., 741 n
Szwajkowski, Eugene W., 726 nn

Taber, Carol, 444
Taber, T., 369 n, 735 n
Tannenbaum, Robert, 372 n
Tansik, David A., 731 n, 743 n
Tasini, Jonathan, 738 n
Taylor, A., 745 n, 746 nn
Taylor, B., 730 n
Taylor, Charlotte, 252 n
Taylor, Frederick W., 40–41, 399, 737 n
Taylor, John, 729 n
Teece, David J., 728 n
Teets, John, 379, 383
Telling, Edward R., 731 n
Tenopyr, M. L., 734 n
Terpstra, David E., 733 n
Tharp, Mike, 740 n, 744 n
Thayer, P. W., 734 n
Theoret, A., 729 n
Therrien, Lois, 738 n
Thomas, Howard, 729 n
Thompson, James D., 726 n, 743 n
Tichy, Noel M., 736 n
Tjosvold, Dean, 739 n
Tolchin, Susan J., 726 n
Tosi, Henry L., 737 n
Trachtenberg, Jeffrey A., 744 nn
Trautlein, Donald, 28–29
Tregoe, B., 729 n
Tretter, Marietta J., 744 n
Trevino, Linda Klebe, 738 n
Treybig, James, 433, 445
Trice, Harrison M., 739 n
Trone, Thomas, 602 n
Truell, Peter, 744 n
Tsuruoka, D., 745 n

Tuckman, Bruce W., 739 n
Tuggel, Francis D., 727 n
Turban, Efraim, 742 n
Turborg, J. R., 745 n
Tushman, Michael L., 732 n, 735 n, 738 n
Tversky, A., 730 n
Tyson, John, 742 n

Udall, John, 731 n
Ulrich, David O., 726 n, 736 n
Ulvila, J. W., 730 n
Urwick, Lyndall, 725 n

Vachani, Sushil, 744 n
Vamos, Mark N., 729 n
van Breda, Michael F., 741 n
Vancil, Richard F., 741 nn
Van de Ven, Andrew H., 729 n, 732 n, 733 n
Van Fleet, David D., 371 n, 725 n, 731 n, 735 nn, 736 n, 739 n
Van Horn, Richard L., 742 n, 743 n
Vecchio, Robert P., 737 n
Verdin, Jo Ann, 83 n
Vessels, Gordon, 732 n
Vettner, J., 730 nn
Vincze, Julian W., 144 n
Volcker, Paul, 470
von Glinow, M. A., 736 n
Vroom, Victor H., 383–385, 384 n, 386 n, 387, 408, 736 nn, 737 n

Wagner, Harvey M., 657 n
Wagner, John A. III, 548 n
Wagner, S., 733 n
Walleigh, Richard C., 743 n
Walters, Timothy R., 224 n
Walton, Richard E., 541 n, 740 n
Wankel, Charles, 724 n, 731 nn, 738 n, 741 n, 742 n
Wanous, J. P., 734 nn, 746 n
Want, Jerome H., 727 n
Warren, E. K., 746 nn
Wasson, C. R., 728 n
Waterman, Robert H., Jr., 505, 725 n, 738 n, 739 n, 740 n
Waters, Craig R., 655 n, 740 n, 741 nn, 743 nn
Watkins, Paul R., 742 n
Watson, Hugh J., 604 n, 730 n, 742 n
Watson, T. J., Jr., 495
Watson, Tom, 495
Wax, Alan J., 146 n
Weber, Max, 45, 240, 725 n, 731 n
Weick, Karl E., 740 n
Weil, Denise, 746 n

Weiland, Michael, 602 n
Welch, Jack, 413–414
Welsh, John J., 741 n
Wexley, K. N., 734 nn
Wheelen, Thomas L., 728 n, 740 n
Wheelwright, S. C., 629 n, 730 nn, 743 n
White, R. K., 735 nn
Whiteside, David E., 742 n
White, Ted, 261
Wight, D. T., 745 n
Wiig, Karl W., 742 n
Wilcox, Ethel M., 738 n
Wilcox, James R., 738 n
Wiles, Q. T., 156
Williams, Brian K., 742 n
Williams, P., 730 n
Willis, Rod, 739 n, 740 n, 743 n
Wilson, Ian, 726 n
Wilson, M., 735 n
Wilson, Sloan, 20, 724 n
Wind, Yoram, 744 n
Wisocki, Bernard, Jr., 736 nn
Withey, Michael, 731 n
Wojahn, Ellen, 731 n, 737 n, 740 nn
Wolf, William B., 725 n
Wolfe, Joseph, 727 n
Wolfe, M. N., 340 n
Wood, Robert A., 727 nn, 741 n
Wood, Robert E., 61–62
Wood, William P., 657 n
Woodward, Joan, 256, 257 n, 731 nn
Worthy, Ford S., 728 n
Worthy, James C., 62 n
Wozniak, Stephen, 251
Wrege, Charles D., 725 nn
Wren, Daniel A., 724 nn
Wright, H. A., 725 n
Wriston, Walter B., 699
Wyman, John, 742 nn

Yancik, Richard F., 217 n, 730 n
Yasai-Ardekani, Masoud, 731 n
Yetton, P. W., 383–385, 387, 736 n
Yukl, Gary A., 369 n, 382 nn, 735 nn, 736 nn

Zajonc, R. B., 739 n
Zaltman, G., 733 n
Zander, Alvin F., 735 n, 739 n
Zawacki, Robert A., 623 n
Zedeck, S., 734 n
Zeithaml, Carl P., 728 n
Zetlin, Minda, 737 n, 738 n
Zimmerman, John H., 353, 734 n
Ziyang, Zaho, 20
Zmud, Robert W., 743 n

Company Index

A. H. Robins Company, 84–85
A. O. Smith, 527–528
Aahs!, 562
Adolph Coors Company, 163, 189
Aerospace Corporation, 9 *illus.*
Aetna Life and Casualty Company, 605
Air Canada, 538
Alcan Aluminum Ltd., 55
Alcoa, 157
Allegheny Ludlum Steel Corporation, 527
Allen-Bradley, 630 *illus.*
AMC, 10–11
AMC Jeep, 529, 650–651
American Airlines, 101 *illus.*, 527, 603·
American Cyanamid, 157
American Egg Board, 103 *illus.*
American Express, 537, 592, 666
American Hospital Supply Corporation,
    612–613
American LaFrance, 154
American Steel Company, 721–722
American Telephone and Telegraph
    Company, 140, 494 *illus.*, 501, 537,
    691
AM International, 506 *illus.*, 509–510
AMOCO, 1 *n*, 176 *illus.*, 214 *illus.*, 523 *n*
AMP, 584 *illus.*
Anheuser-Busch, 82 *illus.*, 147, 535 *illus.*
A&P, 513 *illus.*
Apple Computer Inc., 140, 155–156, 251–
    253, 277, 278–279, 430, 587–588,
    634, 678
Appleton Papers, 256 *illus.*
ARCO, 446
Armstrong Rubber Company, 274 *illus.*
Ashton-Tate Inc., 3, 5, 27
AT&E Corporation, 196, 197
Atlanta Tool and Dye Inc., 456
Atlantic Richfield, 90
AT&T, 140, 494 *illus.*, 501, 537, 691
Au Bon Pain Company, 333, 361–362
Avon, 676

Bally Manufacturing Corporation, 416 *illus.*
Banc One Corporation, 389–390, 429
Bank of America, 453, 591, 619, 669
Bausch & Lomb, 6, 240 *illus.*
Baystate Medical Center, 433 *illus.*
Beatrice Companies, 367, 393
Beecham Research International, 665 *illus.*
Beech-Nut, 148
Bell Atlantic, 420 *illus.*
Best Western, 359 *illus.*, 597
Best Western International, 680
Bethlehem Steel Corporation, 28–29
Biggers Corporation, 214–215
Black and Decker, 134, 661, 688–689
Blue Bell Inc., 655–656
BMW, 204 *illus.*, 338 *illus.*
BOC Group, 680 *illus.*
Boeing Aircraft, 500
Borden Company, Dairy Group, 71
Borg-Warner, 123, 444
Braniff Airlines, 4, 6, 7, 8, 9
Briggs & Stratton, 134
Bristol-Myers, 663 *illus.*
Brown Deer Bank, 463
Brunswick Corporation, 507
Buffalo Savings Bank, 375
Burlington Industries, 303, 546 *illus.*,
    615 *illus.*
Burrelle's Information Services, Inc., 75
Burroughs Corporation, 168

Campbell Soup Company, 11 *illus.*, 309–
    310, 310 *illus.*, 601 *illus.*, 606
Campbell Taggart Inc., 525–526, 527
Cannon Mills Company, 360
Canon, 463
Carnation, 132
Carter Hawley Hale, 201
Cartier, 129
Catalog Stores, Inc., 426–427
Caterpillar Tractor Company, 534, 540,
    673 *illus.*

CCC Bakeries, 205–206
Central Soya, 208 *illus.*
CFS Continental, 133 *illus.*
Champlin Petroleum, 603
Chase Manhattan Bank, 6
Chem-Nuclear Systems, 402 *illus.*
Chesebrough-Pond, 666
Chick-fil-A, Inc., 374–375
Chrysler Corporation, 4, 12 *illus.*, 117 *illus.*,
    176, 242, 635 *illus.*, 637
CIBA-GEIGY, 118 *illus.*, 343 *illus.*
Citicorp, 395, 611
Clairol, 78 *illus.*
Cluett, Peabody & Company, Inc., 372
Coca-Cola Company, 132, 180–181,
    678 *illus.*, 681, 683 *illus.*
Coleco Industries, 196 *illus.*
Colt Industries, 703 *illus.*
Columbia Gas, 475 *illus.*
Columbia Gas Distribution Companies
    (CDC), 156 *illus.*, 719 *illus.*
Columbia Gas System, 105, 107, 121
Columbia Pictures, 132
Comerica Inc., 358 *illus.*
Commodore International Ltd., 191
Compaq Computer Corporation, 182 *illus.*,
    271–272, 367, 471
Continental Steel Corporation, 515
Control Data Corporation, 83, 666
Convergent Technologies, 319–320
Corning Glass Works, 650, 685–686
CP Rail, 69 *illus.*
C&P Telephone, 420 *illus.*
Crane Plastics, 285–286
Crescent Engineering Company, 498

Daimler-Benz, 51 *illus.*, 219 *illus.*
Data Products, 4 *illus.*
David's Cookies, 145
Dayton Hudson, 202 *illus.*
Dean Foods Company, 54 *illus.*
Deere & Company, 138–139

Delco Electronics, 459, 486, 642
Deloitte, Haskins & Sells, 699 *illus.*
Delta Airlines, 75, 439, 501, 540
Diamond Shamrock, 113 *illus.*
Digital Equipment Corporation, 331, 592
Disneyland, 667 *illus.*, 714, 717–718
Domino's Pizza Distribution Company, 9, 433
Dow Chemical Company, 76, 77, 675
Duke Power Company, 346
Du Pont, 676
Dynascan, 509 *illus.*

E. F. Hutton, 81
Eastern Airlines, 76, 138
Eastman Kodak, 160–161
Ebasco Services Inc., 328 *illus.*
Electronic Data Systems (EDS), 243, 339, 495, 505, 607
Electronic Realty Associates, 19 *illus.*
Elling Brothers Mechanical Contractors, 557, 586–587
Embassy Communications, 132
Emergency One, 154
Employer's Reinsurance Corporation, 134
Equitable Life Assurance Society of the United States, 452 *n*
Executive Pools, 218
Exxon, 194 *illus.*, 569–570, 603

Federal Express Corporation, 145, 610 *illus.*
Federal Kemper Life Assurance Company, 272
Federal Reserve Board, 470
Fiesta Food Marts, 173–174
Fireman's Fund Insurance Company, 383
First Boston Corporation, 592
First United Bank Corporation, 603
Fleming, 123 *illus.*
Florida Power & Light Company, 245, 314–315
Foote, Cone & Belding, 674
Ford Motor Company, 36, 43, 272–273, 451 *illus.*, 567–568, 634
Fort Howard Paper Company, 149
Franklin Elementary School, 539
Franklin Savings & Loan, 488–489
Frito-Lay Inc., 147, 301
Fujitsu Limited, 504–505

General Dynamics Corporation, 89
General Electric Company, 121–122, 133, 134, 140, 143, 301, 323, 329, 392 *illus.*, 534, 568, 606 *illus.*, 673
  Appliance Division, 625, 653
General Foods Corporation, 132
  Post Cereal Division, 137
General Host, 76
General Mills, 306–307
General Motors, 76, 122–123, 196, 229, 243, 244, 271 *illus.*, 303, 312, 315, 417, 418, 440 *illus.*, 463, 483–486, 505, 506, 554, 606, 630, 639, 644, 673, 716
General Telephone & Electronics Corporation, 320

Gerber Foods, 167 *illus.*
Gerber Products Company, 65, 91–92
Gibson Glass Company, 224
Gillette Company, 142–143, 581 *illus.*, 466 *illus.*
Gillette Thailand, 669 *illus.*
Glidden Paint, 201 *illus.*, 673
Goodyear Tire & Rubber Company, 385 *illus.*, 526 *illus.*, 564 *illus.*, 713 *illus.*
Goulds Pumps, Inc., 120 *illus.*
Graco Inc., 672
Greyhound Lines Inc., 229, 276, 379
Gromer Supermarket Inc., 600–601
Guardian Engineering, 190

H. G. Heinz Company, 150–151
H.I.D., 127–128
Hamilton/Avnet, 235 *illus.*
Hardee's Restaurants, 595
Harley-Davidson, 491, 517, 634
Harris Corporation, 268 *illus.*
Hasbro Inc., 143 *illus.*, 673
Heineken, 671
Hercules Inc., 592, 610–611, 666
Hershey, 131–132
Heublein Inc., 136 *illus.*
Hewitt Associates, 322 *illus.*
Hewlett-Packard, 235, 293 *illus.*, 308, 309 *illus.*, 492, 494, 605, 625, 676
Hickory Farms, 76
Honda Motor Company Ltd., 10–11, 24 *illus.*, 462, 650–651, 669
Honeywell Corporation, 8 *illus.*, 87, 323–324, 356 *illus.*, 475–476
Huffy Corporation, 199–200
Hughes Aircraft Company, 545 *illus.*, 651 *illus.*
Humana Heart Institute International, 243 *illus.*
Human Resources Administration, 294–295

IBM. *See* International Business Machines
IBP, 148
IDS, 444 *illus.*
Illinois Central Gulf Railroad, 562
Ingersoll-Rand Company, 678
Inmed Corporation, 625–626
Integrated Genetics Inc., 320
Intel, 480
INTERCO, 7 *illus.*
International Business Machines (IBM), 72–74, 76, 173, 235–236, 309, 318, 320, 373 *illus.*, 385, 387, 462, 482, 495, 501, 506, 540, 577, 599 *illus.*, 616 *illus.*, 631, 632 *illus.*
International Harvester, 133, 316–317
International Playtex, 676
International Telephone and Telegraph, 133, 140, 572
Interstate Van Lines, 452–453
Iowa Beef Processors, 148
Ito-Yokada, 58 *illus.*
ITT, 133, 140, 572

J. C. Penney Company, 492
J. P. Morgan Investment Management Inc., 71 *illus.*, 90 *illus.*, 221 *illus.*, 482 *illus.*, 608 *illus.*
Jack Daniels Distillery, 94–95
Jaguar, 421, 455
James River Corporation, 133–134
Jay Jacobs Stores, 499
Jim Beam, 135
John Hancock Mutual Life Insurance Company, 156–157
Johnson Controls, 175, 644
Johnson & Johnson, 65, 511 *n*
Jostens Inc., 135

Kawasaki, 546, 645
Kellogg Company, 78–79, 669
Kentucky Fried Chicken, 251–253
KeyCorp, 114 *illus.*
Kidder Peabody & Company, 134
Kimberly-Clark, 68, 348
K mart, 240
Knight-Ridder, 480 *illus.*
Kodak, 534 *illus.*
Kollmorgen Corporation, 275, 482–483, 569
Ko-Rec-Type, 385–387

Lear Siegler Inc., 643 *illus.*
Legrande Stores, 363
Leisure Pools, 218
Leo Burnett, 495 *illus.*
Leprino Foods, 538
Lever Research and Development, 174 *illus.*
Levi Strauss, 87
Lewis Galoob Toys Inc., 611
Lewis Grocer Company, 320 *illus.*
Limited Express, 403 *illus.*
Limited Inc., The, 403 *illus.*
Lincoln Electric Company, 87 *illus.*
Lionel Trains, 665
Lockheed Corporation, 4, 7
Lone Star Industries, 647 *illus.*
Lotus Development Corporation, 75 *illus.*, 229, 260, 716
LSI Logic Corporation, 683
Lucky Stores, 138 *illus.*

Macy's, 304 *illus.*, 349–350, 710
Malard Manufacturing Company, 262–263
Marine Midland Bank, 518–519
Marquette Electronics, 404–405, 542
Marriott Corporation, 138, 180 *illus.*, 258–259, 446, 447
Mary Kay Cosmetics Inc., 69, 410 *illus.*, 493, 496 *illus.*, 499, 540
Maytag, 417
Mazda, 687 *illus.*
McDonald's Restaurants, 496, 501, 636 *illus.*, 665, 677, 688 *illus.*
MCI Communications Corporation, 76, 353
McKesson Corporation, 614–615
Mellon Bank, 715
Memorial County Hospital, 620–621
Mercury Marine, 201
Merrill Lynch, 412

Merv Griffin Enterprises, 132
Metallic Finishes Inc., 588–589
Microrim, 500 *illus.*
Milliken & Company, 483
Millipore Corporation, 123
MiniScribe Corporation, 156
Minnesota Mining and Manufacturing
    Company (3M), 302, 495
Minnie Pearl, 140
Modulate Corporation, 636
Monsanto Corporation, 171 *illus.*, 219, 314,
    443 *illus.*, 666
Morgan Guaranty Ltd., 595 *illus.*
Morgan Stanley, 501
Motorola Inc., 152–153
Mrs. Field's Cookies, 145

N. V. Phillips Gloelampenfabriken, 666
Nabisco Brands Inc., 132, 134
NASA, 605
National Forest Service, 216–218
Nationwide Insurance, 422 *illus.*
Navistar, 133, 316–317
Nestlé, 132
New United Motor Manufacturing Inc.
    (NUMMI), 76 *illus.*, 673
New World Pictures, 33, 60
New York City Transit Authority, 103–104
Nike Inc., 287 *illus.*, 531
Nippon Electric Company, 675
Nippon Light Metal Company, 669
Noxell Corporation, 639 *illus.*
Nucor Corporation, 149, 408
NUMMI, 76 *illus.*, 673
NYNEX, 551 *illus.*

Oceanographics Inc., 564–565
Ohio Bell, 157 *illus.*
Ok Tedi Mining Ltd., 689–690
Olin Ski Company, 421
Omark Industries, 644
Ontario Health Insurance, 538
Ore-Ida, 166 *illus.*
Ortho-Kinetics, 272
Owens-Corning Fiberglass, 307
Owens-Illinois, 100
Oxford Industries, 595

Pacific Gas and Electric Company,
    107 *illus.*
Pan Am, 294 *illus.*, 460 *illus.*
Panhandle Eastern, 469 *illus.*
Parsons Pine Products, 416
Peat Marwick Mitchell, 715
Pennwalt, 463 *illus.*
    Stokes Division, 400 *illus.*
People Express, 34, 159–160, 253, 527
PepsiCo Inc., 20, 125 *illus.*, 251 *illus.*, 446,
    507–508, 678, 680
Perdue Farms Inc., 134, 649 *illus.*
Pfizer Pharmaceuticals, 696 *illus.*,
    702 *illus.*, 715 *illus.*
PG&E, 107 *illus.*
Philip Morris Inc., 90, 132
Phillips Petroleum Company, 454 *illus.*,
    675 *illus.*

Pier I Imports, 110 *illus.*, 478 *illus.*
Pillsbury Company, 105, 106 *n*, 187 *illus.*,
    318 *illus.*
Pitney Bowes, Data Documents Division,
    201
Pittsburgh Brewing Company, 84
Pittsburgh Plate Glass, 14 *illus.*, 147
Pizza Hut, 632
Polaroid, 289, 307 *illus.*
Post Cereal, 137
Potlatch Corporation, 85 *n*
PPG Industries, 141 *illus.*, 147
Price Waterhouse, 370 *illus.*, 566 *illus.*,
    710 *illus.*
Procter & Gamble, 68, 132, 248–249, 532,
    540, 669, 678, 715
Producers Gas and Transmission
    Company, 581–582
Pro Line Company, 30
Prudential Insurance Comapny, 344 *n*

Quaker Oats Company, 570 *illus.*,
    576 *illus.*
    Pet Foods Division, 147 *illus.*
Quaker State Oil, 151 *illus.*

R. H. Macy & Company, 304 *illus.*, 349–
    350, 710
R. J. Reynolds Industries Inc., 132, 134
Ralston Purina Company, 59 *illus.*
Rayovac, 610
RCA Corporation, 76, 133, 134
Republic National Bank, 261–262
Richardson-Vicks, 132
Rockwell International, 537 *illus.*
Rolm Corporation, 76
Rospatch Corporation, 110

S. C. Johnson & Son Company, 312
Safeco Insurance Company, 502
Sakowitz Inc., 131, 158
Saks Fifth Avenue, 149 *illus.*
Salomon Brothers, 367
Salvo Inc., 477
Sanyo, 545
Saatchi & Saatchi, 674
Scandinavian Air System, 135
Scandinavian Design Inc., 452, 535–536
Schering-Plough, 387 *illus.*
Schlitz Brewing Company, 147
Schwinn Bicycle Company, 611
Scott Paper Company, 513, 514 *illus.*
Sealy Inc., 153 *illus.*
Sears, Roebuck and Company, 61–62,
    236–237, 240, 276, 711
Second National Bank, 223–224
Sequint Computers Systems Inc., 493
Sharp Corporation, 76
Sibson & Company, 355
Singer Company, The, 712 *n*
Smith Kline & French, 714 *illus.*
SNECMA, 673
Sonat Inc., 122
Sonoco Products Company, 549–550
Sony Corporation, 304, 494
Sorbee International, 408 *illus.*

Southland Corporation, 325 *illus.*
Southwestern Bell Corporation, 330
Spectrum Control Inc., 525, 526, 552–
    553
Sperry Corporation, 167–168
Star-Kist Foods, 76
Steelcase, 471 *illus.*
Stilwell Foods Inc., 376 *illus.*
Stix & Company, 526
Stotler Associates, 211–212
Sun Petroleum Products Company, 278–
    280
Swissair, 416
Syntex Corporation, 429
Szabo Correctional Services, 233 *illus.*

Taco Bell, 133
Tandem Computer Company, 433, 445,
    499, 532, 540
Tasty Baking Company, 559, 637 *illus.*
Tenneco Inc., 133, 284 *illus.*
Texas Air, 76
Texas Instruments, 307, 502, 576
Textron, 17, 17 *illus.*
Thermo Electron Corporation, 603
3M Company, 302, 495
Thrifty Scott Warehouse Food Inc., 578
Time Inc., 167
Timex, 196
Toyota Motor Corporation, 76, 505 *illus.*,
    673
Training Development Corporation, 447–
    448, 448–449
Traveler's Insurance Company, 319–320
Triangle Equipment, 361–362
Tridon Ltd., 585
Tri-Star Pictures, 132
TRW Inc., 118, 316
Tucker Company, 297–299

U.S. Steel, 17, 169, 236–237
Uniroyal, 104
United Airlines, 134, 495
United Parcel Service, 46
United Technologies, 182–183
United Telecom, 348 *illus.*
United Way, 621–622
USAir, 66 *illus.*, 246 *illus.*, 341, 531 *illus.*
U.S. Caterpillar, 534, 540 *illus.*, 637 *illus.*
USF&G, 316 *illus.*, 350 *illus.*
U.S. Shoe, 418 *illus.*
U.S. West, 512 *illus.*
USX, 117, 169, 236–237

Varian Associates Inc., 354 *illus.*
Volkswagen, 99, 126

W. L. Gore & Associates, 483, 506
W. T. Grant, 147
Walmart, 240, 544 *illus.*
Walt Disney Productions, 119–120, 717–
    718
Warner-Lambert, 571 *illus.*
Waste Management Inc., 80 *illus.*,
    244 *illus.*, 402 *illus.*
Wells Fargo & Company, 172–173

Western Electric Company, 48 *illus.*
Western Engine Company, 599–600
Westinghouse, 532, 684, 716 *illus.*
Wetterau Incorporated, 465 *illus.*
Weyerhauser Company, 169 *illus.*, 170
Wicker Company, 207–209

Wild Things, 381 *illus.*
Woodward Governor Company, 421

Xaloy Inc., 654–655
Xerox Corporation, 265, 297, 722–723

York International Corporation, 185 *illus.*
York's Restaurant, 413 *illus.*

Zales Corporation, 603
Zebco, 646, 650
Ztel Inc., 446–447

Subject Index

Accommodative response, 85
Achievement need, 405
Achievement-oriented leadership, 381
Achieving excellence, 59, 505–507
  compared with other management
    perspectives, 56–57
Acquired needs theory, 405–406
Action, bias toward, 505–506
Action plan, 580
Activity ratio, 564–565
Adaptive mode, 154
Adaptive strategy typology, 145–147
Adhocracy, 294
Adjourning, 469–470
Administrative intensity, 240
Administrative model of decision making,
  170–172
  compared with classical model, 172
Administrative principles, 42, 43–44
Advertising, 77
Affiliation need, 405
Affirmative action, 343
Alternatives
  development of, 175–177
  implementation of, 178–180
  selection of, 177–178
Ambiguity, 167
Analyzer, 147
Analyzer strategy, 147
Ancient management, 37–38
Application forms, 346
Artificial intelligence, 606
Assessment centers, 348
Assets, 562
Authority-obedience management, 327
Autocratic leader, 371–373
Automated offices, 607–608
Autonomous work groups, 482–486
Autonomy, 419–420

Autonomy and entrepreneurship, 506
Avoidance learning, 413

Balance sheet, 561–562
Balance sheet budget, 573
Bargaining/negotiation, to resolve conflict,
  478
Batch-push inventory system, 639
BCG Matrix, 141–143
**Behaviorally anchored rating scale
  (BARS), 351,** 352
Behavioral sciences approach, 50–51
Behavior modification, 412
Belongingness needs, 402
Benefits, 357–360
Bet-your-company culture, 499–500
  heroes in, 500
Birth stage, 250–251
Bottom-up approach, 318
Bottom-up budgeting, 574–575
Boundary-spanning roles, 74–75
Bounded rationality, 170
Brainstorming, 188
Breakeven analysis, 203–206
Budget control. *See* Middle management
  budget control
Budgeting process, 574–578
  advantages and disadvantages of, 577–
    578
  top-down or bottom-up budgeting, 574–
    575
  zero-based budgeting, 575–576
Bureaucracy, 292–293
Bureaucratic control, 537, 539
  compared with clan control, 541–542
Bureaucratic organizations, 45–46
Burnout, 705
Business growth rate, 141

Business-level strategy, 134–135, 144–
  151
  adaptive strategy typology, 145–147
  Porter's competitive strategies, 147–149
  and product life-cycle, 149–151

CAD (computer-aided design), **635**–636
CAM (computer-aided manufacturing), **636**
Capacity planning, 636–637
Capital expenditure budget, 573
Career, 695
  compared with a job, 694–695
Career development, 695–702
  disengagement stage, 701
  establishment and advancement stage,
    700–701
  exploration and trial stage, 700
  mid-career stage, 701
Career ladder, 711–712
Career management, 695, 708
Career management problems, 715–718
  dual-career couples, 716–717
  plateaued employees, 717–718
  women and minorities, 715–716
Career management strategies, 709–714,
  718–720
  career ladders, 711–712
  career paths, 711
  career planning programs, 713
  evaluation of career potential, 709–710
  facilitation of mentoring, 713–714
  focus on career stages, 718–720
  human resource information systems,
    710–711
  succession planning, 713
  training and management development,
    710
Career path, 711

Note: Running glossary terms and the page on which they are defined are set in boldface type in this index.

Career planning, 695–707
 avoiding overplanning, 699–700
 career development stages, 700–702
 managing career stress, 704–707
 mentor relationships, 702–703, 713–714
 steps in, 696–697
Career planning programs, 713
Career plateau, 717–718
Career stages, 718–720
Career stress, managing, 704–706
Carryover behaviors, 474
Case discussion groups, 349
Cash budget, 572–573
Cash cow, 141
Causal modeling, 200
Causes, for decision making, 174–175
Centralization, 236–237, 686
Centralized network, 448–449
Centralized planning department, 121–122
Central processing unit (CPU), 596–597
Ceremonies, 496–497
 as change tools, 512
 in different cultures, 499, 500, 502
Certainty, 166
Chain of command, 233
Chance fork, 216
Change
 external forces for, 303
 implementing, 310–317
 initiating, 305–310
 internal forces for, 303
 managing, 303–304
 need for, 304
 planned, 317–321
Change agent, 325
Change tools, 510–513
 public statements, 510–511
 stories and heroes as, 512–513
 symbols, ceremonies, and slogans as, 512
Changing, 324
Channel of communication, 432. *See also* Communication channels
Channel richness, 435–436
Clan control, 539–542
 compared with bureaucratic control, 541–542
Classical model of decision making, **168**–170
 compared with administrative model, 172
Classical perspective, 39–46
 administrative principles, 42–44
 bureaucratic organizations, 44–46
 compared with others, 56–57
 forerunners of, 39–40
 scientific management, 40–42
Classroom training, 349
Closed systems, 54
Coalition, 111, 182–183
Coalition building, 111–112
Code of ethics, 88–90
Coercion, to implement change, 315–316
Coercive power, 369
Cohesiveness in groups, 470–473

consequences of, 471–473
 determinants of, 471
Collectivism, 668
Command group, 461–462
Command method, 36
Commitment, as a response to power, 369
Committee, 482
Communication, 430. *See also*
 Organizational communication,
 formal channels, informal channels.
 See Communication channels,
 circular nature of
 importance to management, 431–433
 in groups, 448–449
 listening as, 439–440
 "noise" a problem in, 432, 433
 nonverbal, 437–438
 and perception, 433–435
 process of, 432–433
 sender and receiver in, 432
 and task complexity, 449
Communication and education to
 implement change, 314–315
Communication breakdown, as a source of
 conflict, 476
Communication channels, 432, 435–437
 capacity of, 436
 channel richness in, 435–436
 circular nature of, 432–433
 formal, 441–445
 informal, 445–448
 selection of, 436
Compensation, 355–360
 benefits, 357–360
 building wage and salary structure, 356–357
 job evaluation for, 355–356
Competitors, 68
Completeness, of information, **595**
Compliance with power, 369
Compulsory staff service, 39
Computation, 595
Computer-assisted instruction, 349
**Computer-based information systems
 (CBIS), 596**–597
 decision support systems, 601–603
 evolution of, 603–605
 limitations of 615–618
 and management hierarchy, 597–604
 management information systems, 600–601
 transaction processing systems, 598–600
Computer conferencing, 605
Computer use, in Soviet Union, 593
Conceptual skills, 16
Concurrent control, 532–534
Conference discussion groups, 349
Conflict, 476–478
 causes of, 476–477
 resolving, 477–478
Consideration, 373
Consolidating corporations, 514
Constituency, 86
Content theories, 401–406
 acquired needs theory, 405–406

hierarchy of needs, 401–403
 two-factor theory, 403–405
Contingency approach, 376–387
 Fiedler's contingency theory, 376–379
 path-goal theory, 379–383
 Vroom-Yetton model, 383–387
Contingency factors, 247–259
 environment, 247–249
 integrating with structure, 290–295
 organizational, 547–549
 production technology, 253–259
 size and life cycle, 249–253
Contingency view, 55–56
 compared with other management
 perspectives, 56–57
Continuous process production, 254
**Continuous reinforcement schedule,
 414**–416
Contracting corporations, 513–514
Control. *See also* Organizational control
 bureaucratic, 537, 539
 choosing style of, 543–544
 clan, 539–542
 concurrent, 532–534
 and cultural values, 687–688
 feedback, 534
 feedforward, 532
 importance of, 526–529
 of information, 596
 for multinational corporations, 680
 multiple systems for, 534–536
 process of, 526–529
 of quality. *See* Total quality control
 relationship to strategic planning, 529–531
Control and follow-up of decision making,
 180
Controlling, 9
Control process, steps in, 526–529
 compare performance to standards, 527–529
 establish standards, 526–527
 measure actual performance, 527
 take corrective action, 529
Control types, and environmental change,
 529–531
Control Type I, 530
Control Type II, 530
Control Type III, 530
Coordination, 242
Coordination costs, 480–481
Core control systems, 558–561
 financial forecast in, 558
 management information systems
 reports in, 560
 operating budget in, 559
 operations management systems and
 reports in, 559
 performance appraisal in, 559
 strategic plan in, 558
Core job dimensions, 419–420
Core memory, 597
Corporate culture, 492–513
 ceremonies important to, 496–497
 and corporate strategy, 497–502
 heroes exemplifying, 495

Corporate culture *(continued)*
  reshaping, 502–508
  revitalization of, 513–516
  role in control, 540
  slogans expressing, 495–496
  stories reinforcing, 494
  strengthening, 501
  symbols associated with, 493–494
  techniques for changing, 508–513
  types of, 498–502
Corporate ethics, 83
Corporate-level strategy, 134, 139–144
  and corporate culture, 497–502
  formulating, 139–144
  for multinational corporations, 676–680
Corporate performance, evaluating, 81–84
Corporate responses to social demands,
    84–85
Corporate social audit, 88
Corrective action, in control process, 529
Cost, as a design attribute, 631
Cost center, 568
Cost leadership, 148
Countertrade, 672
Country club management, 327
Creativity, 305–307
Critical events, 473
Critical psychological states, 420
Critical success factors (CSF), 618–619
Cultural values, tailoring management style
    to, 686–688
Culture, 492, 667. *See also* Corporate
    culture
Current assets, 562
Current debt, 562
Customer driven companies, 506
Customers, 68
Cyclic pattern, 199

Data, 594
  compared with information, 595
Debt, 562
Decentralization, 236–238, 686
Decentralized network, 448–449
Decentralized planning staff, 122–123
Decisional roles, 22
Decision fork, 216
Decision making, 164
  and ambiguity, 167
  and certainty, 166
  and cultural values, 687
  group approaches to. *See* Group
      decision making
  improving effectiveness of, 187–188
  models for. *See* Decision-making
      models
  quantitative approaches to, 213–220
  and risk, 166
  steps in. *See* Decision-making steps
  and uncertainty, 166–167
Decision-making models, 168–172
  administrative, 170–172
  classical, 168–170
Decision-making steps, 172–181
  control and follow-up, 180–181
  development of alternatives, 175–177

diagnosis and analysis of causes, 174–
    175
  implementation of chosen alternatives,
      178–180
  recognition of decision requirement, 172–
      174
  selection of desired alternatives, 177–
      178
Decision package, 576
Decision requirement, 172–174
Decisions, 164–168
  programmed and nonprogrammed, 165
Decision support systems (DSS), 601–
    603
Decision tree, 215–218
Decode, 432
Defender strategy, 145, 147, 287
Defensive response, 85
Delegation, 238
Deliberately structured organization, 10
Delphi groups, 185
Delphi technique, 202
Demand pull inventory system, 639
Democratic leader, 371–373
Demographic forecasts, 196
Demotivation, 8
Departmentalization, 235–236
Dependent demand inventory, 641
Descriptive model of decision making,
    171
Development, distinguished from training,
    348
Devil's advocate, 187
Diagnosis, 174
Dialectical enquiry, 187–188
Differentiation, 148, 247
Differentiation strategy, 614–615
Diffusion of responsibility, 481
Direct investment, 673
Directive leadership, 381
Discretionary costs, 571
Discretionary responsibility, 84
Disengagement stage, 701
Disseminator role, 21
Distinctive competence, 133–134
Disturbance handler role, 22
Diversification, 140
Divestiture, 140
Divisionalized forms, 293
Divisional structure, 266, 274–277
  advantages and disadvantages of, 276–
      277
  customer based, 275–276
  geographically based, 276
Division of labor, 233
Dog, 141
Downsizing, 335
Downward communication, 440–443
  loss of information in, 442
Dual-career couples, 716–717
Dual roles, 466

Econometric models, 201
Economic dimension, 71
Economic environment, for international
    business, 663–664

Economic forces, 36
Economic order quantity (EOQ), 639–
    641
Economic responsibility, 81
Effectiveness, 10–11
Efficiency, 10–11
Efficiency goals, 287
Electronic bulletin boards, 605–606
Electronic mail, 605
Employee-centered leaders, 374
Employee growth-need strength, 420
Encode, 432
Entrepreneurial leader, 391
Entrepreneurial mode, 153–154
Entrepreneur role, 22
Entrepreneurship and autonomy, 506
Entry strategies, for international
    business, **671**–674
  exporting, 671–672
  foreign production, 673–674
  franchising, 673
  licensing, 672–673
Environment, 53
  external, 66–74
  general, 67, 69–72
  impact on organization structure, 247–
      249
  for international business, 663–671
  organizational, 66–67
  task, 66–67, 68–69
Environmental analysis, for multinational
    corporations, 678
Environmental change, and control types,
    529–531
Environmental discontinuity, 529
Environment/organization relationship, 74–
    79
  adaptation, 74–76
  influence, 77–79
E—P expectancy, 409–410
**Equal employment opportunity (EEO)
    laws, 343,** 360
Equity, 407
Equity theory, 407–408
ERG theory, 402
**Establishment and advancement stage,
    700**–701
Esteem needs, 402
Ethical advocate, 89
Ethical dilemma, 83–84
Ethical responsibility, 82–84
Ethical responsiveness, improving, 87–
    89
Ethics committee, 89
Ethnocentrism, 668
Excellence, achieving, 59
  compared with other management
      perspectives, 56–57
Excellence characteristics, 505–507
Exception goals, 110
Exchange rates, 665
Existence needs, 402
Exit interview, 361
Expectancy theory 408–411
  E—P expectancy, 409–410
  implications for managers, 410

Expectancy theory *(continued)*
P—O expectancy, 410
valence of outcomes, 410
Expected value, 214
Expense budget, 570–571
Experienced meaningfulness of work, 420
Experienced responsibility, 420
Expert power, 369
Expert systems, 606
Explicit statements, 474–476
Exploration and trial stage, 700
Exporting, 671–672
External audit, 565
External environment, 66–74
general, 67, 69–72
organizational, 66–67
task, 66–67, 68–69
External forces for change, 303
Extinction, 413

Facilitating communication, to resolve
conflict, 478
Facilities layout, 632–634
Facility location, 636
Feedback, 53, 420, 432
Feedback control, 524
Feedforward control, 532
Femininity, 668
Figurehead role, 20
Financial analysis, 563–565
Financial audits, 565–566
Financial budgets, 572–574
Financial control
budgeting process as, 574–578
middle management level, 568–574
top management level, 561–568
Financial forecasts, 563
in a core control system, 558
Financial ratios, 563–565
Financial statements, 561–562
Finished-goods inventory, 637
First-line manager, 13
Fixed assets, 562
Fixed costs, 571
Fixed-interval reinforcement schedule, 414–
415
Fixed-position layout, 634
Fixed-ratio reinforcement schedule, 415
Flaming, 609
Flat structure, 235
**Flexible manufacturing system (FMS),
635**
Flexible structure, 75–76
Flextime, 422
Focus, 148–149
Focussed companies, 506–507
Force field analysis, 313–314
Forecasting, 75, 196–203
demographic forecasts, 196
financial forecasts, 558, 563
human resources forecasts, 197
qualitative techniques for, 201–202
quantitative techniques for, 197–201
sales forecasts, 196
technological forecasts, 196
Foreign production, 673–674

Formal communication channels, 441–
445
downward, 441–443
horizontal, 444–445
upward, 443–444
Formal groups, 461–463
Formalization, 240–241
Forming, 468
Four-day workweek, 422
Franchising, 673
Free rider, 480
Friendship group, 463
Frustration-regression principle, 403
Functional-based structure, 684
Functional departmentalization, 235
Functional group, 461–462
Functional-level strategy, 135
formulating, 151–153
Functional manager, 14
Functional structure, 266, **268**–270
advantages and disadvantages of, 269–
270
**Functional structure with lateral
relationships,** 266, **271**–273
advantages and disadvantages of, 273

Game theory, 218
General environment, 67, 69–72
economic dimension, 71
international, 663–666
international dimension, 71–72. *See
also* Multinational corporations
(MNC)
legal-political dimension, 71
international, 666–667
sociocultural dimension, 70–71
international, 667–669
technological dimension, 69–70
General manager, 14–15
Geographical departmentalization, 235
Geographic-based structure, 682–683
GE screen, 143–144
Globalization, 676
Goal characteristics, 109–111
Goal differences, as a source of conflict,
476–477
Goal directed organization, 10
Goals, 100. *See also* Management by
objectives (MBO)
characteristics of, 109–111
criteria for effectiveness, 109–112
developing plans for attaining. *See*
Planning; Plans
exception goals, 110
and goal-setting behavior, 111–112
innovation goals, 110
in organizations, 104–109
problem-solving, 110
relationship with plans, 100–109
types of, 105–109
Goal-setting behavior, 111–112
coalition building, 111–112
participation, 112
Grand strategy, 140
for multinational corporations, 676–678
Grapevine, 446–448

Griggs v. *Duke Power Company,* 346
Group cohesiveness, 470–473
Group communication processes, 448–
449
Group concepts, organizational application
of, 481–487
Group decision making, 181–186
advantages of, 186
disadvantages of, 186
formats for, 184–185
importance of coalitions, 182
task groups for, 183–184
Group development, 468–470
Group norms, 473–476
Group processes, 468–476
group cohesiveness, 470–473
group norms, 473–476
stages of development, 468–470
Groups, 460. *See also* Work groups
autonomous work groups, 682–686
committees, 482
conflict in, 476–478
potential benefits of, 479–480
potential costs of, 480–481
task forces, 481
types of, 461–463
Group task performance, relationship with
leadership style and situational
favorableness, 377–378
Groupthink, 186
Growth needs, 402
Growth strategy, 140
for multinational corporations, 677–678

Halo error, 351
Hands-on leadership, 506
Hardware, 597
Hawthorne studies, 48–49
Heroes, 495
as change tools, 512
in different cultures, 498, 499, 500, 502
Hierarchy of authority, for control, 537
Hierarchy of needs theory, 401–403
and frustration-regression principle, 403
Holding costs, 639
Homogeneity, 351
Horizontal communication, 444–445
Horizontal linkage models, 319
Human relations approach to motivation,
399–400
Human relations movement, 49–50
Human resource approach to motivation,
400
Human resource generalists, 336
Human resource information systems, and
career management, 710
Human resource inventory, 710
Human resource management, 333–334
goals of, 337–361
implications of corporate mergers for,
334
implications of downsizing for, 335
implications of government regulations
for, 335
Japanese perspective on, 503–505
process of, 335–336

Human resource management
(continued)
   sharing responsibilities with line
     managers, 336
   strategic role of, 334–335
Human resource perspective, 46–51
   behavioral sciences approach, 50–51
   compared with others, 56–57
   forerunners of, 47
   Hawthorne studies, 47–49
   human relations movement, 49–50
Human resource planning, 338–342
   forecasting techniques for, 340–342
   job analysis for, 339–340
Human resources forecasts, 197
Human resource specialists, 336
Human skills, 16–17
Hybrid structure, 266, **277**–281
   advantages and disadvantages of, 280–
    281
Hygiene factors, 403

Illegal practices, 79
Implementation
   of decision making, **178**
   for multinational corporations, 680
Impoverished management, 327, 328
Income statement, 562
Indirect-to-direct labor ratio, 240
Individual barriers to communication, 450
Individualism, 668
Informal communication channels, 445–
   448
   grapevine, 446–448
   management by wandering around
    (MBWA), 445–446
Informal groups, 463
Information, 594
   characteristics of, 594–595
   compared with data, 594
   and management, 593–595
Informational roles, 21
Information and control systems, and
   strategy implementation, 156–157
Information systems, 242–243, **595**–597.
   See also Management information
    systems (MIS)
   artificial intelligence, 606
   automated offices, 607–608
   components of, 595–597
   computer-based. *See* Computer-based
    information systems (CBIS)
   manual, 596
   networking, 606–607
   telecommunications, 605–606
Information technology
   impact on organizations, 608–612
   and strategic management, 612–615
Infrastructure, 664–665
Initiating structure, 373
Innovation goals, 110, **287**
Inputs, 53, 595
Inspirational leader, 389–391
Inspirational leadership, 388–391
Integrating managers, 244–245
Interactive groups, 184

Interest group, 463
Intermediate-term planning, 119
Internal analysis, for multinational
   corporations, 679
Internal audit, 565–566
Internal environment, 67
Internal forces for change, 303
International business. *See* Multinational
   corporations (MNC)
International business environment, 663–
   671
   economic, 663–666
   legal-political, 666–667
   sociocultural, 667–669
   summarized, 669–671
International dimension, 71–72
International division, 681–682
International management, 662–663
International markets, entry strategies for,
   671–674
Interpersonal roles, 20–21
Interview, 346, 347
Intrapreneurs, 307–308, 311
Intuition, 171
Inventory, 637
   importance of, 638–639
Inventory management, 637–645
   economic order quantity, 639–641
   importance of inventory, 638–639
   just-in-time inventory, 643–645
   manufacturing resource planning, 643
   materials requirement planning, 641–
    642
Inventory status file, 641
Investment center, 569–570
Iron law of responsibility, 80

Japanese management, 57–58, 503–505
   combined with American in Theory Z
    approach, 503–505
   compared with other management
    perspectives, 56–57
Job, 695
   compared with a career, 694–695
Job analysis, 339–340
   and career management, 710
Job-centered leaders, 374
Job characteristics model, 419, 418–421
Job description, 344, 345
Job design, 417, 416–421
Job enlargement, 417–**418**
Job enrichment, 418
Job evaluation, 355–356
Job matching systems, 710
Job rotation, 417
Job sharing, 422
Job simplification, 417
Joint venture, 76, 673
Jurisdictional ambiguities, as a source of
   conflict, 476
Jury of opinion, 202
Just-in-time (JIT) inventory, 313–314,
   643–645

Kanban systems, 639
Key indicator systems, 618

Knowledge of actual results, 420

Labor supply, 69
Lateral structure, 242–245
   balancing with vertical structure, 245–
    259
   coordination vital to, 242
   and information systems, 242–243
   integrating managers in, 244–245
   liaison roles in, 243
   permanent teams for, 244
   task forces in, 243–244
Law of effect, 413
Laws and regulations, affecting
   international business, 666
Leader behavior, 380–381
Leader-member relations, 376–377
Leader role, 20–21
Leaders
   autocratic, 371–373
   characteristics of, 370–371
   democratic, 371–373
Leadership, 368
   achievement-oriented, 381
   contingency approaches to, 376–387
   and cultural values, 686–687
   at different organizational levels, 392–
    393
   directive, 381
   hands-on, 506
   inspirational, 388–392
   nature of, 368–371
   neutralizers for, 388
   participative, 381
   and strategy implementation, 155–156
   studies of, 371–387
   substitutes for, 387–388
   supportive, 381
   two-dimensional approaches to, 373–
    375
Leadership situations, 376–377
   relationship with style and performance,
    377–378
Leadership style
   relationship with situation and
    performance, 377–378
   selecting, 385
Leadership traits, 370–371
Leading, 8
   vs. managing, 389
Least preferred coworker scale (LPC), 376
Legal-political dimension, 71
   for international business, 666–667
Legal responsibility, 81–82
Legitimate power, 368
Leverage ratio, 564
Liabilities, 562
Liaison roles, 21, **243**
Licensing, 672–673
Line and staff structure, 238–240
Linear programming, 206–210
Line authority, 239
Line departments, 238–241
Line managers, sharing responsibility with
   human resource managers, 336
Linguistic pluralism, 668

Liquidation, 140
Liquidity ratio, 564
Listening
 in communication, 439–440
 to overcome barriers to communication, 451
Long-range forecasting, for human resource management, 341–342
Long-term debt, 562
Long-term planning, 119
Low-cost strategy, 613–614
LPC scale, 376
Lump sum salary increases, 422–423

Machine bureaucracy, 292
Management, 5
 authority-obedience, 327
 classical perspective on, 39–46
 contingency view of, 55–56
 country club, 327
 early history of, 37–39
 functions of, 5–9
 historical forces shaping, 35–36
 human resource perspective on, 46–51
 impoverished, 327, 328
 and information, 593–595
 Japanese, 56–58, 503–505
 management science perspective, 52
 Organization Man, 327–328
 perspectives compared, 56–57
 recent historical trends in, 56–59
 search for excellence in, 59
 and systems theory, 53–55
 team, 327
Management by objectives (MBO), 112–114, **579**–583
 appraising overall performance, 581
 assessing effectiveness of, 582–583
 characteristics of, 112–113
 developing action plans for, 580
 reviewing progress in, 580–581
 setting objectives for, 579–580
 strengths and weaknesses of, 113–114
Management by wandering around (MBWA), 445–446
Management control systems, 537
Management development, 709–710
Management efficiency, impact of information technology on, 608–609
Management hierarchy, and computer-based information systems, 597–604. See also Computer-based information systems (CBIS)
Management information systems (MIS), 52, **600**–601. See also Information systems
 in a core control system, 560
Management science, 194–196
Management science aids
 forecasting, 196–202
 limitations of, 221
 models, 195
 quantitative approaches to decision making, 213–220
 quantitative approaches to planning, 203–213

strengths of, 220–221
Management science perspective, 52
 compared with others, 56–57
Management skills, 15–18
 AT&T study of, 23–24
 conceptual, 16
 human, 16–17
 learning, 22–25
 need for, 17–18
 technical, 17
Management style, tailoring to cultural values, 686–688
Managerial activities, 18–20
Managerial grid, 326–328, **374**–375
Managerial productivity, 650–651
Managerial roles, 20–22
Managers
 activities of, 18–20
 AT&T study of, 23–24
 first-line managers, 13
 functional managers, 14
 general managers, 14–15
 importance of, 3–5
 middle managers, 12–13
 project managers, 15
 roles of, 20–22
 skills needed by. See Management skills
 study of success and failure of, 24–25
 top managers, 12
 types of, 12–15
Managing vs. leading, 389
Manual information system, 596
Manufacturing organizations, 627
 compared with service organizations, 627–628
Manufacturing resource planning (MRP II), 643
Manufacturing technology, 254–256
Market method, 36
Market share, 141
Masculinity, 668
Mass production, 254
Master production schedule, 641
Matching models, 337–338
Materials management, 651
 reporting levels for, 651–653
Materials requirement planning (MRP), 641–642
Matrix boss, 284
Matrix structure, 266, 281–286
 advantages and disadvantages of, 284–285
 for international businesses, 684
 key relationships in, 283–284
Maturity stage, 250, 253
Means-end chain, 109
Mechanistic organizations, 246
Mechanistic structure, 75–76
Mediation, 478
Medieval management, 38–39
Member roles in groups, 465–466
Mentor, 702–703
Mentoring, facilitation of, 713–714
Merger, 76
Merit pay, 421–422
Message, 432

Michigan studies of leadership, 374
Mid-career renewal strategy, 719
Mid-career stage, 701
Middle management budget control, 568–574
 financial budgets, 572–574
 operating budgets, 570–571
 responsibility centers, 568–572
Middle manager, 12–**13**
Midlife stage, 250, 252–253
Minorities, career management problems of, 715–716
Mintzberg's typology of structure, 290–294
 adhocracy, 294
 divisionalized form, 293
 machine bureaucracy, 292
 professional bureaucracy, 293
 simple structure, 291
Mission, 105
Mission statement, 100
Modified work schedules, 422
Monitor role, 21
Monte Carlo methods, 220
Motivation, 398
 content perspectives on, 401–406
 and cultural values, 687
 foundations of, 399–401
 job design for, 416–421
 lump sum salary increases, 422–423
 merit pay used for, 421–422
 modified work schedules used for, 422
 open salary information, 423
 process perspectives on, 407–411
 reinforcement perspective on, 412–416
 and reward, 399
Motivators, 403
Multidomestic strategy, 676
Multinational corporations (MNC), 674–686
 characteristics of, 674–675
 corporate strategy for, 676–680
 organizational structure for, 680–686
Multiple advocacy, 187
Multiple control systems, 534–536

Needs
 acquired, 405–406
 hierarchy of, 401–403
Needs analysis, 349
Negotiation, to implement change, 315
Negotiator role, 22
Network corporation, 611
Networking, 606–607
Networks, 448–449
Neutralizer, 388
New-product approaches to change, 318–320
 horizontal linkage model for, 319–320
Nominal groups, 184
Nonparticipator role, 466
Nonprogrammed decisions, 165
Nonroutine service technology, 257
Nonverbal communication, 437–439
Normative model of decision making, **169**
Norming, 469
Norms, 473–476

Objectives, 102
  hierarchy of, 109
  operational, 109
  tactical, 108
Obstructive response, 84–85
Ohio State leadership studies, 373
On-the-job training (OJT), 349
Open salary information, 423
Open system, 54
Operating budgets, 570–571
  in a core control system, 559
  expense budget, 570–571
  profit budget, 571
  revenue budget, 571
Operational objectives, 109
  for multinational corporations, 680
Operational plans, 115–116
Operations management, 52, 626
  designing systems for, 631–637
  inventory management, 637–645
  productivity management, 646–651
  purchasing, 645–646
  strategic role of, 628–631
Operations management function
  materials management approach, 651
  organizing, 651–652
  structural location, 651–652
Operations management systems
  in a core control system, 559
  designing, 631–637
Operations research, 52
Operations strategy, 628–631
  stages of, 628–630
Opportunity, 137, 172
Ordering costs, 639
Organic organizations, 246
Organic Structure, 75
Organization, 10
  policies and procedures basic to, 252
Organizational barriers to communication,
    451–453
Organizational career, 695
  management strategies for, 707–714.
    See also Career management
Organizational change, 302. *See also*
    Change
Organizational communication, 440–448
  barriers to, 449–453
  formal channels, 440–445
  informal channels, 445–448
  managing, 449–453
  overcoming barriers, 451–453
Organizational constituencies, 85–87
Organizational contingency factors and
    quality circles, 547–549
Organizational control, 526. *See also*
    Control; Financial control
  characteristics showing effectiveness,
    550–552
  by computer, 538
  core control systems, 558–561
  performance appraisal used for, 579–
    586
  simultaneously loose-tight, 507
  types of, 530
Organizational control focus, 532–534

Organizational control methods, 536–543
  bureaucratic control, 537, 539
  clan control, 539–542
  and social responsibility, 538
Organizational design for planning, 121–
    123
Organizational development (OD), 321–
    328
  assumptions of, 322–324
  interventions used, 325–328
    managerial grid, 326–328
    survey feedback, 326
    teambuilding, 325
  steps in, 324–325
Organizational effectiveness, 10–11
Organizational efficiency, 10–11
Organizational environment, 66–67. *See
    also* Environment
Organizational level, and leadership, 391–
    392
Organizational mission, 105
Organizational performance, 9–12
Organization chart, 232–233
Organization life cycle, 250–253
  birth stage, 250–251
  influence on organizational structure,
    250–253
  maturity stage, 250, 253
  midlife stage, 250, 252–253
  youth stage, 250, 251–252
Organization Man management, 327–328
Organizations
  impact of information technology on,
    608–612
  in management efficiency, 608–609
  in organization structure, 610–612
  in social relationships, 609–612
Organization structure, 231. *See also*
    Structural design
  balancing vertical and lateral structures
    environment as a factor, 247–249
    organization size and life cycle as
      factors, 249–253
    production technology as a factor, 253–
      259
  flat structure, 235
  impact of information technology on,
    610–612
  integrating with contingency factors, 290–
    295
  lateral structure, 242–245
  mechanistic vs. organic, 246–247
  Mintzberg's typology of, 290–294
  for multinational corporations, 680–687
  need for change in, 288
  relationship to responsibility centers, 570
  simplified, 507
  size influencing, 249–250
  and strategy implementation, 156
  tall structure, 235
  vertical structure, 232–242
Organizing, 7, 230
  process of, 231–232
Orientation training, 349
Outputs, 53
Outsourcing, 678

Overall strategy development, for
    multinational corporations, 680
Owners' equity, 562

Paper-and-pencil tests, 343
Partial productivity, 647–648
Partial reinforcement schedule, 414–416
Participation, 112
  to implement change, 315
Participative leadership, 381
Path-goal theory, 379–383
  and leader behavior, 380–382
  situational contingencies in, 381
  use of rewards in, 381–382
Pause strategy, 140
Payoff matrix, 213–215
Pay survey, 357
Pay-trend line, 357
Peer group, and control, 540
People approaches to change, 321. *See
    also* Organizational development
    (OD)
People change, 321
Perception, 434, 433–435
Perceptual organization, 434
Perceptual selectivity, 434
Performance, 12
Performance appraisal, 350–354
  behaviorally anchored rating scales
    (BARS) used for, 351–352
  in a core control system, 559
  for control, 579–586
  correcting rating errors in, 351–353
  documentation of, 354
  need for accuracy in, 351
  sources of error in, 351
Performance appraisal interview, 353–
    354
Performance gap, 304
Performance measurement, in control
    process, 527
Performance standards
  compared to actual performance, 527–
    529
  in control process, 526–527
Performing, 469
Permanent teams, 244
Personal ethics, 83
Personality clashes, as a source of
    conflict, 476
PERT (Program Evaluation and Review
    Technique), **210**–213
Physical ability tests, 347–**348**
Physiological needs, 402
Planned change, 302. *See also* Change
  types of, 317–321
Planning, 5–7, **75, 100**
  barriers to, 123–126
  intermediate-term, 119
  long-term, 119
  organizational design for, 120–123
  overcoming barriers, 124–126
  quantitative approaches to, 203–213
  short-term, 119
  steps in, 116
  time horizon for, 119–120

Planning mode, 154
Planning premises, 100
Planning task force, 123
Plans, 100
  developing, 114–119
  operational, 115–116
  relationship with goals, 100–104
  single-use, 117–118
  standing, 118–119
  strategic, 114–115
  tactical, 115
Plateaued employees, 717–718
P—O expectancy, 410
Point systems, 356
Policy, 118
Political activity, 78–79
Political forces, 35
Political instability, affecting international
  business, 667
Political risk, 666
Porter's competitive strategies, 147–149
Portfolio strategy, 140–144
Position power, 377
Position reinforcement, 413
Power, 368–370
Power and status differences, as a source
  of conflict, 476
Power distance, 667
Power need, 405
Preretirement programs, 719–720
Primacy, 473
Proactive response, 85
Problems, 172
Problem-solving goals, 110
Procedure, 118–119
Process culture, 500, 502
  heroes in, 502
Processing, 595
Process layout, 632–634
Process theories, 407–411
  equity theory, 407–408
  expectancy theory, 408–411
Producibility, as a design attribute, 631
Product and service design, 631–632
Product-based structure, 682
Product change, 318
Product departmentalization, 235–236
Production technology, 634–636
  CAD/CAM, 635–636
  flexible manufacturing systems, 635
  influence on organization structure, 253–
  259
Productive output, as a measure of group
  effectiveness, 460
Productivity, 646
  improving, 649–651
  managerial, 650–651
  managing, 646–651
  measuring, 646–648
  partial, 647
  and quality, 648–649
  technological, 649
  through people, 506
  total factor, 647
  worker, 649–650
Product layout, 634

Product life cycle, 149–151
Professional bureaucracy, 293
Professional ethics, 83
Profitability ratio, 565
Profit-and-loss statement, 562
Profit budget, 571
Profit center, 569
Profit-maximizing view, 80
Program, 117
**Program Evaluation and Review
  Technique (PERT), 210**–213
Programmed decisions, 165
Programmed instruction, 349
Project, 117
Project manager, 15
Prospector, 145
Prospector strategy, 145, 287
Prototype, 617
Providing well-defined tasks, to resolve
  conflict, 478
Public relations, 77
Public statements, 510–511
Punishment, 413
Purchasing function, 645–646

Qualitative forecasts, 201–202
Quality
  as a design attribute, 631
  and productivity, 648–649
Quality, of information, **594**
Quality circles, 546–549
Quality control, 544–550
Quantitative approaches to decision
  making, 213–220
  decision tree, 215–218
  game theory, 218
  payoff matrix, 213–215
  simulation models, 218–220
Quantitative approaches to planning, 203–
  213
  breakeven analysis, 203–206
  linear programming, 206–210
  PERT (Program Analysis and Review
  Technique), 210–213
Quantitative forecasts, 197–201
  causal forecasting models, 200–201
  time series analysis, 198–200
Question mark, 141
Queuing theory, 52

Random variation, 199
Raw materials inventory, 638
Reactor, 147
Reactor strategy, 147
Realistic job preview (RJP), 342–343,
  718
Reality shock, 718
Rebuilding corporations, 514
Receiver, 432
Recruiting, 342–344
Referent power, 369
Refreezing, 324
Regression analysis, 200
Reinforcement, 413
  schedules of, 414–416
Reinforcement theory, 412–421

Reinforcement tools, 412–414
Relatedness needs, 402
Relevance, of information, **595**
Reliability, as a design attribute, 631
Reorder point (ROP), 640
Resistance to change, 311–313
Resistance to power, 369, 370
Resource and product markets, for
  international markets, 665
Resource deployment, 133
Resource handler role, 22
Resource scarcity, as a source of conflict,
  476
Responsibility centers, 568–570
  cost center, 568
  investment center, 569–570
  profit center, 569
  relationship to structure, 570
  revenue center, 569
Retrenchment, 140
Retrenchment strategy, for multinational
  corporations, 680
Revenue budget, 571
Revenue center, 569
Revitalization, 513–516
Reward power, 368–369
Rewards, use of, by leaders, 381–382
Risk, 166
Risk propensity, 177
Roles, 20–22
  decisional, 22
  in groups, 465–466
  informational, 21
  interpersonal, 20–21
Routine service technology, 256–257
Rules, 119
Rules and procedures, as controls, 537

Safety needs, 402
Safety stock, 641
Salary structure, 356–357
Sales force composite, 202
Sales forecasts, 196
Satisfaction, as a measure of group
  effectiveness, 460
Satisficing, 170–171
Scalar principle, 233
Schedules of reinforcement, 414–416
Scientific management, 40–42
Scope, 133
Search, 305
Seasonal variation, 199
Secular trend, 198–199
Selection, 344–348
Selection and socialization, under clan
  control, 540–541
Selection, training and control, 537
Selection devices, 344–348
Selective perception, 434
Self-actualization needs, 402
Self-control, 540
Semantics, 450
Sender, 432
Service organizations, 627
  compared with manufacturing
  organizations, 627–628

Service technology, 256, 255–259
Short-range forecasting, for human resource management, 340–342
Short-term planning, 119
Simple structure, 291
Simulation models, 218–220
Monte Carlo method, 220
Single-use plans, 117–118
Situational characteristics, 376–377
Situational contingencies, 381
Situation analysis, 136–139
Size, 249
of groups, 464–465
influence on organizational structure, 249–250
Skill variety, 419
Skunkworks, 309
Slogans, 495–496
as change tools, 512
Small batch production, 254
Social audit, 88
Social contract, 35
Social entity, 10
Social facilitation, 479
Social forces, 35
Social performance, evaluating, 81–84
Social relationships, impact of information technology on, 609–610
Social responsibility, 80
discretionary level of, 84
economic level of, 81
effect on economic performance, 90–91
ethical level of, 82–84
fundamentals of, 79–80
legal level of, 81–82
opposing views of, 80
profit-maximizing view of, 80
Social responsiveness, improving, 87–89
Social values, and international business, 667–668
Sociocultural dimension, 70–71
for international business, 667–669
Socioemotional role, 465–466
Software, 597
Span of control, 235–236
Span of management, 235–236
Spokesperson role, 21
Stability, 140
Staff authority, 239
Staff departments, 239–240
Standing plans, 118–119
Star, 141
State of nature, 213
Statistical process control (SPC), 583–586
Stereotype, 434
Stockless systems, 643
Storage, 595–596
Stories, 494
as change tools, 512–513
Storming, 468–469
Strategic business units, 139–140
Strategic control point, 534
Strategic goals, **106**–108
types of, 107
Strategic management, 132–134

and information technology, 612–615
process of, 136–139
Strategic objectives, using structural approaches to obtain, 287–289
Strategic planning
for multinational corporations, 678–680
relationship to control, 529–531
Strategic plans, 114–115
in a core control system, 558
Strategy, 133. *See also* Business-level strategy; Corporate-level strategy
components of, 133–134
and corporate culture, 497–502
formulation vs. implementation, 135–136
levels of, 134–135
for multinational corporations, 676–680
Strategy formulation, 135–136
human element in, 153–154
Strategy implementation, 136, 154–157
human resources role in, 157
information and control systems role in, 156–157
leadership role in, 155–156
organization structure role in, 156–157
role of technology in, 157
Strengths, 137–138
Stress, 704–706
Structural approaches to change, 320–321
Structural design
approaches compared, 267
and attaining strategic objectives, 287–290
divisional approach to, 266, 274–277
functional approach to, 266, 268–270
functional approach with lateral relationships, 266, 271–273
hybrid approach to, 266, 277–281
impact on employees, 267–268
matrix approach to, 266, 281–287
Mintzberg's typology, 290–295
Structural location, for operations management, 651–652
Structure changes, 320
Substitute, 387–388
Subsystems, 54
Succession planning, 713
Superordinate goal, 478
Suppliers, 68–69
Supportive leadership, 381
Survey feedback, 326
Symbolic manager, 508–510
Symbols, 493–494
as change tools, 512
Synergy, 53, 134
System, 10, 53
organizations as, 10
Systems development life cycle, 616–617
Systems theory, 53–55
compared with other management perspectives, 56–57

Tactical objectives 108
Tactical plans, 115
Tall structure, 235
Task environment, 66–67, 68–69

Task forces, 243–244, **481**
Task group, 183–184, **462**–463
Task identity, 419
Task significance, 419
Task specialist role, 465–466
Task structure, 377
Team building, 325
Team management, 327
Technical complexity, 255
Technical core, 626
Technical skills, 17
Technological dimension, 69
Technological forecasts, 196
Technological productivity, 649
Technology, 253
influence on organization structure, 253–259
manufacturing, 254–256
role in control, 537
service, 256–258
and strategy implementation, 157
Technology change, 318
Telecommunications, 605–606
Telecommuting, 614
Terminations, 360–361
Theory X, 49–50
Theory Y, 49–50
Theory Z, 58, 503–505
Threats, 136–137
Timeliness, of information, **595**
Time series analysis, 198
Timing, as a design attribute for services, 632
Top administrator ratio, 240
Top-down approach, 318
Top-down budgeting, 574, 575–576
Top leader, 284
Top management financial control, 561–568
financial analysis used in, 563–565
and financial audits, 565–566
financial forecasts for, 563
financial statements as basis for, 561–562
management use of controls, 566–568
Top management support in implementing change, 316
Top manager, 12
Total factor productivity, 647
Total quality control, 545, 544–550
emphasis on total participation in, 545
and organizational contingency factors, 547–549
quality circles for, 546–547
Total study, 618
Tough-guy, macho culture, 498–499
heroes in, 498
Trade associations, 79
Traditional approach to motivation, 399
Tradition method, 36
Training
for career management, 719
distinguished from development, 348
Training and development, 349, 348–350
forms of, 349

Training and development *(continued)*
  needs analysis for, 349
  on-the-job training, 349
  training program evaluation for, 349
Training and management development, 710
Training program evaluation, 349
Traits, 370–371
Transactional leader, 389
Transaction processing systems (TPS), 598–600
Transformational leader, 391
Transformation process, 53
Two-boss employee, 283
Two-factor theory, 403–405

Uncertainty, 74, 166–167, 312
Uncertainty avoidance, 667–668
Unfreezing, 324
Unions, 360
Unity of command, 233
Upward communication, 443–444

Validity, 345–346
Value driven companies, 506

Variable costs, 571
Variable-interval reinforcement schedule, 415
Variable-ratio reinforcement schedule, 415
Vendor relations, 646
Venture teams, 308–309
Vertical structure, 232–242
  administrative intensity, 240
  balancing with lateral structure, 245–259
  centralization and decentralization, 236–238
    for multinational corporations, 686
  chain of command in, 233
  departmentalization, 235–236
  formalization, 240–241
  line and staff departments, 238–240
  problems with, 241–242
  and span of management, 234–235
  work specialization, 233
Videoconferencing, 605
Voice messaging, 605
Vroom-Yetton model, 383–387
  leader participation styles described in, 383–384

Wage and salary structure, 356–357
Weaknesses, 138
Whistle blowing, 89
Wholly owned foreign affiliate, 673–674
Women, career management problems of, 715–716
Worker productivity, 649–650
Work force
  attracting, 337–348
  developing, 348–354
  maintaining, 355–361
Work groups
  characteristics of, 463–467
  effectiveness model for, 460–461
Work hard/play hard culture, 499
  heroes in, 499
Work-in-process inventory, 637
Work redesign, 418
Work specialization, 233

Youth stage, 250, **251**–252

Zero-based budgeting (ZBB), 575–576
Zero inventory systems, 643